M

European Human Resource
Management in Transition

European Human Resource Management in Transition

PAUL R. SPARROW

AND

JEAN-M. HILTROP

PRENTICE HALL

New York London Toronto Sydney Tokyo Singapore

First published 1994 by
Prentice Hall International (UK) Limited
Campus 400, Maylands Avenue
Hemel Hempstead
Hertfordshire, HP2 7EZ
A division of
Simon & Schuster International Group

Typeset in 10/12 pt Sabon by
Mathematical Composition Setters Ltd, Salisbury, Wiltshire.

Printed and bound in Great Britain at the
University Press, Cambridge

Library of Congress Cataloging-in-Publication Data

Sparrow, Paul.
    European human resource management in transition / Paul R. Sparrow
and Jean-M. Hiltrop. – 1st ed.
       p.   cm.
    Includes bibliographical references and index.
    ISBN 0-13-202095-5
    1. Personnel management – Europe. I. Hiltrop, Jean-M. (Jean-
Marie) II. Title.
HF5549.2.E9S68   1994   94-6412
658.3″0096–dc20   CIP

British Library Cataloguing in Publication Data

A catalogue record for this book is available from
the British Library

ISBN 0 13 202095 5 (pbk)

1 2 3 4 5   97 96 95 94

Contents

PART ONE
The Context of European Human Resource Management
Perspectives and determinants

CHAPTER ONE
Anglo-Saxon Models of HRM
Theoretical debates from across the water

CHAPTER TWO
The European Perspective on HRM

CHAPTER FIVE

The Organizational Response
Integration of European management

CHAPTER TEN

Internal Resourcing
Employee training and development   361

CHAPTER THIRTEEN
Pay and Benefit Systems   513

CHAPTER FOURTEEN
Performance Management and Appraisal   551

CHAPTER FIFTEEN
Industrial Relations   588

PART FOUR

Future Issues in European Human Resource Management

CHAPTER SIXTEEN

Emerging HRM Issues in the Late 1990s
Thinking European, acting through processes of transition

Preface

▌

This book is intended for general managers who have an interest in, or responsibility for, people management within Europe. It therefore approaches the topic of Human Resource Management (henceforth called HRM) from a business perspective. It is not intended just for personnel managers, undergraduate and postgraduate students, but also for line managers who have responsibility for managing change in European organizations. There are three major themes that we hope will emerge from the wide range of material that we discuss:

1. A need to understand HRM from a European perspective.
2. An underlying process of transition that has generated new patterns of convergence and divergence within European HRM.
3. The emergence of new concepts of organizations and their structure that is driving a new set of HRM imperatives.

We believe that the issues and topics discussed in this book – all of which have implications for the changing nature and shape of European organizations – are of such crucial importance that those personnel managers who do not respond to these business transitions will perhaps no longer have a significant role in their organizations, nor perhaps even a job. However, in considering these issues, a major problem for most European managers is that the vast majority of existing management literature and the tools, techniques and conceptual models in the field, are of North American, or at best British, origin. They emanate from across the Atlantic or the Channel – 'over the water' – for most Europeans and may not necessarily be seen as relevant to continental European practice or business culture.

So how should we create a book on HRM for European managers? At the simplest level, we have 'Europeanized' the literature. This has involved incorporating material and analysis on various aspects of HRM that has been written by European academics or practitioners in order to build on the early Anglo-Saxon work in the area. This immediately raises the question of what we mean by Europe? We include the UK in Europe. Despite its cultural distance from many European countries, the nature of HRM in the UK is significantly different from the US. As a member of the European Union (EU) and a significant target of foreign direct investment, practices in the UK are undergoing as much change as are those in continental Europe. There is a core focus on the countries of France, Germany and the UK throughout many chapters in the book. This is not intentional – although the three countries do represent powerful contrasts in many aspects of HRM – but rather reflects the relative volume of national publications of HRM practitioners and the dominant size of these economies in Europe. However, data are also provided on national practice throughout all the other EU countries, especially where significant differences exist. Given the imminent inclusion of Scandinavian countries within the EU, and the strong HRM traditions in these countries, we have also included examples from, and reference to, Nordic perspectives. From the outset, we acknowledge that in talking about European HRM, we are talking about diversity. Understanding the patterns of convergence and divergence in HRM practice across this diverse continent is the challenge we face.

A second level of 'Europeanization' is to place the discussion and presentation of HRM techniques firmly within the European business context, which is one of radical restructuring of business, increasing competitive threat, competing models of effectiveness, and significant cultural heterogeneity within the European business world. It also involves presenting European case study material. We have deliberately woven examples from and reference to a number of significant European industrial sectors (such as automobiles, chemicals and pharmaceuticals, airlines, consumer products, oil and electronics and computing) and European organizations (such as Philips, ICL, British Airways, Shell, British Petroleum, Bayer, Hoechst, Volkswagen, Nestlé and Suchards) into the various chapters in the book. The book is grounded in current and historical organizational practice, for it is European organizations and their employees that are in the greatest state of transition. A companion casebook to this text is available, again consisting of European case examples of business change, which have implications for the nature of their HRM. This volatile business environment provides us with an opportunity to assess the nature of European HRM in terms of convergence, reliance on core techniques, and our understanding of specific and enduring aspects of cultural diversity in HRM practice. Given the considerable interest in the comparative aspects of HRM in recent years this task too can be achieved without much difficulty.

The third and most difficult level to achieve is that of creating a European theory of HRM. This is the challenge that we have set ourselves. We approach this last task on the basis of grounded evidence rather than prescription. Throughout the early parts of the book we build up an understanding of the common and unique themes in European HRM practice. There has until recently been little agreement about definitions of HRM (or the related concept of strategic HRM which has proved to be a natural development from early discussions on the topic) and even less progress towards defensible theoretical models to help us understand the role of HRM in organizations, the determinants of various HRM practices or their relative importance (Wright and McMahan, 1992). In order to provide a theory we need to be able to state the relations between concepts, the boundaries to our assumptions and their constraints (Bacharach, 1989). This book has to move beyond a simple description of those phenomena that are of interest to the topic of European HRM by also asking questions about how, why and when these phenomena have developed. It also seeks to provide a degree of knowledge about predictions and outcomes as well as an understanding of how the various processes occur. We do this by focusing on the transitions that are taking place in Europe, pointing to their most obvious implications for HRM, noting the constraining impact of national practice or cultural factors, and then highlighting the resulting content of practice. In order to achieve such an understanding, the model of HRM used to structure this book takes a broad and contextual view of the field. The book is therefore divided into four parts.

Parts One and Two contain six chapters which should be read as a whole (see Figure 0.1 for an outline of the main areas of context covered in the book). It is important that the reader draws links between each of the various topics that they cover. Part One compares the Anglo-Saxon approach to HRM with European practices, discusses the

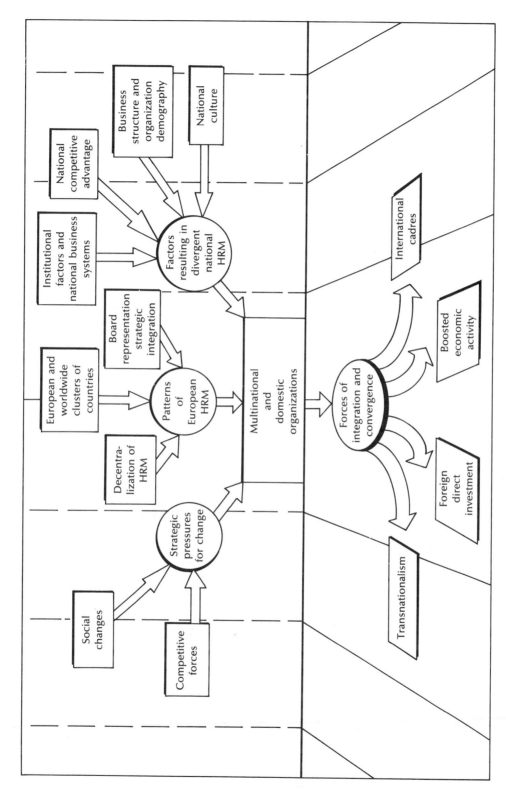

Figure 0.1 A model of the context for European human resource management (HRM).

distinctive features of a European approach, and considers some of the determinants of different HRM practices across Europe. This opening chapter introduces the topic of HRM and briefly summarizes the main approaches that have been taken in the US and the UK. The second chapter introduces European models of HRM. We use Chapter Two to stress and highlight the considerable diversity in European models of HRM. Chapter Two is therefore concerned with description – both conceptual and empirical – of diversity within European HRM. Chapter Three focuses on the main determinants of diversity in European HRM. It is intended to balance the debate about integration of European HRM, lest we become too fixated on change, and considers themes of continuity by describing national business systems and those national cultural forces that are anticipated to slow down and mediate the impact of the forces of integration.

Part Two changes the tenor of the argument. It considers the strategic pressures driving developments in European HRM from both an external (socio-economic) and internal (organizational) perspective and provides the background knowledge and context that is necessary to understand the nature of HRM in Europe. It necessarily represents a substantial proportion of the book as it is used to raise the agenda for and draw connections to more traditional areas of HRM. Chapters Four and Five marshal the evidence that we believe represents an overwhelming force for change at the organizational level. These pressures will create both winners and losers, and for the survivors, there will likely be a much tighter and more coherent integration in their HRM practices on a pan-European basis. Chapter Four deals with the external strategic pressures (competitive forces and social pressures) faced by multinational and domestic European organizations. Chapter Five focuses on how European organizations are responding to these external pressures and outlines the main forces of integration in HRM practice, focusing in particular on transnationalism and foreign direct investment. In Chapter Six we cover the debate about convergence or divergence of European HRM practice and consider the various complex arguments that are used to argue for and against the emergence of a European notion of management in general – and HRM in particular. The changing role of the European HRM function is discussed. We use the description of the changing context for HRM in Europe to highlight those areas of content that have the most relevance.

Part Three describes the actual content of HRM across a range of policy and practice areas and takes on more of a 'how it is done' perspective, whilst still examining the practice of HRM in a European context. The chapters included in Part Three describe the most important areas of comparative knowledge required for HRM practitioners, as defined by two criteria:

1. Their conceptual role and logical connection to the implementation of the various business and strategic changes taking place in Europe.
2. The frequency of their mention and coverage in the business literature by academics and practitioners.

The connection between Parts One and Two of the book and the subsequent chapters in Part Three is shown in Figure 0.2. Using the two criteria listed above it is clear that a book on European HRM must cover topics such as recruitment, training, career development, work design and industrial relations. These have all been influenced by the strategic changes taking place in Europe and dealt with in a comparative manner. General managers will find that they need to understand the importance of these topics, and the extent to which there are different European conceptualizations or norms of practice if they are to implement strategic change successfully.

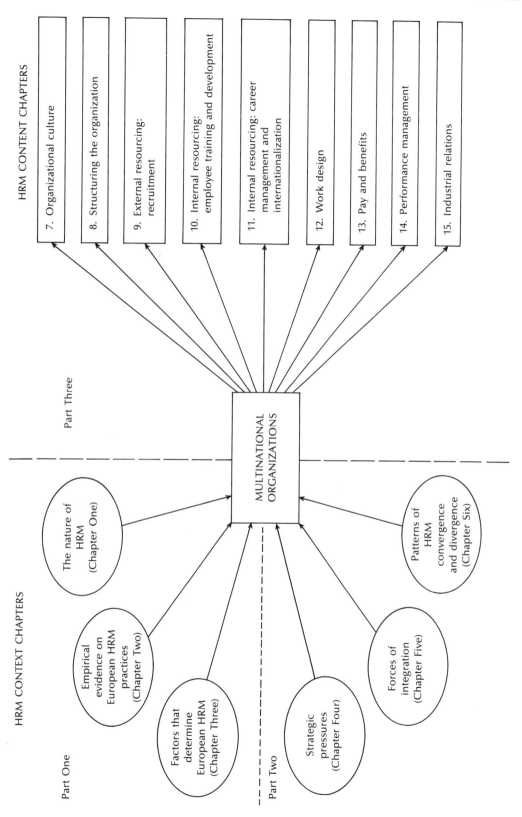

Figure 0.2 Links between Parts One and Two and Part Three of this book.

There are nine main topics that form the core of European HRM in a comparative context:

1. Changing organizational culture.
2. Structuring the organization.
3. External resourcing through recruitment, selection and assessment.
4. Internal resourcing through employee training and development.
5. Internal resourcing and internationalization through career management.
6. Work design.
7. Pay and benefits issues.
8. Performance management.
9. Industrial relations.

These cover most of the topics in the international HRM literature identified by Torrington (1994). In Chapters Seven to Fifteen we therefore analyse the debates in these nine areas, as well as providing a core 'how it is done' level of knowledge. Some of the more esoteric, specialist and generic techniques such as how to conduct a job analysis or build a manpower or human resource plan we leave for other (prescriptive) books on personnel management practice. There is little new to say on such topics; they have been ably described elsewhere, and they have little sensitivity to the European environment. We would refer readers interested in these levels of practice to a number of comprehensive and recent generic personnel management textbooks (for example Bernardin and Russell, 1993; Schuler and Huber, 1993; and Torrington and Hall, 1993). We also do not focus on the organizational behaviour topics of leadership, motivation and communication. Again, these are of more theoretical interest and usually dealt with in separate books.

In Part Four we summarize the findings from the various chapters and introduce a number of future issues within European HRM that will continue to fuel the process of transition. We focus in particular on the latest developments to challenge the HRM function, such as the process of downsizing, business process re-engineering and the emergence of new organizational forms.

Finally, we should comment that we see this book as the beginning of an ongoing venture. In grounding it in the changing context and content of HRM practices, which we clearly demonstrate are in a state of transition, we shall continue to seek examples and developments within Europe. We have learned much during the writing of this book and shall continue to learn. We hope that it will stimulate those who feel they know of new developments, or better examples, to share their insights with us.

PAUL R. SPARROW   *Manchester Business School*

JEAN-MARIE HILTROP   *International Institute for Management Development*
February 1994

Acknowledgements

It is customary to give thanks to the person who helped type the manuscript, but rarely can so much be owed to one person. Our heartfelt thanks go to Vera Vose, whose skills helped create graphics, organize our contacts with other institutions, and keep track of the numerous developments made to the material as the book took shape. We would have been lost without her.

To Prem Nair our thanks for his research assistance. We also appreciate the comments from those people who reviewed the material in the book and must acknowledge the numerous academics, managers and consultants whose ideas about Europe have helped form the core of the book. Our respective institutions, Manchester Business School and the Institute for International Management Development, have helped make it possible for us to take on the commitment of writing this book.

To our families, our thanks for being so understanding about and supportive of this project that took away much of our time with them.

Finally, we owe much to the patience and encouragement from Julia Helmsley, Cathy Peck and the team at Prentice Hall.

About the Authors

PAUL SPARROW is currently a Lecturer in Organizational Behaviour at Manchester Business School. He graduated from the University of Manchester with a BSc (Hons) Psychology and the University of Aston with an MSc Applied Psychology and was then sponsored by Rank Xerox to study the impacts of ageing on the organization for his PhD research. He worked as a freelance consultant for a couple of years involved in projects relating to future patterns of work. He then spent four years as a Research Fellow at Aston University and Senior Research Fellow at Warwick Business School researching problems of strategic change and human resource management in UK organizations. In 1988 he joined PA Consulting Group working as a Consultant and then Principal Consultant in Human Resource Strategy carrying out assignments on human resource planning, organization and role review, team building, people and technology, competency analysis, assessment centre design, career development workshops, appraisal design and training, and individual psychological assessments. In 1991 he returned to academia and took up his Lectureship. He lectures in Human Resource Strategy on the international MBA programme at Manchester and has taught on executive development courses for several leading organizations. His recent publications are in the areas of human resource planning, management competencies, the psychology of strategic management and international human resource management.

JEAN-MARIE HILTROP is Professor of Human Resource Management at the International Institute for Management Development (IMD) in Lausanne, Switzerland. He has been involved in executive education for many years at the Management Centre of the University of Bradford and at the Department of Applied Economic Sciences of the Katholieke Universiteit Leuven in Belgium. He also has extensive experience as a personnel manager and consultant for several large companies in Europe, Asia and the United States. Professor Hiltrop has published in numerous journals and has also published a European casebook of human resource management issues with the same co-author. He is currently leading an international research project, which examines the impact of human resource practices on the global strategy and competitiveness of European organizations.

PART ONE

The Context of European Human Resource Management

Perspectives and determinants

CHAPTER ONE

Anglo-Saxon Models of HRM

Theoretical debates from across the water

INTRODUCTION

Recently several comparative analyses of European and international HRM have been carried out in order to identify the most significant influences that have shaped HRM (see, for example, Brewster, 1993; Brewster, Hegewisch and Mayne, 1993; Brewster and Tyson, 1991; Hickson, 1993; Lessem and Neubauer 1994; Pieper, 1990; Schuler, Dowling and de Cieri, 1993; Sparrow, Schuler and Jackson, 1994; Torrington, 1994; Tyson, Lawrence, Poirson, Manzolini and Vicente, 1993; and a series of articles in *Personnel Management* reviewing European national practice). These studies reveal long histories of HRM in countries other than the US. Mostly they leave aside the often controversial meaning of HRM and start from the perspective of describing the factors that shape national practice as opposed to the practices of specific organizations. There is consequently considerable latitude in the interpretation of what constitutes HRM (Hendry, 1991). The contextual factors that are believed to account for distinctive differences also vary across the studies, which tend to focus around notions of difference and similarity (Brewster and Bournois, 1991) and therefore provide us with a glimpse of the uneven way in which concepts of HRM have been applied across Europe. And yet, as Torrington (1994) observes:

... international HRM has the same main dimensions as HRM in a national context, but with some additional features... in many ways international HRM is simply HRM on a larger scale [but] the strategic considerations are more complex and the operational units more varied, needing co-ordination across more barriers.   Torrington (1994, p. 4).

Torrington (1994) believes that there is a need to develop a technology for international HRM to take the field beyond simply being aware of the different national contexts in which organizations operate, in order for managers to be able to understand what to do and how to do it. This is because managers – particularly those dealing with people issues – develop their competence by comprehending and then mastering the subtle relationships between behaviour, relationships, values and traditions. These relationships are steeped in a national or regional culture. Operating outside this 'learned framework' is a distinct challenge. So what has the existing literature told us? The typical questions that have been analysed are shown in Illustration 1.1.

The majority of reviews have unfortunately been specific to national practice. They have therefore been written to varying levels of detail and sophistication. The most

Illustration 1.1   **Typical questions analysed in comparative studies of HRM.**

- How is HRM structured in individual European countries?
- What strategies are discussed?
- What is put into practice?

- What are the main differences and similarities?
- To what extent are corporate policies and strategies influenced by national factors such as culture, government policy and educational systems?

Source: Pieper (1990).

notable works, country by country, are for:

- United Kingdom (Brewster, Hegewisch, Lockhart and Holden, 1993; Legge, 1989; Storey, 1992a; Tyson, 1993).
- Germany (Arkin, 1992a; Conrad and Pieper, 1990; Eberwein and Tholen, 1993; Gaugler and Wiltz, 1993; Lawrence, 1993a and Staehle and Schirmer, 1992).
- Switzerland (Hilb and Wittman, 1993).
- Denmark (Andersen, Cour, Svendsen, Kiel, Kamp and Larsen, 1993; and Arkin, 1992b).
- Sweden (Söderström, 1993; Söderström and Syrén, 1993).
- Norway (Lange and Johnson, 1993).
- France (Besse, 1992; Bournois, 1993; Poirson, 1993; and Rojot, 1990).
- Belgium (Buelens, De Clercq, Graeve and Vanderheyden, 1993; and Sels, 1992).
- Holland (Hoogendoorn, 1992; Hoogendoorn, Van der Wal and Spitsbaard, 1993).
- Ireland (Gunnigle, 1993; and Hannaway, 1992).
- Italy (Camuffo and Costa, 1993; Caplan, 1992; Cooper and Giacomello, 1993; Hinterhuber and Stumpf, 1990; and Manzolini, 1993).
- Spain (Filella, 1992; Filella and Soler, 1993; Rodriguez, 1991; and Vicente, 1993).
- Portugal (Mendes, 1992).
- Greece (Ball, 1992; and Papalexandris, 1991, 1993).
- Former East Germany (Meyer, 1990).
- Former Czechoslovakia (Landa, 1990).
- Former Yugoslavia (Purg, 1990).

A second set of literature has provided us with descriptions of country by country practice in key HRM practices, such as industrial relations (Baglioni and Crouch, 1991; Ferner and Hyman, 1992b; and Incomes Data Service, 1991), recruitment (Incomes Data Service, 1990a), terms and conditions of employment (Incomes Data Service, 1990b), pay and benefits (Incomes Data Service, 1992) and training and development (Incomes Data Service, 1993a).

Very few textbooks have attempted to consider the whole field in terms of generic topics without resorting to a country by country style. Hendry (1993) highlights the disjuncture this creates. International HRM becomes a description of a series of fragmented responses to a series of distinct national problems. By emphasizing the differences between doing business internationally as opposed to nationally, writers tend to focus exclusively on multinational organizations, and also overlook many of the continuing similarities between domestic and international HRM. Notable exceptions are the studies by Lane (1989) on the management of labour in Europe, Dowling, Schuler and Welch (1994) and Torrington (1994) on the phenomenon of international HRM, and Hendry's (1993) analysis of the processes of internationalization (such as building effective domestic organizations, networking, creating international commitment, learning in alliances, managing complexity and developing intercultural competence). Building on this work is the challenge we address in this book. We have attempted to describe and analyse both the context and content of European HRM, and emphasize the main 'technologies' that managers will need to apply in their organizations in order to operate effectively in Europe.

WHAT IS HRM? A HISTORICAL PERSPECTIVE

First, however, we must develop an understanding of what HRM is in a European context. Throughout the late 1980s and early 1990s there has been a process of 'Europeanization' taking place and this provides us with an opportunity to re-evaluate HRM in a regional context, by examining and interpreting differences in labour markets, participation structures, legislation, rewards, recruitment patterns and the harmonization of qualifications (Brewster and Tyson, 1991). However, the need to take stock and re-evaluate what is meant by HRM in a European context is not just driven by international developments. There has been a growing academic criticism of the generally prescriptive approach taken by many textbooks on HRM which simply provide descriptions of best practice (in traditional personnel management areas such as recruitment and selection, performance appraisal, pay, training and development) without providing any credible framework for the reader (Boxall, 1991; Guest, 1987, 1990; Legge, 1989). In the 1980s many textbooks on personnel management simply added some new material, changed the title to human resource management, yet did not change the structure or premise of the book. In an excellent review of American and British theories, Boxall (1991) argues that this is inappropriate and that readers of textbooks on HRM have to be taught to think about the relevance of specific topics, rather than accept standard prescriptions.

It is necessary to step back in time in order to examine and outline the major developments in thinking about HRM. The important conceptual and methodological points are best made by playing out the various academic debates that have taken place to date. In the 1950s writers such as Drucker and McGregor talked about the need for visionary goal-directed leadership and management by integration. This was followed by a behavioural science movement in the 1960s in which writers such as Maslow, Argyris and Herzberg placed greater value on the human resources in the organization by raising the importance of topics such as needs, learning and motivation. In parallel the organizational development movement, typified by writers such as Bennis in the early 1970s, began to focus on the importance of seeing the organization as a whole. The origins of HRM as a defined school of thought are usually traced back to the 1970s and the development of 'human capital theory' (Flamholtz, 1974). It was argued that it was more appropriate to view human resources as assets as opposed to just a cost. This view remained in the literature throughout the 1970s, but began to gain more widespread support in the early 1980s (Hendry and Pettigrew, 1990).

It is interesting to speculate that few European academics or practitioners would take strong issue with most of the statements of purpose and attitude shown in Illustration 1.2. Such observations would cross most cultures. It was only in the 1980s when things got tough and academics began to theorize about models of HRM that underlying cultural assumptions arose. By this time US organizations were under severe competitive threat from Japan. Management writers began to draw attention to low levels of commitment in Anglo-Saxon organizations and the need for major restructuring and reorganization in order to meet the challenge of the new competition (Abernathy, Clark and Kantrow, 1981; Ouchi, 1981; Pascale and Athos, 1982). The role of quality – and the need to tie people in the organization deeper into the heart

Illustration 1.2 **Early definitions of HRM: a focus on purpose and attitudes.**

The purpose of HRM is to ensure that the employees of an organization, i.e. its human resources '... are used in such a way that the employer obtains the greatest possible benefit from their abilities and the employees obtain both material and psychological rewards from their work'   (Graham, 1978).

The purpose of HRM is to provide '... a process of analysing an organization's human resource needs under changing conditions and developing the activities necessary to satisfy those needs'
(Walker, 1980).

HRM should be '... concerned with the consequences of all organizational decisions for human productivity and for the well-being of the entire workforce'   (Prewitt, 1982).

HRM entails '... a very strong managerial responsibility to HRM in which it draws the most from each asset at its command, with the realization of employee potential being the primary job'   (Fitz-enz, 1981).

Alongside developing general managerial responsibility must come a change in attitude such that there must be '... a move away from seeing employees as a necessary expense of doing business to a critical investment in the organization's current performance and future growth'   (Ross, 1981).

of the business process – was seen as central to achieving this restructuring (Peters and Waterman, 1982).

In order to achieve this tighter link between 'people management' and business transformation, the need to integrate HRM considerations into strategic planning systems was also widely argued (Fombrun, 1983; Walker, 1980). It was this linkage of 'people management' issues and strategic planning processes that was seen to differentiate HRM from personnel management (Sibson, 1983). It shifted the content of personnel management away from traditional concerns with the specialist aspects of recruiting, training, rewarding and managing the 'workforce' towards higher level issues of managing the organizational culture, designing the structure, and resourcing the organization with an appropriate set of competencies. It also focused attention on the identification, analysis and activity scheduling of events which impacted the management of people in the organization of the future. The new debate became how could HRM contribute to developing 'competitive advantage' for such organizations (Baird, Meshoulam and DeGive, 1983)?

The business literature was combined into a series of more generalizable theories that classified the content of HRM and postulated explanatory links between competitive advantage and this content. These theories were supported by reference to numerous case studies (principally large US multinationals) and managerial interviews. They served to establish a 'territorial map' for the realm of HRM and it was at this point that there was a schism in US thinking about HRM (see Figure 1.1). We examine the two models highlighted in Figure 1.1. in the next two sections of this chapter.

Whilst Brewster and Bournois (1991) point out that the topic of HRM is in itself '... more a bundle of overarching notions than a concept in its own right' we can usefully distinguish four significant views of HRM that have emerged from the literature. In the next few sections we summarize the main points of each of these models of HRM. The four approaches discussed in this chapter are:

■ The Michigan and New York Schools: strategic matching theories.
■ The Harvard School: a multiple stakeholders theory.
■ The Warwick School: a political and change process theory.
■ The Schuler School: a behavioural transformation theory.

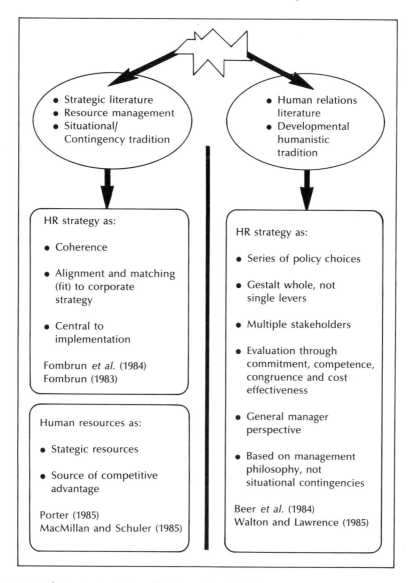

Figure 1.1 A schism in American thinking about HRM.

MATCHING MODELS OF HRM: THE MICHIGAN AND NEW YORK SCHOOLS

One of the most documented sets of concepts about HRM, strongly featured in the American literature, highlights the importance of what has been called a 'matching' model of strategic HRM. Early interest in this approach has been associated with the Michigan Business School and was outlined by Tichy, Fombrun and Devanna (1982) and Fombrun, Tichy and Devanna (1984). Their matching model emphasizes the 'resource' side of the phrase, i.e. human *resource* management. It argues that people need to be managed like any other organizational resource. This means that they have to be obtained cheaply, used sparingly and developed and exploited as fully as possible. The philosophy does not limit itself to direct employees of an organization.

Therefore humans or people – as opposed to just employees – need to be managed in a way that is consistent with broad organizational requirements such as quality or efficiency. Personnel policies and organization structures have to be managed in a way that is congruent with organizational strategy and organizational effectiveness depends on there being a tight 'fit' between human resource and business strategies. HRM strategies are all about making business strategies work and so emphasis is placed on how to best match and develop 'appropriate' HRM systems. The systems that Fombrun *et al.* (1984) felt to be the most important in achieving this match were selection, performance, appraisal, rewards and development (see Figure 1.2). These four areas of HRM policy have to be coherent and consistent and linked to the strategy. This alignment is necessary in order to channel behaviours and create a dominant value or culture in the organization that enables the effective implementation of strategy.

Throughout the 1980s there were a number of variations along this theme of 'strategic fit' (Lengnick-Hall and Lengnick-Hall, 1988). One of the clearest expositions and developments of this sort of theory was given by Schuler and Jackson (1987), referred to here as the New York model. They examined each of the generic competitive strategies outlined by Porter (1980, 1985), i.e. quality enhancement, innovation and cost leadership or reduction. For each strategy they developed a set of 'needed role behaviours' which varied across a number of dimensions and then stipulated a set of hypotheses about the personnel and industrial relations practices that were needed. They identified the most important HRM practices about which strategic decisions had to be made (see Illustration 1.3) and for each practice noted the dichotomous but logical alternatives that could be applied. HRM could be seen as a menu of strategic choices to be made by HR executives intended to promote the most effective role behaviours that are consistent with the organization strategy and are aligned with each other.

'... Just as firms will be faced with inefficiencies when they try to implement new strategies with outmoded structures, so they will also face problems of implementation when they attempt to effect new strategies with inappropriate HR systems. The critical managerial task is to align the formal structure and the HR systems so that they drive the strategic objectives of the organization.'

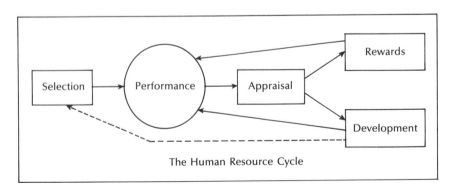

Figure 1.2 The Michigan matching model of HRM. *Source*: reproduced from *Strategic Human Resource Management* by C. J. Fombrun, N. Tichy and M. A. Devanna. Copyright © 1984. Reprinted with permission of John Wiley and Sons, Inc.

Illustration 1.3 **HRM practice menus.**

Planning choices
Informal...Formal
Short-term...Long-term
Explicit job analysis...Implicit job analysis
Job simplification...Job enrichment
Low employee involvement...High employee involvement

Staffing choices
Internal sources...External sources
Narrow paths...Broad paths
Single ladder...Multiple ladders
Explicit criteria...Implicit criteria
Limited socialization...Extensive socialization
Closed procedures...Open procedures

Appraising choices
Behavioural criteria...Results criteria
Low employee participation...High employee participation
Short-term criteria...Long-term criteria
Individual criteria...Group criteria

Compensating choices
Low base salaries...High base salaries
Internal equity...External equity
Few perks...Many perks
Standard, fixed package...Flexible package
Low participation...High participation
No incentives...Many incentives
Short-term incentives...Long-term incentives
No employment security...High employment security
Hierarchical...High participation

Training and development choices
Short-term...Long-term
Narrow application...Broad application
Productivity emphasis...Quality of work life emphasis
Spontaneous, unplanned...Planned, systematic
Individual orientation...Group orientation
Low participation...High participation

Source: Schuler and Jackson (1987), reprinted with permission © Academy of Management Executives, 1993.

Having selected its strategy the organization has to ensure 'behavioural consistency'. For example, an organization that adopts an innovation strategy needs to foster behaviours that are creative, have a long-term focus, a relatively high level of co-operation and interdependence, a moderate concern for quality and quantity, attention to both the process and the results, a high degree of risk taking and a high tolerance of ambiguity and unpredictability. In order to foster these sorts of behaviours, it is argued, the following types of personnel and industrial relations policies are needed: job specifications that define close interaction and co-ordination among groups of individuals; performance appraisal systems that reward group-based achievements; compensation systems that emphasize internal equity rather than market-based pay; and broad career paths to reinforce the development of a wider range of skills. A series of different matches were articulated by Schuler and Jackson (1987).

THE CONTRIBUTION OF CONTINGENCY-BASED MODELS

The contingency-based models of HRM argue that the shape of HRM (in both its content and its form) varies in relation to the strategic business needs. There are two sorts of relationships (Schuler, 1992a). The first is a contingent relationship, in which various triggers result in a predictable, systematic influence. A number of authors have outlined contingent relationships that dictate the shape of HRM (see Illustration 1.4).

The contingency-based models of HRM serve to highlight the importance of ensuring that there is some sort of coherence and consistency across a range of human resource policies and practices in order to speed up the implementation of any strategic change. The prescriptions are, however, highly culture-bound and generally only tested against US organizations. For example, Jackson, Schuler and Rivero (1989) used surveys to investigate the relationship between organizational characteristics and personnel practices in 267 US organizations. As we shall see in the next chapter, such conceptions of HRM tend not to fit easily with the European situation. Moreover, subsequent work revealed an increasingly complex picture in which personnel practices, even within the US, varied with manufacturing technology, industrial sector, the size and structure of the organization, and the degree of unionization (Boxall, 1991).

These matching models have therefore been criticized on a number of counts (see Illustration 1.5). They tend to cast HRM in a reactive mode, seen as only serving the efficient implementation of a preconceived and rational strategy. This asks too little of HRM and ignores the contribution that it can make to the formation of strategy (Boxall, 1991). Matching models also assume that generic typologies of strategy such as those articulated by Porter (1980, 1985) are a valid starting point. They are not. Generic strategies tend not to be as mutually exclusive as asserted and the process of strategy implementation is often one that creates its own learning about HRM. The approach tends to underestimate the importance of incremental processes of strategy making and strategy change (Pascale and Athos, 1982). There is also a problem with the choice of content areas for HRM. For example, the four policy areas of selection, appraisal, rewards and development in Fombrun *et al.*'s (1984) model seem to ignore

Illustration 1.4 **The most important contingent relationships for HRM.**

Top management goals, values and strategic intent (e.g. Ackermann, 1986; Miles and Snow, 1984). Basis of competitive battles in terms of cost, quality and innovation (e.g. Schuler and Jackson, 1987; Olian and Rynes, 1984). Life cycle of the business or industry (e.g. Kerr, 1982; Kochan and Capelli, 1984; Pettigrew, Hendry and Sparrow, 1990).	Nature of the business sector (e.g. HRM implications of strategic change in the information technology sector have been outlined by Kleingartner and Anderson, 1987; Sparrow, 1988 and Sparrow and Pettigrew, 1988b; whilst the banking sector has been analysed by Hendry and Pettigrew, 1987 and Hiltrop, 1991a; and the manufacturing sector has been analysed by Hiltrop, 1992).

Illustration 1.5 **Arguments for and against a matching or contingency approach to HRM.**

Arguments for	Arguments against
Management personalities, skills and styles must be selected to match different situations.	It assumes a rigidity of personality and stereotypes managers
As business needs change, so must people.	It requires an unrealistic precision in selection systems.
Behaviours need to be channelled through appropriate pay and appraisal systems.	It creates an unrealistic requirement for mobility and flexibility
A contingency approach facilitates the use of different approaches to employee relations in different parts of the business.	Training, job rotation and rewards can be used to develop a broad repertoire of behaviours in managers.
It reduces the importance of questions about culture, style and non-economic issues.	The strategy process and business differentiation is never really based on situational contingencies.

important areas such as the design and organization of work and the role of industrial relations (areas that are examined in this textbook). Finally, the whole idea of 'fit' seems inappropriate for a world in which there are high levels of dynamic and unpredictable change (see Part Two for a discussion of the most important changes in the European environment). Strategic planning is in reality a multi-stage and multi-level process. At what point and at what level is an assessment of fit best made? It is not surprising that in reviewing this first approach Hendry and Pettigrew (1990) conclude:

... the contingency framework readily led to prescriptive theorising, especially when linked to typologies of strategy, 'culture' itself tended to be treated as a manipulable variable, and people tended to get excised from the equation.   Hendry and Pettigrew (1990, p. 23).

Academics have focused more recently on a series of 'non-contingent' influences on HRM (Schuler, 1992a) which may be organizational or non-organizational (see Figure 1.3). The non-organizational factors include social and economic factors,

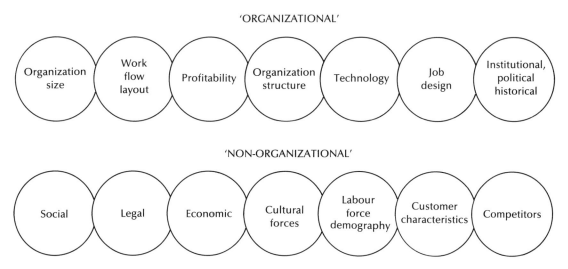

Figure 1.3 Non-contingent determinants of HRM. *Source:* after Schuler (1992a).

the legislative environment, cultural forces, the nature of the labour market, customer characteristics and the behaviour of competitors. Organizational influences include the size of organizations, the work flow layout, levels of profitability, structure and job design. By saying the relationship is 'non-contingent' it does not mean that such factors do not determine HRM. They do. However, with our current level of understanding the various factors involved are seen to trigger new developments in HRM, but have an unpredictable, undiscriminating, or unknown effect, either across countries or across organizations. A primary function of this book is to develop our understanding of many of these 'non-contingent' factors in Europe so that in future they may be more formally included in theories of HRM.

THE HARVARD MODEL OF HRM: MULTIPLE STAKEHOLDERS

A second – and less rational or prescriptive – view about HRM emanates from the Harvard Business School. This model was first articulated by Beer, Spector, Lawrence, Mills and Walton (1984) and Beer, Lawrence, Mills and Walton (1985) and has tended to find greater favour in Europe, particularly in the UK (Guest, 1987; Hendry and Pettigrew, 1990; Poole, 1990). It concentrates more on the softer issues of strategic management, and given its roots in the human relations tradition, stresses the 'human' aspect of human resource management. In defining HRM as involving all those management decisions and actions that affected the nature of the relationship between the organization and the employee, the model argues that historical problems of personnel management can only be solved when general managers develop a philosophy or viewpoint about how they wish to see employees involved in and developed by the organization. This central philosophy can only be provided by general managers and ensures that personnel management activities do not simply become a set of unco-ordinated activities, each guided by their own tradition.

The model postulates a range of different stakeholder interests such as shareholders, management, employee groups, government, the unions and the community. Although management are seen as having the upper hand, the importance of 'trade-offs' between the owners, employees and various employee groups is recognized, as are mechanisms for reconciling employee interests with the objectives of management. The model is not solely limited to the American experience (Boxall, 1991) as, for example, some attention is given to European models of co-determination.

It also builds on the matching model of Fombrun *et al.* (1984) by describing a much broader range of content for HRM policy co-ordinators. The actual content of HRM is described in relation to four policy areas (see Illustration 1.6). Each policy area represents a series of major tasks that managers must attend to. The attraction of the model lies in both the breadth of content covered by these policy areas and the emphasis it gives to developing broad patterns of activity.

The outcomes that the design of these four human resource policies need to achieve are:

- Commitment.
- Congruence.
- Competence.
- Cost effectiveness.

Whilst these all sound sensible enough, this specification of desired outcomes makes the model become more prescriptive, since not all organizations would use this language or would wish to achieve these particular outcomes. However, the model

Illustration 1.6 **Four policy areas of HRM.**

Human resource flows
Activities involved in managing the flow of people at all levels into, through and then out of the organization i.e. recruitment, selection, placement, promotion, appraisal and assessment, promotion, termination and various other forms of outflows. Broadly akin to a 'resource development' set of policies intended to ensure the organization has the right number of managers with the right mix of competencies.

Reward systems
Activities necessary to ensure that reward systems are designed and operate in a way that attracts, motivates and retains employees at all levels in the organization. It includes pay systems, motivation, and benefits.

Employee influence
Management of levels of authority, responsibility and power that are voluntarily delegated or involved in decision making within the organization.

Work systems
Definition and design of work and the way in which people, information, technology and activities are arranged in order to provide the most appropriate outcomes.

Source: Beer *et al.* (1984).

allows for analysis of these outcomes at both the organizational and societal level. It also acknowledges a broad range of contextual influences on management's choice of HRM activities. The employment relationship is seen as a blending of business and societal expectations. Although business strategy has a major role to play, a number of other factors such as socio-cultural considerations – including patterns of unionization, labour market regulations, workforce characteristics, and community values are included in the equation. Unlike the 'matching' models which point to a strong determination of HRM action by the situation and the environment, the Harvard model argues that managers are major actors, capable of making unique contributions and altering the organizational and environmental parameters that influence HRM activities.

However, because it acknowledges the role of societal outcomes Poole (1990) argued that the Harvard model provides a useful basis for comparative analysis of HRM. Although most of the case development used to support the Harvard model was US-based, the importance of comparative learning was recognized by the original researchers:

… variations in HRM policies and practices across countries offer useful alternatives for US managers to learn from. This comparative perspective allows managers to examine and question the ideology and assumptions that underlie their own HRM practices. Looking at what managers in other countries do can also suggest alternative models for integrating people and organizations.
                                                            Beer *et al.* (1984, p. 35).

THE ARGUMENTS BEHIND THE US APPROACH TO HRM

The arguments that the Michigan, New York and Harvard models forwarded for greater integration between the content and process of HRM and organizational strategy (see Illustration 1.7) were summarized by Lengnick-Hall and Lengnick-Hall (1988).

Lengnick-Hall and Lengnick-Hall (1988), however, also note that despite such a rationale for an HRM approach, there are a number of common characteristics to the

Illustration 1.7 **The rationale for an HRM approach.**

- Provides a broader range of solutions to solve complex organizational problems.
- Ensures that human, financial and technological resources are given consideration when setting goals or assessing capabilities.
- Forces an explicit consideration of the individuals who comprise and implement the strategies.

- Encourages a two-way link between strategy formulation and the people implications and thereby avoids problems that might occur through:
  (a) subordinating strategic considerations to HR preferences, and
  (b) neglecting human resources as a vital source of organizational competence and competitive advantage.

Source: Lengnick-Hall and Lengnick-Hall (1988).

approaches to HRM emanating from the US at this time. In considering the need for strategic integration they emphasize the increasing importance of the implementation of strategy over its formulation, by either assuming that HRM considerations only occur once the strategic direction has been decided, or that whilst the two domains learn from each other, strategic issues typically remain unchanged throughout implementation. As people are more adaptable than organizational strategies, the match between people and strategy is generally seen as unidirectional – from strategies, to HRM practices that elicit employee role behaviours, to changes in resultant organization performance (Wright and McMahan, 1992). HRM is not then really portrayed as a measurable capacity from which strategic choices can be derived easily. The models also place great emphasis on the external dominance of organizations – by factors such as the organization or product life cycle – and managers are therefore seen at best as having only limited choices or influence over their strategic options. Such a summary invokes a number of business and cultural assumptions.

THE ASSIMILATION OF HRM CONCEPTS INTO THE UK

We noted earlier that the language and theoretical concept of HRM (if not the practice) moved into continental Europe via the UK. In the 1980s there was a vigorous (and academic) debate about the nature of the American models of HRM described above and their relevance to the UK situation. Guest (1990) argued that the concepts were as American as apple pie. The views of HRM discussed so far reflect the US value system which is not truly reflected in the UK – and is certainly not reflected in continental Europe. The case studies used to demonstrate the existence and benefits of HRM presented a favourable 'new frontier' ethos without mentioning the harsh realities of cowboys in the 'Wild West' or the 'Massacre of the Indians'. Emotive criticism, but a view widely held in the more collective and less individually competitive Europe.

There were a number of similarities in the 1980s between the UK and the US. The UK was also experiencing a period of extreme competitive threat. However, interest in HRM developed under a different set of influences than seen in the US (Beaumont, 1991a; and Hendry and Pettigrew, 1990). Hendry and Pettigrew (1990) provided an excellent summary of the historical antecedents of HRM in the UK. In the early 1980s Britain faced endemic problems associated with a short-term perspective in personnel and industrial relations matters, and a non-strategic approach to management (Gospel and Littler, 1983; Thurley and Wood, 1983; and Tyson, 1983). The US focus on quality was therefore reinforced (Goldsmith and Clutterbuck, 1984) and considerable attention was paid to Britain's very poor comparative record of training and development (Constable and McCormick, 1987; Handy, 1987; Martin and Nicholls, 1987).

There was also a fundamental schism in British thinking about HRM – which was seen as an American import of unproven relevance (see Figure 1.4). Academics from the 'industrial relations' tradition debated the concept of HRM in the context of political change in the UK, a shift in power from unions towards management, and the threat of a mere re-labelling (with little substantive change) of the role of the personnel function. In contrast, there was an 'excellence' tradition which focused on

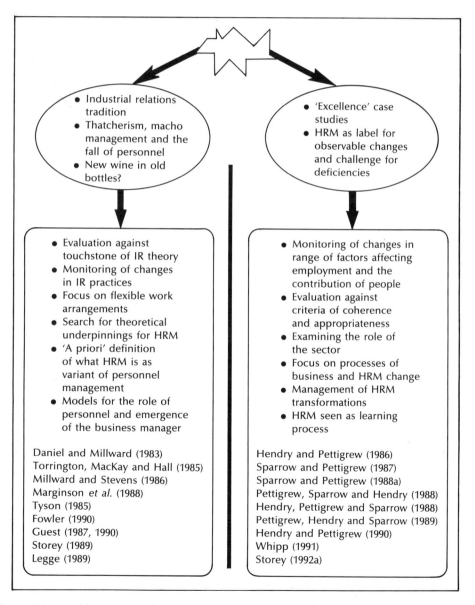

Figure 1.4 A schism in British thinking about HRM.

case studies of strategic change, using HRM as a label to explain the observable changes in people management or as a challenge for the observed deficiencies in management. This latter approach was guided by an increasing focus of attention on the role of leadership, the political nature of management of change processes, and the range of strategic triggers that were creating an unavoidable pressure for change in personnel management (Grinyer, Mayes and McKiernan, 1987; Pettigrew, 1985).

Arguing from the industrial relations tradition, Torrington (1988) felt that the concept of HRM reflected a decline in the importance of collectivism in Europe, the greater opportunities afforded to personnel management as organizations were faced with significant strategic changes, and the need to focus more on the management of the individual. However, the concept of HRM was directed solely at management needs and driven by their interests. As personnel management adapted to the new circumstances it would again rise in importance as a mediating discipline that balanced management demand with issues of supply and the employee interest. He made a distinction between managing human resources (the philosophy embedded in the US models) and ·managing resourceful humans (a philosophy that crossed the Atlantic more easily). Merit (1992) neatly outlined the philosophical unease felt by the British academics. Whilst on the one hand they appreciated the difficulties faced by organizations that had to '. . . behave like a gentleman while having its vitals savaged by competitive rottweilers' they believed that '. . . the resourceful individual resists being resourced. . . being treated like the supplied goods the firm buys in'.

Another line of debate was that HRM was in fact no more than a re-labelling of personnel directors' job titles and a re-packaging of an old product (traditional personnel management activities). HRM, this school of thought argued, is just good personnel management practice and there was no real change in the content of what was happening in organizations (Armstrong, 1987). Given the ferocity of the philosophical debate above it was never likely that this was really the case, and increasingly many of the originally sceptical academics and researchers began to accept that there was a fundamental shift taking place in the nature of personnel management in the UK − if not totally along the lines prescribed by the US models of HRM.

A CONTEXTUAL MODEL OF HRM

There are a series of implications for HRM raised by the earlier criticisms of the situational contingency and stakeholder approaches (Hendry and Pettigrew, 1990; Pettigrew, 1985):

- Strategy should not really be seen as a ready-formed output to which HRM can be easily moulded. It is quite possible that changes in structure, culture or other areas of HRM can precede strategic change and therefore shape the way that the organization thinks about strategy.
- Changes in strategy and HRM tend to occur over a long time frame. This makes the process of change of as much interest as the content of change. HRM systems should not be designed in an overly rational way when the processes that raise the need for them are anything but rational.

Building on the human resource policy framework provided by the Harvard group, researchers at the Centre for Corporate Strategy at Warwick Business School therefore developed an understanding of strategy-making in complex organizations and related it to the ability to transform HRM practices (see Figure 1.5). They conducted empirical investigations of over twenty leading UK organizations (including ICL, Wang UK,

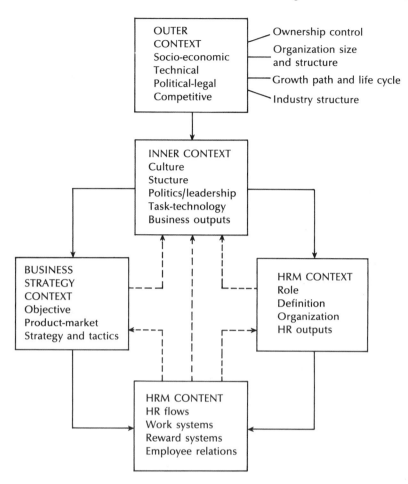

Figure 1.5 Strategic change and HRM. *Source*: Hendry and Pettigrew (1990), reprinted with permission of © *International Journal of Human Resource Management*, 1993.

Honeywell-Bull UK, Halfords, Asda Stores, Trustee Savings Bank, Barclaycard, Pilkingtons, GKN, and IMI) in order to examine the link between strategic change and transformations in the way in which people were managed (Hendry and Pettigrew, 1986, 1990; and Hendry, Pettigrew and Sparrow, 1989). This view of HRM argues that it is not appropriate to label HRM as a single form of activity. Organizations may follow a number of different pathways in order to achieve the same end result. Any analysis of HRM requires a sensitivity to management of change processes, as well as an understanding of the history (often over a 15 to 20 year time period) of how the organization has developed.

The model adopts the Harvard researcher's description of HRM content (see the four policy areas outlined previously), includes the need to consider the external business environment and strategy, and builds in a requirement to understand the culturally-unique role of the HRM function in terms of:

■ The definition of its responsibilities.
■ Its perceived competence across a range of activities.
■ The way the function is organized.

The researchers demonstrated that a number of leading UK organizations were indeed undergoing a transformation in the way they managed people. However, there were also a number of important political and process considerations to bear in mind. Business change was the 'necessary condition' and primary driving force behind new patterns of HRM. Business changes brought about by acquisitions, mergers, internationalization, new technology, new products or customer requirements for quality and service acted as 'triggers' for new HRM activities, as did large scale reductions in headcount to achieve productivity improvements, labour market shortages, high levels of employee turnover, the need to upgrade recruitment or a requirement to meet rising career aspirations. The patterns of HRM became both more obvious and aptly described as 'strategic' once organizations had:

- Recognized the increased complexity of their environment.
- Perceived the centrality of people skills.
- Re-labelled their HRM activities by looking back over initial changes and identifying common patterns.

The contours of the strategic changes in HRM experienced by UK organizations in the 1980s were generally unclear at the outset. For many organizations there was a strong element of 'learning by doing' (Hendry, Pettigrew and Sparrow, 1989). The role of corporate leadership and 'HRM champions' in bringing about successful change was also significant (see Illustration 1.8). Whipp (1991) later extended the analysis to

Illustration 1.8 **The role of HRM champions in creating change.**

- Engage and involve top management as a whole.
- Build concern and commitment for the new practices.
- Mobilize support within their organizations.
- Maintain initiative.

- Use their power and authority to link human resource systems to other business processes.
- Bring about changes in information systems, commercial policies and financial control mechanisms where they stood in the way of HRM change.

Illustration 1.9 **Managing change in HRM: the necessary conceptual and process skills.**

A perception and understanding of the connections between business and HRM needs.

Diagnostic skills to audit and take stock of existing skill bases in organizations in the light of anticipated business and technological changes.

Ability to identify and advise on the business opportunities afforded by the existing skill base of the organization, creating a business case for why human resources are a perceived source of competitive advantage.

Preparedness to initiate new styles and patterns of HRM activity in advance of business changes.

Sufficient cultural understanding to be able to preserve what is valuable from previous missions and values, meet new task requirements and be sensitive to individual satisfaction and career needs.

Development of the power base of the personnel management function by linking its activities to overarching information, commercial and financial policies.

Sensitivity to the changing internal situation during major periods of change.

Political skills to mobilize the internal and external forces of change, creating increasingly self-reinforcing patterns of HRM.

Recognition of the wide range of pressure points within HRM that can be brought to bear in a strategic change.

Ability to initiate timely adjustments in HRM agreements and practices.

Source: Hendry, Pettigrew and Sparrow (1989).

organizations such as Chrysler UK/Peugeot Talbot, Kleinwort Benson, Longman Publishing, Prudential Corporation and Jaguar Cars.

Responsibility for the new HRM activities was devolved increasingly to line management. However, in order for the changes to 'take root' in the organization and become 'stabilized' organizations had to have already established a number of activities such as: appraisal systems to identify development needs; human resource planning systems; integrated recruitment and training; graduate intakes to accelerate development in the organization; open and continuous career paths; and HRM budget relief mechanisms.

Of direct relevance to this book, the research revealed a range of conceptual and process skills that were necessary in order to be able to both understand the importance of HRM and manage the changes it implied (see Illustration 1.9). These characteristics helped managers change the patterns of HRM within their own organizations. They are applicable to understanding HRM in the European context, mainly because HRM is more decentralized in many European countries and most organizations are undergoing a major change in their business environment.

STRATEGIC INTENT: THE SCHULER MODEL AND PEOPLE-RELATED BUSINESS ISSUES

It is possible to see a number of enduring patterns that cut across the story of theoretical development we have laid out in this chapter. There are three connecting themes that provide important lessons for all organizations, no matter what their geographical location or cultural preference:

- The nature of strategic intent.
- Behavioural consistency.
- The devolvement of responsibility for HRM to the line.

Recently, the US models of HRM have been developed and modified as the authors have extended their analysis into human resource strategy and international management (Schuler, 1992a; Schuler, Dowling and de Cieri, 1993; Walker, 1992; Wright and McMahan, 1992). Schuler (1992a) has incorporated and answered many of the criticisms levelled at HRM theorists in his revised theory about the nature of strategic human resource management, which he defines as:

... all those activities affecting the behaviour of individuals in their efforts to formulate and implement the strategic needs of the business resulting from the organization's strategy.

At the organizational level, his model would seem to help explain strategic organizational behaviour in a way that does not specify the actual solution. It is less culture-bound than many of the early US theories. Schuler (1992a) points out that successful efforts at more strategic HRM begin with the identification of strategic business needs. These needs are typically expressed as mission statements. During times of turbulence organizations define and re-define these needs in order to reflect management plans for survival, growth, adaptability, productivity or profitability.

They are usually developed into more actionable strategic business objectives, expressed as objectives or vision statements.

The factors that act as triggers for change in HRM arise in organizations either as a result of their formal strategy, or from other pressures. These pressures may emerge from within the organization, or from the external environment and the focus of these pressures may be from top management or the grass roots of the organization. Both the external factors (such as the state of the economy or critical success factors in the industry) and internal factors (such as the culture of the organization, its home country, and the nature of the business systems) may be different from one country to another, but regardless of nationality, these are the factors that necessitate developments in HR activity.

Schuler and Walker (1990) argue that as business goes, so does human resource strategy. In the same way that planning in organizations in the turbulent 1990s has become more tentative, short term and issue focused, so has human resource strategy. It is no longer possible for organizations to determine with any certainty long-term courses of action through sophisticated planning systems (and comprehensive links to HR activities). The 1980s bore witness to more rapid and dramatic changes than at any other time in recent history. Heightened competitiveness, demographic shifts, more complex technologies and changing work patterns and employee needs all have significant implications for HRM. The past is no longer seen as any guide to the future. The rising importance of people to the very success of the business has developed hand in hand with human resource strategy becoming a more streamlined activity that involves a shorter term set of processes and activities. Specific HRM concerns are seen as 'people-related business problems' that have to be jointly shared and solved by the HRM function and line management.

... Strategies are being shaped as guides to help organizations recognize and address important changes and give them opportunities to manage the changes effectively.

Schuler and Walker (1990, p. 6).

At the same time in the UK, Whipp (1991) was pointing to the role of learning in HRM. He argued that the learning from such strategic change was becoming acute because the rate at which competitive bases were altering was both rapid and accelerating. For example, in the early 1980s quality was seen as a prime differentiator, yet by the late 1980s Japanese organizations simply assumed it was a basic qualification for membership of an industry. Under such circumstances the ability to learn faster than competitors is the only sustainable competitive advantage. This ability requires organizations to have both:

- The capacity to identify and understand the competitive forces at play in their industry.
- The competence to mobilize and manage the resources necessary for their chosen response through time.

The most important people-related business issues for US organizations in the 1990s are detailed in Illustration 1.10. As we shall see in Part Two, the issues faced by European organizations are essentially identical. They too represent a basic transformation of the bases of competition. Despite the current differences in perspective between Anglo-Saxon and European models of HRM discussed in the next chapter, many of the learning points raised from models discussed in this chapter will have relevance for European organizations as they experience radical transformations in their business.

BEHAVIOURAL CONSISTENCY

A second common feature of most HRM theories is the need to create behavioural consistency and coherence. The behavioural perspective taken by the US theories in particular stresses the role of employee behaviour as a mediator between strategy and

Illustration 1.10 **People-related business issues for the 1990s.**

Cost competitiveness
- Keeping down the costs of utilizing personnel.
- Downsizing through analysis versus headcount reduction.
- Eliminating work, not just people.

Delegation
- Increasing the capacity to react through streamlined approval processes.
- Increased employee involvement.
- New measurements under delegation.
- Risk compensation.

Organizational changes
- Considering spans of control.
- Centralization versus decentralization.
- Restructuring through internal growth, acquisitions and divestitures.

Enhanced competitiveness
- Working with an eye towards customer satisfaction.
- Quality of products and services.
- Productivity.
- Customer service excellence and other total quality efforts.
- Safety.
- Innovation.

Organizational effectiveness
- Building flexibility, efficiency, integration and differentiation.
- Interdependence and team effectiveness.
- Clarity and relationships of roles.

Employee competence
- Training in leadership development.
- Staffing.
- Appraisal.
- Development beyond traditional, institutional management education.

Managing workforce and cultural diversity
- Increasing the capability and motivation of the workforce.
- Focusing on work-life issues posed by an increasingly diverse workforce.

Global competitiveness
- Taking a global business perspective.
- Managing multinational careers.
- Looking for points of global corporate integration.

Source: Schuler and Walker (1990).

organizational performance. Different HRM practices serve to elicit and reinforce the appropriate behaviours in the organization. These 'role' behaviours cut across the specific skills, knowledge and abilities that are required to perform particular tasks. Instead, they are instrumental in the implementation of competitive strategies. Consistency needs to be achieved in two directions (Wright and McMahan, 1992):

- Vertically, so that HRM practices are linked with the strategic management processes of the organization, as outlined in the previous section.
- Horizontally, in order to emphasize the co-ordination and creation of congruence among various HRM practices.

... The need for consistency... arises because all strategic human resource management activities influence individual behaviour. If they are not consistent with each other... sending the same messages about what is expected and rewarded, the organization is likely to be an aggregation of people pulling in somewhat different directions. Hardly a situation for successful implementation of strategic business needs.   After Schuler (1992a).

To achieve these types of consistency the organization needs to plan its actions. The model builds on the behavioural perspective by differentiating five different levels or facets of a more strategic approach to HRM: philosophy, policies, programmes, practices and process. It categorizes the activities that should traditionally be covered by an organization's HRM and linked back to its strategic business needs. Figure 1.6 outlines how each of these aspects of HRM are typically represented and the contribution they make.

The philosophy, policies and programmes tend to express the culture, values and goals of the HR function. It is the specific practices that have the most powerful influence in motivating employees to exhibit the appropriate behaviour. For this reason we shall place most emphasis in this book on the various HRM practices, giving more limited attention to HRM programmes. The model serves to indicate the numerous ways in which HR activities interact with and actually influence individual and group behaviour.

Actually achieving linkages between the strategic business needs and HR activities tends to be the exception, even during non-turbulent times, and when linkages are formed they tend to be driven by efforts to formulate as well as implement a particular strategy. Nevertheless, by specifying the range of connections possible the model shows just how powerful an effect can be created in organizations if a successful link between strategic business needs and HR activities is achieved.

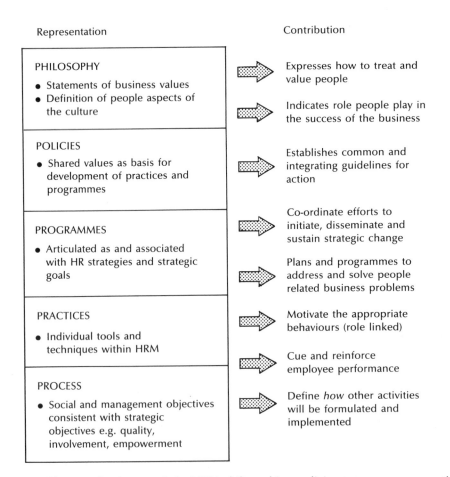

Representation   Contribution

PHILOSOPHY
● Statements of business values   Expresses how to treat and
● Definition of people aspects of   value people
  the culture
                                                 Indicates role people play in
                                                 the success of the business

POLICIES
● Shared values as basis for   Establishes common and
  development of practices and   integrating guidelines for
  programmes   action

PROGRAMMES
                                                 Co-ordinate efforts to
● Articulated as and associated   initiate, disseminate and
  with HR strategies and strategic   sustain strategic change
  goals
                                                 Plans and programmes to
                                                 address and solve people
                                                 related business problems

PRACTICES
                                                 Motivate the appropriate
● Individual tools and   behaviours (role linked)
  techniques within HRM
                                                 Cue and reinforce
                                                 employee performance

PROCESS
● Social and management objectives   Define *how* other activities
  consistent with strategic   will be formulated and
  objectives e.g. quality,   implemented
  involvement, empowerment

Figure 1.6 The contributions made by HRM philosophies, policies, programmes, practices and processes. *Source*: after Schuler (1992a).

DEVOLVEMENT OF HRM TO LINE MANAGERS

The third generic element of the Anglo-Saxon models of HRM is their emphasis on the devolution of responsibility for HRM to line management. We consider this issue in a purely European context in the next chapter. However, it is argued that the HRM department is being presented with the opportunity to make a significant contribution in top management teams (Schuler and Jackson, 1988; Schuler, 1990). An implication of the important people-related business issues outlined in Illustration 1.10 is that line managers are reaching out to take both control and ownership of the HR function, especially where HRM departments have remained focused on functional as opposed to business issues. HRM functions in US and UK organizations face the challenge of 're-positioning' themselves if they are to survive:

> ... The real role of HR is in the areas of human productivity, quality and performance, yet these are being done increasingly by line managers, especially in the highly innovative successful mid-sized companies. The HR staff just do the administrative stuff which could be downloaded someday to the accounting and legal departments.
>
> US Personnel Manager, in Schuler (1990, p. 49).

Several US organizations – such as IBM, General Electric and Digital Equipment – have already begun developing these new HRM roles. It is interesting to note that the new roles and key competencies for HRM departments identified by Schuler and Jackson (1988) and Schuler (1990) bear a striking similarity to those listed in Illustration 1.9 and identified in the UK by Hendry, Pettigrew and Sparrow (1989).

For comparative purposes, HRM is best considered as a range of policies which have strategic significance for the organization (Brewster and Tyson, 1991). HRM policies are typically used to facilitate integration, employee commitment, flexibility and the quality of work as well as meeting broader business goals such as changing organizational values, structure, productivity and delivery mechanisms. Therefore, in order to explain the various 'brands' of HRM across Europe in sufficient detail, any textbook must include '... subjects which have traditionally been the concern of personnel management and industrial relations... as well as... more innovative and strategic approaches to people management' (Brewster and Tyson, 1991, p. 1). As will become apparent throughout the various chapters in this book, there are very different institutional and legal environments, histories and levels of sophistication in HRM, and therefore unique approaches to practice, tools and techniques across Europe. All such differences have to be accommodated. Yet there are also clear areas of commonality and a reliance on use of core techniques. The need to consider HRM at a European level is also driven by the imperative of deep and widespread business change. The book must therefore also help to demonstrate the clear links between such business change and the process and content of HRM.

In the 1990s and beyond the imperative for HRM departments is to increase their value to the organization by significantly enhancing the quality of their products and services, expanding their skill base and providing a series of bottom-line improvements to their businesses. Walker (1992) points out that human resource strategies are much the same as any other management strategy in this regard. They involve a set of activities that help to define the nature of HRM issues, develop the ways in which the response will be implemented, and manage the HRM function accordingly. These activities have to be developed continually, but must include:

- Aligning employee expectations with the strategic realities for the organization.
- Designing the organization.

- Defining the staffing needs.
- Strategic resourcing policies.
- Developing capabilities.
- Developing effective managers.
- Enabling performance.
- Evaluating performance.
- Sharing successes.

THE RELEVANCE OF HRM FOR EUROPEAN MANAGERS

We consider these activities within the European context. However, this agenda still represents the picture as it is seen from 'over the water'. To many European managers the underlying assumptions in this chapter and the description of priorities for the way people are managed are not just separated from their own experience by the Atlantic Ocean or the Channel, but also by deeper differences in national culture. Are the learning points from this chapter of any relevance to European HRM or personnel functions? Yes, of course they are. Why? The topic of HRM developed from work in the US in the 1960s and 1970s and has since become a fashionable topic. The concept of HRM was initially taken up in related cultures to the US, such as the UK and Australia. Terminology then spread into Scandinavia and finally it is being taught on courses in Continental Europe. It is highly visible in the academic and business literature, with the number of scientific articles, books, new journals, conferences, and business school courses set up to discuss and analyse the concept increasing dramatically (Brewster and Bournois, 1991; Pieper, 1990). The same competitive pressures that engulfed the US in the 1980s are now threatening Europe. The same general principles of people being a key to competitive success apply to European brands of capitalism as well as Anglo-Saxon capitalism. However, there is a distinctly different starting point for European organizations, and the paths they will follow to achieve greater linkage between their HRM and strategic change will naturally reflect their own existing processes. In order to develop our understanding, in the next chapter we consider some of the specific differences between American and European concepts of HRM.

CONCLUSIONS

Whilst attention has been devoted to international comparisons of production systems and management strategies for many years, the comparison of people management systems has until recently been overlooked (Brewster, Hegewisch and Lockhart, 1991; Pieper, 1990). In most business situations the technical solution to specific issues has been understood, yet the associated implementation problems of how to change behaviour, improve performance, predict future performance and make the best use of available talents remain the most significant obstacles. Moreover, Bournois and Metcalfe (1991) argue that in widening an organization's strategic focus beyond the confines of their national boundaries, the human element becomes paramount. The HRM function has a vital contribution in helping organizations adapt to changes in the European business arena (these changes are detailed in Part Two). HRM practitioners can aid European organizations during the current period of uncertainty and rapid change by creating new flexible structures, patterns of strategic thought, and enhanced adaptability of employees (Smiley, 1989).

Nevertheless, we have argued that HRM, whilst an American management concept, also has a long history in many other countries, and especially in Europe. Most comparative books on HRM have avoided defining the common content of HRM practices across countries and have instead described the factors that account for distinctive differences in practice based on country-by-country reviews of national practice. The current process of 'Europeanization' provides us with an opportunity to re-evaluate HRM in a regional context and address some of the shortcomings of both academic criticism and simple managerial prescriptions forwarded in the area of HRM. In many ways European HRM has the same dimensions as descriptions of national practice. It differs only in the extent to which attention is given to strategic considerations and the problems of dealing with high levels of complexity and a requirement to co-ordinate activity across national barriers. In understanding the issues associated with HRM, however, we need to both understand the processes by which European organizations are becoming more international, and the way in which thinking about the nature of HRM has developed. In this chapter we have started to create this understanding by outlining the original Anglo-Saxon concepts of HRM. The most important learning points are summarized below.

LEARNING POINTS FROM CHAPTER ONE

1. There has been a shift in attention away from the traditional and specialist areas of personnel management towards broader strategic issues of changing the organizational culture, designing the structure and resourcing the organization with an appropriate set of competencies.

2. This focused concern on the need to link the processes through which human resource issues are considered and organizational strategy is planned. This integration of HRM into strategic planning systems was felt to differentiate the topic from personnel management. It also established a much wider territory for the topic.

3. American thinking about HRM evolved down two separate paths. The first concentrated on the need to achieve a match between the organizational strategy, and the resultant parameters for HRM, i.e. a contingency perspective. Depending on the nature of top management goals, the basis of competition in the industry, the life cycle of the business or the nature of the business sector, a series of either/or choices about HRM practices in terms of planning, staffing, appraising, compensating and training and developing were recommended, based on empirical investigation of US organizations.

4. A series of determinants of HRM practice were identified. In addition to those factors above which were felt to be strong determinants of practice, social and economic factors, cultural forces, the nature of labour markets, customer behaviour, the size of the organization, levels of profitability, the structure of the organization and jobs and institutional factors were also felt to play an important role.

5. A second view concentrated on the softer issues of strategic management, and stressed the human dimension of HRM. It highlighted the existence of multiple stakeholders in decisions about HRM, including shareholders, management, employee groups, governments, unions and the community. It also identified a much broader range of HRM policies that had to be considered, including the flow of people into, through and out of the organization, the nature of reward systems, employee influence, and the design of work systems.

6. The UK also faced considerable strategic pressure. For different reasons it was also attracted to the HRM philosophy. There was, however, a fierce debate about the benefits of HRM. One group saw HRM as an American import intended to break collectivism in the workplace, and to hasten a shift of power from unions to employers without making any real change in the nature of responsibilities given to personnel managers. Another group used HRM as a label to explain the changes taking place in UK organizations. Despite the debates, considerable development in the tools of personnel practice occurred in this period.

7. A third, British, view emerged which focused on the importance of understanding the business context within which HRM was developed. The importance of political influences, the level of leadership within the organization, the history of personnel management and the perceived credibility of functions were all highlighted through extensive case studies. The model demonstrated how organizations could follow very different paths in terms of HRM practice but still achieve the same end strategic result.

8. A fourth model concentrates on the importance of linking strategic intent in organizations to the underlying people-related business issues, the ways in which organizations can create some consistency in the behaviours of employees in order to implement strategic change consistently and rapidly, and the necessary devolvement of responsibility for these issues to line managers.

9. Most of these people-related issues, such as cost competitiveness, changes in structure, the need to enhance competitiveness, the need to develop employee competence, and manage workforce diversity, apply to European organizations. So too do the lessons about creating consistency in behaviour and line management responsibility.

10. Whilst clearly relevant to the European context, in the same way that American concepts of HRM were adapted to the British situation, it is essential to adapt the current Anglo-Saxon models of HRM to the European situation. This is best done by considering both the determinants and the content of European HRM practice in the context of the process of business integration and the process of internationalization.

CHAPTER TWO

The European Perspective on HRM

... The international character of human resource management can be said to rest on three things:

(1) the increasing internationalization of business which brings organizations into contact with different national cultures and promotes the spread of management practices across national boundaries;

(2) underlying economic and technological trends, arising in part from the activity of multinational firms but mediated also by international institutions, which may produce similar patterns of adjustment in the organization and management of employment at the national, sectoral and firm level; and

(3) the processes whereby businesses become progressively international.

... Present trends towards increasing globalization and the threatened dominance of many industries by global oligopolies bring into even sharper relief the tension between national systems and cultures and corporate pressures for convergence.

Hendry (1991, p. 415).

INTRODUCTION

In the previous chapter we defined the concept of Human Resource Management (HRM) and outlined the principal features of four popular models – all American or British in origin – that have been used to both define the 'territory' of the subject and its importance to the implementation (and reformulation) of strategic change. We hinted throughout Chapter One that whilst the topic is of clear relevance to European managers, there is a need to place the Anglo-Saxon perspective into a European context. In this chapter therefore we focus on distinguishing European approaches to HRM from those taken in the US and assess the extent to which, given such composite differences between Europe and the US, there is also a common European approach to HRM.

This immediately requires us to specify what we mean by Europe. Despite considerable discussion of Anglo-Saxon versus continental European models of business in the business literature, it would be foolish to exclude the UK from any discussion of European HRM. Although there are many similarities between the UK and the US, and, in relation to Europe, the UK really is a mid-Atlantic country, the

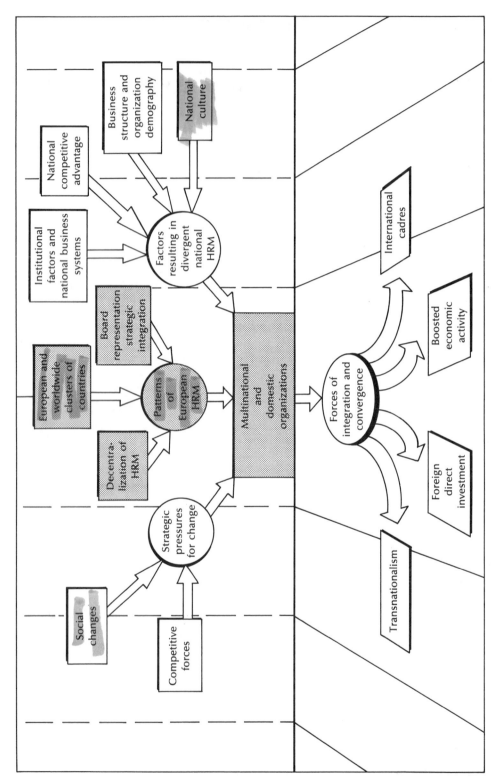

Figure 2.1 Areas of context covered in Chapter Two.

nature of HRM in the UK is significantly different from that of the US. As a member of the European Union (EU) and a significant target of foreign direct investment, practices in the UK are undergoing as much change as are those in continental Europe. There is therefore a core focus on the countries of France, Germany and the UK throughout many chapters in the book, reflecting both the relative volume of national publications of HRM practitioners from these countries and the dominant size of their economies in the EU. However, data are also provided on national practice throughout all the other EU countries, especially where significant differences exist. Given the imminent inclusion of Scandinavian countries in the EU, and the strong HRM traditions in these countries, we have also included examples from, and reference to, Nordic perspectives. From the outset, we acknowledge that in talking about European HRM, we are talking about a continent of diversity. Understanding the patterns of convergence and divergence in HRM practice across this diverse continent is one of the most important challenges that European managers face. Figure 2.1 places in context the analysis of European patterns of HRM that forms the basis of this chapter.

EUROPEAN INTEREST IN HRM: CRITICISM OF US MODELS

Our first core task is to distinguish European approaches (in the composite) to HRM from those taken in the US and outlined in the previous chapter. In the same way that mass production, marketing and corporate strategy were adopted as standard business school teaching topics based broadly on the American experience, there is a temptation to assume that having 'invented' management, all other specialisms (including HRM) can be extrapolated to other countries, analysed and made the subject of generalization (Lawrence, 1992). Although it is widely acknowledged that much of the business and HRM literature within Europe is rooted in US thinking and HRM is largely seen as an American invention, sophisticated application of personnel management and HRM concepts has a long and often ignored history in European countries (Pieper, 1990). Paternalistic personnel management in the early period of European industrialization, comprehensive welfare policies, and integration of personnel management as a teaching topic in general business administration make it clear that HRM should not be considered as a purely American invention.

> ... European-style class consciousness, a serious socialist movement ... penetration of Marxist ideology in 'old Europe' ... have variously served to structure both the perception and reality of superior-subordinate and management-worker relations in industry.
>
> Lawrence (1992, p. 12).

As attention has shifted to developments in Europe, the American models of HRM outlined in the previous chapter have come under increasing criticism (Brewster, 1993; Guest, 1990). Lawrence (1992) argues then that HRM is essentially an Anglo-Saxon construct that has been 'grafted on' – rather than 'taken root' – in Continental Europe. However, classic HRM functions such as recruitment, socialization, training and development are determined by different conceptions of management in Europe, and underpinned by a related set of values. Historically, HRM has not had the same élan in Europe and in part it has been socially and culturally bypassed. When compared with American (or indeed British) concepts of HRM, a more European model needs then to take account of a number of factors (see Illustration 2.1).

Illustration 2.1 **In relation to American concepts of HRM, continental European concepts suggest . . . .**

1. More restricted employer autonomy:
   - hiring and firing decisions,
   - lower geographic and professional employee mobility,
   - stronger link between type of education and career progression.

2. Less stress on market processes:
   - human social life not viewed totally as an economic transaction,
   - lower emphasis on the contractual sale of labour by an employee.

3. Less emphasis on the individual, more emphasis on the group:
   - strong sociological rather than psychological traditions,
   - less importance on interactions between individuals,
   - lower importance given to controlling individuals through competition.

4. More emphasis on workers rather than managers:
   - raison d'être for managers derived from people,
   - less emphasis on decisive managerial heroes,
   - management effectiveness dependent on workers.

5. Increased role of 'social partners' in the employment relationship:
   - role of trade unions' influence in the setting of HRM policy,
   - collective bargaining at the state and regional level,
   - direct co-determination at the company level.

6. Higher level of government intervention or support in many areas of HRM:
   - state role in education through public school and university systems,
   - formal certification systems influencing personnel selection and careers,
   - comprehensive welfare policies.

Sources: after Brewster and Hegewisch (1993); Hofstede (1993); Guest (1990); Pieper (1990).

EUROPEAN MODELS OF HRM: A RICH ARRAY OF SITUATIONAL INFLUENCES

A major aspect of the context highlighted by the Warwick Model of HRM is the historical role of the HRM function, its perceived goals and mission, focus of activity, and levels of competence and credibility (Hendry, Pettigrew and Sparrow, 1989). A number of factors differentiate European business systems from the US model, and indeed also differ between European countries (these are developed in Chapter Three), and there are also a number of competing arguments for and against the notion of European management (summarized in Chapter Six). These factors are reflected in different national models of HRM across Europe, such that within an organization, management agendas get reinterpreted at the local national management level (see Illustration 2.2).

It is extremely important to note that different political, economic, social and cultural considerations lead to a reinterpretation of management agendas at a local level. Different national models of HRM practice–and conceptual frames to reinterpret strategic organization issues – are still very much in evidence. Every European country has a different historical and legal inheritance and so European HRM must remain an ambiguous concept. Bournois (1991a, 1991b) also makes an essential distinction between HRM in Europe and European HRM. He argues, however, that:

... a detailed knowledge of the specific practices of each country as well as the common independent variables greatly limits the risk of lapsing into incoherence when building up an international system of human resource management. It is a preliminary stage which is all the

Illustration 2.2 **Reinterpretation of management agendas at the local level.**

In carrying out the pilot studies for a survey on European HRM, the researchers noted that identical questions about specific HRM tools or issues were interpreted by respondents within their national cultural and legal context. For example, the issue of flexible working in Britain and Germany has been linked to demographic change and the need to reintegrate women into the labour market, whereas in France flexible working is seen as a response to general changes in lifestyle and nothing to do with female labour force participation. Similarly, the issue of health and safety is seen in Britain as a narrow manufacturing-related issue but in Sweden it is seen with general reference to the working environment and is placed at the forefront of the personnel management role over the next ten years.

Source: Brewster, Hegewisch and Lockhart (1991).

more essential since the international development of the firm is based on ... global and local requirements [that] have to be integrated rather than simply a global form of management [in which] ... the values and the culture of the firm itself are emphasized.

Bournois and Roussillon (1992).

Before we move towards an understanding of European HRM, we must first fully consider the national patterns of HRM in Europe. In the remainder of this chapter we identify some of the most important features that currently distinguish European national practice.

HISTORICAL COMPETENCE, ROLE AND DEVELOPMENT OF THE HRM FUNCTION IN EUROPEAN ORGANIZATIONS

In Chapter One we discussed the increasing devolvement of HRM functions in US and (supposedly) UK organizations and pointed to the critical importance of the historical competence, role and credibility of the HRM function for understanding the likely impact of changes in HRM. The historical role and development of HRM professionals varies considerably across European countries (see Illustration 2.3). For example, in Italy or Holland many HRM professionals have a financial background (Filella, 1992; Hoogendoorn, 1992) reinforcing a focus of attention on cost control and labour savings, whilst in Germany legal backgrounds are evident (Arkin, 1992a) creating a focus on interpreting rules and regulations.

There are not only differences in the professional allegiances and traditional roles of personnel departments. Career paths for personnel specialists also vary widely across Europe (Brewster and Hegewisch, 1993). In European countries HRM specialists rarely reach the very highest positions in employing organizations (Coulson-Thomas, 1990; Coulson-Thomas and Wakeham, 1991). HR specialists leading organizations appear to be most common in Scandinavia (Brewster, 1993). The greatest level of HRM experience (specialists with more than five years personnel experience) is found in Germany, Ireland, France, the Netherlands and the UK. In countries like Denmark and Ireland, top personnel specialists are most likely to come from non-personnel functions in the organization (reflecting their high levels of decentralization) whilst in most countries they have come from other organizations, i.e. personnel managers are promoted by changing their employer. Only in Portugal do more than three out of ten personnel specialists come from within an organization's own ranks.

There are differences in the extent to which personnel activities are contracted out.

Illustration 2.3 **A legalistic framework for German HRM functions.**

The German personnel function is characterized as more reactive, legalistic, and concerned with training, and less autonomous and professional than many other European HRM functions. The more reactive role of personnel managers in Germany is due in part to their payment systems. In contrast to UK and US personnel managers, most German personnel managers are not involved in pay negotiations although they are involved in the implementation and execution of pay policies. The co-determination system is another factor that reinforces the reactive role by creating a climate of restraint, shared responsibility, and higher levels of trust compared, for example, to the more adversarial industrial relations systems in the UK.

The German situation is more legalistic than elsewhere in Europe. More activities are encoded by legislation (such as rights and duties of trades unions, co-determination, and annual wages contracts). There is also a system of labour courts. Rules, regulations and procedures are also treated more legalistically. The institution of the Works Council structures the deployment of time and professional knowledge of the German personnel manager. The traditional qualification for personnel managers is the 'Dr Jura' – a German equivalent of an LLB plus a PhD in law. The Anglo-Saxon business culture of getting things done through a 'nudge and a wink' or by 'fudging' is simply not part of a German personnel manager's mindset.

Source: Lawrence (1991, 1993a).

In Holland and Belgium this is particularly high and has led to criticisms that inhouse personnel functions have become too specialized to meet the needs of line managers (Hoogendoorn, 1992; Sels, 1992). The actual date from which significant personnel management activities historically became prevalent in a country also influences the current shape and focus of activity.

The extent to which HRM activities have been devolved to line managers also varies widely, and this has shaped different roles for personnel management functions. Brewster and Hegewisch (1993) found that most European organizations with more than 200 employees determine HRM policies centrally, but share responsibility for most issues between the HRM function and the line. From 1990 to 1992 there was a slight trend in the direction of devolved responsibility to the line (see Figure 2.2). Whilst the UK tends to be at the more decentralized end of the personnel management spectrum (Brewster and Hegewisch, 1993) the most decentralized country by far is Denmark (Arkin, 1992b). It gives the greatest line responsibility on all issues. Despite considerable debate about and claims for decentralization in the UK, senior personnel specialists consistently report that primary responsibility is least likely to be given or shared with line managers on a range of issues.

In fact, about half the European countries covered in the Price Waterhouse/ Cranfield Project (PWCP) studies (summarized in Table 2.1 and described later in this chapter) have been increasing line management responsibility faster than in the UK. In France the HRM function has increasingly had an advisory role (Besse, 1992), whilst in Spain integration of HRM activities into line management is low despite a high level of board-level HR Directors (Filella, 1992). This is also the case in Italy.

The strategic role of the HRM function can (to some extent) be gauged by three proxy measures (Brewster, 1993):

- An organizational structure which provides for the head of the HRM function to be present at the key policy-making forum.
- Perceived involvement in developing corporate strategy.
- The existence of a written personnel/HRM strategy.

Data from the PWCP study for 1991–92 indicate that the highest level of board-level

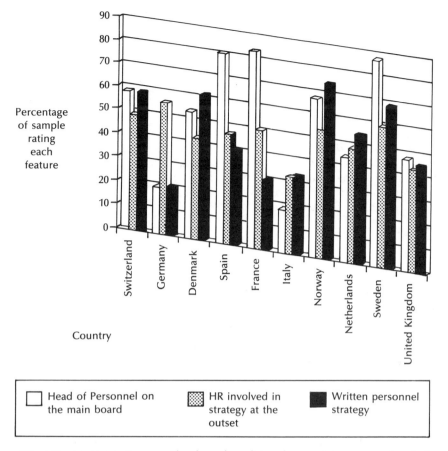

Figure 2.2 HR representation on the board and involvement in corporate strategy in European HRM functions. *Sources*: Brewster and Hegewisch (1993) and Brewster (1993), reprinted with permission, © C. Brewster, 'European human resource management: reflection of, or challenge to, the American concept?', in P. Kirkbridge (ed.), *Human Resource Management in the New Europe of the 1990s*, Routledge, 1993.

representation is in France (eight out of ten organizations consistently report that they have an HR director or equivalent at board level) and Spain (seven out of ten organiz-ations). In most other countries, including the UK, about half of the organizations have board-level HR directors (Brewster, 1993; Brewster and Hegewisch, 1993; Brewster and Larsen, 1993). We consider the main mechanisms of corporate governance in Chapter Eight.

In Germany the figure is only two or three out of ten. However, the German system of co-determination clearly influences the strategic role of the HRM function (see Illustration 2.4) and the lower figure reflects both the more administrative role of personnel functions as well as the linkage between personnel issues and corporate thinking through other mechanisms such as top-level employee representation. There are linguistic and cultural assumptions in management theories. These are reflected in the German academic literature on HRM, and the way personnel management is distinguished from HRM:

... The closest German equivalent to the linguistic distinction between personnel management and HRM is between 'Personalwesen' or 'Personalverwaltung' (-administration) and

Illustration 2.4   **Achieving strategic influence: co-determination versus HR directors on the board.**

The co-determination system muddies the issue of strategic influence of personnel directors in Germany. The two-tier board system results in a supervisory board (*Aufsichtsrat*) consisting of shareholders' representatives and around 33–50 per cent of employee representatives and an executive committee (*Vorstand*) to set policy and run the company, consisting of full time senior managers. The *Aufsichtsrat* has power of veto and appoints members of the *Vorstand*. In most large public companies there has to be a labour director (*Arbeitsdirektor*) on the *Vorstand*. In the iron, steel and coal industries the *Arbeitsdirektor* is seen as a genuine representative of employee interests as s/he has to be chosen by the majority of the employee representatives on the *Aufsichtsrat*. The 1976 co-determination law officially strengthened the personnel function and created career personnel managers with special responsibility at board level for industrial relations and personnel matters.

Source: Lawrence (1991).

'Personalmanagement'; this differentiation is much weaker and concentrates more on the shift from administration to management, rather than emphasizing a different valuation of employees.

Brewster (1993).

Brewster and Hegewisch's (1993) data show greater uniformity across European HRM functions on the perceived involvement of the HRM department in corporate strategy from the outset. Around half of the senior personnel executives felt they were involved in France, Spain, West Germany and the UK. The lowest strategic role is found in Italy, with less than two out of ten organizations having board-level HR directors. Indeed, the whole topic of HRM tends to lack theoretical sophistication in Italy, in that there is no specific HRM discipline taught in business schools. Rather, the topic is subsumed under several economic disciplines (Hendry, 1991). It has been argued that this opens up Italian management education on the topic to US influences.

Brewster and Larsen (1993) have recently argued that HRM practices in the ten European countries involved in their study can be categorized quite distinctly by:

■ The degree of integration of HRM into business strategy.
■ The degree of devolvement, i.e. the degree to which HRM practice involves and gives responsibility to line managers rather than personnel specialists.

These two theoretical elements of HRM were discussed in detail in Chapter One. To some extent the elements of integration and devolvement seem inconsistent and paradoxical. Integration may be seen to be associated with centralization and senior management responsibility whilst devolvement is associated with decentralization and the passing of responsibility to junior levels in the organization. Brewster and Larsen (1993) explain the paradox by pointing out that integration is an issue of policy which necessitates close involvement of HRM specialists with senior line management.

On the basis of such policy-level involvement it is possible (and desirable) to allow greater devolvement and decentralization of the actual HRM practices so that they may be more easily understood and implemented by line managers. There are four relative positions of HRM as a general managerial activity (see Illustration 2.5). Figure 2.3 shows the relative integration and devolvement rankings for the ten European countries and classifies them on the Integration/Devolvement matrix. It should be made quite clear that this classification represents the position for the typical organization in each country, but by no means all organizations. In each country there will be

Illustration 2.5 **Four positions of HRM as a general management activity.**

Mechanics (low integration and low devolvement)
- Specialist, but limited skills and interests of HRM practitioners.
- Professional personnel manager with 'higher' imperatives than the organization.
- Belief that specialist knowledge is beyond the scope of untrained people.
- Focus on the mechanical requirements of the function.
- Increasing isolation from strategic interests of the organization.

The wild west (low integration and high devolvement)
- Individual manager free to develop his/her own employee relationship.
- Increased power to hire and fire, reward and develop employees.
- Potential for incoherence, inconsistency and strong employee reactions.

Guarded strategists (high integration but low devolvement)
- Specialists powerful figures in the organization.
- Close liaison with senior managers to develop strategy.
- Large and influential departments with centralized control of policies.
- Better line managers frustrated with lack of control, poor managers welcome lack of responsibility.

Pivotal (high integration and high devolvement)
- Senior personnel managers act as catalysts, facilitators and co-ordinators.
- Small, but powerful departments.
- Monitoring of and internal consulting on HRM developments.
- Responsibility and authority devolved to the line.
- Problems with resourcing high-calibre business-orientated HRM managers.

Source: Brewster and Larsen (1993).

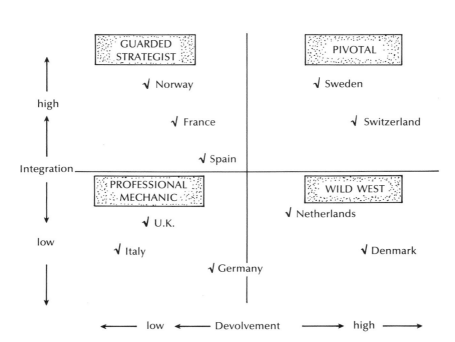

Figure 2.3 The integration/devolvement matrix: models of HRM in ten European countries. *Source*: Brewster and Larsen (1993), reprinted with permission of © *International Journal of Human Resource Management*, 1993.

organizations that fall into each category. Nevertheless, country tendencies were clear. When aggregated at the national level: Sweden and Denmark have 'Pivotal' HRM functions; Denmark and the Netherlands fall into the 'Wild West'; Italy, the UK and Germany have 'Professional Mechanic' HRM functions; whilst Norway, France and Spain have HRM functions that may be classified as 'Guarded Strategists'.

Brewster and Larsen (1993) conclude that American (or Anglo-Saxon) models of HRM do not fit comfortably with the reality of HRM in Europe and therefore consider their findings in relation to other research on national culture. It is clear then that the status and strength accrued by line managers versus personnel managers, and the dynamics of the trade off, are not consistent across Europe. In contrast to the Anglo-Saxon theories of HRM which focus on the importance of the direct integration of

---

Illustration 2.6 **Evolution in the role and capabilities of Swedish personnel management.**

Personnel management in Sweden had its roots in the Social Workers within Industry and Business (SAIA) movement, founded by the Liberal MP Kerstin Hosselgren in 1921. The Sveriges Personal-administrative Forening (SPF) grew out of this body. The role of the SAIA was to campaign for better working conditions and social welfare on health and safety grounds. Operational personnel issues were handled by line managers and supervisors.

The 'individual' period followed on from post-war expansion. The role of personnel changed rapidly as the Swedish economy entered sustained growth of 3 per cent a year in GNP for 25 years. A free Nordic labour market was established to cope with labour shortages. The 'Swedish model' of industrial relations was based on co-operation and negotiation at national and company level, a nationwide training system, and state role in economic and labour market planning. Personnel departments were set up in most organizations, drawing on the disciplines of psychology, social work, union officials and retired army officers. They became specialists in procedures, pay and benefits, negotiation and planning for recruitment and training.

In the late 1970s and 1980s Swedish personnel management entered a period of 'structured change'. A rise in industrial disputes in the early 1970s triggered a trend towards legislation for industrial relations policies and employee protection. This coincided with structural unemployment under pressures from international competition. Dismissals, retirements and retraining became new activities. A new academic programme for personnel managers call P-linjen integrated behavioural science, business studies and labour law. HRM gained greater acceptability as a profession, with SPF membership increasing from 3,000 to 10,000 from 1980–1990.

In the 1990s Swedish personnel is in 'the period of fate' and a struggle for survival of a professional personnel function. Internal recession and a decline in domestic productivity sharpened economic pressures. The labour market shifted from manufacturing to services and service strategies focused on customer relations, quality, training, corporate culture, motivation and work organization. Decentralization and a market orientation meant another new role for personnel managers. A study by the Uppsala Institute of Human Resources Management identified the shift across three roles from 1990–92 in 60 Swedish organizations:

- Strategic (20 per cent increasing to 32.5 per cent).
- Internal standardized service (48 per cent decreasing to 30 per cent).
- Non-standardized internal consultancy (32 per cent increasing to 37 per cent).

There was also a newly discovered connection between economics and HRM, with the use of cost/benefit models and HRM variables in balance sheets. The debate now is whether simple economic contributions about costs and benefits will be enough to justify the cost of the large personnel management infrastructure. Conversely, will the new economic situation force Swedish personnel managers to throw away their culture and focus on human values and social welfare merely for short-term accountancy? Unclear values may make for unclear HRM, and although the map for the new role for personnel managers seems clear, the direction of travel is not.

Source: Söderström (1993). Reprinted with permission. © M. Söderström.

HRM into corporate strategy, integration and decentralization of responsibility for HRM at the corporate level in Germany (still a highly successful world economy) is a less significant issue because personnel issues are integrated in the collective consciousness of the organization and also in legislation.

It should be pointed out that the dynamics of the trade-off in roles are not always consistent even within the Integration/Devolvement Matrix developed by Brewster and Larsen (1993). The United Kingdom and Germany are both classified as having 'Professional Mechanic' HRM functions. However, in the UK although there is generally a lower level of devolvement than in Germany, line managers do have to handle minor conflicts on a day to day basis and also have influence over pay policy and planning. The shift of control over such activities from personnel to the line has significant implications for HR strategies. In Germany, line manager roles are quite different because conflicts are rooted in the Works Council process. However, the lack of involvement of personnel managers in pay bargaining also diminishes their strategic profile to one of execution and implementation only (Hutton and Lawrence, 1979).

Changes in the strategic profile of HRM functions in Europe are in many cases so powerful that it becomes of little importance where the existing national functions stand on the Integration/Devolvement matrix. This is clear from Illustration 2.6 which describes the evolution in the role of Swedish personnel management, and the extent to which its current role – characterized by Brewster and Larsen (1993) as 'pivotal' – is under threat from the strategic pressures we outline in more detail in Chapter Four.

LATIN, CENTRAL EUROPEAN AND NORDIC MODELS OF HRM?

The analysis of the different models of HRM across Europe in the previous section helps to provide an understanding of the different practices and priorities that exist. However, we argue in Chapters Four and Five that we are living in a rapidly changing world. Are we already witnessing a process of convergence or divergence between currently different models of European HRM? What is the empirical evidence on comparative HRM practices?

Until recently, there has been little empirical evidence and even now few quantitative data exist to allow a systematic analysis of international and European trends in HRM (Brewster, Hegewisch and Lockhart, 1991). Comparative labour market statistics tend to be too broad in their approach and case studies tend to concentrate on larger, more 'advanced' organizations from which it would be dangerous to generalize. In the last sections of this chapter we consider the overview findings from two major comparative studies of HRM:

- The Price Waterhouse/Cranfield Project (PWCP) on European HRM (e.g. Brewster, 1993).
- The IBM/Towers Perrin worldwide study of HRM practices for achieving competitive advantage (IBM/ Towers Perrin, 1992).

We compare the main areas of investigation in these studies in Table 2.1. The areas of HRM listed have been categorized according to the Harvard Model of HRM outlined in Chapter One. It can be seen that between the two studies – very different in their nature and intent – we now have some extremely useful empirical points of comparison.

Throughout this chapter we have referred to the Price Waterhouse/Cranfield Project (PWCP) on European Trends. This has been the most comprehensive pan-European survey of HRM practices whose results are in the public domain. Survey data relevant

Table 2.1 **Major areas of HRM under comparative empirical investigation.**

	PWCP project	IBM/Towers Perrin
Comparative coverage		
European countries	UK, France, Germany, Italy, Spain, Switzerland, Denmark, Norway, Netherlands, Sweden	UK, France, Germany, Italy
Other countries		USA, Canada, Australia, Brazil, Mexico, Argentina, Japan, Korea.
Years of survey	1990, 1991, 1992	1991
Human resources flows		
Recruitment policies	√	√
Recruitment methods	√	
Training expenditure	√	
Training volume	√	
Requirement for continuous training		√
Emphasis on management development		√
Identification of high potential		√
Multiple and parallel career paths		√
Outplacement, retirement		√
Rewards management		
Pay determination systems	√	
Merit or performance related pay	√	√
Other benefits: profit sharing	√	√
Reward for customer service, quality		√
Reward for innovation/creativity		√
Reward for enhanced knowledge		√
Pay systems promoting sharing		√
Employee relations		
Collective bargaining trends	√	
Equal opportunities policies	√	
Communication of business plans		√
Facilitation of employee involvement		√
Provide full employment/lifetime job		√
Corporate responsibility		√
Work systems		
Part time work	√	
Temporary/casual work	√	
Fixed term contracts	√	
Impact of changes in working hours	√	√
Requirement for employee flexibility		√
Requirement for autonomy, self monitoring		√
Flexible cross functional teams		√
Increasing spans control/fewer levels		√
Specialized/directed workforce		√
Cultural shifts		
Corporate culture based on equality		√
Peer/subordinate customers service		√
Context of HRM function role		
Devolvement of HRM and policy decisions	√	
Integration of function with strategy	√	
Responsibility for implementation	√	

to specific chapters will be introduced in the appropriate sections. We have already discussed the survey in relation to the Integration/Devolvement model developed by Brewster and Larsen (1993). However, it is useful at this stage to consider some other findings from this stream of research (see Illustration 2.7 for an outline of the methodology).

The first overall pattern in HRM we shall discuss is the existence of different emphases between the Nordic, Central European and Latin countries. Filella (1991) analysed the data from Brewster, Hegewisch and Lockhart's (1991) PWCP study in an attempt to delineate three different patterns of HRM within the European Union. Hofstede's (1980) data on world cultures in organizations (see the next chapter) suggested the presence of a Latin, Anglo-Saxon and North European culture. Similarly, the World Competitiveness Report (World Economic Forum, 1990) identified a set of Latin Mediterranean nations as a distinctly different group to other parts of Europe. Were there discernible cultural patterns of HRM activity and issues across Europe within the PWCP data?

Filella (1991) created a Latin grouping of countries (geographically comprising all those European regions surrounding the western Mediterranean basin, i.e. Portugal, Spain, southern France, Corsica and Sardinia, Italy). The inclusion of France in any Latin grouping is always problematic because of the proximity of its northern regions to the main EU industrial belt. He combined the data from the PWCP study for Italy, Spain and France to create descriptive statistics for a Latin grouping. The central European cluster included the UK, the Netherlands, Germany (what was the FRG) and Switzerland. The Nordic cluster included Denmark, Norway and Sweden. Rigorous statistical comparisons were not carried out, but the analysis did provide some powerful impressions of the three geographical groups. Some of the most telling 'impressions' to consider as a prelude to Chapters Seven to Fifteen are shown in Table 2.2.

Within the Latin countries it was important to note that the data for France (and Spain) followed a different path from those of Italy (Filella, 1991). This separation of France from both Latin (and Central European) attitudes on HRM is also picked up by the IBM/Towers Perrin (1992) survey discussed in the next sections of this chapter. France has a unique position with regard to training expenditure, with legislation prescribing that organizations devote at least 1.2 per cent of their salary and wage budget on training. It appears that legislation does make a difference as in fact 75 per cent of French organizations spent over 2 per cent of the salary and wage budget on training

Illustration 2.7 **The Price Waterhouse/Cranfield study of European HRM.**

This project was set up to monitor the impact over time of the Single European Market (SEM) on HRM and to ascertain the degree to which a strategic (i.e. planned, coherent and interactive) approach was being adopted. It has involved three annual surveys to date. In the first year data were gathered for France, Germany, the UK, Sweden and Spain. In the second year Denmark, Italy, the Netherlands, Norway and Switzerland were added to the study. The project uses a postal questionnaire to collect hard facts from senior personnel managers in relation to the areas shown in Table 2.3. To date 16,000 questionnaires have provided data on the views of senior personnel specialists in all sectors of fourteen European countries over three years (1990, 1991 and 1992). The samples were broadly representative of employment size, country of origin and sectoral distribution in the economy. Response rates however varied from 42 per cent in Sweden down to 10 per cent in Italy. Most response rates were around 14–16 per cent.

Source: Brewster and Hegewisch (1993).

Table 2.2 **Key differences in HRM practice across three clusters of European countries: Latin, Central and Nordic.**

Area of HRM practice	Latin	Central	Nordic
HR policy decisions at HQ			
Expansion or reduction	64	45	41
Pay and benefits	79	68	66
Training and development	60	46	37
HR department responsible for implementation of ...			
Recruitment/selection	12	7	3
Health and safety	26	19	15
Industrial relations	40	31	29
Management recruitment methods			
Sourced from own employees	60	63	54
By word of mouth	37	20	21
From publicity	52	78	83
Collective bargaining for payment agreements			
At management level	37	24	51
At technical/professional level	41	28	60
Training (excluding France)			
More than 2 per cent of salaries/wages spent on training	24	38	38
More than five days management training/year/manager	57	38	48
More than five days clerical/manual training/year/employee	31	14	12

Source: reprinted from J. Filella, 'Is there a Latin model in the management of human resources?', *Personnel Review*, **20(6)**, 14–23, © 1991, with kind permission of MCB University Press Ltd.

– far outstripping the other countries in the analysis. Eighty-three per cent of French organizations had HR directors on the board compared to only 18 per cent in Italy. We discussed the charge that the title 'Human resource director' may just represent 'old wine in new bottles' in Chapter One. Whilst most countries preferred the traditional name of Personnel Department (the use of the title Human Resource Department varied from 0 per cent in Norway to 15 per cent in the UK), in France 49 per cent of organizations reported a preference for the title 'Human Resources' in preference to 'Personnel'.

In all countries recruitment from amongst their own employees was used quite consistently, although countries in central and northern Europe rely more heavily on the use of newspapers and advertising. Filella (1991) concluded from the impressionistic analysis shown in Table 2.2 that Latin countries were in the process of revising their views and unconscious assumptions on how organizations could usefully match individual talents and aspirations with business success. Central European and Scandinavian countries in particular have a higher sensitivity to the human issues within organizations. However, it was not possible to conclude whether such differences represented different models of managing steeped in cultural constraints (as

Illustration 2.8 **PWCP study conclusions about European HRM models.**

1. The HRM issues that are being dealt with in Europe are remarkably similar. However, whilst the issues have much in common there are clear national differences in the way they are handled.

2. The way in which personnel departments are organized and operate varies widely across Europe, with distinctive roles, status, and functions that reflect cultural, traditional, legislative and labour market factors.

3. Some models and concepts of HRM (in particular those that reflect a strong US influence) do not fit well with existing European practice.

Source: Brewster and Hegewisch (1993).

discussed in the next chapter) or merely different stages in the industrialization process, or both. The conclusions that Brewster and Hegewisch (1993) later came to in summarizing the PWCP studies are shown in Illustration 2.8.

WORLDWIDE PATTERNS IN THE RELATIVE IMPORTANCE OF HRM PRACTICES FOR COMPETITIVE ADVANTAGE

Tyson and Brewster (1991) argue that the spread of common ideas about HRM occurs because global information sharing has become more possible and multinational organizations prefer to distribute common policies. Therefore, they believe, we are seeing some convergence in HRM practices that is most notably evidenced by the acceptance of common technical languages in areas such as job evaluation, employee appraisal and development. Although there is no clear model for European HRM, it is clear that many major European multinationals (for example, Shell, Olivetti, and Siemens) and some cross-border, medium-sized organizations already display some pan-European HRM principles in a distinct form (Thurley, 1990). However, much of the data from the PWCP studies showed that from 1990 to 1992 there was a high degree of consistency in the responses – with areas of communality remaining so – and areas of national variation persisting (Brewster and Hegewisch, 1993).

To explore patterns in the relative importance of HRM practices on a worldwide basis Sparrow, Schuler and Jackson (1994) conducted secondary analyses on data obtained as part of a larger international survey introduced earlier and conducted by IBM and Towers Perrin (IBM/ Towers Perrin, 1992). A major topic addressed in one section of the questionnaire was the human resource concepts and practices for gaining competitive advantage. Respondents indicated the degree of importance attached to 38 different aspects of HRM in their organization's attempt to gain competitive advantage through HRM policies and practices for both the year 1991 and for the year 2000. This allowed a comparison of the extent to which future plans and expectations within the organizations surveyed are likely to converge (see Illustration 2.9 for a summary of the methodology used).

The dependent variables for the analysis were the percentages of respondents (from each country) stating that each of the 38 items (human resource concepts or practices) were of critical importance or importance in order to achieve competitive advantage by the year 2000. The dendogram shown in Figure 2.4 illustrates the results of the cluster analysis carried out by Sparrow, Schuler and Jackson (1994) and the successive fusions of countries, starting from the most similar. Each fusion decreases by one the number of country groupings or clusters and occurs at a point where increasingly

Illustration 2.9 **Sample details for the IBM/Towers Perrin worldwide survey of HRM practices for competitive advantage.**

The organizations included were those identified jointly by IBM and Towers Perrin as being the most effective firms in highly competitive environments in each of several countries. Given the increasingly global nature of organizations major employers in one country were, in some cases, subsidiaries or divisions of organizations headquartered in other countries. Respondents included the chief operating officers and the senior HRM managers (2961 respondents or 81 per cent of the sample). Of these respondents 22 per cent were from organizations that employed over 10,000 employees, 46 per cent were from organizations employing 1,000 to 10,000 employees and 32 per cent were from organizations employing less than 1,000 employees. The other 19 per cent of the sample comprised leading academics, consultants and individuals from the business media. The total sample of respondents were located in twelve countries throughout the world (the figures in brackets denote the sample size for each country): Argentina (42), Brazil (159), Mexico (67), France (81), Germany (295), Italy (212), the United Kingdom (261), Canada (120), the United States (1,174), Australia (94), Japan (387) and Korea (69).

dissimilar countries are being combined (i.e., more and more 'mathematical force' is required to fuse them). The differences in importance attributed to various HRM policies and practices between the five resultant clusters of countries were analysed across fifteen underlying areas of HRM. These areas identified elements of culture change, structuring the organization, performance management, resourcing, and communication and corporate responsibility and therefore broadly correspond with current conceptualizations of strategic human resource management (see, for example, the models of Schuler, 1992a and Walker, 1992 in Chapter One).

There are five resultant clusters of countries. The first cluster initially comprises the Anglo-Saxon business culture countries of the UK, Australia, Canada, and the US. This reinforces many of the points made in the opening chapters of this book. These

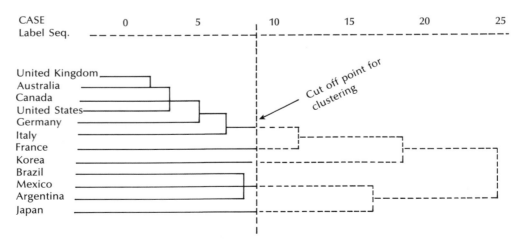

Figure 2.4 Rescaled dendogram showing the average linkage within the twelve countries. *Source*: reprinted with kind permission of Routledge. P. Sparrow, R. Schuler and S. Jackson, 'Convergence or divergence: human resource practices and policies for competitive advantage worldwide', *International Journal of Human Resource Management*, © 1994.

countries (the most similar) are, however, subsequently joined by Germany and then Italy. The second cluster (a cultural island) consists solely of France. The third cluster is another cultural island consisting of Korea. The fourth cluster reveals another set of cultural allies comprising the South American or Latin countries of Brazil, Mexico, and Argentina, whilst the fifth cluster represents another cultural island consisting of Japan alone.

It is useful briefly to compare and contrast the national clusters of countries found by Sparrow, Schuler and Jackson (1994) to other clusters of countries associated with cultural stereotypes (Adler, 1991; Phatak, 1974; Hofstede, 1980; 1993) or the management of change (Moss-Kanter, 1991). Their Anglo-Saxon cluster contains very similar members to those identified by Moss-Kanter (1991) in a worldwide survey of 12,000 managers. The US, Australia, the UK and Canada have a common business culture, united through the primacy of the English language and stereotypes of behaviour based on openness and equality.

It is interesting to note, however, that in Moss-Kanter's (1991) study, Germany formed part of a North European cluster of countries, and Italy formed part of a Latin cluster of countries. In contrast, the Sparrow, Schuler and Jackson (1994) study suggests that where people management issues are concerned, the relative emphasis these countries expect to give in the year 2000 to the fifteen dimensions of HRM places them in the Anglo-Saxon camp. Similarly in Moss-Kanter's (1991) study France formed part of a North European cluster of countries. The only difference noted in the study by Sparrow, Schuler and Jackson (1994) is that Germany does not share the same pattern of HRM emphases as France. This finding seems to reinforce the distinctions made earlier in this chapter by analysts of French HRM (Besse, 1992; Poirson, 1993 and Rojot, 1990). The results obtained for the French cluster strongly reflect Hofstede's (1980) findings on culture (see the next chapter).

The study also indicated that both Japan and Korea stand alone with unique clusters of HRM emphases – cultural islands – as was also the case in Moss-Kanter's (1991) study. Finally, Moss-Kanter (1991) identified a Latin cluster of countries consisting of South American nations, Italy and Spain. Sparrow, Schuler and Jackson (1994) similarly found that the South American countries of Mexico, Argentina and Brazil clustered together. The one difference was that Italy seems to adopt an Anglo-Saxon perspective on future HRM practices for competitive advantage. Recent analyses of HRM in Italy and the European Latin countries (Camuffo and Costa, 1993; Filella, 1991) support this finding.

EMPIRICAL EVIDENCE ON DIFFERENCES IN HRM BETWEEN THE US AND EUROPEAN COUNTRIES

So empirical analysis suggests that there are five clusters of countries in relation to their future HRM practices, and organizations in two of the European countries (Germany and Italy) are adopting similar perspectives to the Anglo-Saxon countries. In this penultimate section, we present some new analyses of these data. The first and most striking finding by Sparrow, Schuler and Jackson (1994) was that the perceived importance of all 38 HRM practices in the future was higher across each individual practice than the organizations' current assessment of their role in helping them achieve competitive advantage. This trend was evident across all twelve countries sampled in the study. The importance of HRM practices is moving on an upward trend across Europe. Such views have yet to be converted into practice and the reality may still of course turn out to be somewhat different, but the intention to improve HRM across European organizations and the recognition of its potential value is quite clear.

There are strong clusters of countries that are more alike than unalike in their HRM practices, and one of the clusters suggests that by the year 2000 Germany and Italy will be moving into the Anglo-Saxon camp. Nevertheless France remains outside this cluster and there are still marked differences within the Anglo-US cluster and across the European countries in general. For example, it is clear that although Germany forms part of the Anglo-Saxon cluster of countries in the analysis conducted by Sparrow, Schuler and Jackson (1994), it was, of course, one of the least similar countries within the cluster. A number of significant differences in HRM practice will still exist between the European countries (and also in comparison to the US) over the next few years. Many of these differences are shown in Figures 2.5 and 2.6. It is also apparent that in many areas of HRM practice there is considerable agreement and convergence.

Two aspects of culture change were examined in the study: the importance of promoting cultures based on empowerment and/or diversity and equality. These variables revealed some quite distinct scores. There was no real difference in the degree of importance given to the need to promote culture change aimed at greater empowerment. The average rating for the importance of this area of HRM practice varied little for most countries (from 71 per cent for the US, 69 per cent for the UK, and 64 per cent for Germany and France). Only Italian organizations placed less emphasis on the importance of this area of HRM activity, scoring lower on their desire to promote both an empowerment culture and a diversity and equality culture than French, German, British or American organizations. Given the emphasis given to the importance of culture change and the management of ethnic diversity in the American management literature, it was not surprising that US organizations scored higher

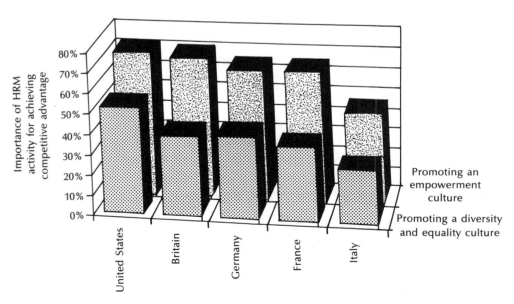

Figure 2.5 Differences in HRM practices for culture change between the US and four European countries. Original survey data from IBM/Towers Perrin (1992), reprinted with permission, © Towers Perrin, 1993.

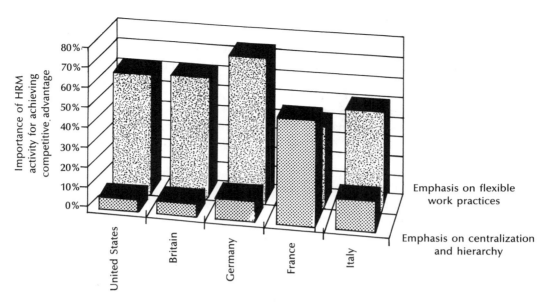

Figure 2.6 Differences in HRM practices for flexible work practices and vertical hierarchy between the US and four European countries. Original survey data from IBM/Towers Perrin (1992), reprinted with permission, © Towers Perrin, 1993.

(53 per cent) on this second aspect of culture change than all the other European countries, i.e. Germany (41 per cent), the UK (40 per cent) and France (37 per cent).

Data on a number of HRM practices related to structuring the organization were also analysed. Again, there are a number of areas on which the respondents from the five countries place a similar emphasis. The importance of focusing on aspects of horizontal management is both high and consistent across countries. Whilst the highest emphasis is seen in the US (62 per cent), high ratings are also given by the UK (59 per cent), and France (56 per cent). There is a lower importance attached to horizontal management by Germany (42 per cent) and Italy (41 per cent). As shown in Figure 2.6, German organizations place a significantly higher emphasis than all other countries (the UK, US, Italy and France) on flexible work practices. Again, the respondents from Italian organizations rate this issue of lower importance than the US, whilst French organizations also rate the issue of significantly less importance than do US and UK organizations. French organizations stand out most clearly in terms of their emphasis on centralization and the vertical hierarchy. They score significantly higher than Italy, Germany, the UK and the US. The degree of emphasis placed on this aspect of HRM by Italy, though lower, at only 15 per cent is still significantly higher than the extremely low scores shown by the UK and the US.

Some important variation is also found across Europe in the HRM practices linked to performance and business process management. In general, Italy scores lowest on most of these variables (such as the emphasis placed on measuring and rewarding customer service, rewarding innovation, and forging a link between pay and performance) whilst either France or Germany score highest. For example, the respondents from French organizations placed the highest emphasis on measuring customer service (82 per cent), followed by Germany (73 per cent), the UK (69 per cent), the US (68 per cent) and Italy (44 per cent). However, respondents from German organizations placed the most emphasis on rewarding innovation and creativity

(85 per cent), with the US, UK and France following (with scores from 63 per cent to 70 per cent). A similar pattern is observed with the importance attached to linking pay to performance. The most marked differences, however, between the US and other European countries are in the importance attached to the need for individual employees to have a share in both the benefits and risks associated with the organizations' performance. Reflecting the greater focus on collectivism in Europe referred to earlier and the higher autonomy of US organizations, the US respondents rated the need for shared benefits and risks and pay for team performance significantly higher (71 per cent) than the UK (52 per cent) and then France (50 per cent), Germany (44 per cent) and Italy (39 per cent).

There are fewer significant differences between the European countries and the US on the areas of HRM concerned with resourcing, such as the emphasis on external resourcing, on training and careers and on managing outflows of staff. Those differences that do exist are generally of a fairly small nature. All the countries placed more importance on internal resourcing (through training and career management) as opposed to external resourcing (through recruitment and selection). Also of note is the finding that France scores significantly lower than Germany on the importance given to internal resourcing through training and careers (60 per cent versus 73 per cent). Germany, not surprisingly, places the highest emphasis on training and careers, although it is closely followed by the UK (73 per cent), perhaps reflecting the emphasis on closing the comparative training gap which spurred on developments in UK HRM in the 1980s (see Chapter One). Virtually no significant differences are found between European countries and the US in terms of the importance given to external resourcing, although Italy once more scores lower than the US and Germany. The US places the highest emphasis on recruitment and selection. The importance given to managing outflows of staff also varied.

Finally, Germany scored highest and the US second highest on areas of HRM related to corporate responsibility. The German score was significantly higher than France, the UK and Italy, whilst the US score was also significantly higher than the UK and Italy. Although the variation on the scores for the importance of communication was less marked (most countries see this area of HRM as extremely important) there were nevertheless some significant differences. Germany again scored highest in comparison to the US, the UK and Italy.

It therefore is quite clear that organizations in the five countries are following different pathways towards the same overall HRM goals (see Table 2.3). There are a number of common areas of focus and importance in HRM across the five countries (the identification of these forms part of the rationale for the structure of Part Three of the book) discussed here – such as:

■ The emphasis on promoting empowerment cultures.
■ The role of communication.
■ The need to improve horizontal management processes.
■ The use of information technology (IT) to help structure organizations.
■ The role of recruitment.
■ The importance of training and career management.
■ The increasing link being forged between pay and performance.

The areas of most contention and diversity of practice across Europe would appear to be:

■ Promoting a culture based on diversity and equality.

Table 2.3 **Future emphasis given to HRM practices for the US and four European countries. Original survey data from IBM/Towers Perrin (1992) reprinted with permission © Towers Perrin, 1993.**

	US	UK	Germany	France	Italy
Empowerment culture	High	High	High	High	Low
Diversity and equality culture	Medium	Low–medium	Low–medium	Low–medium	Low
Flexible work practices	Medium	Medium	High	Medium	Low
Centralization and vertical hierarchy	Low	Low	Low	High	Medium
Horizontal management	High	High	Medium	High	Medium
Customer service measurement	Medium	Medium	Medium	High	Low
Rewarding innovation	Medium	Medium	High	Medium	Low
Pay for performance	Medium	Medium	High	Medium	Low
Shared benefits and risks	High	Medium	Medium	Medium	Low
External resourcing	High	Medium	Medium–high	Medium	Low
Training and careers	High	High	High	Medium	Medium
Managing outflows of staff	Low	Low	Medium	Medium	Low
Communication	High	High	High	High	Medium
Corporate responsibility	Medium	Low	Medium–high	Medium	Low

- The emphasis on centralization and vertical hierarchy.
- The role of flexible work practices.
- The emphasis on measuring and rewarding customer service.
- Rewards for innovation and creativity.
- Emphasis on corporate responsibility.

The only clear differences between the US and the UK (as representatives of the Anglo-Saxon approach to HRM discussed in Chapter One) and the other European countries are seen in relation to the desirability of sharing organization benefits and risks with individuals and paying for team performance. In most other areas the US is like all the other countries – a shade more or less importance being given to the various areas of HRM. Is it possible that future patterns of HRM are converging?

We consider this question in Chapter Six. Next, however, we need to outline the main determinants of the different patterns of HRM that currently exist across Europe. This forms the topic of the next chapter.

CONCLUSIONS

Currently, there are still some marked differences across Europe, and between Europe and the US, in terms of HRM practices and policies. It is quite clear that for any HRM strategy to succeed – in any context, but especially in a European context – it has to be highly responsive to local cultures, national legal and institutional frameworks, business practices and ownership structures, i.e. the major determinants of local HRM practice (Forster, 1992; Smith, 1992). The main learning points from this chapter are summarized below.

LEARNING POINTS FROM CHAPTER TWO

1. Whilst there is no such thing as a European pattern of HRM, with marked differences existing across European countries in terms of practice, as a composite, European countries are sufficiently alike to be distinguished from America. In order to adapt models of HRM to the European context, far more consideration has to be given to restricted employer autonomy, a lower importance of market processes, a greater emphasis on the role of the group over the individual, consideration of workers and not just managers, the increased role of social partners in the employment relationship, and higher levels of government intervention.

2. Within larger European organizations, most management agendas are reinterpreted at the local, national level.

3. The historical competence, career paths and professional background of managers in HRM roles varies across Europe. In Germany HRM professionals have a strong legalistic background, creating a very different mindset amongst personnel professionals in comparison to less formal Anglo-Saxon personnel professionals. Financial backgrounds dominate the thinking of many Dutch and Italian HRM professionals. HRM specialists are likely to have more experience in Germany, Ireland, France, the Netherlands and the UK. They are more likely to reach board positions in Sweden. In countries like Portugal, most HRM managers come from within the organization's own ranks.

4. Devolution of responsibility for HRM issues to line managers varies considerably, as does the level of strategic influence (as measured by organization structures that place HRM professionals in the top policy-making forum, perceived involvement in developing organizational strategy and the existence of a written HRM strategy). The level of strategic integration and devolvement to line management can be used to identify four separate positions of HRM across Europe.

5. However, the current standing of many national models of HRM is under extreme threat from changes in the business environment, particularly in the case of Sweden or Germany.

6. The HRM issues being dealt with in Europe are remarkably similar, although these common issues are being handled along different lines across countries. There is little empirical evidence to compare European HRM functions. What there is provides some support for the existence of Latin, Central European and Nordic models of HRM. Central European and Nordic countries had a higher sensitivity to HRM issues within organizations. The inclusion of European countries in this three-fold classification is difficult. For example, some parts of France would be characterized by the Latin model, whilst others would be central European. It is not possible to tell whether these

differences are steeped in cultural constraints, or simply represent different stages of the industrialization process.

7. Patterns of European HRM showed a high degree of consistency from 1990–92. The same patterns of national variation and similarity persisted. However, the differences in HRM do not seem as stark when organizations are asked about their future objectives for HRM practices. This suggests that there may be some patterns of convergence taking place over the longer term.

8. Indeed, on a worldwide basis, there are at least five different clusters of countries in terms of their HRM practice. The Anglo-Saxon countries have similar intentions for HRM policies and practices. German and Italian organizations appear to share these intentions. Within Europe, the distinctness of French approaches to HRM was found to be most marked. Anglo-Saxon and French approaches both differed from a Japanese cluster, which were different again from approaches in South American countries, or Korea.

9. Within Europe, there is a growing common emphasis on the need to promote levels of empowerment, the role of communication, the need to improve horizontal management processes, the use of information technology to help structure the organization, the role of recruitment, the importance of training and career management, and an increasing link between pay and performance. The areas of most diverse practice, both now and in the future, appear to be the promotion of organizational cultures based on diversity and equality of opportunity, the emphasis on centralization in organizational structures, the role of flexible work practices, the emphasis on measuring and rewarding customer service, rewards for innovation and creativity, and the importance of corporate responsibility.

10. In facing these patterns of convergence and divergence, organizations need to consider whether they wish to create a European form of HRM, or a form of HRM that will be effective in Europe. There is a difference. The determinants of these differences have to be understood.

CHAPTER THREE

Factors that Influence European HRM Practice

INTRODUCTION

In the previous chapter we established that there are clear differences between European and US concepts of HRM. We have argued that in order to appreciate HRM from a European perspective it is necessary to adopt a 'contextual' model. In this chapter we describe the most important contextual factors that shape the nature of HRM in Europe. Brewster and Hegewisch (1993), in reporting on their series of surveys from 1990 to 1992 carried out as part of the Price Waterhouse/Cranfield Project (PWCP) studies on strategic HRM in Europe, note that their data show considerable stability over time but also considerable variation between countries. In order to understand and interpret local action, as well as what is distinctive and intractable about HRM in the different countries as distinct from what is not, an

Illustration 3.1 **Important contextual determinants of European HRM.**

Institutional factors
- National business systems.
- Level of provision for social security and welfare.
- Scope of labour legislation.
- Recency of labour legislation codification.
- Employer/employee bias in labour legislation.
- Corporate responsibility/penalization for redundancy.
- Employment philosophy.

National competitive advantage
- Factor conditions.
- Demand.
- Related and supporting industries.
- Firm strategy, structure and rivalry.

Business structure
- Degree of state ownership.
- Organizational autonomy.
- Size of organizations.
- Level of single family stakeholders.
- Fragmentation of industrial sectors.

National culture
- Management styles.
- Attitudes to authority.
- Value differences.
- Pay systems and distributive justice.
- Career mobility.
- Approaches to cultural diversity.

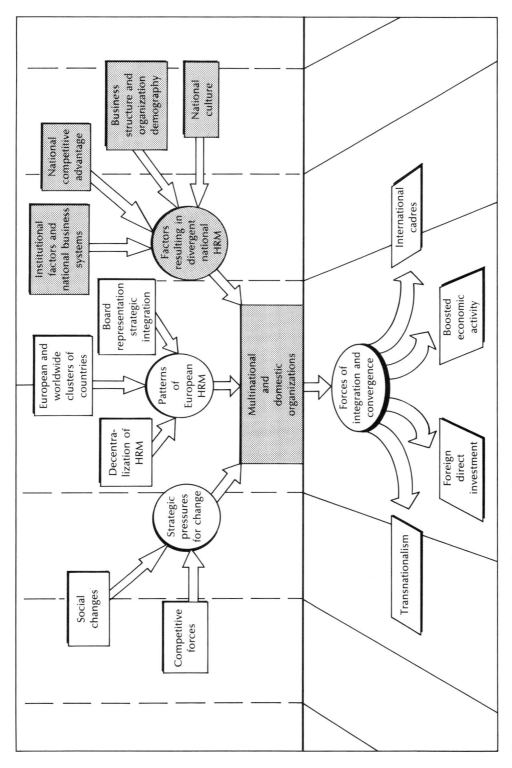

Figure 3.1 Areas of context covered in Chapter Three.

appreciation of the factors that characterize national practice is essential. Figure 3.1 places in context the analysis of factors that result in divergent national HRM. There has now been enough investigation into the European context for us to be more specific about the contextual factors that need to be examined (see Illustration 3.1, p. 50).

INSTITUTIONAL FACTORS

Business systems

The first – and perhaps most significant – contextual factor that helps shape and determine European HRM is the existence of different systems of business, and indeed models of capitalism, across Europe. In terms of the Schuler and Warwick models of HRM described in Chapter One, these differences constitute one of the internal factors that help define the strategic needs of the business. They therefore have significant implications for all five levels of HRM: the philosophy, policies, programmes, practices and process (see Figure 1.6). At the level of national institutions the argument for a European concept of management – or any process of convergence or integration – appears difficult to sustain. The organizational sociologists tend to take a sceptical view about European integration. Whitley (1992) notes that as organizations move towards greater integration there is increasing recognition of national differences in higher level European business systems. Despite increasing internationalization within many European industries, national institutions remain quite distinct. The role of the state and financial sectors, national systems of education and training, and diverse national cultures, employment expectations and labour relations all create 'national business recipes' each effective in their particular context but not necessarily elsewhere. These different national business recipes carry with them a 'dominant logic of action' that guides management practice. This logic of action is reflected in specific management structures, styles and decision-making processes, growth and diversification strategies, intercompany market relationships and market development.

> ... As long as national institutions continue to be more influential in structuring systems of economic organization than pan-European ones, ... differences will remain significant and the development of pan-European forms of firms and markets will remain unlikely.
>
> Whitley (1992, p. 1).

The institutional argument against European integration runs broadly as follows. There are a number of different and equally successful ways of organizing economic activities (and management) in a market economy (Whitley, 1992). These different patterns of economic organization tend to be a product of the particular institutional environments within the various nation states. The development and success of specific managerial structures and practices (such as HRM) can only be explained by giving due cognisance to the various institutional contexts across Europe. Not all management methods are transferable. The effectiveness therefore of any universal or pan-European conceptualization of HRM will very likely be constrained by the different institutional contexts across Europe.

Whitley (1992) identifies sixteen characteristics of 'national business systems' or 'recipes' that together constitute the major dimensions along which (European or indeed any other) comparisons of the nature of management practice should be based (see Illustration 3.2). Many of the factors are interconnected such that a number of distinctive configurations across countries can be determined. These different

Illustration 3.2 **Comparative characteristics of business systems.**

1. **The nature of the firm**
   - The degree to which private managerial hierarchies co-ordinate economic activities.
   - The degree of managerial discretion from owners.
   - Specialization of managerial capabilities and activities within authority hierarchies.
   - The degree to which growth is discontinuous and involves radical changes in skills and activities.
   - The extent to which risks are managed through mutual dependence with business patterns and employees.

2. **Market organization**
   - The extent of long-term co-operative relations between firms within and between sectors.
   - The significance of intermediaries in the co-ordination of market transactions.

   - Stability, integration and scope of business groups.
   - Dependence of co-operative relations on personal ties and trust.

3. **Authoritative co-ordination and control systems**
   - Integration and interdependence of economic activities.
   - Impersonality of authority and subordination relations.
   - Task, skill and role specialization and individualization.
   - Differentiation of authority roles and expertise.
   - Decentralization of operational control and level of work group autonomy.
   - Distance and superiority of managers.
   - Extent of employer–employee commitment and organization-based employment system.

Source: Whitley (1992).

configurations represent alternative responses to three fundamental issues:

1. How economic activities and resources are controlled and co-ordinated.
2. How market connections are organized between authoritatively co-ordinated economic activities.
3. How activities and skills within firms are organized and directed through authority relations.

The various European nation states represent an obvious starting point for comparison. The Anglo-Saxon societies have business systems with many common characteristics, such as a strong finance function, and preference for internalizing risk (given the absence of close bank–firm connections). These characteristics are less apparent in continental European business systems (Horovitz, 1980; Lane, 1992; Lawrence, 1980). A number of comparative analyses of European business systems – along the lines outlined by Whitley (1992) – have been carried out to compare Britain and Germany (Lane, 1992), Holland (van Iterson and Olie, 1992), Denmark (Kristensen, 1992) and Finland (Lilja, Räsänen and Tainio, 1992). The example given in Table 3.1 compares the effects of institutional differences in Britain and Germany.

Such comparisons serve to provide a basis for explanation of differences in management style, culture or behaviour that may be observed between the managers or organizations from the two countries. Lane (1992) also considers the degree of distinctiveness, internal consistency and stability across the twenty-four points of comparison. The tight integration of the elements in the German case suggest the system is stable. The British national business system, as generalized by Lane (1992) is, however, much more loosely fitted together. The management attachment to an ideology of worker involvement and commitment she argues is more recent and still fragile. It is not supported by institutional arrangements which tend still to be steeped in a 'minimum involvement' and purely contractual philosophy. On this analysis, the recent growth of HRM approaches in Britain described in Chapter One must remain fragile and is possibly subject to becoming 'unlocked' and 'dislocated' by the marked changes in markets and technology that will be discussed in the next two chapters (Knights, Morgan and Murray, 1992).

Table 3.1 **Effects of institutional differences in Britain and Germany.**

	Britain	Germany
The State		
Decentralization of economic policy making	Low	High
Reliance on intermediate organizations and self-regulation of industry	Low	High
Stability of economic framework	Low	High
Legitimacy of policy-making	Medium	High
Degree of State involvement:		
■ Risk sharing	Low	Low
■ Regulatory	Low	Medium
The financial system		
Degree of pressure for high short-term return on capital	High	Low
Participation in rationalization of firms/industries	Low	High
Ease of takeover	High	Low
Impact on industrial concentration	High	High
Attention to 'small firm' needs	Low	Medium
The system of education and training		
(a) Vocational education and training		
Prestige of VET	Low	High
Availability of highly skilled, flexible deployable human resources	Low	High
Homogeneity of competences/orientations within firms	Low	High
(b) Management education		
Availability of managers with high level of technical competence	Low	High
Availability of managers with high level of 'generalist' training	Medium	Low
(c) Scientific research		
Degree of industry–university co-operation	Low	High
Degree of industrial self-administration	Low	High
Trade Associations and chambers		
Degree of industrial self-administration	Low	High
Degree of formalization of interfirm relations	Low	High
The system of industrial relations		
Effectiveness of conflict resolution	Low	High
Degree of flexibility in labour deployment	Low	High
Union recognition of 'the right to manage'	Medium	High
National homegeneity of negotiated bargains	Low	High

Source: Lane (1992). Reprinted with permission, © 1993, Edward Elgar Publishing Ltd.

The social, legislative and welfare context

The social, legislative and welfare context also cannot be ignored when considering European HRM. Financial and taxation practices will have an important bearing on the pace of integration. For example, in Denmark the onus for funding social welfare is on the individual rather than on the organization (Arkin, 1992b). This possibly is a reflection of the high level of foreign ownership in the Danish private sector noted in Chapter Five. It makes it easier for organizations to make staff redundant and has led to objections by Danish citizens that they will have to bear the financial brunt of greater national mobility. In Belgium it has been argued that the taxation system blunts the impact of incentives and fringe benefits (Sels, 1992) and thereby limits the use of rewards as an integrating mechanism for HRM or the adoption of performance management techniques (see Chapter Fourteen). It also places more emphasis on the ingenuity of HRM managers to invent tax-friendly benefits.

A major difference between HRM in America and Europe, and indeed between European countries, is the degree to which HRM is influenced and determined by state regulations. The detail of differences in this emphasis is not covered at this point, mainly because it varies for each area of HRM. We consider aspects of legislation in Chapter Nine when we discuss recruitment and employment contracts. At this point, it is sufficient to note that there are differences in the scope of legislation covering a wide range of areas that might be involved in HRM strategies (see Illustration 3.3).

Such differential national labour legislation reflects different biases along the continuum from employees to employer. For example, Portuguese legislation incorporates a high employee bias (Mendes, 1992) whilst in the UK the bias is strongly towards employers. The proliferation of generally protectionist labour legislation, high levels of state ownership and a reliance on internal regulation are all expected to slow the progress towards European HRM, particularly in Italy (Caplan, 1992), Ireland (Hannaway, 1992) and Spain (Filella, 1992). Similarly in Greece, historically hostile employer–employee industrial relationships militate against rapid integration of HRM practices, as does the bewildering complexity of laws and inefficiency of public administration (Papalexandris, 1991).

Not only does the degree of emphasis on legislation differ across Europe, but so does its recency. Continuing with the Greek example, the complex labour legislation and the recency with which it was codified means that the HRM function spends considerable time and effort in an administrative role simply ensuring compliance rather than focusing on human resource development (Ball, 1992). In contrast, Denmark has exceeded the minimum standards of social and employment legislation being set by the European Union for a long time with its highly structured welfare system (Arkin, 1992b).

Related to the issue of legislation is that of organizational autonomy (see Illustration 3.4). We have already noted that the issue of organizational autonomy is one that

Illustration 3.3 **Major areas of differential employment legislation across Europe.**

■ Recruitment and dismissal. ■ Health and safety.
■ The formalization of educational certification. ■ Working environment and hours of work.
■ Quasi-legal characteristics of industrial relations. ■ Forms of employment contract.
■ Rights to union representation.
■ Pay. ■ Consultation and co-determination rights.

Source: Pieper (1990).

Illustration 3.4 **Impact of organization autonomy on HRM.**

High autonomy (US)	Low autonomy (Europe)
Low levels of industrial support, subsidy and control.	State intervention and role of organizations in social engineering.
Private enterprise culture.	Greater corporate and social responsibilities.
The 'right to manage'.	The right to employee participation.
Antagonism of management towards unions.	Co-determination.

Source: Brewster (1993).

separates European HRM from American concepts in that there is less freedom and autonomy of organizations from the state in Europe. High organizational autonomy from the state is clearly reflected in a number of important areas in relation to HRM. Whilst these factors may have some limited acceptability in the UK, in countries such as Germany and Sweden such assumptions are only held by a small minority of the population. Organizational autonomy is more constrained in these countries by national culture and legislation.

Corporate responsibility

A final institutional determinant of HRM practices stems from differences in corporate responsibility. The extent to which taxation practices or legislation encourage corporate responsibility for making employees redundant – and the relative burden on individuals and organizations – varies considerably. Although many European countries such as Germany, France and Spain have made moves towards a flexibility model (Britain has made the most marked moves in this direction) by relaxing the 'hiring and firing' rules and making it easier to recruit staff on a part-time or temporary basis, most member states have only made revisions at the margin (Teague, 1991). The prevalent employment philosophy also influences the shape of HRM with employer–employee relationships typically collegial and participatory in Germany (Arkin, 1992a) and paternalistic or patriarchal in Greece (Ball, 1992).

NATIONAL COMPETITIVE ADVANTAGE

Questions about national culture and the relative strength of underlying 'business recipes' has given rise to discussion of the competitive advantage of nations. International strategic management traditionally brings with it a focus on differences in national environments and the ways in which the host organization has to cope with, and benefit from, this diversity. For many organizations strategy is still formulated in a European context, and given that the need to improve competitiveness lies at the heart of the process of European integration (see Chapter Four), it is important to consider questions of national competitiveness. We have established that there are distinct national business systems across Europe. There are broadly two contrasting conclusions that may be drawn from this:

1. There are different business systems across Europe, but they merely constitute different ways of reaching the same final goals.

2. The different institutional environments shape business systems and give some European nations a competitive advantage, particularly in specific industries.

What is the answer? Porter (1990, 1992) has been associated with the latter argument. He argues that we have traditionally explained the competitive advantage of nations in terms of 'factors of production'. These are becoming more and more fleeting in their duration (see the comments made by Whipp (1991) in Chapter One). The behaviour of organizations is a far more important determinant of competitiveness. Porter (1990) asked the question: why do organizations in one nation achieve international success in distinct segments and industries? He pointed to four determinants in each national environment:

1. 'Factor conditions' such as production factors.
2. 'Demand conditions' such as the level of home demand for products and services.
3. 'Related and supporting industries' such as the presence or absence of internationally-competitive sectors.
4. 'Firm strategy, structure and rivalry' such as differences in the way organizations are created, organized and managed, and the nature of domestic rivalry.

Porter (1990) uses the relative attractiveness of the 'national diamond' (as represented by the four conditions above) to account for differences in performance across Europe such as the German lead in the printing press industry or the Italian lead in ceramic tiles, although he points out that organizations can improve their conditions by investing in their home base and influencing appropriate government policies. While many of the unique strengths of the German business system outlined in the previous section are well known, it is perhaps less appreciated that Germany has few natural resources. Porter (1990) argues that much of Germany's success has been powered by pressure from such a disadvantage. Indeed, Porter (1990) argues, for example, that the combination of highly skilled workers, advanced technology, engineering skill and high research and development intensity gives German organizations an edge in machine tool and car industries whereas British organizations fare better where mass production of standardized products supported by marketing skill is required, such as in retail goods and drinks, electronics and data processing. Using similar reasoning, Porter (1990) also believes that Europe as a whole is no longer the locus of competitive advantage.

Indeed, to say that Germany's greatest asset is her people is no mere platitude (Hendry, 1991). German concepts of HRM, whilst not in line with US models, are nevertheless in tune with the need for a highly motivated, flexible and trained workforce. Moreover, high wage levels reinforce the pressure to improve productivity through enhanced skill levels and technology. Seen in this light, HRM is neither a new nor alien concept for German organizations (Hendry, 1991).

THE INFLUENCE OF BUSINESS STRUCTURE

Another powerful set of current differences in the role of HRM functions across Europe are linked to the existence of different national business structures. Many aspects of the business structure clearly influence the shape and nature of HRM. The relative size and strength of the private and public sectors is important because both the concentration of ownership and the average size of organizations varies substantially across Europe (Brewster, Hegewisch and Lockhart, 1991). For example, public sector employment in the PWCP study varied from 15 per cent to 40 per cent of total employment in the ten European countries. In countries such as Denmark, Norway, the Netherlands and Sweden, public and private sector personnel management are fairly integrated with considerable overlap in professional bodies, training courses and educational routes. However, in countries like Spain and Italy there are particularly large public sectors that are institutionally separate to the private sector – leading to a 'social engineering and responsibility' focus in public sector personnel management (Caplan, 1992; Filella, 1992). However, Brewster (1993) points out that state ownership does not necessarily imply the same thing. For example, in Germany most major organizations are owned largely by a tight network of a small number of substantial banks, whose interlocking shareholdings and close involvement in management create less pressure to produce short-term profit and a positive disincentive to drive competitors out of the market place (Randlesome, 1990b). The net result is akin to public ownership in many respects. In Chapter Four we discuss one of the strategic pressures – privatization – which may lessen the current influence of this institutional difference on HRM.

Organizations are also only likely to have a formalized approach to HRM if they employ over 200 employees (Semlinger and Mendius, 1989; Brewster, Hegewisch and Lockhart, 1991). Although the small firm sector is less significant in Britain and Sweden, in countries like Denmark, the Netherlands and Spain this definition excludes at least half of the working population from any analysis of HRM. In 1981, for example, 16 per cent of the French workforce were employed in small businesses compared to only 6 per cent in the UK.

To some extent these differences have levelled in the 1990s, particularly in the UK. By 1991, 23 per cent of employees worked in organizations with fewer than ten employees, compared to 22 per cent in France. However, in Spain the figure was 41 per cent and in Italy, 40 per cent. Table 3.2 shows the percentage of employees in nine European countries who work in organizations with 0–9 employees, 10–499 employees or over 500 employees (Sisson, Waddington and Whitston, 1991).

The industrial structure in Britain is characterized by a few very large organizations.

Table 3.2 **Proportion of employees by organization size in nine European countries.**

Country	Percentage of employees in organizations of 0–9 employees	Percentage of employees in organizations 10–499 employees	Percentage of employees in organizations with over 500 employees
Belgium	31.03	40.49	28.48
France	22.30	41.50	36.20
Germany	18.21	46.00	35.79
Italy	40.31	42.53	17.16
Luxembourg	26.36	49.39	24.26
Netherlands	19.40	41.90	38.70
Portugal	35.70	45.20	19.00
Spain	41.30	50.60	8.10
UK	23.17	46.80	30.03

Source: reprinted from *Human Resource Management Journal*, **2(1)**, K. Sisson, J. Waddington and C. Whitston, 'Company size in the European Community', © 1991, by kind permission of John Wiley and Sons, Inc.

Out of the thirty-five undertakings with over 100,000 employees in Europe, the UK has eighteen, Germany ten, France four and Italy two (Sisson, Waddington and Whitston, 1991). Even when organizations of over 100 employees are considered (8,447 in Europe), Britain has 3,024 of them, Germany 2,449, France 873, the Netherlands 700 and Italy 479.

In general, however, the prevalence of small businesses in Europe is still widespread. Of the 18 million businesses in the EU fewer than 15,000 employ more than 500 people (Millen, 1990) and the importance of small businesses increases in European countries with less developed economies. Italy and Portugal rely heavily on small businesses. In Italy, just under 70 per cent of workers in the industrial private sector are employed in businesses of less than 100 employees (Hendry, 1991). Similarly, in Spain just over 2000 businesses employ more than 100 people and over 300,000 employ fewer than 100 people.

In countries like Greece the extremely small size of most organizations (and therefore personnel departments) and the highly fragmented range of industrial sectors is felt to constrain the role of HRM (Ball, 1992). It means that HRM as a professional or functional need has had a relatively low level of development. The ability to survive with low productivity, the family ownership structure of many businesses, the lack of separation between ownership and management control and the high centralization of decision-making are all also associated with a continuance of poorer management (including HRM) practices. HRM developments in France have also been very strongly influenced by the small size of organizations, the late process of industrialization and a preference for centralization (see Illustration 3.5).

The pace of industrial restructuring across Europe detailed in the next two chapters is expected to affect HRM practices in different ways. For example, in Ireland there is a perceived threat to indigenous organizations in that they may not be able to keep pace with competition from other EU organizations, thereby slowing down the pace of internal industrial restructuring (Hannaway, 1992).

Illustration 3.5 **HRM developments in France: the influence of small organizations, late industrialization and centralization.**

The economy of France is also characterized by a large number of small to medium-sized organizations, mainly of family origin. There are only 6,000 organizations with more than 200 personnel in France, and even the large industrial groups such as Peugeot, Renault, Rhône-Poulenc and Péchiney are small in comparison to their competitors. In France, industrialization was only completed after World War Two in 1950. This has meant that HRM has developed in the context of both a large number of small organizations and a high level of family ownership. In 1971, 125 of the top 200 French organizations were still family-owned or managed. By 1987, 57 per cent of the largest privately-owned organizations still had a single individual or family as the majority stakeholder. Given this high level of family ownership, the French government has traditionally created a protected reserve of small businesses walled off from competition by special rules and tax laws. In UK organizations the senior managers are still felt to be employees and therefore identify more with general life in the organization but historically in many French organizations the higher level of family ownership has created a greater distance between 'le patronat' and the employee. This distance has characteristically produced a more centralized approach to HRM and is reinforced by the strong link between management seniority and the elitist education system in France (see Chapter Ten).

Source: Poirson (1993).

CULTURAL CONSTRAINTS IN MANAGEMENT PRACTICE AND THEORIES

One of the major dangers of any discussion of HRM is that it is easy to fall into the trap of ignoring the difference between national cultures. In recent years several management writers have adopted a cultural perspective on life in organizations by focusing in particular on the concept of organizational culture (Davis, 1984; Deal and Kennedy, 1982; Frost, Moore, Louis, Lundberg and Martin, 1985; Kilmann, Saxton and Serra, 1985; Ouchi, 1981; Pascale and Athos, 1981; Peters and Waterman, 1982; Sathe, 1985 and Schein, 1985). We devote Chapter Seven to the topic of organizational culture and make some distinctions between organizational culture and national culture in that chapter. However, from Chapter Two it is apparent that identical personnel policies and practices may have different effects both across countries and for different subgroups of employees within countries. National culture may impact the culture of an organization by selecting and framing the particular sets of organizational values, norms and artifacts that managers perceive as being consistent with the basic assumptions that are developed within their countries as a product of national patterns of early childhood and formative experiences and education, language, religion and geography (Derr and Laurent, 1989).

As part of this general review of determinants of European HRM it is important to consider the argument that there are national cultural constraints to management theories. These constraints even apply to the concept of organizational culture itself (Hendry, 1991). Hendry (1991) notes that the topic of HRM places the contrast between continuing national differences or convergence in a particularly stark form because, more than any other set of management practices, HRM impacts directly on culturally-specific ways of doing things and is buttressed by national institutions and value systems. We therefore need considerable historical and cultural insight into local conditions to understand the processes, philosophies and problems of national models of HRM (Hofstede, 1993).

As we have seen, the US literature embodies its own cultural assumptions about the ability of people to change the environment, presuming that cultural differences, once recognized, may be modified or overridden, since the individual is dominant rather than societal culture. In Europe, the reverse is true. Societal culture dominates the individual. It is not surprising that it is European writers who have concentrated on the cultural constraints of management theories.

Hofstede (1993) is strongly associated with the contention that there are no such things as universal management theories or management practices. Although diversity in management practices has long been understood, Hofstede (1993) argues that the validity of many management theories (including HRM) stops at management borders. He points to linguistic differences even in the way we use the term 'management' as an indication of the subtle, but significant shades of meaning, we attribute to theories.

> ... The linguistic origin (of management) is from Latin 'manus', via the Italian 'maneggiare' which is the training of horses in the 'menege': (the meaning was) subsequently... extended to skilful handling in general... however, the word also became associated with the French 'menage'... as an equivalent of 'husbandry' in the sense of art of running a household. The theatre of present day management contains elements of both 'manege' and 'menage' and different managers and cultures may use different accents.   Hofstede (1993, p. 82).

All great ideas have travelled from one country to another and have been enriched by foreign influences. Hofstede (1993) points out that the roots of American management theories originate largely in European writers such as Adam Smith,

John Stuart Mill, Leo Tolstoy, Max Weber, Henri Fayol, Sigmund Freud and Kurt Lewin. These theories were 'replanted' in the US, developed locally, and bore fruit. The same may happen again with concepts of HRM. However, we should not automatically expect one country's theories of management to apply abroad without testing the assumptions.

As Hofstede (1991) says, 'often, the original policy will have to be adapted to fit the local culture and lead to the desired effect'. This was clearly the case with Management by Objectives. In a book of case studies about the topic – probably the single most popular management technique 'made in the USA' – it was stated:

MBO has acquired a different flavour in the German-speaking countries, not least because in these countries the social and political pressures towards co-determination has forced management to adjust the basic principles of MBO. Thus, in Germany MBO has been transformed into Management by Joint Goal Setting, which is in line with the lower individualism and willingness to take risks.   Ferguson (1973).

Pieper (1990) argues that descriptions of HRM must be sensitive to the different meanings that people in European countries attribute to specific HRM practices, such as:

- Attitudes to, and definitions of, managerial skill (see Chapter Ten, Internal Resourcing: Employee Training and Development).
- The giving of face to face feedback (see Chapter Fourteen, Performance Management and Appraisal).
- Readiness to accept international assignments (see Chapter Eleven, Internal Resourcing: Career Management and the Internationalization of Managers).

The brief overview of national culture in this chapter cannot do justice to this vast subject. However, we highlight those aspects of national culture that are most crucial to our understanding of international HRM issues today. We will consider these aspects of national culture and the issues they raise in succeeding chapters.

WHAT IS NATIONAL CULTURE?

The problem of adequately defining and measuring national culture is one of the key challenges confronting cross-cultural research (Ronen, 1986). It is a problem that has attracted considerable attention. Aijeruke and Boddewyn (1970), for example, suggest that culture is one of those terms that defy a single all-purpose definition and that there are almost as many meanings of culture as people using the term. After analysing 164 different definitions of culture, Kroeber and Kluckhohn (1952) concluded that:

Culture consists of patterns, explicit and implicit of and for behaviour acquired and transmitted by symbols, constituting the distinctive achievement of human groups, including their embodiment in artifacts: the essential core of culture consists of traditional (i.e. historically derived and selected) ideas and especially their attached values; culture systems may, on the one hand be considered as products of action, on the other as conditioning elements of future action.
                                                        Kroeber and Kluckhohn (1952).

Culture also embraces the concept of morality as it determines for each person in the group what is 'right' and 'proper' – and it teaches individuals how things 'ought' to be done. As such, it forms the basis of communal life. In Europe, for example, a person may begin a career in one organization, move to another organization after a number of years, transfer to still another one later, and go to yet another organization before

Illustration 3.6 **Aspects of national culture.**

- Something that is shared by all or almost all members of some social group.
- Something that the older members of the group try to pass on to the younger members.
- Something (as in the case of morals, laws and customs) that shapes behaviour, or structures one's perception of the world.

Source: Adler (1986).

retiring. This career pattern is common within specific national cultures and is governed by the overall understanding that such movements are acceptable and even desirable. But in other societies, such job hopping may be quite unacceptable. We discuss differences in job mobility in Chapter Ten. Adler (1986) has identified three aspects of national culture (see Illustration 3.6).

HOW DO NATIONAL CULTURES VARY?

Although Kroeber and Kluckhohn's (1952) definition of culture provides an overall picture of the many factors that affect national cultures, it does not provide a very practical or structured method for analysing national cultural differences; nor does it enable us to know how management practices differ across cultures and what specific cultural factors are responsible for such differences.

A more appropriate and potentially useful method for defining and comparing national cultures focuses on their value systems (Ronen, 1986). Research over the past two decades has produced fairly convincing evidence that values differ significantly among countries and that these differences can, in fact, be measured. As such, several 'national value profiles' have been developed (see, for example, Hofstede, 1980; Ronen, 1986; Ronen and Shenkar, 1985; Trompenaars, 1993).

Ronen and Shenkar (1985) identified eight generic clusters of countries based on language, geography and religion. The Anglo-Saxon cluster included the USA, the UK, Australia, Canada, New Zealand, Ireland and South Africa. The Latin American cluster included Argentina, Venezuela, Chile, Mexico, Peru and Colombia. The

Illustration 3.7 **Example questions examining national culture as a determinant of behaviour.**

1. You are riding in a car driven by a close friend. He hits a pedestrian. You know he was going at least 35 miles per hour in an area of the city where the maximum allowed speed is 20 miles per hour. There are no witnesses. His lawyer says that if you testify under oath that he was only driving 20 miles per hour it may save him from serious consequences.

   What right has your friend to expect you to protect him?

   (a) My friend has a definite right to expect me to testify to the lower figure.

   (b) He has some right as a friend to expect me to testify to the lower figure.

   (c) He has no right as a friend to expect me to testify to the lower figure.

2. What do you think you would do in view of the obligations of a sworn witness and the obligation to your friend?

   (d) Testify that he was going 20 miles an hour.

   (e) Not testify that he was going 20 miles an hour.

Source: Trompenaars (1993).

Near-Eastern cluster included Turkey, Iran and Greece. The Arab cluster included Bahrain, UAE, Kuwait, Saudi Arabia, Oman and Abu-Dhabi. The Latin-European cluster included France, Belgium, Italy, Portugal and Spain. The Germanic cluster included Germany, Switzerland and Austria. The Nordic cluster included Sweden, Denmark, Norway and Finland. Finally, the Far Eastern cluster included Malaysia, Hong Kong, Singapore, Philippines, South Vietnam, Indonesia, Thailand, and Taiwan. Brazil, Japan, India and Israel could not be classified and stood out as 'cultural islands'. The argument is that since each cluster is based upon key cultural values and attitudes, organizational behaviours (and accepted HRM practices) should be more similar within clusters than between them (Wilson and Rosenfeld, 1990).

Percentage of respondents opting for a universalist system rather than a particular social group

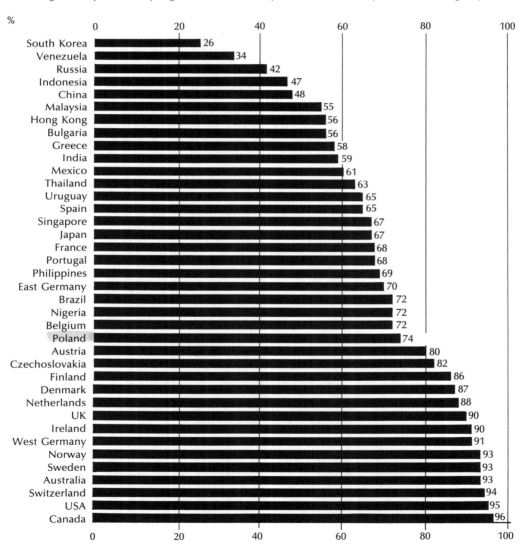

Figure 3.2 The car and the pedestrian. *Source*: from *Riding the Waves of Culture* by Fons Trompenaars, published by Nicholas Brealey Publishing Ltd, London, 1993.

Unfortunately, however, researchers have used a great variety of different instruments to measure values. There is little agreement regarding any definitive value scale suitable for measuring cultural differences among nations. A typical example of value differences was provided by Trompenaars (1993). He asked 15,000 managers from fifty different countries the two questions shown in Illustration 3.7. Figure 3.2 shows the result of putting these two questions to a variety of nationalities. The percentage shown in the graph represents the proportion who answered that the friend had no right or some right and would then not testify, i.e. answered 1(c) or 1(b) and 2(e). As Trompenaars (1993) points out, North Americans and most North Europeans emerge as almost totally 'universalist' in their approach to the problem. This approach is roughly 'What is good and right can be defined and always applies'. The proportion of people in this category falls to under 70 per cent for the French and the Japanese, while in Russia, Venezuela, Indonesia and China more than half of the respondents said they would lie to the police to protect their friend. They seem to reason that 'my friend needs my help more than ever now that he is in serious trouble with the law.'

Another striking example appeared in a systematic survey of upper-middle managers attending INSEAD's executive programmes (Laurent, 1991) (see Figure 3.3). Participants were asked to respond to the following statement: 'It is important for a manager to have at hand precise answers to most of the questions that his subordinates may raise about their work.' Responses were scored on a five-point scale from 'strongly agree' to 'strongly disagree'. Although only a minority (13 per cent) of both Swedish and American managers agreed with the statement, a majority (59 per cent) of both French and Italian managers did agree. The number of managers from the UK, Germany, Switzerland and Belgium who agreed with the statement varied between

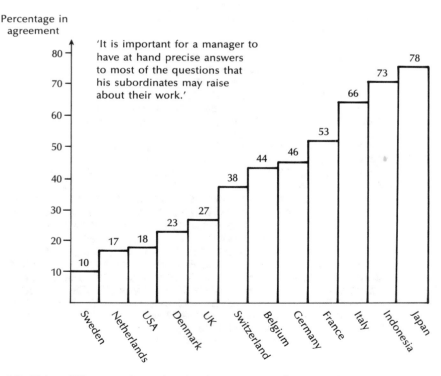

Figure 3.3 Value-differences in national cultures – attitudes to authority. *Source:* Laurent (1983).

30 per cent and 50 per cent. Thus, whereas most French and Italian managers expect the boss to have the answers, American and Swedes apparently do not. As a result, French and Italian managers must often pretend to know more than their subordinates even if they do not. If they are found to know less than their subordinates about the task, their authority base could suffer and their credibility may be lost.

Different attitudes toward authority among national cultures have been observed in other studies. For instance, in the 1970s, Stevens, in Laurent (1991) asked MBA students from Germany, France and the UK to write their own diagnosis and solution for a small case study of an organizational problem – a conflict between two department heads within a company. The results were strikingly different among the

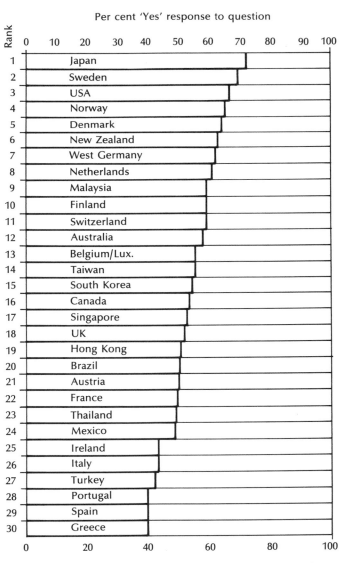

Figure 3.4 Willingness of managers to delegate authority in selected countries. *Source*: Hampden-Turner (1990). Copyright © 1990 The Economist Books Ltd. Text copyright © 1990 Charles Hampden-Turner.

three groups of students. The majority of French students recommended that the conflict be taken to the general manager, who should issue orders for settling such conflicts in the future. The Germans typically diagnosed the case as a lack of structure, and proposed to establish clear rules and procedures for solving interdepartmental problems. The British attributed the conflict to a lack of interpersonal communication and proposed to send the two heads to a negotiation training course.

Stevens, in Laurent (1991) interpreted the results as a fundamental difference in the 'implicit organizational models' of managers from different countries. The French view the organization as a 'pyramid' where the power to organize and control the members stems from their positioning in the hierarchy. The Germans, Stevens felt, see an organization ideally as a 'well-oiled machine' in which management intervention is limited to exceptional cases because the rules should be clear enough to handle day to day operations. The implicit model of the British managers is that of a 'village market' in which neither hierarchy nor rules, but situational demands and interpersonal networks determine what gets done.

Table 3.3 **The qualities most demanded in European advertisements for executives.**

Quality	N	Sweden 225	Denmark 153	Norway 162	Germany 161	UK 146	France 164
Ability to co-operate (interpersonal ability)		25	43	32	16	7	9
Independence		22	22	25	9		
Leadership ability		22		16	17	10	
Ability to take initiatives		22		16	0	0	
Aim and result orientation		19	10	42		5	
Ability to motivate and inspire others		16	11				9
Business orientation		12					
Age		10	25		13		12
Extrovert personality/ contact ability		10	8	12	11		4
Creativity		9	10	9	9	5	
Customer ability		9					
Analytic ability			10				
Ability to communicate			12	15		23	
High level of energy/ drive				12		8	
Enthusiasm and involvement				14	14		
Organizational skills					7		6
Team builder						10	5
'Self motivated'						10	
Flexibility						5	
Precision							7
Dynamic personality							6

N = total number of advertisements analysed in each country. Each entry represents the percent of the total advertisements requested by each quality.
Source: Tollgerdt-Andersson (1993). Reproduced with permission of the publishers. Management Education and Development, © 1993.

Figure 3.4 (p. 65) shows the willingness of managers in several national cultures to delegate authority. These figures are consistent with Stevens' (in Laurent, 1991) observations. Swedes and North Americans are again the least hierarchical, whilst Italians and Frenchmen are the most reluctant to let authority move down the line. Surprisingly, Japanese managers are at the top of the delegation scale, despite being most concerned about being able to answer subordinates' questions (Laurent, 1983). Perhaps delegation in Japan does not imply escape from the manager's own responsibility for the decisions made by subordinates. In any event, the results from these studies are striking examples of the extent to which managers in different cultures have very different views about leadership and organization.

To further illustrate this point, Table 3.3 shows the qualities most mentioned in newspaper advertisements for executive positions in six European countries in 1992. In general, it can be said that the demands placed on executives vary a great deal from one country to another. Some kind of personal or social quality such as 'ability to cooperate' is mentioned in 80 per cent of the 540 executive advertisements in Nordic countries. These qualities were mentioned in only 66 per cent of the (West) German advertisements. In France, personal or social characteristics were mentioned in 54 per cent of the 164 advertisements analysed.

FOUR DIMENSIONS OF NATIONAL CULTURE

In a landmark study of national cultures, Hofstede (1980), who defines culture as the collective programming of the mind which distinguishes the members of one group or category of people from another, analysed survey data from 116,000 employees of IBM in 48 different countries. The data consisted of responses by individual employees to standardized paper-and-pencil attitude and work-related value questionnaires. He undertook his study by utilizing two chronologically different questionnaire surveys during the period 1967–1973. Whilst some core business values – such as productivity and individual abilities – remained the same across countries, nationality does affect many cultural assumptions and business practices. These in turn affect appropriate managerial conduct and behaviours and assessments of employee effectiveness. Hofstede (1980) concluded that differences in responses can be explained to a large extent by four key factors, which he defined as:

1. Power distance.
2. Masculinity.
3. Individualism.
4. Uncertainty avoidance.

Power distance

This indicates the extent to which a society accepts and expects that power in institutions and organizations is distributed unequally. More specifically, power distance is associated with the degree of centralization of authority and the extent of autocratic leadership. In cultures with 'high power distance' scores, bosses have much more power than their subordinates, power-holders are entitled to privileges, and subordinates consider superiors as a different kind of person. Examples of such cultures are Portugal, Greece, France, and Belgium. In low power distance countries, such as Denmark, Norway and the UK, employees expect superiors to be accessible and bypass their boss frequently in order to get their work done.

Masculinity

This is the extent to which the dominant values in society are 'male' – values such as assertiveness, the acquisition of money and goods, and not caring for others. Masculine societies also define gender roles more rigidly than do 'feminine' societies. As Hofstede defines it, Scandinavian countries are the most feminine; the US, slightly masculine; and Japan and Austria, highly masculine.

Individualism

This is the opposite of collectivism and describes the extent to which individuals are

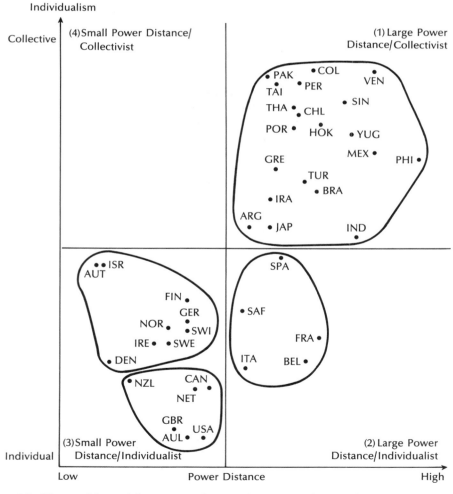

Figure 3.5 The position of forty countries on the power distance/individualism scales. *Source*: Hofstede (1980).

integrated into groups. Where individualism is high, people expect to take care only of themselves and their immediate families, their relatives to look after them, and be more loyal to them in exchange. In addition, members of individualistic societies place important emphasis on self-respect; members of collectivist cultures place more importance on fitting in harmoniously and face-saving. Individualism is highest in Anglo-Saxon countries, Italy, Belgium and France; it is much lower in Spain, Greece, Portugal, Latin American countries, and Japan. Hofstede (1980) states that a country's degree of individualism is related statistically to its wealth. There is a 0.82 correlation between individualism and wealth as measured by GNP per capita. There is also a relationship between individualism and the other cultural dimensions. The power distance index, for example, correlates negatively with individualism (see Figure 3.5).

There are some exceptions, though. Latin European countries such as France, Belgium and Italy have a combination of high power distance and high individualism scores. Hofstede suggests that in these countries people have a high need for dependence on superiors; at the same time, they stress their personal independence

Illustration 3.8 **Culture specifications for selected European countries.**

The following brief paragraphs give a flavour of the country-specific characteristics identified in Hofstede's work.

Belgium
Emphasis is on duty but risk tolerance is low. Importance is placed on being sharp witted; less importance is placed on tolerance or thoughtfulness. Belgians are high on uncertainty avoidance, moderate in masculinity, and relatively high in power distance.

Germany
Low in tolerance to risk, with an emphasis on self-realization, leadership, and independence as life goals. (West) Germans are highly competitive, with little regard being placed on patience and reliability. They are relatively high on masculinity but low on power distance.

The Netherlands
Concerned with expertness and duty, and less concerned with self-realization. The Dutch are high in tolerance of risk and content to be reactive rather than proactive, with an emphasis on being sharp witted.

France
Strong emphasis on logic and rationality, with stress on individual opinions, and élan are essential to organizational success. It is important to be sharp witted as well as mature, steady and reliable. One-way communication is relatively acceptable.

Self-perception is one of tolerance of conflict. France is high on uncertainty avoidance, relatively low on masculinity, and high on power distance.

Italy
Low in risk tolerance and high on uncertainty avoidance. Italians are willing to accept affection and warmth but are high on masculinity. They are highly competitive but prefer use of group decision making and are moderate on the power distance index.

Denmark
Like other Scandinavian countries it is above average in risk tolerance; emphasis is on maturity and steadiness, with premium placed on tolerance and sociability. Femininity is combined with weak uncertainty avoidance and low power distance.

Britain
Strong social class traditions. Security is an important goal, yet pleasure is emphasized as a life goal. Resourcefulness, logic, and adaptability are considered important; the British people are highly competitive. They are low on indexes of power distance and uncertainty avoidance, high on individualism, and relatively high on masculinity.

Source: Ronen (1986).

from the organization to which they belong. In many ways the two orientations trade off individual freedom against collective protection.

Uncertainty avoidance

This factor measures the extent to which people in a society feel threatened by ambiguous situations and the extent to which they try to avoid unstructured situations by providing greater career stability, establishing more formal roles, rejecting deviant ideas and behaviour, and accepting the possibility of absolute truths and the attainment of expertise. High uncertainty avoidance indicates that people like to control the future. It is associated with dogmatism, authoritarianism, traditionalism and superstition.

Plotting the uncertainty avoidance index for fifty countries against the power distance index reveals several clusters of countries that are characterized by strong uncertainty avoidance and large power distance. For example, most Latin American and Latin European countries fall into this category of countries. On the other hand, countries such as Singapore, Hong Kong and India combine large power distance with weak uncertainty avoidance, while Scandinavian and Anglo-Saxon countries are typically countries with small power distance and weak uncertainty avoidance. The cultural specifications for a number of European countries based on Hofstede's work are shown in Illustration 3.8 (p. 69).

NATIONAL CULTURE AND THE CONCEPT OF TIME

Recent work by King and Bond (1985), Trompenaars (1993) and Laurent (1981) shows some clear national cultural differences between the attitudes to time in different countries. Bond (1988) analysed data from a questionnaire designed with a deliberate Eastern bias to measure the values of students in twenty-three countries. From these data he was able to reproduce three of the factors identified by Hofstede (1980), but he also found a fourth factor unrelated to anything found by Hofstede. He named it 'Confucian Dynamism', referring to a long-term versus short-term orientation in society and to whether one is mainly preoccupied with the future or with the past. Bond chose the name 'Confucian' for this factor because nearly all its values seem to be taken straight from the teachings of Confucius. Respondents with a long-term orientation emphasized the values of:

- Perseverance.
- Ordering relationships by status.
- Thrift.
- Having a sense of shame.

By contrast, respondents with a short-term orientation stressed:

- Personal steadiness and stability.
- Protecting your 'face'.
- Respect for tradition.
- Reciprocation of greetings, favours and gifts.

Moreover, it would appear that the values of respondents with a long-term orientation are more concerned with the future (especially perseverance and thrift), while the values of those with a short-term orientation are more concerned with the past.

Past-oriented people believe that plans should be evaluated in terms of the customs and traditions of society and that innovation and change are justified only according to past experience. By contrast, future-orientated people believe that plans should be evaluated in terms of the projected future benefit to be gained from a specific activity or project. Future-oriented people justify innovation and change in terms of future economic pay-offs, and have less regard for past social and organizational customs and traditions (Adler, 1986).

After positioning the twenty-three nationalities on the Confucian dimension, King and Bond (1985) found that in contrast with West Europeans and North Americans, most East Asian respondents have a long-term orientation and are more concerned with the future (see Table 3.4). However, some non-Asian countries such as Brazil and the Netherlands also score relatively highly on this dimension. The most short-term oriented countries are the UK, Canada, Nigeria and Pakistan.

The concept of time is also viewed as a factor that differs between cultures in the Trompenaars (1993) study.

... The way in which societies look at time also differs. In some societies what somebody has achieved in the past is not that important. It is more important to know what plans they have developed for the future. In other societies you can make more of an impression with your past accomplishments than those of today. These are cultural differences that greatly influence corporate activities.   Trompenaars (1993).

To measure these cultural differences in relation to time, Trompenaars (1993) asked his respondents to draw three circles representing the past, present and future. In some

Table 3.4 **Long-term orientation (LTO) index values for twenty-two countries.**

Score rank	Country or region	LTO score
1	China	118
2	Hong Kong	96
3	Taiwan	87
4	Japan	80
5	South Korea	75
6	Brazil	65
7	India	61
8	Thailand	56
9	Singapore	48
10	Netherlands	44
11	Bangladesh	40
12	Sweden	33
13	Poland	32
14	Germany FR	31
15	Australia	31
16	New Zealand	30
17	USA	29
18	UK	25
19	Zimbabwe	25
20	Canada	23
21	Philippines	19
22	Nigeria	16
23	Pakistan	00

Source: Hofstede (1991), reprinted with permission © McGraw Hill, 1993.

Past, present and future

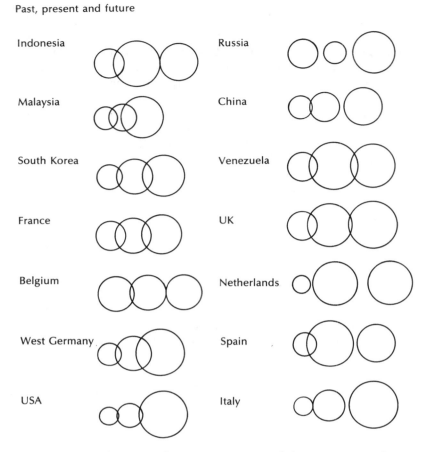

Figure 3.6 Connections between the past, present and future across cultures. *Source*: from *Riding the Waves of Culture* by Fons Trompenaars, published by Nicholas Brealey Publishing Ltd, London, 1993.

cultures, such as Russia, the typical response was to draw three separate circles; there is no connection between the past, present and future, though the future is considered more important than the past and the present (as indicated by the size of the circles). Belgians typically see a very small overlap between the present and the past. In this they are not dissimilar to the British who have a rather stronger link with the past but see it as relatively unimportant. Both groups are very different from the French, for whom all three time zones overlap considerably. The Germans think the present and the future are strongly interrelated. The connections between the past, present and future across national cultures are shown in Figure 3.6.

ARE NATIONAL CULTURES BECOMING MORE SIMILAR?

Are countries becoming more similar culturally or are they maintaining their cultural dissimilarities? This question of convergence versus divergence has puzzled the international management field for years. As Adler (1983) notes, if people around the world are becoming more similar, then understanding cross-cultural differences will become less important. If people remain dissimilar, then understanding cross-cultural differences in organizations will become increasingly important. According to Hofstede (1980), there is no evidence of convergence.

When people write about national cultures in the modern world becoming more similar, the evidence cited is usually taken from the level of practices: people dress the same, buy the same products, and use the same fashionable words (symbols); they see the same television shows and movies (heroes); they perform the same sports and leisure activities (rituals). These rather superficial manifestations of culture are sometimes mistaken for all there is; the deeper, underlying levels of values, which moreover determine the meaning for people of their practices, are overlooked. Research about the development of cultural values has shown repeatedly that there is very little evidence of international convergency over time, except an increase in individualism for countries that have become richer. Value differences between nations described by authors centuries ago are still present today, in spite of continued close contacts. For the next few hundred years countries will remain culturally very diverse.

Hofstede (1980).

To examine this issue, Child (1981) compared organizational research across cultures. He found one group of highly reputable researchers repeatedly concluding that the world is growing more similar, and another group of equally reputable researchers concluding, like Hofstede, that cultures are maintaining their dissimilarities. Looking closer, Child discovered that most of the studies supporting the convergence hypothesis were focusing on macro-level issues, such as the structure and technology of organizations, while most of the studies supporting the divergence hypothesis focused on the behaviour of people within organizations. Thus organizations in Germany and the US may increasingly become similar in terms of having the same structure and systems, but Germans and Americans continue to behave differently within them.

The debate over convergence versus divergence continues to rage. Ultimately, the issue will require longitudinal empirical research to reach a conclusion. As Ronen (1986) suggests, the research has, to this point dealt almost exclusively with how nations cluster according to values held by the workforce in each country. We should note, however, that these studies have been able only to isolate the clusters; they have not yet been able to measure the distances between them. Consequently, the empirical verification of the convergent or divergent movements separating or drawing together national cultures remains to be accomplished.

HOW DO NATIONAL CULTURAL DIFFERENCES AFFECT HRM IN ORGANIZATIONS?

The implications of these national cultural differences are far-reaching. For example, when there are several national cultures operating within an organization – as is the case of a multinational enterprise – an important aspect of the HRM manager's role is to ensure that people from different cultural groupings both understand and respect each other's customs and traditions. If one cultural group dominates, it may suppress others, leading to conflict and inefficiency.

In Illustration 3.9 we highlight some national cultural differences in the practice of international negotiation (Guptara, 1989). Such cultural differences have implications for HRM policies and practices of multinational organizations. For example, some of the policies and practices that are used by organizations as a means of attracting, rewarding and motivating employees at headquarters may not be transferable to subsidiaries in other countries given the specific beliefs, values, and norms of the environment in which the subsidiary is embedded. HRM practices that are considered appropriate in one culture may appear biased, illogical and unfair when implemented in a different culture. For example, when large Japanese firms recruit employees, they tend to prefer friends and relatives of people already working for the organization. Since the commitment of both parties is for life, the recruits' prime qualifications are trustworthiness, loyalty, and compatibility with co-workers. However, many Europeans see Japanese hiring practices as nepotism because they are only seeing these practices from their individualistic, short-term perspective.

Illustration 3.9 **Under negotiation.**

It has been estimated that managers spend up to 60 per cent of their time in negotiations. Negotiating is difficult enough when it is with somebody you have known since before the day you were married. It is much more difficult when the counterparty is from a completely different culture and has a different way of interpreting signals. How you shake hands, say 'hello', the distance at which you choose to stand, the pattern of body movement and eye contact, what sort of gifts you give (or don't give) and when – all these contribute to getting a negotiation off to a good or bad start.

The situation becomes more complex when it involves a group of people. Variations in customs can be unexpectedly wide. Take the case of an Englishman on his first business trip to the Netherlands. His plane was delayed and he phoned through that he would be five minutes late. Being British he was surprised to find on arrival that the meeting had begun without him. However, he was taken round the table and introduced to the other people present, each of whom warmly shook hands with him.

Two Dutch latecomers who arrived after him cheerfully went round the table and shook hands with everybody. The late arrivals were not treated as pariahs. In a British meeting, of course, the latecomers would have slunk in as quietly as possible. Even in neighbouring West Germany latecomers would behave like the British.

What makes someone a good negotiator in one culture may well not work in another. Different social groups have different ideas of what is proper protocol and procedure. The emphasis placed on preliminaries varies, and the order and spirit in which the different elements of negotiation are approached can be radically different. The English, for example, are perceived as sociable, flexible, and under-prepared. Working with Italian and other Mediterranean cultures has a much stronger social aspect, but negotiation with Meditarranean cultures can turn sour remarkably quickly.

By contrast, Germans have a reputation for coming to negotiations thoroughly prepared, of bidding strongly and early, and of being unlikely to move from their bids once made. They tend to regard anybody who shifts position as unreliable.

The French, too, are perceived as firm. They tend to adopt a broad-front approach, going from an outline agreement to an agreement in principle, to heads of agreement, etc., in contrast to Americans in Europe who go for piece-by-piece negotiations. Northern Europeans come across as more shy, but wonderfully open and with a great deal of mental flexibility and imagination.

These are, of course, broad-brush pictures which ignore regional, class or personal distinctions. Swedes, for example, are more influenced by American practices than are Norwegians or Finns. And bureaucratic organizations everywhere have to be handled differently from entrepreneurial ones.

Despite the additional factors that come into international negotiations, the fundamental skills of negotiation should not be forgotten: that they be handled in such a way that neither side feels manipulated; that the negotiators should be flexible; and that they should be 'tuned in' to the person they are negotiating with. Such skills are still too widely ignored when negotiators of any kind are being trained.

Source: Guptara (1989). Reprinted with permission of the author, © 1989.

CULTURAL DIFFERENCES IN PAY SYSTEMS: DISTRIBUTIVE JUSTICE

Recent events within Europe have created demands for HRM policies that people in different nations believe are fair and equitable across national borders. Perhaps the most difficult of these new policies will be the harmonization of workers' rights and the reconciliation of benefits and wage rates within the European Union. As the 1993 pay dispute in (East) Germany showed, establishing fair and equitable pay levels will be especially difficult given the diversity in current average wages within Europe, and the large differences in the compensation expectations of individual workers in the various EU countries. People in Belgium, France, Greece, Portugal and Spain seem to prefer equality-based pay policies that reward group-level effort and efficiency. By contrast, Danish, German, Irish and British employees appear to prefer equitable pay policies that reward individual levels of performance.

The relative importance of cash and non-monetary rewards, such as company cars, holidays and office space, also varies across countries and affects the motivating potential of reward systems. For instance, one compensation and benefits manager told Schneider (1988) that for the Germans, a big Mercedes was not enough; a chauffeur was also needed (because of status concerns). Also, in Sweden, monetary rewards were viewed as less motivating than providing vacation villages, in part as a result of the taxation system and inflation.

As Miles and Greenberg (1992) state, the creation of unified pay policies that are perceived to be fair by all involved will be one of the most important and controversial issues facing the European Union over the next decade. Following changes in social legislation, HRM managers may soon be forced to consider differing values and morals (or what psychologists call 'distributive justice' norms) when creating resource allocation policies to meet the needs and expectations of people for fair pay beyond their own national borders.

However, as a whole, Europe also has some pay norms that differ from American organizations. Henzler (1992b) noted the phenomenon of 'socially healthy' top pay levels. European organizations usually set top pay levels at no more than 12 to 15 times the average salary or wage, whereas in the US the multiple may be as much as 100 times the average. In general, European organizations have a more middle class workforce than their American counterparts.

CULTURAL DIFFERENCES IN CAREER MOBILITY

Many career management systems assume international mobility of the workforce. As we shall see in Chapter Eleven, expatriate transfers are often used as a development tool designed to create a 'cadre' of international managers (Edstrom and Galbraith, 1977). However, cultural differences affect the use of expatriates (such as local acceptance of outsiders), as well as the availability of people who are willing to take up international assignments. As Schneider (1988) points out, Europeans are considered more internationally mobile than Americans, but one Belgian manager stated that the biggest problem in developing leadership was getting people to move from one part of the country to another. 'Belgians would rather commute two hours a day to Brussels than to leave their roots. How can you get them to go abroad?' Derr (1987) found that over 60 per cent of European managers expressed difficulty in relocating geographically due to their wives' careers. The rise of dual career and family constraints is now a key issue for human resource managers, as changing social values increase the likelihood of women having professional careers. Through its influence on basic underlying assumptions, national culture also influences the internal career maps that managers create (see Chapter Eleven) and the way in which managers perceive the impact of change in the outside world on their organizational roles.

ORGANIZATION CULTURE AS A MAGNIFIER OF NATIONAL CULTURAL DIFFERENCES

Differences in national culture are also important to HRM because of their potential impact on organizational culture. Managers and researchers have increasingly

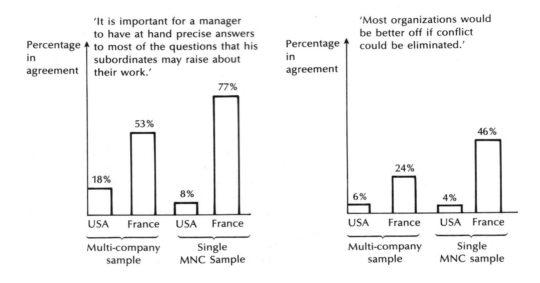

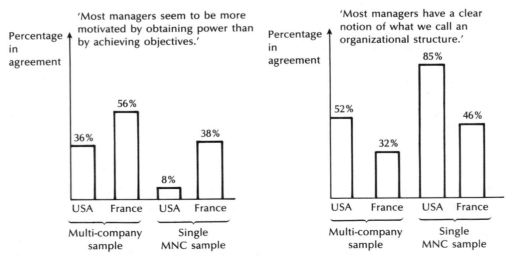

Figure 3.7 Organization culture magnifies cross-cultural differences. *Source*: Laurent (1981). Reproduced with permission from International Studies of Management and Organization, © 1981, M. E. Sharpe Inc.

recognized the importance of organizational culture as a source of competitive advantage and the role of HRM practices in creating and maintaining this culture. Many researchers and managers believe that the creation of a strong organizational culture erases or moderates the influence of national culture. They assume that the values of employees working for the same organization – even if they come from different countries – are more similar than different. However, the evidence suggests that our national culture is so deeply ingrained in us that by the time we reach adulthood it cannot easily be erased by any external force (Adler, 1986). For instance, after observing significant cultural differences between managers from nine Western European countries and the US who were working for organizations in their native countries (e.g., Italian managers working for Italian organizations), Laurent (1981) replicated his research in one multinational organization with subsidiaries in each of the ten original countries. He assumed that employees working for the same organization would be more similar than their domestically employed colleagues, but instead found cultural differences more pronounced among foreign employees working within the same multinational organization than among employees working for organizations in their native countries. Within the European affiliates of a US multinational, for instance, only 25 per cent of the German managers agreed that 'the main reason for having a hierarchical structure is so that everyone knows who has authority over whom', while 50 per cent of the Italian managers did so. On the other hand, only 25 per cent of the Italians believed that 'in order to have efficient working relationships, it is often necessary to bypass the hierarchical line', while 70 per cent of the British agreed to this statement. Finally, while only 15 per cent of the Swedes thought it was important to have ready answers to most of their subordinates', questions, 65 per cent of the Italians did so. The unambiguous conclusion is that employees maintain and enhance their culturally specific ways of working when placed within a multinational organization (Adler, 1986). Thus when working for a multinational corporation, the Germans become more German, the British become more British, the Italians more Italian, and so on (see Figure 3.7).

Similarly, Hofstede (1992) found that employees did not abandon their culturally specific ways of working when placed within a multinational organization. Far from reducing national differences, the pressures to conform to a strong organizational culture appeared to maintain and enhance them. We highlight the emergence of the transnational organization in Chapter Five. It should be made clear that the idea of the transnational organization that is beyond nationality in terms of employees' attitudes and values remains, in reality, a myth, and is likely to do so for many years to come.

APPROACHES TO MANAGING CULTURAL DIVERSITY

Most of us act, think and dream in terms of the norms and standards we have absorbed from the culture in which we are reared. That which our culture values, we value; that which our culture abhors, we abhor. By education or experience some of us become aware that there are other values and beliefs that make sense too – as much or more than our own. But we see them hazily and all too often, with age, the awareness slips away. A few, a very, very few, are able to escape, overcome parochialism and see the world more objectively. But escape is by no means entirely desirable. We can feel alone and unsure when the comfortable values of our old culture fall away, become irrelevant and are replaced by nothing.   Weber (1969).

Finally, cultural differences are important to HRM because they suggest that our ways of perceiving, thinking, reasoning, communicating, leading and problem solving are not random or haphazard, but are profoundly influenced by our cultural heritage.

There are fundamentally three approaches to managing cultural diversity in an organization (see Illustration 3.10 and Table 3.5).

Lee (1966) sees the ethnocentric approach as the root of most international business problems. He says that American organizations have long assumed that they are blameless in matters of chauvinism or nationalism. However, members of most nationalities probably hold this view as well (Ronen, 1986).

The extent to which organizations recognize cultural diversity and its potential advantages and disadvantages defines the organization's approach to its HRM. If managers believe the impact of national culture to be minimal, as in the case of the parochial organizations, the policy is to ignore differences in employee values, norms and preferences. On the other hand, if the managers view all other ways of doing things as inferior, as in the ethnocentric organization, then their policy is to minimize the impact of cultural diversity; for example, by recruiting a homogeneous workforce. Finally, if managers recognize both the cultural diversity and its potential positive impacts, as in the case of the synergistic company, the human resource policy will be to create a truly international workforce and to use the similarities and differences among the nationalities to create new forms of management and organization. In a survey of 145 international executives from around the world, Adler and Laurent (1986) found that 83 per cent of respondents preferred the synergistic approach to international management, yet only 33 per cent described their organizations as currently using this approach to problem solving.

There are several reasons for this. First, as Adler (1986) points out, although most organizations clearly recognize the existence of cultural differences, managers involved in international business often view such differences as a handicap to global operations. As a result they continue to dream of uniformity and universality – of the best way of doing things across the whole organization – when it comes to managing their foreign operations. In addition, it may be that most managers do not recognize their own peculiar way of managing and organizing as being influenced, if not determined, by their own cultural habits. Because we learn cultural behaviour early in life, it frequently affects us on an unconscious level.

...our own cultural traits are so much part of ourselves that we cannot see them any more. As we become blind to our own cultural norms, we often assume others to be similar to ourselves and we become greatly surprised (and most often upset) when others, coming from different cultures, do not behave or act as we do. Cultural myopia – the inability to see one's own cultural make up – leads to implicit ethnocentrism in management, a tendency to hold one's own way

Illustration 3.10 **Three approaches to managing cultural diversity.**

Parochial
Parochial approach does not recognize the existence of cultural differences. In the parochial firm, managers believe that 'our way is the only way' to manage and that management theories and practices transfer easily from one country to another.

Ethnocentric
Ethnocentric approach managers recognize diver-sity, but only as a source of problems. They believe that 'our way of managing is the best way' and regard their own values as superior to those of others.

Synergistic
Synergistic approach managers believe that 'our way and their way differ, but neither is inherently superior to the other'.

Source: Adler (1983).

as being the best and to expect it from, or to impose it on, others. Basically other cultures are implicitly perceived as unfortunate deviations from the norm – the norm being obviously that of our own culture.   Laurent (1991).

The tendency to holding one's own way as being the best and to expect it from others is often reinforced by stereotypes of other cultures and nationalities. For instance, in the interaction between Germans and Americans, certain stereotypes recur with a high degree of predictability. As Meyer (1993) notes: Americans see Germans as 'logical, thorough, well-educated', but also as 'distant, cold, and brooding'. Germans see Americans as 'friendly, open, flexible', but also as 'insincere, uncritical and shallow'.

Table 3.5 **Perceiving and managing the impact of cultural diversity on the organization.**

Type of organization	Perception: What is the perceived impact of cultural diversity on the organization?	Strategy: How should the impact of cultural diversity on the organization be managed?	Most likely outcomes: What can be expected with this perception and this strategy?	Frequency: How common is each of these perceptions and strategies?
Parochial	No impact	Ignore differences	Problems	Very common
Our way is the only way.	Cultural diversity is seen as having no impact on the organization.	Ignore the impact of cultural diversity on the organization.	Problems will occur but they will not be attributed to culture.	
Ethnocratic	Negative impact	Minimize differences	Some problems and few advantages	Common
Our way is the best way.	Cultural diversity will cause problems for the organizations.	Minimize the source and the impact of cultural diversity on the organization. If possible, select a monocultural workforce.	Problems will be reduced as diversity is decreased while the possibility of creating advantages will be ignored or eliminated. Problems will be attributed to culture.	
Synergistic	Potential negative and positive impacts	Manage differences	Some problems and many advantages	Very uncommon
The combination of our way and their way may be the best way.	Cultural diversity can simultaneously lead to problems and advantages for the organization.	Train organization members to recognize cultural differences and use them to create advantages for the organization.	Advantages to the organization from cultural diversity will be realized and recognized. Some problems will continue to occur which will need to be managed.	

Source: Adler (1983), reprinted with permission © 1993 *Academy of Management Review*.

ENGLISH
Sociable, flexible and under-prepared   *EuroBusiness*

FRENCH
Rude, chauvinistic, even greedy   *The Economist*
Friendly, humorous and sardonic   *International Management*

GERMANS
Warlike, folkloric, relentlessly efficient, humourless   *International Management*

SPANISH
Dramatic, jealous, lazy   *International Management*

ITALIANS
Operatic, subtle, romantic, hard-headed   *International Management*
La dolce vita minus all that *Angst*   *The Economist*

BELGIANS
Formal, *petit bourgeois*, materialistic   *International Management*
Each book's [romantic] hero will be
from a different EU country. Yes, even Belgium   *The Economist*

DUTCH
Stingy, philistine [!]   *International Management*

SWISS
'Mauschwyzerdütsch'   *unidentified*

AUSTRIANS
Devious, snobby, xenophobic   *unidentified*

SCOTS
Drunken, feckless depressives   *The Economist*

IRISH
Amiable, ignorant   *International Management*

SWEDES
Naive, cautious, weakwilled   *Communication World*

PORTUGUESE
Quiet, law-abiding, introverted   *New York Times*
Easy-going, smiling, patient, good-natured   *Insight Guide to Portugal*

GREEKS
Mercurial, poetic, devious, hospitable   *International Management*
Slow, loquacious, impulsive, irrational, chaotic   *La Vie en Grèce*

GENERAL
Not all Americans are loud, lazy, overbearing and overweight, nor are we all preachy, pompous, naive bullies. The Germans are not all obnoxious, arrogant lager louts. The French are not all baguette-munching xenophobes. The Japanese are not all myopic, camera-wielding lemmings. And the English, thank God, are not all gray, humorless, supercilious, patronizing twits.
                                        Letter to *International Herald Tribune*

Figure 3.8 Some examples of verbal violence perpetrated on different European nationalities. *Source*: reprinted with permission from Europublications, © 1993.

While the existence of such stereotypes can prevent serious misunderstanding between different cultural groups, they can be very misleading.

The French, in describing the British as 'perfidious', 'hypocritical', and 'vague', are in fact describing the Englishman's typical lack of a general model, or theory, and his preference for a more pragmatic, evolutionary approach. This is hard for the Frenchman to believe, let alone accept for a viable alternative, until, working alongside one another, the Frenchman comes to see that there is usually no ulterior motive behind the Englishman's vagueness, but rather a capacity to think aloud and adapt to circumstances. For his part, the Englishman comes to see that, far from being 'distant', 'superior', or 'out of touch with reality', the Frenchman's concern for a general model or theory is what lends vision, focus and cohesion to an enterprise or project, as well as leadership and much needed authority.   Adler (1986).

To be effective, international managers must therefore be aware of their cultural biases and learn to set them aside when faced with different cultural groups. Some examples of stereotypes and verbal violence against different European nationalities are presented in Figure 3.8. Awareness of cultural differences does not necessarily mean that organizations can easily overcome their effects; however, knowledge at least provides a chance to avoid some of the problems that result from cultural blindness in international business. Adler (1983) published trends in cross-cultural management for the 1970s. Only 4.2 per cent of research articles focused on organizational behaviour issues from a cross-cultural or international perspective. Despite the dramatic increases in international business in the 1980s, a number of more recent investigations have shown that the proportion of publications on this topic have not increased (Godkin, Braye and Craunch, 1989; Peng, Peterson and Shyi, 1990; and McEvoy, 1991), although Adler and Bartholomew (1992) found that around 9 per cent of all organizational behaviour articles are now international in perspective. In concluding on the implications of recent cross-cultural research, they commented:

... Global competition requires firms and their members to continually work with and learn from people worldwide. As more firms become transnational, business relationships will take place increasingly within networks of equals rather than within hierarchies of dominance and subordination. Discourse on international organizational behaviour and HRM in the 1990s therefore requires a conceptual shift: from a hierarchical perspective of cultural influence, compromise and adaptation, to one of collaborative cross-cultural learning.
                                                    Adler and Bartholomew (1992, p. 566).

Figure 3.9 shows the extent to which management in different countries are perceived as having such cross-cultural awareness. It draws upon research in the World Competitiveness Report (World Economic Forum 1993), introduced more fully in the next chapter. According to this survey, the Swiss, Dutch and Belgians have the highest level of intercultural understanding. By contrast, the French, British and North Americans are judged as having the lowest level of intercultural understanding. It is interesting to note that in the same survey, the North American respondents also rated their senior managers as being least experienced in international business. Over 69 per cent of respondents from Switzerland, Sweden, Belgium, Germany and Denmark said senior management in their company typically has more than ten years' experience in international business.

The knowledge of foreign languages is also very unevenly distributed across countries. For example, a public opinion survey among the twelve EU countries (see Table 3.6) shows that the ability to participate in a conversation in a second or third language is highest among the Germanic and Nordic countries. Italians and the native English-speaking people are least versed in foreign languages. Paradoxically, having

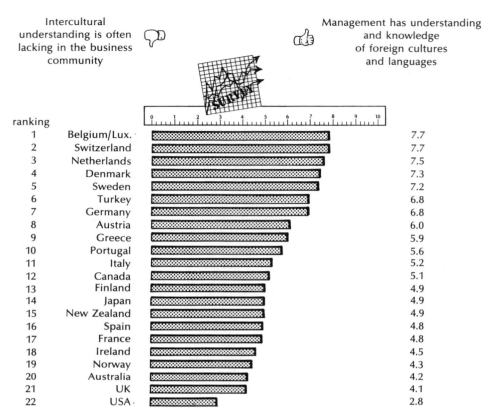

Figure 3.9 Intercultural understanding in twenty-two OECD countries. *Source*: World Economic Forum (1993), reprinted with permission, © World Economic Forum, 1993.

Table 3.6 **Ability to converse in foreign languages in twelve EU countries.**

Country	Percentage speaking the following number of foreign languages				
	None	One	Two	Three	Mean number
Luxembourg	1	10	47	42	2.3
Netherlands	28	29	32	12	1.3
Denmark	40	30	25	6	1.0
Belgium Dutch	46	22	20	11	1.0
Belgium French	56	23	16	6	0.6
Germany FR	60	33	6	1	0.5
Greece	66	27	5	2	0.4
France	67	26	6	1	0.4
Spain	68	26	5	1	0.4
Portugal	76	14	8	2	0.4
UK	74	20	5	1	0.3
Italy	76	19	5	1	0.3
Ireland (Republic of)	80	17	3	0	0.2

Source: based on various data from Eurobarometer (1987), the opinion polling unit of the EU.

English, the world trade language, as one's first language may be a liability in international business.

All international business activity involves communication. Within the international business environment, activities such as exchanging information and ideas, decision making, negotiating, motivating, and leading are all based on the ability of managers from one culture to communicate successfully with managers and employees from other cultures. Achieving effective communication is a challenge to managers world-wide even when the workforce is culturally homogeneous, but when one company includes a variety of languages and cultural backgrounds, effective two-way communication becomes even more difficult.   Adler (1986).

Without knowing the foreign language one misses a lot of subtleties of a culture and is forced to remain a relative outsider. Native English speakers do not always realize this (Hofstede, 1991).

There are, then, marked differences in national factors such as business systems or recipes, relative competitive advantage, business structure, the legal framework for HRM, and cultural differences. These have all helped determine existing differences in HRM practices across Europe. However, there are very significant business pressures taking place which, we argue, are likely to accelerate a process of convergence in HRM practice. This topic forms the core of the next two chapters.

CONCLUSIONS

Many of the differences in European HRM practices discussed in the previous chapter arise from a complex set of determinants. There are strong institutional factors, such as the existence of unique national business systems, differences in the level of provision for social security and welfare, the scope of labour legislation and employment philosophies. European countries may also be judged as having relatively different levels of national competitive advantage. The business structure – in terms of state ownership, levels of organizational autonomy, the size of organizations, level of family stakeholders and degree of fragmentation in industrial sectors have all helped to create differences between countries. Finally, and perhaps most importantly, there are different patterns of national culture as reflected in management styles, attitudes to authority, value differences, pay systems and the importance of distributive justice, levels of career mobility and approaches to cultural diversity. In order to appreciate the determinants of HRM practice in Europe, there are a number of important learning points to consider.

LEARNING POINTS FROM CHAPTER THREE

1. Despite the increasing internationalization of European organizations, many national differences in institutional systems remain. The role of the state, financial sectors, national systems of education and training, and labour relations systems combine to form a dominant logic of action in each country. These guide both national business systems and management practice. They represent different positions in terms of the way economic activities and resources are controlled and co-ordinated, how market connections are organized, and how activities and skills within organizations are directed.

2. Certain European business recipes, such as that operational in Germany, appear more tightly integrated and consistent, and therefore are likely to be more enduring of

external pressures for change. For example, German concepts of HRM, whilst culturally different from those of the US, are in tune with the need for a highly motivated, flexible and trained workforce and form the basis of a national competitive advantage. The British national business system is less stable, and therefore recent advances towards HRM may not be as certain as was previously felt.

3. The social, legislative and welfare context influences many areas of HRM, such as: the topics of recruitment and dismissal; the formalization of educational qualifications; aspects of industrial relations, pay, health and safety; the working environment; the nature of the employment contract; and levels of co-determination and consultation.

4. Levels of organizational autonomy in Europe are lower, increasing levels of co-determination, requiring greater levels of corporate and social responsibility, and more state intervention and attempts to socially-engineer organizations.

5. Many aspects of the business structure influence the shape of HRM, such as the relative size and strength of the private and public sectors, which ranges from 15 per cent to 40 per cent of employment across European countries. Public and private sector management are quite integrated in the Nordic countries, the Netherlands or France, but less so in Italy, Spain and the UK. Business structures that contain a greater number of large organizations (such as those found in the Netherlands, France, Germany and the UK) are associated with more formalized patterns of HRM. France, however, also has a strong family-owner tradition with paternalistic attitudes to personnel management.

6. Management theories and practices are also clearly constrained by national cultures. We need to develop considerable historical and cultural insight into the various processes, philosophies and problems of national models of HRM in Europe.

7. National culture consists of both explicit and implicit patterns of behaviour that may be transmitted by symbols and artefacts. They are evidenced in historically derived ideas about organization which are shared by all, or most of, the members of the country. It shapes behaviour and structures the perception managers have of the world. National cultures have been compared along a number of dimensions, but most managerial studies have focused on the underlying value systems of managers. Clear differences exist in relation to attitudes to authority and the extent to which managers will delegate authority. This leads to differences in the qualities that job advertisements for executives mention.

8. The most notable study of national culture identifies four dimensions along which countries differ: the extent to which societies accept and expect power to be distributed equally (power distance); the importance of values such as assertiveness, acquisition of money and goods and not caring for others (masculinity); the extent to which individuals are integrated into groups or not (individualism); and the extent to which people in society feel threatened by ambiguous situations and try to avoid unstructured situations (uncertainty avoidance).

9. There are also clear national differences in the importance attached to time, and the degree of long-termism or short-termism.

10. The question of convergence or divergence in these national cultures has puzzled international management researchers for many years. It may be that convergence is occurring in relation to the macro-level issues (such as the structure of technology and organizations), whilst diversity remains strong at the level of individual behaviour within organizations. Only longitudinal research will determine the truth, by which time the answer will no doubt be obvious anyway.

11. Differences in national culture affect organizations in many ways. They influence attitudes in international negotiations (which themselves may determine the outcome of investments, trade and ownership within organizations). They also create assumptions about appropriate pay systems and the importance of distributive justice; the importance of centralization and hierarchies within organizational structures; the extent to which the manager–subordinate relationship facilitates effective performance management; and attitudes towards job and career mobility. Most of the chapters in Part Three of this book contain reference to the impact of national culture on HRM practices.

12. Organizational cultures appear to magnify differences in national culture. The pressure to conform to a strong organizational culture often enhances national differences. The idea of a transnational organization that moves beyond nationality in terms of employee attitudes and values is likely to remain a myth for several years to come.

13. Organizations can take three stances toward managing such cultural differences. A parochial approach focuses on 'our way is the only way', forcing managerial practices into different countries. An ethnocentric approach recognizes diversity, but only as a source of problems. A synergistic approach assumes that cultures differ, but none is inherently superior to others. Most organizations take an ethnocentric approach and this creates difficulties. The extent to which organizations recognize cultural diversity defines its approach to HRM. Most managers would prefer a synergistic approach, yet believe that their organizations are ethnocentric.

14. Global competition is forcing organizations to work continually with and learn from people worldwide. International organizational behaviour and HRM in the 1990s therefore has to shift from a perspective of cultural influence, compromise and adaptation, to one which leads to more collaboration and cross-cultural learning.

PART TWO

The Context of European Human Resource Management

Strategic pressures driving developments

CHAPTER FOUR

Strategic Pressures Driving Developments in European HRM

In Part One we discussed the nature of human resource management (HRM), the extent to which patterns of HRM differ in Europe from the US, the range of institutional and societal factors that help determine these national models of HRM across Europe, and the need to develop more contextual models of HRM that take account of different social and economic environments. Towards the end of Chapter Two we also presented some empirical evidence which suggested that the historical differences in HRM – at least in terms of the HRM issues that European organizations wished to address – are perhaps now beginning to disappear. This chapter will provide an understanding of the main social and economic factors that will influence future European HRM (see Figure 4.1). These factors represent some of the most important 'non-contingent' determinants of HRM (see Hiltrop, 1993; Schuler, 1992a). They help to explain some of the reasoning behind the ratings given by managers in the IBM/Towers Perrin (1992) survey.

We shall therefore develop the argument for increasing integration by describing the range of strategic pressures facing European organizations. In so doing, it should become evident that there are two trends that are likely to lead to greater HRM convergence:

1. A pan-European requirement to create organizations (and HRM systems) that are capable of surviving rapid and 'discontinuous' change.
2. A collection of powerful economic and social forces – such as globalization, rationalization, business integration and demographic shifts – that will re-shape and possibly supersede national differences in HRM implementation at the organizational level.

In recent years, European organizations have come under increasing pressure to change. Ferner and Hyman (1992) point out that since the 1970s European countries have faced a number of common economic developments and structural transformations. Increased international competition, slower growth and, in some cases, declining markets are forcing organizations to reduce costs, improve the availability and deployment of resources, and achieve dramatic improvements in productivity.

At the same time, changes in workforce demography, technology and other aspects of the environment are creating the need for new structures and management practices

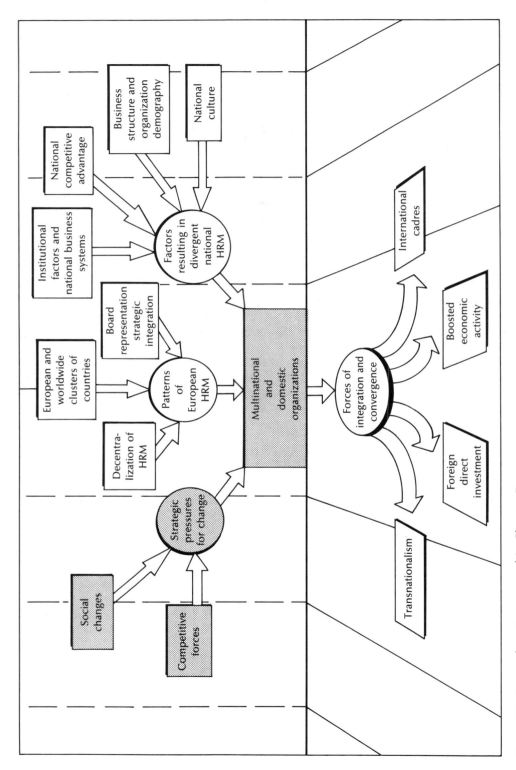

Figure 4.1 Areas of context covered in Chapter Four.

which increase organizational commitment and flexibility whilst ensuring a long-term supply of people with necessary competencies and skills (Beer, Spector, Lawrence, Mills and Walton, 1984). Even in banking and insurance, where organizational change has traditionally been slow and incremental, macro changes in the social and competitive environment of the late 1980s and early 1990s have been of such significance that a wholly different approach to selling products and services is required (Luffman, Sanderson, Lea and Kenny, 1991). Clearly, the old ways of managing organizations and the people who work in them have ceased to be either effective or profitable, reflecting the fast-changing environment in which organizations now operate.

This chapter looks at some of the major trends and developments in the business

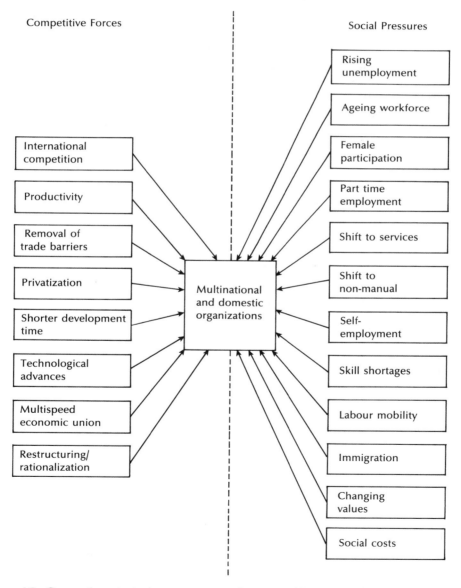

Figure 4.2 Competing strategic pressures on European HRM.

environment (see Figure 4.2). Particular attention is given to the economic, demographic and technological changes that are affecting European organizations and their implications for the management of human resources. This chapter raises a number of key issues and topics which will be elaborated on throughout the book. We believe the powerful strategic pressures discussed here will not only shape the context of European HRM, but will increasingly determine its content. To support the argument, we attempt where possible to provide comparable international statistics as suggested by Bamber and Whitehouse (1992).

ECONOMIC PRESSURES

A review of recent books, surveys and publications by organizations, government agencies, consulting firms, academics, and specialist magazines suggests that several important trends and developments in the social, political and economic environment are having a significant effect on organizations. Stanton (1992) points out that the task of strategically-minded HR specialists, personnel directors and senior managers is to propose and implement the policies that will continuously improve their organization. This demands that they understand the matters dealt with in this chapter. Anticipating and understanding these trends will place them in a better position to capitalize on opportunities and to minimize or avoid problems. We analyse the strategic economic pressures on European organizations and their HRM in the next nine sections of this chapter.

INCREASING INTERNATIONAL COMPETITION

The traditional focus of comparison for European competitiveness is against Japan and the US. Stanton (1992) argues that the process of converting the European collection of nation states into an integrated economy carries major implications for the management of its most critical resource base – the people. The European Union (EU) has a population of 323 million producing 4.1 trillion ECU* (US$ 5.0 trillion) in Gross National Product (GNP). The United States' 250 million people produce 4.2 trillion ECU (US$ 5.2 trillion), and Japan's 125 million people produce 2.6 trillion ECU (US$ 3.2 trillion). Europe's lower productivity stems in part from its fragmentation into nation states. The EU trade deficit with Japan has also reached huge proportions. In 1992 the deficit was 25.9 billion ECU (US$ 31.2 billion) – almost as large as the total value of European exports to Japan of 26 billion ECU (US$ 31.3 billion).

> . . . The key (to competitiveness) is the management of change: for countries and companies that have grown complacent with the existing state of affairs, adapting to a changing global environment may be painful. Different competitive means may now be required. . . a redefinition of the problem. . . a radically new way of looking at the company–customer interface. The real test of managerial skills comes then in rendering a qualitative shift in corporate behaviour.
> Välikangas (1992, p. 10).

Some of the evidence on European competitiveness in this chapter is drawn from the *World Competitiveness Report* (World Economic Forum, 1993). This publication acts as a strategic tool for senior managers. It is researched by the World Economic Forum and the International Institute of Management Development and analyses thirty-seven

---

* All prices have been converted into ECU based on currency cross-rates on 8 June 1993.

key economies. National competitiveness is defined as '. . . a country's ability to create and sustain value-added economic activity in the long term relative to its competitors' (Välikangas, 1992). The study assumes that every national economy has at its disposal a series of inputs – or factors of competitiveness – which include domestic economic strength, internationalization, government, finance, infrastructure, management, science and technology and people. These factors are assessed in relation to their degree of excellence in strategic implementation. The 'hard' side of competitiveness is analysed through statistics on factors such as Gross Domestic Product (GDP), growth, and balance of trade. The 'soft' side of competitiveness assesses aspects of motivation, education, attitudes and values. These aspects of competitiveness have become more important in the knowledge economy, where only 15 per cent of the working population physically touches their organizations' product whilst the other 85 per cent add value through the creation, management and transfer of information.

Figure 4.3 shows the relative competitiveness in 1993 of twenty-two OECD countries, as measured by the World Competitiveness Report's (1993) consolidated rankings across all measures. It demonstrates the difficulties in treating Europe as a single source of competitiveness. Germany, Switzerland and Denmark are Europe's leading countries, followed by the Netherlands, Austria and Sweden. Belgium, France, Ireland, Norway and the UK fall in the mid-range, whilst Italy, Portugal and Greece are clearly the least competitive. Finland has suffered a major decline due to a loss of its export markets in eastern Europe (see Illustration 4.19 later in this chapter). France

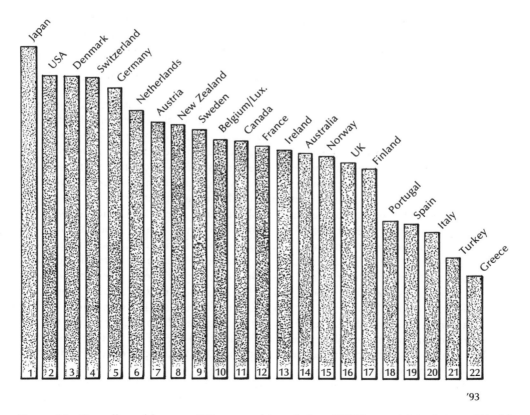

'93

Figure 4.3 Overall world competitiveness of twenty-two OECD countries. *Source*: World Economic Forum (1993), reprinted with permission, © World Economic Forum, 1993.

has overtaken the UK largely due to Britain's weak domestic economy. The most significant change has been the demise of German competitiveness, falling from a position of second in 1992 to fifth in 1993. Despite the fact that Germany has a relatively tightly-integrated national business model (see Chapter Three), it has been hit by the cost of reunification and its high wage, high social cost employment model is under severe threat. Japan has held onto its number one slot with a clear supremacy in domestic economic strength, management and science and technology. Its dominance in five of the eight composite factors, including confidence amongst managers, is however under threat, and an underlying shift from collective to individual values in its younger managers is seen as a powerful background force. Nevertheless, Japan outperforms even Europe's best, and the US has once more moved ahead of Europe's leading pack of countries (i.e. Germany, Switzerland and Denmark).

In addition to long-term economic and structural developments in Europe, there have been major international recessions in the 1980s and 1990s. The latest set of economic crises – with the deepest recession for 60 years – have hit European optimism hard. Much of the discussion in this chapter reflects the emerging economic and social crisis and its impact on organizations. The statement below by Carlo de Benedetti could have been applied to his own situation within a year of utterance.

... Western business had great hopes for the 1990s. The euphoria... and the prospect of an apparently never-ending cycle of growth led many to proclaim the coming of a new golden age for the world economy... the picture could not be more different today. The confidence and optimism of the 1980s have been eroded by anxiety and pessimism... this sudden reversal in the economic and political climate is the outcome of an extraordinary acceleration of history... in every area events are unfolding at a relentless pace. Discontinuity and contradictions fuel the sense of uncertainty and confusion.

Carlo de Benedetti (1992), Chairman of Ing. C. Olivetti.

In recent years the nature of competition has become more intense. A number of factors have contributed to this situation. The break up of the communist bloc and the fragmentation of the Soviet Union destroyed in less than two years a great command economy which supported (albeit in varying degrees of deprivation) more than 400 million people. By the time the independence process has worked its way through this massive region, the world economy is likely to have gained more than a dozen new nations, all fully recognized by the international community and varying in size from 3 million to 150 million people. In the short term, these new nations will need considerable aid from Western economies to achieve even second-world standards of living. In the longer term, however, some of these countries could become powerful competitors to the West, if they are able to capitalize on their basic natural and human resources, traditional industrial and agricultural strengths, good scientific education and, in some cases, very low labour costs. The Russian Tu-204 airliner, powered by Rolls Royce engines, is built by 36,000 employees at Russia's most modern manufacturing facility – the Ulyanovsk aviation complex. It costs 30 per cent less than comparable European and US airliners at a time when the 'peace dividend' is leading to the loss of 60,000 direct workers and another 40,000 indirect workers in the French aerospace industry alone.

On the other side of the world, Japan, Korea, Taiwan and other countries of South East Asia are continuing to build up their strength. The EU countries' share of the global market outside Europe fell from 25.5 per cent in 1980 to 21.4 per cent by 1990

(Hofheinz, 1992) and their combined share of the world export market has fallen by 20 per cent since 1980. Central to the Far East's economic and industrial expansion has been the success of Japan in combining economic resilience with skilful diplomacy, but the whole region has begun to assert itself more widely (even Japan has lost market share to new nation states such as Hong Kong, Taiwan, Singapore and South Korea). For example, amongst the industrialists of the East, new names of emerging regions are discussed with great regularity: Riau in Indonesia, Guangdon and Fujian in China, Johore in Malaysia, and others as yet unfamiliar in the West. Moreover, South Africa is rapidly returning from its isolation to the international business scene and over the next decades could again become a significant trading force, provided that it is able to create a stable political environment. It has massive natural resources, good labour supply and a competitive culture and will start re-establishing commercial links with the business community worldwide.

PRODUCTIVITY PRESSURES

Increasing international competition is driving developments in European HRM mainly though the pressure it is creating on productivity levels. There is a growing consensus amongst industrialists that the economic slowdown in Europe of the early 1990s could turn into a more serious long-term decline that will cut into Europe's high standard of living and dent its competitive performance in the global economy even further (Hofheinz, 1992). After 47 years of economic growth, Europe's productivity trails both the US and Japan. Although the gap has narrowed, Germany is still 20 per cent behind the US in purchasing power parity (calculated as the value added in the manufacturing process divided by the hours worked), France lags by 24 per cent and the UK by 39 per cent. Manufacturing productivity growth in Europe as a whole since 1980 has been on average 1 per cent below the US and 2 per cent below Japan, with this particular productivity gap expected to widen.

Producing or creating goods or services in Europe is seen by globally-minded industrialists as becoming more expensive. With virtually universally available health insurance, generous unemployment benefits and free education, much of Western Europe enjoys perhaps the world's best standard of living (Hofheinz, 1992). However, the higher level of taxation, stronger role of trades unions, and web of employment legislation that together defined a European model of HRM (see the discussion in Chapter Two) result in some of the highest labour costs in the world, which, when passed on to consumers, make more expensive and less competitive products. The argument that these goods are better quality and so can demand a price premium becomes increasingly hard to sustain given the competitive performance of other nations.

The problem is seen to be most serious in Germany (see Table 4.1). German labour costs in 1990 were 50 per cent higher than those in the US and 70 per cent higher than those in Japan. They were seven times higher than in Singapore and twelve times higher than in Mexico. It has been estimated that if Western Europe and Japan reached complete convergence with US productivity levels, they would increase their output by 23 per cent and 26 per cent respectively, for a total economic gain of about 1.24 trillion ECU or US$ 1.5 trillion (Lewis and Harris, 1992). This is, of course, a positive estimate, for it takes no account of the respective economies failing to meet the competitive challenge, or indeed the short-term rationalization engendered if globalization turns into a process of de-industrialization.

Table 4.1 **Manufacturing labour costs in 1991.**

US ($ per hour) average	Pay for time worked	Holiday pay and bonuses	Non-wage labour costs (a)	Total labour costs (b)	(a) as a % of (b)
EU	9.92	2.95	4.08	16.95	24.1
Germany	12.67	4.63	4.87	22.17	22.0
Italy	8.66	3.04	5.48	17.18	31.9
France	8.34	2.56	4.36	15.26	28.6
UK	9.88	1.60	1.94	13.42	14.5
Spain	9.03		3.62	12.65	28.6
Non-EU countries					
US	11.33	1.00	3.12	15.45	20.2
Japan	8.38	4.14	1.89	14.41	13.1
Asian NIES*	3.82		0.38	4.21	9.0

* Hong Kong, Korea, Singapore.
Compiled from various CBI staff estimates and US Bureau of Labour Statistics.

REMOVAL OF TRADE BARRIERS AND THE SINGLE EUROPEAN MARKET (SEM)

Globalization – defined as '. . . the spread of economic innovations around the world and the political and cultural adjustments that accompany the diffusion' – is a force that is unlikely to be stopped, barring economic catastrophe (Lewis and Harris, 1992). In response to this global competitive and productivity threat, Europe has embarked down two paths that may prove to be related (or may become separated): agreeing to a liberalization of world trade, and creating an open internal market within a wider Europe.

There has been a continuing movement towards deregulation of trade worldwide, through structural reform and the dismantling of barriers to free trade. A number of supranational institutions, such as the EU and the General Agreement on Tariffs and Trade (GATT) are setting the ground rules under which international trade is conducted and determining the pervasiveness of forces of demand and supply, the transfer of technology, industrial structures and the organization of employment (Poole, 1990). The GATT talks continue to meet obstacles at every round, but despite fears that globalization of the 'Triad powers' (Europe, the US and Japan) may unravel into economic wars, Lewis and Harris (1992) believe that economic convergence and technology transfer will prevail, driven in large part by the action of transnational organizations (discussed later in this chapter) and the expectations of consumers. Such overwhelming economic factors tend to prevail within a generation, and within one or two political cycles, i.e. five to ten years. Indeed, progress was made in the 1980s, and there is little doubt that, in time, trade barriers will be lowered universally, since the participants in these negotiations have such great vested interests in ensuring their success that there is little doubt they will eventually succeed. This will expose European organizations to both the widest range of international opportunities to sell products and services abroad and the widest range of competitive threats ever known.

A Canadian study of the Uruguay Round of the proposed GATT arrangements conservatively estimated an additional injection of 97.9 billion ECU (US$ 118 billion) a year into the world economy, with net gains of 29 billion ECU (US$ 35 billion) for the US, 23.2 billion (US$ 28 billion) for Japan, 23.2 billion ECU (US$ 28 billion) for Europe and 22.4 billion ECU (US$ 27 billion) for the rest of the world. However, such gains in the levels of trade will not be experienced until the end of the decade. In the meantime there will be many losers. Free trade will result in trade imbalances being ironed out as countries fall back on the goods and services they are best at providing. The economic theory on which GATT stands was developed by David Ricardo in the nineteenth century based on competition in natural resources. The premise that all countries will prosper under GATT is not proven.

In parallel with this development, within the EU discussions are now dominated by the consequences of the 1992 programme and the Single European Market (SEM). The intention of the programme is to create a single market of over 323 million people based on a tight definition of economic union. Indeed, the suggested European Economic Area of the twelve EU countries plus Scandinavia, Switzerland and Austria, would be the largest single trading bloc on earth, with more than 40 per cent of the world's GDP (Rappoport, 1992). Switzerland withdrew from this grouping in the short term but may still align itself in the future.

Monetary union was a central part of EC/EU strategy until 1993, since which time its achievement has become less certain. In order to meet European Monetary Union (EMU), the twelve European economies had to meet a strict set of conditions by the year 2000: inflation rates within 1.5 per cent; interest rates within 2 per cent of the three best performing countries; stable exchange rates for two years preceding union; low budget deficits, with annual deficits below 3 per cent of GDP and ratios of government debt to GDP not exceeding 60 per cent. As discussed later in this chapter, the possibility of currency union introduces a new ingredient into European competitive dynamics (Dixon and Hedley, 1992).

The final decisions on monetary and political union are still under debate and the final 'economic architecture' of European business is yet to emerge. The Brussels co-ordinated twelve Western European nation model, as enshrined in the Maastrict Treaty, is only one scenario. European governments still have a long way to go before the full impact of deregulation will be felt. Many goods and services – such as food and insurance – are yet to be released from national regulations which restrict organizations from trading freely in other parts of the EU. There also remains a great deal of work to do in harmonizing key areas of legislation. At present, it is unlikely that the various directives outlined in the White Paper that initiated the 1992 programme will be implemented at the time stated. The SEM legislation requires the implementation of 282 directives. On 1 January 1993, only 79 directives had been fully adopted in all twelve EU countries.

The optimistic view of the SEM, expressed in the Cecchini Report (Cecchini *et al.*, 1988) is that market completion may trigger a virtuous circle of economic growth whereby market integration provides a major supply-side shock to the economies of Europe, leading to lower costs and prices. The resulting increase in purchasing power and the improved competitiveness of European organizations in world markets would lead to significant increases in both European GNP and employment similar to the ones enjoyed by the Common Market in its formative years (Teague, 1989). European industry, despite its declining competitive position, has many strengths. Its workforce remains one of the most highly trained in the world, it has a strong capital base, and commanding market shares in sectors such as automated tools, commercial vehicles and heavy machinery. In the words of one EU official, 'by choosing a large, frontier-free market by 1992 as its goal, the EU has undoubtedly hit upon the venture most likely to rekindle a forlornly glittering flame'. For instance, the Cecchini report predicts an increase in EU-wide employment of between 1.3 and 2.3 million jobs in the medium

Illustration 4.1 **The benefits of the SEM for Philips.**

Philips has long operated large assembly plants that source from factories across Europe and dispatch finished goods to distribution centres. A TV factory in Belgium receives tubes from Germany, transistors from France and plastics from Italy. However, centralized manufacturing, whilst efficient, is made cumbersome and expensive by internal trade barriers. Trucks spend 30 per cent of travel time idling at customs posts. To avoid closing assembly lines when deliveries are late, factories keep extra stock. Philips' inventories are 23 per cent of annual sales versus 14 per cent for producers in the US and Japan. The SEM will enable Philips to cut inventories, close warehouses, reduce clerical staff and save several million ECU a year. Concentration around fewer technical standards will also enable it to shrink its vast range of washing machines, fluorescent light bulbs and TV sets.

Source: Shapiro (1991).

term, and 5 million in the long term. How does the creation of a SEM aid the competitiveness of European organizations (see Illustration 4.1)?

However, the EU as a whole experienced GDP growth rates of less than 1 per cent in 1992–93 and any gains in GDP growth from the SEM are anticipated to be delayed until 1994 at the very earliest. Therefore, in contrast to the anticipated improvements in productivity outlined above, the pessimistic view emphasizes the negative employment and related effects of the SEM as organizations rationalize and restructure their operations in an attempt to improve competitiveness in a Europe without frontiers. The strategic response to these economic pressures and the specific impact of the wave of acquisitions and mergers on employment in Europe are discussed in Chapter Five. The impact of the main outcomes of this strategic response, i.e. the related process of restructuring and rationalization, is discussed in the next section.

COMPETITIVE THREAT, RESTRUCTURING AND RATIONALIZATION

In response to the fears of Europe being faced with a long-term decline in its competitiveness, and with increasing external pressures, many large organizations have been forced to undergo major structural transformations, involving bureaucracy-reducing and cost-cutting measures and large-scale reductions in the number of people and jobs (Hofheinz, 1992).

During the late 1980s, many multi-national enterprises rationalized their global production and distribution systems in response to the increasing pressures of global competition. The same trend has recently become evident in a European context. The removal of internal trade barriers and closed economic integration within Europe will significantly reduce the need for a market by market approach to plant location. As a consequence, many multi-nationals are beginning to rationalize their European production and logistics networks by consolidating activity into fewer, larger plants serving multi-country markets.   Hamill (1992b, p. 335).

Many recent examples of the impact of this trend towards production and logistics rationalization can be identified (Hamill, 1992a). For example, Europe is now the largest market in the world for cars and the health of the industry significantly affects national economies. It accounts for 2.2 per cent of total EU GDP – ranging from 1.5 per cent of UK GDP to 4.2 per cent of German GDP. Total direct employment in the industry in Europe is 1,800,000 rising to 4,000,000 (accounting for 7 per cent of European GNP) when all related businesses are considered (Very, Berthelier and

Illustration 4.2 **Competitive threat and rationalization in the European car industry.**

Despite the advent of the SEM, quotas are still in place for Japanese car imports. By 1999 these will be phased out. However, Japanese producers currently take 3 years to develop a new model. In contrast, Peugeot takes 4.5 years. The total Japanese market share was 11.9 per cent in 1992, anticipated to grow to 14.53 per cent by 1998. There are no quotas on cars produced within the EU with significant EU-sourcing. All three Japanese producers – Nissan, Toyota, Honda – have located plants in the UK. These Japanese 'transplant' plants are making cars at productivity rates well above European standards. European plants take 36.2 hours per vehicle (55 hours in the worst plants), US plants 25.1 hours per vehicle, and Japanese transplant factories in the US take 21.2 hours per vehicle. Average absenteeism rates in Japanese plants are 5 per cent compared to 15 per cent in European plants. The productivity issue is no longer one just of assembly. It affects the whole business process. The number of defects per 100 cars in the first three months is 180 for European-manufactured cars compared to 110 for Japanese ones. European car manufacturers are emulating Japanese production methods. As a consequence 150,000 jobs are expected to be lost by European manufacturers by the year 2000, from assembly, marketing, design and development engineering, distribution and sales functions. Industry analysts feel there is no longer room for all six of the main European and US manufacturers. These manufacturers therefore face significant problems in both the immediate and medium-term future. All six are expected to have a reduced market share by 1998, but already face significant problems.

Volkswagen currently has the largest market share (16.5 per cent in 1992). It approved a spending programme of 38.9 million ECU (DM76 million) as part of a rapid expansion programme into Eastern Europe. However, by 1992 the expansion programme and the increasingly expensive German cost-base had created a significant fall of profits. Cost cutting measures led to 7,000 job losses in 1992, with another 30,000 jobs anticipated to be lost by 1994.

In contrast, General Motors Europe has the second largest market share at 12.7 per cent. It is the most profitable of the six, and is expanding capacity by 25 per cent from 1990–95. Fiat has suffered both in terms of profits and market share (down to 11.54 per cent in Europe, and fallen from 60 per cent to 45 per cent in Italy) because of high inflation, Italian wage rates and the impact of the recession, but it too is attempting to face competition with a 22.7 billion ECU (12,000 billion Lire) investment programme in new technology, new plants and new models.

Renault embarked on a significant restructuring of its European production operations aimed at reducing the number of factories, increasing plant integration and consolidating production volume into larger plants to achieve greater scale economies. Major changes have included the phasing out of the Billancourt assembly plant in France and the transfer of operations to other facilities in France and Spain; the closure of the No. 1 plant at Valladolid in Spain with operations transferred to two other Spanish assembly plants; a reduction in volume at the van assembly plant at Chausson and an increase in volume at the Maubeuge, Flins and Batilly plants. Although it gained market share in 1992, cost pressures still led to the loss of 4,000 jobs. The failure to link up Renault and Volvo is discussed in Chapter Five. Whilst Peugeot–Citroen has also gained market share (12.3 per cent by 1992) it cut its workforce by 5 per cent in 1993 in order to boost productivity and reduce product development times.

Finally, Ford of Europe announced in 1989 a major restructuring of its operations with the aim of becoming the lowest cost producer in Western Europe by the early 1990s. Its market share declined by 2 per cent to 11.45 per cent in 1992. In 1992 it shed 22,000 jobs, announcing a further 10,000 redundancies in 1993. Cars produced in high-labour cost Germany have become more expensive in currency-devalued countries. Ford spent 4.9 billion ECU (US$ 6 billion) on its new world car, the Mondeo.

Calori, 1993). In Germany it has been estimated that the industry secures employment for 4,000,000 once related service industries, repair shops, professional drivers, petrol stations, dealers, road workers and administration jobs are included. In Italy Fiat accounts for 3 per cent of total Italian GDP and 13 per cent of Italy's R&D activity. Nearly 200,000 jobs out of a total 1 million are expected to be lost from the motor components sector by the year 2000, as both Ford and Volkswagen are cutting back their number of European suppliers. Most of the losses are expected in Germany which dominates the car components sector, with other losses in France and Italy. There will be some gains in employment in Spain as manufacturers locate new jobs in low wage economies.

Mueller and Purcell (1992) have pointed out that convergent forces in terms of globalization of markets, European legislation, cross-border shipments of components or half-finished products have created remarkably similar operational requirements across Europe in management and HRM policies. The industry therefore provides a representative example of the scale of restructuring and rationalization in European business over the next decade (see Illustration 4.2). Rehder (1992b) argues that the industry is going through the most radical shift in paradigms this century (see Illustration 4.3). This competitive threat even places a question mark over, for example, the Swedish humanistic model of HRM at Volvo, as was seen in Swedish objections to the merger of Renault and Volvo. This issue is discussed in Chapters Five and Twelve.

A number of other key industrial sectors are also felt to be in severe difficulty. Europe is losing out in high-tech growth industries which have fuelled economic recovery in other countries – such as computers and semi-conductors. European exports in these sectors from 1980–90 increased only at an average rate of 2 per cent (less than aggregate growth in GDP) whilst imports grew by 8 per cent. For example, Toshiba sells more semi-conductor products around the world than the Dutch Philips, French–Italian SGS-Thomson, and German Siemens added together. Even within Europe, the troubled IBM outsells rival computer firms Siemens–Nixdorf, Groupe Bull and Olivetti combined (Hofheinz, 1992). Despite a high-quality technological base, European organizations are on the whole failing to bring innovative products onto the market quickly enough, as illustrated by evidence in Figure 4.4 from the World Economic Forum (1993).

Illustration 4.3 **The time for radical change in Daimler-Benz.**

In order to bring about change in German management, consensus has to be built. Timing in initiating 'radical change' is of the essence. That time has come in many German organizations. Edzard Reuter, Chairman of Daimler-Benz, has set about transforming the strategy and culture of Germany's largest industrial group, which includes Mercedes-Benz, Daimler-Benz, AEG and Deutsche Aerospace. Dramatic increases in competitive pressure from worldwide manufacturers working on different cost assumptions have obliged the Mercedes-Benz car division to produce outside Germany for the first time (Mexico, the US and South Korea are likely candidates). Other changes induced by cost pressures are a shift towards decentralization and team management. Forty thousand job losses have been announced. The strategy entails greater responsibility and participation for the remaining workforce, and is supported by Deutsche Bank (Daimler's biggest shareholder). The Daimler-Benz experience is anticipated to be repeated across German industry. By the end of 1994 the German motor industry will employ 300,000 fewer workers.

Source: Parkes (1993).

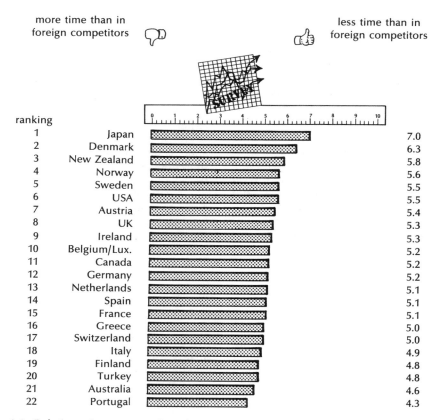

more time than in foreign competitors

less time than in foreign competitors

ranking			value
1	Japan		7.0
2	Denmark		6.3
3	New Zealand		5.8
4	Norway		5.6
5	Sweden		5.5
6	USA		5.5
7	Austria		5.4
8	UK		5.3
9	Ireland		5.3
10	Belgium/Lux.		5.2
11	Canada		5.2
12	Germany		5.2
13	Netherlands		5.1
14	Spain		5.1
15	France		5.1
16	Greece		5.0
17	Switzerland		5.0
18	Italy		4.9
19	Finland		4.8
20	Turkey		4.8
21	Australia		4.6
22	Portugal		4.3

Figure 4.4 Relative time to market in twenty-two OECD countries. *Source*: World Economic Forum (1993), reprinted with permission, © World Economic Forum, 1993.

The trend towards rationalization has not, however, been restricted to firms or sectors in immediate trouble. European multinationals like ICI, Unilever, Nestlé, Cadbury Schweppes and BSN, to name but a few, have recently gone through similar changes aimed at reducing costs and improving efficiency through the closing of inefficient plants, the reduction of manpower levels, and the consolidation of production into fewer, larger facilities.

Job losses and labour dislocations may provide powerful incentives for European governments, organizations and trades unions to appeal to nationalist emotions and protectionist policies (see Illustration 4.4). However, short-term retrenchments aside, the target for these job reductions has changed. Middle management has been a particular target for recent headcount reductions. For example, the recent wave of rationalizations at Philips (described in the previous section) as it addresses the SEM have been particularly significant at the middle-management levels. By reducing the number of hierarchical levels, organizations like Philips are hoping to become leaner, faster and more flexible. Others view these reductions as a method of putting employees in closer contact with customers.

In addition, within virtually every sector of the economy, there is now a greater reliance on subcontracting for the supply of goods and services. For example, Marks & Spencer, a British retail company, contract out all their production to specialized firms. The company philosophy is to concentrate on 'core' activities – activities in which the management have expertise – and to leave 'peripheral' activities to others.

Illustration 4.4 **The export of jobs outside the EU.**

A related issue is the transfer of jobs outside the EU. Percy Barnevik, CEO of Asea Brown Boveri (ABB) the Swiss–Swedish builder of transportation and electric generating systems argues that it is a fallacy to believe that industry will increase employment overall in Europe or indeed the Western world. He foresees a massive move to non-EU countries. By 1992 ABB had 25,000 employees in former communist countries doing the jobs that used to be done by many more West European workers. Employment in Thailand expanded from 100 in 1980, to 2,000 by 1992, and a planned 7,000 by the year 2000. Barnevik argues that Western European and American employment will shrink and shrink in an orderly way, rather like farming at the turn of the century.

Similarly, in Sweden SKF, the world's largest producer of steel bearings, has disclosed plans to increase manufacturing in low cost areas in Eastern Europe and Asia. Some 13,000 jobs have been lost since 1989 with another 3,000 anticipated. The brunt of job losses has been in the company's German factories. Responding to the need to improve margins and reduce labour costs, SKF is negotiating to start operations in Poland, Hungary and the Czech and Slovak republics, China and Malaysia.

Source: B. O'Reilly (1992); *The European Business News* (1993).

Illustration 4.5 **Norwegian Telecom: new structure to cope with internationalization.**

The solution to these competitive pressures for rationalization need not always be negative. Norwegian Telecom, the state-owned PTT, was under pressure from deregulation and new carriers in related sectors. As an employer of 18,000 people in a small country, it was not believed that becoming internationally competitive by making large numbers of people redundant in times of high unemployment was a viable strategy. President Tormod Hermansen came up with a unique solution. A streamlined Norwegian Telecom was broken down into a matrix-structure core organization of three service divisions and seven geographical regions. A separate company was set up for non-core businesses like publications and information services and other enterprises. It will generate employment and educational efforts for people whose skills are surplus to the main business. Norwegian Telecom has promised its staff and the Norwegian parliament that everyone will be looked after.

This can sometimes avoid the need for rationalization. Indeed, the solution to these competitive pressures may not always be negative (see Illustration 4.5). We develop the theme of flexibility later in this chapter.

MERGERS, ACQUISITIONS AND STRATEGIC ALLIANCES

One major consequence of the SEM programme has been a significant increase in the number of cross-border mergers and acquisitions in the EU. We examine this topic more fully in Chapter Five but make some general points about the phenomenon in this chapter. There were a total of 3410 cross-border mergers and acquisitions in the EU in 1989 and 1990 (Hamill, 1992b). These included both takeovers of European organizations within the EU and a large number of European acquisitions by non-EU companies. United States organizations have been the largest acquirers in Europe, followed by French, Swedish and British organizations. In the food industry, for example, corporate giants like Unilever, Nestlé, BSN and United Biscuits have recently been acquiring hundreds of smaller firms in each of the twelve member countries of the

EU. The number of European mergers and acquisitions exceeded the number of domestic takeovers for the first time in the twelve months to the end of June 1990. This is an important phenomenon with potential as an integrating force for European management. Related to the whole issue of mergers, acquisitions and alliances is the increasing globalization and transnationalization of businesses. All these forces are discussed in more detail in Chapter Five under the topic of integration.

Even more popular than mergers and acquisitions has been the forming of strategic alliances. The last few years have witnessed a significant increase in the use of strategic partnerships, with reports of their successes and failures to be found in the financial press almost daily (Hamill, 1992b). In banking, for example, Germany's Commerzbank took a 10 per cent stake in Spain's Banco Hispano Americano, which, in turn, has a 5 per cent stake in Commerzbank. Both banks are also members of Europartners, a wider grouping that includes Italy's Banco di Roma and France's Crédit Lyonnais, and which allows member banks to form relationships in local markets and to sell their goods and services through their partners' branch network. Similar deals have been made in industries as diverse as electronic engineering, packaged food and insurance. Looser cross-border alliances such as the attempted link-up between France's Renault and Sweden's Volvo also became more popular in the 1980s. According to the EU, the number of this type of arrangement involving organizations from different member states rose from 16 in 1986–87 to 55 in 1989–90.

Taken together, all of these mergers, acquisitions and strategic alliances have led to the emergence within Europe of a number of very large organizations which operate on a worldwide basis. For example, in 1986–1987 there were 87 mergers and acquisitions in the EU which created new organizations with a turnover of more than 5 billion ECU. In 1989 and 1990 there were 257 such deals valued in excess of 63 million ECU.

SHORTER DEVELOPMENT AND LIFE CYCLES OF PRODUCTS AND SERVICES

There has been a shift from standardized price competitive production towards customized quality competitive production (Sorge and Streeck, 1988). As foreign competition is increasing and production is becoming global, organizations do not have as much time to get new products or services developed and into the marketplace. Once they are in the market, their useful lives tend to be shorter. For example, most innovations are now rapidly diffused. It took an average of only 2.5 years for all the major semi-conductor innovations to spread throughout the Triad powers (Lewis and Harris, 1992). Time is of the essence. This increasing concern for efficiency has fuelled the application of evermore sophisticated technology to address the needs of customers on a global scale.

... Rapid technological changes have transformed the time dimension of competition. Where in the past new entrants had years of monopoly to exploit their technological advantages, such windows of opportunity have shrunk to mere months today (contrast the worldwide expansion of Xerox with that of Apple, or consider Japanese and Korean entry into the electronics field). Speed and quality in addressing the needs of worldwide customers will greatly influence who the next winning firms are going to be. Pucic (1992, p. 1).

Evidence from the World Economic Forum in Figure 4.5 shows the relative competitive performance of European and other countries in terms of their speed to market with products.

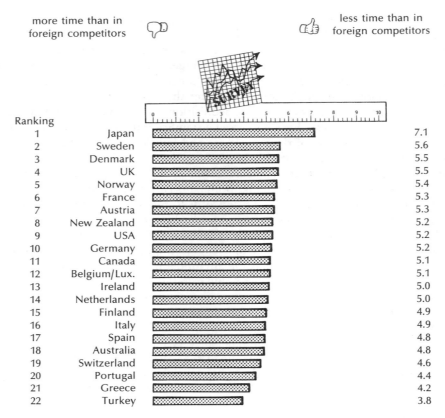

Figure 4.5 Time to innovate for twenty-two OECD countries. *Source*: World Economic Forum (1993), reprinted with permission, © World Economic Forum, 1993.

PRIVATIZATION OF STATE ENTERPRISES

At the political level the balance of power has shifted towards the right since the 1980s. Social-democratic approaches (highlighted in Chapter Two as being a factor that distinguished European and US models of HRM) are generally in retreat in Spain, France and Scandinavia (Ferner and Hyman, 1992). The economic context has encouraged policies (from European governments of the left or the right) of retrenchment, control of public expenditure, restructuring of labour markets and privatization.

In Chapter Three we pointed out that differences in state ownership of industry have helped shape unique patterns of HRM in a number of European countries. However, another major and pan-European trend in the international business environment has been the privatization of nationalized industries. European industry is pushing back the frontiers of the State. An analysis of Europe's top organizations showed that by 1989 the ten largest private sector groups employed more people than the ten largest state enterprises for the first time ever (Eurobusiness, 1989). Indeed, the whole world is set upon a trend of increasing change in ownership and control of national markets and national enterprises (Dixon and Hedley, 1992). According to the World Bank, fewer than 1000 state-owned companies were privatized throughout the world between 1980 and 1987. However, the shift over the past decade away from nationalized industries is unmistakable, as one government after another is selling off its public sector corporations to institutional and private investors.

As in the industrial revolution, Britain led the way. Under the prime ministership of Margaret Thatcher, the British Conservative government raised 41.2 billion ECU from the sale of nationalized industries and almost halved the state-owned industrial sector. From relatively small beginnings, involving Cable and Wireless, and Amersham International, the government moved on to sell large public sector organizations such as British Telecommunications, British Gas and British Airways. Although the UK programme developed more by accident than by plan (Mullins, 1993) economists at Morgan Stanley see the trend continuing and estimate that European governments plan to sell off more than US$ 150 billion (equal to 2.5 per cent of total GDP) of state assets over the next five years, despite poor market conditions.

Between 1986 and early 1988 the French government pursued a vigorous policy of privatization, although seven of France's top ten companies remained in state hands at the time of the 1993 elections. These companies behave like independent profit-driven businesses. However, the election of the centre-right wing coalition in 1993 heralded a potential US$ 30 to US$ 40 billion privatization programme involving twenty-one companies over the next five years (see Illustration 4.6). After the privatization of Banque National de Paris in October 1993, further candidates for privatization in a twenty-one company sell-off campaign aimed at releasing the high levels of savings in the French economy included: Banque Hervet, UAP, AGF in the finance sector, Air France, Rhône-Poulenc, Elf Aquitaine, Renault, Electricité de France, France Telecom and SNCF (Poole, 1993). Nationalized industries account for some 30 per cent of French GNP. A further 16.6 billion ECU (US$ 20 billion) of privatization is planned for the UK, 8.3 to 12.4 billion ECU (US$ 10 to US$ 15 billion) in Italy, 8.3 billion ECU (US$ 10 billion) in Sweden, 6.6 billion ECU (US$ 8 billion) in Germany, 4.1 to 6.6 billion ECU (US$ 5 to US$ 8 billion) in Spain, 4.1 billion ECU (US$ 5 billion) in both the Netherlands and Finland, and 2.5 billion ECU (US$ 3 billion) in both Belgium and Austria. Sales of telecommunications utilities accounts for 25 per cent of European privatization alone. British Telecom still employed 246,000 people in 1990 (1 per cent of total British employment) but this figure fell by 75,000 from 1990–93, with an annual downsizing of 15,000 per year for the next few years planned.

This, then, is an age of great transition for the public sector and no-one really knows where the balance will finally rest. Many of the distinctions between European HRM practices that stemmed from the business structure and different levels of private ownership (see Chapter Three) will erode under these pressures. What is also clear,

Illustration 4.6 **New industrial policy in France.**

The French privatization programme represents a partial dismantling of the last command economy in Western Europe and the programme may end up as the largest privatization process in Europe. Associated with privatization in France is the emergence of a new industrial policy which is anticipated to herald massive changes for many organizations. Groupe Bull has to introduce a new financial strategy that does not rely on state finance or friendly financing from the Franco-Italian semi-conductor giant SGS-Thomson or from Alcatel-Alstorn. This may entail a restructuring of the organization and a greater level of shareholding from Nippon Electrical. Similar changes were announced for Air France. Existing cost cutting measures entailing 5,000 redundancies are insufficient and new financial rigours are anticipated to have major HRM implications.

however, is that there remains a good deal of work to be done in making those activities which remain in the public sector as efficient as possible, and in ensuring that the customer gets a high quality service from the state. Initiatives such as the UK's Citizen's Charter demonstrate the political importance of not allowing the public sector to become a twilight zone for those services which are inherently or momentarily unattractive to the private sector, or unsuited to market exposure.

TRANSFORMATION OF CENTRAL AND EASTERN EUROPEAN ECONOMIES

It is also a period of transition for Central and Eastern Europe. While during the late 1980s and the early 1990s much attention was given to the increased competition from Japan and the uncertainties and distortions of the SEM programme for the economies of Western Europe, the spotlight now is on Central and Eastern Europe, which is taking privatization into uncharted territory (see Chapter Five for a discussion of acquisition in East Europe). This move has been driven by financial expediency more often than ideological conviction.

For example, the governments of Hungary and Poland have both said they want to privatize half their state assets within three years – an enormous task (International Management, 1992a). In Poland the coalition government intends to privatize some 600 organizations each with a turnover of more than 8.4 million ECU. In order to wipe out the 80–90 per cent stake of the state industry, East Germany has to privatize 8000 firms, Poland 7000 firms, the CFSR 4800 firms and Hungary 2500 firms. By 1996 foreign owners are expected to hold 25 per cent of all Hungary's industrial assets (Welfens, 1992). In May 1993 the first privatization laws in Slovenia took effect. Public enterprises employed 84 per cent of the workforce and the already high unemployment rate of 12 per cent was expected to rise. Therefore, part of the problem is that these governments have to be sensitive to their constituents, many of whom depend on only one or two main enterprises for their jobs. Existing enterprise managers look for solutions that bring new resources into the company in order to avoid hard decisions on redundancies, and selling off or scrapping part of the equipment base. In addition, many managers suffer 'technocratic tunnel vision' and understand neither marketing, HRM or organizational analysis. Such problems with existing enterprises have led some authorities to suggest the cause of most state enterprises is hopeless. Instead of trying to privatize and revive these organizations, according to this approach it would be better to 'push them aside' and focus reform efforts on newly organized private enterprises. Thus, a major issue is whether existing organizations can be privatized or must be broken up, with new blood injected into them.

The transformation of East European economies has engendered a high price. Inflation rates in 1990 climbed to levels varying from 30 per cent in Hungary to 60 per cent in Poland and the former USSR (Nikas, 1991). Industrial output and investment fell by up to a third in Poland and future forecasts leave little room for optimism, with unemployment expected to reach up to 12–15 per cent of the workforce. The unification of Germany has equally resulted in an economic drain (see Illustration 4.7) on already stretched resources as well as marked industrial unrest, as evidenced by the 1993 action taken by I.G. Metall.

By 1993 there were still marked pay disparities between Eastern and Western German wages, with workers in the Bischafterade potash mines actually going on hunger strike over perceived unfair conditions. Wages in Eastern German white collar

Illustration 4.7 **German unification: a slow transition.**

The unification of Germany has presented immense economic and social difficulties. In 1991 nominal incomes in Eastern Germany were roughly half those in Western Germany. East Germans owned about 20 per cent of the private assets owned by Western Germans. Public facilities (roads, railways, airports, museums, housing construction) were all to lower standards. From 1991–93 Eastern German employment fell from 6.5 million to 4.5 million owing to redundancy, early retirement, emigration and women giving up work. The former East German government employed 2.2 million people. The new bureaucracy employs 1 million less. Manufacturing employment used to be 3.2 million. It will drop to 0.8 to 1.4 million. Only 25 per cent of the Eastern German jobs in existence in November 1989 are expected to survive the transformation process. There are 1.6 million people who are working short hours, 400,000 are in government sponsored temporary jobs, 300,000 in retraining programmes and 400,000 are commuting to Western Germany. In order to avoid continued mass unemployment, Eastern Germany will have to create almost three times as many jobs as it currently is doing in industry and service sectors. This task is not made any easier by the fact that Western German industry is efficient enough to satisfy all the Eastern German demand for industrial goods by running one additional half day shift per working week. Germany was channeling 71.7 billion ECU (DM 140 billion) a year into the reconstruction of Eastern Germany. The argument is whether unification will result in de-industrialization – as with the German steel, engineering and electrical industries – which by 1993 employed only 450,000 against 1.5 million before unification. The German experiences of redressing East–West imbalances will serve as a model for the rest of Europe.

jobs were only 43 per cent of those in Western Germany, and construction wages only 66 per cent of the Western equivalents, even though prices were harmonized. Although labour costs are lower, a study by the Institut der Deutsche Wirtschaft (IW) estimated productivity to be only 40 per cent of Western levels, making labour costs in the east 70 per cent higher than in the West. A further 750,000 jobs were estimated to be at risk before 1996 if wages were harmonized. However, where new technology has been used, as in the Opel car factory at Eisenach, East German workers achieve productivity levels higher than anywhere in Europe. Nevertheless, the general situation is bleak. If Western German environmental law had been applied in 1992 about 70 per cent of Eastern German industry would have had to be shut down (Henzler, 1992a). Transformation of the East European economies is likely to be a slow process, creating a surplus of labour and pressures in migration (see the section on Immigration on p. 131).

THE MULTI-SPEED EUROPE SCENARIO: COMPETITIVE REALIGNMENT AND DEVALUATIONS

The Maastricht framework was dependent on the rapid alignment of divergent economies under the stable anti-inflationary regime of the Bundesbank. In 1992 the twelve EU countries were still far from reaching most of the tight economic conditions stipulated by EMU. For example, the target of 60 per cent government debt to GDP ratios were not being met by Belgium (132 per cent), Italy (112 per cent), Ireland (108 per cent), Greece (87 per cent), the Netherlands (79 per cent), Portugal (62 per cent) and Denmark (61 per cent). Public sector deficits in EU member states were forecast to rise to 6 per cent by the end of 1993 – twice the Maastricht convergence criteria – and drastic cuts in public spending were anticipated. After the severe economic downturn of the early 1990s, the currency crises of 1992 and 1993 and variable referendum results, the reality of the Maastricht Treaty for European organizations and nations was less positive than originally envisaged. Europe was turned upside down after the signing of the Maastricht Treaty. With open trade borders, unfettered flows of capital from state to state and a deregulated 1.24 trillion ECU (US$ 1.5 trillion) a day global currency market, the price for an unhealthy economy can be de-industrialization. The brute power of unsentimental money upset the grand plan for a single currency. European economies faced an even more painful period of restructuring to withstand the onslaught of a globalizing market. By the end of 1992 it was being suggested increasingly that in order to avoid the threat of de-industrialization (as European currencies lost out and were devalued in a power struggle against currency markets and the German domestically-led Bundesbank) Europe would move towards a *de facto* multi-speed arrangement for economic union – a *deux vitesses* or two-speed Europe (Rappoport, 1992).

In August 1993, within eight months of the SEM, the European Exchange Rate Mechanism (ERM) was essentially dismantled as the currency bands were broadened effectively to allow 15 per cent variation. In total US$ 100 billion was spent defending currencies, with a net cost to European banks of US$ 52 billion. With the additional costs of defending high interest rates, US$ 65 billion was spent – equivalent to 1 per cent of European GDP or the entire EU's annual budget. The year of turmoil on currency markets cost each EU citizen US$ 150. French industrialists, worried about the competitive devaluation of other European currencies, pointed out that staying in the first tier in 1993 meant real interest rates of over 9 per cent in France compared to 3.9 per cent in Germany and 0.2 per cent in the US. In order to bring French interest rates on a par with those of Germany, the franc needed to devalue by 15–20 per cent, just as the UK pound had. It fell in value by just 8 centimes. In the year before the collapse of the ERM, Spain's government deficit grew by 46 per cent in one year and unemployment soared to 22 per cent. Then came the cost of devaluation with the highest losers being Spain (US$ 26 billion), Portugal (US$ 10 billion), Britain and Germany (US$ 3 billion each), Italy (US$ 2.7 billion), and France (US$ 1.8 billion). Greece and the Netherlands broke even and Ireland and Denmark made minor gains. On the day that the ERM became a relic of history, Britain ratified the Maastricht Treaty, and a new political agenda was set for Europe as belief that monetary union could be achieved by 1997 waned. Political divisions between countries became more exposed and inward-looking as anti-recessionary attitudes took over from the early momentum towards integration, and nationalist and ethnic forces were given a new lease of life.

The devaluation of currencies brought the opportunity for a reduction in interest rates but without a twelve nation single currency organizations will not be able to eliminate fully exchange rate risks and second-tier neighbours may only be able to compete by raising costs or lowering margins. The changing dynamics between the performance of organizations and countries has a direct effect on decisions about global pricing, marketing strategies, international sourcing and manufacturing, financial performance and resource allocation (Dixon and Hedley, 1992). The increased uncertainty over these dynamics has global implications. Three days after France's ambiguous 'Oui' to the Maastricht Treaty, and the defence of the European currencies costing tens of billions of ECU, the US dollar also hit its postwar all time low of 119.65 Yen as investors headed for the comparative calm of Asia (Javetski, Glasgall, Melcher, Oster and Kiefer, 1992).

The two-tier Europe scenario suggests that whilst the scrapping of internal trade barriers and free trade would continue, a new 'economic architecture' could dominate European business. Europe would split into a hard-currency (Deutschemark) bloc of Germany, Switzerland, Austria, Denmark, Belgium, Holland, Luxembourg and (possibly) France, whose share of trade would increase. Germany is a magnet for exports, accounting for 39 per cent of Austrian, 28 per cent of Dutch, 27 per cent of Hungarian, 21 per cent of Luxembourg and 20 per cent of Danish exports. The Deutschemark makes up 35 per cent of Poland's currency basket and all three Baltic states have large Deutschemark components in their currency targets. High wages in the first tier would be paid for by high performance products but layoffs in other areas would occur as the rest of Europe offered cheaper labour. A second more loosely integrated and soft currency trading block of Britain, Ireland, Italy, Spain, Portugal and Greece would see new investment, but only for low-skilled and low-wage production, achieved at the expense of higher inflation, fluctuating interest rates and uneven growth (Melcher, Levine and Oster, 1992). The emergence even of these two tiers is by no means certain. The debate by 1993 was whether the whole of Europe needed to devalue competitively.

Therefore, after years of preparing for unity, involving many changes in HRM in anticipation of a complete SEM, many European organizations will end up redrawing their strategic blueprints. There could be a further shake-out of the currently less competitive organizations. Short-term gains for the currently most competitive organizations in the second tier (for example, through increased margins afforded by cheaper exchange rates) would be offset by a longer term shift in underlying competitiveness towards the larger European industrial groups. We have already described the competitive pressures facing the European car industry. Currency instability further eroded the position of the industry. For example, the devaluation of sterling, the lira and the peseta against the franc in 1992 cost Renault, the French state motor manufacturer 450 million ECU (FFr 3 billion) because it had to reduce its car prices to maintain local market shares. Volkswagen similarly has significant export markets in Italy, Spain and the UK. Devaluation cost it 102 million ECU (DM 200 million), exacerbating cost pressures.

In a two-tier scenario the larger of the first-tier organizations would need to re-assess their risks. Several multinationals may find their longer term strategies unsettled and less effective. For example, Unilever, Proctor and Gamble and Whirlpool all centralized production of some products, anticipating economies of scale and currency stability. As a consequence they removed their future flexibility to cope with the more variable cost base entailed by a multi-speed Europe, having already re-located many of their assets in the run-up to the creation of the SEM. The two-tier scenario remains a significant threat to organizations and some European nations. However, it also raises the prospect of 'competitive devaluation' within Europe – a situation not experienced since the 1930s. HRM conditions and practices in the softer currency bloc would also be devalued (see Illustration 4.8).

Similar concerns were raised when Grundig moved production of electronic goods from France to Austria. Such events also raised the spectre of 'social dumping' with claims that organizations will be encouraged to pursue tactics aimed at locating jobs in areas offering the cheapest labour and lowest demands in terms of conditions of employment. We discuss the effect of fears about 'social dumping' on industrial relations within Europe in Chapter Fifteen. Under the multi-speed Europe economic scenario, splits between North and South would be exacerbated and European integration, particularly in the realm of HRM, would follow a slower and far less predictable path.

Illustration 4.8 **Hoover relocation of jobs from France to Scotland.**

In May 1989 the Maytag Corporation acquired Chicago Pacific Corporation, thereby taking ownership of the loss-making Hoover Europe. In May 1993 the Maytag Corporation confirmed its decision to close the Hoover plant in Dijon, France, and transfer production to Cambuslang, Scotland. The home appliance market (including Hoover) accounts for around 95 per cent of Maytag's sales. Maytag has 20 manufacturing operations in six countries and employs around 21,400 employees. Hoover Europe consisted of four manufacturing plants: Merthyr Tydfil and Cambuslang in the UK; the Dijon plant in France; and a small operation in Lisbon. Hoover's losses in the UK were reported to be three times as great as those of Hoover France by the French publication *Usine Nouvelle* and the Dijon plant had reduced production costs by 8 per cent. However, Hoover's European business relied heavily on the UK as both a market and as its major production centre. The French government argued against the enticement of investment away from France towards the recently currency-devalued UK. French workers in Dijon only found out about the decision from Scottish newspapers. The relocation resulted in the loss of 600 French jobs for the gain of 400 Scottish jobs. It was also associated with a change (lowering) of employment rights. The European Parliament adopted a resolution by 198 to 42 votes that 'condemns governments which, by focusing on economic competition without the necessary social rules, are willing to make workers the victims of current developments'.

Source: European Parliament News (1993); McDermott (1993).

NEW FORMS OF ECONOMIC COMPETITION

As economic competition between communism and capitalism has finished, the new competition is between Anglo-Saxon and Germanic/Japanese forms of capitalism (Thurow, 1992), or what were referred to as 'national business systems' or 'business recipes' in Chapter Three. Each form of economic competition has significant implications for HRM. The Anglo-Saxon approach champions the responsible individual, with an underlying emphasis on large scale earnings differentiation, profit maximizing policies and mergers and takeovers that serve the interests of individual shareholders. The Germanic or Japanese forms of capitalism have a group-orientated focus on business clusters, teamwork, social responsibility for skills, company loyalty and industrial strategy. The primary field of economic tension over the next few decades lies between these two business philosophies and their associated management practices. Moreover, the seven key industries of the next few decades – microelectronics, biotechnology, new materials, civilian aviation, telecommunications, intelligent machine tools and information systems and technology – all rely on information. Each industry could be located anywhere in the world depending on the appropriateness of the organizational, educational and cultural philosophies of the host countries. Hampden-Turner and Trompenaars (1993) argue that in the same way that capitalism is constantly evolving, so are the values which engage it to best advantage. European HRM lies in the centre of a cultural and technical battlefield.

Europe's smaller countries in particular face significant threats to their national business systems (Marceau, 1992). In the emerging world economic order they have found that changes in generic technologies and the products in which they are embedded are increasingly being dominated by large organizations from large countries, as was seen in Norway in the late 1970s when it lost its consumer electronics industry. Small countries also risk losing their domestic market shares to low labour cost industrializing nations. Consequently, the previously distinct national business systems (which it was argued in Chapter Three have helped created unique patterns of

HRM in these countries) are under threat of dissappearing. As national business systems go, so will national patterns of HRM.

TECHNOLOGICAL ADVANCES

Sharp (1990) has analysed the role of technology in European integration. She points out that concerns about technological dependence in Europe first started to surface in the 1960s when it was feared that US multinationals were beginning to dominate Europe. By the late 1970s the very fast advances made by US and Japanese organizations in microelectronics and associated technologies caused consternation, but by the 1980s a far more deep-rooted 'technology gap' was being acknowledged. It is difficult, however, to generalize about the position of Europe as a whole. Pavitt and Patel (1988) analysed change in R&D expenditures as a proportion of industrial output from 1967 to 1985. In the US it fell slightly from 2.35 to 2.32 per cent (but still remained quite high). In Japan it more than doubled from 0.92 to 2.11 per cent and in Europe as a whole it crept up from 1.27 to 1.81 per cent. However, the European picture hides very different levels of progress. Sweden managed to double its proportionate R&D expenditure from 1.29 to 3.03 per cent and Germany increased from 1.31 to 2.42 per cent. Against these advances, the UK maintained a static 2.01 per cent of output, as did the Netherlands at around 1.50 per cent, while France caught up slightly with the leading European countries, increasing from 1.36 to 1.78 per cent.

However, existing skills and equipment are rapidly becoming obsolete and the entry of Japanese organizations has intensified competition enormously. Europe has increasingly relied on the US for transfer of process technology. Hagedoorn and Schot (1988) of the Studiecentrum voor Technologie en Beleid (TNO) in the Netherlands have analysed technological co-operation agreements in information technology and biotechnology (two key technologies). The majority were conducted after 1983, with most being between domestic US organizations, followed by agreements between US organizations and European organizations. Slow European progress in technological re-equipment and retraining, and legislative uncertainty in key areas of technological innovation (see Illustration 4.9) present European organizations in a dangerous

Illustration 4.9 **Biotechnology, competitiveness and employment creation.**

In much of this chapter we have focused on rationalization. Biotechnology, however, is widely believed to represent a core employment-creating technology for the twenty-first century. It holds the promise of boosting competitiveness in sectors such as agriculture, pharmaceuticals, healthcare, food and drink, and the EU estimates the industry could create another 2 million jobs by the year 2000. Annual sales for low-technology bio-products are already 14.5 billion ECU (US\$ 12 billion) with sales of 108 billion ECU (US\$ 90 billion) forecast for the year 2000. Europe's pharmaceutical giants are investing heavily to gain a lead, but claim they are hampered by varying national restrictions on biological research. The US has 1200 successful genetic companies compared to Europe's 250. Biotechnology has become an exportable commodity, as have the jobs associated with it. The three largest Swiss pharmaceutical and chemical organizations – CIBA, Hoffman La Roche and Sandoz – have moved facilities outside local Swiss jurisdiction. CIBA spends 10 per cent of it R&D budget on biotechnology, mostly outside Switzerland and is about to open its new 'Biotechnikum' plant in France. Bayer has responded to strict German legislation by broadening the geographic spread of its activities into the US, Japan and China.

Source: Hasell (1993), Parry (1993).

situation – squeezed by the cheap labour-intensive countries at one end, and by escalating R&D costs and US protectionist moves towards intellectual property at the other end (Sharp, 1990).

However, regardless of who owns and innovates the technology (and so is more likely to gain employment benefits) all European organizations are adopting new technologies that now have the potential radically to shift patterns of HRM. In addition to the radical economic transformations already described there has been a dramatic increase in both the types and amount of new technology used in organiz-ations, with no sign whatsoever of this advance slowing down. The pace of innovation is as great as ever, and the price–performance ratios of technologies such as computing and communications continue to improve exponentially.

When mobile telephones emerged in the late 1980s they were first seen as an executive luxury, then as a useful way of doing business, and finally as a personal convenience for the individual user. Further examples of technological transformations are found in manufacturing organizations. The increasing popularity of Computer Aided Manufacturing (CAM) and Computer Aided Design (CAD) technologies, and their combination into Computer Integrated Manufacturing (CIM) is revolutionizing the production process in the car manufacturing industry. In General Motors, for example, technological advances in information technology have revolutionized the way in which assembly line work is being done. Shopfloor workers are increasingly required to engage in activities of a non-manual nature, as an increasing proportion of traditional assembly line work is being done by robots. Similarly, the manufacturing of textiles, shoes, and other consumer products has been widely automated. In fact, research shows that more than 25 per cent of European manufacturing organizations rely on robot technology and other computer equipment to carry out the most routine and repetitive jobs (Hackett, Mirvis and Sales, 1991).

Computers are used on a broad basis in organization management, business analyses, electronic communication, accounting tasks, order entry, inventory control (see Illustration 4.10), and work scheduling as well as for design, production activities, and word processing. Xerox, for example, uses computers to help executives co-operate in planning the future. The computer combines individual forecasts and budgets so that each individual can see how his or her plans affect the group and

Illustration 4.10 **The technology pay-off: re-engineering work at Sweden's ICA.**

Sweden's ICA Handlarnas found information technology had done little to help the bottom line. Three sales regions still could not share data and so movement of retail goods to stores was inefficient and marketing campaigns were often conflicting. Andersen Consulting 're-engineered' the business process by linking together all 3350 retail stores and making inventory data more readily available. A third of warehouses and distribution centres were closed and costs were halved. The workforce of 5,000 was reduced by 30 per cent. Over a three year period revenues grew at 15 per cent per annum. ICA now focuses its information technology on the best way to organize work, fine tuning its marketing efforts with data and eliminating invoices. Similar re-engineering initiatives have been carried out at Reuters, Rolls Royce Motor Cars, Union Bank, Siemens and Ciba-Geigy. The pattern that is emerging, however, is that there are strong cultural impediments in countries like Germany (craft work traditions) and Italy (strong role of unions) and so different countries and different industries do not just adapt the North American model of business process re-engineering, but are finding their own paths to the productivity targets that are being set by their competitors.

Source: Guterl and Gross (1993).

vice-versa. Similarly, Royal Dutch/Shell has been experimenting with a yet more ambitious technique by involving executives in planning as a sort of do-it-yourself business simulation. Ideally, it would like executives to build their own models of how the company might react to various events, and test and improve their ideas by bringing scenarios to life inside the computer. Thus, computers not only automate aspects of work; they also 'informate' every facet of running a business (Ginzberg, 1982; Zuboff, 1988).

Evidence from the World Economic Forum (1993) indicates some significant differences still across Europe in the extent to which senior management feel that information technology is being fully exploited by their organizations. Whereas over 70 per cent feel that information technology is being fully exploited in their organizations in Finland, Sweden (and Japan) and over 60 per cent felt this was the case in Switzerland, Germany and Denmark, the figure falls to under 50 per cent in the UK, Turkey, France, Greece and Italy and under 40 per cent in Spain and Portugal. Many organizations have been surprised by the effort and time that it takes to implement new technology in the workplace and by the way employees react to and make use of it. However, a growing body of studies (and some 25 years of experience in industry) suggest that new technology offers many significant advantages to people and organizations by making certain aspects of work more interesting and enjoyable while adding to the user's task efficiency, autonomy, flexibility and motivation (Hackett, Mirvis and Sales, 1991). BMW reports that completely automated processes have led to an increase in the proportion of skilled production workers over the last 10 years from 30 to 50 per cent. Another example is robot technology, which can be used to automate the dirtiest and most dangerous jobs in manufacturing organizations and to relieve operators of repetitive, tedious tasks. Similarly, in the office, the jobs of secretaries and clerical workers can be enlarged with computers offering them more variety, the chance to learn new skills, more flexibility about the location and timing of work, and the opportunity to assume additional responsibilities (Buchanan and Boddy, 1982).

Computers can also help push down decision-making power in an organization. In 1958, the Harvard Business Review predicted that by the end of the 1980s important decisions would be made by a handful of executives with access to the firm's single, big computer (Economist, 1990a). In predicting that information technology would increase centralization, this journal was merely propagating the conventional wisdom of the 1950s. The argument boiled down to the idea that computers would enable top executives to keep better track of more information, to make wiser decisions and to disseminate them more widely. In actual fact, the exact opposite has occurred. Instead of centralizing decision making, most big organizations have taken advantage of new technology to push responsibility down to the lowest hierarchical level. Increasingly, first-line supervisors are given access to information on markets and production that enables them to make decisions once reserved for upper management and staff (Ranney and Cardner, 1984). All this adds up to the notion that employees and managers have many reasons to welcome new technology and be ready to change their work methods to gain full advantage of computerization. It would appear that, by replacing people in routine jobs with machines doing the same work, organizations can cut their wage bills, increase productivity, improve speed and quality of customer service, decentralize decision making, and improve morale.

Yet, research in organizations that have introduced computers over the past two decades suggests important caveats to this conclusion. As Hackett, Mirvis and Sales (1991) point out, there are also side effects to consider and some, such as increased social isolation, remote monitoring of work, and a loss of operator control, can easily cancel out the benefits of new technology in manufacturing operations. There can also be problems with office automation. A major concern among clerical workers, for example, is job loss. Clearly, information technology can eliminate the least skilful aspects of administrative work, reducing the need for clerical workers. In addition, automation, whether in the office or the factory, can make work more stressful. It can detract from the employee's control over the pace of their work or force lower skilled employees to make a significant leap in training and education, something many may feel is beyond them (Ettlie, 1986). However, given the rise in education standards (discussed later) 47 per cent of young Europeans aged between 15–24 years claim to know how to use a computer.

SOCIAL AND DEMOGRAPHIC TRENDS

On top of economic and technological changes there is a third stream of pressure. Over the past two decades there have been a number of significant and interrelated changes in the social and demographic environment that are transforming the European labour market. Predicting the final impact of social factors on the shape of HRM in European organizations is a difficult task. It is possible that European organizations will have to tackle economic problems, whilst simultaneously addressing the social and demographic shifts. It is equally possible, given the highly volatile political situation in the 1990s, that the social and demographic pressures already faced will lead to a counter-reaction to economic pressures for globalization, cost competitiveness, and rationalization. All the social and demographic pressures described in this chapter (if mobilized in conjunction with increasing nationalism) may serve to simply slow down the economic transformation, make it more complex to implement, or actually derail the whole process. There can be few certainties about the final impact of social and demographic pressures in the 1990s. There is, however, a clear consensus over what the pressures are (see Illustration 4.11).

SOCIAL COSTS OF EMPLOYMENT

In the section on competitive forces we highlighted the issue of productivity and the increasing focus on the direct and indirect social costs of employment. Social costs are, of course, only one factor used by employers to make decisions about the location of investment. Noble Lowndes (1993) point out that the degree to which skill and

---

Illustration 4.11 **Social and demographic pressures in the 1990s that will shape European HRM.**

- Social costs of employment.
- Rising unemployment.
- Demographic pressures and an ageing workforce.
- Increasing participation of women in the labour force.
- Increase in part time and temporary employment.
- Rising level of education.

- Shift from manufacturing to service employment.
- Shift from manual to non-manual jobs.
- Rise in self employment.
- Increasing skill shortages.
- New patterns of labour mobility.
- Rising concern over immigration.
- Changing values and expectations of the workforce

technology requirements can be met, the general fiscal climate, access to research, the state of the infrastructure and communications and the size of the local market all make a significant contribution to competitiveness. However, Noble Lowndes (1993) have responded to the prospect of multinationals shifting operations from one country to another and the debate on differing social costs of employment across Europe by analysing the real costs. Simple comparisons of social security contributions are misleading. These suggest that Italy is expensive as an employment site but Denmark is cheap but this is only so because Denmark funds social security costs through taxation rather than direct contributions. More realistic comparisons need to tap those factors that influence pay levels and expectations and therefore should include estimates of:

- Social security contributions by employees and employers.
- Income tax paid by employees.
- Mandatory supplementary benefit contributions by employees and employers.
- Voluntary (but virtually obligatory through custom and practice) pension plan contributions by employees and employers.

On this basis, for each S Kr. 100 of take-home pay in Sweden an employer must allocate a further S Kr. 105 to cover social costs. Similar high costs are evident in Italy, France, the Netherlands and Belgium, whilst in contrast employers in Greece only have to add Dr. 53 for every Dr. 100 of take-home pay. When considering the proportion of add on social costs to basic pay costs, Switzerland (S Fr. 48 for every S Fr. 100 of pay) and Japan (Yen 52 for every Yen 100 of pay) are low social cost countries. However, local currencies are associated with different purchasing power. The data shown in Figure 4.6 adjusts total pay and social costs to take account of the purchasing power of local currencies and deviations in the amount of public holidays from the norm of 30 days. It reflects the true costs to investors wishing to set up operations in Europe and is therefore a more realistic reflection of the league table of social costs.

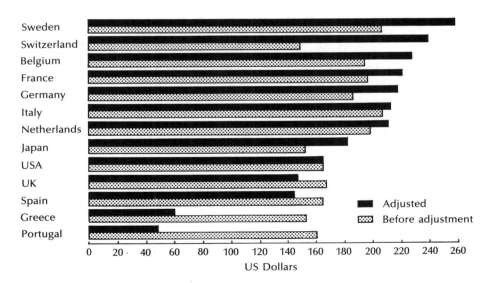

Figure 4.6 Pay and social costs of employment adjusted to reflect purchasing power. *Source*: reproduced with the permission of Noble Lowndes & Partners Ltd, using comparative compensation costs in US dollars and OECD average 1992 exchange rates adjusted for GDP purchasing parities relative to those in the USA.

Table 4.2 **Comparison of holidays, productivity and absenteeism data to reflect indirect social costs in Europe.**

Country	Holidays* per year	Productivity**	Average hours lost per worker per year due to sickness
Germany (West)	42	100.0	148
Netherlands	41	102.0	–
Belgium	–	120.1	–
Italy	40	97.7	–
Austria	39	–	–
Spain	38	75.2	–
Portugal	36	26.1	–
Denmark	35	78.9	–
France	35	81.2	144
UK	35	73.8	119
Japan	25	91.9	–
USA	23	83.3	57

* average holiday days plus national holidays
** relative productivity in 1991 calculated from working costs per hour where West Germany = 100.
Source data: from Datastream and the Institute of German Economy (IW), Cologne.

... We have accumulated a lot of ballast in the past 40 years... we have the shortest working week, the oldest students and the youngest pensioners in the industrial world.

Statement by Chancellor Helmut Kohl to the Bundestag, March 1993.

Related to concern over the direct social costs of employment across Europe there has been an increased focus on indirect social costs incurred as a result of differences in such things as absenteeism rates and levels of paid holiday. The costs of absenteeism and sickness to organizations are not insignificant. For example, BMW reports an annual cost of 109 million ECU (DM 212.7 million) in 1991 for sickness and other time off work. Research by Heiner Flassbeck at the German Institute for Economic Research (DIW) in Berlin has attempted to assess the background to the statistics on holiday sickness and pay disparities (see Table 4.2). In 1991 the average work hours lost per worker due to sickness were 148 hours in Germany, 144 hours in France and 119 hours in Britain compared to only 57 hours in the US. However, despite high levels of holiday entitlement and absenteeism productivity per hour in West German industry is still amongst the highest in the world (although East German productivity lags by around 30 per cent).

RISING UNEMPLOYMENT

Rising levels of unemployment have helped increase the social costs of employment in Europe. The general level of employment from 1977 to 1990 increased across the EU by 35 per cent in the Netherlands, 19 per cent in Portugal, 10 to 12 per cent in France and Germany, 9.6 per cent in the UK and 2.7 per cent in Spain (Euromonitor, 1993) and between 1983 and 1990 the EU created no fewer than 9 million new jobs. Supply-side economic policies aimed at improving labour market flexibility rather than stimulating economic demand created a low-inflation boom from 1983 to 1990 – the longest inflation boom in Europe since the 1960s. However, only 1.2 million of the new jobs went to people actively seeking work whilst 7.8 million went to new entrants into the labour force. Therefore, unemployment levels hardly changed (International Management, 1992a). Employment increased in the 1980s because GDP growth outpaced labour productivity gains (see Table 4.3). Despite labour saving technology it took more people to produce the higher output.

After five years of the most sustained job creation (between 1985 and 1990) unemployment in the EU started to rise again in the latter half of 1990 and by 1992 stood at an average of 11 per cent or 18 million unemployed people (see Table 4.4). Economic forecasts suggest a continuance at or around these levels in most European countries. Only 60 per cent of Europeans of working age have a job, compared to 70 per cent in the US and 75 per cent in Japan. European GDP needs to grow at 3 per cent each year simply in order to service current unemployment, whilst similar growth rates in the US create four times as many jobs as in Europe. The latest increase in unemployment occurred because the labour supply grew at a faster rate (on average 0.8 per cent more a year) than the demand for labour. The 1991 rate of 9.5 per cent was higher than the USA at 7.0 per cent, Japan at 2.4 per cent and the rest of Europe at 2.3 per cent.

There are large differences in unemployment between sectors and regions. For example, the Italian state is characterized by a deep North–South divide. The industrial triangle of Genoa–Turin–Milan is less affected by unemployment, whilst in the South unemployment rates were twice as high at 19.2 per cent in 1987 (Hinterhuber and Stumpf, 1990). The trend has not been reversed. Similarly, although the four poorest EU-states (Portugal, Greece, Spain and Ireland) had a 4 per cent higher growth in employment in industry and the service sector than the more developed member states, they also had a heavy loss of agricultural jobs (19 per cent) leading to an overall increase in their unemployment (Mill, 1991). According to the EU annual report on the employment situation and patterns within the EU, these four member states would need to create four times as many jobs in the service sector and industry as other EU states in order to compensate for the decline in agriculture.

Specific industrial sectors have problems, with, for example, the defence, automobile and textile, leather and clothing industries facing particular issues. General cuts in government defence budgets are leading to dramatic reductions in the defence industry, which employs about 1.5 million people in the EU, largely in France and the UK. As already discussed, the automobile industry – which employs three million – is in serious recession and is suffering from fierce external competition and lower productivity than the USA and Japan. The textile, clothing and leather industries provide 3.5 million jobs, but are also suffering from strong external competition, with

Table 4.3 **Output, productivity and employment from 1980 to 1991 in the three main trading blocs.**

	Real GDP growth	Productivity growth	Employment growth	Unemployment rate
EU	2.2%	2.0%	0.5%	9.5%
US	2.2%	0.5%	1.4%	7.0%
Japan	4.1%	3.0%	1.3%	2.4%

Source: International Management (1992a), reprinted with permission © International Management, 1993, Reed Business Publishing.

Table 4.4 **Standardized unemployment rates percentage of total labour force.**

	1965	1970	1978	1979	1980	1981	1982	1983	1984	1985	1986	1987	1988	1989	1990	1991
Austria*	1.9	1.4	1.8	1.8	1.6	2.2	3.1	3.7	3.8	3.6	3.1	3.8	3.6	3.1	3.3	–
Belgium	1.8	2.1	7.9	8.2	8.8	10.8	12.6	12.1	12.1	11.3	11.2	11.0	9.6	8.1	7.3	7.1
Denmark*	–	–	7.3	6.2	7.0	9.2	9.8	10.4	10.1	9.0	7.8	7.8	8.5	9.2	9.5	–
Finland	1.4	1.9	7.2	5.9	4.6	4.8	5.3	5.4	5.2	5.0	5.3	5.0	4.5	3.4	3.4	7.4
France	1.5	2.5	5.2	5.9	6.3	7.4	8.1	8.3	9.7	10.2	10.4	10.5	10.0	9.4	8.9	9.3
Germany	0.3	0.8	3.5	3.2	2.9	4.2	5.9	7.7	7.1	7.2	6.4	6.2	6.2	5.6	5.1	4.3
Greece	–	–	1.8	1.9	2.8	4.0	5.8	7.8	8.1	7.8	7.4	7.4	7.7	7.5	7.2	–
Ireland	–	–	–	–	–	–	–	13.7	15.4	16.8	17.1	16.9	16.3	15.0	13.7	15.1
Italy	5.3	5.3	7.1	7.6	7.5	7.8	8.4	8.8	9.4	9.6	10.5	10.9	11.0	10.9	9.9	–
Luxembourg*	–	–	0.8	0.7	0.7	1.0	1.3	1.6	1.7	1.6	1.4	1.6	1.4	1.3	1.3	–
Netherlands	0.5	1.0	5.3	5.4	6.0	8.5	11.4	12.0	11.8	10.6	9.9	9.6	9.2	8.3	7.5	7.0
Norway	1.8	1.6	1.8	2.0	1.6	2.0	2.6	3.4	3.1	2.6	2.0	2.1	3.2	4.9	–	5.5
Portugal	–	–	–	–	–	–	–	7.9	8.4	8.5	8.5	7.0	5.7	5.0	4.6	4.1
Spain	2.7	2.4	6.8	8.4	11.1	13.8	15.6	17.0	19.7	21.1	20.8	20.1	19.1	16.9	15.9	16.0
Sweden	1.2	1.5	2.2	2.1	2.0	2.5	3.1	3.5	3.1	2.8	2.7	1.9	1.6	1.3	1.5	2.7
Switzerland*	–	–	0.3	0.3	0.2	0.2	0.4	0.8	0.9	0.8	0.7	0.6	0.7	0.6	0.6	–
UK	2.3	3.0	5.9	5.0	6.4	9.8	11.3	12.4	11.7	11.2	11.2	10.3	8.5	6.9	6.9	8.9

* Non-standardized definitions.

Source: Ferner and Hyman (1992), OECD statistics, reprinted with permission © 1993 *Industrial Relations in the New Europe*, Basil Blackwell.

Illustration 4.12   **Different incentives for the long-term unemployed.**

Incentives to encourage the long-term unemployed back to work vary widely across Europe. In insurance-based systems (related to what the employee has paid in) in countries such as Germany, France and Spain, assistance drops sharply after the first year of unemployment, whereas in the welfare-based systems (linked to perceived need) in the UK and Ireland benefits for the long-term unemployed are higher than those for the short-term unemployed. Most EU countries provide benefits ranging from 50 per cent to 70 per cent of the last previous wage for a limited initial period. Whereas in Ireland the figure is 41 per cent, in the UK it is only 26 per cent (excluding social security top-up payments). In countries like Denmark, the Netherlands and Belgium an unemployed man can receive 50 per cent of his last wage for an unlimited amount of time under some circumstances. Roughly two to three times as much money is spent on unemployment protection in these countries as in either Germany or the UK. Countries like Italy, Portugal and Greece spend proportionately less on unemployment benefit and protection.

survival relying on restructuring and development of the high value-added quality end of the market (Mill, 1991).

It is also worth noting that the proportion of long-term unemployment in the EU has not changed in the last five years, despite extensive programmes at both national and community level (see Illustration 4.12 for an outline of the different incentives for the long-term unemployed). In 1992, five million EU citizens had been unemployed for over a year. There is a particular problem with youth unemployment with the unemployment rate for the 20–24 age group at least double that of the over-25 year olds. In January 1993 the lowest youth unemployment rates were 4.5 per cent in Germany, but, typically, rates varied from 10.7 per cent in the Netherlands, 17.8 per cent in the UK, 22.3 per cent in France, to a staggering 35.5 per cent in Spain. Approximately 70 per cent of Italy's three million unemployed are aged 14 to 29, most of them looking for their first job (Hinterhuber and Stumpf, 1990). In Southern Italy one in two under-25 year olds cannot find a job. There is also a high level of female unemployment in the EU. In Greece, Belgium and Portugal, 60 per cent of unemployed are female whilst in the UK and Ireland the rate is between 35 and 40 per cent. The UK is the only EU country where the rate of unemployment is lower for women than for men.

DEMOGRAPHIC SHIFTS AND AN AGEING WORKFORCE

The EU Social Affairs directorate acknowledges that from 1972 to 1992 the overt and covert policy of European governments was to trigger a mass expulsion of older people from the labour force in order to help solve the unemployment crisis. However, Europe is now faced with a rapidly ageing workforce and has the highest proportion of elderly people in the world. People also live longer than before. In 1960, the average life expectancy across the whole of Western Europe was 68 years for men and 72 years for women. By 1980 it was 72.5 years for men and 79 years for women. From 1970 to 1990 the life expectancy at birth has increased from 70.5 years to 76.1 years in West Germany, from 72.9 years to 77.1 years in France, from 71.8 years to 75.5 years in the UK, and from a relatively low 67 years to an average of 74.7 years in Portugal. As a consequence of longer life expectancy, one person in 15 in the EU is now aged over 75 years and almost 20 per cent of the population is aged over 60 years.

Illustration 4.13   **Declining birth rates in Europe.**

Probably the best known demographic problems are the declining birth rate and the increasing life expectancy of the EU population. There has been a substantial drop in the annual birth rate during the past three decades. The fertility rate in the EU needed to maintain population levels is 2.1. It has now fallen below this level. According to the Council of Europe, just six of its 26 member states (Cyprus, Ireland, Iceland, Poland, Sweden and Turkey) have birth rates that will lead to an increase in population. In 1960 the EU average was 2.63 children per woman, compared to only 1.6 by 1986. In the Catholic south of Europe (Spain and Italy) fertility rates have fallen as low as 1.28. In Greece the birth rate has fallen from 2.2 to 1.4 within a decade. As a result of social and economic upheaval in East Germany the number of births halved in two years while fertility rates also fell in the Baltic States, Slovenia, Croatia, Romania, Russia and Ukraine. Exhortations and financial incentives to increase the birth rate do not appear to have worked (for example, the provision of high child benefits in France failed to shift the birth rate). In 50 years time, the population of Europe's twenty largest nations will fall from the current 449 million people to 342 million people – a drop of over 100 million. A more immediate consequence of this trend is a shrinking supply of young workers. By the end of the century, people aged twenty-one years or less will make up one fifth of Europe's population whereas in 1950 they accounted for one quarter.

A decline in the birth rate (see Illustration 4.13) is creating even more pressure on social costs in Europe. We have already discussed the different social costs of employment across Europe. However, average EU expenditure on pensions and other old-age benefits was 9 per cent of GDP by 1988 rising to 12 per cent by 1992 (and considerably higher in countries like Italy). By 2020 the proportion aged over 60 will be 37 per cent – resulting in a markedly higher pension provision requirement for national states and organizations. This trend is likely to continue until 2040, when 21.9 per cent of the total EU population will be over 65 (an increase of 63 per cent on present levels).

The release of pension funds seems increasingly likely (see Illustration 4.14). Across Europe pension systems are starting to stare into the abyss as a growing army of retired people depend for their living on the funds provided by dwindling battalions of workers (Carson, 1992). The demographic problem is so marked that government finances, the current pay-as-you-go provision for retirement (in which today's active workforce pay the pensions of today's retired workers), and the welfare state are all anticipated to come under significant pressure. Indeed, they may become untenable. A massive shift in the dependency ratio is in store (see Figure 4.7). For example, in France in 1970 there were three workers working for every dependent relative and the average contribution from the pay packet to support pensions was 17 per cent. By 2010 there will be only 1.7 employees per relative. Demands on the fund will amount to 89.3 billion ECU (FFr 587 billion) with receipts totalling only 58.4 billion ECU (FFr 384 billion). Contributions will need to rise to 40 per cent (Heath, 1993b) and by 2020 there will be more retired people than workers (Carson, 1992). In Germany the situation is even more marked. There are currently four times as many people aged from 15 to 64 than aged over 65. By 2035 the proportion will be one to one (Carson, 1992). This shift is reflected in the EU as a whole where there are two people of working age for every person aged over 60. By 2020 there will be just one. The imbalance becomes alarming when the number of children and unemployed (see the previous section) is added to the equation.

Some European governments are already responding to the crisis. For example, in Germany the Nursing Care Bill, due to be phased in from 1994 to 1996 will result in

Illustration 4.14 **Freeing up pension funds.**

The EU is making considerable efforts to free up the massive nationally-based private sector pension funds for European-wide investment (Carson, 1992) and to harmonize pensions rights. As noted above, Italy currently has the most generous provision. An individual earning 1.5 times the national average wage before retirement can expect 79 per cent of pre-retirement income as a pension. Social security contributions to fund pensions already consume 14 per cent of GDP, up from 5 per cent in 1960. The pay out exceeds contributions by 9 per cent. Italian employers pay insurance contributions at a rate twice that of other EU countries. We have already discussed the impact of privatization, but the shift from state to private pension provision may turn out to be the largest and most significant pan-European privatization. Funded-pensions are valued at a massive 600 billion ECU in the EU (Carson, 1992), with the UK accounting for 350 billion ECU, the Netherlands 145 billion ECU and Germany 36 billion ECU. In France, the UK and the Netherlands the value of pension fund and life insurance assets exceeds each countries GDP. The largest pension fund in Europe is that of the Dutch civil servants – the Algemeen Burgerlijk Pensioenfonds (ABP). The release of pension funds across borders would fuel economic growth. The value of such pension funds can also become an important element in takeovers and privatizations. Most of the assets tied up in pension funds are locked within national boundaries. The pension fund of British Coal alone (targeted for privatization in the UK) is worth 2 billion ECU (£1.6 billion) – a potentially richer seam than any found underground. In France and Germany industry-wide occupational plans are more prevalent, and retained contributions by companies can be invested in friendly companies. Such cross-shareholdings are, however, coming under increasing pressure (see Chapter Five).

an additional charge of 1.7 per cent of salary, split 50:50 between employee and employer. In order to avoid raising social employment costs too much, the employer contributions will be offset by reducing the number of paid sick days by six a year. Difficult decisions will have to be made, but social expectations in Europe are high. Surveys consistently show the majority of citizens wanting their governments to spend more on old age pensions and healthcare, with many of the most exposed countries (such as Italy and the UK) having the highest expectations for such spending (Knights, Morgan and Murray, 1992). Although financial security in Italy has long been based on the art of *'l'arrangiarsi'* – arranging security for yourself and your family through

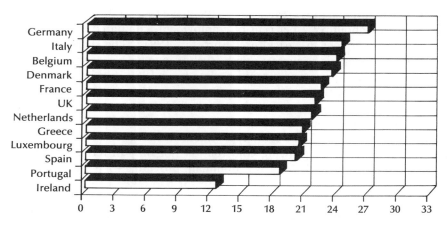

Figure 4.7 Projected increases in the proportion of over 60s in the EU population by the year 2010. Data from various publications from the Statistical Office of the European Union.

Illustration 4.15   **Projected impacts of an ageing workforce on Europe.**

- Competition between young and old generations for dwindling social resources.
- Increases in the age at which state pensions are paid.
- Acute labour shortages in key areas.
- Reduced levels and ratios of saving.

- Lower liquid savings leading to higher interest rates, slower investment and lower economic growth.
- Higher demand on and cost of social services.
- Greater pension fund pressure on management boards.

associative memberships based on occupation, locality, party or ideology – the state has long been seen as the ultimate patron. When states cannot deliver, workers will begin to object strongly.

Pension planners now face the double challenge of meeting the needs of fit and healthy over-50 year olds (already one EU citizen in three is aged over 50) who are increasingly being pushed out of the workforce and caring for the growing number of people aged over 75 who need greater medical attention and care. It is unfortunate that at the same time that the workforce is ageing, 'ageism' and employment discrimination are still major features of the labour market (Davies and Sparrow, 1985). Even the EU still attaches an upper age limit of 35 to its external job adverts.

The impact of this ageing workforce (see Illustration 4.15) will result in a combination of tighter belts for pensioners and greater burdens of pension provision for employees. Another side effect of the pensions deficit is that private funds are expected to grow as employees attempt to reduce the shortfall in their living standards. Pension funds will then become such large shareholders in organizations that they will have a considerable say in how they are run (the impact of increasing shareholder power on corporate performance is discussed in Chapter Five).

SHIFT FROM MANUFACTURING TO SERVICES

Another structural transformation (see Figure 4.8) has been the continued shift from manufacturing to service employment (Ferner and Hyman, 1992b). According to the EU, almost all additional jobs created since 1985 have been in the service sector, which now accounts for about 59.2 per cent of employment, compared to 33.2 per cent in industry and 7.6 per cent in agriculture (Eurostat, 1991). The share of employment in the service sector tends to increase with level of income per head. Employment in the industrial sector experienced a rapid decline from 1980, but began to stabilize in 1985. However, the picture is different in Germany, where the proportion employed in industry (over 40 per cent) is the highest in the EU. In Greece and Portugal over 20 per cent of total employment is in agriculture, whilst the Netherlands, Luxembourg and Denmark have over 67 per cent employment in the service sector.

The service sector has a growing contribution not only in terms of employment. Whilst in 1970 the industrial sector was dominant providing 42 per cent of total value added at market prices, by 1986 the service sector had taken first place providing 45 per cent of value added (Eurostat, 1989). The US is more developed still, with 54 per cent of value added coming from the service sector. The figure for Japan is 42 per cent. However, although the 62 per cent growth rate in value added in the EU service sector from 1970–85 was high, it was outpaced by a 109 per cent growth rate in Japan. We

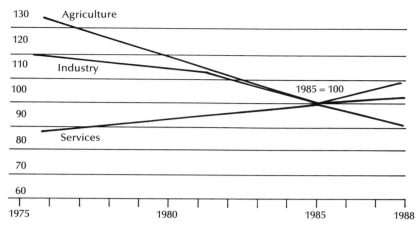

Figure 4.8 Fluctuations in EU employment by economic sector. *Source*: Eurostat (1991), reprinted with permission, © 1993, report on *A Social Portrait of Europe*, Eurostat, 1991.

have already questioned the ability of the service sector to grow fast enough to reduce unemployment significantly.

Linked to the growth of the service sector and the increased levels of education has been a trend from manual to non-manual occupations. In the UK, for example, the number of non-manual workers overtook the number of manual workers for the first time in 1981. However, this was due in large part to a faster than average decline in manufacturing employment in the UK. From 1977–1990 the number of manufacturing jobs in the UK fell by 30.3 per cent, compared to falls of 20 per cent in France, and 13–14 per cent in Spain and Italy. In Germany manufacturing jobs remained static, and in Portugal they actually grew by 31 per cent (Euromonitor, 1993).

INCREASING PARTICIPATION OF WOMEN

The total working-age population of the EU is 225.4 million of whom 134.7 million are employed. It is often suggested that women are under-paid, under-represented and under-achieving in the EU. Research by the International Labour Organization (ILO) in Geneva suggests that on present trends women will only hold an equal number of management posts to men by the twenty-fifth century! Only 51 per cent of women in the EU are working or are actively seeking work compared to 78 per cent of men, and female employment rates are less than 30 per cent in many of the Mediterranean countries. However, at a European level there is a strong self-interest in raising the levels of economic participation. If the EU could raise female participation rates from the current 50 per cent to the figure of 60 per cent seen in the US, then the EU labour force would acquire an extra 6 million workers (Carson, 1992), which is an attractive proposition given the the demographic and ageing problems and the need to fund pension provision, as already discussed. The UK has one of the highest proportions of women at work, although 45 per cent of employed women are in part time jobs which are invariably low status and with little opportunity for career progression (see the next section). In Germany, only 25 per cent of the workforce are women.

Female participation rates have been growing in every EU country, but still vary widely. Participation rates for women aged from 15 to 64 years range from 81 per cent and 78 per cent in Sweden and Denmark (rates unrivalled anywhere in the EU), 65 per cent in the UK, between 51 per cent and 56 per cent in Austria, Belgium, France, Germany, the Netherlands and Switzerland, and as low as 40 per cent in Spain (Economist Intelligence Unit, 1991). Participation rates are clearly influenced by the availability of childcare and the existence of flexible work arrangements. Paid maternity leave entitlement depends upon the contribution history (except in the UK where it is granted irrespective of the length of job service). Attempts to introduce a minimum parental leave entitlement in the EU have been blocked by the UK, which has the least generous arrangements. The heightening professional profile of women has much to do with effective childcare provision. Dutch and British women have the highest fallout rate from work after their first child, whereas in France, where 95 per cent of pre-school children have nursery places, the fallout of women from the workforce does not begin until after the third child. Female participation rates have only approached those of men in countries where public arrangements for the care of pre-school children are widely accessible, such as in Scandinavia and Eastern Europe. The disruption of mothers' employment by childbearing and rearing varies in degree and pattern across Europe. Joshi and Davies (1992) have explored the relationship between day care in Europe and forgone earnings for mothers and created detailed reconstructions of women's lifetime earnings for Britain, Germany, Sweden and France. The earnings loss due to having children has three components:

1. Lost years' earning in the labour force.
2. Fewer hours worked upon return to work due to childcare.
3. Diminished employment record reducing future earnings' power.

Comparisons on this basis show that in Britain and Germany the lost earnings associated with one child are well over half the loss associated with having two children. The lifetime earnings costs (loss) of having two children (expressed as a percentage of earnings of childless women) amount to 58 per cent in Britain, 49 per

Illustration 4.16 **Women as managers in Europe.**

The number of female professionals is increasing, if slowly. Comparative figures on women in management provide conflicting evidence, largely due to different definitions of what constitutes a management job. For example, when considering all management jobs, the UK has the highest representation of women at 27 per cent. However, Belgium has the highest proportion of female executives in the EU. In Spain a mere 9 per cent of management posts are occupied by women, but for a country that entered the equality race late, rapid progress is being made. The number of female professionals in sectors such as computing and banking more than doubled from 1987–1992. In the public sector more than 12 per cent of executives are women – a higher proportion than in the UK or Norway for instance. In Greece, however, the number of women in management jobs has actually fallen since 1985. The Centre of Research in Organizational Behaviour in Milan has recently investigated the progress of women in Italian industry. Only 5 per cent of employed women worked in managerial positions. The typical Italian female manager was found to be aged 45 years old, has 16 years service having started work at 21 and reached a managerial position at the age 37. Average income is 48,600 ECU (25.7 million lire). Across the whole of Europe there are still marked inequalities in pay. Female executive salaries are only 75 per cent of equivalent male salaries in Belgium, 78 per cent in Germany, 82 per cent in Spain and 83 per cent in the UK. In the US 40 per cent of senior business executives are women, whilst in some Asian economies – such as the Philippines – 35 per cent of management jobs are held by women.

Source: Hinterhuber and Stumpf (1990); Wassell (1993a).

cent in Germany, 16 per cent in Sweden and only 1 per cent in France (Joshi and Davies, 1992). Even more marked differences are seen once three children are born. Therefore, although an increasing number of women are interested in joining the workforce, doing so is not always easy.

However, according to the EU statistics, two-thirds of new jobs between 1985 and 1990 were taken by women, and the female employment rate grew at 9 per cent, as opposed to 4 per cent for men. The growth rate was lowest in France at 4 per cent and highest in Spain and the Netherlands, where it was over 25 per cent. Unfortunately, there is a relatively low priority given to the need to employ more women by European HR Directors (see Table 6.1) and notably the EU itself, where 46 per cent of the 13,000 workforce are women, yet women account for 80 per cent of the clerical posts, 50 per cent of the interpreters and translators, but only 12 per cent of the A-grade administrative staff, and only 2 of the 53 Director Generals. The experience of women as managers in Europe is summarized in Illustration 4.16.

INCREASING NUMBER OF PART-TIME AND TEMPORARY WORKERS

The pan-European trend towards more flexible forms of employment can be seen now in countries like Germany. Except for a rise in unemployment, the employment situation had changed little in Germany from the 1970s. In the mid-1980s the average length of employment in German organizations was second only to that in Japanese organizations (Streeck, 1987) and the part time quotient remained relatively low. Lane (1989) has analysed the debate on flexibility that preoccupied German employers and authors in the early 1980s. She points out that even in Germany – which had not demonstrated the same problems of unemployment or levels of reliance on flexible patterns of work as were found in many other EU countries – significant change has been fuelled by the 1985 Employment Protection Act (EPA) which radically attacked 'employment rigidity' in Germany in an attempt to reduce unemployment, increase the availability of part time work and make it easier to issue fixed termed contracts (if they employed the unemployed or retained apprentices). The experience in Germany since the EPA (Bosch, 1988; Kern and Schumann, 1989; Lane, 1989) has been a growth in part time work, more rigid segmentation of the labour force (although still less pronounced than is found in France and the UK), an opening up of internal labour markets to entrants from occupational markets, a growing substitution of skilled workers for unskilled or semi-skilled workers, and closure of the internal labour market to unskilled workers (see the section on Skill Shortages on page 130).

Table 4.5 provides comparative figures on part time working from the OECD Employment Outlook 1991. These figures show that part time work increased throughout the 1980s, especially for women. Vickerstaff (1992) notes that 'part time' covers a wide range of different employment situations in terms of hours worked and degrees of job security. Unfortunately, part time work has typically been seen as low status, marginal employment with lower pay and career prospects. As a proportion of total employment, part time work is highest in the Netherlands (33.2 per cent), Norway (26.6 per cent), Denmark (23.7 per cent) and Sweden (23.2 per cent), and lowest in Greece (5.5 per cent), Italy (5.7 per cent), Portugal (5.9 per cent) and Spain (4.8 per cent). It is particularly prevalent in the services sector (18.6 per cent of all jobs) and in agriculture (14.8 per cent of all jobs). Only 5.3 per cent of industrial employees work part time (Eurostat, 1991).

In the last five years, across the EU as a whole, 30 per cent of new jobs created have been part time. More women than men work part time: over 80 per cent of people

Table 4.5 **Size and composition of part time employment, 1979–1990 (percentages).**

| | Total employment | | | Part time employment as a proportion of | | | | | | Women's share in part time employment | | |
| | | | | Male employment | | | Female employment | | | | | |
	1979	1983	1990	1979	1983	1990	1979	1983	1990	1979	1983	1990
Australia	15.9	17.5	21.3	5.2	6.2	8.0	35.2	36.4	40.1	78.7	78.0	78.1
Austria	7.6	8.4	8.8b	1.5	1.5	1.6b	18.0	20.0	20.0b	87.8	88.4	88.8b
Belgium	6.0	8.1	10.2b	1.0	2.0	1.7b	16.5	19.7	25.0b	88.9	84.0	89.6b
Canada	12.5	15.4	15.4	5.7	7.6	8.1	23.3	26.1	24.4	72.1	71.3	71.0
Denmark	22.7	23.8	23.7c	5.2	6.6	9.0c	46.3	44.7	41.5c	86.9	84.7	79.4c
Finland	6.7	8.3	7.2	3.2	4.5	4.4	10.6	12.5	10.2	74.7	71.7	67.8
France	8.2	9.7	12.0	2.4	2.6	3.5	16.9	20.0	23.8	82.2	84.4	83.1
Germany	11.4	12.6	13.2c	1.5	1.7	2.1c	27.6	30.0	30.6c	91.6	91.9	90.5c
Greece	–	6.5	5.5c	–	3.7	2.9c	–	12.1	10.3c	–	61.2	65.7c
Ireland	5.1	6.6	8.1c	2.1	2.7	3.8c	13.1	15.5	17.1c	71.2	71.6	68.2c
Italy	5.3	4.6	5.7b	3.0	2.4	3.1b	10.6	9.4	10.9b	61.4	64.8	64.7b
Japan	15.4	16.2	17.6b	7.5	7.3	8.0b	27.8	29.8	31.9b	70.1	72.9	73.0b
Luxembourg	5.8	6.3	6.5c	1.0	1.0	2.0c	17.1	17.0	15.1c	87.5	88.9	80.0c
Netherlands	16.6	21.4	33.2	5.5	7.2	15.8	44.0	50.1	61.7	76.4	73.3	70.4
New Zealand	13.9	15.3	20.1	4.9	5.0	8.5	29.1	31.4	35.2	77.7	79.8	76.1
Norway	25.3	29.0	26.6	7.3	7.7	8.8	50.9	63.3	48.2	83.0	83.7	81.8
Portugal	7.8	–	5.9b	2.5	–	3.1b	16.5	–	10.0b	80.4	–	69.8b
Spain	–	–	4.8b	–	–	1.6b	–	–	11.9b	–	–	77.2b
Sweden	23.6	24.8	23.2	5.4	6.3	7.3	46.0	45.9	40.5	87.5	86.6	83.7
UK	16.4	19.4	21.8b	1.9	3.3	5.0b	39.0	42.4	43.8b	92.8	89.8	87.0b
US	16.4	18.4	16.9	9.0	10.8	10.0	26.7	28.1	25.2	68.0	66.8	67.6

a. For sources and definitions, see Annex 1.B *OECD Employment Outlook 1989* and Annex 1.C *OECD Employment Outlook 1990*, except as indicated below for the Netherlands.
b. Data are for 1989.
c. Data are for 1988.
d. Break in series in 1985.
e. The 1990 data for male employment include conscripts, contrary to the situation for earlier years.

Sources:
Australia: Australian Bureau of Statistics, *The Labour Force Australia.*
Austria: Central Statistical Office, *Mikrozensus.*
Belgium, Denmark, France, Germany, Greece, Ireland, Italy, Luxembourg, the UK: EUROSTAT, *Labour Force Sample Survey.*
Canada: Statistics Canada, *The Labour Force.*
Finland: Central Statistical Office of Finland, *Labour Force Survey.*
Japan: Bureau of Statistics, *Labour Force Survey.* Data refers to non-agricultural industries.
New Zealand: Labour and Employment Gazette.
Netherlands: Data were provided by the Central Bureau of Statistics.
Norway: Central Bureau of Statistics, *Labour Market Statistics.*
Sweden: National Central Bureau of Statistics, *The Labour Force Survey.*
United States: US Department of Labor, Bureau of Labor Statistics, *Employment and Earnings.*

Source: S. Vickerstaff (1992) (ed.), *Human Resource Management in Europe: text and cases,* Figure T3.1 pp. 86–87, reprinted with permission © Chapman & Hall.

employed part time in the EU in 1988 were women, 64 per cent of whom were married. The figure for men was 18.2 per cent (Eurostat, 1991). Part time work accounts for between 10 and 12 per cent of female employment in Greece, Portugal, Italy, and Spain, but over 40 per cent of female employment in the UK and Denmark and 62 per cent in the Netherlands. The proportion of men working part time is around 5 per cent on average in most EU member states, except in the Netherlands where it is 16 per cent.

Sparrow (1986) has argued that in the UK at least part time work has fuelled the pauperization of employment. Over the period 1951 to 1981 the proportion of part time to full time jobs rose from 1 in 23 to 1 in 5. A simple substitution process took place in the UK economy in which 2,375,000 full time jobs were lost (81 per cent of the loss being experienced by men) and 3,700,000 part time jobs were created (82 per cent of the gain being experienced by women). Up to 70 per cent of the female part timers were employed for less than 16 hours a week, and the majority were paid beneath the threshold for National Insurance contributions. On average part time employees work a little over 19 hours a week in the EU. However, this ranges from 16.7 hours for women in the Netherlands, 17.9 hours in the UK, to 23.1 hours in Italy.

Part time employment has, then, increased dramatically across Europe. In 1975, 14 per cent of Dutch jobs were part time. In the subsequent fifteen years the proportion more than doubled to 33 per cent. As with unemployment, part time work tends to be concentrated in particular sectors. Forty-six per cent of all Dutch jobs in health and welfare are part time, as are 43 per cent of retail jobs, compared to only 7 per cent of manufacturing jobs (Visser, 1990).

Results from the PWCP Project show that there have been marked increases in forms of flexible working across many European countries (Brewster, Hegewisch and Mayne, 1993). The Nordic countries appear to be an exception. The percentage of organizations reporting an increased reliance on part time work over the last three years versus a decrease is 80:1 per cent in Switzerland, 58:3 per cent in the Netherlands, 49:6 per cent in Italy, 48:6 per cent in the United Kingdom and 47:5 per cent in Germany. Only in Sweden did more organizations report a decrease in reliance on part time work (24:17 per cent). Similarly reliance on temporary and casual work is generally rising (see Illustration 4.17), with the ratios of increase to decrease being 66:5 in the Netherlands, 58:5 in Switzerland, 51:9 in Spain, 46:12 in the UK and

Illustration 4.17   **The spread of temporary work.**

Every year, almost 10 per cent of Europe's workforce is involved in temporary work ranging from seasonal agricultural labour to filling in in an emergency at a family-owned company. The Netherlands again has the largest army of formal temporary workers (or 'uitzendkrachten') in Europe. At any given moment, some 2 per cent of the Dutch labour force is temporary, compared to 1.5 per cent in the US, 1 per cent in Belgium, France and the UK and 0.5 per cent in Germany. Temporary work is highest in the Netherlands because of its high growth in productivity, strict employment laws for permanent staff and the presence of several highly organized temping agencies. It is also argued that the prevalence of temporary work in the Netherlands is linked to the high degree of specialization in Dutch organizations, i.e. a lower level of structured overmanning. One in three people of working age in the Netherlands has worked for a temping agency at some point. Social security protection is relatively good, with cover for illness and holiday pay mirroring salaried permanent employees. In Germany, the spread of temporary work is limited by legislation barring temps from working longer than six months in one job.

Source: Krol (1993).

40:14 in France. Again, in only one country (Denmark) did more organizations report a decreased reliance on temporary/casual labour. Fixed term contracts are on the increase mainly in Germany, Spain, France and Italy, with the Netherlands being the dissenting country in this area.

There is then an emerging dichotomy between protected and unprotected workers (Baglioni, 1991). We discuss the industrial relations implications of this in Chapter Fifteen. The spread of part time work is generally in response to the needs of employers who see it as an additional element of flexibility (discussed in more detail at the end of this chapter). In Belgium, which has lagged behind in the shift to part time work, most of those working part-time are doing so because they cannot find full time jobs (Spineux, 1991). Related to the development of part time work has been an increase in a number of forms of non-core work as discussed towards the end of this chapter. Including the growing number of part time jobs between 33 and 50 per cent of Dutch wage and salary earners are employed in jobs that deviate from the concept of a full time job (Visser, 1990). It was also estimated that by 1986 about 6 per cent of the French labour force were in 'interim' employment while waiting to obtain a steady job (Segrestin, 1990).

RISING LEVEL OF EDUCATION

Public expenditure on education varies widely across Europe, ranging from over 1245 ECU (US$ 1500) per capita in Sweden and Norway, to 754 ECU (US$ 908) in France, 690 ECU (US$ 832) in Germany, 573 ECU (US$ 691) in the UK, 432 ECU (US$ 521) in Italy, 308 ECU (US$ 371) in Spain and only 102 ECU (US$ 123) in Greece (World Economic Forum, 1993). These figures distort national patterns such as the funding of training in Germany primarily by employers and we discuss the impact of education systems on training and work in Chapter Ten. At this point it is important to note that secondary education merges into training for work. In Belgium and the Netherlands around 45 per cent of secondary pupils are on vocational courses, compared to under 10 per cent in the UK and Switzerland (Economist Intelligence Unit, 1991). There are also marked differences in the educational attainment of the working age population. Over 70 per cent of women and 50 per cent of men in the UK, Italy and Spain have completed less than upper secondary education. In Germany the figures are 40 per cent and 20 per cent respectively.

The situation is, however, changing dramatically. The demographic shift (already discussed) has led to an overall fall in pupils studying at the first level in the EU from 29.1 million in 1970/71 to 22.7 million in 1986/87, whilst the numbers in higher education have increased from 3.5 million to 6.6 million (Eurostat, 1991). The rise in higher education has been due chiefly to the growth in the number of female students.

Throughout the EU, there has been a shift towards more and higher levels of education as shown in Table 4.6. The highest education participation rates are in France, Belgium and Spain whilst the lowest are in Luxembourg and the UK. In Italy, for example, 86 per cent of men aged 55 years or more left school before they were 14 years old. In contrast, only 58 per cent of their grandchildren left school so early. The greatest progress in the level of education has been for women as noted above. Among European women, nine out of ten aged 55 years or more in 1991 had no higher education, compared to only half of those aged between 20 and 24 years. The proportion of female graduates at universities is 54 per cent in Sweden and Spain, 50 per cent in France, 43 per cent in the UK but only 32–33 per cent in Switzerland and the Netherlands (Economist Intelligence Unit, 1991). Several European countries have

Table 4.6 **Percentage of 5–24 year olds who are in education as pupils and students in EU countries.**

	1970/71	1980/81	1986/87
Belgium	78.4	77.6	81.0
Denmark	61.3	72.5	73.1
Germany	59.7	68.9	66.9
Greece	63.3	65.6	70.8
France	73.2	79.4	82.8
Ireland	69.7	70.4	73.3
Italy	66.1	72.2	68.9
Luxembourg	62.1	59.0	61.7
Netherlands	68.2	74.5	72.3
Portugal	47.7	54.6	63.0
Spain	60.2	74.6	79.6
UK	63.4	65.8	62.0

Source: Eurostat (1991), reprinted with permission © 1993 Report on *A Social Portrait of Europe*, Eurostat, 1991.

set targets for raising the number of school-leavers with university degrees even further. France, for example, hopes to double the proportion of teenagers with a grade to get to university to 80 per cent by the end of the decade. In Germany, the problem is one of over-populated universities. From 1966–90 the number of students starting at colleges rose by nearly 350 per cent. In 1993 the Ludwig–Maxmilian University in Munich and Free University in Berlin both had twice their official number of students. The *Fachhochschulen* (technical colleges) were even fuller. As a symptom of overcrowding, the German education system suffers from a 25 per cent drop out rate.

The fields of study have also shifted. The proportion studying social sciences in higher education has increased from 11.8 to 20.0 per cent, whilst the proportion studying engineering sciences has fallen from 12.3 to 11.2 per cent. We are also observing the advent of free foreign education. A little noticed EU Directive (90-364) allows children from the EU to study in any other EU country for one year without paying for their education and without their parents (who only need to pay for accommodation).

RISE IN SELF-EMPLOYMENT

Staber and Bögenhold (1993) have analysed changes in self-employment across 17 OECD countries. They note that historical decline in self-employment was halted and generally reversed in most countries in the 1970s. Self-employment in the EU increased by two million between 1979 and 1989 to 21 million or 16 per cent of the workforce, with particular growth in the UK. Structural changes in the economy, changes in the labour market, employment policies by organizations and governments, technological changes and the tightening of general economic conditions have all played a role. Of these factors, government policies were found to have a powerful role, but the job and wealth creation potential of the self-employed was limited. Most job creation came from a small handful of rapidly expanding businesses. As can be seen in Table 4.7, self-employment is most important in the less developed regions of the EU. In Greece and Portugal it accounts for a third and a quarter of all employment respectively.

Table 4.7 **Self-employment as a percentage of total employment in US, Japan and Europe.**

	1979	1983	1989
US	7.1	7.7	7.5
Japan	14.0	13.3	12.0
Austria	8.9	8.1	6.6
Belgium	11.2	12.3	12.9
France	10.6	10.5	10.5
Germany	7.7	–	8.4
Ireland	10.4	10.7	13.0
Luxembourg	9.4	8.8	7.4
Netherlands	8.8	8.6	7.8
UK	6.6	8.6	11.5
Greece	32.0	27.9	27.4
Italy	18.9	20.7	22.4
Portugal	12.1	17.0	17.2
Spain	15.7	17.0	17.6
Denmark	9.2	8.5	6.9
Finland	6.1	7.0	8.7
Norway	6.6	6.8	6.4
Sweden	4.5	4.8	7.1

Source: S. Vickerstaff (1992) (ed.) *Human Resource Management in Europe: text and cases* Figure T3.2 pp. 88–89, reprinted with permission © Chapman & Hall.

INCREASING SKILL SHORTAGES

Despite the rising level of unemployment, the general shortfall in skilled labour particularly in the scientific and technical fields is affecting the development of manufacturing and service businesses in all member states, with small firms finding it particularly difficult to recruit skilled staff. Several manpower studies and reports have emphasized the need for improved education and continuous vocational training if the EU is to compete effectively in the world marketplace. Lane (1989) quotes a study in *Industriemagazin* that analysed the changes in qualification structure in German production facilities associated with the adoption of advanced technology and flexible specialization. The general result is one of up-skilling and an increasing demand for skilled employees at all levels of production, as well as a decline in employment opportunities for the unskilled. The proportion of employees needed without any initial apprenticeship training will fall from 38.1 per cent in 1982, to 31.1 per cent in 1990 and only 24.4 per cent by 2000. The proportion with short- or long-term apprenticeships and initial training will rise from 54 per cent in 1982, to 59.9 per cent in 1990 and 65.9 per cent in 2000. Similarly, the proportion with Certificate of Foreman (*Meister*) rises from 6.9 per cent in 1982 to 8.3 per cent in 2000, and the proportion with a degree from polytechnic (*Fachhochschule*) or university rises from 1 per cent in 1982 to 1.5 per cent in the year 2000 (Industriemagazin, 1987). In some countries there has been a stark change in employment strategy (see Illustration 4.18).

NEW PATTERNS OF LABOUR MOBILITY

One specific objective of the SEM programme is to achieve the free movement of EU nationals to work wherever they wish in the Union, similar to the labour market

Illustration 4.18 **Stark changes in employment strategy in Finland.**

In the 1980s Finland attempted to reduce its vulnerability to international economic fluctuations by diversifying into high technology and advanced production technologies. However, the collapse of markets in the former Soviet Union helped fuel an increase in unemployment from 4 per cent in 1990 to nearly 20 per cent by 1992. 'Quality of working life' and 'job enrichment' initiatives have been abandoned in favour of employment creation and wage control measures.

Internationalization and potential EU membership have led to a review of labour legislation and fears of a 'brain-drain'. Once the recession is over, post-recessionary labour shortages will be more difficult to resolve because women already play a prominent part in employment. More flexible work practices and multifunctionalism are expected to form the core of the future skills-shortage strategy.

Source: Seppänen (1993).

situation that exists in the US. A 1988 report by the EU on labour mobility suggests that a new pattern of migration has emerged in recent years. This involves transnational organizations moving their staff across different geographical (national) sites inside the EU. Given that a substantial proportion of EU trade is between member states, and given that mergers, acquisitions and joint ventures between organizations in different member states are increasing, it is likely that this more fluid form of labour mobility will become more widespread (Teague, 1989). Yet, as Mill (1991) argues, language difficulties, cultural differences, and various legal and fiscal practices are likely to keep migration at a low level. Mass movements of labour are not considered to be likely as a result of the SEM.

In 1993 the first ever study by the EU's statistical office Eurostat on inter-EU mobility showed that mobility levels have increased little since the mid-1980s, when there were around 5 million EU citizens living in other EU countries. By 1991 the figure had only risen to 5.5 million. Some 862,000 Portuguese (8.1 per cent of the workforce) seek a better future abroad (most going to France), whilst 391,500 Greeks (3.8 per cent of the workforce) go north (mainly to Germany).

RISING CONCERN OVER IMMIGRATION

In the past, some intra-European migration has occurred although today this type of migration has more or less dried up, as the demand for unskilled labour has abated or been moved to the Pacific Rim (Torrington and Hall, 1991). The inflow of foreign labour (including workers from other EU countries) from 1977 to 1986 halved in Belgium and in France, but increased by 26 per cent in Germany and 49 per cent (from small numbers) in Switzerland (Romero, 1990). The national make-up of immigrant labour varies from country to country. In order of size, the largest groups of foreign nationals in 1986 were: in Belgium – Italians, Moroccans and Turks; in France – Algerians, Portuguese, Moroccans, Italians and Spaniards; in Germany – Turks, Yugoslavians, Italians and Greeks; in the Netherlands – Turks and Moroccans; and in Sweden Finns. Such figures do not visualize the large and rapidly expanding phenomenon of illegal immigration in these traditional receiving countries, but most notably in southern Europe. Romero (1990) estimates that there are at least 2 million illegal workers in Europe, with half in Italy (accounting for 5 per cent of the Italian labour force). Nikas (1991) has analysed the postwar intra-European movements of people. They have occurred in three phases (see Illustration 4.19).

Illustration 4.19   **Historical movements of labour within Europe.**

- A massive inflow of East European refugees from 1945–61. West Germany received 7.8 million refugees (mainly ethnic Germans) from 1945–50. By 1955 immigrants represented 17.4 per cent of the population. These movements were triggered mainly by political factors.
- An inflow of labour from Mediterranean European countries (Greece, Spain, Portugal, Turkey, Yugoslavia and Italy) from 1961–74. For example, in the 1950s and 1960s, many Italians moved to the coal-mining regions of Belgium in search of work. From 1975 until recently, such immigration decreased. These movements were triggered mainly by economic factors, were more regulated, and the size of movements evolved in relation to demand for labour.
- A projected increase of immigrants from East Europe and Russia during a prolonged period of economic and political disintegration.

According to the World Economic Forum (1993) the proportion of senior managers who think that their national immigration laws do *not* prevent their organization from employing foreign skills is high in countries like Denmark (83.5 per cent), the Netherlands (83.5 per cent), Sweden (80.6 per cent) and Germany (80 per cent), moderate in the UK (72.5 per cent) and France (71.5 per cent), but markedly lower in Spain (52.9 per cent), Finland (48 per cent) and Switzerland (33 per cent). Although fears were expressed during these periods that the inward flows of labour could not be absorbed in productive employment, the unprecedented levels of economic growth more than accounted for immigrants, such that after 1961 West Germany had to import labour from other countries. Indeed, even the large flows of people from one country to another were insignificant in comparison to the drift of people from the country to the cities within countries (Nikas, 1991). For example, after 1945 in Italy approximately 5 million people from South Italy went looking for work in the North Italian cities and beyond (Hinterhuber and Stumpf, 1990). The outbreak of economic crisis in the 1970s led to the suspension of bilateral agreements, the minimalization of inflows and the repatriation of existing immigrants.

Therefore, on average, in 1989, 2.5 per cent of the people living in the EU were citizens of countries outside the Union. The majority of these migrant workers were manual workers, with over 45 per cent working in industry. There are regional variations, with there being less than 1 per cent of non-EU citizens in Spain, Ireland, Wales, and Southern Italy, but more than 4 per cent of non-EU citizens in Corsica, Provence, Paris, Southern Belgium and the Central German states. However, the influx of migrant workers into the EU is likely to rise under three main pressures:

- Recent political changes in Eastern Europe.
- The unification of Germany.
- Progress towards economic integration in Western Europe.

The anticipated mass exodus of labour after the collapse of communism did not really materialize. Most migration has not been East to West, but has involved a redistribution of groups within Eastern and Central Europe. Emigration from the Russian Federation is only around 100,000 a year. Germany (which has by far the most liberal immigration laws in Western Europe), however, has felt the impact. The number of refugees worldwide in early 1993 was estimated at 18 million, 8 per cent of whom headed for Germany. Sixty-five per cent of all asylum-seekers to Western Europe applied to live in Germany. Following the collapse of the Communist regime in Eastern Europe, by early 1993 Germany had already taken in more than 1.5 million immigrants (or 2 per cent of its population of 61 million) since 1989, chiefly from Poland, Yugoslavia, Romania, and the Soviet Union.

In several EU countries, the development of immigration has led to political upheaval. For example, in Belgium's general election of November 1991, the anti-immigrant Vlaams Blok won a quarter of the votes in the Antwerp region. Similarly, nearly a quarter of the French electorate tell opinion pollsters they agree with the leader of the National Front on tougher immigration controls and deportation. In Germany anti-foreigner crimes rose from 2,400 in 1991 to 6,000 in 1992 (still less than reported levels in the UK which has a lower level of immigration) directed mainly at the 1.85 million resident Turks.

However, forecasts for the net yearly immigration to the EU during the 1990s range from 200,000 to 700,000, ethnic Germans excluded. Even the higher figure would add only 0.3 per cent a year to the total EU population. In some quarters therefore it is being suggested that Europe should take the opportunity to address its demographic imbalance by providing a more open door to immigrants. Anatoli Tchernyschov, the Deputy Employment Minister of Russia, suggested a scheme in 1991 whereby 6 million Russians could work in the West in skill shortage professions (paramedics, nursing, construction, agriculture) on two year contracts, paying local taxes in return for payment in hard currency. The maximum guest work period would be seven years (as a prelude to full citizenship). Belgium agreed to an initial 500 guest workers a year, and Germany to 15,000 workers. Italy considered a scheme for temporary legal workers from North Africa. Russian graduates have been offered to UK organizations at a salary of only £2000 a year. As and when recessionary pressures ease in Europe, such schemes will again be considered.

CHANGING VALUES AND EXPECTATIONS OF THE WORKFORCE

Sparrow (1986) analysed the erosion of employment in the UK pointing to the conflict between the use of employment to distribute work, leisure and wealth, and the emerging patterns of advanced industrialization that was creating poverty amidst wealth, disenfranchizement within democracy and idleness in a world of unprecedented need. Drastic reductions have been achieved in the employed working life. In 1851 a man worked for wages for 200,000 hours over a lifetime. By 1971 this had halved to 100,000, or 47 hours a week, for 47 weeks a year, for 47 years (Handy, 1984). To effect a further halving only requires this base number to fall to 37. By 1986 male employment had already fallen to 84,000 hours over a lifetime, and another 16 per cent fall to 70,000 hours is forecast by the year 2001 (Armstrong, 1984). Only a minority of the population actually have 'jobs' (full time or part time). By 1981 only 43 per cent of the UK population were employed (Sparrow, 1986). The rest were at school, disabled, on government schemes, unemployed, married housewives or retired. The centrality of employment is diminishing.

The time freed from employment has not all become leisure. Free time has been exchanged for higher earnings and consumerism. From 1850 to 1950 the proportion of increased productivity taken in the form of reduced work hours as opposed to higher wages was 33 to 67 per cent. From 1950 to 1978 it was 8 to 92 per cent. The higher wages were spent on consumer goods which increased the amount of domestic work and the productive capacity of households (Gershuny, 1985). This has made it more economic in many sectors to use domestic time to produce a service that once provided employment for others.

. . . Rather than pay the Great Western Railway to travel, we bought a car of our own; instead of going to the cinema we bought a television and video; and instead of paying for a decorator we went to the DIY superstore and bought the tools to fix it ourselves.

Sparrow (1986, p. 103).

The result has been (as we discussed in the section on unemployment) jobless economic growth, structural de-industrialization, and a pauperization of much employment. Although still politically unpalatable, there are more forward looking solutions such as work sharing (through shorter working weeks, reduced overtime, voluntary job sharing schemes, employment-creating part time jobs, shiftwork innovations, extensions to flexible worktime, increases in holiday entitlement, flexible retirement patterns and the institutionalization of longer bridges from school to work). Recessions aside, we are seeing developments in all these areas, as with the EU Directorate on the 48 hour week which created such debate in 1993.

Therefore, in addition to the workforce changes already outlined, there is evidence to suggest that during the 1980s there was a significant shift in employees' attitudes relating to career management, leadership style, rewards and motivation, working hours, and so forth. Some experts suggest that work has become a less important aspect of people's life. Indeed, a study in France showed that after paying taxes and social security contributions by 1990 only 45.4 per cent of the average household disposable income came in the form of wages. Capital investment brought in 13.4 per cent of income and 33.7 per cent of income came from payments such as family allowances, state benefits and pensions.

According to Hammett (1984) there is also a new generation of highly educated workers who want more opportunities for development, autonomy, flexibility and meaningful work experiences. They want to participate fully in the work environment, react adversely to rigid hierarchies and emphasize the lack of involvement in decisions affecting them. Recent surveys carried out by Stephen Harding of International Survey Research in Britain show that young people brought up in 'an atmosphere of peace and relative affluence' are more concerned with their quality of life, are more critical of employers and authority, and seek jobs which are useful for society as well as challenging. Older workers, particularly those over 50, are more likely to emphasize the Protestant work ethic, whereas the young value independence, imagination, tolerance and responsibility. In other words, with the changing composition of the workforce has come a new set of work standards and values. Apparently, the ideal job is seen as offering flexibility, autonomy, responsibility, variety and opportunities for self-development and growth. In fact these are all attributes long recognized by psychologists as providing job satisfaction and performance.

DECLINING WAGE DISPARITIES AND DECENTRALIZATION OF BARGAINING STRUCTURES

In addition to the economic, technological and demographic trends, three other developments that affect the European business environment are worth highlighting. In the opening sections of this chapter we discussed the external pressures on European wage and productivity levels. There is a second dimension to the wage issue, and this is the level of internal wage disparities. Conventional wisdom argues that greater economic integration within the EU, and later under a possible single currency (discussed earlier in this chapter), will cause a shift in the cost of labour. In particular, increased trade and cross-border investment within the EU should cause a convergence of national wages. A study in 1992 by Professor McWilliams of the London School of Economics confirms this hypothesis. For example, Spanish wages rose from 29 per cent of German wages in 1970 to 68 per cent in 1991; Italy's wage disparity decreased from 58 to 26 per cent. Non-wage costs now range from 22 per cent of total labour cost in Denmark to 102 per cent in Italy. However, as more and more organizations employ people across Europe, and as eleven of the twelve EU countries move to harmonized workers' rights and benefits, such wide disparities are also unlikely to survive.

Another clear trend in European HRM is towards the decentralization of bargaining structures. Brewster, Hegewisch and Mayne (1993) note that both countries with highly centralized systems of pay such as Denmark and Sweden and countries with already higher levels of decentralization (such as the UK and France) are moving in this direction. Only a minority of private sector organizations in the UK and France negotiate over basic pay at national or industry level. Even in Sweden, where over 60 per cent of employers still bargain at industry or national level, there has been a shift to industry level bargaining and greater scope for company implementation. Only in Germany has there been a relatively low level of decentralization in pay bargaining. We consider pay and benefits issues in Europe in more detail in Chapter Thirteen.

CHANGING ROLE OF THE TRADE UNIONS

Similarly, detailed consideration is given to European industrial relations in Chapter Fifteen. However, at this point it is worth noting that during the 1980s there has been a perceptible decline in the legitimization and representativeness of trade unions. Due to declining membership and the prevailing political and ideological climate, unions have been forced to retreat, and their influence has declined, not as dramatically as some observers have contended, but still significantly, both in actions and in underlying conditions (Baglioni and Crouch, 1991). There are differences across Europe in the level of union affiliation and perceptions of union strength. For example, in the PWCP Project described in the last chapter, Filella (1991) analysed the data for three clusters of European countries: Latin, Central and Nordic. Fifty-six per cent of Latin organizations had affiliation rates of less than 25 per cent, compared to 44 per cent in Central European organizations and only 4 per cent in Nordic organizations. However, in response to the question of whether in the eyes of the HR Director the influence of the unions had increased in the last three years, the vote was 4 to 1 in favour in Spain, 2 to 1 in favour in the Nordic countries, a split 1 to 1 in Central European countries, but 6 to 1 against in France and Italy. Even in countries (like Spain) where unions had gained in influence around the bargaining table, they had lost much credibility in the eyes of employees. Although this trend is more general, the change is most evident in Britain, for three major reasons:

First, the almost complete rejection by the Conservative government of the search for national compromise in industrial relations that had characterized the policy of all parties since at least 1940 and, arguably, since the early twentieth century. Secondly, the installation of a tough legal framework for trade union action, marking the final end of the so-called 'voluntarist' tradition that dates back to 1871. Thirdly, in several sectors of the economy, the emergence of the company as the most important level for industrial relations activity, replacing the branch, shop-floor and state levels that had previously competed for importance with the British system.

Crouch (1991 p. 326).

INCREASING AMOUNT OF EMPLOYMENT LEGISLATION

We noted in Chapter Two that one of the significant differences between HRM in the US and Europe is the level of organizational autonomy and employee legislation. During the past two decades, there has been a general increase in the amount of legislation in Europe affecting employment and labour relations. One example is the Community Charter of the Fundamental Social Rights of Workers – or the Social Charter as it is more commonly known. This seeks to avoid 'social dumping' (discussed earlier in this chapter) as a possible threat to European integration by regulating the free movement of workers within the EU. In particular, there are proposals for worker participation in public limited liability companies, maximum working times, minimum standards of health and safety, disclosure of information to employees, atypical contracts for part time work, and minimum wages. For example, with regard to the draft directive on working hours, the Social Charter would entitle every worker to at least 11 hours of rest in 24 hours, and an average of one rest day per week. Night work would be limited to eight hours per day, averaged over two weeks. This directive's potential impact is huge: it affects 14 per cent of the total EU workforce. Although initial reactions from certain countries and institutions (such as Britain and UNICE, the European employers' federation) have been hostile, it is generally expected that the arguments for and against increased European employment legislation will eventually be reconciled.

CONCLUSIONS

In this chapter we have provided an overview of the key trends and developments that are taking place in the European business environment today. Some of these trends are long term and are likely to produce a gradual shift in the economic, technological and demographic conditions experienced by organizations. Other developments, such as the creation of the SEM and the political transformation of Eastern Europe, happened more quickly. These various changes have not only brought about a very different competitive environment, but have also had a direct and immediate impact on the size and complexity of organizations. In addition, new technology and ongoing changes in workforce demography are causing managers to re-examine the structure of their organizations. Some are reducing the number of middle management levels whilst others are trying to break down traditional demarcations and to move towards new organizational structures that are more flexible, putting managers and employees in closer touch with customers and clients. Obviously, all these changes have implications for HRM across the whole of Europe. Internationalization of business alliances, the move towards greater decentralization of decision making, and the changing values and expectations of the workforce are creating a number of major issues and challenges in managing human resources.

Although experience has shown that managerial understanding of, and responsiveness to, these issues generally is low, research shows that a number of European organizations are addressing the challenges raised in this chapter and are taking actions that will dramatically change their approach to managing people. These organizations and their actions are the focus of the chapters in Part Three on the content of HRM but we also attempt to provide information that places this description of organizationally-driven HRM in its national context in these chapters. However, there is another major set of forces that are having an integrating effect on HRM in Europe. In the next chapter, therefore, we consider these forces and the extent to which there is a process of integration taking place within European business. The key learning points from this chapter are shown below.

LEARNING POINTS FROM CHAPTER FOUR

1. A wide range of pressure points in the business environment are combining to create an irresistible force for change in Europe. European HRM is in a period of transition. We are likely to see greater convergence in patterns of HRM as European organizations respond to two imperatives: a pan-European requirement to create organizational structures and HRM systems that are capable of surviving rapid and 'discontinuous' change; and a collection of strategic pressures (such as globalization, rationalization, business integration and social and demographic problems) that will re-shape and possibly supersede national differences in HRM as organizations implement new policies and practices. These pressures for change will not only shape the context for European HRM, but will increasingly determine its content.

2. The task of strategically-minded HR specialists, personnel directors and senior line managers will be to anticipate the business trends outlined in the chapter, understand the implications, and implement new policies and practices to continuously improve their organizations. They will need to maintain sensitivity to the issues covered in Part One, but respond to the pressing agenda for change, i.e. think globally, act locally.

3. Europe (as a whole) is plagued by lower levels of productivity in comparison to its worldwide competitors, due in part to its fragmentation into nation states. The EU trade deficit with Japan has reached huge proportions. National competitiveness involves a country's ability to create and sustain value added economic activity in the long term relative to competitors, but the key to competitiveness lies in the management of change. Many European organizations now believe that different competitive means may be required as they redefine their problem of poor competitiveness.

4. It is, however, difficult to treat Europe as a single source of competitiveness. Germany, Switzerland and Denmark are Europe's most competitive countries, followed by the Netherlands, Austria and Sweden, whilst Italy, Portugal and Greece are the least competitive. There is considerable change in this competitiveness, placing national business models under threat. France has overtaken the UK, whilst German competitiveness has fallen markedly as it bears the cost of reunification with a high wage, high social cost employment model. Japan outperforms even Europe's best and the US has once more moved ahead of Europe's leading pack of countries. Major international recessions – the latest recession has been the deepest in Europe in 60 years – have hit European optimism hard.

5. European organizations are therefore under considerable pressure to improve their productivity. Producing goods and services in Europe is expensive. High levels of taxation, strong trade unions, a web of employment legislation and high levels of social welfare provision have combined to produce perhaps the world's best standard of living and quality of life. However, the removal of trade barriers and globalization of trade is leading to pressures to justify high labour costs. The underlying quality differential can no longer be guaranteed as many technological innovations now sweep around the world within a three year period.

6. There is also an internal restructuring of the European economic architecture, driven by attempts to create monetary union and a Single European Market. Whilst the final economic architecture is yet to emerge and the full impacts of deregulation have yet

to be felt, the benefits to European organizations through the centralization of manufacturing, more efficient distribution, lower levels of stock inventories, reduction in variety of technical standards, range standardization and employment efficiencies have combined to create a process of asset redistribution on a pan-European scale. This has triggered new developments in HRM as the organization structure, work practices, employee training and development needs, levels of international mobility, career development patterns and performance management requirements have changed.

7. There has also been an extensive process of restructuring and rationalization as European organizations have at the same time attempted to respond to the growing competitive threat. The car industry provides a good example of the changed work practices, rationalization of employment, and knock-on effect on supplier and R&D activities that has followed this restructuring. Despite national differences in HRM, all the European car manufacturers have pursued similar operational changes and HRM policies. In the process, distinctive national models of HRM, such as the Swedish humanistic model, have been threatened. The lesson is that industrial sector competitive dynamics are challenging national models of HRM.

8. Radical changes have been implemented in leading European organizations. For example, several German organizations are in the process of transforming their strategies and culture. At the same time some transnational organizations are exporting jobs across the EU to cheaper wage economies, and especially to countries outside the EU, on the grounds of relative labour costs, market expansion or technological deregulation.

9. The historical differences across Europe of levels of state ownership in industry are being eroded as a massive process of privatization has swept across Europe and beyond. This has led to policies of retrenchment, control of public expenditure, and restructuring of labour markets. A new industrial policy has been introduced in France, which although qualitatively different from the British experience of privatization, is nevertheless leading to reductions in employment and new patterns of HRM, as well as industrial unrest. Privatization continues in the UK, Italy, Sweden, Germany, Spain, the Netherlands, Belgium, and Finland.

10. There has also been a massive transformation of Central and East European economies, with massive levels of privatization, deregulations and foreign direct investment. The social costs, as evidenced by East Germany, have been extremely high and the process of change is expected to be long, slow and painful. This has created changes in the HRM policies of West European countries and organizations as they have pursued international expansion but have also borne the high costs of investment. At a time of world instability it has led to an increase of social tensions and divisions within Europe.

11. The failure of early attempts to create monetary union has added more cost to European economies as exchange rates were defended. It is also leading to the creation of a two-tier Europe, in which high wages in the first tier countries would be paid for by high performance products, but in other areas jobs would be lost to the cheaper second tier countries. The second more loosely integrated tier would, however, only be able to attract investment for low-skilled, low-wage production which would be achieved at the cost of higher inflation, fluctuating interest rates and uneven economic growth. The overall position of Europe could deteriorate further.

12. Technological advances carry the ever-tantalizing promise of job creation or job destruction. There are differences across Europe in the extent to which information technology is being used effectively. The time and effort taken to achieve the benefits from investment in technology is extensive. In a period of retrenchment and

rationalization, the temptation is to use technology to assist in the 're-engineering' of key business processes, and possibly to design out the need to re-employ redundant workers in an effort to transform productivity radically. In this regard, national differences in HRM do appear to be mediating moves down this route in the short term.

13. There are a series of social and demographic pressures, such as the high and variable social costs of employment, rising levels of unemployment, demographic shifts, an increased participation of women in the labour force, higher levels of part time and temporary employment, a shift from manufacturing to service employment and from manual to non-manual jobs, a rise in self-employment and levels of education, increasing skills shortages, new patterns of labour mobility, concern over immigration and changing values and expectations of the labour force, that are leading to a mosaic of influences on European HRM policies and practices.

14. Social costs of employment vary significantly across Europe and attention has been directed not just at pay levels, but at holiday entitlement, working time, pension and social benefit levels and absenteeism. Conflicting arguments abound as to whether Europe should equalize these differentials, reduce working time in an attempt to share out what employment there is, or significantly reduce entitlement in a response to competitive pressure. Most likely, all three processes will take place, changing HRM policies and practices all the more.

15. Unemployment levels have risen across Europe, creating at least 18 million unemployed people. Only 60 per cent of Europeans of working age have a job compared to 70 per cent in the US and 75 per cent in Japan. There are large differences in unemployment between industrial sectors, geographical regions, and demographic groups. The incentives for the long-term unemployed vary across Europe, as do levels of social protection. However, in most countries concerted efforts at job creation have done little to dent the rising tide of unemployment and the increasing pressure on social costs and social unrest.

16. Declining birth rates in West European and East European countries will reduce the supply of young people onto the labour markets, easing unemployment pressures in the short term, but increasing them in the longer term as skills shortages are experienced and the size and purchasing power of domestic markets is reduced. Linked with the process of ageing in industrial workforces and earlier withdrawal from labour markets, the age–dependency ratios are set to increase significantly. Pension funds and employee contributions to social funds are coming under immense pressure, and few analysts believe that current social welfare systems can sustain the drain on their funds. The social, employment and HRM implications of theses 'age wars' are only just beginning to dawn on Europeans.

17. More women are joining the workforce, although on current trends women will not reach equal representation in management jobs for hundreds of years. Female participation rates, and the target jobs they have moved into, vary across European countries. Nevertheless, substantial changes have occurred in the number of women managers in European industry and this has helped fuel pressure on the need for more flexible time patterns of employment and nursery provision. In the longer term it will influence management styles and career patterns within European organizations.

18. There has been a pan-European trend towards flexibility of employment. Historical differences in employment protection and social legislation are being eroded as processes of deregulation, attacks on employment rigidity and the availability of new (in many cases more attractive) patterns of work have both attracted new entrants to the labour force and opened up internal labour markets. Levels of part time

employment still vary significantly between countries, especially between the North and the South of Europe, but in all countries the trend is upwards. However, there has been an almost one-for-one substitution of male full time jobs for female part time jobs and at a societal level this organizational flexibility may result in a pauperization, not just peripheralization, of employment. The division between socially-protected workers and those in unprotected jobs is increasing.

19. Paradoxically, we are also witnessing a period of increased skills shortage as scientific and technical changes place a premium on certain skill combinations. In general, levels of education and training are increasing as societies cope with these skill shortages, although investment in education still varies considerably across countries. Coupled with complex patterns of skills shortage in some areas, and a marked over-supply of labour in others, new patterns of labour mobility are emerging. Job migration levels are still relatively low, despite the creation of the Single European Market, and many concerns over economic immigration seem overstated (most mass movements of people have been outside the EU to the East and South). Nevertheless, employee attitudes are hardening towards immigration and the transfer of employment.

20. The values and expectations of the workforce in Europe are also changing. Economic recessions aside, employment is playing a less central role in many employees' lives. Conflicting pressures are creating both a new generation of highly educated workers who want more opportunities for development, autonomy, flexibility and meaningful work. The denial of such opportunities bears a higher price. At the same time, levels of commitment and job satisfaction are falling. The net result is an increasingly instrumental attitude to work, which will make the process of creating change in European organizations all the more intricate.

21. The combination of social and economic pressures is leading to numerous changes in HRM provision across European organizations. In general, wage disparities are being reduced, bargaining structures decentralized, the role of trades unions is changing, and organizations are faced with paradoxical trends of deregulation in some areas but increasing employment legislation in others. The most pressing HRM issues are the need to create flatter and more flexible European-wide organization structures, a stronger emphasis on external customers, and greater sensitivity to national cultural differences whilst attempting to converge HRM policies. In response to these issues, European organizations are pursuing common policies aimed at enhancing their management skills, promoting flexibility, encouraging participation, creating new career paths, building international workforces and attempting to develop an organizational capability for the future.

CHAPTER FIVE

The Organizational Response
Integration of European Management

... Forces of convergence are at work within and across national boundaries. Managers under pressure to change and improve will look for and adopt ideas that are currently considered as contributors to excellence.... An international cross-synthesis is emerging in those countries which are at a similar stage of industrialization, share common technology and are part of an international competitive economy.   Kidger (1991).

The process of European integration is reinforced by a number of related factors (see Figure 5.1). In this chapter we focus in particular on the organizational response to the external strategic pressures outlined in the previous chapter by discussing issues of transnationalism and foreign direct investment. Competition among European organizations through foreign direct investment (FDI) is becoming more and more crucial in ensuring that the gains from the SEM, such as boosted economic activity, are achieved (Thomsen and Woolcock, 1993).

Is there a process of industrial restructuring taking place across Europe in which we are witnessing the emergence of increased integration and convergence of European management? There are two essential but separate questions to consider. First, are we seeing industrial integration? Second, will the end point of such a process be the likely emergence of, or convergence around, an identifiable concept of European (or any other) management that will be reflected in the HRM practices and policies of European organizations? The first question is dealt with in this chapter and the second question is dealt with in the next chapter.

GLOBALIZATION AND TRANSNATIONALIZATION OF BUSINESSES

Ferner and Hyman (1992b) note that European economies are becoming increasingly integrated into a global economy dominated by large multinational organizations. These organizations have become large employers of labour, as outlined in the last chapter. In 1986 more than 13,000 EU organizations had more than 500 employees. Although they numbered only 0.1 per cent of EU enterprises they accounted for 28 per cent of employment. Sisson, Waddington and Whitston (1991) established that by

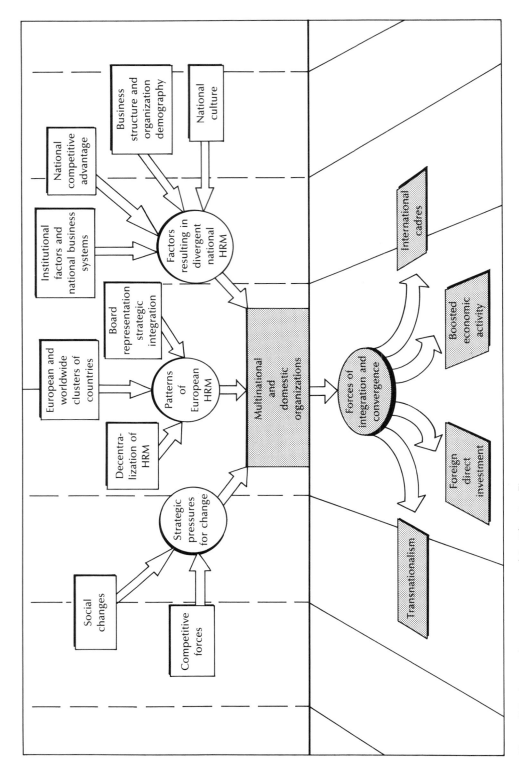

Figure 5.1 Areas of context covered in Chapter Five.

1991 there were:

- Over 8,000 organizations in the EU employing over 1,000 people.
- Over 900 multinational corporate groups with at least 1,000 employees in two countries.
- At least 280 non-EU multinationals with over 1,000 employees.
- Forty-three non-EU multinationals with over 1,000 employees in two or more EU countries.

The most notable large non-EU multinationals include: Digital, IBM, Honeywell, Esso, Exxon, Mobil, Hertz, Ford, General Motors, Goodyear, Motorola, Kodak and Mars from the US; Fujitsu, Sony and Nissan from Japan; Ericksson, Electrolux, Norsk Hydro and Volvo from Scandinavia; and Du Pont, Asea Brown Boveri and Nestlé from Switzerland. The UK is the country of registration of 133 of the 280 non-EU multinational organizations, with only 50 being in Germany and 26 in France.

We drew attention to the phenomenon of internationalization of business in the last chapter. Transnational organizations are providing the engine for this process of internationalization (see Illustration 5.1). Contact between those organizations who know how and those who want to know is being generated increasingly by the web-like interconnections between modern organizations (Ohmae, 1990). There has been a tendency for European organizations to internationalize their operations by moving their production and co-ordination centres to a strategically important market with low labour costs and/or a high level of local competency.

In addition, large chemical firms like Smith Kline Beecham and ICI have worked hard over the past two decades to 'go global'. All now have more than three-quarters of their assets outside their home country. In fact, some estimates suggest that by the year 2000, manufacturing will account for only 20 per cent of GNP in most of the industrialized nations (Fombrun, 1984).

Bartlett and Ghoshal (1989, 1992) have argued that the globalization concept is being superseded by the need for a 'transnational' organization. Bartlett and Ghoshal (1992) interviewed 236 managers from three industries in Europe, the US and Japan. Their research demonstrated that the management of cultural diversity presents organizations with both opportunities and threats. Organizations tend to move through three successive stages when they think about the management of foreign operations (see Illustration 5.2). Bartlett and Ghoshal (1992) note that in comparison to organizations elsewhere in the world, European organizations (notwithstanding differences between the UK, France, Germany and Sweden) were generally the first to expand internationally. They built worldwide markets giving them strengths in terms of their closeness to and understanding of the political and cultural aspects of their

Illustration 5.1 **Examples of the trend towards globalization of business.**

- IBM's decision to transfer worldwide responsibility for its communications systems division to Europe.
- Apple Computer's major expansion of its manufacturing facility at Cork.
- Motorola's announcement of a new manufacturing and headquarters facility in Swindon.
- Ford Europe's decision to end the production of the Sierra at the Dagenham plant in the UK and transfer the production to the Genk plant in Belgium.
- Philips' decision to shift the traditional multi-domestic approach of local production for local markets to highly efficient factories across the globe through the establishment of 'international production centres'.

Source: Hamill (1992a).

Illustration 5.2 **Three types of international businesses.**

1. Multi-domestic organizations which manage a portfolio of multiple national entities, with strategy and organization being very sensitive to different local environments.
2. Global organizations which strive to achieve cost efficiency through centralized and globally scaled strategies.
3. International organizations which rely on export-based strategies and the international transfer of parent company knowledge and technology to foreign markets.

Source: Bartlett and Ghoshal (1989).

markets. However, the markets were mainly colonial and the tendency was to centralize and control foreign subsidiaries.

According to Bartlett and Ghoshal (1989) these three main approaches to international business have become increasingly inappropriate in the new economic environment of the 1990s. What is now required is an 'integrated network configuration', which achieves national responsiveness, global economies of scale, and worldwide diffusion of knowledge simultaneously. This configuration is called the transnational solution. A transnational organization recognizes other resources and capabilities, captures them and then leverages them on a worldwide basis.

Although, to date, there are few examples of truly transnational organizations, there is a clear trend towards greater geographical dispersion of traditional headquarter responsibility for one or more of the company's main lines of business. For example, IBM's global responsibility for communications systems is now based in London, rather than in the US. According to Hamill (1992), the decision to transfer this decision making power from the US to Europe was motivated by the rapidly growing European market for telecommunications as a consequence of deregulation, the SEM programme, and the prospects created by political developments in Eastern Europe.

TRANSNATIONALISM AS A SOURCE OF EUROPEAN COMPETITIVE ADVANTAGE

Bosch and Prooijen (1992a, 1992b) take issue with the description of the relative competitive advantage of nations outlined by Porter in Chapter Two. They argue instead that the emergence of an identifiable brand of 'European management' could provide European organizations with a new asset that lies at the heart of competitiveness, i.e. the ability to foster innovation in a transnational context. Truly transnational organizations have to establish complex mechanisms and procedures to co-ordinate the range of interdependent and differentiated units within the organization. In doing this they have to recognize the importance of differences between national environments. Transnationalism is essentially a model of organization towards which a variety of the leading organizations are evolving (Bosch and Prooijen, 1992a, 1992b). Bartlett (1992) believes that many European organizations have – and will continue to in the future – adapted their historical limitations and learned to compete in transnational industries. He points to Nestlé, Unilever, Ericsson, Alcatel, Siemens, Shell, B.P., Ciba-Geigy, ABB, ICI, Rhône-Poulenc and SKF as holding their own in business sectors that are increasingly transnational. In the early stages of the process such organizations show an increasing awareness of – and then openness towards – European diversity. As the process gathers pace, organizations learn how to integrate such diversity into their structures and business processes (van Dijck, 1992).

Such a transnational approach to management lies at the heart of innovation – itself a major determinant of long-term competitiveness. Innovation requires the generation, acceptance and implementation of new ideas, processes, products and services. The fusion of the different European models of business and HRM – with the need to consider increased complexity, a wider range of relationships, more sources of information, and more angles on problems – will create a climate steeped in cultural diversity in the European organizations that go down this path. It is exactly the type of climate just described that fosters innovation (see Illustration 5.3).

It is argued that successful adoption of transnational management will lead to:

- The emergence of a European model of management.
- A spur to performance that can break the limits on national competitiveness often assumed by economists.

In essence, the argument from the 'transnationalists' is that in order for Europe to respond to the relative competitive threat of the US and Japan it has to come to terms with its different national cultures and institutional inheritance. A number of European academics (for example, Hofstede, 1991) reinforce the view that whilst European organizations will inevitably have to find out about intercultural co-operation the hard way, what they have already learned will become a source of competitive advantage over the other economic superpowers during the next ten years. To the extent that European organizations can convert their learning about cultural and institutional diversity into a European style of management, then the next ten years will present them with powerful opportunities. However, this integrating force in European HRM still sounds distant, and perhaps speculative. Most certainly, its final impact will be relatively slow (although as we argue in the next section fundamental changes in HRM are already taking place in the leading European organizations) and the implementation problems associated with it will provide plenty of scope for localized patterns of HRM – and therefore plenty of scope for patterns of HRM steeped in national continuity.

Illustration 5.3   **Transnationalism: competitive success at Airbus Industries.**

Airbus Industries began life in the 1970s as a consortium of French (Aérospatiale), German (Deutsche Aerospace), Spanish and British (British Aerospace) organizations. Armed with $13 billion of subsidies over 20 years, it adopted an early competitive edge against US competitors such as Boeing and McDonnell Douglas by developing superior technology. Airbus is seen as one of Europe's most effective tie-ups in the sense that it broke up America's dominance of the civil aircraft market. However, the consortium experienced a number of difficult problems, particularly in relation to cross-functional areas of management. Having to manufacture parts in different countries and assemble them centrally created a range of internal and cross-cultural management difficulties. However, Airbus gradually overcame the severe management difficulties that arose from the diverging national cultures. It then benefited from the increased levels of innovation. By 1992 Airbus Industries represented a serious threat to Boeing and McDonnell Douglas in terms of its worldwide growth rates in new orders. Whilst Boeing still had just over half the market, Airbus had grown to a 25 per cent market share, overtaking McDonnell Douglas. With the loss of $8 billion of business during the recession in 1993, Deutsche Airbus reduced its workforce by 13 per cent whilst Boeing had to eliminate more than 20 per cent of its entire civil production workforce.

Source: Bosch and Prooijen (1992b); *The Economist* (1993).

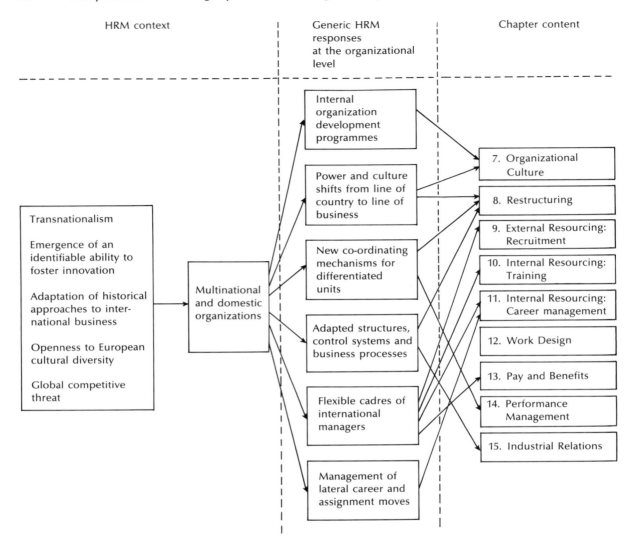

Figure 5.2 Links between transnationalism and European HRM.

FLEXIBLE CADRES OF INTERNATIONAL MANAGERS AS THE VANGUARD OF DEEP STRUCTURAL CHANGES IN PATTERNS OF HRM

... Companies have been trying to implement third generation strategies through second generation organizations with first generation managers. We are now attempting to describe and construct the skills, particularly of general managers, necessary to manage in the transnational organization.   Bartlett (1992, p. 274).

The HRM implications of this evolving form of transnational organization appear initially to revolve around the emergence of a highly flexible international cadre of transnational managers capable of implementing the very complex strategies involved (see Figure 5.2 for an outline of the impact of transnationalism on different areas of European HRM). We deal with the development of an international cadre of managers in more detail in Chapter Eleven on career management and internationalization. However, in general, these managers will have weakened loyalty to any one organization – and will hence have to be retained through more attractive and progressive HRM policies (Bartlett, 1992). Organizations face the prospect of coping with powerful elites, fluctuating alliances, continuous groupings and regrouping of teams, and global movements of a small cadre of executives. Moreover, these managers will need to be developed in very different ways to the existing systems. Instead of having careers that are driven by vertical moves up the hierarchy, the focus will shift to managing lateral moves aimed at broadening and sharpening experience. The way in which managers are allocated to assignments and temporary projects will need to be aligned and managed more tightly, and these projects will become more cross-functional, cross-business and cross-geography.

The HRM implications of this transnational integration run much deeper than just creating a mobile international cadre of managers. European organizations will need to create strong co-ordinating centres (see Chapter Eight on structuring the organization) – no longer wielding centralized command and control policies – but providing a vision, a purpose and a set of principles that help create a 'binding glue' (Bartlett, 1992). Classic matrix organizations that create diversity within operations and then have it all report to a central co-ordinator will become ill-suited to the environment. Highly diversified organizations like Unilever or highly acquisitive organizations like Asea Brown Boveri are being forced to make important decisions about what to manage centrally, what to manage locally, what to co-ordinate in a globally-integrated fashion and what to manage in a dispersed fashion. Within the same organization, the answers to these questions are typically different from business to business.

Therefore, patterns of HRM within organizations are being driven more and more by sector and business solutions than by national solutions. Several organizations, such as Kodak and Hoescht, in reconfiguring their matrix structures have changed their European structures in ways which have taken power away (by reducing the influence of the dotted reporting lines) from the line of country and have vested more power for HRM issues in the line of business segments. The need to manage significant cultural change in the organization (see Chapter Seven) will become paramount. There are significant implications for training as well (see Chapter Ten). Lower down the organization (where the current technical expertise lies) new skills and competencies are being created. Managers will no longer just learn through sophisticated organizational structures and systems, but through the development of people. Greater emphasis will be placed on the need to become coaches of learning, more creative, and more entrepreneurial.

In driving all these changes forward, Bartlett (1992) argues that European organizations will not wait for Business Schools to create an intellectual basis for the phenomenon of transnationalism. Instead, they will lead the way towards new patterns of HRM in Europe (perhaps without realizing all the consequences and pressures this will create) by:

- Recruiting managers of this new persuasion.
- Developing and shaping internal management development programmes.
- Re-orientating matrix structures away from a line of country towards line of business focus.
- Redirecting training and career development moves.

It can be seen from this description of the likely HRM implications of transnationalism, why we believe that the field of HRM is inevitably becoming a central focus for European organizations and will become a strategic capability and core competence.

EUROPEAN MANAGEMENT INTEGRATION THROUGH FOREIGN DIRECT INVESTMENT

Is there a more immediate and widespread process of European integration taking place? In this section we present some compelling evidence that there is by examining Foreign Direct Investment (FDI). FDI is an investment made to acquire a lasting interest in an enterprise operating in an economy other than that of the investor with the aim of having an effective voice in the management of the enterprise. It includes mergers, acquisitions, majority or minority participation, greenfield investments, joint ventures and parental to subsidiary transfers of equity capital, intercompany debt and retained earnings.

In the narrow sense, FDI is simply capital transferred between an organization and its foreign affiliates. In its broadest sense it represents competition among workers, governments, organizations, markets and economic and business systems. Thomsen and Woolcock (1993) focus on the role FDI plays in increasing competition and providing a foretaste of potential competitive winners and losers. We devote considerable attention to FDI because of this link to competitiveness, as well as its ability to shape significantly patterns of HRM in Europe.

Nicolaides (1992) of the European Institute of Public Administration in Maastricht examined the impact of FDI on management. It provides a significant impetus to management integration in the manufacturing sector through associated gains in productivity, new production systems, working practices and relationships with suppliers and distributors. In service sectors integration is achieved through the hiring of personnel with comparable skills and the transfer of existing skills through training. More than two-thirds of Japanese and German FDI in other countries since 1985 has been in services. From 1985–91 FDI has grown faster than exports, consistent with a new phase of globalization in which organizations are crossing borders to deliver services to customers locally, whilst export markets are approaching saturation (Lewis and Harris, 1992). For example, US-owned organizations in Europe now sell almost five times as much locally as America exports to Europe (Thomsen and Woolcock, 1993) and the greatest source of transatlantic tension in the GATT talks is in those sectors with low levels of FDI. In the second half of the 1980s FDI grew at annual rates three times as high as international trade (Welfens, 1992).

The 1980s witnessed rapid globalization of organizations. This resulted in increased competition among organizations as they ventured beyond their own sheltered markets, and has also triggered a competitive race between governments within and outside the EU as they created policies aimed at attracting 'footloose' organizations (Thomsen and Woolcock, 1993). The world stock of FDI doubled as did the annual flows of inward and outward investment. Since 1980 FDI by transnational organizations and capital goods exports have both grown at a compound annual rate of 14 per cent. Eighty per cent of FDI from Triad countries was in other countries in the Triad (Lewis and Harris, 1992). By 1990 annual flows of FDI were in excess of 76 billion ECU (Turner, 1991). The largest foreign investor (by value of investment) was the US. However, 87 per cent of the world stock of inward foreign direct investment is located in the seven industrial countries of the US, the UK, Japan, Germany, the Netherlands, France and Canada. Of these, the four European countries hosted 40 per cent of the world stock of FDI (Akimune, 1991). Inward flows of FDI

Table 5.1 **Contribution of FDI to national economies.**

Country	Stock of inward investment as a percentage of GDP	Percentage of sales accounted for by foreign owned firms	Proportion of exports from foreign owned firms
US	7%	10%	23%
Japan	4%	n/a	n/a
Netherlands	31%	n/a	n/a
UK	22%	19%	30%
Germany	8%	19%	24%
France	6%	27%	32%

Sources data: Nicolaides (1992). Reprinted data with permission, Oxford University Press, © 1992, Business Strategy Review.

to the European Union rose nearly sixfold from 9.3 billion ECU in 1985 to 55.1 billion ECU by 1990.

There are several ways in which the contribution of FDI to national economies may be measured. Table 5.1 shows some alternative contributions.

Foreign involvement in national economies is even more potent and subtle than the FDI statistics suggest. The global web of corporate alliances (including joint ventures, collaborative research, subcontracting and original manufacturer equipment agreements) has also seen an increase in direct foreign involvement in national economies, leading to fears that national firms may lose their corporate identities and control over decisions (Reich, 1991; Thomsen, 1992). We address the strategic integration options available to European organizations later in this chapter.

THE MERGER AND ACQUISITION PHENOMENON IN THE EU

... Cross-border mergers and acquisitions within Europe and relentless investment by Japanese, American and other non-EU firms in the EU are reshaping the European economy.

Nicolaides and Thomsen (1991).

In Chapter Four we briefly introduced the role of mergers and acquisitions. Attempts to increase organizational integration through mergers and acquisition represent just one way – but an increasingly prevalent way – of achieving the desired business benefits from the Single European Market. The impact of mergers and acquisitions and FDI on European economies is not, of course, a new phenomenon. In the 1970s there were fears that US investment would threaten European independence (Servan-Schreiber, 1967). Amoroso (1990) points out that by as long ago as the end of the 1970s about 33 per cent of private Danish organizations (accounting for 16 per cent of Danish employment and 26 per cent of corporate turnover) were partially or totally foreign owned. Nevertheless, one of the most visible signs of more recent business integration through FDI has been the marked growth of cross-border mergers and acquisitions in Europe – both friendly and hostile (Hamill, 1992). Shenton (1992) has pointed out that there is nothing specifically European about cross-border mergers and acquisitions and that business will steadily become more global, not just European, through this process. The removal of capital controls in the UK and US in the late 1970s enabled organizations in liberal countries to compete in foreign markets, which in turn led to policy changes by countries that had hitherto supported national champions. As some organizations were allowed to compete globally, more restrictive governments were obliged to follow suit (Thomsen and Woolcock, 1993).

Therefore, mergers and acquisitions have become more intense in Europe as economic space is being re-organized at a supranational level. This is because in 1990 Europe overtook the US as the world's leading market for international mergers and acquisitions (Mergers and Acquisitions Europe, 1991a) and between 1988 and 1991 European organizations were involved in three-quarters of all international cross-border merger and acquisition activity (Strongin Dodds, 1992). A report by the London Business School (1990) argues that this has happened because European organizations see mergers and acquisitions as the centre-piece of their European strategy. The European market will become increasingly dominated by large organizations enjoying economies of scale. Single European Market takeovers are seen as the means of promoting restructuring between and within organizations (Cecchini *et al.* 1988). Thompson, Wallace and Flecker (1992) point out that considerable strategic hope is riding on the power of mergers and acquisitions as a change agent. They set out to investigate to what extent they trigger transformations, or under what circumstances they have the most potent effects on work organization, industrial relations and management systems in a series of case studies in Austria and the UK.

There were two phases of internationalization in the run up to the creation of the SEM (Thomsen and Woolcock, 1993). In the first phase, European organizations invested heavily in the US. The 1980s represented a strong break with the past in terms of European integration. The first three postwar decades were characterized by growing intra-EU trade and American FDI in Europe. However, by investing 50 billion ECU in the US, Europe invested four times as much in America as it received in the second half of the 1980s. The UK provided 41 per cent of Europe's investment in the US. In the latter half of the 1980s the bulk of the investment was focused around Europe, and between one-half and two-thirds of most European countries' investment remained in Europe.

Nicolaides and Thomsen (1991) estimated that during 1985–89 cross-border mergers in the EU almost quadrupled in number (from 52 to 197) while national mergers increased by only 60 per cent. In 1988–89, 73 per cent of the mergers for which motives were specified were undertaken either to facilitate expansion or to strengthen the organizations' market position. This was the motive for only 20 per cent of the mergers in 1985–86 (when the dominant motive was rationalization in the aftermath of the recession in the early 1980s). Merger and acquisition activity peaked in 1990 (see Figure 5.3), with disclosed cross-border mergers valued at 46 billion ECU (Mergers and Acquisitions, 1992a). This figure was considered to be a 23 per cent underestimate given the undisclosed value of many mergers and acquisitions (Hindle, 1989). Even though domestic turnover in the US and UK fell by 40 per cent in 1990 the value of cross-border transactions in Europe grew by 20 per cent to set a new record (Mergers and Acquisitions, 1991a). However, the harsher economic climate brought a seedchange in the European mergers and acquisition market with activity falling 45 per cent from a value of 46 billion ECU in 1990 to 31 billion ECU in 1991.

The recession of the early 1990s saw an absence of mega-deals and focused management attention more sharply on the need to boost productivity, expand market share and secure economies of scale. In the UK, although merger activity overall declined by 70 per cent (in terms of value) during 1989–90 as a result of the recession, acquisition of EU companies by UK companies declined by only 4 per cent (Nicolaides and Thomsen, 1991). Similarly, despite the currency crisis of October 1992 and the difficulties this presented in predicting the cost of purchase and resulting profits, the pace of merger and acquisition activity in Europe did not fall.

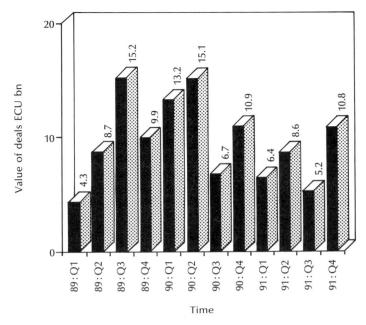

Figure 5.3 Quarterly value of European cross-border mergers and acquisitions. Data from various editions of *International Mergers and Acquisitions*.

JAPANESE ENTRY INTO EUROPEAN MARKETS THROUGH ACQUISITION

In Chapter Four we highlighted the competitive threat for European organizations represented by Japan. Japanese cross-border merger and acquisition activity grew rapidly from 31 per cent of all Japanese merger and acquisition activity in 1984 to 61 per cent in 1990 (Lewis and Harris, 1992). Cumulative Japanese investment in Europe nearly tripled between 1987 and 1990, reaching a level of $60 billion. The advent of the SEM was accompanied by predictions of a Japanese onslaught on 'Fortress Europe' before the end of 1992. This was not actually realized (Mergers and Acquisitions Europe, 1992b). In spite of the attention that Japanese investment received in Europe, it paled into insignificance compared with the activities of European multinational enterprises (MNEs) both at home and in the US (Thomsen and Woolcock, 1993). It was also greatly exceeded in value by FDI by organizations from EFTA. The value of Japanese acquisitions in EU countries peaked at 4.2 billion ECU in 1989, falling back to 2.17 billion ECU by 1991 (the same level as 1988). Declining share prices, tighter credit and shrinking profits all constrained Japanese merger and acquisition activity with the larger companies. However, Japanese companies are expected to continue with strategic acquisitions of mid-size companies (14 to 42 billion ECU acquisitions). Abranavel and Ernst (1992) cite a McKinsey survey that indicates that Japanese executives across all industries view Europe as the major geographical area for expansion in the 1990s. The percentage of Japanese executives citing the US as their main focus for expansion fell from 60 to 32 per cent, whilst Europe rose from 20 to 27 per cent. Indeed, in the run up to the SEM the UK was a pre-eminent target for Japanese acquirers, although in the future Japanese acquisition is expected to be more widespread. Many economic and business forecasters expect to see much more two-way traffic between Europe and Japan in the mergers and acquisition field.

The continued Japanese influence and impact on the competitive position of European organizations does not only flow from their level of acquisitions and mergers. For example, continuing with the example of the automobile industry discussed in Chapter Four, profitability of European car manufacturers used to be twice that of Japanese car manufacturers on average, but has since fallen dramatically. In addition to the pressures on profitability, the next few years will see considerable pressure put on customer satisfaction. By 1992 only 45 Japanese car models were available in Europe compared to 90 in Japan. Simply by expanding existing distribution systems Japanese car manufacturers intend to enhance the choice of models and put pressure on measured customer satisfaction for European car makers (Abranavel and Ernst, 1992).

HOSTILE TAKEOVERS: A NEW EXPERIENCE FOR EUROPEAN MANAGERS

The first hostile takeover bid in French stock exchange listings was actually in the 1960s by the glassmaker Boussois-Souchon-Neuvesel (the bid failed). Acquisitions for the next twenty years were friendly. Since 1985, however, takeover activity began to take off again highlighting a delicate debate between the defence of European organizations against destabilizing raiders and the interests of shareholders (Aboud, 1992).

The early 1990s then saw the phenomenon of hostile bids clearly move into the European market from the UK and US. Of 26 hostile takeover bids in Europe in 1988, 23 were in the UK, with one each in France, Italy and the Netherlands (Hindle, 1990a). The UK continued to be the most popular target for hostile takeovers, accounting for almost 50 per cent of all deals by value in 1989. Europe incorporates a range of national economic and policy environments: from high-cost locations in Germany and the Netherlands to low-cost Spain and Portugal; from liberal FDI policies in Northern Europe to the more restrictive France and Italy; from active competition policies in Britain and Germany to the absence of policies in Italy or Greece; and from the Anglo-Saxon approach to capital markets in Britain to less liberal markets elsewhere in Europe (Thomsen and Woolcock, 1993).

The conventional wisdom up until the late 1980s was that hostile takeover battles – along the lines well trodden in Britain and the US – were not a feature of European merger and acquisition activity because of the complex shareholding structures, a less liquid market in equity, and a less developed regulatory framework. However, conventional wisdom was turned on its head in March 1988 with a wave of aggressive bids (see Illustrations 5.4 and 5.5) concentrated on Belgium, France and Holland (Dickson, 1988). Dickson (1988) documented how the phenomenon moved into mainland Europe.

Such events, whether eventually successful or not, tend to force organizations to re-examine their respective managements. The attempted takeover of SGB led several executives to reveal later that they gained ten years' advance in management thinking in the process as they questioned management practices and organization design features (Franck, 1990). There was a lot of questioning about management practices across Europe in the late 1980s and early 1990s. During the same period Assurances Générales de France (AGF) raised its stake in Aachener und Munchener Beteiligungs (AMB) to 25 per cent, Nestlé and Gianni Agnelli tustled over Perrier, and Krupp

Illustration 5.4 **Abortive bid for Société Générale de Belgique.**

Italian financier Carlo De Benedetti made an (unsuccessful) bid for Société Générale de Belgique (SGB), Belgium's largest holding organization. SGB had interests in more than 600 Belgian companies and acted as a centre of decision making for large areas of the Belgian economy. A lack of coherent takeover rules meant it was easy for De Benedetti to build up his launching pad unnoticed. A defensive alliance led by a Flemish businessman, and then a Franco-Belgian alliance led by Compagnie Financière de Suez (France), Group AG (Belgium) and Stella Artois (Belgium) was able to defeat De Benedetti's offer to double the value of his bid for a critical 7 per cent of capital when Groupe AG, the insurance subsidiary of SGB bought shares in its parent company.

Illustration 5.5 **Pirelli versus Continental, 1991.**

The difference between UK–US methods of hostile takeover and the way in which they are fought in Europe was demonstrated by Pirelli's unsuccessful proposal to merge with German tyre maker Continental. In the UK once a predator buys up 30 per cent of a company's stock it has to make an offer for the rest of the company. In Europe there is usually no requirement to bid at a specified level. Germany felt no need for a takeover code or regulatory framework. Each company's super-visory board (the upper tier of the two-tier German board system) was charged with protecting share-holders' interests. Pirelli moved on the healthier Continental after winning the support of arbitrageurs who claimed to have amassed a 50 per cent stake. Continental was able to mount its defence because of the network of cross shareholdings and interests. Deutsche Bank held 5 per cent of Continental shares and advised clients to reject the merger. Volkswagen (Continental's largest customer) followed the advice of the bank as did Daimler-Benz (another customer that was 28 per cent owned by Deutsche Bank). Though a merger may have brought many advantages, Continental felt these were outweighed and rejected the bid. Pirelli failed to win approval at the extraordinary meeting of shareholders amassing only 38 per cent of the stock.

Source: Strongin Dodds (1992).

(a German steelmaker) launched a successful bid for Hoesch (a domestic rival) as a prelude to the rationalization of the German steelmaking industry.

SHAREHOLDER DEMOCRATIZATION AND LEGISLATIVE REFORM

This globalization has led to a wider and more diverse shareholder base for many European organizations. Between 20 and 30 per cent of the stock in the largest quoted companies in Europe is now held by overseas institutional investors whose demand for improved performance, coupled with the threat of sell out to bidders, is anticipated to herald a new set of pressures for many European managers. They are having to develop an 'unregulated' perspective through which they view former partners as competitors, former competitors as global allies, and traditionally friendly national customers as more demanding stakeholders. As shareholder demands reinforce and increase the intensity of competition between the more and less protected countries within Europe, convergence will be accelerated by the strategies and actions of global organizations already inside Europe (Abranavel and Ernst, 1992). For example, in France, moves to reduce regulation and control of inward investment, the lifting of foreign exchange controls and the liberalization of tax laws led to an eight-fold increase of FDI from 1976 to 1988 (Aboud, 1992).

In response to this trend European countries began to tighten their legislation on disclosure of shareholdings and mandatory offers to protect minority shareholders. In the UK purchasers now have to reveal a 3 per cent as opposed to 5 per cent stake in a company and have to declare their interest within two days instead of five days. In May 1992 France ruled that bidders must make an offer for all outstanding stock once they have acquired more than 33 per cent (previously it was only a further 33 per cent) in response to the battle over Perrier. Indeed, even after the 1993 French election, despite the advent of increased privatization, the French government intends to maintain considerable influence in organizations like Renault and Air France through such mechanisms as:

- The retention of golden shares to fend off takeovers.
- Encouragement of loyal institutions to become investors.
- Reliance on a management corps that is tied to the state (45 per cent of French CEOs in the mid-1980s came from government backgrounds).

Italy and Spain also changed the rulebooks to make bids more transparent whilst Belgium passed a law to permit subsidiaries to buy 10 per cent of voting right shares in the parent company. However, the EU's internal market council decided to amend the Second Company Law Directive restricting a company's control over its own capital (preventing defence from takeovers through the purchase of parent voting shares by subsidiaries). In smaller European countries cross-share holdings are part of the corporate culture and the directive is seen to represent an Anglo-Saxon approach to management. The amendment to the Second Company Law Directive to take effect from 1995 will have radical implications for the corporate landscape in smaller European countries (Arbose, 1992).

The hostile takeover phenomenon should not be overstated, however. Nor should the openness of UK capital markets lead to the misconception that British organizations are still more vulnerable to hostile takeovers than European competitors. Only a small proportion of the wave of cross-border acquisitions that hit Britain in 1988 to 1990 (see the later section on acquirers and targets on page 160) were hostile. Nicolaides and Thomsen (1991) estimate the proportion as 5 per cent in 1988, 1 per cent in 1989 and 3 per cent in 1990.

ATTRACTIVENESS OF THE MERGER AND ACQUISITION OPTION

Since the initial burst of restructuring there has been a continuance of strategically-motivated mergers and acquisitions (but with a more cautious approach) and greater attention given to joint ventures, strategic alliances and minority stakes. Nevertheless, the industrial restructuring process feeds on itself and the fall in activity only masked the continued urge to unite (*The Economist*, 1992a; Mergers and Acquisitions, 1992a). The wave of mergers and acquisitions has been, and will continue to be, fuelled by the pressures shown in Illustration 5.6.

There are a wide variety of motives for takeovers, including: limiting risks, control of resource dependencies, tax advantage, transaction costs, hostile takeover defences, diversification, and cheaper and faster expansion (Napier, 1989; Larsson, 1989; Schweiger and Weber, 1990). The synergy achieved can range from a loose combination effect, including the blending of resources without any significant integration of functions or practices, through to a tight bonding in which organization

Illustration 5.6   **Forces fuelling integration through merger and acquisition: asset sharing and asset creation.**

- Industrial restructuring in which organizations are prepared to compete on a continental basis.
- Disposal of assets in non-core businesses to free up capital in areas (such as brand or market share) where organizations can be the top five or ten players.
- Knock-on effects in related industrial sectors (for example, supremacy of brands across European markets will accelerate rationalization in the retail sector).
- Opportunities to consolidate and cut capacity within national industries.
- Geographical diversification leading to expansion of core businesses across borders to offer economies of scale.

- A need to ensure closeness to principal customers in regional markets.
- Creation of the Single European Market to reinforce this process leading to liberalization in many sectors and the reshaping of traditionally fragmented national markets.
- Realization of vast assets through privatization in both the East and West of Europe.
- Changes in stock market rules making friendly mergers more expensive, but hostile bids more possible.
- Integration of capital markets leading to an increased profit motive and need to consider the most appropriate mix and portfolio of businesses to be in.

structures, systems and cultures are redirected towards new goals. Whatever form the desired synergy may take, it is usually aimed at achieving benefits such as economies of scale and scope, rationalization of resources, price co-ordination and redeployment of capital. In order to achieve these benefits, many acquired organizations are managed at a distance through tight and powerful financial controls such as profit targets, detailed monetary indicators and managerial reward systems.

Nicolaides and Thomsen (1991) point out that many of the motives and desired outcomes that fuelled mergers and acquisitions within Europe are just as likely to result from the process of global restructuring that is also taking place. It is difficult to tease out global reasoning and motivation for FDI from those associated specifically with Europe. The influence of the SEM has been more important for intra-European mergers, whilst American and Japanese acquirers have been attracted by the enhanced prospects for growth in European markets and a reaction to the potential closure of European markets after the SEM.

DIFFICULTIES IN ACHIEVING INTEGRATION THROUGH MERGERS AND ACQUISITIONS

However, pan-European acquisition and merger strategies are fraught with difficulties. For example, Crédit Lyonnais pursued an international diversification strategy from 1987 to 1992. Its Chairman, Jean-Yves Haberer, doubled its assets from FFr. 887 billion to FFr. 1587 billion by combining a global acquisition policy with aggressive lending policies. This culminated with the purchase of Germany's Bank für Gemeinwirtschaft, seen as a ten year investment. Ten years is a long time in business, and after lending exposures to MGM, the Maxwell empire and Olympia and York, profits at Crédit Lyonnais declined by 92 per cent placing considerable strains on its acquisitions. Similarly, having acquired an assortment of industrial interests from La Société Générale de Belgique (mentioned earlier in relation to hostile takeovers), the French holding company Compagnie Financière de Suez made FFr 11 billion of

Illustration 5.7 **Factors limiting the pace of integration through mergers and acquisition.**

- Whilst acquisition can bring fast growth it is not necessarily the best way to build global businesses. Alliances may be more favourable.
- The European-wide recession in the early to mid-1990s will generate a significant amount of rationalization and de-merger pressure.
- Mergers and acquisitions can exact a high toll on staff and frequently fail for HRM reasons.
- Cultural and attitudinal differences exist. In the UK–US shareholder interest is paramount and the role of managements subject to hostile takeovers is to either defeat the bid completely or secure the best price for their shareholders. Despite changing rules and regulations in Europe greater attention is given to the interests of the business as a whole and the needs of the workers.

disposals in 1992, FFr 5.5 billion of which were from the originally acquired stock. Reviews of the stock market performance of the high profile acquirers in the 1980s indicated that there were more losers than winners (Mergers and Acquisitions Europe, 1992c). The restructuring tactics of the more successful organizations such as Guinness, Asea Brown Boveri, BSN, Electrolux and Michelin were associated with demergers, spin-offs, related acquisitions and non-core disposals.

The business literature is generally fairly sceptical or pessimistic about the track record of merged or acquired companies. In the US, Lefkoe (1987) estimated that up to 50 per cent of all mergers and acquisitions failed to meet the expectations of the acquirers; and over one third of acquired companies are sold off in the first five years. This organizational literature tends to focus on the negative aspects of behaviour that are created (Marks and Mirvis, 1985; Jemison and Sitkin, 1986; Buono and Bowditch, 1989) and points to the low managerial attention given to people problems and under-management of the post acquisition processes that result. Business history is therefore littered with examples of organizations that grew large through mergers and acquisitions but did not achieve the desired improvements in efficiency or competitiveness because, as they grew in size, they grew in complacency. Therefore, despite the apparent inevitability of continued integration of European management under the pressure of mergers and acquisitions (both friendly and hostile) a number of factors will also dampen activity (see Illustration 5.7).

The wave of restructuring in Europe naturally raises questions about winners and losers. Which companies, corporate styles and national economies will prevail? In order to answer this question we have to consider:

- Which country's organizations are the highest performing?
- What is the true geographic scale of the top European organizations?
- Which countries were the most acquisitive or were the targets of acquisition?

WHICH COUNTRY'S FIRMS HAVE THE BEST CORPORATE PERFORMANCE?

Anglo-Saxon and continental forms of capitalism continually reassess their efficiency (see the discussion on European business systems in Chapter Two) and FDI has made this competition more immediate. Countries which do not enact business-friendly policies towards FDI run the risk of losing their organizations to locations elsewhere through an exodus of FDI. Similarly, host countries run the risk of depriving themselves of vital technologies, management and marketing skills (Thomsen and

Woolcock, 1993). For example, Germany worries that it will lose factories to lower-wage locations such as Spain and the United Kingdom, while Spain and Portugal worry about the appeal of Eastern Europe.

Mergers and acquisitions have, not surprisingly, resulted in considerable movement and change in the various league tables of European organization performance (Eurobusiness, 1989). Comparative measures of corporate performance are difficult to agree because of the diverse range of European organizations. Private sector, public sector and co-operative organizations all feature prominently in Europe's top 500 companies when measured in terms of turnover and employment (Eurobusiness, 1989), in contrast to the US where the private sector dominates. Oil organizations like Royal Dutch Shell and British Petroleum; car manufacturers like Fiat, Daimler-Benz, Volkswagen and Renault; technical giants like Seimens and Philips, and public sector employers feature strongly on such measures of size. However, ranking by turnover exaggerates the significance of trading companies that may add little value. Consideration of profits brings a different set of organizations into the frame.

There is considerable debate over which European management styles will prove to be the most enduring over the next decade and beyond. Indeed, in Chapter Two we examined some empirical evidence from the IBM/Towers Perrin survey which indicated that some European countries such as Germany and Italy were moving into the 'Anglo-Saxon camp' in terms of the relative importance they perceived for 37 HRM issues. In part, the debate over the most appropriate management style may be determined by future levels of corporate performance. This immediately raises questions about what is meant by good performance.

A survey of the performance of the 250 largest European organizations compiled by P-E International (Hindle, 1990b) showed that 28 out of the first 50 organizations were British. Using a triple measure of pre-tax profit as a percentage of turnover, return on total assets and added value as a multiple of pay – nine out of the top eleven profit makers in 1989 were British or Anglo-Dutch organizations (Eurobusiness, 1989). Similarly, according to a series of benchmarks drawn up by Professor Schmidt of the Kiel University and simultaneously published in *Management Today* and *Management Magazine*, British companies are the best performers in Europe and the British corporate style may come to dominate the European competitive arena (Lloyd and Skeel, 1992). These benchmarks use five-year weighted averages of three qualities, each by two variables: *Rendite* (profitability), *Sicherheit* (financial solidity) and *Wachstum* (growth). Profitability is weighted as four times more important than the

Table 5.2 **Expected and actual national portfolios of Europe's top 500 companies.**

Country	Percentage GDP (out of 15 European countries)	Prosperity index	Expected portfolio (out of 500)	Actual portfolio (out of 500)	Anomaly (%)	Average RSW score
Germany	24.2	126.3	153	94	−39	−6.5
France	18.4	106.6	98	87	−11	16.2
Italy	14.9	85.1	77	28	−64	−6.6
UK	12.7	90.1	58	141	+143	21.6

Source: Lloyd and Skeel (1992), reprinted with permission © 1993 *Management Today* and *Manager Magazine*.

other factors (hence the more favourable scores of British companies). Despite the fact that British Gross Domestic Product is only the fourth largest in Europe, it has 28 per cent of the top performing companies. Irish and Belgian firms also scored highly.

Table 5.2 shows the expected portfolio of companies (out of Europe's top 500 companies) based on the proportion of GDP for each country (size) and the relative prosperity (GDP per head ratioed against the average) for the UK, Italy, France and Germany. Whilst British organizations have poor performance in terms of growth (*Wachstum*), they have high returns on equity and good cash flow (recessions apart).

THE BATTLE BETWEEN COMPETING MODES OF EUROPEAN CAPITALISM

In Chapter Three we highlighted the existence of competing national business systems in Europe. One aspect of the process of European integration is the dissolution of barriers between national capital markets. This is likely to have a significant impact on the management and HRM philosophies across Europe, but also on the German model of capitalism in particular. An increasingly international shareholder base is demanding greater influence over operating decisions made by company management (Popper, 1993). In the short term, shareholder power appears to be on the march in Germany and equity investors – particularly the small domestic shareholders and foreign investors – are campaigning to persuade German directors and managers to implement policies which will maximize the stock market value of their companies (Heath, 1993a). Recessionary pressures are exacerbating the situation. From 1981 to 1991 total return on German equities was 16.4 per cent compared to 21.2 per cent in France, 27.5 per cent in Italy, 19.8 per cent in the Netherlands and 20.9 per cent in the UK. By 1992 German equities were providing a return of under 4 per cent – the lowest of all the European industrial states (Heath, 1993a). In order to avoid German savings moving to higher performing UK and US funds, German companies will need to push for greater profitability at the expense of *Wachstum* or *Sicherheit* (Lloyd and Skeel, 1992).

The Anglo-Saxon model of capitalism is competing with, and attempting to replace the German (and Continental European) system (Henzler, 1992b; Popper, 1993). European capitalism and all its corporate and managerial philosophies are coming under pressure (see Illustration 5.8).

Another pressure on the German model of capitalism is coming from the German banks themselves (Saunderson, 1993b) as they fight to make Frankfurt the centre of Europe's financial system. Whilst cross-holdings are forbidden in the UK and the US, share ownership in German industry lies at the heart of its universal banking system. In Illustration 5.9 we point to the emergence of radical change in Daimler-Benz. This is linked to increasing exposure to new bases of capital.

Illustration 5.8 **Sources of pressure on European capitalism.**

- Regulatory accommodation and shareholder democratization.
- Capital-hungry managers in recession-weakened economies.
- Common strategy and tactics in takeovers.
- Uncompetitive cost structures in the face of competitive devaluation and rationalization in some parts of the EU.

Source: Popper (1993).

Illustration 5.9 **An opening up to capital at Daimler-Benz.**

The Deutsche Bank shocked Germany when it declared that it was giving active consideration to the sale of its 28 per cent stake in Daimler-Benz (worth around 4.1 billion ECU). In 1993 Daimler-Benz also abandoned a powerful protection against hostile takeover. Mercedes Holding (set up to protect Germany's largest company from a bid for 39 per cent of its shares by the Shah of Iran in 1975) is to convert its shares into Daimler shares. Before these moves half of Mercedes Holding was controlled by Stella Automobil and Stern Automobil, themselves owned by leading German banks and industrial groups.

If Germany's largest banks (such as Deutsche, Dresdner, Commerzbank and Bayerische Vereinsbank) do cut or dilute their stake in major German companies (unthinkable in the 1980s but a distinct possibility in the 1990s) the implications for corporate performance would be enormous. Coupled with the pay and productivity pressures, pensions and demographics problems and the costs of unification outlined in Chapter Four, such issues provide additional pressure on the German model of capitalism, its concepts of corporate performance, and the unique aspects of its HRM.

Strong leading organizations do not then necessarily mean strong national economies (see Illustration 5.10) and nationalist sentiments may yet block the shift towards *Wachstum* as a measure of corporate performance. Moreover, the study by Lloyd and Skeel (1992) must be qualified because the dominance of the UK organizations (in terms of overall corporate performance) reflects a number of specific factors (shown in Illustration 5.11).

The study by Lloyd and Skeel (1992) does, however, raise a fundamental question. What kind of corporate performance pattern will dominate in Europe? The process of European business integration and the convergence of world capital markets make it hard to believe that all the present institutional and cultural differences between countries outlined in Chapter Three can survive for long. To the extent that organizations become driven more by the balance of qualities suggested by Schmidt,

Illustration 5.10 **Germany's *Mittelstand* – a reverse process of integration?**

Clearly the long-term consequences of a shift in German management thinking towards profitability are still unknown and hard to predict, as are the hidden strengths of Germany's *Mittelstand* (the pool of 2.5 million small and medium-sized companies, each employing under 500 people, but together employing over 60 per cent of private sector workers). Despite the detailed discussion of competitive threat to European industry discussed in Chapter Four, many medium-sized German organizations still have commanding world market shares. For example, Hauni (cigarette machines), Krones (bottling machines), Fischer-Poege (textile preparation machines) and Tetra (tropical fish food) all have worldmarket shares ranging from 70–100 per cent. Such organizations demonstrate the inner strengths of the German economy and educational infrastructure. It is also argued that the *Mittelstand* structure, with its proximity of management to products and customers, focus on a single technical skill, labour flexibility and high participation offers a model that the larger European organizations may do well to move towards. Given the discussion we have already had about transnational organizations, large organizations could well restructure by providing a *Mittelstand*-type of environment based on decentralized profit structures sharing services within the framework of a larger entity. Processes of integration can always work both ways.

Illustration 5.11 **Factors that may overstate British corporate performance.**

- The UK's possession of a few very successful organizations (rather than any industrial depth).
- Measurements of profits through different accounting practices which inflate UK scores.
- The inherently profitable nature of the traditional UK sectors (services, media, food and beverages and chemicals and pharmaceuticals). In low-profit sectors such as building, paper, machinery and steel, French, Irish, German and Swedish organizations turn in a better performance than UK organizations.
- Intense pressure from UK financial institutions for high levels of short term performance.

and that German organizations become more open to external shareholder pressure, then the Anglo-Saxon corporate style may be favoured.

GEOGRAPHIC SCALE OF THE TOP EUROPEAN ORGANIZATIONS

Regardless of such management style issues however, all organizations have had to consider what is the most appropriate mix and portfolio of businesses that they should be in. We discussed the emergence of transnational organizations earlier in this chapter. As part of the evolution to transnational management it is increasingly apparent that global organizations will supersede the multinationals (Gray and McDermott, 1987). The underlying assumption of the 1990s is that 'big is better'. Organizations will attempt to build strength upon strength in order to survive and attain market leadership. Geographical diversification has become instrumental in attaining this market leadership.

However, one of the early lessons of the industrial restructuring process in Europe was that institutional investors and capital markets prefer to diversify their own portfolios rather than entrust managers to do it for them. There has been a shift in power from European managers to the capital markets which becomes more evident when the advent of hostile takeovers is considered. The result of this shift in power and the underlying 'urge to merge' has been a series of considerably larger, more focused but less diversified (in terms of products and services) organizations. An analysis of the geographical source of sales revenues of the top 75 European organizations in 1990 (Abranavel and Ernst, 1992) showed that only 22 were truly global, 31 could be characterized as pan-European and 22 were local national businesses (see Figure 5.4).

WHO WERE THE ACQUIRERS AND WHO WERE THE TARGETS?

Given the competition over FDI, it is important to consider the geographical and sectoral flows of investment, as it might provide a foretaste of the future location of various economic activities throughout Europe. A clear geographic pattern emerged in the industrial restructuring (see Figure 5.5). About three-quarters of the continental organizations targeted since 1985 were in the UK, France, Sweden, Italy and Germany. The UK, France and Germany were the most acquisitive nations. Figure 5.5 shows the main targets of the wave of cross-border mergers and acquisitions. During 1989 and 1990 the value of acquired organizations in the UK was £31,103 million – or 49 per cent of all cross-border acquisitions by value. This was more than the value of acquired

31

Aerospatiale
Alcatel Alsthom
BASF
BMW
BP
Bertelsmann
British Aerospace
Cadbury Schweppes
Continental
Daimler-Benz
Dalgety
Ferruzi
GEC
Grand Met
Huls
ICI
Lafarge Coppee
L'Oreal
MAN
Mannesmann
Metallgesellschaft
Norsk-Hydro
Olivetti
Pechiney
Philips
Saab-Scania
Saint Gobain
Siemens
Thorn EMI
Usinor-Sacilor
VW

22

Akzo
Asea Brown Boveri
BAT
DSM
Degussa
Henkel
LM Ericsson
Michelin
Pirelli
RTZ
Repola
Roche
Rolls-Royce
Sandoz
Smith Kline Beecham
Solvay
Stora Kopparbergs
Svenska Cellulosa
Tate & Lyle
Thompson
Total
Volvo

22

Allied-Lyons
Australian Industries
BICC
BSN
British Steel
CEA-Industrie
Elf-Aquitaine
Eni
Fiat
Fried Krupp
Hachette
Hanson
Hillsdown Holdings
Hoesch
INI
Peugeot
Preussag
Procordia
Renault
Thyssen
United Biscuits
VIAG

| Home country less than 30% | Home country is 30–50% | Home country greater than 50% |

Figure 5.4 Home versus foreign revenues in the top 75 European companies in 1990 that reported country breakdown of sales. *Source*: Abranavel and Ernst (1992) and Fortune 500 data, reprinted with permission of *Mergers and Acquisitions Europe*, © 1992, DDD Inc.

organizations in (West) Germany, France, Spain, Italy, the Netherlands, Belgium and Denmark combined (Hamill, 1992a). This represented an 84 per cent increase in the number (207 per cent increase in the value) of European acquisitions within the UK (Nicolaides and Thomsen, 1991). In 1991 the UK remained the largest European target, but the proportion of acquisitions in other European countries was larger, and by 1992, in fact, France was the main target for acquisitions (Holmes, 1993).

The targeting of the UK for acquisitions in part reflected the sluggish economic performance of many of its organizations, but is also a reflection of the relative size of its stock market. Nicolaides and Thomsen (1991) point out that the UK stock market is about 33 per cent larger than the combined total of all other EU stock markets, so more organizations are listed.

Hamill (1992a) noted that during the peak period of cross-border acquisitions (1989 and 1990) the largest acquirers (by value) were the US (£12,193m), France (£11,287m), Sweden (£7,350m), the UK (£6,864m) and (West) Germany (£3,883m). A similar pattern re-emerged in 1992 as the level of mergers and acquisitions increased again (Holmes, 1993).

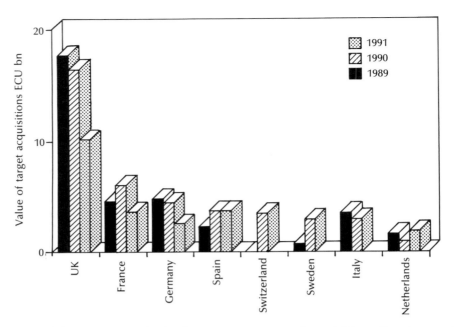

Figure 5.5 Main target countries for European mergers and acquisitions. Data from various editions of *International Mergers and Acquisitions.*

Table 5.3 shows two contrasting ways of viewing the acquisitive countries. The first column adjusts the data for the relative size of economies by calculating the ratio of foreign merger and acquisition spending to national GDP over the period from 1989 through the third quarter of 1991. This reveals a different picture. When the ratios for all sixteen countries are averaged, Sweden was the largest acquirer spending 3.3 times the average. Switzerland, Ireland and the UK are also large acquirers, spending 3.0 times the average. France and the UK are the largest European acquirers by value. In 1990, a survey of 171 British organizations found that 62 per cent planned to expand their business interests into Europe (Wood and Peccei, 1990). The next two largest acquiring nations by value are Germany and the Netherlands. For France, Germany and the Netherlands it has been argued that the close relationship of banks (as suppliers of capital) to the boards of organizations has had both a liberating and constraining effect on their acquisitions activity. On the one hand it gave them access to lower-cost finance (enabling them to pay a higher price for targets and to take a long-term view of markets, investments and pay back periods). The relatively high showing of the UK reflects the strong corporate performance of its large organizations (although small in number) discussed in the previous section. Three of the most prolific restructurers of European industry – Asea Brown Boveri, Nestlé and Electrolux – are based in Switzerland and Sweden. Although a large spender by value, relative to the size of its economy the US spends only half the average. The second column of Table 5.3 shows the total value of acquisitions made by each country during 1990 and 1991 (billion ECU). France was the most acquisitive nation in both 1990 and 1991, spending 9.2 billion ECU on foreign mergers and acquisitions.

However, institutional investors are increasingly looking at the most fragmented and previously protected industrial sectors as opposed to countries and smaller medium-sized companies are also targets for increased merger and acquisition activity. Many

Table 5.3 **The main acquiring countries.**

Country	Ratio of foreign merger and acquisition spending to GDP (average = 1.0)	Total value of foreign mergers and acquisitions (billion ECU)
Sweden	3.3	9.2
Switzerland	3.0	1.6
Ireland	3.0	0.4
UK	3.0	8.8
France	2.2	17.1
Netherlands	2.2	4.5
Finland	2.0	0.8
Australia	1.6	2.0
Norway	1.1	1.1
Japan	0.7	3.4
Belgium	0.7	0.8
Germany	0.7	5.0
Denmark	0.6	1.5
USA	0.5	11.5
Spain	0.4	0.3
Italy	0.4	3.7

privately owned companies are currently looking for buyers, particularly in Germany and Italy, and the number of acquisitions in these countries is expected to increase in the future (Abranavel and Ernst, 1992; *The Economist*, 1992a). However, in general, Germany has remained a bulwark against incursions by foreign organizations. As the largest economy in Europe it only received 6 per cent of incoming FDI to the EU in the 1980s. This has sparked fears that Germany might face an industrial exodus in the face of rising labour costs, a strong currency and stringent environmental legislation (Thomsen and Woolcock, 1993).

PAN-EUROPEAN INTEGRATION IN KEY INDUSTRIAL SECTORS

Behind the various statistics and projections for future levels of merger and acquisition activity there lie several stories of a prolonged phase of integration already seen within numerous sectors of European business. The chemical industry alone has accounted for over 25 per cent of intra-EU mergers, with the food products sector representing another 12 per cent (Thomsen and Woolcock, 1993). In this section we consider two examples: pan-European integration in the confectionery and paper sectors. The Nestlé acquisition of Rowntree in 1988 formed part of a sustained period of integration in the confectionery sector (Hyde, Ellert and Killing, 1991). Since the Nestlé takeover of Rowntree-Mackintosh (see Illustration 5.12) we have had five years to assess the impact of the acquisition. At the time of acquisition, several parties warned of dire consequences. How justified were the fears? History shows that Nestlé has shown a general sensitivity as it has absorbed and refashioned the enterprise (see Illustration 5.13).

Illustration 5.12 **Nestlé's acquisition of Rowntree.**

Since 1981 Helmut Maucher, the Managing Director of Nestlé S.A. made confectionery a strategic priority, believing that by the year 2000 there will be only three or four global players. Over the period 1982–1987 several major producers acquired smaller, national chocolate companies. Between 1986 and 1988 Jacobs Suchard acquired six confectioners including E.J. Brach (the US), Van Houlen (Holland) and Cote d'Or (Belgium) and Cadbury acquired Chocolats Poulain (France) in 1988. As the world's largest food company Nestlé also had diverse interests. Between 1983 and 1985 it acquired 20 companies (including Carnation and Buitoni) as part of a strategic plan to strengthen its market position in individual countries and product groups. By 1987 there were six major producers worldwide with market share dominated by Mars (18 per cent), Hershey (9 per cent), Cadbury-Schweppes (7 per cent), Rowntree (7 per cent), Jacobs Suchard (5 per cent) and Nestlé (4 per cent). Consumers demonstrated considerable brand loyalty but as research and development and distribution costs were high considerable synergies were available for organizations with complementary brands and products. Maucher concluded that it would take Nestlé 25 years to develop a major stake in the confectionery industry. Acquisitions were the best way of accelerating development. Rowntree, in the meantime, invested £100 million in continental Europe but only achieved modest returns. Its highly valued brands and improving operating performance were not reflected in its share price after the Stock Market crash of 1987. A hostile takeover attempt by Jacobs Suchard was successfully defended and Nestlé approached Rowntree with a more palatable merger. The acquisition by Nestlé consolidated previous co-operation between the two organizations. Nestlé saw Rowntree as a perfect fit. Its strength in countline bars complemented Nestlé's strength in block chocolate. Rowntree also had a strong position in distribution outlets, well established world brands and good marketing skills. The merger made eminent business sense, creating an immediate 11 per cent market share (No. 2 position in the industry) with a complementary range of products, and providing cost savings of between 5 and 15 per cent through synergies in research and development, administration and the sales force. Nestlé's turnover of 7.2 billion ECU in 1991 amounted to nearly 15 per cent of Swiss GDP.

Source: Hyde, Ellert and Killing (1991).

Organizations have been prepared to pay handsomely for strategic acquisitions. Another organization in the confectionery sector, Kraft General Foods, is part of Philip Morris (Europe's fourth largest food manufacturer and owner of Jacobs Suchard). It offered $1.5 billion (twenty-five times earnings) for the Norwegian sweet producer Freia Marabou, because it dominated its regional market (Baxter and Bollen, 1992). Long-term market thinking has driven such integration. Similarly, there was a strong business rationale for integration in the paper industry, as highlighted by Illustration 5.14.

We have provided two examples of the merger and acquisition process in this chapter: Nestlé's acquisition of Rowntree, and Arjo Wiggins Appleton. Several other significant events have been documented by European researchers. The most notable include the creation of Asea Brown Boveri (Kennedy, 1992); the acquisition and integration of Zanussi by Electrolux (Ghoshal and Haspeslagh, 1990, 1993); the creation of CMB Packaging from Carnaud of France and Metal Box Packaging of the UK (Gibson, 1990; Hamill, 1992b); strategic integration in the European brewing industry (Steele, 1993) and Brasseries Kronenbourg (Calori, 1993); and the strategic acquisitions made by French organizations such as Hachette, Rhône-Poulenc, BSN, Michelin, Bull, Elf Aquitaine, Thomson and Alcatel in the late 1980s (Franck, 1990; Mergers and Acquisitions Europe, 1991b; 1992d).

Illustration 5.13　**The absorption of Rowntree-Mackintosh by Nestlé: fears and reality.**

Fears expressed in 1988	*Reality by 1993*
Nestlé plan to cut 1,600 of Rowntree's UK staff.	■ Overall employment levels generally the same, but re-location of jobs. ■ Factory shut in Glasgow, 550 jobs moved to Dijon and Newcastle. ■ Administrative cuts. Loss of 400 jobs through natural wastage. ■ Shifts in working practice and contract out of non-core activities. ■ Closure of packaging unit with 160 jobs lost. ■ Offset by new hirings. ■ Spectacular productivity gains. One thousand Kitkat workers produce twice the tonnage that 800 did five years ago.
Shift production abroad and starve investment.	■ Capital spending increased from £9 million in 1987 to £19 million by 1989, reaching a cumulative £100 million by 1994. Invested as much in 5 years as Rowntree did in 20 years. ■ Exports from the UK risen by 56 per cent in two years.
Dismantle research and new brand development.	■ Research centre has doubled in size and recruited 40 top quality scientists from around the world. ■ Wages lower but still above average.
Finish Rowntree's proud history as a benevolent employer.	■ Profit-sharing arrangements have been extended to embrace all Nestlé UK. ■ Company pension arrangements improved for early retirement at 50. ■ Community relations budget maintained at £670,000 a year.
Shift decision making and senior management functions to Switzerland.	■ Transfer of financial functions to London. ■ York-based international strategy function quietly withered away. ■ Nestlé Rowntree Division now reports to Switzerland via Newcastle, UK. ■ Some two-way traffic. Computing functions moved to York.

Source information: in Wilsher (1993).

Illustration 5.14　**Pan-European integration in the paper industry: Arjo Wiggins Appleton.**

During the mid-1980s, Arjomari of France grew rapidly through fifteen acquisitions in France, Spain, the UK, Germany and Italy. Net sales more than doubled from 1983 to 1988 supporting an average ROE of 32 per cent. In 1990 BAT in the UK divested Wiggins Teape Appleton. The two organizations merged to create Arjo Wiggins Appleton (AWA) with worldwide sales of $4.5 billion, a strong paper distribution network in Europe, added scale in manufacturing, greater purchasing power, and the option to rationalize and specialize production across twenty European paper mills.

Source: Abranavel and Ernst (1992).

ACQUIRING IN EASTERN EUROPE

Similar long-term thinking lies behind Western European acquisition in Eastern Europe. The restructuring of industry in Eastern Europe was heralded by the unification of West and East Germany (see Illustration 5.15).

Compared to the former GDR other East European countries are facing a much more complex transition. External transfer of resources will remain modest. The massive know-how transfer between West and East Germany achieved by dispatching senior management consultants and experienced civil servants is not feasible, and the loss of management as organizations are dismembered before privatization will slow down integration even more (Welfens, 1992). Nevertheless, many European organizations are focusing heavily on opportunities in Eastern Europe. The ten largest ventures announced by European organizations in 1991 in Poland, Hungary and Czechoslovakia alone absorbed nearly 33 per cent of all their cross-border merger and acquisition expenditure in that year (Abranavel and Ernst, 1992). Ackermann and Lindquist of the Boston Consulting Group (*op. cit.* Mergers and Acquisitions Europe, 1992a) conducted a study of 80 equity participations in existing East European companies from January 1989 through to March 1992. They found that foreign acquisitions of equity stakes accelerated as privatization schemes generated investment opportunities. Over 200 deals were completed in this period with nearly half of these being in Hungary. Foreign acquisitions in Czechoslovakia (CSFR) jumped four-fold from March 1991 to March 1992.

In general French and German organizations were the leading acquirers in Eastern Europe, followed by the US and Austria. Together they accounted for over 60 per cent of all deals although they concentrated their efforts in different sectors and countries. German and Austrian acquirers focused strongly on Hungary and Czechoslovakia whereas French acquirers focused on Poland. Manufacturing accounted for around half of all transactions (with German firms being the main acquirers) with the largest deals in the automotive sector. Volkswagen took a 25 per cent stake in Skoda and 80 per cent stake in BAZ and Mercedes-Benz invested in Liaz and Avia. These investments triggered further acquisitions in the auto components sectors in both Poland and Czechoslovakia. Chemicals, textiles and pharmaceuticals have attracted only a handful of investors due to uncertainties around environmental liabilities. In these sectors

Illustration 5.15 **The Treuhandstalt experiment.**

The five year role of the *Treuhandstalt* government agency to privatize the state-owned companies of East Germany represented a unique experiment in social and economic history. In 1989 the *Treuhandstalt* became the world's largest company, taking over responsibility initially for nearly 9,000 companies and 9 million employees in East Germany. From 1990–93 nearly 12,000 whole companies or parts of companies have been sold off generating an income of 16.8 billion ECU and guaranteeing 1.5 million jobs. However, despite subsidies of 58.6 billion ECU (Dm 30 billion) a year, total debts amounted to 586 billion ECU (Dm 300 billion), 2000 companies employing 250,000 workers have been closed down and 3000 were facing financial difficulties. Most survivors experienced radical reductions in employment, in some cases maintaining only 10 per cent of the workforce. West German organizations picked up most of the companies on offer. Only 450 companies were bought by foreign organizations. Nearly 3000 companies were disposed of through management buy-outs. The restructuring process is likely to continue throughout the 1990s as uncertain financing, poor quality of local management and slow growth in East European markets takes their toll on the less attractive ventures.

greenfield investments or joint ventures were the preferred method of entry. Over 40 per cent of acquisitions in East Europe were in the service sector (and in particular the media) with intense acquisition activity in this sector by French, UK and Swiss investors. Most Western investments involved strategic stakes of 40–60 per cent of equity. Outright majority stakes were fewer than expected as Western investors seemed intent on sharing the risk with national governments.

Future projections in 1992 indicated that the period 1992–1995 would see a high and steady level of merger and acquisition activity, although there will be changes in the country mix as investor perceptions of political and economic risks develop. Macroeconomic stability, the long industrial tradition and proximity to Western markets made the former Czechoslovakia a powerful magnet for investment. Notwithstanding the split in the federation, the prospects for the future indicated a growing level of acquisition in the Czech Republic through to 1993 (Mergers and Acquisitions Europe, 1992b). Poland's political instability, fragile economic condition and centralized privatization programme is expected to limit its attractiveness as a low-cost manufacturing base with a large domestic market. In Hungary merger and acquisition activity will be steady or declining, although new sectors such as oil and gas, transport and telecommunications are being deregulated and earmarked for privatization. Outside these three countries merger and acquisition activity by 1992 was still minimal. Bulgarian and Romanian opportunities are anticipated to emerge by 1993 followed by the first real wave of Russian and Ukrainian acquisitions by 1994.

The collapse of communism was followed by the creation of massive trade imbalances. EU exports to Eastern Europe rose by 22 per cent, benefiting recession-hit Western producers and Eastern consumers, but knocking the economic health of the region as trade barriers back into the EU failed to come down. FDI flows into East Europe will not be sufficient to unfreeze its industrial structure, which relies on the heavily-protected agriculture, steel, chemicals, textiles, footwear and clothing sectors. The true extent of continued acquisition in East Europe will be subject to many short-term economic forces, as demonstrated by Volkswagen's experience. In Chapter Four we used the European car industry to exemplify competitive pressures on organizations. The example of Volkswagen in Illustration 5.16 demonstrates some of the problems with East European expansion.

Indeed, even if East Europe, the remains of the former Yugoslavia and the ex-USSR were to attract 5 per cent of all Western and Asian FDI flows, not more than $5 to 6 billion of investment per year could be expected (Welfens, 1992). The European Bank for Reconstruction and Development estimates that Eastern Europe and the

Illustration 5.16   **Volkswagen's reversal of East European investment.**

After a cost cutting programme in 1987, the fall of the Berlin wall saw Carl Hahn take Volkswagen into a massive spending spree as it expanded into East Germany and Czechoslovakia. However, the emerging economic recession in Germany in 1993 led Volkswagen to postpone plans for the production of 30,000 Passat cars at Bratislava in the Czech Republic by three years. The planned investment of Dm 860 million by 1995 could no longer be guaranteed. The German recession, overcapacity in the automobile industry, and continued productivity problems (productivity at Volkswagen's Emden factory by 1993 was around half that of its competitors) all conspired to force Volkswagen to reduce its costs. Out of a global workforce of 276,000, 30,000 jobs were cut in October 1992. Net profits fell by 200 per cent and a further 7–8 per cent of the workforce faced the prospect of redundancy.

Source: Saunderson (1993a).

former countries of the Soviet Union will take 35 years to achieve half the level of income of the West, unless it can achieve growth rates on a par with those in the Far East.

Nevertheless, some remarkable changes in fortune have been achieved, with some notable winners as well as losers. Investments by Volkswagen, Opel, Fiat and Suzuki fuelled an increase in total car production in the Czech Republic and Slovakia. It rose by 10 per cent in 1993, with a further 60 per cent rise forecast by the year 2000, mainly for export.

Volkswagen originally planned an investment of Dm 7 billion in Skoda over the 1990s, supported design changes to the local Favorit car model, and encouraged changes to the Czech supplier network. Despite a cut back in this investment, enhanced productivity levels in Skoda meant that original targets could still be met. Volkswagen gains from cheaper parts whilst the Czech Republic gains a vibrant mechanical engineering section. Similarly, the production figure of 12,000 cars produced in Hungary in 1992 was expected to rise to 1,200,000 by the year 2000.

STRATEGIC INTEGRATION OPTIONS FOR EUROPEAN ORGANIZATIONS

In the longer term, cross-frontier restructuring within the EU may shift away from takeover bids towards 'international assets mergers'. The proposal for a Regulation on the Statute for a European company published by the Commission in May 1989 lays down a possible legal form for a 'European Company' which would stand apart from companies recognized by national laws (Thurley and Wirdenius, 1991). Such a recognized international company would form the basis of new joint subsidiaries and holding companies. As the previous two sections demonstrated, acquisitions can be a painful way to grow (Hindle, 1990). Whilst organizations are going through this painful process, their European competitors may be generating growth internally from retained profits and hidden reserves.

In Chapter Four we pointed out that the number of strategic alliances in Europe has grown every year since 1984. Estimates from the EU Directorate-General for Competition show an 83 per cent increase from 1985 to 1989 (Beaumont, 1991b). The difficulties encountered with integration problems for pan-European mergers and the relatively minor increases in scale achieved indicate that they might not be as effective in delivering performance improvements as other options, such as alliances with non-European partners (Abranavel and Ernst, 1992). In countries like Germany and Italy, where many acquisition targets are closely held family firms, alliances offer an attractive form of partnership and an entry route to fuller control (Holmes, 1990). Entering into joint ventures and strategic alliances has proved an attractive way to access markets and skills quickly. Strategic alliance or partnership is a term loosely applied to several forms of corporate link up, as driven by growing internationalization of competition (see Illustration 5.17). Alliances between European national champions are also problematic because they are still natural competitors. Therefore, for European organizations with truly global aspirations forging alliances with a single non-European partner has been used by many as a way to develop global market presence and fill critical gaps in their core businesses.

As the process of industrial restructuring continues European national champion organizations (i.e. those with more than 33 per cent of total revenues and profits earned in their home country) are, therefore, faced with a number of strategic questions. Before they determine the attractiveness of alliances or acquisitions, decide

Illustration 5.17 **Forms of strategic alliance and partnership.**

Distribution agreement.	Licensing or cross-licensing.
Joint venture (multi-purpose).	Partial merger.
Corporate venturing.	Sub contracting or OEM sourcing.
Cross-marketing.	R&D co-operation.
Joint acquisition.	Minority investment.
Joint purchasing.	Cross-shareholdings.

Source: Holmes (1990).

whether to lead the process of restructuring or exit from markets and select potential partners, organizations and European managers need to learn when and how to use both instruments and to assess:

- The dynamics of competition in their industry.
- The industry's true geographic scale.

Figure 5.6 shows the menu of alliance and acquisition options open to organizations, as argued by Abranavel and Ernst (1992). In industry sectors that are operating on a truly global scale (such as automobiles, computers and electronics) mergers and acquisitions within Europe are less attractive than joint ventures with single non-European partners.

However, as we noted earlier in the chapter, in industrial sectors that are less developed and are currently becoming pan-European as opposed to local (such as

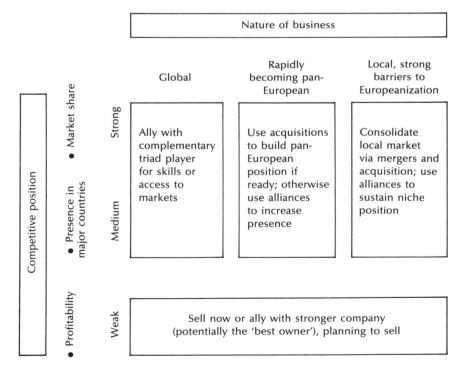

Figure 5.6 Menu of alliance and acquisition options. *Source:* Abranavel and Ernst (1992), reprinted with permission of *Mergers and Acquisitions Europe*, © 1992, IDD Inc.

paper, white goods, confectionery, chemicals and process industries) then acquisition within Europe is seen as an attractive way to generate meaningful scale economies or leverage of skills. Consequently, many European national champion organizations are now being threatened in their home country one way or another (see Illustration 5.18). For example, in the white goods sector Whirlpool-Philips and Electrolux-Zanussi are challenging Thomson of France, Merloni of Italy and Siemens-Bosch and AEG in Germany. Indeed, in 1992 Electrolux entered into a long-term strategic partnership with AEG Hausgeräte (the white goods arm of AEG, the Daimler-Benz subsidiary) for product development and manufacture. European airlines have also entered a fevered series of alliances. Air France linked up with Sabena of Belgium and the Czech CSA; Alitalia with Hungary's Malev; British Airways with regional airlines in France and Germany; and Lufthansa with Austria's Lauda Air and the DHL International courier service. Similarly, in the chemicals sector, Hoechst merged its agro-chemicals activities with Schering and put its viscose and acrylic fibres business into a joint venture with Courtaulds; BASF and ICI considered a swap of their acrylic and polypropelene activities.

This challenge will continue, since strategic alliances meet numerous strategic objectives (see Illustration 5.19), such as access to new markets, technologies or resources; economies of scale and scope; sharing of costs and risks; industry rationalization; exits from non-core business; or the creation of barriers to takeovers (Holmes, 1990).

They also offer an elegant exit route from industries (Holmes, 1990). We have already argued that the 1990s will be littered with winners and losers as organizations acquire, digest and divest business operations. Many organizations seeking to withdraw from non-core businesses with no immediate buyers find alliances attractive (see Illustration 5.20). Having secured a partner who is committed to remaining to the business, the traumas of shutdown may be avoided. In 1993 Bayer announced that it

Illustration 5.18 **The Dresdner Bank/BNP alliance.**

Two of the largest banks in Germany and France took unprecedented steps in 1993 towards establishing the first pan-European global banking group. Germany's Dresdner Bank and France's Banque Nationale de Paris (BNP) gained share-holder approval to exchange 10 per cent of shares and extend joint activities. The combined Franco-German grouping, with a balance sheet of $490 billion, would be a serious competitor to the largest financial institutions which are Japanese.

Illustration 5.19 **Objectives of strategic alliances.**

Time advantage: Faster responses to changes in the environment, reduced product development times.

Know-how advantages: Mutual learning to overcome knowledge deficits as product technology increases in complexity whilst life cycles shorten.

Access to markets: To overcome potential protectionist moves.

Cost advantages: Combination of value-chain activities.

System competence: Combining specific strategic competencies in core areas with complementary organizations to provide a new market capability.

Source: Bronder and Pritzl (1992).

Illustration 5.20 **Elegant exiting from businesses: AT&T – Philips Telecommunications.**

Philips followed the alliance option as an exit route from the public telephone exchange business. In 1984 it struck an alliance with AT&T, then a newcomer to European markets. Each took a 50 per cent share in the Dutch-based AT&T – Philips Telecommunications. The alliance was not overly successful and in 1987 Philips reduced its stake to 40 per cent, dropping its name from the venture.

By 1989 it cut its stake to 15% and in 1990 gave up even this residual holding. AT&T, far from discouraged, recruited new European strategic partners in STET in Italy and Telefonica in Spain. Philips may have taken a similar route with its domestic appliance business with the Whirlpool relationship.

Source: Holmes (1990).

was seeking alliances for a number of its mature, downstream chemicals businesses. In the words of its Chairman, Manfred Schneider, this was '. . . a good method for dealing with structural problems' (Hasell, 1993).

MAKING STRATEGIC ALLIANCES WORK

Like acquisitions, alliances are fraught with risk and the failure rate is high. Holmes (1990) cites a survey which found that less than 50 per cent of alliances were deemed successful by both participants. Sixty per cent expired within four years and only 14 per cent survived for more than a decade, whilst Beaumont (1991b) reports failure rates of 30 to 40 per cent. General problem areas with international joint ventures (IJVs) typically involve strategic shifts, conflict over scope, uneven levels of commitment, power imbalances concerning resources or access to information, unequal benefits, premature trust, conflicting loyalties, under-management, insufficient integration or internal corporate politics (Moss-Kanter, 1989).

To better understand what is required to make cross-border alliances work, Bleeke and Ernst (1992) analysed 40 alliances made by 150 of the top organizations in the US, Europe and Japan. The success criteria were two-fold: both partners needed to achieve their ingoing strategic objectives and also recover their financial costs of capital. Both cross-border alliances and acquisitions were good vehicles for international strategy and had similar success rates (51 and 57 per cent respectively). These rates were twice as high as achieved by domestic diversification strategies. Both options worked well for expanding core businesses, but when existing businesses were being moved into new geographic regions, cross-border alliances worked better. Where there was minimal geographic overlap 92 per cent of the mergers and acquisitions resulted in failure for the acquirer. Only 6 per cent of acquisitions failed when the overlap was high. However, minimal geographic overlap only resulted in 24 per cent of the strategic alliances failing (Bleeke and Ernst, 1992).

Alliances will continue to be an important strategic option within the European context. As organizations share costs, senior managers have to learn to design relationships with other European (and global) organizations (Ohmae, 1992). This typically leads to a reconsideration of corporate structures (Bronder and Pritzl, 1992). It also focuses attention on designing corporate relationships, which depends as much upon effective communication as it does upon the legal relationships. The ease of this communication depends on shared values, and the flexibility to adapt approaches and tactics to the local country and culture.

THE HRM IMPACT OF THE FORCES OF INTEGRATION

In Chapter Two we outlined the various different notions of European management that still persist and the extent to which empirical data suggests that there is a process of convergence in practice, whilst in this chapter we have described the phenomena of transnationalism, international cadres of managers, and foreign direct investment (FDI) – involving a range of options from mergers and acquisitions through to alliances. All these forces are associated with a process of industrial restructuring that is taking place within Europe. The central question to be determined therefore is as follows: will the phenomenon of industrial restructuring in Europe precipitate 'leakages' between national economies and their management practices and thereby strengthen the linkages between previously different notions of European HRM?

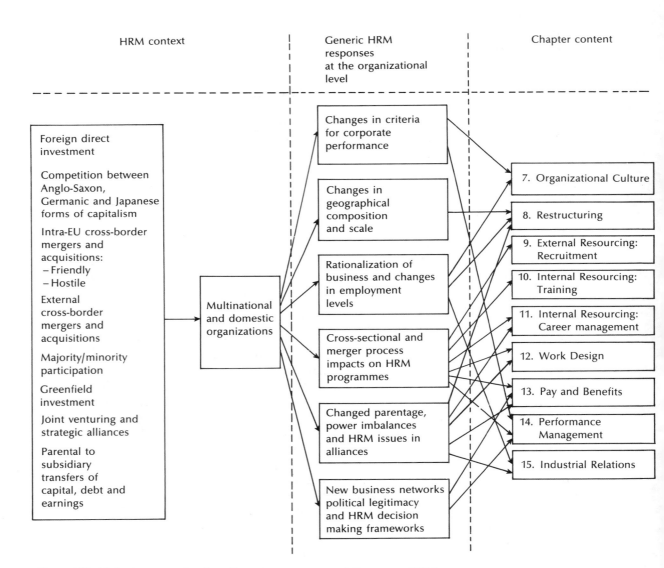

Figure 5.7 Links between foreign direct investment and European HRM.

We have pointed to a number of significant forces of integration in this chapter (see Figure 5.7), but have also made it clear that each one brings with it a host of very significant HRM issues and problems. We first described the HRM implications of transnationalism. However, understanding and managing the HRM implications of both mergers and acquisitions and strategic alliances is an equally important critical success factor for European organizations. Above and beyond the important questions we have considered of competing modes of capitalism, measures of corporate success and management philosophies, if we simply consider mergers and acquisitions, there are four broad ways in which they will influence European HRM:

1. Changes in overall employment levels and the structure of industry.
2. The creation of new dynamics of business networking, changed mindsets and contexts for HRM decisions.
3. Differences in patterns of HRM between foreign-owned and domestic organizations.
4. The need to tackle specific HRM problems associated with the actual process of merging and integration.

EMPLOYMENT EFFECTS OF CROSS-BORDER MERGERS AND ACQUISITIONS

Young and Hamill (1992) point out that the wave of cross-border mergers and acquisitions in Europe raises important issues about its economic impact. There will clearly be a trade-off between gains in competitiveness and reduced competition. International competitiveness *vis-à-vis* Japan and the US may be achieved through stronger products and brands, geographical market portfolios, economies of scale, and synergies through shared R&D and technology costs (Hamill, 1992a). Although there is recognition that mergers and alliances between European organizations may be needed for achieving global economic advantages, widespread concern exists regarding the monopolistic effects of such deals through increasing industry concentration. Reflecting this, the EU was given the power in September 1990 to vet mergers involving firms with a joint turnover of more than 5 billion ECU, providing that at least 250 million ECU of these revenues are in the EU. In its first year of operation, this commission was notified of 54 deals and made 48 final decisions. In 1990, for example, there was a joint plan by France's Aérospatiale and Italy's Alenia to share in the acquisition of De Havilland, a Canadian aircraft manufacturer. This deal was blocked by the competition commissioner, on the grounds that the new company would have controlled 67 per cent of the EU market for commuter aircraft.

The employment effects of the wave of cross-border mergers and acquisitions are harder to quantify (see Illustration 5.21). Even the optimistic Cecchini Report on the employment effects of the SEM predicted the loss of 250,000 to 500,000 jobs between 1992 and 1994 as a result of industrial restructuring (Cecchini *et al.* 1989). It is anticipated that job losses will occur across a wide range of manufacturing and non-manufacturing sectors. However, it is virtually impossible to disentangle job losses (or gains) that result from cross-border mergers and acquisitions as opposed to other multinational organization strategies and environmental pressures discussed in the previous chapter, such as transnationality, Japanese FDI, industry deregulations, rapid technological change and world recession. Multinational strategies in Europe will have major implications for employment. The negative and positive trends are summarized in Table 5.4.

Illustration 5.21 **Sources of job losses through post merger consolidation and integration in Europe.**

- Consolidation of HQ staff.
- Closing down of unnecessary or inefficient facilities.
- Eliminating redundant executive and other staff positions.
- Centralizing volume leverage functions such as purchasing, insurance, and data processing.

- Integrating operations such as raw materials, manufacturing and production, distribution and marketing.
- Integrating R&D and technology development.

Source: Hamill (1992a).

Table 5.4 **Employment effects of changing MNE strategies in Europe.**

Positive	Negative
Possible long-term increase in employment as a consequence of the improved international competitiveness of European MNEs	Plant closures and rationalization of production as a consequence of global/regionally coordinated strategies
Direct and indirect employment generated by 'new wave' of greenfield FDI in Europe	Locational shift of production from periphery to core regions
Employment effects of enhanced plant status over time in Japanese and US subsidiaries	Employment losses as a consequence of post-M&A rationalization and integration
Improved quality of employment through establishment of European centres of excellence	Indigenous displacement effects of Japanese FDI in Europe

Source: Hamill (1992a), reprinted from *European Management Journal*, **10**(3), Hamill, J. 'Employment effects of changing multinational strategies in Europe', 334–40, © 1992, with kind permission from Pergamon Press Ltd, Headington Hill Hall, Oxford OX3 0BW, UK.

EUROPEAN BUSINESS NETWORKS AND NEW CONTEXTS FOR HRM DECISIONS

Bressand and Nicolaïdis (1990) point out that the levels of business integration that we are observing in Europe bring with them their own dynamics. New networks of connections are established in what has become a narrower area of economic space. This makes it legitimate to make changes that may hitherto have been unacceptable. It used to be the case that German managers would resent working under French bosses, or French under Italian ones. Whilst such prejudices die hard, they are on the decline. For example, Alain Minc, a pure product of the French elite school system was no longer seen as a maverick when working under Carlo de Benedetti. French financial companies like Victoire and Suez in acquiring Colonia (the number two German insurance company) and then launching hostile takeover attempts at one another were able to achieve what would have been unthinkable only five years ago. The political legitimacy is now there for European organizations to network with each other in many areas. This brings with it a process of mutual recognition in which national governments and the public are gradually educated into the behaviour and norms of the other countries. Bressand and Nicolaïdis (1990) quote the example of controversy over the Peugeot chairman's salary and self-approved pay rise which was disclosed in the middle of a strike by low-paid French automobile workers (given the discussion in Chapter Four we can expect further rationalization in this industry). Five years ago public discussion would have limited itself to issues of wage inequality in France, but by 1990 it was conducted with explicit reference to the German wage structure. The basic yardsticks and references that are central to each set of national HRM practices can be seen to be converging as a result of the increasing interconnections of legal, regulatory and business networks. And networks, as opposed to institutions, learn from each other.

FDI AND NEW PATTERNS OF HRM

In order to help answer the question of 'leakage' of HRM practices, there are two broad sets of studies that need to be described. These can be characterized as:

1. Cross-sectional studies that compare and contrast the HRM practices of indigenous national organizations versus those subjected to foreign direct investment (for example, a subsidiary of a foreign multinational).
2. Studies that have directly analysed various HRM aspects of the merger and acquisition process.

The cross-sectional studies show that although the higher productivity often associated with FDI leads to resources naturally being targeted on the more productive and technologically progressive sectors, there is nevertheless a clear link between the FDI process itself and new patterns of HRM. Greece is a good example of a European country where foreign ownership appears to have brought new patterns of HRM. Early studies of the impact of EU membership (Hassid, 1980) indicated that there was limited use of modern management techniques, although the problem could be improved if more attention was given to the management of human resources. The establishment of multinationals challenged Greek company-owners' attitudes as did the return of European-educated Greek managers to their domestic companies. Papalexandris (1991) compared five Greek organizations (large by Greek standards with over 500 employees) to similar sized and matched multinationals and examined various HRM practices under the topics of policy and planning, recruitment and selection, appraisal and promotion and managerial training. Every aspect of practice in the firms was rated on a five-point scale (measuring the extent to which the practices were systematically used) based on respondent and researcher opinions. The multinationals outperformed their Greek counterparts in all areas (except the reliance on outside training bodies). The reason behind the poorer levels of HRM systematization was that the Greek-owned firms were more adversely influenced by the local political, social, and economic framework.

Evidence that FDI is associated with new patterns of HRM is also found in Spain. For example, Incomes Data Service (1993a) report the annual survey of collective agreements carried out by the Spanish Economics Ministry which showed that whereas 54 per cent of Spanish-owned private organizations provided training, the figure rose to 80 per cent for foreign-owned private sector organizations.

Data from a survey of 143 organizations in Britain in 1985 (Marginson, Edwards, Martin, Purcell and Sisson, 1988) also indicated that foreign-owned organizations used more advanced HRM techniques, devoted more resources to personnel management and were more likely to use a variety of new communication and work design methods in order to gain employee loyalty. However, it was appreciated that in many cases the differences in HRM may still have had as much to do with the specific sector, or the strategy being pursued by the organization, as it did with the fact that FDI took place.

In order to test for this, Hiltrop (1991b) compared the HRM practices of multinational organizations in Belgium with those of indigenous organizations in the same type of industry (see Figure 5.10). Multinational organizations clearly have to engage in additional HRM activities – such as relocation, extended induction, international job rotation programmes, employee relations and complex equity issues – when compared to indigenous organizations. There are a broader series of options open to senior management in choosing how to plan, acquire, appraise, compensate and train human resources (Schuler and Jackson, 1987) and it was these that formed the basis of the study. Hiltrop (1991b) obtained data from 117 personnel managers in the largest Belgian enterprises. The study demonstrated differences in HRM that resulted directly from foreign ownership. Nine HRM practices were found to differ significantly between the 52 Belgian subsidiaries of foreign-owned organizations and 65 indigenous organizations with head offices in Belgium (see Table 5.5).

Whilst the personnel practices used by the organizations studied also varied with their management philosophy and industry sector, these factors were not found to be as important as national ownership and competitive strategy (Hiltrop, 1991b).

Table 5.5 **Impact of FDI on areas of HR practice in Belgium.**

	Occurrence in % of firms	
Human resource practice	Domestic N = 65	Foreign-owned N = 52
Creativity assessment in the selection process	34	62
Internal promotion policy	21	63
Socialization of new employees	71	47
Personnel manager involved in strategic planning	41	72
Formal manpower planning	34	72
Performance appraisal interview	44	83
Performance related pay	15	58
Special rewards for outstanding performance	1	23
Job evaluation	11	63
Relocation assistance programmes	26	47
Quality circles	16	28
Formal grievance procedures	61	77
Decentralized decision making	16	37
Systematic communication of corporate decisions to all employees	30	53
Communication of corporate goals and priorities to all workers	28	60
Employee shareholding scheme	37	70
All differences were significant at the 0.01 level (Chi-square test with 1 Df)		

Source: Hiltrop (1991b), reprinted from *European Management Journal*, **9**(4), Hiltrop, J.M. 'Human resource practices of multinational organizations in Belgium', 404–11. © 1992, with kind permission from Pergamon Press Ltd, Headington Hill Hall, Oxford OX3 0BW, UK.

THE MERGER PROCESS AND NEW PATTERNS OF HRM

So how is this transfer of management techniques and practices achieved? The second set of studies that focus on the actual merger process can help provide the answer. Given that the merger and acquisition phenomenon has long been a mainstay of Anglo-Saxon business culture it is inevitable that the majority of research into the actual process is of US and UK origin. There have been over 75,000 takeovers and mergers in the US alone in the last 25 years. However, recently there have been some notable contributions from academics and consultants from mainland Europe.

Although it has been argued earlier in this chapter that there is an inevitable and continuing process of industrial restructuring taking place in Europe, driven in part by a wave of acquisitions and mergers, there are good reasons to doubt the success of acquisitions and mergers on HRM grounds (Jemison and Sitkin, 1986). They often fail to deliver against expectations. Two-thirds of the corporate acquisitions examined by McKinsey earned less for the acquirer than if the money had been invested in a bank deposit account (Magnet, 1984). This chapter has shown that the stock market performance of many of the large European restructurers has also not performed well. Baker, Miller and Ramsperger (1981) reported an international survey of top executives that indicated 80 per cent of acquisitions and mergers failed to meet financial or organizational expectations with 84 per cent of the sample believing that HRM problems were most likely to affect long-term success or failure. Hunsaker and Coombs (1988) found that in 33 to 50 per cent of acquisitions and mergers it was specific personnel problems that resulted in the venture failing to meet financial expectations. Grindley (1986) has outlined the most obvious personnel problems encountered (see Illustration 5.22).

Despite the plethora of US research into the financial returns and strategic fit of acquisitions and mergers, until recently there has been a very low understanding of the organizational processes and implications involved. A merger can be defined as the fusing together (in an organizational and behavioural sense) of some or all of the central functions of two organizations, whilst an acquisition involves the purchase of more than 50 per cent of a vendor's equity (Hunt, Lees, Grumbler and Vivien, 1987). Mergers are felt to be different to other organization change processes because they involve a critical mass of the unknown and an accelerated tempo of change. Acquisitions and mergers clearly need to be better understood from an HRM perspective.

ALLIANCES, POWER SHARING AND NEW PRESSURES ON NATIONAL MODELS OF HRM

Alliances may also have significant implications for HRM in Europe. Problems in international joint ventures ultimately stem from their mixed parentage (Beaumont,

Illustration 5.22 **Frequently encountered personnel problems with acquisitions and mergers.**

- Reduced productivity due to unexpected change, uncertainty or perceived betrayal.
- Acts of sabotage e.g. IT systems.
- Unsystematic cost consolidations, staff reductions and transfers.
- Unwanted turnover or staff loss.
- Unexpected employee benefit costs.
- Dysfunctional leadership struggles.
- Ill thought out management development.
- The wrong mix of human resource skills.

1991a). The AT&T–Philips experience provided a range of national influences on HRM: US, Dutch, Italian and Spanish. Few HRM systems will prove immune to these transformations, since the essence of an alliance is the creation of a subtle management style based on power sharing (Holmes, 1990). A good example of this is the Renault and Volvo partnership, outlined in Illustration 5.23. The failure of this alliance makes it clear that there are marked HRM implications associated with most joint ventures. All stages of the negotiation were marked by concerns over national issues.

For many organizations, particularly those with an Anglo-Saxon corporate culture that places a high value on self-reliance and strong central control mechanisms, the subtler power-sharing management style will not come easily (Holmes, 1990). Even continental organizations more accustomed to exercising influence through minority

Illustration 5.23   **The failed Renault/Volvo partnership and marriage: a threat to Swedish job design?**

The logic of the original partnership in January 1991 was that it would bring together two of Europe's smallest independent car makers, with Volvo in the specialist, low volume and luxury market and Renault in the high volume mass market. In less than two years the alliance developed into a formal merger. Whilst other luxury car-makers such as Jaguar and Saab became American owned, Volvo followed Swedish foreign policy and opted for a European partner. The companies had a twenty year history of collaboration. The expected benefits were the achievement of a critical mass in R&D, a reduction of purchasing costs and geographical complementarity of sales. The combination of truck operations would allow them to compete for first place in the market. Potential savings of $5.1 billion by the year 2000 were estimated. However, the alliance also carried the risk of Renault being forced into an expensive rescue of Volvo, which lost nearly 3.5 billion Swedish Krona in 1992, and eventually led to a formal merger proposal in 1993. The new combined Renault–Volvo became one of the world's largest industrial groupings, with over 200,000 employees. It would have moved Renault from ninth position worldwide to sixth in the car industry, and second only to Volkswagen in Europe. It was seen as evidence that despite the traumas of the Maastricht Treaty, vital industrial restructuring in Europe would proceed apace.

Under the initial strategic alliance between Renault and Volvo, championed by Raymond Lévy (the former Renault Managing Director), Renault owned 25 per cent of Volvo's car operations, 45 per cent of the truck division and 8.2 per cent of the holding company. Volvo in turn owned 20 per cent of Renault (with an option to raise to 25 per cent) and 45 per cent of its truck and bus operations. The intention of Renault was to move towards a fuller merger in a structure that guaranteed French majority holding of Renault. The merger was intended to bring simplicity and speed to decision making. However, an increase in stake in Renault by Volvo above 25 per cent would require a change in French law. A painstaking equity structure was derived which maintained respect for each others' products and national identities whilst fusing the automotive interests.

The new Chairman was the former head of Renault, Louis Schweitzer, and three out of five management board positions were French. The French state directly or indirectly controlled 65 per cent of Renault–Volvo's capital. Banque National de Paris was expected to play a significant role in controlling French interests if Renault was privatized in late 1995. In the run-up to the merger, Volvo production in Europe fell by 10 per cent in 1992 whilst Renault's increased by 10 per cent. As the fortunes of Volvo continued to decline in the 1990s when US sales and export markets were lost, Pehr Gyllenhammar, the then Chairman, announced the closure of two out of three plants in Sweden. The Uddevalla and Kalmar plants were to be closed with the loss of 4,500 jobs (10 per cent of the workforce) by 1995. The Uddevalla plant was conceived and built on a grand scale in the mid-1980s on the back of US export profits. Despite the fact that the Volvo plants are better equipped than those of Renault, they were the ones most at risk, as was the participatory style of working and job designs they experimented with.

Illustration 5.24 **Potential HRM problem areas in international joint ventures.**

Differences in desired and actual staffing levels.	Complex decision-making processes.
Promotion blockages for direct recruits.	Communication difficulties.
Conflict of loyalties.	Dissatisfaction with compensation from parent
Limited delegation of decision-making authority.	companies.

Source: Shenkar and Zeira (1987).

stakes and cross-shareholdings may be inhibited by the desire to maintain their national identity and ultimate control of mainstream operations.

Early in the chapter we described the Airbus Industries case. This alliance initially had major HRM problems, such as a requirement to devise a set of employee–management consultative arrangements which was acceptable to both the West German and French workforces but which ultimately involved court proceedings (Beaumont, 1991a). A number of generic HRM problems are frequently associated with international joint ventures (see Illustration 5.24).

THE LESSONS OF INDUSTRIAL RESTRUCTURING FOR EUROPEAN HRM

Given the scale and scope of industrial restructuring taking place in Europe, as outlined in this chapter, what broad lessons should be drawn? Shapiro (1991) argues that European corporate management should look to the American experience of deregulation since 1975 to understand the competititve challenges that will result from European integration and new entrants into once restricted markets (see Illustration 5.25).

In short, Shapiro (1991) argues that the early years of European integration and

Illustration 5.25 **Competing dynamics at work during periods of industrial restructuring.**

Reduced profitability
- Industry becomes more competitive.
- Profitability deteriorates rapidly as strong firms expand and low cost suppliers enter markets.
- Falling profits spur staff reductions and cost cutting measures.
- The weak get weaker and many fail.
- The strong do not get more profitable for several years.

Changed sources of profitability
- High profit market segments come under severe price pressure.
- Low profit segments become more attractive as protected organizations leave the market.

Acceleration of mergers and acquisitions
- Weaker firms combine to gain size.
- Scales of economies do not materialize.
- Stronger firms merge selectively to fill out gaps in product portfolios or customer segments.

Reduced number of firms
- Only a handful of firms survive as broad-based competitors.
- Precise understanding of cost structures and pricing enables them to offer new services.
- Most firms have to narrow product ranges and withdraw from non-core activities.
- Industry becomes more segmented.

Source: reprinted from *European Management Journal*, **3(3)**, 3–18, A.C. Shapiro, 'Competitive implications of Europe 1992', © 1991, with kind permission of Elsevier Science Ltd, The Boulevard, Longford Lane, Kidlington, OX5 1EB, UK.

deregulation – in response to the strategic pressures we have outlined in the last two chapters – will be characterized by shake-outs, restructuring and the consolidation of positions by the survivors. Moreover, the new entrants that European organizations will be forced to compete with are already large globally-minded competitors. Therefore, the shake-out and consolidation phases are likelier to be even bloodier than the US experience in the 1970s. Given that the early 1990s will be associated with a 'profit drought', those organizations that have spent too much money on the wave of acquisitions and mergers will find themselves with too little cash to weather the competitive storm.

A clear lesson has emerged from this chapter. It will be those European organizations that address fundamental gaps in competitiveness – by developing appropriate skills and global geographic scale – that will survive and prosper in the 1990s. In order to do this these organizations, and their managers, need to appreciate the new dynamics of competition within their industry, and the continued viability of their position in terms of changes to profitability, the attractiveness of products to customers, market share and the levels of customer satisfaction. Sounding a note of warning, Abranavel and Ernst (1992) note that nearly 30 per cent of the 500 largest European organizations in 1989 were no longer on the list by 1991. Many had been merged or sold. They had perhaps not appreciated that a new competitive era has engulfed European management. Franck (1990), who is based at HEC-ISA in France, described the impact of a number of significant European mergers, acquisitions and joint ventures such as the Rhône-Poulenc–Union Carbide combination, and Thomson Consumer Electronics' series of joint ventures.

... If this method of worldwide expansion is to be a success ... these companies must acquire ... new and needed management skills. It is their capacity for taking advantage of a merger and acquisition and the cultural shock that accompanies it, by inventing a new corporate identity with its inherent new management processes, that will open the door to long-term success or failure.   Franck (1990, p. 43).

The context of strategic change and European integration that we have outlined in the last two chapters will have enormous ramifications for European organizations. It simply is not credible to believe that there will not be significant changes in the content of European HRM practices (see Illustration 5.26).

CONCLUSIONS

In Part Three of this book we shall outline the differences and similarities across a range of European HRM practices and issues. There are a wide range of HRM problems involved in the transitions outlined so far. Most areas of HRM will be directly influenced by the transitions described in this chapter. However, the issues of organizational culture change, the fit of structures, managerial philosophies, values

Illustration 5.26 **Driving forces behind the integration in European HRM in the 1990s.**

- Attempts to positively address the new strategic imperatives.
- A reaction to business restructuring.
- Common techniques to facilitate the implementation of change.
- Accommodating and learning from national and cultural differences in personnel practice.

and ethics and the various HRM tools and techniques available, are still bound up in national culture. The two themes of convergence and divergence of national HRM practice are dealt with in the next chapter, but are also reflected throughout the rest of the book. A number of important learning points have emerged from this chapter.

LEARNING POINTS FROM CHAPTER FIVE

1. There is competition between European countries through their foreign direct investment. This has led to a process of industrial restructuring which is generating new patterns of HRM. European economies are becoming increasingly dominated by large multinational organizations. These organizations are reinforcing the process of internationalization through a series of interconnections.

2. The new economic environment of Europe in the 1990s is creating the need for a new form of organization – the transnational organization – which recognizes new resources and capabilities, captures them and then leverages the advantages on a worldwide scale. Although there are few examples of such organizations as yet, there is a clear trend towards greater geographic dispersion of business activities. The prospect of transnational organizations is seen by many as a possible new source of European competitive advantage, because it may spur performance that can break the limits of national competitiveness. It may also lead to a new European model of management.

3. One of the HRM implications of this trend is the emergence of a flexible cadre of international managers, capable of implementing complex strategies. European organizations will also develop strong co-ordinating centres and will be forced to make decisions about what to manage centrally and what to manage locally. The answers are typically determined on an industry basis, again superseding national models of HRM.

4. A more immediate process of integration of European industry is being driven by high levels of foreign direct investment. In its broadest sense this represents a competition between workers, governments, organizations, markets and business systems, with clear winners and losers. Mergers and acquisitions have become more intense as European economic space is reorganized. In the mid-1980s cross-border mergers within the EU quadrupled and Europe became the focus of worldwide FDI transfers.

5. Clear geographical and sectoral patterns of capital flow can be detected. Three-quarters of European organizations targeted from 1985 to 1992 were in the UK, France, Sweden, Italy and Germany. Nearly half of the value of acquired organizations was accounted for by the UK. However, the UK, along with France, Sweden and Switzerland, was also a significant acquirer. Significant levels of pan-European integration have taken place in industrial sectors such as chemicals, food products, and consumer goods.

6. Hostile takeovers became a new experience for many European managers. There has been a process of shareholder democratization and legislative reform which is bringing a new set of pressures for European managers. The basis of effective corporate performance is being questioned within European organizations as a battle between competing forms of capitalism, such as the Anglo-Saxon and the Rhine-Alpine model, has ensued. National management philosophies are being challenged.

7. Significant investments have been made in Eastern Europe. The external transfer of resources is more modest. In general, German and French organizations were leading acquirers in Eastern Europe, followed by the US and Austria. These investments are highly vulnerable to employment problems and economic pressures in Western Europe.

8. Despite the many attractions of mergers and acquisitions, there are many factors that will limit the pace of integration through mergers and acquisitions. Various forms of strategic alliance have proved a popular option. Many European national champion

organizations are being threatened in their domestic markets one way or another. Strategic alliances are being created in order to access new markets, technologies or resources, create economies of scale, share the costs and risks of technological innovation, create barriers to takeovers, or slowly exit from non-core businesses.

9. This integration of European business through foreign direct investment, either in the form of mergers and acquisitions or strategic alliances, is impacting patterns of European HRM in four ways. There are changes in the overall employment level and structure of industries. New dynamics of business networking have created different mindsets and reference points for HRM decisions. Different patterns of HRM practices are created in foreign-owned organizations as core techniques are transferred from the acquirer. Finally, the need to tackle specific HRM problems that are associated with the actual process of merging and integration generates new policies and practices.

10. There may be lessons for Europe to draw from the process of industrial restructuring that took place in the US since the mid-1970s. As industry becomes more competitive, profitability deteriorates as strong organizations expand and low-cost suppliers enter the market. Weaker organizations fail and many try to combine in order to regain market share. The stronger organizations merge selectively in order to fill out gaps in product portfolios and customer segments. Overall there is a reduction in the number of surviving organizations and employment levels fall. The 1990s may be characterized by a period of industry shake-outs, restructuring and a consolidation of the position of the survivors. The new dynamics of competition within each industrial sector will further accelerate transition in national models of HRM.

CHAPTER SIX

An Emerging European Style of Management?

Patterns of Convergence and Divergence

INTRODUCTION

The rapid internationalization of organizations has been one of the most significant economic and sociological developments in global markets since the Second World War (Forster, 1992). It is important to establish whether, given the differences in attitudes to HRM between the US and Europe discussed in Chapter Two, there is any significant communality in this process of internationalization and the approaches taken across Europe. Brewster (1993) feels that despite a number of differences in the role of European HRM functions, a European approach to HRM is discernible. However, it would be foolish to assume that progress towards European HRM is an absolutely inevitable process that will completely override national practices or indeed that the process is likely to be rapid. Like all strategic changes, there will be some rapid adopters and many laggards, both at the national and organizational level. There are good reasons why there will be a different pace of integration. Where there is an absence of the most powerful forces for integration then progress will be slowed. In dealing with this issue, most textbooks or articles on European HRM tend to treat it as an extension of domestic HRM (Hendry, 1991). They present an existing Anglo-American model, note some significant differences in the European context, and then draw a further box around the model labelled 'international context'.

It is useful to draw a link back to the previous chapters in Parts One and Two and summarize the main arguments that are typically used to suggest that the end point of the integration process will indeed be the emergence of a European style of management, with its inevitable reflection in HRM practices (see Illustration 6.1).

In considering the issue of integration and convergence within European HRM, Kidger (1991) highlighted a series of questions outlined below. These questions should be applied to the subsequent chapters in this book, but also have relevance when considering the forces that are leading to greater integration within European organizations (see Illustration 6.2).

So, to what extent is there sufficient similarity in Europe to enable us to speak sensibly – either now or in the near future – of 'European HRM'? We consider this

Illustration 6.1   **Key arguments that industrial integration will result in a European style of management.**

- Differences that have arisen historically from contrasting beliefs and value orientations within national cultures are being superseded by the logic of technology.
- Whilst culture is an important variable that often provides the context in which to understand management practices, over time cultural differences are diminishing in importance.
- Countries are faced with similar problems in a unified market place and it is these business pressures that will dictate future developments in management, reinforcing integration.
- International best practice, management education and the influence of multinationals are creating an international management culture.
- A process of industrial restructuring is taking place – driven by mergers, acquisitions, joint ventures and new market entries – from which there will be natural winners and losers. The winners' concepts of HRM will spread.

Illustration 6.2   **Key HRM questions about the process of integration.**

- Will the development and exchange of ideas and practices across national boundaries result in an international consensus of good management?
- To what extent is such development constrained by the diversity of national culture, history and political structures?
- Are management practices culture-bound or culture free?
- Can management policy developed in a multinational's home country be transferred elsewhere?
- Are national culture and corporate culture potentially opposing forces within the organization?
- What are the implications of developing internationally orientated managers?
- Should HRM specialists develop policies that can accommodate multiple value systems?

question by addressing three issues in this chapter:

1. To what extent is there a notion of European management?
2. Is there any evidence that European HRM priorities are converging, and if so, around what concerns?
3. Is there any agreement amongst personnel specialists and line management that the role of HRM managers is changing?

THE NOTION OF EUROPEAN MANAGEMENT

We first need to assess the extent to which a common approach to European management is emerging. The development of the notion of the European manager (or Euro-manager) is a relatively recent phenomena. Like all new ideas in management, it has only gained legitimacy because of a series of shock waves (mainly economic) which have undermined the currency of dominant ideas. In 1990, Bournois and Chauchat (1990) commented:

... We now have a better idea of what is meant by the European dimension, but there is still a great deal of controversy as to what really makes a manager. What are the similarities between the concepts of 'cadre', 'manager', 'fürungskraft', 'quadro', 'Kader', 'dirigenti', 'quadri'. . .?

Bournois and Chauchat (1990, p. 5).

We consider some of the practices behind the making of European managers in Chapter Ten. In this chapter we generally review the debate about the notion of the usefulness of the term 'European management', which has grown in intensity as the implications of the Single European Market (SEM) have become more apparent (Thurley and Wirdenuis, 1989, 1991). A series of social champions from politics, business and education have argued that we are witnessing the creation of a cadre of Euro-managers as we proceed through this transition in our socio-economic environment. However, not all management writers believe that the emergence of a European style of management is possible or indeed desirable and there are competing arguments for and against the emergence, existence or utility of the concept of European management. European academics are therefore asking the following sort of questions:

- Is there a specific European identity in social structures and cultural values or is there just a mosaic of conflicts?
- Are European organizations moving closer together, or merely converging around a generalized model of post-industrialism?
- Does European management really exist?

The notion of 'European management' tends to be seen in extremes. The positive view argues that it is necessarily hard to observe, describe and define, not only because of the cultural diversity and range of management styles from which it must be synthesized, but also because, in large part, it is emerging through the process of specific responses to the new business priorities. Nevertheless, by analysing the cultural synthesis and business priorities that are emerging and by searching for the people and organizations that are creating the new skills, new awareness and new mindsets, then a definition of 'European management' will emerge (Shenton, 1992). He points out that in asking such questions, there are two distinct notions of 'European management' (see Illustration 6.3).

Thurley and Wirdenius (1989) argue that it is both possible and necessary to define the '... assumptions and strategies which might categorize an approach to management which is peculiarly and distinctly European'. European managers are different to those from, for example, the US or Japan, in terms of shared beliefs and values and the specific skills and competencies they see as being important to cope with a changing industrial environment (Shenton, 1992). Questions about the nature of 'European management' can still be considered without tackling the deeper (but separate) issue of whether a closed Europe-centered or an open international view of business activity is the most appropriate for the future competitive success of European organizations.

... Something different is happening in Europe, with shared beliefs and values... specific skills and competencies necessary for coping with a new environment... cultural diversity is no longer

Illustration 6.3 **Two notions of European management.**

- The definition and description of features that distinguish management in Europe as opposed to management elsewhere (for example, the US).
- The sum or synthesis of the mosaic of national styles (for example, French management or German management) in which different national styles are examined critically alongside each other.

Source: Shenton (1992).

experienced as radical differences, as separation, as superiority over others. It is not a source of fragmentation and partitioning, but has come to be seen as a value, as an added richness and a potential for progress.   Shenton (1992).

As evidenced by the discussion of national models of European HRM in Chapter Three and reflected throughout Part Three of the book, European management is rooted in cultural diversity and managers are obliged to operate in a multicultural environment. Given the high pace of integration and change in domestic markets throughout the EU, an important feature of Europan management is a heightened ability to manage change in comparison to the more protected home markets of Japan and the US. Being a European manager is not something divorced from the (clearly acknowledged) national management styles. European management is an added dimension to management – not a culturally different style (see Illustration 6.4). A key element of it has to be the ability to 'read and interpret the complex and diversified social, cultural and political European business environment' (van Dijck, 1990).

In this chapter we review the main arguments both for and against the concept of European management. The debate covers a range of levels (see Illustration 6.5).

Socio-economic factors

The socio-economic arguments for European management point to the gradual convergence of lifestyles in Europe and the impact this will have on various business sectors and market dynamics (Tijmstra and Casler, 1992). We examined the strategic pressures on organizations that are resulting from changes in the socio-economic environment in Chapter Four. Such trends are often used to create a case for the emergence of a European style of management by drawing attention to the convergence of values in European societies (especially North European) in terms of: a decreasing importance of religion as a source of moral obligation, a fairly stable attitude towards democratic political systems, and an increasing democratization of norms and values. This process of modernization is impacting all aspects of economic, social and political life (van Dijck, 1990).

The quality of life is becoming a new religion in European countries (as noted in Chapter Four) indicating a deep re-orientation of attitudes in Europe, with senior

Illustration 6.4 **Europe-specific management skills.**

■ Technical skills to deal with laws and regulations at a regional level.   ■ Language ability.
■ Skills in cross-frontier activities like mergers and project teams given the intensity of European business restructuring.   ■ Intercultural skills.

Source: Shenton (1992).

Illustration 6.5 **Dimensions to the argument for and against a European style of management.**

■ Socio-economic.   ■ Technological.
■ Political.   ■ Competitive and strategic.
■ Cultural.   ■ HRM and managerial practice.

managers and specialists demanding increasingly that they be provided with international careers in a European context. The counter argument presents Europe as more fragmented than either the USA or Japan in terms of economic factors like price controls, investment incentives and the social costs of employment. A convergence of socio-economic trends does not necessarily result in expectations of new patterns of HRM, it is argued.

Political and institutional factors

In Chapter Three we pointed to the existence of marked political and institutional differences across Europe. The importance of these cannot be understated. Nevertheless, there are some political and institutional arguments in favour of there being a European notion of management. They run as follows. The European Union (EU) exists as a growing influence, drawing in Eastern European and Scandinavian countries. In some functional and geographic areas we can expect stricter European-level controls to develop (Thurley and Wirdenius, 1991) and these will be followed by political pressures from European institutions to reduce the economic fragmentation by building a new socio-economic and political framework. Such political pressures will help transform the business environment and will lead to a fundamental change in the mentality of European managers (Tijmstra and Casler, 1992). For example, the Social Chapter is seen by some as the first step in a long process of transition towards a European framework which will take precedence over national systems and rules. Although there are still institutional differences within Europe, Tijmstra and Casler (1992) argue that the national patterns of historical and legislative factors that are needed to make business decisions are now more similar (and hence learnable) within the European context than between, say Japan and the USA.

The counter argument points to the currently widely different social institutions across Europe, and argues that these will at best hinder the pace and ultimate depth of integration across Europe (Whitley, 1992) or indeed ultimately derail the process. For example, under the Social Chapter qualification systems, minimum wage legislation, social welfare provision and collective bargaining procedures will not be harmonized and nation states will therefore preserve considerable powers to retain local systems of social security and employment law. Moreover, the EU is a relatively novel political entity and very unlike existing federations, such as the USA. Because the precise framework and membership of the EU cannot be stabilized in the face of the political and economic transformations raging through Europe, the contours of the business environment will remain uncertain and in a state of flux for several years to come (Thurley and Wirdenius, 1989). The reality may be that multinational organizations – particularly US and Japanese ones – will exert considerable power during this period of transition, resisting EU legislation. Of course, in resisting the institutional pressures from the EU they may put in place their own changes and thereby still fuel the process of convergence.

Cultural factors

There are also a number of cultural arguments that support the notion of European management. Child (1981) believes that differences in national culture – although an important determinant of national management practice – are clearly eroding over time as international recognition of best practice, management education and the growing influence of multinationals create an international management culture. Van Dijck (1990) argues that even the current (marked) cultural diversity across Europe offers many new opportunities to learn, create new wealth and new management mindsets. Indeed the issue of cultural diversity can be presented in contrasting ways. Some present it as a positive value (see, for example, the discussion of transnationalism in Chapter Five) – an added richness and a potential for progress – rather than as a source of fragmentation and partitioning. As part of this new management mindset, European corporate culture will place a greater emphasis on managers with cross-cultural awareness, skills and abilities to operate in different cultural contexts, multiple languages and an attitude to work and life that is based on mobility (Tijmstra and Casler, 1992) not nationality. Increasing numbers of professionals and managers are becoming involved in international activities such as task forces, project groups and conferences. They are learning and adapting their management styles accordingly (Dadfar and Gustavsson, 1992). Many European organizations have also recognized the importance of having strong corporate images at the European level and are using this to define a new European-wide management style.

The counter argument points to the prospect of cultural fragmentation and polarization. There are few examples of truly European organizations in terms of their culture and identity. Philips, for example, whilst genuinely European in its employment of managers and engineers, still has a clear Dutch identity. Indeed, most European multinational organizations – such as Fiat, Thompson and Siemens – whilst having a high degree of geographic spread retain a strong home market and culture (Thurley and Wirdenius, 1991). This retention of local identity is important, because it means that:

- The choice of senior managers is still often guided by national concerns or preferences.
- Existing social and cultural differences in the definition and concept of management are reinforced.

Moreover, as was argued in Chapter Three, in relation to HRM practices the cultural needs of employees in terms of work, organization and society are substantially different between the Northern European and Southern European countries (van Dijck, 1990). Therefore those who argue against cultural integration also warn that the existing social and cultural diversity within European society may pose a challenge to attempts to develop any new management style (Tijmstra and Casler, 1992).

Differences between management systems are such that even culturally sensitive executives will struggle to understand them. Greater mobility across frontiers may just bring new problems of motivation, identity and commitment (Thurley, 1990). Finally, it must be pointed out that creating a small cadre of internationally mobile and cross-culturally aware managers only means European management for the few and by the few. Creating a reliance on such small cadres of managers may result in organizations actually avoiding the need thoroughly to internationalize their management.

Technological factors

Technological arguments for the emergence of European management stress the strong trends towards the harmonization of technology and work systems within Europe (Tijmstra and Casler, 1992). This logic of technology is increasingly superseding historical differences in beliefs, value orientations and national cultures.

Competitive and strategic factors

The competitive and strategic arguments are perhaps the most strongly asserted and convincing reasons for convergence. In Chapters Four and Five we presented some compelling evidence showing that European organizations are facing similar strategic problems in a unified market place. Global market pressures will force organizations to adapt their management practices and will dictate common developments in management models. Until recently the global model of management has been, by default, an American one although it is recognized that this is not necessarily the most appropriate. A European alternative is developing. Trends towards greater industrial concentration and business integration within Europe will continue to erode differerences in management style between sectors and European countries (Tijmstra and Casler, 1992). Merger and acquisition activity, which has become more intense in Europe, will focus attention on different management approaches and the need to internationalize management teams and the ability to work across very different cultural systems will give the best European management teams a source of competitive advantage (Shenton, 1992). The current phase of European business integration means that European organizations are probably ahead of the game in terms of cross-cultural learning, and the skills they are learning (for example, most European managers have at least one foreign language) are ones that the Japanese and US organizations will not so easily acquire (Shenton, 1992).

Moreover, the creation of effective trans-European business structures will also create the need for new management approaches and systems at a European level (van Dijck, 1990). Transnational product development, production and marketing will lead to greater international and European awareness, sensitivity and competence amongst European managers and the development of this European awareness will represent a new source of competitive advantage in world markets (Tijmstra and Casler, 1992).

Effective strategic decision making requires a cadre of managers with broad cognitive frames of reference (see Illustration 6.6). Many European organizations are developing a group of senior employees and exposing them to pan-European careers. On top of these pressures, the presence of intense competition and the need for survival will drive a management of change culture (and its associated policies) into more and more managerial levels of all European organizations (Thurley and Wirdenius, 1991).

The negative and more defensive view argues that the reality of the SEM has always been rooted in the need for improved economic competitiveness, not the need for social or management integration. The search for economic competitiveness will happily see unemployment continue to rise whilst skill shortages persist. Internationalization – and

Illustration 6.6 **Developing a European perspective: new management cadres.**

Rhône-Poulenc and Henkel, the French and German chemicals companies, have 'Europeanized' their personnel strategies, headhunting executives who are trilingual and can work anywhere in Europe. Nokia, the Finnish conglomerate, runs a European manager programme which is open to executives from other European organizations. The intention is to expose students to different corporate and national cultures whilst on the course. It includes two operational assignments within the organization. The European Roundtable of Industrialists, an association of around 40 of Europe's largest organizations, promotes executive mobility by arranging for its members to swap managers for short periods. In 1993 it commissioned a study by ESC Lyon into the notion of European management.

Source: The Economist (1992).

transnationalization – of management may just produce more conflict in Europe, not tolerance (Thurley, 1990). Multinationals in fact demonstrate that the most successful strategy is an international – not just a European – perspective. Finally, for many organizations that have traditionally competed on national characteristics – for example, the association with German quality engineering skills – a shift to pan-European structures may actually dilute the perception of their competitive advantage.

Management practices

Finally, we should consider the conflicting arguments about managerial practices. Tijmstra and Casler (1992) argue that European organizations have developed strong links with European Business Schools and are recruiting significant cadres of like-minded managers into their ranks, armed with the same kitbag of the best management practices. Internal education and training is also reflecting a wider European focus, reinforcing a European specialism at middle management levels. Sparrow and Hendry (1988) also pointed out that in any process of industrial restructuring – especially one driven by mergers, acquisitions and joint ventures – there are clear winners and losers. Usually, it is the winners' set of management concepts and techniques that prevail and spread. We examined evidence suggesting there were national changes in HRM practices as a result of foreign direct investment (FDI) in Chapter Five. Indeed, the proposal for a Regulation on the Statute for a European company published by the European Commission in May 1989 lays down the possible legal form of a company which would stand apart from companies recognized by the laws of the twelve EU nations (Thurley and Wirdenius, 1991). This would enable organizations to carry out cross-frontier restructuring by means of an international asset merger rather than by use of a takeover bid. This will form the basis of joint subsidiaries and holding companies of international groups and will also provide for new choices in the form of employee involvement, controls over policies for disclosure of information and for auditing accounts.

Organizations also tend to desire some predictability in their local markets and so will plan and structure themselves at the most appropriate level. This is becoming a European level. In response to the development of transnational structures, European organizations may create central planning processes and co-ordination centres in order to create better internal links between their manufacturing and selling operations, and better external links with joint-venture partners and subcontractors (van Dijck, 1990; Thurley and Wirdenius, 1991). Again, there will be a wave of new and homogeneous management tools and techniques to manage this process that will supersede national management styles. Moreover, local European operations will increasingly use management tools and techniques aimed at integrating their foreign nationals and ensuring their effectiveness, leading to a broader management style.

The counter argument to these developments points out that there has never been any tried and tested European model of management (whilst certain national models have proved to be effective). By contrast, many US and Japanese management techniques have been tested at home and abroad. Organizations may therefore choose existing and competing US or Japanese management techniques (Tijmstra and Casler, 1992). Indeed, it is argued that at present there are few management education centres that provide a genuinely European response to corporate management requirements.

FORCES OF INTEGRATION WITHIN EUROPEAN HRM

The previous section has served to summarize the ambivalent arguments about the emergence of a European style of management (see Figure 6.1 for a summary of the competing forces). Most of the points made will be developed throughout Part Three of the book. However, whilst some writers (see, for example, Lane, 1992; and Whitley, 1992) feel that national business systems have an overarching and dominant impact on effective management, it must also be acknowledged that there is considerable variety within national business systems. Distinctive patterns of HRM can emerge at other levels of analysis. Räsänen and Whipp (1992) point to the collective action that occurs across industries, sectors, districts, regions, production systems, crafts, professions, and corporations. National and international economies can be seen as combinations of a number of economic and competitive sectors that more or less dominate the various national economies. For example, changes in HRM in Finland may be driven as much by developments in the timber and electronics sectors as by supranational institutions such as the EU.

By moving down a level of analysis – to that of industrial sectors – and by appreciating the dynamics of internationalization, studies of business recipes and their associated logic of action tend to provide us with a more positive perspective on pan-European developments in HRM. The growth of international organizations and markets has modified the significance of purely national institutions (and national institutional differences). These institutions are being opened up to external influences and models.

This is called the convergence thesis. It argues that the context of business (in this instance the European business context) operates independently of national culture and in fact predominates over it (Wilson and Rosenfeld, 1990). Organizations are becoming increasingly alike in terms of their strategic implementation, structure, technology, levels of bureaucratization, HRM policies and practices and role of the HRM function, it is argued. Therefore in the European context, although strong control over foreign direct investment, legislation and regulatory frameworks limits the internationalization of organizations, many of these constraining factors are being removed within Europe and leading to greater convergence amongst organizations. The collapse of the ERM in 1993 demonstrated this. In Chapter Five we outlined the remarkably deep and swift process of industrial restructuring in Europe that has been reflected in a large increase of foreign direct investment. There are a number of factors contributing to the internationalization of organizations.

These factors are eroding the boundaries between industries such that a core set of associated HRM and technology requirements are gradually confronting all industrial sectors, leading to more homogeneous management adjustment strategies (Lane, 1992). Some observers have stressed the role of common economic and structural changes across Europe in eliciting similar responses in HRM strategies (Grahl and Teague, 1991). Indeed, Brewster and Tyson (1991) argue that there are increasingly few distinctions between the realm of what is national and what is international. The internationalization of trade and business has brought with it 24-hour stock exchanges, information exchange through satellite, computer and television, customers and suppliers that cross national boundaries, and international marketing, manufacturing, research and development functions within organizations. This has led to the convergence thesis:

. . . There are universal truths about the management of human resources which can be applied in the same way as truths in other areas of management. Effective manpower planning,

Competitive/Strategic Arguments

For	Against
Similar strategic problems (customer service, flexibility, cost competitiveness, innovation) are being pursued in a unified market place.	Global models of management, whether US, Japanese or pan-European, do not reflect highly successful national business recipes.
The dominant logic of top teams is associated with common perceptions of the strategic environment. Clearly defined management cadres provide a more focused target for educational change.	National differences exist in the cognitive maps and levels of sector understanding of European managers.
HRM developments are driven by sectoral and not just national developments.	The most successful strategy is international and not just European.
Merger and acquisition activity creates winners and losers and the eventual subordination of national HRM practices.	
The creation of transnational and pan-European business structures is leading to common management processes and systems.	

Management Technique Arguments

For	Against
There is a dominant philosophy and culture of managing change. This is leading to a core set of management techniques which are slowly working through all management levels and cadres.	Tried and tested US or Japanese management techniques will be adopted first, reducing the possibility of any unique European approach.
Education and training centres are being co-ordinated on a European basis.	
Planning systems and organizational structures are being co-ordinated at a European level.	

Cultural Arguments

For	Against
International recognition of best practices in management education is developing an international cadre of managers who are culturally-sensitive, multilingual, and mobile.	Different cultural needs of employees in terms of work, organization and definition of the management task will result in only an internationalization of the few.
Cultural diversity provides new opportunities to learn and to create new wealth.	Cultural diversity becomes a source of fragmentation and polarization.

Figure 6.1 (*Continued*).

There is a redefinition of corporate images taking place at a European level.

International project teams, task forces and conferences provide new social contexts for the development of management styles.

Most organizations currently still have strong national identities, reflected in their senior management appointments.

Technological Arguments

For

Harmonization of technology and work systems, driven by a technological logic, is superseding historical differences in job design and creating new cultures and organizational values.

Against

Common technologies are utilized in different ways in practice, depending on the different core capabilities of the organization. These are linked to national business systems and cultures.

Socio-economic Arguments

For

Dominant supranational economic pressures and institutions, such as the collapse of the ERM or agreement on GATT, demonstrate the limitation of national business models.

There is a convergence of lifestyles and social values.

Against

The dominant logic of the SEM is improved competitiveness, but the co-existence of high levels of unemployment with skills shortages, will exacerbate national divisions and lead to decisions in the national interest.

Fragmented economies, price controls, investment incentives and social costs of employment will remain in place.

Political/Institutional Arguments

For

Growing institutional influence and membership of the EU will lead to stricter controls in some areas of management.

The evolving framework of the SEM has created a new internationally-sensitive management mentality in Europe.

The presence of already highly-regulated labour markets will make the adoption of institutional reform an easier process.

Against

Different social institutions, such as qualification systems, minimum wage legislation, collective bargaining and social welfare provision, will mean that considerable local powers are retained.

Non-European multinationals will exert considerable power and influence during the period of transition. They will forward global solutions.

Figure 6.1 Convergence or divergence of European management: a force field analysis.

recruiting, training and development, work allocation, motivation and control of the workforce are requirements for any successful organization and, while they will of course need to be adapted, for example, to local labour markets, the basic principles hold true in any country.

Brewster and Tyson (1991).

The presence of common strategic pressures at the organizational level – such as quality issues, the need to decentralize, innovation and the linking of HRM with the strategic management of the organization – will facilitate greater integration of HRM largely because each issue tends to have a clear pattern of HRM practices associated with it (see Illustration 6.7). The more that European organizations are faced at the sector or national level with common strategic pressures, the more they will learn from each other and move towards common HRM solutions (Grahl and Teague, 1991).

High levels of foreign direct investment at the organizational level (either as acquiring or acquired organizations) can also accelerate the harmonization and integration of existing HRM practices or lead to new practices and innovations in key areas. For example, HRM in Ireland has been particularly subject to new practices in TQM and JIT as a result of foreign direct investment (Hannaway, 1992). In other countries it is the process of industrial restructuring and the creation of larger organizations that is having a dominating influence. This increase in scale and restructuring entails the need to develop a model of HRM – often for the first time – and these new models are more likely to be influenced by the current level of European development and thinking on the topic.

Although we saw in Chapter Three that the pattern of HRM in France stands out amongst the European countries in terms of its uniqueness, Besse (1992) argues that the presence of a highly regulated labour environment in France may also facilitate integration because of its ability to absorb many of the legislative requirements of the SEM more easily. Similarly, it has been argued that the existence of a clearly identified management cadre has facilitated the development of HRM in Denmark (Arkin, 1992b) and France (Besse, 1992) because the common background of the management cadres aids transfer of functional knowledge and could potentially lead to HRM being seen as a key career advancement post. To the extent that European organizations adopt similar HRM solutions to common problems, then strong internal labour markets will tend to accelerate the dissemination and transfer of European 'know-how' in the HRM area because the lessons are directed at a captive workforce. Finally, high historical exposure to cultural diversity at the national or organizational level, as seen for example within Belgium, or in Anglo-Dutch organizations like Shell or Unilever, can lead to a more flexible and open approach in terms of adjusting HRM practice to the necessities of European integration (Hoogendoorn, 1992).

Illustration 6.7 **Forces or factors facilitating integration of European HRM.**

- The presence of common strategic pressures – such as decentralization, quality issues, innovation and globalization – each associated with its own package of required or associated HRM practices.
- Foreign direct investment (both within the EU and from external sources) in the form of acquisitions, mergers, and joint alliances.
- The emergence of transnational organizations.
- Boosted economic activity leading to a restructuring of organizations into larger units requiring new models of HRM.
- A highly regulated and balanced labour environment.
- Strong identity of the management population as an identifiable cadre, and positioning of HRM as an important area of functional expertise and career development.
- High exposure to cultural diversity at organization or national level.

An important lesson to draw from a discussion of the convergence thesis is that individual European nations (and their major organizations) may find that they integrate their HRM under a different set of influences. Acquisitions, mergers and joint ventures may be leading forces of integration in the UK and Ireland (Hannaway, 1992) – because of their attractiveness as a target – and also in many of the Latin countries such as Portugal (Mendes, 1992), Spain or Italy – because of their large-scale privatization programmes. In countries like Greece it may be the simple boost to economic growth caused by the SEM that stimulates business restructuring (Ball, 1992) and forces fragmented and small organizations to combine and create a critical mass that becomes capable of developing standalone HRM. In countries like France it may be the fact that its highly regulated and balanced labour environment enables it readily to absorb new EU legislation that fosters integration (Besse, 1992). The various experiences of European countries and the different features of their HRM will inevitably mean that European integration encroaches down different pathways. However, one way or another, encroach on management practices (including HRM) it will. Is there any empirical evidence to support the convergence thesis?

CONVERGENCE OR DIVERGENCE IN EUROPEAN HRM PRACTICE?

In the final sections of this chapter we return to some of the more recent empirical evidence. Evidence for convergence comes from two main sources:

- The IBM/Towers Perrin survey on worldwide HRM practices.
- An IMD/European Association of Personnel Management survey on the role of the HRM function.

The study by Sparrow, Schuler and Jackson (1994) outlined in Chapter Two revealed that there are at least five clusters of countries worldwide in terms of the importance they attach to their various HRM practices and concepts. Although there were several areas of HRM which were receiving a common focus – such as the emphasis on promoting an empowerment culture, the importance of communication, the need to improve horizontal management processes, and the roles of recruitment and training – there were also a number of areas in which there was still considerable diversity in HRM practice across Europe. These included the extent to which cultures that promoted diversity and equality were actively being pursued, the emphasis on centralization, the role of flexible work practices, the emphasis on measuring and rewarding customer service, rewards for innovation and creativity and the degree of corporate responsibility. Nevertheless, the fact that Germany and Italy formed part of the same cluster as the Anglo-Saxon countries in terms of their HRM priorities for the year 2000 not only flies in the face of the theoretical differences in HRM in Europe and the national determinants of practice discussed in Chapter Three, but it also suggests that there may be a degree of convergence taking place.

A final question to consider is the extent to which, despite some remaining inter-European differences in HRM focus, the data analysed by Sparrow, Schuler and Jackson (1994) indicates either an overall pattern of convergence or one of divergence in the various areas of HRM priority between the four European countries examined: the UK, Germany, France and Italy. There are significant correlations between the percentage of respondents in each country who think the 38 human resource policies/concepts are critically important or important. Reflecting the results of the original cluster analysis – Germany, Italy and the UK (as members of the US–European cluster) show the highest intercorrelations, whilst the communality between

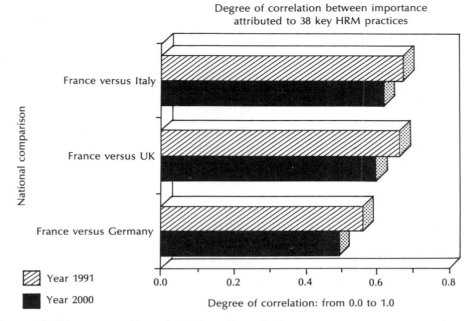

Figure 6.2 Divergence of French HRM profile and other European countries over the years 1991 and 2000. *Note*. This secondary analysis is based on data contained within the IBM/Towers Perrin (1992) survey.

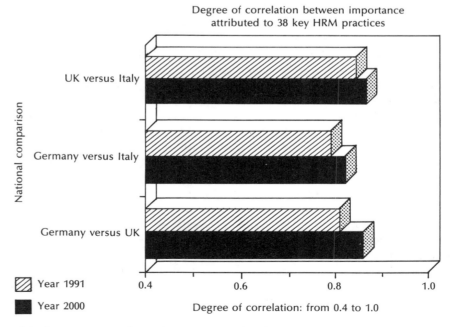

Figure 6.3 Convergence of British, German and Italian HRM profiles over the years 1991 and 2000. *Note*. This secondary analysis is based on data contained within the IBM/Towers Perrin (1992) survey.

the French profile and the other European countries never exceeds more than 36 per cent of the variance.

But what path are these countries on? Do the responses of the managers suggest that the European countries will get more or less alike in terms of their profile on the 38 areas of HRM? By comparing the degree of correlation in the year 1991 data to the degree of correlation in the year 2000 data there is evidence of both differentiation and integration (see Figure 6.2 for the divergence of the French profile). The correlation between the French and German profile in 1991 was 0.5608, falling to 0.4946 for the Year 2000. Similarly the correlation between France and the UK falls from 0.6650 in 1991 to 0.5990 in 2000, and between France and Italy it falls from 0.6751 in 1991 to 0.6206 in 2000. The other European states show a trend in the opposite direction (see Figure 6.3). The correlation between the German and UK profile increases from 0.8103 in 1991 to 0.8594 in 2000. Germany versus Italy increases from 0.7947 to 0.8236. The UK and Italy are also integrating, with the correlation increasing from 0.8499 to 0.8688. Therefore, despite some significant differences in HRM focus between the European countries described in the previous section, those European organizations within the overall US–European cluster (Britain, Germany and Italy) are on a path of convergence in their HRM, whilst France may be expected to continue to pull apart.

IMPLICATIONS OF STRATEGIC PRESSURES FOR HUMAN RESOURCE MANAGEMENT

Part Two of the book has built up a picture of mounting economic and social pressure on the previously discrete European models of HRM. In recent years, much has been written about the macroeconomic consequences of the various environmental changes. For instance, there has been a large number of publications about the economic impact of the SEM and what actions organizations need to take to survive and take advantage of it. Much less has been written about the social implications and how organizations are dealing with the numerous HRM issues and challenges created by changes in the environment. Nevertheless, competitive pressures and changes in the labour market have highlighted a number of fundamental and sometimes provocative questions about what HRM policies and practices organizations use to attract, keep, utilize, motivate and reward high-quality people and how effective these activities are in helping to achieve corporate goals. These changes also have implications for the roles and functions of HRM or personnel managers and for the legal and membership position of trade unions. In this section, we briefly introduce and explore some of the general implications for HRM managers. We do not examine the issues in depth here, but raise them in order to help establish and reflect the emerging HRM agenda both for European organizations and for Part Three of this book (see Figure 6.4 for an overview of the links between the strategic and social pressures described in Chapter Four and the various chapters in Part Three).

Table 6.1 summarizes the results from a recent survey of 59 HR executives working in 14 countries and 21 industries in Europe by Coopers and Lybrand (*op. cit.* Stanton, 1992). It found that the major concerns were for:

- Flatter, more flexible Europe-wide organization structures.
- Structures that were more customer-focused.
- A more strategic and international policy-making role for the HRM function.

- Greater sensitivity to national cultural differences and agreement to reach goals by a number of different routes.
- Convergence of HRM policies.
- The emergence of a cadre of Euro-managers to act as the glue between subsidiaries and headquarters.

There are distinct national cultural differences and institutional and business system differences (see Chapter Three) that will ensure that the social reaction to the pressures outlined in this chapter will vary in intensity from country to country. However, because all organizations operate under broadly the same capitalist system (see Chapter Five) their response will be forced towards similar goals (the actual practices and techniques used to meet these goals may of course still vary). We saw some evidence

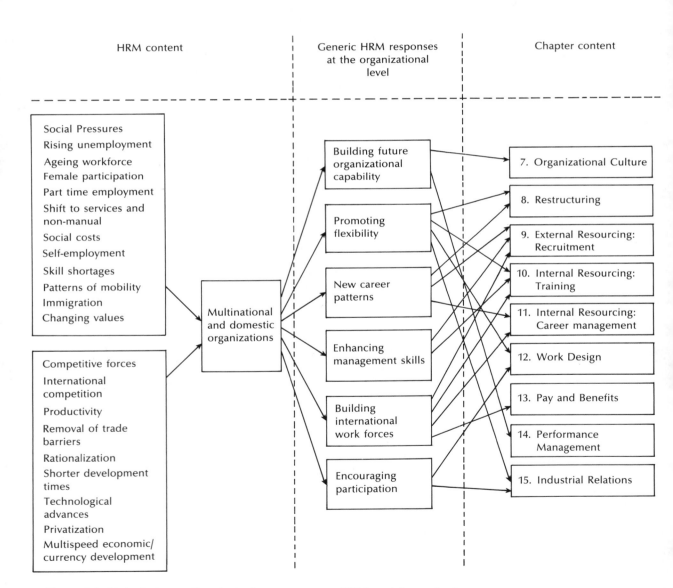

Figure 6.4 Links between the strategic pressures on HRM and its content.

Table 6.1 **Ten most urgent challenges facing European HRM managers.**

	Score
Enhancing management skills	2.8
Skills shortages	3.6
Promoting flexibility	4.3
Training	4.6
Encouraging participation	5.6
Containing wage rises	6.1
Work/family issues	6.7
EU social charter	6.8
Hiring more women	7.1
Industrial unrest	7.6
Rank 1 = extremely urgent	
Rank 10 = relatively unimportant	

Source: Stanton, M. (1992), reprinted with permission © 1993, M. Stanton, *Organization and Human Resource Management: the European Perspective*, Kogan Page.

of this convergence towards the end of Chapter Two and in the previous section. Despite the national differences in HRM systems outlined in Chapter Three, then, there is considerable agreement between academics and practitioners in the HRM area about the significance of a number of issues and challenges at the organizational level that are created by the environmental pressures and business decisions described in Part Two of the book. In particular, there is considerable consensus around the following goals for HRM managers:

- Enhancing management skills.
- Promoting flexibility.
- Encouraging participation.
- Creating new career paths.
- Building international workforces.
- Building organizational capability for the future.

Enhancing management skills

Globalization and commercial pressures for international acquisitions and joint ventures are also requiring HRM managers and their organizations to rethink the type of managers that will be needed in the future and the career paths and other incentives that need to be offered to attract and develop them. In the past, most multinational organizations were content to delegate responsibility for products and services to functional specialists at national and local level. Therefore, there was little point in trying to 'internationalize' recruitment, training and development programmes, unless there was a very specific need for expatriates at middle management level. Today, however, a great many pressures are demanding more multiculturally sensitive managers who are not blinkered by work exposure in only one national culture (Clark, 1992). Geographical spread, particularly into Asia and Eastern European countries, presents new challenges in managing human resources in diverse cultures and societies where laws, customs and prevailing social values are quite different from those at home. Hence, an increasing number of organizations, such as Hoechst, Siemens, Elf Aquitaine and Thomson, are recognizing the necessity for future top managers to take a global and cross-cultural perspective. This implies not only fluency in a second or third language, but also understanding of different cultural values, political and economic infrastructures, and business practices.

Promoting flexibility

Lane (1989) points out that trends towards increased external and internal flexibility in organizations have been initiated by both European organizations and governments. Organizations have pursued flexibility in order to increase business competitiveness in international markets, whilst governments have pursued it in order to reduce unemployment. Although some of the trends towards flexibility were already underway in the 1970s, particularly in the UK and to a lesser extent in France, it was only from the mid-1980s onwards that there has been a sustained attack on 'employment rigidity' across Europe. This is a notably new and qualitatively different phenomenon to that experienced in the past, Lane (1989) argues, because the attack is on so many fronts and we have seen the simultaneous emergence of a large variety of forms of labour market flexibility (see Illustration 6.8 for a description of future employment strategies in the UK).

Indeed, atypical work patterns or contracts, such as temporary, casual, fixed term, home based and annual hours contracts are continuing or are now on the increase in all the countries covered by the PWCP survey (see Chapter Two) despite the differing legal, cultural and labour traditions (Brewster, Hegewisch and Mayne, 1993). More than half the organizations in countries such as Switzerland, the Netherlands and Denmark have increased their use of particular forms of flexible working, indicating

Illustration 6.8 **Long-term employment policies in the UK.**

Evidence from a recent British Institute of Management/Manpower survey suggests that the employment scene in the UK is changing permanently and provides direct evidence of a shift towards the core/periphery model. The drive is to concentrate on core businesses, contracting out peak workloads and support functions to maximize productivity. CEOs believe that flexible working, contracting out of non-essential activities and part time employment will become the norm, not the exception. Key statistics in the survey show that:

- Nearly 90 per cent of Britain's largest organizations have carried out a restructuring exercise since 1985.
- Seventy three per cent anticipate further significant restructuring by 1996 with 63 per cent predicting future job losses.
- In 76 per cent of organizations one or more management layers had been eradicated and 66

per cent of organizations had lost jobs at all levels.

The survey also provided figures on the current expectations for increases in reliance on flexible work practices and planned reliance in 1996. Working life in the UK is undergoing dramatic change with less job security but more autonomy over decisions on working hours, retirement and work arrangements. The figures below show the percentage of organizations *expecting to make more use* of categories of flexible practice in 1992 and 1996.

Practice	1992	1996
Temporary workers	47%	60%
Contracting out of non-core work	55%	71%
Flexible work times	55%	75%
Flexible retirement	45%	67%
Part time work	46%	52%

Source: British Institute of Management/Manpower (1992), reprinted with permission © British Institute of Management, 1993.

a levelling out of and more widespread use of flexibility across Europe. Increasing international competition is creating the need for dramatic improvements in human productivity (Beer, 1984). As noted earlier, this has led to a search for new organizational structures that are flat, flexible and highly responsive.

J. O'Reilly (1992) has recently examined the employment strategies in the retail banking sector in both Britain and France. She warns that cultural and institutional factors (such as those discussed in Chapter Two) should not be overlooked when describing what appears like a stark and dichotomous choice between core and peripheral forms of employment. Flexibility, she suggests, is not universal. For example, although the banks in both countries experienced similar pressures in terms of competition and technological change – there were still important differences in employment strategies and the way the banks from France and Britain organized their systems and response. For example, part time employment accounted for 14 per cent of the bank's workforce in Britain but only 9.6 per cent in France. Stricter definition by law of employment rights for part time employees meant the trend was less well developed in France (and it was also a more expensive option than in Britain). The French banks, however, made more use of temporary work, of functional flexibility, and numerical flexibility (4.5 per cent in France compared to 2.4 per cent in Britain). It is of course difficult to assess whether such findings are specific to one sector, or just to the French situation (which as was seen from the IBM/Towers Perrin survey in Chapter Two is pursuing a less integrated approach to HRM when compared with the UK, Germany and Italy). Nevertheless, we should draw attention to the fact that European countries may follow different paths towards the same goal of flexibility.

... Firms have found themselves under pressure to find more flexible ways of manning. They have put a premium on achieving a workforce which can respond quickly, easily and cheaply to unforeseen changes, which may need to contract as smoothly as it expands, in which worked time precisely matches job requirements, and in which unit labour costs can be held down.

Atkinson (1984, p. 37).

We discuss the evidence on the importance of flexibility across Europe, and different approaches to it, in Chapter Twelve. However, at this point we draw attention to the fact that it has been suggested that, in order to compete internationally, organizations will need to achieve flexibility in at least three areas relating to employees:

1. Functional.
2. Numerical.
3. Financial.

Functional flexibility facilitates the quick redeployment of staff to different activities and crafts. Numerical flexibility enables the total number of employees to be easily adjusted for short-term fluctuations in the demand for labour through a more individualized contractual relationship between the company and employees. Financial flexibility as a third option allows, among other things, an organization's remuneration system to be sensitive to differences in the performance of employees and to reflect the state of the market (Clark, 1992).

A number of authors have proposed a possible organization structure that enables these three types of flexibility to co-exist. Handy (1989), for example, talks about the emergence of the 'shamrock organization' as an alternative to the traditional hierarchy. This consists of three groups of people. First is the 'core' group consisting of professionals, managers and technicians who constitute the primary labour market. They are full time, highly flexible, well paid and involved in those activities that are unique to the firm or give it a distinctive character (Torrington and Hall, 1991). These employees have invested heavily in terms of time and effort to reach the core group and their rewards are closely related to individual performance. Then there are two peripheral groups; first, those who have skills that are needed but not specific to the particular firm, such as secretarial, clerical, routine maintenance and lesser skilled manual work. Their payment is for specific tasks and in fees rather than for time and in wages. The second peripheral group is made up of people whom the organization employs as and when the need arises, for example, temporary staff from agencies, participants in job training schemes, and self-employed subcontractors.

It is unclear to what extent this type of structure has been adopted and whether it is likely to become more common. Yet, from the HRM manager's viewpoint, such a trend has major implications. Within the core group, for example, there would need to be a strong commitment by the organization to provide suitable rewards and career prospects because, due to the declining workforce, it will be more difficult to find replacements of people with critical company-specific knowledge and skills. In order to achieve functional flexibility, employees would also need to carry out a wider range of activities. This implies the ability to perform cross-functional work in multidisciplinary teams, and the willingness to keep training and retraining as the situation requires new skills.

Finally, Handy (1989) argues that to keep costs down, organizations will concentrate more resources on people and activities that are at the core of the business, either by employing more part time workers (as already discussed and evidenced) or by contracting out activities that are at the periphery. This implies the emergence of two categories of workers. One group consists of highly professional workers, who benefit from the organization's investment in their training and career development and enjoy greater job security in return for the willingness to carry out a variety of tasks. The second group will be made up of people who provide the organization with 'numerical flexibility'. Such employees have less access to career opportunities, little or no company investment in their training, and even less job security than those in the first group. For many people, this development may be an unwelcome situation as it makes workforce reductions relatively easy by decreasing the number of employees in the second group. For others, however, it provides the attraction of working part time, being able to have a variety of work experiences, taking extended career breaks, becoming self-employed, or maintaining a mix of activities without the single minded preoccupation with one job (Torrington and Hall, 1991).

In 1993, British Telecom was seeking a further 15,000 voluntary redundancies after an already protracted period of 'downsizing' that had delivered 60,000 voluntary redundancies. In order to keep the flow of voluntary redundancies going, British Telecom introduced a scheme whereby it offered half the one-off redundancy payment to those workers who were willing to cut their hours by half and become part time workers. Engineers could change to full or part time voluntary work. Four thousand engineers expressed an interest in the full time clerical jobs and 1,000 expressed an interest in the part time jobs. We consider aspects of flexibility in both Chapters Eight on organization structuring and Chapter Twelve on job design.

Encouraging participation

We also discuss changes in work design, including flexibility and participation in Chapter Twelve and the pressures on industrial relations in Chapter Fifteen. The ongoing changes in the labour market, particularly rising unemployment and the changing values of the workforce, are creating pressures on organizations to re-examine their assumptions about the management of human resources. In particular, there are significant problems to be faced in encouraging participation.

... With widespread unemployment, much temporary and part time working, a gradual reduction in normal working hours and a shortening of the working lifetime, the workplace is not quite as significant as a source of personal self-esteem and as an arena for achieving personal objectives, as it was 10–15 years ago. When full time employment is an experience shared by all people for most of their adult lives, then it is the source of most opportunities and the means of self-actualization. Now it is an experience which a significant minority do not share at all ... Even those employed full time probably spend no more than twenty per cent of their time for half their lifetime at work. In this situation the meeting of personal goals at work is a prospect denied to many and an instrumental orientation to work becomes more common.

Torrington and Hall (1991, p. 17).

HRM managers will need to find new ways to attract, motivate, develop and retain people in the late 1990s and beyond. Reflecting the greater instrumentality that people have to work, they will probably face a number of changes:

- More and different types of specialists with different values, career insights, and lifestyles.
- More people looking for work away from the traditional office setting.
- More people looking for flexible approaches to work, such as flexible hours, job sharing, and part time employment.
- Decreased loyalty to organizations, as people are changing jobs and organizations more often.

These changes, in turn, will create new pressures on organizations (see Illustration 6.9).

Alternative career paths for managers

At the same time, slower growth and in some cases declining markets have dramatically reduced an organization's ability to offer advancement and career opportunities to employees and managers (Beer *et al.* 1984). These changes have also led to a questioning of traditional employment policies, whether they are necessarily applicable to all. The notion of 'a career for life', in particular, has come to be seen as neither the only nor the desirable option, for organizations and employees alike. However, as Clark (1992) points out, when you talk to personnel managers and those involved in management development about careers in their organization, before too long the

---

Illustration 6.9 **Pressures on organizations resulting from an instrumental orientation to work.**

- Increase job satisfaction by increasing job variety, autonomy in determining methods of work, challenge, responsibility for problem-solving, and knowledge of the actual results of the work activities.
- Find new ways to attract, keep and reward high-quality human resources.
- Re-examine how much involvement employees should be given and what mechanisms for employee participation and representation need to be provided.
- Provide broader and more flexible career paths to take into account employee needs and lifestyle.
- Re-examine the capacity of employees to contribute and therefore the amount of training and development opportunities they should be given.

conversation will expand into many related areas of HRM and business strategy. Therefore this issue is picked up directly in Chapter Eleven on Career Management, but is also reflected in all the chapters on resourcing issues. Clearly, because of the downsizing and restructuring taking place in many organizations (see Chapters Eight and Sixteen), HRM personnel managers will have to anticipate possible career implications far enough in advance. Career planning and development in the 1990s will have to become much more proactive than it has been in the past.

Building international workforces

Globalization and organizational responses to changes in their competitive environment also have raised questions about the adequacy of traditional HRM policies and practices used to manage worldwide operations. We discuss the impact of internationalization on recruitment in Chapter Nine and on career management in Chapter Eleven. However, a large range of HRM policies and practices can have a significant effect on building an international workforce. For example, Unilever uses its personnel policies not only to develop human resources, but also to shape the organization's decision processes and to influence corporate values. Its selection policies emphasize the need for team players rather than soloists; its management development process moves high-potential managers across product lines, between countries, and from national companies to corporate headquarters, thereby broadening their perspectives while developing their skills and knowledge; its education and training programmes reinforce corporate values and provide numerous opportunities to foster informal personal contacts across organizational lines; and its performance evaluation process considers not only measurable output, but also co-operation with colleagues and adherence to organizational values.

... Building a complex structure and flexible process is difficult enough, but, as we have continually emphasized, the development of a transnational organization requires more than multidimensional capabilities and interdependent assets. It is crucial to change the mentality of members of the organization. Diverse roles and dispersed operations must be held together by a management mindset that understands the need for multiple strategic capabilities, views problems and opportunities from both local and global perspectives, and is willing to interact with others openly and flexibly. The task is not to build a sophisticated matrix structure, but to create a matrix in the minds of managers.   Bartlett and Ghoshal (1989, p. 212).

Building organizational capability for the future

Finally, more concern with customer responsiveness, quality, and long-term relationships with clients and suppliers is causing organizations to build organizational capability through the strategic management of human resources. The main elements of organizational capability are shown in Illustration 6.10. To build and sustain organizational capability, an organization has to integrate these four elements into a coherent system that will become a competitive weapon. We discussed the changing competencies needed by HRM managers in Chapter One. Writers who focus on organizational capability focus on the ability and competency to meet the criteria shown in Illustration 6.11. With these criteria, personnel professionals and line managers can develop a coherent HRM policy that contributes to corporate performance. Unfortunately, experience suggests that this does not happen in many organizations. All too often, HRM is an unco-ordinated collection of practices based

Illustration 6.10 **Four critical elements of organizational capability.**

- *A shared mindset.* Shared mindset stems from organizational culture. This means that the people within the organization and the stakeholders outside it have a common way of thinking about goals and the means used to reach these goals.
- *Management and human resource practices.* Managers have tools with which to create organizational capability, and thus competitive advantage. These tools, or levers, comprise the formal processes for governing how employees think and behave.
- *Leadership.* Organizational capability is driven by leadership, from individuals with vision at all levels of an organization.
- *Capacity for change.* This derives from individuals being empowered and able to influence others.

Source: Ulrich and Lake (1990).

Illustration 6.11 **Key competencies and criteria for human resource specialists to deliver organizational capability.**

- Become strategic business partners and gear their activities to the strategy and goals of the organization. Development and training activities, for instance, must be viewed as means for improving individual and corporate performance, not as ends in themselves.
- Spend time with line managers both within and outside the organization to develop a good working knowledge of their service needs.
- Actively participate in business planning meetings and offer informed insights on the competency requirements of the organization, and the actions taken for acquiring those competencies.
- Provide the organization with the right mix of talent to meet current and future needs of the business.

Source: Ulrich and Lake (1990).

on little more than outmoded habits, current fads, pet ideas of functional specialists, and patched-up responses to former crises (Beer *et al.*, 1984). Perhaps this explains why a number of companies, such as ICI, Shell and Unilever, have begun to appoint line managers rather than specialists to the most senior personnel post in the organization. HRM issues, it seems, are much too important to be left largely to HRM or personnel managers. The need to build organizational capability is most clearly reflected in Chapter Seven, Changing Organizational Culture, and Chapter Fourteen, Performance Management and Appraisal.

THE HRM ISSUES FACING EUROPEAN ORGANIZATIONS: AN AGENDA

The empirical data on convergence are limited to one (albeit quite large-scale) survey and further empirical testing of the convergence and divergence hypotheses is required. Clearly, however, European organizations are re-examining their human resource policies and practices and the issues they face are both urgent and critically important. They may be forced to act quickly – perhaps in a way that flies in the face of much of their history and traditional cultural values. It will be the management practices of leading European organizations, not just national institutions, that will shape the future of work for most European citizens.

Illustration 6.12 **The organizational agenda: human resource issues for the 1990s.**

Issue 1 Self-directed teams are emerging as the organizational norm, but geographical distance, language differences, management level differences and multiple social, political and professional cultures have the potential for both increasing conflict and co-operation.

■ *The challenge*: how can we develop and encourage the positive consequences of self-directed teams?

Issue 2 Economic circumstances may necessitate a crisis situation where 'action' is needed. Often, as the circumstances diminish in magnitude and importance, the crisis situation and action bias diminish as well.

■ *The challenge*: how can we maintain a sense of urgency in a continuous manner?

Issue 3 Information sharing and communication are components of our corporate values. Yet, it remains unclear if the values are shared by the workforce and acted upon.

■ *The challenge*: how can we ensure that corporate values are both communicated and used as guidelines for action?

Issue 4 Cross-functional, multiple level, and geographically distant teams provide an excellent opportunity for significant changes in the business

system. Such advantages are becoming evident; yet, the performance review process may not reflect such new behaviours.

■ *The challenge*: how can you take into account the total performance of an individual in numerous roles including teams?

Issue 5 New management roles include leadership, coach, evaluator, negotiator, co-ordinator and trainer. With these additional roles comes an increasing need for personal interaction; yet, the economic realities suggest less time is available for multiple roles with an interpersonal orientation.

■ *The challenge*: how can we more effectively manage ourselves to accomplish more with less and still fulfil these multiple roles?

Issue 6 Self-directed teams, autonomy, empowerment, information sharing, decreasing management levels, and increasingly complex management roles have not removed or reduced the pressure on results and accountability. In fact, the reverse may be true. The pressure for results and accountability is even more intense.

■ *The challenge*: how can we best manage the complex environment in which we find ourselves to meet our mutual personal and professional goals?

The nature of the agenda being pursued is therefore perhaps best described by a leading European multinational manufacturing organization. It ran a workshop and conducted a series of interviews with its managers to identify the set of issues for their HRM in the 1990s. The issues, highlighted in Illustration 6.12, reflect the practical problems and contradictions associated with the development of a pan-European approach.

THE FUTURE ROLE OF EUROPEAN HRM MANAGERS

So has Europe adopted an HRM perspective? We argued in the first chapter that historically there have been marked differences in the European context and that of America, the developer of an HRM perspective. The empirical evidence suggests European personnel managers are getting there, although not without much heart-searching.

In 1988 a survey by the former IMI found that more than two-thirds of European Chief Executive Officers concluded that '. . . the purpose of the HRM function needs to be redefined'. Given the rapid social, economic, technological and political changes around European organizations, what will be the future role of the personnel or HRM manager? This was the research question that the European Association of Personnel

Management set itself in the early 1990s (Derr, Wood, Walker and Despres, 1992). An innovative IMD/EAPM study involved an extensive literature review, pilot interviews in Switzerland and Sweden, a survey of over 15 countries involving 1530 responses (85 per cent from HR managers and 15 per cent from non-HR managers), and a series of 36 in-depth interviews in Germany, Spain, the UK and France (conducted in the national language, analysed through the use of computer-driven content analysis, and involving senior and mid-level HRM managers, a line manager and an employee or worker representative). The average size of the organizations involved was 1,000 employees.

One of the themes to emerge from the study was that the European personnel function is a function in conflict and the conflict concerns its territory, both within the function and between the function and line managers. The tension involves issues of both power and territory. There are differences of opinion about the identity of European personnel managers. In Chapter One we indicated the academic debate that took place in the UK in the 1980s about the split between personnel management and HRM which has now moved to the core of European organizations. Only around a third of the sample felt that European personnel departments were able to fulfil the more strategic, innovative HRM role forming the core of an organizational change process. The majority felt the function was caught between the legal system, the management board, the workers' council and the individual employee.

... HRM is more important than ever but I can't trust my personnel people to do it. Most of them seem to prefer a traditional administration role and I need sparring partners, change agents and members of top teams who help us understand how to make use of our people so we can be more competitive.   Swiss CEO, quoted in Derr *et al*. (1992, p. 9).

Consequently, there were territorial disputes over who will control the organizational changes that form an HRM approach. Who is best suited to manage the HRM agenda outlined in Illustration 6.12? Senior line managers felt the agenda was too important to be left in the hands of existing personnel or HRM departments. Chief Executives and circumstances will increasingly demand that senior personnel/HR managers have significant business knowledge, skills and experience as well as professional experience in the personnel and HRM field.

Earlier in the chapter we argued that the existence of a core set of HRM, strategic and technology requirements will act as a force of integration. There was general agreement among countries about the importance of nineteen external challenges faced in the 1990s in the IMD/EAPM study. Some international variations were found, in that the impact of technological innovation was most marked in Spain and Portugal, but felt to be less significant in Finland and Sweden. Similarly Spain and Portugal saw most threat from increased competition, whilst Germany and Ireland attributed most importance to customer service pressures.

There was significantly less agreement as to what knowledge and skills were needed to meet the challenges. The analysis of these areas of knowledge showed that managers most wanted hands-on tools. Following change and change management skills were concepts of individual values and motivation, knowledge of working in teams and consultation skills.

Our results reveal personnel/HR to be a field in transition. External forces such as quality, customer service and technology are considered important influences across organizations in our study. In addition, management development, organizational development and strategic HR planning are the three areas viewed as increasing in importance in the future ... We have found that the differences between the personnel/HR professionals within an organization and other functional professionals will narrow over the coming decade. The personnel/HR function is in a unique position to help engineer the changes necessary to bring the function in line with the main business of the organization.   Derr *et al.* (1992).

This uncertainty about the competencies needed by international HRM managers has spurred the British Institute of Personnel Management (IPM) to initiate a study of the skills, knowledge, experience and personal characteristics required to work effectively across borders in areas such as international compensation, recruitment, organization and management development, international assignments, mergers and acquisitions and employee relations. Five hundred organizations from Australia, Canada, France, Germany, Hong Kong, Ireland, Italy, Japan, New Zealand, Singapore, South Africa, Sweden, the UK and the USA will be involved in the study.

Ultimately, the view one takes on the transferability or convergence of the concept of management and HRM practices within Europe depends on the extent to which management is felt to be a science or an art. The scientific approach to management – concentrating on the specific tools and practices adopted and the causal links between national institutions and managerial behaviour and culture – tends to lead observers to focus on some apparently irreconcilable differences between the European nation states and their HRM. This scientific perspective tempts managers to think that the same results can only be produced if the same (or similar) conditions exist and therefore managerial practices – rather like precise scientific laws – will not work properly when taken out of their context.

But is management really so scientific? Those who conceive of management as more of an art form do not see the issues of convergence and transferability in black and white terms. If art can cross national boundaries so can management practices. To continue with the artistic metaphor, by applying a few tints and hues to reflect the national and local differences that currently colour our view of European management, then best practice will be adapted and will transcend the sociological and institutional differences. It is our view that European HRM leans more towards being an art form than to being precisely scientific and therefore, under the weight of the economic, competitive and social pressures described in earlier chapters, we shall see even more convergence than divergence within European HRM over the 1990s.

As many other writers have been forced to conclude, there are elements of truth in both the convergence and institutional-difference perspectives on European HRM. Whilst undoubtedly there are elements of economic and business life that are converging or are at least less disparate than in the past, deep rooted cultural and institutional factors will clearly mediate the effects of convergence and integration of European management. Brewster and Tyson (1991, p. 5) make a valuable observation on the debate. They note that '. . . researchers who focus on the content of management tend to find similarities; researchers who focus on the process tend to identify cultural variations'.

CONCLUSIONS

Change in HRM is afoot. In order to improve on this generalization, it is necessary to marshal the evidence on European HRM practices (and their appropriate business context) and examine questions about best practice, core and pan-European activities, and important situational practice. We endeavour in this book to bring together a wide range of material to enable firmer conclusions to be drawn. In so doing it is important remind ourselves that since the late 1980s Europe has seen unprecedented change. During the writing of this book the European economy nose-dived into a deep recession, two revolutions took place in Russia, communism began to reappear in East

Europe, the ERM system collapsed in all but name, the Italian political system was overhauled, and marked political changes occurred in France. Many previously cherished practices and assumptions will continue to be under threat, and significant change is on the agenda for most European organizations. Carlos Ferrer, president of the Union of Industrial and Employers' Confederations of Europe (UNICE) forewarns us of some of the changes in store. In introducing UNICE's study on European competitiveness, he argues:

... We are now living in a real revolution and we need a flexible society. If we are not able to adapt to the dramatic changes taking place every day then we shall perish... Europe can no longer afford the developed welfare state, with its benefits of all kinds and strong rigidity in the labour market that had been constructed over the past 40 years... Europe is a highly protected island with storms on all sides... our competitiveness study will stress the need for better training, more research and reform of the labour market. We must be able to adapt very quickly.

Carlos Ferrer, President of UNICE, quoted in Watson (1993).

LEARNING POINTS FROM CHAPTER SIX

1. Progress towards a European model of management is not absolutely inevitable. Nor is the process likely to be immediate. National models of management will persist for many years to come. Nevertheless, despite remaining national models of management, it may still be possible to discern a generic European approach.

2. The notion of European management tends to be seen in extremes. The positive view argues that whilst it is necessarily hard to observe and difficult to describe, new modes of thinking are emerging as European organizations respond to different business priorities. The definition of European management will be based around those people and organizations that create the new skills, awareness and mindset for survival throughout the 1990s and beyond and the assumptions and strategies that characterize their behaviour.

3. European management may be seen as a description of those features that distinguish management in Europe as opposed to other areas of the world, or it may be viewed as the synthesis of the diverse management styles in which national styles are critically analysed alongside each other. Questions about European management do not preclude taking a truly global and international perspective.

4. A host of arguments, both for and against the emergence of a distinctly European style of management can be marshalled. They range across socio-economic, political, cultural, technological, competitive and strategic and managerial practice factors.

5. Distinctive patterns of HRM can emerge at the level of industrial sectors and the organization. It is at this level that patterns of integration are emerging most clearly. Common strategic pressures, high levels of foreign direct investment, the emergence of transnational organizations, boosted levels of economic activity associated with a restructuring of organizations, the ability of highly-regulated labour markets to absorb new institutional pressures, clearly defined and educatable management cadres, and high levels of exposure to cultural diversity are all significant factors that will facilitate the integration of European HRM.

6. There is some empirical evidence to suggest that HRM policies and practices across some European countries – such as the UK, Germany and Italy – are converging. Countries like France appear to be on a separate path. The different priorities and experiences of European countries during the 1990s will mean that integration will be

driven down separate pathways. Nevertheless, considerable convergence appears to be demanded by organizations.

7. This is reflected in views about the role of the HRM function in European organizations. The majority of European CEOs believe that the purpose of the HRM function has to be redefined. There is considerable conflict over the relative power and territory that will remain in the hands of HRM specialists as opposed to line managers. HRM in European organizations is a field that is in transition.

PART THREE

The Content of European Human Resource Management

CHAPTER SEVEN

Changing Organizational Culture

INTRODUCTION

In Chapter Three we discussed the topic of national culture and noted that the topic of organizational culture has also received a great deal of attention in the last two decades. What gave this subject most impetus was the popularity of some practice-orientated management books (such as Pascale and Athos, 1982; Deal and Kennedy, 1982; Kotter and Heskett, 1992; Peters and Waterman, 1982; and Smircich, 1983). Pregnant with practical and theoretical promise, these books depicted organizational culture as:

- One of the primary keys to organizational effectiveness.
- An all-encompassing metaphor for the organization.
- A 'master contract' forming the social reality of organizational members.

In Parts One and Two of this book, attention was drawn to a number of factors that are driving a change in the culture of European organizations (see Figure 7.1). Increasing levels of female participation and a general change in workforce values have created social pressures for change. The move towards transnational organizations has created power shifts in structures, from the line of country to the line of business, and several internal organization development programmes have been aimed at changing the organizational culture. National culture differences have required greater intercultural sensitivity. The process of business restructuring and foreign direct investment has brought new criteria for corporate performance, rationalization of businesses, and pressures for continued downsizing and delayering. General competitive forces have seen common trends in privatization, adoption of new technologies, and pressures for higher quality, customer service and rapid response. These all have significant and increasingly common implications for the type of organizational culture in European organizations. The relevance of the topic of organizational culture for European organizations has recently been critically analysed (see, for example, Kreiner, 1989; Schultz, 1992).

As a result, the creation and maintenance of a strong organizational culture has become the cornerstone of employee relations strategies in many European organizations. The underlying assumption is that a strong organizational culture enables people to feel better about what they do, so they are more likely to work

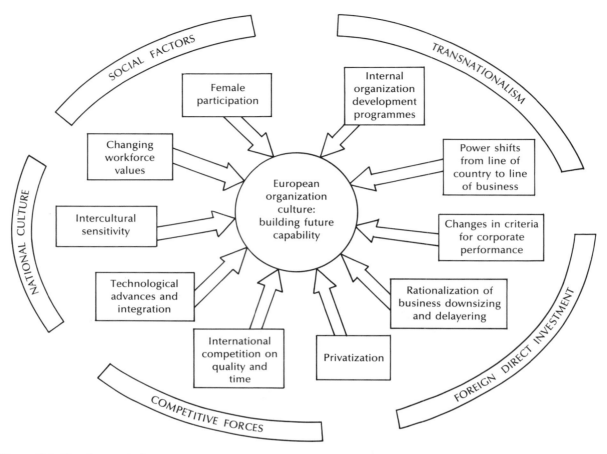

Figure 7.1 The factors influencing change in European organization culture.

harder, achieve high targets, and otherwise make a significant contribution to the goals and success of the organization that employs them.

In a world in which economic systems are in state of constant redefinition, as emphasized in Chapter Four, managers in general and HRM managers in particular, have to understand the extent to which an organization's culture can be changed and how the changes can be made. In order to develop this understanding this chapter is divided into five sections. We begin by considering the international interest in issues of organizational culture change and then present some of the definitions and models of organizational culture, building on these in the third part to explain how a strong organizational culture can be created and maintained and considering the consequences of a strong organizational culture. In the fourth part we examine the various mechanisms through which organizational culture may be managed, ask whether organizational culture can be managed, and examine the link between HRM and organizational culture change. We conclude with a discussion of the various attempts to change organizational culture, using examples of European organizations in which having the right organizational culture is seen as crucial to achieving good service quality.

IMPORTANCE OF ORGANIZATIONAL CULTURE CHANGE ISSUES: SOME COMPARATIVE EVIDENCE

In this first section we consider why there has been international interest in the topic of organizational culture. In Chapter Two we pointed out that there is a process of integration taking place within European HRM. Data were analysed from the Towers Perrin worldwide survey of HRM practices (Towers Perrin, 1992; Sparrow, Schuler and Jackson, 1994) across a number of dimensions. Three of these dimensions involved organizational culture:

- Promoting an empowerment culture.
- Promoting diversity and an equality culture.
- Measuring and promoting customer service.

The results are shown in Figure 7.2. We have conducted some further analysis for this book. It reveals some interesting differences but also shows a high degree of similarity on this issue between many European countries and the US. There is no significant difference between the US, the UK, Germany and France in the extent to which they rate the importance of promoting an empowerment culture. All four countries provided a high rating (ranging from 64 to 71 per cent). Only Italy scored significantly lower on this issue (45 per cent of the sample felt that promoting an empowerment culture was critical to competitive success).

In relation to the promotion of diversity and an organizational culture based on equality, there were three levels of significance. The greatest significance was given to this by the US (53 per cent). The UK and Germany rated the issue of medium

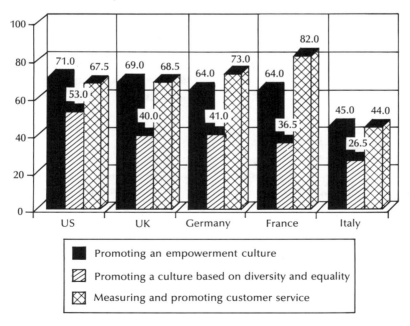

Figure 7.2 The importance of organizational culture change issues in the US, UK, Germany, Italy and France. Data show the percentage of the sample who rate the issue of importance or critical importance in achieving competitive advantage. Reprinted with permission, © Towers Perrin, 1993.

importance (from 40–41 per cent). France and Italy were least concerned about the importance of this aspect of organizational culture (36 and 26 per cent respectively). The work by Hofstede on national culture described in Chapter Three can help explain these differences.

Finally, there were differences in the emphasis given to the need for measurement and promotion of customer service. Interestingly, France was the most concerned about this issue (82 per cent rated it as of importance or critical importance in achieving competitive advantage). The US, the UK and Germany show a similar level of concern (between 67 and 73 per cent). Italy again shows a lower level of concern over this issue (44 per cent). But what exactly is it that organizations from these countries are concerned about? What is organizational culture?

WHAT IS ORGANIZATIONAL CULTURE?

In this second section we consider the various definitions and models of organizational culture. Despite these differences in focus, it seems that interest in organizational culture issues has well and truly crossed the Atlantic. However, most of the theoretical work on defining organizational culture has been American. These concepts, too, seem to transfer to European organizations quite easily. There are many definitions of organizational culture, creating difficulties in reaching consensus on measurement and operationalization (see Illustration 7.1). Sociologists, anthropologists, psychologists, and many others who write about it emphasize different perspectives and together they produce a cacophony which serves to confuse the concept, making it imprecise and ambiguous. Louis (1986) has likened the many grasps at conceptual clarity to the allegory involving an elephant and the truth-seeking blind. Reviews and consolidations of existing works have been attempted by Schein (1983), Smircich (1983), Wilkins (1984), Ott (1989) and others, yet the concept continues to elude theoretical precision and managerial instrumentality.

The 1980s taught most managers that direct efforts to change organization culture are extremely difficult. It is difficult to identify, therefore impossible to affect in a controlled manner, and results of any attempt to change organizational culture are

Illustration 7.1 **Definitions of organizational culture.**

- The pattern of basic assumptions that a given group has invented, discovered, or developed in learning to cope with its problems of external adaptation and internal integration (Schein, 1981).
- An historically transmitted pattern of meaning embodied in symbols, a system of inherited conceptions expressed in symbolic forms by means of which men communicate, perpetuate, and develop their knowledge about attitudes towards life (Geertz, 1973).
- A system of informal rules that spells out how people are to behave most of the time (Deal and Kennedy, 1982).
- The collective programming of the mind which

distinguishes the members of one organization from another (Hofstede, 1991).
- An interdependent set of beliefs, values, ways of behaving, and tools for living that are so common in a community that they tend to perpetuate themselves, sometimes over long periods of time (Wilhelm, 1992).
- The way people are chosen, developed, nurtured, interrelated, and rewarded in the organization (Mintzberg, 1983).
- A shared set of beliefs about how people should behave at work and matter, and a shared mindset which largely influences the way they perceive the environment (Sadler and Milmer, 1993).

hard to measure. However, concern and interest in the topic have been based on three enduring motivations:

- How do similar organizations perform better than others?
- 'Soft' management issues such as quality, customer service and human resource management have markedly increased in importance.
- Interest and awareness of differences in national and organizational cultures, and problems of transferability, have increased.

A series of fads have attracted management attention. In the 1950s management by objectives was in vogue. In the 1960s the debate was about organization structure, moving to corporate strategy in the 1970s. Organizational culture, quality, customer service and empowerment became international buzz words in the 1980s. Kilmann, Saxton and Serra (1985) argue that the interest in organizational culture is not a fad. Why? They see organizational culture as the social energy that either drives or impedes change in the organization.

. . . to ignore culture. . . is to assume. . . that formal documents, strategies, structures and reward systems are enough to guide human behaviour in an organization – that people believe and commit to what they read or are told to do. On the contrary, most of what goes on in an organization is guided by the cultural qualities of shared meaning, hidden assumptions, and unwritten rules.   Kilmann, Saxton and Serra (1985).

The view began to emerge that organizations could be characterized as quasi self-contained organizational cultures, and that these could be used to explain differences in organizational design, behaviour and performance. Control and understanding of an organization's culture is seen as a key responsibility of leaders and a vital human resource management tool. It provides leaders with an insight into the appropriate behaviours, bonds and motivations of individuals. It can be used to assert solutions where there is ambiguity, and has a significant role in governing the way an organization processes information and conducts its internal relations (Hampden-Turner, 1990).

DIFFERENT LEVELS OF ORGANIZATIONAL CULTURE

Although there is no agreement about the definition of organizational culture, the model proposed by Kotter and Heskett (1992) helps to understand the nature of the concept. According to this model, organizational culture is represented at two levels, which differ in terms of their visibility and their resistance to change.

At the deeper and less visible level, organizational culture refers to values and beliefs that are shared by the people in a group and that tend to persist over time even when group membership changes. At this level organizational culture can be extremely difficult to change, in part because group members are often unaware of many of the values and beliefs that bind them together. After some time, employees may no longer be aware of how much their communications, justifications and behaviour are influenced by their shared basic assumptions. Like the process of breathing, internalized beliefs and values have a powerful influence on organizational life that normally escapes the attention of those it most affects (Sathe, 1985).

At the more visible level, organizational culture represents the behaviour patterns or style of an organization that new employees are encouraged to follow by their fellow employees. For example, employees in one group are quick to respond to requests from customers, while those in another are often slow to respond to customer complaints.

Table 7.1 **Diagnosing the culture of an organization: some useful questions.**

(a) Stories
1.   What core beliefs do stories reflect?
2.   How pervasive are these beliefs (through levels)?
3.   Do stories relate to:
     ■ strengths or weaknesses?
     ■ successes or failures?
     ■ conformity or mavericks?
4.   Who are the heroes and villains?
5.   What norms do the mavericks deviate from?

(b) Routines and rituals
1.   Which routines are emphasized?
2.   Which would look odd if changed?
3.   What behaviour do routines encourage?
4.   What are the key rituals?
5.   What core beliefs do they reflect?
6.   What do training programmes emphasize?
7.   How easy are rituals/routines changed?

(c) Symbols
1.   What language and jargon is used?
2.   How internal or accessible is it?
3.   What aspects of strategy are highlighted in public?
4.   What status symbols are there?
5.   Are there particular symbols which denote the organization?

(d) Organizational structure
1.   How mechanistic/organic are the structures?
2.   How flat/hierarchical are the structures?
3.   How formal/informal are the structures?
4.   Do structures encourage collaboration or competition?
5.   What type of power structures do they support?

(e) Control systems
1.   What is most closely monitored/controlled?
2.   Is emphasis on reward or punishment?
3.   Are controls related to history or current strategies?
4.   Are there many/few controls?

(f) Power structures
1.   What are the core beliefs of the leadership?
2.   How strongly held are these beliefs (idealists or pragmatists)?
3.   How is power distributed in the organization?
4.   Where are the main blockages to change?

(g) Overall
1.   What is the dominant organizational culture (defender, prospector, analyser)?
2.   How easy is this to change?
3.   Are there any linking threads through the separate elements?

Adapted from Johnson and Scholes (1993, p. 163). Reprinted by permission of Prentice Hall.

Organizational culture at this level is still tough to change, but not nearly as difficult as at the level of basic values because group members tend to behave in ways that teach these practices and values to new members, rewarding those that fit in and sanctioning those that do not.

This two-level model of organizational culture is very similar to an earlier model developed by Schein (1985). According to Schein, organizational culture is represented at three levels:

1. *Behaviours and artifacts*, i.e. easy to observe but difficult to decipher visible manifestations of an organizational culture such as behavioural patterns, dress codes and the way in which time and space are organized.
2. *Beliefs and values* about the world and how it actually works, i.e. the guiding beliefs, preferences and norms, and manifest or espoused values of the organization.
3. *Underlying assumptions* regarding the nature of human relationships and the relationship with nature, i.e. invisible, preconscious or unconscious cognitive structures that determine how group members perceive, think and feel.

These levels are arranged according to their visibility such that behaviours and artifacts are the easiest to observe, while the underlying assumptions need to be inferred. Although changes in behaviour may result in changes in underlying assumptions over time, this is most difficult as assumptions are considered to be taken for granted and out of awareness. It is the basic assumptions that confer meaning on the more manifest values and overt behaviour in the organization (Derr and Laurent, 1989). Although the most difficult to uncover, these assumptions help explain how managers interpret the social reality of their organizations (see Table 7.1 for questions to diagnose organizational culture).

Conceptualized in this way, organizational culture is not the same as a firm's 'ideology' or 'identity', although these terms (and others such as 'philosophy', 'climate' and 'recipe') are often used almost interchangeably by academics and practitioners because they can all play an important role in shaping people's behaviour (Kotter and Heskett, 1992). As Trice and Beyer (1984) point out, the culture of any organization is built around a shared ideology which binds some people together and helps members make sense of decisions. However, problems of interest to managers are better understood and addressed if a distinction is made between organizational culture and other concepts or organizational characteristics that influence how people think and behave (Sathe, 1985).

ORGANIZATIONAL CULTURES VERSUS NATIONAL CULTURES

Clearly, the topics of organizational culture and national culture overlap. In Chapter Three we described the phenonemon of organizational culture frequently acting to magnify differences between national cultures. Derr and Laurent (1989) argue that Schein's model of organizational culture can best be understood by linking it to the broader societal contexts that constitute national culture. Whilst organizational cultures are important in influencing and creating change in the upper levels of the organizational culture edifice, i.e. the individual behavioural norms, values and artifacts of organizations, national cultures have a more profound impact on underlying assumptions. The formative and homogeneous patterns in a manager's life – the early educational experience, family patterns, institutional arrangements, religious experiences and language – serve to develop Schein's underlying assumptions

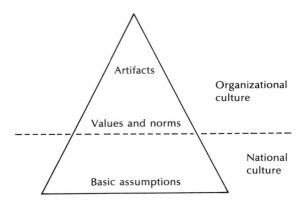

Figure 7.3 The relationship between different levels of organizational culture and national culture. *Source:* reproduced from C. B. Derr and A. Laurent, 'The internal and external career: a theoretical and cross-cultural perspective', in Arthur, Lawrence and Hall (eds), *Handbook of Career Theory.* Reprinted with permission of the publishers, Cambridge University Press, © 1989.

along national patterns. Multinational organizations may be able to change the upper levels of organizational culture (see Figure 7.3) through efforts at socializing employees and the various practices outlined in this chapter, but stand less chance of influencing the fundamental assumptions their employees have about life and work as these are rooted in the broad cultural settings of nations. We discuss the implications of this model for career management and the internationalization of managers in Chapter Eleven.

CLASSIFYING ORGANIZATIONAL CULTURES

The content of a culture refers to the relative ordering of basic values, which determines what policies and practices should prevail when conflicts arise between different sets of assumptions. For example, two organizations may each value teamwork and individual performance, but one organization may emphasize teamwork more in the decision making process and in its system of promotion and rewards, and individual performance may predominate in the other. The cultures of these two organizations consequently have quite different content, even though some of their basic values are the same. Handy (1976; 1987) describes four very different types of organizational culture which '. . . are founded and built over the years by the dominant groups in an organization', and '. . . turn organizations into cohesive tribes with distinctly clannish feelings'.

The power (Zeus) organizational culture

This type of culture is frequently found in small entrepreneurial organizations. The organization depends on a central power source, the spider in the centre of the web with colleagues on the same wavelength, and rays of power and influence spreading out from that central figure. There are few rules and procedures, little bureaucracy. Control is exercised by the centre largely through the selection of key individuals and by occasional forays from the centre or summonses to the centre. It is a political organizational culture in the sense that decisions are taken very largely on the balance of influence rather than on procedural or purely logical grounds.

The role (Apollo) organizational culture

This type of organizational culture is often stereotyped as bureaucracy, where the role, or job description, is more important than the individual who fills it. Individuals are rewarded for satisfactory performance of the role. Performance over and above the role prescription is not required, and indeed can be disruptive at times. Position power is the major power source in this organizational culture. Rules and procedures are the major methods of influence. Individuals are managed scientifically with precise and mechanical instructions. The efficiency of this organizational culture depends on the rationality of the allocation of the work and responsibility rather than on the individual personalities.

The task (Athena) organizational culture

This type is job or project orientated. The whole emphasis of the organizational culture is to get the job done. To this end, the task organizational culture seeks to bring together the appropriate resources, the right people at the right level of the organization, and to let them get on with it. It is typical of interdisciplinary project groups. Influence is based more on expert power than on position or personal power. This organizational culture is extremely adaptable. Groups, project teams, or task forces are formed for a specific purpose and can be reformed, abandoned or continued. Decisions over work methods are decentralized and formalized through joint disciplines. Individuals find in this organizational culture a high degree of control over their own work, judgement by results, easy working relationships within the group with mutual respect based on capacity rather than age or status.

The person (Dionysus) organizational culture

In this organizational culture the individual is the central point. If there is a structure or a formal organization it exists only to serve the interests of the individuals within it. Control mechanisms or management hierarchies are impossible in this organizational culture except by mutual consent. Relationships are characterized by bonds of respect. Influence is shared and power, if needed, is usually expert-based. Individuals do what they are exceptionally good at and are listened to on appropriate topics. Professional partnerships, volunteer organizations, and small consultancy organizations often have this type of organizational culture.

Deal and Kennedy (1982) developed a quadrant of organizational cultures, classifying organizations as either high or low in terms of the amount of risk, and speed of feedback. Regardless of the classification adopted, according to Handy (1976), the individual orientation of the key people in an organization will have a large say in determining what the dominant organizational culture is, irrespective of what it should be. In general, certain types of people will be happy and successful in one type of organizational culture, not in another. Time and success leads to a match between organizational culture and an individual's psychological contract.

THE ISSUE OF SUBCULTURES

Although we usually talk about organizational culture in the singular, most organizations have multiple cultures – usually associated with different functional groupings or hierarchical classifications (Louis, 1986). Even within a relatively small organization, there may be multiple and even conflicting subcultures (Kotter and Heskett, 1992). For example, research and development people may have different values towards risk taking than finance people, depending on the different requirements for success in their basic functions. Older employees may see the world differently than youngsters; mature businesses probably set different standards than the newest divisions.

Balancing the legitimate differences of subcultures with the legitimate and desirable elements of an organization's culture as a whole is one of the trickiest parts of diagnosing and managing organizational culture. A healthy tension among subcultures is desirable, but when the tension becomes pronounced and destructive, they can begin to work to the detriment of the organization as a whole. At a minimum, managers must know what is happening in existing subcultures and be alert to new ones that may emerge (Deal and Kennedy, 1982).

To gain a better understanding of the types of subculture existing in so-called 'talent-intensive' organizations, a research team from the Economist Intelligence Unit interviewed managers in large organizations. Three main subcultures were identified in the course of the study (see Illustration 7.2).

In addition to these three types of subculture, the researchers also found that different organizations had developed cultures in which different subcultures were the dominant ones in terms of influencing and exemplifying the organization's values, and in terms of receiving the highest rewards and the chances of moving into the organization's top jobs (see Table 7.2). Based on highly subjective classifications, the managerial culture appeared to be the dominant one in such organizations as ABB, J.P. Morgan, Unilever and Baxter Healthcare. The organizations dominated by a scientific, professional organizational culture included Glaxo Group Research in the UK, GSI in

Illustration 7.2 **Three functional subcultures.**

Managerial
Key values are efficiency, profit, growth, competitiveness, quality and service. Managers lean towards tight controls, particularly financial controls, clear structures, formal systematic procedures, measurement and quantification, certainty and acceptance of authority. Managers like money, power, status and upward mobility through a career structure. They behave and dress soberly and conventionally. They respect analytical ability, planning skills, numeracy, communication skills, decision making skills and so on.

Sales and marketing
Values relate primarily to competitiveness, growth and individual achievement. Less regard than among managers for formal procedures and tight financial controls, and little interest in quantitative analysis. In common with managers, this group is motivated by money and status. They allow more scope for individuality in dress and behaviour. The skills they respect are those that make for the successful salesperson, in particular communication, negotiation and interpersonal skills.

Professional, technical and scientific
Values are more determined by the professional group identified with than with the organization which employs them. Money and position in the hierarchy are relatively unimportant, compared to the challenge of the job and a sense of freedom and achievement.

Table 7.2 **Strengths and weaknesses of subcultures in talent-intensive organizations.**

	Strengths	Weaknesses
Managerial subculture	1. Clear strategic direction 2. Focus on the market and the customer 3. Strong systems and procedures	1. Inadequate understanding of core technology 2. Slow to innovate 3. Failure to attract/retain/motivate top technical/professional talent
Marketing subculture	1. Focus on the market and the customer 2. Responsive to changes in demand 3. Responsive to competitor behaviour	1. Inadequate understanding of core technology 2. Failure to attract/retain/motivate top technical/professional talent 3. (Sometimes) weak financial controls
Technical/ professional/ scientific subculture	1. Leadership in technical innovation 2. Strongly motivated technical/professional employees	1. Lack of clear business strategy 2. Failure to focus on market/customer need 3. Failure to focus on the bottom line 4. Often poor man management

France and SAS Institute in the USA. The marketing culture predominated in ICL, IBM and Coley Porter Bell.

WHAT MAKES SOME ORGANIZATIONAL CULTURES STRONGER THAN OTHERS?

In this third section of the chapter we consider what makes some organizational cultures stronger than others and the consequences of strong cultures. The strength of an organizational culture can be defined in terms of:

1. The homogeneity and stability of group membership.
2. The length and intensity of shared experiences of the group.

If a stable group has had a long, varied, intense history (i.e., if it has had to cope with many difficult survival problems and succeeded), it will have a strong and differentiated culture. By the same token, if a group has had a constantly shifting membership or has been together only for a short time and has not faced any difficult issues, it will, by definition, have a weak culture. Although individuals within that group may have very strong individual assumptions, there will not be enough shared experiences for the group as a whole to have a defined culture.

Schein (1981, p. 5).

The strength of an organizational culture is also defined by the intensity of its effects on organizational behaviour. The stronger the organizational culture, the more powerful its effects; the weaker the organizational culture, the less pervasive and direct the effects are. Organizations with strong cultures are usually seen by outsiders as having a certain 'style' – the Proctor and Gamble or Hewlett Packard 'way of doing things'. They often make some of their beliefs and values publicly known in a creed

Illustration 7.3 **Factors influencing the strength of organizational cultures.**

- Business environment and sector.
- Role of founder.
- Size and geographical dispersion.

- Myths, symbols and rites.
- Human resource management practices.

or mission statement such as 'Putting People First' (British Airways) or '24-Hour Parts Service Anywhere in the World' (Caterpillar), and seriously encourage all their employees to follow that statement. Furthermore, the style and values of a strong organizational culture tend to persist when a new leader takes charge – their roots go deep (Kotter and Heskett, 1992).

The strength of a specific organization's culture is determined by a number of factors (see Illustration 7.3). The influence of the business environment in general, and the industry in particular, is one important factor. For instance, organizations in industries characterized by rapid technological change, such as those in computer and electronics manufacturing, normally have organizational cultures that embody the ethic of product innovation to some degree. Those that don't might not survive (Sathe, 1985).

A pervasive role for founders

Although the business environment can have a profound effect on the values and beliefs of the members of an organization, environmental influences do not always push the cultures of companies in the same direction. Systematic differences exist between organizations with regard to values about how people should behave at work and with regard the tasks and goals that really matter, even if they belong to the same industry. The values and belief of the organization's founder may explain some of the differences.

Groups and organizations do not form accidentally or spontaneously. They are usually created because someone takes a leadership role in seeing how the concerted action of a number of people could accomplish something that would be impossible through individual action alone. In this process the founder will have a major impact on how the group solves its external survival and internal integration problems. In my experience, entrepreneurs are very strong-minded in what to do and how to do it. Typically they already have strong assumptions about the nature of the world, the role their organization will play in that world, the nature of human nature, truth, relationships, time, and space.   Schein (1983).

According to Schein (1983), each of the mechanisms listed opposite is used by founders and key leaders to embed a value or assumption they hold, though the message may be very implicit in the sense that the leader is not aware of sending it. Leaders also may be in conflict, which results in conflicting messages. A given mechanism may convey the message very explicitly, ambiguously, or totally implicitly. The mechanisms listed in Illustration 7.4 move from more or less explicit to more or less implicit ones.

Size and geographical dispersion of the workforce

Normally, a smaller workforce and more localized operations facilitate the growth of a strong organizational culture because it is easier for values and beliefs to develop and

Illustration 7.4 **Mechanisms for embedding organizational culture.**

1. Formal statements of organizational philosophy:
   - charters,
   - creeds,
   - materials used for recruitment and selection,
   - socialization material.
2. Design of physical spaces, facades, buildings.
3. Deliberate role modeling, teaching and coaching by leaders.
4. Explicit reward and status systems, promotion criteria.
5. Stories, legends, myths, and parables about key people and events.
6. What leaders pay attention to, measure and control.
7. Leader reactions to critical incidents and organizational crises:
   - times when organizational survival is threatened,
   - norms are unclear or are challenged,
   - reaction to insubordination,
   - threatening or meaningful events.
8. How the organization is designed and structured:
   - the design of work,
   - who reports to whom,
   - degree of centralization,
   - functional or other criteria for differentiation,
   - mechanisms used for integration.
9. Organizational systems and procedures:
   - types of information, control, and decision support systems,
   - categories of information,
   - time cycles,
   - who gets what information,
   - when and how performance appraisal and other review processes are conducted.
10. Criteria used for recruitment, selection, promotion, levelling off, retirement, and 'communication' of people who 'fit' or don't 'fit' membership roles and key slots in the organization.

Source: Schein (1983).

become widely shared. Yet, larger organizations with worldwide operations can also have strong organizational cultures that derive from a continuity of strong leadership, as well as a consistent set of HRM policies.

Myths, symbols and rites

The importance of myths, symbols and rites is seen by the outline of organizational culture at Tandem Computers (see Illustration 7.5). A *myth* is a dramatic narrative of imagined events, usually to explain the origins or transformation of something. It is also an unquestioned belief about the practical benefits of certain techniques and behaviour that is not supported by demonstrated fact (Trice, 1985). For example, in almost any organization, there are stories that go around the grapevine about how someone saved the day by extra-ordinary initiative and dedication to customer service (Torrington and Hall, 1991). How much truth and how much fiction there are in the myths and stories is not important. They are a way of transmitting feelings and values in the organization and are part of the organizational custom and traditions.

Symbols are objects to which organizational meaning has been attached. They include things such as titles, special parking places, special eating facilities, company cars, office size, carpets, furniture, and other expressions of position and power within the organization (Pfeffer, 1981). In addition, the company logo often provides a symbol of corporate identity, which everyone can see, understand and share. For example, the Nestlé logo, a nest of birds, stands for childhood, family, tradition and security, the core values of the organization's founder and his successors up to this day.

Rites are relatively elaborate, dramatic, planned sets of activities that consolidate

Table 7.3 Types of rite and their role in organizational culture change.

Types of rite	Example	Manifest expressive social consequences	Examples of possible latent expressive consequences
Rites of passage	Induction and basic training, US Army	Facilitate transition of people into social roles and statuses that are new for them	Minimize changes in ways people carry out social roles Re-establish equilibrium in onging relations
Rites of degradation	Firing and replacing top executive	Dissolve social identities and their attendant power	Provide public acknowledgement that problems exist and what their details are Defend group boundaries by redefining who belongs and who does not Reaffirm social importance and value of role involved
Rites of enhancement	Mary Kay cosmetics seminars	Enhance social identities and their attendant power	Spread good news about the organization Provide public recognition of individuals for their accomplishments and motivate others to similar efforts Enable the organization to take some credit for individual accomplishments Emphasize social value of performance of social roles
Rites of renewal	Organizational development activities	Refurbish social structures; improve the ways they function	Reassure members that something is being done about problems Disguise nature of the problems Defer acknowledgement of problems and away from others Legitimate and reinforce existing systems of power and authority Deflect attention from solving problems
Rights of conflict reduction	Collective bargaining	Reduce conflict and aggression	Compartmentalize conflict and its disruptive effects Re-establish equilibrium in disturbed social relations
Rites of integration	Office Christmas party	Encourage and revive shared feelings that bind people together and keep them committed to a social system	Permit venting of emotion and temporary loosening of various norms Reassert and reaffirm, by contrast, moral rightness of usual norms

Source: reprinted with kind permission of the publishers, Jossey-Bass, Inc., from H.M. Trice and J.M. Beyer, 'Using six organizational rites to change culture', in R.H. Kilmann, M.J. Saxton, R. Serra and associates, Gaining Control of the Corporate Culture, Table 1, pp. 374–5. Copyright 1985 by Jossey-Bass, Inc., publishers.

Illustration 7.5 **Tandem computers: a strong organizational culture.**

Tandem Computers was 'founded on a well ordered set of management beliefs and practices'. The organization is said to have 'no formal organization chart and no formal rules', yet employees keep 'off each others toes' and work productively 'in the same direction' because of the 'unwritten rules and shared understandings'. This condition is maintained 'because top management spends considerable time in training and in communicating the management philosophy and the essence of the organization, because achievements consistent with the organizational culture are regularly recognized on bulletin boards as Our Latest Greatest, and because rituals such as the Friday afternoon beer-bust symbolize that organizational culture. All this makes employees feel like they belong to an exclusive club. Most develop great respect for and loyalty to that club, a feeling which often translates into long hours of hard, productive work'. The strong organizational culture is also maintained by a relatively stable and long-tenured work force. Tandem's staff turnover is one third the national average for the computer industry.

Source: Deal and Kennedy (1982).

various forms of cultural expressions into one event, which is carried out through social interactions, usually for the benefit of an audience. Trice and Beyer (1984) have identified four types of rite that they believe occur in organizations (see Table 7.3 also):

1. 'Rites of passage' intend to facilitate transition of persons into social roles and statuses that are new for them. For example, new employees are told on their first workday what are the organization rules and regulations, to do particularly unpleasant tasks, or to undergo certain ordeals before they are really 'one of us'.
2. 'Rites of enhancement' increase the status or position of a person after he or she is in the organization, such as awarding symbols of achievement or announcing promotion at office parties or during social events.
3. 'Rites of renewal' refurbish social structures and improve organizational functioning. These rites often take the form of different types of training and development programmes.
4. 'Rites of integration' are intended to encourage and revive common feelings that bind members together and commit them to the organization. Examples are office parties and annual picnics.

THE LINK BETWEEN ORGANIZATIONAL CULTURE AND HRM PRACTICES

Why should organizational culture form the opening topic in our discussion of the content of HRM practices? The logic of how HRM relates to organizational culture involves three ideas (see Illustration 7.6). The first concerns goal alignment. In an organization with a strong culture, methods of recruitment and selection as well as appraisal and promotion give important signals to employees about the values of the

Illustration 7.6 **Contribution of HRM practices to organizational culture.**

- Goal and value alignment.
- Organizational cohesion.

- Structure and controls.

organization. In organizations like Procter and Gamble, the process of communicating core values to new employees begins even before they enter the organization. During the recruitment and selection process, there are systematic opportunities for both the organization and the prospective employees to gauge whether they are going to get along. Well conceived orientation programmes facilitate the communication of core values. These programmes present important facts about the organization, its goals, its functions, its history and its mission. Most importantly, these messages are delivered by trained people. Once hired, guidelines for acceptable and rewardable behaviour are introduced, and new members begin incorporating these into their personal value system.

HRM practices also help form and support organizational culture by creating a higher level of organizational cohesion. One example of this is the growing use of training and development programmes to increase the level and frequency of communication between different parts of the organization. Traditionally, training and development activities have been viewed as a method of improving skills and knowledge of workers. Recently, however, organizations have begun increasingly to use these activities to deliver organizational philosophy and to increase the exchange of ideas and experience among members. The ultimate objective is very often to improve individual and organizational performance by breaking down barriers to intergroup co-ordination.

Finally, HRM practices are sometimes said to strengthen organizational culture by providing needed structure and controls without having to rely on bureaucratic methods of supervision that can stifle flexibility and innovation. When the human resource function can recruit, select, and place employees in ways that create a high degree of 'fit' between the individual and organizational values, there is less need for the use of rules, procedures and other bureaucratic mechanisms to control behaviour and assess performance.

CAN ORGANIZATIONAL CULTURE BE MANAGED THROUGH HRM?

In this fourth section we consider the link between HRM and organizational culture and the various mechanisms involved in changing organizational cultures. Can organizational culture be managed through HRM? Research and case study experience reveals four perspectives. Empirical observation has often pointed to the failure of planned change (Beer *et al.*, 1990; Deal and Kennedy, 1982). A second perspective points to the probability of making minor alterations in limited areas (Martin and Siehl, 1983). A third perspective, based on best practice case studies, points to the achievement of cultural metamorphoses on the back of time consuming, expensive and difficult interventions (Johnston, 1991; Scholz, 1987). Finally, the fourth perspective argues that organizational cultures inevitably change as part of a natural process of management initiation and shaping. By understanding the dynamics of the learning process, it is possible to help direct and steer this evolution (Payne, 1991; Schein, 1989; Trice and Beyer, 1986). Indeed, Pascale (1985) has pointed to the important role of socialization of new members in steering and maintaining organizational cultures (see Figure 7.4).

It is difficult to separate the topic of organization culture from that of leadership. Corporate leadership can never be a passive observer when organizational cultures are changed. Leaders are both a prime artefact and shaper of such change (Ott, 1989). Consequently, planned intervention in the selection, development and retention of leaders becomes a central element of any effort to change the organizational culture.

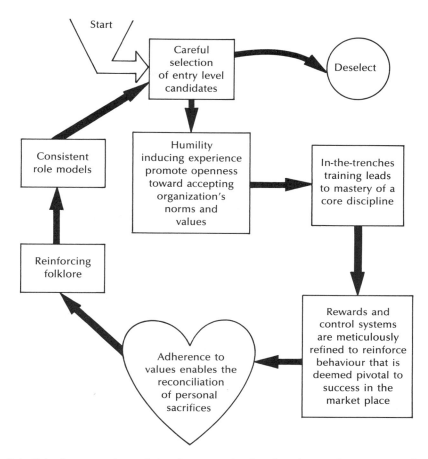

Figure 7.4 Bringing members into the organizational culture. *Source*: Pascale (1985). Copyright © 1985 by the Regents of the University of California. Reprinted from the *Californian Management Review*, Vol. 27, no. 2, 26–41, by permission of the Regents.

However, there are many who would be concerned that a strong focus on using HRM policies to 'socialize' and 'enculturate' the newly recruited leaders of the future will merely serve to recreate the grey-suited, conforming, conceptually-bereft 'organization men' favoured in the 1950s and 1960s. We cannot think about such socialization attempts without also re-examining the skills and competences that should be 'enculturated' into the organization.

Payne (1991) believes that organizational cultures evolve through a series of stages: conception, conversion, consolidation, change or collapse (see Figure 7.5). Whilst the organizational culture is determined initially by senior managers, HRM managers can advise on the suitability of actions and HRM policies to the organizational culture, acting as 'stewards'. The HRM function has control over many of the processes which help senior managers develop and nurture an organizational culture suitable to long-term goals (see Illustration 7.7). These can help develop organizational cultures through three processes:

1. Leading.
2. Communicating.
3. Controlling.

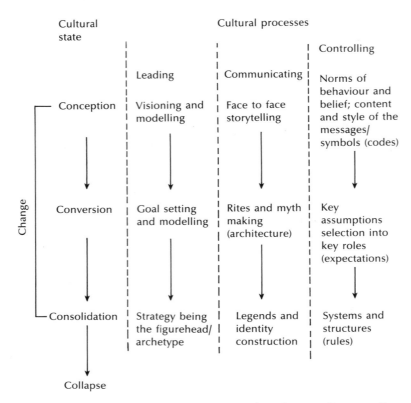

Figure 7.5 Development/creation of organizational cultures. *Source*: Payne (1991), reprinted with permission, © R. Payne, 1993.

A technique used by many organizations to make HRM interventions in order to help steer cultural change is to perform some form of 'organizational culture gap analysis'. This is usually facilitated by the use of a questionnaire or inventory which can be used to represent the existing and desired organizational culture in terms of the overall organization climate, the values, attitudes and behavioural norms that are prevalent. Whilst this only represents one level of organizational culture, it is often the most easily understood and accepted side for managers. Such instruments usually measure this level of organizational culture along several dimensions. The data gathered can be used to identify the most notable gaps between the organizational culture as espoused, and the organizational culture as actually experienced. The information is often used to set in place a variety of HRM responses (see Illustration 7.8).

Illustration 7.7 **HRM processes which may steward the evolution of organizational culture.**

- ■ Selection, recruitment and induction.
- ■ Career development and promotion.
- ■ Coherent training and development.

- ■ Control of communication messages and images.
- ■ Influence on reward system.

Source: Payne (1991).

Illustration 7.8 **Typical HRM interventions informed by an organizational culture gap analysis.**

- Measuring the progress of organizational culture-change programmes focused on customer service, total quality management or empowerment, and targeting further action.
- Developing a total rewards management approach, designing rewards systems (remuneration, direct benefits and indirect benefits) to close negative organizational culture gaps.
- Designing team building interventions to address significant cultural mismatches arising after organization change events, such as mergers and acquisitions.

- Strategy articulation processes, helping top teams to describe what a new strategy or change in organization structure may well look like in behavioural, value and management style terms.
- Setting cultural imperatives for the design and introduction of new technology, by providing system designers with targeted cultural changes that the new technology must help produce.
- Establishing the requirement for future management competencies, skills, attitudes and behaviours.

Pettigrew (1985) believes HRM managers should be wary of attempting such precise measurement and intervention. He believes that organizational culture is manageable, but only with extreme difficulty (see Illustration 7.9). The difficulties arise because they vary in terms of:

- The level at which they are visible, from core beliefs through to behaviours.
- Their pervasiveness in terms of breadth and depth.
- Their implicitness, and the extent to which they are built into patterns of thinking and ways of doing things that are taken for granted.
- The amount of imprinting, with difficulties in attempting to rewrite the heavy hand of history.
- Their plurality, with the presence of numerous subcultures.
- Their interdependency, with connections into other systems in the organization such as politics.

Illustration 7.9 **Key management tasks in changing organizational culture.**

- An external business context creating pressure for change coupled with the internal management skill to mobilize this context and create a receptive climate for the difficult messages.
- Leadership behaviour from high ranking new blood, from both internal resource routes or external recruitment.
- The existence of a vision for the business that is still imprecise and open to further articulation, i.e. malleable.
- Use of deviants and heretics to say the unsayable and think the unthinkable.
- Releasing avenues and energy for change by moving people around and changing business portfolios.

- Creating new meetings and other arenas that bypass the formal organization and help articulate the change and focus energy.
- Altering management processes from the top to ensure they are cohesive and coherent.
- Reinforcing early cultural shifts through closely matched changes to the structure, and public use of the reward systems.
- Finding and using role models to display the organizational culture and 'walk the talk'.
- Use of training and development strategies to carry new processes deep into the organization.
- Transmitting new beliefs and behaviour by revamping communication mechanisms.

Source: Pettigrew (1985).

CLUB MÉDITERRANÉE (CLUB MED): SELECTING FOR CUSTOMER SERVICE

Under the leadership of Gilbert Trigano, Club Med was the innovator of the village vacation concept in which vacationers pass their time in a location where everything is provided. Food, lodging, entertainment and access to sports facilities are all included in the price and are paid for in advance. At Club Med, the HRM policies and practices are all orientated towards achieving total customer satisfaction. This philosophy comes from its history. When the Club Med started up in the 1950s, it was truly a club and had a non-profit status. The objective was for members to enjoy a vacation together in a beautiful location.

The spirit of the Club in the 1950s was to live side by side with our guests; we wanted them to be happy. The Club's organizers became so involved in the managing of the Club that they became full time organizers, calling themselves 'gentil organizateurs' (GO) or kind organizers. The other participants and their guests subsequently became the 'gentils membres' (GM) or kind members.

Michel Perchet, Human Resources, Club Med in Horovitz and Jurgens-Panak (1992).

To reinforce its philosophy, Club Med has a policy that no GO is ever off duty. As long as he or she is at the Club, the GO is always available to the members and prepared to help them, play with them or party with them. Moreover, GOs have total freedom to ensure that the guests have as nice a vacation as possible. Gentil organizateurs need autonomy to give good service and have to be able to step out of the mould and treat each customer as an individual. The ratio of GMs to GOs is four to one.

The HRM practices of Club Med support its organizational culture. GOs are recruited for their outgoing personalities and are tested using psychometrics on how they are likely to react in certain situations and on their customer service attitude.

We look for people who have a welcoming way about them. We also want people who can adapt rapidly to different situations, different cultures, different people. Then they are trained. GOs are trained even before they are officially hired. Some don't make it through the training; they decide that the Club is not for them. But, even the greenest GOs any GM will meet have been trained for over a month.   Horovitz and Jurgens-Panak (1992).

To improve GOs' work performance, Club Med has developed a system of employee evaluation which pushes GOs to attain ever greater customer satisfaction. Customer satisfaction is measured every week for each individual GO and the results go directly to the village chief. It is called a 'Barometer'. Each GO's individual performance is also measured by performance appraisal. GOs are also evaluated on their contributions to improving service, mainly through their participation in error chasing groups in which employees identify the cause and possible solutions to incidents.

In addition, the organization believes that staff should spend no more than one year in any location; sometimes they stay as little as six months. In between postings or 'seasons', GOs are trained, sometimes for two months, in one of Club Med's training centres. In this way, employees learn to keep an eye on their customers and to ensure the same kind of service quality wherever they go with the group.

IS THERE A LINK BETWEEN STRONG ORGANIZATIONAL CULTURE AND PERFORMANCE?

A specific organization's culture will be strongly influenced by the various factors discussed above. But does organizational culture make a difference in terms of the attitudes and motivation of employees and long-term competitiveness? Jacques Solvay, chairman of the Belgian chemical company, claims that a strong organizational culture is essential.

I am convinced, together with all those who are interested in the success of a company, that what is most important today within a company or a group is neither what it does nor where it is located. It is the way in which it works which makes all the difference and distinguishes it from its competitors. And the way in which the company carries out its operations is precisely its company culture. It is this which enables it to motivate its personnel, which leads them to work together in a climate of trust and reliance and with the desire to complete an interesting project in which all its members are involved. This is the vital ingredient for success.

This view is echoed by Horovitz and Jurgens-Panak (1992) in *Total Customer Satisfaction*.

Having the right culture is crucial to achieving good service quality. In all the companies we looked at, this was the element that managers cited as contributing the most to good customer service. It directed employees' efforts when no points of reference were available, it motivated them towards ever greater achievements and it kept them thinking of the customer.
Horovitz and Jurgens-Panak (1992, p. 1).

Several studies have supported this assertion. For instance, Sheridan (1992) examined the retention rates of 904 college graduates hired in six public accounting organizations over a six year period. The data showed that organizational culture has a significant effect on the rates at which the newly hired employees voluntarily terminated employment. Individuals hired in the organizations emphasizing the interpersonal values of teamwork and respect for people stayed fourteen months longer than those hired in the organizations emphasizing the work task values of detail and stability. The estimated cost of this effect was over 6 million dollars in revenues and replacement expenses.

Going far beyond previous empirical work, Kotter and Heskett (1992) examined the relationship between organizational culture and economic performance in more than 200 worldwide organizations and found that shared values and unwritten rules can profoundly enhance economic success, but only if the resulting actions fit an intelligent business strategy for the specific environment in which the organization operates. As they point out:

Performance will not be enhanced if the common behaviors and methods of doing business do not fit the needs of a firm's product or service market, financial market, and labor market. Strong cultures with practices that do not fit a company's context can actually lead intelligent people to behave in ways that are destructive – that systematically undermine an organization's ability to survive or prosper.
Kotter and Heskett (1992).

To test this idea, Kotter and Heskett (1992) asked a group of investment analysts to rate a large number of organizations by how much each valued customers, shareholders and employees (see Illustration 7.10). Managers and employees at the organizations were also interviewed. From this data, twelve organizations were identified whose organizational cultures valued all of the three major stakeholders. A

Illustration 7.10 **Performance of multi-stakeholder culture organizations.**

The results showed that, over an eleven-year period, in the 12 organizations in the first group:

- Revenues increased, on average, by four times as much compared to the 20 organizations in the second group.
- Workforces expanded by eight times as much.

- Share prices increased by twelve times as much.
- Net profits soared by an average of 756 per cent during the period, compared with an average increase of only 1 per cent for the organizations in the second group.

Source: Kotter and Heskett (1992).

further twenty were identified which did precisely the opposite; whose managers, according to the analysts, cared mostly about 'themselves'.

This research shows that even contextually or strategically appropriate organizational cultures will not increase performance over long periods unless they contain norms and values that can help organizations adapt faster and better to a changing environment. Organizational cultures that are not adaptive take many forms. In large organizations, they are often characterized by some arrogance, insularity and bureaucratic centralization, all supported by a value system that cares more about self-interest than about employees, shareholders and customers (Kotter and Heskett, 1992). In other words, cultural strength is an important asset that can become a liability.

Illustration 7.11 **Nestlé: maintaining organizational culture and performance throughout growth by acquisitions.**

Nestlé was founded in 1867 by Henri Nestlé, a German chemist who came to live in Switzerland. The company makes chocolate and coffee, but it is also a worldwide group active in practically every segment of the food manufacturing industry selling hundreds of different brands.

When Helmut Maucher became Managing Director in 1981, he made a number of significant changes. For example, he banned the existing monthly twenty-five page reports and quarterly profit and loss statements, in favour of a monthly one page report which highlights key numbers such as turnover, working capital and inventories. 'With quarterly reports all managers care about is the next three months', he explained, 'and they manage for the next quarter instead of for the next five years'.

Under Mr Maucher's direction Nestlé also made significant product line and geographic changes, divesting low profit businesses like Libby's $1800 million canned food business and acquiring twenty companies (at a price of $5 billion) between 1983 and 1985. The largest acquisition was the US-based Carnation, purchased in 1985 for $2.9 billion. Since then, the organization has grown regularly by successive mergers and acquisitions of more than sixteen major companies (see the case in Chapter Five).

In spite of the pace of its acquisition programme, Nestlé has been able to retain a strong organizational culture. Its logo, a nest of birds, is almost the same as it was in 1867, standing for the values of the organization and its founder. Mr Maucher strongly believes that any acquisition that Nestlé made needed to fit into the company's strategy and culture. 'We are not portfolio managers', he once said. 'Acquisitions are part of an overall development strategy. That's why we cannot leave acquisitions decisions to purely financial considerations. Of course, you must have some figures to evaluate an acquisition, but more important is the feel you have about what you can do with the brand and the people.'

Source: James Ellert and Peter Killing, IMD Case Study GM 432 (1992).

Culture becomes a liability when important shared beliefs and values interfere with the needs of the business and of the company and the people who work for it. To the extent that the content of a company's culture leads its people to think and act in inappropriate ways, culture's efficiency will not help achieve effective results. This condition is usually a significant liability because it is hard to change culture's content.   Sathe (1985).

Horovitz and Jurgens-Panak (1992), describe fifty examples of European organizations recognized for the quality of service they provide. In all the organizations they looked at, organizational culture was the element that managers cited as contributing the most

Illustration 7.12 **The Bekaert Group: implementing a total quality culture through communication and training.**

N.V. Bekaert is a Belgian multinational company with forty-eight manufacturing facilities in fifteen countries producing steel wire and related products. The largest manufacturing unit and headquarters of the company are located in West Flanders, where the company was founded by the Bekaert family in 1880. The Bekaert Group sells its products through twenty-eight sales offices and a large number of agencies located throughout the world. In 1993 the consolidated revenues amounted to BF 73 million.

The international expansion of the Bekaert Group started in the 1920s as a survival strategy in the face of crisis and protectionism. Steel wire and steel cord represent 96 per cent of the total turnover. The remaining 4 per cent are realized in engineering products, new industrial products and services.

During the late 1970s there was a growing awareness and consensus among Bekaert managers that high quality of products and services was essential to make the company successful in the international marketplace. Therefore, after running a highly successful pilot project for quality improvement in Belgium, in November 1983 a Total Quality Management programme was launched for all the operating units of the company. This resulted in the establishment of TQM Steering Committees at the unit level and the development of a Beliefs and Mission Statement which emphasizes quality, customer satisfaction, safety and innovation.

Bekaert employees typically describe the culture of the organization as open, energetic, communicative and results-oriented. This view reflects the Group's policy which strives to establish relationships among employees that are based on honesty, trust, teamwork and joint problem solving.

Human resource management played an important role within the Bekaert Group as a tool for stimulating and guiding the cultural shift towards improved quality and performance. For example, at the managerial level, the reward system was changed in 1988 to emphasize and recognize the importance of teamwork. This change also resulted in a new performance appraisal system which evaluates the competencies of managers. In addition, special training programmes have been created for workers, supervisors and managers. The company has now progressed to the point where every new employee receives five days' training as part of his or her induction process.

To achieve the cultural changes needed to support the quality improvement efforts, Bekaert managers also rely on direct communication and participation. For instance, throughout the change programme, informal lunch meetings were organized between Mr Karel Vinck – the CEO – and a group of employees randomly chosen from all levels and parts of the organization. During these meetings, Mr Vinck explained the strategy of the Group and asked employees for their suggestions and ideas regarding the implementation of the TQM programme. In addition, the CEO and members of the Executive Committee regularly organized meetings with managers, employees and representatives of the work force on major issues or barriers for continuous improvement.

In 1988, fourteen European companies (including multinationals such as Bosch, British Telecom, Ciba-Geigy, KLM, and Nestlé) formed the European Foundation for Quality Management. In recognition of its initiatives and efforts to strengthen the role of management in quality improvement, Bekaert was the first Belgian company to become a member of this group.

to good customer service and effective corporate performance. For Nestlé, as with many other European organizations given the discussion in Chapter Five, the difficulty has been maintaining its organizational culture throughout a sustained period of acquisition (see Illustration 7.11, p. 234).

The Bekaert Group – a Belgian company with 48 manufacturing facilities in fifteen countries producing steel wire and related products – relied heavily on training and communication to introduce its Total Quality Management programme throughout the organization (see Illustration 7.12, p. 235). This method of managing organizational culture is particularly important in a large manufacturing organization like the Bekaert Group where a large proportion of the workforce is unionized and continuous improvements in quality, safety and productivity are essential to achieve long-term goals.

WHY LARGE-SCALE CHANGE PROGRAMMES FREQUENTLY FAIL

In this fifth and final section of the chapter we consider why many change programmes fail and provide some case examples of attempts to change organizational culture. Recent studies underscore how incredibly difficult it is to change organizational culture. For instance, in a four year study of organizational change at six large corporations in the US, Beer, Eisenstat and Spector (1990) found that most organization-wide change programmes (mission statements, organizational culture programmes, training courses, quality circles, and new pay-for-performance systems) had virtually no impact or transfer into behaviour. In actual fact, the researchers found that exactly the opposite is true:

... the greatest obstacle to revitalization is the idea that it comes about through company-wide change programs, particularly when a corporate staff group such as human resources sponsors them. We call this 'the fallacy of programmatic change'. Just as important, formal organization structure and systems cannot lead to a corporate renewal process.

> Beer, Eisenstat and Spector (1990).

Illustration 7.13 **Why large-scale programmes do not produce change.**

Based on the experiences of six large US organizations where top management was attempting to revitalize the corporation, there are seven major reasons for the failure of organization-wide change programmes.

1. They focus exclusively on global business issues and have little to do with short-term critical issues.
2. They rely heavily on education and training methods that raise expectations and frequently lead to increased frustration when employees get back on the job.
3. They facilitate the use of new buzz words like 'quality', 'empowerment', and 'participation' rather than changes in what people do.
4. They are driven by an exclusive project team with little devolved control.
5. They focus exclusively on one or, at best, two of the factors that need to be changed for corporate revitalization, such as the organization's patterns of co-ordination, new competencies and employee commitment.
6. They are vulnerable to changing business priorities.
7. They are guided by a theory of change that is fundamentally flawed, such as the belief that changes in attitudes will automatically lead to changes in individual behaviour.

Source: Beer, Eisenstat and Spector (1990).

Illustration 7.14 **Six steps to successful change.**

1. Mobilize commitment to change through joint diagnosis of business problems.
2. Develop a shared vision of how to organize and manage for competitiveness.
3. Foster consensus for the new vision, competence to enact it, and cohesion to move it along.
4. Spread revitalization to all departments without pushing it from the top.
5. Institutionalize revitalization through formal policies, systems, and structures.
6. Monitor and adjust strategies in response to problems in the revitalization process.

Source: Beer, Eisenstat, and Spector (1990).

Yet, competitive pressures are causing organizations in Europe to move to change the thinking, the attitudes and the behaviour patterns of employees inside their organizations, as we made clear in Chapter Four.

In the last ten years, dozens of large corporations have undergone some version of a culture change initiative. Labelled revitalization, renewal, large scale systems change, transformation, or reengineering, many executives have attempted to alter fundamentally how work is done in their companies. Porter and Parker (1992).

But while senior managers understand the necessity of change to cope with new competitive realities, they often misunderstand what it takes to bring it about (Beer, Eisenstat and Spector, 1990). Many organizational culture-change programmes are open to the short-term pragmatists and cynics in the organization, who can claim with some evidence: 'this too will pass' (see Illustration 7.13). The more successful tactics are shown in Illustration 7.14.

METHODS OF ORGANIZATIONAL CULTURE CHANGE

Although organizational change has been written about extensively and in various ways, no one model has been articulated which defines precisely how organizational culture can be changed (Porter and Parker, 1992). Some writers have taken a rather mechanistic approach. For example, Pettigrew and Whipp (1991) suggest that there are a set of 'levers' for change which managers can employ (although in so doing go on to stress the highly political and context-sensitive nature of organizational culture change). Other writers have emphasized the role of the manager as change agent, sometimes laying particular stress on the charisma and vision of the leader (Johnson and Scholes, 1993; Wilson, 1992). Most writers focus on three aspects of managing change in organizational cultures: people, management systems and structures (see Illustration 7.15). These are topics that are covered throughout the rest of this book.

Illustration 7.15 **Main methods for changing organizational culture.**

- Changing people.
- Changing structure.
- Changing management systems.

Source: McBeath (1990).

Changing people

This approach is reflected in new methods of recruitment, selection, transferring employees and releasing them. For example, if a number of key managers are removed and replaced by strong supporters of the new organizational culture, it is likely that the message will be clearly understood and employee attitude and behaviour will be reshaped on the new course. In one example of this sort, McBeath (1990) refers to an organization in which the externally recruited chief executive decided that the only way a strong people-orientated organizational culture could be changed was by wiping out the existing top management completely. The combination of the 'alien' action of getting rid of the top people and introducing a deliberately intensive 'achieve or be fired' message 'unfroze' and destroyed much of the old organizational culture quickly and enabled the organization to respond more alertly to its rapidly changing environment. However, surviving old employees insist that the organization is no longer a good employer, but it is expanding and profitable after near bankruptcy.

Changing structure

We consider the role of changing organizational structure in the next chapter. As will be shown it tends to include four types of changes. Restructuring typically involves:

1. Changes to the composition of the organization's stakeholders.
2. Decentralization.
3. Job redesign to increase role flexibility.
4. Introducing new structures to cater for new needs (see Illustration 7.16).

Changing management systems

The most frequently changed systems are:

1. Budgeting and control systems
2. Human resource management systems such as rewards, training and appraisal (see Illustration 7.17).

What are the key factors that separate successful from less successful change efforts? While it is useful to identify the levers and mechanisms of organizational culture change, managers in general and HRM managers in particular need to know which are the critical success factors associated with organizational culture change. To understand better how organizational culture change can be successful in large

Illustration 7.16 **Creation of Alcomm as an independent business unit within Ciba-Geigy.**

The aim at Alcomm was a change in values, attitudes and behaviour. It wanted its people to be market-oriented, business-like, to take initiatives, and be willing to take risks. Alcomm felt that the only solution to achieve this was to give the workforce more responsibility because traditional, centralist organizations react too slowly to change.

Source: Wissema (1992).

Illustration 7.17 **International Service Systems.**

International Service Systems (ISS), a Danish multinational organization with an annual turnover of DKr10 billion and over 115,000 employees in the professional cleaning, security and building maintenance businesses, has relied heavily on training as the principal method of improving the quality awareness of its people and to implement its high-standard service strategy. There are basically three types of training being done at ISS:

■ Introductory training, done when the employee first joins the organization.

■ Specialized skills training, done to prepare an employee for a specific and specialized task.
■ Promotional and managerial training which qualifies employees to advance to higher levels of responsibility within the organization.

Overall, ISS sees training as an absolute necessity. As one employee put it, 'If you don't train people, you don't deliver the product. It's as simple as that.'

Source: Horowitz and Jurgens-Panak (1992).

organizations, we outline the change process at four famous European organizations that have tried recently to change fundamentally the way in which employees think and behave. The first example of how training and other HRM practices can be used intensively to change the culture of an organization is the well known British Airways case. It emphasizes the possibility of creating transformational change.

BRITISH AIRWAYS: A CASE OF TRANSFORMATIONAL CHANGE?

A number of writers have focused on the British Airways case (Hampden-Turner, 1990; Garratt, 1991; Goodstein and Burke, 1991; and Lauermann, 1992). When Sir Colin Marshall took over as Chief Executive of British Airways (BA) in early 1983, the pressures to change exerted on the organization by the external environment were broad and intense. The growing deregulation of international air traffic, the decision to convert the organization from government ownership to private ownership, and the rising cost of labour in Britain in the late 1970s all required fundamental change to the existing structure and organizational culture in order to make the organization profitable and ensure survival. The pressures became critical when Britain's worst recession in fifty years reduced passenger numbers and raised fuel costs substantially. Marshall made customer service a personal crusade from the day he entered BA.

It was really Marshall focusing on almost nothing else. The one thing that had overriding attention in the first three years he was there was customer service, customer service, customer service, nothing else. That was the only thing he was interested in, and it's not an exaggeration to say that was his exclusive focus. Goodstein and Burke (1991).

The methods used by Marshall to achieve this organizational culture change were massive and widespread. They included:

■ A large scale programme of briefings and training.
■ Strong internal communication of new sets of values and expected behaviour.
■ Significant downsizing of the workforce.
■ Changing organizational structures and systems.
■ Redefinition of the business priorities.
■ Continued commitment of top management.

Getting the right people into key jobs was a further element. Inevitably, over a period of several years there were many people changes; plus a massive investment in team building and process consultation to heighten involvement. For example, in 1983 the organization began to put a third of its staff through a training programme called 'Putting People First' in which groups were shown 'how their own attitudes towards the customer, and towards their own colleagues, affected the way in which customer saw them' (Sir Colin Marshall, Turnaround). Some 40,000 employees attended these sessions between November 1983 and June 1985, with the organization spending several million pounds on the programme. In the end the course was so popular that practically every employee at BA went through it. A follow-up programme was launched in 1986 called 'A Day in the Life'. This was designed to give employees an understanding of the work done by others in different parts of the organization. It was also succeeded by 'To Be the Best', which focused on competition, and 'Managing People First', which helped managers to motivate, take responsibility, delegate, plan and create a vision. It was designed to develop a consensus among managers of where the organization was heading.

We realized that a clear definition of strategy and what customers desire were the foundation which enabled the organization to redesign its change approach and grow. We had to articulate clearly what we were trying to accomplish in the organization and what customers value in products/services as well as in other areas, so that all the changes could be tied to implementing the strategy and delivering customer value.

Sir Colin Marshall, CEO British Railways. *Source*: Kotter and Leahey (1990).

Table 7.4 **Applying Lewin's model to the British Airways change programme.**

Levels	Unfreezing	Movement	Refreezing
Individual	Downsizing of workforce (59,000 to 37,000); middle management especially hard-hit New top management team 'Putting People First'	Acceptance of concept of 'emotional labour' Personnel staff as internal consultants 'Managing people first' Peer support groups	Continued commitment of top management Promotion of staff with new BA values 'Top flight academies' Open learning programs
Structures and systems	Use of diagonal task forces to plan change Reduction in levels of hierarchy Modification of budgeting process	Profit sharing (3 weeks' pay in 1987) Opening of Terminal 4 Purchase of Chartridge as training center New, 'user friendly' MIS	New performance appraisal system based on both behaviour and performance Performance-based compensation system Continued use of task forces
Climate/interpersonal style	Redefinition of the business: *service*, not *transportation* Top management commitment and involvement	Greater emphasis on open communications Data feedback on work-unit climate Off-site, team building meetings	New uniforms New coat of arms Development and use of cabin-crew teams Continued use of data-based feedback on climate and management practices

Table 7.5 **The British Airways change programme.**

	1982	1987
Ownership	Government	Private
Profit/(loss)	($900 million)	$435 million
Culture	Bureaucratic and militaristic	Service-oriented and market-driven
Passenger load factor	Decreasing	Increasing – up 16% in 1st quarter 1988
Cargo load	Stable	Increasing – up 41% in 1st quarter 1988
Share price	N/A	Increased 67% (2.11.87 – 8.11.87)
Acquisitions	N/A	British Caledonian

Source: Goodstein and Burke (1991). Reprinted by permission of the publisher from *Organizational Dynamics*, Spring 1991, © 1991, American Management Association, New York. All rights reserved.

Table 7.4 presents an overview of the BA change programme in terms of Kurt Lewin's three-stage change model (Goodstein and Burke, 1991). The many and diverse initiatives involved in the programme are categorized both by stages and by level of intervention (individual, structures and systems, and climate/interpersonal style). The success of these efforts over a five-year period is clearly shown in the data presented in Table 7.5. Together, the various efforts transformed the BA organizational culture from what managers described as 'bureaucratic and militaristic' to one that is now described as 'service-oriented and market-driven'.

The general atmosphere of the company is a much more positive one. There is an attitude of 'we can change things, we are better than our competitors'. I'm not certain if there's a relationship which is that a good culture leads to a successful company, but there is certainly the converse of that, that a successful company leads to a better culture. We are a more successful company now, and as a result of that it's easier to have a positive culture.

Goodstein and Burke (1991).

The organization today is at a stage where most of the fundamental changes have been achieved. In 1991, BA was voted 'Best Airline Overall' by Business Traveller magazine for the fourth year in a row. Now they must maintain what has been achieved while concentrating on continuing to be adaptable to changes in their external environment.

The real challenge in a people culture and a service culture is when the pressure's on. How do you manage change which requires you to get more productivity or more cost-efficiency or whatever, but still maintain a degree of trust, a respect for the individual, which I still think underpins service?

Human Resource Manager, British Airways in Goodstein and Burke (1991).

Yet without increasing the value the organizational culture placed on productivity and profits, while maintaining or increasing the value placed on customer service, Colin Marshall and BA could not guarantee the airline's continual success in an increasingly competitive global marketplace (Kotter and Leahey, 1990).

SAINSBURY'S: A RELIANCE ON PROGRAMMATIC CHANGE

A number of writers have focused on Sainsbury's (Horovitz and Jurgens-Panak, 1992; McBeath, 1990). Sainsbury's is the largest food retail chain in the UK. It employs nearly 100,000 people in 315 stores, of whom 62,000 work part time. In 1990 group sales amounted to £7.3 billion (compared to £4 billion in 1987), with pre-tax profits of £450 million (compared to £268 million in 1987). Sainsbury's has one of the lowest employee turnover rates in the industry. A recent survey showed that 1,300 staff have been with the organization for over 25 years and 30 for over 40 years.

Sainsbury's has a strong reputation. Within the UK, the stores are a byword for high-quality products, cleanliness and good service. The stores are spacious, well lit and well designed. To run each store, the organization uses a heavy concentration of HRM resources. Each store has a personnel manager who co-ordinates training and a number of instructors who carry out the training of sales staff.

However, the 1980s saw an increase in customer expectations. Competitors were catching up with Sainsbury's image. Consequently, the board of directors decided to set up an organizational culture change programme, called 'Building Better Business' (BBB), to improve the quality of the customer service offered by the sales staff. It felt from the outset that the key to changing the behaviour of sales staff was to change their attitudes towards the customer, their colleagues and their job. The programme was aimed at the discretionary part of the job and not the mandatory parts stated in the job descriptions, i.e. the focus was on 'how' staff did their job and not on 'what' they did (McBeath, 1990). We examine the impact of such changes on performance appraisals in Chapter Fourteen.

In May 1986 two training videos were developed and piloted in five stores as the basis of the BBB programme. One called 'Out in Front' concentrated on the role of the front-end check-out staff, and the other called 'Counting on Service' was aimed at the counter sales staff. After some fine tuning the programme began to run through all branches, 25–30 branches at a time. This approach kept the resources required to manageable proportions and also served to reinforce and keep the programme alive. In May 1987 a further three videos and a new introductory video began touring the branches. These encouraged positive attitudes towards the job and colleagues, reinforced the five reasons for customers to choose Sainsbury's (Friendliness, Responsiveness, Enthusiasm, Sincerity and Helpfulness), and showed the importance of body language and first impressions. In addition, a number of supporting activities were undertaken to encourage employees to put the lessons into practice, such as a poster competition where employees were asked to design posters for the BBB programme. The purpose of these activities was to reaffirm and reinforce the customer service and BBB message (see Illustration 7.18).

In recent years, the BBB programme has become a vehicle for more than customer

Illustration 7.18 **Sainsbury's objectives.**

- To discharge the responsibility as leaders in our trade by acting with complete integrity, by carrying out our work to the highest standards, and by contributing to the public good and to the quality of life in the community.
- To provide unrivalled value to our customers in the quality of the goods we sell, in the competitiveness of our prices and in the range of choice we offer.
- In our stores, to achieve the highest standards of cleanliness and hygiene, efficiency of operation, convenience and customer service, and thereby create as attractive and friendly a shopping environment as possible.
- To offer our staff outstanding opportunities in terms of personal career development and in remuneration relative to other companies in the same market, practising always a concern for the welfare of every individual.
- To generate sufficient profit to finance continual improvement and growth of the business whilst providing our shareholders with an excellent return on their investment.

Source: Horovitz and Jurgens-Panak (1992).

service training (McBeath, 1990). Product knowledge, customers with special needs, and telephone training courses have been developed and run under the BBB banner, but in a drastically altered form. The training has become:

- Shorter.
- Less participative.
- More focused on behaviour than attitudes.

In line with the recommendations made by Beer *et al.* (1990), greater emphasis has been placed on the monitoring and formal control of training and behaviour. Managers and supervisors are requested to monitor customer service in stores, and to act as role models in order to 'set a first class example'. It is too early to tell whether the new approach is going to be more successful than the original at changing customer service behaviour. The original BBB videos are now included as part of the organization's extensive post-induction training programme.

There is no real end to building better business. It is an ongoing training programme which is to be developed for the future and will grow and encompass different areas.
Sainsbury's Inhouse Journal in Horovitz and Jurgens-Panak (1992).

HOFFMANN-LA ROCHE: A CUSTOMER FOCUS

Hoffmann-La Roche is one of the leading organizations in the pharmaceuticals and health care industry. It was founded in 1896 in Basle. It now has operations in over 100 countries, employing 55,000 people in four main divisions of activity: Fragrances and Flavours, Pharmaceuticals, Vitamins and Fine Chemicals, and Diagnostics. Roche is probably best known for its drugs which are used to control the central nervous system. The most famous of these is Valium, introduced in 1963.

Hoffmann-La Roche is very much a people and service oriented company. Key elements built into its business approach include service to the customers, respect for the individual, motivating leadership, obligation to shareholders and employees, obligation to society and openness to change.
Horovitz and Jurgens-Panak (1992, p. 270).

With these elements in mind, the organization was restructured in 1986 and this was accompanied by an organization-wide culture change programme called Customer Focus. The objectives were to bring the organization closer to the customer and to change attitudes in the entire organization.

We felt that the customer focus was not enough in the forefront. We wanted to orient the company further toward the outside and toward the market.
Dr Markus Altwegg, Director, Hoffmann-La Roche, in Horovitz and Jurgens-Panak (1992).

The Customer Focus programme was overseen by the Executive Committee of the organization, but operationally managed by each division as it saw fit. It was felt that a blanket improvement programme would be too unwieldy and have little real impact. Hence, managers in the various countries and divisions were free to develop their own approach for achieving the overall aims set by the executive committee.

Since launching the programme, Roche's Diagnostics Division has gone the furthest in terms of setting up a structured approach to increasing the customer focus within the organization. From its origins, the programme represented a cultural revolution within the organization, because it implied change in values. It represented one of the most marked changes in the division in recent history.

A major part of the change programme has been an ongoing communications effort.

The launch was a half-day event held in a large congress hall to which all of the employees in the Diagnostics Division were invited. Each employee received a special invitation letter which informed them of the event, reminded them of the importance of the programme to the organization's future and was signed by the head of the division. In addition, prior to the launch, quality group leaders were selected. They were responsible for leading interdepartmental teams that would work on improving service quality problems. They were trained to perform that function and were strongly committed to the objectives of the programme.

These activities were accompanied by an ongoing communications effort. The major focus of the change programme was communicated to the workforce through regular articles and internal reports on the progress made in the quality groups. These initiatives made a strong impact on the workforce. As one employee said: 'We had never done anything like this before. It drew a great deal of attention' (Horovitz and Jurgens-Panak, 1992).

The results of the Customer Focus programme have been encouraging. The most recent developments at Roche Diagnostic Systems show an increasingly focused approach to service quality improvement. However, the responsibility for improving affiliates' and customers' satisfaction is gradually shifting from the interdepartmental quality groups to the line managers.

SCANDINAVIAN AIRLINES (SAS): THE ROLE OF CRISIS, LEADERSHIP AND SYMBOLIC CHANGE

SAS is the national carrier of Denmark, Norway and Sweden. Although the organization is operating in a high labour cost situation with strong unions and a small domestic market, SAS has managed, thanks to the entrepreneurial spirit of Jan Carlzon, to become a successful organization. In 1986, SAS came fifth in Europe on the basis of the number of passengers. In terms of the number of paid passenger kilometres, the organization stood in sixth place, indicating that a relatively low proportion of its flights fell within the profitable long-haul category.

When Carlzon was appointed president and CEO of SAS in 1981, the airline's profits and its market share had been falling since the mid 1970s. However, the real financial crisis had already hit in 1979. After 17 profitable years, the organization suffered a loss of $17 million on a total revenue of $861. With hindsight Carlzon suggested that this crisis was necessary for him to step in and implement drastic changes.

Carlzon's most immediate task involved creating a new organization philosophy by:

■ Focusing his people and systems on the marketplace.
■ Implementing a new organizational structure.

'In this business', he said, 'we don't fly planes, we fly people' and aligned the organization structure and culture accordingly (Vandermerwe, 1992). Carlzon's 'little red book' as it came to be known, was the first step toward involving all employees in the new way of thinking. He wanted to find a way to communicate to all levels in the organization that the organization was in a serious crisis, fighting for its life, and make them understand what he wanted to do about it. To achieve these goals, he created a booklet in cartoon form called 'Let's Get In There and Fight' that detailed the airline's financial position, the vision of the future, and the plan for delegating responsibility to frontline employees.

At the beginning, people were somewhat surprised by this unusual form of communication, but they got used to it in time and even came to expect it. Resistance came mainly from the technical side of the operation, especially from the older pilots. It became clear early on that, culturally, many Scandinavians regarded the service concept as 'not professional'. Anxieties were lifted by internal marketing and morale steadily improved. In fact, employees became excited by the new strategy and the attention it was getting in the press.

Carlzon and his team personally visited 'frontliners' throughout the organization. A training organization was hired to put 20,000 managers and employees through a two day training programme designed to give them a sense of the organization's purpose and their role in the new concept of customer service. Before launching the mass training phase, Carlzon hosted an intensive gathering of his top 120 executives and 30 of the senior union representatives. Training for middle managers proceeded more or less in tandem with the frontline programme, with supervisors joining a large session of over 100 people.

In the organization structure introduced in August 1981, Carlzon erased the pyramid and implemented his concept of the new organization as a kind of wheel with the CEO at the hub and operating departments revolving around him. Whereas frontline workers with the most customer contact were formerly at the bottom of the chart, Carlzon put them on top. It became everyone else's responsibility, including his, to 'serve' those who directly served the customer. Strong emphasis was given to delegating responsibility down the line. Carlzon believed competent result-oriented managers should be well informed people who could work without supervision. In his own words, he wanted to 'put workers in charge and have management serve as consultants to the organization' (Vandermerwe, 1992).

Carlzon actively tried to encourage initiative on the part of the staff to think outwardly about customers instead of inwardly about the head office. He knew that a badly managed 'moment of truth' had a terrible effect on the customers. For example, on one occasion he applauded a pilot whose plane was grounded by a strike on the Copenhagen airport, and responded by opening the bar, taking passengers on a guided tour of the airport perimeter and pointing out interesting sights. This kind of initiative, he believed, could never happen by simply giving instructions.

Telling people what to do only succeeds in putting limitations on them. Information, on the other hand, permits them to know their opportunities and possibilities. To free someone from the rigorous control of instructions, policies and orders, and to give that person freedom to take responsibility for his ideas, decisions and actions, is to release hidden resources which would otherwise remain inaccessible to both the individual and the company. A person who has information cannot avoid taking responsibility.   Vandermerwe (1992).

By the end of 1982, SAS had achieved a totally changed image. It had become the most punctual airline in Europe as well as the preferred airline for Scandinavian businessmen. The financial situation had also changed. Corporate overheads were reduced by 25 per cent and, from a $10 million loss, the organization achieved a $76 million profit. Although the profits of the 1980s were followed by losses in the early 1990s, after divesting Amadeus and the Intercontinental hotels SAS was making profits again in August 1992.

BOWING TO CULTURAL REALITY: ADAPTING HRM PRACTICES TO LOCAL CONDITIONS

Finally, one of the themes throughout this book is the need for organizations to bow to cultural reality, adapting their core HRM practices to local conditions, thereby

Illustration 7.19   **Wine on the tables at Eurodisney.**

Many analysts believe that Walt Disney erred in believing that what worked in the US would work in Europe. Every aspect of the project was controlled by managers from the US with 300 Americans on site in Paris. The impact of European tastes, seasonal weather and vacation habits were not assessed sufficiently. When Walt Disney opened the first theme park in Los Angeles in the late 1950s the consumption of alcohol was forbidden. American managers stuck to their homegrown business formula and insisted that alcohol could not be served in Eurodisney. Within six months the American president and chairman of Eurodisney was replaced by Frenchman, Philippe Bourguignon. By June 1993, little more than a year after opening, diners at the Auberge de Cendrillon (Cinderalla's Inn) found they could order French or Californian wine with their meal. Financial losses forced the change of heart. In the first half of 1993 losses hit FFr 1 billion on a turnover of FFr 1.8 billion. Wine on the tables signalled a deeper shift in HRM practice. By 1993 labour disputes over long working hours and poor pay were being addressed with a French industrial relations approach rather than the imported US techniques, recognizing French job classifications, setting a maximum working week and introducing annual hours, in return for greater flexibility from the workforce. The management team has now become roughly one-third US, one third French and one-third UK, Ireland and the Netherlands, as part of a planned transition under the 'expatriate partnership scheme'. The result is a European management core steeped in Disney practices but with the freedom to experiment with changes and innovate. Eurodisney will develop its own organizational culture, not reflecting the US as strongly, but not typically French either. This pattern may be the way forward for many European organizations.

Source: Sasseen (1993).

achieving a balance between organizational imperatives and successful local implementation. Eurodisney provides a useful illustration of this (see Illustration 7.19).

CONCLUSIONS

This chapter has shown why organizational culture is seen by many as the primary mechanism for achieving organizational effectiveness. Despite the fact that as a concept it continues to elude theoretical precision, it frequently represents an all-encompassing metaphor or master contract within an organization from which the social reality of living and working in that environment stems. This is why it has formed the first chapter in our analysis of the content of European HRM. However, organizational culture change is a long-term process which takes several (often three to ten) years to accomplish. Somehow people must continue to operate while the culture of the organization is being modified. Employees cannot be disciplined for being resistant to change, especially in the first year of the programme and impatience with behavioural change has to be avoided. Indeed, since behaviour patterns are so hard to change, employees should be rewarded for adopting new ways of working through financial rewards, promotions, and public recognition. This is why changes in so many other areas of HRM tend to flow out from attempts to engineer the organizational culture. The lessons and conclusions drawn from both the theoretical discussion and the various case examples are not complex or particularly surprising, but illustrate what researchers and practitioners have learned and said about changing the culture of an organization. The key learning points from this chapter are shown below.

LEARNING POINTS FROM CHAPTER SEVEN

1. A wide range of social, competitive and economic pressures are driving the need for change in the social reality in European organizations. The creation and maintenance of a strong organizational culture has become the cornerstone of many HRM strategies. Interest in the topic of organizational culture has crossed the Atlantic. Comparative data show a high degree of similarity between US and European organizations in the degree of importance they attach to many cultural changes. Certainly, there is a common focus on the need to create organizational cultures that foster higher levels of empowerment and also focus on the measurement and promotion of customer service. The importance of creating cultures that are based on diversity and equality is recognized in the US, the UK and Germany, but less so in France and Italy.

2. The attention given to organizational culture is unlikely to represent a short-term fad. To ignore organizational culture assumes that formal strategies, changes to structure and alterations to employment conditions can by themselves change the way people behave. Employees tend not to commit readily to what they are told to do. The shared meanings, hidden assumptions and unwritten rules across countries or organizations provide the real energy that will either progress or impede change.

3. Organizational culture can be defined in many ways. It has variously been defined as patterns of basic assumptions that arise from learning about and coping with the need to adapt, historically transmitted patterns of meaning through which knowledge and attitudes to life are transmitted, informal rules that spell out how people should behave, and shared mindsets that lead to a collective programming of the mind which distinguishes members of one organization from another.

4. Organizational culture exists across a series of levels. At the deepest levels it refers to underlying assumptions about the nature of human relationships. Above this may be a set of shared values and beliefs that create an understanding about how the organization works. Finally, there is the most visible and explicit level of behaviours and artefacts. Concepts of HRM that only deal with this surface behavioural level are unlikely to have much impact on organizations. National culture is probably responsible for determining many of the deepest level aspects of organizational culture.

5. The organizational culture is frequently evidenced and diagnosed by examining a collection of stories, routines, rituals, symbols, organizational structures, control systems and power structures. On this basis many writers have created classification systems that attempt to capture the different assumptions, policies and practices. A variety of mechanisms can be use to embed organizational cultures, including statements of philosophy, the design of the physical environment, role modelling, explicit use of reward and status systems, stories, legends and myths, leader behaviour, the design and structure of the organization, its systems and procedures, and the criteria for HRM systems. It is clear what an important linking mechanism it can represent.

6. Classifications of organizational cultures can be no more than generic descriptions. Whatever system of classification is used tends to reveal the existence of strong subcultures within an organization. These subcultures tend to reflect functions and hierarchies, such as managerial, sales and marketing and professional, technical and scientific groupings. Balancing the legitimate demands of subcultures with the needs of the overall organization is a delicate task.

7. Some organizational cultures are stronger than others, either in terms of the homogeneity and stability of group membership, the length and intensity of shared

experiences within the organization or the intensity of its effects on behaviour within the organization. The business environment and sector, role of the founder, size of the organization and geographic dispersion and HRM practices can all influence the strength of organizational cultures.

8. Efforts to change organizational culture involve a number of rites and rituals, including rites of passage, degradation, enhancement, renewal, conflict reduction and integration. Direct efforts to change organizational culture are extremely difficult. The organizational culture change programme within an organization or division must be owned and personally led with high levels of involvement from the top managers. Control and understanding of the organization's culture is a key responsibility of leaders. If not, the credibility of the change programme and the probability for success is greatly reduced. The change programme has to be applied to the entire business unit and be systematic, not fragmented. If the structure, systems and jobs of the organizations are not 'aligned', people will probably continue to operate as they did before the change programme was started.

9. Employees must know where the organization is going and how it is trying to get there. Frequent and repetitive communication is needed. Every employee from the bottom of the organization to the top needs to understand what the objective of the change programme is, what are the underlying reasons for changing. The need for change should be recognized by those who will be affected by the change. This implies that the change programme must be based on a level of dissatisfaction with the status quo of the business. People must believe that things can and must get better.

10. Although ultimately all employees undergoing the change programme have to be involved, it is important to form an 'organizational culture change' team consisting of representatives from all levels of the organization. The role of the team is to link with the general manager or business unit head, and help him or her manage the transition process. Care has to be taken to reduce the uncertainties accompanying change programmes, particularly those threatening the security of jobs and existing rewards. A variety of methods can be employed to achieve this, including training, direct participation of individual employees in the decision making process, and where appropriate, the early consultation and negotiation with employee representative bodies.

11. Organizational culture contributes to HRM practices through providing a structure to assist the alignment of individual goals and values. HRM practices can also help to create and support organizational cultures by creating a higher level of organizational cohesion. There are fundamental differences between management thinkers and organizations as to whether organizational culture can be managed by HRM. Empirical observation points to the failure of much planned change. Others point to the likely prospect of making minor alterations in certain areas of behaviour. A smaller number of best practice case studies point to the achievement of cultural metamorphoses through time consuming and expensive interventions. Finally, some writers point to the natural evolution of organizational cultures, pointing to the management role of initiating and shaping this evolutionary process.

12. Several organizations have attempted formal HRM interventions by carrying out 'culture gap' analyses. However, managers have to be wary of attempting such precise measurement and intervention. Organizational culture is manageable, but only with extreme difficulty. A series of key management tasks in changing organizational culture can be identified. These point to the highly political nature of most change processes.

13. The link between strong organizational cultures and organizational performance has been asserted by a number of writers. Organizational culture has a significant effect on voluntary turnover rates and may possibly be linked to other measures of economic performance. However, improvements in organizational performance only seem to follow when the shared values and unwritten rules of the resulting actions fit an intelligent business strategy for the specific environment the organization is in. However, even contextually or strategically appropriate cultures will not increase performance over a sustained period unless they can help the organization adapt faster and better to a changing environment. Creating organization cultures for adaptability and change is a process that is leading to more convergence in HRM practices across Europe.

14. This is leading organizations to change the way they manage their people – by bringing in new methods of recruitment, selection, transferring employees and releasing them. Management systems – including budget and control systems, rewards, training and appraisal controls – are also being changed. Finally, structures are being changed in terms of the composition of stakeholders, levels of decentralization, job redesign to increase role flexibility, and the creation of new temporary structures to cater for special needs. In attempting these changes in order to influence organizational culture, it must never be forgotten that many of these efforts, one way or another, still have to bow to national culture.

CHAPTER EIGHT

Structuring the Organization

INTRODUCTION

In Part Two we pointed to a number of transitions that are focusing the attention of HRM managers on the structure of European organizations. The forces for change are both powerful and varied. The social and competitive pressures outlined in Chapter Four have resulted in new career patterns and higher levels of flexibility in European organizations. The emergence of transnational organizations has been accompanied by power shifts away from the line of country towards the line of business. It has also required new co-ordinating mechanisms and changes in the structure, control systems and business processes of the organization. Increased levels of foreign direct investment have focused around three major trading blocs (Europe, the US and Asia/Pacific). It has shaped world trade, and increased intra-continental dependence. Foreign direct investment has brought with it changes in the geographic composition and scale of organizations, a rationalization of business activity, changes in the employment levels, changed national parentage, power imbalances and a range of other issues involved in strategic alliances. Finally, greater cultural sensitivity has led to an appreciation of national differences and has highlighted the cultural assumptions that influence the way managers think about structuring their organizations (Amado, Faucheux and Laurent, 1991; van Wijk, 1987). These transitions are highlighted in Figure 8.1.

This chapter covers many strategic issues that will have a significant impact on the focus of European HRM. It has to cover a series of complex issues, and is therefore divided into four sections:

1. The key concepts and ideas in the topic of organization design.
2. A comparison of European management structures, corporate governance, and cultural preferences for organization.
3. A description of the approach taken to organization by the European multinationals, outline of the main co-ordination options and example case studies.
4. An outline of the challenge faced in creating pan-European structures.

We begin by discussing organization design from a general perspective, conveying the main ideas that are influencing the thinking of European managers. It is argued that structural change will become a continuous process throughout the 1990s. It is therefore necessary to consider in more detail what exactly is meant by structure. Some of the main ideas about organization structure are presented, as well as a series of principles that tend to govern the way in which people are organized into small units.

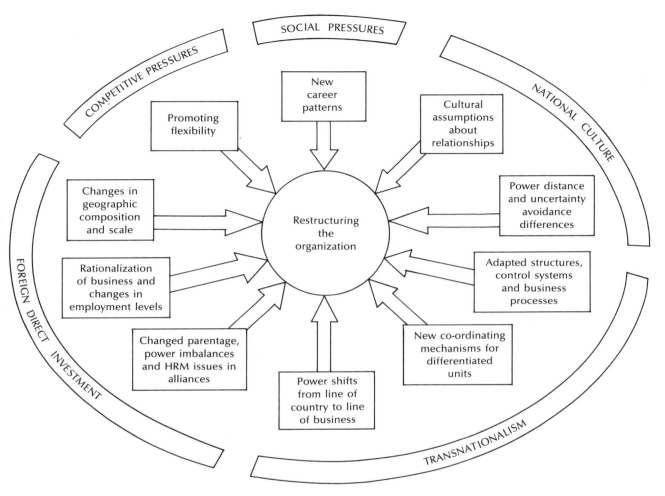

Figure 8.1   The forces precipitating changes in organization structure in Europe.

This discussion is used to highlight the true purpose of organization design. Having described the aims of organization design, we introduce an HRM perspective. A series of key HRM considerations when changing organization structures are highlighted, and some of the behavioural and social problems associated with change are discussed.

Having conveyed an understanding of what is typically involved in structuring organizations, the second section of the chapter is devoted to providing a comparative analysis of some key areas of difference in organization structures in Europe. We describe a series of studies on European manufacturing plants that highlight a number of differences, and relate these back to the IBM/Towers Perrin survey described in Chapter Two. Important differences in corporate governance are described, as is the impact of national culture on preferences for co-ordination.

In the third section we consider the approaches taken to structuring the organization by leading European multinationals. These organizations have evolved their structures and so we take a historical perspective, outlining the main developments to date. The main options taken by organizations, such as international divisions, functional structures, product divisions, matrix structures and cluster structures are explained.

We also develop understanding of the strategic issues involved in restructuring by providing examples of structural change from Bayer, British Petroleum, Philips and Jacob Suchard. These cases enrich the points made in general discussion, and also demonstrate how changes in organization structure create a range of interlinked HRM problems in such areas as culture change, management development and performance management. These issues are dealt with in other chapters.

Finally, we consider the latest challenge to organizations – the need to develop pan-European structures. The forces that are spurring the creation of the pan-European organization are outlined. A number of difficulties and causes of failure in this latest challenge are highlighted, and best practice solutions pointed to. In conclusion, we raise the main paradoxes that are faced by organizations as they attempt to design their structures and manage change.

STRUCTURING THE ORGANIZATION: MULTIPLE PERSPECTIVES

Given this range of pressures, it is not surprising that the topic of 'organization structuring' is complex. Numerous concepts are used by management writers in order to explain the nature of organization, the role of structure and its impact on the people. Recently, a number of authors (see, for example, Bartlett and Ghoshal 1992; Humes, 1993; Ulrich and Lake, 1990) have argued that, within the bounds of their history and inheritance, many European multinationals are being driven towards similar organizational designs and solutions. Our discussion of specific modes of operation and co-ordination later in this chapter reinforces this view. Any trend towards convergence of organization designs would have very significant implications for HRM because the organization design and structure has a powerful impact on HRM and vice-versa. The topic is, however, very complex and we need to consider the arguments across a number of levels of analysis and from a variety of perspectives (see Illustration 8.1).

Figure 8.2 models these various perspectives on organizational structuring and links them to human resource management and the underlying employee behaviour. The model summarizes much of the material described in more detail throughout this chapter. We have argued that there are a number of both powerful strategic pressures for change and cultural constraints that have implications for the structure of organizations in Europe. In order to cope with these pressures, organizations have debated the importance of and their ideal positioning along a number of 'primary design criteria'. These primary design criteria are most usefully expressed as complementary opposites (Evans and Doz, 1989). The typical decisions that have to be made are where to place the organization along a continuum from domestic and

Illustration 8.1   **Perspectives on organization structuring.**

1. Principles of organization: metaphors and frames of reference.
2. Social and behavioural impact on individuals and groups.
3. Co-ordination mechanisms and modes of operation for large organizations, international divisions, functions, product, geographic market, matrix.
4. Primary design paradoxes: along continua such as centralized–decentralized, global–local etc.

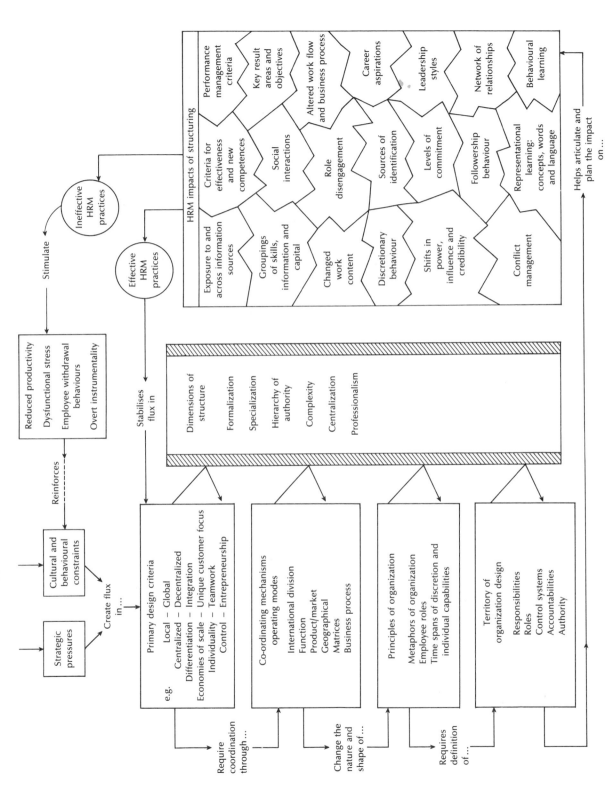

Figure 8.2 A theoretical model of organization structuring and human resource management.

local to global, whether to be centralized or decentralized, whether to operate in competition or partnership, whether to be driven by a business logic or a technical logic, and so forth. The relative balance across these design criteria is in a constant state of flux and necessarily creates tensions within the organization. These tensions create the need for effective co-ordination mechanisms. A number of these co-ordination mechanisms or models of organization have emerged over the twentieth century. The most notable are the international division, function, product/market, geographical area, matrices, and the core business process. It is at this level – the co-ordination mechanisms – that we are seeing most convergence across European organizations, or at least common solutions within specific industrial sectors.

These modes of organization are used to co-ordinate smaller units of the organization. These smaller units tend to be designed around a variety of principles or ideas that serve to shape managers' thinking and determine how tasks actually get done. The most easily discernible and influential of these principles is to consider the generic roles played by employees. Other principles consider the key communication nodes and interactions within the organization, the decision making that is required, and the time span of managerial discretion at various levels of work activity. Both the need to create clear, co-ordinated changes in these units and the frame of reference (or image of how the organization works) help to define the scope and territory of organization design, as both a topic and a management practice. This territory has typically been seen to include the need to outline the impact on responsibilities, roles, control systems, accountabilities and levels of authority for both specific organizational units and the individuals within them (Galbraith, 1977).

All these features of organization structure – the primary design criteria, the modes of operation and co-ordinating mechanisms, the principles used to structure the units of the organization and the territory and scope of organization design practices – eventually have a simple physical reflection. It is this reflection that researchers typically try to measure and compare. The structure of organizations has traditionally been compared along a number of common dimensions such as the level of formalization, specialization, standardization, hierarchies of authority, and so forth (Daft, 1992). Certainly, much of comparative work on European structures has taken this perspective.

These composite dimensions of structure, and the various interventions made by organizations in order to change them, result in a host of impacts on employees, all of which require a co-ordinated HRM response. These changes are detailed in Figure 8.2 but include such things as social interactions, changed career aspirations, power shifts, new requirements for the management style, changed work content, new groupings of skills and new competency requirements, and the creation of both representational and behavioural learning. If these impacts on employees are managed effectively, through appropriate HRM practices, then the net result reinforces the achievement of the organizational goals. If the changes are poorly managed, then the net impact becomes dominated by the more negative behaviours associated with an instrumental attitude to work and all the associated withdrawal behaviours. These negative behaviours bear both high (and hidden) costs to the organization and frequently derail the implementation of strategic change. Getting the structure right creates the bedrock for most HRM practices.

The need to get it right and to understand the various elements of Figure 8.2 has never been more pressing, largely because changes in organization structure are becoming a universal and continuous phenomenon.

STRUCTURAL CHANGE WILL BE A PERVASIVE AND CONTINUOUS PROCESS IN THE 1990S

Restructuring in organizations is becoming an increasingly continuous process (Bandrowski, 1991). There was a wave of restructuring in the early 1980s (largely intended to undo diversifications that took place in the 1970s) and the 1990s is seeing continued pressure for structural changes. The money required to invest in such change is coming from the sale, rationalization and downsizing of non-core businesses. The fact that the money is available is an indication of the pervasive size of the world's largest organizations, with many earning revenues larger than the GDP of medium-sized countries. Foreign countries' subsidiaries have become increasingly important in the industrial and economic life of many nations. Dominant economic interests are no longer in the hands of the local population. If nations and organizations are ranked by GNP and total sales respectively, 48 out of the first 100 on the list are large industrial organizations. For example, in 1990 Royal Dutch Shell ranked twenty-third in the world league of organizations and nations (down from twenty-first in 1981) according to GNP or total sales (Ball and McCulloch, 1990; Morgan, 1986). Its sales were almost as large as the total Norwegian GNP, and were larger than countries such as South Africa, Saudi Arabia or Turkey. British Petroleum ranked fortieth in the league, with sales larger than Portuguese GNP, closely followed by IRI of Italy and Daimler-Benz of Germany.

A worldwide survey by Harvard Business School (Moss-Kanter, 1991) confirmed many of these developments and also pointed to the pervasive impact of organization restructuring (11,678 managers from twenty-five countries were surveyed between November 1990 and January 1991). As was the case in the Towers Perrin survey data on worldwide HRM practices (see Chapter Two), Moss-Kanter's (1991) study revealed a number of separate clusters of similar countries when their attitudes to the focus, content and management of change were examined. There was an English-speaking (mainly Anglo-Saxon) cluster consisting of managers from the US, the UK, Australia, Canada, New Zealand and Singapore. The Latin cluster consisted of managers from Argentina, Brazil, Mexico, Venezuela, Italy and Spain. The North European cluster contained managers from Austria, Belgium, Finland, France, Germany, the Netherlands and Sweden. A number of 'cultural islands' also existed – namely Japan, South Korea, India and Hungary (representative of Eastern Europe). Some of the key survey findings are shown in Figure 8.3.

The most pervasive changes experienced were reorganizations, downsizings, changes in leadership and mergers and divestitures. The prevalence of restructuring cut across international boundaries. For example, 60 per cent of managers from German organizations (representative of the North European cluster) had experienced a major restructuring from 1989–1991, and an almost identical figure – 59 per cent – of American managers (representative of the English speaking cluster) reported a similar experience. There was still some ambivalence about internationalism and global economics had not triumphed over politics, but less than a quarter of all the managers surveyed wanted business owners to care more about the success of their country than the success of their organization. The most internationalist managers in outlook were from German, Swedish, Finnish, Dutch and Belgian organizations.

Although the level of restructuring is high worldwide, restructuring linked to reductions in employment has been most prevalent in the Anglo-Saxon countries such as the US and UK and in Eastern Europe. The main reasons for this high level of restructuring have a financial motive (see Illustration 8.2) reflecting some of the

Question: Which of the following changes has your organization experienced in the past two years?

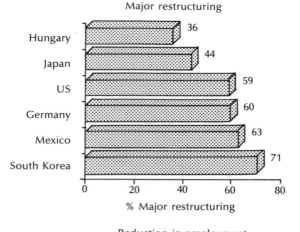

Major restructuring

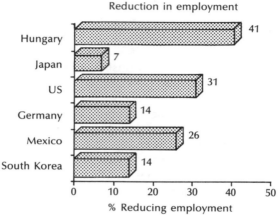

Reduction in employment

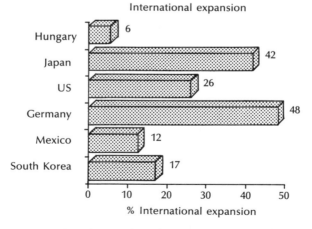

International expansion

Data for the US are representative of scores from the UK, Australia, Canada, New Zealand and Singapore

Data for Germany are representative of Austria, Belgium, Finland, France, The Netherlands and Sweden

Data for Mexico are representative of Argentina, Brazil, Venezuela, Italy and Spain

Data for Japan, South Korea and Hungary are representative of the single countries

Figure 8.3 An international comparison of the sources of change. *Source*: Moss-Kanter (1991).

Illustration 8.2 **Reasons for restructuring in Anglo-Saxon organizations.**

- Purchase absorption, rationalization or sale of businesses in order to sustain growth and financial performance, maintain high returns to shareholders, and achieve productivity improvements.
- A retreat to core operations and business processes in order to undo previous diversification.
- Streamlining towards new business where prospects for core businesses are poor, sales are lagging, or a global competitive threat has emerged.
- Shifts in markets and technologies.

- Shortfalls in operating volumes or profits due to a business downturn, sale of under-performing assets or scale back of operations.
- Flotation of successful subsidiaries to improve management incentives, accomplish equity carve-outs or achieve greater visibility of high performing units.
- Superior break-up value of specific parts of the organization in comparison to the whole.
- Leveraged buy-outs in mature industries to fend off or prevent takeovers, reduce cash flows to service debts and streamline expenses.

Source: Bandrowski (1991).

differences in the Anglo-Saxon and Germanic models of capitalism introduced in Chapter Five.

WHAT IS ORGANIZATION STRUCTURE: PHYSICAL TRAITS OR DIMENSIONS?

But what exactly is involved in restructuring? Indeed, what is organization structure? In his detailed work on the design of organizations, Daft (1992) summarizes seven dimensions or traits of an organization that may be used to describe the structure in much the same way that personality or physical traits label people. These dimensions are essentially derived from the Aston studies in the 1970s (Pugh, 1976; Pugh, Hickson and Hinings, 1969) which were themselves informed by Weber's factors of bureaucracy. The seven structural dimensions (see Illustration 8.3) can provide a basis

Illustration 8.3 **Seven structural dimensions of organizations.**

Formulation	Amount of written documentation i.e. procedures, job descriptions, and policy manuals.
Specialization	Degree to which tasks are subdivided into separate jobs, i.e. division of labour.
Standardization	Extent to which similar work activities are performed in a uniform manner.
Hierarchy of authority	Reporting relationships and spans of control of individuals.
Complexity	Number of activities or subsystems within the organization in terms of: ■ number of levels (vertical complexity), ■ number of job titles or departments (horizontal complexity), ■ number of geographic locations (spatial complexity).
Centralization	Hierarchical level that has authority to make a decision.
Professionalism	Level of formal education and training of employees.

Source: Daft (1992).

for measuring and comparing organizations, but are, of course, themselves dependent on a number of contextual dimensions such as size, technology, environment, goals and strategy. Many – but not all – of these dimensions of structure are reflected in the organization chart. Organization charts tend to highlight the 'vertical' aspects of an organization's structure, i.e. the chains of command, the departmental groupings and the information linkages that have become the traditional concern of organizational designers. An often overlooked, but increasingly vital, aspect of organizational design is the creation of 'horizontal information linkages' that overcome barriers between departments, provide opportunity for co-ordination of employees and facilitate the implementation of strategy. These include flows of information and documentation, direct contact, liaison roles, task forces, integrator roles and project teams. Rarely drawn on organization charts, these are nevertheless part of the organization structure (Galbraith, 1977).

The advantage of viewing organization structure in terms of these seven dimensions is that they describe easily observable and comparable physical aspects of the structure. The disadvantages are that they:

- Have little to do with the underlying intention or motivations behind the organization design.
- May each be caused by several different factors.
- Tend to promote a very hierarchical and static view of the structure.
- Reflect an increasingly dated perspective on organization structure.
- Are extremely dependent on the technology within the organization.

WHAT IS ORGANIZATION STRUCTURE: METAPHORS AND IMAGES?

The structure of an organization is only an instrument that is created to achieve other (usually strategic) ends. Given that the work by Moss-Kanter (1991) has shown so much change is taking place, what kind of thinking about the nature of organization structure is influencing managers? In this section we highlight the many ideas that managers might consider.

Morgan's (1986) seminal work, *Images of Organization*, explores our understanding and ideas about organization and management. He uses a series of metaphors (see Illustration 8.4) to convey the principles and images that we often take for granted when we think about, and see, organizations, but which powerfully shape the options managers believe they have open to them when they restructure organizations. By exploring these metaphors, Morgan (1986) highlights why we need to create new ways of thinking about management and the design of organizations.

Organizations. . . (and their structures) are very complex and paradoxical phenomena that can be understood in many different ways. . . we frequently talk about organizations as if they were

Illustration 8.4 **Eight metaphors of organizations: organizations as . . . .**

- Machines.
- Organisms.
- Brains.
- Cultures.
- Political systems.
- Psychic prisons.
- Flux and transformation.
- Instruments of domination.

Source: Morgan (1986).

machines, designed to achieve predetermined goals and objectives, and which should operate smoothly and efficiently. And as a result of this kind of thinking we often attempt to organize and manage them in a mechanistic way, forcing their human qualities into a background role ... by using different metaphors to understand the complex and paradoxical character of organizational life, we are able to manage and design organizations in ways that we may not have thought possible before.   Morgan (1986, p. 13).

All of these metaphors can be seen to influence the ways managers think about the design and structure of their organizations. We give consideration to the five most relevant metaphors. Three metaphors (machines, organisms and brains) are clearly visible in the physical structure of most current organizations, and represent the more rational influences on management thinking about organization designs. Two other metaphors (political systems and psychic prisons) reflect the more irrational influences. Morgan (1986) goes on to detail other metaphors, but these are of most relevance to the topics of culture, the management of change and the impact of organizations on society and so are not considered here.

A pervasive image is that of the machine bureaucracy (Fayol, 1949; Taylor, 1911; Weber, 1947). Organizations have largely become mechanized – with precise requirements for work hours, tasks to be completed, activities to be planned, and procedures of operation. When managers think of organizations as machines they tend to focus on the need to design them like machines – with a series of top-down controlled interlocking parts (Drucker, 1954) that each have a defined role in the overall function of the organization. This type of image has become ingrained into our thinking, despite frequent criticisms. A second image views organizations and their structures as living organisms and uses biological metaphors to structure our thinking. This makes managers focus on the needs of the organization in relation to its environment (Beer, 1980; Emery, 1969; Katz and Kahn, 1978). Different types of organization (species) are seen to cope better with and suit specific types of environment (Burns and Stalker, 1961; Lawrence and Lorsch, 1967; Miller and Friesen, 1984; Mintzberg, 1979). The dimensions of structure identified in the previous section are an example of this type of thinking. Ideas about life cycles emerge (Freeman, 1982; Kimberley and Miles, 1980) as managers are encouraged to think about organization structures in evolutionary terms, in order to understand how one type of structure has developed out of another (Moss-Kanter, 1983; Peters and Waterman, 1982) and contains more enduring advantages.

A third and highly influential metaphor draws upon frameworks from information processing, learning and intelligence. Managers are encouraged to view and design organizations as brains in order to enhance these qualities. This focuses attention on two ideas: information processing and self-organization. The information processing image suggests an organizational design akin to a computer, in which information has to be transmitted through various pathways, and millions of pieces of separate data inform human decision making (Cyert and March, 1963; Galbraith, 1974, 1977; Simon, 1947). The purpose of an organization design is then to fragment, routinize and place boundaries around the decision making process in order to make it manageable. Various jobs, departments or divisions of the organization serve to structure work activity, compartmentalize responsibilities and simplify the domain of interest. Of course this focuses attention, interpretation of information and decision making. This image of organization means that as new information processing capacities emerge – as we now see with information technology – then new forms of organization become possible. The design of the organization rests *in* the information system (Beer, 1972). Like all brains, the question raised is: can it become more intelligent? Therefore, managers consider how they can build in mechanisms for learning such as better ways to scan the environment, compare incoming information against operating performance, question the business process and implement changes (Argyris, 1982; Schön, 1983). Closely associated with this idea that organization designs and structures should work as the brain of the organization is the concept or metaphor of holograms. A hologram has all the information necessary to produce a complete image in each of its parts. This type of thinking encourages managers to design, organize and structure in a way that facilities learning, self-organization and duplication, such that the complete system can function effectively even when specific parts of it are removed (Susman, 1976).

These three metaphors or images of organization have clearly had the most powerful influence on the way managers deal with the rational or logical aspects of designing organizations and their structures. Two other metaphors are covered in this section. These reveal some of the more irrational – but none the less influential – impacts on management thinking. They have an important influence on the design of organizations and the practice of restructuring. A fourth metaphor (Morgan, 1986) considers organization structures as a product of political activities – shaped by the attempts of various interest groups, group conflicts and power plays – and used as an attempt to legitimize different kinds of rules (Jay, 1967; Pettigrew, 1973; Pfeffer, 1978). Political rules in organizations may be exercised according to absolute government (autocracy), the use of written word or law (bureaucracy), knowledge and expert power (technocracy); joint management of mutual interests (co-determination), elected mandates (representative democracy) or equal rights in decision making (direct democracy). Each type of rule is associated with day to day political activity and conflicts of interest, usually resolved through differences in power such as superior control of scarce resources, decision processes, knowledge and information or technology. Decisions about organization structure may be designed to shift such sources of political power.

A somewhat more abstract metaphor presents organizations – and their structures – as 'psychic prisons' or products of our own mindsets. Their design is preoccupied by the unconscious drives in the minds of managers, such as desires for control or to minimize anxiety-provoking situations (Burrell and Morgan, 1979). The organization becomes trapped by favoured ways of thinking, for example, its historical success or consensus group processes. The structure is therefore designed in a way that represses the uncomfortable. Shaped by human personality, the structure adopts a series of recognizable defence mechanisms such as repression, denial, displacement, fixation, projection, rationalization and so forth (Hampden-Turner, 1981), dominated by a patriarchal set of values and structures.

THE MAIN WAYS OF ORGANIZING PEOPLE

By detailing the most influential metaphors of organization design it becomes clear that managers have to consider the creation of a new structure from a range of perspectives. Another perspective on the analysis of organization structuring is to consider some simple ways in which people are organized into smaller organization units. In practice, as we have seen, changes in the shape of an organization may be triggered by:

- Proactive decisions to change the business strategy.
- The need to accommodate the business vision of key personalities within the organization.

Illustration 8.5 **The bases for grouping people in the structure.**

- Employee roles.
- Communication and co-ordination nodes and patterns of interactions.
- Time spans of discretion and levels of individual capability.

- Gradually disclosed needs to change the structure in order to implement the business strategy resulting from formal business planning processes.
- Changes in customer or supplier practice which necessitate new ways of operating.
- Evolutionary responses to internal strains resulting from new (and initially informal) processes of communication and co-ordination, decision making, employee roles and individual capabilities.

Given such constant 'background noise' it is often difficult to detect any clear underlying logic in the way in which units of people are brought together. There are however a number of simple principles that have informed the way many organizations determine this feature of their structure. We discuss three of the most popular ways of grouping people into small units (see Illustration 8.5). They can be applied to all European organizations, and are heavily influenced by the machine, organism and brain metaphors already outlined.

Generic employee roles

Organization designs tend to differentiate between a series of generic roles played by groups of employees. Mintzberg (1979) presents a role based taxonomy and outlines six basic building blocks of an organization (see Illustration 8.6). The relative size and importance of these building blocks varies with circumstances and depending on these circumstances, different sorts of co-ordination mechanisms are needed.

Nodes, communications and interactions

Vernon and Wells (1991) focus on another way in which people are grouped, i.e. to act as communication nodes. All organizations contain pools of resources (devoted to specific business functions, products or markets, countries or areas) between which interactions of one kind or another have to take place. These basic groupings are called 'nodes'. This approach takes an information processing perspective. It argues that the fundamental challenge to the organization is to devise a structure in which the necessary interactions between nodes take place with the highest degree of efficiency. Efficiency is important because people are seen to act as information filters, distorting and weakening information as it passes through their 'node'. There are some general rules to guide these interactions:

- The fewer nodes the interaction has to pass through between sender and receiver, the more efficient and powerful it will be.
- Nodes that have wide spans of control have a higher 'cost of passage', reducing efficiency. Wider spans of control necessitate fewer levels.
- Efficiency is a function of group size, with several originating points within one node or group creating inefficiencies.

Illustration 8.6 **Six role-based building blocks in organization design.**

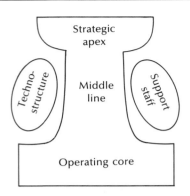

Operating core Location of basic work, e.g. factory floor, retail outlet, operating theatre. Most important in professional organizations, operating in a complex but static environment with control exercised by standardized skills. Also important to young organizations in a dynamic environment relying on expert control.

Strategic apex Location of general management activities. Most important in small, young organizations in a simple environment that allows direct supervision or where professional control and networking contacts are required.

Middle line Management roles that stand between the strategic apex and operating core. Most important in old, very large organizations with diverse but divisible tasks and standard outputs.

Technostructure Analytical roles used to design systems whereby work processes of others are delivered and controlled e.g. systems analysts, engineers, accountants. Most important in old large organizations with regulated tasks, standardized work and a simple or static environment.

Support staff Roles required to support the work of operating core e.g. secretarial, clerical, catering. Important to young organizations in a complex and dynamic environment relying on expert control.

Ideology Overarching paradigm, consisting of the organization's values and core beliefs, that glues the other roles together. Most important in maturing organizations with simplified systems where control can be exerted by missions and standardized norms.

Based on Mintzberg (1979).

The ideal (most efficient) shape of the organization using this type of organizing principle is influenced greatly by the anticipated pattern of interactions that should take place. The interactions or communications needed within an international organization tend to evolve, and as the organization grows, so does the diversity of its integration problems.

Time spans of discretion and individual decision making capabilities

A third way of grouping people together highlights the fact that there are different levels of decision making systems within an organization that operate across different time spans. The Brunel Institute of Organizational and Social Studies has based its approach to organization design and career paths on the work of Elliot Jacques. When studying organizational structures and pay systems in organizations across the world and from public or private sectors it became apparent that the time span during which the consequence of a decision became known (or the time span of discretion) lengthened the further up the management hierarchy you go. Moreover, each successive time span of discretion was associated with a specific level of individual capability in terms of the judgement and decision making requirements. Long time spans are associated with higher responsibility for the individual and greater risk and vulnerability for the organization (because it relies on the judgement of the decision maker). Jacques identified a series of distinct decision making levels within any organization that reflect these times spans. Ensuring a match between the time spans of discretion built into the organization structure, and the decision and judgement making capabilities of the individuals who operate at that level is an essential building block of organization. Whilst this match may be better achieved in some European countries than others because of differences in national training provision for example, the levels of decision making capability are based on individual differences and are, therefore, applicable across Europe. The work has been developed by Stamp (1990) and applied to career management under the title of 'career path appreciation process'.

Having identified the seven different time spans of discretion, the model summarizes the typical working relationships for each level in terms of:

- The roles associated with the activity.
- The complexity of typical reporting relationships.
- The main responsibilities for the individual.
- The judgement making capabilities that the individual must have.

These features are summarized in Table 8.1. Stamp (1990) has also identified the creativity capabilities required at each level, the sorts of collaboration involved, and the most obvious pitfalls and problems that are associated with each time span of discretion. Each of the seven levels has been given a label to reflect the sorts of theme involved. These labels are the least powerful aspect of the model because they may serve to confuse. The theme of quality, for example, actually applies to all levels of discretion, and most first line workers also have to attend to service. However, taken as a whole, most managers would accept that the seven themes of quality, service, good practice, development, mission and strategic intent, corporate citizenship and corporate prescience should apply to, and be built into, their organization structure.

Jacques originally used the seven levels to reinforce the existence of hierarchies in organizations, and to link these to pay systems on a justifiable basis. There is sometimes confusion that the seven levels should represent a top-down description of the management hierarchy. It is tempting for managers to conclude from Stamp's (1990) work that no organization should ever reduce itself to less than seven levels, i.e. to assume that each different time span of discretion should be associated with a single grade or level of the structure. This of course is not the case. The seven levels are an abstraction. Whilst Stamp (1990) would argue there are seven generic and unchangeable levels of discretion that can be applied to most organizations, any one layer of the organization may combine one or more of them.

The framework is, therefore, most useful for organization structuring when applied in one of the following ways:

- Informing decisions about the size of units and whether to centralize or decentralize decision making.
- Ensuring a match between all seven time spans of discretion and the physical levels of the organization structure.
- Shaping thinking about the most appropriate objectives and responsibilities for individuals in a new structure.
- Making assessments about individual capability to perform each type of role.

Table 8.1 A matrix of working relationships.

Time span of discretion	Typical roles	Objective	Responsibilities	Judgement-making	Theme	Complexity model
I Up to three months	First line worker responsible for direct operating tasks	Make or do something concrete that can be fully specified beforehand and can assure viability	Manage self and resources to optimum effect; use continuous practical judgement	*Touch and feel* practical watchfulness in direct response to immediate tasks	Quality	
II Up to one year	First line manager or supervisor, first level technician; professional specialist	Demonstrate the purpose of organization in response to particular situations/ cases/customers	Comprehend and resolve situations; explain why and how work is to be done	*Accumulating* Gather information step-by-step to reveal underlying complexities of each particular situation; imagine outcomes of possible responses	Service	
III Up to two years	Middle manager, principal specialist, principal officer	Maintain various ways purpose is being realized in provision of services/ production of goods i.e. the means	Imagine all possible practices and systems; select in the light of local conditions; make the most of people, finance and technologies to realize those chosen	*Connecting* Scan series of activities; Look for trends or principles that link plan and reality to make or improve a coherent whole	Good practice	
IV Up to five years	General manager; head of function; chiefly specialist or professional	Manage the relationship between mission and means	Develop new means; resource established means; terminate means that are no longer effective	*Modelling* Retain mental contact with a starting point that exists, detach from it, shape information and 'noise' in that detachment to produce something completely innovative	Development	

	Time span	Role/position	Viability	Represent		Mission
V	Up to ten years	Managing director of a corporate subsidiary, chief executive officer of a free-standing strategic unit; director of a national voluntary organization; group specialist	Ensure the long-term external and internal viability of executive organization in financial and social terms	Represent organization to external socio-economic context; represent organization to itself; source of current and new technologies; relate functions of Level IV	*Weaving* Draw on sense of interconnectedness to relate apparently discrete issues, events or matters	Mission/strategic intent
VI	Up to fifteen or twenty years	Corporate group executive; corporate counsel, treasurer or strategic analyst	'Read within' economic, political, social, technological and religious contexts	Obtain and shape intelligence; alert and protect strategic units against excessive turbulence; priorities for investment and divestment; represent the organization in the transnational arena	*Revealing* Extend curiosity beyond recognized areas of potential influence on events to probe for unexpected sources of opportunity or instability	Corporate citizenship
VII	More than twenty years	Chief executive officer, chief operating officer or president of a very large organization	Sustain viability for future generations	Define and disseminate vision and values; design contexts for strategic advantage >25 years ahead	*Previewing* Interpret shifting configurations of economies, politics, nations, religions, ideologies and mould into desired futures	Corporate prescience

The Operation Matrix			The Organization Matrix		The Strategic Matrix	
Level I	Level II	Level III	Level IV	Level V	Level VI	Level VII

Source: Stamp (1990), reprinted with permission © Brunel Institute of Organization and Social Studies, 1993.

The time spans of discretion are also relevant to work on downsizing and empowerment. We discuss downsizing in detail in Chapter Sixteen. One of the most common pitfalls is to eradicate whole layers of management without due regard to redesigning the structure and management process. The time spans of discretion have wide applicability and may be used to assess where, and with what level of accountability and responsibility, the seven roles still take place in the redesigned structure. In many cases it is only several years after a reorganization that it becomes apparent that certain levels are missing and have not been re-allocated. There are useful modern applications for old ideas about organization structure that have a long heritage.

PURPOSE OF ORGANIZATION DESIGN

From the preceding section it is clear that the organization structure has important implications for the main roles that employees play, for the sorts of communications and interactions they perform, for the decisions they make, and the judgement skills they possess. Organization structure is a critical element in the process of managing human resources (Walker, 1992). Many managers are tempted to believe that there is an ideal and enduring design for their organization. Ulrich and Lake (1990) argue this is no longer the case. We pointed out that structural change will become a continuous process in most organizations throughout the 1990s. Managers therefore have to establish a stable process of ongoing organization design. Only by recognizing that organization designs have to be fluid (and cannot realistically be perfected) will managers find it easier to implement the changes suggested in Part Two. However, whilst organization designs cannot be perfected, they can be 'engineered' to meet some quite exacting performance criteria. Mastering this process of design has to allow for continuous:

- Modification of the organization.
- Clarification of reporting relationships, responsibilities and control systems.

The structure of an organization needs to send clear messages about the management philosophy. In this respect, we can summarize the lessons from the first part of this chapter by highlighting the most important aims of an organization design (see Illustration 8.7).

Ulrich and Lake (1990) stress that the primary purpose of an organization design is

Illustration 8.7 **The aims of organization design.**

- Shape the organization in terms of the number of levels, spans of control, roles, reporting relationships and division of labour.
- Establish a mechanism for governance.
- Shape the way people think and behave.
- Create an organization identity and grouping of activity that lasts beyond the tenure of individuals.
- Provide and sustain the most appropriate combination of personal competencies in order to improve the total organization's capability.
- Ensure a match between the time spans of discretion and the individual capabilities.
- Provide boundaries for, and consistency and stability in, business operations.
- Provide a rationale and basis for the formal interactions between individuals.
- Design systems to ensure efficient and effective communication, co-ordination and integration of effort.

Illustration 8.8 **The scope and territory of organization design from a mechanistic, biological or information processing perspective.**

■ Establishing the processes by which responsibility is allocated.	■ Creation of control systems.
	■ Identification of accountabilities.
■ Definition of roles.	■ Delegation of decision making authority.

Source: Galbraith (1977).

to create the most appropriate combination of individual skills and competencies in order to build an 'organizational capability' that is better than that of competitors. In combining these personal competencies, the organization design should ensure that they endure and persist over time. The way in which an organization is structured helps sustain this capability by offering institutional support to individuals who display the appropriate competencies.

In order to achieve these aims, and to help articulate the impact that changes in structure have on employee behaviour, writers who view the organization in mechanistic, biological or information processing terms have identified a clear scope and territory for approaches to organization design (see Illustration 8.8).

ASKING IMPORTANT QUESTIONS ABOUT APPROPRIATE BEHAVIOUR

The HRM perspective on organization structuring builds on this approach by focusing on the social and behavioural impact of the organization design. We have already described how the organization design has a profound effect on the relationship between business activities, the flow of information and the decision making necessary for work to get done. The structure of an organization provides an essential order to the business process and helps co-ordinate the activities of employees. This is why it is so essential that the structure in some way reflects the strategy of the organization. There are dangers, however, in always assuming that a change in the structure is the best solution. Heyer and Lee (1991) point out that for many organizations changing the structure is the first response they think of, often regardless of long-term strategic needs, or the short-term social and behavioural consequences.

When an apparently well-crafted and coherent business strategy is not working, companies usually respond by reorganizing or restructuring to become 'leaner and meaner' ... 'flatter', purging 'excessive bureaucracy', acting 'like a small company' and locating decision making 'close to the customer'. Such well-intentioned responses can be completely wrong.

Heyer and Lee (1991).

Figure 8.2 has already shown the pervasive impact that changes in the organization structure have upon the behaviour of employees and the social structure of the organization. There are undoubtedly many problems with re-organizations. They can often be:

■ Costly and confusing.
■ Abandoning the real benefits of the existing structure in return for speculative benefits of a new one.
■ Treating symptoms rather than causes.
■ Introducing undesirable side effects of their own.

Illustration 8.9 **Why change the structure? Key HRM considerations.**

- What exposure to new sources of information is desired?
- Information, skills or capital to be collected in a single grouping?
- Resources that should be used by the grouping?
- Performance indicators that should be monitored?
- Discretion in goals and action setting?
- Which interactions should be controlled or co-ordinated? i.e. Who needs to talk to who?

- What new relationships are intended to be developed?
- What new work content is expected?
- What are the new role requirements, and why are they necessary?
- What new accountabilities are involved?
- What improvements to the business process can be affected?

Given the likely scale of future organizational change within European organizations we clearly need to develop a better understanding about the topic from a behavioural and social perspective if these pitfalls are to be avoided. The most important questions to ask from this viewpoint are shown in Illustration 8.9.

Having clarified the answers (in clear observable and actionable terms that managers can understand) the organization can then make more appropriate decisions about the actual form of the structural change, i.e. will it be achieved by reducing levels, decentralizing, creating new levels, using project teams and task forces, or perhaps relying on voluntary or informal associations?

SOCIAL PROCESSES PRECIPITATED BY STRUCTURAL CHANGE

Changing the structure also precipitates a host of awkward social processes that have to be managed. In the previous chapter we discussed the work of Michael Beer on the strengths and weaknesses of programmatic change. Changing an organizational structure is a classic example of the need to manage several very complex social processes. Figure 8.4 shows seven successive phases of social processes involved in a typical major organizational change such as creating a new structure. HRM managers need to manage all seven phases actively if the answers to the questions in Illustration 8.9 are expected to be converted into changes in behaviour (which lie at the heart of effective HRM). In reality a few organizations attempt to manage the first three phases. A smaller proportion put sufficient thought into the design of the delivery phase and only a handful attempt to manage the critical social processes that occur after the new organization has been designed and implemented i.e. the endings and unlearning that are required, the legitimization, and the requirements for new learning. These issues are often only encountered (once it is too late) two to three years after the new design is in place. It is not surprising that Heyer and Lee (1991) found that changes in organization structure are notable mainly for their failure.

Unfortunately, as Peters (1979) concludes, organizational restructuring is frequently a short-term measure used to respond to external and internal pressures in an attempt to enhance effectiveness. Rarely does it achieve a sense of consistency and internal balance (Mintzberg, 1991) and few organizations can be credited with objectively identifying all the structural needs, contingencies and impacts on behaviour. All European organizations need to bear these lessons in mind as they continue down their path of restructuring. We now turn our attention to the nature of organization structures in large European organizations.

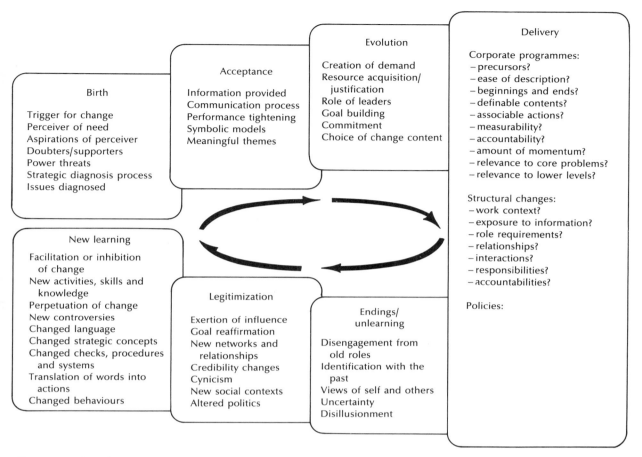

Figure 8.4 Social processes involved in successful management of change.

NATIONAL DIFFERENCES IN ORGANIZATION STRUCTURE

Having reviewed the most important ideas about organization, ways of grouping people together into small units, the purpose of organization design, the important questions to ask about changing behaviour and the various social processes precipitated by changing the structure, we return to the European context. In this second section of the chapter we examine some differences that exist in work structuring, co-ordination and the shape of organizations across three European countries: Germany, France and Britain. The evidence for these differences tends to come from studies of manufacturing activities and factory organization (Bessant and Grunt, 1985; Finlay, 1991; Lutz, 1981; Maitland, 1983; Maurice, Sorge and Warner, 1980; Sorge and Warner, 1986). We then consider the differences in mechanisms for corporate governance, and cultural preferences for different types of co-ordination.

It should be stressed that as the manufacturing sector continues to erode as a proportion of employment, so might some of the distinctions drawn in this section. However, since the underlying reasons for differences in work structuring and the shape of organizations are generally felt to be linked to underlying cultural factors that are often expressed in institutional arrangements such as qualification and promotion systems, skills profiles and industrial relations practices (i.e. more enduring factors), then their continued influence on organization structure seem guaranteed for a while. We link some of the empirical findings on European HRM practices from the IBM/Towers Perrin study (see Chapter Two) to material reviewed in this part of the chapter to support some of the points made.

Given that the structure of a business organization is highly dependent on a number of factors in the environment, marked variations are always found across societies, industrial sectors and size of enterprise. Nevertheless, there are some clear natural patterns that cut across such factors (Lane, 1989). These tend to result in distinct national differences in a number of areas (see Illustration 8.10) which cover all seven dimensions of structure identified by Daft (1992).

Maurice, Sorge and Warner (1980) analysed nine matched production units in Britain, Germany and France. They found that organizations from the three countries had a number of common structural features (see Illustration 8.11). However, although there were common structural features, the size of each category relative to other categories differed significantly between the three countries (see Figure 8.5).

Work tasks and processes of supervision

There are differing national patterns of structuring and co-ordinating work between France, Britain and Germany that tend to result in different organizational configurations. In France, features of organization structure include both a large number of hierarchical layers and a compartmentalization along horizontal lines. In contrast to stereotypes of a highly bureaucratized and formal German organizational style, in structural terms their organizations are the most personal and career-friendly ones (Maurice, Sorge and Warner, 1980). In Germany there is a relatively flat organization structure and a blurring of differentiation across horizontal parts of the structure. In Germany, given the greater balance of economic activity in the

Illustration 8.10 **National differences in organization structure.**

- Division of work tasks and design of jobs (Specialization, Professionalism, Standardization).
- Distribution of work tasks across the hierarchy (Hierarchy).
- Processes of co-ordination, supervision and spans of control (Complexity, Formulation).
- Structures of business governance, top-level hierarchies and strategic decision making (Centralization).

Source: Lane (1989).

Illustration 8.11 **Common structural features in production organizations.**

- Similar categories of employees divided according to task performance:
  - staff versus works employees,
  - conceptual work versus executing plans,
  - controllers and those who submit to control.
- Categories of employees arranged in the same hierarchical manner.
- Greater horizontal division of labour as the complexity of the organization increased.

Source: Maurice, Sorge and Warner (1980).

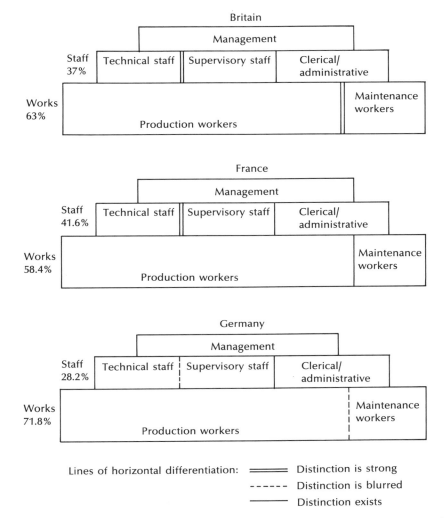

Figure 8.5 National organizational configurations. *Source*: Lane (1989), reprinted with permission, © 1993, Edward Elgar Publishing Ltd.

manufacturing sector, the production department has a central role and other departments tend to be at its service (Lane, 1989). More flexibility is required and boundaries between departments are more fluid, co-operative and interactive. The IBM/Towers Perrin survey found that 84 per cent of German managers saw the requirement for employee flexibility as important to achieving competitive advantage, compared to 78 per cent in France and 77 per cent in Britain. In contrast, the greater specialization and compartmentalization between departments in Britain and France is associated with production departments more dominated by, and in competition with, technical services.

The IBM/Towers Perrin (1992) survey found that 81 per cent of German managers saw flexible cross-functional teams and work groups as important in achieving competitive advantage, compared to 65 per cent in Britain, but only 22 per cent in France. Similarly, 65 per cent of German managers valued flexible work arrangements compared to 52 per cent of British managers and only 19 per cent of French managers.

British organization structures tend to have higher horizontal differentiation between roles and functions in comparison to German structures. These horizontal divisions tend to create higher levels of conflict between functional groups, perceptions of dual authority, communication blocks and lower integration of work roles (Bessant and Grunt, 1985). Historically, this has presented British organizations with problems of production quantity and quality, and after sales service. Lane (1989) points out that such inbuilt deficiencies often have as much to do with national education, qualification and training arrangements and industrial relations systems, as they do with pure decisions about organization design and structure. These features are summarized in Figure 8.5.

In Chapter Two we examined some empirical evidence on European HRM practices. The IBM/Towers Perrin survey data revealed a distinct pattern of French concepts and practices (Sparrow, Schuler and Jackson, 1994) and one of the most marked differences between France and other European countries was the greater importance attached to centralization and vertical hierarchy (see Figures 2.6 and 8.6). Lane (1989) points out how the French organization is the epitome of the bureaucratized and highly formalized structure. Such organization creates a heavy administrative load, bypasses supervisory staff, and can lead to communication and morale problems at lower levels. Communication tends to be impaired by distant management–worker relations linked to stark differences in social origin and education and pronounced pay differentials in French organizations. Tall hierarchies within French organizations do, however, carry certain benefits such as greater emphasis on on-the-job training as opposed to formal development, clear progression from job to job within the enterprise, better career prospects and rewards for desired managerial behaviour. The heavier reliance on supervision and control has been associated with higher productivity. Grünberg (1986) found that efficiency and productivity in matched British and French plants was clearly superior in French ones, although at a price of higher employee disaffection. This

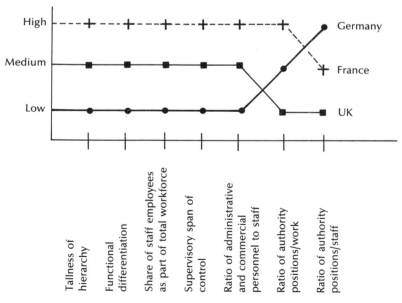

Figure 8.6 Contrasting features of organizational structures in France, Germany and UK.
Source: after Lane (1989), based on Sorge and Warner (1986), reprinted with permission, © 1993, Edward Elgar Publishing Ltd.

aspect of structure – specialization – may remain different between French organiz-ations and other European organizations for the forseeable future. The IBM/Towers Perrin survey found that only 7 per cent of British managers, 11 per cent of German managers and 15 per cent of Italian managers saw the maintenance of specialized and directed workforces as being of value in achieving competitive advantage. The figure was around four times as high – 53 per cent – for French managers.

Corporate governance

Humes (1993) points out that the different compositions of American, European and Asian corporate boards mirrors and reinforces the perspective they each have to oversee corporate operations and international opportunities. We have pointed out that one of the triggers for structural change may be changes in leadership and the articulation of new business strategies. The way in which a multinational organization structures the two main bodies of corporate governance (the corporate board of directors and the corporate executive team) determines the impact that corporate leadership may have in managing the different perspectives that managers use to shape the organization and its structure. Who comprises the corporate governance, the interests they represent, the responsibilities they shoulder, and how issues are dealt with individually and collectively all have a significant impact on the corporate strategy and structure. In this section we answer these questions by considering national differences in:

- The proportion of insiders and outsiders on boards.
- Unitary and dual board structure.

One significant difference between American, British, European and Asian corporate boards is the extent to which they are composed of executive 'insiders' and non-executive 'outsiders'. Most of the larger American, British, Swiss and Italian multinationals mix 'outsider' directors with 'insider' executives on their boards. American corporations tend to have 40 per cent of seats held by 'insiders'. In British corporations the figure is 60 per cent, whilst in Swiss and Italian multinationals only a handful of top officers are on the board (Mills, 1985). Only 'outsiders' are included in German 'supervisory boards' (*Aufsichtsrat*). These are separate to the members of the corporate executive team on the Management board (*Vorstand*). The larger French and Dutch multinationals have a similar two-tier arrangement. In contrast, in Japanese and South Korean multinationals the senior executives generally hold all of the seats.

These differences in the inclusion of 'outsiders' as part of corporate governance tend to reflect national cultural differences. The lack of outsiders on Japanese and South Korean boards reflects the emphasis on group homogeneity, the inclusion of workers' representatives on German boards reflects Germanic social values, whilst the fact that 59 per cent of US corporations had women board members and 31 per cent included minorities in 1989 (Korn-Ferry International, 1990) reflects an equal opportunity consciousness. Home cultural values, until recently, have taken priority over the development of more globally representative mechanisms of corporate governance. We discuss the internationalization of top boards in Chapter Eleven, Career Management.

The corporate executive team tend to share top management leadership responsibilities. In continental European organizations with a two-tier structure, the second tier is the executive team. It is often labelled differently, known as the Vorstand in the Bayer Group, Management Committee in Philips, Committee of Managing Directors in Royal Dutch/Shell and the Office of the Chairman in DuPont.

As well as differences in the proportion of insiders versus outsiders involved in corporate governance, there are both unitary and dual board systems. British organizations only use the unitary system where executive and non-executive directors sit on one board. This combined board is the supreme decision making body, with power to elect and dismiss the chief executive and considerable delegated responsibilities. British unitary boards are considered to be more powerful than in Germany (Wilpert and Rayley, 1983) although their active involvement in strategic policy making varies considerably. In Germany, the unitary system is found in the smaller private limited companies (such as the GmbH type). This single tier board consists of managers (*Geschäftsfürer*) and directors elected by shareholders (Lane, 1989).

The two-tier system, instituted in Germany in 1870 to recognize the close relationship between industry and banking (Dyson, 1986) provides financial institutions with a more powerful instrument of control. It is a legal requirement for larger private and public limited companies (*AG* or *Aktiengesellschaft*) in Germany and is also widely adopted by French and Dutch corporations. The supervisory board (*Aufsichtrat*) represents shareholders and employee interests. It mirrors the organizations' business relationships, also consisting of other industrialists whose organizations are either customers or suppliers. The function of the supervisory board has shifted from one of control towards administration, and the two boards are increasingly linked (Dyson, 1986). The banks still exert considerable influence over restructuring in German organizations. The management board (*Vorstand*) consists of 3–15 top managers. Members bear a collegiate responsibility (Dyas and Thanheiser, 1976) and there is no managing director. Rather, the chairman represents the organization, but with varying degrees of personal power. However, top management are on five year contracts, reviewed by the supervisory board. Since 1971, by law, German corporations cannot vest corporate management authority solely in the chairman (chief executive), although certain individuals, such as Edzard Reuter of Daimler-Benz, still manage to demonstrate powerful leadership.

In France company articles determine whether a single or two-tier board is established. The majority of large limited companies (*Société Anonyme, SA*) have single tier boards. The board (*conseil d'administration*) has 3–12 directors (*administrateurs*) presided over by an elected chairman and managing director (*président directeur-général, PDG*). The PDG has considerable delegated power, frequently being the only management representative on the board (Horovitz, 1980). The two-tier alternative has a supervisory board (*directoire*) which appoints directors on the management board. Private limited companies are usually owner-managed (*Société à responsabilité limitée, SARL*) with similar powers to the *directoire* (Mills, 1985). Control in larger organizations is exerted through technocratic power, with former high civil servants being prominent due to the system of *pantouflage* (an old boys' network whereby senior civil servants get rotated into senior management positions in industry). The role of these ex-civil servants is similar to that of bankers in German organizations.

THE IMPACT OF NATIONAL CULTURE ON CO-ORDINATION PREFERENCES

From an organizational perspective, Europe is a collection of cultures, and European integration is unlikely to overcome the markedly different histories, languages, traditions and education systems for many years to come (Humes, 1993). It is easier to note distinctions and dissimilarities than commonalities. Hence, the British business culture tends to attribute organizational success to a resourceful pragmatism and adaptability, whilst the German business culture attributes organizational success to logic and rationality. In France a sense of *élan* and educational pedigree, shared values and elitist networks are important. The Italian business culture prizes charisma, spontaneity, and a degree of chaos (Humes, 1993). When viewed as a whole, these European business cultures have historically been reflected in a less formal or carefully defined approach to organizational structuring than seen in US organizations, with a preference for loosely defined arrangements and job descriptions in contrast to the desire for organizational structures with closely defined distributions of authority, responsibility and job duties in US organizations.

Despite such general historical differences, Humes (1993) makes four useful observations about the impact of national culture on decisions about organizational structure:

1. Within countries and sectors, there are marked differences seen between organizations. For example, British Petroleum undertook rapid and revolutionary changes in its structure, whilst Shell adopted a more deliberate evolutionary approach.
2. In the face of global competition, organizational values associated with the US approach to structure have begun to replace the traditional European ones.
3. European multinationals have historically accommodated a greater variety of national cultures and approaches and have therefore not pursued a path of creating strong corporate-wide cultures.
4. Occupational cultures, steeped in the specializations, predispositions and priorities of professions (such as engineers, marketeers and accountants) or industries (such as motor vehicles, chemicals or oil) have as powerful an influence on thinking about organization structure as do national cultures.

These observations should be borne in mind when considering some of the findings on national cultural preferences for particular organization structures. In Chapter Three we discussed the impact of national culture on aspects of European HRM. Cultural factors – and particularly their reflection in institutional arrangements in such areas as training and promotion systems, qualification structures, industrial relations systems, and the relationship between financial and industrial capital – can be expected to influence decisions made by managers about organization design.

> . . . Although the design of organizational structure has to take account of environmental factors, managers can usually exercise a degree of choice between alternative designs. Such choice can be influenced by knowledge about alternative and more effective designs of organizational structure.   Lane (1989, p. 39).

Nevertheless, given that culture consists of a shared and commonly-held body of general beliefs and values that define many of the 'shoulds' and 'oughts' of managerial life, facets of it should be expected to be reflected in preferences for particular types of organization design (Lane and DiStefano, 1988). This is particularly the case given the nature of organization design outlined in this chapter, i.e. a series of metaphors used to reflect underlying mindsets about the purpose of organization, decisions about employee roles, patterns of communication and interaction, time spans of discretion in decision making, and co-ordination mechanisms used to control the vertical and horizontal dimensions of structure. These all represent ripe territory for national cultural differences.

European countries differ along a number of cultural dimensions. One is in terms of the responsibility one has for the welfare of others. As we discussed in Chapter Two, Anglo-Saxon approaches to HRM are influenced by more individualistic attitudes, whilst Mediterranean cultures (such as in Italy and Spain) place more emphasis on a group orientation, with allegiance extended to the group (or tribe) to which one belongs. A third type of relationship is hierarchical (as found, for example, in France) in which the relation is to others in a group that is nested in a stable hierarchy. Organizational structures, communication and influence patterns, reward systems and many managerial processes are all influenced by these three relationship orientations (Lane and DiStefano, 1988), as shown in in Table 8.2.

In Chapter Three we described the work of Hofstede on national culture, and presented one of the maps for power distance × individualism. Lane and DiStefano (1988) believe that from a cultural perspective the most important map to consider when structuring organizations is the power distance × uncertainty avoidance map (see Figure 8.7). It can be related to many of the dimensions of structure outlined by Daft (1992). Other factors being equal, people in large power distance cultures (for example, France, Belgium and Turkey) prefer decisions to be centralized whilst people from small power distance cultures (for example, Denmark, Sweden, Austria and Ireland) want decisions to be decentralized. Whilst power distance relates to centralization, uncertainty avoidance relates to formalization (the need for formal rules, specialization and assignment of tasks to experts). Work by O.J. Stevens whilst at INSEAD (in Lane and DiStefano, 1988) examined the organizational solutions preferred by German, British and French MBA students to a conflict and problem within an organization's structure. Most French MBAs referred the problem to the next highest authority, the German MBAs attributed it to a lack of written policy, whilst the British MBAs attributed it to a lack of interpersonal communication, best cured by

Table 8.2 **Relationship orientation and behaviours associated with organization structure.**

Relationship orientation	Example countries	Reflection in organizational structure
Individual	US UK	■ Considerable attention given to the structure ■ Focus on leadership ■ Informal attitude to the arrangement of relations, i.e. report to who needs to know ■ Flexible behaviours within the structure ■ Instrumental attitude to interpersonal relationships ■ Two-boss relationships possible e.g. matrix structure
Group	Italy Spain	■ More attention to horizontal differentiation ■ Structures of work; organizations reflect differences between groups ■ Within-group communications
Hierarchical	France	■ Rigidly obeyed structures ■ Preference to report to a single boss, i.e. matrix not favoured ■ Authority-based communications ■ Emphasis on both vertical and horizontal differentiation ■ Interpersonal relationships valued as ends in themselves

Source: after Lane and DiStefano (1988).

group training. Managers, therefore, carry 'implicit models' about the workings of organization structures in their heads. Nevertheless, these 'implicit models' may easily be open to modification. Laurent (1991) found that the high power distance in French organizations means that French managers strongly disbelieve the feasibility of matrix organizations (defined and discussed later in this chapter). Yet, in the French subsidiary of a multinational corporation that had a long history of successful matrix management, the French managers were quite positive toward it. Cultural barriers to organizational innovation can be overcome (Lane and DiStefano, 1988).

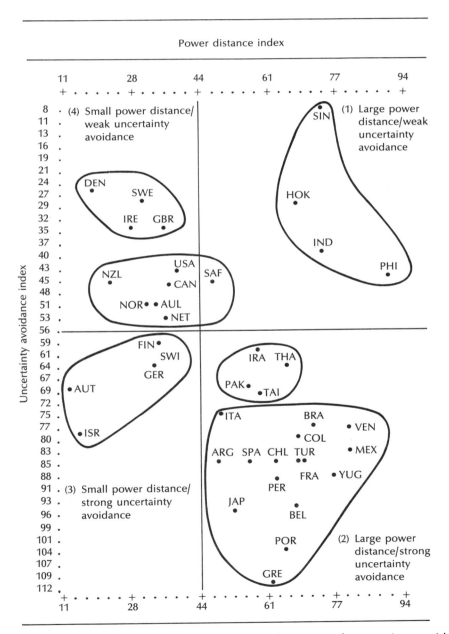

Figure 8.7 Position of forty countries on the power distance and uncertainty avoidance scales. *Source*: Lane and DiStefano (1988), after Hofstede (1980).

Illustration 8.12 **Pan-European pressures leading to convergence of structures in larger organizations.**

- Increased market/competitive pressure on performance resulting in an equalization in the number of management layers.
- Requirement for higher levels of workforce commitment.

- Higher levels of communication, consultation and empowerment associated with redesigned business processes.
- Requirement for more collaborative organization cultures.

Despite these national differences in the shape of organizations, the high level of organizational change appears to be associated with the intention at least (if not the eventual practice) to converge as far as the number of managerial levels is concerned. The IBM/Towers Perrin survey of worldwide HRM practices found that only 38 per cent of German managers – already working in flat, delayered structures with broad spans of control – saw the need to eliminate layers and increase spans of control as being important to achieve competitive advantage. However, sitting in their taller, more hierarchical structures, this figure rose to 62 per cent of British managers and 63 per cent of French managers. Lane (1989) acknowledges that despite some deep-rooted institutional differences accounting for organization structure differences in Germany, Britain and France, several European-wide developments in the relationship between management and labour in the larger organizations at least may result in greater convergence in structures at the middle and lower levels (see Illustration 8.12).

THE INTERNATIONAL DIVISION: EMERGENCE OF MULTINATIONAL STRUCTURES

In the third section of this chapter we take a historical and evolutionary perspective on the development of the large multinationals in Europe. In order to co-ordinate smaller units within the organization, a number of mechanisms or modes of organization have emerged over the twentieth century. Bartlett and Ghoshal (1989) observe that multinational organizations, built up over decades, develop a distinct heritage (above and beyond the cultural factors just discussed) which is both difficult to change and also shapes their future organization. The ability to change an organization's structure and its principal co-ordinating mechanisms is usually severely constrained. In the next sections of this chapter we shall describe the main forms of co-ordination and organization structure by placing their development into a description of the historical evolution of multinational organizations in the US and Europe. In so doing we intend to explain both the detail and nature of organization modes of operation within Europe, and the emerging HRM issues and paths of change. The discussion draws strongly on the excellent comparative analysis of multinational organization recently provided by Humes (1993). He has studied the collective histories of twenty-six organizations from the US, Europe and Asia and analysed the strategies employed in reorganizing their international activities.

In general, the basic co-ordinating mechanisms and modes of operation of international organizations correspond to those of domestic ones, although, of course, the greater the degree of internationalization, the more complex this aspect of structure becomes (Czinkota, Rivoli and Ronkainen, 1992). There have been four successive eras of organizational change that have left their 'imprint' on modern multinationals (Humes, 1993):

- Pre-1945 – emergence of big industrial corporations and the international division.
- 1945–59 – American domination.
- 1960–74 – European redevelopment.
- 1975–89 – Asian emergence.
- 1990–?   – towards transformation and new organizational forms.

Useful historical reviews of the emergence of large industrial corporations have been provided by Chandler (1990) and Wilkins (1974). They first emerged in the latter decades of the nineteenth century. In the early decades of the twentieth century there were more modern enterprises in the US than Britain or Germany, and organizations like Standard Oil, Ford and General Electric began to directly invest overseas. International expansion accelerated after the First World War. In order to manage international operations a new structure was needed, and this has widely become known as the international division. General Electric formed an international division in 1919, General Motors in 1924, Standard Oil in 1927, and IBM created a foreign department in 1939.

European organizations also expanded beyond their domestic markets during this period. They chose a different organizational design and tended to create clone-like, relatively self-contained and autonomous affiliates – what Humes (1993) calls 'daughter companies'. The parent exerted strategic control over groups of such companies. Nestlé began assembling its international empire before the First World War, and Philips developed eighteen European affiliates by 1930. Similarly, the Anglo-Persian Oil Company (now British Petroleum) developed European affiliates before the Second World War. The European philosophy was to rely on trusted associate organizations which were well understood, thereby allowing significant levels of autonomy. This reliance on geographically disparate and highly autonomous national affiliates influences restructuring in European organizations to this day (Mitchell, 1993). It led to a reliance on the 'man on the spot' (the country manager), lower local management costs because of low co-ordination, but fragmented markets, complex and over-staffed headquarters, and high central costs needed to maintain separate subsidiaries in each country.

In the years immediately following the Second World War, the US firms capitalized on their network of operations controlled by international divisions and well developed, war-propelled productive capacity and domestic markets. The US approached a near world domination in several industries such as electrical equipment, motor vehicles, oil, chemicals and food. By 1959 all but six of the world's largest multinationals were American, the other six being European. These were the two Dutch–British organizations of Royal Dutch/Shell and Unilever, British Petroleum and Imperial Chemical Industries from Britain; Nestlé from Switzerland and Philips from Holland (Humes, 1993).

Moves towards the international division therefore only began to occur on a large scale in the 1950s, led by US organizations expanding worldwide. It represented a fundamental shift in philosophy, signalling that foreign countries were no longer just markets for domestic exports, but locations for an expanding business presence in terms of sales, service, warehousing, manufacturing, product design and research (Taoka and Beeman, 1991). It also reflected a different US philosophy to European operations. US managers were used to a large domestic market, liked to be able to have 'hands on' control, and placed little weight on national differences (Mitchell, 1993).

However, it is important to outline the nature of the international division for two main reasons:

1. Historically it formed the antecedent of many current multinationals.
2. For current domestic organizations that are just beginning to internationalize, it is often the first mode of operation they develop.

As well as having a historical pedigree, the international division is relevant to organizations currently internationalizing. Early work on international modes of operation and organization structure took the logical approach of relating it to the life cycle of organizations and the growth of international activity (Beamish, Killing, Lecraw and Crookell, 1991). The first organizational stage for currently internationalizing organizations is the establishment of export departments to handle the technical task of exporting products (see Figure 8.8). If successful, the greater awareness of global opportunities leads to establishing an international division to control both exports and foreign investments. The point in establishing international divisions so early in the internationalization process is to protect emerging sales and profits from core domestic concerns, and provide a basis for building future international activity. The key challenge in internationalizing organizations is for the manager of the international division to understand the product-market strategies of each product division and adapt them to international markets.

The international division has therefore been used as a way of centralizing all of the responsibility for international activities. The structure is intended to eliminate the possible biases against international operations that emerge when domestic divisions independently serve international customers. International expertise, information flows on foreign market opportunities and authority over activities are all concentrated into one area, although manufacturing and other related functions may remain with domestic divisions in order to maintain economies of scale. Co-ordination of the domestic divisions and the international division is achieved through joint staffing functions or strategic planning processes and frequent interaction of personnel.

Organizations tend to outgrow this type of structure once international sales and products grow in diversity. Historically, many US organizations shifted from

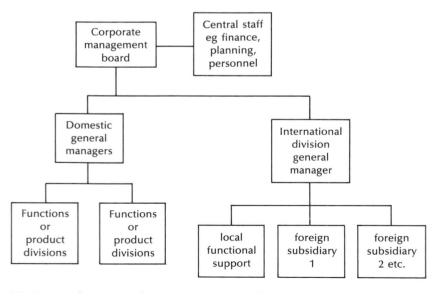

Figure 8.8 A typical structure for an international division.

independent international divisions in the 1970s. However, for medium-sized European organizations in early stages of the internationalization process it is a common mode of operation. Size in itself is not a limitation on this type of co-ordination mechanism, with some of the world's largest organizations relying on international divisions.

EVOLUTION TOWARDS THE GLOBAL ORGANIZATION: THREE PRINCIPAL CO-ORDINATING CATEGORIES

To return to the historical perspective, it was during the years 1960–74 that the major European multinational groups grew dramatically. Siemens, Daimler-Benz, Volkswagen and Fiat all secured places in the Fortune Global 50, soon joined by BASF, Hoechst, Bayer, Renault and British American Tobacco (Humes, 1993). In fact the number of European multinationals in the Global 50 tripled to twenty by 1974.

As these organizations grew they also diversified into new products and markets. It was at this point that significant differences in co-ordination mechanisms and modes of operation began to emerge between European organizations as the industrial sector began to shape options more than national culture. Philips, for example, continued to rely on international affiliates to develop worldwide activities and started a process of rationalization in manufacturing that was to last decades. Fiat became a loosely administered conglomerate, whilst Bayer undertook a re-organization that would lead to the adoption of a product-based structure. Similarly, US organizations, whilst continuing to expand, declined from forty-four to twenty-four of the Global 50. As they downsized international operations and made sizeable investments they began to replace their international divisions with other forms of co-ordination (Humes, 1993).

Most organizations are built around co-ordinating mechanisms or modes of operation that represent 'top level dimensions' which are used to group departments. They tend to represent common or shared identities (Vernon and Wells 1991). The primary concern at this level of analysis is how best to group business activities (not people). Organizations usually align themselves to either customers, markets or business processes in order to provide some basis for differentiation (Walker, 1992). As overseas operations increased in importance and scope, most managements felt the need to eliminate international divisions and establish worldwide organizations based on one of three types of shared identity and co-ordination (Ball and McCulloch, 1990):

1. Functions which are generally defined in terms of production, finance, marketing, human resources, research, and so forth.
2. Businesses within the organization: which are generally grouped according to a key product or market characteristic.
3. Countries or areas: which are generally grouped on a common principle of maximum homogeneity.

In essence, these forms of co-ordination define the overall shape of most multinational organizations. They were seen as being more attractive than the international division because they would help organizations develop competitive strategies to confront new global competition, allow lower production costs by promoting worldwide standardization and manufacturing rationalization, and would enhance the transfer of technology and allocation of resources. The three organizational prototypes are shown in Figure 8.9.

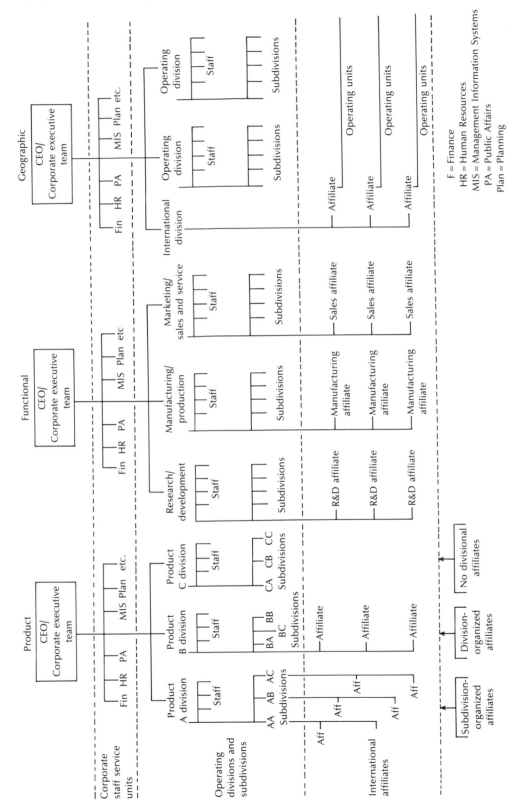

Figure 8.9 Three international organizational prototypes. *Source:* Humes (1993). Reprinted by permission of Prentice Hall.

FUNCTIONAL CO-ORDINATION

A very common mode of co-ordination in domestic organizations is to specialize parts of the organization according to function. Each function – such as production, marketing, finance, sales, and research and development – has its own hierarchy with a chain of command running from top to bottom. From any place at the bottom of the structure there is only one route back up to the top such that each employee has only one immediate superior. This form of structure is more common in domestic European organizations than US ones (Taoka and Beeman, 1991). Each functional head has worldwide line and staff responsibility for those activities. This mode of operation and co-ordination is significantly influenced by what Morgan (1986) called the

Context		Internal systems	
Environment:	Low uncertainty, stable customers and product requirements	Operative goals:	Functional goal emphasis, centralized decision making
Technology:	Routine, low interdependence	Planning and Budgeting:	Cost basis, statistical reporting
Size:	Small to medium	Formal authority:	Functional managers
Goals:	Internal efficiency and cost control Technical quality		

Strengths	Weaknesses
• Least complex structure	• Slow response time to environmental changes
• Allows economies of scale with functional departments	• May lead to decision overload at higher levels of hierarchy
• Enables in depth skill development	• Poor horizontal coordination among departments, excessive meetings
• Enables the organization to achieve functional goals	• Lower levels of innovation
• Best for small to medium size organizations	• Restricted view of organizational goals
• Clear accountability for functional failure	• Not fitted to growth, flexibility or change
	• Excessive levels of bureaucracy through operating procedures and planning systems
	• Professional or craft loyalty rather than customer orientation
	• High levels of conflict and political behaviour

Figure 8.10 Functional structure. *Source*: after Butler (1991), reprinted with permission, © 1993 R. Butler, *Designing Organizations: A decision-making perspective*, London: Routledge.

'mechanistic' image of organization. The advantages and disadvantages of a functional structure are shown in Figure 8.10.

A functional approach is still seen in many Japanese multinationals. Sales operations have long been separated from production divisions. International expansion was accommodated by relying on trading partners at Mitsui & Co. and the Mitsubishi Corporation, international trading and sales subsidiaries at Matsushita and Toyota, international divisions at Sony and Nissan, or a combination of these options at Hitachi (Humes, 1993). In general, Japanese production divisions developed their own international manufacturing affiliates, extending their function split. Canon is organized into three functional global systems for research and development, product and marketing.

Excepting Japanese organizations, few other worldwide organizations are structured by function at the top level. Those that are, have to believe that worldwide functional expertise is more significant than product or geographical knowledge. This tends to be the case for organizations with a narrow and highly integrated product mix, such as aircraft manufacturers or small computers (Ball and McCulloch, 1991). The disadvantages include duplication of geographic expertise, conflicting development of goals and difficulties dealing with product lines (Taoka and Beeman, 1991) and so most European multinationals have abandoned this form of co-ordination.

PRODUCT CO-ORDINATION

From 1975–89 both European and US organizations began to feel the presence of Japanese and then South Korean organizations. By 1989 there were twenty-one European, seventeen US and twelve Asian multinationals in the Global 50. The emergence of three continental trade blocs led to the need for dramatic organizational changes. Many US and European multinationals restructured themselves into product-driven multinationals, although in general they were coming from different backgrounds. US multinationals were increasing and then rationalizing operations across continents, strengthening product co-ordination and localizing their support functions as they transformed international divisions into global product structures. European multinationals such as Philips and ICI were attempting to convert daughter companies into product-driven multinationals. By the beginning of the 1990s most US multinationals relied on highly structured product divisions with only a handful – such as Proctor and Gamble or 3M – keeping international divisions. Similarly, an increasing number – but by no means all – of the European multinationals relied on product divisions to manage international affiliates. A few organizations, such as Royal Dutch/Shell and Nestlé, still relied on globally-dispersed daughter companies (Humes, 1993). A considerable degree of convergence in co-ordinating mechanisms has taken place.

A product structure provides each division with responsibility for a line of related products. The advantages and disadvantages of product or divisional structures are shown in Figure 8.11. Corporate staff provide support for the various business functions and area specialists remain in the corporate headquarters. The product division plans and controls worldwide activities for its line of products and can choose how activities are conducted, i.e. through subsidiaries, branches, licensees or distributors (Taoka and Beeman, 1991).

Context		Internal systems	
Environment:	Changing, moderate to high uncertainty	Operative goals:	Product line emphasis
Technology:	Non-routine, high interdependence among departments	Planning and Budgeting:	Profit centres, cost and income
Size:	Large	Formal authority:	Product managers
Goals:	External effectiveness, adaption, client satisfaction		

Strengths	Weaknesses
• Suited to fast change in an unstable environment	• Duplication of resources across self-contained operating divisions
• Clear product responsibility and contact points, and higher client satisfaction	• Eliminates economies of scale in functional departments
• High co-ordination across functions	• Poor marketing co-ordination across product lines
• Allows units to adapt to differences in products, regions, and clients	• Eliminates in depth competence and technical specialization
• Encourages growth of new products	• Makes integration and standardization across product lines difficult, wasteful of variety
• Suits large organizations with several products	• Inability to adapt to cost controlling environment
• Decentralizes decision making, encourages autonomy, economical on top management decision making	• Divisional rather than corporate loyalty
	• Promotes competitive rather than co-operative culture, especially when resources become scarce
	• Lower diffusion of innovations

Figure 8.11 Product or divisional structure. *Source*: after Butler (1991), reprinted with permission, © 1993, R. Butler, *Designing Organizations: A decision-making perspective*, London: Routledge.

FROM FUNCTIONAL TO PRODUCT CO-ORDINATION AT BAYER GROUP

Given some of the distinctions between British and German organizations discussed earlier in terms of the levels of horizontal communication, tallness of hierarchies and relations between departments (Lane, 1989), it might be expected that German organizations, driven by a faithful adherence to achieving *Termintreue* (deadlines promised to customers), would not find functional structures so problematic. However, a number of leading German multinationals are following the US trend of creating product divisions with global responsibilities. The Bayer Group is the world's fourth largest chemical company with revenues of $970.2 million. In 1993 it employed 154,000 people, operating in 150 countries and six sectors covering polymers, organic products, industrial products, healthcare, agrochemicals and imaging technologies (Hasell, 1993). Reflecting the discussion in Chapter Five on joint ventures, Bayer has pursued a strategy of concentrating on core businesses and co-operating in areas of low strength.

Bayer was founded in 1863 as a manufacturer of synthetic dyes. By 1900 it was a highly diversified organization, having expanded into the US and Europe, and into pharmaceuticals and photographic products. The 1925 consortium between Bayer, Hoechst and BASF to form I.G. Farben was confiscated by the Allies in 1945 and broken up into its three constituent parts in 1951. Until 1965 Bayer was divided into functions headed by members of the *Vorstand*.

Bayer has undertaken three re-organizations since 1965 in order to co-ordinate its group of diversified international businesses. The net effect of the changes were to transform Bayer from a functionally driven domestic management to a set of product groups with worldwide responsibilities (Humes, 1993), and the reputation of being highly innovative and the best organized of the three major German chemical organizations of Bayer, Hoechst and BASF (Hasell, 1993). Product co-ordinating committees were introduced to the functional structure with *Vorstand* members having dual responsibilities, directing one function and one product division. The result was a halfway house with a lack of objectivity in the board (Humes, 1993). In 1971, under advice from Du Pont, Bayer developed a multidivisionalized structure, rejecting the option of setting up an international division and moving straight to product divisions with worldwide responsibilities. The *Vorstand* were relieved of direct operational responsibilities. The change in German corporate law changed the position of Chief Executive Officer from a 'one-above-others leader' (*Führerprinzip*) to that of 'primus inter pares' who needed the support of at least one half of the board for a major decision.

Thirteen years later, in 1984, Bayer again re-organized, dividing into nine divisions and twenty-four business groups (themselves forming six sectors) and a smaller *Vorstand* with nine members. The business groups were regrouped and restructured, responsibilities classified, many responsibilities of the *Vorstand* were delegated to lower levels, and many foreign activities and subsidiaries were integrated into Bayer World. Each business group had its own headquarters, mostly in Leverkusen in Germany. By 1992 one of the nine *Vorstand* members was a non-German, and six of the twenty-five business groups were non-German. The structure is shown in Figure 8.12. Nevertheless, the German-orientated staffing policies and organizational culture may hamper further internationalization (see Chapter Ten for a discussion of similar policies in Hoechst) and the structural change process will continue throughout the 1990s (see Chapter Sixteen and the discussion of delayering).

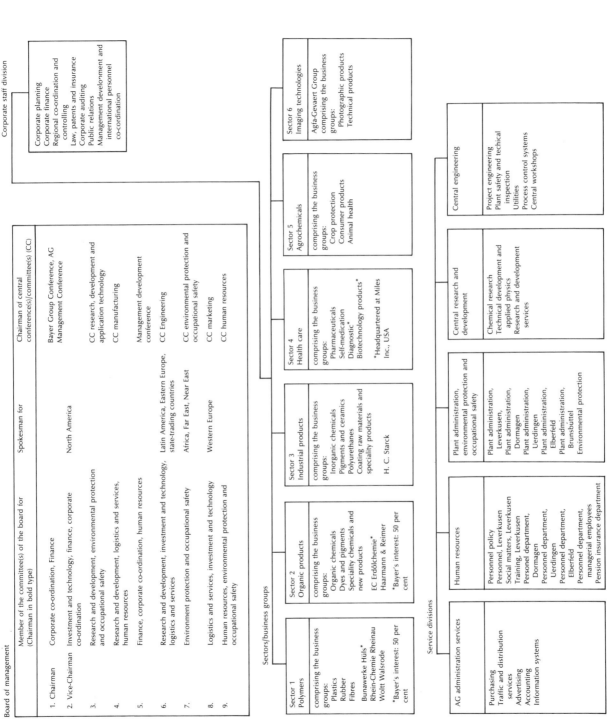

Figure 8.12 The Bayer Product division-based structure in 1988. *Source:* Humes (1993). Reprinted by permission of Prentice Hall.

COUNTRY CO-ORDINATION

A third form of co-ordination is on a country-by-country basis. During the 1960s many US multinationals invested significantly in Europe, acquiring former distributors and setting up full subsidiaries (Mitchell, 1993). Many multinationals continued to rely on international affiliates to conduct multifunctional management of their foreign operations. European multinationals such as Royal Dutch/Shell and Philips also divided responsibility for international operations by continent.

The regional structure places primary responsibility for all activities across a series of countries under a general manager. Each region has its own marketing, product and finance functions, which received support from specialist staff in corporate headquarters (Taoka and Beeman, 1991). The regional and subsidiary management have greater independence and autonomy, frequently acting as a separate profit centre. Such a set-up allowed a highly responsive organization, with a strong 'small is beautiful' organizational culture, an entrepreneurial spirit and sense of leadership among country managers and a balance between authority and accountability (Blackwell, Bizet, Child and Hensley, 1991). The co-ordination approach was relatively simple. In practice it means that the country manager reports to headquarters, but is emperor of his or her own domain. Tight financial disciplines (budgets and audits) are applied in conjunction with regular reviews of performance by headquarters staff (Mitchell, 1993).

Whilst sales outgrew expenditure, this co-ordination mechanism proved quite effective (especially in US multinationals based in Europe). It is suited to organizations that manufacture low or stable technology products that require a strong marketing capability, or organizations with diverse products operating under different competitive environments. Consumer products (goods, pharmaceuticals and household) adapt to this form of co-ordination. It facilitates regional economies of scale, and a prompt and informed response to regional issues. It suits many domestic industries, but does not help to co-ordinate diverse product lines or rapidly changing technology as effectively (Taoka and Beeman, 1991). Since the end of the 1970s the combination of slower growth and stiffer (mainly European, but also Asian) competition resulted in low profitability for US multinationals. Costs became more significant than sales and US organizations began to look for new solutions. For some, the matrix design seemed the answer.

MATRIX CO-ORDINATION

Most organizations have found that some variation of either a functional or product structure provides them with a set of reporting relationships and horizontal linkages sufficient to meet their goals (Daft, 1992). However, once organizations begin to differentiate both in terms of products and functions a high degree of tension is created. The desire for economies of scale and expertise within the business process tends to push the organization towards a functional structure, yet the desire for greater accountability to the market and customers tends to push the organization towards a product structure (Butler, 1991).

Matrix organizations originated in the aerospace industry and spread to other sectors such as computing and pharmaceuticals where the technology was complex and changing rapidly and the highly capital-intensive manufacturing or research and development processes required a pooling of resources. European organizations, with scattered national affiliates and poor communication, were slower to adopt the matrix than US multinationals (Mitchell, 1993)

A matrix organization superimposes a structure based on one dimension onto a structure based on another dimension. A matrix organization therefore has a dual, sometimes even triple or quadruple, hierarchy which can be represented by a grid or matrix of interconnecting responsibilities. One dimension represents business functions, resources or processes, with a series of groups headed by a functional head. The main responsibility of functional heads is to ensure that the necessary skills and resources are available and people are up to date with their skills. The function heads are controlled internally through the allocation of budgets. A second dimension of hierarchy is formed by product/market heads. This manager has to manage complete outputs (products, services etc.) and ensure that it is manufactured and delivered to the customers' complete satisfaction. The product heads are controlled internally by a mixture of profit and cost centres.

The product and functional heads have equal authority and therefore both hierarchies are implemented simultaneously. Neither manager has complete control over subordinates. There are a series of cells within this two dimensional matrix, occupied by the traditional operators, groups or departments. Most participants in a matrix structure have to report to two heads: function and product. This is the unique feature of matrix structures, and it tends to violate the classic features of management (Daft, 1992). Over the whole organization there is a Directorate with the role of ensuring an equal balance of power between the two hierarchies, allocating resources, conducting central planning and co-ordination, delegating decisions and information sharing. Planning committees comprising the Directorate and all functional and product heads develop overall strategy. In regional markets like Europe, the matrix was frequently also between country managers and product managers.

If an international organization can create the desired advantages and avoid the disadvantages implied by both hierarchies, then a matrix structure will endure for several years (Taoka and Beeman, 1991). Working within matrix structures has proved difficult for most managers and it has necessitated a new set of skills such as conflict management, team building, performance management, communication, influencing skills and decision quality management. Matrix structures require matrix minds and organizational cultures in order to make them work effectively (see Figure 8.13).

Matrix structures tend to highlight a number of 'behavioural failures' which although present in the other formal structures, are amplified by this mode of operation (Butler, 1991; Naylor, 1985; Peters, 1979). The ambiguities inherent in the approach tended to allow assertive executives to exact undue power. Travel costs ballooned, meetings soaked up time, central analytical managers divided and delegated their activities and the number of middle managers mushroomed (Mitchell, 1993). Many organizations found that they began to lose their cost advantages, barnacled by overhead costs. European organizations are searching for subtler mechanisms to provide a sense of cohesion and balance.

. . . Many decisions had to climb wearily up several levels, a heavy burden of rapidly decaying analysis, before final assent was obtained. Cost became increasingly uncompetitive, and decision times increasingly out of phase with requirements.   Mitchell (1993, p. 54).

Context		Internal systems	
Environment:	High uncertainty, pressure for flexible use of people and resources across product lines; requirement for both technical quality and frequent new products	Operative goals:	Equal product and functional emphasis
		Planning and Budgeting:	Dual systems by both product and function
Technology:	Non-routine	Formal authority:	Joint between functional and product heads
Size:	Medium		
Goals:	A few product lines		

Strengths	Weaknesses
• Focuses on both economies of scale and product development	• Causes participants to experience dual authority leading to frustration and confusion
• Achieves coordination and balance of power to meet dual demands from the environment	• Conflicts of role or ideology
	• Requires good interpersonal skills and extensive training
• Flexible sharing of human and other resources across products	• Higher levels of bargaining and political behaviours
• Suited to complex decisions and frequent changes in unstable environment	• Time-consuming with frequent meetings and conflict-resolution sessions
• Opportunity for functional and product skill development	• Requires strong horizontal, collegial, rather than vertical relationships
• Suits medium-sized organizations with multiple products	• Requires dual pressure from environment to maintain power balance
• Less costly than product organization	• Poor quality of decisions: more compromises
	• Slow decision making with large and complex coalitions
• Facilitates allocation of scarce technical expertise	• Re-negotiation of matrix with each management change
	• Need for strong directorate and an overarching mission ideology or culture

Figure 8.13 Matrix structure. *Source*: after Butler (1991), reprinted with permission, © 1993, R. Butler, *Designing Organizations: A decision-making perspective*, London: Routledge.

EVOLVING THE MATRIX: PRODUCT OVER COUNTRY IN PHILIPS ELECTRONICS

The problems associated with matrix organizations have meant that many European organizations have either shunned it, or have adapted their initial matrices. Some European organizations have, however, developed an extremely complex matrix. For example, Ciba-Geigy, the Swiss chemical and pharmaceutical multinational, has an organization structure based on three dimensions: product, function and geographic region. Lines of communication therefore flow both vertically and horizontally across these three dimensions (Ball and McCulloch, 1990). Final authority rests with the executive committee, whose role is to maintain two way communication between the home office and lower units. Matrix co-ordinating mechanisms of one form or another have become important for a number of European multinationals such as Shell, British Petroleum, Hoechst and Philips. US multinationals with this kind of structure include Eastman Kodak, Dow Chemicals and 3M.

The matrix structure is a good example of the biological or organism metaphor of organization (Morgan, 1986). It has evolved as the difficulties experienced by many European multinationals with their matrix structures (in terms of diluted priorities, slow decision making, unclear responsibilities and high levels of conflict) have led to a series of adaptations (see Illustration 8.13).

Philips Electronics, the Dutch electronics organization, exemplifies the process of learning about matrix co-ordination mechanisms. It has grown from a small Eindhoven-based electric lamp producer in 1891 to the sixth largest electronics company in the world by 1992, employing some 252,000 people with a turnover of $33,270 million. Its products range from lighting, small and major domestic appliances, and consumer electronics and its chief competitors include General Electric, Siemens, Hitachi and Toshiba. As a typical diversified European multi-national, Philips also covers telecommunications and data systems, electronic components, medical and scientific equipment and software.

Before the Second World War, Philips had developed a series of autonomous national affiliates, each developing products specific to their national environments. The occupation of the Netherlands served to reinforce the autonomy of the national affiliates. The emphasis has gradually shifted towards the product division. From 1945 onwards, Philips began to diversify and its product divisions began to develop matrix co-ordinating mechanisms with the national organizations. National organizations negotiated for the technical know-how and support for manufacturing and marketing that resided in the product divisions. The matrix arrangements were formalized in 1972, but in practice were relatively unchanged from the 1940s through to the 1980s. As Europe-wide competition increased in the 1960s and 1970s, Philips began to standardize products and establish international production centres. The 1972 change

---

Illustration 8.13 **Typical adjustments to the matrix.**

- One arm of the matrix should lead in order to minimize the risk of paralysis by analysis.
- Allocation of workloads for individual managers is not balanced across all arms but tilted in one direction.

- Senior levels of the matrix have to be resourced by managers with collaborative styles and a tolerance of uncertainty.

Source: Johnson and Scholes (1993).

began the shift of power away from national affiliates towards product divisions. Product divisions were made responsible for creating profit potential through product marketing, manufacturing, research and development strategies, whilst national affiliates realized profits through sales and service (Humes, 1993).

The matrix co-ordinating structure at Philips has been described by a number of writers (van Houten, 1989; Czinkola, Rivoli and Ronkainen, 1992; and Humes 1993). It has serviced Philips well for many years. In the late 1980s Philips managed four principal elements in its matrix structure (see Illustration 8.14).

The simplified picture of the organizational structure in Figure 8.14 does not highlight the complex management processes that result from the multiple interfaces of activity within Philips. A typical manager has to report to a functional, product and resource manager. The whole co-ordination mechanism depends on high levels of teamwork and considerable specialization within areas of expertise. Van Houten (1989) explained how a typical factory manager could no longer excel in just the technical aspects of operating a factory but had to be skilled in communication and managing complexity. He or she would be responsible to the local national management, for sales and production, the product policies and strategies emanating from the product division, and the staff department's requests for co-ordination of design, development and component sourcing. Most project decisions are made in informal meetings, driven by career-long networks of contacts and learning about the rules and boundaries to behaviour. Such learning takes two to five years to develop (Humes, 1993).

The response to pressures for globalization within Philips were met by a series of modifications to the matrix structure, initiated in 1972 and accelerated in 1987. Technologies converged and created the need for integrated applications. Many existing product boundaries became less important, new expertise was needed, and research and development costs increased dramatically. The shift in macroeconomic power from the Atlantic to Pacific Rim meant that Philips had to shift its concentration of resources from Europe in order to reflect the more dynamic markets and greater technological strength of the US and Far East. The 'centre of competence' – seen as the need to access technological and commercial expertise – shifted dramatically. International product centres were assigned worldwide responsibilities.

By the mid-1980s worker productivity doubled as factories were modernized, production was reallocated and the workforce was reduced. By 1985 more than half the employees still worked in Europe with 22 per cent still in the Netherlands (despite

Illustration 8.14 **Four co-ordinating mechanisms in the Philips matrix structure.**

- A board of management with nine members to set policies. Each member is assigned a portfolio closely related to either corporate functions, product policies or national organizations.
- Eight product divisions, headed by senior managing directors with global responsibility for major product categories and participation in joint ventures.
- Twenty-three corporate departments or staff functions located at the HQ in Eindhoven, and responsible for co-ordinating activities such as finance, product design, marketing, human resources.
- Sixty national organizations where business is conducted. These vary in size in relationship to the local market, but each carries the full complement of activities such as manufacturing, marketing and in some cases research.

Source: Johnson and Scholes (1993).

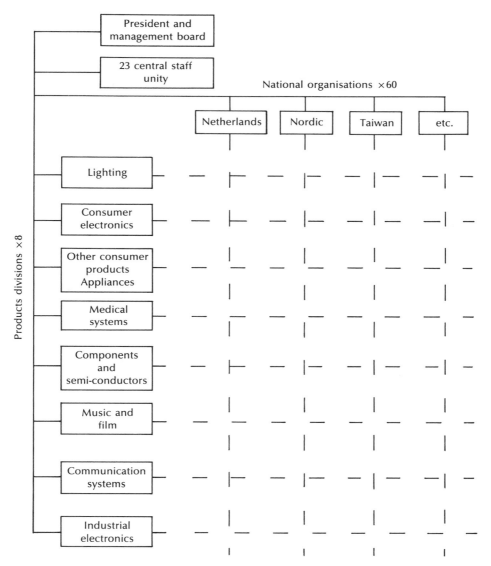

Figure 8.14 The global matrix structure at N. V. Philips. *Source*: Philips Group annual report, 1992.

Holland representing only 6 per cent of the total sales). From 1985 to 1992 total employment fell by 92,000 (a 27 per cent reduction in manpower).

The global strategy had significant implications for the delicate balance between centralization and decentralization. Lines of authority and accountability had to be clarified, decision making skills improved and the communication of goals increased. Philips chose to centralize, through focused product management, regional co-ordination and integration of divisions. Responsibility and power shifted away from the geographically orientated axis to the product division axis of the matrix structure, with all product divisions operating under a single managing director and a centralized product management team. Several product divisions were integrated as electronics technologies converged. For example, audio and video divisions merged into a consumer electronics division, data system and telecommunications were integrated,

Illustration 8.15   **HRM implications of restructuring at Philips.**

- Management teams needed a more international outlook to reflect the shift in geographic scope and regional management.
- The performance appraisal and career potential assessment systems had to be adapted.
- A corporate wide education programme was started to focus managers' minds on the new goals and profits.
- Supplementary formal training was used and more team-based projects introduced.
- Job rotations became increasingly important as a tool to develop interdisciplinary skills and an international perspective.
- International career assignments and placements in joint ventures were used to develop cross-cultural experience.
- Pay and benefit policies in key regions such as Europe were integrated to facilitate mobility.
- A human resource planning process was used to co-ordinate the HRM implications of the revised organization structure.

Source: van Houten (1989); Humes (1993).

and so forth. From 1987–92 the defence division was sold to Whirlpool and much of the computer systems division was sold to DEC. As well as spinning off some divisions, it was also recognized that whilst some of the product divisions were stand alone, others were linked in terms of marketing and technical synergies. Decision making in linked divisions was co-ordinated through new regional managements.

The increased centralization created significant cultural change problems, and was counteracted by attempts to stimulate entrepreneurial attitudes and responsibilities in the various units of the organization. Centralized planning and co-ordination was balanced with decentralized decisions in national operations where local factors were important. Philips therefore retained a matrix structure to balance the conflicting pressures to co-ordinate global activities, whilst still being responsive to national markets (van Houten, 1989). Global co-ordination has been met by adjusting the product-related aspects of the structure, whilst responsiveness to cultural and market differences has been met by adjustments to regional co-ordinations.

The HRM challenge will remain for several years (see Illustration 8.15). More than 85 per cent of middle and higher managers have only worked for Philips, 70 per cent within only one product division, and product divisions are responsible for recruitment and career postings (Humes, 1993). The loss of job security has influenced corporate loyalty at a time when more commitment is needed.

At the beginning of the chapter we pointed out that restructuring organizations has a very significant and broad impact on the behaviour of employees and usually entails a complex set of HRM policies and practices to ensure that the desired changes are implemented effectively. This is clearly the case in Philips. Some of the most marked HRM changes associated with the restructuring are detailed in Illustration 8.15. Van Houten (1989) concludes that although HRM in Philips was still in its infancy by the late 1980s, the new macroeconomic realities and implications of globalization had increased its recognition and legitimacy within the organization.

SIMPLIFYING THE MATRIX: THE BRITISH PETROLEUM EXPERIENCE

At a corporate level, BP also made changes to its matrix structure in the early 1990s, broadly aimed at simplifying the structure. The British Petroleum case has been examined by Humes (1993) and Sparrow and Bognanno (1993). British Petroleum was originally founded in 1909 as the Anglo-Persian Oil Company (APOC). In 1914 the

British government invested £2 million in the company and gained a majority shareholding, and guarantee of oil supplies in the First World War. From 1917 to 1929 the APOC expanded its refining and marketing activities in Europe and Australia and substantially strengthened its position in Europe by acquiring control of Deutsche Petroleum and Deutsche Erdol. The Iranian government nationalized local oilfields in 1951 and by 1955 the company was renamed British Petroleum (BP). BP developed its refining capacity near its main markets in Western Europe and sought new sources of oil. Major finds in the Persian Gulf, the North Sea and Alaska accelerated the spread of geographic activities. In 1969 BP purchased a share of the Standard Oil Company Ohio to expand its downstream sales outlets, and by 1978 it gained a majority shareholding. The oil crises of the 1970s forced BP to diversify into chemicals, mining and petrochemicals. In 1987 BP was privatized by the UK government.

Until the 1960s BP retained a functional structure, with each function internally divided on a regional basis and co-ordinated at main board level (Humes, 1993). In 1970 line responsibilities were shifted to an area-division basis, with four regional directors responsible for around seventy trading companies. In 1981 another reorganization was implemented to introduce a series of checks and balances at the headquarters and up and down the hierarchy. There were a series of international divisions with their own boards and financial relationships. Bureaucracy and administration costs grew significantly throughout the 1980s as the matrix structure had to co-ordinate eleven business streams with seventy national trading companies. The structure was felt to impede operational flexibility and collaboration between managers and businesses.

The heir-apparent managing director, Robert Horton, established 'Project 1990'. BP launched a corporate reorganization in 1990 as part of a major change to its structure, culture and management processes. The re-organization was intended to:

- Simplify the existing 11×70 matrix structure into a 4×3 matrix.
- Revise the role of the headquarters by redistributing power in the board of directors.
- Reduce the executive power of the headquarters by removing large numbers of support staff.
- Strengthen the global role of the four business streams by increasing the stress on products.
- Shift towards regional management for Europe, America and Asia/Pacific.
- Shift power away from national companies towards international business streams.

BEYOND THE MATRIX: CLUSTER ORGANIZATION AT BRITISH PETROLEUM ENGINEERING CENTRE

Under the new regime some areas of BP attempted to move beyond the matrix structure. The need for openness to outside ideas, becoming more responsive to customers and understanding how their desires are changing had a significant impact on how the organization was structured (Mills and Friesen, 1992). British Petroleum's engineering centre had four successive structures from 1988–1992 as it attempted to put employees in direct contact with customers and clients and facilitate a 'learning organization' approach. In 1988 the Group Engineering and Technical Centre employed 1400 engineers and support personnel in a typical functionally-structured hierarchy. These were re-organized into sixteen semi-autonomous business units with no direct reporting relationship to other parts of the organization. Instead, they had a direct contact with their customers and were supported by technology development and business services structures (which still had a formal hierarchy). The second transformation built on this concept of customer-facing semi-autonomous business units and attempted to clarify the concept. The organization chart was redrawn (see Figure 8.15) showing the business units at the centre of the chart (to acknowledge their role as the central supplier of services). The management units were shown in supporting positions, nearer the boundary of the organization (i.e. facing out to the customer), whilst all elements reported to a managing director (shown at the top of the diagram). This type of organization chart was a good reflection of the delayered organization (we discuss this topic in Chapter Sixteen).

The third transformation was the most revolutionary. It is nicknamed the 'egg structure'. The large business units (business service, engineering resources and technology development) were broken down into smaller ones based on very specific functions. Even managerial units were represented as non-hierarchical teams. No direct reporting lines were shown on the chart (see Figure 8.16) in order to suggest the requirement for close communication between teams. A contact person for each team was named to facilitate close interchanges both within the organization and externally with customers. Each section has a series of key results areas. The organization was designed to operate with a relatively small number of managers in order to limit the overhead costs associated with traditional matrices or hierarchies (Mills and Friesen, 1992). The structure consists of a series of 'clusters' of teams. These clusters are typically run without any formal designation of job responsibilities or career ladders. Collaboration and communication patterns emerge as and when they are needed to get jobs done. Middle management functions are delegated down to team members or are assigned to computer expert systems.

The HRM issues and problems associated with the new delayered cluster organization adopted by British Petroleum Engineering Centre were both marked and varied. Table 8.3 shows that a simple shift in organization structure can have a radical impact on the nature of HRM. It can also totally shift the balance of responsibilities and role requirements for the HRM function. As more European multinationals adapt their structures in the directions outlined in this chapter, the pressure to resolve the HRM issues sensibly will increase. Most observers would acknowledge that for European organizations it will be the HRM implications of both the matrix and cluster structure that drives future HRM requirements, and no longer just the historical patterns of national HRM practice outlined in Chapter Two. Many areas of HRM in Europe are in transition. We pick up these themes in later chapters.

In Europe, part of BP headquarters was moved to Brussels. The re-organization was facilitated by a change in resourcing strategy (see Chapter Eleven), but was primarily driven forward by an attempt to change the organizational culture.

... To make the re-organization work will require a fundamental change in the mandate and mode of managing. For managers who have got to the middle or the top by behaviour for years like stereotype military commanders who are always controlling and checking subordinates; it is different to start delegating real power and trusting the recipient to use it well.

Humes (1993, p. 271).

BP has taken the lead amongst European multinationals in establishing continental co-ordinating offices in the three areas of triad power (Europe, Asia/Pacific and the U.S). It also took the lead in moving towards a much flatter structure and decentralized approach to decisions on how to implement Project 1990.

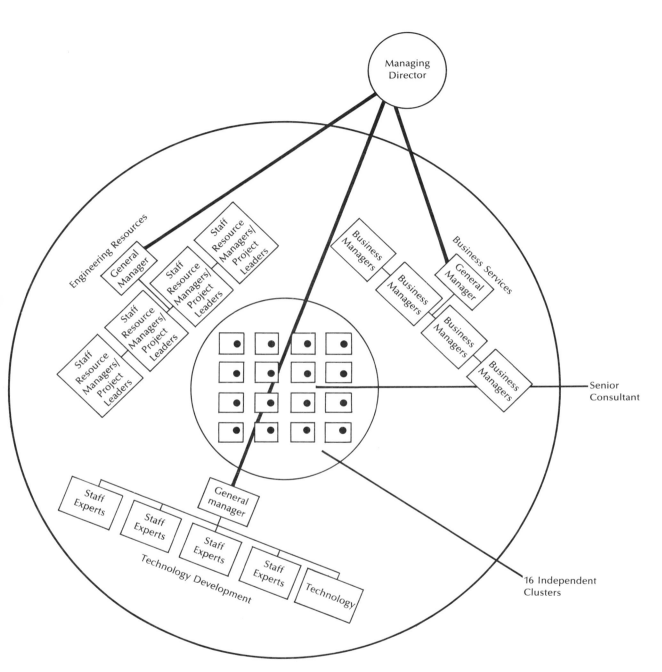

Figure 8.15 1990 organization chart for Group Engineering and Technical Centre, British Petroleum. *Source*: Mills and Friesen (1992), reprinted from *European Management Journal*, **10(2)**, D. Q. Mills and B. Friesen, 'The learning organization', 146–56, © 1992, with kind permission from Pergamon Press Ltd, Headington Hill Hall, Oxford, OX3 0BW, UK.

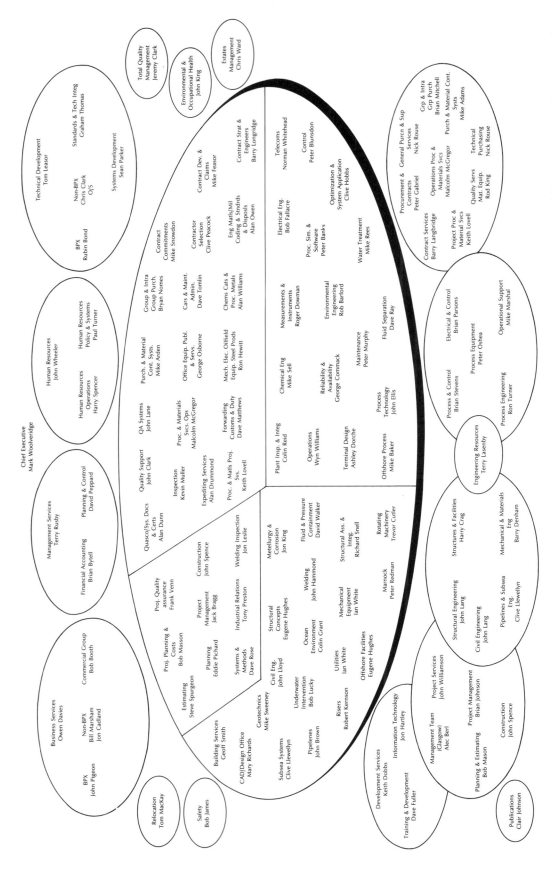

Figure 8.16 1992 organization chart for Engineering Centre, British Petroleum. *Source:* Mills and Friesen (1992), reprinted from *European Management Journal* **10(2)**, D. Q. Mills and B. Friesen, 'The learning organization', 146–56, © 1992, with kind permission from Pergamon Press Ltd, Headington Hill Hall, Oxford OX3 0BW, UK.

Table 8.3 **The HRM implications of flat structure organizations.**

	Hierarchical structure	Cluster structure
Recruitment	Carried out by supervisor and personnel function	Devolved to members of the team cluster
	Assessment centres and realistic job previews developed to test technical skills	Testing on the basis of ability to fit into the group and perform in the environment immediately
	Low immediate costs (automated process) but high indirect costs (expensive supervision or staff turnover)	Higher immediate costs (multiple interviews) balanced by lower staff turnover and improved productivity
	Assess technical work skills and learning ability	Assess social skills and interaction ability
Managerial control	Confidence in performance based on willingness of subordinates to carry out directives	Confidence in performance based upon competency (knowledge and professionalism) of team
Rewards and incentives	Strong reliance on direct benefits	More power given to indirect benefits around opportunity, growth and development
	Compensation fixed by rank and determined by length of service, teamwork and/or productivity	Rewards given on the basis of knowledge, performance, quality
	Pay grades set on analysis of carefully defined 'comparison' jobs	Tighter link between pay and performance
Culture	Used to control and define behaviours	Used as a means of communicating and influencing behaviours
Career management	Advancement through rank	Advancement through leaving the team
	Perception of greater promotion opportunity	Recognition of career plateaux
	Career reward through climbing ranks	Career reward through successive projects, i.e. broadened scope of work, greater opportunity for diversity and challenge, wider network of contacts
Performance appraisal	Personnel function driven performance criteria	Senior manager designed performance criteria
	Clear defined job descriptions; appraisal measures based on achieving set outputs	Appraisal measures that are not all job-specific, i.e. can earn a good rating in several different ways to encourage multiple skill use
	Limited sources of information; supervisor focus	Varied sources of information; external focus

After: Mills and Friesen (1992), reprinted from *European Management Journal*, **10(2)**, D.Q. Mills and B. Friesen, 'The learning organization', 146–56 © 1992, with kind permission from Pergamon Press Ltd, Headington Hill Hall, Oxford OX3 0BW, UK.

PAN-EUROPEAN STRUCTURES: BALANCING INTERNATIONAL CO-ORDINATION AND LOCAL CONTROL

In the fourth and final section of this chapter we consider the latest challenge to European organizations, i.e. how to create pan-European structures? We discuss some of the pressures that have made this an issue and then examine how organizations such as Jacobs Suchard, Cap Gemini and ICI have dealt with the problem. This last case highlights the difficult decisions and paradoxes that have to be dealt with when designing organizations.

Since 1989 the decline of US organizations and the rise of those from Europe and East Asia has continued. Table 8.4 shows the number of organizations in the Fortune 50 in 1992 country by country. It also includes three current performance measures: the biggest increase in sales, highest profits and largest number of employees. The number of Global 50 organizations from the US fell from seventeen in 1989 to fourteen by 1992, replaced by Japanese organizations who increased their presence from twelve to fifteen over the same period. Europe maintained a stable twenty-one organizations. A different picture emerges between the Triad blocs when current performance measures are considered. In terms of the highest profits, the Anglo-Saxon culture (including Britain), organizations win hands down. The US has twenty-six of the fifty most profitable organizations whilst East Asia only has two. When the number of employees is considered, the reverse situation applies. Europe has twenty-six of the largest employing organizations and the US (after a significant period of downsizing) has twelve, with eight from East Asia. Of most note is Europe's record when performance is considered in terms of increase in sales. Fuelled by the Single European Market (SEM), Europe claimed twenty-six of the fifty largest revenue-growth organizations with organizations from Spain (and Turkey) bursting into the Global 50 rankings. The US had only twelve of the top fifty sales-growth organizations and East Asia eleven. History never allows winners for long. The attempts to link European currencies through the ERM in the early 1990s led to an overvaluation of European currencies, once more increasing the relative competitiveness of US organizations. Nevertheless, the SEM has clearly had significant organizational implications, reflected in structural pressures, since 1989. The original formation of the EEC (now the European Union) was largely ignored by European organizations as far as their structures were concerned, with a continued reliance on national affiliates. However, regardless of the eventual success or not of the SEM, it has recently triggered a series of 'strategic repositionings' (see Illustration 8.16) in European multinationals as they attempt to gain viable market shares in all the major European countries (Mitchell, 1993).

In Chapter Five we pointed out that acquisitions became the main chosen instrument for this. As many multinationals continued to expand globally, they set up continental centres in Europe to co-ordinate and rationalize the efforts of local affiliates in order to convert global product strategies into country specific efforts (Humes, 1993). IBM started the trend, followed by Far Eastern organizations such as Canon, Nissan, Matsushita, Sony and Samsung. In the 1990s British multinationals BP and ICI attempted to do the same. Nestlé, Shell, Bayer, BP, Philips and ICI have given corporate executive team members specific Europe-wide responsibilities.

From an international marketing perspective organizations have been designed around 'fine and specific differences in tastes, preferences and buying criteria of national customers' within limited geographic areas but now several new questions have been evoked by the shift towards a single market that all have implications for the 'construction and architecture of corporations' (Vandermerwe, 1993). Traditional

Table 8.4 **Global 50 organizations by country 1959–92 and 1992 performance.**

	Global 50 ranking by sales, five year benchmarks								1992 performance measures		
	1959	1964	1969	1974	1979	1984	1989	1992	Biggest increases in sales 91–92	Highest profits 1992	Most employees 1992
North America *Total*	44	37	36	24	22	21	17	14	12	26	12
USA	44	37	36	24	22	21	17	14	11	26	12
Canada	0	0	0	0	0	0	0	0	1	0	0
West Europe *Total*	6	13	13	20	20	19	21	21	26	19	26
UK	2	3	4	4	3	3	3	1	3	6	2
UK/Netherlands	2	2	2	2	2	2	2	2	0	2	2
France	0	0	0	3	4	3	4	5	5	3	4
Germany	0	5	4	7	7	6	6	7	8	3	10
Italy	0	1	2	2	2	3	3	3	0	0	3
Netherlands	1	1	1	1	1	1	1	1	0	0	1
Switzerland	1	1	0	1	1	1	2	2	2	4	2
Norway	0	0	0	0	0	0	0	0	1	0	0
Sweden	0	0	0	0	0	0	0	0	1	1	1
Spain	0	0	0	0	0	0	0	0	4	0	1
Turkey	0	0	0	0	0	0	0	0	2	0	0
East Asia *Total*	0	0	1	4	6	6	12	15	11	2	8
Japan	0	0	1	4	6	6	10	13	10	2	7
South Korea	0	0	0	0	0	0	2	2	1	0	1
Other *Total*	0	0	0	2	2	4	0	0	1	3	4
Iran	0	0	0	1	0	0	0	0	0	0	0
Kuwait	0	0	0	0	0	1	0	0	0	0	0
Brazil	0	0	0	1	1	1	0	0	0	0	0
Mexico	0	0	0	0	0	0	0	0	0	1	1
Venezuela	0	0	0	0	1	1	0	0	0	1	0
Australia	0	0	0	0	0	1	0	0	1	1	1
Malaysia	0	0	0	0	0	0	0	0	0	0	0
South Africa	0	0	0	0	0	0	0	0	0	0	0
India	0	0	0	0	0	0	0	0	0	0	1
Zambia	0	0	0	0	0	0	0	0	0	0	1
Total overall	50	50	50	50	50	50	50	50	50	50	50

Illustration 8.16   **Spurs to the creation of the pan-European organization.**

- After a brief resurgence of European multi-nationals, small to medium sized US organizations have become more competitive.
- Asian organizations continued to advance with high quality and low cost, with newcomers from Malaysia, India and potentially China.
- European organizations had developed serious cost problems, and had inherited structures that were difficult to adapt.
- Specific customer and consumer markets are converging around new patterns of economic,

demographic and lifestyle factors shaping purchasing behaviour.
- Scale economies are being realized beyond traditional products such as cars, in product areas as diverse as drugs, yoghurts and telecommunications.
- Information technology is allowing interfaces between organizations to be redesigned in order to remove face-to-face contacts and national cultural constraints.

geo-political and cultural barriers are disappearing, according to the product marketeers. Moreover, manufacturing techniques can offer flexible alternatives and information technology has eradicated the constraints of time, space and distance.

The integration between businesses (discussed in Chapter Five) is creating a new economic balance of power and a convergence in consumer markets (see Illustration 8.17). Collaborative alliances between manufacturers and suppliers, and service and goods organizations and their customers are stretching across traditional national and competitive borders. Organizations are centralizing their buying activities and sourcing from strategic centres for the whole of Europe. This is made easier by remote technological infrastructures that facilitate cross-border buying and eliminate the need for face-to-face contact. Such face-to-face contact was previously a cultural constraint on integration. Customers are also identifying increasingly with pan-European brands. Economic and geographical space is being re-shaped and instead of a single homogeneous market or a collection of small specialized markets, the most likely model is a series of regional Euro-clusters based on similar geographical, economic, demographic and lifestyle characteristics. Similarity of needs and purchasing behaviour will shape European organizations, not cultural and national boundaries. Location becomes an important issue, but the question of location is not just where to locate each element of the system. Factories, service points, distribution centres, and sales outlets will be relocated, as might leadership in specific organization functions such as information technology, HRM, research and development and marketing (Vandermerwe and L'Huillier, 1989; Vandermerwe, 1993). For example, Philips is moving from twenty-two to four warehouses in its consumer electronic business, Apple

Illustration 8.17   **Customer-driven questions about pan-European organization.**

- Who are the future European customers, both industrial and consumer?
- What drives their purchasing decisions?
- Which new European markets (as opposed to countries) should be served?
- Where are they geographically clustered?
- How can we reconfigure the new market into a meaningful format?
- What are the organizational implications of getting to these customers in a cost effective manner?
- How should activities between the countries involved be co-ordinated?
- How can the people (and their HRM) be reorientated to produce the pan-European result?

Source: Vandermerwe (1993).

is replacing thirteen national warehouses with two European distribution centres, and Jacobs Suchard is rationalizing from seventeen factories across Europe to six (Blackwell, Bizet, Child and Hensley, 1991).

This process of reconfiguration of economic and geographical space has been called the 'Europeanization' of structures. Asea Brown Boveri re-organized in 1993, administering Europe as a homogeneous region, and a business area with more direct responsibility for global profit targets. For many organizations, such as Jacobs Suchard, 'Europeanization' is best dealt with by creating new management networks (see Illustration 8.18), whilst other organizations, such as Cap Gemini of France, have taken a more centralized approach (see Illustration 8.19)

It is important, therefore, that European managers do not assume that there is one clear-cut model to follow in creating a pan-European organization structure. The real choice in the 1990s has less to do with national cultural characteristics, but more to do with finding the right balance between international co-ordination and local control in each function, business unit and national organization (Blackwell, Bizet, Child and Hensley, 1991). Moreover, the process of change and of getting 'there' from an organization's historical structure, is extremely challenging.

Even when in strict economic terms it is clearly in the interest of the business to participate in a European-wide organization, cultural traditions and human nature do still get in the way. Therefore whilst the task of designing an effective pan-European organization is difficult in itself, it is not as problematic as being able to get the organization to operate effectively across geographical, political, cultural and

Illustration 8.18 **Europeanization of the structure: developing European networks at Jacobs Suchard.**

Jacobs Suchard, despite a history of nearly 170 years, is a newly emerging and fast growing European coffee and chocolate company. By 1990 it had a turnover of 3.5 billion ECU, and recognized brands with Cote D'Or, Van Houten, Suchard-Tobler, Jacob's and Jacques Vabre. It was still small compared to the likes of Nestlé, and with 80 per cent of its sales volume in Europe, it had to face up to a global challenge.

It made a policy decision to develop European networks to help shift orientation. Several layers were removed from the structure, with the 50-person corporate office in Zurich becoming a single layer. National headquarters were removed and several business unit general managers per country reported directly to Zurich. Managers and staff were encouraged to make direct contact with other managers anywhere to get a problem solved. A process of 'Europeanization' was introduced into every function. Rather than adopt a centralized approach, with the HQ providing the force for standardization, planning, co-ordination and control of the move towards pan-European networks were decentralized. All local units were

given the staff resources to support a European lead management role; for example, the French chocolate operation leads the European Milko brand, the German HRM function leads the Europe-wide job evaluation system. The objective of Europeanization is to encourage local diversity whilst promoting a common culture reflected in a consistent approach to products, systems and management transfers. Every qualified business unit has some lead-functions. Each unit has the problem of getting its initiatives and controls accepted by others and is ready to accept the co-ordinating activities of others. The structural changes were supported by internationalizing the corporate governance, with seven Swiss, six Germans, one French, Dutch, British, American and Brazilian members of the management committee. European task forces and project teams were used extensively, along with multi-country interest groups tasked with tackling strategic issues. European mobility amongst management was encouraged, and English was adopted as the business language as long ago as 1973.

Source: Jakob (1990).

Illustration 8.19 **Cap Gemini: balancing acquisition, corporate structure and HRM.**

By 1991 Cap Gemini, the French computer services supplier, had become the European market leader. Its turnover of 1.5 billion ECU was roughly twice that of its nearest competitors of Finsiel (Italy), ICL (UK/Japan) or Sema (France) and made it the world's fourth largest IT services organization. A joint venture with Debis Systemhaus, Daimler-Benz's IT subsidiary, will make Cap Gemini no. 2 in the world. However, it faces enormous challenges in order to blend a widely disparate array of Europe-wide companies. It originally relied on a highly decentralized organization structure and tight financial controls. However, in the light of its acquisitions this led to poor communications problems and the continuance of a national, as opposed to European, image. In order to build a pan-European service the decentralized structure gave way to a new international organization in January, 1993. Seven new geographic business units were created, each responsible for a specific sector. The aim is to build up strong sectoral expertise that can be sold across borders. For example, the UK will oversee worldwide banking activities whilst Paris will oversee telecommunications. In order for this new structure to work, and to avoid Daimler-Benz taking full control, Cap Gemini focused on three key HRM issues in the early 1990s:

- Ensuring uniform levels of quality across subsidiaries.
- Developing an international salesforce to cater for multinational clients.
- Installing greater co-operative working practices into a workforce of 19,000 so that managers are not driven by short term (local) revenues but will be prepared to develop business for other parts of the structure.

Source: Sasseen (1992).

economic contours of Europe (Blackwell, Bizet, Child and Hensley, 1991). Well intended designs frequently come to grief for often very simple and human reasons (see Illustration 8.20).

Blackwell *et al.* (1991) argue therefore that the key to creating pan-European structures is achieving the right balance between alternative integrating mechanisms, between central control and autonomy. They identify six intermediate stages of integration that can be used to achieve sufficient co-ordination across pan-European structures without necessarily shifting formal lines of accountability from national marketing managers to new European managers (see Figure 8.17). The choice of co-ordination level can reflect the cultural history and style of the organization and its ability to work with less formal accountabilities.

Blackwell *et al.* (1991) also illustrate what these six levels of co-ordination look like for seven different types of business unit and five corporate headquarter functions, pointing out that each may require different levels of co-ordination and may have a smaller or larger co-ordination gap (or need for change). Blackwell *et al.* (1991) also described some of the HRM lessons that could be learned from organizations that have attempted to build more integrated pan-European structures (see Table 8.5).

Illustration 8.20 **Factors constraining the creation of pan-European structures.**

- Multiple business languages and national management account systems.
- Promotion and compensation systems that reinforce behaviours tied to local objectives and measures, not cross-border synergies.
- Cultural threat as the powers of 'national barons' and long standing traditions of decentralization are threatened.

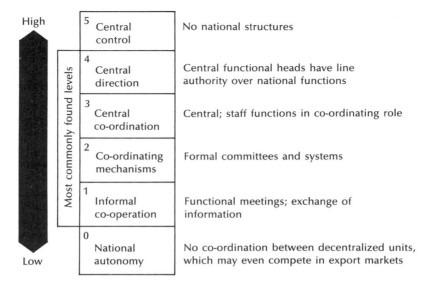

Figure 8.17 Levels of international co-ordination in the pan-European structure. *Source:* Blackwell, Bizet, Child and Hensley (1991). Reproduced from 'European organization: corporate design' by J. Nielsen and J. Rötiss in *McKinsey Quarterly*, 1991(2), 94–111. Reprinted with permission of the publishers, © 1991, McKinsey & Co. Inc.

Based on consulting experience at McKinsey, the authors noted that the smoothest examples of implementing pan-European organizations occurred when the issues of purpose, power, people and process were resolved in a synchronized way. In general, the first step was to build commitment and general understanding, followed by building up capability, then addressing the power structure, and finally implementing changes to business processes.

PRIMARY DESIGN CRITERIA: PARADOXES AND DUALITIES

In the previous sections considerable reference has been made to the need for 'balance' between features such as central control and local autonomy. Such decisions reflect 'primary design criteria'.

... The test of a first-rate intelligence is the ability to hold two simultaneous ideas in mind and still keep the ability to function.   F. Scott Fitzgerald in Evans and Doz (1989).

At the highest level of design, managers usually consider a number of primary criteria. Unfortunately, these primary design criteria are becoming more paradoxical and managers increasingly have to make trade-offs between them. The paradoxes often continue long after an organization design has outlived its usefulness. Evans and Doz (1989) of INSEAD have developed this argument and pointed to the problem of 'dualities' faced by complex organizations around the globe. Whereas once conventional wisdom swung from one alternative to another over a generation, the unprecedented levels of competition between organizations, waves of foreign direct investment and strategic partnerships have accelerated the change in desired qualities for organizations. Simple, either/or alternatives have become obsolete (Räsänen, 1991). Using distinctions originally drawn by Hedberg, Nystrom and Starbuck (1976), they argue that the maximization of anything – decentralization, teamwork,

Table 8.5 **HRM implications of creating pan-European organization structures.**

Systematic reason for structural failure	Best practice solutions
Purpose: insufficient commitment to move beyond national structures, traditional domestic markets and established customer relationships	Compelling business logic for pan-European operation Articulation through fact-based justification of the benefits of integration Communication programme to ensure consistent messages to European managers *Ad hoc* pan-European task forces to build recognition of need for change and deal with lead functions
Power: barriers resulting from perceived threats to national management roles, responsibilities, influence and career routes	Avoiding short-cuts such as imposing functional 'Heads of Europe' who lack power Accommodating gradual shifts in power structures Involving IT to develop groups in the planning and responsibility for change Using IT to develop centralized and integrated control systems for production, distribution or customer handling Identifying individuals with high potential for broad international careers
People: low levels of skill and capability such as strategic and lateral thinking, language skills and culture skills to maintain informal contacts and communication	Creating precedents for international careers through international re-assignments Recruiting staff in countries where the organization is weak and training them in countries where it is strong
Processes: An inadequate or inflexible infrastructure of shared systems and processes such as accounting procedures, cost and performance measurement and inconsistent personnel management	Introducing important changes to accounting, management information and personnel systems early Identifying and correcting problems in key processes such as order processing, quality testing, and transfer pricing

Source: Blackwell, Bizet, Child and Hensley (1991). Reproduced from 'European organization: corporate design' by J. Nielsen and J. Rötiss in *McKinsey Quarterly*, 1991 (2), 94–111. Reprinted with permission of the publishers, © 1991, McKinsey & Co. Inc.

formality – is inappropriate for organizations. They identify a series of 'complementary opposites', many of which may act as primary criteria to help guide an organization design. Like a seesaw on a fulcrum, there is a gentle oscillation from side to side which has to be delicately maintained. This balance between opposites requires the creation of a minimal amount of contentment, satisfaction and consensus within the organization about the desirability of the various attributes. This minimal threshold ensures that key actors stay with the organization, but also means that organization designs do not become road maps that are blindly implemented (see Illustration 8.21).

Morgan (1986) also draws attention to the theme of contradictions and flux in thinking about organization, talking of 'self-generating oppositions' (where one side of the phenomenon tends to produce the existence of the other) and the need for more 'dialectical imagination' (where we see the seeds of the future enfolding in the oppositions shaping the present, rather than thinking in straight causal lines). Man's mastering of nature turns back on him with problems of pollution and resource depletion and leads to subordination of man, the dehumanization of work produced the human relations movement, but then the success and power of unions fuelled the internationalization of labour and substitution of robots for labour, and so forth. This

Illustration 8.21 **Common dualities or complementary opposites that organization designs must accommodate.**

Decentralization	– Centralization
Economies of scale	– Unique customer needs
Domestic/local	– Global
Large	– Small
Competition	– Partnership
Differentiation	– Integration
Loose	– Tight
Delegation	– Control
Control	– Entrepreneurship
Planned	– Opportunistic
Formal	– Informal
Vision	– Reality
Business logic	– Technical logic
Analysis	– Intuition
Individuality	– Teamwork
Action	– Reflection
Change/flexibility	– Continuity/stability
Top-down	– Bottom-up
Tolerance	– Forthrightness
Flexibility	– Focus

Source: reproduced from *Human Resource Management in International Firms* by P. Evans, Y Doz and A. Laurent (eds). Reprinted by kind permission of the publishers. The Macmillan Press Ltd, © 1989.

kind of analysis forces managers to consider which tensions and oppositions are primary, and which are subsidiary.

The paradigms that have guided management thinking have shifted since the Second World War (see Figure 8.18) and this has had a profound effect on the way we think about organizations and their design. We have moved through three stages of thinking. First, we thought organizations should consist of some form of rational architecture, intended to bring order to a relatively stable business environment. The typical questions being asked were: what is an appropriate span of control? Are there limits to size and economy of scale? Is a product organization superior to a functional organization? Then, as competition increased and the business environment changed incrementally, the metaphor became one of fit, matching and consistency between strategy and management processes. The 'one-best-way' search for effective structure was replaced by the notion that specific structures suited specific business environments and the focus therefore shifted to management processes – such as strategic planning, human resource management and job design – that could be used to assess this fit. By the mid-1980s the highly turbulent, complex and competitive environment forced another shift in thinking, which Evans and Doz (1989) characterize as creating a 'dynamic balance between dualities'. Creating a tight fit resulted in rigid organization structures and the perception by senior managers that they were always behind, always feeling the need to catch up, or facing barriers to competitive and strategic development.

Evans and Doz (1989) believe that the dualities described in Illustration 8.21 will remain for the foreseeable future. They should not therefore be seen as threats to consistency and coherence, but as opportunities that can be used to create an optimal

+	50s–60s	70s–early 80s	mid-80s–90s
Management metaphor	Structuring (providing order)	Fit, matching, consistency	Dynamic balance between dualities
Nature of the environment	Relatively orderly and stable	Incrementally changing with increasing competition	Turbulent, complex, highly competitive
Focus of management attention	Structure and systems Planning systems Budgeting systems Organizational structure Information systems Job evaluation	Strategy and management processes Strategic management: *matching* environmental threats and opportunities to internal strengths and weaknesses Organization: ensuring *consistency* between the 7Ss Human resource management: *fitting* jobs to people Job design: *matching* technical and task specifications to social needs	Innovation, flexibility, and organizational capabilities Channelling entrepreneurship Focusing diversity Integrating decentralized subsidiaries/business units Creating teamwork among strong individuals Planning opportunism Partnerships between competitors

Figure 8.18 Three paradigms of management in the period after 1950. *Source*: reproduced from *Human Resource Management in International Firms* by P. Evans, Y. Doz and A. Laurent (eds). Reprinted with kind permission of the publishers, The Macmillan Press Ltd, © 1989.

level of tension within the organization. An example of having to cope with these competing tensions whilst restructuring is afforded by ICI (see Illustration 8.22). It is quite clear that the 1990s will continue to witness several major changes in organizational structure amongst the largest multinationals as they attempt to resolve the many paradoxes presented by their structure. In Chapter Sixteen we discuss some of the key structural concepts that are emerging as organizations face the challenges of the 1990s.

SUMMARY: WHAT IS SUCCESSFUL ORGANIZATION STRUCTURING?

Humes (1993) detects three communalities emerging towards the end of the twentieth century (see Figure 8.19).

1. Globalization of marketing, manufacturing, research and development, support services and management infrastructures.

Illustration 8.22 **European sales synergies versus streamlined business processes: competing restructuring pressures at ICI.**

Sometimes the potential synergies to be gained from re-organizing on a European basis are outweighed by competing pressures. ICI is the world's fourth largest chemicals company. In September 1990 it opened ICI Europe. However, influence had been shifting away from its regional organization towards global businesses since the 1970s. The European structure was therefore taking primacy only at the end of a slow power shift. ICI announced in late 1991 that it was reshaping the organization to face the challenge of the Single European Market. It created a new 60-person regional organization based in Brussels.

ICI was tempted by the 'supermarket' theory of inter-business purchasing. The motivation had been to source large European manufacturers like BMW from a single point as opposed to customers dealing with four separate ICI businesses. The new structure was to be transnational. It had to achieve the orderly transfer of sales from 15 national companies to three European sub-regions (Benelux, Nordic and mid-Europe) and six sub-regional support services centres were established.

However, ICI's profits continued to fall and takeover pressures emerged from the Hanson Group. An even stronger imperative than European integration therefore took hold. This was the need to simplify the overall structure, cut costs and improve responsiveness. ICI, like many European multinationals, was under pressure to speed up decision making and streamline the complex 'matrix' structures established in the 1960s. In early 1991 ICI's businesses were combined into eight large units, each with over £1bn of revenues.

The role of ICI Europe began to cause problems, increasing the cost of selling into Europe, and limiting the larger businesses' ability to control the whole business process (from the customer through to the factory). A study group decided that ICI Europe had achieved much of its original remit (to encourage transnationalism) and should now be shut down. The European reorganization therefore proved to be only a temporary structure. Only sixteen months after its initiation, the lights went out in Brussels. The shared service centres were transferred to the strongest businesses in each European sub-region and geographic 'head office' responsibilities were dispersed amongst senior manager roles on a part time basis. Cost savings of around 20 per cent were achieved. However, this informal networking of an essential transnational task was seen as potentially slowing down ICI's ability to develop a strong cadre of international managers capable of moving across businesses.

Source: Lorenz (1993).

2. Localization of activities on a continental basis to compete more effectively on a local and worldwide basis.
3. Strengthening of cross-border linkages to create greater coherence.

The historical preference of European organizations for national companies with geographical territories, of US organizations for product divisions with global responsibilities, and of Japanese organizations for a function-driven approach is being superseded by increased complexity and diversity of design choices.

... While the traditions of American, European and Asian multinationals have differed, the recent re-organizational transitions of many leading American, European and Asian multinationals have indicated an increasing convergence that points to a prospective synthesis ... the re-organizational initiatives driving this convergence – more cross-border enabling structures, more power-sharing, linchpin managers, and more corporate-concerting core values ... provide the ideas comprising the prospective emerging trends.   Humes (1993, p. 352).

Organization structures are extremely fluid and should not be viewed as permanent. However, whilst not permanent, there are a number of clear success indicators that characterize successful organization designs (see Illustration 8.23).

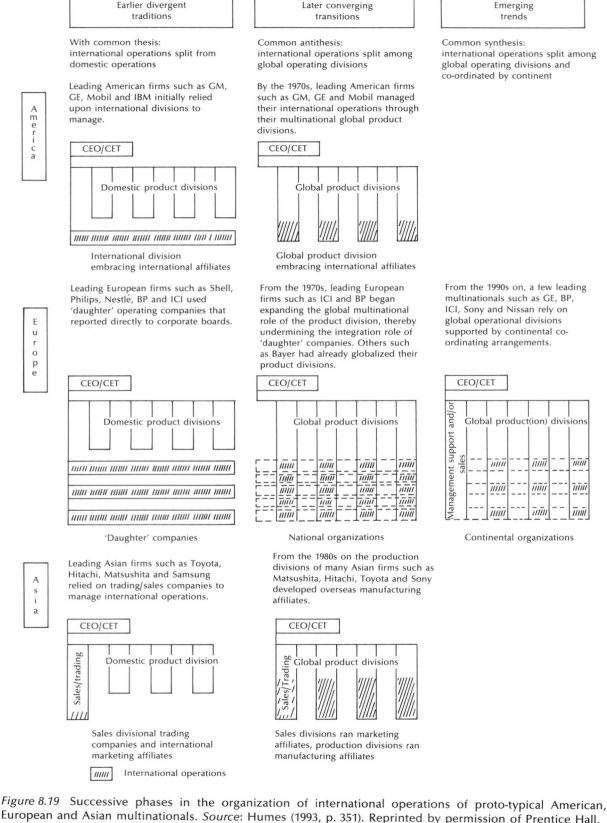

Figure 8.19 Successive phases in the organization of international operations of proto-typical American, European and Asian multinationals. *Source*: Humes (1993, p. 351). Reprinted by permission of Prentice Hall.

Illustration 8.23 **Success indicators for organization design: key questions.**

- Clarity of purpose (as opposed to simplicity)?
- Economy of effort to maintain control and minimize dysfunctional conflict?
- Decision making concentrated on correct issues, i.e. focused on achieving the result rather than the process involved?
- Ability to survive turmoil?
- Adaptable enough (not rigid) to learn from turmoil and open to sources of new ideas?
- Extent to which customer values are reflected in the organization design?
- Correct number of layers to meet criteria of efficiency and responsiveness?
- Organization costs and benefits favourable in comparison to competitors?

- Degree of control over individual behaviour through shared values between employees and managers?
- Decision making carried out at the lowest possible level of management?
- Culturally-appropriate mechanisms to allocate decision making responsibility?
- Level of employee understanding of the process used to arrive at the organization design?
- Consistency and integration in the signals of how people should act?
- Employee understanding of their tasks?
- Involvement of HRM professionals in pre- and post-change social and behavioural processes?

Source: Ulrich and Lake (1990).

CONCLUSIONS

We hope this chapter has made it clear that there is no such thing as the 'right' organizational structure. Most organizations do not conform totally to pure forms (such as functional, product or matrix approaches to co-ordination) but have mixed structures. There is a continual conflict between specialization of units and co-ordination requirements. Moreover, developments in the business environment and information technology are leading to totally new concepts for organization design, whilst a more sophisticated understanding of human resource strategy is focusing attention on the social and behavioural change aspects of restructuring. A number of complex considerations have been discussed in this chapter. The key learning points are shown below.

LEARNING POINTS FROM CHAPTER EIGHT

1. The topic of organization structuring is complex and includes numerous concepts. There are four perspectives that need to be understood. The first is the various principles by which work may be organized, i.e. the frames of reference used by managers to organize work. The second is an understanding of the social and behavioural impact of organizing on individuals and groups. The third is the various co-ordinating mechanisms and modes of operation that large organizations tend to adopt, and the way in which these have evolved. The fourth need is to understand the design paradoxes that managers have to resolve, such as the balance between centralization and decentralization.

2. Structural change is becoming a pervasive and continuous process in European organizations. Many of these organizations are as large as small national economies. There was a wave of restructuring in the early 1980s to undo the diversifications of the 1970s. In the 1990s the money to invest in future organizational change is coming from the sale, rationalization and downsizing of non-core businesses.

3. The formal and visible aspects of organization structure may be considered along seven dimensions: formality, specialization, standardization, hierarchy of authority, complexity, centralization and professionalism. These tend to be reflected in organization charts. They tend to emphasize the vertical aspects of an organization's structure, i.e. the chains of command, departmental groupings and information linkages. They may be used to compare and contrast organizations. However, this way of viewing organizations provides little understanding about the motivations behind an organization design, tends to promote a hierarchical view of organization and a very static view of organizations.

3. Many of the principles and images that managers use to think about their organization can be expressed as metaphors. These metaphors express new ways of thinking about management and the design of organizations. These metaphors can help explain the operation of organizations' machines, organisms, brains, cultures, political systems, psychic prisms, systems of flux or instruments of domination.

4. Decisions to reorganize may represent a proactive decision to change the business strategy. Other motivations typically include the need to accommodate the business vision of key personalities, a gradual realization that structural changes are needed in order to implement the strategy, changes in customer or supplier practice which necessitate new ways of operating, or internal strains in the flow of information, decision making and understanding of employee roles.

5. Organizations are often structured around generic employee roles, such as the operating core, a strategic apex, a middle line, a technostructure, and support staff. Another way of grouping people is to determine the important communication nodes and interactions that have to take place. Finally, there are different levels of decision making which are afforded different time spans of discretion. These ideas are often used to create basic building blocks and working relationships within the organization. They can inform decisions about the size of units, whether to centralize or decentralize decision making, a match between the time span of discretion available and the capabilities of people within the organization.

6. The basic organizational design serves a number of purposes. It shapes the structure in terms of levels, spans of control, roles, reporting relationships and the division of labour. It establishes a mechanism for governance and shapes the way that people think about tasks. It can create an identity within the organization, or provide some boundaries for and consistency in business operations. It provides a rationale for the basis of formal decisions, and can also ensure that systems create the most efficient and effective communication.

7. However, few re-organizations are designed well. They frequently carry high cost and create confusion. They may involve abandoning known benefits in the existing organization for speculative benefits of a new one. They may just treat symptoms of organizational problems and frequently introduce undesirable side effects of their own. This is because a series of social processes are precipitated by structural change.

8. There are also some national differences across Europe in organization structures. Many of these differences have been observed in the organization of manufacturing activities. The basic division of activity into functions, and splits between staff and workers is the same. However, there are differences in the way work is divided and jobs are designed, the way in which work is distributed across the hierarchy, the main processes of co-ordination and the structures of business governance, top level hierarchies and strategic decision making.

9. The main mechanisms of corporate governance also vary across European

organizations. The main differences are in terms of who comprises the corporate governance, the interests they represent, the responsibilities they shoulder, whether issues are dealt with individually or collectively, the proportion of insiders or outsiders on the board, and the structure of the board system. These structural differences have a significant impact on the way strategies are formulated and implemented.

10. National cultures also influence the attitudes that managers have and the approaches they take to formalizing the organization structure. European organizations tend to prefer more loosely defined arrangements and job descriptions in contrast to US organizations, who prefer to use organizational structures to define tightly and distribute authority and responsibilities. A number of cultural dimensions, such as the interpersonal relationship orientation, power distance and uncertainty avoidance, have a bearing on the way managers think about organization structure. However, there are large differences between organizations within countries and sectors.

11. Occupational cultures, steeped in their own specializations, predispositions and professional priorities can have as powerful an influence on thinking about organization structure as does national culture.

12. In the face of global competition and culture changes intended to foster Anglo-Saxon values, the approaches taken by European organizations to structuring are beginning to change. A number of pan-European pressures are leading to convergence of thinking about structures in larger organizations. These include increased market and competitive pressure equalizing the number of management layers in organizations, a requirement for higher levels of workforce commitment, higher levels of communication, consultation and empowerment associated with redesigned business processes, and a requirement for more collaborative organizational cultures.

13. This gradual process of convergence is most evidenced in the co-ordinating mechanisms adopted by large organizations. These include structures based on international divisions, functions, product markets, countries or areas, or a matrix system of control. These modes of operation are essentially the same as those adopted by domestic organizations, but the greater the degree of internationalization, the more complex the structural problems become.

14. There have been successive eras of organizational change, each of which has left its imprint on the structure of modern multinationals. Before the Second World War large industrial corporations first emerged. US organizations adopted international divisions to manage foreign operations, whilst the early European multinationals created highly autonomous daughter companies. Immediately after the Second World War the international division emerged as a successful structure during a period of American domination.

15. As organizations began to internationalize, the sector as opposed to national country of origin began to shape decisions about co-ordinating mechanisms. The various structures – functional, product or geographical – each had a number of strengths and weaknesses. As a general trend, European organizations began to respond to competitive pressures from Japan in the late 1970s. Many European and US organizations began to adopt product-driven organizational structures. A few European organizations retained globally dispersed daughter companies. The 1980s saw a considerable degree of convergence in co-ordinating mechanisms, dependent on the need of the industrial sector. In some technological sectors, matrix forms of co-ordination began to develop.

16. Matrix structures have also evolved in recent years, with some European organizations shunning this type of co-ordination mechanism, some building in greater complexity

and others simplifying the matrix. Matrix structures have also highlighted a number of significant HRM problems in making structures work.

17. The HRM problems associated with existing co-ordination systems have encouraged organizations to experiment with new organizational forms. Decentralized and delayered units, with greater horizontal co-ordination and more team-based working, are being adopted by more organizations. These new organizational forms also carry significant HRM implications. These cover the role played by organizational culture, rewards and control systems, recruitment needs, employee training and development needs, career paths and performance management. The evolution and development of the structure of European organizations has become a significant driver of developments in HRM.

18. The resurgence of competition from US and Asian organizations has created serious cost problems for European organizations. The inherited structures are proving difficult to co-ordinate, and new customer and consumer markets based around changes in economic activity, demographic characteristics and purchasing behaviour are leading to the adoption of pan-European structures. New scale economies and information technology links are breaking down many previous national boundaries. The Europeanization of organization structures is growing around the development of new management networks.

19. Well intended organizational designs, however, frequently come to grief for human reasons. It is becoming even more important for European organizations to identify the right balance between co-ordinating mechanisms, central control and autonomy. There are a series of intermediate stages that can be identified in this transition process, providing organizations with choices about the level of integration they wish to adopt, dependent upon the cultural traditions and history of the organization. However, the role of the business sector and nature of the business process within the organization is becoming an important determinant of organizational structures.

20. In managing this transition there are a series of primary design criteria that have to be considered. These include determining the balance between centralization and decentralization, economies of scale or unique customer needs, domestic and local or global, competition or partnership, delegation or control. The paradigms that managers are using to make decisions about the organization structure are shifting markedly. The levels of structural tension within organizations and the levels of change and uncertainty are rising. This is creating the need to resource organizations with different sets of skills and competencies. Recruitment and selection systems are also being developed.

CHAPTER NINE

External Resourcing
Recruitment, selection and assessment

INTRODUCTION

The transnationalization of business, increasing sophistication of communication technologies and growing number of international managers are changing the shape of the knowledge, skills and abilities that are required for effective managerial performance. Rather than maintain local and fragmented recruitment and selection policies, European organizations are rapidly trying to establish best practice throughout their European (and worldwide) operations (McCulloch, 1993) and are searching for a more internationally co-ordinated, standardized and justifiable approach to selection and assessment.

Boerlijst and Meijboom (1989) argue that European organizations now appreciate that their survival depends on the quality of their people and that their human resource management (HRM) therefore requires a conscious and specific direction of effort in both the short and long term. Employee resourcing is the main way in which organizations can achieve this co-ordinated direction of employees. It involves all the processes and activities that are aimed at managing the stock and flow of an organization's human resources throughout their joint relationship. Typically, this includes the topics of manpower planning, recruitment, training and development, and career management. We cover the topic of recruitment and selection in this chapter. Employee training and development (ETD) forms the basis of Chapter Ten, and career management forms the basis of Chapter Eleven.

Having realized that more attention has to be directed at the way in which the organization resources its employees, the selection and assessment of people becomes a central issue. Effective recruitment, selection and assessment practices provide the organization with a powerful basis for influencing and organizing human behaviour in line with the strategic direction of the organization.

[Assessment involves] . . . collecting and processing relevant information in a systematic and reliable manner with a view to realizing and maintaining adequate matching between the organization and its surroundings . . . [and] the sub-systems of the organization.

Boerlijst and Meijboom (1989, p. 26).

Shimmin (1989) observes that within the context of the significant restructuring taking place in Europe, the topic of selection and assessment has shifted from one which used to focus on matching past performance to a defined job which an individual could hold until retirement, to the need to estimate a person's probable adaptability and ability to learn new skills and tasks. In the new environment, European organizations have three strategic selection options (see Illustration 9.1).

The factors influencing change in European recruitment and selection are shown in Figure 9.1. Organizations are attempting to build international workforces, enhance their management skills, develop alternative career paths and cope with the impact of mergers on their recruitment processes. Demographic and skills shortages and increased participation of women in the labour market call for new recruitment methods. Finally, there are strong cultural differences within recruitment legislation, labour markets and workforce values.

Selection and assessment in European organizations in the 1990s will be fundamentally concerned with dealing with problems of change (Dachler, 1989) and not only dealing with change in the business environment, but as we argued in the last chapter, changing the perspectives held by managers on both the nature of organization and the meaning and practice of employee recruitment and selection. The currently accepted assumptions in recruitment, selection and assessment will need to be re-assessed. These assumptions tend to have emerged from experiences based on organization structures that have now passed. The future will involve far more complexity, greater ambiguity, more rapid change and a challenge to the methods that made sense to those managers who constructed the old organizations. This challenge will reduce the meaning and usefulness of traditional methods of recruitment and selection.

It is clear that European HRM managers will no longer face clear-cut selection situations. Instead, they are seeking enormous flexibility. In a period of high technological change and low economic growth, combined with low voluntary turnover rates and a highly legislated environment, new employees, when appointed, have to be able to perform a series of jobs over time, with job changes no longer linked to promotion (van Ham, Paauwe and Williams, 1986). The challenge is immense, mainly because such 'new' selection decisions still have to be made in the existing context of national legislation, particularly in relation to fairness and the avoidance of discrimination. The need to accommodate such legislation will encourage a different approach to selection. Traditional 'go/no go' decisions, based on information and data relating to a specific job, will be replaced by decisions to manage a gradual entry of people into the organization (via probationary periods, fixed term contracts, part time work, and so forth). These 'phased entry' selection decisions will be made on grounds of adaptability, social and personal values, and trainability (Shimmin, 1989).

Textbooks on recruitment, selection and assessment often tend to focus on 'what should be done' and how to devise effective systems. This requires a discussion of the principles of job analysis, test construction, regression analysis, validation and assessment of utility. Meanwhile, most managers are interested in 'what is actually done'. They want to know how to improve existing tools, how to find out about new

Illustration 9.1 **Strategic selection choices for European organizations.**

1. Select for short-term proficiency and accept the possibility of high levels of turnover if, and when, employees cannot cope with change.
2. Select for longer-term adaptability to change, but accept that the limited knowledge of future priorities and changes will make it difficult to assess 'adaptability' as the criteria change.
3. Make continuous adaptations to the selection system (when there is a high reliance on the external labour market) or to the vocational training and development systems (where there is a high reliance on an internal labour market).

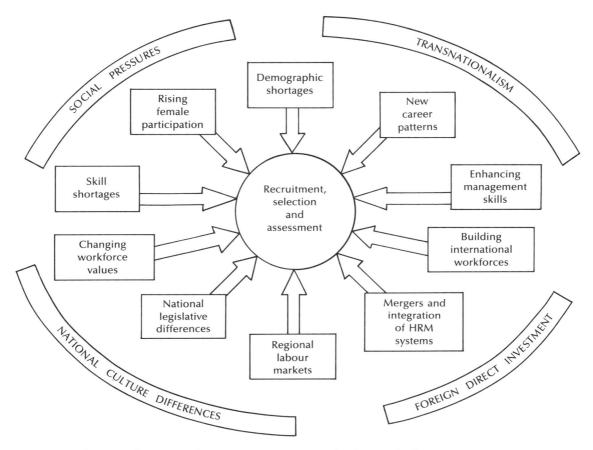

Figure 9.1 The factors influencing change in recruitment and selection in Europe.

tools, and what their colleagues are doing (Roe, 1989). By taking the middle ground, this chapter focuses more on the underlying issues. The majority of research and writing about European recruitment and selection systems has focused on the distinctive features of each national labour market, the legislative environment and the ethical context, as opposed to the actual uptake of the various tools and techniques that typically constitute a selection system. In this chapter we give consideration to these issues of national labour markets, legislation and ethics, but also attempt to redress the balance by providing a description and analysis of the main elements of recruitment and selection systems on a pan-European basis. This chapter is therefore split into three main sections:

1. The nature of recruitment systems:
   ■ The legislative environment.
   ■ Distinctive features of the labour market.
   ■ Methods of recruitment.
2. The nature of selection systems:
   ■ Methods of selection.
   ■ The cost-benefit of recruitment and selection systems.
3. Key issues in recruitment and selection for European organizations:
   ■ The reliability and validity of selection predictions.
   ■ Social and ethical issues and the democratization of selection systems.

THE NATURE OF RECRUITMENT SYSTEMS

Schuler and Huber (1993) define recruitment as the set of activities used to obtain a pool of qualified applicants – i.e. the future human resources who will assist the organization in achieving its strategic aims. Recruitment has to serve a variety of specific purposes (see Illustration 9.2). It is a significant and time-consuming activity in many European HRM departments. In Britain it has been estimated that over 41 per cent of personnel managers spend more than a quarter of their time involved in recruitment activities (Curnow, 1989) and 54 per cent confirmed that the proportion of their time required to service these activities had increased in the last two years of the 1980s.

... Recruitment involves the searching for and obtaining [of] qualified job candidates in such numbers that the organization can select the most appropriate person to fill its job needs. In addition to filling job needs, the recruitment activity should be concerned with satisfying the needs of the job candidates. Consequently, recruitment not only attracts individuals to the organization but also increases the chance of retaining the individuals once they are hired.

Schuler and Huber (1993, p. 189).

LEGISLATIVE CONTEXT FOR RECRUITMENT IN EUROPE

A second topic to consider when discussing the nature of recruitment systems in European organizations is the most important features of the legislative context. The UK is unique in the developed world for having a system of HRM which remains largely unregulated by legal requirements (Brewster, Hegewisch and Lockhart, 1993), relying instead on a tradition of 'voluntarism'. This topic has to receive considerably more attention in the European context because some countries (such as Germany, Norway, France, Belgium, the Netherlands and Italy) are renowned for their high levels of public domain legislation or collective agreements in the recruitment sphere. The breadth of potential legislation affecting recruitment is large (see Illustration 9.3). The nature or source of the law is also quite varied, ranging from codified legislation, constitutional rights, national or sectoral collective agreements, to codes of best practice that have set precedents in labour courts.

Illustration 9.2 **The purposes of recruitment.**

- To determine the organization's present and future recruitment needs in conjunction with human resource planning and job analysis.
- To increase the pool of qualified job applicants at minimum cost to the organization.
- To help increase the success rate of the [subsequent] selection process by reducing the number of obviously under-qualified or over-qualified job applicants.
- To help reduce the probability that job applicants, once recruited and selected, will leave the organization after only a short period of time by providing applicants with sufficient information about the organization and target position to allow them to self-select themselves out of the process before being engaged.
- To meet the organization's responsibilities, legal and social obligations regarding the composition of the workforce.
- To increase organizational and individual effectiveness in the short term and the long term.
- To evaluate the effectiveness of various techniques and locations of recruiting all types of applicants.

Source: Schuler and Huber (1993).

Illustration 9.3 **Sources of law affecting recruitment in European organizations.**

- ■ Use of employment exchanges and job centres
- ■ Outplacement
- ■ Temporary work
- ■ Fixed term contracts
- ■ Hours of work
- ■ Time off work
- ■ Termination of employment
- ■ Unfair dismissal
- ■ Redundancy
- ■ Maternity leave
- ■ Discrimination and equal opportunities
- ■ Health and Safety
- ■ Recruitment codes of practice
- ■ Use of psychological testing
- ■ Disclosure of information

Constitutional employment rights can be seen in both Nordic and Latin countries. For example, paragraph 110 of the Norwegian constitution of 17 May 1814 expresses the nation's social view on employment. It is reflected in the Employment Act of 27 June 1947. It states that every every citizen has the right to make a living and that the government is obliged to supply every citizen with a job and an income (and therefore follow an active policy of avoiding unemployment). Whilst not tested in the courts, strictly interpreted the government breaks the law by allowing unemployment to exist. Recent public opinion and media pressure suggest that modern politicians have not fully realized the implications of this law (Lange and Johnsen, 1993).

Similarly, Article 1 of the Italian constitution defines Italy as a democratic republic established on labour and this is reflected in one of the most protective structures of workers' rights in Western Europe (Cooper and Giacomello, 1993). The employer is defined as the provider of work (*datore*) whilst the employee or worker is the lender of labour (*prestatore*):

> ... In Italy [employment legislation] is rooted in Roman law and enshrined at the highest level of the constitution and at a secondary level in 'legislazione ordinario' (statutory law)... Italian labour law is extensive and highly structured... it is essential that any company which is unfamiliar with the Italian legal system, and labour law in particular, seeks professional, preferably local or regional, advice before establishing any work contract.
>
> Cooper and Giacomello (1993, p. 316–17).

The topic is complex and detailed. In this chapter therefore we only draw attention to the most pertinent recruitment and selection issues influenced by the legislative environment, i.e. sources of labour supply, equal opportunities and discrimination, and termination of employment. We consider legislation and codes of practice pertaining to the use of psychological testing later in the chapter. Legislation and other sources of law in areas not dealt with here are fully covered in specialized source books (for example Incomes Data Service, 1990a).

The source of law varies considerably and even in countries where there is now relatively little direct regulation in the area of recruitment, such as Denmark, the climate of industrial co-operation still encourages employee involvement in the elaboration of workplace personnel policies. In Denmark there are over 3,000 joint workplace 'co-operation committees' (jointly staffed by members of management and employees) which draw up personnel policies. The long tradition of agreements directly between parties in the labour market, common to many Nordic countries, is therefore a major source of labour market regulation, in the form of collective agreements, arbitration courts' interpretations and custom and practice. However, the trend is for public domain laws, secondary legislation and EU directives gradually to replace these collective agreements (Andersen, la Cour, Svendsen, Kiel, Kamp and Larsen 1993).

National agreements on recruitment and selection procedures are a common feature in European countries. For example, in Belgium there is a national collective agreement established in 1983 (*Convention collective de travail No. 38 concernant le recrutement et la sélection de travailleurs*) which although only morally binding and in an unsatisfactory format to legislate over selection decisions (Shimmin, 1989) nevertheless serves to provide a framework and set of guidelines within which most recruiters operate in the main (Incomes Data Service, 1990a). In addition to requiring the provision of information about job duties, location, and the application procedure, employers have to disclose whether the recruitment exercise is being conducted in order to build up a labour reserve. A respect for privacy is included in the agreement, with questions about marriage plans, or starting a family deemed unacceptable in a recruitment interview.

In France, organizations need to be aware of a remarkable range of collective agreements – which may exist at a national or industry level. These typically require organizations to follow certain set procedures, or limit what they can and cannot do in the recruitment process. For example, in distribution and retailing all vacancies have to be advertised internally to give existing staff priority for recruitment. In the chemicals sector employers must inform all interested parties of general staff needs and appointments, and where employment levels fluctuate, have to give priority in recruitment to employees terminated in the last twelve months. In the hotels and catering sector existing employees have preference for newly arisen vacancies, followed by employees terminated in the last twelve months (Incomes Data Services, 1990).

In Germany regulations governing recruitment, selection, transfer, re-grading or dismissal require the agreement of the works council in plants with more than 1,000 employees (Gaugler and Wiltz, 1993). Works councils also have to agree to the use of personnel questionnaires during the recruitment process. In practice, the works council only sees personal information on shortlisted candidates, but it has the right to see job descriptions, suggested grading, and application forms. It can veto appointments within one week of job offer.

Labour supply

Recruitment and the supply of labour is to some extent regulated by the significant role played by national employment offices (discussed later in this chapter). Another set of laws deal with the stimulation of labour supply and incentives to recruit from particular sources of labour. The debate raised by such interventions in the labour market is the extent to which the increased flexibility given to employers and training provided in return can be felt to outweigh the scope given to employers to use cheap labour and exert a downward pressure on salaries and labour costs. There is also debate over whether it is more important to focus national government legislation on the reduction of overall levels of unemployment, or to address specific areas of skills shortage.

For example, since the oil shocks and economic crises of the 1970s, Belgium has attempted to use employment law to control and stimulate the supply of labour, with benefits and incentives (such as work placements) to hire new (and especially previously unemployed) employees (Buelens, de Clerq, de Graeve and Vanderheyden, 1993). In Italy, employers recruiting more than ten workers are obliged to maintain a statutory minimum level of 12 per cent of their workforce taken from the lists of unemployed workers looking for their first job or workers receiving extraordinary support from measures used prior to the possible liquidation of companies (Cooper and Giacomello, 1993). In most countries, labour supply is also influenced by a vast array of incentives for establishing new businesses, undertaking specific types of training, and enticing high levels of mobility.

Equal opportunities

In France employment legislation bans employers from discriminating in the availability of jobs or hiring of employees on the grounds of origin, ethnic background, race, religion, state of health, handicap, sex or family situation (Bournois, 1993). Similar broad regulation of opportunities is found in Belgium, where the constitution and collective agreement No. 38 prohibits discrimination on the grounds of sex, marital status, race, past health record, political opinion or religion, and the same criteria and conditions of employment must be applied throughout the term of employment for both men and women. Women are to receive the same pay for equal work and are protected from dismissal whilst in the process of receiving this right (Buelens, de Clerq, de Graeve and Vanderheyden, 1993).

In most countries, sex may only be a qualification for employment in certain occupations (for example, personal care services, nightwork or the performing arts), but positive action may be taken in areas where women are under-represented (Incomes Data Service, 1990a). In Ireland, the Employment Equality Agency's code of practice recommends that interview panels should consist of both male and female members, with records kept of interviews to ensure that where personal questions are asked, they are asked of both men and women (Gunnigle, 1993). In Denmark, whilst the Equal Opportunities Act places restrictions on employers to provide equal treatment of men and women in recruitment of jobs, transfer or promotion, there are no special rules for the employment of older people, ethnic minorities or disabled persons (Andersen, la Cour, Svendsen, Kiel, Kamp, and Larsen, 1993). In Germany the Civil Code requires job advertisements to be gender-neutral.

Despite this legislative environment, organization practice is often still discriminatory. Bournois (1993) notes that in France discrimination still affects immigrants, the unemployed, women and disabled people. The emerging practice – declared or not – is for vacancies to be first offered to people already in stable jobs, then to people coming onto the market for the first time, then to women returners. Such a hierarchical strategy is probably followed in many other countries. Breaking into the labour market for people not already employed in the core of organizations is going to be a very difficult task throughout the whole of the 1990s.

Terms of notice and termination of employment

Terms of notice and termination of employment are dealt with in this chapter because decisions by organizations to resource externally from the labour force are strongly influenced by the degree of flexibility they feel they have over the termination of the employment contract. Where it is difficult to terminate employees, organizations are more circumspect about who they recruit and from what source. Levels of financial compensation associated with termination of employment can also have a dampening effect on recruitment. For example, in Spain rigid hiring regulations and an indemnity rate of forty-two months' salary when making an employee redundant is a disincentive to multinationals to invest in the country and have proved a constant source of irritation to employers (Filella and Soler, 1993; Vicente, 1993).

Typically, the different levels of entitlement exist on the basis of:

- The type of worker (defined by rank or industrial sector).
- The length of service and employment.
- The age of the employee.

In countries such as Denmark, Norway, the UK, Ireland and Switzerland notice for salaried employees depends on seniority in terms of time with the employing organization. For example, in Denmark there is a minimum notice of one month for new recruits, increasing by one month for every three years of service up to a maximum six months after nine years' service (Andersen, la Cour, Svendsen, Kiel, Kamp, and Larsen, 1993). The Irish system provides for a minimum notice of one week with under two years' service, rising to eight weeks' notice after fifteen years' service (Gunnigle, 1993) whilst in the UK after a qualifying period of two years, periods of notice increase up to a maximum of twelve weeks dependent on service (Brewster, Hegewisch and Lockhart, 1993).

In countries such as Belgium and Italy a combination of the type of work and length of service is applied. In Belgium the position on termination of employment differs for blue and white collar employees. White collar employees with more than five years' service must be given three months' notice per five year period (three months' notice only is required if service is under five years). Blue collar workers with less than twenty years' service only receive twenty-eight days' notice, rising to fifty-six days after 20 years' service. Termination of employment for executive and management employees can only be settled by mutual agreement. There are generally long periods of notice, with a three year period not uncommon (Buelens, de Clerq, de Graeve and Vanderheyden, 1993). Sales representatives, union representatives and members of works councils or safety committees are even more protected. In Italy, withdrawal from a labour contract by either party is marked by extensive job security guarantees for the worker (Cooper and Giacomello, 1993). In organizations with more than sixteen employees, dismissal can only be on the grounds of 'just cause' (*giusta causa*) such as prolonged absence, theft of company goods and so forth, or the more difficult to prove 'justifiable reason' (*giustificato motivo*) such as incompetence without deliberate intent by the employee (*soggettivo*), or the making of a point of the production process into a superfluous, unprofitable or detrimental activity (*oggettivo*). This latter cause for dismissal is the nearest Italian labour law comes to making someone redundant, although few claims succeed in court. Only since the introduction of the EU directive on collective dismissals in July 1991 has a clear definition of redundancy existed in Italian labour law (Cooper and Giacomello, 1993).

Finally, Sweden has an age-based system, with the minimum period of notice of one month increasing at ages 25, 30, 35, 40 and 45 up to an entitlement of six months. Only in a handful of European countries, such as Greece, is there very little employee protection. Employers in the private sector in Greece may dismiss workers with either advance notice or by immediate termination of the employment contract. No advance notice is required for manual workers and technicians (Papalexandris, 1993).

LABOUR MARKET CHARACTERISTICS

Another important feature to consider is the nature of European labour markets in relation to recruitment and selection. We have considered many aspects of labour markets elsewhere in the book. For example, levels of unemployment, the demographic crisis, the proportion of women returners to the labour market, shifts in employment by industrial sector, labour productivity and social employment costs were dealt with in Chapter Four, education and training levels are dealt with in Chapter Ten, and the breadth and structure of unions is dealt with in Chapter Fifteen. Many of these differences are expected to slow down the pace of integration of HRM practices in Europe. In this section we consider a number of other aspects of the labour market that have a bearing on recruitment and selection:

- The extent to which European organizations have internal or external labour markets.
- Skills shortages.
- The presence of strong regional characteristics and labour markets.

Internal versus external labour markets

There are two general sources of recruiting: internal and external. Internal recruiting seeks candidates from among the ranks of those currently employed for all but a handful of 'entry-level' positions. External recruiting attracts labour from outside the organization. Brewster (1993) points out that both internal and external labour markets are used to some extent by all organizations. However, we should point out that the more that a European organization or country relies on an internal labour market, the easier it becomes to control the definition of what makes an effective manager and to apply national cultural stereotypes, i.e. the more resistant the organization may be (initially) to adopting some of the changes in HRM highlighted in Chapter Six and at the beginning of this chapter. We give detailed consideration to the assumptions of what makes an effective manager and internal labour market in the next chapter.

Internal markets are assumed to be easier to control than external markets and most of the HRM literature described in Chapter One assumes the workings of an internal labour market (see for example Illustration 1.5 and the four policy areas used by Beer *et al.* (1984) to define the scope of HRM) although with different cultural assumptions about what skills to resource. Reliance on an internal labour market involves a greater emphasis on recruitment from the bottom and retention of employees to develop a high length of company service. There are a number of alternatives to recruiting externally (Schuler and Huber, 1993; Torrington and Hall, 1991) and in the context of the structural changes outlined in the previous chapter, and the level of downsizing discussed in Chapter Sixteen, these will be capitalized on by European organizations regardless of their historical traditions. As Illustration 9.4 shows, there are plenty of alternatives to explore before recruiting externally.

Relying on an internal labour market tends to lead to the following benefits:

- It improves the morale, commitment and job security of employees through higher job security and career opportunities.
- It provides for more opportunity to assess the abilities of employees accurately given the accrued knowledge gathered over the employment relationship.
- It is a cheaper way of resourcing labour than external recruitment and selection.
- It concentrates external recruitment activities on single entry levels (typically school leavers and graduates), allowing for more specialization of skill in the HRM department.

Illustration 9.4 **Internal alternatives to recruiting externally.**

Promote from within Relying on existing qualified employees familiar with the culture, policies, and procedures.

Transfers Transferring current employees without promotion.

Job rotation systems Temporary exposure to alternative job roles.

Re-hire arrangements Local collective agreements to give preference to previous (usually redundant) employees.

Job posting systems Open invitation for internal applications in preference to external candidates.

Skills inventories Formalized data on employee skills used to assist rotation, transfer or re-hire systems.

Work reorganization Changes to arrangements of jobs, roles or business process that ensure leavers do not need to be replaced or new resource requirements can be managed.

Automation Mechanization, automation or robotization of the work requirement.

Shift to part time Achieving marginal reductions in staff time and costs and/or facilitating employee requirements for more flexibility.

Subcontracting Avoiding ongoing costs and obligations of employment and transferring these to another employer.

New work patterns Manpower economies created by introducing new shifts or flexible working patterns.

Overtime To accommodate short-term shifts in work requirements, such as maternity cover. Usually subject to collective agreement.

- It affords more opportunity to control salary levels (because there is less need to accommodate external salaries).

The disadvantages are higher levels of 'political' behaviour associated with advancement and the danger of complacency as a single mindset besets the organization (Mathis and Jackson, 1992). It can lead to the development of workforces ill-suited to current technological or market demands because old ways of doing things become perpetuated (unless there is a very active management development policy). Units within the organization may raid each other for the best personnel and it is easier for an organization to become stuck with the wrong person in the job. It can lead to the growth of informal 'glass ceilings' or 'glass walls' whereby employees (for example, women) tend to find that movement through the internal labour market is restricted to certain levels in the hierarchy or functions in the organization. Finally, it often means that changes to HRM systems have to be conducted at the macro-level – bringing about alterations in the whole training or development system – whereas external recruitment may afford a more immediate and localized solution.

In general there is a high reliance on internal labour markets across all Europe (see Illustration 9.5 for an outline in Germany and Sweden and Illustration 9.6 for a description of resourcing at Bayer). For example, 66 per cent of Spanish employers prefer to recruit their professional and clerical staff from amongst their current employees (Filella and Soler, 1993) and a similar proportion of Swiss organizations fill their professional and technical vacancies from their own apprentices (Hilb, 1992; Hilb and Wittmann, 1993).

There are notable variations and exceptions to this rule. In Britain there has always been an active external labour market, with lower levels of organizational tenure, high mobility and low internal investment. Similarly, in Belgium most organizations resort to the external labour market to fill vacancies, although in recent years the tighter

Illustration 9.5 **Strong internal labour markets in Germany and Sweden.**

Results from the PWCP studies showed that two-thirds of European organizations recruit less than 30 per cent of their senior managers externally. However, in Denmark and Germany, well over half the organizations recruited the majority of their staff into clerical work (at least partially through apprenticeships) and then resourced most positions from these cadres. Private recruitment agencies for clerical and manual staff are unlawful in Germany and Sweden. A study by APEC (the Association pour l'Emploi des Cadres) in 1993 found that during the 1980s French organizations recruited only 28 per cent of their senior executives internally, compared with 36 per cent in Germany, 37 per cent in Britain, 45 per cent in Spain and 51 per cent in Italy. The economic recession in the early 1990s reversed this trend, with fewer French executives obtaining promotion by changing employer. This shift towards an internal labour market is changing recruitment policies, career assessments and rewards packages.

Source: Brewster (1993); Harding (1993).

Illustration 9.6 **An internal labour market at Bayer Group: managing recruitment at the entry point.**

Relying on an internal labour market makes it all the more important to manage recruitment at the entry point effectively. The Bayer Group focuses its recruitment on young people with a year to go at university. Each year some 200 graduates spend three months gaining work experience and 6,000 students work with Bayer during summer vacations. Professors at universities nominate their best doctoral students, who then attend a three-week all-expenses-paid course at Bayer. University projects are often sponsored by Bayer and the best scientists – around 50 to 60 Bayer staff – give lectures in universities. Mortgages are provided at low interest rates and rented accommodation is provided for over 20,000 employees.

Source: Sadler and Milmer (1993).

labour market has seen more organizations put resources into their inhouse training programmes (Incomes Data Service, 1990a).

External recruitment and selection are considered to be the two most important issues facing personnel professionals in Greece (Kanellopoulos, 1990; Papalexandris, 1988, 1993) although only a handful of organizations have formalized and systematic policies. In Greece, recruitment and selection policies are being re-examined in relation to their bearing on management development strategies (Lorbiecki, 1993). Given their shortage of management talent, Greek organizations have the option of either developing their existing workforce or seeking talent that has been developed elsewhere. Subsidiaries of multinational organizations often find it cheaper to import specialized managers from other parts of the organization. The risks of ignoring the importance of national culture to resourcing policies are discussed at length in the next chapter. However, in Greece, the government and national management development institutions are taking local action to improve the recruitment and selection process so that local talent may also be identified.

In Denmark, although the trend is for large organizations not to increase their levels of external recruitment but rather to rely on internal systems of training and career planning, there is still a very high level of mobility. Only 31 per cent of Danish organizations favour promoting internal candidates instead of external people for vacant management positions (Hilb, 1992). Around 700,000 Danes (a quarter of the workforce) switch between employment and unemployment in any one year creating a significant external labour market (Andersen, la Cour, Svendsen, Kiel, Kamp and Larsen 1993). Naturally, methods of external recruitment and selection are more prevalent and more developed in those European countries that rely more on an external labour market. These organizations have developed quality approaches to external recruitment (see Illustration 9.7).

Skills shortages

We alluded to the problem of skills shortages in Chapter Four. Even organizations that make more use of internal labour markets need to resource at basic entry points. As the young and the qualified become scarcer and more expensive, finding and retaining people will become a critical success factor within European business. After the boom in employment in the late 1980s, many European organizations found themselves facing labour shortages. Immediately prior to the recession that hit Britain first in 1990, many British organizations were searching for recruitment strategies to overcome the demographic crisis and related skills shortages. Switzerland has found that a policy of technological investment has resulted in a 'tighter' labour market. It has the lowest level of unemployment in Europe and the biggest recruitment problems. Ninety-four per cent of employers report recruitment problems, particularly in technical areas. Skills shortages are leading to innovations in HRM practice, not just in terms of recruitment and selection systems. In order to cope with recruitment problems, Swiss organizations have introduced a variety of measures: 84 per cent have introduced flexible working; 87 per cent part-time work; 52 per cent are recruiting from abroad; and 36 per cent have introduced job sharing (Hilb and Wittmann, 1993).

In France, INSEE (the *Institut National des Statistiques et des Études Économiques*) statistics show that the proportion of manufacturing organizations experiencing difficulties in recruiting all categories of staff has risen from 25 per cent in 1976 to nearly 50 per cent by 1989 (Bournois, 1993). The greatest problems are in the managerial and technical labour markets, where the channelling of investment into new computers and machinery, increase in production capacity, new organization methods have all been associated with a requirement for more qualified personnel. For example, the number of operators for computerized machines rose by 23 per cent in 1988–89 alone in France (Bournois, 1993).

Illustration 9.7 **A quality recruitment function in British Airways.**

British Airways claims to have the largest centralized commercial recruitment operation in the UK. There are 159,000 unsolicited enquiries for employment. Ninety full time staff process some 72,000 job applications each year, conducting some 13,000 interviews and making between 3,000 to 5,000 appointments. In response to skills shortages in IT, finance and engineering and the demographic downturn in the supply of young people, four recruitment marketing teams were set up. Each team focused on the needs of internal departments and applied customer service standards to both their dealings with the internal departments and the external recruitment operation. The quality, quantity, timing and cost of services were assessed and guidelines established for response targets in order to improve administration and communication of the recruitment process.

Source: Sadler and Milmer (1993).

Although in many European countries the high levels of unemployment of the early 1990s are expected to lessen such pressures in the short term, skills shortages will persist in the face of record levels of unemployment throughout the 1990s. In Belgium, despite the economic downturn, recruitment problems are expected to increase due to a number of 'structural imbalances' (skills shortages) within the economy (Incomes Data Service, 1990a). The most marked shortages exist for physics technicians, metal workers, electricians, welders and cutters, maintenance workers, bricklayers, sales representatives, machinists, carpenters, and engineers. Similarly, despite large inflows of Eastern German and East European workers, West Germany continues to experience labour market shortages for craft workers, engineers and managers. In the Eastern *Länder*, migration out of the region has led to shortages of people with technical, business administration and management skills (Gaugler and Wiltz, 1993). To the extent that such skills shortages do persist, then regardless of the level of 'downsizing' in European organizations (see Chapter Sixteen), there will be a continued need for significant levels of external recruitment and continued transformation in the nature of HRM practices.

However, it should be noted that in some countries the pressures associated with skills shortages appear not to be as great (see Figure 9.2). For example, the Price Waterhouse Cranfield Project found that in Denmark 62 per cent of organizations report no major skills shortages, even in a growing labour market. The exception is in small Danish organizations that are expanding and seeking middle managers with broad skills or technical specialists with upgraded and specialist skills (Andersen, la Cour, Svendsen, Kiel, Kamp and Larsen, 1993). In Norway an investigation by the

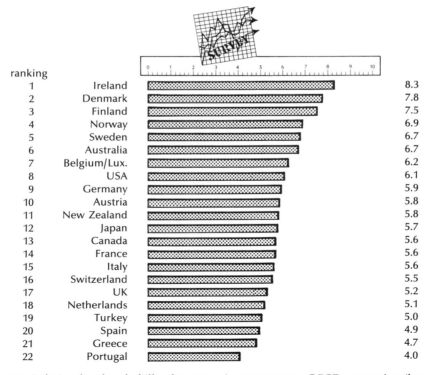

ranking			
1	Ireland		8.3
2	Denmark		7.8
3	Finland		7.5
4	Norway		6.9
5	Sweden		6.7
6	Australia		6.7
7	Belgium/Lux.		6.2
8	USA		6.1
9	Germany		5.9
10	Austria		5.8
11	New Zealand		5.8
12	Japan		5.7
13	Canada		5.6
14	France		5.6
15	Italy		5.6
16	Switzerland		5.5
17	UK		5.2
18	Netherlands		5.1
19	Turkey		5.0
20	Spain		4.9
21	Greece		4.7
22	Portugal		4.0

Figure 9.2 Relative levels of skills shortages in twenty-two OECD countries (low score reflects greater skills shortages). Source: World Economic Forum (1993), reprinted with permission, © 1993, World Economic Forum.

Ministry of Employment in 1989 found an average of eighteen applicants for each registered vacancy, with there being no marked shortages in specific job categories (Lange and Johnsen, 1993). Similarly, in Ireland the high birth rate, high levels of unemployment and well educated workforce generally results in an adequate supply of labour for prospective employers (Gunnigle, 1993).

In many European countries the proportion of foreign nationals is slowly increasing, but often as immigrant workforces as opposed to cross-border workers. For example, in Belgium, the number of Belgian residents of foreign nationality rose from 368,000 to 881,000 from 1946 to 1989, and is forecast to increase to over 1 million by the year 2,000 (Belgodata, *op. cit.* Buelens, de Clerq, de Graeve and Vanderheyden, 1993). The majority of these foreign nationals are Italian, Moroccan or French working in the Walloon or Brussels regions. The proportion of cross-border workers in Belgium fell from 56,000 in 1970 to 29,000 by 1988, with no increase foreseen by the Belgian Department of Employment.

Strong regional labour markets

There are a number of other labour market issues or anomalies that have an impact on recruitment and selection in Europe. In some parts of Europe there are strong regional or geographic labour markets. This is reflected in:

- Regional differences in recruitment behaviour in terms of mobility, sexual equality.
- Strong divisions on the grounds of religious, ethnic or cultural traditions.
- A strong economic focus on particular regions within countries.

For example, there is little or no geographic mobility for non-executive employees in Spain (Vicente, 1993) and trade unions are fiercely opposed to an opening up of the labour market and moves from one part of the country to another. In Norway most recruitment takes place within local villages. Taxation policies may also produce local labour market phenomena. For example, in Denmark any reward incentive or assistance from employers to employees to help them change residence in connection with a new job is taxable, and the resulting tradition of low mobility has led to the creation of strong regional labour markets (Andersen, la Cour, Svendsen, Kiel, Kamp and Larsen, 1993). Large differences in HRM conditions also exist between West and East Germany. Gaugler and Wiltz (1993) note that the employment of women continues to grow in Western *Länder* but has fallen in the East (having had 90 per cent participation rates before unification).

In Belgium, the labour market is still split between the French- and Flemish-speaking communities (Incomes Data Service, 1990a). Over half the population live in the North, speaking Flemish, and around a third of the labour force live in the Southern Walloon region, speaking French. Many regional and community administrative functions have been devolved to each region and many organizations have reflected this in their structure (operating autonomously in both regions or just in one) and in their legal instruments, documentation and communications to staff (which must be in the official language of the region). The Flemish are more likely to be bilingual (with French or English as a second language) than the French-speaking Walloons and therefore tend to have greater employment opportunities in the international context (Incomes Data Service, 1990). Multinational organizations recruiting in Belgium need to be aware of the separate recruitment networks.

In other countries the regional issues are connected to different levels of economic growth. In Sweden, around 75 per cent of all recruitment takes place in four regions: Stockholm/Uppsala, Lund/Malmö, Gothenburg and Linköping/Norrköping (Söderström and Syrén, 1993).

METHODS OF EXTERNAL RECRUITMENT

Recruiting internally may not always produce enough qualified applicants, especially if the organization is growing rapidly or is undergoing rapid technological change. Recruiting from the outside then becomes a necessity (Schuler and Huber, 1993). There are a number of motivations to recruit externally (see Illustration 9.8).

The price to be paid for relying on external recruitment is the possibility of recruiting employees who do not 'fit', the potential creation of morale problems for internal candidates, and the lengthy adjustment and socialization times (Mathis and Jackson, 1992). Costs are also quite high once indirect factors such as management time and resources are calculated. In a human resource accounting exercise for a major European engineering organization, Sparrow (1992) found that the typical cost of recruiting a single graduate into what was an efficient recruitment process was £10,000 (more than the initial starting salary of the graduate) once the managers' time, travel, advertisement costs and so forth had been priced. This figure made no assumption about the lost productivity of those involved in the process.

There is a considerable range of recruitment methods available (see Illustration 9.9). Most organizations use multiple methods, although in practice advertisements, personal contacts and interviews form the core of most recruitment and selection systems. There has been considerable development in the breadth of techniques used, particularly in response to the demographic crisis in Europe. For example, in France an estimated 200,000 managers change their job each year (these vacancies do not include larger numbers of technicians and manual workers) and the skills shortages of the late 1980s were reflected in increases in most company recruitment budgets and

Illustration 9.8 **Motivations to recruit externally.**

- Bring 'new blood' into the organization, perhaps as part of a broad culture change programme.
- Provide insights into competitor organizations.
- Provide a cheap way of acquiring a skilled employee, particularly when there is an immediate demand for scarce skills.
- Resource a temporary or short-term need for employees in order to achieve more flexibility to expand or contract the overall workforce.
- Assist in meeting equal legislation requirements.

Source: Mathis and Jackson (1992).

Illustration 9.9 **The main sources of recruitment in Europe.**

- National employment offices.
- Advertisements in the press.
- Recruitment consultancies, temping agencies and executive search.
- Direct targeting of schools and colleges.
- Personal contact.
- Radio, direct marketing, posters, electronic mail.
- Graduate recruitment through visits and fairs.

attempts to improve the sophistication of selection methods, particularly for managers (Bournois, 1993).

Organizational demography also has a large influence on the nature of recruitment methods. For example, the majority of Norway's 14,000 companies have fewer than 50 employees and a high number of companies are dependent on local recruitment in small villages (Lange and Johnsen, 1993).

NATIONAL EMPLOYMENT OFFICES

National employment offices play a major role in resourcing employment and filling vacancies in many European countries. They have had a historical role of regulating the labour market, motivated by constitutional rights or custom and practice concerned with ensuring objectivity in practice and employee rights (see Illustration 9.10).

Similarly, in Norway, under the law only the state labour market authority (*Arbeidsdirektoratet*) may serve as a mediator in the labour market. This situation is in a state of transition in many European countries. In the North this is due to deregulation and the impact of supranational legislation, whilst in the South it has been fuelled by the impact of democratic rule after periods of dictatorship. EU membership is changing the situation in Nordic countries. For example, in Denmark the state employment agency AF (*Arbejdsformidlingen*) until recently had a monopoly on placements. Liberalization of placement activities in 1990 was intended to strengthen the service, which is offered free in most cases. The service is used to analyse the qualifications and work experience of the job seeker and match this against an analysis of the requirements in the job. The AF recruitment service fills between 15 and 20 per cent of Danish vacancies (Incomes Data Service, 1990a). In Germany, the Federal Department for Employment (*Bundesanstalt für Arbeit*) has a monopoly on the placement of labour. Organizations can publicize their vacancies through their own

Illustration 9.10 **Recruitment process in Italy: maintaining objectivity through the** *collocamento.*

Until recently the recruitment process in Italy placed considerable restrictions on the freedom of employers to select and contract employees. The new process introduced in July 1991 provides wider discretion to the employer. The hiring and placement process (*collocamento*) obliges all prospective employees to register at district employment bureau (*ufficio di collocamento*) and all employers to request labour through these offices. Run by the Ministry of Labour these bureaux have a central role in the hiring process, reflecting the constitutional responsibility to further the rights of citizens to work. Intermediary private placement or employment organizations are restricted to an 'advisory' role. The old system of recruitment by number (*richiesta numerica*) where employers were allocated a certain number of employees of a particular category has become moribund, with recruitment of named individuals to fill specific positions (*richiesta nominativa*) becoming customary. The employer makes a hiring selection in advance of reference to the placement office, and the employee is then directed to the '*ufficio di collocamento*' for official registration. Only then does the employer make a request to the placement office for the employee as a direct hire. Failure by an employer to follow the '*collocamento*' procedures can result in fines from 1 million to 5 million lire, with a prison sentence or 15 million lire fine if the intention was deliberate and for financial gain.

Source: Cooper and Giacomello (1993); Folletti, Giacomello and Cooper (1991).

channels and private recruitment agencies can assist in the design of job adverts and selection process (but not the actual placement).

In Belgium, job placement has been devolved to three regional regional authorities. VDAB (*Vlaamse Dienst voor Arbeidsbemiddeling en Beroepsopleidung*) is responsible for placement and training in the Flemish-speaking areas, accounting for 45 per cent of manual job placements and 7 per cent of managerial posts (Incomes Data Service, 1990a). FOREM (*Formation-Emploi*) performs the same function in French-speaking Wallonia. These institutions retain a monopoly on placements in the public sector and also cover many placements at the low-skill end of the private sector. A survey reported by Buelens, de Clerq, de Graeve and Vanderheyden (1993) estimated that around 57 per cent of employers use such employment offices as a recruitment source whilst 70 per cent of prospective employees become aware of vacancies through this channel.

In France, the public bodies include ANPE (*Agence Nationale pour l'Emploi*), which provides recruitment services for blue and white collar workers and managerial staff, and AFPA (*Agence de la Formation pour Adultes*), which has encouraged organizations such as Sligos, Bull and Société Generale to sign employment contracts for new recruits aged under twenty-six years old and provide special management training in order to make up for their shortfall in computer operators. However, public bodies represent a minor source of employment. As in Denmark, until relatively recently (1986) ANPE possessed a monopoly of placements. Now French organizations wishing to recruit externally may use ANPE or registered private employment agencies, although all vacancies must still be notified to local regional offices of ANPE. ANPE still handles significant numbers of vacancies, for example in 1989 filling 70 per cent of the 310,000 unskilled and semi-skilled vacancies notified, 55 per cent of the 713,000 skilled blue and white collar vacancies and 37 per cent of the 54,000 managerial vacancies notified. However, only 9 per cent of French organizations turn to ANPE to help them recruit managers (Incomes Data Service, 1990). The state executive placement service, APEC (*Association pour l'Emploi des Cadres*) assists small French organizations with between 200 and 300 employees, and fills 37 per cent, 21 per cent and 23 per cent respectively of their middle management, senior management and executive posts.

In Britain 71 per cent of organizations use Job Centres as a source of recruitment (Curnow, 1989), but of these 25 per cent were making less use of the service than a couple of years ago. The advantage of national employment offices is that they can select applicants from nationwide computer-based data sources, are socially responsible and secure and can produce applicants very quickly. The disadvantages are that the registers tend to consist mainly of the unemployed and under-represent people in employment seeking a new organization (Torrington and Hall, 1991). These observations apply to most other European countries. Recruitment consultancies, employment agencies and executive search consultancies are therefore becoming more popular.

ADVERTISEMENTS IN NEWSPAPERS AND MAGAZINES

The use of advertisements is a very popular source of recruitment in most European countries. Expenditure on advertisements is difficult to compare because it is closely associated with the overall economic cycle in each country and linked to changes in legislation of placement services. For example, expenditure grew by 70 per cent from 1987–91 in Belgium (i.e. due to general expansion of the labour market before the economic recession) whilst from 1990–91 the number of job adverts in Danish newspapers fell by 50 per cent. In France, newspaper advertising by recruitment consultancies increased by 17 per cent from 1988–89 because of their increasing role after deregulation, with the same happening in Sweden.

A major source of recruitment is advertising in national or local newspapers and magazines. A survey of over 1,000 HRM professionals carried out in Britain by the Institute of Personnel Management and MSL recruitment consultants found that 87 per cent of organizations use advertisements in regional newspapers, 80 per cent advertise in specialist press and 78 per cent in the national press (Curnow, 1989). In Belgium, a research project by VUM – a major newspaper publisher – found that 89 per cent of employers used newspaper advertisements and 29 per cent used magazine advertisements as a source of recruitment whilst 82 per cent of prospective employees heard of vacancies from newspapers, and 40 per cent from magazines and local newspapers (Buelens, de Clerq, de Graeve and Vanderheyden, 1993). Public authorities have to advertise vacancies in the press. Well qualified clerical staff, sales representatives, lower and middle management are usually recruited through adverts in 'semi-national' regional newspapers angled at the Flemish or French regions. There is no national newspaper and so national campaigns require the use of newspapers in both regions.

In Denmark around one in three executives is recruited through advertisements and direct advertising in the press remains the main form of recruitment. The main business daily *Berlingske Tidende* carries some 80 per cent of all private sector recruitment advertisements. Specialist magazines and trades union publications are also used to attract graduates in Denmark (Andersen, la Cour, Svendsen, Kiel, Kamp and Larsen, 1993). A similar proportion of Spanish organizations (39 per cent) use external advertisements to recruit managers (Filella and Soler, 1993).

In most European countries, such as France, Denmark, Belgium and Germany, advertisements comply with the spirit of race discrimination and sex equality legislation or civil code. Advertisements in France cannot mention upper age limits, discriminating statements on the grounds of race, religion or sex, or indeed use any foreign expression where an equivalent French word exists. Pay rates are also rarely mentioned in advertisements across Europe, except in Britain or by Anglo-Saxon organizations advertising in Europe (Incomes Data Service, 1990a).

Although newspaper advertisements are also the traditional source of recruitment in many countries, they are becoming increasingly ineffective as a method of recruitment. For example, in France acute competition for school leavers has reduced their cost effectiveness and organizations are looking for alternatives such as radio and electronic mail (Bournois, 1993). More details on the most important newspapers and advertising media are provided for Britain by Torrington and Hall (1991) and for continental Europe by Incomes Data Service (1990a).

RECRUITMENT CONSULTANCIES, TEMPING AGENCIES AND EXECUTIVE SEARCH

As we have noted, in many European countries such as Germany, Norway and Italy, recruitment agencies are forbidden to do recruiting work for private organizations. Nevertheless, given the increasing deregulation of national placement services, the use of recruitment agencies of various forms has taken off in other parts of Europe than just Britain, such as Ireland, Denmark and France. In Denmark, until the 1990 legislation on placement services (ILO Employment Services Convention No. 88), the state placement service AF (*Arbejdsformidlingen*) had a monopoly on placements and private employment agencies were generally prohibited. Recognized trade union placement activities (mainly for employees with academic qualifications) and clerical agencies were the exception. Since deregulation, some trades unions such as Dansk Metal have set up 'jobs banks' holding information on employed and unemployed metalworkers and a national newspaper – *Berlingske Tidende* – has set up a database job service (Incomes Data Service, 1990a).

The use of recruitment agencies and consultancies in France also needs to be seen in a historical context. From 1974 to 1982 the low levels of economic growth meant that French organizations took on relatively few employees. As their personnel departments stagnated, recruitment was contracted out to external agencies. By 1990 the increasing volumes of recruitment in France and skills shortages once more created a situation in which recruitment is being contracted out. The use of search and selection consultancies is increasing again, growing at around 10 per cent a year and accounting for around 16 per cent of all executive placements (Incomes Data Service, 1990a). Moreover, in the 1990s these consultancies, which used to deal exclusively with top management, are now being used to help French organizations recruit middle management and younger executives (Bournois, 1993).

In Britain, employment agencies and recruitment consultancies have long provided a major source of recruitment, with 62 per cent of organizations using employment agencies, 61 per cent using recruitment consultancies and 36 per cent using executive search consultancies (Curnow, 1989). Fifty-seven per cent of those using recruitment agencies had made more use of them than in the past. Torrington and Hall (1991) have outlined some of the advantages and drawbacks in Britain of these sources of recruitment. Employment agencies have the advantage of reducing the administrative chores of the recruitment process, but may resource staff who will only stay for a short time. Recruitment consultancies afford the opportunity to elicit applicants anonymously and to use their expertise in an area where the organization may not

Illustration 9.11 **Selection methods used by executive search consultancies in four European countries.**

Executive recruitment and selection assignments may be indigenous (where assignments are confined to one country), transnational (when an assignment originates in one country but is conducted in another), or multi-country (where an assignment is conducted simultaneously in a number of countries). Although the majority of consultancies are locally owned, the personnel are drawn from a number of countries. There are around 820 executive recruitment and selection consultancies in the UK. A recent study identified all the officially listed consultancies through entries in relevant directories, institutional contacts and HR directors, and then asked each consultancy to identify its known competitors, thereby expanding the total population of companies. Using a similar approach, the study found that there were only 60 consultancies in Germany, 26 in Italy and 54 in France. Postal surveys and face-to-face interviews were used to examine the selection methods used by the consultancies. Response rates of 43, 25, 65 and 44 per cent were achieved for the UK, Germany, Italy and France respectively. The low response rate in Germany reflected the legal uncertainties surrounding executive search activities in that country. The survey found widespread use of selection methods with low validities. However, apart from greater use of graphology in French organizations, and a higher reliance on references in the UK, international executive search consultancies adopt a very similar approach. The data below show the percentage of consultancies using each selection technique.

	France	Germany	Italy	UK
Interviews	100	93	100	100
References	57	60	75	88
Psychological testing	35	40	38	40
Graphology	48	13	6	3

Source: Clark (1993). Table reproduced with permission of the publishers, Blackwell Publishers, © 1993.

always be active. The drawbacks are the high costs and the exclusion of internal candidates. Executive search consultants or 'headhunters' can approach known individuals directly and are useful for recruiting specialist skills or candidates from overseas, but conversely are limited to their own networks of contacts and new recruits may therefore be subject to further approach. Subsequent to the study by Curnow (1989) the recession in Britain severely depressed the use of recruitment agencies. A comparative study is outlined in Illustration 9.11.

Switzerland is notable for the lack of labour market regulation and around 61 per cent of employers use recruitment agencies for managerial staff (Hilb and Wittmann, 1993). Small organizations in Belgium also make extensive use of recruitment agencies and consultancies to source white collar employees and executive staff, and there are over 110 executive search and selection companies. Large organizations are also increasingly using recruitment consultancies as they subcontract out parts of their selection process. Buelens, de Clerq, de Graeve and Vanderheyden (1993) report that in Belgium, only 11 per cent of employers use recruitment agencies as a source of recruitment (rising to about 40 per cent of the smaller organizations), whilst 34 per cent of potential employees hear of vacancies through temping agencies (which must be recognized by the government and provide details of their ties with other organizations or institutions) and 4 per cent through headhunting consultancies (which are not regulated).

TARGETING SCHOOLS AND COLLEGES

Many European organizations recruit direct from schools, colleges or universities. For example, 22 per cent of Belgian employers recruit directly from schools and 17 per cent of prospective employees hear of vacancies this way (Buelens, de Clerq, de Graeve and Vanderheyden, 1993). Similarly, 21 per cent of Danish employers specifically target school-leavers for recruitment (Andersen, la Cour, Svendsen, Kiel, Kamp and Larsen, 1993) whilst in Spain 75 per cent of organizations target school leavers as a source of recruitment (Vicente, 1993). In France, a consortium of thirty industrial concerns are attempting to forge closer links between businesses and educational organizations in order to increase the output of engineers in postgraduate study. Such practices are indicative of a more long-term approach to the management (planning two to three years ahead) of recruitment being taken in European organizations (Bournois, 1993).

PERSONAL CONTACTS

Despite some of the recent innovations in recruitment methods (see Illustration 9.12) a reliance on personal contacts is still a strong source of recruitment. Forty-four per cent of Belgian organizations rely on personal contacts whilst 39 per cent of prospective employees hear of vacancies this way (Buelens, de Clerq, de Graeve and Vanderheyden, 1993). In Italy the personal recommendation system (*raccomandazione*) is still a widespread source for qualified and skilled personnel in small and medium-sized enterprises (Cooper and Giacomello, 1993) and in Greece extensive use is still made of personal contacts (Papalexandris, 1993). Where all other information is equal, preference will be given to a friend's recommendations. In countries where there is always an over-supply of labour, such as Ireland, unsolicited applications submitted on a speculative basis prove to be a cheap and effective source of recruitment.

Illustration 9.12   **Innovation in recruitment methods in France.**

Radio   There are a number of radio programmes, such as Challenge broadcast on France Inter at 8.15 am, on which organizations advertise vacancies and invite listeners to apply. Radio and TV are becoming an increasingly popular source of hearing about vacancies. Twenty-five per cent of Belgian job-hunters hear of vacancies this way and 17 per cent of larger British organizations use radio to attract staff.

Direct marketing   Compagnie Bancaire pioneered a direct marketing approach in 1989, and has received a 5–15 per cent rate of return for an investment of 100,000 Francs.

Poster advertising   Spie-Batignolle ran an adver-tising campaign in 1988 in which it advertised for staff on 1,800 posters and received 3,000 telephone calls and 1,200 letters.

Electronic mail (Minitel)   The computerized information service is regularly used by 30 per cent of French households. Candidates complete a short 'pre-selection' test devised by the company, which if they pass, allows access to more information. Minitel research shows that out of 100 candidates accessing information about a post, 60 complete the pre-test, 25 are pre-selected and 10 actually apply for the job. The method is inexpensive and saves employers and candidates time by weeding out the utterly unsuitable.

This reliance on informal personal contacts is, however, being capitalized on in more sophisticated ways by many organizations. In Denmark a high proportion of employees contact organizations where they know someone if they wish to change employment and several organizations have now established systematic databases on would-be employees (Andersen, la Cour, Svendsen, Kiel, Kamp and Larsen, 1993). The use of graduates in the graduate recruitment and induction process to help market the organization has been common practice in British organizations for several years. However, in France, organizations such as Bouygues in the construction sector and Hewlett Packard in the computing sector have adopted 'co-opting schemes', whereby low-service employees are promoted to recruitment positions and rewarded for their ability to become good recruiters (Bournois, 1993). Bournois (1993) feels there are dangers inherent in using young managers, inexperienced in general business and given only fifty hours training in recruitment techniques. Such concerns reflect the different composition and capabilities of managers in HRM departments across Europe. In Britain fifty hours training on recruitment techniques would be a rare gift.

GRADUATE RECRUITMENT

There are substantial differences in the methods of graduate recruitment in the UK, continental Europe and the US (Sadler and Milmer, 1993). The representation of graduates amongst managers is 85 per cent in the USA, 60 per cent in France and Germany, but only 20 per cent in the UK (although what constitutes a graduate and the quality of the different national patterns of education is not reflected in such statistics).

In Britain graduate recruitment is a significant activity for the larger organizations, as graduates seek to secure employment before the end of their studies. Twenty-one per cent of larger organizations use systematic visits to universities (called the 'milk round' and the main source of new graduates) and 32 per cent use recruitment fairs (frequently attended by graduates) as a source of recruitment (Curnow, 1989). ICL provides a typical example of the approach taken by the larger British organizations. It recruits 300 graduates a year from a pool of 5,000 applicants (Sadler and Milmer,

1993). Having cut back on graduate recruitment in the 1979–82 recession, it suffered for six years from a negative image and inherited resourcing problems (Sparrow, 1992). The flow of graduates into the organization is now based on manpower planning rather than what can be afforded year by year. Sponsorship has become an important way of attracting graduates, with around half the intake receiving some form of sponsorship from ICL. Ninety per cent of the sponsored graduates receive and accept job offers. A 'schools connect' programme links senior managers into local schools, and particular colleges and universities are targeted for recruits. Assessment centres are used to select graduates for the organization. As well as being more reliable in predicting success, it is felt they send a message of professionalism and fairness to the graduates applying for a job.

Ireland has a similar approach to Britain, with many colleges and universities offering 'sandwich' courses involving a period of placement (Gunnigle, 1993). In France, the 'milk round' does not exist. We detail the unique attributes of the French graduate system in the next chapter when discussing management development. Employers instead rely on direct applications from graduates and networks of links between senior managers and specific educational institutions. For example, Thomson receives around 6,000 spontaneous graduate applications a year, whilst the European Space Agency (ESA) receives around 8,000 to 10,000 (Sadler and Milmer, 1993). Because the ESA is a public body, it has more formalized procedures concerning the use of application forms and the collation of applicant information on its databases than might be found in other organizations. Similarly, in Belgium most individuals who are destined for senior management or technical positions are recruited directly from the higher educational institutions (Incomes Data Service, 1993), with one third of all degrees awarded in science and engineering (the figure is 39 per cent in France). Attracting graduates is becoming an increasingly more important topic across Europe. In Denmark an increasing number of graduates from non-technical backgrounds have taken managerial positions (Andersen, la Cour, Svendsen, Kiel, Kamp and Larsen, 1993).

In Greece most large multinationals are trying to find young graduates with management potential in order to allow themselves to shift from an external labour market to an internal one, with higher levels of internal potential and capability (Papalexandris, 1993). The reliance on personal recommendations often means that in order to get a first job many Greek graduates go abroad to gain a postgraduate qualification to make up for their lack of professional skills. In general, military service in Continental Europe frequently serves to create a clear bridge between education and job-seeking behaviour. The direct recruitment of graduates into mainline organization posts is also more limited and blurred by closer links between the education and vocational training systems. In Italy, although customs are changing, exams take place in summer and winter and so there is no formal graduation period (Cooper and Giacomello, 1993).

In Chapter Eleven we discuss the development of a cadre of 'Eurograduates' that are expected to play a significant role in the 'Europeanization' process taking place in many organizations. In this section we draw attention to the increasing competition over graduates and the particular recruitment methods used to attract them into organizations. The importance of graduates in European labour markets will only increase. According to BIPE (*Bureau d'Informations et de Prévisions Économiques*) the number of jobs requiring graduate skills in France is set to virtually double, from 5 per cent in 1982 to 11 per cent by the year 2000 (Incomes Data Service, 1990a).

Differences in the structure of management education have a bearing on recruitment strategies. In Belgium, for example, there are no business schools and although MBAs have only recently started to be taught at the universities, the qualification is not particularly sought after.

Graduate fairs have become a popular way of attracting graduates and they are often the only occasion when employers make direct offers to graduates in countries such as Belgium, France and Britain. In France there are over ninety recruitment fairs held for graduates every year, and each fair is often subscribed by five times as many organizations than there are stands (Bournois, 1993). However, the utility of such fairs is being questioned as organizations that use them have to sort through thousands of indiscriminately submitted curricula vitae in order to make a small number of appointments at a time when the price of attending the fairs has increased. The focus of graduate recruitment for European organizations is therefore best understood in the context of their internationalization strategies. The move towards international resourcing through foreign recruitment (see the section on Eurograduates in Chapter Eleven, page 439) should not be overstated.

THE NATURE OF SELECTION

The second major section of this chapter covers selection. Recruitment and selection are clearly overlapping processes, with, for example, advertisements serving the purpose of screening out potential applicants on a variety of grounds. Selection, however, covers that part of the process that gathers '. . . legally defensible information about job applicants in order to determine who should be hired for long- or short-term positions' (Schuler and Huber, 1993). The selection process also involves the need for assessment and final placement, which is concerned with matching individual skills, knowledge, abilities, preferences, interests, and personality to the job. Robertson and Smith (1989) point out that the topics of selection and assessment are fundamentally concerned with the prediction of job performance, or more recently a broader set of organizational requirements. The main purposes of selection, assessment and placement are outlined in Illustration 9.13.

The history of personnel selection is also dominated by the concept of individual differences (de Wolff, 1989). The field has therefore been the preserve of psychologists. Psychologists have been concerned with trying to identify, describe and measure differences between individuals in terms of their aptitudes, personality traits and interests. The approach involved studying jobs in order to find out what incumbents were required to do and then devising various tests or indicators to measure the desired qualities. For a long time (whilst organizations and the jobs within them were stable

Illustration 9.13 **The main purposes of selection, assessment and placement.**

- To obtain appropriate information about jobs, individuals and organizations to enable high quality decisions to be made.
- To transform this information into predictions about future behaviour and resulting contributions to organizational goals.
- To contribute to the organization's bottom line through efficient and effective production or delivery of service.
- To ensure that there is a cost-benefit to the financial investment made in employees.
- To evaluate, hire, and place job applicants in the best interests of both the organization and the individual.
- To enable organizations to fulfil their strategies.

Source: Schuler and Huber (1993).

Illustration 9.14 **Pressures requiring greater attention to selection systems in European organizations.**

- Selection systems usually involve high costs, which are now being incurred at at time when competitive and cost pressures are at their highest. Managers want to ensure bottom-line benefits result from the system.
- Reduced job mobility and a greater reliance on

the internal labour market means that selection errors will stay with the organization for longer.

- Legislation promoting equality of opportunity, and the democratization of the selection process, require sounder and well validated selection procedures.

and unchanging) psychologists were able to assist managers in making decisions about selection and determining which job category the individual should pursue. Selection became a science, and psychologists defined selection as a problem of prediction. Two problems have emerged for this paradigm. First, the nature of jobs has become extremely fluid, so many of the old predictions no longer hold. Second, by defining selection as a problem of prediction, many other problems (such as dignity and discrimination) were overlooked (de Wolff, 1989).

Torrington and Hall (1991) point out that whilst the search for the perfect method of selection continues, HRM managers continue to use a variety of imperfect methods in order to cope with the demands of the job. Attitudes to selection are changing, however, under the influence of more sophisticated recruitment methods introduced in the 1980s and recessionary pressures in the 1990s. There are a number of diverse pressures forcing organizations to devote more attention to the efficiency and validity of the selection system (see Illustration 9.14).

A TYPICAL SELECTION PROCESS

Shackleton and Newell (1991) point out that selection involves a sequence of activities, beginning with some kind of job analysis. Job analysis is used to title a job accurately, establish its purpose and position in the organization, the duties and responsibilities, limits to authority, and working relationships involved. This stage is followed by the recruitment stage, which as we have already outlined is intended to attract potentially suitable candidates, so that time and money are not wasted examining the credentials of candidates whose experience does not match the job requirements. Recruitment focuses on finding an appropriate source to locate candidates. It is followed by the selection process, which usually involves a series of methods to improve the information available about a candidate so that a decision can be made. These methods tend to be used in two ways – they either work as initial screening, whereby the focus is on identifying who to reject from the process, or they work as decision aides for the final selection decision, whereby the focus is on identifying relative strengths and weaknesses. Finally, the last stage is the selection decision. These decisions may be:

- Actuarial (statistical).
- Clinical.

The first approach is considered the most scientific, and uses objective, statistical analysis of data about candidates. The second, clinical approach, relies more on a 'gut feel' or intuitive judgement. In practice, the vast majority of organizations use methods which result in a clinical decision.

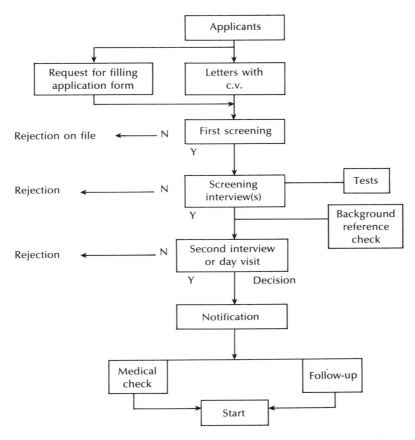

Figure 9.3 The recruitment and candidate handling process at Proctor and Gamble.

The final product of the design process is the description of the complete selection process. This makes it quite clear what activities should be undertaken, by whom, when and with what tools and techniques. A flow description of the whole process helps to make it clear which activities are involved in their chronological order, and the logical relationships between them (see Figure 9.3). Such a flow description is usually supported by a description of the techniques used, their validity and reliability, the facilities needed, instructions on their administration, and other work aids that are necessary (Roe, 1989). We now consider the various techniques used.

METHODS OF SELECTION

Despite there being a diverse range of selection methods – or 'predictors' – most European countries rely on only very traditional systems of selection. The main predictors available are shown in Illustration 9.15. The situation is complicated by the fact that some of these predictors can be mixed, as in assessment centres, to produce a combination which becomes a method in its own right (Robertson and Smith, 1989). Most of these predictors have been available for the last twenty years, with the exception of situational interviews, accomplishment records and computer assisted testing. Also, in most countries the use of recruitment and selection methods varies

Illustration 9.15 **The main selection predictors available.**

- Interviews:
  - unstructured,
  - structured,
  - situational,
  - behavioural description.
- Analytical tests:
  - cognitive ability (general or specific),
  - perceptual-motor,
  - personality,
  - interests.
- Analagous or sample tests:
  - work sample,
      - situational (intrays, role plays, simulations),
      - trainability tests.
- Computer-assisted tests.
- Repertory grids.
- Biodata and accomplishment record.
- Future autobiography.
- References.
- Graphology.
- Astrology.
- Self-assessment.
- Supervisors/peer assessment.

Source: Robertson and Smith (1989).

markedly with the size of the organization. The high number of small organizations means that in practice recruitment and selection may be a very informal affair.

INTERNATIONAL COMPARISONS OF SELECTION METHODS

There is a paucity of hard, reliable empirical evidence on the relative uptake of these various selection methods across European countries and organizations. The evidence tends to rely on a handful of academic studies (for example, Clark, 1993; Shackleton and Newell, 1991) which have compared the use of selection techniques in a few countries or organizations, some comparative results produced in consultancy reports (Arkin, 1993), and local national surveys of variable reliability reported in national summaries of recruitment and selection (see, for example, contributions in Brewster, Hegewisch, Holden and Lockhart, 1993; Incomes Data Service, 1990a). We draw upon all these sources to place the discussion of the various methods of selection in their national context where possible, but without a large-scale study, the comparative data can only be treated as a series of snapshots and insights into national practice.

In Britain the relative use of selection techniques has been examined and data established on the frequency of use of various selection techniques in 1984 (Robertson and Makin, 1986). Using a similar methodology, a recent study compared the methods used to select managers in seventy-three British and fifty-two French organizations (Shackleton and Newell, 1991) and provided some insights into the advance of selection techniques in Britain from 1984–89 and a comparison to the situation in France. The British sample were drawn from the Times 1000 and the French sample from *Les 200 Premières Groups des Echos*. They found a series of common themes in the selection methods used in France and Britain, as well as numerous distinct national characteristics. The authors caution against generalizing the results to wider national practice because of the difficulties that arise from postal surveys and small sample sizes. With this caveat, findings from these studies are incorporated into the ensuing description of selection methods.

Data from the Price Waterhouse Cranfield Project on HRM suggested some differences in preference for particular selection methods across European countries. These are highlighted in Table 9.1.

Table 9.1 **Selection methods in European countries.**

	Sweden	France	Netherlands	Portugal	Switzerland	UK
Application form	87	95	94	83	15	97
Interview	85	92	69	97	69	71
References	54	73	47	55	96	92
Graphology	8	57	2	2	0	1
Work sample tests	72	28	53	17	14	45
Biodata	12	26	20	62	69	8
Psychometric tests	60	22	31	58	24	46
Team selection	22	10	2	18	3	13
Assessment centres	18	9	27	2	5	18

Data drawn from various reports from the Price Waterhouse/Cranfield Project and ESC Lyon.

CURRICULUM VITAE AND REFERENCES

So what techniques are available? What do selection systems typically involve? In many cases initial screening is achieved through the use of the curriculum vitae (c.v.) only, followed by extensive interviewing. In France and Belgium it is common for job adverts to specify the submission of handwritten curricula vitae and supporting letter of application (for later analysis by graphologists). Indeed, in Denmark curricula vitae are so prevalent that application forms are rarely used and in Spain selection at the managerial level is usually based on the provision of a c.v. and a photograph.

Another source of information is the reference report, which is known by a number of terms such as letter of reference, recommendation reference check, referee report, employer's reference or testimonial. They all involve an assessment of the individual by a third party. References vary considerably in the range of information that is gathered, and the way in which it is collected, i.e. a written report or verbal report by telephone. Britain has a strong tradition of selectors using references as a method of selection, irrespective of the organization size or level of management intake. In their comparative study Shackleton and Newell (1991) found that 74 per cent of British selectors use references compared to just 11 per cent of French selectors (mainly from small to medium-sized organizations with small intakes). In Ireland formal reference-checking is the most popular source of selection (Gunnigle, 1993) and in other countries, such as Belgium, it is customary to take up references by telephone. References may be used as the whole basis for a clinical selection decision, or more usually, as part of the information available.

APPLICATION FORMS AND BIODATA

Application forms are commonly used in France and Britain, with Shackleton and Newell (1991) finding usage rates of 98 per cent and 93 per cent respectively. In Germany, the involvement of works councils and formalized vocational training systems means that many organizations ensure uniformity of information by using standard application documents. In Ireland, application forms are favoured over c.v.s as a selection device (Gunnigle, 1993) yet in other countries such as Denmark, the use of the curriculum vitae seems to preclude widescale use of application forms.

It is often remarked that what a person will do in the future is best predicted by what they have done in the past. Biodata represent a systematic way of using information about past events to predict future job success (Drakeley, 1989). There are a number of advantages to the approach. The same questions can be asked of everybody, read and assessed in the same way, items that discriminate against social groups can be eliminated and the link between questions and job performance can be demonstrated and defended. Biodata is then essentially a collection of items that might be found on a biographical questionnaire or application form (such as age, marital status, educational attainment, job history, or hobbies) that enable the respondent to describe him or herself in demographic, experiential or attitudinal terms (Drakeley, 1989). Biodata differs from traditional items on an application form in that the respondent's answers are combined to produce a score analogous to that established by a test. This score is used for selection purposes. A distinction can be made between 'hard' items, typically representing historical and verifiable information, and 'soft' items, which may be more abstract in nature and include multiple choice questions on value judgements, aspirations, motivations and expectations. Biodata is a relatively recent method of selection in the European context and its use has developed most rapidly in Britain. Shackleton and Newell (1991) found that 19 per cent of British organizations used the technique compared to 4 per cent of (mainly very large) French organizations. However, only a small proportion of British organizations used this technique in more than half their selection processes. Biodata scoring keys tend not to be indefinite and typically need to be re-assessed every two to three years. They are most cost effective when used for pre-selection, particularly for organizations that routinely need to recruit from large labour pools.

UNSTRUCTURED INTERVIEWS

By far and away the most popular method of selection is the recruitment interview which has been described as a '... conversation with a purpose' (Armstrong, 1988). Considerable store is set on this 'conversation' in most European countries – most notably the UK, France, Belgium, and Spain – although it is difficult to generalize about the intensity of interviewing across European countries. The number of interviews varies between organizations and the level of seniority of the job, and also depends whether the interviews are integrated with other selection procedures (Incomes Data Service, 1990a).

Vicente (1993) estimates that the personal job interview is used by 80 per cent of Spanish organizations as the main method of selection. In the UK around 80 per cent of organizations always use interviews as part of the selection process (Bevan and Fryatt, 1988; Institute of Manpower Studies, 1988; Robertson and Makin, 1986). In their comparative study, Shackleton and Newell (1991) found that interviews were used widely in both Britain (93 per cent) and France (94 per cent), although there was a striking contrast in the number of interviews used in the selection process. Only 60 per cent of British organizations used more than one interview. Responsibility for decentralization of decision making was handled by using more panel interviews. In France, 93 per cent of organizations used more than one interview, and the preferred form was a series of one-to-one interviews. A study by the Psychology Laboratory of the University of Bordeaux (Bournois, 1993) estimated that 98 per cent of French organizations used interviews in their selection process. The French preference for using more than one interview was linked by Shackleton and Newell (1991) to Hofstede's (1980) analysis of national culture. The higher scores on Uncertainty Avoidance found in French managers is reflected in a preference to have their own views supported by views from their colleagues. Even in L'Oréal, which has an atypical organizational culture for a French organization in that it is 'fervently anti-bureaucratic', the recruiting process is seen as a 'co-option', with the decision to recruit made with participation and input from all levels of the organization and based on consensus. Recruitment policies are neither dictated from above nor written down (Sadler and Milmer, 1993). In most other French organizations, which are more formalized than L'Oréal, the managers' higher Power Distance scores are reflected in a desire to seek approval from seniors before accepting candidates. In Greece too, the final decision for appointment often resides with the Managing Director after a strict initial screening and selection process.

The majority of research by psychologists suggests that interviews are an extremely unreliable method of selection, but more recent work has argued that interviews may still form an extremely useful part of the selection process if used in the right way (Arvey, Miller, Gould and Burch, 1987). Despite their limitations in predicting job success accurately, they may serve a variety of other purposes such as selling the organization to the candidate, providing an opportunity to assess cultural, attitudinal and personality fit (rather than aptitude for the job) in the broad.

STRUCTURED INTERVIEWS

Interviews are not a uniform selection procedure (Arnold, Robertson and Cooper, 1991) and structured interviews which utilize job-related questions tend to be much better predictors of subsequent performance. In structured interviews candidates are asked a series of predetermined questions, minimizing the chance for irrelevant information to be gathered, and for prejudice and bias to influence the choice. The interviewer has advance knowledge of the best answers, based on the analysis of responses from superior performers in the job. Structured interviews are quite effective in predicting subsequent job performance. This type of system is proving attractive to organizations who want to improve the objectivity of their selection system at a relatively low cost, as for example in Spain (Vicente, 1993), where studies have indicated that employees recruited through this method make a greater contribution to bottom-line profit, change jobs less frequently and are rated higher in terms of customer satisfaction.

SITUATIONAL INTERVIEWS

A situational interview is a specific type of structured interview that was developed in the mid-1980s in order to increase the predictive power of interviews (Latham and Saare, 1984). They are based on the premise that managerial performance can be predicted, in part, by the way in which applicants say they will tackle an example problem or task that is taken from the task or job itself. Critical incidents involving examples of particularly good or bad performance are identified, and job experts used to provide realistic behavioural examples. These are used to develop a series of behavioural observation scales (often established for a number of competencies). A measure of effective and less effective responses is devised, and used to assist in selection decisions. The scales provide benchmarks for interviewers to score candidates, and have increased the reliability and validity of interviews as a selection method.

HANDWRITING ANALYSIS/GRAPHOLOGY

Graphology is the art or science of deducing personality descriptions or behaviour predictions from a sample of individual's handwriting (Clark, 1993). It is felt by some European selectors to be an additional tool to personality testing (not an alternative) because it potentially adds additional information to psychological tests. Proponents of the technique argue that it elicits 'self-generated' and therefore more expressive behaviour, handwriting features such as size, slant, word and line spacing lend themselves to detailed analysis, an individual's handwriting is unique to their personality and remains recognizable across media and mood swings, and samples can be obtained cheaply and with ease. Critics point to the shaky evidence on its effectiveness, which we discuss later in this chapter.

Handwriting analysis, or graphology, is a very commonly used selection technique in France, with more than 77 per cent of French organizations (although not the larger ones) using it to select managers (Shackleton and Newell, 1991). A study by the Psychology Laboratory of the University of Bordeaux (*op. cit.* Bournois, 1993) estimated that 97 per cent of French organizations used the technique. Many of the French recruitment and consultancy agencies employ graphologists as selectors (Shimmin, 1989). In comparison, only 3 per cent of British employers used graphology for selection purposes. Buelens, de Clerq, de Graeve and Vanderheyden (1993) report that French speaking organizations in the Walloon region of Belgium also use graphology, although its use in Belgium is more controversial. Nevertheless, graphology tests are widespread both as a pre-selection procedure or as a back-up to impressions gained through other parts of the selection procedure (Incomes Data Service, 1990a). Although there is mounting criticism of the use of such techniques on the grounds of their poor validity, the skills shortages being experienced by French organizations, mounting cost pressures on their recruitment budgets, and contracting out of activities to agencies are all combining to encourage the use of '. . . quick and cheap selection techniques such as astrology, numerology and graphology' (Bournois, 1993).

PSYCHOLOGICAL TESTS

However, other more valid selection techniques are also quite widely used in France. A study by the Psychology Laboratory of the University of Bordeaux (*op. cit.* Bournois, 1993) estimated that 62 per cent of French organizations used personality tests in their selection process, 55 per cent used aptitude or intelligence tests and 21.5 per cent used projection tests such as Rorschach. These seem to be rather high estimates, however, and probably reflect the practice of the largest organizations only. In their comparative study of leading organizations, Shackleton and Newell (1991) found that no French organizations with less than two hundred employees reported using either personality or cognitive tests. Across the whole sample, 17 per cent of French organizations used personality tests compared to 10 per cent of British organizations, and 49 per cent of French organizations used cognitive tests compared to 70 per cent of British organizations. The French public sector until recently had a strong tradition in the use of psychometrics (Shimmin, 1989). Many of the national placement services, such as ANPE in France, offer pre-selection psychological testing of candidates.

For the purposes of personnel selection, psychometric tests are divided into two categories: cognitive tests (assessing attributes such as general intelligence, spatial ability, and numerical ability) and personality tests (assessing individual traits against a model of underlying personality factors). In Britain, the psychological testing agency Saville and Holdsworth found in a survey of 361 large organizations that between 57 per cent and 71 per cent used personality questionnaires and 63 per cent and 68 per cent used cognitive tests at some point during management recruitment (McCulloch, 1993). There are, however, clear differences in the overall level of use. Smaller organizations make less use of tests, as does recruitment for other than management jobs. Whilst organizations may have tests at their disposal, they often limit their use to smaller-scale management assessments. The deciding factors are company size, volume of recruitment and level of staff assessed. Therefore two surveys of total usage of psychological tests (the first by Robertson and Makin, 1986 and the second by the Institute of Manpower Studies, 1988) found respectively that between 64 per cent and 78 per cent of respondents did not use personality tests and between 71 per cent and 84 per cent did not use cognitive tests.

Social, economic, political and religious influences have resulted in marked differences in the uptake of psychological testing. In the predominantly Catholic South of Europe, such as in Spain, the Catholic Church tends to disapprove of psychological tests, whilst the unions do favour their use in order to counter patronage and nepotism (Shimmin, 1989). The use of psychological testing in such countries is, however, increasing. Large Spanish organizations are making more use of testing in order to improve the objectivity of their selection systems (Filella and Soler, 1993; Vicente, 1993). Indeed, in Italy the 1970 law on the rights of workers (*Statuto dei lavoratori*) forbade the use of selection tests and attitude surveys (Shimmin, 1989). In the Protestant North, for example Sweden, the objections are on social and ethical grounds and psychologists are becoming more critical of their use on grounds of validity (Poortinga, Coetsier, Meuris, Miller, Samsonowitz, Seisdedos and Schlegal, 1982) or the invasion of privacy.

In some countries, therefore, psychological tests are used only in very specific situations. For example, in Belgium they are frequently used by organizations in graduate recruitment (because of concerns about the gap between theoretical education qualifications and employers' desire to recruit adaptable, mobile and linguistically-skilled students) or for older candidates who have applied for particularly sensitive posts (Incomes Data Service, 1990a).

In Germany psychological tests must be conducted by qualified psychologists, must be linked to the job, and can only be used if the candidate has been informed about their nature and content and has given their explicit agreement. In other countries, such as Belgium, the recruitment culture is such that most organizations provide candidates with information about the tests they intend to use in the selection process and also obtain candidates' consent to use the tests.

However, once corrections are made for different research methodologies, many of the differences between European organizations (apart from the use of graphology and references) disappear (Smith and Abrahamsen, 1992). Indeed, throughout Europe there has been a marked trend to import psychological tests, mainly from the US and Britain, and this has had a profound effect on selection processes in many organizations. An area of concern is that as more and more European organizations follow this trend, and import tests developed in a foreign language and using Anglo-Saxon cultural assumptions, there will be many problems of linguistic inaccuracy, poor cultural relativity, and uncontrolled application. In Norway, a survey by the Norwegian Institute for Personnel Management in 1990 found that thirty-one different tests were being used by organizations but most were simple translations using tests norms from other countries and cultures (Lange and Johnsen, 1993). In some countries individual psychologists or institutions have even produced different versions or translations of imported tests. Shimmin (1989) points out that such practice has spurred European psychologists towards the establishment of:

- Professional competences for selectors.
- Quality control procedures for the use of tests.
- Levels of training and codes of ethics.

The key issues surrounding multinational assessment using psychological tests are the choice of language for the test (particularly personality questionnaires where linguistic subtleties prove difficult for non-native speakers). Culturally-sensitive translation that reflects intended meaning is also important (Hambleton and Bollwark, 1991). There are more similarities than differences in the personality scores of European managers, but some variations are important enough for managers to be compared only against their fellow nationals. Saville and Holdsworth report that their experience in Southern European countries (for example Italy and France) shows that response patterns of managers on certain personality scales varies. On some scales which in Britain had a 'normal distribution' of response, Italian and French managers tended to cluster only towards one end of the scale (McCulloch, 1993). For example, Italian managers describe themselves as being more innovative and conceptual, and less traditional or emotionally-controlled than British managers. To cope with such differences, Saville and Holdsworth have developed an International Testing System which administers and interprets tests in eleven languages. They have also initiated a research project in the US, UK, France, Germany and Australia to examine the effectiveness of a range of tools for selection of managers in an international context (Gibbons, 1993).

ASSESSMENT CENTRES

A number of writers have outlined the nature of assessment centres (Feltham, 1989; Woodruffe, 1990). The term 'assessment centre' does not refer to a place where managers go to be assessed, but rather to a process that is used to assess individuals within organizations (see Illustration 9.16). This process involves multiple, trained observers using a range of selection techniques (most of which have already been outlined) to make judgements about behaviour. Participants in an assessment centre are generally evaluated against a number of predetermined and job-related criteria, usually called 'dimensions' (but sometimes also measuring skills, characteristics, abilities, attributes, qualities or competencies). They are particularly prevalent and useful when assessing moves into positions that demand a significant new set of skills

Illustration 9.16 **General characteristics of assessment centres.**

1. Use of multiple assessment techniques.	4. Training of assessors in how to record and observe behaviour impartially.
2. Development and use of tailored simulations and work samples.	5. Separation of the process of observation from the final evaluation.
3. Observation by multiple assessors.	

Source: Iles (1992).

(for example, a move into first line management positions, senior management jobs, or a shift from scientific or engineering roles into project management).

The method was first used by the German army before 1939 to identify leadership potential and was subsequently developed by the British War Office Selection Board and US Office of Strategic Services. After the war British and American approaches diverged (Iles, 1992). Development in Britain was mainly for public sector organizations (civil service, army, navy, air force and police), a tradition which allowed the use of lengthy interviews, extended written exercises, physical tasks, accompanied by references, cognitive tests, one-to-one interviews, group exercises and 'in tray' simulations. In the US, exercises simulated actual work content less closely, and made less use of personality testing or role plays. As with many other HRM developments, British commercial organizations re-imported the American tradition of assessment centres in the early 1960s and late 1970s and adapted the model to local use. The approach has been adopted to serve a variety of purposes, with use in recruitment and selection systems being only one. Given that most of these purposes will help bring about many of the changes outlined in Part Two of this book, we can expect to see greater use of the approach within HRM systems of European organizations (see Illustration 9.17). But what is the current uptake of the approach across Europe?

The use of assessment centres (mainly by multinational organizations) is reportedly increasing in countries such as Denmark (Incomes Data Service, 1990a), where they are being used for a wider range of jobs. The uptake of assessment centres for selection purposes has also been most marked in Britain, and less so in France. Mabey (1989) found that in 1988, 37 per cent of British organizations used behavioural simulations such as group exercises, in tray exercises and role play exercises. From 1984–89 the proportion of British organizations using assessment centres grew from 7 to 25 per cent (Robertson and Makin, 1986; Shackleton and Newell, 1991). By 1989, 59 per cent of the top British organizations reported that they used the technique compared to only 19 per cent in France (Shackleton and Newell, 1991). In France the approach was only used in organizations employing over five hundred people. However, even where assessment centres were used it was still for less than half of all candidates. On-the-job work sample tests are used by 28 per cent of French organizations as part of their selection system (Bournois, 1993). In Spain, only a handful of organizations use assessment centres because of the high costs involved (Vicente, 1993). The use of graduate assessment centres at Shell is outlined in Illustration 9.18.

Illustration 9.17 **Purposes of assessment centres.**

Selection Selection of appropriate candidates for intake into a target job or career stream.	*Organization development* Creation of a language to identify key competencies and convey expectations about current and future operations in the organization.
Identification of potential Identification of long-range potential with a view to subsequent development and upward advancement of a cadre of high fliers.	
Developmental/diagnostic Facilitation of managers' personal development on the basis of detailed behavioural feedback.	*Cultural change* 'Auditing' of whole groups or sections of the organization in order to identify generic strengths and weaknesses and plan changes or remedies to widespread deficiencies.

Source: after Iles (1992).

Illustration 9.18 **Graduate assessment centres at Shell International Petroleum Company.**

Assessment Centres (ACs) require a considerable amount of detailed work and significant resources. Shell investigated the ability and personality profiles of 299 of its graduate applicants. This showed that the selectors were using limited sets of criteria. For example, some personality characteristics associated with creativity were found to be associated with poor performance in the recruitment interview but a positive contributor to the work of the organization. Shell wanted its selectors to make more comprehensive judgements and introduced ACs into the recruitment of graduates in order to identify senior management potential. A job analysis identified twelve dimensions all associated with competent handling of critical situations. These included analysis and judgement, divergent thinking, business aware-ness, persuasiveness, communication skills and sensitivity. ACs were run in each area of significant graduate recruitment, e.g. commerce, finance and engineering. They involved a range of assessment procedures designed to simulate executive work and to provide opportunities for observing and measuring relevant behaviour. These included case studies of problem situations requiring written answers and role plays, group exercises, presentations and computer-administered psycho-logical tests of creativity, work values and personality preferences. Each behavioural dimension was rated on a six-point scale. ACs were attended by twelve participants and six assessors. Assessors were all senior executives trained in assessment techniques and behavioural observation.

Source: Feltham (1989).

CHOOSING SELECTION METHODS

Why do employers persist in using poor methods of selection? An important part of the selection process is the choice of selection method to be used. Usually a combination of the various methods outlined in the previous sections is used, and we have noted the various advantages and disadvantages of each method. Above and beyond such information, the choice of method is usually dependent on a number of other pragmatic factors (see Illustration 9.19).

In making these decisions, a much more sophisticated style of thinking and analysis is needed than simply considering such pragmatic factors.

RELIABILITY AND VALIDITY OF SELECTION SYSTEMS

In the last section of this chapter we outline the main technical points and management debates about three essential considerations for European recruitment and selection systems:

1. The reliability and validity of the selection predictions that are made.
2. The cost-benefits of the various methods used.
3. The democratization of the recruitment and selection process.

The standards by which selection systems are evaluated can be related to their impact and benefit on the organization. This is called the 'psychometric' approach (see Illustration 9.20). It assumes that selection is a 'neutral' process, in which it is possible to codify the job tasks, and then objectively observe and assess the individual against these requirements. Candidates are viewed as objects to which a range of selection methods are applied in order to elicit individual differences in job performance and ensure that negative organizational outcomes such as staff turnover or high costs are

Illustration 9.19 **Pragmatic choices about selection methods.**

Selection criteria for the post to be filled Detailed match between the job requirements as revealed by the job analysis, and the characteristics assessed by each method.

Acceptability and appropriateness of method Match between the expectations of candidates and added value provided by the selection method. For example, the use of intelligence tests for senior positions is sometimes seen as offensive by the candidate.

Abilities of the staff involved in the selection process Particularly applicable to the choice of testing or assessment centres, or recruitment of specialist skills, which require specific competencies on behalf of the selector which may not be available.

Administrative ease The organization of a series of interviews as opposed to panel interview may reduce the impact of the recruitment task.

Time factors A balance between the immediacy of the recruitment need versus the length of the selection method.

Accuracy and validity Accuracy generally increases with the number of methods, but the utility of this may be outweighed by other options such as improved induction systems to overcome selection inaccuracies, deliberate targeting of over-qualified staff, and so forth.

Cost A balance between the greater accuracy and added information achieved by the method (such as assessment centres or testing), the cost of errors and the immediate and long term running costs of the selection system.

Source: Torrington and Hall (1991).

reduced. Objective assessment in these terms is therefore judged by its ability to reduce selection errors, help recruit more efficient staff, and improve productivity (McCulloch, 1993).

Although trade unions and works councils have shown considerable interest in the social and ethical aspects of selection systems in Europe, they have shown little interest in the need to investigate the validity of the process (Levy-Leboyer and Sperandio, 1987; Shimmin, 1989). The amount of research on the topic in universities has fallen in recent years and there is a relative lack of systematic research on the evaluation and assessment of adults in a work setting in Europe. During the 1960s and 1970s students of business or work psychology in Continental Europe were reluctant to be employed in, or on behalf of, industry. This situation was changing by the late 1980s. Consequently, formal data on the comparative use of European selection practices or their validity is difficult to obtain.

Subjectivity in selection, whilst caused in part by behavioural failures of the assessor, such as bias in the interview, is also caused by systems which are based on the applicant having the right connections, holding the right opinions and various forms of nepotism (Shimmin, 1989). The extent to which such forms of subjectivity are legislated against, socially deplored, tolerated or actually encouraged varies markedly across Europe and is deeply entwined in historical and cultural management practice.

Beyond the pragmatic choices about selection systems outlined in Illustration 9.19, there are a series of extremely important, but unfortunately rather technical, factors that have to be considered and decisions that have to be made. We have outlined some of the most pertinent factors that help determine the relative usefulness of the different selection methods in earlier sections. Another aspect to consider is the reliability and validity of the predictions made. Most selection decisions are made on the basis of predictions about how well the applicant, if selected, will perform. The usefulness of these predictions is determined by two main factors: their reliability and validity (see Illustration 9.20 for an explanation of these terms).

Illustration 9.20   **Important concepts and psychometric properties in the evaluation of selection systems.**

Correlation coefficient   This is used to determine whether the score from a selection technique can predict an aspect of performance. The result is summarized in a single number, or coefficient. If one measurement does not predict another, then the value of the correlation coefficient is zero (0.0). If one measurement more or less perfectly predicts another, then the value of the correlation between the two measures increases to a maximum of one (1.0). Degrees of prediction between these two extremes have coefficients between zero and one. A correlation of only 0.2 would be seen as weak. Better predictors tend to produce correlations of over 0.4. Coefficients over 0.7 are rarely achieved.

Predictive validity   This is the extent to which a specific selection technique can predict a range of performance criteria, such as supervisor rating, level of turnover.

Construct validity   An abstract concept. Tests for an empirical link between the constructs or qualities purportedly assessed by the selection method, and the performance criterion. If a psychological test of analytical ability is being used, do differing amounts of this ability help to explain why people perform better or not in the first place? Knowledge of the validity of these constructs usually helps judge the predictive validity.

Face validity   Even if measuring an appropriate construct with the right range of content, is the knowledge required to answer questions felt to be relevant to the workplace, so that respondents are motivated to give their best performance?

Concurrent validity   There may be a substantial time lag before it can be established if a selection method has predictive validity. Does the method help predict the performance of current job holders? A correlation between selection scores and immediate job performance is called concurrent validity.

Convergence/divergence of indicators   Does the selection method measure something different to other parts of the total system, or is it another measure of the same qualities? To improve cost effectiveness it is often better that the scores do not correlate with other measures.

Test/retest reliability   The extent to which the same group of candidates get the same scores in the selection method when it is given on two separate occasions.

Parallel reliability   The extent to which respondents get equivalent scores on similar (parallel) versions of the selection method

Internal consistency   The degree of correlation between single items on a test with performance on all the other items.

Source: Bethell-Fox (1989).

The predictor problem

In recent years the focus of attention has shifted from determining the relative ability of various selection methods to predict accurately, to issues of fairness, evaluation criteria and the utility of various approaches. Robertson and Smith (1989) point out that research on the validity and reliability of the various predictors has taken place over the last twenty years, but more recent mathematical techniques, such as meta-analysis, have allowed more systematic comparison of the various predictors. Several reviews have confirmed the overall picture (Hunter and Hunter, 1984; Muchinsky, 1986; Reilly and Chao, 1982; Schmitt, Gooding, Noe, and Kirsch, 1984) which seem to be consistent regardless of the approach used. In terms of 'predictive validity', work samples are the best selection method, closely followed by composite measures of ability and assessment centres. Interviews, references and graphology are poor predictors of performance (see Figure 9.4).

Interviews are relatively poor selection methods, as are personality tests, and the results obtained from studies of graphology are nothing short of abysmal. Although unstructured interviews have very poor validity coefficients of around 0.15, work in the 1980s provided more positive findings on the predictive power of situational interview questions and behavioural description interviews, with validity coefficients reaching 0.54 (Janz, 1982) and 0.61 (Arvey, Miller, Gould and Burch, 1987).

Despite their popularity, the predictive value of references is low, with average validity co-efficients of only 0.14 (Reilly and Chao, 1982) and 0.23 (Hunter and Hunter, 1984). Low reliability, a tendency towards leniency and poor response rates all serve to reduce the value of references. The validity of biodata is best summarized in three studies (Hunter and Hunter, 1984; Reilly and Chao, 1982; Schmitt, Gooding, Noe and Kirsch, 1984). Biodata are among the best predictors of turnover (0.21) and wages (0.53) and have a mean validity across a range of performance criteria of from 0.24 to 0.46.

The effectiveness of graphology is even less impressive than interviews. Successive reviews have concluded that it has low validity as a selection tool (Ben-Shakar, 1989; Klimoski and Rafaeli, 1983) with average correlations between 0.14 and 0.19 for both graphologists and non-graphologists. In compared tests the graphologists made worse predictions than the psychologists, and even the low validities were attributed to the

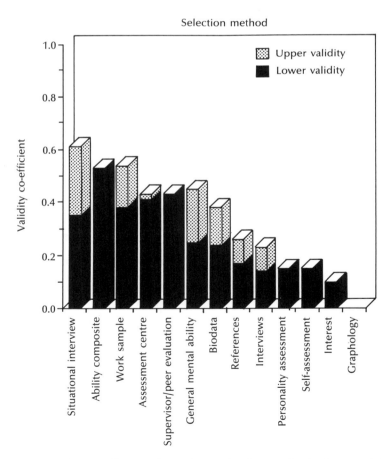

Figure 9.4 Mean validity co-efficients for various selection methods. *Source*: data for graph provided by Robertson and Smith (1989).

influence of other factors contained in the scripts, such as biographical data. When neutral scripts are used validities of graphology are near zero (Ben-Shakar, Bar-Hillel, Bilu, Ben-Abba and Flug, 1986; Reilly and Chao, 1982). Commenting on the use of graphology in his own country, Bournois quips:

... In Germany, a recruiter will look at a candidate's qualifications and work experience. In the United States, professional references and the opinions of previous employers are used to form a consensus about the candidate; the occult has never been particularly popular. That these pseudo-scientific techniques ... are so big in France has perhaps something to do with the fact that the French invented them in the first place.   Bournois (1993, p. 147).

Irrespective of the accuracy of individual techniques, it was apparent by the 1970s that there was a 'ceiling' for the validity of most techniques, with predictions of training performance averaging around 0.50, and job performance (measured by supervisor ratings) averaging around 0.35. The search for new predictors proved elusive (de Wolff, 1989). In addition to considering the reliability and validity of various selection methods, organizations may also be influenced by the number of applicants per vacancy, and the probable cost of making a mistake (Shackleton and Newell, 1991). The more applicants per vacancy (high selection ratio), the more likely simple selection techniques will be used. However, the probable cost of making a mistake is important. These costs might arise from higher initial training costs, human error in operating, loss of vital information through high staff turnover and so forth. The factors influencing methods of selection and likely outcome are summarized in a 2 × 2 matrix in Figure 9.5.

Cultural traditions in the psychometric approach

It should be noted that there is a distinct cultural tradition in the psychometric approach. Psychologists have been under far less pressure in Continental Europe to demonstrate the empirical, scientific and purely psychometric benefits of selection systems than is observed for example in the UK, where until recently the focus was mainly on issues of reliability, validity and utility (Cherns, 1982). The empirical tradition in Anglo-Saxon countries has shaped the nature of selection research, reflected in the relatively higher use of the more valid and reliable selection techniques

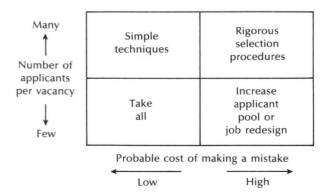

Figure 9.5 Factors influencing methods of selection. *Source*: reproduced from 'Selection procedures in practice' by V. Shackleton and S. Newell in *Assessment and Selection in Organizations* by P. Herriot (ed.), p. 222, copyright © 1989. Reprinted by permission of John Wiley and Sons, Inc.

in Britain in comparison to many European countries. French attitudes to selection, for example, tend towards a more intuitive, interpretative and clinical model, and as such encourage wider use of personality questionnaires, multiple one-to-one interviews and graphology. French selection research is more concerned with the process of selection than its outcome. The idea is more important than hard confirmed evidence. Hence Bournois's (1993) comments on the use of graphology.

However, if the international mobility of managers does increase, then the 'cultural fingerprint' of national selection systems will be more widely felt, with, for example, British managers feeling rather aggrieved at losing their job because of their handwriting, and French managers bemused by the impersonal nature of cognitive tests and biodata, and the time-consuming rigour of assessment centres (Shackleton and Newell, 1991).

The criterion problem

We have said that selection systems have essentially been steeped in the prediction of performance. But what do the system designers consider is a good measure of performance? The criterion is that aspect of job performance which is actually measured. Is the classic model relevant to the selection decisions in the 1990s? As well as the problem of reaching a ceiling on the validity of different predictors, another problem with validity studies is that the performance criterion often only samples a narrow spectrum of employee behaviour. Potentially, selection methods might be evaluated in terms of their ability to predict a variety of criteria (Landy and Rastegary, 1989):

- Ratings of performance on a number of dimensions (usually from supervisors) either in the field or retrospectively.
- Objective measures of productivity which lend themselves to unambiguous counting or measurement.
- Ancillary measures of performance, such as absenteeism, turnover and accidents.
- Hands-on measures of work samples chosen for their frequency or criticality to the organization.
- Knowledge tests or measures of task mastery.
- Multiple indicators.

The range of selection methods or predictors described in this chapter have only been systematically evaluated in terms of their ability to predict a handful of these performance criteria (Robertson and Smith, 1989), and indeed many managers may feel that they wish to achieve different outputs from their selection systems, as we highlighted at the very beginning of this chapter.

Returning to these arguments, Dachler (1989) points out that in a period of rapid change, unfolding events and circumstances and high flexibility, recruitment and selection systems based on an analytical, *a priori* system of defined job requirements that form part of a well designed organizational machine no longer fit reality. The debates about reliability and validity of techniques become less meaningful when predictive validity has been measured against an inappropriate end point. In other words, the technical and measurement issues of validity and reliability have taken precedence over worrying about the meaning of the performance criterion. There is an increasing discrepancy between the meaning of success as implied by the changing nature of European organizations, and those aspects that are actually assessed. Rather than focus on the effectiveness of people who have the best requirements and qualifications with respect to successful performance in a predefined job, European selection systems should focus on the future orientated potential. Selection systems need to assess:

> ... the extent to which the individual fits the ... [general purpose] ... an organization has in the context of its strategies, history and culture, in addition to the specific momentary requirements of a given job.   Dachler (1989, p. 58).

COST-BENEFIT OF RECRUITMENT AND SELECTION SYSTEMS

Another way of evaluating how useful selection systems are is to consider their impact on the organization in broad cost-benefit terms. We noted earlier that increasing levels of competition and rising cost pressures on European organizations have created a need to ensure cost effectiveness of the selection system. The utility of recruitment practices can be tested by placing a value, or costing out, each method in terms of the short- and long-term benefits and costs that result from it (Schuler and Huber, 1993). Illustration 9.21 shows a typical set of assessment criteria that might be used to evaluate each selection method.

For example, de Witte (1989) analysed a series of studies that compared the effectiveness of three recruitment channels (references of employees, spontaneous applications, and advertising) in terms of the subsequent turnover rates of employees. The least effective channel in terms of subsequent high levels of staff turnover was advertisements (turnover rates ranged from 24 to 84 per cent). Spontaneous applications fared a little better, with subsequent turnover rates of between 13 and 75 per cent, and references from other employees produced the best results, with turnover rates from 17 to 61 per cent. Informal recruitment channels can provide a much more realistic job preview.

Illustration 9.21 **Evaluation criteria to assess recruitment and selection systems.**

Stage of entry	Type of criteria
Pre-entry	Total number of applicants.
	Number of minority or female applicants.
	Cost per applicant.
	Time to locate job applicants.
	Time to process job applicants.
Offers and hires	Offers extended, by source.
	Total number of qualified applicants.
	Number of qualified female, minority or handicapped applicants.
	Costs of acceptance versus rejection of applicants.
Entry	Initial expectations of newcomers.
	Choice of the organization by qualified applicants.
	Cost and time of training new employees.
	Salary levels.
Post-entry	Attitudes toward job, pay, benefits, supervision and co-workers.
	Organizational commitment.
	Job performance.
	Tenure of hires.
	Absenteeism.
	Referrals.

Source: Schuler and Huber (1993).

Table 9.2 **Cost-benefits of selection techniques: cost savings per £1,000 of salary for different validities and selection ratios.**

Validity coefficient	Selection ratio		
	1 in 3	*1 in 6*	*1 in 10*
0.1	39	45	61
0.2	77	91	122
0.3	116	137	183
0.4	154	182	245
0.5	192	228	306
0.6	231	273	368
0.7	270	368	429

Source: Reproduced with permission of the author, © Mike Smith, 1986.

Where the validity coefficient and the selection ratio can be estimated, then it is possible to estimate the utility of different selection techniques in terms of cost savings per £1000 of salary (Smith, 1986). Such cost utilities show that the highest gains are accrued when both validity and high selection ratios apply, but of the two criteria, improvements in the validity of selection techniques yield the most striking cost benefits (see Table 9.2).

DEMOCRATIZATION OF EUROPEAN SELECTION SYSTEMS

In the previous chapter we highlighted the existence of 'opposites' in the development of HRM, competing forces and challenges that result in a new balance of activity. This is also the case in European recruitment and selection. We began this chapter by drawing attention to the shift of power towards employers as they grapple with restructuring of business and the need for a different basis of selection. We end it by describing a paradoxical development, which is the growing awareness of the importance of the individual in European selection systems (as both an applicant and as an employee), which is part of a wider philosophy in Europe that human resources (and HRM) should not be treated like material resources, totally at the disposal of the organization, but should rather have the right to object to HRM decisions that affect them (Shimmin, 1989). There is then a pan-European trend towards an emphasis on the perceptions, attitudes, reactions and rights of the applicant in the recruitment process. HRM specialists are increasingly having to work 'with' applicants rather than work 'on' them (Anderson and Shackleton, 1986). Countries such as the Netherlands, Sweden and Germany have led a move towards the democratization of the selection process, with the introduction of the more interactive procedures and constructive feedback to candidates, and co-decision rights vested in works councils to formulate the regulations and principles of personnel selection (Koopman-Iwema and Flechsenberger, 1984).

The use of psychometrics in Europe serves to illustrate some of the distinctly European debates in relation to recruitment and selection practices. It is also another example of an advanced HRM technique being absorbed into diverse European cultures and treated quite differently. It has increasingly become the subject of legislation and issue of best practice guidelines by professional bodies. In the US concerns over legislation forced many organizations to rethink their use of tests, with fears about being able to justify any 'adverse impact' which results in proportionately fewer members of one ethnic or gender group being able to meet the criterion or advance to the next stage of the selection process. As early as the 1960s it was argued in the US that many psychological tests measured the knowledge and capacities of advantaged groups (white, middle class citizens) and discriminated against minorities. This issue has never formed a central part of the European debate (Drenth, 1988; 1989) although the increase in foreign native speakers and immigrants in many European countries has made the problem more acute.

In Europe the issue was more one of dignity than discrimination (de Wolff, 1989). In the Netherlands, the final report of the Hessel Committee, a 1977 government-appointed commission into the use of psychological tests, was titled *An applicant is also a human being* and described a number of rights that the commission considered applicants should have (see Illustration 9.21). Although these rights were not enacted by the Dutch government, they were incorporated into the codes of practice of the Dutch Institute of Psychologists and Dutch Association of Personnel Officers (see Illustration 9.22). In part they were intended to redress the balance of power between the employer and the employee, informed by the European preference for participation.

In France, although there is no employment code to deal with ethical issues, the three recruitment agency unions Syntec, CSNCR and Aprocerd have set up a single confederation to establish an ethical code, and CNIL (Commission Nationale Informatique et Libertés) has confronted abusive selection practices that threaten individual liberties (Bournois, 1993). This awareness of the rights of the individual is also exemplified by the selection situation in Sweden. Ekvall (1980) points to the advance of industrial democracy in which decision making for personnel selection is made by a larger group of people, not just HRM specialists and senior management. Employee representatives are now present when psychologists report on the results of testing. Applicants have been given greater control over the results of psychological testing. They must be informed about the results before the employer is given the information, may back out of the selection process and have their test results and protocols destroyed, and can request that the psychologist use the results as a basis for vocational guidance. Similar conditions exist in the Netherlands.

In other countries such principles represent more of an ideal than actual practice, but these views are gaining ground and reflect the fact that the selection systems in European organizations should be seen as social processes, subject to national cultural traditions, but on a common path towards providing greater assistance to the individual in order to increase self-awareness, self-selection and more realistic job previews.

Illustration 9.22 **Dutch code of practice for selection procedures.**

- Right to a fair chance to be engaged.
- Right to information about the procedure, the job itself and the work organization.
- Right to information gathered about the applicant and reasons for rejection.
- Right to privacy, tempered only by the seeking of information pertinent to the job.
- Right to confidential treatment of personal data.
- Right to an efficient, instrumental selection system that is valid and reliable.
- Right to lodge a complaint about treatment and the eventual decision made.
- The subjection of test administrators to legal disciplinary procedures.

Source: Shimmin (1989).

CONCLUSIONS

In this chapter we have argued that European organizations are faced with the need to change the basis of their recruitment systems. The coming decades will be characterized by a continuous and dynamic process of matching individuals to the organization. However, at a time of increasing competitive pressure, the high costs of recruitment will demand a more targeted and effective approach. Selection errors are becoming more costly as organizations need to recoup their investments in people at an increasing speed. Moreover, the actual basis on which people have traditionally been recruited – the possession of technical and vocational knowledge in the context of tightly defined jobs and a lifelong career – is disappearing. Selection and assessment systems will need to deal fundamentally with the problems of change, moving towards much more tightly defined phases of 'entry' into the core of the organization, and promoting advancement through these phases in terms of more transferable expertise such as an assessment of trainability. However, there is a considerable historical inheritance that will have to be dealt with by organizations, notably, the powerful legislative environment which although of differing focus and intensity from one European country to another, represents a common philosophy of the need to regulate the labour market and balance employee interests with the needs of the organization. There are some common patterns of convergence in this recruitment legislation and regulation, notably in the area of recruitment sources and the abolition of monopolies held by state placement services. We are therefore witnessing a period of innovation in recruitment practice, and a convergence around best practice as organizations are co-ordinating their approach on an international (and European) scale. There is clearly much room for improvement as organizations are adopting similar approaches, with many of the most valid and predictive selection methods still only being used by a handful of the better organizations. There are also a number of cross-cultural issues to deal with. These range from technical points such as the creation of national language versions of psychological tests and more culturally-sensitive norms, through to deeper philosophical differences in the purpose of recruitment and selection systems. Again, we see a process of convergence, as continental European organizations take more account of the strong Anglo-Saxon focus on the need for empirically-validated selection tools and techniques whilst British organizations are accommodating the long-standing European trend to greater democratization of the recruitment and selection process. Legislation promoting more equality of opportunity and greater democratization of the selection process reinforces this need to consider the validity of selection procedures. Continued skills shortages in the face of high unemployment, high levels of cultural change, and the redesign of much managerial work in European organizations will shape developments in recruitment and selection practice for many years to come. There are a number of learning points that have emerged from this chapter.

LEARNING POINTS FROM CHAPTER NINE

1. The nature of skills, abilities and competencies needed by organizations is being changed by several processes including the transnationalization of business, increasing sophistication of information technology and the need for an international perspective. In order to cope with this, European organizations are co-ordinating local and fragmented recruitment and selection systems in order to absorb best practice and

develop a more international approach. Effective recruitment, selection and assessment practices provide a powerful basis for influencing human behaviour in line with the strategic direction of the organization.

2. The topic of selection and assessment has shifted from one based historically on matching past performance to a defined job which was held for life, to the need to estimate a person's probable adaptability and ability to learn new skills and tasks. In order to do this European organizations may select for short-term proficiency and accept higher levels of staff turnover, select for longer-term adaptability to change by accepting limited knowledge of future priorities and changes, or make continuous adaptations to the selection system. Selection and assessment in European organizations will be fundamentally concerned with dealing with problems of change. Decisions will no longer be clear cut.

3. Recruitment is the set of activities used to obtain a qualified pool of applicants. It serves several purposes, including the need to determine present and future staffing needs, increasing the pool of qualified applicants, reducing the number of clearly over- or under-qualified applicants, reducing the probability of subsequent staff turnover, meeting legal responsibilities and increasing organizational effectiveness in the long term.

4. The legislative context is extremely important for recruitment in Europe. Numerous sources of law and rulings, covering areas as diverse as use of employment exchanges, temporary work, fixed term contracts, unfair dismissal, maternity leave and use of psychological testing, affect the recruitment process. The most important implications are in terms of the supply of labour, equal opportunities, and terms of notice and termination.

5. Labour markets also vary markedly. A principal difference is the extent to which the labour market is internal or external. Internal labour markets are more common in many European countries than in Anglo-Saxon cultures. There are numerous internal alternatives to having to recruit externally, and relying on an internal labour market can improve morale, commitment and security. It provides for a longer period of assessment of capabilities, is cheaper than external recruitment, concentrates external recruitment on single entry points and affords more opportunity to control salary levels. However, it also carries dangers of complacency, workforces ill-fitted to technological change, dysfunctional internal competition for labour, and informal career ceilings. Germany, Sweden, Spain and Switzerland have strong internal labour markets. Britain, Belgium, Denmark and Greece have stronger external labour markets.

6. Other important attributes in labour markets are the marked differences in the levels of skills shortages across Europe and the existence of strong regional markets in many areas.

7. There are many motivations to recruit externally, such as the need to bring in new blood, often as part of an organizational culture change programme, or the need to provide people who have new insights into the organization. It can often be a cheap way of acquiring skilled labour, or may be used to resource short-term or temporary skill needs. The disadvantages include recruiting ill-fitted employees, a lengthy socialization process and morale problems, and high indirect costs once management time has been accounted for.

8. The main sources of recruitment in Europe include national employment offices, advertisements in the press, recruitment consultancies, direct targeting of schools, personal contacts, radio and direct marketing and graduate recruitment. Each carries

its own advantages and disadvantages and tends to be relied upon to different levels across Europe.

9. National employment offices have played a significant part in resourcing employment in Europe, having had a historical role of regulating the labour market in conjunction with constitutional rights, custom or practice. However, in many European countries, such as Italy, Germany, Denmark and France, these offices are being deregulated, providing more scope for organizations to pursue alternative sources of recruitment, such as recruitment consultancies, temping agencies and executive search. There is some variation in the selection methods used by these agencies.

10. Selection covers the process by which legally defensible information about job applicants is used to make hiring decisions. It is closely associated with the recruitment process, but involves the need for assessment and final placement and the creation of a match between individual attributes and the organizational requirements. Selection is intended to obtain appropriate information about jobs, individuals and organizations to improve the quality of decision making by creating predictions about future behaviour and contribution to organizational goals. It also ensures that there are cost-benefits to the subsequent financial investment made in employees and that the interests of both the organization and employee can be met.

11. The field has historically focused on identifying individual differences and so became the preserve of psychologists. However, traditional paradigms are being challenged as the nature of jobs has become more fluid and as the dominant focus on prediction ignored other issues in the selection process such as dignity and discrimination. Attitudes towards selection are changing.

12. A typical selection process involves a sequence of activities, from job analysis, through the location and targeting of appropriate candidates, information gathering and initial screening, selection decisions, and job placement. The final selection decision may be actuarial (statistical) or based on a more qualitative clinical judgement. Despite there being a wide range of possible 'predictors' available, most European organizations use a narrow range of traditional methods.

13. The main 'predictors' available include interviews, analytical tests, work sample tests, behavioural event investigation techniques, biographical data, references, graphology, self-assessment and peer assessment or multiple-method assessment centres. There have only been a few international comparisons of selection methods. Evidence is limited to a few academic studies, consultancy publications and local national surveys. These tend to demonstrate a number of common themes and a series of distinct national differences. Application forms, references and c.v.s and unstructured interviews form the core of most systems. National culture may play a role in influencing the number of selection interviews used and in determining the degree of importance attached to hard, empirical supporting data, i.e. the balance between actuarial or statistical decisions.

14. These predictors have different psychometric properties in their validity and reliability. In reality, there are a number of very pragmatic considerations in making selection decisions, such as the surface acceptability of the methods involved, the abilities of the staff involved in the process, administrative ease, time factors and cost. However, there is a slow shift towards using the more predictive and efficient techniques.

15. A more protracted problem is that of the performance criterion that selection systems may use as a basis of their predictions. Performance may be judged by current or retrospective ratings from supervisors or other stakeholders, objective measures of productivity, related measures such as absenteeism or staff turnover, frequent or

critically important work samples, or measures of task mastery. The classic selection model no longer seems relevant for today's decisions. In a period of rapid change, recruitment systems based on *a priori* definitions of job requirements no longer fit reality. Rather than focus on the effectiveness of people who have the best requirements and qualifications with respect to job-related successful performance, selection systems are in transition. They are assessing the extent to which the individual fits the general purpose of the organization in the context of its strategies, history and culture.

16. There is also a pan-European process towards the need for greater democratization of selection systems. Whilst employers have more power through their ability to redefine the nature of future selection systems in line with the process of business restructuring, paradoxically, there is a growing awareness of the importance of the individual in selection decisions. The perceptions, attitudes, reactions and rights of the applicant have become more dominant and HRM specialists are working with applicants, rather than working on them.

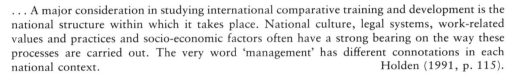

CHAPTER TEN

Internal Resourcing
Employee training and development

... A major consideration in studying international comparative training and development is the national structure within which it takes place. National culture, legal systems, work-related values and practices and socio-economic factors often have a strong bearing on the way these processes are carried out. The very word 'management' has different connotations in each national context.   Holden (1991, p. 115).

... There is a need to understand what is causing the convergence between different ways of organizing and managing... an overall conclusion that can be reached... is that European management development needs to be conceived and implemented in a way that is distinct from any of the national models that currently exist.   Lorbiecki (1993, p. 5).

INTRODUCTION

Employee training and development (ETD) forms an important part of an organization's overall human resource management (HRM) strategy. It implies transition – transition in skills, knowledge, attitudes or social behaviours (Cascio, 1982) and involves the analysis, design, implementation and evaluation of relevant activity to this transition, usually focused around two types of initiative:

- Attempts to improve current or future employee performance in the context of organizational goals by increasing the ability of individuals and groups to perform.
- Planned efforts to facilitate and organize learning experiences and the acquisition of job-related knowledge and skills.

Why do European organizations need to train and develop their employees? To a large extent their success in completing the process of integration depends on their ability to prepare and train their workforces for the new challenges they will meet. In general, there are several possible motivations to pursue such employee development initiatives. The most obvious motivation is to remove current or anticipated deficiencies in performance that result from increased global competition. The organization may have identified an immediate or future demand for skills which job applicants from the external labour market do not possess (Schuler, 1992b; Schuler and Huber, 1993). Changes in the technology associated with their products, process or markets may have created the need for employees to use new skills or knowledge in response to new operations, job designs or work flows (Bernardin and Russell, 1993). The organization structure may have changed or jobs may have been redesigned. The general increase of demands on management time may require more decisive and competent individuals. Finally, it may be desirable to respond to the desire for more self-development by improving the performance and achievement of work goals and enhancing the knowledge, skills, enthusiasm and learning ability of individuals at all levels of the organization (Harrison, 1992).

In Parts One and Two of the book we highlighted a number of pressures that are creating a change in the internal ETD systems of European organizations (see Figure 10.1). The development of a more transnational approach to organization has brought about the need to train and develop a more flexible cadre of international managers and has increased the importance of cross-cultural awareness and sensitivity skills. The increased level of foreign direct investment and impact of mergers and acquisitions has often entailed the need for long-term training plans and an increased training load as new strategic and business plans are communicated and new teams are built. A range of competitive pressures have led to developments. The need to promote employee and work practice flexibility has seen an increase in the amount of cross-functional training and a general enhancement of management skills. Quality and customer service pressures have often been associated with an increase in the level of management education as part of large scale change programmes and this has also frequently changed the focus of training provision in the organization. Social pressures have led

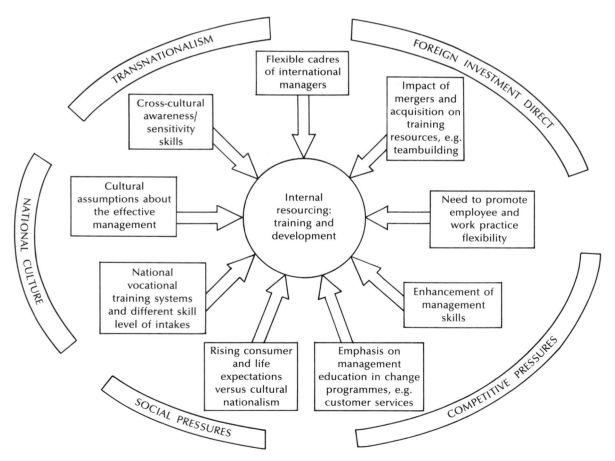

Figure 10.1 The factors influencing change in training and development.

to conflicting demands on national training systems, as changes in occupations caused by the changing nature of the economy and the shift from manufacturing to service industries have required flexible training policies to prevent lower productivity and increased turnover of employees. At the same time the existence of different cultural assumptions between countries about what makes a manager effective and differences in the relative skill level of recruits into the organization as a result of different national vocational education and training systems have heightened the impact and awareness of national culture on organizational ETD systems. Given the breadth of these issues, not surprisingly employee training and development (ETD) covers a wide range of topics (Naulleau and Harper, 1993), ranging from:

- Training managers and other vocational groups.
- Improving the qualification and competence of the workforce.
- Ensuring adequate employee mobility.
- Reducing high levels of staff turnover.
- Motivating managers.
- Career planning.
- Modifying a dominant culture.

It is best approached as part of a wider business strategy intended to align the organization's corporate mission and goals with the capabilities of its people, and vice-versa. In dealing with the topics identified above, most definitions of ETD draw upon four separate individual processes: education, training, development and learning. Illustration 10.1 presents dictionary definitions of these related concepts.

ETD, frequently also called human resource development (HRD), is then the primary process through which individual and organizational growth over time can achieve its full potential. It involves integrating the four elements of education, training, development and learning into the wider framework of an 'employee resourcing' policy and strategy. Whereas the topic of recruitment, discussed in the last chapter, may form part of an internal or (primarily) external resourcing strategy, employee development is a purely internal process. ETD is one topic within the overall

Illustration 10.1   **Definitions of four individual processes that take place within ETD.**

Education
Definition: bringing up individuals and groups so as to form habits, manners, intellectual and physical aptitudes.
Contribution: directly and continuously affects the formation of knowledge, abilities, national culture, aspirations and achievements.

Training
Definition: instruction and discipline in or for some particular art, profession, occupation or practice; the making proficient by such instruction and practice.
Contribution: shorter-term systematic process which helps to master defined tasks or areas of skill or knowledge to predetermined standards.

Development
Definition: to unfold more fully and bring out all that is potentially contained in the individual or group.
Contribution: facilitates actions towards maximum levels of performance and achievement of the individual and the organization.

Learning
Definition: relatively permanent changes in behaviour that occur as a result of practice.
Contribution: provides the mechanism for transferring training and development activities into actual practice.

Source: after Fisher, Schoenfeldt and Shaw (1990); Harrison (1992).

concept of 'employee resourcing', but given its complexity frequently forms a subject in its own right in professional HRM syllabuses and examinations.

ETD is of central importance to the evolution of Europe in the 1990s. Using evidence from the Price Waterhouse/Cranfield Project (PWCP) studies, Hilb (1992) summarizes the overall position of Western Europe as follows. In most countries and organizations, the selection, appraisal, reward and development of people are neither strategically orientated nor integrated with each other, and yet as we argued in Chapter One, this strategic orientation and integration is a precondition of effective HRM. Nevertheless, the evidence suggests that HRD or ETD is seen as the most important personnel function in all the main European countries.

We have drawn attention to the fact that ETD may be conducted for a variety of reasons. It is a very systematic activity that is best described by considering a number of sequential stages. This chapter is therefore divided into seven main sections:

1. The identification of appropriate ETD needs.
2. The matching of ETD programmes and policies to other (internal) areas of HRM.
3. The relationship between ETD activities and the external (institutional and national cultural) environment of the organization.
4. The main trends in ETD practice at the organizational level.
5. The impact of the trend towards more flexible employment relationships and management structures on the quality of ETD and the HRM issues that may arise from the process of internationalization of internal resourcing systems.
6. The nature of effective management and the underlying competencies.
7. The nature of competencies for the effective Euro-manager and the shape of future competencies for organizations.

THE IMPORTANCE OF ETD NEEDS ANALYSIS

In this first section of the chapter we consider how European organizations should identify appropriate ETD needs. The first step in establishing viable ETD activities is to decide whether training is really needed by assessing the underlying needs of the organization and its employees (Bernardin and Russell, 1993; Fisher, Schoenfeldt and Shaw, 1990; Schuler, 1992b; Schuler and Huber, 1993). Evidence from the US suggests that less than 33 per cent of organizations conduct formal training needs analyses (Saari, Johnson, McLaughlin and Zimmerle, 1988), yet, without such assessment there is no guarantee that the right training and development activities will be put in place, despite the topics' importance (Schuler and Huber, 1993). Within Europe, the figures appear to be higher. Eighty-five per cent of French organizations claim to systematically analyse their ETD needs (reflecting the needs for legislative reporting). The figures for the UK are 80 per cent, 79 per cent for Italy, 76 per cent for Sweden, 74 per cent for Switzerland, 72 per cent for Spain, 68 per cent for the Netherlands, 63 per cent for Norway, 56 per cent for Denmark and 55 per cent for Germany (Holden and Livian, 1992). However, the European data are based on a small sample of the largest organizations, and so is an overestimate of typical national practice.

Effective ETD needs analysis can have a powerful impact in financial terms. Bernhard and Ingolis (1988) estimated that US organizations wasted around $30 billion in 1988 because they had not addressed the fundamental issue of analysing their

ETD needs in the context of the short-term and long-term business plans. Similar stories are found in European organizations. A prominent French banking organization made a massive investment in an extensive training programme, but failed to analyse its ETD needs. The programme led to '... less than beneficial results' (Courpasson and Livian, 1991, *op. cit.* Holden, 1991). ETD needs assessment has to be linked to the overall business and HRM strategy. It therefore has to be conducted at three levels of analysis (see Illustration 10.2) in order to identify whether training is needed, and if so where, what and how? Usually, the ETD needs assessment process takes organizations through a systematic series of choices about the following:

- The most appropriate instructional objectives.
- The criteria that should be used to evaluate the outcomes of ETD.
- The best design for the learning environment based on principles of learning and the characteristics of the target population.
- The development of training materials and methods.
- The conduct of the actual training.
- The evaluation process for the ETD systems.

These are standard personnel management techniques which cannot be documented in this comparative book, but are detailed in a number of other sources (see, for example, Bernardin and Russell, 1993; Goldstein, 1986; McAfee and Champagne, 1988; Moore and Dutton, 1978; and Rossett, 1990). These sources stress that, in essence, the identification of ETD need is achieved through considering the issue at three different levels of analysis (see Illustration 10.2). This reduces the consideration of ETD needs to four questions which echo many of the issues considered in the previous chapter on

Illustration 10.2 **Three levels of ETD needs analysis.**

Organizational
- Examination of the short- and long-term objectives of the organization and trends that will affect the objectives.
- Analysis of overall human resource needs, efficiency indices (e.g. cost of labour, quantity of output, quality of output, waste, equipment use and repairs), organizational culture, corporate-level competencies, customer data.
- Translation of organization objectives into accurate estimates of demand for human resources and location of ETD resources into units of the organization.

Jobs, role or career stream
- Examination of the content of present or anticipated jobs, roles, or career streams through job analysis techniques.
- Collation and prediction of information on the operating problems, tasks performed, skills and competencies necessary, and minimum acceptable levels of performance.

- Tailoring of training programmes to job, role or career stream content.

Person
- Comparison of actual current job performance and minimum standards to identify employee performance discrepancies.
- Evaluation of employee proficiency on each required skill or competency with the desired level of proficiency to identify future development needs.
- Consideration of 'needs' in terms of measures of:
  - output (e.g. performance data, work sampling and job knowledge tests),
  - self-assessed training requirements,
  - attitudes as assessed by a variety of stakeholders (e.g. customers, subordinates),
  - competencies (e.g. underlying characteristics of an individual associated with effectiveness).

Source: Bernardin and Russell (1993); Schuler and Huber (1993).

recruitment and selection (Torrington and Hall, 1991):

1. What are the organization's goals?
2. What tasks must be completed to achieve these goals?
3. What behaviours are necessary for each job holder to complete his or her assigned tasks?
4. What deficiencies, if any, do job holders have in knowledge, skills or attitudes required to perform the necessary behaviours?

A variety of methods are used for analysing training needs. In addition to training audits, analysis of business plans is used by between 10 and 41 per cent of European organizations (Holden and Livian, 1992) and line management or employee requests are also common methods. The use of performance appraisal to identify ETD needs is discussed in Chapter Fourteen.

A CHANGE IN THE FOCUS OF ETD NEEDS

The solutions and answers to all four questions about ETD needs are changing. Why is this the case? The pressures for change identified in Figure 10.1 have naturally been reflected in a change in the focus of ETD and the related educational approaches taken in Europe. Lorbiecki (1993) provides the following analysis. In the 1970s there was relative economic prosperity. The focus of development was on challenging the status quo, freedom of individual thought and a concentration on personal experience. From 1979 we entered a period of what the sociologists call 'modernity'. A harshening economic climate saw management development revert to more traditional and scientific methods, a focus on ensuring economic survival, the use of experts who knew the secrets of success and wanted to help you transplant them into your organization. From the end of the 1980s onwards management development has been in a period of 'post-modernity'. In practice this meant that a further deterioration in the economic situation provoked questions about the traditional way of thinking. Management was no longer conceived as an activity that could be separated from its cultural context. As globalization increased the focus on international management joined forces with the economic paradigm. The concept of the 'Euro-manager' first came into consideration, and the accent shifted to the need to understand a plurality of meanings, identifying and praising differences between countries, rather than denying their importance. The 'one best way' paradigm gave way to a diversity of opinion, the need to tolerate ambiguity, accept uncertainty, the ability to cope with change and a quest for creativity. Business schools and management centres are also becoming more internationalized, moving from a national to an international context for teaching purposes, making language training a central part of the curriculum in many countries, offering work or study placements abroad, exchanging faculty and teachers, and offering joint programmes across Europe (Hale and Tijmstra, 1990). Whether these changes in course titles and curricula also develop an understanding of national styles of learning and management is under debate.

Reflecting this shift in the nature of management development, a report on 'Managers for the 21st Century' by the American Assembly of Collegiate Schools of Business (AACSB) and the European Foundation for Management Development (EFMD) described by Finney and Von Glinow (1988) identified five formidable challenges to management (see Illustration 10.3).

Illustration 10.3 **Five critical management problems for the twenty-first century.**

1. Moving from a period of relative abundance to scarcity of natural resources and the impact of scarcity and increased costs of materials and energy on management decision making.
2. Necessity for managers of international organizations to understand foreign cultures and national aspirations and adapt their decision making accordingly.
3. An increase in the number and effectiveness of claimants and stakeholders who will make demands on the business.
4. Continuous external change which will necessitate greater flexibility of organizational structures.
5. Interdependence within a global economy leading to an increase in the vulnerability of international (and domestic) business to political and economic instability.

Source: Finney and Von Glinlow (1988).

THE RELATIONSHIP BETWEEN ETD SYSTEMS AND OTHER AREAS OF HRM

A second area of attention in this chapter is the relationship of ETD systems to other areas of HRM within the organization. Not surprisingly, given the change in focus discussed in the previous section, the training department of organizations can have a powerful influence on the strategic impact of HRM. The central role of ETD in performance improvement can bring a series of important benefits to the organization (see Illustration 10.4).

It is important to appreciate the inter-relationships between ETD systems and other areas of HRM (Cherrington, 1987; Fisher, Schonfeldt and Shaw, 1990). The provision of ETD opportunities can reduce the need to recruit highly qualified applicants, whilst careful recruitment and selection may reduce the need for ETD (see Chapter Nine). ETD may help employees to perform better, reducing the need for sophisticated performance management systems (see Chapter Fourteen), but then performance appraisals can be a powerful source of information for assessing ETD needs. ETD should improve performance and result in higher levels of reward and benefit (see Chapter Thirteen), yet financial incentives can create higher levels of motivation and participation in ETD activities and training may also be seen as an attractive benefit

Illustration 10.4 **The role and contribution of ETD in relation to HRM.**

- Improving stagnant productivity.
- Rapid incorporation of new technologies and fulfilling skill needs in the light of technological change.
- Adaptation to new competitive conditions.
- Contribution to long-term strategic manpower planning.
- Informing decisions over human resource allocation.
- Development of skills for the present and the future.
- Information for management succession and career planning systems.
- A means of substituting for the need to resource externally.
- Developing managerial attitudes.
- Modifying management and leadership styles.
- Building creative and effective teams.
- Improving communications.
- Increasing levels of commitment and the perception of being a good employer.
- Reduce turnover and absenteeism, indirectly improving productivity.

in its own right. Finally, by creating a more trained, effective and motivated workforce, performance levels should rise and the probability of grievances and industrial relation issues decrease (see Chapter Fifteen), but unions in many areas of Europe participate in the design and presentation of ETD activities. Harrison (1992) draws attention to a number of other topics that strongly influence the effectiveness of ETD:

- *Leadership*, which may provide the vision and values that drive training and development initiatives within the organization.
- *Teamwork*, which can either provide continuing development opportunities that facilitate a return on the investment in people, or erect barriers that rapidly cause the value of people to depreciate.
- *Learning activities and organizational culture*, through which learning and work may be integrated as mutually-reinforcing activities, or positively discouraged.
- *Employer philosophy and national legislation* in areas such as equal opportunities, which may remove barriers to individual and organizational growth or put obstacles in their path.
- *Termination policies and procedures*, which may or may not facilitate continuous development after the exit point from the employment relationship is reached.

CONFLICTING PRESSURES: CONVERGENCE AND DIVERGENCE OF ETD PRACTICES

In the third section of this chapter we discuss the relationship between ETD systems in the national context within which European organizations have developed them. It is important to appreciate that whilst most organizations recognize that ETD has a central role in their internal HRM strategy, there are differing national interpretations of how to implement the systems. Whilst some aspects of ETD may be standardized, such as job and training needs analysis techniques, job descriptions and the creation of an organizational labour market, most areas are not so readily generalizable (Naulleau and Harper, 1993). Therefore, despite the fact that there are common pressures for change and powerful arguments for the central role of ETD to HRM systems, European countries have had separate paths of industrial development and there are marked national differences in education institutions and practices, work structuring and management styles. Although Europe is endeavouring to become a more powerful political and economic group, its countries are at different stages of transition both in terms of ability to deal with global competition and how their managers are developed (Lorbiecki, 1993). This has had a marked impact on the HRM policies and practices of European organizations, but particularly in relation to internal resource development practices.

Moreover, there has been a psychological reaction to the pace of transition that has created competing and paradoxical forces reinforcing both homogeneity of culture and lifestyle as well as national awareness and sentiment. In times of transition and high change, underlying values are threatened and we seek assurance in the patterns of continuity that mark out what are perceived to be our enduring differences and identities. As the pace of business change has increased, so has the output of academic literature pointing to the uniqueness of management across different countries in Europe. Naisbitt and Aburdene (1990) referred to this paradox of 'cultural nationalism' and predicted that '. . . in 1992 an economically integrated Europe will be accompanied by an outbreak of cultural assertiveness for the rest of the 1990s'. Why? Because on the one hand we are witnessing the development of an international youth culture based around a consumer-driven global lifestyle:

... [young managers are] drinking cappucino and Perrier, furnishing the apartment with IKEA, eating sushi, dressing in the United Colours of Benetton, listening to US/British rock while driving the Hyundai over to McDonald's.   Naisbitt and Aburdene (1990, p. 102).

Yet, on the other hand, the more homogeneous lifestyles are becoming:

... the more steadfastly we shall cling to deeper values – religion, language, art and literature. As our worlds grow more similar, we will increasingly treasure the traditions that spring from within.   Naisbitt and Aburdene (1990, p. 104).

Reflecting on this psychological reaction to the onslaught of international products and the globalization of world markets and the debate by Hofstede (1993) on the cultural relativity of management theories (see Chapter Two), several writers have analysed how internal resourcing practices (and in particular management development practices and national vocational training systems) reflect our deeper cultural values and assumptions. Immediately following the creation of the SEM, a stream of articles from management developers from France, Greece, Hungary, Italy, Spain, Sweden, the US and the UK demonstrated the rich variety of perspectives and a gradual unfolding of a European view on management development (Lorbiecki, 1993; Fox, 1992b). Most have taken a historical perspective, describing the emergence of distinctive ways of managing over time. The challenge to European managers will be to create a system of management development that is simultaneously inward and outward looking – inward in terms of providing national arrangements which consider work organization in its local setting, and outward in terms of providing international arrangements which focus on foreign markets and developments in the business environment (Lorbiecki, 1993).

SHOULD ORGANIZATIONS MAKE MANAGERS FOR EUROPE OR MAKE MANAGERS IN EUROPE?

We therefore need to consider the problems initially raised in Chapter Six about whether we are seeing convergence or divergence in the notion of European management in more depth. Should European organizations build teams that play to national strengths, or should they develop the 'Euro-manager'? The process of internationalization is proceeding apace, but because a large part of this process is accounted for within the European continent, the notion of developing European managers has become a legitimate sub-question (Storey, 1992b). As European organizations began to prepare for the SEM and generally pursued strategies of mergers, acquisitions, joint ventures and minority stakeholdings in order to gain a critical mass of revenue, financial leverage and market share, they also began to consider the human dimension. National systems of ETD were challenged in the late 1980s and the concept of the 'Euro-manager' (see Illustration 10.5) came into vogue (Bournois and Chauchat, 1990; Storey, 1992b).

A major lesson from the previous chapter is that many European recruitment and selection systems currently operate on a national basis. However, the 'making of European managers' invokes a much wider set of issues than initial recruitment and selection. It does not involve, for example, just training and developing British, Swedish or German managers to operate in Europe, but also recruiting German, French, Spanish and other nationalities into the management stock of the organization or acquiring overseas national teams (Storey, 1992b). There are two fundamentally

Illustration 10.5 **What is a Euro-manager?**

1. Any manager from a member state of the European Union (or soon to be associated countries).
2. A manager working in his home country for an organization based in another European state.
3. A manager working outside the frontiers of his home country for an organization based in his own country.

4. A manager who has undertaken a career spanning several European countries, working for a large organization that operates far beyond the frontiers of the country where it was originally registered.

Source: Bournois and Chauchat (1990).

different philosophies to consider:

- Making managers *for* Europe, i.e. resourcing the organization with a new breed of managers who are able to operate across national boundaries and possess a distinctive set of competencies.
- Making managers *in* Europe, i.e. highlighting the distinctive approaches to management development found in the different countries and resourcing the organization with multinational teams designed to operate to the strengths of various national systems.

These are two profoundly different perspectives and philosophies. Do we make European managers or make managers more European? We consider the first option – making European managers – later in this chapter. Before we can do this it is essential to highlight the ways in which managers are made in Europe and the distinctive approaches to management development. This option is the one which, after the initial euphoria of European integration, has started to gain ground again. The argument is that European multinationals should take advantage of the various national systems and strengths creating pan-European teams. The solution is to create stronger systems of Euro-management, not elusive Euro-managers, and this necessitates the development of coherent resources in multinational management based on a matrix of complementary cultural, linguistic and professional skills. In relation to the ETD needs of the organization, the key questions that have to be answered are shown in Illustration 10.6.

There is, as yet, no hard, reliable evidence to answer any of these questions. We have to rely on managerial anecdotes, emerging European multinational practice and sociological analysis of the various management development systems and organizational impacts on the qualities of managers.

Illustration 10.6 **Key cross-cultural questions about the creation of optimum European management.**

- Do the affinities and attributes that managers perceive to be linked to national cultures have any substance in actual skills and competencies in management tasks?
- Do cultural and educational traditions predispose managers from different countries to excellence in different fields of management?

- Do educational curricula and underlying value systems encourage the development of mind-sets that are more naturally attuned to different management disciplines?

ETD IN ITS NATIONAL CULTURAL CONTEXT

Can organizations sensibly combine and matrix different combinations of European managers to optimum advantage? The challenge of making managers more European is formidable, because in the European context even the word 'management' has differing connotations. Dictionary definitions do not convey the historical and socio-economic background that give linguistic meaning (Brewster and Tyson, 1991; Evans, Lank and Farquhar, 1989; Gospel, 1991; Lane, 1989; Lawrence, 1991). For example, the word *'cadre'* in France holds more meaning than the word 'manager' suggests (Boltanski, 1982), whilst to Swedish managers the word 'competence' is conceived in a wider strategic context than seen in the British view of the word (Holden, 1991). These differences have implications for the topics covered in the next two chapters, and in particular:

- The various notions of what it means to be a manager.
- The management development traditions.
- Selection criteria for entry into the internal management labour market.
- The psychological constructs used to think about career paths (see Chapter Eleven).
- The nature of performance management (see Chapter Fourteen).

A number of writers point to the salutory lessons that emerge and therefore criticize what they see as facile trends towards 'internationalism' (Barsoux, 1992; Bournois, 1992; Bournois and Roussillon, 1992; D'Irbane, 1989; Lane, 1989; Lawrence, 1993b). The arguments are powerful and the concerns they highlight will inevitably slow the development of common practice in training, development and career management. It is critical that these cultural traditions be understood before interpreting the various comparative empirical evidence on training and development. We therefore develop this chapter by discussing these different cultural notions and systems and draw attention to the fact that this topic has implications for most of the other chapters on HRM in Part Three of this book. Some of the questions that managers are grappling with as a result of these different cultural traditions are shown in Illustration 10.7.

In order to answer some of these questions, we need to consider two features of the external context for ETD systems:

1. Different notions and models of management development.
2. National vocational education and training practices.

Illustration 10.7 **Key cultural questions about the standardization of ETD systems.**

- How far should the organization go in its attempt to standardize training and management development programmes?
- At what level can the need to establish standardized programmes in worldwide subsidiaries in order to ensure that the right issues are addressed in each local subsidiary be balanced with the need to ensure adaptation to local custom and practice?

- How can the financial and cost attractions of standardized training and development packages be balanced against the risk of unexpected and costly outcomes associated with making cultural assumptions and imposing stereotypes?
- How important is it to take into account the cultural and social assumptions of managers when they work together?

Potential development:
Functional ladders
- functional careers, relationships and communication
- expertise based competition
- multifunctional mobility limited to few elitist recruits, or non-existent
- little multifunctional contact below level of division heads and *vorstand* (executive committee)

Potential identification: Apprenticeship
- annual recruitment from universities and technical schools
- 2 year 'apprenticeship' trial
  – job rotation through most functions
  – intensive training
  – identification of person's functional potential and talents
- some elitist recruitment, mostly of PhDs

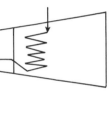

Functional approach to management development: the 'Germanic' model

Potential development:
Management potential development
- careful monitoring of high potentials by management review committees
- review to match up performance and potential with short and long term job and development requirements
- importance of management development staff

Potential identification: Unmanaged function trial
- little elite recruitment
- decentralized recruitment for technical or functional jobs
- 5–7 years' trial
- problem of internal 'potential identification' via assessments, assessment centres, indicators
- possible complementary recruitment of high potentials

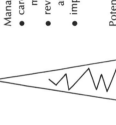

Managed development approach to management development: the 'Anglo-Dutch' model

Potential development:
Time-scheduled tournament
- unequal opportunity, good jobs to the best
- 4–5 years in a job, 7–8 year up-or-out
- comparison with cohort peers
- multifunctional mobility, technical–functional track for minority

Potential identification:
Managed elite trial
- elite pool or cohort recruitment
- recruitment for long-term careers
- job rotation, intensive training
- regular performance monitoring
- equal opportunity

Elite cohort approach to management development: the 'Japanese' model

Potential development:
Political tournament
- high flyers
- competition and collaboration with peers
- typically multifunctional
- political process (visible achievements, get sponsors, coalitions, read signals)
- if stuck, move out and on
- the 'gamesman'

Potential identification: Elite entry, no trial
- at entry
- elite pool recruitment (non-cohort)
- predictive qualities
- from schools specialized in selecting and preparing future top managers
  – *Grandes ecoles*
  – MBAs
  – Scientific PhDs

Elite political approach to management development: the 'Latin' model

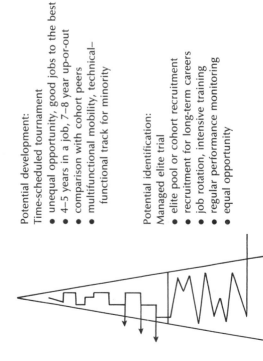

Figure 10.2 Four international models of management development. Source: Evans, Lank and Farquhar (1989). Reproduced from *Human Resource Management in International Firms* by P. Evans, Y. Doz and A. Laurent (eds). Reprinted with kind permission of the publishers, The Macmillan Press Ltd, © 1989.

NATIONAL MODELS OF MANAGEMENT DEVELOPMENT

The cultural assumptions about the nature of effective management outlined in Chapter Three and the introduction to this chapter make it quite clear that there is no one best way of tackling management development. Managers' roles and practices are deeply embedded in their social and cultural environment. Evans, Lank and Farquhar (1989) mapped out the most marked competing traditions and labelled them in terms of their national stereotypes into four categories:

1. The Japanese model.
2. The Latin European approach.
3. The Germanic tradition.
4. The Anglo-Dutch model.

These models are only stereotypes, reflecting the main patterns of homogeneous practice in the countries. Evans, Lank and Farquhar (1989) emphasize a number of caveats, which bear upon the discussion of cultural stereotypes of management in this chapter:

■ Within the US there is considerable variety, with different organizations adopting different elements of each of the four models.
■ Within certain European countries there are marked differences (for example between the large established organizations and the *Mittelstand* in Germany, or between the establishment and self-made entrepreneurs in France).

With such caveats in mind, the four cultural models of management development are summarized in Figure 10.2. We do not detail the Japanese model in this chapter beyond the information in Figure 10.2, given the focus of this book on Europe. The approach taken in any one set of related countries, such as the Anglo-Saxon approach, not only reflects its own particular set of underlying values, but also the different configurations of educational, political and economic institutions that impinge upon management and the different understandings about what 'management is all about' (and therefore the different qualities that managers should bring to it). We explore these issues in the next four sections and analyse:

■ The cultural and historical determinants of the notion of management and the response of élites to the introduction of management practices and ethos.
■ The impact of organization structure on the role of managers.
■ The implication of these notions for the selection of managers.
■ The national management training and development schemes.

CULTURAL AND HISTORICAL DETERMINANTS OF THE NOTION OF MANAGEMENT

Some observers use the existence of national assumptions about the nature of management and different patterns of development to argue that it disproves the idea of international convergence. Others acknowledge the powerful mediating influence of these national models, but argue that historical differences do not make convergence impossible. Regardless of such black-and-white debate, there is clearly a differential underpinning of HRM and view of the nature of managerial priorities across both Anglo-Saxon countries and Continental Europe. Many of the major determinants of management roles, such as the process of socialization, education and vocational training systems, social and organizational structure, are associated with distinctive national solutions and ways of coping with the challenges presented by the business environment (Naulleau and Harper, 1993). Whilst these distinctions and national solutions should not be viewed in 'black or white' terms and only reflect matters of relative importance and national emphasis, some historical and cultural reference is required in order to draw out the lessons for ETD.

The Anglo-Saxon concept of management

The idea of 'management' was first identified and labelled in the USA. Lawrence (1993) characterizes these origins of the Anglo-Saxon model of management as follows. The early period of expansion into an unclaimed continent (from 1783–1890) was characterized by an over-supply of space and resources coupled with too few people and too little time. In such circumstances the need for drive, entrepreneurialism, versatility, adaptability, opportunistic exploitation of circumstance and resource became paramount. They also became the focus of a subject (management) that was felt to be generalizable to other activities and teachable. The focus on the 'teachability' of management was a reflection of other American values such as proactivity, a drive to efficiency and equality of opportunity. The world's first business school was established in 1881 in Wharton, Pennsylvania. Without the pre-structuring of thought prevalent in Europe (which had more class-consciousness, socialist history and ingrained superior–subordinate, or management–worker, relations) the Americans approached the social side of the equation with an open mind. Rejecting European élitism, people were seen as having primary importance as individuals, either in groups or in organizations. Therefore having invented management, the Americans went on to espouse all its specialisms, inventing mass production, marketing and corporate strategy before the end of the Second World War, and creating most of the theories of motivation, leadership, group dynamics, supervisory effectiveness, informal organization, work group behaviour and organization theory and analysis in the period after the war.

But what of the UK – the 'intermediate state' as Lawrence (1993) calls it? There has been a parallel development in the notion of management, and yet in the context of management training and development the only thing that Britain shares with the USA is not being Continental European. In part, in recognizing its weaknesses in industry and management the British sought more effective role models. Until the 1970s the USA as the dominant trans-Atlantic economy was the centre of British admiration. The historical fascination with 'great men' who had turned the country round in times of trouble produced a natural affinity with the US focus on leadership and individuals. However, a number of writers point to a series of negatives that induced British adoption of US business models (Lawrence, 1993; Naulleau and Harper, 1993) by a series of 'gifted amateurs':

1. The British gentry class were challenged by the scientific management movement which espoused an ethos of organizational order based on meritocracy, performance and expertise, not social class (Merkle, 1980).
2. As an anti-industrial culture and society which portrays industry as soulless, depersonalizing, calculating and overly materialistic (Wiener, 1981), Britain was attracted to HRM on the grounds that it had the mission of re-personalizing a dreary and mechanistic world and forced managers to build their interpersonal skills, communication and leadership.

3. The low status of engineering and under-valuation of *Technik* portrayed engineers as interpersonally inadequate and in need of playing up the human side of the organization.
4. Class consciousness, unprofessional industrial relations and poor communication across authority lines pointed to the need to coach and train people, managers and supervisors in areas of leadership and communication.

The Germanic concept of management

Management development traditions in Germany are virtually a mirror image of the Anglo-Saxon norms. As we discussed in Chapter Two, the law counts for more than the diffuse expectations, custom and practice that dominate Anglo-Saxon attitudes to management development. The reactive role of personnel managers in Germany has historically militated against the raising of the management development function to a more organizationally-specific and strategic level. In addition to the legal context associated with recent statehood, in cultural terms there is a much lower tolerance for ambiguity in Germany (Hofstede, 1980). Because wage negotiations are conducted at a level above the individual organization (see Chapter Thirteen) wage agreements have created numerous pay scales into which managers must be fitted, in turn necessitating complicated systems of job-grading which are seen to have validity above and beyond the characteristics of the particular job incumbent (Lawrence, 1993).

Cultural traditions in Germany placed great value on the entrepreneur and not the manager. The word 'manager' has only recently come into widespread use. Lawrence (1993) notes that the Germans still cannot quite bring themselves to say 'managerial' which should be *managerhaft* in German. They say *unternehmerisch* (entrepreneurial) which has very positive connotations and reflects the long survival of owner-managers in many medium-sized and large organizations. This relatively weak concept of management, together with a relatively recent emergence of general management education, has limited the attention given to management development in Germany.

The French concept of management

The recent phenomenon of industrialization in France (only completed in the 1950s) and subsequent thirty year period of growing prosperity (*les trentes glorieuses*) meant that industry was 'civilized' from within the prior development of the educational system. Industry did not need to combat the negative image of early industrialization prevalent in Britain and was able to present itself as an attractive career for intelligent and educated people (Lawrence, 1993). Moreover, élites were consistently valued as a source of management wealth and industrial activities were historically pursued for reasons of social prestige as opposed to profit-only motives (Naulleau and Harper, 1993). Managers were, however, seen to have special needs within the education system and a strong distinction developed between the skills of both the manager in the recent private, profit-making sector and the long-standing public-sector administrator and other areas of society. The heroes of French history have been authoritarian centralizers – Richelieu, Louis XIV, Robespierre, Napolean and de Gaulle – with power vested in a state bureaucracy (Crozier, 1971; Lawrence, 1993). Management, coming later, was not seen as needing to be differentiated from civil administration and state service was regarded as a plausible model for industrial organization. The preference for a more rational social order, as opposed to one based on ascribed status, created a strong expectation amongst the French industrial élite that management could be the science of organizational life. Management offered an avenue for the technical middle class to promote its position in organizational life. In 1916, Fayol's *Traité d'Administration Générale et Industrielle* focused on the systematic analysis of the functions and roles of command. From such roots the view in France was that organizations should be staffed by a bright 'cadre' of experts and managed by the application of rationality (Naulleau and Harper, 1993). The education system apparently already provided for this.

WHAT DOES IT TAKE TO BECOME A MANAGER? THE IMPLICATIONS FOR ENTRY-POINT SELECTION DECISIONS

In Chapter Eight we also drew attention to the fact that most European organizations are essentially structured in the same way, making distinctions between production and management, and basic functions (Lane, 1989), yet in our discussion of the different selection techniques that a European manager might be subjected to as he or she moved from one country to another (see Chapter Nine) we noted that a British or Dutch manager might be somewhat aggrieved by being rejected for a job on the basis on an analysis of their handwriting, whilst a French manager would be bemused by the wasted sophistication of a behaviourally-based assessment centre. One of the key responsibilities of senior European managers is the delicate task of identifying 'high potential' in other managers and then managing the careers of these managers. The decisions that are made have a significant impact on the performance of the organization by influencing the renewal of management teams and the replacement of those in key positions (Bournois and Roussillon, 1992). However, it is impossible to consider the topic of 'management potential' by divorcing it from national culture. Why is this? There are two differentiating factors between a manager and a non-manager, both strongly embedded in the national patterns of business development, institutions and culture outlined in the previous section (Bournois and Chauchat, 1990):

1. The nature of the work itself and the responsibilities which are linked to it.
2. The initial training of the individual.

The situation is, then, more complex than we hinted in the previous chapter. As this chapter has shown, there are very different cultural assumptions about what makes a manager, and these are naturally reflected in selection systems used at both entry-points to the management ranks, and key development points. In the following sections we analyse the British, German and French systems as the prime examples of Anglo-Saxon, Germanic and Latin models.

The Anglo-Saxon notion that management is something separate, definable and objective means that management ability is seen to be a general and transferable skill, with a strong emphasis placed on interpersonal skills (Barsoux and Lawrence, 1991; Barsoux, 1992). The British system emphasizes empirical thinking (the impact of this on approaches to recruitment and selection was discussed in the last chapter). It also places a premium on personal experience rather than the codified judgements of previous generations. Self-regulation in all things, rather than statutory control, are the preferred mechanisms of control, as is a liberal education with less emphasis on vocational skills (Hill, 1993). The basis for selection into the management labour market is therefore driven by assumptions about the basic character of the individual in terms of personality and behaviour. These personality and behavioural assumptions are seen to underly the most important skills, which are typically felt to be man-management, social, political and leadership skills. Derr (1987) was one of the first to point out the basic differences that exist in European concepts of the 'high potential' executive. In a study conducted at INSEAD of the kind of employees most valued by multinational organizations, he found that British managers attached most importance to recruiting and developing people with a classical education and a broad general approach to management. During the 1980s, management as a career became more professionalized and therefore attracted much more credibility.

In Germany the considerable status of the *Unternehmer* has meant that membership of the management class has always carried a strong sense of collective identity. German executives have difficulty with the idea of management as something general, something that can be taken in the round, analysed and generalized to the organization (Lawrence, 1993). Reflecting the high levels of uncertainty avoidance, a manager's power of analysis is emphasized. This reinforces a preference for compartmentalizing problems around building block principles (*Baukastenprinzip*). German managers therefore do not 'manage' in the round but are instead seen to manage 'something'. Consequently they are selected primarily for their professional and expert knowledge which is required for the variety of traditional functions and departments. Inter-organization mobility is not viewed as bad, but it is expected to take place only within the same industry or sector, or between contiguous technical functions (such as design, production, maintenance, engineering and quality control). If you forfeit your functional expertise or knowledge in a career move, you forfeit ten years. This was supported by Derr's (1987) study which found that German and Swiss managers relied more on formal authority and attached a higher value and degree of respect to technical competence and functional expertise than did managers from other European countries.

Management in France is regarded '... more as a state of being than as a result of fashioned development processes within the company. It connotes an identity, more than an activity or set of capabilities' (Lawrence, 1993). Managers are collectively known by the term '*cadres*' – legally recognized as '... a *grande-école* or university graduate with five years study after the *Baccalauréat* or A levels holding a position from which he can exercise authority over subordinates which is delegated by his employer' (Bournois and Chauchat, 1990). A similar legal definition of middle manager exists in Italy, where the 1985 Clause 190 established a new professional category of *quadri* – salaried employees who are responsible for certain functions in the organization which are of major importance for its growth and the realization of objectives. The French concept of the *cadre* is really untranslatable: '... it is full of magic and promise for those who do not belong to this category' (Bournois and Roussillon, 1992). The term was adopted in the early 1930s when troubled relations between organized labour and the *patronat* class of business owners created the demand for a group of disinterested, impartial technocrats who were distinct from the owners but dedicated to the efficiency of the organization. The French therefore see management as an intellectually (rather than interpersonally) demanding task (Barsoux and Lawrence, 1990; Lawrence, 1993). Job advertisements reflect this by asking for qualities of *réception*, *la rigueur* and *l'esprit de synthèse* (i.e. powers of analysis, synthesis, evaluation, articulation and mental agility). According to Barsoux (1992) this emphasis on the intellectual side tends to 'crowd out' and diminish the attention given to *émission* (i.e. charisma, pugnacity, capacity to communicate and motivate). Managers are selected more on the basis of their intelligence, but the high status attached to qualifications such as the *grande école* diploma and the gaining of *cadre* status is difficult to attain.

... [In France] the emphasis is on formal learning, the development of educated cleverness, numeracy, literacy and a stylish competence with the French language, together with a high level of formal reasoning ability and 'culture générale'. All this fits very nicely in a milieu that conceives of management as being about ordering and deciding on the basis of analysis and synthesis, rather than about interpersonal manoeuvring, motivating and implementing.

Lawrence (1993, p. 19).

Does the empirical evidence support this picture of French management? In a study of the criteria used by seventy large French organizations to identify 'high potential' managers, i.e. managers who have the ability to rise through the hierarchy, Bournois and Roussillon (1992) found that performance in the present post is the most important criteria (see Table 10.1). Only 18.6 per cent of managers mentioned degrees or diplomas. However, entry into entry-level posts is determined by educational qualifications and so it would be expected that they play less of a role once this assessment has been made. The importance of being part of the 'old boys network' is evidenced by the fact that being 'discovered' by a top manager and the intuition of the HRM manager are signicifant criteria. A more important criterion is refusal of geographic mobility which essentially removes the manager from the list of high-potential executives.

The study of managers' perceptions of valued employees conducted by Derr (1987) found a more balanced approach in Sweden between the need on the one hand to differentiate between high-potential candidates and future leaders who need special developmental experiences, and an adherence, on the other hand, to strong cultural norms of equality, social democracy and collaboration where no individual is singled out for special treatment. Nordic and Dutch traditions emphasize a participative and consensual approach to life and the role of managers as team members and links within the organizational hierarchy (Hill, 1993). What then is the recipe for European management (see Illustration 10.8) suggested by this analysis?

Illustration 10.8 **Moulding diverse skills into a multinational team: a recipe for European management?**

What conclusions would a European HRM manager draw from the national concepts of management and the different selection criteria that are implied? How should the team be composed? Rather like selecting the best European football team, the HRM manager of one European multinational suggested that the organization should utilize the following blend of resources. The British should act as team leaders, HRM specialists, marketeers and operational managers, reflecting their generalist traditions. The French make the best company planners, naturally at home with the need for strategic thinking. The Germans represent the best technicians and engineers, given their depth in analytical and technical skills. The Scandinavians and Dutch make the best team players and middle managers. The Italians provide the best designers and public relations people. But who should be the captain? Who has the best CEOs? There's the rub ! In reality, the skills are at such a honed pitch that only individuals (with an international mindset) should be distinguished between. It also depends on which form of capitalism and measures of corporate performance win out (see Chapter Five). But not wanting to duck the issue, the European HRM manager picked Germany as the source of the best general managers, despite the fact that it has not had a professional general management culture until very recently. Dissenters to the team please vote!

Source: after Hill (1993).

Table 10.1 **Essential criteria for qualifying as a high-flier in French organizations.**

Criteria for qualifying as a high-flier	% of respondents
Performance in the present post	81.4
Personality traits	69.5
Readiness to move	66.0
Executive's own motivation and aspiration	48.0
Management training received during career	32.2
'Discovered' by a top manager	30.5
Intuition of the HRM or career manager	20.3
Degrees or diplomas	18.6
Time spent in the company's head office	11.9

Source: reprinted from *Human Resource Management Journal*, **3(1)**, 37–56, E. Bournois and S. Roussillon, 'The concept of high-flier executives in France: the weight of national culture', copyright © 1992, with kind permission of John Wiley and Sons, Inc.

THE IMPACT OF ORGANIZATIONAL STRUCTURE ON THE ROLE OF MANAGERS

Of course, it is not as simple as this. Given the discussion in Chapter Eight about the relationship between the metaphors and mental models of managers and the choices they make about organizational design, it is difficult to determine whether different national concepts of what management is determine the structure of organizations or the existence of different structures reinforces differences in the understanding of the management task.

There are some clear links between the topics of organization structure and the notion of management. We need to know the nature of this relationship, because as we outlined in Chapter Eight, the overall structure of European organizations is undergoing major transformation. Will national notions of management change accordingly? The Anglo-Saxon tradition displays a fascination with the organization itself. As a man-made creation it can be improved, endlessly tinkered with and ultimately perfected in order to achieve improvements in efficiency, effectiveness and enhanced interpersonal co-operation (Lawrence, 1993). In contrast, the Germans see the organization as only a secondary consequence of the primary task – which may be engaging in a specific activity such as manufacturing. The consequence of such differences in attitude is that aspects of the organization structure can be seen strongly to influence the notion and role of the manager.

For example, whilst the tall vertical structures of French organizations naturally reinforce the development of an internal labour market (Lane, 1989), in the UK, the structure of organizations tends to emphasize large 'horizontal' differences. The more rigid job demarcations and emphasis on individual structures therefore leads to more inter-organization career mobility and an external market-based labour system. Lower levels of education are also associated with a higher reliance on supervisors and technical foremen in career structures. France has a very bureaucratic work system with many layers of hierarchy in the organization, more supervision and less autonomy than many other European countries. The tall vertical structures in French organizations have given opportunity for an internal market-based labour system. In contrast, many studies of German management only define two levels of authority below board level (Maurice, Sorge and Warner, 1980): the *Hauptabteilungsleiter* (head of division); and the *Abteilungsleiter* (head of department). This is a reflection

Table 10.2 **A comparison of British and French management cultures.**

1. The hierarchy of managerial functions

Britain
The most valued functions are finance, accountancy and law

The statuses of production management and R&D are lower

Principally, functions with a professional status outside the company are the most valued

France
There is no strict hierarchy of functions. In the most traditional French companies, R&D and production management are, however, the valued functions

Principally, functions with high intellectual content are the most valued

2. Access to top management

The principal criteria are:

Britain
The 'right' social network

Practical achievements and job performance
Social skills

An accountancy or legal qualification is an asset

Management with technical qualifications are under-represented in senior management positions

France
Diplomas usually from *Grandes ecoles*
Strict hierarchies of diplomas

Importance of the 'old boy' network

Political skills

In large companies, appointing of managers to top management coming from the civil service ('pantouflage')

3. Education and training of managers

Britain
Not of primary importance
Emphasis is on pragmatism and learning by doing
Training might be seen as a sign of weakness
Empirical approach values

Low status attached to applied studies, for example in engineering and technology

France
Considered as very important
Strong emphasis on analytical and deductive qualities
Low training in social skills

Theoretical approach valued

High status attached to engineering, technology and those subjects taught in the *Grandes ecoles*

4. Leadership and patterns of authority

Britain
Paternalistic attitudes are common. Consensus is important for decision making

Fragile nature of the top manager's authority since it is derived from his social position rather than based on merit or technical competence

Leadership style is more orientated towards persons than towards tasks

Conflict avoidance is prevalent

Pseudo participative attitudes are common in decision making, often coloured with manipulative overtones

France
'Autocratic' attitudes are common. Reduced participation of intermediate and low management in decision making
Consensus is not the point in decision making

Authority from top management is not challenged
Leadership style is more directed towards tasks than persons

Conflict avoidance is prevalent

Fragile nature of the authority of intermediate management

5. Communication patterns and styles

Britain
Oral communication preferred, with a high premium placed on face-to-face interpersonal relationships

Communication is pragmatic and non-didactic

Informality is strong, e.g. use of first names, and a general informality of manner

France
Written communication preferred
Face-to-face interpersonal relations are difficult

Communication is abstract and didactic

Formality is strong, for example the use of family names, and a general formality of manner. Strong perception of 'power distance' (Hofstede, 1980). Hierarchical bypassing is common

Source: Naulleau and Harper (1993). Reproduced with permission of the publishers, Management Education and Development, © 1993.

of the shorter organizational hierarchies. Similarly, because German managers tend to understand the management task in specialist terms the organization tends to be structured into large functional units with only a thin level of general management on top (Lawrence, 1993).

Considerable attention has been given to the differences between the British and French systems, as archetypal examples of Anglo-Saxon and Continental European systems (Easterby-Smith, 1992; Lane, 1989; Naulleau and Harper, 1993). Table 10.2 describes a series of historical and cultural differences between French and British managers in terms of the relative hierarchy given to management functions, access to top management, the education and training of managers, the patterns of leadership and authority, and patterns of communication and management style (Naulleau and Harper, 1993). Despite such differences, the discussion in Chapter Eight about the convergence of organizational structures in the largest European organizations should not be forgotten. This convergence will clearly have a significant impact on the desired qualities for managers and this will place considerable pressure on national development systems and notions of management (Dopson, Risk and Stewart, 1992). These systems are summarized in the next section.

DIFFERENCES IN NATIONAL MANAGEMENT EDUCATION AND TRAINING SYSTEMS

The historical differences discussed so far in the notion of what an effective manager is and the impact of the structure of organizations have created profound differences in the way managers are made and in the process by which knowledge is transmitted to them across Europe (Lawrence, 1993). In this section we consider the most important features of the British, German and French management education and training systems. Direct comparison between national vocational education and training systems is difficult because there are many economic, cultural, industrial and educational differences between countries (Harrison, 1992).

The British system

The philosophy more prevalent in Anglo-Saxon organizations (the UK and US but being increasingly adopted in Holland and Scandinavia according to Evans, Lank and Farquhar, 1989) focuses on the generalist notion of management development. Entry into management positions is not based on élitist principles. For example, 80 per cent of the graduate intake at Shell have technical qualifications, and 99 per cent of all IBM executives have come from non-management entry positions (Evans, Lank and Farquhar, 1989). Managers climb up through functional or technical hierarchies over a period of around eight years, frequently moving through key career-anchor jobs which have to be mastered. Formal programmes are then used to evaluate a notion of general management potential based on a series of techniques. Career development is in practice a series of deselection decisions, hopefully made before the individual reaches their level of incompetence.

Lane (1989) has argued that British industry is structured in relation to its educational system, and that it has a managerial culture based on a highly individualistic university education system, relatively narrow access to top quality education, which emphasizes theoretical disciplines such as pure sciences, little on-the-job training or education, a narrow definition of job responsibilities, relatively short-term minded management caused by greater shareholder interest. Promotion is gained by moving between organizations, with management seen as a profession, and early promotion to management positions (often without experience of lower line positions).

In the UK, the 1980s saw the publication of a stream of reports which focused on the paucity of vocational training for managers and the poor quality of what was provided (Handy, Gordon, Gow and Randlesome, 1988; Constable and McCormick, 1987; Pye and Mangham, 1987; Barham, Fraser and Heath, 1987). Holden (1991) also draws attention to similar calls for an improvement to the level, quality and focus of training for managers in France, Germany, Sweden and Spain (Amblard, Abramovici, Livian, Poirson and Roussillon, 1989; Barsoux and Lawrence, 1990; Bruton, 1990; Courpasson, 1989; Forsberg and Söderström, 1991; Hayes, Anderson and Fonda, 1984; Pinaud, 1992; and Randlesome, 1989, 1990a).

The German system

The Germanic tradition (considered also to include many Swiss, and certain Scandinavian and Dutch organizations by Evans, Lank and Farquhar, 1989) relies on more formalized apprenticeships, job rotation and training, even for graduates. Apprenticeship is a well-rooted historic German tradition for skilled and blue collar workers. Two to five year periods of on-the-job training coupled with courses on company practices and policies and training partnerships with local technical or trade schools form the core of the system. Graduates undergo a two-year apprenticeship which uses a series of job rotations to both provide broad exposure to the organization and help identify the most suitable job or function for the individual. This decision is not made until the individual is in their late twenties. However, the higher the position within the organization hierarchy, the greater the percentage of university or college graduates encountered. The proportion of managers or middle managers, executives (on the level directly under the executive board), and managing directors who are graduates is 44 per cent, 54 per cent, and 62 per cent respectively. Thirty-one per cent of the executives with an academic background have doctorates (Lane, 1989; Roomkin, 1989). The prestige of executive jobs in manufacturing is high and organizations have less of a problem attracting highly qualified staff into a management career.

In contrast to the Anglo-Saxon tradition, management is not seen as a unified profession, and so there exists little general management education in Germany. In 1990, 700 business schools in the USA conferred some 75,000 Master of Business Administration (MBA) degrees. In the same year 10,000 graduates emerged from about 120 business schools in Western Europe and the number of European MBAs is set to double by the year 2000. However, none of these MBAs formed part of the official German education system (Randlesome, 1993). Why do German educators resist the American model? As well as the cultural factors outlined above, there are markedly different educational traditions between Germany and the USA. Management education in Germany has a long history, with the first college of commerce (*Handelschochschule*) established in 1898 and many of the most respected economic journals emanating from Germany. The history of business teaching in Germany shows a long tradition of erudition in *Volkswirtschaftslehre* (economics) and *Betriebswirtschaftlehre* (business economics). The prevaling attitude amongst the economically-educated decision makers in the federal ministries of education is 'if it isn't broken, don't fix it' (Randlesome 1993). Consequently, Germans apply to attend business schools in other countries. Germans formed the second largest contingent of overseas students at Cranfield School of Management in 1992. Some changes have recently taken place, with an MBA Center established in Frankfurt am Main to assist applications to foreign business schools and help prepare for the Graduate Management Admission Test (GMAT) exams. Koblenz School of Corporate Management teamed up with University of Texas to make an MBA available whilst the University of the German Army has made Henley distance learning packages available (Randlesome, 1993).

The French system

The Latin European system is exemplified by France. With parallels to the Japanese system of strict recruitment criteria forming a small élite, followed by limited screening but high performance monitoring until seven or eight years into the organization, career progression in France is a competitive struggle of achievement (Evans, Lank and Farquhar, 1989). Managers attend selective parts of secondary schools (*lycée*) and work towards their *baccalauréat* exam at the age of eighteen. University entrance is accessible to most high school graduates providing they hold a *baccalauréat* but significant choices have already been made because of the different groupings of subjects. Able and ambitious managers-to-be take the 'bac C' option that includes mathematics and natural science, since these are seen as the best test of intellectual and reasoning ability (Lawrence, 1993). There is then a two-tier system of higher education, with the majority of universities having lower prestige (except in the subjects of medicine or computer science) in comparison to the superior *grandes écoles* – which restrict admission to socially élite *cadres moyennes*. *Écoles préparatoires* offer intensive two year preparatory courses (the most testing time of a manager's life) leading to *concours* – or nationally competitive exams that admit students into the *grandes écoles*. The *grandes écoles* are élitist and exclusive, admitting only small numbers. Although there are 140 to 160 establishments, they are arranged in a prestige order. The most prestigious engineering school is the *École Polytechnique* and the most prestigious commercial or business school is *Haute École de Commerce* (HEC) in Paris. The inordinate attention in France to an élitist system of training means that institutions are invariably able to place graduates in leading areas of responsibility. Graduates usually develop an expertise in engineering disciplines and reach high positions in both public administration and industry. Barsoux and Lawrence (1991) claim that 90 per cent of presidents and chief executives are graduates of the *grandes écoles*. A 1990 survey of 108 French chief executives by *L'Expansion* found that 31 had come from *École Polytechnique* alone. Sixty-five were from the top four *grandes écoles* and only four were educated at state universities. Only one CEO had risen through the ranks – an *autodidacte* (Incomes Data Service, 1993). A small number of CEOs follow up with an MBA or a spell at one of the US 'Ivy League' universities. In France, top management in both the private and public sectors are strongly linked:

- Senior posts in both state service and private industry are staffed by people with the same educational background.
- There is a system of *pantouflage* with high mobility of civil servants in mid-career to posts at or near the top of private sector organizations.
- Board directors typically hold seats in the private and public sectors and tend to run both in the same bureaucratic style.

Most of the larger French organizations recruit exclusively from the *grandes écoles*.

Entering an organization in this way means achieving *cadre* status early and being on the *voie royale* or royal road to success. Although university graduates outnumber graduates from the *grandes écoles* by a ratio of 10:1, they represent only 10 per cent of new managerial recruits (Incomes Data Service, 1993a). Naturally, there is then a diminished role for management development. The management development process tends to be one of grooming and validating experience. Young graduates are sent on international assignments, serve as an attaché to senior managers and are sent to the provinces on fact finding assignments (Lawrence, 1993). Diagonal promotion routes from research and development into general management can also be a useful proving ground. Nevertheless, the task of management development is to allow the public demonstration of generalist responsibilities in the knowledge that the important qualities were selected long ago at the *concours* (entrance to the *grandes écoles*).

The homogeneity of the *cadres moyennes* and the distinctiveness of the French manager may, however, present French organizations with problems in the new global environment outlined in Part Two of the book (Barsoux and Lawrence, 1991). They quote the self-made executive who asks in despair: '. . . for how many more decades are we going to sit idly by while great talents and potential are permanently stifled?'. There is, then, currently a wide process of discussion in France about the nature of high potential management, posed against this backdrop of national culture (Bournois and Roussillon, 1992). It is dominated by three arguments:

1. Some writers point to the waste of potential by ignoring all those individuals who do not belong to the élite.
2. Others claim to be satisfied with the system and point to its efficiency in selecting executives with potential at an early age.
3. More recently, analysts point to the failing of French organizations in not providing high quality career paths, not the national education system, by questioning whether any organization that makes use of graduates should believe that managers are produced spontaneously and are automatically prepared for difficult and demanding careers, even if recruited from the best sources (Bournois, 1991a, 1991b; Gentil, 1988).

Perhaps in recognition of this, in the late 1980s there has been greater concern in France for new industrial priorities and the number of Business Schools in France has

Table 10.3 **The level of concern with the management of high potential managers in Europe.**

Country	% of managers concerned
France	44
Sweden	41
Spain	39
Norway	38
Switzerland	33
UK	29
Denmark	28
Italy	28
Holland	24
Germany	21

Source: reprinted from *Human Resource Management Journal*, **3(1)**, 37–56, F. Bournois and S. Roussillon, 'The concept of high-flier executives in France: the weight of national culture', copyright © 1992, with kind permission of John Wiley and Sons, Inc.

increased (Easterby-Smith, 1992; Usunier, 1990) and the term *Mastères* is now commonly used for advanced qualifications. Bournois and Roussillon (1992) draw attention to the paradox revealed by the Price Waterhouse/Cranfield Project. Data from the studies reveal that French managers are deeply concerned with the issue of high potential managers (see Table 10.3). They show the highest level of concern amongst European managers about the topic.

The differences between Anglo-Saxon and other European systems of management education are very marked (Easterby-Smith, 1992). Spain also exemplifies a Latin approach. The first business school was established in Bilbao in 1916, although most business schools were established from 1955–65 (Hale and Tijmstra, 1990). Courses lead to a diploma after three years, or a *licendiado* qualification after five years. This is a prerequisite for admission to an MBA degree. The two most prestigious institutions, IESA and ESADE in Barcelona, have religious links (the Opus Dei and Jesuits respectively). The curriculum was for many years centralized, but has recently been released from central control. In Italy, university entrance is without examination and there is consequently a high dropout rate. There is little link between the education system and the needs of specialized industry. There are ten business schools, which are not well established. The two leading schools are SDA Bocconi in Milan and ISTUD on Lake Maggiori (Easterby-Smith, 1992). The system is influenced by the role of small business in the Italian economy.

Table 10.4 **What makes an effective European manager? Student perceptions from four countries.**

	Sweden	Belgium	Germany	Spain
Most desirable skills				
Decision making	174	146	169	182
Conflict resolution	162	139	133	137
Planning and evaluation	140	159	107	172
Directing	154	122	138	155
Negotiation	132	129	136	159
Problem solving	139	135	137	119
Organizing	117	125	101	138
Forecasting	97	142	96	93
Diplomacy	110	109	90	93
Interpersonal relations	167	118	55	51
Aspects of knowledge and learning				
General knowledge	152	168	119	116
Pertinent technical knowledge	90	83	166	135
Social forces impacting the organization	152	156	87	125
Theories of human behaviour	120	86	101	120
Socio-economic-political developments in the country	118	132	81	97
Developments in other countries	105	94	115	92
Scientific and technological developments	92	84	128	86
Management theories and techniques	77	119	58	136
Theories of social and political behaviour	69	97	73	91
History of the organization	64	63	−7	64

Source: Boldy, Jain and Northey (1993). Reproduced with permission of the publishers, Management International Review, © 1993.

Table 10.5 **Comparison of European systems for apprenticeships and initial vocational training.**

Belgium	Denmark	France	Germany	UK
Part time education obligatory until age 18, usually on TSO or BSO courses in schools	182,000 pupils in VET and apprenticeships	Most initial training in state educational institutions. 1.3 million students. Apprenticeships less important	One year of basic pre-vocational school education, compulsory for unemployed or those without apprenticeship place. 105,000 trainees	Underperformance in VET area is a long-standing policy concern. System based on encouragement of industry to offer training. Only 33% of workforce have a vocational qualification
Vocational apprenticeships administered along linguisitic lines	Around 48,000 receive instruction from 112 commercial and technical schools in two 20 week courses separated by work placement	Vocational training certificate (CAP) is principal initial qualification. 3 years duration. 2 years for less specialized BEP	State-controlled apprenticeship system, with 1500 special vocational schools, covering 70% of young people. 1.5 million trainees, 42% women	VET system revolves around craft apprenticeships. Only 13,564 craftsmen and technicians in basic training
Most apprenticeships for craft training or self-employed and closely legislated	86 courses, with training lasting from 3–4 years. Certificated to NVQ level 3	230,000 apprenticeships for 16–25 year olds. 50% classroom taught and 50% company placement, 1–3 years. Registered providers. Low job offer ratio after apprenticeship	Dual system. Mostly on the job training with instruction in state-run vocational schools. Close connection between the two	Combination of on-the-job training and day release college instruction
Industrial apprentice contracts for 18–21 year olds from 6 months to 2 years	High involvement of social partners in both policy-making and administration of VET	Apprentices paid from 30% to 80% of national minimum wage	Standard curricula for 380 vocational qualifications, linked to access to more advanced schools and training courses	Youth training in practice limited to unemployed. Number of other schemes for the unemployed, and start-up business growth companies
Duration from 1–3 years for over 25 years olds. From 28–32 hours a week with the company. 120 hours per year formal instruction	82,000 EFG students, 43,000 apprenticeships and 30,000 basic technical and commercial diplomas	Number of schemes for the unemployed as 'formation en alternance' or sandwich courses. Qualification, return to work, solidarity or orientation contracts	319,000 manufacturing apprenticeships registered in 1990. Only 172,000 applicants	National Vocational Qualification scheme set up in 1986 to reform and rationalize system. Four levels of qualification, based on on-the-job training and distance learning. System of basic job competence accreditation. No independent examination. No requirement for training of accreditors
	Recent attempts to co-ordinate VET across industries		Schemes with different requirements at Technical Colleges, vocational schools, specialist secondary schools and chambers of commerce set standards for facilities, trainer qualifications. 50% of trainees take a permanent job, 85% with organization that trained them	

Greece	Italy	Spain	Netherlands	Portugal
New legal framework for a National System of VET and qualifications introduced in 1992	Bulk of initial VET provided through state education system and a limited number of apprenticeships in small firms for young people aged 15–20	All levels of education under reform	Egalitarian higher education system, high decentralization and organization on religious grounds	VET systems currently the centre of political debate
Officially recognized professions and levels of qualification still regulated through presidential or ministerial decree	State-run technical and vocational training institutes. Low linkage between vocational education and education syllabus. 380,000 school leavers attend Regional Centres. 1.3 million in technical institutes	VET takes place within school system	490,000 students enrolled on MBO and KMBO vocational education courses	Decentralized system of training colleges with 11,000 students
Initial VET takes place primarily in public institutions through technical and vocational education and apprenticeships	No centralized system for certification of courses or institutional network with nationally-accepted standards or resources	National Training and Development Plan oversees training schemes	Young people aged over 16 and not in F.T. education have to attend VET establishment for 1–2 days a week	Framework for VET only recently established
Low level of integration between education system and attitudes of employers	Vocational courses for 2 years at 1st level, and one year at 2nd level	312,000 trainees (the majority unemployed) on schemes under the plan	Apprenticeships regulated by law. 3 levels. First level lasts for 2–3 years. Nationally recognized diplomas	15,500 on state vocational courses and a similar number on apprenticeships
		260,000 young people aged 16–20 employed on fixed-term training contracts from 3 months–3 years	136,000 apprenticeship contracts	
		184,000 people on work experience contracts		
		Specialist courses for under represented groups		

Table 10.6 **Comparison of European systems for continuous training.**

Belgium	Denmark	France	Germany	UK
Advanced technical training kept inhouse	Open education policy. No age limits. Legislative requirement for outside-work hours provision	5 million people (25% of working population) undertake VET. Access varies across industries. Most supplementary training organized by employers	Comprehensive inhouse post qualification training. Quality assurance standards (FUU) applied to private training providers	Around 8% of UK organizations provide an average of 10 days training/per employee/per year
Continuing and higher vocational training provided inhouse with frequent resort to public institutions	Widespread in-company training programmes. 40% of workforce participate in some retraining, spending 2.5% of working hours	14% of continuing VET conducted inhouse by companies	80% of employees in trade and industry sectors take part in further training	Less than 33% provide over 5 days training per year
Work training contracts for 18–25 year olds below degree or technical secondary education level. 1–3 years with at least 500 hours per year	Internal career development and education the norm for large organizations	Entitlement to a minimum of 3–4 days training a year in the public sector	18% of all Germans take part in some form of continuing VET, rising to 40% of those with tertiary education	
Over 34,000 work placements for under 30 year olds with less than 6 months employment, equal to 3–4% of workforce. Pay at 90% of worker with equal skill	Courses at vocational training institutes and further education centres	100% pay for training leave caused by departmental restructuring	Most collective agreements stipulate minimum training levels for grading purposes	
Advanced technical training run by VDAB or FOREM (employment offices) in some 400 centres. 325 courses for supervisors and managers run at VDAB or FOREM centres	Training courses for skills refreshment. 100,000 trainees in courses for skilled/unskilled		Assessments of organization training needs, provision of retraining for socially warrented rationalization, may form part of agreements	
	60,000 participating in 1 to 4 week modular courses for skilled workers			

Greece	Italy	Spain	Netherlands	Portugal
On-the-job training for young people practically non-existent	Although continuing VET carried out by state system, regions have legal responsibility	Skills shortages led to a proliferation of private training providers	Complex adult education and training systems being harmonized	Level of training and qualifications of managers linked to their age
Very low level of continuing inhouse training in bulk of small to medium-sized companies	Regional centres deliver around 20,000 courses a year, with the majority in the South	52% of companies with under 500 employees and 75% with over 500 employees have training programmes	Rauwenhoff Commission in 1990 led to a number of reforms	Number of firms involved in training doubled from 1986–1989
Rising level of training in large and export-orientated companies	External training providers growing as organizations modernize, subcontract and streamline	Foreign-owned companies have higher levels of training provision	28 regional services, employment and careers centres	Low levels of management education
Wide variety of training providers offering short and long-term training programmes, e.g. ELKEPA, EEDE, EOMMEX and OAED	Employers' associations and some industry associations offer courses	Unmet demand in management training e.g. 10,000 MBAs	Continuous training for the unemployed	MBAs are rare
Courses for adults and unemployed provided in technical-vocational centres		17 Business Schools	Larger organizations have inhouse training facilities, smaller companies share facilities	
		In-company accounts for 75% of company training budgets	Substantial company training effort	

These differences in the nature of management education clearly create different perceptions amongst young managers about what makes a manager effective. The International Project on Culture and Management has provided data on the perceptions of 870 university students in business disciplines from Sweden, Belgium, Germany and Spain (Boldy, Jain and Northey, 1993). They were presented with a variety of items describing: skills, knowledge and learning; beliefs and values; and personality characteristics. They were asked to rate the extent to which these items would help managerial effectiveness. The results are shown in Table 10.4 (p. 385).

The findings from the study provided some support for the North/South European hypothesis. This postulates that North Europeans are more instrumental in their view of management. They emphasize the rational organization of tasks. The South European or Latin cultures emphasize the social dimensions of managing groups of people (Ashton, 1986). For example, the study highlights the German emphasis on the importance of technical knowledge and the Spanish emphasis on being supportive. However, a simple North–South cultural divide hides many other conflicting results. For example, Swedish students also emphasized the importance of interpersonal relations. The research is clearly subjective and taps into student perceptions of what they think makes a manager more effective. However, it serves to highlight the need to develop culturally-appropriate management education and ETD systems within organizations.

EDUCATION AND VOCATIONAL TRAINING SYSTEMS IN EUROPE

The last topic to consider whilst outlining the relationship between ETD activities and the external institutional and cultural context of the organization is the nature of vocational education and training systems across Europe. Vocational education and training (VET) in the European Union is marked by a very high degree of diversity both in terms of the role of public institutions and the degree of formalization in the training systems (Incomes Data Service, 1993a). The only evidence of convergence is in the degree of interest in the 'German model' in those countries that are overhauling their VET systems. Such convergence is, however, a long way off. We summarize the key points in three areas: systems for apprenticeships and initial vocational training (see Table 10.5, pp. 386–7); systems for continuous training (see Table 10.6, pp. 388–9); and levels of subsidies, funding and expenditure systems for VET (see Table 10.7).

There are a number of common features that serve as useful points of contrast between systems. The first common feature is the system of funding and mandatory training. Some European countries, such as France, have mandatory levies to ensure that minimum levels of training are complied with. In France, the state has low direct influence on vocational education and apprenticeships, but nevertheless imposes laws on organizations such that 1.2 per cent of wages must be spent on training. This legislative control has apparently had a beneficial impact on organizational behaviour (Holden and Livian, 1992; Dayan, Gehin and Verdier, 1986). However, because of the low levels of mobility in France, vocational training mainly takes place within organizations, is carried out on an *ad hoc* basis and is on-the-job. In Germany, training services provided by chambers of trade and commerce are partly subsidized by membership fees, payment of which is compulsory for most businesses, and in Greece there is a levy of 0.45 per cent of wage costs (Incomes Data Service, 1993a).

However, the existence of mandatory funding and targets does not cause improved organizational behaviour. Some countries, like Germany, can rely on a well developed training culture to ensure effective participation. Germany has no mandatory training

Table 10.7 **Comparison of European subsidies, funding and expenditure systems for VET.**

Belgium	Denmark	France	Germany	UK
Funding for VET largely the responsibility of the regions	Compulsory employer contributions for initial school-based VET. Grants awarded for open education courses covering 80% of operational expenditure	F.Fr. 79 billion spent on continuing vocational training	Costs of training borne solely by organizations. No levies or mandatory requirements for level of training expenditure	Provision, content and financing of VET is largely the responsibility of organizations
Organizations spend from 1.4% to 8% of wage bill on continuing training, with 0.25% devoted to 'at risk' groups	Wage compensation for adult vocational trainees	Minimum of 1.2% of total gross salaries per year contributed by employers. 0.6% of salary bill used to fund apprenticeship system	Dm. 26.7 billion spent by organizations on inhouse training through dual system	Responsibility for financing split between employer and individual and devolved to local regions through 104 TECs
Social security reductions to induce employers to provision of work training contracts	DKr. 2 billion spent on Adult Vocational Training each year	Many training arrangements incorporated into industry collective agreements, allocating training 'capital' e.g. 400 hours for non-qualified staff in insurance industry	Further Dm. 39 billion spent on continued training, compared with Dm. 9 billion from public funds	18% of organizations spend over 4% of wage bill on training
Belgium spends 6% of GDP on education	13% of organizations spend more than 4% of salary bill on ETD	Clauses for higher training spend quite common	Average of 34 hours further training per employee/per year in trade and industry sector	
45% of organizations have a training budget		Average spending of private sector companies is 3.2% of the wage bill	16% of organizations spend more than 4% of salary bill on ETD	
19168 BFr. spent on training per employee/per year		32% of organizations spend more than 4% of salary bill on ETD		
4–5 days training per employee/per year				

Greece	Italy	Spain	Netherlands	Portugal
Increased funding from EU funds for a range of agencies, including local authorities, private schools and government organizations	Funding of initial VET is by the State	Average time spent on training is 59 hours per employee (3% of working time)	NFl.2.8 billion spent on adult education and vocational training	European Union funding for the Specific Programme for Industrial Development
Many programmes jointly funded by employers, unions and EU finances	Concessions on social security contributions for apprenticeship or training contracts	Average training costs 1% of wage bill	Average of 3% of wage bill spent by companies on training	Lowest proportion of qualified personnel in the EU
	9% of organizations spend more than 4% of salary bill on ETD	40% of collective agreements stipulate training provision	NFl.8 billion spent by companies on training in public and private sector	1.25 million Ecu from Social Fund earmarked for adult training
		10% of organizations spend more than 4% of salary bill on ETD	16% of organizations spend more than 4% of salary bill on ETD	
			Widespread inclusion of training schemes in collective agreements in recent years	

requirements for organizations, but the support and involvement of strong employers' organizations and unions and the equation of training with capital investment as opposed to a part of wage cost has ensured an over-supply of training places. An integrated system can also be found in Sweden, where three government commissions have analysed the participation patterns and distribution of VET and continuous training. Whilst some imbalances still exist, with men, technical specialists, well educated 25–40 year olds, and public sector employees receiving more training, continuous adult education is freely available and provides a key strand in a training system that has a low cost to trainees. Continuous education forms the basis of adult education. Voluntary study associations and folk high schools form a system for labour market training, with evening classes and distance learning quite prevalent. Some 18 per cent of blue-collar workers, 37 per cent of white collar workers and 45 per cent of academics and professionals receive continuous education and training.

The institutional context for education and training varies. We discussed the different levels of educational provision in Chapter Four. Countries with a strong education and training record integrate training with the upper level of secondary education. In Germany this takes the form of requiring people aged under 18 to continue in some form of general education. In the Netherlands and Denmark the bulk of initial training is carried out within the public education system. Belgium, Germany and the Netherlands stream secondary school students into either vocationally-orientated or academically-orientated institutions. In many European countries possession of a vocational or technical qualification serves as the basis for entry into higher education. Britain is one of the few countries in Europe to have a comprehensive education system at both lower and upper secondary level.

TRENDS IN ETD WITHIN EUROPEAN ORGANIZATIONS

Having described the different notions about management development and national systems of VET across Europe, in the fourth section of this chapter we focus on trends in ETD within European organizations. As part of the Price Waterhouse Cranfield Project (PWCP) research project (outlined in Chapter Two), Holden (1991) analysed the training needs of organizations from Britain, France, the former Federal Republic of Germany, Sweden and Spain in order to identify the main trends in their training and development activities and to assess how strategic the implementation of the training process was. The analysis was later extended to all ten countries involved in the study (Hilb, 1992; Holden and Livian, 1992). The main trends are summarized in Illustration 10.9.

Accordingly, there were considerable increases in training investment from 1988–91 (see Table 10.8). Much of this increased ETD investment has been focused on the upper echelons of organizations and managers (Holden and Livian, 1992), although, of course, the figures in Table 10.8 do not reflect the substantial state apprenticeship and VET schemes in Germany, France and Sweden (Holden, 1991). French organizations emerged as leading this trend towards greater ETD expenditure, with 70 per cent of organizations increasing their budgets for all staff groups (71 per cent for *Etam* – professional, technical and clerical; 67 per cent for *Ouvriers* – manual). A similar even distribution of expenditure was found in the Netherlands. German, Swiss and Danish organizations continued to adopt their traditional approach, with more limited resources being devoted to unqualified staff. This focus of ETD resources only on the top echelons of the organization is seen by many as hampering the ability of European organizations to implement major organizational culture

Illustration 10.9 **The main trends in ETD within European organizations.**

- After a considerable increase in the investment in training from 1987–1990, all ten countries listed an area related to training as their main objective for the early 1990s.
- Reflecting the discussion of labour markets in Chapter Nine, many European HRM managers are using ETD much more as a recruitment strategy. In all countries except Germany and Sweden, training for new employees was cited as the most popular means to aid recruitment.
- Internal resourcing in the form of retraining existing employees was the second most popular recruiting option in Denmark, Spain and the UK (shown to have a strong reliance on external labour markets in Chapter Nine) and third most popular option in France.
- Most ETD resources are focused on the upper echelons of organizations and the management

- structure. On average European organizations spend around 2 per cent of their wage and salary bill on ETD.
- The majority of organizations monitor the effectivness of their ETD. The proportion varies from 58 per cent to 84 per cent for all countries, except for Denmark, where the figure is 35 per cent.
- Responsibility for ETD is being decentralized to line managers. The proportion of organizations who see ETD as a responsibility of solely line managers, or line managers in conjunction with HRM managers, ranges from only 14 per cent in Italy, 29 per cent in the UK and 32 per cent in Spain, up to 66 per cent in Sweden and 64 per cent in Denmark. These figures have all increased from 1988–1991.

Source: Holden (1991); Holden and Livian (1992).

change programmes, such as Total Quality Management or Customer Service, effectively.

When training expenditure is considered in relation to the total wage and salary bill, the picture is less optimistic. Only France and Sweden have more than 25 per cent of organizations spending more than 4 per cent of their wage bill on ETD (see Table 10.7). Most European organizations spend around 2 per cent of the wages and salary bill on ETD (Holden and Livian, 1992). However, many European HRM managers do not know how much their organizations really spend on ETD (the figure is 44 per cent of Swedish HRM managers, 42 per cent in Germany, 38 per cent in the UK and 33 per cent in Denmark). Moreover, those reporting systems that do exist often measure very different items, making most organizational statistics highly suspect.

Table 10.8 **Increases in training investment 1988–91 (in percentage terms) in ten European countries.**

Country	Management	Professional	Technical	Clerical	Manual
Switzerland	74	68	66	35	34
Germany	61	68	43	39	17
Denmark	51	50	icl	39	33
Spain	61	70	icl	58	50
France	64	65	icl	icl	60
Italy	62	74	icl	58	50
Norway	49	43	icl	33	36
Netherlands	63	66	icl	54	65
Sweden	70	48	58	46	49
UK	66	59	icl	46	41

Icl = included in category to the left
Source: reprinted from L. Holden and Y. Livian, 'Does strategic training policy exist?', *Personnel Review*, **21(1)**, 12–23, © 1992, with kind permission from MCB University Press Ltd.

The volume of training can be assessed in part by the time spent on training. Even at management level, the majority of organizations in most countries only provided five or less days training. Over ten days training for managers was provided by 29 per cent of Spanish organizations (reflecting their vibrant economic growth in the late 1980s and the high levels of skills shortage in the lead up to the SEM), 12 per cent of Norwegian organizations and 11 per cent of German, Danish and Dutch organizations.

Many of the cultural differences discussed earlier are reflected in the existing types of training provided for managers. For example, reflecting the importance given to the topic of motivation, between 55 and 76 per cent of organizations from Switzerland, Germany, Sweden and Norway claim to have trained over a third of their managers in the topic. This falls to only 33 per cent of French organizations (Holden and Livian, 1992). A similar pattern can be found when training in delegation is considered, with France again providing the least attention with only 22 per cent of organizations training more than a third of their managers in this topic. Despite the espoused focus of Anglo-Saxon organizations on interpersonal skills, the figure was a middle range 47 per cent for motivation training and 40 per cent for delegation training in British organizations. Team building training was most popular in British and Swedish organizations, followed by Swiss, Dutch, Norwegian and Spanish organizations. It was least popular in Danish and German organizations. Such findings obviously cannot be interpreted without considering other aspects of HRM, such as job design (see Chapter Twelve). In German and Danish organizations, team building training may be unnecessary because of the greater concentration on horizontal aspects of organizational structure (see Chapter Eight).

However, whilst the current focus of ETD provision varies across European organizations, there appears to be a greater degree of communality in plans for future training. The areas of people management, business administration and management of change emerged as clear preferences, with little deviation between countries (Holden and Livian, 1992). For example, in a more limited comparison of the UK, France, Spain, Sweden and Germany (Holden, 1991), 'people management' was ranked as the most important training requirement by all the countries except Spain (where it was ranked last). Computers and new technology was ranked top by Spain and second by the UK, France and Germany and the management of change was ranked second or third by the UK, France and Sweden. However, despite these trends at the organizational level, the authors of the Price Waterhouse/Cranfield Project surveys concluded:

> ... It is clear that in Europe few organizations can be said to act strategically in the use of their training function and most tend to rest on the national training and educational structures which operate externally to, or in best practice, in co-ordination with the organization. In this sense both Sweden and Germany, and to some degree France, with their strong legislation and national training infrastructures can help organizations in their efforts to develop their training function.
>
> Holden (1991, p. 129).

LABOUR FORCE MOBILITY, JOB SECURITY AND THE QUALITY OF ETD

In the fifth section of the chapter we consider some of the main issues that have been created by the trends discussed in the previous section. The pressures for change in European management development and vocational training systems have created three main issues:

1. Will the trend towards more flexible employment relationships and management structures have an adverse impact on the quality of training and development?
2. What will be the HRM issues that arise from the process of internationalization of internal resourcing systems?
3. What is the nature of effective management, now, and in the future?

We discussed the development of the flexible organization in Chapters Four and Twelve. It has become increasingly apparent to European organizations that the shift towards more flexible contracts for hiring employees and the desire to create a more mobile workforce have produced a number of more negative side effects. Concerns about the impact of low job security on the long term quality of the labour force led to a study in 1993 by the Organization for Economic Co-operation and Development (OECD) on the link between job security and training (*The Economist*, 1993). The level of mobility in the labour force tends to be looked at in two ways:

1. The average length of tenure of employees and the percentage of the labour force who have been with the employer for one or five years.
2. The average tenure of employees across different age groups.

The frequency with which people change jobs varies considerably between countries (see Figure 10.3). In Germany, the average tenure of employees in 1991 was 10.4 years, which was only marginally less than the 10.9 years found in Japan. More than half the workforce have been with their current employer for over five years. A similar situation applies to France. In Spain, the average tenure is 9.8 years and in Switzerland it is 8.8 years. A more mobile labour force exists in Britian, where the average tenure

Figure 10.3 Comparative labour market turnover. *Original data: The Economist* (1993).

of employees in 1991 was 7.9 years, with less than 45 per cent of employees having over 5 years' service with their employer. The most fluid labour market in Europe is found in Holland, where average tenure is only 7.0 years and less than 38 per cent of employees have over 5 years' service. The Dutch labour market is almost as fluid (and flexible) as the US labour market, where average tenure is only 6.7 years. It should be noted that figures on average tenure and length of service with the current employer tend to exaggerate labour market turnover because they do not measure how much longer existing employees will stay with the organization (i.e. they do not take account of the eventual completed spells of employment).

Another way of examining mobility is to consider the average length of job tenure (length of service) with age. The duration of average tenure falls off earlier in Japan because most workers have to retire at 55 and then take up another job. Until this age, however, Japanese employees are more likely to stay with employers for most of their working lives. This is broadly paralleled in the German experience. American employees (and similarly British and Dutch) aged 45–49 have been with their current employer for an average duration of 12 years, in comparison to a tenure of 19 years for Japanese and German employees of the same age. Given the shift of employment strategy in Britain (see Illustration 6.8) towards a flexible model, the average tenure of most employees should be expected to fall sharply throughout the 1990s.

The OECD study focused on the link between such mobility (and the associated lack of security) and training, and found that where labour mobility is high, not surprisingly, the level of formal organization training was more limited. For example, in the US only 10 per cent of young recruits have any formal training from their organization compared to 70 per cent in Japan and Germany. The level of formal training was correlated with the length of time with the employer. Does high mobility cause low levels of training, or do low levels of training cause high mobility? Unfortunately, correlation does not prove causality, and many employers (particularly in Britain) argue high labour mobility (induced by a minority of employers who prefer to poach employees rather than train them themselves) reduces their motivation to invest in training employees for the benefit of other employers. On the evidence of correlations, the OECD concluded that there is a clear link between employment stability and skill training, acknowledging that the two mutually reinforce each other.

European organizations will become caught between a vicious circle where higher labour turnover produces a less trained (and less committed and loyal) workforce, thereby discouraging investment in employees even further, and a virtuous circle where lower mobility is associated with higher tenure, more investment in training, and the resultant levels of commitment to ensure that the changes in organization culture and structure outlined in Chapters Seven and Eight are implemented effectively. Improving management development and developing career systems that get the balance right will be one of the most significant challenges for European organizations through the late 1990s.

ETD AT THE HOECHST GROUP: A SYSTEM IN TRANSITION

Clearly, the transitions taking place in ETD are having an impact on HRM systems of European organizations. In order to examine this, we describe the way in which the Hoechst Group has responded to the need for greater international training and career development within the context of its German-influenced tiered training strategy. Hoechst Group is a major European chemicals and pharmaceuticals organization that employs over 170,000 employees worldwide. Founded in Frankfurt, in 1863, by 1991 nearly 75 per cent of its sales were from outside Germany. EU countries, however, provide 58 per cent of its sales and approximately two-thirds of its production output originates in EU countries. Hoechst Group is the seventh largest German organization in terms of turnover (eighteenth largest in Europe) and eighth largest German employer (twentieth in Europe). It employs 170,000 people worldwide, with 80,000 in Europe and 30,000 on the Frankfurt site. Like several European organizations discussed in Chapter Eight, Hoechst focuses on the three world markets of the US, Europe and the Far East.

After several years of growth in revenues and market capitalization, sales at Hoechst Group in 1989 were 22 billion ECU. In 1990 sales fell by 2.3 per cent whilst profits after tax fell by 20 per cent to 0.83 billion ECU, largely due to a series of acquisitions and record levels of capital expenditure coming hand in hand with political and economic change, a declining value of the dollar, lower sales prices, and increasing raw material prices. Labour costs, at 6.43 billion ECU represented 29.2 per cent of sales. In 1991 sales recovered and grew 5.2 per cent to 23.13 billion ECU, but profit after tax fell a further 20 per cent to 0.67 billion ECU as employment costs continued to rise in the face of continued economic recession. The result was a process of streamlining of product ranges, production facilities and organization structure. In the late 1980s Hoechst shifted the emphasis in their structure from one of national control to control through strategic business units and the line of business.

There are a number of pressures at lower levels that require a greater international focus in training. As European integration increases it is likely that Hoechst Group will rationalize production around fewer sites. Demographic pressures in Germany will increase the need for more international sourcing, and work on vocational qualifications is increasing the 'transferability' of skills and the creation of a common job language. The worldwide growth in Hoechst was accompanied by significant changes in the business portfolio, and as a result, much greater attention is paid to planning the manpower development. Hoechst Group adopts a tiered approach to training and career development, very much reflecting its German origins. Four tiers are applied:

1. Basic vocational training.
2. Advanced vocational training.
3. Management training.
4. General management development.

Vocational training

Training is mainly on-the-job and is seen as a lifelong process. It focuses on employees' knowledge, skills, attitudes and personalities. Personal responsibility is encouraged. Because training is seen as an investment, Hoechst Group has been happy to incorporate a more international element at lower levels within the organization than is justified by immediate business need. Hoechst spent 73.5 million ECU on vocational training in 1991, or 11,130 ECU per employee. Training places are offered in eighty different scientific, technical and commercial disciplines. More than 5,200 German and 5,700 UK employees were undergoing training in 1991. The dual system of training and education was introduced for British management trainees in 1991 (Harrison, 1992). Approximately 2,000 trainees join the various Hoechst schemes each year. The pass rate is 97 per cent, and 84 per cent remain with the company (most of those who leave go on to do a degree).

Over half of all inhouse staff have attended advanced vocational training with the major areas of interest being information technology, process engineering and languages. Hoechst has its own language laboratories open to any member of staff (Personnel Management, 1991). Intercultural exchanges are common and an industrial scholarship and exchange programme for junior executives and young employees is run in co-operation between seven West European subsidiaries. In 1991 some 20,000 employees participated in some additional training. In five to seven years it is possible to obtain a degree via intermediate qualifications. About 50 per cent of those completing the Chemical Engineering course in the last twenty years are now in senior management positions whilst 30 per cent occupy management jobs in production or in the laboratories. A total of 8.3 million ECU is spent on advanced vocational training.

Management training and development

Management training is the responsibility of the manager and includes periods of on-the-job training, working with the field force, stays abroad, job rotation and participation in project and product teams. This is supported by language training and intercultural seminars for employees with overseas contacts. Around 11,000 employees attend inhouse Hoechst training schemes each year whilst 5,000 take advantage of external management training courses. In 1984 Hoechst Group started a development scheme to cover staff suitable for international middle and top management tasks. There are over 1,000 jobs (out of the 150,000 jobs worldwide) at this level and above, and over 2,000 people have now been actively considered. The Committee is headed by the Chairman and its members come from a variety of disciplines. A systematic process is used to identify those individuals with potential to think and act in corporate and international dimensions. The results of these 'trawls' for potential are discussed and used to make centrally-managed decisions about job appointments and general management seminars (such as programmes run at INSEAD, IMD and Harvard).

Greater international experience was created by managing four types of assignments: cross-European project teams; two year secondments; two to eight year delegations and permanent transfers. We discuss such processes of internationalization in the next chapter. In order to achieve senior positions in line functions, employees must have spent a two year assignment in Germany, not just for language training but for contacts, knowledge and experience.

The internal resourcing problem: an ageing population

The tiered approach to management training came under pressure in the 1990s from two areas: demographic and structural change. By 1990 Hoechst became aware that as a result of its ageing management structure, and demographic pressures on recruitment in Germany, within a ten-year period it would need to replace 60 per cent of top management positions. This represented both a remarkable opportunity to 'internationalize' its management but also a significant resourcing problem. The resourcing problem was exacerbated by Hoechst's 'fill from within' policy.

In many cases senior managers were being developed for international positions at a time in their careers when for personal reasons their mobility was low. There was a need to identify internationally mobile managers at an earlier point in their careers. The first response by Hoechst Group in 1990 was to hold general management seminars for junior executives from throughout the world. The seminars are in English and are aimed at promoting understanding amongst staff on a worldwide basis. Written reports covering degree of specialist orientation, intellectual potential, entrepreneurial attitude, leadership and personality are produced. Every two years round table discussions are held to plan career development. Hoechst Group therefore managed the careers of the top 1 per cent of the company whilst the national operations took an interest in the top 10 per cent.

By the early 1990s Hoechst had put management training and career systems in place that resulted in a more systematic identification, evaluation and fostering of talent. The evidence indicated a successful strategy. The number of job changes had increased, appraisals were more widely available, employees were more mobile, young managers gained more experience in different jobs, the management base had been broadened and international awareness had been sharpened.

New structures, new international skill demands

A renewed pressure for greater international management in Hoechst Group and a second pressure on internal resourcing stemmed from structural changes made in January 1991. Since the 1970s the organization had been structured into divisions. It was sales driven with strong supporting functional groups. Each national company was a mirror of the German parent. By the late 1980s, however, these divisions resembled large companies in themselves. They were split up into a series of autonomous business units operating in three worldwide geographical markets.

In Chapter Eight we pointed out that changes in organizational structure often bring a series of associated developments in HRM. For Hoechst, the new structure meant that each national organization in Hoechst effectively became a holding company and a reporting centre for corporate profit. The decentralized business units, however, now had to operate within their sector (such as fibres and plastic film, polymers or health) across the whole of Europe. This shift entailed the need to develop managers who had expert functional knowledge into more general managers and created two fundamental skill requirements within each business unit:

1. The need for a larger pool of mobile, internationally-orientated managers within each sector specialism or product group.
2. A new emphasis on cross functional experience for those who ran the business. Sales experience was no longer paramount. Each business unit also had to draw upon production, research and other disciplines.

The international resourcing priorities therefore required a move from a technological to a general management and a national market to international product group focus.

The role of personnel: managing career tensions within the internationalization process

Shortly afterwards the support functions, including personnel, were decentralized. Within each national holding company, the corporate centre was made responsible for human resource strategy, policy and control. Pay policy, performance management, pensions, manpower planning and management development all became central matters managed by monthly meetings and supported by a corporate database. Each business unit also has its own personnel manager who sits on the boards of the respective companies as well as reporting to corporate personnel management. Moving to such a decentralized (on a product basis) structure, whilst bringing market benefits, also entails short-term pressures and obstacles that work counter to an internationalization process. It relieves the pressure on the corporate centre to manage effectively a cadre of 2000 international managers but places greater responsibility on line managers to maintain their knowledge and awareness of international managers and take responsibility for their transfer. In the short term, however, the net result (in Hoechst, and in many other organizations) was to reinforce a vertical or tunnelled view of career development needs. Business unit managers felt obliged to keep their hands on people they had invested in and continue to grow managers within single functions. The Hoechst system is based on 'pushing' an international cadre of managers into a corporate centre. To accelerate the process and move to a 'pulling' or demand strategy from within the decentralized business units, Hoechst Group has not only to manage career processes but also tackle obstacles such as entrenched attitudes, perceived loss of functional power, and greater need for international outlook.

The next stages therefore will be to reinforce the corporate-wide management of a central pool of international management talent with internal resourcing initiatives aimed at identifying and reinforcing those skills and competencies associated with effective international management. Such initiatives will probably draw upon the local strengths of each national personnel operation, but be managed within the decentralized product-based business units. The challenge is to examine the tremendous amount of human resources and to find those equipped for an international career. This requires looking at managers in new ways.

Capitalizing on national differences in personnel practice

Knowledge of HRM techniques is shared across the European personnel teams through two-monthly meetings focused on pan-European issues such as works councils, trade union positions, employment law changes, and international job rotations. These meetings act as bipartite exchanges of experience and expertise. For example, Hoechst UK is the largest German employer in the UK. Several years ago the UK personnel function instituted a competency-based personnel system based on 39 'job attributes' applied to various jobs (the nature of competencies is defined later in this chapter). These criteria, however, did not help identify those with international potential. The UK personnel function then built on its own work with Assessment and Development Centres, and identified a series of attributes (such as adaptability, coping with culture change, emotional stability) that enabled its managers to survive and make the most of foreign assignments in the more regimented and structured national culture of Germany. A psychometric battery was used to identify a small number of young managers suitably equipped for an international career who would otherwise be overlooked by the centrally managed career management system. These managers have been nominated for the centrally managed top management career pool.

Each national personnel function can, then, choose how best to develop its managers to reach the top centrally managed pool of international managers, and can also decide which competencies are most appropriate. The race between national European personnel systems, in the context of the German tiered approach to management development, is now on as each unit tries to get as many of its own managers nominated for the central pool.

THE NATURE OF MANAGEMENT COMPETENCIES

What should ETD systems be developing in managers?

In the previous section we saw how Hoechst UK began to develop a competency-based HRM system, whilst the German HQ learned and transferred knowledge of core techniques across its operations. In the sixth section of this chapter we develop an understanding of the underlying nature of management competencies and outline the general trends in thought about the nature of management effectiveness at the organizational level and their impact on ETD strategies across Europe. Organizations tend to categorize the deficiencies in their ETD systems by identifying the knowledge, skills and attitudes required for effective performance.

In the previous chapter we pointed out that the whole question of management effectiveness is being questioned. Many traditional selection and assessment techniques appear not to be able to predict final job or organizational performance. The ultimate objective of any organization is to link its ETD system to the creation of a series of desired behaviours that are causally linked to improved performance (Cascio, 1982). Whether these behaviours should reflect the individual dimension or that of collectives depends on national cultural characteristics. Despite a range of methodologies being available to practitioners to examine these deficiencies, practitioners have recently focused on identifying the most desirable managerial 'outputs' (couched in terms of what an individual achieves and produces from a situation by managing it effectively).

The 1980s saw the development of the idea of 'management competencies' (Boam and Sparrow, 1992). The language of 'competency' in the singular, and 'competences' or 'competencies' in the plural has become one of the 'big ideas' in HRM, on a par with management by objectives (MBO), total quality management (TQM) and empowerment. A number of organizations have focused significant parts of their HRM systems around sets of 'competencies' for managers (Boam and Sparrow, 1992; Dale and Iles, 1992; Fletcher, 1992; Iles, 1992; Salaman, 1991, and Spencer and Spencer, 1993). They have attempted to define the behaviour of employees in the context of a broad view of management effectiveness, and have then used this definition of effective performance to choose the right people to join, appraise and manage their performance, assess their career readiness or potential and diagnose appropriate training and development.

What is involved in identifying competencies?

Competency-based approaches are related to a clear set of performance criteria and are directed at identifying the outputs associated with achieving these criteria. The validity of the approach lies in its use of 'criterion samples', i.e. people who have clearly had success in their jobs. It also lies in the identification only of those behaviours that are causally related to a successful outcome (Spencer and Spencer, 1993). The behavioural competencies that are identified are specific to each organization. An example of the approach in British Airways is provided in Illustration 10.10. Identification of behavioural competencies relies on one or more of a range of job analysis techniques (such as repertory grids, critical incidents, structured skills questionnaires, observations, diaries, and behavioural event interviews) used to gather data from either a neutral stance (tapping the employee's constructs of 'effective' performance without specifying what sort of criteria the organization believes are most appropriate) or a

Illustration 10.10 **Management competencies at British Airways.**

British Airways uses a set of management competencies to assess management potential and determine ETD needs. Competencies have been identified for specific positions within the organization, as well as a set of corporate-wide competencies to set standards at various levels of management. At senior management level it took a group of 24 of the most senior and successful managers who showed the desired performance characteristics and developed a set of competencies based on an analysis of their behaviours. Seven primary competencies were identified: vision; direction; business orientation; results orientation; managing interpersonal relations; resources management; and sensitivity to the complex interdependencies of a large organization. Each competency is defined through a descriptive statement, and is further elaborated by outlines of the essential behaviours that evidence the competency. The seven competencies embrace a total of 64 desired behaviours in order to illustrate the complexities of performance and ETD needs in high-level management jobs.

Source: Sadler and Milmer (1993).

values-driven stance (specifying performance criteria that the organizational culture or strategy suggest are most appropriate). These outputs may be expressed in terms of desired performance outcomes (Torrington and Hall, 1991; Torrington, 1994) and are typically operationalized as a series of overt, observable and measurable behaviours, evidenced by positive and negative indicators (Sparrow and Bognanno, 1993).

What distinguishes competency-based approaches from other methods of identifying ETD needs is that rather than use some predetermined framework of management skills or effectiveness (which may or may not transfer from one culture to another) the approach makes no assumptions as to what characteristics are required to perform effectively. It focuses only on those behaviours associated against some defined criterion of effectiveness or performance using open-ended techniques. All these

Illustration 10.11 **The various components that constitute a competency.**

A behavioural competency is 'an underlying characteristic of a person which results in effective and/or superior performance in a job' (Boyatzis, 1982). However, behaviour without intent is not a source of competency. Competencies are therefore comprised of a series of elements:

Body of knowledge What the employee needs to know in order to achieve the goals the job specifies. Information in specific content areas.

Skills What the employee has to possess in order to do the job. The ability to perform a physical or mental task and demonstrate a sequence of behaviour that is functionally related to a performance goal and can be applied to a range of situations.

Attitudes, values and self-image What the employee needs to display in connection with achieving the tasks. Attitudes that predict behaviour in the short or long term.

Traits Characteristics or qualities of a person that are associated with effectiveness. Physical characteristics and consistent responses to situations or information.

Motive A drive or thought that is related to a particular goal. The things a person consistently thinks about or wants that cause a desired action or goal.

Self-image The understanding individuals have of themselves in the context of values held by others.

Social role The perception of social norms and behaviours that are acceptable and the behaviours that a person needs to adopt in order to fit in.

Source: Torrington and Hall (1991); Boyatzis (1982); Spencer and Spencer (1993).

behaviours are identified, and only then are clustered and interpreted into underlying dimensions of 'competency'. However, competencies have to include a 'causal intent' that generates action towards the desired outcome (see Illustration 10.11). A characteristic is not a competency unless it predicts something meaningful in the real world (Spencer and Spencer, 1993).

Are there different types of competencies?

Couched in terms of behaviours – what people actually do as opposed to what they say they do – competencies have proved an attractive way of linking effective performance to the strategic direction of the organization, whilst maintaining sensitivity to the sharp end of operational practice. In his pioneering work, Boyatzis (1982; 1991) studied 2,000 managers holding 41 different jobs in twelve (mainly Anglo-Saxon) organizations. He recognized that using a *post hoc* labelling process meant that competencies drew upon a variety of individual attributes such as personality traits, skills and abilities (see Illustration 10.11). He distinguished between 'threshold' management competencies which usually means the minimally acceptable level of work (see Illustration 10.12) and 'superior' management competencies, defined as the level achieved by one person out of ten (see Illustration 10.13).

Should competencies be trained or selected for?

Considering the various competencies shown in Illustrations 10.12 and 10.13, it is clear that some may be measured, some may be developed, some may be modified, whilst some have to be selected. Competency frameworks, such as that developed by Boyatzis (1982), are really best treated as templates against which whole teams should be assessed and resourced. Individuals are unlikely to have strengths against more than three or four competencies and so they serve more as a guideline for coaching, training and development. Illustration 10.14 shows the different types of behavioural competency. The surface knowledge and skill competencies are the easiest to develop, with ETD activities being the most cost effective way to improve employee abilities.

Illustration 10.12 **Seven threshold competencies.**

Threshold competencies are those which are 'essential to performing a job, but not causally related to superior job performance' (Boyatzis, 1982).

- *Use of unilateral power*: using forms of influence to obtain compliance.
- *Accurate self-assessment*: having a realistic or grounded view of oneself, seeing personal strengths and weaknesses and knowing one's limitations.
- *Positive regard*: having a basic belief in others; that people are good; being optimistic and causing others to feel valued.

- *Spontaneity*: being able to express oneself freely or easily, sometimes making quick or snap decisions.
- *Logical thought*: placing events in causal sequence; being orderly and systematic.
- *Specialized knowledge*: having usable facts, theories, frameworks or models.
- *Developing others*: helping others to do their jobs, adopting the role of coach and using feedback skills in facilitating self-development of others.

Source: Torrington and Hall (1991).

Illustration 10.13   **Five clusters of superior competencies.**

Superior competencies are those which are causally linked to excellent performance. Boyatzis (1982) identified fifteen competencies, grouped into five clusters, for Anglo-Saxon organizations.

Goal and action management cluster

- *Concern with impact*: being concerned with symbols of power to have impact on others, concerned about status and reputation.
- *Diagnostic use of concepts*: identifying and recognizing patterns from an assortment of information, by bringing a concept to the situation and attempting to interpret events through that concept.
- *Efficiency orientation*: being concerned to do something better.
- *Proactivity*: being of a disposition toward taking action to achieve something.

Leadership cluster

- *Conceptualization*: developing a concept that describes a pattern or structure perceived in a set of facts: the concept emerges from the information.
- *Self-confidence*: having decisiveness or presence; knowing what you are doing and feeling you are doing it well.
- *Use of oral presentations*: making effective

verbal presentations in situations ranging from one-to-one to several hundred people.

- *Logical thought*: (see threshold competencies).

Human resource management cluster

- *Use of socialized power*: using forms of influence to build alliances, networks, coalitions and teams.
- *Managing group process*: stimulating others to work effectively in group settings.
- *Accurate self-assessment*: (see threshold competencies).
- *Positive regard*: (see threshold competencies).

Focus on others cluster

- *Perceptual objectivity*: being able to be relatively objective, avoiding bias or prejudice.
- *Self-control*: being able to inhibit personal needs or desires in service of organizational needs.
- *Stamina and adaptability*: being able to sustain long hours of work and have the flexibility and orientation to adapt to changes in life and the organizational environment.

Directing subordinates cluster

- Threshold competencies of developing others, spontaneity and use of unilateral power.

Source: Torrington and Hall (1991).

The core motive and trait competencies, at the base of personality, are more difficult to assess and develop. Organizations find it most cost effective to select for these characteristics (Spencer and Spencer, 1993). The type or level of competencies identified therefore has significant implications for HRM managers.

On this analysis it becomes apparent that many European organiations tend only to select, train and develop the 'surface' competencies. The Anglo-Saxon preference for MBA and generalist managers, the French focus on qualities of *réception*, *la rigueur* and *l'esprit de synthèse* and the Germanic attention to technical bodies of knowledge are all surface-level, and therefore more developable, qualities. These should form the basis of ETD systems, whilst selection systems should focus on some of the deeper qualities that cannot really be developed and should therefore be selected for.

Do competencies transfer across cultures?

By considering the nature of effective management at the level of underlying individual characteristics, in the context of social roles, and expressed in terms of behaviours, competency-based approaches have the potential of being sensitive to the different national cultural notions of what makes an effective manager as discussed at the

Illustration 10.14   **Different levels of competency.**

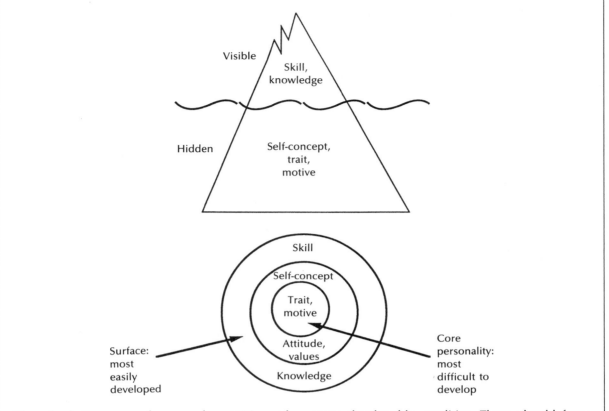

The Anglo-Saxon preference for MBA and generalist managers, the French focus on qualities of 'réception', 'la rigueur' and 'l'esprit de synthèse' and the Germanic attention to technical bodies of knowledge are all surface-level, and therefore more developable, qualities. These should form the basis of ETD systems, whilst selection systems should focus on some of the deeper qualities that cannot really be developed and should therefore be selected for.

Source: reproduced from *Competence at Work: Models for superior performance*, by L.M. Spencer and S.M. Spencer, copyright © 1993. Reprinted by permission of John Wiley and Sons, Inc.

beginning of this chapter. The competencies shown do not just reflect the nature of the management task based on Anglo-Saxon notions (Jackson, 1993). The McBer consultancy group re-analysed the data for more than 286 jobs for which competency models were available. The sample included 187 US studies and 98 studies from twenty other countries, covering a wide range of jobs. Approximately 760 separate 'behavioural indicators' were identified. Of these, 360 indicators defining 21 competencies accounted for 80–98 per cent of behaviours reported in each model. The competencies associated with superior performance were found to be the same all over the world. For example, the characteristics associated with entrepreneurs were the same in Latin America, Africa and South Asia (Spencer and Spencer, 1993). The tools and techniques used in the competency approach, as well as the distinctions between threshold and superior competencies made by Boyatzis (1982), are all valid in the European context, despite the different notions about what makes an effective manager. Only the resultant competencies would differ across nations. However, because management competencies vary from one organization to another anyway, they are usually never generalized across organizations, let alone nations. The approach, whilst initially popular mainly in Anglo-Saxon organizations, is being transferred into other countries in the Asia/Pacific region (Armstrong, 1991; Glass, 1990; Macleod and Wyndham, 1991, and Murdoch, 1992), Scandinavia (Hansson, 1988) and Contintental Europe (Hooghiemstra, 1990). We consider the issues of generalizing competencies across Europe by examining the approach taken by BP later in the chapter.

THE SKILLS AND COMPETENCIES OF THE EURO-MANAGER

In this last section of the chapter we consider the nature of competencies for the Euro-manager and the competencies that are helping organizations deal with the future. We now return to the question of whether to make managers more European, or whether to make European managers. What are the competencies associated with effective management in Europe? Are they any different to the ones identified by Boyatzis (1982)? European management may be understood as a set of competencies which are developed in response to the specific challenge of managing organizations in Europe. Whilst it is too soon to prescribe the art of European management, the main characteristics of a distinctive approach already seem apparent. The skills or competency approach to European management argues that it should not be divorced from national management styles. Some HRM specialists argue that good European managers are first and foremost good national managers who have an additional set of skills or competencies which characterize the individual and organizational response to change (Shenton, 1992). Others would argue that the competencies required to work effectively in a range of European countries and to work in countries outside Europe are broadly the same (Storey, 1992b). The Euro-manager may not be any different to the international manager. Another view is that by focusing on competencies, organizations may not gain a sufficient understanding of the requirements for managing across cultures (Davison, *op. cit.* Jackson, 1993). For example, the ability to deal with frustrations, isolation, failure; learning how to network, gain support and anticipate differences may be overlooked by competency profiles. Other qualities, such as the ability to fly a helicopter, take an overview, or intuition and cultural sensitivity, are difficult to express in behavioural terms, to teach or to acquire.

A review of the literature suggests that the main additional skills may be those included in Illustration 10.15. They represent a composite of recent research. In addition to the obvious qualities that create a willingness to be geographically mobile, to assume responsibility, to handle different time zones, to possess stamina for foreign travel, a set of deeper skills are needed. Whilst considering the 'add-on' skills and competencies in Illustration 10.15, a related set of important competencies for ETD systems to develop are discussed in the next chapter when we consider the characteristics associated with effective performance on international assignments. Project management skills are also likely to have a bearing.

Some writers take a more fundamental view. Jackson (1990, 1993), based at the European School of Management, argues that the lessons of new technology, globalization and deregulation in the 1980s showed that rigid organizational structures and procedures and an emphasis on training for predefined technical and administrative skills were not applicable to the new HRM imperatives faced by European organizations. Flexibility demands education of European managers, not just training, as well as a broad set of competencies to manage change. John Stopford

Illustration 10.15　**Additional skills and competencies needed for effective Euro-managers.**

- Technical skills to deal with expansion of European laws and regulations, international finance, marketing and strategic awareness.
- Gathering and handling of information from new sources and outside immediate business concerns.
- Dealing with nationals from other European countries through new customer–supplier relationships, strategy alliances, mergers and project assignments and having the ability to understand the basis on which they behave.
- Communication and interpersonal relationship skills to get ideas across to people from other cultures and ensure their understanding.

- Cross-cultural sensitivity to understanding the debating rules, negotiation, conventions, argument, non-verbal communication, humour, and awareness of own culture.
- Ability to work in international teams.
- Strategic awareness.
- Management of change skills and adaptability to new situations.
- High task orientation and self-reliance.
- Linguistic abilities and skills in at least two European languages, possibly with English as a core.

of London Business School and Philippe Naert of INSEAD also believe that the process of European business integration throughout the 1990s will result in profound changes in the skills and competencies required by senior managers (*op. cit.* Syrett and Gratton, 1989). There are very few managers who will not be confronted with the challenge to enlarge their skill-base and redefine their activity in order to manage in a European context. Their knowledge-base will need to include a detailed understanding of the many markets in which their organization operates, as well as the systems and procedures used by their competitors. They will have to have a sensitivity to different cultures, and a personal knowledge of key contacts and managers in different countries. Perhaps most importantly, they will need to be able to keep their options open and to encourage diversity where appropriate.

ORGANIZATION STRATEGY AND DIFFERENT APPROACHES TO THE EURO-MANAGER

So is there such a thing as the Euro-manager? Can a single specification be drawn up? In considering the skills and competencies for the Euro-manager, we must acknowledge that we are not talking about some single entity around which European organizations should base their ETD systems. Recent discussion of the topic suggests that, in practice, different specifications will be needed depending on four main factors:

1. The organizational strategy in relation to the SEM, the role of foreign direct investment and the potential for the sharing of resources (including managers).
2. The degree of pressure down the supply chain to match the Europeanization process of suppliers and customers.
3. Variable cultural attitudes and preference for either making European managers, or making managers more European, linked to the existing level of internalization within the organization.
4. The specific international role played by the manager.

Bournois and Chauchat (1990) conducted structured interviews with forty large European organizations across industrial sectors located in Milan, London, Madrid, Paris, Barcelona and Frankfurt. They interviewed chairmen, managing directors and

Table 10.9 **Four frameworks for the Euro-manager in large European organizations.**

Contextual variables	Global multinationals	Europe first	Repositioning for Europe	Supranationals
Organizations	BMW Saint Gobain Branche Vitrage Sanofl Bayer AG Pechiney BAT Industries	Midland Bank Commercial Union Beecham Products Merlin Gerin Rhône-Poulenc Agro Chimie CGE Air France Lagarge Coppee Rhône-Merieux Total LVMH Philips	Casino SAE Thomson BSN SAP Credit Agricole Dumez Henkel Glaxo Holdings	Crédit Lyonnais France Renault Crédit Lyonnais Italie Lufthansa
Strategy towards SEM	Improve European ranking within business sector, but Europe may be only part of operations	Distinctive European strategy within a global approach Successful adaptation to European focus	Powerful organizations but a focused strategy on Europe represents a new phenomenon	Strong national position, but intent to excel in Europe due to feelings of vulnerability or deregulation
Main concerns	Little concern with behaviour of competitors and attempts to manipulate uncertainties which threaten others	Little concern with behaviour of competitors	Concerned with the behaviour of competitors	Concerned with the behaviour of competitors
Function with greatest influence on strategy	Human resources	Production marketing and sales	Production and human resources	Marketing and sales
Concept of the Euro-manager	Euro-manager has special aptitude to work in European context	Euro-manager has special aptitude to work in European context	Meaningless concept. Managers limited to strong national perspective or already global in outlook	Euro-manager has special aptitude to work in a European context

Recruit managers on a European basis?	100%	92%	60%	25%
Recruit young graduates as Euro-managers?	17%	75%	40%	50%
Management of Euro-managers is centralized?	33%	17%	40%	75%
Careers of managers co-ordinated at a European level?	83%	33%	30%	50%
Pay systems cause problems for Euro-managers?	0%	33%	0%	0%
No particular problems for Euro-managers?	83%	17%	40%	0%
Openness to other cultures is a key characteristic of the Euro-manager?	50%	67%	10%	100%
Are the managers attuned to Europe?	100%	92%	10%	100%

Source: reprinted from *European Management Journal*, **8(1)**, 3–18, F. Bournois and J.-H. Chauchat, 'Managing managers in Europe', © 1990, with kind permission from Pergamon Press Ltd, Headington Hill Hall, Oxford, OX3 0BW, UK.

HRM directors in order to establish their approach to the concept of Euro-managers. The methodology for grouping the organizations was similar to that outlined in Chapter Two in the study of national patterns of HRM. Organizations were clustered according to their answers on eighteen questions about their approach to Euro-managers (see Table 10.9). The analysis revealed four different approaches to the Euro-manager, determined more by the organizational strategy than any pattern of national ownership or culture. The four approaches were labelled:

1. Global multinationals.
2. Europe first.
3. Repositioning for Europe.
4. Supranationals.

Nearly all the organizations agreed on their objective to recruit new managers on the basis of their European calibre, to organize greater numbers of transfers at management level and to make Europe-wide experience the basis of future rapid career advancement. However, if the objective of creating European managers is clear, the means to be used to attain this objective are more variable. The recruitment and management of the Euro-manager was not the same across the board, with there being 'no one best way' to solve the problems (Bournois and Chauchat, 1990).

The approach taken to the ETD issues raised were governed by organizational strategy towards the SEM. The 'global multinational' organizations (such as BMW, Bayer, Pechiney and BAT Industries) were the strongest at recruiting managers on a European basis and co-ordinating careers at this level. They studiously avoided relying on young graduates as Euro-managers, tended to adopt a decentralized approach to their management and clearly felt they had no particular problems in managing their Euro-Managers.

A second group of organizations (such as Midland Bank, Commercial Union, Rhône-Poulenc, Air France, Total and Philips) adopted a 'Europe first' strategy and a distinctive approach to the management of their Euro-managers. They were quite keen on recruiting managers on a European basis, but relied very strongly on a cadre of young graduates. They were quite poor at co-ordinating the management of careers on a European basis and so adopted a very decentralized (localized) approach. This created a significant number of problems in managing Euro-managers, particularly in terms of pay systems.

For a third group of organizations (such as Thomson, BSN, Henkel and Glaxo Holdings) who were repositioning themselves for Europe, the concept of the Euro-manager was quite meaningless. Whilst a small majority recruited managers on a European basis, and a minority relied on young graduates, they were the poorest at co-ordinating careers on a European basis and were the least likely to see openness to other cultures as a key characteristic of the Euro-manager.

Finally, a fourth group of organizations (such as Crédit Lyonnais, Renault and Lufthansa) were characterized as 'supranationals'. They had an intention to excel in Europe because of concerns over their market vulnerability or deregulation, but really approached the Euro-manager from a strong national position. They were the least likely to recruit managers on a European basis, but for those Euro-managers that were recruited, they adopted a centralized approach to their career management. They experienced the greatest number of problems with Euro-managers and were therefore the strongest group in support of the idea that openness to other cultures was a key characteristic of the Euro-manager. It should be noted that this four-fold categorization could not be applied to eight of the forty organizations studied (including Daimler-Benz, Petrofina, Assurance Generale de Belgique, ICI and Olivetti) who presumably adopted a mix of all the strategies or fell somewhere in between the four archetypal strategies.

When the four strategies were considered in detail, the diversity of practices adopted was quite large (Bournois and Chauchat, 1990). There were, however, two clear philosophical stances taken towards the development of Euro-managers:

1. A technical management stance focusing on issues related to the efficiency of the HRM system – such as pay structure techniques, manpower planning, rules for expatriation – when managing the Euro-manager.
2. A motivational management stance focusing on the attributes and behaviour of the management hierarchy, reflecting the value stance on the importance of participative management and the attention to the career objectives of the Euro-manager.

The multinationals, reflecting their higher levels of internationalization, were more concerned with the technical aspects of managing the Euro-manager. However, most CEOs and HRM Directors who were concerned with the motivational aspects of Euro-managers were firmly of the view that the development of mobility and career paths across Europe could not be facilitated through the development of rigid, centralized HRM techniques. We consider the career management dimension to the process of internationalization in the next chapter.

Another determinant of the specification for the Euro-manager is linked to the customers and suppliers. Coulson-Thomas (1992) points out that the need for international skills has to be seen in the context of the value chain and customer needs and preferences. Whilst in some cases customer behaviour may constrain the need for new skills and competencies, in many cases it may also drive it. For example, when ASEA of Sweden merged with Brown Boveri of Switzerland to form ABB, Digital Equipment quickly merged its account teams for the two organizations and responded with an assessment of their new requirements. Bournois and Chauchat (1990) sum up the situation when there is little pressure down the supply chain to Europeanize management as follows:

. . . For a few companies the notion of the 'Euro-manager' has no meaning; for others, it is sheer nonsense. In fact there are some top executives who feel that a national manager will be much more competent in his own country than an expatriate; this attitude will continue to exist even after the Single Market Act has completely taken effect. . . even though your strategy is European, your customers' attitudes may still be very regionally entrenched.

Bournois and Chauchat (1990, p. 9).

Illustration 10.16 **Different roles and different specifications for the Euro-manager?**

- *Home-based manager*: who has a central focus on international markets and players.
- *Multicultural team member*: who works on a series of international projects.
- *Internationally mobile manager*: who undertakes frequent but short visits to numerous overseas locations, but remains loyal to the parent organizational culture.
- *Traditional expatriate*: who carries the parent organizational culture but spends lengthy assignments in a limited number of host countries representing the parent organization.
- *Transnational manager*: who moves across borders on behalf of the organization and is relatively detached from any single organization HQ.
- *Specialist non-management roles*: which involve international activity, e.g. sales staff, trainers, buyers and technical experts.

Source: Storey (1992b) based on a categorization by David Buchanen.

Finally, the ETD needs of the organization will depend on the different roles to be played by Euro-managers. The different roles, each of which may require a subtly different blend of competencies, are shown in Illustration 10.16.

FUTURE MANAGEMENT COMPETENCIES

As we have argued throughout this book, the nature of management competencies is changing. In the previous section we have analysed the need for more European managers or management and its impact on the competencies that will form the basis of ETD systems in European organizations. In this last part to the chapter, we consider another more generic pressure for change – the future competencies related to general developments in the shape and role of organizations. Since the original work of Boyatzis (1982), there has been a shift in thinking about the nature of 'competency', particularly as the relationship between organizations and their managers has evolved (Sparrow, 1994a). In an empirical study of strategic change in eight UK organizations, Whipp (1991) found that their ability to compete rested on:

- Their capacity to comprehend the competitive forces at play and how these had changed over time.
- The ability of the organization to mobilize and manage the resources necessary for the chosen response.

In the future, HRM will be linked to the process of competition through the issue of learning. Many writers see the ability to learn faster than competitors as the only sustainable advantage: '. . . the ability of the organization to reconstruct and adapt its knowledge-base (made up of skills, structures and values) should be a key task for managers' (Whipp, 1991). As product life cycles (and the technical skills associated with them) shorten, the management skill development life cycles become relatively longer. Therefore actively managing the skill-base of the organization will become a mainstay of competitive strategy (Klein *et al.*, 1991). The strategic HRM literature now points to the need to educate, mobilize and then integrate managers into the strategic change process. In the past, managerial competency was equated with the possession of specific skills and abilities. In the future it will rest in '. . . the development of attitudes, values and "mindsets" that allow managers to confront, understand and deal with a wide range of forces within and outside their organizations' (Morgan, 1989).

Identifying the competencies needed for the 1990s is an educational and values-driven process, rather than one based solely on traditional job analysis techniques. Why is this the case? An increasing number of HRM thinkers argue that organizations can no longer continue to 'drive through the rear-view mirror', analysing what they and other excellent organizations have done in the past to be successful (or indeed what their national assumptions of effective management have traditionally been). In practice, as a consequence of the methodologies employed, the competencies identified by many organizations are orientated towards the skills that allow them to continue doing what they already do (Pedler, Burgoyne and Boydell, 1991; Boam and Sparrow, 1992). Such backwards looking analysis can be dangerous. If existing competencies are used as part of an ETD strategy, they may only serve to reinforce and cement the current or historical ways of doing things into the organization, dragging the cloak of the old business into the new. A more pro-active, future-orientated approach, intended to anticipate likely strategic changes and the position of the organization and its members to address these challenges, is required. Unfortunately, the paradox faced by

European organizations is that their need to understand new competencies comes at a time when their job holders' knowledge of the competency is probably at its lowest.

... The stream of mergers, acquisitions and 'grand alliances' [in the 1980s] ... has left many organizations as little more than a variety of sub-businesses with different and often conflicting management needs. The combination of rapidly changing markets, new technologies and shorter business time cycles has meant that these needs are often difficult to predict in advance. That leaves future executive jobs with parameters and demands that are unknown. Yet most traditional succession strategies have been based on the assumption that executive roles are relatively stable and predictable over time, and grounded in a development programme that may take 15 years to complete.   Syrett and Gratton (1989, p. 33).

Syrett and Gratton (1989) argue that to cope with this issue, European organizations are trying to move beyond internationalization. An examination of some competency models in use by leading Anglo-Saxon organizations reveals a series of assumptions about the most appropriate performance criteria for management competencies in the 1990s. These break down many of the traditional assumptions about management development that permeated thinking in Anglo-Saxon organizations until the late 1980s. The same messages are being considered by European organizations. Two main routes have emerged:

1. Accepting that the future organization is unlikely to have a single, identifiable, strategy, but will be made up of sub-businesses each requiring its own set of management competencies.
2. Designing ETD programmes so that they produce senior managers who are flexible, adaptable and able to work in situations of continual change.

Linking management competencies to the life cycle of the organization

The Prudential Group, a UK insurance organization, identified its general business position in order to indicate the core skills and competencies needed by its senior managers. It then identified future business paths for each of its subsidiaries, which signalled the requirement for five separate sets of skills. For example, a senior manager with entrepreneurial skills works best in a start-up venture, which requires a different set of competencies than those required to manage a more established business that has to maximize its profits (Syrett and Gratton, 1989). Senior managers were developed through training and career management interventions so that they were able to work in two or three of the business scenarios. A similar approach was taken by a British utility organization that was in the process of privatization and understood that the various businesses within the organization were at different levels of maturity and would need managers with different competencies if they were to be managed effectively (Boam and Sparrow, 1992). The managerial characteristics (as opposed to the underlying competencies) that are associated with success in different business scenarios linked to the life cycle of the organization are shown in Table 10.10.

The message that managers need to change their style in relation to the business life cycle perhaps also has some relevance to the smaller European organizations that are in the process of internationalizing (Lindell, 1991). In a study with 502 observations of managers from four Finnish manufacturing and five service organizations, three management styles were identified: change-orientated, development-orientated and task-orientated. Managers were evaluated by their subordinates, with managers using the development- and change-orientated styles given better ratings for their ability to

Table 10.10 **The managerial characteristics associated with business life cycle scenarios.**

	Start up	Turnaround	Dynamic growth	Extracting profit	Redeploying efforts
Scenario demands	■ High financial risk ■ Limited management team cohesiveness ■ Few organization systems or procedures in place ■ Little operational experience ■ Endless workload: multiple priorities ■ Generally insufficient resources to satisfy all demands ■ Limited relationship with suppliers, customers and environment	■ Time pressure for results ■ Need for rapid situational assessment and decision making ■ Limited resource; skills shortages; some incompetent personnel ■ Re-evaluation of business position ■ Inappropriate reporting channels ■ Re-orientation of organization mission; cost/profit	■ High financial risk ■ New markets, products, technology ■ Multiple demands and conflicting priorities ■ Rapidly expanding organization in certain sectors ■ Inadequate managerial/technical/financial resources ■ Unequal growth across sectors of the organization ■ Likely shifting power bases ■ Constant dilemma between doing current work and building support systems for the future	■ 'Controlled' financial risk ■ Unattractive industry long term ■ Need to invest selectively ■ Internal organizational stability ■ Moderate to high/managerial technical competence ■ Adequate systems and administrative infrastructure ■ Acceptable to excellent relationships with suppliers, customers and environment	■ Moderate short-term risk ■ Unknown long-term risk ■ Resistance to change ■ Bureaucracy in some sections ■ High mismatch between some organization skill sets ■ Highly operational orientation in executive team
Management characteristics	■ Vision of finished business ■ Hands on orientation ■ In-depth knowledge in critical technical areas ■ Organizing ability ■ Staffing skills ■ Team building capabilities ■ High-energy level/stamina ■ Personal magnetism/charisma ■ Broad knowledge of all key functions ■ Creating vision of business ■ Establishing core technical and marketing expertise ■ Building management team	■ 'Take charge' orientation ■ Strong leader ■ Strong analytical and diagnostic skills, especially financial ■ Excellent business strategist ■ High-energy level ■ Risk taker ■ Handles pressure well ■ Good crisis management skills ■ Good negotiator ■ Rapid accurate problem diagnosis ■ Fixing short-term and ultimately long-term problems	■ Excellent strategic and financial planning skills ■ Clear vision of the future ■ Ability to balance priorities ■ Organizational and team building skills ■ Good crisis management skills ■ Moderately high-risk taker ■ Excellent staffing skills ■ Increasing market share in key sectors ■ Managing rapid change ■ Ability to build toward clear vision of the future	■ Technically knowledgeable ■ Knows the business ■ Sensitive to changes ■ Ear to the ground ■ Anticipates problems ■ Strong administrative skills ■ Orientated to systems ■ Strong relationship orientation ■ Recognizes need for management succession ■ Stresses efficiency ■ Works towards stability ■ Senses signs of change	■ Good politician/master of change ■ Highly persuasive – high interpersonal influence ■ Moderate risk taker ■ Highly supportive, sensitive to people ■ Excellent 'system thinker' ■ Good organizing and executive staffing skills ■ Establishing effectiveness in managing change ■ Supporting the dispossessed

Source: reprinted from R. Boam and P. Sparrow, *Designing and Achieving Competency*, with permission of the publishers, McGraw-Hill Book Co. Europe, © 1992.

manage effectively in today's environment (Lindell and Rosenqvist, 1990). In balancing these styles, can the three styles be achieved in different stages of the business life cycle? Based on a case study of a small entrepreneurial organization that had 50 per cent of the world market for ski sticks and 30 per cent for windsurfing boards, Lindell (1991) found that development and change-orientated styles were found to dominate the early business growth (and internationalization) stages, with a control style only appropriate once the business had reached maturity. He linked the changes in patterns of managerial style to successful and unsuccessful patterns of transformation in CEO and top management behaviour.

Is this attention to matching management style (and competencies) to the business life cycle moving beyond the problem of internationalization, incorporating some of its business principles, or simply ignoring it? Do the managerial characteristics shown in Table 10.10 reflect the local national characteristics of management sufficiently well? Most certainly the approach reflects the contingency-based perspective to strategic HRM (see Chapter One) that has a strong history in Anglo-Saxon thinking. Nevertheless, as European organizations continue to restructure their operations through FDI and strategic alliances (see Chapter Five), rationalization (see Chapter Four), and pan-European changes to the organization structure based on local market characteristics (see Chapter Eight), then forging a closer link between the business life cycle of the various organizational units and the skills and competencies of the managers may become a more widely practiced option. Indeed, Ohmae (1990) has suggested five sequential stages of internationalization, moving from a home-based exporting organization through various stages of overseas production presence to a final stage where functions such as R&D, finance and engineering are transferred around the world as duplication becomes less of a concern than market share. Each stage of this organizational process of internationalization requires different types of international managers (Storey, 1992b) and a unique set of ETD needs. In the final stage of this development – transnational managers – have to be able to 'think globally and act locally' which necessitates the development of a new 'mental set' or 'management mentality' (Bartlett and Ghoshal, 1989). In this sense, the transnational organization is not just a specific strategic posture or organizational structure, but is a new management mentality and set of ETD needs, which acts as a form of 'corporate glue' that combats parochialism.

High performance competencies for an uncertain world

European organizations may take a second route towards future competencies – designing ETD programmes that produce flexible managers capable of adapting to continuous change. These organizations have tried to avoid the problem mentioned above of incorporating the old ways of thinking about the business by building in a learning element to their more future-orientated competencies (Sparrow, 1994b), either by:

- Recognizing aspects of learning (such as creativity, mental agility and balanced learning habits) as specific competencies to be trained and developed in managers.
- Recognizing future forecasting as a competency, and incorporating the behaviours and skills associated with reading the future (such as spotting major 'fracture lines' and discontinuities) into organization criteria for training and development.

Schroder (1989) derived a set of eleven high performance competencies based on complex experimental simulations of team performance and assessment centre experiences. They focus on the competencies involved in reacting to and capitalizing on change and have been applied to managers operating in dynamic, high change (unknown) turbulent environments in decentralized organizations, such as the National Westminster Bank. These competencies highlight the cognitive and interpersonal dimensions of adaptability (we discussed the need to recruit and select on this basis at the beginning of Chapter Nine). Information search, concept formation, conceptual flexibility, interpersonal search, managing interaction and personal impact have all been operationalized by National Westminster for assessment purposes at senior levels in the organization (see Illustration 10.17). Again, these competencies reflect Anglo-Saxon assumptions about team behaviour, but their emphasis on the cognitive and interpersonal requirements of coping with uncertainty would be considered valid for all European societies by occupational psychologists.

Competencies for flexibility and the implementation of change

A second approach has been to focus on those competencies that enable organizational

Illustration 10.17 **High performance management competencies at the National Westminster Bank.**

- *Information search (to make decisions)*: gathers many different kinds of information and uses a wide variety of sources to build a rich informational environment in preparation for decision making in the organization.
- *Concept formation (on basis of information)*: builds frameworks or models or forms concepts, hypotheses or ideas on the basis of information; becomes aware of patterns, trends and cause/effect relations by linking disparate information.
- *Conceptual flexibility (consideration of alternatives)*: identifies feasible alternatives or multiple options in focus simultaneously and evaluates their pros and cons.
- *Interpersonal search (understanding others' ideas and feelings)*: uses open and probing questions, summaries and paraphrasing to understand the ideas, concepts and feelings of another; can comprehend events, issues, problems, opportunities from the viewpoint of another person.
- *Managing interaction (team building)*: involves others and is able to build co-operative teams in which group members feel valued and empowered and have shared goals.
- *Developmental orientation (creating a developmental climate)*: creates a positive climate in which individuals increase the accuracy of their own awareness of their own strengths and limitations and provides coaching, training and developmental resources to improve performance.
- *Impact (to gain support for ideas and initiatives)*: uses a variety of methods (e.g. persuasive arguments, modelling behaviour, inventing symbols, forming alliances and appealing to the interest of others) to gain support for ideas, strategies and values.
- *Self-confidence (confidence for implementing own ideas)*: states own 'stand' or position on issues; unhesitatingly takes decisions when required and commits self and others accordingly; expresses confidence in the future success of the actions to be taken.
- *Presentation (communicating ideas)*: presents ideas clearly, with ease and interest so that the other person (or audience) understands what is being communicated; uses technical, symbolic, non-verbal and visual aids effectively.
- *Proactive orientation (implementation)*: structures the task for the team; implements plans and ideas; takes responsibility for all aspects of the situation.
- *Achievement orientation (ambitious yet attainable goals)*: possesses high internal work standards and sets ambitious yet attainable goals; wants to do things better, to improve, to be more effective and efficient; measures progress against targets.

Source: Cockerill (1989); Jackson (1993).

change to happen. For some organizations, the challenge is how best to create a central resourcing policy for devolved businesses that face very different strategic scenarios. In this situation, British Petroleum (BP) defined effective performance as the ability to implement change, no matter what that change might be. The competencies for change were driven, and labelled, according to a series of culture change dimensions and included behavioural indicators under the headings of open thinking, networking, empowering and personal impact. BP undertook a detailed study to ensure that it could convert these corporate competencies into a meaningful framework for its European subsidiaries.

ENSURING CROSS-CULTURAL VALIDITY OF COMPETENCIES: THE BRITISH PETROLEUM EXPERIENCE

BP are one of the few organizations to use a competency-based approach as part of a human resource strategy (Bognanno and Sparrow, 1994; Sparrow and Bognanno, 1993). Important lessons were learned about using a competency-based approach to implement corporate strategy, and the need to address the impact of diverse national cultures on the behaviours associated with effective management. By the late 1980s, BP faced ominous problems, after having diversified in the 1970s away from the core upstream and downstream oil activities and into minerals and coal production, consumer products and information systems. To manage such diversity, BP created a strong matrix organization (see Chapter Eight for a discussion of matrix structures and the organizational changes at BP) around a series of eleven business streams and seventy national associates. Rather than leading to the desired decentralization, the structure actually created enormous additional complexity (Mills and Friesen, 1992) at the same time that BP undertook a major acquisition programme and was privatized (we discussed the impact of acquisitions and privatization in Part Two of the book). An internal analysis of the organization by the incoming (and soon to be departed) Chairman, called 'Project 1990', revealed that BP had to:

- Reduce complexity throughout the organization.
- Redesign the central organization.
- Reposition the management style and culture.

In a period of intense activity, BP attempted fundamentally to change its structure, management processes and organizational culture. There was a gap between the Chairman's Vision and Value Statement (based on espoused values of openness, care, teamwork and empowerment) and actual practice (which required the reduction of management layers and costs). A series of culture change workshops allowed managers to express their concerns. They asked questions that many European managers will ask over the 1990s as their organizations are transformed:

- What exactly is the new culture?
- What does it look like?
- What do I do differently?
- Do we need a single corporate culture?

To answer these concerns BP created an organization-wide 'competency' framework. The process of decentralization and downsizing meant that implementation strategies would vary across business streams and countries. Therefore BP chose a generalizable performance criterion against which competencies were to be established: the ability to enable change to happen, whatever that change might prove to be. A competency model was developed by comparing BP to other multinationals on the consultants' database and creating a set of 'behavioural indicators' that reinforced the organizational culture. Sixty-seven 'essential behaviours' were identified in relation to the organizational culture dimensions involved in 'Project 1990', i.e. open thinking, personal impact, empowering and networking (OPEN). The model was communicated throughout the business and awareness of the new competencies grew amongst senior managers. The competencies were then devolved to the national businesses.

The 'OPEN' competencies (and the sixty-seven behaviours that evidenced them) had been designed to express BP's organizational culture, yet had to be adapted to suit a wide range of national cultures. The cross-cultural validity of the essential behaviours was challenged by non-British or non-American managers. They had been developed by a team of Anglo-Americans. Were they transferable to other countries? BP conducted its investigation by:

- Consulting experts in the field of cultural diversity.
- Using 'focus groups' of non-Anglo-Saxon employees to adapt the behaviours.

The expert reviews conducted by external academics and consultants sampled twelve countries. It was concluded that the competencies (i.e. the essential behaviours) were capable of cross-cultural implementation and represented a cogent statement of the shift required in management behaviour. However, the behavioural anchors used to describe specific competencies were in some instances unnecessarily directive and contained a 'culturally provocative bias'. The greatest challenge came from competencies contained in the Personal Impact (Bias for Action, Knows What Makes Others Tick, Concern for Impact and Self Confidence) and Empowerment (Coaching and Developing, Building Team Success and Motivating) clusters. The recommendation was that BP step back from the behavioural detail of the proposed OPEN competencies and encourage people in different countries to offer their own illustrations of how they might change behaviours and organizational culture.

The process demonstrated that the OPEN competencies were capable of crossing cultural barriers in their essential meaning and purpose (reinforcing their use as a 'corporate glue' to integrate human resource policies and practices) but also that their implementation and assessment would require greater effort in order to customize and translate the behavioural indicators to fit the culturally different groups involved. The feared barriers to cross-cultural implementation did not materialize.

The customization process, however, had to avoid any misinterpretation or fundamental change to the meaning of the competencies. BP ran a series of 'focus groups' in France and Germany, each with ten to twelve local employees who spoke English as a second language. The intended objective of the behaviours contained within each competency and the intended meaning behind the English words were presented in local language. The groups were facilitated by consultants operating in the area of cross-cultural management and fluent in English, French and German. The groups adjusted the behavioural indicators around each competency so that they were appropriate for their own national culture and organization. Local business trainers and facilitators were given instruction on how to present the OPEN competencies as part of change programmes being carried out in Europe and Asia-Pacific. Local trainers fashioned the training process used to introduce the competencies themselves. Finally, role plays were run as part of 'Awareness Building Workshops' in which managers who would be responsible for assessing the competencies enacted them out in role plays, during which further lessons were learned about the behavioural enactment of specific competencies across the national cultures. After this lengthy cross-cultural implementation process BP was confident that its OPEN competencies could be applied throughout the organization and across national operations.

STRATEGIC CAPABILITIES AND ORGANIZATIONAL-LEVEL MANAGEMENT COMPETENCIES

There is a thin line between intuitive deduction about future management competencies, and simple speculation. However, the logic for determining the nature of management effectiveness is shifting from national notions of the management role, to a business logic that analyses the management role in the context of organization capabilities. For example, Shell Canada has focused its HRM systems on a series of competencies at the organizational level which it feels facilitate the comprehension and management of complexity and uncertainty. The competencies identified included building bridges and alliances, reframing problems, scanning, forecasting, identifying fracture lines, visioning, empowering, skills of remote management, creativity, learning and innovation (Morgan, 1989).

The second source of discussion about 'competency' comes from the strategists (Barney, 1991; Fiol, 1991; Grant, 1991; Grønhaug and Nordhaug, 1992; Hamel and Prahalad, 1991; Klein, Edge and Kass, 1991; Mahoney and Panadian, 1992; Reed and DeFillippi, 1990 and Roos and von Krogh, 1992). Strategy has become difficult to formulate and plan in the 1990s because most organizations see themselves facing rapid discontinuous change and intense competition. Traditionally, strategists consider the organization's internal resources – the assets, capabilities, organizational processes, firm attributes, information and knowledge that enable it to conceive of, and then implement, its goals (Barney, 1991). In order to provide some fixed points to help deal with high levels of turbulence, strategists are translating the strategic capabilities of organizations into underlying competences (Grant, 1991) and as management skills have become organization-specific, then the concept of 'organization-level' skills and capabilities becomes a central source of differential and sustainable competitive advantage. As cost and quality advantages lose their potency Hamel and Prahalad (1991) stress the importance and exploitation of 'core competences' (viewed as static attributes which senior managers need to seek out in order to capitalize on opportunities). Whilst Hamel and Prahalad (1991) view organization level competences as distinctly technical, marketing or strategic capabilities, Grant (1991) builds on this view by examining what lies beneath such organization competences (such as the ability to innovate and the development of a learning organization). He sees organization competences and capabilities as a meshing together of organization resources such as the skills of individual people, leadership, and more tangible assets such as capital resources, brand reputation and patents held. Similarly, Klein, Edge and Kass (1991) view 'corporate skills' as strategic combinations of individual (human) competencies, hard organizational factors (such as equipment and facilities) and soft organizational factors (such as culture and organization design). The focus is shifting more towards the individual and soft organizational factors. The richer the connection between the capabilities and skills of the organization's human resources, the distinctive areas of high performance and technical know-how of the organization, and the dominant logic or mental models of the top management teams, then the more effective the strategy will be (Reed and DeFillippi, 1990; Sparrow, 1994b).

The strategists view management skills in the context of strategic key success factors – evidenced by both the organization's behaviour and the skills of the total pool of human resources. Although strategic competences are clearly distinguishable from the concept of behavioural competencies, there is a meeting of the minds between strategists, HRM practitioners and psychologists (see Table 10.11). The core competences considered in the strategic management literature impact management competencies in two ways:

1. There is a behavioural reflection of the specific technical and marketing capabilities they tend to describe.
2. There must be a set of conceptual abilities that are associated with the identification, modification and management of strategic competences.

Table 10.11 **Distinctions between individual behavioural competencies and strategic organization competences.**

Element of definition	What are behavioural competencies?	What are strategic organization competencies?
DESCRIBE...	Behavioural repertoires which people input to a job, role or organization context	Resources and capabilities of the organization linked with business performance
IDENTIFIED THROUGH...	Behavioural event investigation techniques	Market analysis methods Strategic and business planning evaluation
WHICH FOCUS ON...	Person centred analysis of jobs that reflect effectiveness	Internal resources (such as tangible technical or capital assets as well as strategic management skills)
AND INDICATE...	What people need to bring to a role to perform to the required level	What makes the organization more successful than others i.e. long-term and fixed sources of competitive advantage
PERFORMANCE CRITERION BASED ON...	Characteristics of superior (excellent) individual performance, i.e. more senior management levels	Superior records of innovation, learning, quality and other long-term business criteria
APPLIED TO...	Tailored excellent behaviours to integrate all areas of HRM, i.e. reinforce distinguishing characteristics	Marketing and product strategies, selection of best economic rent generating activities, underlying business processes
LEVEL OF ANALYSIS...	Job level, or across the management hierarchy	Organization level and underlying business process
OWNERSHIP...	Competency held by the individual and brought to the organization	Competence held by the organization and jointly developed by individuals
ASSESSMENT ONUS...	Identification of potential to ensure best internal resourcing decisions	Articulation of key success factors and unique proprietary know how
INDIVIDUAL MOTIVATION...	Internally rewardable achievement and recognition	Organizationally-sustainable employment and security

Source: Sparrow (1994a).

SHIFTING THE MANAGEMENT DEVELOPMENT FOCUS TO TOP TEAMS

In taking a more strategic view of ETD needs and the underlying management competencies, we must also consider the issue of team-based competencies, not just individual competencies. Kakabadse (1993) has examined the training and effectiveness of senior executives and questions the Anglo-Saxon predilection for individualism, i.e. focusing on the leader, the characteristics of successful leaders and their management styles. The prevalence of mergers and acquisitions, the emphasis on product quality, quality of service, customer care and responding to change have been commonplace in mid-to-large sized organizations. These pressures all suggest that the team who run the business have become the unit for management development, not the individual manager. They are the prime mechanism to consider and implement policies and strategies. One of the most important factors for management effectiveness is:

... the creation of a framework of values and beliefs that enable a team's members, collectively and individually, to accommodate and work well with contrasting philosophies, attitudes and cultures.
Syrett and Gratton (1989, p. 32).

Kakabadse (1993) consulted, interviewed and surveyed 1,100 top managers from 740 organizations covering sectors such as banking, high technology, consultancy, manufacturing and privatized utilities.

The Cranfield Executive Competencies Survey found that 52 per cent of UK chief executives felt uncomfortable about the effectiveness and performance of their top teams and 63 per cent recognized that substantial problems existed in these teams that were preventing their organizations from achieving their objectives (Kakabadse, 1991). Despite the cultural differences in the structure of corporate governance and management boards discussed in Chapter Eight, this was a pan-European problem (see Table 10.12), with difficulties about the quality of relationships in top teams most marked in Germany and Spain, but remarkably prevalent across Europe:

... the strategic concerns of top management in mid-to-large sized European corporate organizations are shared, irrespective of nationality. In effect, differences and acrimony are a natural part of the process of addressing difficult and complex issues... the challenge for top management is how to address sensitive issues, such as reconciling strategic options and negotiating to improve the quality of relationships and dialogue amongst members of the senior executive.
Kakabadse (in press, p. 2).

Table 10.12 **Development problems in European top management teams.**

Country	Proportion of the top team who feel that senior executives hold different views as to the future direction of the organization	Proportion of the top team who believe there are issues which should be discussed but which are too sensitive to be discussed by the top team
Germany	34%	80%
Spain	46%	66%
France	56%	39%
Austria	67%	31%
UK	51%	30%
Sweden	51%	20%

Source: Kakabadse (1993). Reproduced with permission of the publishers. MCB University Press, © 1993.

This creates a significant problem. Hilb (1992) points out that ETD is worthless unless there is a clear strategic organization vision. ETD can only affect the strategic implementation significantly when such clarity exists across the whole management team, based on consensus. However, although individual senior managers currently know the nature of the issues and problems facing their organization, most seem to have different views on the appropriate way forward to combat these challenges. When these insights are not utilized due to sensitivities that disrupt relationships and dialogue, organizations hit severe problems.

In order to develop the capability of the organization to manage difficult transitions, developing the competence to action the insights becomes critical. Kakabadse (1993) argues that this actioning *process* is common to all nationalities (the actual *behaviours* used to talk to each other, tease out sensitivities, avoid disruption, offer feedback and counsel may differ from country to country, but the requirements to work through the process are common). In addressing these difficulties, Kakabadse (1993) argues that we should not be seduced by the '. . . myth of national differences'. There is no one country or culture better adjusted or more naturally gifted in management than any other. Getting the best out of people through recognizing the circumstances of the organization and realistically addressing each situation with tact and maturity is a prerequisite for all European managers.

Some of the key top team capabilities are shown in Illustration 10.18. The survey suggested that on average, high calibre executives attain a senior management position by the age of 32 and the average age on appointment to the board was 39.4 years in the US and 41 years in the UK. As discussed in the previous chapter, there was a critical eight to nine year period of development before managers were considered suitable for top positions. Despite closeness between US and UK management development traditions, there were some notable differences between the two in the factors that they saw as being critical to career success. Table 10.13 shows the top six factors for managers from both countries.

We consider the phenomenon of the impact of national cultural differences on the careers of European managers in the next chapter. It appears that not only are there differences in the critical success factors that managers believe account for their career success, but there are also some marked differences in the competencies of top teams between countries, in part reflecting the impact of historical work styles, structures and national cultures on management development discussed earlier in the chapter. The Cranfield Executive Competencies survey found that only 41 per cent of top French managers were recognized as being sensitive to people, falling to only 26 per cent of top German managers. In both countries between 14 and 16 per cent of managers

Illustration 10.18 **Key top team capabilities.**

Shaping
- The future: vision.
- The team: team mechanics, shaping the people, styles of management.
- The business.

Influencing
- Spreading the message.

- Hearing what's said: openness, feedback, managing ambiguity.

Sustaining momentum
- Success culture; quality, damage limitation.

Source: Kakabadse (1991).

Table 10.13 **Critical career success factors for US and UK managers.**

Critical career success factors	US	UK
Need to achieve	1	3
Ability to work with a wide variety of people	2	1
Challenge	3	–
Willingness to take risks	4	–
Early overall responsibility/leadership experience early in career	5	4
Width of experience in many functions before the age of 35	6	5
Substantial responsibility for important tasks	–	2
Ability to do deals and negotiate	–	6

Source: reproduced from *The Wealth Creators* by A. Kakabadse. Reprinted with kind permission of the publishers, Kogan Page, © 1991.

practised a power-orientated style, but only 19 per cent of top French managers respected the rules and regulations of the organization, compared to 31 per cent of top German managers.

... the level of maturity and sophistication of behaviour required to invite and accept feedback, grow strong collegiate relationships in order to ensure quality of service to customers and not respond to the parochial concerns when pressure is on, has still not substituted the void of traditional functional management... effective interfacing is crucial to the process of adjusting to changing market circumstances. That lesson still has to be learnt across Europe.

Kakabadse (in press, p. 9).

CONCLUSIONS

In this chapter we have argued that ETD will form a central part of the HRM strategies taken by many European organizations. The very nature of ETD, with its focus on skills, knowledge, attitudes or social behaviours, implies transition. ETD centres around the efforts made by organizations to increase the ability of individuals and groups to perform, and the management of planned learning experiences that facilitate the acquisition of job or organization-related knowledge and skills. The success of European organizations will in large part be determined by their ability to train and develop their employees to meet the challenges of business integration and change. In meeting this challenge, there are a number of important learning points to consider:

LEARNING POINTS FROM CHAPTER TEN

1. The topic of employee training and development (ETD) is broad in its scope. It covers issues related to the training of managers and other vocational groups, improving the qualifications of the workforce, ensuring adequate employee mobility, reducing high levels of staff turnover, career planning and modifying a dominant organizational culture. It is best approached as part of a wider organizational strategy. ETD is one topic within the overall concept of employee resourcing.

2. In dealing with the topic of ETD, there are four underlying individual processes that are involved: education, training, development and learning. By integrating these four processes, ETD is the main way in which both individual and organizational growth can achieve its full potential.

3. The first step in establishing viable ETD activities is to identify whether training is really needed, and if so, what training. This training needs analysis establishes the most appropriate instructional objectives, the criteria that should be used to evaluate the effectiveness of ETD, the best learning environment, the development of training materials and the content of training. It is not always conducted by organizations, nor linked to strategic objectives. It covers three levels of analysis: organizational; jobs, role or career stream; and individual.

4. There has been a change in the focus of these ETD needs. Most organizations need to tolerate diversity in their methods. The challenges faced by ETD systems are to develop managers who can manage in a period of resource scarcity, to understand foreign cultures and national aspirations, to satisfy a wider range of stakeholders in the organization, cope with continuous levels of change and the increased vulnerability and exposure of their organizations to international business and political instability.

5. In addressing these challenges, ETD systems can make a central contribution to the effectiveness of HRM. They can improve stagnant productivity, speed up the incorporation of new technologies and adaptation to new competitors, inform long-term manpower planning, help develop more future orientated skills, substitute the need to recruit externally, modify management styles and develop new attitudes and improve the communication process. ETD systems are therefore highly interrelated with other areas of HRM.

6. The effectiveness of ETD systems is also highly dependent on the national context within which organizations operate. European countries have followed different paths of industrial development and have cultural differences in education practices, work structuring and management styles. Internal resourcing policies reflect many of these deeper values and assumptions. This presents European organizations with two separate choices. Should they make Euro-managers and develop a new set of competencies that allow managers to operate across national boundaries, or should they make the most of the distinctive approaches to management development across Europe and create a matrix of teams that capitalize on the different strengths?

7. The challenge is formidable. The very notion of management differs across European countries, reflecting the separate paths to industrial development. This different understanding of what management is will slow down the pace of integration and limit the attractiveness of many standard HRM tools to organizations. It also raises fundamental cross-cultural problems such as how far organizations should go in attempting to standardize ETD systems, at what level should standardized programmes be introduced, how can the advantages of both global HRM systems and local HRM systems best be balanced, and how important are the cultural and social assumptions of managers when working together?

8. Within the European sphere, three distinct concepts of management can be identified: Anglo-Saxon, Latin and Germanic. Each has its own reflection in management education systems and institutions. Each also suggests a different set of characteristics or capabilities that are taken into account when organizations consider selecting people to join their stock of management. These national characteristics may be associated with the creation of mindsets and attitudes that create natural strengths in specific functional areas. They are reflected in the perception that students have about desirable management characteristics.

9. It is difficult to determine whether national concepts of management determine the structure of organizations, or whether the existence of different structures reinforces differences in understanding about the nature of the management task. The two are

related, however, such that the convergence in overall mechanisms of co-ordination discussed in Chapter Eight is likely to influence national assumptions about the nature of the management task.

10. Vocational education and training systems also differ across Europe. Common points of reference – such as systems for apprenticeship and initial training, provision for continuous training and funding arrangements – highlight very different principles in terms of the role of the state, the link between education and vocational training, the responsibility of organizations to fund training, the degree to which there is a training culture, and the depth of training provision. These differences will take many years to be reduced.

11. There are, however, some common trends in ETD at the organizational level. In most countries and organizations the majority of resources are directed at the upper echelons of the organization. Current differences in the focus and content of management training are being eroded as organizations are prioritizing training around the areas of people management, the accommodation of new technology and the management of change. More responsibility for ETD within organizations is being decentralized to line managers.

12. Such changes have led to debate around three main areas. Are the trends towards more flexible employment relationships and management structures going to have an adverse impact on the quality of ETD in Europe? What are the main HRM issues associated with the process of internationalization of internal resourcing systems? Can any common frameworks be identified to suggest the nature of effective management in the future? There are marked differences in the average tenure of employees across Europe and this is linked to the level of training. The OECD believes there is a clear link between employment stability and level of skill training. This makes it essential for European organizations to develop management development and career systems that balance changes in structure and culture with the necessary levels of employee commitment.

13. The ETD systems of most European organizations are in transition. This is creating several HRM problems such as the need to cope with internal career blocks, the apportioning of responsibility for employee development between lines of country or lines of business, the need to identify high potential early, the identification of the new skill demands associated with European organizational structures, the role of HRM functions in transferring national best practice and the need to avoid internal competitions for resources and career placements between national operations.

14. One way of maintaining a degree of coherence in ETD systems is to identify underlying sets of management competencies. This provides a behavioural description of excellent performance against a broad view of management effectiveness. Such competencies include bodies of knowledge, skills, attitudes and values, traits, motives, self-images and social roles. Although originally popular in Anglo-Saxon cultures, the approach is slowly being transferred to other countries. There is some evidence to suggest that it can create descriptions of effectiveness that are sufficiently generic to form the basis of corporate resourcing systems, but also sufficiently context-specific to be tailored to local operating environments.

15. Some attention has been paid to identifying the competencies that may be associated with the effective Euro-manager. Various views exist about this development, ranging from those that believe that the nature of management effectiveness will be profoundly affected by the process of Europeanization, to those that see the need only for an additional set of skills and competencies that can be tacked on to national managers,

those who believe that many of the skill requirements are too subtle to be described and developed, and those who believe that the whole concept is inappropriate.

16. In practice, both the need for Euro-managers and the specification of skills and competencies required is dependent on a number of factors. The most important of these are the organizational strategy towards the Single European Market, the degree of pressure down the supply chain (from customers and suppliers) and the actual role to be played by the Euro-manager.

17. On top of changes in the nature of management skills (and focus of ETD systems) caused by the process of Europeanization, more fundamental changes are being caused by the need to develop a more future-orientated set of competencies. The ability to compete depends on the capacity to comprehend the competitive forces at play, how these have changed over time, and the ability of the organization to mobilize and manage the necessary resources. HRM is becoming linked to the process of competitiveness through the process of learning.

18. This is reflected in three main approaches towards identifying future competencies. The first involves linking the development of management competencies to the life cycle of the organization or its stage of internationalization. The second involves identifying those competencies that are associated with high performance in a highly uncertain environment. The third involves developing competencies that are associated with high levels of flexibility and the ability to implement changes, no matter what those changes may be. These new models of effectiveness require a fairly sophisticated effort in ensuring cross-cultural validity. They also represent a significant challenge to national models of management development.

19. There is a growing common understanding between the approach being taken by organizational strategists in identifying the core strategic, technical and marketing competences of the organization, and the reflection of these in softer high-level corporate skills. As cost and quality advantages have lost their potency and the life cycle of technical skills continues to shorten, then the importance of effective ETD systems that can reduce the time to develop managers and resource organizations with managers who have a set of capabilities that are both flexible and attuned to the strategic pressures facing the organization becomes paramount.

20. In doing this, it is becoming more important to ensure that organizations also focus on the top team, the extent to which they can address difficult and sensitive issues through reconciling strategic options. This has placed a premium on the quality of relationships and dialogues amongst members of the top team, identifying the most important capabilities that allow them to tease out sensitivities. In addressing these differences, there is no one European country or culture that is better adjusted or more naturally gifted. However, there are marked differences in the success factors that managers from European organizations believe will be rewarded and a clear need to internationalize many career development mechanisms. The issues associated with this are covered in the next chapter.

CHAPTER ELEVEN

Internal Resourcing

Career management and the internationalization of managers

INTRODUCTION

Despite the economic recession in the early 1990s, European, US and Asian organizations saw an increasingly higher proportion of sales coming from international markets. Many European organizations have not yet developed international HRM strategies, although it is argued that within the next decade they will become an inevitable feature of European multinationals (Hogg, 1988), largely because of the integration that has already been achieved (see Chapters Four and Five). They face the challenge of internationalizing their personnel, usually by exposing them to decision making experiences that require an awareness of the cultural, economic and political systems of other countries. Hendry (1991) has argued that it is a mistake to view internationalization as a static or structural phenomenon, limited simply to considering how global organizations manage international units and internationally mobile managers. It is more important to understand the internationalization of organizations in terms of the processes by which it is brought about.

International careers are becoming a common feature of the working life of many European professionals (Forster, 1992). The study of emerging career management strategies that facilitate the process of internationalization provides a 'realistic preview' of common patterns of HRM. In the last chapter we described a number of features of employee training and development (ETD) systems of organizations. One of the topics that can be considered in relation to ETD systems is the process of career management. Traditionally, careers have been defined as the advancement within a profession or occupation, made possible within an organization by the provision of a cradle-to-grave employment philosophy. Fundamental to the management of careers is the idea of 'progression' or the achievement of increased levels of competency and fulfilment of experience by both the individual and the organization. Pursuing a career is fundamental to the achievement of new goals and competencies, and therefore the management of careers becomes a strategic HRM activity (Pearson, 1991). Indeed, in leading European organizations (particularly in complex and global sectors such as telecommunications, computers, chemicals and banking) career development has become the number one challenge in international HRM (Evans, 1992b).

Before we can understand how careers can be managed, we need to have a clear idea of what careers are. Careers have traditionally been evidenced by a series of indicators such as entry criteria linked to educational attainment or vocational training, the provision of specific job experiences, a recognized structure of promotional steps, progressive status or salary, and membership of a professional body that is independent of (external to) the organization and requires a commitment to its own codes of practice (Pearson, 1991). However, the task of defining and managing careers has become more difficult because of the continuing demise of cradle-to-grave employment philosophies across Europe. Yet, at the same time the push towards the Single European Market (SEM) and the requirement for Euro-managers have spurred European organizations to internationalize many of their employees (Bournois, 1991a) and those organizations with a clear strategy aimed at 'Europeanization' (usually articulated as a desire to improve their European market ranking) are doing their utmost in this respect and feel that the human factor is decisive (Bournois and Chauchat, 1990).

A number of conflicting pressures, then, are leading to a transition in career management systems within European organizations. These were highlighted in Parts One and Two of the book and are summarized in Figure 11.1. What is the nature of this transition? The move towards transnational structures has created the need to manage the career paths of a flexible cadre of international managers and provide more

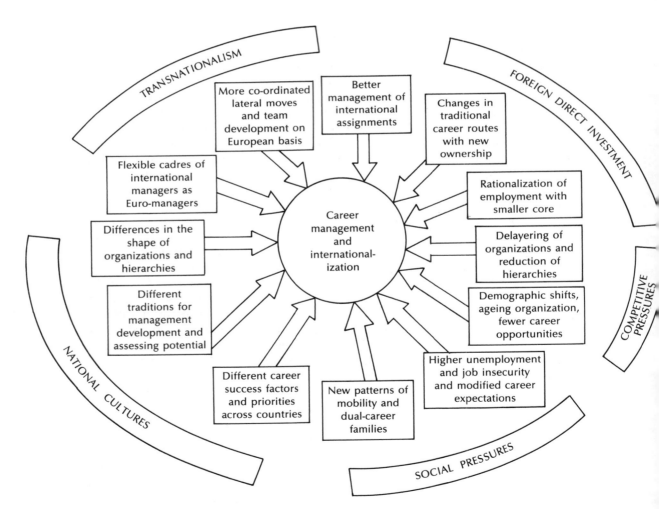

Figure 11.1   The factors influencing change in career management.

co-ordinated management of lateral moves and project assignments. Long standing difficulties with managing expatriate staff have led to greater experimentation with new methods of internationalizing managers. The increase in foreign direct investment and mergers and acquisitions has led to changes in traditional career routes in organizations. The associated rationalization of employment, delayering of organizational structures and peripheralization of employment has had a marked impact on the nature of management careers, as has the fact that an ageing workforce has reduced the opportunities for career advancement for younger managers. Rising levels of unemployment and job insecurity are also modifying expectations of career advancement. The situation is complicated by differences across national cultures. Notably, as discussed in the previous chapter, there are very different national models and traditions of management development, and also national differences in structure of organizations in terms of their functional divides and vertical hierarchies. Clearly, we need a greater understanding of the transition taking place in career structures and processes in European organizations and amongst their managers.

This chapter is divided into five main sections. In the first part we discuss the important theoretical concepts that have been used to describe management careers. We also present some cross-cultural evidence on career success criteria. In the second part we concentrate on the two most important mechanisms that have been used to internationalize career development in organizations: creating international top teams and mechanisms of corporate governance and the introduction of a new cohort of internationally-minded graduates. In the third part we describe the central role played by the management of international assignments and expatriate managers. We then consider some aspects of planned career management systems, the identification of high potential, and the management of career mobility. Finally, in the fifth part of the chapter we outline how European multinationals are broadening the HRM agenda and pursuing new methods of internationalization as they attempt to accelerate the transition.

THE INTERNAL CAREER: INDIVIDUAL DIFFERENCES, CAREER ORIENTATIONS AND CAREER ANCHORS

Careers concern the sequence of jobs people hold and the attitudes and behaviours associated with them. The impact of these changes on careers will therefore be quite pervasive. Theory and research into careers tends to have developed against two frames of reference (see Illustration 11.1):

1. The internal career.
2. The external career.

It is useful to separate these two frames of reference because they highlight the two foci of career dynamics: individual aspirations and occupational realities (Derr and Laurent, 1989). However, each frame of reference is based on its own set of findings and priorities.

Most of the literature about careers can be organized around individuals deciding and managing their internal career. This internal career is typically described in terms of career orientations, career anchors, decisions between personal and professional life, dual-career marriages, and progress through psychological life stages. Work psychologists define a career as '... any sequence of attitudes and behaviours associated with work-related experiences and activities over the span of a person's life' (Hall, 1986). The internal career therefore reflects an individual's own subjective idea

Illustration 11.1   **Two frames of reference for the topic of career management.**

Internal career
- Assumes that people make careers.
- Examines careers from a psychological or personal point of view.
- Focuses on self-development within a career, career motivation, career orientations and the psychological transitions that take place.
- Argues that careers are socially constructed and so considers the cognitive constructs and phenomenological views that illustrate how managers' make sense of their careers.
- Key question: What do I want from work, given my perceptions of who I am and what is possible?

External career
- Assumes that careers make people.
- Examines careers from a sociological and organizational point of view.
- Focuses on career paths and occupational streams, career stages within organizations, the nature of occupations in society.
- Argues that careers link the individual to the social structure and so considers observable, structural and measurable facts about how managers' interpret their career experiences.
- Key question: What is possible and realistic in my organization and occupation, given my perceptions of the world of work?

Source: after Derr and Laurent (1989).

or map about work life and his or her role within it (Schein and Van Maanen, 1977).

We have argued throughout this book that the 1990s will bring a series of novel work demands for most European managers. This is because the external career is under considerable threat. Although many espoused the importance of offering a career to employees, in practice most Anglo-Saxon organizations began to withdraw from the promise of offering an external career in the 1970s and 1980s when the economic going got tough. High levels of unemployment and redundancy, a rejection of organizational responsibility for cradle-to-grave employment and the rise of a more individualistic work ethic all made the management of external careers by organizations something of a fiction (Pearson, 1991). This fiction may begin to permeate European organizations given the pressures shown in Figure 11.1.

As the external career changes, a major transition in the 1990s will be that the 'internal' career will begin to dominate managerial behaviour. As external careers are devalued, then the economic and psychological importance of upgrading skills and competencies becomes more the responsibility of the individual. In abdicating responsibility for providing a traditional external career, during the process of transition organizations will be presented with a new challenge. As (some) individuals both take on responsibility for and seek opportunities to enhance their personal skills and knowledge, whether these coincide with the interests of the organization or not, will organizations be able to ensure their own interests are not damaged?

... Instead of fruitlessly trying to prevent turnover of skilled and creative people, human resource planners should turn to accepting and managing it. Designing a satisfying and profitable short-term assignment for a highly motivated but temporary member of staff presents... a motivating challenge.   Pearson (1991, p. 203).

Both individuals and organizations need to understand the nature of the internal career in order that it may be managed more strategically. Psychologists point to the high levels of change in facets of personality, self-concept and cognitive functioning that will follow such a transition. They also highlight the role of individual differences in mediating the impact of this transition. Individual differences tend to determine both the choice of career (see Illustration 11.2) and the subsequent development of careers. What is the evidence for the role of individual differences? Historically, internal careers

Illustration 11.2 **Making effective career decisions.**

Psychologists have identified a series of factors that are associated with making effective career decisions:

- Self-awareness
  - accurate appraisal of own strengths and weaknesses
  - knowledge of values, likes and dislikes.
- Knowledge of occupations.
- Putting self-knowledge and occupational knowledge together.

- Readiness for effective decision-making
  - level of career planning
  - use and evaluation of resources in exploration
  - knowledge of decision making principles
  - knowledge of career development principles.
- Decision making style.
- Self-esteem and self-efficacy.

Source: Arnold, Robertson and Cooper (1991).

have been analysed empirically and theoretically in terms of social class (Roberts, 1981), personality differences (Holland, 1985), phases or stages of career activity (Super, 1957, 1980), and the key life roles linked with the biological and cultural development of the individual (Levinson, Darrow, Klein, Levinson and McKee, 1978). Arnold, Robertson and Cooper (1991) argue that the internal career is therefore concerned with:

- The pattern (change and stability) of attitudes and behaviours over long periods of time.
- Subjective as well as objective assessments of success.
- Movements within and across a broad range of occupations.

Internal careers are also described in terms of individuals' career maps or 'career anchors'. Driver (1980, 1982) postulated that individuals' build career maps – which may be:

- Linear (conceived in terms of vertical moves 'up the ladder' in the same occupation),
- Spiral (remaining in the same occupation for seven to ten years and then choosing another which builds on past skills and experience).
- Steady state (representing a life time's commitment to an occupation).
- Transitory (frequent changes in occupation with variety being the main driving force).

As promotion opportunities become few and far between and the demographic problems associated with an ageing workforce take hold in organizations, then managers who think of their careers in 'spiral' or 'transitory' terms (and therefore in terms of accomplishment as opposed to advancement) will remain the most satisfied. An individual's own cognitive style serves to guide their long-term career maps and choices. We consider another framework for career success maps, developed by Derr (1986), in a cross-cultural context in the next section.

An important concept that guides career development is that of 'career anchors'. Schein (1975, 1978) developed the concept of career anchors as a way of establishing an individual's internal career orientation. People begin their working life with a set of ambitions, fears, hopes and illusions. Early work experience uncovers these initial interests, motives, values and skills. These gradually coalesce into a 'career self-concept' or 'career identity' as work and life experience, feedback on what they are good at, and the development of skills and abilities critical to their work creates a

Illustration 11.3 **Major employee transitions that reshape the internal career.**

1. Initial employee entry into the organization.
2. Transition from from being a specialist to a generalist.
3. Transition from technical work to management.
4. Transition from from being fully work-involved to being more accommodating with regard to family concerns.

5. Transition from being 'on the way up' to 'levelling off',
6. Transition from being employed to becoming (partly or fully) retired.

Source: Schein (1978).

clearer picture of what they need and like. On-the-job time brings a clearer career identity through a reciprocal process of learning and focus on those things they are best at. An individual's career anchor is an:

... overriding concern or need that operates as a genuine constraint on career decisions. The anchor is the thing the person would not give up if she or he had to make a choice.

Schein (1982, p. 8).

Career anchors may reflect managerial, technical or functional, autonomy, creativity, security, service, pure challenge or lifestyle identities. Organizations need to be aware of their existence and try to cater for people with different anchors.

During their working lives individuals move through a series of 'career transitions' (see Illustration 11.3), the major events that trigger shifts in their internal career map or career anchor. The changes in working life signalled by the discussion in Parts One and Two of this book will clearly influence all these transitions. In managing these transitions, people are either changed by their work environment (socialization) or change the environment (innovation). In a period of transition, the 'people-processing' strategies of the organization can have a powerful impact on the ultimate shape of careers (Van Maanen and Schein, 1979). Some organizations adopt very formal socialization strategies, with centralized approaches to training for newcomers and structured off-the-job development for both individuals and groups. Those individuals that have a tendency to accept job requirements as given (called career custodians) find their careers shaped by this organizational socialization process. However, there are also individuals with a 'role innovation' orientation (Schein, 1971). These individuals redefine the goals of their job and shape the work environment. In the long run, the role innovators are the most vital managers for societal advance. However, in the short run whilst many organizations will claim to value these role innovators, they prefer to reward the career custodians (Arnold, Robertson and Cooper, 1991). The approach taken by individual European organizations towards their socialization process (and the shaping of their managers' internal careers) will have a major impact on their long-term success.

CAREER DYNAMICS AS A REFLECTION OF NATIONAL CULTURE

Whilst the internal career revolves around the individuals' career self-concept, the external career is based around individuals' perception of the organizational and work context (Derr and Laurent, 1989). It is driven by the realities, constraints, opportunities and actual job sequences in the world of work, including changes in the job market, demographics, skills obsolescence and employment opportunities. The discussion of social and economic changes in Chapter Four presented evidence of significant change in all these 'drivers'. The external career tends to be discussed in organizational and occupational terms. It encompasses career stages, career development systems, the importance of internal and external labour markets, patterns of career mobility, and career planning models for organizations. We consider these issues later in this chapter.

First, we examine the relationship between careers and national cultures. The traditional concept of careers is deeply ingrained in the industrial culture of European countries. Why is this the case? Clearly, the external careers offered to managers are influenced by the factors outlined above. However, the underlying constructs that managers use to perceive their careers are also culturally-specific. Derr and Laurent (1989) argue that both internal and external careers can be considered as psychological constructs and social typifications. Even the 'objective' external career is really subjective, influenced by the way individuals perceive the ambiguous, complex and fast-changing phenomena discussed in Chapters Four and Five. It represents a construction and interpretation of selected external events and stimuli. The internal career is influenced by the external career in that most people change aspects of their internal career (maps, anchors, orientations) to fit their perception of the requirements of pressures on the external career.

However, in Chapter Three we argued that national culture should be expected to influence managers' careers. Why? Because the foundations of individual behaviour lie beyond the realm of the person. We discussed the impact of national culture on management development traditions in Europe in the previous chapter. Derr and Laurent (1989) believe that career dynamics are also embedded in the cultural characteristics of social groups and institutions, such as nations and organizations, and that careers cannot be understood in isolation from their cultural context. However, much of the career management literature has remained acultural or blindly unicultural (reflecting Anglo-Saxon assumptions about internal and external careers).

Derr and Laurent (1989) developed a cultural model of career dynamics in an attempt to integrate the internal and external career perspectives. As a personal and subjective map, the internal career operates at the deepest level of organizational or national culture, i.e. that of basic assumptions (see Figure 7.3 and the discussion in Chapter Seven on levels of culture). Derr and Laurent (1989) argue that the internal career is critically influenced by national culture. A career has different meanings in different cultures and will therefore evidence different patterns of career dynamics across countries.

... National cultures have a significant impact on career dynamics in two major ways. First, national cultures shape the individual's self-definition of a career – the internal career – through fundamental ideas about self and work that the individual acquires from early experience in families and schools – the prime carriers and reproducers of a culture. National cultures shape the filters of individuals so that they perceive the world of work – the external career – through the same cultural lenses as their compatriots. Second, national cultures also shape the institutional context or design of work and the individual's perception of it – external career – through the norms, values and assumptions that the individual has already learned in the culture. Thus, careers link individuals to their cultures through their socialization experiences in various institutions. This may help us to understand that careers make people as much as people make careers.
                                                            Derr and Laurent (1989, p. 466).

Experience however also tells us that individuals who are socialized in one particular culture may adjust quite successfully to the requirements of other cultures. Derr and Laurent (1989) provide the anecdote of a French engineer whose internal career may have been shaped by French national culture and management development practices, but may still be able to operate successfully within the context of the organizational culture of an American multinational, and therefore conform to the requirements of a US-orientated external career. This is because individual differences serve to mediate the relationship between the two. As we have pointed out, individual differences in career decision making, choice and orientation exert a powerful influence.

CULTURAL DIFFERENCES IN THE EXTERNAL CAREER

What empirical evidence is there to allow us to assess the validity of the theoretical model of cultural career dynamics forwarded by Derr and Laurent (1989)? As they themselves comment, understanding the meaning and concept of career in different national cultures represents '... virgin territory in the garden of career theory'. However, some empirical data do exist.

The external career can also be studied by collecting and analysing the various perceptions that individuals have about their careers and how they are managed by employers. Asking employees what they believe their employers value and reward in employees, what traits, attitudes or behaviours are seen as valuable, and what are therefore the perceived determinants of career success, is a useful way of investigating cultural differences in the external career of managers across Europe (Laurent, 1981). Studies of the collective perceptions of external career dynamics have been conducted by Derr (1987) and Laurent (1986). Laurent (1986) studied a US-based multinational corporation operating in Europe. For several years the organization had operated a standardized worldwide system for the multiple assessment of managerial potential and performance. Would such a system also standardize managers' perceptions of career success criteria across European countries? A hundred upper-middle managers produced a list of sixty career success criteria. These items were then used to construct a questionnaire, administered to matched samples of 50 managers from France, West Germany, the Netherlands, the UK and the US. A total sample of 262 managers chose the ten items shown in Illustration 11.4 as the most important factors determining

Illustration 11.4 **Ten most important indicators of career success that managers believe are valued by organizations.**

Rank	Career success criteria	% selecting item
1.	Ambition and drive	82
2.	Leadership ability	77
3.	Skills in interpersonal relations and communications	75
4.	Being labelled as having high potential	72
5.	Managerial skills	69
6.	Achieving results	69
7.	Self-confidence	65
8.	Creative mind	60
9.	Ability to handle interfaces between groups	58
10.	Hard work	58

Source: Human Resource Management, A. Laurent, 'The cross-cultural puzzle of international human resource management', **25(1)**, 91–102, copyright © 1986. Reprinted by permission of John Wiley and Sons Inc.

external career success. These represent the aggregate perceptions of the whole sample about desired employee characteristics.

When Laurent (1986) conducted a comparative analysis there were some important differences between the five national groups, in spite of the fact that the standardized career system should have created a high degree of convergence. Eighty per cent of the American managers, culturally closer to the career system designers, agreed on the top six criteria. An eighty per cent agreement level could only be achieved around the top three items for British managers, one item for the French and Dutch managers, and none for the German managers. There were marked differences in the degree of perceptual clarity, fit and comfort between the national managers and the career system designers.

The results also showed that the collective perceptions of one aspect of the external career – indicators of career success from an organizational perspective – varied markedly according to national culture even when the occupational, administrative and organizational contexts were similar. Reflecting the strong Anglo-Saxon emphasis on the need for interpersonal skills (discussed in the previous chapter), 87 per cent of British managers selected this item as the most important determinant of career success, compared to only 57 per cent of the Dutch managers. Reflecting the élitism of French management development systems, being labelled as 'high potential' was perceived as being the most important indicator by 81 per cent of the French managers compared to only 54 per cent of the German managers. Self-confidence is not necessary in managing an external career for French managers (confidence is implicit in being high potential). Only 42 per cent of French managers selected self-confidence as a predictor of success, compared to 82 per cent of American managers, where projected image plays a more obvious role. Job visibility was chosen as an indicator by 73 per cent of British and 71 per cent of American managers, compared to only 30 per cent of Dutch and 18 per cent of German managers. Similarly, reflecting the short-termism of the Anglo-Saxon culture, achieving results was selected by 88 per cent of American managers compared to 52 per cent of French managers. Finally, having a creative mind was ranked the most important indicator by German managers and selected by 77 per cent of managers, compared to only 40 per cent of French managers (who ranked it 21st out of 60 items).

In a similar study Derr (1987) also focused on cross-cultural perceptions of career success. However, he asked managers to rate their personal definitions of career success rather than the organizational point of view, i.e. internal career orientations. The most important internal career orientations of the European managers are shown in Illustration 11.5. Derr (1986) has used research on these orientations to isolate five internal career success maps, using his Career Success Map (CSM) questionnaire:

1. Getting ahead (upward mobility).
2. Getting secure (company loyalty and sense of belonging).
3. Getting free (autonomy).
4. Getting high (excitement of the work itself).
5. Getting balanced (finding an equilibrium between personal and professional life).

The comparative results of Derr's (1987) study are subject to a number of qualifications. The subjects were executives on an INSEAD course who had been away from home for several weeks and had been instructed on the importance of 'getting balanced'. The importance of this orientation is likely to be over-estimated. Moreover, the sample represents an overt group of high-fliers and so their orientations should be skewed towards the perceptions of such individuals and may not be representative of lesser national mortals. Nevertheless, are there still national differences in internal

Illustration 11.5 **Internal career orientations of European managers.**

1. Being influential enough to get exciting and challenging assignments.
2. Being in the 'inner circle' regarding important decisions.
3. Being able to influence events and policies in support of my values and philosophies.
4. Achieving a balance in my progress at work, in my relationships (family life, friendships) and in self-development activities.
5. Being able to keep personal and professional life in equilibrium.

6. Becoming a general manager (e.g. director, vice-president).
7. Working for a firm whose values are congruent with mine
8. Being able to sell my ideas to others.
9. Using my creative talents.
10. Creating new products, ideas, services or organizations.

Source: Derr (1987).

career orientation between individuals selected in their own countries as high-fliers? Yes, and these are quite significant (see Figure 11.2).

British and Swedish managers showed a higher 'getting ahead' orientation than did French managers, whilst French and German managers had a higher 'getting balanced' career orientation. The high 'getting ahead' orientation of the Swedish managers runs counter to the outline of management development traditions given in the previous chapter. Derr and Laurent (1989) explained this by acknowledging that the Swedish executives represented a self-selected and counter-cultural élite who were willing to opt for life on the high-potential track, relocate geographically and upset their spouse's career. This is not typical of most Swedish executives.

Clearly, there is a need for more generalizable research that truly reflects the internal and external career aspirations of managers from representative national samples of managers (and indeed non-management populations). However, the early evidence

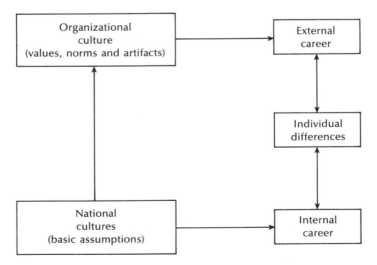

Figure 11.2 Cross-cultural differences in internal career orientations. *Source*: after Derr (1987), reprinted from *European Management Journal*, **5(2)**, C. B. Derr, 'Managing high potentials in Europe: some cross-cultural findings', 72–80, © 1993, with kind permission from Pergamon Press Ltd, Headington Hill Hall, Oxford, OX3 0BW, UK.

Illustration 11.6 **Key cross-cultural questions about managing careers.**

- Do managers view the same organization through different cultural lenses and arrive at different subjective interpretations of reality?
- Do various national affiliates of multinationals operate a standardized career system and also reward managers differently within their cultural settings?

- What is the best way to manage a culturally diverse workforce?
- How can career policies and practices allow for the existence of cultural diversity?
- Are there any ways of building on cultural and career similarities to enable more effective development of staff in a global economy?

Source: Derr and Laurent (1989).

suggests that career success from an organizational point of view, whether assessed by European managers or by the career system designers, is no more culture free than other facets of management or the organizational world (Derr and Oddou, 1993). This conclusion presents a challenge to European organizations. The most important questions to address are highlighted in Illustration 11.6. In Chapter Three it was pointed out that the cultural diversity represented in many European multinational organizations can offer a unique way of increasing competitiveness. However, cultural differences also present major potential pitfalls, as well as opportunities. One of the greatest challenges of international management is '... to help those responsible for managing multicultural teams to understand some of the difficulties they may come across in their work, by recognizing the myriad subtle differences in the behaviour and outlook of the people they manage' (Phillips, 1992).

INTERNATIONALIZATION OF TOP TEAMS AND THE MECHANISMS OF CORPORATE GOVERNANCE

In the second section of this chapter we consider the main internationalization strategies that have a bearing on career management and development systems. There are three main approaches:

1. Internationalizing the mechanisms of corporate governance of the organization.
2. Internationalizing the resourcing policies and developing a new cohort of young internationally-minded managers at lower levels in the organization.
3. Relying on the effective management of the international career assignment mechanism.

Unfortunately, in many European organizations, whilst the principle of European strategy is espoused, only one nationality (that of the main shareholder) is represented at board level. In order for the roads to Europe to be paved with more than good intentions, corporate boards need to demonstrate that more than one nationality can excel in the top echelons and mechanisms of corporate governance (Bournois and Chauchat, 1990). Therefore, one of the first ways in which European organizations responded to the pressures and challenges outlined in Part Two of the book has been to internationalize the very top echelons of their management, i.e. the mechanisms of corporate governance. Within Anglo-Saxon organizations, the percentage of chief executive officers (CEOs) recruited externally over the last few decades has been on the increase (Hogg, 1988). In the late 1960s less than 10 per cent of US CEOs were external recruits. By the early 1980s the figure was 25 per cent. In the UK, the

Illustration 11.7 **Attracting foreign national non-executive directors.**

Foreign national non-executive directors (FNEDs) are being enticed onto European boards in order that domestic organizations may benefit from their expert advice and intimate knowledge of the structural and cultural issues involved in making deals in European countries. Whitehead Mann, an executive search consultancy, found that by 1993, 59 of the top 100 UK organizations were interested in recruiting FNEDs (with 40 already employing at least one FNED) compared to 33 per cent of the US organizations. In many cases, such appointments followed in the wake of foreign direct investments – whether successful or not. For example, after the German mail order house Quelle made an unsuccessful bid for the UK's Littlewoods Home Shopping, its retiring director Harald Schroff joined the Littlewoods board. Hans Reischl, the CEO for German supermarket chain Rewe, joined the board of British food retailer Budgen after Rewe took a 26 per cent stake in Budgen.

Source: Carty (1993).

executive search firm Korn Ferry found that the proportion of CEOs in Britain promoted from within fell from 79 per cent in 1986 to 68 per cent in 1987 (*op. cit.* Hogg, 1988).

The thrust towards multinational top management teams is, however, coming from Continental Europe (Hogg, 1988). It featured in the internationalization strategies of many European multinational corporations (MNCs). For example, in the late 1980s, Nestlé appointed five out of its fifteen directors from outside Switzerland (Hogg, 1988). Forbo, another Swiss organization, has directors from all the countries it had factories in, whilst ICI appointed three foreign executives (from Japan, the US and Germany) to its board, and Philips appointed six non-Dutch managers (all from different countries) to its board. Linked to such changes is the phenomenon of recruiting foreign national non-executive directors (see Illustration 11.7).

This may become a peculiarly European practice, although as we noted in Chapter Eight, the ability of some German and Austrian MNCs to recruit foreigners onto their dual boards may be constrained by their legislation (Carty, 1993). It is not yet a strong feature in the US. A survey by headhunters Korn-Ferry (*op. cit.* Hogg, 1988) found that the proportion of foreigners on US boards fell from 15 to 11.2 per cent from 1981–87. Similarly, Japanese organizations retain control over local subsidiaries and have a higher proportion of expatriate middle managers.

EUROPEAN EXPERIENCE FOR NON-EUROPEAN MANAGERS

Historically, a career move into Europe for an American manager was disastrous. It resulted at best in a sideways move on return to the US or falling from the corporate ladder altogether. However, as European business integration progresses and as US organizations continue to lose out in terms of worldwide competitiveness, international business and management experience has become critical for career management success (see Illustration 11.8).

Finding good international managers who are eager for European experience is as fraught with difficulty as is encouraging mobility within Europe. Only 30 per cent of the US managers desire foreign duty, although 60 per cent would be willing to accept foreign duty if the incentives were right. Key changes asked for were increased willingness of spouses to move abroad, a 50 per cent increase in pay and guarantees of career advancement after international assignments.

Illustration 11.8 **Organizing for global success in US multinationals.**

As part of a study on 'Organizing for global success', McKinsey management consultants surveyed 43 of the top US consumer organizations and found that international transactions were increasing faster than domestic business in all consumer sectors except services. In 1991 home sales provided US organizations with 70 per cent of their turnover. Sales growth for 1991–96 in the US was expected to be 5 per cent, but whilst European sales accounted for 15 per cent of turnover, sales growth was expected to be 9 per cent. The ability to manage trouble-free cross-border alliances and the recruitment of local nationals to lead country subsidiaries were accepted as successful indicators of globalization and 91 per cent of US Chief Executives saw the development of a cadre of international managers as the most significant organizational challenge.

Source: Riley-Adams (1993).

Illustration 11.9 **Tapping global talent at Compaq.**

Eckhard Pfeiffer, a German national, was recruited by Compaq in 1983 as their first European employee. He built up European operations whilst based in Munich into a series of subsidiaries that accounted for 46 per cent of group turnover. In 1991 he moved to Houston as vice-president, soon becoming president and chief executive. He repositioned Compaq with new product launches and delivered a 25 per cent increase in turnover and 65 per cent increase in profits by 1993. The career appointment was not seen as reflecting a premium on European management skills, but rather part of a natural logic of tapping global talent in order to recruit managers who have a skill set and global comprehension, regardless of their nationality.

Source: Craggs (1993).

Indeed, international headhunting organizations such as Russell Reynolds Associates and Egon Zehnder International point out that 'reverse movers' (see Illustration 11.9) – European managers moving into US organizations – find themselves being consulted not only as executives who can counter provincial attitudes in US organizations, but also as international 'gurus' or 'mentors' who can educate others about how Europe works (Riley-Adams, 1993). McKinsey notes that in the last ten years the top European positions in several US multinationals have been taken over by Europeans: the top position moved from an American to a German national at Proctor and Gamble, a Frenchman at Honeywell-Bull, and a Belgian, then an Englishman and finally a Frenchman at IBM (Belgium).

INTERNAL RESOURCING THROUGH EURO-GRADUATES

A second strategy to internationalize the organization is through changes to the career development systems and in particular the entry-point resourcing policies, i.e. graduate recruitment. In the last chapter we saw how several European organizations see 'Euro-graduates' as a key tool in their search for the 'Euro-manager'. By ensuring that an international dimension is built into the recruitment of new graduates – the pool from which future top managers will be resourced – the top European organizations hope they can foster senior management teams that are adaptable, cosmopolitan and laterally-minded (Syrett and Gratton, 1989). Some 30,000 students graduate each year in Europe with the experience of mobility and destined for managerial jobs in Europe. If the UK received a proportionate share (5,100 per year), within twenty years there would be 100,000 Euro-graduates in the UK management pipeline queueing up for senior management jobs. They would comprise roughly 1 per cent of the middle management population (Fox, 1992a). If the ranks of middle management are decimated through 'downsizing' then this process of internationalization will be accelerated.

To a large extent the current low levels of internationalization amongst European managers represent generational differences. Derr and Oddou (1993) argue that it is vital for the younger generation of European managers to have more international exposure. They expect to see the numbers of mobile Euro-graduates rising rapidly during the 1990s. There is some evidence that a cadre of Euro-graduates is emerging as many European organizations adopt this slow-fuse strategy of internationalization

Illustration 11.10 **British and French approaches to the Euro-graduate.**

A survey of 137 British graduate recruiters (36 per cent response rate) and 62 French graduate recruiters (18 per cent response rate) examined perceptions about the impact of the SEM on graduate recruitment activities and strategies and the qualities that were valued in the new; 'European' graduates. There was no difference in the expected impact of the SEM on organizations, with 68 per cent of French recruiters and 74 per cent of British recruiters anticipating practical changes in their organizations. Despite the anticipation of change, only a handful had rethought their graduate recruitment strategy (10 per cent in France and 14 per cent in Britain). Nevertheless, significant differences were found in both existing practice and proposed graduate recruitment activities. Less than 20 per cent of the British sample recruited graduates from other European countries compared to 45 per cent of the French sample. Of those already recruiting Euro-graduates, 60 per cent of French respondents intended to increase the volume compared to 40

per cent of British respondents. Sixty per cent of French organizations not currently active intended to become so, compared to only 23 per cent of the British organizations. To a large extent the British and French recruiters were looking for the same qualities. Both nationalities identified a set of general abilities (knowledge of the business environment, communication skills, good interpersonal skills, commitment to work, technical and scientific ability and intellectual abilities) and gave them equal weighting. A second set of 'European orientation' factors included fluency in a foreign language, knowledge of European cultures, experience of living abroad, willingness to work in different cultures, educated in more than one country and knowledge of EU legal frameworks. In all cases, the French recruiters placed greater emphasis on these qualities than the British recruiters. The impact of not possessing these skills on performance on the job and career prospects was also seen as more detrimental by the French graduate recruiters.

Source: Keenan (1992).

Illustration 11.11 **Relying on an internal market at Bosch to cope with international resourcing.**

Bosch is best known for automotive equipment and domestic appliances. It is one of ten largest German organizations with 147,000 employees (48,000 overseas). The organization has a strong international orientation. Over half its turnover is outside Germany, as are 50 manufacturing sites and distribution and after sales representatives in 130 countries. It would be characterized as pan-European (see Figure 3.3). This organic growth has led to a stronger internal focus in its resourcing.

Although locals are employed where possible in subsidiaries, there is a heavy reliance on 250 German expatriates with three to five year postings, and CEOs in subsidiaries. The 13-member board consists entirely of Germans and most graduate level recruits are from German universities. However, as a matter of policy it is slowly moving towards recruiting MBAs across Europe and more overseas employees are receiving training.

Source: Hogg (1988).

Illustration 11.12 **International resourcing centred around German headquarters: Henkel KGaA.**

Henkel KGaA would be characterized as an international company with headquarters in Germany (see Figure 3.3). More than 50 per cent of turnover comes from overseas. It has operations in 40 countries, and 35,000 employees worldwide (18,500 based outside Germany). It manufactures consumer products (e.g. Persil) and industrial chemicals. It grew through acquisitions in the 1980s but is now consolidating. Large pay differences are allowed across subsidiaries to remain competitive. The national composition of boards varies country by country and all CEOs are local (but capable of speaking German). However, most operational HQ staff speak English. Special programmes have been developed for recruiting graduates from France, and an increasing percentage of local nationals are receiving centralized training in Dusseldorf. Short-term assignments are also increasing.

Source: Hogg (1988).

(see Chapter Nine for an introduction to graduate recruitment). For example, 40 per cent of large French organizations intend to increase the proportion of graduates in their high potential management pool (Bournois and Roussillon, 1992).

There are differences in the current proficiency of organizations in European graduate recruitment (see Illustration 11.10). The sample in Keenan's (1992) study is heavily skewed to UK graduate recruiters and should not be generalized, but nevertheless provides some useful insights. Hogg (1988) provides two contrasting German examples at Bosch and Henkel (see Illustrations 11.11 and 11.12).

THE CAREER ASPIRATIONS OF THE EURO-GRADUATE

But are the career aspirations of young future high-potential managers the same as their predecessors? A study conducted by Taillieu (1990) of Tilburg University in collaboration with MSL Europe and the Euro-managers Association examined the career orientations and aspirations of the next generation of Euro-managers – graduates aged between twenty-two and thirty. The study was tapping the internal career orientations described at the beginning of this chapter. Data were obtained from

Table 11.1 **Most preferred nationality of parent organization for European graduates.**

Country	National background of graduates (% of sample)	Most preferred nationality of parent organization (% of sample)
Britain	5.7	79.6
France	18.6	69.5
Germany	23.9	60.4
Italy	4.8	43.3
Spain	3.0	37.9
Holland	15.5	35.7
Switzerland	1.3	32.9
Belgium	15.1	32.0
Scandinavia	1.1	19.4

Source: after Taillieu (1990).

1733 graduate applicants to a career conference. The population represented a strongly motivated and internationally-orientated group of graduates. Of these, 78 per cent preferred to work for an organization that operated worldwide with only 19 per cent wanting a solely European operating base. Also, 68 per cent had lived in two or more foreign countries, 52 per cent had two foreign languages, and 28 per cent had three languages.

Table 11.1 shows that despite the majority of graduates not being English, nearly 80 per cent saw English-owned organizations as the most preferred destination. French and German organizations were also seen as very attractive, whilst the least preferred destinations were in Southern and East Europe. The internal career orientations for the Euro-graduate of the future seem to be quite clear from Taillieu's (1990) study (see Table 11.2).

However, if European organizations are going to use such cadres of internationally

Table 11.2 **Career orientations of Euro-graduates.**

Mean score for career orientation	Description of orientation
10.48	*Managing people* The process of supervising, influencing, leading and controlling people at all levels, integrating their efforts (questions 2 and 6)
10.33	*Service and dedication* The use of one's interpersonal and helping skills in the service of others; commitment and devotion to an important cause in one's life (questions 3 and 5)
10.04	*Life style* Developing a life style that balances career and family needs, being able to lead one's life in one's own way (questions 1 and 10)
9.56	*Pure challenge* Confronting, working and solving tough problems, no matter what they are (questions 4 and 7)
7.97	*Entrepreneuring* Working with own products and ideas, being on the look-out to start or build one's own enterprise (questions 8 and 13)
7.92	*Autonomy* Concern about freedom and independence, not being constrained by organizational rules, doing things one's own way (questions 9 and 12)
6.37	*Technical-functioning expertise* Concern for developing one's expertise and specialization, building a career in some specific technical or functional area (questions 14 and 15)
6.33	*Job security* Concern for stability and guaranteed employment, security, benefits and good retirement conditions (questions 11 and 16)
3.50	*Geographical stability* Being able to remain in one's country or geographical area for a full career (questions 17 and 18)

Source: after Taillieu (1990).

Illustration 11.13   **Internationalization at ICL: the Euro-graduate programme.**

ICL has worldwide revenues of $4 billion and has been the only consistently profitable European computer manufacturer during the late 1980s and early 1990s. In 1987 the strategic plan reaffirmed the need for ICL to make Europe its home base. Despite a long presence in twelve European countries ICL's human resource strategy had failed to focus on internationalization. The European personnel function had the delicate task of defining the extent of its responsibility within the strategic framework. There were parallel developments to cover:

- A mergers and acquisition strategy.
- Building a European corporate culture.
- Remuneration and benefits.
- Resourcing and development.

In 1988 ICL restructured the organization. Its non-UK Information Systems business was split into ICL International and ICL Europe in order to plan European investment, focus on niche markets where it had created an international focus (e.g. No. 1 supplier of retail systems to French hypermarkets) and derive the benefits from a series of acquisitions (such as Denmark's Regen Centrale Computers) and joint ventures (principally in Spain and Denmark). At the same time it revised its European Strategy Board, demonstrating top management commitment to Europe, and revised its business planning process. The relationship between the European headquarters and subsidiary operations was strengthened by eliminating intermediate structures. The business strategy was supported by a major communications programme. A tiered communication strategy to all levels of staff was used to cover European events and developments, awareness of ICL's operations, awareness of national cultures and opportunities for international communication. Strategic and business planning information was provided for senior managers to incorporate 1992 sector analysis reports, scenario models and information letters from Brussels. A quarterly 'Europe Sans Frontières' magazine was published in English, French and German to describe the purposes behind the SEM, organization ventures, the 'people' aspects of Europeanization (such as student placements, international career moves and language courses), personal interest items and country profiles. This communication strategy was seen to bring benefits by increasing staff awareness, identifying specific skills and knowledge in the organization

that would otherwise have remained hidden, and highlighting the information that would be needed to create a European HR system.

A number of core activities were involved in the effort to 'Europeanize' the organization's home base (where the majority of product development and manufacturing took place) and to create a 'mobility' culture. The move towards a pan-European corporate culture involved the recognition of a series of common language blocks (Nordic countries, Benelux, Germany and Southern Europe). In each of these blocks, a lead country was appointed to co-ordinate activity, share cross border expertise and break down cultural barriers within the block. The corporate values handbook, initially devised in the UK in the early 1980s, was relaunched in all languages to refocus the key messages. Organization wide quality material was made available in all languages.

A common European-wide philosophy for objective setting, appraisal systems, people development programmes, recruitment and selection and manpower planning was established and applied to all countries under the theme 'Investing in people'. Finally, a European-wide opinion survey was used to assess understanding and feeling.

Only tentative developments were made in the field of remunerations and benefits. The intention was to establish a common approach across European operations, with a common grading system for technical and managerial staff. As a precursor to this move, ICL kept a close watch on pay movements in relevant fields throughout Europe and participated in sectoral 'salary clubs'. A common policy was put in place for executive bonus plans and share option schemes. International career placements were made to reflect local market rates, but the financial incentives were seen as less important than the career development benefits that resulted.

ICL also participated in ERASMUS, COMETT and language-linked university and polytechnic courses. However, a key feature of the internationalization effort was an attempt to internally resource the organization with a cadre of European minded mobile graduates. ICL had a tradition of resourcing based on graduates and had boosted representation of foreign nationals in the UK by recruiting INSEAD MBA graduates. In 1989 it formalized this process into the Euro-graduate Programme. Selected European graduates were brought to the UK for ten months' centrally-funded intensive training. Advertising for recruits took place in several countries. The recruits had to be fluent in English as they were put through the same technical and specialist induction training as the home nationals. Employment Conditions Abroad provided a Cultural Awareness Workshop for the Euro-graduates. They were set work-related objectives, formally appraised and were monitored by a regional country manager. Great reliance was made on exposing the Euro-graduates to a network of peers from Europe and key managerial and professional staff.

The success of ICL in 'Europeanizing' its culture and operations made it an attractive acquisition for Fujitsu of Japan. Fujitsu has sales of $21 billion and is the second largest information technology organization in the world. After long standing technical collaborations Fujitsu took an 80 per cent stake in ICL in 1990. However, ICL's managerial independence was reaffirmed by 1992 as it moved towards flotation on the London stock exchange and was given control over Fujitsu operations in the US and Europe through three joint ventures.

Source: Pinder (1990); Sparrow (1991; 1994c); Mayo (1991).

Illustration 11.14   **The British Airways approach: preparing fertile ground for Euro-graduates and selling the need for diversity.**

British Airways also introduced a European graduate resourcing policy in the early 1990s. Picking up some of the concerns outlined in Illustration 11.13, they identified a series of challenges related to this policy:

- How to generate an understanding and appreciation of cultural differences amongst managers.
- How to 'Europeanize' the thinking of managers (British Airways was a typical Anglo-Saxon organization which had revered American business schools and management consultants).
- How to persuade managers to learn foreign languages.
- How to integrate elements of the Social Charter into personnel policy making (on the assumption that if they were not the best in Europe they could not retain graduates in the UK).
- How to develop their understanding of the industrial relations implications of EC legislation.

They tackled the problem of encouraging interculturalism in two ways. First, they put all their senior managers through a training programme which explained Hofstede's (1980) model for understanding the culture of different nationalities. However, after 18 months it was difficult to find managers whose thinking had been altered by this knowledge. There was no immediate requirement to change behaviour. The second approach involved co-opting an existing corporate programme – called Equal Opportunity 2000 – which broadened the base of resourcing policies to include all forms of diversity (sex and race). This programme opened the door to valuing the difference that European recruits could bring to the airline. The programme does not change attitudes, but changes the mindset of lead opinion formers by exploring the value of diversity through carefully posed questions. As a result, managers began to set objectives for the recruitment of European graduates.

As well as selecting the right person, British Airways recognized that work had to be done in preparing the receiving department. Air Cabin Crew and Customer Service Staff had been recruited throughout Europe for many years, but worked from their home countries. Mentors have been adopted to help graduates through their early days with the organization. Recruitment procedures have been adapted to meet cultural norms, as have personnel policies for pay rates, pensions, allowances, and housing.

Source: Lauermann (1992).

mobile Euro-graduates as a primary resource their for internationalization, it becomes extremely important that they:

- Adjust and adapt their career management processes in order to both retain these individuals and accommodate their internal career orientations.
- Ensure that the receiving departments are culturally-aware and prepared to effectively manage the incoming graduates.
- Build a formal system of identifying continuing potential and managing career aspirations until the cadre reach senior levels within the organization.

We deal with the first two requirements now and consider the third requirement in the following sections. The ICL case study (see Illustration 11.13, pp. 443–4) exemplifies how a UK organization attempted to internationalize itself. The strategy was broad based and covers initiatives in culture change, remuneration and internally resourcing key positions through graduates. It is considered at this point because of the novel internal resourcing initiatives, and its demonstration of two of the methods found by Derr and Oddou (1993) to be highly important, but currently less frequent:

1. Bringing a cadre of foreign nationals into the world headquarters.
2. Making use of a network of international contacts.

Similarly, Olivetti created a 'No Frontiers' programme in the late 1980s with the short-term objective of recruiting up to 1,000 systems-support specialists capable of working in international environments and a longer-term aim of developing a pool of talented young managers with the potential to become top managers (Syrett and Gratton, 1989). In one year's intake, for example, 58 recruits from 13 different nationalities were attracted from a worldwide advertising campaign run in English. Once organizations embark on this type of internationalization strategy, it becomes essential to ensure that the receiving parts of the organization are equipped to deal with the Euro-graduates (see Illustration 11.14).

THE INTERNATIONAL CAREER ASSIGNMENT AS A UNIT OF ANALYSIS: OBJECTIVES OF EXPATRIATION

International assignments have become one of the most important ways of internationalizing managers and a major unit of analysis in international career research (Peltonen, 1993). In this third section of the chapter we describe the main issues involved in the use of international assignments. There has been an increase in the complexity of expatriate employment, a greater mix of nationalities employed overseas, and a general shift away from creating long-term career expatriates, towards managing short-term overseas project-based expatriates. As product cycles have collapsed, especially in service industries, organizations are thinking in shorter time frames, making the use of long-term international assignments more difficult (Carter, 1989).

Managing an international assignment is a highly complex exercise, full of pitfalls for the unwary manager (Hogg and Tugwell, 1988). Unfortunately, the sophisticated systems put in place by the larger multinationals are often inappropriate for smaller organizations that may only have a handful of overseas employees. The problems of managing the assignments depend on the employer, the type of contract, the nationality of host countries and the length and type of assignment. In the following sections we summarize the available research on the topic.

International assignments are the most frequently used method for making managers aware of differences among countries, cultures, and markets. They are usually discussed in relation to the topic of expatriation, or sending home-country nationals on two-to-four-year assignments to manage parts of the business outside the country of origin. International organizations frequently categorize managers as 'locals' (citizens of the country in which they are working) or 'expatriates' (non-citizens). Expatriates can be further categorized as home-country nationals (citizens of the country where the organization has its head office) or third-country (citizens of any other country) (Wilson and Rosenfeld, 1990). Torrington (1994) uses a more understandable way of classifying 'cosmopolitan' managers: 'international managers' (who are continually mobile across national borders); 'expatriates' (working on an international assignment); 'engineers' (involved in short-term technical projects);

Table 11.3 **Reasons for international assignments.**

Type of assignment	Organization justification
A. Transfer of skill or knowledge	
A1. Use of a worldwide skillpool	Sharing and full use of highly specialized talent globally
A2. Development of local knowledge/skill by secondment to a more developed centre	Local assimilation of skills on a permanent basis
A3. Meeting a local lack of skills by seconding a person out from a developed centre	Local need resourced quickly
A4. Meeting a local management need because existing capability inadequate	Local need resourced quickly
A5. Bringing international understanding into the homebase	Ensuring international needs are built into organization's products/services/plans
A6. Staffing an extension of an existing homebase function in another country	To take a function closer to a market, or to deliberately build a more international mix
A7. Representation of parent company in a local subsidiary	Safeguard of the organization's interest
B. Individual personal growth	
B1. Training young entrants for local country in homebase	Efficiency of learning curve through using homebase facilities; creating early international attitudes
B2. Personal development of local nationals	Development of specific knowledge, skills, attitudes, experience and wider organization understanding as part of career plan
B3. Development of high-flyers	Development of specific knowledge, skills, attitudes, experience and wider organization understanding as part of career plan

Source: this table is taken from *Merging Careers: Strategies for organizations* by A. Mayo, and reproduced with permission of the publishers, the Institute of Personnel Management, IPM House, 35 Camp Road, Wimbledon, London, SW19 4AX, © 1991.

Illustration 11.15   **Reasons for the growing focus of attention on expatriation and international assignments.**

- There has been an increase in the size, number and importance of multinational organizations (Ronen, 1986).
- Globalization of market competition, increased levels of mergers, acquisitions and joint ventures have increased the need for co-ordination of international activities (Zeira and Banai, 1985).
- In the context of management development, international assignments offer excellent learning possibilities and can represent a powerful source of new knowledge, skills and attitudes (Mayo, 1991).
- High levels of historical failure have heightened sensitivity to the financial and emotional costs associated with expatriation (Zeira and Banai, 1985).

and 'occasional parachutists' (who make a number of overseas trips a year for their organization).

In a review of expatriation and international assignments, Hiltrop and Janssens (1990) noted that the 1980s witnessed an upsurge of interest and available research in the topic. A number of reasons have been put forward to explain this increase in importance (see Illustration 11.15).

International assignments therefore tend to be initiated for a variety of reasons (see Table 11.3). These are usually intended to provide a degree of transfer of control, skill or knowledge from one organizational unit to another, or to provide individual managers' with personal development. Most organizations view international moves as important management development experiences for high-potential managers, giving them broader and more global perspectives. Such experiences have the additional advantage of carrying the organizational culture, personified in the expatriate, out to the field (Mayo, 1991). As a further benefit, this trusted contact can report accurately on field conditions and circumstances affecting the local business, a form of corporate spying. However, Mayo (1991) recommends that line managers and HRM specialists use the framework in Table 11.1 periodically to analyse where their international assignment costs are being spent and re-establish a balance between assignments for development versus expedient needs.

RECRUITING AND SELECTING EXPATRIATES

Peltonen (1993) argues that international assignments tend to follow a clear cross-national set of transitions, involving career cycles of recruitment and selection, training and briefing, adjustment and performance, assignment closing and re-entry (see Figure 11.3).

The quickest way to obtain personnel for foreign operations is to acquire a local organization and use their stock of human resources. However, organizations such as Royal Dutch-Shell, Unilever and Nestlé have attempted to develop an international cadre of managers for several years. However, most of the HRM research into the behaviour of managers and organizations during international assignments is of US origin, reflecting the high reliance of US organizations on the international division structure (see Chapter Eight). A preliminary question to be resolved before organizations consider recruiting and selecting managers for expatriate assignments is: do we need to send an expatriate in the first place? The factors to consider in choosing a local or expatriate manager are shown in Illustration 11.16.

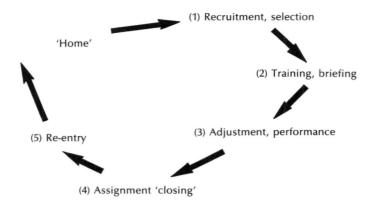

Figure 11.3 The overseas assignment career cycle. *Source*: reprinted from *European Management Journal*, **11(2)**, 248–57, T. Peltonen, 'Managerial career patterns in transnational corporations: an organizational capability approach', © 1993, with kind permission from Pergamon Press Ltd, Headington Hill Hall, Oxford, OX3 0BW, UK.

Illustration 11.16 **Factors to consider in choosing local or expatriate staff for assignments.**

- *Knowledge of local operating conditions*: trade-off between local knowledge, business acumen and technical expertise versus the need for worldwide standards of production and close coherence to corporate directives.
- *Incentives to local personnel*: importance of reducing high turnover amongst local staff through the provision of financial and career incentives; importance of promoting a local image; legal or social restrictions restricting local operations; level of risk-avoidance by using expatriate managers.
- *Cost*: cost of transferring expatriate managers; moving and settling-in expenses; residential costs.

- *Legal restrictions*: laws favouring home-nationals; level of skill required for the assignment; time-consuming process for gaining permission to import staff.
- *Control*: level of head office control required; degree of corporate acculturation required.
- *Long-term focus*: difficulty of short-term focus engendered by expatriate assignment versus long-term factors.
- *Management development*: importance of training in overall corporate system; ability to adapt to differing social systems.

Source: Wilson and Rosenfeld (1990).

The issues involved in selecting and training managers for international assignments have received detailed attention in recent years (see Black and Mendenhall, 1990; Black, Mendenhall and Oddou, 1991; Church, 1982; and Stening, 1979 for reviews). Most candidates for assignments are usually selected from within the organization, although organizations are increasingly using executive search consultancies to identify senior executives (Hogg and Tugwell, 1988). The techniques used for expatriate selection tend to be much the same as those used for local employees (see Chapter Nine). This presents an immediate problem, because if international organizations are to succeed with expatriate managers then they need to recruit truly international managers (Wilson and Rosenfeld, 1990). Recruitment policies need to transcend factors of nationality and job location because selecting managers for international merger assignments or secondments represents a special case. Moreover, it is becoming the norm to recruit complete teams or groups of managers for international projects as opposed to individual managers (Carter, 1989).

Unfortunately, there is often a substantial mismatch between the selection criteria employed by organizations and those that are really needed for international assignments. The immense personal difficulties associated with international assignments (described in the subsequent sections) mean that preventing selection mistakes in sending people on international assignments has become a priority for organizations (Mendenhall, Dunbar and Oddou, 1987). Organizations need to select the most effective, rather than marginal, managers on the basis of a well thought out selection system. Hiltrop and Janssens (1990) have outlined both the factors that cause expatriate failure and the factors that are linked to effective expatriate assignments (see Illustration 11.17). These factors should serve as a basis for selection for international assignments. It is interesting to note that they do not reflect the traditional skills and abilities built into most selection systems or assessments of career potential.

Whilst early studies of personal characteristics of expatriate managers focused on the role of superior intelligence, self-confidence and a strong drive for completion of the task (Miller, 1972), such qualities actually failed to predict expatriate performance to a significant degree. Most discussions of the competencies needed for international assignments point to the famous caricature of the successful expatriate (Phatak, 1974) and then point out that the appropriate attitudes may not be translated into actual behaviour.

... Ideally, it seems, he (or she) should have the stamina of an Olympic swimmer, the mental agility of an Einstein, the conversational skill of a professor of languages, the detachment of a judge, the tact of a diplomat, and the perseverance of an Egyptian pyramid builder. And if he is going to measure up to the demands of living and working in a foreign country he should not be too rigid; he should be able to merge with the local environment with chameleon-like ease and he should show no signs of prejudice.   Phatak (1974, p. 183).

Several studies have shown that the managerial skills needed to be effective in a domestic position are different to those required for success on an international assignment (Samovar, Porter and Jain, 1981; Whetton and Cameron, 1984). Certain skills and characteristics have been found to be useful in predicting success. Experienced expatriates use effective and creative mechanisms for coping with stress and intercultural adaptation (Adler, 1986; Torbiorn, 1982). Simple practices such as

---

Illustration 11.17 **Important selection considerations: personal characteristics associated with effective completion of international assignments.**

- *Technical ability*: technical knowledge and skills to do the job; confidence in ability to accomplish the purpose of the overseas assignment.
- *Stress tolerance*: ability to deal with personal anxieties, cultural adaptation, and social dislocation; ability to manage on incomplete information from novel sources and gaps in information from previously reliable sources.
- *Emotional maturity and flexibility*: ability to cope with role conflict; to replace and substitute interests and activities; flexible social tastes.

- *Communication, listening and relational skills*: effective social and business relations; ability to get along with people well; willingness to work with others; broad basis of respect for religious and political beliefs; ability to learn and use local language.
- *Cultural empathy*: understanding of foreign cultural behaviour patterns; ability to differentiate between idiosyncratic behaviour and behaviour that reflects a cultural pattern; heightened individual awareness.

Source: after Hiltrop and Janssens (1990).

forbidding complaints and only allowing positive comments about the new environment during meals and creating a rhythm of engagement and withdrawal from the local culture by using 'stability zones' that recreate home life and form a basis of retreat (such as playing a musical instrument, keeping a diary, watching videos in native language) can be remarkably effective. Having the flexibility to substitute hobbies with similar yet different activities, or learning the local language and picking up 'conversational currency' such as anecdotes, jokes, proverbs, and the names of sports stars are also effective strategies (Abe and Wiseman, 1983; Hiltrop and Janssens, 1990).

In summary, technical factors may form the basis of individual selection when cultural differences between the two countries are insignificant and the degree of interaction is low (Tung, 1988). In these situations an important contingency to consider is the type of information and control required by the assignment (Pucik and Katz, 1986). Technically competent expatriates are most effective when the information available is objective and understandable regardless of national origin, and when control is bureaucratic. In most expatriate situations, however, personal attributes associated with adaptability, flexibility, maturity and emotional stability, communication and relational skills should be the dominant factors in selection decisions (Tung, 1988).

The selection decision also needs to consider the position of the manager's spouse and family (Tung, 1982) and yet this is a surprisingly under-utilized criterion. Few organizations assess the adaptability of the spouse or conduct any family screening process. The impact of expatriation is often greater on the spouse. Not only may partners find their own friends and jobs lost and career broken, they have more time on their hands and frequently become more immersed in the local culture and dealing with realities of life in the country on a day-to-day basis, creating an even stronger challenge to adaptation (Harvey, 1985). Loneliness and isolation have to be coped with, as does the need for greater levels of companionship from (busy) partners in a foreign environment and the reality that the international assignment may be one of many, making it difficult for the expatriate to engage the local culture in any depth or to create a meaningful life. Despite the clear impact of the spouse on the effectiveness of an international assignment, Tung (1988) found that only 40 per cent of organizations interviewed the spouse of the candidate.

Given these personal, family and organizational factors, although selecting a young manager for an international assignment offers an excellent learning opportunity, Mayo (1991) observes that in practice many organizations find that sending the most dynamic, young and bright managers into such a sensitive situation is generally not appropriate. This raises a number of questions about the appropriateness of relying on a strategy of internationalizing the organization through the use of 'Euro-graduates'. Managers with considerable service and seniority and little to prove on a personal level often make the best ambassadors. There are usually some key technical support roles on such assignments that can provide excellent development opportunities for the younger managers.

TRAINING AND BRIEFING OF EXPATRIATES

Even the most careful selection does not eliminate the need for training. Many of the personal factors associated with successful expatriate assignments shown in Illustration 11.17 are in fact more a matter of training than selection. Once the screening process is completed, organizations need to offer formal training programmes to prepare expatriates and their families for the international assignment (Hiltrop and Janssens, 1990).

Two studies of US expatriate managers revealed the startling fact, however, that 65 per cent of expatriated managers received no training or orientation before departure. Only 35 per cent felt that their organizations had made an effort to prepare them to maximize their experience by on-site orientation, and only 26 per cent of this group felt that such training was effective or adequate (Derr and Oddou, 1991; Tung 1981). Despite the clear need to minimize the expatriate managers' culture shock, few organizations offer formal training programmes (Tung, 1988). Only 27 per cent of UK organizations had any formalized international briefing courses for employees in 1988 (Forster, 1992). There is some evidence to suggest that European strategic managers are looking beyond national boundaries as they focus on the global marketplace (Bartlett, Doz, and Hedlund, 1990). If the sample is restricted to those organizations that already have significant expatriate operations, then Handy and Barham (1989) reported that 60 per cent of organizations in the UK, 59 per cent of those in West Germany, and 59 per cent of those in France were already using cross-cultural training programmes in their expatriate management training. However, much cross-cultural training is limited to environmental briefs which are inadequate for assignments that require extensive local contact. More comprehensive culture assimilation training (Brislin, Cushner, Cherrie and Young, 1986), identification of critical incidents, sensitivity training and field experiences need to form the core of training preparation (Hiltrop and Janssens, 1990). When the intercultural competencies of expatriate managers are analysed, affective, cognitive and behavioural aspects have to be developed (Gertsen, 1990).

MANAGING ADJUSTMENT AND PERFORMANCE ON INTERNATIONAL ASSIGNMENTS

One of the largest problem areas with international assignments is the need to establish clear terms and conditions and to manage the compensation and reward issues. Terms and conditions vary widely. Documentation usually covers a host of related issues, such as basic salary, details of allowances, how they are paid, responsibility for payment of tax and social security coverage, education provision, benefit implications, leave and housing arrangements, insurance and sale of personal effects, limitations on shipment of goods, definition of family dependents, and terms and conditions for the termination of the assignment (Hogg and Tugwell, 1988).

Beyond agreeing and understanding the contractual and compensation issues, completing an international assignment presents expatriate managers and their families with a number of other difficulties and challenges (Hiltrop and Janssens, 1990). International assignees usually have to operate in an environment which is culturally, politically, economically and legally different from that experienced in the home country. Social customs are frequently at odds with their own value systems and living habits. When expatriates face host-country nationals and their different behavioural norms and expectations, tensions may rise (Feldman and Tompson, 1992). Whilst successful expatriates learn not to apply the assumptions that guided their behaviour at home, many are not so flexible. Early studies of international staffing highlighted a series of adjustment problems (Brooke and Remmers, 1977; Zeira and Harari, 1977; Ronen, 1986), with managers showing symptoms of:

- Transfer anxiety.
- Culture shock (usually in stages of honeymoon, disillusion and adjustment).

- Social dislocation.
- Adaptation problems.
- Feelings of abandonment and exile.
- Frustration and disappointment.

The US literature on the management of international assignments might not truly capture the European experience. Recent research demonstrates this. Understanding of the adjustment issues experienced by European managers has been advanced by a series of studies by Janssens (1994a, 1994b) in Belgium. Study of 162 expatriate managers from four Belgian multinationals, and a UK-owned Belgian subsidiary by questionnaire showed 57 per cent of the sample were Belgian, 23 per cent British, 8 per cent North American and the other 5 per cent Brazilian, Australian and Asian. Nearly all were male and were accompanied on their assignment by their spouse and family. A 32-item scale was used to study cross-cultural adjustment in terms of:

- Intercultural interaction (knowledge of cultural values and norms of host country and interaction with local nationals).
- Personal adjustment (general satisfaction and feeling at home).
- Work adjustment (satisfaction with organizational and job issues).

The managers scored highest on adjustment to work and lowest on intercultural interaction. However, intercultural interaction was significantly related to the length of time in the host country and location of international assignment. The relationship between the degree of adjustment to a foreign country and time has been described as a 'U', as managers go through four stages of honeymoon, disillusionment, recovery and positive adjustment (Oberg, 1960; Black and Mendenhall, 1991). The longer the time in the host country, the greater the intercultural adjustment (see Figure 11.4). Work adjustment bore no relationship to the time spent on the assignment.

The relationship between the location of the foreign assignment and intercultural interaction was intriguing. The 'cultural novelty' hypothesis argues that the more

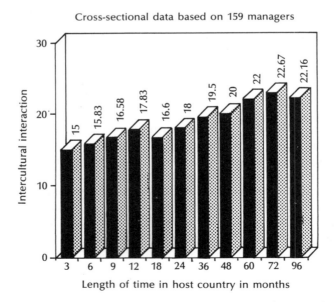

Figure 11.4 Relationship between time in host country and intercultural interaction amongst Belgian expatriate managers.

distant or different a host culture from one's own; the more difficult the adjustment (Church, 1982). The prediction from Janssens's (1994a) study would be that European managers on assignment to North America or Asia would experience the lowest level of intercultural adjustment. In fact, the opposite happened. European managers on assignment in North America and Asia showed higher levels of adjustment than when they had assignments in other European countries. Why? Perhaps because when they are on assignment in Europe, the smaller distances and possibility of weekend vacations, visits and family contacts reduce the degree of effort they put into learning about the host culture and making local friends.

The implications of this finding, were it to be replicated in other European multinationals (or more importantly by longitudinal tracking), are very significant for the process of industrial integration in Europe. It suggests that the cultural determinants of managers' careers may remain relatively intact, as European managers learn to cope with higher levels of mobility by avoiding the need to increase their intercultural adaptation.

Janssens (1994a) also studied levels of work adjustment. The expatriates were asked to list three major problems in adjusting to work. Then 423 separate problems of work adjustment were content analysed, revealing 16 separate types of problem (see Table 11.4). Of these problems, two were significantly related to the level of work adjustment. High levels of role ambiguity and lack of understanding from the parent company reduced work adjustment on the assignment. This may help explain the finding that managers on assignments showed lower levels of work adjustment, but also had lower levels of job discretion because they were more likely to be working with fellow countrymen and third countrymen.

The findings on work adjustment in Janssens's (1994a) study clearly indicated that organizations can be active participants in helping international managers adjust to their work, in particular by matching the objectives and expectations of both parties

Table 11.4 **Problems of adjusting to work in international assignments in a group of Belgian multinationals.**

Problem	% of sample
Relationship with locals	19
Value differences of locals	15
Work overload	14
Way of doing business	14
Language	13
Lack of skills of locals	13
Role ambiguity[**]	11
Lack of organizational clarity	11
Working conditions/infrastructure	10
Divergent objectives between parent and host organization	9
Lack of information	9
Culture of the host company	9
Communication with parent company	8
Lack of understanding from parent company[*]	8
Difficulty of foreign assignment	7
Understanding behaviour of locals	6

Source: Janssens (1994b). Reproduced with permission of the author, © M. Janssens: 1994.
[*] denotes significant at <.01
[**] denotes significant at <.001

by creating a clear psychological contract which specifies the transactional and relational obligations of both parties (Rousseau, 1990).

To minimize the risk of expatriate failure organizations need to allow managers sufficient time to adapt to the local environment rather than creating pressure for immediate high levels of personal productivity. Zeira and Harari (1977) recommended an induction period of up to six months' exemption from active management duties for long-term assignments. Such induction periods of course add to the cost and reduce the practical utility of choosing to create an international assignment. The provision of co-ordinated local support systems designed to meet the needs and aspirations of expatriate employees is a cost-effective way of increasing the chance of assignment success (Tung, 1988). Such systems have to focus on the provision of a social network for expatriates and monitor the training and development needs whilst on the assignment (which tend to be overlooked but are nevertheless high). The requirement for an extended induction period, time devoted to personal support systems and top-up training has implications for the performance management criteria, which need to be linked to long-term objectives and measures of profitability. However, the continued assessment and appraisal of performance and early identification of future career opportunities is of paramount importance (Hogg and Tugwell, 1988).

In the emerging less hierarchical organizational structures of multinationals the linkage between operations depends even more on the interactions of individual managers. Janssens's (1994a, 1994b) studies of Belgian expatriates showed the importance of role clarity. International managers operate in 'boundary spanning' roles. A decision has to be made about which boundary has responsibility for managing the performance of the international manager: the home country or local operation.

There is no obviously correct way to assess the performance of international managers, principally because the appraisers in the home country cannot be sure whether local managers are carrying the expatriate, local conditions may be favourable, or local problems may be poorly comprehended. The decision to be made is when best to exercise centralized performance appraisal, or when to allow local appraisal. The theoretical connections are shown in Figure 11.5.

The assignment of managers abroad is a difficult process and one that generally cannot be deemed successful (Kobrin, 1988). Numerous studies have demonstrated high failure rates amongst expatriates. Although failure rates appear to be falling, they are still high. Early studies in the US reported failure rates (the expatriate returning home early before the task was completed) of 50 per cent in developed countries, rising to 70 per cent when the assignment was in developing countries. More recently it has been estimated that between 16 and 40 per cent of expatriate US managers do not complete assignments because of poor work performance or adjustment problems (Black and Mendenhall, 1990; Sperl, 1988), whilst between 50 and 80 per cent of US managers perform under par. Little data is available for Europe, but a 1986 study suggested that less than 60 per cent of British expatriates in the Middle East completed their assignments (Findley and Stewart, 1986). A large scale study of 639 Swedish expatriates in 26 countries found that 25 per cent returned home before the assignment was complete, usually citing problems of cultural adjustment. There are notable psychological costs to the manager associated with such failure (Mendenhall and Oddou, 1987) including a loss of self-esteem, a severe career set-back and the loss of prestige amongst peers.

Hiltrop and Janssens (1990) warn that it is difficult to define failure precisely and such estimates should not be treated as hard data. Nevertheless, although both US and European expatriates show high failure rates because of adjustment problems, it is evident that their experience and competence at managing expatriates are different.

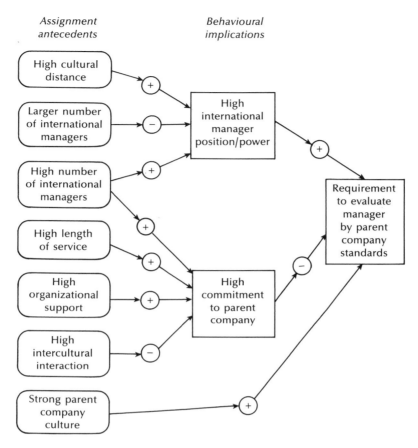

Assignment antecedents

Behavioural implications

Figure 11.5 Theoretical relationship between assignment antecedents, behavioural implications and centralized performance control. *Source*: Janssens (1994c). Reproduced with permission of the author, © M. Janssens 1994.

Tung (1982) has also demonstrated that European and Japanese organizations tend to have lower expatriate failure rates than US multinationals (only around 5 per cent for Japanese managers in the US). In large part this is because they manage expatriate assignments as part of socialization process, actively encourage familiarity with local markets and cultures, and test for language competence prior to foreign assignments (Pucik, 1988).

EXPATRIATION AS A SOURCE OF CONTROL AND EXTERNAL CAREER SOCIALIZATION IN EUROPEAN MULTINATIONALS

Although European organizations readily identify with the same issues experienced by US multinationals, the American attitude to expatriation has not been shared in Europe. The original need for expatriate assignments in European organizations was similar to those practised by US multinationals, i.e. to:

- Exercise control.
- Provide specific skills that the local organization did not have.
- Find career opportunities for a cadre of bright, ambitious managers.

- Develop a stronger managerial (as opposed to technical or functional) orientation through greater mobility.

Reflecting the pressures for strategic and structural change, the reasoning behind using expatriate assignments to develop European managers is changing (Evans, Lank and Farquhar, 1989). This is evidenced by the attitude of the Head of Management Development at Unilever:

... Over the years, the reasons for wanting expatriates have changed. Originally... you didn't have a local who could do the job, so let's find someone who has the skills... a further feeling has grown that the top managers ought to get international experience because they are going to hold top jobs; therefore they need experience of working in different cultures... several group directors... would like an expatriate on the board of their local company... because it would be good for the company to have a bit of challenge to the one best way of doing things.
Head of Management Development, Unilever, in Evans, Lank and Farquhar (1989, p. 122).

In an unpublished survey of over a hundred Business Association organizations (mostly European) of the International Institute for Management Development (IMD) in Lausanne, Derr and Oddou (1991) report that in response to the statement, 'In our firm, international assignments are now mandatory to reach senior management positions', 36 per cent of the respondents answered 'always', 21 per cent replied 'often', 13 per cent specified 'sometimes', 3 per cent answered 'rarely' and 27 per cent answered 'never'. The last figure reflects the fact that 22 per cent of those surveyed were large national (domestic) organizations operating only in their own home markets.

European multinational organizations are now trying to use international assignments to develop their managers and improve the overall 'organizational capability' (Derr and Oddou, 1991; Oddou, 1991; Prahalad and Doz, 1987; Tung, 1989). Within Europe, organizations like BP, Shell, Philips and IBM Europe have considerable experience of managing international career paths and mobility (Forster, 1992). Shell took the policy to its limits, transferring employees in far greater numbers than its competitors, more frequently and at all levels. Edstrom and Galbraith (1977) called this 'control through socialization'. Rather than relying on the more formal and bureaucratic systems of control such as procedures, hierarchical communication and surveillance, they observed that the Shell approach to expatriation created an informal information network – a 'nervous system' – in the organization that facilitated:

- Corporate strategic control.
- Communication and the flow of information between headquarters and the subsidiaries and throughout the organization.
- Identification with the corporate culture without compromising local subsidiary cultures.

This approach was not without problems and these were exacerbated for European oil companies in the early 1990s by falling oil prices and profit levels (Sparrow, 1990). Shell was renowned for its effective system of expatriation, but changes in the organizational structure, joint ventures and mergers all shifted the focus of the employment policy and put pressure on the formalized career planning system (see Illustration 11.18). Indeed, mature organizations such as Unilever, ICI, Philips and Shell are reducing the number of expatriates in line with a policy of increasing the localization of management (Storey, 1992b). However, as Scullion (1992) found in his sample of British and Irish multinationals, whilst formal policies may shift towards favouring host country managers, in practice the reliance on expatriates remains

Illustration 11.18 **Mounting pressure on expatriate career planning systems: the Shell experience.**

In the early 1990s Shell operated in over 100 countries, with refineries in 34 countries and 138,000 employees. Historically, success relied on two policies: strong decentralization (a triple-matrix structure produced a high level of national identity and devolved discretion for local General Managers); and a philosophy of long-term planning. A gradual process of regionalization meant that local General Managers were less open to placing expatriates on their teams, preferring to develop more local managers. This created problems for the expatriation policy, which was tied into a cradle-to-grave employment policy. High levels of historical recruitment coupled with contraction in overall employment had created a large pool of managers with international aspirations but fewer senior-management positions and promotion opportunities. Expatriate managers were the 'glue' that held Shell together and the central career planners were the 'glue' that held the expatriate system together. A central personnel and career planning unit ran assessment centres and managed a coherent planning system for career placements, job evaluation and merit appraisals for 10,000 British and European managers. Managers moved within the same function. One career planner was responsible for recruiting an individual into a function, then acting as a 'parent' and finding a suitable international placement. Career planners acted as 'job-brokers' negotiating, lobbying, prioritizing and co-ordinating the career moves of around 400 managers, who moved every two to three years. A rating of 'estimated potential' (indicating the hierarchical job grade the manager could currently achieve) was assigned to each manager. Each year a formal manpower review considered the performance and development actions for the pool of 10,000 managers, matching men for jobs and jobs for men. This system came under considerable pressure. Regionalization and high costs of expatriate assignments required a more judicious placement system. Contraction in expatriate posts raised the importance of development on the job and indirect international development. Increasing numbers of joint ventures required placements of managers who were adaptable, had good interpersonal skills and a tactful leadership style, yet such qualities were not measured as part of the 'estimate of potential'. Finally, acquisitions and mergers were draining the pool of managers with good marketing and general management abilities, forcing career planners to break the functional barriers previously applied to career moves and enter into difficult negotiations for the release and return of staff.

strong. The response that Shell made to these pressures is outlined later in the chapter (see Illustration 11.24).

A similar approach is adopted by Philips (van Houten, 1989). The entire workforce is ranked into twelve hierarchical levels. Employees with high potential are identified, as are a quota of 2 per cent of management staff deemed capable of rotation to other divisions. International job rotation lies at the heart of Philips' approach to management development. Candidates with the highest potential for top management positions can expect to be sent abroad for at least three or four years and increasingly Philips managers are assigned to its joint ventures with other companies. The system for ranking is based on two assessments, shouldered by line managers, but centrally co-ordinated and tracked by the 'corporate staff bureau':

1. Performance appraisal to evaluate objective, demonstrable job-related criteria.
2. Potential appraisal to generate judgements and hypotheses about the future.

The importance of the corporate staff bureau is reflected in the direct reporting relationship between its director and the president of the board of management, with the top 120 positions in the company under presidential control (van Houten, 1989).

REPATRIATION

Repatriation or the management of 're-entry' is the process of recycling the internationalized manager back into the organization mainstream. Premature repatriation is costly both to the organization and the manager. However, even planned repatriation seems to be a problem (see Illustration 11.19).

Black, Gregersen and Mendenhall (1992) point out that although much has been written about the issue of adjusting to international assignments, little attention has been paid to the topic of repatriation and what has been written has been theoretical and anecdotal (see Adler, 1981; Black and Oddou, 1991; Clague and Krupp, 1978; Harvey, 1982, 1985; Howard, 1980; Kendall, 1981 and Napier and Peterson, 1991). We need to understand the factors involved in successful adjustment by managers during repatriation because:

- The frequency of international assignments will increase.
- International experience is fast becoming an essential stepping stone to career success.
- Given the high failure rate of ongoing assignments, mismanagement of the repatriation process can destroy the considerable efforts put into managing the survivors.

The most pressing motivation to improve the management of repatriation and post-assignment transitions is to allow a joint learning process to take place. Given the centrality of international assignments to the process of internationalization in many European organizations, managers have to be debriefed and their knowledge and learning has to be incorporated into the organization's systems and operations. The organizational learning dimension to international assignments seems to have been completely ignored by researchers.

A major reason for this repatriation failure is that many organizations adopt a 'home and host' system, whereby responsibility for the management and career development aspects of the assignment, the basic administration during the assignment, and facilitation of re-entry all reside with the original 'home' unit (Mayo, 1991). Given the high levels of change in most organizations, the home unit frequently gets restructured or even eliminated whilst the manager is on assignment. A significant majority of

Illustration 11.19 **Difficulties encountered with repatriation.**

Financial

Many of the financial benefits provided in foreign assignments are taken away upon return. Coming to terms with loss of allowances, understanding the impact of inflation and exchange rates on remuneration, and readjustment to home standards of living are all problems.

Organizational

The organizational structure may have changed. Career prospects tend to deteriorate after overseas assignments. Peers have been promoted whilst expatriates have been away, and returners have less autonomy in replacement jobs. Status and credibility may have changed for unexplained reasons, and job expectations and opportunities have to be reconciled.

Personal re-acclimatization

Adjustment back to new schools and lifestyles for families can be as difficult as the original move abroad. The reality of life in the home country has often changed (for the worse). The experience of time overseas has a subtle but slow impact on attitudes and values.

Source: Hogg and Tugwell (1988); Wilson and Rosenfeld (1990).

repatriated employees are dissatisfied with the process (Gomez-Mejia and Balkin, 1987; Napier and Peterson, 1991). Hazzard (1981) found that fewer than half of returning expatriates were promoted upon their return. In many cases repatriation can lead to redundancy and outplacement. Approximately 25 per cent of repatriated US employees leave their organization within one year of returning home (Black, Gregerson and Mendenhall, 1992). Carter (1989) found that more than 50 per cent of expatriates from US organizations eventually ended up in outplacement. Even the survivors typically take between six to twelve months to return to full productivity (Adler, 1991). Similar problems are found by UK employees (Johnston, 1991). Not surprisingly, the main concern of repatriating managers is that their next job should be identified and agreed at least six months before their return (Hogg and Tugwell, 1988). As European organizations come under increasing pressure to rationalize and downsize their operations, one can only expect international managers to become even more uncertain about retaining jobs back in the headquarters once an assignment is complete. The discussion in Chapter Sixteen has considerable bearing on this problem. Excessive repatriation problems can only be avoided where:

- A thorough debriefing system is used, which may involve joint evaluation of the assignment, but also gives recognition to the experience gained abroad and helps managers become aware of how the experience has changed their attitudes.
- Progress in the organization is understood to depend on international service and there is therefore a managed career process with a strong corporate stake in assignments.
- The organization is very centrally driven and directive and operates a succession planning system.

Despite the staggering investment of money and employee time to provide the expatriate experience, most respondents in the Derr and Oddou study (1991) basically agreed with the pungent assessment of one participant: '. . . terrific for me personally but a really lousy career move'. Organizations seem to have only a vague idea of what to do with their internationalized managers after repatriation. Only 23 per cent of managers reported being promoted upon their return; 18 per cent were actually demoted; and 59 per cent ended up in positions of less personal independence and less impact on their organization than they had earlier. In fact, 46 per cent of those surveyed reported that they were not consulted about the type of assignment they would like to have when they returned. 'It was like starting over again when I got back', reported one repatriate, whilst another commented '. . . I realized that I'd learned a foreign language and that nobody in the home office was speaking it − in more ways than one'.

DEMONSTRATING THE BENEFITS: AN EVALUATION OF MANAGER PERFORMANCE VERSUS THE COSTS

Perhaps not surprisingly, international assignments have proved to be an expensive way of internationalizing managers. Expatriate managers typically earn substantial allowances in the form of premiums for relocation, cost-of-living differentials, travel expenses, children's education (Hiltrop and Janssens, 1990). These allowances may increase base salaries by between 25 and 100 per cent. Most multinational organizations also make up any monies lost to the employee through higher taxes. Tax equalization costs, relocation costs, and the cost of travel between subsidiary and parent organizations make the cost of employing expatriate managers significant.

Illustration 11.20 **Typical benefits that accrue from international assignments.**

- Wider understanding of operations, people, organization, strategy, technology, available help and political constraints from inside another 'centre of excellence'.
- Understanding of local environments, constraints, requirements, capabilities and cultures outside the 'home' centre of excellence.
- Enhanced skills in planning, organizing, communication, interpersonal relationships.

- Direct experience aimed at increasing independence, initiative, adaptability, stress tolerance and resilience.
- Attitudes shaped by international thinking, flexibility, realism and multicultural understanding.

Source: Mayo (1991).

When all things are considered, Andrew Mayo, the Director of Personnel for ICL Europe, cites the rule of thumb that the cost of employing a foreign national (depending on the method of calculation) is usually around 300 per cent that of employing a local (Mayo, 1991). A similar figure was found by Sparrow (1992) as part of a human resource planning exercise in a European automobile manufacturer. The human resource productivity loss and replacement costs can really be quite staggering. Failed international assignments severely hamper organizational effectiveness, with the costs to US industry having been estimated at $2 billion (Copeland and Griggs, 1985).

This creates a number of conflicting difficulties for international organizations that target business units and senior managers on their profit and loss, or who delegate significant autonomy to such units in HRM matters. Who cares if it benefits the individual manager or the organization as a whole if it dents my budget? Not surprisingly, there has been a concerted effort to:

- Demonstrate the broader advantages of international assignments, and to tighten up their management and evaluation (see Illustration 11.20).
- Use broader internationalization strategies which complement international assignments with other activities.
- Adopt much higher levels of local management resourcing.

One way around this problem is for organizations to establish 'strategic pots' of money that are used to seed-corn international development and to pay the difference between the assignment costs and the costs of employing a local person. Such seed-corning should only really be necessary where the assignment is mainly intended for personal development and carries less immediate organizational benefit.

CAREER MANAGEMENT SYSTEMS

In this fourth section of the chapter we outline the main issues involved in creating career management systems, identifying high potential and managing mobility.

There is often a lack of strategic integration between the management of mobility, succession planning and the assessment of career potential (Forster, 1992). Succession planning is best considered under three headings (Hirsh, 1984):

- Inputs.
- Outputs.
- Processes.

The most appropriate inputs that need to be considered in an effective career management system are shown in Table 11.5. On the basis of these data, the system typically uses a series of processes (such as matching people to jobs, sequencing career moves, assessing succession strength and creating plans, and creating lists of people according to specific information search criteria) to provide useful outputs that the organization can use to make decisions about career development (see Table 11.6). There are differences across Europe in the use of various career development techniques and processes. Succession plans are the most popular process used. They are used by between 41 and 50 per cent of organizations in Switzerland, Germany, Norway, Sweden and the UK, falling to between 11 and 17 per cent of Danish, French and Dutch organizations. Formal career plans are used by between 20 and 28 per cent of Swiss, Spanish, Italian, Dutch, Swedish and British organizations. This falls to 12–13 per cent of German, Danish and Norwegian organizations, and only 7 per cent of French organizations (Holden and Livian, 1992).

Table 11.5 **Inputs to a career management process.**

Type of input	Type of source
Individual data	
Personal details; name, date of birth, sex, date of joining, qualifications	Personnel information database (preferably an automatic link)
Career history post, grades, time in each	as above or written c.v. if special coding needed
Training history	ditto
Earliest date for move	These come from appraisal information or supplementary discussions/assessments
Last performance rating	
Current potential code	
Mobility	
Knowledge, skills, attitudes and experience; languages	Personal growth profile
Career plan including plans for significant training	From development review with individual
Other information (textual)	Careers manager's input
Organizational data	
Characteristics of posts	Organization charts
Division, department	
Post identifier	
Title(s)	
Development post identifier	
Manpower category	
Location(s)	
Earliest date available	
Grade/level	
Current post holder and date appointed	
Essential knowledge, skill, attitude and experience requirements	Person specifications for jobs
Other textual data	Careers manager's input

Source: this table is taken from *Managing Careers: Strategies for organizations* by A. Mayo and reproduced with permission of the publishers, the Institute of Personnel Management, IPM House, 35 Camp Road, Wimbledon, London SW19 4UX, © 1991.

Table 11.6 **Key processes and outputs in career management systems.**

Process	Output
1. Job/people matching	Options of candidates for posts available
2. Move sequencing	Chains of planned career moves
3. Succession strength assessment	Availability of potential in specified areas
4. Succession plans	Successors for particular posts or types of post – with 'ready dates'
5. Order, list, search	Lists of people according to specified search or ordering instructions
	Manpower planning data, such as percentage of people with potential, ratio of women, etc.

Source: this table is taken from *Managing Careers: Strategies for organizations* by A. Mayo and reproduced with permission of the publishers, the Institute of Personnel Management, IPM House, 35 Camp Road, Wimbledon, London SW19 4UX, UK, © 1991.

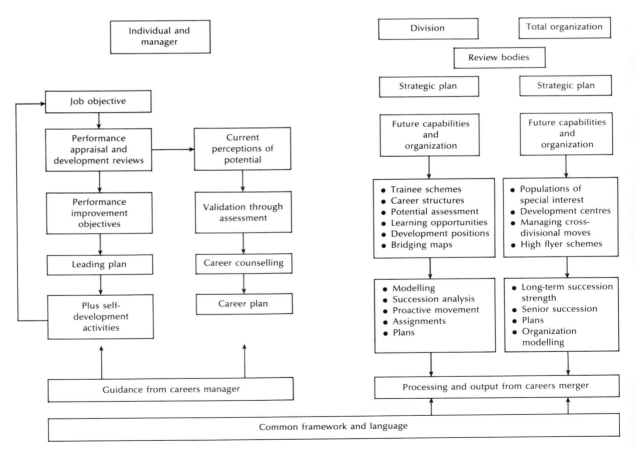

Figure 11.6 Framework for career development in an organization. *Source*: this figure is taken from *Managing Careers: Strategies for organizations* by A. Mayo and reproduced with permission of the publishers, the Institute of Personnel Management, IPM House, 35 Camp Road, Wimbledon, London, SW19 4UX, UK, © 1991.

Illustration 11.21 **Career development tools and techniques.**

- Approaches involved in the identification of high potential.
- Career succession planning.
- Self assessment tools, e.g. career planning workshops.
- Individual counselling, e.g. by internal or external specialists.

- Information on the organization's internal labour market, e.g. internal vacancy lists, skill requirements of particular posts, career path planning.
- Development programmes, e.g. mentoring systems, job rotation/sharing, time off or financial assistance for an educational course.

Ideally, career management systems are linked into personnel information databases. They have the capability of processing information in a defined and usable way. They operate at three levels: the individual or manager, the division or business unit, and the total organization career management system. The various features of an organization career management system are shown in Figure 11.6. The main tools and techniques are listed in Illustration 11.21.

IDENTIFYING HIGH POTENTIAL: ASSESSMENT CENTRES OR CAREER DEVELOPMENT WORKSHOPS

. . . There is a growing obsession to detect HIPOs (High Potential Employees) from the very start. A 'high potential employee' is often defined as a manager who is able to climb up two levels in the hierarchy before reaching a given age. Because of cultural differences, the systems used to detect HIPOs are designed differently.   Bournois and Chauchat (1990, p 8).

The Price Waterhouse/Cranfield Project has found some evidence to support this contention. High-flier schemes were used regularly by 44 per cent of French organizations and 41 per cent of Swedish organizations (the sample was biased towards larger employers). The figure was between 33 per cent and 39 per cent for organizations from Switzerland, Spain, and Norway, and 28 to 29 per cent of Danish, Italian and British organizations. High-flyer schemes were least popular in organizations from Germany (21 per cent) and the Netherlands (24 per cent).

Assessment centres are mainly used in relation to recruitment and selection, career assessment, or occasionally as part of an appraisal system, particularly when the emphasis is on identifying 'high potential'. In Chapter Nine we outlined the use of assessment centres in recruitment, noting the Anglo-Saxon emphasis on the use of detailed and empirically-validated techniques to make resourcing decisions. In this chapter we consider the use of assessment centres in the context of career management. When used as part of career management systems, they are more normally called 'career development workshops' (CDWs). This method typically involves a series of exercises in which employees are required to show their ability or potential for taking up more responsible positions. These involve various job practice simulations (group exercises, in tray exercises, presentations), interviews and often also psychometric testing (personality questionnaires, occupational interest surveys, etc.). Each element of the CDW is designed to assess critical skills or specific competencies (see Chapter Ten), which are assessed by trained observers, usually psychologists, who use the various tests, tasks and assignments to predict the individual's performance if and when promoted to a higher level. CDWs produce more accurate and reliable information about employees than most traditional methods of potential assessment. However, they are relatively expensive and time consuming and are not used by all European organizations.

Within Europe, CDWs are most popular in Britain, Scandinavia, the Benelux countries and Germany. In these countries the method is mainly used as a diagnostic tool in the evaluation of potential, career planning, and management development. In Britain, for instance, it is estimated that nearly half of all organizations with more than 1,000 employees use CDWs at some level or another for the assessment of career potential. Electrolux, the Swedish white goods manufacturer, assesses the potential for senior management responsibility using a series of international CDWs that use an agreed set of criteria and an international group of line managers as assessors (Syrett and Gratton, 1989). However, in Danish organizations, despite the high level of formal training, there is a strong belief in experiential learning processes (on-the-job development). A heavier emphasis is put on stimulating learning opportunities within the environment, and notably less emphasis on the use of formal career plans, planned job rotation and high-flier schemes. Earmarking and formally training only the most talented employees is felt to be a waste of resources (Andersen *et al.* 1993). The high level of job mobility allows high-fliers to be recruited, rather than specially developed.

We noted the paradox in Chapter Ten that although French managers show the highest concern in Europe for the identification of high potential, there is very little literature on the topic (Bournois and Roussillon, 1992). Differences in the use of particular assessment techniques may reflect different ways of thinking about the problem of identifying high potential managers. Bournois and Roussillon (1992) argue that a hidden assumption of CDWs is that it is possible to identify managers who are innately capable of effective performance at senior levels and those who are not (in practice most Anglo-Saxon organizations use CDWs for the identification and discussion of strengths and weaknesses and coaching purposes as opposed to definitive promote/don't promote decisions). Given this assumption of innate abilities, one might expect that CDWs could find a role in French organizations, although, as we pointed out in the last chapter, the decision about qualities of leadership (as measured by intellectual qualities) for French managers tends to be made on entry to the organization.

Bournois and Roussillon (1992) carried out a postal survey of seventy French private sector and nationalized organizations employing more than 2,000 employees. The questionnaires were completed by HRM managers and line managers responsible for executive careers. Some organizations were domestically owned and others were subsidiaries of multinationals. The proportion of organizations using different methods (including assessment centres) to identify high potential is shown in Table 11.7. In general, the importance of line management formal decisions and interpersonal relationships is stressed, with very little emphasis on the psychological assessments of potential favoured by Anglo-Saxon organizations. In France, it is the process as opposed to the method which is more important.

It seems that the whole concept of identifying a series of separate 'competencies' against which managers may be assessed may be counter-cultural to French organizations. Gentil (1988) quotes a French specialist in the identification of potential, Marcel Husson, to explain that the notion of 'high potential' in France refers to '. . . a unique phenomenon made up of basic and evolving fundamental possibilities as well as acquired forms of competence, of yet unsounded talents, of traits, of character and of regular habits, of taste and of different motivations and aspirations'. Potential in France is seen as a complex unity '. . . that is impossible to reduce to a sum of its separately identifiable parts and capacities' (Bournois and Roussillon, 1992). In a study on the identification and management of potential in French organizations,

Table 11.7 **Methods for identifying high potential executives in French organizations.**

Method for identifying high potential	% considering technique as satisfactory or very satisfactory	Predictive value
Annual performance appraisal	70.2	74%
Other information from superiors	57.9	75%
Career guidance interviews with DHR	57.9	72%
Being 'discovered' by a top manager	17.5	43%
Psychological tests	3.6	25%
Assessment centres	8.7	44%
Simulation exercises	1.7	n/a
Graphology	1.7	n/a

Source: reprinted from *Human Resource Management Journal*, **3(1)**, 37–56, F. Bournois and S. Roussillon, 'The concept of high-flier executives in France: the weight of national culture', copyright © 1992, with kind permission of John Wiley and Sons, Inc.

Vermot-Gaud (1990) only devotes five pages to the topic of assessment centres, pointing to the problem of conflicting interests amongst groups of employees in France and the difficulties experienced in arriving at a consensus about the nature of effectiveness from all those involved. Paradoxically, one of the greatest selling points of competency-based approaches to management potential in Anglo-Saxon organizations is their ability to create a joint understanding and language for effectiveness amongst various employee groups. The rejection of a joint manager–subordinate problem-solving approach also has implications for the topic of performance management, which we discuss in Chapter Fourteen.

DEVELOPMENT OF POTENTIAL THROUGH PLANNED CAREER PROGRESSION

A number of essential qualities in managers are developed through career mobility. For example, Evans (1992b) argues that as European organizations continue to decentralize and segment their structures, and as they attempt to adjust to new competitive threats and pursue continuous improvement, then leadership qualities become more important at lower levels, and certainly amongst middle managers. Historically, poor leadership abilities at this level have hampered the implementation of change, and it can be expected to create difficulties again in the 1990s. In developing these qualities, the traditional ETD techniques outlined in the previous chapter are of limited value. Cross-functional mobility aimed at transferring the person to another job where he or she has to produce results through people who have more expertise than they have themselves is a core management development process. An important rule in career mobility is that no manager should become a member of a cross-functional management team unless they have proved themselves in a job in the other function. This creates three benefits to the organization, improving its underlying capabilities by:

1. Ensuring senior executives have improved their leadership qualities through having to deliver results through people who have different skills and cultural norms.
2. Guaranteeing that the management team understand the importance of collaboration and personal networks that facilitate co-ordination.

3. Changing the culture down the functional hierarchy by demonstrating career prospects are damaged without cross-functional collaboration.

The use of planned job rotation as a way of developing managers varies across European organizations. The approach is used by between 21 and 32 per cent of organizations from Italy, Norway, Sweden, Denmark, the Netherlands and Spain (listed in order of use of planned job rotations). It is least well developed as an approach in organizations from France (only 8 per cent use the technique), Germany (12 per cent) and Switzerland (13 per cent). Two examples of career development through planned career progression (which is not the same as job rotation) are provided at Asea Brown Boveri (Illustration 11.22) and Philips (Illustration 11.23). As with all HRM approaches, a sense of balance in the breadth and pace of career or job mobility is needed:

... excessive rotation may develop zig-zag management, where able newly-appointed general managers lead their subsidiaries or business units in new directions, to be replaced three years later in the implementation stage by a successor who leads the unit off in a different direction. Driven by a questionable logic that high potential individuals have to occupy ten or twelve different jobs before reaching positions of strategic responsibility at the age of 45, these persons spend about 18 months in each job ... they develop skills in starting things off, but not in finishing them. They develop good networking skills, but are shallow in their people management competences because they have never been long enough in a position for the consequences of their actions to catch up on them.   Evans (1992b, p. 6).

LIMITED EURO-MANAGER MOBILITY

The advent of the SEM and the rapid process of internationalization of organizations is expected to accelerate present levels of job mobility across Europe (Forster, 1992),

Illustration 11.22 **Management development through planned career progression at Asea Brown Boveri.**

In the Swiss/Swedish organization of Asea Brown Boveri management development is based on learning on-the-job in the context of a planned increase in the scope of responsibility. Considerable attention is given to identifying talent and ensuring that managers are exposed to upper-level management, although this is a difficult task in an organization with 1,300 companies operating in 120 countries. 'High-fliers' are identified around the age of thirty, by which time they typically have a university degree and three to six years' service and will have a post such as a production planning manager. By their mid-thirties managers will become a functional manager, in preparation for running a division or small company by the age of thirty-seven. Three years later, the high fliers are capable of taking charge of a division of a large company or running a similar smaller company. Development through these stages is monitored through discussion with superiors. There is no group-wide appraisal scheme or system of identifying potential. The organizational structure is too complex and diversified. Local HRM managers create their own succession plans detailing the next seven or eight managers below company president level, and a further pool of around twenty managers who are successors to the level below president. Within the Swedish group of 30,000 employees, there would be forty-five managers who are candidates for the very top and 200 candidates for running smaller companies. In this process line managers are seen as the real HRM managers. However, this process is open to the different skills and motivations of line managers. The 'givers' are very good at attracting, training and developing managers for the organizational good, whilst 'receivers' tend to take the best talent and try to keep it.

Source: Sadler and Milmer (1993).

Illustration 11.23 **Corporate interest groups and planned career scenarios at Philips.**

Philips, based in the Netherlands, employs 240,000 people worldwide. It is creating new formal systems to manage career development and the identification of high potential. The HR function meets at least once a year for a formal management development review process that considers succession into key positions and the pool of young high-potential managers in both the product divisions and the large national organizations (see Chapter Eight). Action plans are drawn up after the review meeting. About five years after joining, at the age of 28–30, a corporate potential appraisal system identifies a number of characteristics that were shown to be predictive of future career success several years ago (and have now been updated to incorporate changed views of relevant managerial behaviour). Development is managed in three main ways:

1. Use of challenging assignments to foster knowledge of the business.

2. Management of career paths with planned rotations.
3. Formal management training.

The appraisal system is operated with varying degrees of effectiveness across the organization. However, a corporate-level career approach is being introduced, with the top 200 people (whom the board appoints), 600 successors to these posts, and a further 1,000 young high-potential managers receiving special 'corporate interest'. Further assessments of potential are made through a standard corporate appraisal, and 'career scenarios' are painted for each individual. The skills of line managers are essential to the process, and the need to build an assessment of their people-management skills into their own appraisal is a likely future development.

Source: Sadler and Milmer (1993).

although most career movement will be limited to skilled professional and managerial employees (Thom, 1992). However, whilst international HRM involves the worldwide management of people and appreciation of the cultural determinants of their internal career, as we have seen, the traditional focus of (principally US) writing has been on the selection, training and development, performance appraisal and rewarding of internationally mobile personnel (Adler and Ghader, 1989). European organizations need to manage mobility, since it holds the key to leadership development, international management skills and organization capability (Evans, 1992b). Although many of Europe's larger organizations (such as Philips, BP and Shell) have developed considerable experience in managing international career paths and mobility, only a small proportion of European organizations in other sectors have systematically understood the impact that their integration strategies will have on the future careers of their employees, their commitment to higher levels of mobility, the preparation they need in terms of employee training and development (ETD) for international careers, and the knock-on effects this will have on employment practices in other areas – such as recruitment, performance management and pay and benefits (Forster, 1992; Mosley, 1990; Smith, 1992). Few social scientists have considered the management of job mobility and careers in an international context, or examined the sociological and psychological dimensions of these transitions, the learning processes that take place in organizations in an international context, the individual adaptability, cultural transition and acclimatization processes that take place; nor have they considered the competency profiles that are associated with effective international managers. In short, a lot more research is needed.

It is also realized increasingly that the requirement for higher levels of mobility within Europe presents a number of challenges:

- Many managers are seeking a form of international management that does not lose sight of national practice (Lorbiecki, 1993).
- There are limitations on this mobility, making integration of management through increased job and career mobility a slow process (Forster, 1992).
- Whilst frequent moves may help in individual career development and may be a useful tool for internationalizing the organization, they often leave managers without a deep level of business knowledge of the markets they have worked in, may remove their sense of personal achievement, and may eventually dilute the 'core competence' of the organization (Hamel and Prahalad, 1989).
- Lifting barriers on the transfer of labour may mean that the international 'cadre' of executives that has been so painfully developed may begin to see themselves as mobile, rather than linked to one organization, especially during periods of skills shortage (Syrett and Gratton, 1989).

Lorbiecki (1993) believes that we cannot afford a world of rootless managers, who move from job to job because the price is right. We have to encourage them to stay because their depth of understanding of the local culture is critical to future success. Not only do some writers believe that managers should not become overly mobile, there are good practical reasons why they will not. The notion that the Euro-worker will move from one country to another in pursuit of jobs seems ill-founded. It is unlikely that this type of lifestyle would appeal to more than a couple of per cent of any large multinational organization (Jackson, 1990).

Mobility will be weighed against an increasing demand for quality of life. Spouses and families have a marked impact on international mobility and the profile of mobile employees is changing. In Europe approximately 85 per cent of mobile families are 'headed' by a male employee (Brett, Stroh and Reilly, 1990; Forster, 1990), rising to 90 per cent of US managers (Black and Gregersen, 1991) and 100 per cent of Japanese managers (Black, 1990). Employees with families are less enthusiastic about accepting international assignments (37 per cent of the managers identified by Brett *et al.* (1990) would not accept international transfers unless severely pressured). European managers are even less enthusiastic about mobility. Moreover, the rapid growth in the number of women in management positions (see Chapter Four) has created dual-career families in European labour markets. The male-headed nuclear family with a compliant female partner prepared to uproot is rapidly disappearing. There are also local issues that deter mobility. For example, in the early 1990s a key deterrent to many German managers moving was the cost of housing. The national accommodation crisis since reunification saw rents rise across Germany by 14 per cent from 1989–92 compared to only 2 per cent from 1980–1989. Attracting good managers to the *Länder* in the East became extremely difficult (International Management, 1992b).

Evans (1992a), based on his INSEAD experiences, takes a pragmatic stance. He argues that it is not a question of creating the 'Euro-manager' by making national managers more European. The challenge will be to create appropriate cohesion among diverse European cultures which must work together (see Chapter Ten for a discussion of the impact of this need for cohesion in top teams). This will occur through a broadening of the HRM agenda to:

- Build more face-to-face relations.
- Create international project groups solving common business issues.
- Build management competency and corporate identity around sets of internationally-shared values.

BROADENING THE EMPLOYEE TRAINING AND DEVELOPMENT AGENDA

In this fifth and final section of the chapter we consider the ways in which European organizations have broadened the HRM agenda in an attempt to accelerate the process of internationalization. In Chapter Six we made the point that when considering the issue of internationalizing careers, most European organizations link management of the issue to the need to adapt a range of related HRM processes, such as external resourcing, deployment practices, aspects of work and organization structure and the cross-cultural fertilization of culture. The need to consider career management issues in this broader (and long-term) framework is made clear by the situation at Shell (see Illustration 11.24).

EUROPEAN MNC STRATEGIES TO INTERNATIONALIZE THEIR MANAGERS

There is, then, still much to be done by European organizations in their attempts to internationalize their managers. The PWCP study of HRM in Europe reported a

Illustration 11.24 **Long-term issues associated with internationalization at Shell: the agenda for the HRM managers.**

A large multinational and culturally diverse European organization such as Shell is likened to a State. It needs a cadre of employees loyal to the organization as a whole rather than its constituent parts, and who transfer the organization's technology, methods and culture to every division and unit. In addressing the need for long-term staffing, Shell concentrate on four challenges:

1. Recruiting people of sufficient quality in sufficient numbers.
2. Deploying managers around the world.
3. Developing new kinds of managers.
4. Retaining good people.

The proportion of highly skilled people to the total number of staff will increase. However, this shift needs to be achieved when external demographics are leading to a 20 per cent fall in the population of eighteen year olds in the Netherlands and a fall in university entrants. Internal demographic problems complicate matters as the people recruited in the growth years of the 1960s and 1970s retire en masse around 2000. Shell therefore needs to place even more emphasis on internal mobility in order to transfer technology and culture and enhance cohesion. Mobility, however, can no longer be taken for granted. By 1995, 81 per cent of US managers will be dual career partnerships. As more managers are women, mobility decreases. Eighty per cent of expatriate men are still accompanied by their spouses, but only 25 per cent of women are. Family and quality of life issues are leading to a reluctance to move or demands for more compensation.

Continued expansion through mergers, acquisitions and new ventures, coupled with a continued contraction of the core of the organization is creating new organizational structures. Small, flexible and decentralized units will blur the differences between supervision and execution and staff and line. Expatriate managers will be deployed as consultants and investors rather than as supervisors and operators, requiring highly developed business skills and cross-cultural awareness. Retention of such managers will be made more difficult because of poaching from unexpected competition, pressures to offer internationally competitive remuneration packages, and the prospect of managers reaching career plateaux sooner in flatter-structured organizations. As the focus in European organizations moves to uncertainty and flexibility, HRM managers must become the facilitators of change within their organizations. Continuous organization change is likely to set the pace for long-term management and career development.

Source: Vanderbroeck (1992), Human Resource Manager, Shell Research, Schwahenheim, Germany.

marked gap between principle and practice (Brewster and Bournois 1991). The mergers and acquisitions, joint ventures, and strategic alliances with organizations headquartered in other European countries force virtually all European multinational organizations to deal with different national cultures and operate in diverse national settings. Although most European organizations acknowledge the importance of preparing their managers to operate effectively in the SEM, according to the study, comparatively few have functioning programmes to internationalize their managers (Derr and Oddou, 1993). Most top executives in global organizations are concerned about speeding the process up.

... we can't wait around for years while someone goes abroad and then adjusts back [after repatriation] and internalizes the whole international experience. We have to find ways to speed up this whole process.   A Shell executive, in Evans, Lank and Farquhar (1989, p. 122).

Derr and Oddou (1993) argue that it is only after a more rapid process of broadening through career management strategies that managers can develop business strategies that are sufficiently influenced by the various European national contexts to be appropriate and successful in the long term. European governments have attempted to foster a cadre of 'European management thinkers' through programmes such as ERASMUS, COMETT and Lingua aimed at encouraging student and business person exchanges between countries. However, until recently the breadth of methods used by organizations to internationalize their managers (i.e. beyond simple expatriation) has not been clear. Derr and Oddou (1993) analysed questionnaire data from sixty-nine international HRM directors on the International Institute of Management Development's (IMD) list of business associates. The sample covered multinational corporations (MNC's) ranging in size from 1,000 to 200,000 employees. A range of industrial

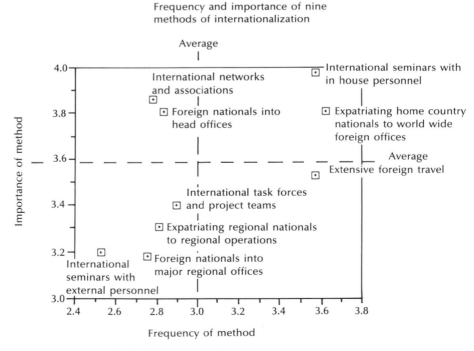

Figure 11.7 Nine methods of internationalizing managers in European MNCs. *Source data*: Derr and Oddou (1993).

sectors were covered including chemicals, pharmaceuticals, banking, finance, computers, manufacturing, mining, petroleum and natural resources. Twenty-two of the organizations were classified as Anglo (UK, Canada, Australia or US origin), fifteen were Germanic (Germany, Austria, Switzerland), fifteen were Scandinavian (Finland, Norway, Sweden, Denmark), six Benelux (Holland, Belgium, Luxembourg) and four were Euro-Latin (France, Spain and Italy). Seven organizations did not claim a single country of origin. Derr and Oddou (1993) felt that, excepting an under-representation of Euro-Latin organizations, this was a representative European sample. The HRM directors were asked to rate questions about methods of internationalizing managers and future trends on a 1–5 point scale. The survey points out several alternatives to the problem of '. . . waiting around for years' for the benefits of internationalization highlighted by many European executives. Figure 11.7 contrasts nine such methods in terms of frequency and importance.

Importing foreign nationals

According to Derr and Oddou (1991), the most important future organization trend for internationalizing executives was importing expertise by bringing foreign nationals into the head office for a one-to-three-year assignment that would involve them in decision making, provide a forum in which they could share their more global perspectives, and expose more nationals to international views and values. In Derr and Oddou's (1993) study, 73 per cent of the respondents identified the practice of importing expert foreign nationals to corporate headquarters as a key to future internationalization. Twenty-five per cent said their use of this approach was remaining constant, and only 2 per cent saw the trend as decreasing. The three major reasons for its future importance were that it:

1. Brought a 'different perspective' to headquarters.
2. Used top people more effectively worldwide, irrespective of their nationality.
3. Trained foreign nationals in the organizational culture so that, when they were again living in their home regions, they would have better connections to and with the home office.

For example, a British Steel respondent noted that the current balance between UK and non-UK personnel in head office management was 90 to 10; but '. . . in the future . . .head office management will become increasingly non-UK'. The respondent at Tetra-Pack International, the Swedish paper and packaging organization, expressed a similar policy: '. . . we will increasingly bring foreign nationals to the head office and run more internationally formulated projects'. Ericsson, the Swedish electronics organization, has also announced a policy of increasing the percentage of non-Swedes assigned to top management positions.

International task forces

Working in international project groups is another excellent way to accomplish needed and important tasks. Internationalization is a side benefit of such assignments, but a side benefit that is being increasingly capitalized on and consciously managed by the more forward-thinking organizations. Eighty-four per cent of those surveyed predicted that such task forces would increase in the years ahead. In Chapter Eight we gave the

Illustration 11.25 **Octagon teams at Philips.**

For two decades, Philips has used cross-national teams (the 'Octagons') as part of its managerial training and development. Three task forces of eight people each work together for six or eight months on specific study assignments. After a two-week seminar in Eindhoven, senior management presents a number of important global projects; each group chooses one. The task force participants devote about 20 per cent of their time to these projects, meeting regularly in various European locations. At the project's end, the group presents its report to Philips's top-level managers, who consider carefully the possibility of implementing their recommendations. In a significant number of cases, the work of the octagons has become the basis for important new directions and emphases for Philips. This meaningful, on-the-job approach not only benefits the organization but internationalizes the participants in the process.

example of Jacobs Suchard using such teams to Europeanize the structure. Philips is another organization that has made use of this approach (see Illustration 11.25).

Attending cross-cultural seminars

A significant number of organizations plan inhouse seminars and external training sessions for their managers that constitute, in effect, cross-cultural classrooms. Seventy-seven per cent of the respondents noted that management seminars (in-company, multi-company or public) with multinational participants were growing in popularity. A respondent from a European-based Australian banking organization explained: '... growth and development of overseas business operations are booming, and we will continue to rely on... international executive programmes to get our people up to speed'. The respondent from a large Dutch paper organization commented: '... our in-company seminar... is indispensable to our international expansion strategy'. The respondent from Montedison, the large Italian chemical and pharmaceutical organization, corroborated: '... we plan to increase group international culture through our inhouse education programs'.

Long business trips

Another important internationalizing tool of the future, according to the survey respondents, was an increased use of the 'long' business trip (see Illustration 11.26). Typically, a mid- or senior-level manager would spend two or three months abroad conducting business, perhaps at a single regional or organization headquarters office or perhaps at several different locales within a region. As more strategic business units and companies within the larger organization locate their head offices away from corporate headquarters, more business has to be conducted at these locales.

INTERNATIONALIZATION OF MANAGERS THROUGH THE CREATION OF EURO-NETWORKS

A number of respondents answered an open ended question asking them to list 'other methods' of internationalization by mentioning global teleconferencing as an

Illustration 11.26   **Advantages and disadvantages of long business trips.**

The advantage of the long business trip is that it gives a manager an international experience without dislocating the family by a disruptive move. Furthermore, the deliberate pacing of the visit, while supplying a flood of information, still allows enough time for the executive to process information, form hypotheses, collect impressions as well as statistics, and make contacts. One short-coming is that the visitor may never get beneath the surface and, hence, may not really end up knowing much detail about another market or culture. A second potential problem, particularly with a visit that moves the executive quite quickly from one location to another, is that the senior manager's experience can be over-controlled. In this situation, called 'festival touring', everything is prettied up for the visiting dignitary, the proportion of ceremonial appearances and banquets to actual work and observation is high, and the visitors' contacts are sufficiently limited that he or she receives only the 'party line' as they pass through.

alternative to extensive travel. Gulf War travel restrictions in early 1991 made this method newly important. In some instances, they said, it was effective in allowing some 'face-to-face' contact, and it was far superior in saving time and money. Some organizations said they plan to continue using teleconferencing as a way of saving executive time and travel expenses. For the same reasons, organizations also keep up international contacts through other methods. A Caterpillar International respondent cited faxes, telephone calls, memos, and reports as ways to move a great deal of information across borders and thereby assist the internationalization process. Several other respondents went beyond the choices of the survey to describe their array of internationalization services. For example, the respondent at NESTE, the Finnish petroleum products and chemical organization, identified an interlocking network of strategies and policies that created an increasingly internationalized management system.

... We believe in using more local nationals, building close contacts with special international consultants, using internal experts and their networks, building international teams and task forces, using external customers as experts, and moving expatriates from their present job to another international location, not back to Finland.   Executive from NESTE.

A clear development in the European approach to internationalization of managers has been the development of stronger internal and external 'networks'. In relation to career management, three other practices on the cutting edge of the challenge of internationalization were identified. These all highlighted the importance of informal management networks (see Illustration 11.27).

Finally, the organization may deliberately design itself so that the combination of decentralized and international organizational structures emphasizes the organizational culture (see Chapter Eight). A respondent from Elf Aquitaine, the French petroleum products organization, commented: '... we move people worldwide in order to share our common culture and know-how'. Organizational culture was seen as '... the glue that holds the diverse pieces of the global puzzle together'. Such organizations achieved their goal of internationalization by the extensive deployment (expatriation) of senior managers. These individuals thoroughly understood the organization culture, could act as role models and mentors for younger foreign national managers and employees, and could articulate the key principles and values from the culture that acted as the most appropriate basis for decision making.

Illustration 11.27   **Internationalizing managers through informal networks.**

Consultants

Some organizations have found it helpful to use consultants specializing in the internationalization of managers. Some persons and consulting organizations help multinational corporations design international training seminars, expatriate/repatriate programs, and international compensation and pension plans. Consultants also serve organizations in delivering specific services to expatriates, such as programs for relocating families with a minimum of disruption, cross-cultural and language training, and finding jobs for working spouses.

In-company networks

Some organizations also create extensive in-company international networks by designing 'invitation only' cross-cultural course meetings, task forces, and seminars within their own organization. Getting more key people within the organization to meet one another and 'connect' is the goal of this intervention.

Senior managers

Some respondents reported making better use of senior managers with extensive international experience. These globally savvy managers are called on in the organization's national offices to give presentations, coach younger up-and-comers, and present the non-dominant perspective at important meetings.

General trends in approaches to internationalization

There is a clear trend of increasing importance across the various methods outlined in the previous sections. Despite a continued reliance on expatriation, methods to integrate knowledge and culture across organizations through the use of more temporary but diverse contacts are coming to the fore. Eighty-one per cent of the sample in the Derr and Oddou (1993) study felt they would make greater use of international task forces and project teams, 78 per cent would increase seminars with inhouse foreign nationals. These approaches are both currently less frequent but highly important methods of internationalizing. Fifty-six per cent would increase seminars attended by foreigners from outside the organization and 44 per cent would increase travel to foreign operations (a frequent, but unimportant, method of internationalizing managers). Although significant differences were found between methods across industrial sectors, on the whole there was surprisingly little variation in approach across European countries. The only notable differences in emphasis were that the Anglo and Germanic organizations brought more foreign nationals to regional headquarter positions than Scandinavian or Benelux organizations.

Despite the pan-European approach to internationalizing management indicated by such trends, Derr and Oddou's (1993) study also indicated relatively low levels of current internationalization on these nine methods at present. Only 28 per cent of the top 200 staff managers and 35 per cent of the top 200 line managers had experienced at least one international assignment. Not surprisingly, 75 per cent of European MNC's felt that in-company expertise was insufficient. The most international function was marketing, whilst members of the Personnel function were the least internationalized. Derr and Oddou (1993) find the low levels of internationalization surprising given the close geographic proximity of European countries. It is also extremely worrying. The limited exposure of important decision makers to global business operations may cast doubts over the wisdom of some of their decisions about restructuring European management (reviewed in Chapter Five).

LATERAL DEVELOPMENT OF MANAGERS: NEW CAREER PATHS AND NEW JOB DESIGNS

As organizational values continue to change (see Chapter Seven) and structures become flatter (see Chapter Eight) then the definition and scope of ETD will broaden. The value of promotion as an incentive is becoming less powerful as managers comprehend the realities of the transition taking place in organizations and the economic environment (Hilb, 1992). Two new career paths are emerging in European organizations:

1. Geographical, functional and divisional job rotation within the organization or with outsiders such as suppliers, customers or joint-venture partners.
2. Permanent job enrichment governed by controlling HRM policies.

Hilb (1992) argues that too many European organizations still provide development opportunities for only a handful of international managers and therefore do not fully utilize their talents. As European organizations move beyond developing this small cadre of international managers, towards a more coherent overall development of their human resources, then HRM policies and processes will begin to encourage reviews of the personnel structure every time a vacancy arises. The considerations that will take place will be whether the position can be eliminated in part or in full by:

- Enriching other jobs with the important elements.
- Automating as much of the routine elements of the job as possible.
- Discounting the unnecessary portions of the job.

The changes in career development and management discussed in this chapter have significant implications for the nature of job design and the shape of future jobs. We therefore move on to discuss the topic of job design in the next chapter.

CONCLUSIONS

This chapter has highlighted a number of extremely important developments in the nature of career management and the process of internationalization in many European organizations. A number of clear transitions can be detected. Conflicting pressures, driven by FDI, transnationalization, competitive forces, social changes and national cultural constraints, are leading to a transition in career management systems. The task of defining 'external' careers for managers has become more complex as cradle-to-grave employment philosophies continue to decline. As the shape of 'external' careers changes, the 'internal' career will begin to dominate managerial behaviour. Consequently, the economic and psychological importance of upgrading skills and competencies will come to the fore. In this period of transition towards the management of internal careers, the career management strategies of organizations will powerfully determine the ultimate progress of their efforts to internationalize themselves.

The mindset of European managers is also in transition. It is being challenged by several processes of internationalization. The most immediate impact is being created by the internationalization of the mechanisms of corporate governance, and new resourcing strategies that are bringing in internationally mobile young graduates. The nature of international assignments and expatriate management is also shifting towards the management of learning through personal networks, team-based learning and shorter term exposure to different cultural environments. However, not all of the lessons from the heavy reliance on expatriate managers in Anglo-Saxon organizations seem to apply to the experience of European multinationals, particularly in terms of cross-cultural adaptability. There is therefore a shift taking place towards a broadening of the HRM agenda in order to manage the internationalization process. Achieving this shift will be very difficult at a time of high rationalization and increasing demands to balance work life with the need for family life and dual-career families. Clearly, in order to manage careers and truly internationalize themselves, there are a number of key learning points from a HRM perspective.

LEARNING POINTS FROM CHAPTER ELEVEN

1. International careers are becoming a more common feature of working life for European managers.

2. In managing these careers, organizations need to consider both the internal career (the psychological perceptions that drive managers' career decisions) and the external career (the career paths, stages and sequence of jobs through which managers progress).

3. The external career is under considerable threat as cradle-to-grave employment philosophies diminish in number.

4. Individual differences play a strong role in determining the internal career and choice of career paths. Effective career decisions are based on self-awareness, knowledge of occupations, readiness for effective decision making, decision making style and self-esteem.

5. The career dynamics within organizations also strongly reflect national culture, as managers are socialized into believing the different indicators of career success across European countries.

6. Individuals who are socialized in one particular culture can adjust successfully to the requirements of other cultures, but European managers tend to have distinctive career orientations depending on their nationality.

7. Organizations are internationalizing their mechanisms of corporate governance by recruiting CEOs and directors from non-traditional sources and foreign countries. Multinational management teams are developing faster in continental Europe than in Anglo-Saxon organizations. Foreign national non-executive directors are becoming a more common feature.

8. European experience is also becoming an important stepping stone in the career development of senior US managers.

9. Several European organizations (and particularly in France) are internationalizing themselves by recruiting new cadres of internationally-mobile graduates. There is fairly high agreement on the important characteristics to look for.

10 These Euro-graduates appear to have a different set of career orientations to existing European managers. They place a greater emphasis on the need to manage people, provide service and develop a balanced lifestyle.

11. Bringing cadres of Euro-graduates into the organization places considerable pressure on the receiving departments. The need for diversity has to be sold to managers.

12. International assignments have long been the most common way of internationalizing managers, but they have become more complex, shorter term and team-based, placing

a greater emphasis on the decision whether to use a local manager or not, and the need to consider the high costs.

13. The selection criteria used to assign expatriate managers often have little to do with those factors that are associated with effective performance on assignment. The managerial skills needed to be effective in a domestic position are different to those needed for international assignments. The adaptability of spouses and family factors need to be considered.

14. Only a small number of European organizations provide effective training, preparation and cultural briefing for assignments.

15. Significant adjustment problems including transfer anxiety, culture shock, social dislocation, adaptation, feelings of abandonment and frustration result in high failure rates in international assignments. However, early evidence suggests that European managers fail to put as much effort into cultural adaptation when posted to other European locations as they do when working outside Europe.

16. Expatriation represents a significant force for socialization and control of managers' careers in large European organizations, but the motivation is shifting towards the need to create management development and learning opportunities.

17. The repatriation process is equally difficult, and is plagued by high levels of career disruption, redundancy or outplacement. Managing larger numbers of international assignments at a time of high rationalization and redundancy in headquarters will be a difficult balance to achieve for European organizations.

18. Most career management systems revolve around succession plans, career mobility and the identification of high potential managers. Planned mobility is one of the best tools for developing leadership competencies. Tools such as Career Development Workshops are popular in Britain, Scandinavia, the Benelux countries and Germany, but less so in France. The notion of 'high potential' is different across Europe, as are the processes used to identify it.

19. The management of career mobility is fraught with practical problems and is made more complex by the emergence of dual-career families. From an organizational capability perspective, it also has to be managed in a balanced way.

20. As a consequence of these developments European organizations are developing much broader internationalization strategies in order to link the recruitment of people with new skills and competencies, measured deployment of people around the world, the development of new kinds of managers and the retention of the best managers.

21. Importing foreign nationals to the HQ, using international task forces and project teams, attending cross-cultural seminars and long business trips are all helping to create strong internal and external networks within organizations. In some instances, the organization structure is attempting to mimic these networks in order to cope with the pressures of internationalization.

22. The increasing reliance on lateral development of managers is forcing the development of new career paths and raising the attention that has to be given to job design.

CHAPTER TWELVE

Work Design

INTRODUCTION

A job is one or more tasks that an individual performs in direct support of the organization's purpose (Wilson and Rosenfeld, 1990). Work design (also called job design, job redesign and work redesign) is therefore the conscious, deliberate and purposeful planning of these tasks, including their structural and social aspects (Lane, 1989; Umstot, Bell and Mitchell, 1976). It also involves the allocation of tasks among organizational roles (Cooper, 1974). As such, work design is often seen as a 'technostructural intervention' that can be applied to the design of jobs and work groups in order to achieve high levels of employee fulfilment and productivity (Cummings and Huse, 1989). It is concerned with the strategies that organizations use in order to bring the technology and the people more into line with each other.

Davis (1966, 1979) introduced the notion of organizing (or structuring) a job in order to satisfy the business and technical requirements of the work and the human requirements of the person performing the work. Tasks or elements within work can be designed by specifying their range, content, the method of performing them, and their combination into specific jobs. The concept of job design therefore involves a systematic and conscious ordering of activity according to a preconceived pattern or plan, in order to utilize human resources effectively and control the relationships between them.

Work design may form part of a broader cultural change – such as a quality of working life (QWL), the redesign of business processes (called 'business process re-engineering' or BPR) or an empowerment programme – or it may be part of a more localized and independent change to the nature of work. Since the 1980s, organizations have tended to combine work design changes with associated changes in rewards and benefits (see the next chapter), performance management (see Chapter Fourteen), and organizational structure (see Chapter Eight). These factors play an important role in structuring and reinforcing the desired work behaviours during a period of transition.

In many organizations traditional jobs have become both routine and repetitive. Important interactions between people and their various stakeholders (such as internal and external customers or suppliers) have become hidden and obscured and employee satisfaction and productivity have become difficult to achieve. However, there are a wide range of factors that are changing the nature of work designs in European organizations (see Figure 12.1), as discussed in Parts One and Two of the book. A range of competitive pressures are changing the shape of jobs in organizations.

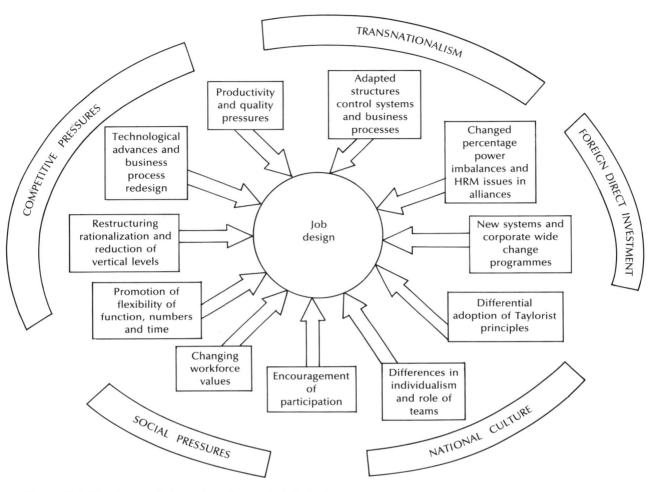

Figure 12.1 The factors influencing change in job design.

Productivity and quality pressures are leading links with new stakeholders as understanding about internal and external customers develops. Technological advances are facilitating the redesign of many business processes, eradicating many simple functions in jobs and divisions between them. We are witnessing a radical restructuring within organizations, with whole management layers being removed and operations being rationalized, affecting the shape of remaining jobs. Moreover, at the organizational level there is a shift towards much greater flexibility, in terms of the time patterns, functions and centrality of many jobs. Foreign direct investment and transnationalism have led to adaptations in organizational structures and control systems, producing new job designs, whilst corporate-wide organizational culture change programmes and shifts in the relative power of management layers or technical functions have often followed in the wake of acquisitions, mergers and joint ventures.

Social pressures, including changes in workforce values and a desire for higher levels of participation, have brought new demands that job designers have to satisfy. Finally, in all this change, there are a number of ways in which national cultures across Europe exert a mediating influence. Notably, there has been a difference in the extent to which work has been specialized and there are differences in the preference for working on an individual or team basis. In times of change and flexibility, where employee commitment is severely tested, overlooking such cultural factors can make the difference between effective and ineffective implementation. Job designers are confronted with four questions:

1. What is the need for technical interdependence (the extent to which the technology requires co-operation among workers to produce a product or service)?
2. What is the level of technical uncertainty (the amount of information that has to be processed and decisions that have to be made by employees in order to produce the product or service)?
3. What are the social needs of employees (their desire for significant social relationships)?
4 What are the growth needs of the employees (their desire for personal accomplishment, learning and development)?

The challenge for job designers has always been how to reconcile the underlying technological and individual needs with the employers' drive to achieve the highest utilization (which in turn is influenced by developments in the social and economic environment). In general, the level of technical interdependence determines whether work has to be designed for individual jobs (low technical interdependence) or for work groups (high technical interdependence). The degree of technical uncertainty determines the extent to which work has to be designed for external forms of control such as supervision, scheduling or standardization (low technical uncertainty) or for worker self-control (high technical uncertainty). However, such simple technological determination of job or work design has to modified by individual needs (Cummings and Huse, 1989), which may be social or growth. Again, in general, the higher the social needs the more attractive will be work group designs, and the higher the need for personal growth, the higher the level of complexity and challenge (job enrichment) that needs to be designed into work.

In order to address some of these issues, this chapter is split into six parts. In the first part we consider some of the institutional and cultural differences that still exist across Europe and that have shaped much of the present thinking about work design. This includes a discussion of the impact of national business systems on work design and the differential impact of the scientific management movement. In the second part of the chapter we address the way in which work designs diverged across Europe and identify four different work design strategies. In the third part of the chapter we concentrate on the developments in work design that stemmed from thinking about the psychological motivation of individuals and the need to match both social and technical systems to job design. In this section we consider whether theories of motivation can be applied across Europe. In the fourth part of the chapter we consider recent developments in flexibility in terms of the time, function and numbers of people employed, and in terms of the product market strategy and production process. In the fifth part of the chapter we review the Swedish model of work design, with its emphasis on participation, quality circles, structural decentralization and work groups. Finally, we review some of the latest developments in work design, the linking of incentive bonuses to team working and the attractions of lean production systems.

THE IMPACT OF NATIONAL BUSINESS SYSTEMS ON WORK DESIGN

However, whilst the technological determinants of work design are converging in relation to the adoption of standardized technologies, there are numerous ways in which the design of jobs varies across countries (and sectors):

> ... Job design is guided by an underlying notion of what goals are to be achieved by a given design. The definition of these goals is influenced by an estimation of the interests of the two parties involved in the employment relationship.   Lane (1989, p. 138).

This reconciliation of interests is bound up in the different paths of industrial development seen across Europe. Jobs are not performed in a vacuum. The organizational, technical and institutional context, whilst not totally determining the shape of jobs, represent important contexts that the job designer has to be aware of. To the extent that there are different individual and social needs and expectations, which in turn are a product of the different national business systems (discussed in Chapter Three), then national business systems have a major influence on the design of jobs across Europe. The most marked differences concern the way in which economic differences are co-ordinated and controlled, the nature of managerial authority and the way it is exercised, and the ways in which commitment to organizations is both developed and maintained (Whitley, 1992). We discussed how the work of different departments, subsidiaries and divisions is systematically organized and integrated under the influence of national business systems in Chapter Eight. At the level of individual work or job design, there are five main factors along which international differences are observed (see Illustration 12.1).

Moreover, each of these dimensions carry deeper cultural assumptions about the nature of managerial authority, with obvious implications for other parts of the HRM system. For example, the degree to which an individual's job is formally specified influences the way in which:

■ Competency is perceived to be an individual or group attribute, and the nature of its assessment (see Chapter Ten).

Illustration 12.1 **Dimensions along which jobs vary from country to country.**

Specialization Extent to which the job varies from single execution or operation to completion of whole product or process.

Formalization of control procedures Level of formally defined procedures for and systems for co-ordinating the work of specialists, e.g. shared values and commitments, common job experiences and knowledge, job rotation (informal control) or contractual rules and governed authority relations (formal).

Decentralization of operational control and participation Distinctions between 'direct' management control, level of trust between employers and employees, levels of long-term employer–employee commitment.

Discretion or autonomy Extent to which execution of tasks allows:

■ Employee to make own decisions about how it is done.

■ Task performance to be prescribed or con-

trolled by employee rather than an outside agent.

Degree to which tasks all have the same degree of complexity (horizontal) or differ (vertical).

Nature of managerial involvement and competence Extent to which managers are expected to play a major part in task performance and become involved in subordinate's knowledge.

Body of technical knowledge and practical competencies relevant to job performance.

Internal or external labour market High level of mutual dependence between jobs, segmentation of labour force into core and non-core groups, development of organization-specific and polyvalent skills (internal or organization-based employer–employee relationship).

Low levels of organization-specific training, limited flexibility within organizations, standard skill sets, publicly certified competency.

Source: after Lane (1989); Whitley (1992).

- Technical skills are separated from the operational task, requiring dedicated co-ordination and centralization of HRM decisions (see Chapter Eight).
- Rewards are allocated (see Chapter Thirteen).
- Performance is assessed (see Chapter Fourteen).

Given the relationship between work design and other areas of HRM, then international variations in work design principles will be reflected in different HRM issues.

INTERNATIONAL DIFFERENCES IN THE ATTRACTION OF SCIENTIFIC MANAGEMENT OR TAYLORISM

There are many theories and ideas that have shaped modern thinking about how best to relate various jobs to each other and how they are influenced. Frederick Taylor, a US engineer, provided a scientific theory aimed at eliminating wastage of resources and enabling management to utilize labour in the most efficient and effective way possible. Scientific management (variously referred to as 'Taylorism', 'industrial engineering' or 'Fordism') was centred around the principle that efficiency and productivity increase in line with the division of labour. Jobs can be divided into their smallest elements or components. This results in an ideal combination of body movements that can execute tasks in the shortest time without increasing the labour intensity. Physical equipment and the environment may then be designed around these reduced tasks. The tasks and work methods for each component are specified. This principle of maximum 'decomposition' of work tasks generally implies deskilling. The scientific management approach introduced two main divisions of labour:

1. Mental (conception and planning) from manual (execution and doing).
2. Direct (production) from indirect (setting up, preparation and maintenance).

In order to encourage employees to participate, two 'motivators' were highlighted:

1. The provision of precise standards to enable judgement of progress and close supervision to control.
2. The linking of pay to the amount of effort invested.

It involved a narrow view of human nature and capability. For example, Henry Ford, who developed scientific management principles to the operation of specialized machinery, is quoted as observing that out of 7,882 different kinds of job in his plants, 4,034 did not require full physical capacity. Another 670 could be filled by legless men, 2,637 by one-legged men, 2 by armless men, 715 by one-armed men and 10 by blind men (Littler and Salaman, 1984). However, the pursuit of equal opportunities was not at the forefront of Ford's mind! The approach resulted in massive gains in efficiency and productivity through the control of the labour process (see Illustration 12.2 for the advantages and disadvantages). Until very recently, it remained a widespread practice.

Lane (1989) has reviewed how scientific management principles were diffused around the world and how jobs were designed and work structured in Britain, Germany and France. She draws attention to differences in the specialization of tasks, skills and roles in organizations. As scientific principles spread around the world they were adapted to local economic and skill traditions. A minimum definition of scientific management traditions is that they involve (Lane, 1989):

- A high degree of division of labour.
- A low degree of worker discretion.

Illustration 12.2 **The advantages and disadvantages of scientific management principles in work design.**

Advantages of greater specialization
- Increases in workers' dexterity skills.
- Less time spent switching from one task to another.
- Less time needed to change machinery set-ups.
- Hiring of cheaper and more readily replaced labour.
- Shorter (and cheaper) training times.
- Development of specialized single-function machinery.
- Facilitation of mechanization and automation of manual operations.
- Easier measurement of work performance.

Advantages of reduced discretion
- Allows managers and not the workforce to establish new work methods.
- Allows managers to establish standards of performance.
- Reduces lost time in worker consultation.
- Consistent with the hiring of cheaper labour.

Disadvantages of scientific management
- Economic gains not realized through problems with higher absenteeism, turnover.
- Reduced production quality in line with higher levels of boredom and frustration.
- Potential for higher wages where workers could control the provision of skilled labour in difficult to automate tasks.

- Close task control.
- A 'minimum interaction' employment relationship based on cash.

Scientific management spread around the world rapidly as technology became an international commodity and was accepted in Europe – in modified form – as early as the 1930s (Littler, 1982; Merkle, 1980). As scientific management adapted to the different national economic strategies, managerial cultures, industrial relations systems and qualification structures of European countries, it did not penetrate Germany, France and the United Kingdom to the same extent.

In France, the intellectual and technically-minded education system (discussed in Chapter Ten) created a receptive environment for scientific management principles. European industrialists, such as the Michelin brothers, strove to emulate Ford's techniques (Lane, 1989). The centralist and rational approach inherent in both French industry and government meant that Taylorism was adopted as a revolutionary system of technical and societal organization. The high prevalence of small, family owned firms producing for small quality goods markets meant that Taylorist principles met with opposition from both the owners and workers. Only the mass production needs of the First World War and postwar commitments to redistribute surplus wealth led to greater acceptance. Until the 1960s, when rapid industrialization led to the creation of large production units serving mass markets, Taylorism had penetrated French organizations more in broad form than in substance.

In Germany the Taylorist notions of scientific study of organizations, emphasis on productivity and efficiency and class collaboration found greatest intellectual acceptance, particularly when applied to overall organizational design and the structure of complete industries (as opposed to changing production methods, where strong craft traditions seemed to diffuse the impact of Taylorism). In Britain, the strong preference for individual solutions to industrial problems, absence of a technical élite, anti-management culture (see Chapter Ten), strong and militant labour movement and presence of liberal thinkers (such as the Quakers) on owner-obligations would all indicate rather infertile territory for Taylorism (Lane, 1989). As with France, the First World War provided the opening for Taylorism, as did the economic depression and

Table 12.1 **Employer strategies on work organization in Germany, Britain and France until the early 1980s.**

	Responsible autonomy		Taylorism
	Germany	*Britain*	*France*
Division of labour	Large proportion of highly skilled	Deskilled (pockets of high skill in craft sector)	Deskilled
	Low formalization of both horizontal and vertical boundaries	High formalization of both horizontal and vertical boundaries	High formalization only of vertical boundaries
	High level of discretion	Low level of discretion	Low level of discretion
Structure of control	Predominantly ideological control	Weak task control	Strong task control, remnants of ideological control
Employment relationship	High degree of employment security for the core labour force	Complete substitutability of workers	High degree of employment security for the core labour force
Shaping factors	High skilled and publicly certified domestic workforce	Co-existence of small high discretion craft sector with large mass production	Low reserve of skilled labour with only narrow artisan sector
	'Polyvalent' skills with knowledge and capability in two areas acquired through rotation	High degree of control over organization of labour process residing with unions	Rapid expansion of industry under state guidance required accelerated move to mass production and absorption of new workers
	Immigrant unskilled and skilled workforce to meet demands of mass production	Low level of technical training of managers and low task/production orientation	
	Easier resourcing of industries requiring large inputs of high level skills	Skills associated with granting of job territory	Preference for making workers adapt to predefined jobs rather than mould jobs to worker
	Craft and scientific origins of management support a continued apprenticeship philosophy	Large representation of large organizations raised the importance of firm-specific skills	Cultural fit of division of labour, split between planning and implementation and educational training of managers
	Legislation on employee rights since 1945 and centralized wage bargaining		

Source: after Lane (1989). Reprinted with permission, © 1993, Edward Elgar Publishing Ltd.

awareness of declining British competitiveness in the run up to the Second World War. A modified form of Taylorism, focused more on cost-cutting as opposed to output maximization motivations, and softened by an emphasis on individual worker health and psychology, took hold.

DIVERGING EMPLOYER STRATEGIES ON WORK ORGANIZATION IN GERMANY, FRANCE AND BRITAIN

A series of empirical studies have shown that the goal of capital accumulation and control over employees can be pursued by a series of strategies, without recourse to overarching bureaucratic or ideological arguments. In the 1960s and early 1970s employer strategies in Germany, France and Britain began to diverge (Littler, 1982). Until the early 1980s clear differences existed (see Table 12.1) in terms of:

- The continued division of labour.
- The structure of control.
- The nature of the employment relationship.

The outline in Table 12.1, of course, hides many subtleties. Many German organizations began to emulate American patterns of mass production in the 1960s after a period of rapid expansion, and the car, metal and chemicals sectors in particular began to divide skilled jobs into semi-skilled ones (Sengenberger, 1984) and a tendency towards skills polarization began. Unlike in Britain and France, however, elements of the model in Table 12.2 were never destroyed (Lane, 1989). Similarly, in France, the continued presence of a sizeable family owned small-firm sector has seen higher levels of casualization of labour (Berger, 1980).

FOUR DIFFERENT WORK DESIGN STRATEGIES

Since the 1960s and early 1970s, many organizations found that problems with absenteeism, labour turnover, recruitment and industrial relations presented as many control problems as Taylorist job design principles solved (Lane, 1989). Increases in education levels, raised employee expectations and a tighter labour market increased employee demands for meaningful jobs:

... Their dissatisfaction became heightened during this period because the intensification of economic growth, technological advance and productivity increases threw the constraints of Taylorism into sharp relief.   Lane (1989, p. 156).

Organizations found that they actually had considerable scope over the kind of work design, even within an apparently fixed technology. For example, technical interdependence could be reduced by breaking long assembly lines up into discrete groups, although modifying people's needs was subsequently found to be more complex. At the organizational level, there are, in fact, four different kinds of work design that tend to be developed:

1. Traditional jobs resulting from scientific management traditions.
2. Traditional work groups resulting from scientific management traditions.
3. Job enrichment strategies (which result from psychological and socio-technical traditions).
4. Self-regulating work teams (which result from 'responsible autonomy' traditions).

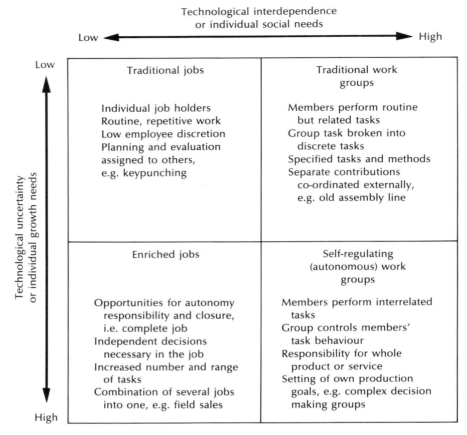

Figure 12.2 The match between four work designs and technological and individual contingencies. *Source*: after Cummings and Huse (1989).

The four generic work design strategies that may be pursued are shown in Figure 12.2. We have outlined the traditional approach to job design in our discussion of scientific management. The demands of the existing work designs were reflected in the recruitment criteria of organizations, with employees placed into the work designs that they were most competent for. When new experiments were run, they were usually staffed on a volunteer basis, with work practices negotiated between the organization and the employees (which, in turn, were dependent on the level of trust and co-operation).

JOB ROTATION, ENLARGEMENT AND ENRICHMENT

The job enrichment movement began in the 1950s, based on the work of Walker and Guest, in response to the limited outlook on the design of work. Wilson and Rosenfeld (1990) define job enrichment as '. . . the practice of building motivating factors into job content'. Enriched jobs provide employees with the opportunity to increase the range of tasks performed. Simply increasing the range of tasks performed is frequently achieved by job rotation – where individuals move from one job to another across time in a pre-planned manner. This approach has been criticized as simply moving individuals from one boring job to another (Herzberg, 1968). Job enlargement refers to increasing the scope of a job by increasing the number of activities and processes involved – frequently achieved by combining a series of narrow jobs into one larger job. Unlike simple job rotation, the job enlargement movement was associated with the creation of higher levels of employee satisfaction and motivation, especially where the increased task complexity was comprehended. More recently organizations in the US have begun to design 'enriched' jobs. These differ from enlarged jobs in that they contain greater levels of employee autonomy, control, feedback of results and task variety. The main principles and motivational assumptions behind job enrichment work design strategies are shown in Table 12.2. The approach focuses on the need to satisfy individual needs for responsibility, growth, advancement, recognition and achievement. Thinking about job enrichment was clearly influenced by three developments in the psychological and organizational behaviour literature:

1. Socio-technical systems understanding of the fit between individual needs and technological constraints.
2. Orthodox job enrichment ideas based on studies of job motivation.
3. Studies of job characteristics, tracing the development of satisfaction back to the psychological state of employees and the design of jobs.

Socio-technical considerations first came to the fore in the 1950s as organizations began to experience difficulties when they introduced new technologies into work systems. In the UK, for example, it was found that new technology conflicted with strong work cultures and social systems in the coal mining and textile weaving industries (Rice, 1958; Trist and Bamforth, 1951) and resulted in a deterioration in both productivity and satisfaction. Similar problems were found in the automobile industry, where resistance to the introduction of new technology resulted in higher levels of sabotage, absenteeism and productivity problems (Gyllenhammar, 1977). The socio-technical systems movement emphasized the need for work designs to optimize the social outputs (such as job satisfaction and commitment) from the system with the technical outputs (such as products and services). In order to achieve this 'joint

Table 12.2 **Principles and motivational assumptions of job enrichment work designs.**

Principle	Motivation involved
Assignment of specific or specialized tasks and knowledge to allow individuals to become experts	Responsibility, growth and advancement
Increasing the accountability of individuals for their own work	Responsibility and recognition
Removing some of the controls while retaining accountability	Responsibility and personal achievement
Granting additional authority to an employee in their activity and promoting job freedom	Responsibility, achievement and recognition
Giving people a complete natural unit of work	Responsibility, achievement and recognition
Making periodic reports directly available to employees without feeding them through the supervisor	Internal recognition

Source: after Torrington and Hall (1991). Reprinted by permission of Prentice Hall.

optimization', clear 'boundaries' have to be established between the work system and the (ever changing) outside world to protect the system from outside disruptions. The US became increasingly aware of European efforts to enhance the design of work and developed its own Quality of Working Life (QWL) traditions. From 1969 to 1974 interest in improving the quality of experiences of people in the workplace became widespread (Cummings and Huse, 1989), such that the number of publications on QWL issues has doubled every five years since. From the mid-1970s onwards, problems with lagging productivity, high energy costs and international competition shifted the focus of attention in the US, UK, Germany and France towards other management systems (notably Japanese) and the role of participative management techniques such as quality circles, participative problem solving, improvements in the work environment and innovative reward systems. In Germany, the reform movement went under the name of 'Humanization of Working Life' (*Humanisierung des Arbeitslebens*) and was pursued in a co-ordinated way, whilst in France the slogan was 'The Improvement of Working Conditions' (*Amélioration des Conditions de Travail*). British attempts to mobilize work redesign around QWL principles were more piecemeal and never reached the level of a major movement.

The job enrichment movement was also influenced by the work of Herzberg (Herzberg and Zautra, 1976) who linked his two-factor theory of motivation to the improvement of motivational factors in the job, such as achievement, recognition,

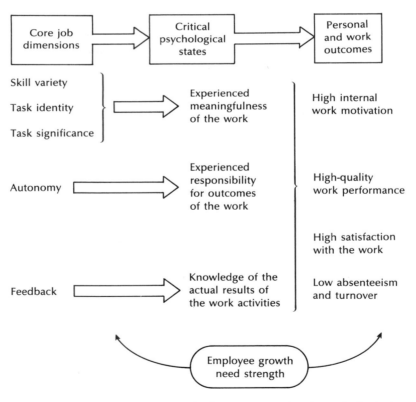

Figure 12.3 Relationship between core job dimensions, critical psychological states and on-the-job outcomes. *Source*: reproduced by permission of the publisher from J. Hackman and G. Oldham, 'Development of the job diagnostic survey', *Journal of Applied Psychology*, **60** (April 1975), 161.

responsibility, advancement and opportunity for growth. Organizations such as AT&T, Texas Instruments and ICI were early pioneers of this movement. However, simply focusing on motivational factors ignores the individual characteristics – such as the strength of their growth needs – which determine whether they respond well or not to job enrichment. A number of individual factors influence the success of job designs, such as age, education, self-assurance, and work ethic (Wanous, 1974).

A second major psychological influence therefore was the work of Hackman and Oldham (1976, 1980) who analysed the attributes of the job itself and developed the Job Diagnostic Survey (JDS). The JDS categorized a series of job characteristics, based on analyses of over one thousand employees in about 100 jobs in thirteen organizations and identified a series of core job dimensions. These job dimensions produced three resultant critical psychological states and a series of personal and job outcomes that flowed from these psychological states (see Figure 12.3).

Over twenty-eight studies have supported the model proposed by Hackman and Oldham (see reviews by Cummings and Molloy, 1977; Loher, Noe, Moeller and Fitzgerald, 1985; McEvoy and Cascio, 1985). The job characteristics shown in Figure 12.3 are positively related with job satisfaction and particularly for individuals who have high personal growth needs. Job enrichment also appears to be quite successful in reducing employee turnover. Improvements in quality and costs were reported slightly more frequently than improvements in employee attitudes and production. Many of the studies suffered from methodological weaknesses and likely over-estimate of the impact of job characteristics on performance (Cummings and Huse, 1989).

DO THEORIES OF MOTIVATION APPLY ACROSS EUROPE?

Are the theories of motivation that underlie these ideas on work design portable across Europe? Hofstede (1991) found that there was a correlation between McClelland's (1987) scores on 'achievement motivation' and his cultural dimensions of 'uncertainty avoidance' and 'masculinity'. Essentially, high 'achievement motivation' is correlated with low 'uncertainty avoidance' and high 'masculinity'. This means that in Anglo-Saxon countries such as the UK, the US, Canada and Australia, provision of opportunity for individual achievement would be a key feature of job design, whilst in countries like Portugal, Spain and France (where high 'uncertainty avoidance' is combined with low 'masculinity') this would not be such an important factor (Jackson, 1993). The motivational factors in work are likely to vary across cultures (see Figure 12.4).

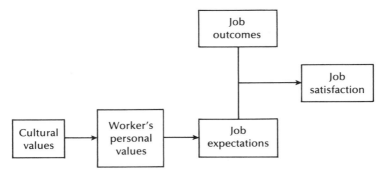

Figure 12.4 A discrepancy model of job satisfaction. *Source*: Hui (1990). Reprinted with permission of the publishers, © 1993, Butterworth-Heinemann.

Why is this so? A person's expectations of a job are influenced by work values, which reflect both life goals and personal goals. The degree of dissatisfaction with work derives from a perceived discrepancy between the actual outcomes of the job and the job holder's expectations. Job satisfaction is seen as a subset of overall motivation.

International Survey Research have developed a series of norms in the area of job satisfaction, based on data from over 750 organizations in forty-six countries. The cultural norms for the various items shown in Figure 12.5 are based on national samples of employees in full time employment structured in terms of geographical distribution, type and size of employing organization, employment status, age and sex (Harding, 1991). Standard questionnaire items have been translated locally. National data are supplemented with client organization data. Cross-sectional data for 1991 suggest that excepting the high levels of acceptance with work designs found in the Netherlands and Switzerland, there is little difference between Britain, France, Belgium, Germany and Italy, with slightly lower levels of satisfaction in Spain. More variation is found in the items on working relationships and job satisfaction.

Historical trend data from this database suggest that, in the UK at least, there has been little change in attitudes about work organization (measured as the extent to which employees feel that their department is well organized, have a clear idea of what is expected of them, are not bothered by excessive pressure, and feel that there are enough staff to handle most workloads). In 1977 64 per cent of British employees showed a favourable response (i.e. agree or tend to agree) to the work organization items, compared to 65 per cent in 1991 (Harding, 1991). Levels of job satisfaction (measured as the extent to which employees feel they are doing a job they feel is worthwhile, which provides opportunity to use abilities, is not dull and monotonous

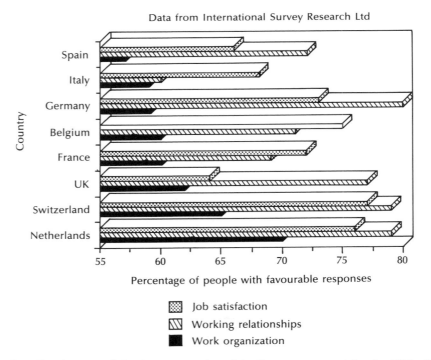

Figure 12.5 Employee satisfaction scores for eight European countries in 1991. *Source*: Harding (1991), reprinted with permission of International Survey Research.

and results in high morale) also appear to be both high and stable, according to this database, rising from 62 per cent in 1977 to 65 per cent in 1991.

Life goals – which are more generalized measures of motivation – also clearly depend on national culture but also show a high degree of consistency. Harris and Moran (1987) found that different motivational factors existed between East Asian organizations (where concerns for equity, the group, saving, extended family relations, a highly disciplined workforce, protocol, rank and status and the avoidance of conflict dominated life goals) and Western organizations (where wealth, the individual, consumption, the nuclear family, low work ethic, informality and the management of conflict dominated life goals), despite differences in national culture within these broad regions. Several studies have shown that individuals from different cultural backgrounds have different attitudes to their work (see de Boer, 1978; Elizur, Borg, Hunt and Beck, 1991; Harpaz, 1989; Hui, 1990; and Warr, 1982).

However, in considering the issue of the degree of work ethic and commitment to work, Warr (1982) distinguished between the instrumental reasons that we have for working (primarily economic) and the non-instrumental reasons. The strength of non-financial commitment to work has been assessed over the decades by asking the 'lottery question'. If you won a considerable amount of money tomorrow, would you continue to work? Data from the Meaning of Work Project based on 8,763 respondents from seven countries has been analysed (Harpaz, 1989). The data showed that, despite reports of various changes in workers' values and attitudes towards work, the proportion who state the intention to continue work beyond financial need is high. The figure was 93 per cent in Japan, 88 per cent in the US, 87 per cent in Israel, 86 per cent in the Netherlands and 84 per cent in Belgium. The proportion fell quite markedly for Germany (70 per cent) and Britain (68 per cent). Other trend data from the Meaning of Work project from 1982 to 1990 showed that importance of work in Japan, the US and Germany had become less important but the relative order of the countries remained the same (Meaning of Work, 1987; Misumi, 1993). The figures are not too different from the data on job satisfaction shown in Figure 12.5. On this basis, work appears to play a more central role in some cultures than in others. Of course, the intention to remain at work may be quite different from the actuality! Perhaps the British are more dissatisfied, or perhaps they are more honest!

Whilst what motivates people may vary across cultures, the way in which people are motivated is more universal. Although some life goals are culturally-dependent, work and family life goals do not seem to vary as much as might be imagined (Kelly, Whatley and Worthley, 1991). Elizur, Borg, Hunt and Beck (1991) have analysed data on work values from 2,280 managers and employees from Germany, Holland, Hungary, Israel, the US, Korea, Taiwan and China. Using the Work Values Questionnaire, they determined the underlying structure of work values. Interestingly, they found that this underlying structure was basically the same across all countries. The outcome of work was divided into items that were cognitive, instrumental and affective (emotional). Cultural differences did have an impact, however, on the relative order of importance of specific work values (see Table 12.3). For example, Hungarian respondents rated supervisor, recognition, and meaningful work and pay higher than other countries, whilst German workers rated co-workers, benefits and security very high, but responsibility as quite unimportant. Such differences, however, only represented minor variations around a much broader pattern of similarity in work values across the countries studied.

. . . Static-content theories [of motivation] do not travel well between cultures. . . [but] process theories are perhaps more portable, because they focus on certain 'universals' in the way

Table 12.3 **Rank order of work values for Germany, Holland, the US and Hungary.**

Source of work value	Germany	Holland	US	Hungary
Job interest	1	1	1	7
Co-workers	2	3	18	14
Meaningful work	3	13	13	14
Benefits	4	19	16	17
Supervisor	5	9	11	1
Security	6	14	10	10
Independence	7	5	7	16
Use of ability	8	8	6	6
Achievement	9	2	2	2
Work influence	10	7	14	18
Personal growth	11	4	4	13
Pay	12	18	15	5
Feedback	13	16	9	8
Esteem	14	15	5	9
Advancement	15	6	3	24
Convenient hours	16	21	22	12
Recognition	17	12	12	3
Work conditions	18	20	20	11
Interaction	19	10	21	19
Responsibility	20	11	8	15
Organizational influence	21	17	19	22
Company	22	22	17	21
Contribution to society	23	23	24	20
Status	24	24	23	23

Source: reprinted from R. Elizur, I. Borg, R. Hunt and I. N. Beck, 'The structure of work values: a cross cultural comparison', *Journal of Organizational Behaviour*, **12(1)**, 21–38, with kind permission from John Wiley and Sons, Inc.

motivation works, rather than focusing on what motivates people. . . managers, especially those managing across cultures, should look very closely at what motivates people working under them and with them. . . motivation is an important aspect of job performance. Without motivated individuals, despite high levels of competence and the opportunity within the organization to perform, nothing will move in an organization.   Jackson (1993, p. 83).

SELF-REGULATING WORK GROUPS

Another important contribution to the socio-technical movement has been the development of self-regulating work groups (also called autonomous or self-managing work groups). The formation of self-regulating work groups was inspired by the aim of achieving the advantages of job enrichment (which had been focused at the individual level) at the team level. It also attempted to design broader advantages into work groups, such as individual's social needs and the organization's requirement for flexibility (Torrington and Hall, 1991). Team members are generally expected to learn all the tasks within the control of the group. Pay is frequently based on performance, as applied to the whole group. Tasks usually performed by separate units, such as quality control, maintenance, industrial engineering and HRM, are included in the responsibilities of each individual (Cummings and Huse, 1989). Self-regulating groups usually have three key characteristics:

1. The task of the group is autonomous and forms a relatively self-completing whole.
2. Employees can influence transactions with their task environment, i.e. the types and rates of inputs and outputs. The work area is well defined and there is responsibility for decisions about their boundary as well as sufficient cross-training of team members to take on all tasks.
3. Regulation and control of the behaviour needed to convert the incoming materials into a finished product. This task control includes the freedom to choose work methods, schedule activities, influence production goals and modify output in order to cope with unpredictable situations, and provide feedback on relevant measures of group performance to allow employees to modify their goal-directed behaviour as necessary.

THE FLEXIBLE ORGANIZATION

. . . Since the beginning of the 1980s there has been considerable movement towards flexibility, affecting most aspects of the employment relationship. The factors underlying this trend have been the focus of much attention. On the employers' side, the main reason for seeking flexibility is the need to be able to adapt more speedily to turbulent and competitive international markets. On the employees' side, the issues are less clear-cut, but there is certainly a feeling that some form of flexibility might meet the needs of new patterns of living and working, as well as favouring greater security of employment.   Treu (1992, p. 509).

The topic of job and work design cannot be considered without discussing the development of the flexible organization, which occurred in conjunction with the experiments in job design outlined in the previous section. The move towards greater flexibility has two main characteristics:

1. A significant role of legislation aimed at removing traditional rigidities within the employment relationship.
2. A consensual approach to seeking a solution based on collective negotiation.

As greater flexibility has been created, many European organizations have pursued two opposing strategies, either relying heavily on the external labour market and low levels of employee involvement, or favouring internal mobility and the development of multiple skills amongst existing employees.

Labour flexibility first became an issue in Europe in the mid-1970s as a result of the economic crises that followed the rises in oil prices (Lane, 1989: Treu, 1992). A preoccupation with changed (more adverse) market conditions began to stand out as a counter-pressure to the earlier focus on the need for more worker control of the variety, speed and sequence of tasks, and the creation of more holistic work structures. From the mid-1970s onwards the argument that Europe suffered from a number of 'institutional rigidities' which greatly reduced the ability of organizations to adapt to turbulent market conditions began to grow (see Chapter Four). In order to achieve international competitiveness and reap the benefits of new information technologies, European employers and governments began to argue that structural changes to both the design of organizations and work were needed (Boyer, 1988). The counter-argument claimed that the economic crisis was not just due to institutional rigidities. Rather, these rigidities stemmed from the need for Taylorist modes of production to create organizational structures and management methods to regulate labour relations.

Institutional rigidities were felt to be more the result of the crisis in production techniques inherent in Taylorism and specialization rather than the origin of the crisis.

In the 1980s a more pragmatic approach, buoyed up by the improved economic and employment performance of the then European Community, appeared. Acceptable compromises were found as unions underwent a decline in their power (see Chapter Fifteen) and profound changes took place in the economy, leading to an increase in service employment, changes in the composition and attitudes of the workforce and a new equilibrium in industrial relations (see Chapter Four). The bleak economic outlook for the 1990s will likely see many of the original (extremely polarized) arguments being replayed as many organizations make even more urgent strides for flexibility.

Numerical flexibility

In Chapter Six we made some basic distinctions between functional, numerical and time flexibility and argued that European organizations are pursuing different paths towards the same goals. Numerical flexibility is the employers' ability to alter the size of their workforce. In Chapter Nine we highlighted the restrictions placed on employers and their access to sources of labour, requirements for equal opportunities, practices associated with the hiring of employees and protection against dismissal in many national recruitment systems. European attitudes to numerical flexibility stand in stark contrast to those of US employers (Grenig, 1991) and the process of deregulation and increased numerical flexibility had only had a limited impact on European HRM systems by the early 1990s (Treu, 1992). However, a number of alternative measures to mass dismissals such as greater internal and external job mobility, short time working on rota systems, temporary wage reductions, recruitment freezes, overtime reductions and early retirements have been pursued in relation to full time workforces.

Associated with this there has been a trend towards higher levels of 'atypical' or 'peripheral' employment (see Chapter Four). The introduction of different types of employment contract has been the major force in increasing labour market flexibility since the late 1970s (Kravaritou-Manitakis, 1988). It has been achieved by:

- A gradual widening in the acceptable reasons for use of fixed-term contracts built into legislation.
- Provision of public subsidies to encourage 'atypical' contracts.
- Reductions in minimum wage levels in relation to the balance of work and training activities.
- Extension of temporary employment contracts to new age brackets.

Consequently, temporary work has become the normal mode of entry into the labour market for most young Europeans. For example, between 1985 and 1988 in Italy some 1.2 million young workers were hired on employment training contracts, with 75 per cent subsequently being given regular (indefinite) employment contracts (Treu, 1992). An enlarged peripheral workforce has now become a stable part and officially authorized part of a dual labour market in Europe. Coupled with related developments, such as intermediate types of semi-independent work through self-employment, or various forms of external collaboration such as subcontracting, outworking, telework and just-in-time methods of supply, the task for work and job designers in European organizations has become more complex.

Time flexibility

Far reaching changes have also taken place in working time flexibility. As the proportion of women in the labour force grew along with the range of service employment, unions became less defensive about new patterns of working time. Employers' requirements for more flexibility were driven by the need to adapt to increasingly variable production needs and styles. They were met by union requests for reductions in overall working hours in a number of European countries. European employers decided that rather than take a purely negative stand that insisted on compensating wage reductions in return for reductions in the working week, they could achieve cost reductions through a more socially-acceptable demand for flexibility in working schedules. There followed a similar process of deregulation as was seen for numerical flexibility (Blanpain and Köhler, 1988; Treu, 1992), with collective bargaining agreements assisting the implementation of time flexibility through:

- A liberalization of restrictions on part time work (e.g. in Italy).
- The easing of standards concerning daily and weekly maximum work hours.
- Greater flexibility in employers' rights to organize working time over the year (e.g. in Spain).
- An individualization of work schedules (e.g. in France).
- The abolition or relaxation of restrictions on night work and compulsory rest periods for women workers (e.g. in Italy and France).

In some cases, as with the Belgian Act of 17 March 1987, attempts were made to match deregulation with other promotional objectives. The Belgians permitted the adoption of flexible working time and the extension of working hours only on condition that the measures had positive employment effects. However, by the end of the 1980s the trend towards time flexibility had developed further than many of the social partners had intended. The trend towards time flexibility has been accelerated by local and decentralized collective bargaining, even in traditionally centralized systems in the Nordic countries, the Netherlands and Germany (Treu, 1992). The net result of time flexibility has been a '... personalization of working time – for the first time there is a clear distinction between the working time of the individual employee and the operating hours of the production unit' (Treu, 1992, p. 505). Most new developments, such as new shift-work arrangements, part time work patterns, weekend-working, job sharing and non-standard distribution of working time over longer periods (e.g. sabbaticals, phased retirement or occasional leaves of absence), tend to be tentative and occurring on a trial-and-error basis in European employers.

Functional flexibility

The persistence of employment protection, underpinned by legislation and industrial relations practice, has seen organizations pursue a third form of flexibility – functional flexibility. Functional flexibility involves reversing the traditional production line model with its division of labour and fragmentation of work organization by extending the range of tasks and skills involved in a job and increasing internal mobility between jobs. The rigidities that functional flexibility is intended to overcome concern both managerial and union practice. The form that functional flexibility – and the work redesign and job reassignment that it entails – has taken has varied across the European Union, largely determined by the strategies of organizations. Functional flexibility has been furthered by many changes in work practice. The most important of these include:

- The relaxation or abolition of restrictive work practices.
- The reduction of job demarcations and the number of grades in the organization.
- Job enlargement and enrichment.
- Experiments with teamwork.
- Job and organization redesign against underlying business processes.
- New forms of participation, such as sophisticated selection, training and performance appraisal; communication programmes and quality circles.

Innovations in functional flexibility and participative management and direct relations with the workforce outside union channels have been most marked in countries where they enjoy government approval (such as the UK) or in weakly unionized industrial sectors such as the service sector or high technology organizations. In countries such as Belgium, Germany or Italy, where unions are more entrenched, then moves towards greater internal flexibility have been matched with guarantees of employment security for the core workforce or closer involvement in company-level decision making (Treu, 1992). Most comparative research in both Europe and Japan suggests that flexibility and innovation in the nature of employment and work design is more likely to succeed where management styles and labour relations are more participative.

Clearly, moves towards the flexible organization have occurred across Europe. We discussed much of the evidence for the shift towards flexibility and free market capitalism in Chapters Four and Five. This phenomenon has significant implications for HRM policies and practices. Lane (1989), despite her critical analysis of this drive towards flexibility based on a detailed consideration of the institutional differences in Britain, France and Germany, concludes that we are witnessing a shift in power from employee to employer that is both qualitatively and quantitatively different to previous trends.

However, despite this trend, there are three main arguments levelled against the continued advance of the flexible organization in Europe that need to be acknowledged:

- There are different limitations to and inequalities in the move towards numerical flexibility across European countries and organizations, suggesting that it may not become a totally pan-European phenomenon (see Chapter Four).
- There are criticisms of the logic that flexibility is automatically associated with improved competitiveness (see the discussion of concerns over the quality of training in Chapter Ten).
- Difficulties may be encountered in sustaining differential HRM policies for the various arms of the flexible organization (i.e. between the core and periphery).

FLEXIBLE SPECIALIZATION OR CUSTOM-MADE WORK ORGANIZATION

In the 1980s European writers began to realize that new developments in technology, the internationalization of markets and new ways of deploying labour, meant that organizations and their production activities have to be structured in radically different ways. Mass production of standardized goods using special-purpose machines and semi-skilled labour requires large and stable markets. As the international division of labour has shifted (see Chapters Four and Five) it has become clear that low wage economies in the Far East and Latin America can produce high-quality standardized goods more cheaply than Europe will ever be able to. The production of more high-quality, specialized and customized goods, with a rapid change in product lines, aimed at smaller domestic markets, presented itself as a sustainable alternative. Such a new market strategy required a new industrial strategy, called 'flexible specialization' (Piore and Sabel, 1984; Sabel, 1982). It is facilitated by the deployment of computerized equipment to the production process (such as numerically-controlled machine tools, computer numerically-controlled machine tools, robotics, and flexible manufacturing systems) and information technology to the redesign of managerial roles, organization functions and business processes. The new model of production currently exists in experimental form and in early strategic adopters, side by side with more traditional production methods. It forms the basis of a 'second industrial divide'.

The model suggested by Piore and Sabel stresses the need for 'functional' flexibility outlined in the previous section (also called 'custom-made work organization' by Streeck, 1987). The new work design requires the assignment of more holistic work tasks, enriched jobs, higher levels of autonomy and responsibility, but also requires a high degree of overlap between specialisms, coupled with flexibility of deployment and the exercise of 'craft' judgement and skill. These latter elements are not seen as employer concessions to a workforce driven by social needs for more fulfilling jobs, but represent a conscious choice by organizations to design work in a way that fits the new market imperatives. Only countries that have a surviving craft tradition and reliance on skilled all-round workers operating in a high-trust environment, Piore and Sabel argue, will be equipped to adopt this new industrial strategy and the associated work designs. A new form of industrial community, based on a new balance between competition and collaboration, will be needed to instigate innovation in work design. It would be interesting to view the massive transfer of ownership and control through mergers, acquisition and joint ventures (see Chapter Five) in this light.

In their estimation, based on empirical examination of work practice, Germany, Italy and Japan will lead the transition to 'flexible specialization'. The US, UK and France will struggle. Lane (1989) points out that hybrid forms of work organization may emerge in the non-craft advanced countries such as France and Britain, as they pursue flexibility in different ways. In a comprehensive review of supporting evidence, Lane (1989) concludes that Taylorism has not been completely abandoned in Germany, but fundamental organizational and technological innovation has occurred. The labour market has made it easier to adopt the strategy and relatively smooth industrial relations have eased the introduction of new methods and Taylorist principles have been ousted from core industries such as automobile manufacture, machine tools, chemicals, shipbuilding and food processing. Continued progress down this route is open to question as Germany faces broader social issues and pressure on social employment costs. Levels of industrial unrest are also on the increase (see Chapter Sixteen). In Britain, there have been some moves towards 'flexible specialization', but rarely as part of an industrial strategy or committed efforts at technological innovation. Hesitant management, a shortage of skilled labour, a haphazard training system, low levels of employment security and an adversarial industrial relations system will all need to be corrected before significant progress is made. In France, managers show more professional technological innovation, but skills shortages still exist and employment security has come under extreme threat in the early 1990s. The strong emphasis on hierarchical management control will also not be conducive to new forms of work organization.

PARTICIPATION AND QUALITY CIRCLES

Work or job design has the aim of improving motivation and efficiency at work. However, as the debate on 'flexible specialization' reveals, there is also a growing need for much higher levels of trust and involvement in industrial and work practice decision making. The introduction of quality circles has demonstrated the connection between quality management and worker participation. Thinking about job design has therefore recently been influenced by developments in participation practices. Participative decision making involves several components: individual autonomy, group responsibility and organization-wide influence. These components all serve to increase the commitment to change and encourage more responsibility and accountability. There are a number of important questions to be determined about participation in organizations (see Illustration 12.3).

There are two main forms of participation: indirect and direct (see Table 12.4). Indirect (or representational) forms of participation, such as works councils and consultation, will be discussed in Chapter Fifteen in the context of industrial relations. In this section we concentrate on direct forms of participation, such as problem solving groups, quality circles and total quality management, which have a considerable influence on job design, training and technological innovation. They are therefore discussed in the context of job design and work structuring. The scope of participative management at Aérospatiale is outlined in Illustration 12.4.

Most quality circles operate at the work group or operational level, focusing on isolated issues of job or product improvement with little involvement from managers. In many cases quality circles were found to reinforce the inherent structural and work

Illustration 12.3 **Key questions about workforce participation.**

- Is it necessary to have worker involvement to improve quality?
- How best can workers be involved?
- What sort of decisions are open or suitable for participation?
- Where in the decision making process should participation occur?
- How far down the organization should participation go?
- Who should be involved in the participative process?
- Do the interests of all those involved in quality improvement converge?

Source: Cressey (1991).

Table 12.4 **Direct and indirect participation methods.**

Informal (direct) system: participative management	Formal (indirect) system: industrial democracy
Focus: Individual	*Focus:* Representation
Informal sharing of decision making at the workplace	*Collective bargaining through representatives*
Briefing groups	Collective bargaining
Attitude surveys	Joint consultation
Problem solving groups, e.g. quality circles	Works councils
Job enrichment	Worker directors
Autonomous work groups	Staff committees

Illustration 12.4 **Participative management at Aérospatiale.**

Aérospatiale is an aeronautical construction organization that employs some 33,000 workers across thirteen plants. The largest plant is at Toulouse, employing over 8,000 technical and administrative, engineering and manufacturing staff. Activities range from the design, purchase of parts and technology, manufacture and after-sales service of aircraft. A variety of methods have been used to increase employee participation. The exchange of information in production units is handled through 'companion meetings' (briefing groups) where heads of units present on the goals and operations of units and then field questions. Working groups solve problems concerning working hours, communication and the production environment. Following legislation on self-expression in France, in 1983 Aérospatiale set up over 450 'exchange and progress fora', in which nine work hours a year are set aside for bi-monthly meetings. The fora shifted from an original question-and-answer focus to one of economic and social information exchange. Under pressure from increased competition, Aérospatiale decided that it needed to motivate and involve the whole workforce in both the organization's economic goals and its ways of achieving them. In 1985 a new participation charter under the theme of 'ideas' (IDÉES) was set up. All managers were provided with a week's training in psychology, face-to-face interaction, delegation and leading meetings. The role of leader became one of *animation*. Quality circles were set up to deal with technical matters. Initially unions felt these would rival or sabotage the expression fora. Senior managers were appointed to help facilitate the *animateurs* in resolving problems. Original fears subsided and the number of circles has increased. Around thirty quality circles now exist. Each solution undergoes detailed financial analysis to assess its profitability potential. No financial rewards exist for ideas, but indirect rewards (such as trips, exchange visits or articles in inhouse journals) are used to highlight good ideas. The current debate centres on how best to involve circle members in the financial outcome of the decisions made.

Source: Frère (1991).

design problems of the organization (Cressey, 1991). The main weaknesses in implementation include their restriction to a narrow set of issues, an instrumental rather than truly participative approach to involvement, short-term and cyclical activity patterns, a lack of sufficient training of team members, a hostile reaction at lower and middle management level as traditional responsibilities were undermined, a separation from the rewards system of the organization, and a perception of being marginalized in relation to the most powerful decision making forum in the organization. In many cases, quality circles also produced quite powerful resistance. This resistance was often because there was a fear of loss of power, despite the fact that quality circles were not integrated into existing structures. Changes were frequently felt to be decreed from above, results were expected too quickly whilst the implementation of solutions took too long, and often only the hard, calculable advantages were taken into consideration (Marciniak, 1991). Therefore, although quality circles caught on in Europe (by 1980 it was estimated that 63 per cent of industrial workplaces ran them), they have waned in importance. By 1989 only 10 per cent of industrial workplaces ran quality circles (Ramsay, 1992). Quality circles have nevertheless proved to be quite resilient, but face many severe difficulties (Cressey, 1991). Failure rates are reported to be around 20 per cent in the UK and 50 per cent in the US. However, many organizations have maintained their quality circles and indeed developed the approach (see Illustration 12.5 for an outline of the Volkswagen experience).

Over this period there was a re-orientation of the quality management movement towards total quality management (TQM) as European organizations began to learn from Japanese inward investors (such as Komatsu, Hitachi and Nissan). According to the European Foundation for Quality Management, most European managers now

Illustration 12.5 **Evolution of quality circles at Volkswagen: the Volkswagen-zirkel.**

Quality circles at Volkswagen grew out of many years' experience with small group activities. Throughout the 1970s and early 1980s small group activities were introduced at plants in Brazil, Wolfsburg, Hanover, Brunswick, Emsden and Kassel. In August 1986 a company agreement between the board and the group works council laid down the aims of quality circles in detail. Volkswagen learned from previous failures and followed an early participation model of implementation. Circles were not introduced on a plant basis, but on a phased basis into areas with no more than 2,000 employees, so that disputes could easily be resolved. Circles cover all level of the company's operations from top management down to semi-skilled operatives. They are in-tended to prepare employees for the transition from Taylorite working methods to flexible specialization, and solve problems of competitiveness under the headings of information flows, creativity, motivation, job satisfaction, team-working, training and problem solving. Only issues regulated by law or collective agreement cannot be discussed by the circles. Everything else is open for consideration. Once a specific issue has been discussed, solved and action taken, the circle is dissolved. Any employee involved in the circle must be directly affected by the problem being worked on, but participation is voluntary. Circles frequently involve related work groups and suppliers, helping to build new collaborative structures.

Source: Marciniak (1991).

recognize that quality is not an isolated issue to be dealt with on such a localized basis, but is instead an issue for the total organization, involving all operational and management units. This emphasis on the 'total' nature of quality addresses many of the criticisms and failures of quality circles. TQM is felt to have a greater chance of success because, by its very nature, it is intended to solve some of the strategic problems that quality circles cannot (see Illustration 12.6). As an approach it is less employee-orientated and concentrates more on issues of management restructuring. As TQM has become a part of the corporate strategy and one of the keys to organizational success, then worker participation in the earliest stages of job design has been shown to be a critical factor. The long preparation and lead times involved in a TQM programme necessitate a top-down approach to implementation, which in turn makes it easier to provide the necessary training, consultation and co-ordination across management levels and functions.

Illustration 12.6 **The main features that distinguish total quality management from quality circles.**

- Quality is seen as a strategic rather than operational issue.
- It includes the whole of the innovation process.
- It includes horizontal improvements, such as those related to the customer, as well as vertical ones.
- Quality is seen as a senior management issue.
- It demands a change in organizational culture, with the principle components being:
  - open communications,
  - greater employee involvement in decisions,
  - creation of high-trust relations,
  - internalization of quality,
  - greater responsiveness to customer satisfaction,
  - systematic approach to quality.

Source: Hill (1990).

THE SWEDISH MODEL: STRUCTURAL DECENTRALIZATION AND GROUP WORKING

European postwar history has been littered with examples of attempts to introduce self-regulating and participative teams. There has been a relatively rapid development of decentralized group working and this form of work organization has also grown in strategic and economic importance (Cressey, 1992). Organizations have moved towards more cellular production methods and integrated work groups in order to gain:

- Economic advantages in terms of costs, response time, quality and productivity.
- Organizational gains in terms of workable decentralization and the use of new production methods.
- Social gains in terms of improved commitment, satisfaction and identity at work on the basis of involvement.

The rationale behind the appearance of integrated teamwork is shown in Illustration 12.7. But does the recent growth of teamwork represent a renewed effort to implement socio-technical principles, or is it a qualitatively different process? We need to examine the historical record of working in teams to answer this question, and there is no better location than Sweden. Group working was introduced in Sweden around 1970 and is now quite widespread amongst Swedish employers, although the original concepts of teamwork came to Sweden from Norway (Hart, 1993). Labour market agencies took responsibility for teamworking developments, and it became the main means by which Swedish organizations achieved their structural decentralization. Initiatives spread from the state sector (mining, shipyards and tobacco) and local authorities (the health sector) to private industry. Saab first introduced self-regulating groups in 1969, with the number of teams growing to 130 production groups by 1973. A continuous conveyor belt with twenty car assembly operators was replaced by eight parallel bays in which two or three people completely assembled an engine, extending job content from two to twenty minutes. Experiments at other plants showed Saab that operator performance deteriorated once job content was expanded to forty minutes (Jones, 1991). The success of these early experiments was attributed to (Hart, 1993):

- Early and close involvement of employees during the design and development stages.
- Use of small-scale experiments to start with.
- Consolidation of new working systems through formal agreements only once learning had taken place.

Illustration 12.7 **The rationale behind the appearance of self-regulating teams.**

- A response to wider market changes (flexible specialization) and even faster product adaptations.
- Changed production methods requiring new forms of labour interaction.
- Requirement for all-round skills and multiple competencies.
- A requirement for more networking, co-operation and integration of functions.
- A need to decentralize decision making as lower and middle management is re-ordered.
- The pervasive need for quality to be implemented and the use of teams (which learn more quickly).
- A requirement to value and use human resources differently, because old disciplinary formats have proved unproductive and demands for participation have increased.

Source: Cressey (1992).

With few exceptions, the early experiments focused on the social organization of work. Early in the history of group working it was appreciated that people would react differently to the challenge. Attainment of more advanced group working has been a progressive and evolutionary phenomenon in Sweden (see Illustration 12.8). The evidence suggests that group working in Volvo has the active involvement of the majority of workers.

This focus on the social organization of work meant that progress was made by focusing on the technological components – the cycle of production processes, range of tasks and stress levels. Work designers assumed that the more skilled employees would then be equipped to mobilize ideas about the level of decentralization and degree of control over the work. In practice, they did not, and throughout the 1970s many of the physical conditions of work were found to deteriorate, not improve (Hart, 1993), despite improvements to the psycho-social working conditions. Teamwork had been introduced within the existing technological framework, simply dividing a production line into bit-sized sections. Delegation of decision making was constrained by what was possible in the old layouts. It was not until the late 1970s that teamwork was seen in its broader context, when the Swedish Employers Confederation (SAF) co-ordinated the New Industries Programme. The original programme concentrated on using new technology as a vehicle for improving work conditions. A range of related programmes have addressed issues of preventive health care, the development of leadership potential, the design of more human-orientated computer interfaces, equal opportunities and skills and training issues. Attention has shifted from designing work groups to solve problems of autonomy and involvement towards issues of exploiting technological change:

> ... Recent developments reveal that work groups today are not autonomous as such but form an integrated part of decentralized planning and production systems. In this respect, new technology has provided a strong incentive to reform the basic principles of the organization of production.   Hart (1993, p. 16).

Self-regulated work groups have since been introduced by many organizations outside Sweden, including Procter and Gamble, Shell, Johnson and Johnson and Honeywell. Jones (1984, 1986, 1991) has documented approaches to job design and motivation in Swedish organizations. Industrial policy in Sweden has the goal of

---

Illustration 12.8 **Evolving stages of group work at Volvo plants.**

In order to provide targets for the most interested employees, Volvo determined 5 successive levels of group working at its Kalmar plant. Each level is typically based on the attainment of four to six new elements. At Level 5 the new elements include correcting the group's own mistakes, reporting via a terminal, choosing and training reserve operators and solving economic questions. In 1978 only one group had obtained Level 5 (increasing to three groups by 1982 and 5 per cent of the production workforce by 1987) and 80 per cent of the groups were at Levels 2 or 3. By 1985, 94 per cent of groups were at Levels 3 or 4 and by 1987 all production groups had attained at least Level 3.

Level 1: Working as a group.
Level 2: Job enlargement.
Level 3: Increases in responsibility for planning.
Level 4: Job rotation.
Level 5: Increased possibility of making own decisions.

Source: Jones (1991).

Illustration 12.9 **The four concepts within the Swedish approach to work design.**

- Structural decentralization.
- Evolution of small autonomous working groups.

- Re-introduction of incentive bonus schemes.
- Joint approach to motivation through the Development Agreement.

Source: Jones (1991).

producing quality goods with sound technology. This requires a well motivated and educated workforce. In turn, the working environment and jobs need to be designed and organized in order to secure commitment throughout the organization. Although Sweden has a long history of such an approach to job design, the recent competitive threat from Japan and challenges to specific organizations (such as Saab-Scania and Volvo) because of the Single European Market (SEM) have served to renew efforts in the area of job design and motivation. The Swedish approach actually involves four concepts (see Illustration 12.9). The role of incentive bonus schemes is discussed in the next chapter and the industrial relations aspects of the Swedish Development Agreement are covered in Chapter Fifteen. In this chapter we focus on the topics of decentralization and small group working in relation to job design.

We discussed the impact of organizational structure on behaviour in Chapter Eight. Swedish organizations recognized the influence that structure has on attitudes and motivation (see Illustration 12.10). There has been a swing away from total decentralization common in many Swedish organizations in the 1970s (with some functions such as finance or corporate marketing becoming more centralized), but the overall aims of decentralization remain the same in the 1990s. It has four main aims:

1. To provide shorter lines of communication so that production can respond quickly to market change.
2. To facilitate greater communication and awareness of the need for profit and survival.
3. To provide feedback on performance in order to foster personal responsibility.
4. To enable purposeful delegation to autonomous profit centres.

Illustration 12.10 **Decentralized participation at Volvo.**

In Swedish organizations the influence that formal structure has on the attitudes of workers is recognized. The structure is intended to involve people in the performance of the company at many levels. In 1991 Volvo consisted of nine divisions, each with a Managing Director and considerable autonomy. People are involved at several layers of the structure. Within the car division, each of the six main works in Sweden made their own decisions on several issues, including the structure of the wage systems. Each foreman at the Kalmar plant is responsible for twenty to thirty people, drawing up budgets and targets to monitor progress and discussing how figures will be estimated.

Source: Jones (1991).

DO AUTONOMOUS WORK GROUPS IMPROVE ORGANIZATIONAL PERFORMANCE?

So have self-regulating or autonomous work groups been successful? Most of the published reports on self-regulating work teams show favourable results (Cummings and Huse, 1989). Reviews of different studies generally support results. An analysis of sixteen studies found that productivity, costs and quality measures improved in 85 per cent of cases, whilst significant improvements in employee turnover, absenteeism and attitudes were reported in 70 per cent of cases (Cummings and Molloy, 1977). Another review found improvements in hard performance measures in 67 per cent of the cases (Nicholas, 1982). The relative impact of self-regulated groups was equal to that of job enrichment (discussed earlier in the chapter), especially when job enrichment is accompanied by increased participation. The major benefits of self-regulating groups are clearly economic, resulting from the need for less supervision. The longer-term impact of self-regulating groups on job motivation, performance, organizational commitment, voluntary turnover and mental health, whilst positive, is also mixed and dependent on a number of other factors (Wall, Kemp, Jackson and Clegg, 1986).

Saab-Scania conducted extensive research on self-regulating groups. These groups have generally shown improvements in productivity, unplanned work stoppages, employee attitudes and staff turnover (Norsted and Aguren, 1975). Studies of Volvo have also demonstrated some benefits of self-regulating teams (Gyllenhammar, 1977; Tichy and Nisberg, 1978). Group working was initially intended to overcome problems of absenteeism and labour turnover. In the 1960s Volvo experienced absenteeism and turnover rates of 17 and 30 per cent respectively at its Olofström plant. The expansion of individual job content within a group setting was intended to attack these problems. Labour turnover became more expensive, since an extra six months' training was required. Labour turnover improved as a result of the introduction of group working, falling from 30 per cent in 1970 to 13 per cent by 1972. It then fell progressively to a figure of 2 per cent by 1983. However, despite the innovative work design, staff turnover began to rise again throughout the 1980s at the Olofström plant to a level of 7 per cent (still less than a quarter of the 1970s rate).

The Kalmar plant has experienced mixed fortunes since production started in 1974. Staff turnover fell from 24 per cent in 1979 to 5 per cent by 1990. Higher levels of productivity are achieved (man-hours per car are 25 per cent less than at the Torslando plant) but at the cost of higher electrical, depreciation and interest charges arising from the design of the plant. New recruits have become more mobile between employers and absenteeism still remains at 23 per cent at the Kalmar plant (Jones, 1991). A system of 'godfathers' to help new recruits and a 'labour pool' of mobile workers to cover absenteeism has been introduced. Absenteeism can be more readily absorbed under a group structure. Overall figures for absenteeism in the various plants have not fallen as dramatically as initially hoped (although in Sweden military service and maternity leave are counted under absenteeism figures and therefore obscure the impact on self-motivated absenteeism).

Other evidence on the impact of group working in Volvo may be gleaned from attitude surveys. The surveys gather data on eight 'vectors':

1. Perceived level of interest that Volvo has in its employees.
2. Motivation of employees to do more than the minimum.

3. Effectiveness of leadership and opportunity to influence own job.
4. Clarity of goals.
5. Level of team spirit.
6. Loyalty to Volvo.
7. Level of training and education.

These surveys have produced rather surprising results (Jones, 1991). Around 54 per cent of employees rate the level of teamworking as good or very good. For example, the level of loyalty to the company (Volvo) has risen, whilst the possibility of influencing one's own job remains remarkably low given the experiments with job design. However, surveys produce quite subjective data and as the years have progressed, expectations have been raised and younger workers lack the length of service to understand the benefits of the new work designs.

Has this relative success of autonomous work groups led to common developments in HRM? The success of self-regulated work teams is dependent on external support systems which are quite different from those found in traditional and hierarchical organizations. Bureaucratic and mechanistic organizations are not conducive to self-regulating groups, whilst organic organizational structures with few rules and decentralized responsibility are more supportive. The implementation of self-regulating teams has been associated with different organizational solutions. Their introduction frequently requires changes in communication flows, power relationships, status hierarchies, job evaluation and reward systems and work flows. The relationship of teams to the rest of the organization varies. In some cases the plant manager is only a few levels above production workers, whilst in others the supervisor reports direct to the plant manager with intermediate positions being eliminated. The complex demands of managing self-regulating work groups have led to a number of common developments in HRM systems, particularly as they apply to first-line management positions (see Illustration 12.11). The role of supervisors is changed quite markedly by the introduction of self-regulating work groups, away from one of control towards a focus on working with and developing group members and assisting the group in maintaining its boundaries (Hackman, 1987).

Illustration 12.11 **Developments in HRM resulting from the introduction of self-regulating work groups.**

Recruitment and selection Selection of supervisor skills in order to achieve a balance of technical and social skills.

Training Extensive formal and on-the-job training in human relations, group dynamics, and leadership styles in order to develop understanding of the supervisor role and team building skills.

Evaluation and rewards Links between supervisor rewards and achievements in team development, creation of developmental plans for individual workers, measurable benchmarks for progress, performance appraisals conducted within a group format, and feedback from group members, peers and higher-level management.

Support systems Development of peer support systems, off-site support groups to share personal issues and concerns.

Utilization of capacity Opportunity to apply talents beyond the immediate work group, especially as work groups mature and take on more authority. Role shift towards higher-level planning and budgeting, and training and development activities.

Source: after Walton and Schlesinger (1979).

LINKING INCENTIVE BONUS SCHEMES TO TEAM WORKING

In Chapter Two we referred to the pronounced change in Swedish HRM, which in large part has been due to fears of a process of 'psychological de-industrialization', whereby delegated responsibility and the higher structural costs of decentralization are not matched by sufficiently high improvements in productivity and performance. Whilst the achievements of both group working and decentralization in motivating workers at all levels have been widely acknowledged in Sweden, seen against the challenge from the Far East, new ideas are needed (Jones, 1991):

... Motivation is a key component of success in a competitive world. The design of schemes to improve motivation and commitment to the organization is not a one-off exercise... It is ... a continuous process requiring a topping up with fresh ideas every few years.

Jones (1991, p. 104).

We discuss the topic of rewards and benefits in the next chapter. However, changes in work design are rarely made in isolation and recently incentive schemes have formed an important part of the HRM solution to low motivation or poor productivity. Whilst changes in industrial relations are intended to influence attitudes in the long term, incentive bonus schemes have been introduced in Sweden in order to address some of the problems of motivation within team working in the short term. In the mid-1970s most Swedish organizations operated large incentive bonus payments, but under pressure from the unions, moved to straight time payments. There has since been a process of 'local drift' where workers at individual plants believed they could earn more money through selective incentives, reinforced by the decentralized approach to wage systems. Sophisticated bonus schemes are becoming increasingly common in a variety of Swedish industries. Many of these new incentive schemes are a spin-off from information technology, in that they rely on the provision of fast and accurate data. The Swedish Employers' Confederation, SAF, conducted a survey of the experience of thirteen organizations. The main conclusions are shown in Illustration 12.12.

In 1981 the Volvo Olofström plant introduced a 3 per cent bonus depending on the degree of participation in group working, followed by a 15 per cent maximum bonus for productivity. In some sections of the plant, for each 1 per cent increase in shop

Illustration 12.12 **The effective linking of incentive schemes to work design in a group of thirteen Swedish employers.**

- Increased motivation is the main aim of most incentive schemes, and without exception improvements in attitudes and output were reported.
- Feedback on performance is essential, conveying the reasons behind both good and bad performance. In addition to written information, regular meetings are held to reinforce conclusions.
- Openness on organization objectives and results is an essential element of the change process, generating interest and loyalty and improving motivation.
- The evolution of a sound system takes time, allowing the opportunity to remove defects and sell the system to all job levels.
- Even the best systems are only expected to last for around two to three years. Administrative systems have to be updated speedily and smoothly.
- Bonus schemes have to be based on one or more factors that can be measured and directly influence the prosperity of the organization.
- Good wage systems are regarded as powerful management tools because they force managers to examine their methods and recognize the many factors involved in effectiveness.

Source: Östman (1977).

Illustration 12.13   **Strategic change through teamwork at Vauxhall.**

Vauxhall has been in the UK since 1905 and was purchased by General Motors in 1925. It remained more or less autonomous until the 1970s, leading to internal competition with Opel. European car design and engineering was progressively integrated and by 1982 there was a common product line. From 1987–92 General Motors-Europe re-orientated its operations to become a credible European player. It spent £462 million on new facilities in the UK to increase capacity. This involved major changes in work design in UK operations, picking up much existing best practice. The Luton plant employs 3,941 staff and builds the Cavalier car. Nearly 42 per cent of the output is for export, up from virtually zero in 1990. Like all European car manufacturers, Vauxhall faced considerable competitive pressure and had to address its productivity problems. The solution was to become a 'lean organization'. A series of beliefs and values were established first, and then changes were made in team work to reinforce these values. Vauxhall combined total quality management (TQM) principles, with innovations in team work and a new rewards policy. The plant introduced a TQM approach, which it called the 'Quality Network Process'. This detailed the customer requirements, people implications, team work and continuous improvement process, and customer satisfaction measures. Vauxhall believed that teams were a critical part of the manufacturing system. The objectives of the team concept were to fulfil and optimize individual abilities, maximize the use of facilities, facilitate continuous improvements in productivity and quality, and create a supportive environment for the management of change. It was hoped that improvements in teamwork would both improve long-term viability by raising customer satisfaction and also enable production at competitive cost against world class quality standards. A new team system was negotiated with the unions, under the slogan 'working together to win'. Three new roles were created: supervisors, team leaders and team members. The role of supervisors shifted from that of policeman and monitor, to coach and problem solver. Team leaders were responsible for day-to-day operations. Their role required new skills in problem solving, motivation and control, group techniques, group dynamics, data gathering and team briefing skills. Teams ranged in number from five to fifteen members. The target span of control for supervisors was seven to eight. Team meetings were used for problem solving, communications and continuous improvement suggestions. They

were trained to do all the jobs and so they no longer worked as individual operators. Responsibilities were shared and jobs rotated within the team, according to their own preferences, and the next team was their customer. Under the new team process, team members put ideas forward to supervisors. For minor improvements the supervisor could provide immediate rewards. Expert reviews were used to judge more fundamental improvements and estimate cost savings. The teams shared 20 per cent of the annual savings, up to a maximum of £12,000, deciding themselves how to to share the benefit. In practice, the upper limit doesn't have to be applied. Non-monetary benefits, such as sports evenings or outings, were also used to reward achievements.

The new work design was implemented side by side with the old system (production could not be stopped). There was a gradual transition from one system to another and other changes in HRM, such as a new grading system and promotion systems based on the acquisition of new skills, are under negotiation. An intensive communication and information programme was followed by a cascading process, in which each level of the organization was responsible for training the next level down. A series of benefits resulted. Quality measures and levels of productivity improved whilst costs were reduced. Dramatic improvements in productivity were achieved between 1988 and 1992, with output increasing from 87,000 units a year in 1988 to 171,000 units a year by 1992. The number of cars produced per employee rose from 19.22 in 1986 to 38.55 in 1992. By 1992 cars were being produced at a rate of 47.6 cars per hour. Stock turnovers increased from 20.7 in 1988 to 56.7 by 1992, the best performance in Europe. The number of discrepancies per vehicle was also quickly brought down. A number of softer measures also demonstrated the benefits of the new work practices. The number of improvement suggestions quadrupled from 1988–92. The workforce was more motivated and versatile. Levels of job rotation increased, waste was eliminated and the continuous improvement process was institutionalized as part of the organizational culture. The Vauxhall Luton plant considered the level of absenteeism to be a good proxy measure of the level of commitment. In the wake of increased levels of teamwork, the absenteeism rate fell from 8 per cent in 1986 to 4 per cent by January 1993. Vauxhall benchmarked itself against the Nissan absenteeism rate of 2.5 per cent.

output, workers receive an extra 0.25 per cent in their pay packet. Consequently, productivity is monitored carefully and considerable thought goes into the choice of measure. Remarkable increases in productivity have been achieved (Jones, 1991). The immediate impact of the incentive schemes at Olofström was a 10 per cent increase in productivity, followed by a steady rise to a level 43 per cent over 1981 levels (more than compensating for a 22 per cent rise in the amount of labour needed at the plant since 1981). At the Kalmar plant incentive bonuses are calculated on seven factors, with the two most important being the level of defects on a finished car (which fell by 39 per cent from 1985–1990) and the number of man-hours needed to produce each car (which fell by 40 per cent over the same period). Feedback on such productivity measures goes directly to the workplace almost on an individual basis through the use of Visual Display Units (VDUs). Around 72 per cent of the Kalmar employees regard the bonus system as a positive incentive. Swedish managers believe that the results described in this section demonstrate that well constructed incentive schemes can have a beneficial effect on the level of motivation. The main union, METALL, supports this view, believing that a 'it doesn't matter' mentality is being replaced by a stronger keenness to do the job.

In Chapter Four we highlighted the problem faced by European car manufacturers in the face of superior productivity in Japanese transplant factories and overcapacity in Europe. Because of this threat, many other European car manufacturers (and indeed other sectors) outside Sweden have begun to use principles of employee involvement, teamwork and incentive schemes in order to address their underlying problems of competitiveness, poor productivity and over capacity (see Illustration 12.13 for an outline of the approach taken by Vauxhall in the UK). As we mentioned at the beginning of the chapter, changes in work design have to be coupled with other other HRM initiatives.

THE JAPANESE LEAN SYSTEM VERSUS THE SWEDISH MODEL

... The automobile industry is entering the most competitive, innovative, stressful and paradigm-shifting decade since its very beginnings more than a century ago.

Rehder (1992a, p. 8).

The term 'lean production' was used by the Massachussetts Institute of Technology (MIT) to describe a concept first introduced by Toyota in Japan. The system combines the best features of mass production, such as speed and low unit costs, with some of the best features of craft production, such as flexibility and high quality. Since the ground-breaking International Motor Vehicle programme at MIT in the US, considerable attention has been given to comparisons between the Japanese 'lean production' system and the Swedish autonomous work group model (Adler and Cole, 1993; Bennett and Karlsson, 1990; Berggren, 1992; Ellegard, Engstrom and Nilsson, 1991; Rehder, 1992b; and Womack, Jones and Roos, 1990). The Japanese 'lean system' is rapidly making both the traditional Ford mass production system and the newer humanistic systems of Volvo obsolete. A comparison of the two approaches is shown in Table 12.5. Whilst Japanese just-in-time and quality methods were also based in a wider social setting, they are far more production- and management-orientated than the humanistic Swedish approach and were introduced unilaterally by managements, as exemplified by Toyota. The teamworking content of the two approaches is broadly similar, but the social context places different constraints on the amount of autonomy that the work design affords. Lean production depends on teams

Table 12.5 **Contrasts between the Swedish and Japanese models of work group participation.**

	Sweden	Japan
Origins	Socio-technical model	Quality control productionism
Socio-economic setting	Social democratic government Class compromise Corporatism Management prerogative Tight labour market	Right wing government Enterprise paternalism Dual labour market Tight labour market
Management objectives	Productivity Motivation Control of labour, turnover and absenteeism Avert challenge from below Collaboration with unions	Productivity Motivation Quality control Aid flexibility and labour task mobility Reinforce management
Content	Mixed content – union dissatisfaction – a dominance of management objectives	Management control typical Production and profit dominant
Participation/control	Tacit management control sometimes increased Schemes curtailed if management objectives not met	Minimal autonomy Close management control Management technique, no independent survival
Other benefits to employee	Job variety Job satisfaction?	Sense of belonging Chance to contribute Job satisfaction?
Costs to employees	Job security Intensity of work effort	Work effort Jobs Powerlessness
Performance	Moderate/marginal?	Moderate/strong?

Source: reprinted from H. Ramsay, 'Swedish and Japanese work methods: comparisons and contrasts', *European Participation Monitor*, issue 3, 37–60, © 1992, with kind permission of the European Foundation for the Improvement of Living and Working Conditions.

taking responsibility for their own work and considering every other team as an 'internal customer' as opposed to the next stage of the production process (Roth, 1993). In Japan, teams are seen not only as the smallest unit in the organization structure, but as a social institution in its own right. Each team guarantees a continuous improvement process (known in Japan as *kaizen*). Continuous improvement, with all workers at all levels reducing levels of waste and improving efficiency and innovation, is central to the Japanese concept of management.

There is some evidence of lean production systems moving into Europe. For example, although attempts at job enrichment and flexible specialization in Germany have been introduced very cautiously and have largely been limited to the high technology sectors of manufacturing, some organizations such as Opel have introduced lean production ideas. Notably, in the Opel experiment there were some divergences from the Japanese model. Roth (1993) draws some useful distinctions. In Japan the spokesperson is appointed by supervisors but in Opel the appointment is by free election. The German model also encourages greater freedom to choose subjects for group discussion, greater specialization and more involvement in decisions. Whilst German managers define goals or objectives against which to measure change, Japanese managers stress an accumulation of small steps rather than focus on the end result. German experimentation with *kaizen* has focused on the reduction of waste and elimination of unproductive aspects of work (it has been estimated that savings of up to 35 per cent could be made on the overall costs of the German motor industry) whilst Japanese thinking focuses on both the product and the process (we consider the implications of 'process' thinking in the last chapter). German organizations have introduced *kaizen* assuming that there will be savings in manpower, whilst in Japan it is assumed that savings will be channelled into improving the overall work of the organization. In summary, it has become quite clear that 'foreign' concepts of work design do not necessarily become absorbed into the fabric of organizational life:

> ... The key factor in the social system is not to turn a French worker into a Japanese or Swedish worker but to design a system which incorporates the values, culture and expertise of the workers into the specific industrial environment. The aim is not to set up quality circles 'like the Japanese' but rather to design and implement a joint approach which will generate both quality and results in economic terms.   Regout (1992, p. 31).

There is a growing consensus that tomorrow's most effective organizations will be characterized by their capacity to learn: '... organizations will need to pinpoint innovative practices rapidly, to communicate them to their employees and suppliers, and to stimulate further innovation' (Adler and Cole, 1993, p. 85). There are two competing views about the best work design to support such organizational learning. Proponents of the Japanese-inspired lean production model argue that a system based on specialized work tasks with modest amounts of job rotation and high levels of discipline in defining and implementing work procedures is the most effective system for the future, whilst '... proponents of the human-centred German–Scandinavian alternative argue that adaptability and learning is best served by greatly lengthened work cycles and a return to work forms that give teams substantial latitude in how they perform their tasks and authority over what have traditionally been higher-level management decisions' (Adler and Cole, 1993, p. 85). Whoever is right, one thing is certain. Work designs are changing quite radically.

CONCLUSIONS

Robertson and Smith (1985) point out that in the 1970s there was considerable emphasis placed on the potential of job redesign as a means of improving the motivational content of work (and indirectly organizational performance). Since then, the theoretical basis of much of the work on job motivation and satisfaction came under attack. Yet, even by the more sceptical and culturally-sensitive standards of the 1980s, redesigning jobs to achieve higher levels of employee motivation still remains a powerful management strategy. When we look forward over the next ten years, and consider the potential of information technology to totally reshape the nature of management jobs, the flow and quality of information, the communication and interaction patterns within the organization and the level of feedback on job performance, then lessons from the implementation of previous work design strategies will prove a useful guideline. When we add to this the current restructuring taking place within organizations – with the associated changes related to downsizing, delayering and business process re-engineering (discussed in the last chapter) – then it becomes clear that we shall witness profound changes in the nature and shape of jobs and work. There are a number of key learning points that have emerged from this chapter that may help inform the managers involved in these changes.

LEARNING POINTS FROM CHAPTER TWELVE

1. Work design represents the conscious and deliberate planning of tasks, jobs and the structural and social aspects of organizations. It involves strategies to bring the technology and people into a closer degree of fit. Work design changes frequently to form part of broader strategies such as empowerment, redesign of business processes or quality of working life programmes.

2. A wide range of competitive, social, technological and organizational factors are leading to developments in work design. We are witnessing a radical restructuring of many European organizations.

3. Whilst technological determinants of work design are converging, job designs still vary quite markedly across European countries. Differences exist in the degree of specialization, the formalization of control procedures, the level of decentralization and participation, levels of discretion and autonomy and the nature of management involvement.

4. This is, in part, due to historical differences in the advance of scientific management across Europe. Taylorist principles were adopted most strongly in France and to some extent Britain. In Germany there was only a weak level of adoption in relation to work design. By the 1980s there was considerable divergence in the nature of work design.

5. At the organizational level there are four job designs that tend to be adopted: traditional jobs, traditional groups, job enrichment strategies and self-regulating (autonomous) work groups.

6. The job enrichment movement involved building motivational factors into the content of jobs through job rotations, an enlargement of the scope of activities involved in the job, or an increase in the level of autonomy, control and feedback of results. Such experiments make clear motivational and cultural assumptions.

7. The quality of working life movement, initiated in the US, spread across Europe through Scandinavia, Germany, France and Britain. Some countries adopted a more systematic approach than others.

8. The motivational factors in work vary across cultures in terms of content. For example, levels of achievement motivation vary considerably. However, many cultural norms influence the surface aspects of work design such as attitudes and levels of satisfaction. The importance of work in relation to other life goals and the underlying structure of work values seems relatively consistent across cultures. Whilst there are differences in what motivates people, the way in which people are motivated at work remains the same.

9. Since the early 1980s there has been considerable movement towards flexibility and this has influenced most aspects of the employment relationship. Organizations sought flexibility in order to adapt to a turbulent environment and international markets, whilst employees sought new patterns of work and greater protection in core employment.

10. The transition to flexibility has been characterized by a significant process of deregulation and removal of traditional rigidities in the employment relationship. This

has been pursued through a consensual approach based on collective negotiation.

11. New developments in technology, the internationalization of markets and new ways of deploying labour have led to the rise of a new market and production strategy called flexible specialization. Only a handful of European countries are expected to be able to compete on this basis.

12. This new market and production strategy highlights a growing need for higher levels of trust and involvement in the workplace. Participative management practices are intended to encourage more responsibility and increase commitment to change.

13. Direct forms of participation, such as quality circles and total quality management, have found favour in Europe. The experience of quality circles has not been overly successful, and their use has declined as broader strategic approaches took hold.

14. Many organizations, spurred on by the Swedish approach to management and work design, have moved towards more cellular production methods and integrated work teams. Self-regulating work groups have been designed around autonomous tasks that form a self-completing whole. There is employee influence over the type and rate of inputs and outputs from the work cycle as well as the ability to regulate the behaviours needed to produce a finished product.

15. Group work has evolved through a number of stages. Early work design experiments concentrated on the technological components of work design such as the production cycle and the range of tasks controlled. Later enhancements tackled issues of decentralization and delegation of decision-making. Teamwork is now being introduced into new technological environments that devolve control even more.

16. Recent work design experiments have led to a tighter integration of developments in teamwork and innovative benefits and rewards packages.

17. Self-regulating teams have been relatively successful. Although improvements to the physical environment have been minor, substantial gains in productivity (partially offset by higher costs) have been achieved and levels of staff turnover (but not absenteeism) have fallen. Such gains have been observed in several European countries.

18. In order to make self-regulating teams work effectively, there have been several developments in human resource management practices, especially at supervisor level.

19. Finally, experiments in work design such as self-regulating work groups and lean production systems are now competing head-to-head in terms of the improvements they create in cost, productivity, quality and innovation. The ultimate measure of success will be the extent to which they facilitate organizational learning. The one certainty is that work designs will continue to change rapidly across Europe.

CHAPTER THIRTEEN

Pay and Benefit Systems

INTRODUCTION

In the last chapter we focused on the development of greater numerical, functional and time flexibility in European organizations and its impact on work design. Hand in hand with the process, there has been pressure for greater pay flexibility (Treu, 1992). The management of rewards and compensation was once a relatively straightforward process. Salary and job level went hand in hand. Year upon year, employees would climb the corporate ladder, receive a higher salary, collect more benefits and develop a growing sense of job security and career entitlement. For the employer, this system assured that the employee would be loyal to the organization, serve with long-term commitment and perform the tasks requested by management. Pay was seen more as a fixed cost than an investment.

In recent years, however, a number of strategies, the pressures of increased international competition, slow growth, volatile financial markets, changing demographics, and shifting social values have turned these quiet waters into a still churning whirlpool of change (Berger, 1991). Economic and demographic realities have shattered familiar frameworks, rendering traditional approaches to compensation ineffective or even redundant. According to data from the PWCP study, compensation ranks as the second most important HRM issue after training and development in Germany and Switzerland (Hilb, 1992).

In Parts One and Two we highlighted a number of developments that are transforming the pay and benefits environment in European organizations (see Figure 13.1).

The move towards transnational organizations has brought a requirement to remunerate more expatriate managers, and to reward a flexible, mobile cadre of international managers. The process of business restructuring and foreign direct investment has resulted in a harmonization of pay and benefit systems immediately following mergers and acquisitions, changed remuneration levels once the new international ownership is established, and a different legitimacy for pay comparisons as new business networks are established. There is increased competition in terms of international productivity and unit labour costs, and concern over marked differences in social costs. We also see conflicting social pressures leading to a pauperization of peripheral employment and a contrasting increased value and skill worth in areas of marked shortage. The broader social context is one of changing values and a greater

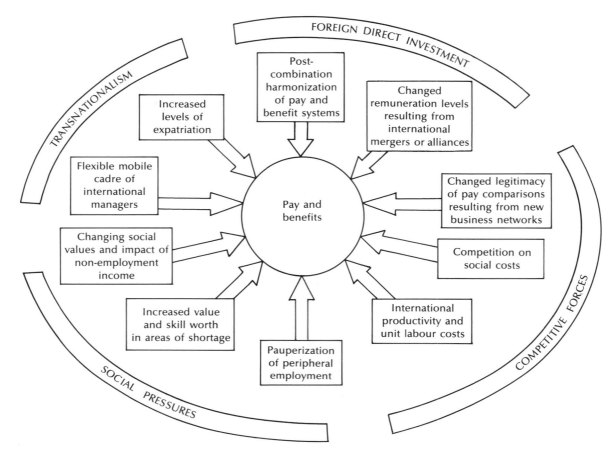

Figure 13.1 The factors influencing change in pay and benefits systems.

impact of non-employment income. All these pressures are influencing decisions on pay and benefits in European organizations.

The need to understand and manage changes in pay and benefit systems is extremely important. Gomez-Mejia and Welbourne (1991) estimate that approximately 90 per cent of the average management payroll for multinational organizations is comprised of compensation for local nationals, principally because of the high costs of maintaining expatriates overseas (as discussed in Chapter Eleven). The challenge to these organizations is not to take advantage of low wage opportunities, but to design compensation strategies that are the most appropriate for the specific cultural traditions. In discussing pay and benefits, this chapter is split into four parts:

- First, we consider some cultural differences in approaches to pay and benefit systems.
- Second, we examine the key reasons for change in the sphere of pay and benefits.
- Third, we examine what is happening to compensation in European organizations today and how these organizations are re-examining their reward policies and practices to meet the challenges of the changing business environment.
- Fourth, we look at some of the key issues and new approaches to compensation, including the equal pay issue and the emergence of skill-based pay.

CULTURAL DIFFERENCES IN PAY AND BENEFIT SYSTEMS

In Chapter Three we noted that national cultural preferences are associated with different perspectives on pay and benefits, most notably through assumptions about 'distributive justice'. We drew attention to the fact that in countries like Belgium, France, Portugal and Spain there is a preference for equity-based pay policies, whilst in Denmark, Germany, Ireland and the UK the preference is for equality-based policies (Miles and Greenberg, 1992). There are also differences in the motivational impact of non-monetary rewards between European countries, and a greater emphasis on the need for 'socially healthy' levels of executive pay (Henzler, 1992b) than would be found in the US business culture.

Recently, Pennings (1993) has examined executive reward systems in a cross-national context. He gathered qualitative data on 51 US executives from twenty organizations, 11 Dutch executives from six organizations and 5 French executives from three organizations and examined the nature of their present executive reward systems, the perceived contribution and function of executive compensation plans, the link between pay and strategic performance and recent changes in reward systems. The American managers showed a greater emphasis on using long-term executive compensation plans. Reflecting the comments of Henzler (1992b) about 'socially healthy' executive remuneration in Chapter Three, in the French and Dutch organizations executive bonuses were smaller and more uniform, typically ranging from 0 to 10 per cent, whilst in US organizations there were sharp differences in executive pay with bonus payments often exceeding the salary by several multiples. This situation reflected very different views about the function of executive pay (see Illustration 13.1).

However, whilst differences in beliefs about executive compensation do surface, Pennings (1993) notes that such beliefs are generally a function of corporate, industry or market culture rather than purely national culture. The positive American view about the efficiency of variable pay is being reflected now by many European organizations that have undergone major re-organizations, despite a national cultural resistance to do so. National resistance to variable pay was strongest in industries where there was also a business logic against the efficiency of it. For example, where an organization has a strong dependence on the business cycle, low research and

Illustration 13.1 **Beliefs about the function of executive compensation in the US, Holland and France.**

- Executives from American organizations express a strong belief in the motivational efficiency of executive compensation systems, whereas the French and Dutch executives tend to be more cautious or even ignorant of such matters.
- Many American divisional managers are evaluated and rewarded exclusively on the basis of profitability, whereas in Holland the relationship between the bottom line, managerial accountability and the internal organization is more complex.

- Money is not felt to be as important a motivator for Dutch senior executives, who prefer instead to focus on intrinsic motivators such as challenge, professional pride, freedom of action from external stakeholders and access to resources.
- In France the topic of executive compensation was taboo, but in the last few years executive pay has become more of an open issue that can be discussed.

Source: Pennings (1993).

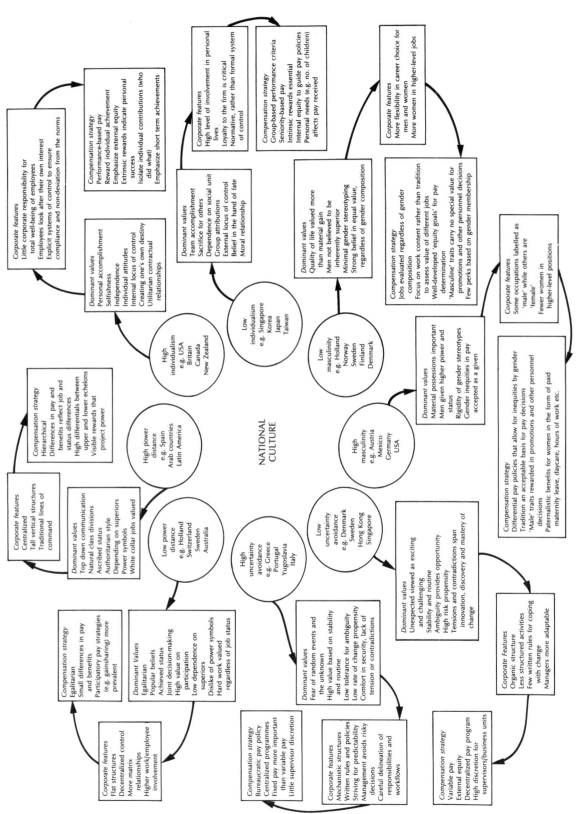

Figure 13.2 National cultures, organizational characteristics and compensation strategies. *Source:* Exhibits 1–4, Gomez–Mejia and Welbourne (1991). Reproduced with permission of the publishers, MCB University Press, © 1991.

development or advertising intensity, then it has little control over short-term efforts to expand demand and supply of products and services, so executive incentives may be misguided. National cultural difficulties simply create a more judicious approach in Europe, dependent on the real contribution to underlying competitiveness, rather than outright rejection. Whereas American managers tend to assume the link between variable pay and corporate performance (given their cultural inclination towards short-term performance measures), European managers (given their cultural rejection of short-termism) need to be convinced of the connection, preferring to proceed in a direction that reflects their 'may be' and 'in certain organizations' philosophy.

Less attention has been paid to the relationship between national culture and compensation strategies at lower levels of the organization. We should not only expect that executive bonus systems will reflect national cultural differences. The connection may be more deep-rooted. Any attempt to develop links between compensation policies and corporate strategies is complicated by the global environment in which it operates. Pay strategies need to be adjusted to meet the unique cultural contingencies of employees within the new environment. Data on national culture are especially relevant given the pivotal role of reward systems in organizations. In the same way that Japanese organizations found it was extremely difficult to transfer their HRM policies and practices into foreign countries, so European organizations will find it difficult to breach cultural assumptions about compensation. Gomez-Mejia and Welbourne (1991) adapt Hofstede's (1980) database on national culture, and, in particular, the four dimensions of power distance, individualism, uncertainty avoidance, and masculinity, to highlight:

- Different dominant values.
- Corporate features.
- Compensation strategies.

This is a theoretical exercise that highlights the connections that would be expected. The result is shown in Figure 13.2. It serves to bring together some of the previous discussion in Chapters Three and Eight and the topic of this chapter – pay and benefits. As with all theoretical frameworks, Gomez-Mejia and Welbourne (1991) highlight four important caveats:

1. An obsessive concern with cultural differences when formulating compensation strategies is more damaging than beneficial. A holistic approach that views national culture as one contingency amongst a multitude of factors is most appropriate. Despite being of the same cultural background, East German workers reacted negatively to incentive schemes that had proved successful in West Germany.
2. The temptation to quickly blame cultural differences for the failure of compensation strategies has to be resisted. Quite often the failure is due to poor management of implementation, not cultural factors (most changes to rewards meet with strong forces of resistance). Other factors, such as the design and flow of work, can have a more powerful influence on the effectiveness of a compensation strategy.
3. The amount of empirical research on the link between compensation strategies and national cultures is minimal. Currently, assessment of the link between the two relies on sociological argument, gut feeling, judgement, and sensitivity. Far more research is needed. Consider the theoretical positioning of the former Yugoslavia in Figure 13.2 as a High Uncertainty Avoidance culture, and subsequent events in Croatia and Bosnia. Events may change national cultures.
4. Even when cultural elements do suggest the need for local compensation strategies, corporate cultural changes may necessitate the imposition of their own value

system, aimed at superseding conflicting national value systems. It is difficult to tease out the difference between corporate and national culture and value systems, and the more general problem of centralized or decentralized control, when considering compensation strategies in international organizations.

Nevertheless, rewards clearly act not only as incentives but also as symbolic divisions between different hierarchical levels within the organization (Lane, 1989). They serve to highlight and reinforce the social distance between grades. In this regard, the pay structure in Britain has historically been more egalitarian than that in France, whilst Germany lies somewhere in between. In the 1970s average earnings of top managers as a percentage of the average income of all workers in industry were 329 per cent in France, 248 per cent in Germany and 207 per cent in Britain. By the 1990s, however, many of these differentials had been eroded, as Britain increased differential earnings.

DISSATISFACTION WITH REWARD SYSTEMS

The transition in reward systems in Europe therefore reflects two potentially competing or mutually reinforcing pressures:

- Compensation practices in European organizations show a slow but discernible trend towards 'de-levelling', with the re-introduction and re-emphasis on wage and salary differentials as a way of recognizing variations in talent, responsibility and performance in an attempt to keep Europe competitive on world markets.
- Many reward systems do not deliver the anticipated results.

Despite their increasing sophistication and importance, the evidence shows that many pay systems fail to deliver the expected results (Lawler, 1981; Moss-Kanter, 1989). For instance, Moss-Kanter (1989) states that 'traditional pay systems ... are under attack for being neither cost effective nor motivating people to do more' and a review of research findings by Beer *et al.* (1984) concluded that:

Despite the enormous amount spent on wages, commissions, cost of living increases, bonuses, and stock options, many studies have shown that in most organizations 50 percent or more of the employees are dissatisfied with pay, and that this percentage is increasing.

Beer *et al.* (1984, p. 116).

These findings are particularly disturbing when one considers that pay has consistently been found to be one of the most important job factors for individuals, usually ranked first or second among all levels of employees. A majority of employees come to work each day believing that their wages are unfair, that pay increases are unfair, and that any improvement in their performance is unlikely to result in better pay. Crowe (1992), a consultant specializing in reward systems, argues that there are two key reasons for this unfortunate situation (see Illustration 13.2).

By way of example, consideration can be given to those organizations adopting Total Quality Management (TQM), which we discussed in the last chapter. Whether applied in manufacturing or services, TQM requires considerable teamwork and flexibility. Most traditional payment systems are in conflict with these requirements because they emphasize individualism and specialization. For those organizations wishing to introduce TQM, a crucial step is to design a new remuneration system. Often, however, there is a considerable time gap between changes in business priorities and major reviews of pay practices. Although new compensation systems are required, they are often not given much top management attention or are not redesigned in conjunction with the enterprise's changing business objectives.

Illustration 13.2 **Reasons why employees feel performance and pay are not linked.**

- Failure to design reward systems that underpin and reinforce business strategies resulting in increasing impatience among business leaders who wish to change the strategic direction of their enterprises but are frustrated by traditional pay systems.

- Failure of reward systems based on so-called proprietary job evaluation techniques to provide an adequate means of paying for skills and experience development or of rewarding contribution to an organization.

Source: Crowe (1992).

At the same time, under TQM, traditional pay systems often fail to support the new business objectives because they do not recognize the contribution of people to the success of the organization. Often the fault lies with the design of the system. As Crowe (1992) suggests, traditional pay systems predominantly strive to achieve internal equity, and to pay individuals fairly and equitably, usually by focusing rewards on the size of the hierarchies controlled by the job holder and on nominal job content, as a proxy for individual contribution to, and impact on, the business. However, most people want to be rewarded in a way that recognizes their real contribution to the business.

The introduction of TQM also requires that the organization must reward key specialists for innovation rather than for the position they hold in the hierarchy. This requirement is totally incompatible with the hierarchical approach of many job evaluation and wage systems. An alternative approach is to introduce parallel career paths so that, for example, software engineers can increase their income by working their way up a technical ladder; they do not have to move into managerial positions in order to gain higher levels of pay. This system already exists in a number of large organizations. Marconi, for instance, has for many years adopted a 'dual ladder' approach to reward its electronics technical staff. The grading structure is based on individual capability and qualification criteria, which are openly discussed and well respected among the employees.

In addition to examining some of the key reasons why traditional reward systems have failed to meet the challenges of a changing business environment, Crowe (1992) argues that a new approach to compensation is needed because of:

1. The increasing inadequacy of conventional sources of external market pay data.
2. The increasing recognition by most employers that they are deriving a poor economic return from the amount spent on their paybills.

The increasing inadequacy of conventional sources of external market pay data is caused by labour market changes. As we suggested in Chapter Four, the demographic forces of the 1980s have led to a fragmentation of European labour markets. The implications of this are shown in Illustration 13.3.

The three factors in Illustration 13.3 pose important new challenges for most European HRM departments. For instance, how can the organization reconcile the company's ability and need to pay with the employee's perception of fairness? Because the employee's perception of fairness is likely to be influenced by a variety of factors (including internal equity, job security, experience, responsibility, working conditions, and so on), the 'fair' wage or salary suggested by the employee can be significantly different from that suggested by the organization's results and by the external labour market.

Illustration 13.3 **Implications of fragmented labour markets in Europe for pay and rewards systems.**

1. Organizations can no longer rely only upon regional or national pay surveys in order to establish their salary scales. International comparisons need to be made.
2. Skill shortages have forced many organizations to modify or manipulate internal pay structures in order to provide salaries in line with those paid elsewhere.
3. The issue of equal pay and conditions of employment for men and women has become more pronounced.

... In most cases it makes sense to focus on external pay comparisons as the major criteria for determining total compensation levels. Both internal and external equity have serious consequences for the organization. However, the consequences of external equity ... are the most severe for the organization and are the ones that deserve primary attention.

Lawler (1981).

Finally, Crowe (1992) suggests that many pay systems, both old and new, fail because of poor communications.

... Too often, employees are left to interpret the meaning and intent of changes in the compensation system on their own. Significant changes in remuneration policy will usually result from a decision by the board to change the strategic direction of the business. Many companies fail to ensure that their new reward arrangements, underlying the purpose, strategy and often values are set out in the organization's mission statement, are given top level commitment and are clearly communicated. Where major cultural change is intended, it is necessary to communicate both the rationale for the changes and the impact that these will have on the staff concerned. Although companies of a certain size may well have written statements on a range of pay-related matters, it is rare to find a document which encapsulates the underlying philosophy that drives the remuneration policy.   Crowe (1992, p. 119).

CONTEMPORARY PRESSURES ON COMPENSATION

In recent years, a number of new approaches to reward management and compensation have been introduced by leading organizations as a means of attracting, retaining and motivating high quality human resources. Flexible reward packages and competency-based pay and compensation have been part of this change. Several reasons have already been listed why organizations have increasingly dropped their traditional approaches to compensation. Illustration 13.4, based on Vickerstaff's (1992) analysis of contemporary pressures on reward practices, expands on this list by considering the main environmental factors that have had an impact upon reward systems in Europe. In the context of these changes, the disparities in standards of living and income between European countries are increasingly highlighted.

Table 13.1, taken from the most recent edition of the World Competitiveness Report (World Economic Forum, 1993), shows the yearly average wages in selected professions for twenty industrialized economies around the world. Clearly, compensation levels are highest in Switzerland, the Benelux and Germany. Within the European Union, the lowest pay levels are found in Portugal and Spain.

Total hourly compensation for manufacturing workers is shown in Figure 13.3. Again, the highest wages and supplementary benefits are found in Switzerland, Germany, and Scandinavian countries. Within the EU, compensation is lowest in

Illustration 13.4 **Pressures on reward systems.**

1. Product market pressures and the need to remain competitive in the labour market are affecting the balance which organizations must tread between keeping costs low while still being able to attract and retain the kinds of staff that the organization needs.
2. Increasing labour mobility in Europe and differences in income levels between European countries (see below) are forcing organizations to keep an eye on the purchasing power and benefits which multinational organizations are offering in different subsidiaries.
3. New technology in manufacturing and in the office have challenged the old demarcations and thus serve to undermine the prevailing pay and grading structures.
4. New forms of work organization with the accent on teamworking, flexibility and multi-skilling make the traditional rate-for-the-job systems of remuneration less applicable.
5. Changing patterns of work, diminishing boundaries between manual and mental labour, and the increasing importance of winning workers' commitment to the objectives of the enterprise have challenged the traditional differences in direct and indirect compensation between hierarchical groups of employees.
6. The spread through Europe of social legislation in areas such as equal pay for men and women, hours of work and part time employment are exerting considerable pressure on traditional compensation policies based on job evaluation and job-related criteria.

Source: Vickerstaff (1992).

Table 13.1 **Yearly average wages in selected professions.**

	Banking: bank teller	Department manager	First level education teacher	Secretary
		US$, 1990		
Australia	16,800	35,700	23,100	20,100
Austria	27,900	51,800	20,700	22,800
Belgium/Lux	69,400	144,300	67,600	49,200
Canada	18,250	50,000	33,050	20,800
Denmark	32,300	51,000	29,100	29,100
Finland	25,200	57,700	31,600	24,200
France	16,500	53,200	21,000	20,700
Germany	31,950	81,250	34,200	29,900
Greece	11,700	18,300	9,400	8,200
Ireland	22,200	43,000	23,300	19,400
Italy	30,500	32,600	19,700	18,800
Japan	33,100	62,500	32,000	21,900
Netherlands	20,700	46,600	21,800	20,900
Norway	27,600	28,200	21,000	24,600
Portugal	7,500	12,800	10,100	6,600
Spain	27,700	27,700	23,600	24,400
Sweden	24,900	38,600	28,100	28,100
Switzerland	54,600	72,850	57,900	38,750
UK	18,500	33,700	26,900	20,200
USA	20,350	56,200	30,400	25,625

Source: World Economic Forum 1993, reprinted with permission © 1993 World Economic Forum.

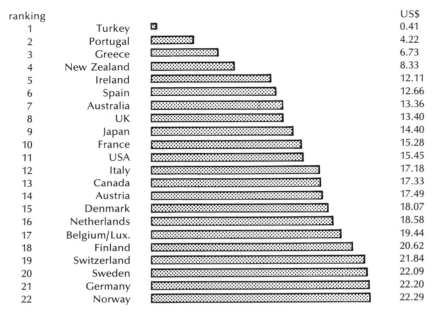

ranking			US$
1	Turkey		0.41
2	Portugal		4.22
3	Greece		6.73
4	New Zealand		8.33
5	Ireland		12.11
6	Spain		12.66
7	Australia		13.36
8	UK		13.40
9	Japan		14.40
10	France		15.28
11	USA		15.45
12	Italy		17.18
13	Canada		17.33
14	Austria		17.49
15	Denmark		18.07
16	Netherlands		18.58
17	Belgium/Lux.		19.44
18	Finland		20.62
19	Switzerland		21.84
20	Sweden		22.09
21	Germany		22.20
22	Norway		22.29

Figure 13.3 Total hourly compensation for manufacturing workers. *Source*: World Economic Forum (1993), reprinted with permission © World Economic Forum.

Spain, Portugal and Greece. These differences in compensation levels between EU member countries have fuelled the debate about the need for a social dimension to accompany the moves to create a unified market for goods, services and capital and labour within the EU by the end of 1992. For instance, advocates of the so-called 'social dumping' thesis have argued that a free internal market without a pan-European foundation of employment rights may lead to a situation in which organizations try artificially to restrain the growth of wages and other benefits in low wage (Mediterranean) countries so as to keep manufacturing costs low vis-à-vis Germany and other North European states (Boyer, 1988). By following such policies peripheral member states would, in effect, be exporting potential domestic unemployment to other EU countries (Teague, 1989), and this might radically change the future growth of wages and social benefits in different member states.

In addition, advocates of the social dumping thesis argue that an internal market without a minimum floor of social and employment standards may further segment the Union's labour market into two distinctive geographical spheres (Lipietz, 1988). Indeed, without such standards, large organizations may re-organize their operations so that complex and technical production tasks are located in Northern Europe, where workers are more expensive and more highly skilled, while the labour-intensive and low-skilled functions are sited in Southern Europe where wages are low (Teague, 1989). This problem was highlighted in Chapter Four.

The entry of Spain, Portugal and Greece into the European Union gave this debate a central role in the run up to the SEM in 1992. Not only were the twelve member states often unable to agree on such matters as health and safety, working hours, equal opportunities and employment rights for part time workers, but frequently their meetings ended in much discord and acrimony (Teague, 1989). In recent years, however, the emerging view has been that national social and labour standards need to be harmonized so that a 'Two-speed Europe' will not be created as a result of some

ranking			%
1	New Zealand		− 2.95
2	Australia		−1.50
3	Norway		−1.28
4	Canada		− 0.57
5	Sweden		− 0.38
6	Denmark		− 0.38
7	Finland		− 0.30
8	USA		− 0.14
9	Greece		− 0.11
10	France		− 0.10
11	Portugal		− 0.09
12	UK		− 0.08
13	Ireland		0.00
14	Spain		0.13
15	Italy		0.13
16	Belgium/Lux.		0.18
17	Japan		0.32
18	Switzerland		0.52
19	Austria		0.52
20	Germany		0.75
21	Netherlands		0.87
22	Turkey		6.25

Figure 13.4 Increase in consumer price inflation. *Source*: World Economic Forum (1993), reprinted with permission, © 1993 World Economic Forum.

member states having more advanced employment conditions than others (Vandamme, 1984).

In any case, the process of reducing the differences in pay and conditions between EU countries is likely to be a slow and difficult one, considering the significant economic, cultural and legal barriers to harmonization of pay and conditions in Europe. Some of these barriers will be removed through the impact of EU law on equal pay and equal treatment of men and women in the twelve member states. However, progress on EU social legislation has been slow, irrespective of whether proposals for harmonization have required unanimity or may be presented to the Council of Ministers through the qualified majority voting procedure. In the mean time, of all the factors influencing pay and conditions of employment, the gap in inflation and cost of living between the different EU countries is likely to remain critical. As shown in Figure 13.4, the consumer price index increased by more than 10 per cent in Portugal and Greece during the 1980s, compared with 6 to 8 per cent in the UK, Italy and Sweden, and less than 4 per cent in Germany, the Netherlands, France and Belgium.

Since wage increases are linked to inflation for many employees in several EU countries (such as Belgium, France and Germany), some of the international wage differences reported in the above table are likely to be maintained.

HOW ARE ORGANIZATIONS RESPONDING TO THESE PRESSURES?

To comprehend just what has happened to pay and benefits in Europe and what it means for the future management of human resources, the PWCP study (see Chapter Two) surveyed organizations in all leading European economies during 1990 and 1991. Their findings suggest that product market pressures and the other factors that affect employee motivation, satisfaction and commitment to the organization have exerted a considerable influence on individual terms and conditions of employment in

Europe. In particular, it appears that there have been a number of significant changes in the reward policies and practices of European organizations. The four main changes identified in the 1991 report are shown in Illustration 13.5.

By far the most marked development has been the move away from rigid towards flexible pay systems. Historically, wages were automatically indexed to measures that had little to do with either individual or organizational performance. Typically wages were linked to the cost of living or to the time served by the individual. This indexation came under attack in the 1980s as a major factor contributing to inflation. Automatic indexation was gradually abolished under the combined influence of legislation and collective bargaining (Treu, 1992). Although it still exists in Belgium and Italy, compensation is only provided up to a given ceiling. Despite the attack on wage increases linked to the length of service, many systems had still been left unchanged by 1990 (Marsden, 1991). The retreat from non-performance methods of indexation has become a pan-European trend.

The widening of pay differentials, which is a separate issue to the breaking of automatic indexing, has not been pursued equally across Europe. In some countries, such as Italy and the UK, pay differentials have increased, as employers believed that a combination of indexing and egalitarian wage policies had compressed differentials to a point where they were considered punitive for skilled workers. Conversely, in Germany, despite a high commitment to productivity and the skilled labour force, there was no real significant change in overall occupational pay differentials. The link between wages and productivity and performance is controversial, but the simple widening of differentials is not necessarily the only way to enhance skill acquisition or organizational performance (Treu, 1992). This move towards pay flexibility is perceived to fulfil two objectives:

First, organizations are exploring whether flexible pay systems can contribute to their economic performance by linking the work performance of employees as individuals, team members or part of a larger corporate unit to business performance. Second, the very tight labour markets, the tailoring of reward packages to meet individual requirements – largely through the provision of more imaginative non-money benefits – plays an important part in recruitment and retention policies.   World Economic Forum (1993).

There are a number of other reasons why variable pay is being pursued. A substantial number of organizations are exploring whether increases in variable pay can contribute to their cost reduction programmes by linking the employees' pay increases more closely to the organization's financial performance. The use of variable pay – largely through the provision of extra rewards for exceptional performance – is assumed to play an important part in motivating certain categories of staff, particularly in the lower wage economies of the South. Given such reasoning, variable pay packages of one form or another are on the increase in all European countries and particularly in Spain and Sweden. The increase in variable pay has been greatest in the retail and distribution sector. Over three-quarters of Spanish organizations in this sector and nearly two-thirds of German, French and British organizations indicated

Illustration 13.5 **Four main challenges to European rewards policies.**

1. Moves towards flexible pay systems.	3. Determination of pay by organizational policy as opposed to national or regional agreements.
2. Development of variable pay packages.	4. Reliance on alternative forms of rewards.

they have made variable pay a more important part of their reward structure from 1988–91.

Pay in European organizations is also increasingly determined by organization policy, rather than national or regional pay agreements. This means that reward packages are centred increasingly on the needs and constraints of the single organization of the individual employee rather than on a regional or national level grouping. Collective pay agreements at the national level are most common in Sweden. They are least used in Spain, where only about a quarter of organizations thought it relevant for managers, professional employees and technicians. One-to-one negotiations with individuals are also on the increase, mostly for managers and professional staff. Two-fifths of British employers use it for managers; less than one in ten negotiate pay individually for manual employees.

An increasing number of organizations have relied on alternative types of rewards and payment systems to compensate workers. Fringe benefits have become an important part of reward packages in most countries except France. Profit-related pay and profit sharing is also readily available in all countries and has received explicit legal sanction in France, mostly to managers and professional staff, although the impact on behaviour of such schemes, given their objective of making employees aware of the economic performance of their organization, has been limited (Della Rocca and Prosperetti, 1991; Marsden, 1991). Bonuses, whether group or individual, and performance-related pay are popular in all countries. However, share options are still predominantly a British benefit.

These differences in payment systems from one country to another are heavily influenced by both their tax effectiveness and their implications for social security contributions by employers and employees. Since social security contributions represent a major component of most businesses' total wage cost in most European countries (see Figure 13.5), many employers have begun to question the true value derived from their current reward structures. In many cases performance-related pay and the provision of non-monetary benefits is seen as a way of reducing the indirect compensation element of the paybill. Performance pay in many different manifestations enables more of the pay package to be targeted upon those individuals who are providing a positive benefit to the organization and may increase the total amount of money received by the employee.

PAYING FOR PERFORMANCE

As a result of the general move towards more variable pay, an increasing number of organizations have introduced performance related pay schemes as a means of making pay reflect contribution, not status, within the organization. Within the broad HRM groupings identified by Sparrow, Schuler and Jackson (1994), there does appear to be a degree of convergence in compensation strategies taking place. Gomez-Mejia and Welbourne (1991) cite a survey by Towers Perrin and Crosby which found that the number of British organizations with American style pay for performance schemes increased five-fold from 1978 to 1984, with similar schemes being introduced in other European countries. These schemes – which typically combine a variable element of between 15 per cent and 40 per cent with a fixed base salary – can take a wide variety of forms, and organizations can select one or more of them. The most frequently used forms are highlighted below.

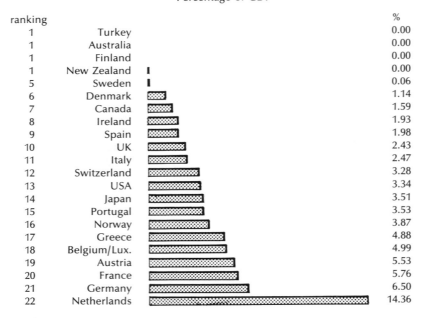

Employer's social security contribution–1990
Percentage of GDP

ranking		%
1	Turkey	0.00
1	Australia	0.00
1	Finland	0.00
1	New Zealand	0.00
5	Sweden	0.06
6	Denmark	1.14
7	Canada	1.59
8	Ireland	1.93
9	Spain	1.98
10	UK	2.43
11	Italy	2.47
12	Switzerland	3.28
13	USA	3.34
14	Japan	3.51
15	Portugal	3.53
16	Norway	3.87
17	Greece	4.88
18	Belgium/Lux.	4.99
19	Austria	5.53
20	France	5.76
21	Germany	6.50
22	Netherlands	14.36

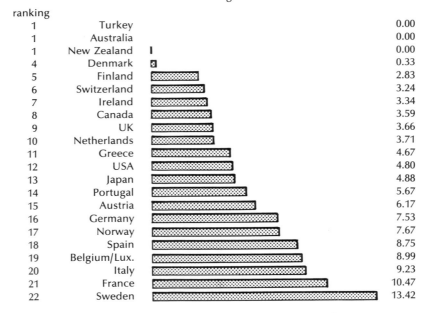

Employee's social security contribution–1990
Percentage of GDP

ranking		
1	Turkey	0.00
1	Australia	0.00
1	New Zealand	0.00
4	Denmark	0.33
5	Finland	2.83
6	Switzerland	3.24
7	Ireland	3.34
8	Canada	3.59
9	UK	3.66
10	Netherlands	3.71
11	Greece	4.67
12	USA	4.80
13	Japan	4.88
14	Portugal	5.67
15	Austria	6.17
16	Germany	7.53
17	Norway	7.67
18	Spain	8.75
19	Belgium/Lux.	8.99
20	Italy	9.23
21	France	10.47
22	Sweden	13.42

Figure 13.5 Social security contributions by employers and employees in EU countries.
Source: World Economic Forum (1993), reprinted with permission, © 1993 World Economic Forum.

Merit pay

Merit pay is that part of the base salary which is determined by reference to individual performance (Wright, 1991). It is the most widespread form of performance related pay in Europe, particularly for the growing number of white collar staff. For example, in 1990 Hay Management Consultants' Industrial and Service Sector pay survey in the UK showed that for managerial and white collar jobs 60 per cent of organizations use 'merit only' pay increases and a further 18 per cent had an element of the base salary increase linked to merit or performance. However, criticism of merit pay has been growing in recent years.

... Because it results in increases to base salary, merit pay can result in an upward drift in fixed pay-roll costs unless there is steady labour turnover. Concern about costs has led some organizations to impose strict control over merit budgets, but the lack of a sufficient pool of money to apply to merit pay and too little discrimination in the distribution can reduce its impact as an incentive. In these circumstances, merit pay can easily be overshadowed by general pay increases (particularly at times of high inflation) or payments from other performance pay schemes.   Wright (1991, p. 92).

Individual bonuses

Unlike merit pay, individual performance or incentive bonuses are designed to link the individual's reward package more closely to his or her performance. Normally, bonuses are paid against achieved measurable outputs. We discussed the use of such schemes in conjunction with changes in work design in Sweden and the UK in the last chapter. Payments are annual, quarterly or, in the case of workers, weekly. Individual bonus schemes fall into two categories (see Illustration 13.6).

The PWCP study suggests that about a third of all European organizations use some kind of individual bonus scheme for managers, and between a quarter and a third for professionals. For manual workers, up to a fifth of all European organizations provide individual bonuses. An example of a variable pay programme at Taco-Bell in the US is provided in Illustration 13.7 based on an analysis by Caudron (1993).

Team bonuses

This type of performance related pay, where a pay-out is dependent on the performance of the whole work unit, has historically been a prerogative of the top and senior management in private sector. In recent years, however, group bonus

Illustration 13.6 **Two categories of individual bonus schemes.**

1. *Incentive schemes*, which provide 'pay-outs' for the achievement of preset targets. For example, many schemes support a focus on improving certain key aspects of individual performance (e.g. sales, profits, units of production, etc.).
2. *Longer term bonuses*, which offer staff the opportunity to increase their income by improving the organization's overall commercial and financial performance. For example, several of the recently privatized organizations offer bonuses to executives for better-than-average performance in areas which are seen as important to customers and shareholders.

schemes have been extended to other categories of staff in, for example, information technology, research and development and customer service. In areas such as these, performance related pay in the form of individual bonuses can be divisive and counter to the team ethos which is a vital component of the work undertaken (Wright, 1991). However, as we saw in the last chapter, many organizations are finding innovative ways to marry team incentives with changes in work design.

According to the PWCP survey, group bonuses are most popular in the UK and France, where approximately one third of organizations provide this type of payment to managers and professional workers. The number of organizations providing this type of benefit to employees in Germany and Spain is considerably lower. In the UK, group bonuses are regularly used in retailing (47 per cent of organizations), in banking

Illustration 13.7   **Variable-pay programme increases Taco Bell's profits.**

Taco Bell Corp.'s upbeat advertisements have been so successful at getting people to 'make a run for the border', that the Irvine, California-based company has opened more than 350 new restaurants in the last two years. Although this is great news for hungry consumers, it was a challenge for the company's HR department to find managers for these restaurants.

'We didn't think we could find all the talent we needed to run those stores', explains Michael J. Rowe, Taco Bell's director of compensation and benefits. 'So we decided to ask existing restaurant managers to start supervising two units instead of one.' Instead of increasing the managers' salaries to correlate to their added responsibilities, Taco Bell did something very interesting. The company kept the managers' base salaries the same, but allowed them to earn twice as much in bonus pay through a variable-pay program.

'To continue to sell 59-cent tacos, we can't have pay programs that are inefficient' Rowe explains. 'We can't afford to give $50,000 in base pay with no performance guarantees. We can, however, afford to pay $30,000 and give managers $20,000 bonus if they drive profits to the bottom line. The way we do this is through a variable-pay program that funds incremental pay out of incremental profits.' Today the 1,600 restaurant managers are evaluated and given bonuses based on three objectives:

1. Targeted profit, which relates to bottom line results.
2. Customer service, which is evaluated by an independent marketing research organization.
3. Actual store sales.

On average, managers receive a bonus worth about 30 per cent of their base pay. But payments

that double the base amount aren't uncommon. However, Rowe is quick to emphasize that not all managers earn a bonus all the time. 'It isn't an entitlement,' he says. 'Between 60 and 70 per cent of managers earn a bonus that's paid every six months. But that means 30 per cent of managers don't get anything in their variable pay for six months' work. Believe me, a person who misses a $5,000 bonus payment twice a year will pay attention to the things that drive profitability: sales and customer service.'

Although Taco Bell's program isn't punitive in nature, it is high-risk. Under the company's previous merit-pay system, about 85 per cent of restaurant managers received $1,000 bonuses four times each year. 'They really had to be bad not to get that money,' Rowe explains, 'whereas under this system, they really have to be good.'

When asked how the variable-pay program fits into Taco Bell's overall corporate strategy, Rowe says that the relationship between both may be irrelevant. 'A bonus program at that level should be reflective of what you want to get out of people in that job,' he says. 'I think it's a mistake for every bonus program in the company to have the same objectives. You have to ask yourself what kind of results are you attempting to obtain from restaurant managers. Hopefully the answer isn't too different from what you want to get out of your president, but clearly I'm not going to expect my president to do customer service at the unit level.'

Taco Bell's program has been implemented for eighteen months, and it seems to be working. Food costs as a percentage of sales continue to decrease, customer service scores for 1992 were the best the company has ever had, and profit records continue to be broken.

Source: Caudron (1993), reprinted with permission © 1993, *Personnel Journal.*

Illustration 13.8 **AAL uses varied approach to compensate teams.**

Aid Association for Lutherans (AAL), a fraternal benefits society, leaves nothing to chance when it comes to compensating members of its insurance service teams. The company, which is based in Appleton, Wisconsin, has devised a four-legged compensation stool, which allows the company to:

■ Recognize individual achievements.
■ Reward team productivity.
■ Compensate employees for the acquisition of new skills.
■ Remain competitive with its salary structure.

AAL has 15 service teams, organized geographically, that perform all services necessary for the company's insurance products. For example, a team, comprising 25 employees, can underwrite a policy, pay a claim, change beneficiaries and modify coverage levels. Furthermore, team members can provide these services for any product, be it life insurance, health or disability insurance.

Before developing the team structure in 1987, the company had organized these services functionally, according to the type of product. Service requests travelled from unit to unit, increasing the amount of time needed to service a customer, and boosting the chance for errors.

'By moving to teams, we were challenging employees to see the whole job, rather than just the piece they performed individually,' explains Jerry Laubenstein, vice president of insurance services.' But we also wanted them to learn additional jobs that could help the team as a whole, and we wanted the team to find ways to boost its overall performance.'

To promote all of these changes, AAL revamped its compensation structure completely to include four main elements.

1. *A skill-based pay program.* The company has implemented a skill-based pay system that compensates individuals for each additional skill they acquire in an effort to help the team. As one of the first organizations to implement skill-based pay for white collar workers, AAL developed a dictionary that describes all the services performed by team members and lists their associated dollar value. Employees are paid a base wage for the primary service they perform, and they can receive incremental pay increases for each service added to their repertoire of skills.

2. *A team-incentive program.* AAL has implemented a team-incentive program through which the entire team is awarded an annual bonus based on three factors:

■ Productivity.
■ Customer satisfaction.
■ Quality of work.

This team incentive can be worth as much as 10 per cent of an employee's annual compensation.

3. *The use of market data.* The company now relies heavily on market data to ensure that employees are paid competitive wages.

4. *An individual incentive program.* AAL has added an incentive component that recognizes outstanding achievement by individual employees. This lump-sum incentive is paid once a year only to those employees who are already paid at market value. This incentive is worth as much as 6 per cent of an individual's compensation.

AAL's compensation structure didn't change all at once, Laubenstein says, and there were several problems along the way. 'We went to teams in 1987 and didn't put any incentives in place until 1989. Then we moved entirely to team incentives, where we didn't recognize individuals at all. This caused a lot of problems with employees who were used to being recognized individually. Finally, in 1991, we modified the program to recognize both individual and team achievements.'

Is the program working? 'We're on a journey, and we haven't reached the destination yet,' Laubenstein cautions. 'But in the five years that we've been in teams, we've increased our productivity by 40 per cent. Surveys reveal that more than 90 per cent of our customers are satisfied with the level of service they're receiving. I'd say things are coming along well.'

Source: Caudron (1993), reprinted with permission © 1993, *Personnel Journal.*

(36 per cent), and in transport and communications (37 per cent). In Sweden and France, group bonuses are particularly popular in the extraction and chemical industry (52 per cent and 36 per cent respectively). An example of a team-based compensation scheme in AAL in the US is provided in Illustration 13.8, based on an analysis by Caudron (1993).

Organization-wide schemes

An organization-wide performance related pay scheme provides extra rewards to all or some employees based on the achievement of one or more organization performance targets. The most common targets are profit, earnings per share, sales turnover, return on investment and cash flow. Payments are typically annual or bi-annual, although some organizations make payments on a more frequent basis. Although the link between individual performance improvements and the overall organization results is tenuous, such schemes are widespread. For example, nearly two-thirds of manual workers in France, about a fifth in Britain and one tenth in Germany and Spain are sharing in their organization's profits.

An important consideration, when it comes to offering profit sharing to employees, is the influence of national legislation. Fiscal rules and regulations vary widely from country to country, and hence the ability of organizations to provide tax-efficient profit benefits to employees. For example, French employment law provides employers with two tax-efficient profit-sharing schemes. One is negotiated with trade unions and works councils and is compulsory for all organizations with over fifty employees as long as the profit made by the company exceeds a level equivalent to 5 per cent of the shareholders' equity. The other is optional and allows for payments to be made available to specific groups of employees. It dates back to 1970 and allows employees and directors of limited companies to subscribe to or to buy shares at a price determined in advance over a certain time. An example of performance related reward in one of the British retail banks, under the pseudonym of United Bank, is provided in Illustration 13.9.

Share option schemes

Like organization-wide schemes, share option schemes provide an opportunity for employees to benefit financially from the economic performance of the organization. As an incentive tool they may not be highly effective because remoteness from influence over the stock price means that employees often regard them as useful extras rather than an integral part of pay for performance. However, share option schemes are popular as a general reward and communication tool for employees, and some of these schemes are felt to increase employee identity with the business.

Table 13.2 compares the different practices with regard to profit sharing and employee participation in company share-holding schemes in the twelve member states of the EU. Historically, British workers have been far more likely to participate in share option schemes than employees in the other European countries. For instance, in 1990, British organizations in the private sector offered such schemes to over half (53 per cent) of their managers, compared to only a quarter of Swedish organizations and a sixth of organizations in Spain, France and Germany. This may change as many European governments are now introducing new laws which provide tax advantages for organizations which offer employee share options.

Illustration 13.9 **Performance related reward in United Bank plc.**

United Bank plc (UB) is a major British clearing bank having a branch network throughout England and Wales. The bank has eight divisions, one of which is our subject: the Domestic Banking (DB) division. The division operates the domestic branch banking network with support from other specialist divisions within the bank.

In 1987, UB introduced a system of performance related reward (PRR), implementing it from the top down. Chief executives of divisions were included in the scheme from July 1987, senior managers from January, 1988, and other management grades from July, 1988. In summer 1988, managerial grades were reduced from ten to seven. Executive and senior managers were graded MA to MC, and the remaining management grades ran from MC down to MG. Within a bank branch are one or more managers on management grades, with more junior employees on staff grades below them. Although extending the scheme to staff grades is being considered, we shall primarily examine how the scheme can be extended to the lower management grades MD to MG, covering a salary range of £16,000 to £36,000 a year (on 1988 salary scales), although we refer occasionally to more senior managers.

The new pay structure's two major elements are merit increments based on an annual salary review, and bonus payments, based on achieving preset performance targets. Merit increments are a permanent increase in salary, which will be maintained into the future, whereas bonus payments are one-time awards with no commitment to continue payment in the future.

Merit increments
The newly implemented PRR scheme has modified the previous salary review system, including formal consideration of individual performance into basic salary calculations. Salary reviews now take place only once a year, in April, and cover both overall individual performance and market comparability. Under this system, the salary rise (merit increment) for an individual is defined with a matrix of possible percentage increments.

Both an individual's present position on the salary range and an assessment of present performance are used to set an appropriate increment; managers at the lower points on an incremental scale are eligible for larger increments. Because this matrix includes an element allowing for general price inflation (a cost-of-living increase), a manager who receives no increment is effectively receiving a salary reduction. A typical matrix, assuming a 5 per cent cost-of living increase, is shown in Exhibit 1.

The rationale behind this part of the system is to allow above-average managers to rise up the salary scale more quickly than was possible before. Previous, increments would be earned by years of service, only exceptional managers receiving accelerated increments. Moreover, the new salary ranges for the grades now have much greater overlap, so that an outstanding manager in the MG grade can earn considerably more than a manager at the bottom of the MF grade, for example. The longer ranges and the overlap seem to help the bank retain outstanding managers in a specific job longer, whereas before, the only method available

Exhibit 1 **Merit increment matrix (including 5 per cent cost-of-living component).**

Position in salary range (percentile)	Performance evaluation rating			
	Outstanding	Good	Fully satisfactory	Less than fully satisfactory
100				
80	5%– 8%			
60	8%–10%	5%– 8%		
40	10%–12%	8%–10%	5%–8%	
20				0%–6%
	12%–14%	10%–12%	8%–6%	

(continued)

for rewarding outstanding performance was promotion to a new job because the pay range was so narrow. Conversely, managers who fail to perform up to expectations can progress only so far up the salary scale, gaining peak salary with fully satisfactory performance at the sixtieth percentile of the grade salary scale. Managers who perform well initially, but whose performance subsequently deteriorates, can be held at a constant money salary until they are once more within an appropriate percentile band.

The bonus system

Beyond the annual salary review, the PRR scheme introduced a once-only bonus for the first time. This payment rewards performance measured against preset performance targets, which are weighted together to give an overall measure of present performance. The period over which bonus payments are assessed is the calendar year, ending in December, making monetary payments in the following February or March. Three performance benchmarks are defined:

Threshold: The minimum level of performance necessary to obtain a minimum bonus payment. This grade is suggested as a financial result of perhaps 10–15 per cent below on-target performance.

On-target: Achieving a stretching but realistic target level of performance.

Ceiling: Achievement justifying payment of the maximum bonus; may be a financial result of about 25–30 per cent above on-target performance.

A bonus payment, expressed as a percentage of annual salary, is associated with each level of performance, and differs slightly between senior and other managerial grades, as shown in Exhibit 2.

The performance targets for managers are referred to as key objectives. Each manager's immediate superior is expected to set two to six key objectives for him or her. These objectives will be assigned numerical weights totalling 100 per cent so that an overall performance measure can be computed. Key objectives are expected to be closely linked to the annual business plan for a manager's unit; they should relate to factors that a manager can directly influence or control; and they should include at least one financial objective, where possible.

The objectives, however, are not necessarily expected to include every aspect of satisfactory

Exhibit 2 **Bonus payments (as a percentage of annual salary).**

Bonus level	Managerial grades	
	MA-MC	MD-MG
Below threshold	0%	0%
Threshold	5%	5%
On-target	15%	10%
Celing	25%	20%

job performance, because other factors will also be considered in the more subjective overall performance review.

Target-setting is evidently an important part of the bonus scheme. Targets are intended to be agreed on by managers and superiors at the start of the year and, as far as possible, to be objectively verifiable, reducing the subjectivity associated with this element of the PRR scheme. The three main types of target are:

Measurable: Targets with a precise numerical measure of achievement (e.g. sales or profit targets).

Testable: Targets which cannot be directly and routinely measured, but which can be subjected to tests such as opinion surveys (e.g. levels of customer satisfaction achieved).

Assessable: Targets for which achievement cannot be measured or tested, but which are subject to a superior's personal judgment (e.g. satisfactory completion of a project).

For each measurable target, the bonus percentage is determined by a straight-line calculation between the various performance levels defined. For non-numerical targets, performance is rated with the marking scale shown in Exhibit 3. The market is then translated into a bonus percentage, using the relevant weighting factor for the objective.

Exhibit 3 **Marking key for non-numerical targets.**

Performance level	Mark	
Unacceptable	1	
Acceptable	2	(Threshold)
Fully satisfactory	3	(On-target)
Good	4	
Very good	5	
Outstanding	6	(Ceiling)

Table 13.2 **PEPPER (Promotion of Employee Participation in Profits and Enterprise Results) schemes in member states of the EU in the late 1980s.**

Country	General attitude	Legislation		Diffusion of PEPPER schemes			
		Specific laws and year of introduction	Tax benefits	Prevalent types	No. of schemes/firms involved	Employees involved	Employee benefits or profit share/employee
Belgium	Mainly unfavourable, but now discussed	Various, but only on ESO (since 1982), including SO (1984)	Rather limited, especially for SO	ESO	Around 30 quoted companies	On average 5% (varying from 1–28%)	Shares reserved for employees: 4% on average of total shares issued
				CPS	Multinationals Insurance Banks Distribution		Around 5% of distributable profits; 8–15% of performance-related pay
Denmark	Mainly favourable and discussed	On SPS and ESO (since 1958)	Some for SPS (shares or bonds) and ESO	CPS	Min. 50 schemes		
				SPS BPS	20 schemes 27 schemes		2% of share capital DKR 3400 per employee
				ESO	32 schemes		Less than 2% of total share capital
				Total	200 or more		
France	Very favourable and intensively discussed	Various: CPS (1959) DPS (1967) SO (1970) ESO (since 1973) Employee invest. funds (1973) EBO (1984) Unique legisl. on all forms (1986)	Substantial for both firms and employees	DPS	12 000 firms and 10 000 agreements	4 500 000 (3 000 000 benefiting)	Profit shares on average 3.4% of the wage bill
				CPS	4600 agreements	1 000 000	Profit shares on average 4.1% of the wage bill
				ESO*	350 firms (2/3 quoted)	600 000*	Free distrib. of shares: 3% of the wage bill
				SO	A total of 40 schemes in 1971–84		
				EBO	10–20 per year in 1980–90		

(continued)

Table 13.2 (Continued).

Country	General attitude	Legislation		Diffusion of PEPPER schemes			
		Specific laws and year of introduction	Tax benefits	Prevalent types	No. of schemes/firms involved	Employees involved	Employee benefits or profit share/employee
Germany	Mainly favourable except for CPS: intensively discussed	Some: on DPS (since 1961) and ESO (primarily since 1984)	Minor until 1984, only for DPS and ESP	ESO and DPS	1600 firms (0.1% of total)	1 300 000 80% usually participate	Employee capital: DM 15 bln (only 5% of firms' annual balance)
				PS in general	Max. 5000 firms, mainly small scale	5.4% of individuals	6.8% of wages
Greece	Not clearly defined; discussions only starting	Non-existent	No	CPS	Very limited; in banking, insurance, clothing, food		Lump sum of GD 30 000–50 000
Ireland	Favourable and discussed	SPS (1982) SO (1986)	Modest	SO	139 schemes	Executives	Probably high
				SPS	87 schemes	35 000	
					All in the private sector		
Italy	Not clearly defined, but some forms discussed	Non-existent, except general provisions (1942 Civil Code)	No	CPS	25% of all large firms; 60 private firms in 1988	400 000; applied to 80% of all employees	3% of average earnings (but can be as high as 10% or more)
				ESO	30 quoted companies		Less than 5% of total share capital
Luxembourg	Not clearly defined	Non-existent	No	CPS ESO	22% of firms mainly in banking		Usually not more than 0.5–2 months' salary

Source: M. Uvalic, 'Profit sharing: different perspectives in Europe', in S. Vickerstaff (ed.) (1992), *Human Resource Management in Europe: Text and cases*, Table T6.1, pp. 206–8. Reprinted with permission. © Chapman & Hall.

EUROPEAN DIFFERENCES IN THE INDIVIDUALIZATION OF PERFORMANCE

There is, then, a process of individualization taking place in the area of pay, with more emphasis being given to merit pay and mechanisms to link a larger proportion of pay to measures of performance. What has been the relative progress towards merit pay and pay for performance across Europe? Incomes Data Service (1992) have reviewed European management practice in this area. They found that in Belgium some 15 per cent of executive pay is currently variable (mainly in larger organizations) and is currently paid on an individual basis tied to performance targets. However, as noted in Chapter Two, the taxation system in Belgium tends to blunt the impact of financial rewards and incentive-based systems (Sels, 1992). Similarly, in Holland progress towards pay-for-performance has been limited. Only 19 per cent of the Dutch working population is paid by some kind of performance-based reward system (van Iterson and Olie, 1992; Thierry, 1987). Most reward systems are tied to position and loyalty to the organization's goals is evoked through the provision of career paths and fringe benefits. For example, in the late 1980s, more than two-thirds of top Dutch managers were working in the same organization in which they started their career twenty-five years ago.

In France it has been common to reward loyalty and obedience in individualized ways such as merit bonuses and promotion into supervisory positions. However, the system for awarding bonuses is very opaque and dependent on management discretion. Until the 1980s it also tended to reward seniority rather than individual merit (Lane, 1989). By the middle of the 1980s there were clear trends, however, towards individualized pay (Schwab, 1987). Similarly, individual performance-related pay systems began to spread in France in the 1980s. A survey of 1,300 private sector organizations by the Ministry of Labour found that the proportion awarding an element of merit-based pay increased from 23 per cent in 1987 to 36 per cent in 1989. In the case of larger organizations (with more than 500 employees) the figure was more than 90 per cent (Incomes Data Service, 1992). However, as in Denmark, the growth of merit-based pay has created problems, usually because there has been a lack of parallel development in adequate appraisal systems.

Differential rewards are also used as incentives to good performance in Germany, based on a meritocratic system that links pay closely to the level of skill exercised and experience within a skill category. Effort bonuses (*Leistungszulage*) are also paid for good performance to around 10 per cent of the workforce on the recommendation of foremen. Works councils participate in working out the arrangements for what is a very transparent system. The individualization of pay was extensively debated in Germany throughout the 1980s, but the practice of industry-level bargaining (see Chapter Fifteen) has acted as a brake on developments in this area.

The Irish Management Institute's 1991 survey found that an average of 22 per cent of chief executives' salaries and 12 per cent of senior managers' salaries were made up of performance-related bonuses triggered by the meeting of individual targets or the meeting of organization targets. In Italy at senior levels the proportion of pay determined by individual elements may be as much as 50 per cent. Organizations tend to use appraisal systems or management by objectives schemes. However, reflecting the highly informal nature of the psychological contract referred to above, Incomes Data Service (1992) note that it is not uncommon for such payments to be awarded on a purely subjective basis.

The progress of performance-related pay has therefore not been universal. Uptake is low in Portugal and Spain, where local organizations tend to award merit-based pay informally, and in the Netherlands, where union resistance to pay-for-performance systems has been strong. However, there has been an increase in pay-for-performance systems and it is now triggering the need for a more systematic performance evaluation and management process in many European organizations. For example, although merit pay has been growing in Denmark, given their high emphasis on equity and objectivity, the lack of a systematic process on which to base merit pay has been a major factor in slowing down the spread of more individualized pay. As organizations go down an individual pay-for-performance route they tend also to have to make developments in their performance management and appraisal techniques (see Chapter Fourteen) in order to satisfy the demands for fairness, equity and objectivity.

FRINGE BENEFITS

Fringe benefits such as company cars, pension contributions, private medical insurance, credit cards, school fee allowances, and low mortgage rates, are an increasing part of reward packages in most European countries. Under the right conditions, such benefits can be a powerful inducement to motivate employees to join a company, and to retain good performers by satisfying their needs for non-monetary compensation, though it is not clear how important minor differences between organizations are.

In several European countries, a marked innovation has been the extension of fringe benefits to the public sector. In Belgium, for example, mixed reward packages containing a number of non-financial benefits are now offered to employees in skill shortage areas (for instance teaching and nursing staff) – a situation which would have been unheard of ten years ago.

Another significant trend in this area has been the 'harmonization' of fringe benefits between blue collar and white collar workers. Traditionally, access to such benefits as private pension schemes and share option schemes was limited to managers. In recent years, however, more organizations have moved to so called 'single status' terms and conditions of employment by extending availability of non-financial benefits to all employees. In a number of European countries this move has been supported by governments through legislation (for example, Sweden and France). In Britain, harmonization of terms and conditions of employment has been slower than in other EU countries and has been influenced strongly by the arrival of Japanese organizations, such as Nissan and Toyota, where single status is seen as reinforcing an organizational culture that stresses teamwork and seeks to minimize conflict between different groups of employees.

We established a number of Human Resource objectives including 'To establish an integrated compensation and benefits package which is designed to properly reward and motivate all employees' and 'To establish policies and procedures... which assist in achieving employee identification with the Organization's aims and objectives'. To attract high quality people we needed to develop a reputation as a good employer, one which trusted its employees, which made demands on them and expected a positive response. One aspect of that reputation is the employment package, and we concluded that common terms and conditions would be one symbol of that approach. While part of a growing trend, we had the opportunity, in a greenfield site, of leap-frogging our competitors.   Wickens (1987, p. 19).

In order to comprehend the availability of fringe benefits in different EU countries, Figure 13.6 shows the results of the annual survey which was mailed to 18,000 executives in twenty-two of the countries covered by the World Competitiveness

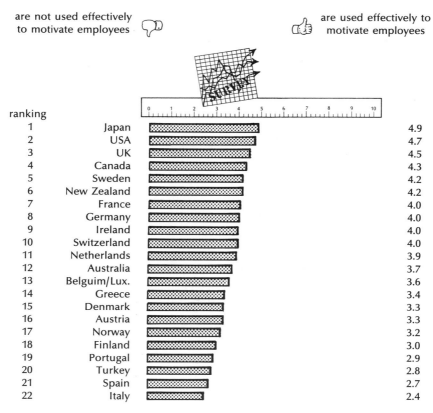

Figure 13.6 Non-wage incentives. *Source*: World Economic Forum (1993), reprinted with permission, © 1993 World Economic Forum.

Report 1993. When asked to what extent non-wage incentives (such as company cars) are used effectively to motivate employees, respondents from Britain, Germany, Sweden and France ranked the highest. Respondents from Portugal, Spain, Greece and Italy consider their organizations to be the weakest in this respect.

Similarly, as Figure 13.7 shows, there is a clear split between mainly English speaking countries that reward managers most on short-term basis in contrast to North European countries such as Germany, Denmark and Sweden, where managerial rewards are more likely to encourage long-term orientation.

FLEXIBLE REMUNERATION SYSTEMS

Flexible remuneration (also known as 'cafeteria benefits'), which allow employees to decide which elements they want in their compensation package and in what amounts, has received much interest in recent years. Employees are thus free, up to an agreed cash ceiling, to make up their own reward packages to fit their needs and desires. Clearly, there are wide individual differences in the preference of people for cash and fringe benefits. There are also differences in the kinds of fringe benefits individuals prefer. Thus, a standardized mix of cash and benefits is unlikely to be attractive to all individuals, so that it may be more effective to allow employees to select individually

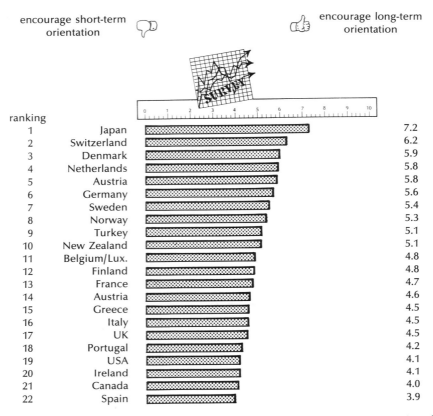

Figure 13.7 Managerial rewards. *Source*: World Economic Forum (1993), reprinted with permission, © 1993 World Economic Forum.

from a (limited) list of mixed packages until they have spent the total allowable compensation cost.

Although the idea of flexible compensation has become widespread in the US (where the number of organizations that use this approach to remuneration is estimated to have grown four-fold in the last five years), acceptance has been slow in Europe. Nonetheless, it would appear that the number of European organizations experimenting with flexible compensation systems is increasing, and this trend is likely to continue for a number of reasons.

Increasingly competitive labour markets, increasing cost pressures on employers and a continuing shift towards greater maturity and independence in corporate attitudes towards employees combine to create an environment where flexible compensation has a lot going for it.   Woodley (1990).

Woodley suggests also that demographic factors, increasing competition, and closer international integration of remuneration policies within multinational organizations may increase the popularity of flexible remuneration systems in Europe, so that this approach to compensation is likely to become as common as it is currently in the US.

USING NON-CASH BENEFITS TO MOTIVATE EMPLOYEES

Traditionally aimed at salespeople, gifts and other non-cash incentives are increasingly used by organizations to add interest to total quality management schemes and encourage money-saving ideas (Hilton, 1992). We considered the contribution of such incentives to team working in the last chapter. Some British examples are shown in Illustration 13.10.

Not all organizations consider such schemes appropriate. For instance, Sun Alliance's staff relations manager comments: 'We concentrate on payment in the form of cash rather than gimmicks'. This view is backed up by the general secretary of the in-company staff association: 'I have worked for a firm which rewarded its top salespeople with a cruise. I can't imagine anything worse than being trapped on a yacht with a lot of other life insurance salesmen' (Hilton, 1992).

In Chapter Seven we pointed out that one of the important roles of compensation policies is to create and reinforce a new organizational culture. An example of this is provided in Illustration 13.11, where compensation was used to unite employees after a merger.

PAYING FOR SKILLS

In addition to linking pay to performance, an increasing number of organizations have relied on alternative types of rewards and payment systems to compensate workers. One of the most recent types, particularly for non-manual workers, is skill or competency-based pay. In skill-based pay systems, employees receive compensation for the range, depth, and types of skills they possess. They are paid for the skills they are capable of using, not for the jobs they are performing at a particular point in time (Ledford, 1991). This is fundamentally different from the conventional system of job-based pay, where employees are paid for the jobs they are performing, not for their ability to perform certain tasks.

In a European context this will increasingly mean designing reward systems appropriate to the employee with pan-European responsibilities, employees who are

Illustration 13.10 **British example of non-cash benefits.**

1. British Telecom offers luxury gift items as part of its 'Living our values' initiative to enable managers to show gratitude to employees for such things as continuous improvement and teamwork.
2. Teams from British Aerospace receive gold pens, watches, ties and scarfs for innovation and creativity. The organization says that one idea alone saved them around £30,000.
3. ICL makes around 2,500 gifts each year to employees who demonstrate excellence, particularly in customer care. Since 1984 the organization has adopted three levels of award which reflect the employee's level of contribution. Those who rise to gold level, the international tier, are presented with their prize in a European city.
4. Abbey Life's top performers are given the opportunity to attend conventions in exotic foreign locations. The location and length of stay depends on performance.
5. Bahlsen Biscuits also sends its top performers to conventions in foreign locations but offers less exceptional staff an opportunity to win individual prizes to boost their selling effort. Most people can win something.

Source: Hilton (1992).

Illustration 13.11 **Compensation unites employees after a merger.**

Compensation isn't just a force that reacts and responds to cultural change. It also can drive that change as well, as Westinghouse Furniture Systems discovered in 1991, following its aggressive acquisition of three other organizations. According to Anthony D. Greco, the organization's director of executive resources and development, within two years, Westinghouse had acquired three other office furniture manufacturers, renamed itself The Knoll Group, and found itself with a diverse workforce of 4,400 employees worldwide. Not only were the employees accustomed to the culture of their previous employers, but they also were accustomed to their compensation practices.

'One big step in unifying these very different organizations during these difficult times was the introduction of a new compensation system,' Greco explains in *Rethinking Corporate Compensation Plans*, published by The Conference Board. 'We couldn't establish a unified strategy if salespeople from the four organizations were compensated in four different ways,' he writes.

The organization began by developing a cross-functional team of individuals to review the four existing compensation plans and combine the best elements of each into one overall program. 'We decided against any one plan, because that could create additional conflict and resentment,' Greco explains. Throughout this process, The Knoll Group solicited extensive feedback from sales employees. This not only helped employees become familiar with the compensation plan as

the organization developed it, but it also allowed the organization to achieve the necessary buy-in. Greco says that the communication effort was successful because the sales managers – not the human resources department – were responsible for communicating the changes to their direct reports.

The second step undertaken to unite the four cultures was an overhaul of the organization's benefits plan. This included shifting all hourly workers to a salary-continuance program. This means that exempt employees are paid even if they're ill and miss work. With the new benefits and sales compensation plans nearly complete, the organization now is dismantling the rigid salary-grading systems that existed in each of the four organizations and is implementing a single broadband structure. By doing this, 'we hope to encourage more movement within the organization, so individuals will expand their knowledge and develop new skills,' says Greco. When complete, the organization hopes to have condensed approximately 30 grades for exempt associates into just five bands.

The process of creating a unified compensation structure has been slow, but The Knoll Group expected a transition period. Extensive employee communications are helping ease the process considerably. In the long run, if these efforts are successful, employees will forget about how things used to be done in the old organizations and realize that they're united under one common vision.

Source: Caudron (1993), reprinted with permission © 1993, *Personnel Journal.*

likely to be required to be mobile across national, fiscal and cultural borders, and the retention of different kinds of specialists who are at risk of cross-national poaching. Traditionally, these employees have been mainly executives, professional staff and technical specialists. Increasingly, they also include skilled craftsmen and technicians.

Skill-based pay has been used to improve the level of customer service (see Illustration 13.12). Among the organizations which first introduced skill-based pay were a few North American pioneers, such as Honeywell Ammunition, Northern Telecom, AT&T, and Polaroid. Recently, however, skill-based pay has spread to European organizations in such industries as insurance, telecommunications, banking, and transport. In Britain, for instance, the National Westminster Bank uses a system of eleven competencies (see Chapter Twelve for a discussion of competencies) which they feel relate strongly to management performance in a turbulent business environment. Cockerill (1989) suggests that these eleven competencies: 'are not concerned with mere competence – with sufficiency or adequacy; rather they are forms of managerial behaviour which will raise performance beyond adequacy to excellence'.

The skills or competencies required to achieve certain outcomes within a job are assessed by a variety of evaluation methods which can range from the simpler non-analytical techniques of ranking and classification to the more elaborate methods of points rating and factor comparison. This approach is based on an assumption that an organization can identify and measure the behaviours people need to display in order to do the job effectively and these behaviours can form the basis of reward packages which encourage the development and use of previously underdeveloped and under-used skills within a job.

A competency-based rating scale is used at a British distribution organization, BSS Ltd. A total of twenty-one competencies were identified together with the behavioural indicators that indicated effective and ineffective performance on each competency. Figure 13.8 shows the behavioural ladder for one of these competencies. Each competency was defined on a 14-point scale and applied consistently throughout the organization. Factors consistent with the core competencies were used for the job evaluation scheme (Mosley and Bryan, 1992). A points system was used to measure performance against the achievement of objectives and the development of skills

Illustration 13.12 **Skill-based pay program improves customer service.**

As a supplier of products to the telecommunications industry, Northern Telecom serves a constantly changing marketplace. Customer demands are high, the pace is rapid and the products made by the company are evolving continually. This constant change puts pressure on all Northern Telecom employees to stay abreast of new product technologies, but the product installers feel the pressure most of all.

To encourage field technicians to keep their skills current and to ensure that they're adequately compensated for their increasing skill levels, Northern Telecom established a skill-based pay program in 1991 for the 1,200 installation-department employees. This program is called *Fast Forward*.

'This is a true pay-for-skills program', explains Dennis Garfield, director of installation at the company's Technical Installation Center in Raleigh, North Carolina. 'The only way our field technicians can receive an increase in their base pay is through the attainment of new skills.'

All of the installation skills that Northern Telecom employees need are listed on a document called the *Skills Capability Record* (SCR). Each skill on the SCR is assigned a point value, based on the difficulty of attaining that skill as well as on how important that skill is to the installation department. Skills range in value from 2 to 40 points, with the high-point skills considered to be the most important.

These points correspond to salary zones that are divided into 100-point increments. As field technicians earn additional points, they move into higher salary zones. 'Now there's no such thing as a dollar per point,' Garfield emphasizes. 'For field technicians to receive an increase in base salary, they must move into a new zone – into another 100-point increment. In other words, someone could go from 699 to 700 points and be eligible for a pay increase.'

Employees receive these points when they demonstrate that they can perform a particular skill on a job site without supervision. When this is done, they are *certified* in that skill by a certification committee that includes:

- The district manager.
- The employee's immediate supervisor.
- A representative from human resources.
- A peer.

In *Fast Forward's* first 18 months, close to 90 per cent of Northern Telecom's field technicians received some sort of skill-based pay increase. What impact has this had on customer service? 'We've heard many positive remarks from customers about our technicians' ability to answer their questions about our products,' Garfield explains.

'Additionally, we have a formal survey that's completed after every job, geared specifically to the installation activity. The surveys are coming back with much higher ratings today than they did two years ago.'

Source: Caudron (1993), reprinted with permission © 1993, *Personnel Journal.*

Motivating others

General description of attribute

Having the skill to gain interest, drive and commitment from others and sustain this over time. Involves viewing motivation in the widest sense, not just as a reward system. The skill comes to the fore in motivating others and managing their work performance even when career development opportunities are not apparent or available.

Level	Description
One	No previous experience of motivating others, does not have the opportunity to demonstrate this skill.
Two	Minimum level of understanding of this skill, or no requirement to motive others in his/her own work.
Three	Tends to be uninvolved, distant and aloof when dealing with others. May not inspire or motivate others.
Four	Begins to demonstrate some attention to motivating others but may lack knowledge of individuals' aspirations. Tends to dominate and impose his/her own standards.
Five	Appreciates individuals' aspirations. May set unrealistic targets.
Six	Sets appropriate targets but does not always provide any positive feedback. May tend to criticize others.
Seven	Is able to, and frequently does, provide positive feedback. Sometimes fails to show or to explain development opportunities.
Eight	Seeks to understand individual aspirations. Demonstrates a sensitivity to morale and levels of individual satisfaction.
Nine	Takes an active interest in what subordinates are doing. Works hard at building a team spirit. Enjoys working with others and listens to their views.
Ten	Builds on team spirit by recognizing good ideas and effort. Is encouraging and able to gain staff commitment.
Eleven	Transfers his/her enthusiasm to others. Gets involved and devotes time to finding interesting things for them to do.
Twelve	Uses the reward system effectively, providing motivating incentives and targets, keeps abreast of motivation techniques.
Thirteen	Is a natural motivator of staff. Finds ways of establishing career development opportunities.
Fourteen	Demonstrates the whole range of skills to motivate others at director level. Is a powerful motivator for all staff.

Figure 13.8 A competency-based rating scale to assess performance at BSS Ltd. *Source*: reprinted from C. Mosley and J. Bryan, 'A competency approach to performance management' in R. Boam and P. Sparrow (eds), *Designing and Achieving Competency*, with permission of the publishers, McGraw-Hill Book Co. Europe, © 1992.

against the competencies. These points were converted into an overall recommended score which was linked to a recommended salary range. BSS Ltd uses a reward system that provided a mechanism to control the structure of their labour costs but was also founded on the mix of competencies that were most likely to bring success. It provided a vehicle for cultural change by clearly rewarding the demonstration of quality values and behaviour.

One potential advantage of this approach to compensation is that it can significantly affect the reward culture within an organization so that individuals will no longer be rewarded simply for moving up a hierarchy but will be encouraged to extend their skills, and should they choose to do so, be rewarded for the additional skills they have acquired through increased pay. In addition, as Beer *et al.* (1984) point out, skill-based payment systems might encourage good specialists to stay in these roles rather than to seek management jobs which pay more but for which they may not have talent.

Torrington and Blandamer (1992) however, argue that:

A competency-based approach may well provide a method of alleviating the difficulties encountered in establishing performance-related pay schemes, but for many jobs its application will be to provide a criterion of minimum standards. To this end it is perhaps more appropriately employed in merit pay systems which generally cover those jobs in an organization that are not sufficiently autonomous for performance standards to be set in business terms.

Torrington and Blandamer (1992).

Skill-based pay systems are fraught with other challenges as well (Caudron, 1993). First, making the transition from traditional systems is tough, especially when there are highly paid employees who possess only one or two skills. Leblanc suggests you can do three things in this situation. First you can reduce their pay. Second you can give them a time requirement to learn the skills they are missing. Third, you can hold the base where it is, but offer those employees a one-time bonus for every new skill they acquire until their pay corresponds with their skill level.

The second concern with skill-based pay is that employees will rush to develop new skills and then plateau on the pay scale (Caudron, 1993). Research conducted by the American Compensation Association supports this, revealing that it takes an average of just three years for a worker to maximize his or her salary in a skill-based system. The answer to this is to institute a variable pay programme that provides bonuses for extraordinary individual or group performance. Variable- and skill-based pay systems can work extremely well together.

The third challenge with skill-based pay systems is that it can increase payroll expenses. For this reason, not many European organizations have been willing to invest in that kind of pay system. However, once employers find out how to assign prices to skills based on their relative worth to the organization, rather than on how long it takes an employee to learn a new skill, this may change.

THE ISSUE OF EQUAL PAY

European Union legislation has so far had modest impact on the determination of individual terms and conditions of employment. However, the directives and the rulings of the European Court of Justice (ECJ) on equal pay and equal treatment of male and female employees are the exceptions (see Illustration 13.13). Indeed, European court cases such as 'Barber' and 'Rinner-Kuhn' have played a decisive role in the implementation of the principle of equal pay for equal work and have compelled several national governments to amend, or consider amending, the national legislation

Illustration 13.13 **The legislative context for equal pay.**

Under Article 119 of the Treaty of Rome, European member states are required to apply the principle that men and women should receive equal pay for equal work, whether they are paid in cash or kind. Later, in 1976, the ECJ decided that Article 119 could be applied in relation to direct and overt discrimination, and in 1987 that it could also be used in circumstances relating to indirect discrimination. The Equal Pay directive elaborates upon the principle of equal pay for work of equal value. The prime example of legislation in the field of equal pay is the UK Equal Pay (Amendment) Regulations 1983, which makes equal pay claims possible for work of equal value, outside of an existing job evaluation scheme. This overcomes the problem of finding a male person within the organization or job evaluation scheme whose work is comparable to that of women.

which the ECJ has found to be incompatible either with existing directives or the equal pay provisions of the Treaty of Rome.

The current objective is to find means of overcoming 'structural' inequalities resulting from the confinement of women workers to low-paid job categories with no career prospects. Draft legislation has now been tabled in Germany to respond to ECJ decisions on remedies for discrimination on appointments, and exclusion from sick pay. The ruling by the ECJ in the 'Danfoss' case in 1989 placed the burden of proof on the employer to show that a pay structure in which there is a statistical difference between men's and women's pay is not based on sex discrimination.

The fact that the majority of 'atypical' employees in most European countries – that is people working on other than full time indefinite contracts of employment – are women, has linked the issues of atypical employment and sex discrimination (see Illustration 13.14). The pioneer case on this issue was referred from a German court to the ECJ (Bilka Kaufhaus *vs* Weber von Hartz) in 1987. The ECJ ruled that an occupational pension scheme whose rules excluded part timers indirectly discriminated against women on the grounds that more women than men were affected by the restriction, and that there were no objective factors to warrant it. ECJ law on indirect discrimination was also developed in 1989 with another German case, Rinner-Kuhn *vs* FWW Spezial-Gebauderreinigung, where the court ruled that any national provision which excluded certain categories of part timers contravenes Article 119 of the Treaty of Rome, unless the exclusion was warranted by objective factors. In making this decision the ECJ rejected a submission from the German government that the employer's duty of care to part time employees was reduced because such employees were 'less integrated in and bound to' the establishment.

The ECJ has also required changes in collective agreements which have been found to be directly or indirectly discriminatory. For example, a 1991 ruling on the German public sector agreement declared that differing qualifying periods for full and part timers for advancement in a pay progression system were indirectly discriminatory and had to be equalized.

In other words, legislation has been a decisive factor in the promotion of the equal pay principle, a principle often flouted in business practice. Where it is a question of combating cases of direct discrimination, the law can establish clearly applicable rules. However, the situation becomes much more difficult when one is dealing with the many and various forms of indirect discrimination inherent in day-to-day HRM practices (Eyraud, 1993). If, therefore, wage comparison and equal pay regulations are broadened to include comparison of opportunities and careers in order to combat discrimination more effectively, the question of women's access to vocational training

---

Illustration 13.14 **Equal remuneration for women welders in Sweden?**

In a Swedish organization one of the women welders demanded the same remuneration as that paid to her male colleagues. The organization had justified the wage difference of which she claimed to be the victim by the fact that she had failed a welding test which would have brought her up to the same skills level as the men. The question having been referred to the Ombudsman, the investigation conducted on his instructions revealed that this failure might very well have been due to the fact that, unlike her male colleagues, the complainant had always been assigned to repetitive jobs. It was subsequently agreed that her supervisor should assign her to more varied jobs in order to provide her with the necessary on-the-job training to give her a better chance of passing the next welding test.

becomes a vital one, and national laws and regulations will have to be amended in this area to cater for this development (Eyraud, 1993).

ARE WE MOVING TOWARDS SINGLE EUROPEAN PAY PRACTICES?

Although EU directives and the rulings of the European Court of Justice on equal pay and employee rights during the transfer of undertaking have had a major impact on corporate pay and benefits policies and have led to a convergence of pay and benefit practice in the member states of the EU, it would be amiss to believe that pay determination in the twelve EU states is homogeneous. To illustrate the very important national differences in the institutions and culture of pay setting, and, in particular, the importance of collective bargaining for determining pay levels and conditions of employment at the workplace level in the twelve countries covered by the EU directives and regulations, let us consider the diversity of minimum wage regulation across the Union.

Minimum wages

Beginning with Britain, the Employment Bill of 1992 abolished twenty-six wage councils, thereby effectively ending the UK's traditional minimum wage system set up by Winston Churchill in 1909. Consequently, Britain now is the only EU country without any legally enforceable minimum wage. At the same time, the UK has the highest proportion of workers earning less than the Council of Europe's 'decency threshold' and nominal wage levels are low compared to the rest of the Union. Hence, the refusal by the UK government to sign the social charter coupled with the abolition of wage councils is seen by many as an attempt at social devaluation, competing on the basis of cheap labour rather than efficiency, quality of service or productivity. Some 90 per cent of the 2.5 million people covered by the old legislation work in retailing and catering, with 10 per cent from hairdressing, clothing manufacture and laundries. Nearly 80 per cent are women.

In contrast with Britain, most other EU countries have either a minimum wage or a structure of enforceable collective agreements which bring about the same result, and most have laws governing collective bargaining which go far beyond the minimum regulation seen in the UK. For example, Belgium, France and Spain all have a statutory minimum wage, although the way it is set and the extent of its coverage varies widely. In Belgium, for instance, the minimum wage only applies to those workers who are not covered by a collective agreement with its own minimum terms; while in France, the 'Smic' (*Salaire Minimum Professionel de Croissance*) covers all employees aged eighteen and over in the private sector and semi-public sector organizations like Renault, but excludes public sector and civil service staff. Greece has a legally binding minimum wage which is agreed each year between the main union and employer organizations; again this does not cover public sector employees. Italy, Germany and Denmark have no statutory minimum wage, but in Germany it is estimated that 90 per cent of employees are covered by legally binding collective agreements which include minimum wage levels. In Italy, industry-wide agreements are legally binding on all organizations operating in that industry. In Denmark, collective agreements are binding on the signatories. Finally, the Republic of Ireland has no statutory minimum wage either, but minimum rates are set for low-paying industries by Joint Labour Committees. The fourteen Committees, set up by the country's Labour Court, cover industries such as hairdressing, hotels and catering and textiles, and make legally binding awards (IPM, 1992).

The determination of pay

There are other significant differences between EU countries with regard to the determination of pay. Compare the two different systems found in Germany and France. We have already noted some marked differences in German personnel management from the French model in Chapters Two and Three. The more legal and formal role is mirrored in personnel's (low) role in pay determination. As the 1990–91 PWCP survey of European HRM practices showed, wage negotiations are not a feature of life for the typical organization or German personnel manager, no matter how senior. Instead, wage bargaining occurs in a formal, procedural and scheduled way between recognized bargaining partners. Typically, one union negotiates with one employer federation on a *Land* basis.

However, although collective agreements are typically made on a regional basis, regional collective agreements in any one sector are largely identical, except for minor variations. Currently approximately 3,500 collective agreements are in force in Germany (Gaugler and Wiltz, 1993). Each general collective agreement is usually subdivided into several sub-agreements, which explains the large number of agreements. There are four categories of collective agreements (see Illustration 13.15). According to Gaugler and Wiltz (1993) this fragmentation of the issues for negotiation under different contracts facilitates the process of collective bargaining. There is no legal obligation to resort to arbitration if the social partners fail to agree, although often there is voluntary reference to outside arbitration bodies.

In France, on the other hand, collective bargaining has traditionally taken place at industry level. Both employer and union organizations preferred such bargaining for ideological as well as tactical reasons. However, the coming to power of the Left induced a different political and legal context for collective bargaining in the 1980s. The policies of the Mitterrand government were outlined in the so called 'Auroux Report', which enumerated a series of deficiencies from which the French system of wage determination was suffering (see Illustration 13.16).

Consequently, the 1982 Collective Bargaining Act followed the Auroux Report. It included many prescriptions, including the obligation to bargain at company level. Moreover, in June 1982 after a second devaluation of the French Franc, the government froze prices and recommended that: the widespread practice of index-linked pay increases should cease, pay increases should not exceed 10 per cent and

---

Illustration 13.15 **Four categories of collective agreements in Germany.**

1. Remuneration collective agreements (*Entgelt-tarifvertrag*), which set wage and salary levels and generally run for one year.
2. Grading and job evaluation collective agreements (*Lohnrahmentarifvertrag*), which determine the grading structure and set guidelines for the grading of different occupations. They generally have a duration of three to five years.
3. Framework or umbrella agreements (*Mantel-tarifvertrag*), which regulate issues such as holiday bonus, overtime rates, shift rates, length of the working week, etc.
4. Special agreements (*Spezialtarifvertrag*), which deal with one-off issues such as payment of a thirteenth monthly salary.

Illustration 13.16   **The Auroux Report: deficiencies in the French wage determination system in the early 1980s.**

1. Many wage earners were not covered by any collective agreements, whether at industry or plant level (i.e. 11 per cent of wage earners in organizations of at least ten employees).
2. Many agreements lacked job classification structures.
3. There was a large gap between basic minimum wages and actual pay (an average of 30 per cent).

4. Collective agreements were highly fragmented (40 of the 1023 national or regional level collective agreements covered more than half of the total number of wage-earners).
5. Only a quarter of wage-earners were covered by a plant agreement.
6. The low density of unionism and the divisions between unions undermined the 'legitimacy' of agreements.

Source: Goetschy and Rojot, 1987.

Illustration 13.17   **Getting Europe back to work: four areas of reform.**

Wage policies
To keep wage increases down, the Spanish, Italian and German governments have sought tripartite deals involving employers, trade unions and government. German unions accepted pay restraint as part of the so-called 'solidarity pact' to spread the cost of unification. 1992 saw the end of the '*scala mobile*' that indexed wage rises to inflation in Italy. In 1993 the Spanish government tried to persuade unions to accept a pay-restraint deal to keep pay increases below inflation. In August 1993, the Dutch government threatened to impose a wage freeze for 1994 if employers and unions failed to restrain wage increases.

Lower minimum wages
Seven EU countries including France, Belgium and Spain have national laws governing minimum wages. This may not last much longer. The Dutch Christian Democrat party proposed to abolish these laws in Holland. Fred Lempers, of the Netherlands Christian Federation of Employers, claimed Dutch organizations would like to reduce the minimum wage, standing at 2,163 guilders a month in 1993, by at least 50 per cent. Although Socialist partners in the ruling coalition government are likely to oppose this, some reduction can be expected.

Fewer unemployment benefits
Social benefits are particularly high in Germany, especially regarding pensions, sickness, and unemployment insurance. In August 1993, Germany's finance minister expressed an intention to cut some benefits, including unemployment pay, maternity pay and child care allowances. The French government is trying to lighten the cost of social benefits to employers. The five-year plan of Michel Giraud, the labour minister, aims to start progressively paying less, reducing the social-security costs now borne by employers for the families of workers earning up to 1.5 times the minimum wage, saving organizations up to FFr.8 billion per year. Organizations will also be freed for a limited period from paying social-security taxes for newly hired employees.

More labour flexibility
As well as making it cheaper to hire new workers, some governments are trying to make it easier to fire them too. In Spain, labour laws are particularly tough on redundancies. The government hopes that by softening employment legislation and offering financial incentives to employers, it can persuade organizations to hire more full time staff. The French government is introducing new labour measures to increase labour mobility and flexibility, including one lifting the 39-hour restriction on the working week, replacing it with an annualized equivalent. In some weeks employees can be asked to work up to 48 hours, providing that they can take more time off when business activity is low.

Source: The Economist (1993a).

should be linked to productivity increases. Whilst this spate of legislation did not induce revolutionary changes, it emphasized a preference for decentralized collective bargaining rather than statutory wage regulation, as Germany currently enjoys.

PAY, BENEFITS AND THE DRIVE TO REDUCE UNEMPLOYMENT

In the 1990s the debate on European pay and benefits has moved on to another agenda, which is the need to restore competitiveness and to get Europe back to work (see Illustration 13.17). At present, EU countries spend between 1 and 3 per cent of their GNP on unemployment benefit, youth training, and other labour market schemes. Pressure to cut the cost of unemployment is likely to grow as more organizations shed jobs and the number of long-term unemployed grows. Governments are concentrating on four areas of reform:

1. Wage policies.
2. Lower minimum wages.
3. Fewer unemployment benefits.
4. More employee flexibility.

Clearly, the topic of pay and benefits will remain one of the most important issues in European HRM for many years to come.

CONCLUSIONS

There have been numerous developments in the area of pay and rewards over the last ten years within the European Union and beyond. Corporate strategies aimed at improving total quality management, levels of customer service or empowerment have all required alterations to pay policies. Productivity pressures, slow levels of economic growth and a shift in the source of economic added value have provided external spurs to the development of more innovative approaches. The increased 'Europeanization' of organizations has brought the need to compensate and reward larger numbers of expatriate managers and to harmonize pay and conditions within a European sphere. Pay costs typically represent the largest single cost (or investment) that an organization has and so it is important that the organization can understand how they work and manage them effectively. In managing pay and benefits, this chapter has emphasized the following key learning points.

LEARNING POINTS FROM CHAPTER THIRTEEN

1. There are different perspectives on the role of pay and benefits and these are linked to underlying concepts of distributive justice. For example, in Belgium, France, Portugal and Spain the preference is for equity-based pay policies, whilst in Denmark, Germany, Ireland and the UK the preference is for equality-based policies. There are differences in the motivational impact of non-monetary rewards across countries. Within Europe, there is more pressure for 'socially healthy' pay levels than found in the US. However, many of these expectations are also part of an organizational, industry or market culture and are not just determined by national factors.

2. Pay strategies need to be adjusted to meet the unique cultural contingencies of employers within countries. Theoretically, there are clear sets of dominant values,

associated organizational features and distinct compensation strategies linked to levels of national culture in terms of masculinity, uncertainty avoidance, power distance and individualism.

3. There is a transition within reward systems within Europe. This reflects a wide range of mutually competing or mutually reinforcing pressures. However, there is a slow but discernible trend to 'de-levelling' and a renewed emphasis on wage and salary differentials as a way of recognizing variation in talent, responsibility and effort. These areas have received attention because, historically, many reward systems have not delivered the desired results.

4. There is a high level of dissatisfaction, both among employees and employers, with reward systems. They are frequently seen as costly to administer and not very motivating. There are two reasons why employees feel performance and pay are not linked effectively: a failure to design reward systems that underpin business strategies and a poor linkage between the design of rewards and the underlying skills and experience that create a real contribution to the organization. Many reward systems are poorly matched to the requirements of teamworking in organizations and over emphasize individualism and specialization. Similarly, many pay systems focus on the need for internal equity, based on an analysis of the number of levels in the organization, the span of control or the nominal job content. These measures frequently have little to do with real effectiveness.

5. The fragmentation of European labour markets has also made it difficult for organizations to rely on regional or national pay surveys in order to establish salary scales. Skills shortages and equal opportunities issues have also posed new challenges for HRM departments. Disparities in standards of living and income in European countries have become more obvious in this context of change. Compensation levels are highest in Switzerland, the Benelux countries and Germany. The need for a social dimension to be built into organizations as they are given the right to create a unified market for goods, services and capital has been raised in order to avoid social dumping.

6. The process of reducing the differences in pay and conditions between EU countries will be a slow and difficult one. There are significant economic, cultural and legal barriers that have to be overcome in order to harmonize pay conditions in Europe. The gap in inflation and the cost of living between different European countries will be critical and will influence developments in pay and benefits significantly.

7. There have been a series of changes in rewards policies and practices of European organizations. The development of flexible pay systems to link variable pay to overall economic performance or company financial performance and the performance of individuals, team members or larger organizational units has become more common. The majority of Spanish, Swedish, British, German and French organizations have introduced variable pay as part of their reward structure.

8. This has meant that pay is increasingly determined by organizational policy, and not national or regional pay agreements. Rewards are becoming focused on the needs and constraints of individual organizations. An increasing number of fringe benefits, individual or group bonuses or forms of profit sharing are being used. Different pay systems across countries are heavily influenced by tax effectiveness and the social security context.

9. An increasing number of organizations have introduced pay for performance schemes in order to make pay reflect contribution and not status. There are a variety of forms used, such as merit pay, individual bonuses, team bonuses, organization-wide schemes and share option schemes.

10. There are cultural differences in the progress of this individualization of pay. Uptake has been relatively low in Portugal and Spain and in the Benelux countries, largely due to union resistance. In Germany the focus of reward is on the level of skill and experience as assessed by a collective system and this has slowed down the development of individual merit elements. In France, the culture has focused on individual pay, but usually reflecting status. Significant changes have taken place. The greatest changes have occurred in Ireland, Italy and the UK.

11. Fringe benefits have become an important element of reward packages across Europe, particularly in skills shortage areas. There have been moves towards a harmonization of fringe benefits between blue and white collar employees and single status terms and conditions. These moves have been supported by legislation in some countries (such as Sweden and France) or by the presence of foreign-owned inward investors.

12. Flexible remuneration or 'cafeteria benefits', which allow employees to decide on the elements in the compensation package has received more attention in recent years, but despite its popularity in the US, acceptance in Europe has been slow in coming. Non-cash benefits have also been used to encourage money saving schemes or to add interest to total quality management schemes.

13. Alternative reward schemes are also being used to compensate individuals for the range, depth and type of skills possessed. Individuals are being paid for the skills they are capable of using and not just the jobs that they are capable of performing at any particular time. This is a fundamentally different concept to conventional systems of job-based pay. In the European context this will mean designing reward systems appropriate to people with pan-European responsibilities. Skill-based pay is moving into Europe in sectors such as insurance, telecommunications, banking and transport.

14. European Union legislation has so far made only a modest impact on the determination of individual terms and conditions of employment. However, the principle of equal pay for equal work and the need to overcome 'structural' inequalities resulting from the confinement of groups to specific labour markets (such as part time work) are issues that will be addressed throughout the 1990s.

15. Although there has been a convergence of organizational pay and benefits policies in Europe, very strong national differences remain and there is a wide diversity in wage regulation practice. Belgium, France and Spain all have statutory minimum wages and most have laws governing collective bargaining. Italy, Germany and Denmark have no statutory minimum wage but legally-binding collective agreements exist. The UK stands alone in its abolition of wage councils. Differences also exist in the determination of pay.

16. Organizational policies on pay and benefits cannot be seen without considering the wider social debate about getting Europe back to work. Pressures to cut the costs of unemployment are reinforcing reforms in Europe in the areas of wage policies, lower minimum wages, fewer unemployment benefits and more labour flexibility. Such external pressures will reinforce dissatisfaction with organization remuneration systems.

CHAPTER FOURTEEN

Performance Management and Appraisal

Performance management is the way forward – for every individual and for the company as a whole. It is therefore vitally important that every individual has a clear understanding of his or her work objectives and responsibilities, because performance will be measured against them.

Extract from *The ICL Way*.

Performance management is an area of human resource management (HRM) which has the potential to make the most significant contribution to organizational effectiveness and growth. Given the wide range of strategic pressures outlined in Chapters Four and Five it is clear that many European organizations will need to focus very strongly on the need to manage their performance if they are going to deliver the improvements to productivity and competitiveness that they seek. There are, in fact, a series of pressures that are focusing attention on performance management systems (see Figure 14.1). In general, interest in the topic of performance management has been stimulated across Europe because of several issues already discussed:

- Increased market competition and associated organizational culture changes (see Chapters Four and Seven).
- Changes in organizational structure associated with a reduction of vertical hierarchies (see Chapter Eight).
- A new agenda for industrial relations and a shift towards more flexible labour markets (see Chapter Twelve).
- Increasing devolution of control to managers (see Chapter Twelve).
- Changes in reward and pay policies and an increasing individualization of reward systems (see Chapter Thirteen).

A series of competitive pressures are reinforcing the need for European organizations to give increased attention to performance management. Exposure to international competition has been increased in most industrial sectors, whilst the process of privatization and reduction of levels of state employment has brought a renewed attention to the need for productivity. As product and service development cycles shorten in duration, a more concentrated co-ordination of effort is required. Rationalization of businesses has in many instances been associated with a reduction in the number of vertical levels in the organization, an increase of spans of control, and a devolvement of accountabilities and responsibilities. These have all placed increased importance on the ability of managers to be able to manage the performance of their staff and teams. Several organizations have redesigned their underlying business

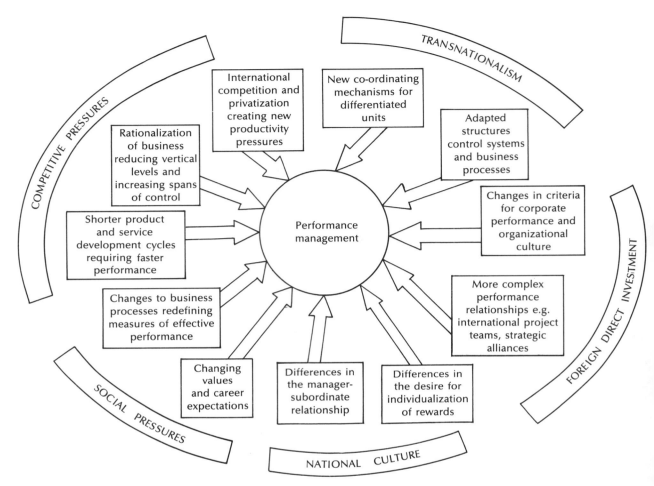

Figure 14.1 The factors influencing change in performance management.

processes, for example increasing the importance of quality or customer service measures, and this has changed the nature (and appropriate performance criteria) of management effectiveness. Social pressures, principally in the form of changed levels of commitment and workforce values, are creating new career and job expectations which have to be managed. The development of more transnational organizations has produced new co-ordinating mechanisms for differentiated units, adapted structures, control systems and business processes. These all have to be absorbed into the organization and reflected in performance priorities. Increased levels of foreign direct investment have led to a change in the corporate criteria for performance and new demands from an altered organizational culture. The performance relationships have also become more complex as the number of international project teams and strategic alliances has increased and organization structures have been evolved into complex forms such as matrix structures. Pitted against these transition pressures there are a number of marked differences in national culture which may shape the way organizations respond to the changes. Most notable amongst these cultural influences are differences in the manager–subordinate relationship which impinge upon the way issues of performance are established and discussed, and differences in the extent to which the process of individualization of rewards has progressed and is seen as desirable.

The topic of performance management (henceforth called PM) is however a difficult one to cover, for three main reasons:

1. There are many different approaches to performance management, ranging from the very simple to the very complex.
2. Discussion of PM systems tends to concentrate on two separate issues. One approach concentrates on reward driven integration, stressing the link between rewards systems (see Chapter Thirteen) and performance appraisal, whilst the other takes cognisance of the whole business process and concentrates on the need to link human resource development (see Chapter Eleven) to organizational performance.
3. The extent to which European personnel and line managers have direct control over some key aspects of PM systems (such as compensation and rewards) varies widely (see Chapter Two). For example, German personnel managers have limited experience of implementing performance management systems. Similarly, cultural differences in aspects of organizational life (such as the manager–subordinate relationship) may make prescriptions for management style inappropriate in some contexts.

PM is then essentially a strategic management technique, with strong roots in Anglo-Saxon management practice, which links business objectives and strategies to individual goals, actions, performance appraisal and rewards through a defined process. To the extent that PM systems are capable of incorporating all these links, then they can provide a very powerful tool for driving change through the organization. The most important feature of an effective PM system is its ability to be seen as a method of continuously securing improvements in the performance of teams and individuals against predefined business strategies and objectives (see Illustration 14.1).

In Chapter Eleven we used ICL as an example of an organization with a defined strategy for internalization and discussed some of the career management implications of this strategy. In this chapter we also consider some of the performance management aspects of HRM at ICL. Peter Williams, Director of Human Resource Development with ICL, says in the opening chapter of the British IPM's *Handbook of Performance Management*:

Ideally, it will provide the basis for managing the business of today and for developing into the future – through the performance of its people. As such, performance management should demand the attention and consideration of both the Chief Executive and the Personnel Director.

Williams (1991, p. 7).

Illustration 14.1 **Links between strategic and individual objectives engendered by a performance management system.**

1. Identifies important business objectives and the factors contributing to their achievement.
2. Assigns key tasks to units and individuals responsible for their attainment.
3. Clarifies what is to be achieved by whom and when.
4. Determines how important results will be achieved.
5. Provides for monitoring and reviewing actual results.
6. Recognizes varying levels of achievement with varying levels of rewards.
7. Encourages learning from experience.

We provide details of the ICL PM system later in this chapter. It is useful at this point, however, to note that Williams (1991) cites a statement of his chief executive to all employees which says:

> By following the performance management process, managers and their staff will be strengthening their working relationship and they will be able to maximize their joint contribution to the long-term success of the company. This will lead to a pattern of growth and achievement, providing good results for the company and a rewarding and satisfying working life for everyone in ICL.
>
> Williams (1991, p. 3).

THE UNDERLYING ASSUMPTIONS OF PERFORMANCE MANAGEMENT

A number of factors therefore impact the attractiveness of performance management tools and techniques across Europe:

- Different levels of HRM sophistication.
- The historical role of the personnel function.
- Cultural differences in management style and the manager–subordinate relationship.

However, one of the points that emerges from some of the case studies is that a number of European organizations that – for reasons of tradition and culture – might have been expected to shy away from a performance management focus, are now, in fact, beginning to embrace the concept. It is therefore important to examine some of the assumptions that underpin a performance management philosophy. According to Fowler (1990) there are two largely unrelated (and sometimes opposing) approaches to performance management: one concerned with work processes; the other with the human element – with people. The *people* approach is based on a number of assumptions detailed in Illustration 14.2.

In contrast, the *process* approach to performance management makes the set of assumptions detailed in Illustration 14.3.

Fowler (1990) argues that almost all the management techniques and systems that have been developed this century, in order to secure a higher level of organizational and managerial performance, fall into one or other of these two categories. For instance, work study, critical path analysis, job evaluation and management by objectives can be seen as predominantly process-orientated approaches, while the people-orientated approach is predominant in a number of other management techniques

Illustration 14.2 **Assumptions behind the people approach to performance management systems.**

- High performance can be achieved only through people.
- The right people need to be selected for the right jobs in the right numbers.
- They need to be trained in the appropriate skills.
- They need to be effectively led and motivated.
- Under such conditions people will inevitably work well.
- By and large, competent, motivated people will evolve their own best methods of working.

Source: Fowler (1990, p. 48).

Illustration 14.3 **Assumptions behind the process approach to performance management systems.**

■ High performance is best secured by analysing the work which needs to be done to achieve a predetermined result. ■ This invariably involves re-designing the most efficient sequence or method of work activities.	■ It is possible and appropriate to find 'the one best way' of doing things. ■ Employees will follow this method because, from an analytically logical viewpoint, it is patently obvious that it is the best way of working.

Source: Fowler (1990, p. 48).

which have also proved popular over the last thirty years, such as quality circles, training needs analysis and performance related pay. Moreover, examination of some of the assumptions in this second approach to performance management – particularly those that infer that there is one best way of doing things – highlights some of the conflicts between some models of performance management and the North European autonomous group work design models discussed in Chapter Twelve.

From Fowler's (1990) viewpoint, the contemporary approach to performance management, which typically begins with identification of critical success factors derived directly from business strategy, is not a totally new system or technique, but rather the latest in a long line of attempts by managers to get the right things done well by subordinates. Despite such a long pedigree, there are international differences in emphasis, which we now consider.

VARIATION IN THE ROLE OF PERFORMANCE EVALUATION AND APPRAISAL ACROSS EUROPE

In Chapter Two we highlighted the fact that there is considerable variation in both the content and context for HRM across Europe, whilst in Chapter Ten we detailed the different assumptions about what constitutes an effective manager. Clearly, this is likely to influence the attractiveness of performance management and appraisal as a management tool as well as the level of sophistication reached by indigenous personnel departments across Europe. An understanding of such international differences can be gleaned from the following areas of writing or research:

■ International and national surveys of practice documenting the use of, or importance of, specific tools or techniques related to performance management.
■ Examination of the cultural aspects of managerial life, particularly the role of the manager–subordinate relationship.
■ Case study examples of best practice, usually focusing on larger organizations that have undergone major change.
■ Comparative manuals documenting the level of take-up of pay-for-performance or merit-pay approaches.

Unfortunately, there is very little quantitative evidence about the take up of specific performance management tools and techniques across Europe. Moreover, it is often very difficult to be sure exactly what sort of practices such surveys are picking up. This chapter clarifies the use of terms such as performance management and performance appraisal and places them in their broader context. Even when survey evidence suggests that an organization has a PM system, this may still hide a multitude of sins in terms of poor practice. Survey evidence may also fail to detect highly relevant practices. Nevertheless, what is the empirical evidence?

The IBM/Towers Perrin (1992) worldwide human resource survey on priorities for gaining competitive advantage (discussed in detail in Chapter Two) provides data on four European countries: the UK, Germany, France and Italy. This survey found that the percentage of organizations that considered performance appraisal to be a top or high priority item by the year 2000 ranged from 78 per cent in France, 57 per cent in the UK, 55 per cent in Germany and 49 per cent in Italy. It is difficult, of course, to establish by survey whether these percentages reflect the existing levels of adoption of performance management techniques, a desire to 'catch up' on competitors or a need to change the focus and content of existing systems. For example, the high proportion of French organizations placing a priority on performance appraisal in this survey probably reflects the latter situation, as made clear in the next section.

Although there was little difference between Germany, France and the UK in terms of the priority given to the need to focus on a merit philosophy and the management of individual performance (seen to be critically important by between 66 and 78 per cent of organizations), the IBM/Towers Perrin survey revealed subtly different emphases in the sorts of criteria that should form a priority for the pay-for-performance link. For example, the proportion of organizations who felt that the reward of employees for high customer service and quality performance was critically important was highest in Germany (89 per cent), followed by the UK (82 per cent), France (80 per cent) and finally Italy (61 per cent). French organizations however were far less concerned about strengthening the link between reward and innovation or creativity performance (54 per cent rating it as critically important in French organizations compared to 90 per cent of German and 71 per cent of UK organizations) or the link between reward and business/productivity gains (52 per cent rating it as critically important in French organizations compared to 81 per cent of German and 77 per cent of UK organizations).

There is very little empirical evidence on the extent to which French organizations have taken up performance management tools and techniques. One source of survey data (*op. cit.* Rojot, 1990), however, indicates that the use of basic management by objective systems in France is now quite widespread. A 1987 survey by Hay France of 220 French organizations employing more than 65,000 managers found that 91 per cent had a policy of fixing individual objectives for managers, 81 per cent evaluated performance in relation to these objectives and 87 per cent had an annual performance appraisal review meeting. The extent to which these practices were formalized was less widespread. Only 58 per cent of the organizations had a corporate-wide process and only 28 per cent imposed a distribution of the levels of rating.

In Italy there is a considerable lag in the adoption of performance appraisal techniques. Reflecting the generally lower ratings (in terms of critical importance) found by the IBM/Towers Perrin survey, Hinterhuber and Stumpf (1990) found that formalized systems of performance evaluation are spread thinly across Italian organizations. In a survey of 116 of Italy's largest organizations by the Centre for Research on Business Organization in Milan, 39 per cent of organizations were found to have no performance evaluation system. Hinterhuber and Stumpf (1990) argue that this lower level of adoption of performance appraisal in part reflects a conscious refusal explicitly to fix aims of an individual's role or job and to document the criteria for evaluation. Italian organizations tend to thrive on maintaining a high degree of flexibility in personnel management matters and motivation and performance evaluation practices tend to be governed by an informal psychological contract between the employer and employee. The situation is changing however. Some 40 per cent of the managers felt their organizations had effective and professional systems of performance evaluation, and 35 per cent of the organizations were modifying their performance evaluation and motivation systems. In Italy there is also increasing evidence that progressive organizations have adopted performance management techniques. For example, Paoletti (1993) describes how as part of a profound revision of its personnel management systems, Telespazio, the publicly owned telecommunications organization, introduced a 'management by objectives' system to bring clarity to its process of restructuring, and subsequently extended the system to executives and managers as a prelude to setting more qualitative customer satisfaction objectives (the growing importance of customer appraisal is discussed towards the end of this chapter). Similarly, Camuffo and Costa (1993) argue that Italian organizations in general made massive organizational changes in the 1980s. Innovative HRM practices, including many of those involved in performance management systems and discussed in this chapter, played a major role in helping organizations such as Benetton, Pirelli and Stefanel achieve their strategic objectives.

Reflecting the process on industrial restructuring in Europe (see Chapter Five) there are often differences between domestically owned and foreign owned organizations within a country, particularly those that on the whole have less developed national HRM functions. In countries like Greece, HRM in the main is less systematic and developed (see Chapter Two) and so their ability to develop the sophistication required to make a performance management system work effectively is more limited. A survey comparing HRM practices in matched pairs of Greek and foreign owned manufacturing companies (Papalexandris, 1991) found that by comparison the degree of systematization of appraisal procedures and the objectivity of results was low in Greek companies yet very high in the foreign owned multinationals.

The legal and social context is also an important determinant of attitudes and approaches towards performance management. For example, the highly legalistic and bureaucratic nature of German personnel management (see Chapter Two), coupled with the lack of control or influence over pay and reward decisions, places appraisal and performance management techniques in a different context to that found in the UK, where the ability to manage performance reflects a stronger link between appraisal and reward under the direct control of the line manager. Despite the evidence of high importance being given to the topic of performance appraisal and pay-for-performance links in the IBM/Towers Perrin survey, it is interesting to note that none of the academic reviews of German HRM practice, or European management guides to pay, benefits, training and development make any specific mention of performance management or appraisal practices. There are clearly cultural differences in the centrality of performance management to the typical management task.

THE EFFICIENCY OF THE MANAGER–SUBORDINATE RELATIONSHIP AS A MODERATOR OF INTEREST IN PERFORMANCE MANAGEMENT

Many of the strategic objectives of European organizations will only be achieved through the creation of highly motivated managers. Whilst managers may dictate the main strategy, they are often not aware of the day-to-day issues. Some recent studies have tended to show that managers in certain countries are less effective than others in leading and motivating their subordinates (Bournois and Chauchat, 1990). Saias (1989) examined the efficiency of the manager–subordinate relationship in a

Estimated management talent

Figure 14.2 Cultural differences in the potential of management as motivators of staff. *Source*: Bournois and Chauchat (1990) who adapted it from Saias (1989). Reprinted from *European Management Journal*, **8(1)**, 3–18, F. Bournois and J. H. Chauchat, 'Managing managers in Europe', © 1990, with kind permission from Pergamon Press Ltd, Headington Hill Hall, Oxford, OX3 0BW, UK.

comparative framework by mapping data on workers' motivation level with estimates of management talent (see Figure 14.2). The efficiency of the manager–subordinate relationship is at its lowest in Portugal, Spain and Greece, making these countries clear targets for improved PM techniques. The UK and Italy also have relatively inefficient relationships, followed by France and Ireland. From this analysis, one might expect that the need for improved PM techniques would be strongest in the Latin countries, whilst the demand for PM techniques would be lowest in the relatively efficient countries such as Switzerland, Germany, Belgium and Denmark.

CULTURAL DIFFERENCES IN THE MANAGER–SUBORDINATE RELATIONSHIP: THE FRENCH PERSPECTIVE ON PERFORMANCE MANAGEMENT

However, whilst the need for PM techniques may be strongest in the Latin countries and in Anglo-Saxon countries, cultural factors seem to obscure this need in Latin countries, as evidenced by the situation in France. The empirical evidence described above suggests a fairly widespread take-up of techniques such as performance appraisal in France, and a high degree of importance being attached to the topic. However, it is important to appreciate that there are philosophical differences in the way PM tools are used. In Chapter Three we discussed the impact of national cultural differences on management practice. Two of the dimensions of national culture identified by Hofstede (1980) have direct relevance to the role of performance management:

1. Power distance.
2. Uncertainty avoidance.

French managers have a higher power distance score (68) in comparison, for example, with British managers (35). This is reflected in the greater differences in formal power across the hierarchy in France and the observation that French managers are more tolerant of these inequalities of power. High levels of uncertainty avoidance should be reflected in greater desire to control the future through planning procedures and contingency arrangements. Given the higher uncertainty avoidance score (86) for French managers in comparison to German managers (65) and British managers (35), one would expect that French managers seek to eliminate uncertainty and ambiguity in their tasks through an emphasis on performance management. The way in which the manager−subordinate relationship enables them to do this nevertheless remains a delicate point in France (Poirson, 1993).

The way in which these cultural differences actually influence attitudes and approaches to performance management is even more subtle than such analyses suggest. Observational studies of comparative management practice, using unstructured exercises and methods, reveal some subtle cultural implications for the practice of performance management systems (Barsoux, 1992; Barsoux and Lawrence, 1990):

. . . Britons learn to expect the unexpected. . . promises are customarily greeted with scepticism, speedy responses with surprise and errors with resignation. British managers. . . feel comfortable with uncertainty. . . Germans, in contrast, expect reliability and punctuality. . . without rules life would become anarchic, hence the national obsession with planning and adherence to plans. . . even linguistically [they] consign their verbs to the end of a sentence, so speakers have to know where they are heading before they set off. . . A French manager analysed a problem and discussed every possible approach to it [and has therefore] . . . relegated the implementation of his plans to a formality.   Barsoux (1992).

A study on the unsuccessful attempt to introduce 'management by objectives' (MBO) in France in the 1970s (Trepo, 1975, *op. cit.* Rojot, 1990) highlighted the fear of face-to-face conflict, the way authority is conceived, and the way in which managers are made (and the mode of selection of senior managers) as powerful cultural forces that made it difficult for French organizations to adopt this Anglo-Saxon management concept. Rojot (1990) pointed out that the French corporate culture creates a situation in which subordinate managers seek more responsibility, but in fact remain passive, fear to commit themselves to specific objectives and mostly look for protection from above. On the other hand, senior managers who rule autocratically see the organization as an élite school in which the boss has to be the most intelligent and subordinates cannot conceivably have valid ideas. Bollinger and Hofstede (1987) point out that the manner in which a manager commands depends to a large extent on the cultural conditioning of his subordinates. French managers are frequently possessive of their individual autonomy. The reaction is: 'I know my job, if I am controlled, this means they have no confidence in me' (Poirson, 1993). Therefore, even where management by objective schemes are practiced in France, they become '. . . the stake of a different game' (Rojot, 1990, p. 98).

For example, the emerging focus of performance management systems in countries such as the UK emphasizing the joint problem solving nature of appraisal interviews (see the discussion later in this chapter) and greater decentralized responsibility over how individual objectives will be met is unlikely to be replicated in the majority of French organizations. There are also differences in the perceived importance of productivity issues. Whilst these issues are to the forefront of British senior management minds, Barsoux and Lawrence (1990) describe how in a typical French organization − L'Oréal − the traditional management style engenders a different perspective on performance management to that articulated above by ICL:

Managing burned out managers in L'Oréal

... A policy of life long employment implies (coping) with individuals whose relative contribution to the company is diminishing... the grounds for keeping on these individuals are often humanitarian: out of tolerance, respect or recognition for having helped the group through difficult times... to help nurture young talent, to preserve the collective memory of the company and pass on the corporate culture... if L'Oréal fails to take care of its ageing cadres, it risks deterring young cadres from even joining the company... L'Oréal is fortunate in that it is large enough to accommodate a fair amount of excess weight... this slack remains invisible because of *un certain flou* (a slight blur) in the organizational chart... territories and responsibilities are ill-defined, re-negotiated daily, with politics and careerism rife.

Barsoux and Lawrence (1990, pp. 172–73).

However, the context within which HRM in France is practised has changed considerably over the last ten years (Poirson, 1993; Rojot, 1990). Increased and globalized competition, the growth of multinational organizations, the shortening of product life cycles, and the growing importance of product quality have all provided a new justification of managerial authority in France, and a new language amongst the employers' associations and bodies has legitimized a number of management and HRM practices, including performance management (Rojot, 1990). For example, in describing the situation at L'Oréal, Barsoux and Lawrence (1990) point out that it would be wrong to assume that such an example is totally representative of French corporate culture. It does serve however to:

- Draw attention to some of the built-in contradictions between what have been defined as traditional French values and the value system underlying the use and successful implementation of some of the newer performance management tools.
- Display some of the distinctive characteristics that may have survived despite increasing internationalization.

In the absence of many comprehensive surveys it is difficult to be certain about the continuance of traditional values in the face of pressures for change. However, as already discussed in the case of Italy, individual case studies of remarkable success with new performance management techniques abound in France (Rojot, 1990). For example, Barsoux and Lawrence (1990) describe another successful French organization – Carrefour – which has a strong tradition of self-made managers and a culture in which graduates rub shoulders with the *autodidactes*. Carrefour therefore places emphasis on the need for individuals to prove their worth and has a stronger performance management culture than many other French organizations. With decentralized responsibility for performance, moves to undermine sacrosanct French salary structures (see Chapter Thirteen) and attempts to link it to individual performance, it is claimed that Carrefour has out-Americanized the Americans (Barsoux and Lawrence, 1990).

MAIN ELEMENTS OF A PERFORMANCE MANAGEMENT SYSTEM

Having described some of the assumptions that underlie the performance management philosophy and drawn attention to the different levels of adoption and cultural importance of the approach, we now consider in detail the various elements of a performance management (PM) system. Will the development of sophisticated performance management systems be more successful than their predecessors –

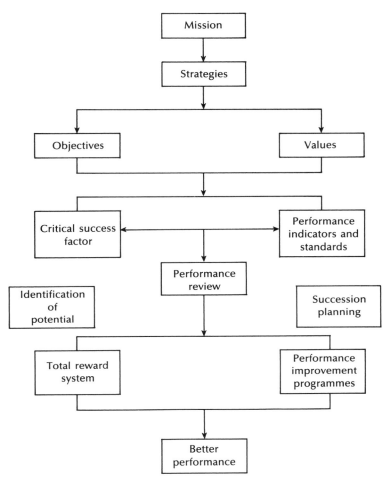

Figure 14.3 The performance management process. *Source*: Philpott and Sheppard (1992), reprinted with permission, © 1993, L. Philpott and L. Sheppard, *Managing for Improved Performance*, Kogan Page.

particularly management by objectives, which performance management resembles most closely? Or will performance management simply be the most recent in a roll-call that also includes management by objectives, total quality management, transformational leadership, zero-based budgeting, empowerment, team briefings and so on? The following sections are intended to help answer these questions.

A generic outline of a performance management system can be gleaned by examining the model suggested by Philpott and Sheppard (1992) shown in Figure 14.3 and the main elements of a performance management system outlined in Illustration 14.4.

DIFFERENCES BETWEEN PERFORMANCE MANAGEMENT AND MANAGEMENT BY OBJECTIVES

Interestingly, Fowler (1990) notes that many of the above features were also present in the much praised management by objectives (MBO) system marketed by Urwick Orr and its derivatives in the 1970s.

Illustration 14.4 **Main elements of a performance management system.**

Elements of system	Contribution to HRM
Development of a mission statement.	Defines the business the organization is in and the direction in which it is going.
Business strategies and objectives.	Provides explicit guidance on the future behaviour and performance required to achieve the mission.
Values statement.	Says what is important to the organization with regard to how it conducts its affairs.
Identification of critical success factors.	Spells out the factors contributing to successful performance.
Performance indicators.	Links the critical success factors and the final results to be evaluated.
Conduct of performance reviews;	Evaluates individual performance, qualities and competencies against relevant objectives.
Pay reviews.	Links rewards explicitly to performance in the form of merit pay, individual bonuses, group bonuses and other variable payments related to corporate or group performance.
Performance improvement.	Concerned with improving performance by means of training, career development, coaching, and counselling.

Source: Philpott and Sheppard (1992), reprinted with permission © 1993, L. Philpott and L. Sheppard, *Managing for Improved Performance*, Kogan Page.

Both systems set objectives within each segment of the job: both distinguish between task-based objectives and personal development goals. Both require the identification of performance measures and the periodic appraisal of achievement against objectives.   Fowler (1990).

However, as Table 14.1 shows, there are also some important differences between performance management and MBO. For instance, full-blown performance management systems are far more cohesive, participative and consistent with the organization's mission, strategy, and objectives than MBO, and consequently stand a better chance of success.

Table 14.1 **Differences between MBO and PM systems.**

MBO	PMS
Packaged system	Tailor-made systems
Applied to managers	Applied to all staff
Emphasis on individual objectives	Emphasis on corporate goals and values
Emphasis on quantified performance measures	Inclusion of qualitative performance indicators
Jobs divided into key results areas (KRAs)	Jobs divided into principal indicators
Objectives set for each KRA	Objectives set for each accountability
Performance measures	Performance indicators
Task and personal goals	Task and personal goals
Annual appraisal including discussion of new goals	Annual appraisal including discussion of new goals
Most schemes used complex paperwork	Some schemes have complex paperwork
Schemes 'owned' by specialists	Schemes owned by line management

Source: Fowler (1990), reprinted with permission © Alan Fowler, 1993.

HRM QUESTIONS AND RESULTING OUTCOMES FROM A PERFORMANCE MANAGEMENT SYSTEM: ZURICH INSURANCE GROUP

Having distinguished PM systems from the MBO approach, we now consider three issues:

1. What are the advantages of using a top-down approach to the setting of performance plans, objectives and milestones?
2. What are the sorts of questions and topics that should typically be addressed by a PM system?
3. What are the typical outcomes and options that result from a PM process?

These questions are best answered by an example. Zurich Insurance Group (ZIG) has established a mission, management principles and long-term objectives which focus on customer strategy. The ZIG vision – which includes the desire to be 'one of the leading worldwide insurance companies with the highest financial ratings providing excellent security to our customers' – is global and sets the course for the individual companies within the Group to follow. Each company and division within ZIG develops 'critical success factors' based on an analysis of the external environment and an internal analysis of the business unit's current resources and capabilities. The PM process continues by translating the key success factors into organizational plans, performance objectives and strategic milestones. Once completed, individual managers are required to cascade the process down the line (see Illustration 14.5).

In order to help managers with the process of effectively assigning objectives and accountabilities to specific individuals within each unit, ZIG set out a list of key questions for line managers to consider (see Illustration 14.6). The contributions that a PM system can make to management thinking become evident by examining these questions.

Based on the answers to such questions, managers can then assess their subordinates' current performance level against the organization's key success factors in order to detect any gaps between actual and current performance levels. In a well designed and flexible PM system, the outputs from such a gap analysis should include a range of options (see Illustration 14.7).

From the list shown in Illustration 14.7, the benefits of a proper PM system should be obvious. However, there are many factors to be considered in determining the most effective way of implementing an appropriate PM scheme. Whatever the system adopted, whatever the external pressures, and whatever the national HRM context, it is important to recognize that implementing performance management is a difficult

Illustration 14.5 **Advantages of cascading performance management systems top-down.**

1. Every person and group has a number of clearly defined objectives and accountabilities that support the strategic goals specific to each unit within the organization.
2. Every employee knows specifically what to do in order to achieve predetermined performance standards.
3. Managers are able to assess performance against relevant goals and monitor progress against clear objectives.
4. Managers are in a position to identify specific factors accounting for over-achieving and under-achieving performance and communicate the need for improvement if performance is not up to standard.

Illustration 14.6 **Key HRM questions covered by a performance management system.**

- What job positions, based upon their purpose and accountabilities, should assume responsibility for executing each of the organizational unit's new plans, objectives and milestones?.
- Given the unit's internal capabilities, which of these specific accountabilities can be executed by individuals?
- Which accountabilities must be executed by groups of individuals working together?
- For those accountabilities assigned entirely to a single individual, what additional capabilities, resources or tools are required to ensure execution?
- What training or development initiatives can be provided for these individuals so that they can successfully execute their assignments during the current planning period?
- For those accountabilities where individuals lack key capabilities, should the organization look outside to procure these capabilities elsewhere? Hire new people? Retain the services of outside advisers? What role can training programmes play?
- Have performance objectives been clearly communicated to each individual? Does each individual understand precisely how he or she will be evaluated against each and every business objective?
- For those objectives assigned to two or more individuals, what tools, work processes and communication mechanisms must be in place to ensure effective and efficient execution?
- Have performance expectations been clearly communicated to the appropriate units? Are they well understood and do the individuals involved understand how they must interact and add value to each other's work?
- What specific activities and tasks will need to be performed in order to execute the assigned accountabilities effectively, efficiently and on a timely basis? What are the top priority achievements?

Source: ZIG Roadmap, First Edition 1992.

Illustration 14.7 **Typical outcomes and options resulting from a performance management process.**

1. Performance improvement plan covering training and any immediate development task or experience needed.
2. Career development plan which defines the most suitable job progression for the employee, taking fully into account the wishes of the individual and the needs of the business.
3. Performance rating, followed, where earned, by a performance related reward.
4. Review of the manpower plan, setting out the new recruitment levels and selection criteria required to enhance the organization's level of skill and knowledge.
5. Review of the performance management process based on the line manager's feedback and experiences.

Source: ZIG Roadmap, First Edition 1992.

process. The indications are that four out of five systems fail in practice (Fletcher and Williams, 1992). In the next two sections we consider the following questions:

- Why is it that so many performance management systems fail?
- What are the conditions under which such systems are likely to work?
- What are the characteristics of 'good' and 'bad' performance management systems?

WHY DO SO MANY PERFORMANCE MANAGEMENT SYSTEMS FAIL?

There are a number of reasons why PM systems fail (see Illustration 14.8). For example, studies have shown that among organizations which utilize performance

Illustration 14.8 **Why performance management systems fail.**

1. The system is not used, modelled and supported at the top of the organization. Senior managers play a game of 'do as I say and not as I do'.
2. Line managers view the system as little more than an administrative burden. They do not see the benefit of energy invested in making the system work.
3. Performance objectives that were established at the beginning of the year seem less important by year end. This typically happens when performance objectives are linked to whatever project or initiative is currently a hot item, rather than being linked to critical success factors.
4. Performance objectives are written so subjectively that performance measurement at the end of the period is not possible.
5. Managers are unable to give feedback and to deal effectively and constructively with the conflict or disagreement surrounding the assessment of employees' performance.

management, 90 per cent of senior managers have not received performance reviews in the past two years. Clearly, the problem here is that performance management is not used, modelled and visibly supported at the top of the organization. Sooner or later people at lower levels catch on and no longer feel compelled to take the time to make performance management work. This typically happens when performance management is introduced or imposed by external sources as a separate technique, rather than within the context of the organization's own business planning and strategy. In truth, a PM system which is not integrated with the objectives of the organization as a whole is as unlikely to work in the longer term as all the management 'quick fix' initiatives that preceded it.

UNDER WHAT CONDITIONS DO PERFORMANCE MANAGEMENT SYSTEMS WORK BEST?

Table 14.2 gives an overview of the conditions under which performance management is likely to work best by listing the characteristics of 'good' and 'bad' PM systems. Essentially, 'good' PM systems have the following qualities:

1. Line managers own the system. Performance management is supposed to be line driven. This requires the development of a shared vision of the organization's aims and purpose.
2. Top managers are visibly committed to the system.
3. To the greatest possible extent, employees are consulted about the design of the system.

Unfortunately, many of the vital qualities listed in Table 14.2 are lacking in the majority of PM system implementations, according to a recent study by Fletcher and Williams (1992) of London University. This study looked at twenty-six organizations in the UK public and private sectors. The main conclusions were as follows:

1. Performance management is often implemented in a reactive way to deal with external pressures rather than as part of a strategic approach to examining and changing the values of the organization.
2 In most cases, there is an excessive emphasis on the bottom line or the delivery of services and not enough concern for the aims and development needs of individuals.
3. Many organizations equate performance management simply with employee appraisal or performance-related-pay.

4. Most organizations are failing to involve line managers in performance management policy. Often the chief executive or external people such as elected council members were the key initiators forcing performance management through. Line management involvement reached significant levels in only a few originations.

The result was a widespread lack of line management commitment which the authors say is one of the main reasons why PM systems are likely to founder.

Table 14.2 **Characteristics of good and bad performance management systems.**

Good	Bad
■ Tailor made to fit the particular needs and circumstance of the organization	■ Lack of strategic direction, with no clear objectives
■ Congruent with the existing culture insofar as they support the achievement of high performance standards but will help to change or reshape that culture if necessary	■ Rivalry and territorialism between departments
	■ Persistent failure to meet objectives and deadlines
■ Support the achievement of the organization's mission and the realization of its values	■ Lack of clear accountabilities and decision making
■ Define the critical success factors which determine organizational and individual performance	■ Confusion over roles in organization
	■ Middle managers feel unable to influence events
■ Clarify the principal accountabilities of managers and staff so that they are fully aware of their objectives, the standards of performance expected of them, and the quantitative key performance indicators which will be used to measure their achievements	■ Absenteeism, sickness and/or overtime out of control
	■ Workforce and middle managers resistant to change
	■ High turnover amongst key posts
	■ Staff appraisal lacks credibility
■ Enable systematic review of performance against agreed criteria in order to establish and act on strengths and weaknesses, identify potential, plan and implement career development and training programmes and provide a basis for motivation through intrinsic and extrinsic rewards	■ PRP scheme regarded as ineffective
	■ Lack of detailed information on costs and contributions
	■ Poor budgetary control and plan
	■ Outdated or inadequate management information systems
■ Develop PRP systems which provide incentives and rewards as motivators for improved performance	■ Lack of structural career and succession planning process
■ Provide an integrated approach to increasing motivation and commitment, which combines the impact of results-orientated performance appraisal and PRP systems with the actions that management and individual managers can take, such as career development and succession planning programmes to develop attitudes and behaviours which lead to better performance	

Source: Philpott and Sheppard, reprinted with permission © 1993, L. Philpott and L. Sheppard, *Managing for Improved Performance*, Kogan Page.

THE ROLE OF THE HUMAN RESOURCE FUNCTION

Given the range of factors that have to be managed with PM systems it is clear that the role of the HRM function or department is obviously related to the success of the approach. According to Williams (1991) the HRM department has five critical roles to play in the design and implementation of PM systems, as detailed in Illustration 14.9. These five roles are vital contributions to be made by the inhouse HRM department in assisting the organization and to achieve business performance and growth through its people. In essence, this is the facilitating role of the HRM function, and one that should not easily be surrendered to external consultancies (Williams, 1991).

... The HR function has a strong facilitating and support role to play that is essential if the policies are to be developed and to function in an effective and equitable way. Without that support, it may be that the additional demands performance management places on line managers would be too great. Where the HR department was trying to act in a facilitating role rather than as a driving force of performance management (as a lighthouse rather than as a World War 1 tank, as one HR director described the change in the way they were seen), they found themselves doing a rather difficult balancing act. It is important on the one hand to be able to offer support and to give guidance where necessary, but not at the cost of taking control and ownership out of line managers' hands.   Fletcher and Williams (1992, pp. 43–44).

In the last couple of years, a number of large organizations have successfully introduced performance management as a means of improving business results in the face of growing competition. The next three sections describe some example applications of PM systems in order to reveal the benefits of the performance management approach. These applications are outlined in Illustration 14.10.

Illustration 14.9 **Five key HRM department roles in implementing performance management systems.**

1. Gaining the commitment of the Chief Executive to utilize performance management as a key strategy in achieving business objectives.
2. Defining the performance management processes applicable to the particular values, culture and strategic vision of the organization.
3. Providing training to managers in the knowledge, skills and attitudes required to implement the processes in a professional manner.
4. Communicating to all employees the mutual benefits and genuinely held organization commitment to the process.
5. Monitoring and evaluating its implementation, particularly in the early years, to keep the processes 'on track'.

Source: Williams (1991).

Illustration 14.10 **Three strategic applications of PM systems.**

1. Providing structured individual guidance and direction in a period of strategic change (ICL).
2. Improving business performance through decentralized responsibility and coaching skills (ICI Pharmaceuticals).
3. Creating a cultural change centred around continuous performance improvement (Powergen).

PERFORMANCE MANAGEMENT SYSTEMS TO STRUCTURE INDIVIDUAL OBJECTIVES: INTERNATIONAL COMPUTERS LTD (ICL)

We have already described some features of ICL's HRM in Chapter Eleven, Internal Resourcing and Career Management. ICL's PM system should be seen in relation to this material. Figure 14.4 shows that the PM system introduced in ICL during the early 1980s consisted of four steps.

We use a description of the ICL system to demonstrate a series of lessons when using a PM system to provide focused individual direction:

- The importance of building a number of supporting processes around the appraisal system.
- Generating a detailed exploration of individual objectives in order to serve a variety of purposes.
- Developing an appraisal system that concentrates on both what is achieved (the objectives) and how it is achieved (the competencies).
- Developing a suitable mechanism for linking pay to performance.
- Linking the system to a human resource planning forum that ties people decisions into the business plan.

The first step of ICL's system involves the determination and setting of individual objectives, ensuring that every employee knows what role they need to play and what results they need to achieve in order to maximize their contribution to the overall

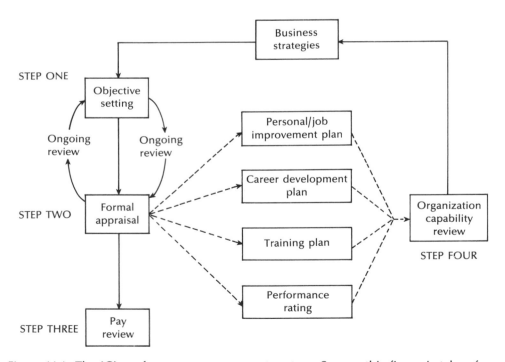

Figure 14.4 The ICL performance management system. *Source:* this figure is taken from *The Handbook of Performance Management* by F. Neale (ed.) and reproduced with permission of the publishers, the Institute of Personnel Management, IPM House, 35 Camp Road, Wimbledon, London, SW19 4UX, © 1991.

Illustration 14.11 **Three types of performance management objectives.**

1. Contribute to the achievement of the business results of the organization (i.e. key results areas).
2. Contribute to an improvement in the performance of the individual job (i.e. performance standards).
3. Contribute to the development of the individual (i.e. performance development).

business. To achieve this the organization uses a cascade process down the organization from the very top through the four or five management levels (we have discussed the advantages of a top-down approach in a previous section). Typically it takes a month to complete the whole exercise for every person in the organization. Each person agrees six to eight ongoing objectives for the year with their manager. The ICL system acknowledges three different types of objectives (see Illustration 14.11). These objectives are not seen as rigid but dynamic, and used as part of the formal appraisal process at the end of a twelve-month period.

The second step comprises the formal performance appraisals (discussed more fully in the second half of this chapter) which are conducted at least quarterly through one-to-one discussions. To aid this process all managers are provided with a descriptive list of about thirty criteria or 'competencies' (discussed in Chapter Eleven) to help classify characteristics. Examples of the competencies used by ICL are initiative, adaptability, communication, delegation and planning. The outputs of the appraisal include a personal improvement plan, a career development plan, a training plan and a performance rating which summarizes performance against the objectives for the preceding twelve months.

The third step is the pay review. At ICL, pay is determined by the line manager of the individual within overall organization-wide pay guidelines, taking into consideration the performance rating, the position of the individual in the salary scale, the person's recent salary history, the market value of the job and factors such as scarcity of skills. The inclusion of such a strong link over compensation and reward reflects the Anglo-Saxon business style of the organization.

The final and fourth step is known as the Organization and Management Review (OMR) and takes place at each management level in the organization on a quarterly basis. The OMR itself covers a number of strategic HRM issues such as organization structure, career development and succession of senior staff, long-term training issues, and any key resourcing issues that have a significant impact on the business. Within ICL this review is seen as one of the major 'added value' roles of the HRM department. Where there are gaps between the present and ideal situation, appropriate actions are taken and reviewed against the business objectives of that activity.

PERFORMANCE MANAGEMENT SYSTEMS AS A COACHING TOOL TO IMPROVE BUSINESS PERFORMANCE: ICI PHARMACEUTICALS

Sheard (1992) has described ICI's approach to performance management. We have described some other aspects of ICI's HRM elsewhere – such as the decision to restructure around the SEM in Chapter Eight. The description of ICI's PM system here is used to highlight:

■ Decentralized ownership of a PM system.

- The importance of coaching and identification of potential when PM systems are used as a tool for improving business performance.
- The need to align job roles and accountabilities with overall business objectives.
- The importance of training support to develop the skills of line managers operating a PM system.

During the 1980s the organization's pharmaceuticals business faced major challenges, such as an expiry of a patent on a major product, competition for resources to support existing products and the race to the markets in a highly competitive industry. In response to growing competition, the chief executive decided that the best way to improve business performance was to improve the individual performance of the people working in it. So, in 1989, a PM system was initiated in ICI with the view that: '. . . the future success of the various businesses depends on developing the talents and performance of its employees' (extract from an ICI group-wide initiative, May 1989). The ICI system focuses on developing people's potential rather than just assessing current performance. The operational system of performance management used in ICI Pharmaceuticals is shown in Figure 14.5.

The ICI PM system was designed to answer the organization's business needs. Therefore another key feature of the system was the aligning of jobs with the business. Evaluated job descriptions – written in a standard format containing job purpose and principal accountabilities – were introduced as part of the wider PM initiative. The task of introducing and integrating performance management in departments was given to line managers throughout the business. These managers, known as 'PM coaches', were selected by their heads of department because of their legitimacy and status with their peers, good interactive skills, and enthusiasm about a shift in business

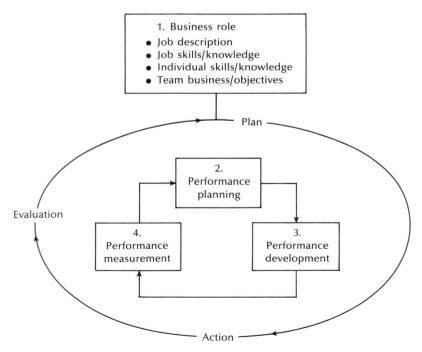

Figure 14.5 ICI Pharmaceuticals' performance management system. *Source*: Sheard (1992), reprinted with permission, © Angela Sheard, 1993.

Illustration 14.12 **Benefits resulting from ICI's focus on performance potential and coaching.**

- Clearer business objectives and personal targets, with an improved correlation between the two.
- Emphasis on developing individuals to help them achieve their targets.
- Closer relationship between individuals and line managers, involving coaching, encouragement and motivation.
- More objective assessment of performance against targets, leading to a more performance related pay system.

Source: Philpott and Sheppard (1992).

culture. Over an eighteen month period they received training (including a two day workshop on coaching skills), and were responsible for delivering training themselves on a local, departmental basis.

Interestingly, under the ICI system, each function and department was free to develop its own reward plan, reflecting its own business goals and objectives. Heads of departments were provided with guidelines for measuring performance and a recommended process for evaluating information on performance. They also had at their disposal a portfolio of reward options and were encouraged to determine the type, scale and timing of rewards. A new module on managing diversity is currently being designed within the performance management framework, focusing particularly on helping staff to achieve their full potential and enhancing teamwork. The ICI system, with its linking of individual potential to business performance, decentralized design and detailed training support, brings a number of benefits as shown in Illustration 14.12.

USING PERFORMANCE MANAGEMENT TO INTRODUCE CULTURAL CHANGE: POWERGEN

We have discussed the topic of organizational culture and the management of culture change in Chapter Seven. Philpott and Sheppard (1992) cite the corporate value statements of organizations such as PowerGen and Ciba Geigy to illustrate the objectives of organizations which have developed a strong performance management culture. We describe some elements of the performance management culture at PowerGen in order to highlight the third and final main application of PM systems (see Illustration 14.13).

Many organizations are using PM systems to manage the culture of the organization.

Illustration 14.13 **Elements of a performance management culture at PowerGen.**

1. Ensures that corporate culture is characterized as one where striving for continuous improvement is the norm.
2. Cascades a clear understanding of what has to be achieved by each individual and the manner in which it is to be achieved down the organization.
3. Facilitates continuous improvement of individual performance against key corporate objectives and leadership practices.
4. Devolves performance improvement responsibility and accountability to individual managers (rather than the HRM function).

Source: Philpott and Sheppard (1992).

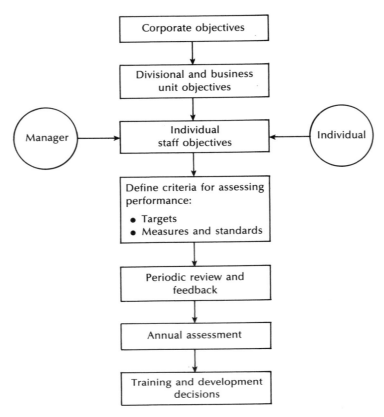

Figure 14.6 The objective setting process at PowerGen. *Source*: Armstrong (1992), reprinted with permission, © 1993, M. Armstrong (ed.), *Strategies for Human Resource Management*, Kogan Press.

To meet its business targets, PowerGen developed a system which focused predominantly on individual performance objectives. Under this system, each division within the organization had to develop its critical success factors and specific objectives which individual managers have to cascade down the organization (in a similar fashion to the ICL system that has already been described). The objective setting process used by PowerGen to help managers set annual performance targets is shown in Figure 14.6.

PERFORMANCE MANAGEMENT SYSTEMS AND THE APPRAISAL PROCESS

The three examples of total PM systems have all highlighted the importance of a strong objective setting and appraisal process at part of the overall system. Indeed, many PM systems have evolved out of rudimentary appraisal schemes. Given that more and more appraisals form part of a full-blown PM system in which rewards are linked to performance, managers must be able to identify and assess employee performance accurately and reliably. Having an effective performance appraisal program is an obvious prerequisite to introducing an effective PM system. Without clarity about the critical task behaviours and valid and reliable measures of such behaviours it is impossible to determine what performance merits a certain level of incentive compensation. Appraisal is therefore an essential element of any PM system, principally because what gets measured gets done. Appraisal is best defined as:

... the systematic description of job-relevant strengths and weaknesses within and between employees.   Cascio (1982).

It is a delicate topic within HRM and is associated with numerous knotty technical problems. There is probably nothing better than a good appraisal system, but nothing worse than a bad one. Formalized staff appraisal started in the 1920s, and for some time was predominantly a characteristic of large, American organizations. Over the past twenty years, however, the use of performance appraisal – at least in terms of expressed organization policy – has become more widespread in Europe, and a particularly strong feature of British HRM. A British survey by Torrington and Mackay (1986) showed that 229 out of a total of 350 organizations have a formal appraisal system for senior management, compared with 251 organizations for middle management, 189 for clerical staff, and 92 for manual unskilled and semi-skilled workers. Over a quarter of the respondent organizations carried out no appraisal at all. It is interesting to note that 140 organizations said they had increased the time that they spent on appraisal over the previous three years, compared with 112 organizations that spent the same amount of time, and only 29 organizations where the time spent had decreased. Given the centrality of the appraisal process to most PM systems, we give detailed consideration in the rest of this chapter to the topics outlined in Illustration 14.14.

PURPOSE OF APPRAISAL SCHEMES

In the context of HRM formal appraisals can serve several purposes (see Illustration 14.15). Without a clearly defined purpose, the different aims of appraisal frequently clash (Livy, 1988). From a management perspective, there are three main groups of appraisal systems. An appraisal system can therefore have several clients. It needs to satisfy the combined needs of individual subordinates, the manager and the organization. It is rarely possible to satisfy all the above purposes in one systematic process. Moreover, in addition to informing personnel decisions about reward, performance or potential, appraisal systems may be called upon to serve other objectives such as communication, culture change, counselling, and identification of training needs.

Illustration 14.14 **Key topics to be considered in connection to appraisal systems.**

- The purpose of appraisal systems.
- Alternative performance criteria: outputs, skills and competencies, task and process or stakeholder expectations.
- Techniques of measurement.
- Behaviourally anchored rating scales.
- Appraisal interview and interviewer style.
- Obstacles to effective appraisal.
- Checklist for effective implementation.
- Upward appraisal and multi-rater systems.
- Self- and peer appraisal.
- Customer appraisal.
- Evolution of appraisal schemes.

Illustration 14.15   **Three main purposes of appraisal.**

Reward reviews

Procedures that relate to the allocation and attribution of awards, rewards and benefits to a particular individual. This does not just include salaries and compensation, but other types of reward that can benefit employees such as power, status, self-fulfilment and freedom.

Performance reviews

Concentrate on improving or at the very least maintaining the performance of employees. Concerned with the development and motivation of staff by looking at what areas are important to the performance of each individual and how well he or she is doing.

Potential reviews

Related to succession planning. Concerned with what an individual will be capable of doing in the future and when he will be ready to do it. Review information is assembled about an individual's past attainments, current performance and personal aspirations. A judgement is made as to his or her future career.

Many of the problems connected with performance appraisal (discussed later in this chapter) can be traced to the confusion in the minds of employees between reward reviews, performance reviews and potential reviews. Although the three types of reviews overlap and interlock to a certain extent, Randall, Packard, Shaw and Slater (1984) recommend that they should be kept separate in practice because each is exceedingly difficult to do well.

… To ask a line manager at one sitting to appraise a person's performance, evaluate it and then predict what he would be capable of in the future is more than a highly trained specialist could be expected to do. The burden on the manager and the risk to the individual should therefore not be imposed. All three reviews certainly need to be achieved and co-ordinated. But if a successful procedure is to have a chance of developing, an organization should break its existing procedures into three.   Randall, Packard, Shaw and Slater (1984, p. 14).

Traditionally, appraisal schemes have concentrated on past and current performance. The main motivation to introduce an appraisal system was to set performance objectives and to provide a basis for wage increases or new levels of merit pay. Today, however, performance appraisal processes are often paired with the identification of training needs and long-term potential. For instance, Torrington and MacKay's (1986) survey suggests that 61 per cent of UK organizations use the performance appraisal system to assess training and development needs of managers, and 57 per cent use it to assess managers' future potential. The study also showed that clerical and secretarial staff are increasingly being included in the appraisal process: 57 per cent of organizations said they were using some form of performance appraisal to assess training and development needs of white collar workers, and 40 per cent used it to assess the future potential of clerical staff. This survey, and many others which have followed, testified to the multiplicity of purposes to which appraisal can be put and for which it is instituted (Holdsworth, 1991).

Demonstrating the interdependence of ETD systems with many other areas of HRM, performance appraisal is a useful source of information to identify ETD needs. Some 38 per cent of Swedish organizations and 35 per cent of British organizations use performance appraisal in this way (Holden and Livian, 1992). The figure is between 21 and 24 per cent for Swiss, Norwegian and Dutch organizations, 13 per cent for Italian organizations and under 10 per cent for German, Danish and Spanish organizations.

WHAT SHOULD BE APPRAISED? ALTERNATIVE PERFORMANCE CRITERIA

Once the purpose of the review has been clarified, the scope of the appraisal has to be determined. Performance is often only considered at the individual level against a set of undefined, generic personal characteristics (e.g. 'leadership') or a set of specific yet narrow technical skills (e.g. 'financial analysis') derived from outdated job descriptions that focus on task execution rather than on outputs. So what should be appraised? If someone is measuring your contribution and strengths and weaknesses in a job, what is the most important measure? There are in essence four different dimensions to consider, detailed in Figure 14.7:

1. What you achieve.
2. How you achieve it.
3. The extent to which you have completed the whole task.
4. The expectations or deliverables for internal and external stakeholders.

The majority of organizations favour the first of these measures: what is achieved. The setting of targets or objectives is often felt to be the simplest and least onerous way of providing a framework for performance. However, given many of the problems with appraisal systems noted in this chapter, the more innovative and committed organizations are adopting broader performance criteria. We discuss the use of customer ratings towards the end of the chapter.

TRADITIONAL TECHNIQUES OF MEASUREMENT

Having clarified the purpose of the appraisal and decided on the most appropriate criteria, a decision has to be made over what techniques and measurements will be used to make the appraisal. In most organizations employees are appraised by their immediate manager on the grounds that those who delegate work and monitor performance are the best placed to assess performance. However, supervisors, line managers and subordinates, either as raters or ratees, frequently do not trust the use

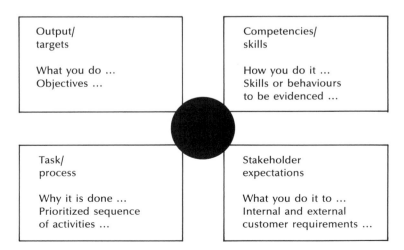

Figure 14.7 Alternative performance criteria used to appraise performance.

Illustration 14.16 **Appraisal measurement techniques.**

1. *Simple ranking.* The manager lists all employees on a sheet of paper and orders them from highest to lowest on one or more criteria.

2. *Pairwise comparison.* Each employee is compared to every other in terms of an overall characteristic such as 'present value to the organization'. The manager's task is to choose the 'better' of each pair, and each employee's rank is determined by counting the number of times she or he was rated superior.

3. *Rating.* A number of employee characteristics such as leadership and initiative are rated on a scale which may range from 'outstanding' to 'unacceptable'. Sometimes the number of employees who can obtain a specific score is predetermined by means of a forced distribution. This method eliminates clustering almost all employees in the middle or at the top of the scale.

4. *Behavioural checklist.* The manager is provided with a series of statements that describe job-related behaviour, and indicates which of these statements, or the extent to which each statement, describes the employee.

5. *Critical incidents.* The appraiser is required to record incidents of the employee's positive and negative behaviour and to give counselling to improve poor performance during a given period. The record of incidents forms the basis of the appraisal report.

6. *Comparison with objectives.* The employees and their manager agree objectives at the beginning of the appraisal period. Individual performance is then reviewed at the end of the period on the basis of how far these objectives have been met.

of information from appraisals. The process of completing appraisals can be as simple as filling out a narrative report once a year about an employee's quality and output of work, or it may involve one or more of a range of sophisticated measurement techniques. The techniques listed in Illustration 14.16 form the core of most appraisal systems. The language used to express the rating scale is critical. It is extremely important to decide what exactly is being rated: the person, the performance, or the match or contribution to job requirements (see Figure 14.8). The last two ratings are the most appropriate. Appraisal schemes that are seen as evaluating the worth of an individual are doomed to failure. It is very difficult to tell someone they are a poor

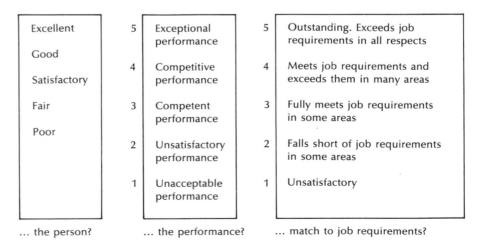

Excellent				
Good				
Satisfactory	5	Exceptional performance	5	Outstanding. Exceeds job requirements in all respects
	4	Competitive performance	4	Meets job requirements and exceeds them in many areas
Fair	3	Competent performance	3	Fully meets job requirements in some areas
Poor				
	2	Unsatisfactory performance	2	Falls short of job requirements in some areas
	1	Unacceptable performance	1	Unsatisfactory
... the person?		... the performance?		... match to job requirements?

Figure 14.8 What is being rated: the person, the performance or the match or contribution to job requirements?

person, and stronger evidence than a manager's rating is needed to allow this. Moreover, real poor performers should have been dealt with through other processes (recruitment and selection, job placement, training and development systems). However, it is easier to assess overall performance against some specified notion, or even more appropriately, to assess the match or contribution to the specified job requirements. Many organizations fall into the trap of allowing a good appraisal scheme to be thrown into disrepute because of a poorly worded rating scale.

BEHAVIOURALLY ANCHORED RATING SCALES (BARS)

This is a comparatively new method which overcomes some of the problems with conventional rating scales. The format consists of sets of statements which describe key aspects of performance in the particular job and have been scaled on a single dimension, ranging from very poor behaviour to outstanding behaviour. For example, for a corporate loan assistant, a rating scale could include 'preparing credit reports' and 'assisting customers with loan applications'. Once the scaling is completed, appraisers use it to evaluate the performance of each subordinate holding the job in question. We provided an example of a rating scale used to evaluate performance across a 'behavioural language ladder' in the previous chapter.

The advantage of BARS is that the scales are directly applicable to the job being evaluated and are therefore more precise than the often vague traits used in conventional rating scales. On the other hand, it is sometimes possible for a job incumbent simultaneously to display behaviours associated with high and low performance. In a situation such as this, it is difficult for the appraiser to determine whether the employee should be rated high or low. In addition, BARS require considerable effort to develop.

APPRAISAL INTERVIEWS AND INTERVIEWER STYLE

Because of the difficulties already outlined, most medium-size and large organizations rely heavily on the interview. They require their managers to set up an annual appraisal interview with each individual. Any such appraisal interview has to gather evidence of what actually happened during the whole of the review period. In theory, the interview should have the following aims:

1. Suggest ways in which the employee's good work can be continued and how he or she can achieve further improvement.
2. Encourage the employee to discuss his or her strengths and weaknesses.
3. Clarify how far agreed objectives have been met.
4. Identify obstacles that are restricting performance.
5. Produce an agreed plan of action that will lead to improved performance.

Increasingly, appraisal is seen as less about judging and rating and more about coaching and counselling; this entails a very different style by the manager or supervisor implementing the appraisal system. Actual appraisal style is clearly very individual, and each style has its appropriate uses, as manifested in the various types of approaches to performance review interviewing described in Illustration 14.17. However, the average behaviour has undoubtedly evolved over the last two decades, and the emphasis on 'joint problem solving' has grown considerably in organizational approaches to performance reviews.

Illustration 14.17   **Four types of appraisal interview styles.**

Tell and sell

Telling the individual what their performance is, spelling out as precisely as possible the nature of the problems hampering the individual's performance during the review period, and then selling the solution. This approach appears authoritarian and stresses that the manager knows best. It is common when a senior manager interacts with a young and relatively inexperienced member of staff.

Tell and listen

The manager describes his or her own observations and thoughts about the individual's performance and then waits until the individual suggests the line of action which the manager has previously decided upon as being the solution to the problem. The manager then directs the discussions to settle on this line of action and encourages the individual to suggest how it can be accomplished.

Listen and support

Talking out a problem, used when the problems raised by the manager unleash a stream of complaints. It is also applicable to situations where nothing can be done about the performance problem except to chip away at it as best one can.

Joint problem solving

Often called 'non-directive interviewing' or even 'counselling'. The manager indicates he or she is willing to listen to all problems put forward by the individual and, in return, the subordinate listens to the performance problems the manager wishes to raise. This approach can be very difficult and time consuming, but when the individual is suffering conflict, frustration and alienation, the situation demands it.

Source: Randall *et al.* (1984).

For a long time it was thought that only specialists (i.e. psychologists) could carry out valid appraisals, and the immediate manager was thought to be rather too close to the individual to be entrusted with this process. Hence, performance appraisal was delegated to the personnel department or the special services of management consultants. The current norm, however, is for employees to be appraised by their immediate manager, with the human resource department playing a more facilitating and advisory role. This means that appraisal often involves a good deal of time and effort on line managers, but it has the advantage that form filling can be kept to a minimum and those who have to operate the system also have an incentive to make it work as effectively as possible.

Randall, Packard, Shaw and Slater (1984) suggest that there are four styles of reviewing an individuals performance. These four styles are not always effective; appraisers must choose the one most appropriate to their plan and subject.

OBSTACLES TO EFFECTIVE PERFORMANCE APPRAISAL

However, the use of appraisal interviews is no guarantee that effective feedback and reinforcement will be offered. Many managers are not skilled enough to adopt the whole range of interview styles. A survey of over 500 organizations by Cascio (1986) found that employees reported a number of general reactions to appraisal interviews. Many employees were less certain about where they stood after the interview than before it. They evaluated supervisors less favourably after the interview than before it and felt that few constructive actions or significant improvements resulted from the appraisal interviews. A survey by Kinnie and Lowe (1990) suggested that only 20 per cent of HRM managers considered their appraisal systems effective and only

11 per cent believed that their system effectively linked pay to performance. This is a disturbing finding when one considers the cost of introducing performance appraisal and reward systems, which is reported to be in the range of 10 to 20 per cent of the first year's salary bill (Torrington and Blandamer, 1992).

It is therefore important to understand the main obstacles to effective appraisals. There is unfortunately much evidence that as a tool to help execute performance management, most employee appraisal systems are woefully deficient.

> ... In many organizations performance measurement and management systems are little more than human resource bureaucracies with forms, rules, and review layers. These paper-driven systems are burdens to managers and hence are completed marginally, if at all. They are typically seen by raters as extra work and by ratees as at best irrelevant, at worst demotivating.
>
> Schneier, Shaw and Beatty (1991, p. 279).

The failure of most traditional performance appraisal systems is reflected in the frequency with which new schemes are developed, modified, and discarded by organizations (Bruns, 1992). Most modern corporations and many other organizations devote considerable resources to the development, maintenance, and perfection of systems to assess and appraise performance and the systems they develop to increase individual performance and productivity are often ingenious. However, what should be measured is often not clear; what should be evaluated is often uncertain; and the assumptions they make about behaviour are often complex and tenuous. Whilst the issues and problems are clear, the solutions tend not to be.

> ... Although most managers acquire a good deal of experience in interviewing techniques during the course of their everyday activities, the performance review discussion tends to be approached with as much circumspection by the reviewer as by the reviewed.   Long (1986).

The biggest obstacle to the operation of an effective appraisal scheme is probably the reluctance or inability of managers to conduct appraisals. Many line managers dislike giving poor ratings, and few have the stomach for passing on the bad news to employees. The main obstacles to effective performance evaluation are shown in Illustration 14.18.

Schneier, Shaw and Beatty (1991) focus on four key reasons why performance appraisal has been of little or no value to most organizations. They argue that most

---

Illustration 14.18 **Obstacles to effective performance evaluation.**

1. Performance appraisals are often a required but unrewarded managerial task so most managers spend no more than minimal acceptable time and effort in evaluating subordinate's performance.
2. Few managers relish giving poor or even mediocre ratings to popular but unproductive subordinates.
3. Performance appraisal systems and processes that were constructed with confidence that they would be effective are frequently modified within a year of their introduction and replaced completely after only a few years.
4. Appraisals are often seen as an unwanted and unnecessary intrusion into working relationships between managers and the workforce.
5. There is ambiguity and inconsistency around the main objectives of the appraisal system, what it takes to achieve high ratings, who does the appraising and whether employees should see their appraisal reports.
6. Most performance appraisal systems use measures that do not truly reflect what is important for success.
7. Many managers do not have the skills to handle poor performers and ratings tend to bunch around the centre of the scale.

appraisal systems have the wrong measures, judgements, owners or results. Performance appraisal systems typically require numerous, finite evaluations that too many managers are unable and unwilling to make accurately on a one-dimensional rating scale. Several studies have empirically demonstrated that such finite evaluations (on a one-dimensional rating scale) are unreliable. The ratings are more reflective of the appraiser's personality and judgement style than the subordinate's actual behaviour.

There is also a tendency to bunch ratings around the average point. Medoff and Abraham (1980), for example, examined the distribution of performance ratings for more than 7,000 managerial and professional employees in two large manufacturing organizations and found that 95 per cent of the employees in each organization were crowded into two rating categories. Rojot (1990) cites a Hay France survey of 220 of the largest organizations in 1987 which found that 30 per cent of managers were rated as 'very good', 56 per cent as 'normal'. Only 2 per cent were rated as 'bad'. Adopting forced-distribution rating systems – in which managers are forced to adhere to a specified distribution of performance ratings – may mitigate managerial tendencies to assign uniform ratings but may also generate important counterproductive side effects (Murphy, 1992).

... The performance measurement and management system is too often viewed as the province of the human resource unit, not the manager's accountability. It is likely that human resource managers designed and implemented the system. (It) is hence seen as extra work by managers, who resent completing forms merely to process a salary increase and are not skilled at providing constructive performance feedback.   Schneier, Shaw and Beatty (1991, p. 282).

In one study, almost half of the executives interviewed indicated they did not receive performance reviews and those that did described it as rushed and vague (Longenecker and Gioia, 1988). While most researchers and practitioners agree that performance appraisal should improve performance, the facts are that the traditional manager-driven appraisal system has failed to produce the expected benefits (Mohrman 1991) and is not a viable force for development in most organizations.

CHARACTERISTICS OF SUCCESSFUL PERFORMANCE APPRAISALS

The best performance appraisal system is one in which an individual's performance and contribution are measured quantitatively and in an objective fashion (Cook, 1991). This is not always possible for some positions because of the nature of the tasks and accountabilities. If the system is to be perceived as effective, the appraisals must be seen by employees to be valid, germane to the job, and free from bias, discrimination, or favouritism.

ACAS has produced a checklist of items (see Illustration 14.19) which need to be considered when a new appraisal system is being introduced. Clearly, to make the new system work, it is important that senior managers support the idea of appraisals. They should fully accept that those who carry out the appraisals are properly trained and have sufficient resources available to complete interviews, fill in the forms and carry out follow-up work. In addition, it is essential to make the system as straightforward as possible. As noted earlier, appraisal schemes often fail because of over-elaborate paper work. The evaluation forms should be designed for and with the collaboration of those who will be using them in order to keep them as simple and as clearly written as possible. Further, a senior manager should be given responsibility for ensuring that the appraisals are held and that they are being carried out properly. Some organizations set an annual timetable for the completion of the various stages of the appraisal process

Illustration 14.19 **Key points for a successful appraisal scheme.**

Advisory Booklet No: 11 of the British Advisory, Conciliation and Arbitration Service (ACAS) states that for appraisal schemes to work effectively it is necessary to:

1. Make sure that senior managers are fully committed to the idea of appraisals.
2. Consult with managers, employees and trade union representatives about the design and implementation of appraisals before they are introduced.
3. Give appraisers adequate training to enable them to make fair and objective assessments and to carry out effective appraisal interviews.
4. Keep the scheme as simple and straightforward as possible.
5. Monitor and update the schemes regularly.

and circulate this timetable to all managers. Another method is to spread appraisals throughout the year, possibly on the anniversary of the employee's appointment. This takes the pressure off the line manager to carry out a large number of appraisals at the same time.

It is also important to give appraisers formal training in setting appraisal criteria, giving constructive feedback on performance, discussing performance problems and difficulties, and so on. Randall *et al.* (1984) suggest that organizations considering the introduction of an appraisal scheme should wait a couple of years, and concentrate first on developing the appraisal skills which would give a subsequent scheme at least half a chance of succeeding. Finally, it is important to monitor the system in order to determine whether it needs to be modified to meet the changing needs of the organization. The views of the users should be obtained about the scheme in general and in relation to any specific problems they have encountered. It is also important to obtain the views of those who are being appraised. All employees should be briefed and told about the overall objectives of the scheme, how the appraisal scheme works and what is expected of them individually. Clearly, schemes will quickly become ineffective if they are not modified to take account of changes in the size of the organization, in products, skills and occupational groupings or if they are not sufficiently flexible to meet the requirements of the individuals

UPWARD APPRAISALS AND MULTI-RATER SYSTEMS

In recent years, a number of new approaches to performance appraisal have been developed by leading organizations in order to eliminate some of the main weaknesses associated with the methods used in traditional approaches. We now consider the main developments. Although performance appraisal remains a largely top-down process, there is a discernible trend towards other types of ratings. In Chapter Eight we described the development of matrix structures and delayered cluster structures. Working in such structures entails having several different stakeholders in an individual's performance.

As part of the trend towards multiple-rater systems, 'upwards' or 'subordinate' appraisal is being introduced in certain countries. The trend is most marked in the US and the UK (Bernardin, 1986; London, Wohlers and Gallagher, 1990; and McEvoy and Beatty, 1989) but has also been documented in Canada, South Africa and the former Soviet Union. Notable organizations that have adopted the process include General Electric, AT&T, American Express and Gulf Oil in the US, and W.H. Smith, BP Exploration, Rank Xerox and Standard Chartered Bank in the UK. From 1977–86

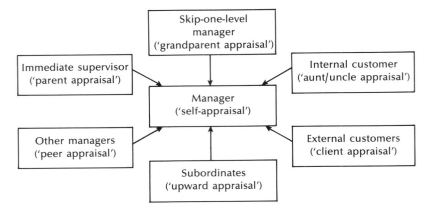

Figure 14.9 Potential appraisers in a multi-rater system. *Source*: reprinted from T. Redman and E. Snape, 'Upward and onward: can staff appraise their managers?', *Personnel Review*. **21(7)**, 32–46, with kind permission from MCB University Press Ltd.

the proportion of organizations using a second reviewer in the UK rose from 7 to 20 per cent (Redman and Snape, 1992). There is no evidence of the extent to which continental European organizations are moving towards multi-rater and upwards appraisal systems but they are likely to become more widespread as Total Quality Management, Employee Involvement and Empowerment programmes develop. There are, in fact, a range of potential appraisers (see Figure 14.9).

As mentioned earlier, there are a number of different performance criteria that may be used to appraise managers. As attention moves away from focusing purely on 'what is achieved' (against targets and objectives) towards 'how it is achieved' and the meeting of 'stakeholder expectations' then the logic of using multiple-rater systems becomes

Illustration 14.20 **Upwards appraisal at Federal Express UK.**

A number of organizations have adopted upwards appraisal as an important feature of two-way communication programmes. In Britain, for example, Federal Express's Business Logistics – which handles the complete distribution needs of the organization's customers and has escaped its parent firm's large-scale redundancies in Europe – conducted an innovative feedback programme in 1992 in which employees had a chance to say formally what they think about the performance of their superiors without fear of reprisal or victimization. As reported in *PM Plus* (1992), the appraisal survey itself consisted of a single form inviting tick-box responses to a series of statements about the individual manager and the organization, such as 'My manager lets me know what is expected of me' and 'Working for Fedex will probably lead to the kind of future I want'. The form was identical for every level of employee from lorry driver to managing director and the response rate was 90 per cent. Completed forms were sealed and sent from Coventry to the worldwide Fedex HQ in Memphis, Tennessee, where they were computer processed to emphasize the anonymity of the procedure. Ian Gordon, the organization's UK personnel director, felt the value of the procedure lay predominantly in the feedback session, where managers discussed the aggregated responses with their group. Low scoring managers were considered as critical groups and were given an extra check every six months. The meetings in these groups could be long and painful and often required a member of the personnel department to sit in as a facilitator. The questionnaire itself may not have always contained the real problem, but simply acted as a medium for making dissatisfaction known.

Source: Ian Gordon, Personnel Director of Federal Express, *Personnel Management Plus* (1992).

Illustration 14.21 **Best practice requirements for an upwards appraisal system.**

1. The personnel department should maintain tight administrative control over distribution and data collection.
2. Subordinates should be assured complete anonymity and confidentiality.
3. The information gathered should be part of a 'multiple rater system' in which the data supplied by subordinates is considered in conjunction with feedback from other sources.
4. Subordinates should rate specific behavioural tasks rather than psychological traits such as leadership, initiative, and dependability.
5. All the parties involved should discuss to information gathered.

Source: Bernardin (1986).

clear. Of all the sources of ratings, upwards or subordinate appraisal has often been suggested as the most obvious means of improving the effectiveness of performance appraisal programmes (see Illustration 14.20). Upwards appraisal places greater emphasis on management style and behaviour, as assessed by those who experience it most often (subordinates or peers). It can provide valuable insights into effectiveness and can help to overcome some of the problems of single-rater bias or over-lenient assessments. Upward appraisal also tends to fit well into an employee involvement or total quality management philosophy. Indeed, it is frequently introduced as a logical development from employee attitude surveys in order to pinpoint problems with individual managers.

As managerial spans of control increase upward appraisal provides a way of maintaining quality in the appraisal process. Bernardin (1986), in particular, has argued that subordinate appraisal is 'one of the most practical and efficient methods for enhancing the quality of an organization's appraisal system by making superiors more aware of their impact on their subordinates'. At times, of course, subordinates may abuse the system by manipulating the evaluation of their superiors, particularly if they feel threatened by them and have no other means of expressing their grievances. In general, however, the advantages appear to outweigh the disadvantages. Nevertheless, in order to keep the system running smoothly and effectively there are a number of good housekeeping rules and these are detailed in Illustration 14.21.

SELF- AND PEER APPRAISAL

Torrington and Hall (1991) argue that there is increasing awareness of the biases that operate when we rate other people and the subjectivity of our judgements. One way of eliminating some of these biases is for people to appraise themselves. On the other hand, self-appraisals tend to be more lenient, less variable, and show less agreement with the judgements of others.

Although self-appraisal is seldom used as a technique for assessing performance, many organizations require individuals to carry out some form of self-appraisal as part of their preparation for the appraisal interview. The difference between the individual's own evaluation and the supervisor's appraisal can then be used as a basis for subsequent discussion during the interview.

Peer appraisal can be a useful method of assessing performance particularly when superiors lack access to some aspects of a subordinate's performance. They are particularly useful when teamwork and participation are key aspects of the employee's performance.

APPRAISAL BY CUSTOMERS

A general tenet in marketing and business today holds that high quality goods and services are favoured in the marketplace (Parasuraman *et al.*, 1991). Both research and organization experience support that tenet and further suggest that high quality service performance produces measurable benefits in profits, cost savings, and market share. As a result of this evidence, some organizations (notably Anglo-Saxon ones) have placed service quality and customer satisfaction at the top of a list of performance criteria for assessing individual and corporate performance (see Illustration 14.22). This reflects the emphasis given to customer service as a key success factor (Moss-Kanter, 1991) by the Anglo-Saxon cluster of countries (see the discussion in Chapter Seven).

Similarly, British Airways routinely has clients rate the quality of its products and services relative to those of competitors, and uses this information to determine salary increases of its employees. In 1991, BA was voted 'Best Airline Overall' by Business Traveller magazine for the fourth year in a row. The success of Rank Xerox (see Illustration 14.23) and others shows that it is possible to achieve big improvements in both service quality and profits in a reasonably short time. The challenge of HRM in such organizations as British Airways, Rank Xerox and IBM UK is to integrate every aspect of performance appraisal into a broader process that is, itself, integrated with

Illustration 14.22 **An appraisal scheme to emphasize customer satisfaction at IBM UK.**

IBM UK introduced a new appraisal scheme in 1993 under which staff were assessed on their contribution to satisfying customers as well as their performance in improving quality. The customer could be internal or external and an employee's contribution could be appraised in relation to a team, a department, a function or a business. Most employees are assigned five or six outputs (key results, services or products for which they agree responsibility) and agree measurable targets with their manager. The rating scale used has five points, measuring 'contri- bution' (from outstanding contributor to unsatisfactory). Key customers contribute to the assessment. The rating on contribution largely determines the salary increase. In 1993, a difficult year for IBM, only staff making an outstanding contribution received a salary increase from a 2 per cent merit pot. An employee's eligibility for promotion (but not the salary award) is also influenced by a ranking of contribution not to targets, but to other groups of employees with broadly similar skills and responsibilities.

Source: Incomes Data Service (1993).

Illustration 14.23 **Linking bonuses to customer satisfaction at Rank Xerox.**

Rank Xerox realized they would have to recast their performance evaluation and rewards system if they were to make their executives and staff more responsive to customers and recoup their lost market share. As a result, in 1988, they purposely linked the bonuses of their top 100 managers to the overall satisfaction scores achieved in their quarterly survey of customers. So successful was the move that now all staff have bonuses related to customer satisfaction measures. Rank Xerox managers say they are recording the highest customer satisfaction and market share scores they have had for years. Employees have become much more sensitive to customer needs than ever before.

marketing, operations and human resource strategies. At all times, the need to take a customer perspective is paramount.

... Having everyone in the company work towards keeping customers and basing rewards on how well they do creates a positive company atmosphere. Encouraging employees to solve customer problems and eliminate the source of complaints allows them to be 'nice', and customers treat them better in return. The overall exchange is more rewarding, and people enjoy their work more. Not just customers but also employees will want to continue their relationship with the business. Reicheld and Sasser (1990).

CONCLUSION: AN EVOLUTION IN THE USE OF APPRAISAL SCHEMES

In conclusion, it is clear that in addition to the emergence of new techniques for appraising employee performance and potential, there have been a number of changes in the goals and content of the appraisal process over the last two decades (see Illustration 14.24). The increased openness of appraisal schemes is a result of the dissatisfaction with the secrecy, and subsequent criticism, of many traditional schemes that as a matter of policy did not allow the employee to scrutinize the appraisal. Shell was an early exception and a shining example of how constructive it could be to share the appraisal of an employee's 'ultimate level of promotability' (Holdsworth, 1991). The majority of current schemes formally require the employee to see most, if not all, of the personal documents and information kept by the personnel department.

George (1986) suggested that the degree of openness that is required in the appraisal process is 'unlikely to materialize without an atmosphere of mutual trust and respect – something that is conspicuously lacking in many employing organizations' (p. 32). The appraisal process, therefore, needs to reflect the culture and climate of the organization for it to be effective. Pryor (1985) also makes the point that organizations should aim to achieve consistency between their normal day-to-day management style and the treatment of people in appraisal interviews and performance management systems. It would be unrealistic to design an appraisal system which requires interactions of a nature and quality which are not evident in the relationships that people normally have at work and this naturally requires a deep understanding of the balance between the impact of national cultural differences (see Chapters Three and Ten and the discussion at the beginning of this chapter) and developments in the organization culture towards a performance management philosophy. Changes in the nature of the appraisal system can be a strong promoter of a performance management culture, despite initial cultural reluctance. Where a performance management culture can be engendered, this chapter has suggested the following key points.

Illustration 14.24 **Main evolutionary developments in appraisals.**

1. Appraisals have become more open.	4. Ownership of the appraisal has tended to shift from the centre to the periphery, from the personnel department to the line manager and the appraiser.
2. The purpose and content of appraisals have changed.	
3. The appraisal style adopted by managers has become more dynamic.	

LEARNING POINTS FROM CHAPTER FOURTEEN

1. Performance management is a strategic management technique rooted in Anglo-Saxon thinking. It has the potential to make a significant contribution to organizational effectiveness and growth because of its centrality to productivity and competitiveness. It links business objectives and strategies to individual goals, appraisal and rewards through a defined process.

2. It has become more important as an area of HRM because of increased market competition, changes in the number of vertical layers in the organization, increased devolution of control to managers, the individualization of pay and benefits and a requirement for more flexible labour markets.

3. Performance management is a difficult topic to cover on a pan-European basis because: approaches to it range from the very simple to very complex, reflecting different levels of HRM sophistication; there are alternative philosophies which create either rewards-driven or human resource development-driven systems; there are cultural differences in management style and the manager–subordinate relationship; the legal and social context determines attitudes to performance management; and there are marked differences in the extent to which European HRM managers have control over the various parts of the system (such as rewards) as a consequence of their historical role.

4. A performance management system helps identify business objectives and the factors contributing to their achievement, assigns key tasks to units and individuals, clarifies what is to be achieved by whom and when, determines how the results will be achieved, monitors results, recognizes achievement and encourages learning from experience. It typically includes mission statements, business strategies and objectives, values statements, critical success factors, performance indicators, performance appraisals, pay reviews and a performance improvement process. A number of important HRM questions are raised by such systems.

5. There are differences in the adoption of key performance management tools such as variable pay and appraisal techniques. Performance appraisal has a high priority in France, but less so in the UK and Germany. Italian organizations lag behind quite markedly and also show a preference for maintaining flexibility in appraisal and objectives. However, the situation is changing rapidly with over a third of large organizations modifying their systems.

6. Managers in certain countries are more or less effective in leading and motivating their subordinates. The efficiency of the manager–subordinate relationship is at its lowest in Portugal, Spain and Greece, quite poor in the UK and Italy but relatively efficient in Switzerland, Germany, Belgium and Denmark.

7. There are philosophical differences in the way in which performance management techniques are used and these are linked to cultural factors such as the level of power distance and uncertainty avoidance. Such factors, if not appreciated, can lead to the failure of techniques, as happened with management by objectives in France. They reflect the fear of face-to-face conflict, the way in which authority is conceived and the way in which managers are made and selected.

8. Many performance management systems fail because they are not used, modelled or supported at the top of the organization, they are seen as administrative burdens, poor objectives and targets are set or there are poor feedback and interpersonal skills amongst the managers.

9. The conditions under which performance management systems succeed are when they are tailor made to suit the organization, fit in with the existing organizational or

national culture, support the underlying values of the organization, define critical success factors and clarify accountabilities, enable a systematic review of performance and provide a way of integrating the motivation and commitment of the workforce to a set of individual or group actions. The HRM function has a critical role to play in this.

10. Appraisal is the systematic description of job-relevant strengths and weaknesses within and between employees. Appraisal can serve three main purposes: a review of performance, the attribution of rewards or an assessment of potential. Confusion typically results if one scheme is used to do all three things. Many performance management systems have evolved out of rudimentary appraisal schemes.

11. There are a range of alternative performance criteria that may be used in appraisal schemes. These range from assessing what is being achieved (the outputs, targets and objectives), how it is being achieved (the skills, competencies, behaviours and values), the expectations of internal and external stakeholders and the extent to which the whole task is being performed against best practice understanding.

12. Performance against these criteria may be assessed using a series of techniques. The most common are simple ranking, rating scales, checklists or critical incidents. The language used to define the rating scale and what is being rated is very important. The extent to which the whole scale is used is linked to whether the rating is about the person, the performance or the match to job requirements.

13. There is considerable variation in the appraisal interview style that may be adopted, ranging from tell and sell, tell and listen, listen and support and joint problem solving approaches.

14. The most common shortfalls in appraisal schemes occur when the wrong measures are used, judgements are inaccurate (for example, ratings tend to converge to the average or avoid assigning poor performance to anyone), the results are owned by the wrong people or the impact on behaviour and future performance is obscured.

15. There have been a number of developments in recent years both to improve the quality of the appraisal process and to fit it more effectively into the strategic needs of a performance management system. These include upwards appraisals, self and peer assessment or customer assessments.

CHAPTER FIFTEEN

Industrial Relations

INTRODUCTION

The past two decades have been a time of widespread change in the nature of European industrial relations. Throughout the 1980s, many trade unions saw their membership decline, established arrangements for collective bargaining came under review, and many employers sought to place greater emphasis on flexibility in hours of work, performance related remuneration systems and direct communication between managers and employees. Furthermore, and perhaps crucially, there is some evidence of significant changes in attitudes among employers and workers, in that significant numbers of companies and employees now are trying to eliminate hierarchical differences between manual and non-manual workers, to look at the working patterns of their foreign competitors, and to increase efficiency by the removal of restrictive practices and by reducing the size of workforces. It is difficult to determine when these trends first began and what were the underlying causes. However, the recent experience of many European organizations suggests that something of a revolution is now getting under way in the management of industrial relations, and this impression seems to be borne out amply by the opinion of many academics and commentators, concerned as they are with practical problems in industry (Bamber and Lansbury, 1987; Blum, 1987; Curson, 1986; Poole, 1986b).

In Parts One and Two of the book we highlighted a series of pressures that are transforming the industrial relations context in Europe (see Figure 15.1). The process of business restructuring and foreign investment has resulted in changed parentage for many organizations, power imbalances in the wake of strategic alliances, and changes in the level of employment after a prolonged period of rationalization. As organizations become more transnational they are negotiating changes in their structures, control systems and business processes. There are conflicting pressures to promote more flexibility in employment practices and contracts, whilst also encouraging higher levels of employee participation and involvement. Finally, there is a gradual evolution in the supra-national legislative context and macroeconomic pressures for competitive devaluation and social dumping. These all have significant implications for industrial relations.

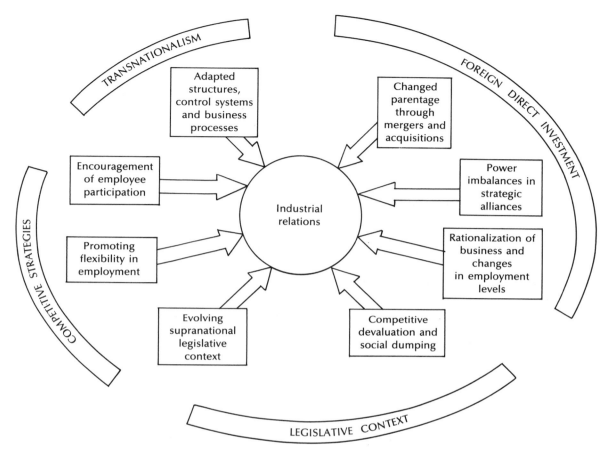

Figure 15.1   The factors influencing change in European industrial relations.

MAJOR TRENDS IN EUROPEAN INDUSTRIAL RELATIONS

The PWCP study discussed in Chapter Two places industrial relations as the second most important HRM function after training and development in France, Italy, Spain and the Netherlands (Hilb, 1992). As we noted in Chapter Four, over the past ten years there has been a dramatic increase in international competition and the competitiveness of newly industrialized countries has improved significantly. At the same time, employment has continued to drop in the manufacturing sector, there has been an increase in the proportion of women, part timers and temporary workers, and the number of large factories and offices, which once employed most of the workforce, has become less significant. Furthermore, and perhaps above all, there has been much more inward direct investment by Japanese organizations in key sectors such as information technology and car manufacturing, as well as a series of European acquisitions and mergers. This has sometimes brought with it an added impetus for structural, cultural and managerial change in European organizations as discussed in Chapter Five.

Not surprisingly, these changes have had implications for the relationship between workers, employers and their respective collective organizations, as borne out by the findings of many recent studies of industrial relations. For example, a cross-national

Illustration 15.1   **Major areas of cross-national difference in industrial relations systems.**

- Political influence of trade unions.
- Level of union membership.
- Unity between and within trade unions.

- Patterns of striking activity.
- Role of the state.
- Levels of collective bargaining.

comparison of European industrial relations systems before and after 1980 shows some remarkable differences between the present state of affairs and that prevailing in the 1970s in most European countries (Baglioni and Crouch, 1991). The main areas in which these differences are most apparent are outlined in Illustration 15.1 and considered in the following sections.

THE POLITICAL INFLUENCE OF TRADE UNIONS

Over the past ten years, there has been a general decline in the political strength and presence of trade unions. As Baglioni and Crouch (1991) point out, in almost every European country unions have been forced to retreat. Their strength has declined, not as dramatically as some observers have contended, but still significantly, both in terms of actions and in underlying conditions. This trend is most evident in Britain (see Illustration 15.2).

The political weakening of trade unions can also be seen, however, in other European countries with more moderate government policies, such as Belgium, Denmark, the Netherlands and even Sweden. In France, Spain and Portugal, unions have been helped by the growth in institutional recognition, but have at the same time been politically weakened by their association with left-wing parties. For example, in Portugal the two national union confederations are linked to the socialist and communist parties (Mendes, 1992).

LEVEL OF UNION MEMBERSHIP

The level of unionization in European countries is shown in Table 15.1. Associated with the foregoing development has been a perceptible decline in the level of union membership. This trend has been most pronounced in countries with already low union density such as Spain and France. For example, Spanish unionization was claimed to be 52 per cent of wage and salary earners in 1977. One provisional estimate gives present union membership in Spain at about 10 per cent (Estivill and de la Hoz, 1991) whilst the Organization for Economic Co-operation and Development (OECD) estimate membership at 16 per cent (see Table 15.1). A number of economic reasons

Illustration 15.2   **Political weakening of trade unions in Britain.**

- Weakening of union influence on government policy making.
- Lower degree of union recognition accorded by employers.

- Reduced role union officials have been permitted to play in serving the needs of their members.

Table 15.1 **Percentage of workforce in a union in twelve EU countries.**

Country	% of workforce belonging to a union
Denmark	73.2
Belgium	53.0
Ireland	52.4
Luxembourg	49.7
UK	41.5
Italy	39.6
Germany	33.8
Portugal	30.0
Netherlands	25.0
Greece	25.0
Spain	16.0
France	12.0

Source: data based on OECD estimates

for this general decline in unionization have been suggested, including economic recession, increased unemployment and other aspects of the business cycle. This is because it is generally assumed that workers will join unions if the expected benefits and returns from the services which unions provide – in the form of relative wage gains, taking up grievances, access to specialized information and the like – exceed the expected costs. These costs comprise not simply membership dues but also such factors as the possibility of employer hostility and retaliation (in the form of job loss or victimization) as a result of taking up membership.

This explanation is not entirely convincing, however, since up to 30 per cent of the rise and fall of union membership typically remains unexplained in studies which concentrate solely upon key components of the business cycle (Bain and Elsheikh, 1976). Furthermore, the assumed negative correlation between union density and economic recession is absent in a number of European countries. In Belgium, for example, the level of unionization has remained high during the 1980s, aided by the stable employment of a large public sector and the important role of the unions in the administration of unemployment benefits and health insurance schemes. Similarly, in 1980 the three Swedish central trade union confederations all reached about 80 per cent density in their respective fields of blue collar, white collar and professional workers. By 1986 they were at about 85 per cent, despite the fact that manufacturing employment went down and there was a significant increase in the (part time) employment of women (Rehn and Viklund, 1991).

Analysis of economic conditions does not suffice for an adequate understanding of the declining levels of unionism during the 1980s. In France, for example, the short periods of union membership growth – interspersed with long periods of stability and decline – seem to have depended more on political events than upon changing economic circumstances (Sellier, 1978). Also, there is evidence that in most European countries, unions have been slow to adapt to the unfavourable demographic and political environment of the 1980s. As one commentator puts it:

The inadequacy of traditional union methods in representing workers with high skills and some individual market power is certainly a problem. Thanks to the historical progress made as a result of the heterogeneity of the wage- and salary-earning classes, the prevailing acceptance of the objective needs of the capitalist economy and the full social and intellectual 'citizenship' attained by employers and managers, the labour movement exerts less attraction than it once did. It is more prosaic, more pragmatic, less enveloped in an emotional aura, frequently not raising dramatic questions. Young workers themselves, except for an activist, politicized minority, make requests of the unions that are less strongly associated than in the past with social and political ideals and militancy and with analogous support for the parties of the left.

Baglioni (1991, pp. 35–36).

This point is reinforced by the trend in Italy, where the overall unionization rate peaked in 1978 at 48.3 per cent and then began to decline rapidly, essentially because of a poor union response to the growth of employment in non-union sectors and industries (Negrelli and Santi, 1991).

DEGREE OF UNITY BETWEEN AND WITHIN TRADE UNIONS

To add to their problems, the trade union movements during the 1980s have been weakened by internal divisions between unions and, in some cases, between workers within the same union or organization. In addition – most notably in countries with a plurality of central confederations – there has been a growth of independent unions, outside the national confederations, for the most part white collar and management unions in the private sector or separate unions in the public sector and the services (Cella and Treu, 1982). One of the most vivid manifestations of this has been the rise of militant rank-and-file organizations, particularly in the private sector, for example, the Italian 'cobas', which have proved a thorn in the flesh of the official trade unions (Ferner and Hyman, 1992b).

According to Baglioni (1991) there have been two main reasons for the lack of unity within the labour movement:

1. The longstanding impact of relations with political parties on the union's posture and strategy.
2. The more recent and multifarious diversity of interests among workers themselves.

The former issue is found chiefly in countries with more than one central federation, with fundamentally political and ideological lines of division such as France, Italy, Spain, Portugal and Belgium. The latter is found in countries with a single central labour organization such as the British Trades Union Congress and the German Trade Union Federation or central organizations that are divided essentially not by ideology but by occupational status such as blue collar and white collar unions (LO and TCO in Sweden). The structure of trade unions varies widely across Europe, as shown in Illustration 15.3.

Given this set of developments, it is easy to predict an increase in the inclination of employers to take advantage of declining union power. Nevertheless, as research by Baglioni (1991) shows, there is no European country in which an employer strategy of outright attack against labour unionism prevails. Instead:

.. in most European countries change at the enterprise level has been achieved in co-operation with rather than in opposition to the workforce and their union representatives. This partly reflects the unions' 'new realism', but it also stems from the fact that the union presence is institutionalized in many countries.   Ferner and Hyman (1992b, p. 33).

PATTERN OF STRIKE ACTIVITY

A fourth significant indicator of the changing nature of European industrial relations is the pattern of strikes. Although international comparisons of this aspect of industrial

Illustration 15.3 **Trade union structure in selected EU countries.**

Belgium

Three trade unions are considered to be representative in Belgium: the Christian trade union (ACCV/CSC); the socialist trade union (ABVV/FGTB); and the liberal (conservative) trade union (ACLVB/CGSLB). These three organizations represent workers who belong to the same sectors. Belgium has no company-based unions. The unions are represented in national economic and social institutions. They play an important role in the political and economic life of the country.

Denmark

In Denmark, there are more than seventy trade unions, who co-operate in several central organizations. The biggest organization is the Danish Confederation of Trade Unions (LO). This represents approximately two-thirds of the workforce and operates in the private as well as the public sectors. There are also close relations with the Social Democratic Party. Approximately 85 percent of the Danish workforce are union members.

France

France has five national multi-professional unions. The Confédération Générale du Travail (CGT) is the largest union, although its membership has shrunk in recent years. Second is the Confédération Française des Travailleurs (CFDT), closely followed by the Force Ouvrière, which rivals the CFDT in certain industries and regions. The Confédération Générale des Cadres (CGC) is clearly smaller than these three, but it is the major union for those in management positions. Lastly, the Confédération Française des Travailleurs Chrétiens (CFTC) is gaining ground, but is relatively weak in relation to the other unions. While French unions and political parties are independent, the links between them are strong. Although the workforce in general is not strongly organized, the unions' role has never seriously been contested, their power and legitimacy deriving from their capacity to represent the social classes from which they have sprung.

Germany

The trade unions in Germany predominantly take the form of industrial associations. This means that employees of an individual company are often represented by a single trade union, irrespective of their occupation. In 1989 there were 16 trade unions, unified in the Deutsche Gewerkschafts-

bund (DGB), as well as a separate trade union for civil servants and the white collar trade union Deutsche Angestelltengewerkschaft (DAG). In addition there were seventeen smaller Christian trade unions, joined in the Christliche Gewerkschaftsbund (CGB). After re-unification in 1990 the West German unions began to organize in the new federal states, and this has had a considerable effect on the overall membership figures. The union density has nevertheless fallen slightly.

Italy

There are three main trade unions in Italy. While all three claim political independence, the largest, the Confederazione Generale Italiana del Lavoro (CGIL) has traditionally had a strong left-wing orientation. The other two are the Confederazione Italiana Sindicati Lavoratori (CISL), which has a Christian Democrat orientation, and the Unione Italiana del Lavore (UIL), with a Social Democratic and Republican orientation. Italian unions cover industrial sectors rather than crafts or occupations. In recent years, however, a growing number of independent unions have been formed, representing the interests of professions rather than industries. Cobas, roughly translated as grass-roots committees, have become active in the public sector, and are generally perceived as a threat to the representative status of the main unions.

The Netherlands

In the Netherlands, unions of nearly all occupations are joined in three federations: the General Workers Federation (FNV), the federation of Christian National Workers' Unions (CNV), and the Council for middle managers and higher-level employees (MPH). Approximately 28 percent of the workforce is unionized. Dutch trade unions are not regarded as militant and do not use strikes as the major way to achieve their goals. They are financed solely through membership contributions.

Spain

Closely following the Latin model, Spanish unions are highly political and ideological organizations. The principal actors are the Comisiones Obreras (CCOO), which closely identify with Marxist ideology, and the Union General de Trabajadores (UGT), which is associated with the socialist government. Union membership is estimated at 10 percent of the workforce. The most recent development is the tentative possibility of a merger between the two organizations, or at least closer co-operation on a variety of issues. This reflects a convergence in policies following the partial estrangement of the UGT from the socialist government.

The UK

In Britain, the national confederation of trade unions is the Trades Union Congress (TUC). It represents seventy-three individual unions and provides a forum in which affiliated unions can collectively determine policy. Trade union structure varies widely in the UK. It is not uncommon to have several unions representing one or more occupational groupings within the same company, office or factory. Where this happens, there will usually be a joint committee formed to discuss matters of common concern or to negotiate jointly with the employer. The reliance on these shopfloor arrangements is a unique feature of the fragmented nature of trade union organization in the UK.

Source: Brewster, Hegewisch, Lockhart and Holden (1993), reprinted with permission © 1993, Academic Press Ltd.

relations are very difficult due to the many idiosyncratic national definitions and distinctions of 'industrial action' (Shalev, 1978), the data derived from such agencies as the International Labour Organization (ILO) and the OECD suggest that three general trends, listed in Illustration 15.4, are emerging.

In Britain, the total number of strikes decreased from 1,538 in 1982 to 903 in 1985, followed by a further decline from 1,016 in 1987 to 781 in 1988, though within this overall decline there have been some major disputes, such as those in the health and civil services (Crouch, 1991). The volume of strikes, as measured by the number of working days lost per thousand employees, has also declined significantly during the 1980s (see Figure 15.2). This trend can be seen most clearly in Norway and Sweden, where despite recent declines in real earnings, the famous 'Saltsjobaden agreement' has been able to avoid 'careless conflict damaging third parties and society as a whole in an irresponsible way' (Rehn and Viklund, 1991, p. 313).

There has also been a significant change in the nature of industrial disputes, as indicated by the emergence of some large and very bitter conflicts (as in the British mining disputes of 1984 and 1992), the high incidence of strikes in the public sector and in the services, the declining number of disputes over 'bread-and-butter' issues, and a greater incidence of short but large 'political' strikes not aimed directly at the employer as a bargaining partner but at the political system and public opinion.

A direct link has been postulated between these developments and key aspects of the business cycle. The underlying assumption is that unions are more likely to press their demands in prosperous periods, when the cost of a strike for their members will be low.

The success of a strike depends on the extent to which workers can minimize costs to themselves while imposing large costs on the employer. Periods of low unemployment increase the bargaining power of workers on both counts; employees have greater alternative sources of work while the costs to the firm both in the form of profits foregone and of difficulty of attracting substitute workers are increased.   Kaufman (1982, p. 479).

Illustration 15.4 **Shifts in the pattern of strike activity.**

- General decline in the number of strikes since the mid-1970s.
- Volume of strikes (number of man days lost per thousand employees) has declined significantly.
- Shift in the nature of disputes.

1991

Working days lost per 1,000 inhabitants
per year

ranking			days	
1	Switzerland	▮	0.04	
2	Austria	▮	0.39	
3	Germany	▮	0.68	[1]
4	Japan	▮	1.42	[1]
5	Netherlands	▮	1.61	
6	Turkey	▮	3.87	
7	Norway	▮	3.99	
8	Denmark	▯	10.31	
9	France	▣	14.25	
10	Ireland	▣	14.35	
11	Portugal	▦	39.21	
12	Finland	▦	41.17	
13	Sweden	▦	48.26	
14	New Zealand	▦	58.40	
15	USA	▦	66.83	
16	Australia	▦	71.44	
17	UK	▦	72.12	
18	Canada	▦	82.97	
19	Spain	▦	96.16	
20	Italy	▦▦▦▦	404.00	[1]
21	Greece	▦▦▦▦▦▦	654.08	[1]
–	Belgium/Lux.		–	
1	Indonesia	▮	0.17	
2	Hong Kong	▮	0.57	
3	Malaysia	▮	1.43	
4	Pakistan	▮	1.71	
5	Thailand	▮	1.81	
6	Mexico	▯	10.39	
7	Chile	▣	23.04	
8	Venezuela	▣	25.51	[6]
9	South Africa	▦	35.89	
10	India	▦	40.23	
11	Singapore	▦	65.33	[1]
12	Korea	▦▦	149.87	
13	Brazil	▦▦▦▦	416.80	[2]
–	Hungary		–	
–	Taiwan		–	

Figure 15.2 Industrial disputes. *Source*: World Economic Forum (1993), reprinted with permission, © 1993, World Economic Forum.

Strikes are expected to peak during periods of economic prosperity and decline during periods of recession. This is indeed what most macroeconomic studies of strike frequency in the UK and the US have found (Ashenfelter and Johnson, 1969). On the other hand, recent studies in Italy, the Netherlands and Germany show that a macroeconomic model of strike frequency is too simplistic to explain the changes in strike activity over the past few years (Soskice, 1978; Bean, 1985). For example, in the Netherlands and Belgium, where a major reduction in the number and volume of strikes has taken place since the mid-1970s, this decline can be explained largely by the growing amount of direct state intervention in the process and substance of wage negotiations. As Spineux (1991) points out, this impasse developed gradually, starting in 1975, and was confirmed in 1981 with the signing of a collective agreement dictated by the government, which drastically limited the scope for wage rises in both the private and public sectors. Similarly, it has been suggested that the decline in strike activity in Norway and Sweden is linked to the permanent mediation agency and the special mediation commissions, appointed by the government in situations where large companies appear to have difficulties in reaching agreement through negotiation (Rehn and Viklund, 1991). In Spain, new legislation requires minimal service to be provided during strikes, and the right to strike is lost if the constitution is subverted, it there is interference with parliament, or if the strike seeks to modify a final settlement (Filella, 1992).

ROLE OF THE STATE

The European economic context of the 1980s was marked by greater, more active and more direct intervention by the state in the management and conduct of industrial relations. This trend has been most visible within the UK, where unions have been forced to retreat and their ability to mount 'official' strike action in support of collective bargaining has been severely limited. As Sisson (1989) puts it:

In its role of legislator, the (Conservative) government has effectively abandoned the commitment of its predecessors to collective bargaining as the most effective method of determining pay and conditions; trade unions – and the collective bargaining for which they are responsible – are seen as major factors in the stickiness of the response of wages to changes in demand and supply. Both the Employment Acts of 1980 and 1982 reinforced the right of individuals to dissociate themselves from trade union membership and imposed stringent requirements for maintaining a closed shop or union membership agreement. There have also been attempts to limit the ability of trade unions to mount industrial action in support of collective bargaining. Following the 1980 and 1982 Employment Acts, trade unions no longer enjoy immunity from the common law where there is picketing other than at the place of work. Secondary action to uphold union recognition practices, and industrial action which has not been 'approved' by secret ballot, have also been outlawed.   Sisson (1989, pp. 25–26).

Similar examples of increased government intervention in industrial relations can be found in almost every European country. For instance, the German Christian Democrat government has recently introduced measures to reduce the role of national collective agreements in favour of local arrangements; the French government (by passing and implementing the notorious Auroux Laws in the early 1980s) has imposed on employers an obligation to negotiate at factory level; and in Italy, the main feature of industrial relations in the 1980s was the government's role transformation from one of spectator or referee to one of active mediator between business and labour (Negrelli and Santi, 1991).

LEVELS OF COLLECTIVE BARGAINING

Not surprisingly, the economic and political transformations of the 1980s also led to changes in the management of industrial relations. The most important of these was the widespread diminution of the traditional representational role played by employers' associations in favour of a more restricted advisory role or totally independent collective bargaining. Another was the general tendency in European organizations to decentralize collective bargaining and employee relations to the lowest possible level. In practice, employers vary in their determination to pursue these two objectives, but they have shown a clear preference in recent years for company, or plant-level, bargaining and generally more participation by local union and management representatives in industrial relations.

In Britain, for example, research has shown that multi-employer negotiations are no longer the major means of pay determination in private manufacturing industry. Two-thirds of manual workers are now covered directly by single employer bargaining (Brown, 1981). The incidence and impact of national and industry-level bargaining between the central labour and employer organizations has been significantly undermined in other countries where this type of bargaining was quite widespread and important in the past, such as Germany, Belgium, the Netherlands, and even Sweden. The rapid decline of centralized industrial relations since 1984 in Italy has meant that any matter can now be discussed at any level and any time. Matters already dealt with in the industry agreement can be renegotiated at shop floor level (Cella and Treu, 1982). Consequently, the May 1986 collective agreement between Conindustrial (the private industrialists' association) and the united union confederations paid less heed to macroeconomic factors than the centralized agreements of 1983 and 1984. It is more adapted to the needs of individual organizations, creating additional room for decentralized bargaining on wages and working hours (Negrelli and Santi, 1991). In France, there is considerable scope for local employer initiatives despite tight central regulation and local industry-wide or national agreements (Besse, 1992).

The reasons for this general trend towards decentralized bargaining have been in part economic (as a result of generally high unemployment) and in part political (as a result of the alteration in the balance of power in favour of management) (see Illustration 15.5).

A significant factor leading towards decentralized bargaining may have been the growing number and influence of multinational enterprises. Although the evidence is limited and based largely on general questionnaire survey data, there is evidence that multinational enterprises, particularly European owned ones, rarely become directly involved in the handling of industrial relations issues by their subsidiaries, believing that there should be minimal central interference on these matters (Hamill, 1984). The effects of increased international competition and the need for flexibility may have encouraged managers in multinational companies to decentralize collective bargaining and to reduce their reliance on central employer confederations.

IMPLICATIONS OF HRM FOR INDUSTRIAL RELATIONS

In Chapter Two we reviewed the empirical evidence for the move towards European HRM. Teague (1991) argues that the advent of HRM does not, in practice, constitute

Illustration 15.5 **Reasons behind the trend to decentralized bargaining.**

- Strong competition for supply of scarce labour.
- Informal agreements to match the ability of more prosperous organizations to pay.
- Greater capital intensity and tighter integration of industrial processes enhancing worker bargaining power.
- Growing number and influence of multi-national organizations.
- Increased international competition and requirement for flexibility.

Source: Bean (1985); Hamill (1984).

a neat or concise set of policies, but rather represents an *à la carte* menu from which personnel managers pick and choose appropriate measures.

The strengthening of internal labour markets, coupled with decentralization of collective bargaining and pay negotiations associated with the development of HRM have played a major role in internalizing the personnel function within the organization, thereby loosening employee relations from many of the wider (and national) labour market institutions and influences. Moreover, more European organizations have introduced *gemeinschaft* arrangements inside the enterprise as they moved away from a collective focus towards the individual – with increased consultation arrangements, more performance related pay and weakened trade unions in an attempt to increase corporate identity and loyalty amongst employees.

Significant changes therefore occurred in the 1980s not only in the coverage of collective bargaining and in the levels at which it is undertaken, but also in its content. It may still be too early to identify definite, general trends in the type of issues governing the process of labour negotiations. In recent years, however, there has been widespread and increasing preoccupation with the following issues:

- Flexibility.
- Demand for shorter hours.
- Demand for employee participation.
- Internationalization of IR.

THE FLEXIBILITY ISSUE

During the 1980s, employers have been experimenting with new forms of employment contracts which allow them to reduce labour costs and to attract the number and type of people their business requires into jobs. The most notable manifestations of this are shown in Illustration 15.6.

In Petrofina, for example, an agreement to reduce weekly hours and eliminate overtime makes provision for the use of outside contractors to meet peak workloads or cover for sickness (Evans and Curson, 1986). Not surprisingly, moves towards greater flexibility have been vigorously opposed by a number of labour organizations. The Intersindicale in Portugal and the Confédération Générale du Travail (CGT) in France have refused to talk about flexibility in labour negotiations. In most cases, however, the initial rejection has given way to a strong propensity to negotiate about the conditions for change. This shift indicates the general alteration in the balance of power in favour of management. It has led to a reduction of restrictive practices, new

Illustration 15.6 **Manifestations of the flexible organization.**

- Annualized hours contracts (in which employees agree to work a certain number of hours each year rather than fixed hours each week).
- New forms of shiftworking (such as five crew shiftworking at Pedigree Petfoods).
- Use of part time workers to provide cover for longer opening hours or weekend working.
- Use of temporary or short term contract staff to meet trading peaks rather than having to resort to overtime.
- Use of subcontractors in preference to full time or part time employees in a growing number of enterprises.

forms of shiftworking, and a range of alternatives to the employment of full time permanent staff.

CHANGES IN LEGISLATION REFLECTING GREATER FLEXIBILITY

The trend towards greater flexibility has been accompanied by changes in the law concerning employment and remuneration. Notable examples are the 1982 Hansenne law in Belgium, the 1985 public employment agreement in Italy, and the French laws of 1986, 1987 and 1991 on the duration and organization of flexible working time. As a result of these initiatives, organizations in both the public and private sector now have more freedom to:

- Recruit and dismiss employees.
- Increase the use of part timers and subcontractors.
- Extend the opening hours of their businesses.
- Use employees' time and equipment to best advantage.

DEMAND FOR SHORTER WORKING HOURS

Another issue that acquired great importance in collective bargaining during the 1980s was reductions in the length of the working week (see Figure 15.3). The debate often led to major disputes concerning the maintenance or improvement of employment levels and in the mid-1980s both the German and British engineering sector saw major industrial action.

In an endeavour to create a more consistent approach to this issue, the European Union recently submitted a proposal for a directive on the re-organization of working time across the community to the Council. Based on article 118a of the EEC treaty (which provides for the improvement and harmonization of the protection of workers' health and safety) this proposal aims to set the framework for a basic set of minimum provisions regarding minimum daily and weekly rest periods, and minimum conditions regarding hours of work, overtime, holidays, shift patterns, and night work throughout the EU. Discussions have not yet led to the establishment of a common position. However, negotiations to reach sufficient agreement between member states for a common position to be adopted by a qualified majority in 1993 are continuing in the Council working group.

DEMAND FOR EMPLOYEE PARTICIPATION

Demand for greater employee participation and workers' requests for direct involvement in management decision making are among the salient features of European industrial relations in the last two decades. They have generally met with strong employer and union opposition, especially in Britain, where unions have sought to extend workers' influence through collective bargaining. Whilst all trade union officers have not acted in this way, those initiatives of managements and workers which have failed to relate to collective bargaining have been met with some suspicion (Poole, 1986b), and hence, forms of participation that do not include a role for union representatives did not progress far during the 1980s.

1991

Hours per week paid per worker in
manufacturing activities

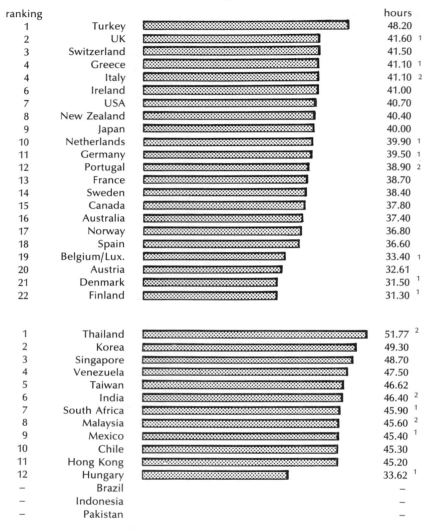

ranking			hours	
1	Turkey		48.20	
2	UK		41.60	[1]
3	Switzerland		41.50	
4	Greece		41.10	[1]
4	Italy		41.10	[2]
6	Ireland		41.00	
7	USA		40.70	
8	New Zealand		40.40	
9	Japan		40.00	
10	Netherlands		39.90	[1]
11	Germany		39.50	[1]
12	Portugal		38.90	[2]
13	France		38.70	
14	Sweden		38.40	
15	Canada		37.80	
16	Australia		37.40	
17	Norway		36.80	
18	Spain		36.60	
19	Belgium/Lux.		33.40	[1]
20	Austria		32.61	
21	Denmark		31.50	[1]
22	Finland		31.30	[1]
1	Thailand		51.77	[2]
2	Korea		49.30	
3	Singapore		48.70	
4	Venezuela		47.50	
5	Taiwan		46.62	
6	India		46.40	[2]
7	South Africa		45.90	[1]
8	Malaysia		45.60	[2]
9	Mexico		45.40	[1]
10	Chile		45.30	
11	Hong Kong		45.20	
12	Hungary		33.62	[1]
–	Brazil		–	
–	Indonesia		–	
–	Pakistan		–	

Figure 15.3 Working week. *Source*: World Economic Forum (1993), reprinted with permission, © 1993, World Economic Forum.

Yet, a growing number of organizations have begun to deal with workers directly, ignoring or cutting across union representatives.

... this constitutes one of the major novelties in current industrial relations and makes a breach with the traditional trade unions and bargaining model. It is a breach that has affected countries with varying past experience of bargaining and has been encouraged by both cultural (that is, Japanese patterns) and structural (changing labour force composition) motives.

Baglioni (1991, p. 25).

Thus in many organizations there has been a growing involvement of workers in decision making through various forms of quality circles. The use of participation to

Illustration 15.7 **EU initiatives to increase participation.**

- A directive in February 1975 covers the case for consultation on collective redundancies.
- The Vredeling Proposal on information disclosure to embrace procedures for informing and consulting employees.
- The Fifth Directive submitted to the council in October 1972 and originally designed to ensure that workers are represented in the governing bodies of all undertakings with fifty or more employees.
- A proposal on 25 January, 1991 submitted to establish a European works council in all undertakings in which the number of employees is not more than 1,000 within the community and with at least 100 workers in each of two member states.

enrich job design is discussed in Chapter Twelve. A number of large organizations have also implemented forms of financial participation by workers such as profit-sharing and the distribution of shares to employees.

During the 1970s and 1980s, there have also been a series of important initiatives for increased participation from the institutions of the European Union (see Illustration 15.7). In practice, it would be up to the employers and trade unions to decide on the nature, composition, functions and powers of the most recently proposed council and only where it proves impossible to reach agreement would a decision be imposed. There are works councils in one form or another in several EU countries outside Germany, such as France, Portugal, Spain and Ireland. There has also been a new EU proposal on financial participation. The objective of the proposal is:

... to encourage wide-ranging usage of the various forms of employee participation in company profits and trading results, either by profit sharing or by equity-shareholding or by a combination of the two.   *Social Europe* (1991, p. 21).

In France, it is compulsory for firms employing more than fifty workers to have a profit sharing scheme (Besse, 1992). It is too early to determine the effects of these proposed directives on the form and degree of employee participation in different European countries and companies. However, judging by the lack-lustre success of their predecessors and the generally hostile reaction from employers to the new set of EU proposals, their impact on contemporary industrial relations is not likely to be very spectacular.

INTERNATIONALIZATION OF INDUSTRIAL RELATIONS

In the past two decades, the emergence of truly global organizations has increased pressure on trade unions to counter the considerable power and influence of multinational enterprises (MNEs). More specifically, Kennedy (1978) has identified the seven characteristics of MNEs as the basis for union concern (see Illustration 15.8). In addition to these concerns, multinational enterprises have sometimes been accused by trade union representatives of 'transplanting' management policies and practices directly from one country to another. Particularly in Britain, there has been concern over the emergence of so-called Japanese management practices, including single union representation, the use of pendulum arbitration to resolve disputes, and the harmonization of working conditions for manual and non-manual employees. In Chapter Five we outlined a significant integration of European management and transfer of practice in the wake of a wave of mergers and acquisitions. This will reinforce the concerns outlined in Illustration 15.8.

Illustration 15.8 **Threats posed to unions by multinational enterprises.**

- Formidable financial resources. This includes the capacity to absorb losses in a particular foreign subsidiary that is in dispute with a national union.
- Alternative sources of supply. This may take the form of an explicit 'dual sourcing' policy to reduce the vulnerability of the organization to a strike by any national union.
- Ability to move production facilities to other cheap labour countries.

- Superior knowledge and expertise in labour relations.
- Remote locus of authority.
- Production facilities in many industries.
- Capacity to stage an 'investment strike' in which the organization refuses to invest any additional funds in a plant, thus ensuring that the plant will soon become obsolete and non-competitive.

Source: Kennedy (1978).

Although there have been attempts by labour unions to exert influence over MNEs decision making through international organizations such as the European Trade Union Confederation (ETUC) and the International Confederation of Free Trade Unions (ICFTU), they have met with limited success. The reasons for this general lack of success are summarized in Illustration 15.9.

In times of economic recession, conflicts of interest become insurmountable barriers to international co-operation within the labour movement. Nevertheless, there have been a few cases in which attempts by trade unions to exert influence over MNEs' behaviour have been successful. The best known of these is the Badger case. In 1976 the Badger organization, a subsidiary of Raytheon, a US company, decided to close its Belgian subsidiary, and a dispute arose concerning redundancy payments (Blanpain, 1974). Badger (Belgium) NV had filed for bankruptcy, so the Belgian unions argued that Raytheon should assume the subsidiary's financial obligation. Raytheon refused, and the case was brought before the Committee on International Investments and MNCs of the OECD. Following a declaration by this committee in favour of the union, the Badger executives and the Belgian government negotiated a settlement of the case.

KEY DIFFERENCES BETWEEN COUNTRIES

In the first part of this chapter we have reviewed the most important developments in European industrial relations. We now turn our attention to examining some of the key differences. Despite a considerable overlap in the overall changes affecting national industrial relations systems, the nature and processes of industrial relations in the

Illustration 15.9 **Reasons for the lack of success of international trade unions.**

- Generally good wages and working conditions provided by MNEs in Western Europe (Hamill, 1984).
- Strong resistance from multinational managements to transnational bargaining and consultations.
- Significant ideological, political and structural

differences between national unions (Jacobs, 1973).
- Differing national laws and regulations in the labour relations area.
- Conflicting national economic interests when dealing with MNEs.

various European countries are fundamentally different and it is difficult to see how these systems are 'converging'.

> ... to presuppose that societies with diverse political economies and at varying stages of development are becoming increasingly convergent in industrial relations structure and process is to strain credibility. *Ceteris paribus*, it is the obverse case which is persuasive. That is to say, unless it can be clearly demonstrated to the contrary, it is to be expected that, as more countries become industrialized and as already complex modes of accommodation of interest amongst the parties are shaped by a progressively diverse range of socio-cultural forms, a rich, heterogeneous and variegated pattern of industrial relations institutions will unfold in future years.
>
> Poole (1986b, p. 11).

Comparative studies by Bean (1985) and by Sorge and Warner (1980) suggest that although organizations in different European countries may be similar in terms of their size, technology and products, they can nevertheless have distinctly dissimilar forms of organization and industrial relations, and that the convergence of national industrial relations systems, where it takes place, is towards a range of alternative solutions to common problems rather than to a particular solution. The corollary of this hypothesis is that differences observed among national industrial relations systems are not simply random, but are rooted in individual country responses to the underlying compulsions of industrial revolution (Doeringer, 1981).

International differences cannot be understood solely in terms of cross-sectional analysis at any point in time. Instead, as Bean (1985, p. 11) suggests 'longitudinal studies incorporating a time dimension are also required for supplying historical perspective, together with a sharper appreciation of change through time and the conditions which generate it'.

What, then, are the key differences between national industrial relations systems in Europe and how can we explain these differences? Bearing in mind that answering such general questions necessarily entails some simplification, it seems that European transnational differences during the 1970s and 1980s have been most marked in the areas outlined in Illustration 15.10.

TRADE UNION DENSITY AND STRUCTURE

As noted above, international statistics of union density are notoriously difficult to compare since methods of counting members vary from country to country and unions have a habit of exaggerating their numbers in order to make their strength seem the more impressive (Jacobs, 1973). In spite of these difficulties it is clear that there are wide differences in union density between the various European countries at the end of the 1980s:

■ There were four countries with densities of 50 per cent or more of the labour force (notably Sweden, Finland, Ireland and Belgium).

Illustration 15.10 **Key differences between European IR systems.**

■ Trade union density and structure. ■ Industrial conflict and strikes.
■ Union responses to the economic crisis. ■ Industrial democracy and employee partici--pation.
■ Managerial styles in industrial relations.
■ Collective bargaining levels.

- There was medium density (between 30 per cent and 50 per cent) in Germany, Switzerland, Italy, and the Netherlands.
- Unionization was lowest in Britain, France and Spain.

At any given point in time these variations may be best explained by cross-national differences in the extent and depth of collective bargaining and in the degree of public support for collective bargaining (Clegg, 1976). The greater the depth of bargaining (in terms of the involvement of local union officers and shop stewards) and union support, the higher the density. This, in turn, moderates managerial and state policies on trade union recognition (Poole, 1986b). In Sweden, for example, 'the catalyst helping to promote extremely high density among salaried staffs was government support in the form of legislation guaranteeing the right of association and negotiation to white collar as well as manual employees since 1936' (Bean, 1985, p. 40).

A comprehensive explanation of variations in union density amongst European countries also has to include the different patterns of trade union structure in Western industrial societies. The assortment of union structures found in the various European countries may be divided, with some simplification, into three traditional types derived from the union's recruitment policy (see Illustration 15.11). Industrial unions feature prominently in Belgium, Finland, Norway, Germany, Italy and Sweden; craft unions in Switzerland, the UK, Denmark and Ireland; and general unions in the Netherlands, Portugal, and France. In addition to these three traditional types of unions, three other types which are commonly found in Europe are white collar unions (for example, the Dutch 'Federatie van Middelbaar en Hoger Personeel'), unions organized on political or religious principles (e.g., the Belgian Confederation of Christian Trade Unions), and unions with strong membership concentrations amongst public sector employees (e.g., the Danish Federation of Civil Servants and Salaried Employees).

How can these variations be explained? The most detailed and influential thesis is that of Clegg (1976), who focused on the state of technology and industrial organization at the time of the birth and growth of a national trade union movement (see Illustration 15.12).

Illustration 15.11 **Three union structures.**

1. Craft unions: restrict membership to those men and women working at a clearly definable trade which normally involves a formal period of training.	2. Industrial unions: recruit all grades of employees in a single industry. 3. Conglomerate (or general) unions: members of many occupations in more than one industry.

Illustration 15.12 **Growth of unionism in Britain.**

In Britain, the new skill requirements of the industrial revolution led to the establishment of craft unions but as white collar jobs increased and collective bargaining became more widespread after the turn of the century, general unions expanded around the previously established craft unions. At the same time, the power and density of craft unions, set up originally to protect the exclusive interests of occupational groups, was diluted by the admission of unskilled workers. As a result many different unions represent identical groups or closely related groups of employees in the same industry and sometimes even in the same organization.

Source: Farnham and Pimlott (1987); Poole (1986b).

UNION RESPONSES TO THE ECONOMIC CLIMATE

The Harvard Centre for European Studies has analysed union strategy in five Western European countries (Lange, Ross and Vannicelli, 1982; Gourevitch, Martin, Ross, Allen, Bornstein and Markovits, 1984), and put a strong case in favour of a 'divergence thesis'. It argues that, in those sectors where it has representation, the union movement has responded to the economic crisis since the early 1970s in quite different ways. In particular, four broad strategies are identified in the responses of Western European unions, as outlined in Illustration 15.13.

These differences do not describe different national union movements with great precision, but they do illustrate how much the strategies and tactics of unions differ both between and within European countries.

MANAGERIAL STYLES IN INDUSTRIAL RELATIONS

As we noted earlier in this chapter, during the 1970s and 1980s, there was considerable pressure on employers in Europe to re-organize and adapt promptly to changes in the economic environment. Moreover, the need for flexibility has perceptibly increased employers' determination to attain and keep greater discretionary power over the rules governing the use of labour. This trend has led to significant changes in the treatment of trade unions, the degree of recognition afforded to them and the role they are permitted to play as representatives of the collective interests of working people. In France there has been a growth in recognition; it has been stable in Sweden, Italy and Spain; it has declined in the Netherlands, Denmark, Belgium and Germany; and in Britain policy has been explicitly hostile to trade unions.

The degree of cross-national variation on this topic is very high, reflecting both the size and importance of cultural differences between European countries and the varying degree of 'trust' or 'good faith' in national labour relations (see Illustration 15.14).

It would appear that, everywhere in Europe, employer support for the 'laissez-faire' approach to labour relations is currently growing, especially in Britain (with a stable, anti-union government). It is worth noting, however, that most employers and managers have not taken advantage of the recent recession and the changed balance of power to marginalize unions and move to a more deregulatory approach. In Italy, for example, major firms such as Pirelli, Zanussi and even the notoriously conflict-

Illustration 15.13 **Four divergent responses by West European unions.**

1. Maximalist response: associated with some of the French unions, especially those on the left, as demonstrated by their refusal to play any role in the 'management of the crisis' at the organization, sectoral or national levels.

2. Interventionist approach: characterizes some of the Italian unions, which have tried to intervene at the organization, sectoral and national levels in order to develop incremental policies to relieve the economic crisis.

3. Defensive–particularistic strategy: occurs where groups of workers seek to protect themselves, in the face of income and job insecurity, using rank and file power bases to veto changes. This is seen as characteristic of some British unions.

4. Corporatist strategy: associated with unions that collaborate with the state and employers in areas such as incomes policies and broader economic and social programmes. Epitomized by unions in Sweden and, to some extent, in West Germany, especially during periods of Social Democratic government.

Source: Bamber and Lansbury (1987, pp. 19–20).

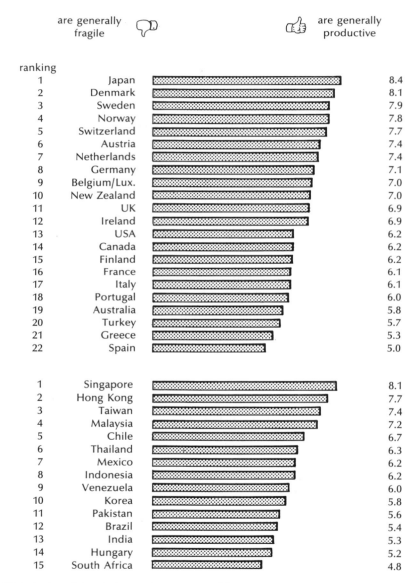

Figure 15.4 Industrial relations. *Source*: World Economic Forum (1993), reprinted with permission, © 1993, World Economic Forum.

Illustration 15.14 **Cultural differences in labour relations.**

- ■ 'Consultative' approach: seeks to achieve strong involvement of employees and strong identification with the organization's goals and culture through direct worker–management communication and ownership in the performance of the organization. Seen fully in Germany, Sweden and the Scandinavian countries, and less widely in the others.
- ■ 'Constitutional' approach: views collective bargaining and dealing indirectly with employees

through unions unfavourably. Most visible in countries where labour organizations are closely intertwined with government institutions, such as Belgium, Spain, Portugal and the Netherlands.

- ■ 'Deregulatory' or 'laissez-faire' approach: formal regulations and collective bargaining are less influential and management tries to maximize discretion and flexibility in the deployment of labour prevalent in France.

Source: Baglioni, 1991; Brown and Sisson, 1984.

ridden Fiat have used an increasingly formalized approach of joint consultation and negotiation to handle a range of industrial disputes (Ferner and Hyman, 1992a). Figure 15.4 shows the degree to which relations between managers and employees are productive in 37 countries around the world.

COLLECTIVE BARGAINING

Closely related to the above topic is the complexity and diversity of bargaining levels across Europe. Despite the overall trend towards decentralization, the main cross-national differences tend to persist and remain relatively stable. As Bean (1985) puts it, bargaining structures 'do not usually break out suddenly from their traditional framework and veer off in a new direction' (p. 85). Thus, collective bargaining remains fairly centralized in Austria, Switzerland, Sweden and France; it is becoming less centralized in Belgium, Denmark, the Netherlands, Germany; and it is decidedly decentralized in Britain. In Portugal and Spain, the entire system of collective bargaining is in transition. Currently, there is a statutory minimum wage (Crabb, 1992). It is too early to predict which model will be adopted by the two countries.

It needs to be remembered, however, that there are marked differences not only between countries but within each country as well (Bean, 1985). Thus, in Sweden, although the Swedish Federation of Trade Unions negotiates with the Employers' Federation (SAF) for 1.4 million workers at the national level, some negotiations also take place at the company- and branch-level about more detailed applications and modifications of the central agreements (Rehn and Viklund, 1991). In France, changes to industry-wide or national agreements are initiated at local employer level (Besse, 1992).

INDUSTRIAL CONFLICT AND STRIKES

Although great caution is required in their use and interpretation, a cross-national comparative analysis of the frequency, size and duration of stoppages, as the most visible and conspicuous indicators of industrial conflict, gives an impression of the diversity in strike patterns amongst countries. Official data tend to measure three

Table 15.2 **Number of employees involved in stoppages in twelve EU countries from 1982–91.**

	Germany	France	Italy	Netherlands	Belgium	Luxembourg	UK	Ireland	Denmark	Greece	Spain	Portugal
1982	40	468	10,483	70	n/a	80	2,103	30	53	224	n/a	
1983	94	617	6,844	20	n/a	n/a	574	30	41	155	n/a	
1984	537	555	7,356	16	n/a	0	1,464	31	51	786	949	231
1985	78	549	4,843	23	34	0	791	169	581	1,106	2,022	81
1986	115	456	3,607	17	n/a	n/a	720	50	57	1,609	7,244	156
1987	155	360	4,273	13	n/a	n/a	887	26	57	449	1,448	296
1988	33	403	2,712	5	23	0	790	10	30	796	776	129
1989	44	298	4,452	15	19	n/a	727	4	27	1,304	1,896	119
1990		278	1,644	25	10	1	290	10	37	477		
1991		408	2,951	42	11	2	176	18	38			

Source: data based on estimates from *Eurobusiness* reprinted with permission © 1993, *The European*.

Table 15.3 **Number of working days lost per 1,000 employees in strikes in twelve EU countries from 1982–91.**

	Germany	France	Italy	Netherlands	Belgium	Luxembourg	UK	Ireland	Denmark	Greece	Spain	Portugal
1982	1	141	1,283	49	n/a	580	248	505	43	809		
1983	2	104	975	27	n/a	0	178	382	36	324		
1984	246	135	611	7	n/a	0	1,278	471	61	275	1,087	145
1985	2	71	266	20	46	0	299	520	1,041	618	546	42
1986	1	109	390	9	n/a	0	90	378	40	712	335	70
1987	1	100	316	12	n/a	0	164	327	58	1,317	692	123
1988	2	109	224	2	75	3	166	177	40	505	1,509	50
1989	4	179	300	4	50	0	182	62	23	702	454	41
1990		69	341	37	38	33	83	266	42	1,720	265	
1991		49	195	17	24	12	34	100	30	452	463	

Source: data based on estimates from *Eurobusiness* reprinted with permission © 1993, *The European*.

aspects of industrial militancy:

1. The number of strikes.
2. The number of employees involved in stoppages (see Table 15.2).
3. The number of working days lost per 1,000 employees (see Table 15.3).

On this basis, Poole (1986b) has distinguished five main clusters of Western industrialized countries, in which a specific type of strike pattern is dominant (see Illustration 15.15). This diversity in strike activity reflects varied political, economic and cultural conditions as well as the distribution of power between the parties themselves. For example, in countries where the strike remains a primary weapon of working class political action (e.g. Italy), frequent and broad-based stoppages dominate (Poole, 1986b). Moreover, there is a strong relationship between the level of strike activity in a specific country and the degree of centralization of collective bargaining systems (Hibbs, 1976). Thus the relatively high number of stoppages in the UK during the 1970s and early 1980s is often explained by the predominance of company-level and plant-level bargaining. With this form of bargaining structure, a strike can more easily be called in particular plants or divisions without

Illustration 15.15 **Five clusters of strike patterns.**

Cluster 1	The United States, Canada and Ireland.	
	■ Long duration of stoppages is dominant.	
Cluster 2	Italy, and to a lesser extent, Finland, Spain and Israel.	
	■ Number of people who participate in stoppages is very high.	
Cluster 3	Australia, New Zealand, France and Portugal.	
	■ Number of stoppages is very high.	
Cluster 4	Belgium, Denmark, the Netherlands, Norway and Sweden.	
	■ Low incidence of strike activity, but duration not insignificant.	
Cluster 5	The United Kingdom and Japan.	
	■ No one strike characteristic is dominant.	

Source: Poole (1986).

Table 15.4 **Militancy league table for twelve EU countries.**

Ranking	Most strikes	Most workers in strikes	Most production days lost in strikes
1	Spain	Italy	Spain
2	France	Spain	Greece
3	Italy	Greece	Italy
4	Greece	France	Ireland
5	UK	Germany	France
6	Germany	UK	Portugal
7	Portugal	Portugal	UK
8	Denmark	Netherlands	Denmark
9	Ireland	Denmark	Belgium
10	Belgium	Ireland	Netherlands
11	Netherlands	Belgium	Luxembourg
12	Luxembourg	Luxembourg	Germany

Source: Wassell (1993b), reprinted with permission © 1993, *The European*.

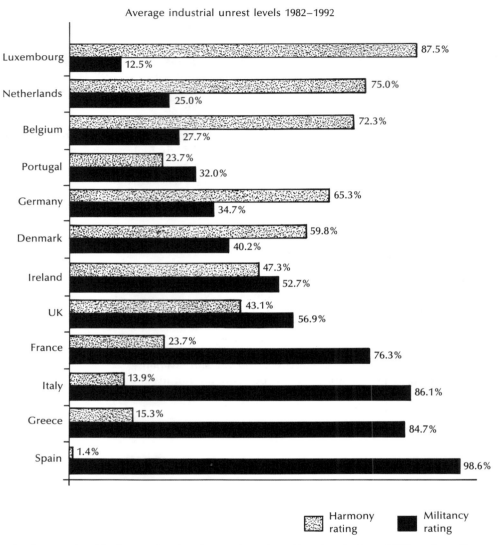

Average industrial unrest levels 1982–1992

Luxembourg — 87.5% / 12.5%
Netherlands — 75.0% / 25.0%
Belgium — 72.3% / 27.7%
Portugal — 23.7% / 32.0%
Germany — 65.3% / 34.7%
Denmark — 59.8% / 40.2%
Ireland — 47.3% / 52.7%
UK — 43.1% / 56.9%
France — 23.7% / 76.3%
Italy — 13.9% / 86.1%
Greece — 15.3% / 84.7%
Spain — 1.4% / 98.6%

Harmony rating   Militancy rating

The Communitywide figures showing the number of working days lost per 1,000 workers, the actual number of reported strikes and the total numbers of workers involved in disputes within each of the 12 member states have been translated here to produce an overall labour militancy and industrial harmony score for each EU country. Figures for the past ten years suggest the comparative national picture painted by the chart has changed little and that employers in some nations face far more disruption than others elsewhere.

Figure 15.5 The harmony and militancy ratings for twelve EU countries based on average industrial unrest levels 1982–1992. *Source*: Wassell (1993b); Graphic by Steve Latibeaudiere, reprinted with permission, © 1993, *The European*.

bringing out all the workers from an entire industry (as in Belgium), or region (as in Germany).

Based on the average industrial unrest levels from 1982 to 1992 using the three measures of number of strikes, number of production days lost per 1,000 workers and the employees involved in stoppages, the EU has produced estimates of the relative harmony and militancy of the twelve countries (see Figure 15.5 and Table 15.4, p. 609). Comparative studies of labour unrest reveal a number of strengths and weaknesses in the various European workforces which make the process of job re-location and foreign direct investment discussed in Chapters Four and Five more complex. For example, whilst Spain has low social costs, it has a high level of industrial unrest, making it less attractive to some organizations.

The old battle lines between unions and employers are being redrawn right across the map of Europe, especially in the wake of the deepening economic crisis of the early 1990s (Wassell, 1993b). This has led to a general undermining of labour bargaining power. In many countries, such as Britain, Greece, and Portugal, lower levels of industrial labour disruption were reported as the recession took hold and unemployment again began to climb. However, as we noted earlier in the chapter, the link between the business cycle and union activity only partially explains events. Despite the European-wide recession, at the beginning of the 1990s the levels of industrial unrest and harmony still varied widely. Industrial labour experts now believe that a wide range of structural factors, above and beyond the basic economic health of the nation, help determine why one country is strike prone whilst another is not. Although cross-border studies into the cultural, legal and workplace traditions of Europan countries have generally failed to identify any universal causes for different levels of disputes, the data in Tables 15.5 and 15.6 show that some industrial relations frameworks are clearly better than others in dealing with and defusing problems. Figure 15.6 shows the connection between the overall level of militancy and the level of unionization. A number of patterns are immediately apparent:

- The five countries with the highest levels of militancy (Spain, Italy, Greece, France and the UK) all have relatively low levels (generally the lowest) levels of unionization.
- Germany, Portugal, the Nertherlands and Ireland have similar levels of militancy and unionization. Excepting Ireland, levels of unionization are quite low but so are levels of militancy.
- Belgium, Denmark and Luxembourg have high levels of unionization and relatively low levels of militancy.

Whilst many factors are involved, there does appear to be a link between the level of militancy in the workforce and the extent to which union activities are actively discouraged by legislation and the governments. Countries which top the league of militancy appear on the whole to have more severe laws governing labour regulations (see Table 15.5). This has significant implications for the extent to which the transition in European HRM discussed throughout this book can be managed smoothly over the 1990s. Two pressures may mediate the relationship shown in Figure 15.6:

1. Calls for greater industrial participation.
2. Movement towards a pan-European industrial relations policy.

Discussion of these trends forms the last part of this chapter, see page 620.

Table 15.5 **The industrial relations framework in twelve EU countries in 1993.**

Country	Official industrial strikes	Wildcat unofficial strikes	Political protest strikes	Disruptive working action	Required strike notice	Staff lock outs	Peace obligations	Penalties
Belgium	Recognized in law	Illegal	Illegal	Legal	7 days	Not recognized within legal process	No compulsory conciliation, mediation or arbitration	Fines and dismissals against individual employees and civil suits against unions in breach of contracts
Denmark	Not recognized within legal process	Illegal	Minor infringement	Illegal	No notice period required	Not recognized within legal process	Compulsory binding legal arbitration	Labour courts may impose fines and sanctions against individual employees and unions
France	Recognized in law	Legal	Illegal	Illegal	No notice period required	Legal in limited circumstances	No compulsory conciliation, mediation or arbitration	Courts can impose a maximum 3-year sentence and fines of up to $3000 on employees and unions preventing non striking employees from working
Germany	Recognized in law	Illegal	Illegal	Legal	No notice period required	Legal	No compulsory conciliation, mediation or arbitration	No legal framework of penalties in force
Greece	Recognized in law	Illegal	Illegal	Illegal	1 day	Illegal	Compulsory binding legal arbitration	Courts can jail union organizers and source union funds if a legal order to settle dispute is not obeyed

Ireland	Not recognized within legal process	Legal	Legal	Legal	Illegal	No notice period required	Illegal	No compulsory conciliation, mediation or arbitration	No legal framework of penalties in force
Italy	Recognized in law	Legal	Legal	Not recognized within legal process	Legal	No notice period required	Legal	No compulsory conciliation, mediation or arbitration	Courts may fine or jail strikers acting in breech of industrial laws
Luxembourg	Recognized in law	Illegal	Illegal	Legal	Legal	Written notice required	Legal	Compulsory binding legal arbitration	Courts may impose token fines on union officials refusing to obey labour court orders
Netherlands	Recognized in law	Illegal	Illegal	Illegal	Illegal	Unspecified reasonable notice period required	Legal	Compulsory binding legal arbitration	No legal framework of penalties in force
Portugal	Recognized in law	Illegal	Legal	Legal	Legal	5 days	Illegal	Compulsory binding legal arbitration in public sector only	Courts may fine and jail employers for sacking striking employees, lock-outs or using coercive methods to settle disputes
Spain	Recognized in law	Legal	Illegal	Illegal	Illegal	5 days in general, 10 days in public sector	Illegal	No compulsory conciliation, mediation or arbitration	Courts may fine employers a maximum $120,000 for engaging in lock-outs
UK	Not recognized within legal process	Illegal	Illegal	Illegal	Legal	No notice period required	Legal	No compulsory conciliation, mediation or arbitration	Employers may dismiss any employee who strikes

Source: Wassell (1993b), reprinted with permission © 1993, *The European*.

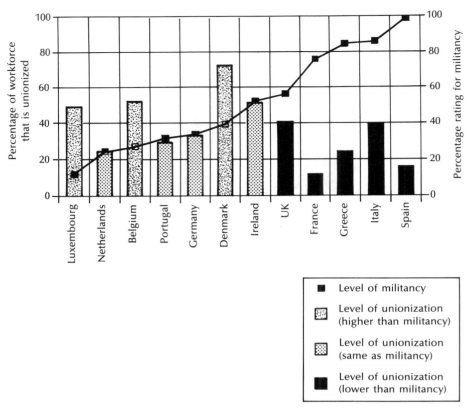

Figure 15.6 The relationship between overall levels of militancy and unionization in twelve EU countries.

INDUSTRIAL DEMOCRACY AND EMPLOYEE PARTICIPATION

Financial participation

The sixth comparative theme to be considered in the analysis of international industrial relations is the practice of employee participation. Although organizations in the US and Japan have been developing financial participation for many years, it is only recently that one can detect an increase of profit sharing schemes in Western Europe. According to the PEPPER report, carried out by the European University Institute in Florence, in 1992, France led the way with approximately 17,000 profit sharing schemes, involving some 18 per cent of the French workforce. The second leading country is the UK, with 7,000 schemes, covering 8 per cent of all British workers and nearly 30 per cent of all UK companies. The amounts of money allocated to profit sharing hardly ever exceed 10 per cent of average employee earnings and 5 per cent of enterprise profits. In the case of share ownership (excluding privatizations), the percentage of shares reserved for employees has generally not exceeded 5 per cent of the total number of shares issued.

Poole (1989) notes that the widespread advance of profit sharing and employee share ownership schemes in the 1980s may be interpreted as part of three distinctive waves of development of industrial democracy during the twentieth century. These waves are characterized in Illustration 15.16. However, if we examine the international practice

Illustration 15.16   **Three waves of industrial democracy in Europe.**

Wave 1
From 1915–55: the rise of statutory or voluntary works councils and similar mechanisms at plant level in both planned and market economies.

Wave 2
From 1920 onwards but especially since 1945: the emergence of board-level co-determination culminating in the EU Social Charter which is aimed to make such arrangements widespread in all European member states.

Wave 3
From the 1980s: the extension of ownership rights to both management and labour. The growth of stock option schemes, management and employee 'buy-outs', stock ownership and wage earner funds, and producer co-operatives.

of employee financial participation, it is clear that development has been uneven and, in many West European countries such as Italy, Luxembourg, Switzerland the Netherlands and Germany, it still remains an uncommon feature of the industrial relations landscape (Poole, 1986a). Moreover, in most countries, the economic impact and penetration of financial participation schemes remains limited, except, in some cases, for those designed for senior executives.

Development of financial participation schemes is strongly related to government action. Implementation of schemes increases rapidly where the legal and fiscal conditions are created for employee share ownership and profit sharing. In France, the government has made deferred profit sharing compulsory in organizations of more than fifty employees since 1967; and in Britain, there has been legal and fiscal support for the implementation of enterprise-level schemes since 1978. In other European countries fiscal and legal incentives for financial participation have only been introduced recently. For instance, fiscal provisions for employee share ownership were made by the Belgian government in the late 1980s. However, these schemes are typically much more limited in scope, and when they provide tax incentives, they tend to be very modest. In Spain, Italy and Luxembourg, no tax incentive at all is currently on offer.

Managerial decision making

Worker participation in managerial decision making within the organization is a multi-dimensional concept. There are therefore a number of ways in which the various schemes used in different European countries may be distinguished from each other (Bean, 1985; Poole, 1986a). Schemes may be classified in terms of their:

- Depth (the degree of authority that is given to workers).
- Breadth (the range of decisions in which workers participate).
- Origin (who are the initiators of the participation process?).
- 'Disjunctiveness' (emphasizing the distinctiveness rather than the communality of workers and management interests).

Where forms of participation initiated by management are concerned, it is also particularly important to make the distinction between 'direct' participation on the one hand and 'indirect' or 'representative' participation on the other in order to identify different levels of worker involvement in decision making within the managerial hierarchy (Poole, 1986a). Thus formal schemes of employee participation may incorporate either the direct involvement of shopfloor in operational decision making through production conferences, semi-autonomous work groups, quality circles and similar arrangements, or be indirect by means of union representatives, works councils or worker directors (as in the German co-determination scheme).

Strauss (1979) makes a basic distinction between three major approaches to the depth of participation:

1. Consultative participation.
2. Co-management.
3. Workers' self-management.

With consultative participation, management makes the final decision but workers or their representatives have the right to be informed and can offer advice and objections. This is the most common form of participation in Western Europe. Notable examples are outlined in Illustration 15.17.

The second approach is that of co-management or joint decision making. Here, workers or their representatives have joint powers on certain matters and the consent of each party is required before action can be taken. For instance, in Holland, when an employer wishes to establish or amend certain rules concerning the organization's social policy and is not bound by a collective agreement, he must first seek the approval of the works council. If the works council disapproves, the employer can ask the industrial tribunal to arbitrate. However, the latter can only decide in favour of the employer if the decision of the works council to withhold approval is deemed unreasonable or if the employer's proposal is dictated by compelling organizational, economic or social reasons. Similarly, in Italy, Germany, Sweden, Norway and Denmark there is legislation preventing employers from implementing decisions regarding matters such as hours of work, vocational training, and health and safety without getting the approval of works councils and similar institutions. The third and most far reaching category, workers' self-management, is found only in a small number of West European organizations in which the employees own the assets of the organization or are represented on the main decision making bodies. These include state enterprises, producer co-operatives, and firms in which the employees are the majority shareholders (see Illustration 15.18).

Finally, in countries like France, participation occurs through Works Councils, which deal with the organization's economic and social affairs, and employee delegate meetings, which discuss individual problems (Besse, 1992).

Illustration 15.17 **Examples of consultative participation.**

- EU directives and regulations governing the procedures for consultation on collective redundancies.
- Irish Worker Participation Acts 1977 to 1991, which provide for formal employee consultation on matters of safety, health and welfare in the workplace.
- Dutch Works Councils Act, which gives employee representatives in all undertakings with thirty-five or more workers the right to financial information and to be consulted whenever the employer wishes to take important organizational decisions.

Illustration 15.18 **Mondragon producer co-operatives.**

The Mondragon producer co-operatives in the Basque region of Northern Spain are a worker-owned group of enterprises established in 1956. They now produce a wide range of manufactured goods and some agricultural products. Indeed, whereas in 1956, there was only a single industrial enterprise, a consistently impressive period of expansion throughout the 1960s and 1970s ensured that, by 1979, there were seventy (currently eighty) factories with an aggregate employment of 15,672 people. Elsewhere in Europe, however, the record of producer co-operatives has been uneven.

Source: Poole (1986a).

Factors behind the development of participatory schemes

A number of studies have tried to explain the development of different participatory schemes. For instance, in a broader comparative analysis of industrial relations systems in continental Europe and the US, Kassalow (1982) suggests that the different forms taken by workers' participation can be explained partially by differences in the ideological background and orientation of their respective labour movements. Thus, in Italy trade unions have traditionally shown an attitude of strong resistance against worker participation in managerial decision making, viewing collective bargaining as the primary way to regulate labour–management relations (Cella and Treu, 1982). Similarly, Blanpain (1974) notes that in Belgium three different forms of participation operate at the enterprise level – a triad which is the result of a compromise between, on the one hand, both the employers and Christian unions (who favour the idea of collaboration between workers and managers through works councils) and, on the other, the socialist unions (who prefer participation through collective bargaining).

. . . the causes of major international variations in formal types of participation may in part be located in the wider political implications, value systems, beliefs and ideologies held by both trade unions and employers' associations and the country at large.   Bean (1985).

Factors such as cultural and political orientations of workers, unions and employers have very little impact on national industrial relations systems when set against the far greater effects of legal and other institutional conditions (Poole, 1986a; IDE, 1981b). The current industrial democracy system in Germany, for example, reflects a long tradition of efforts to improve employee participation within industry. Works councils were first established by law in 1916, in industries which were important for the national economy in the First World War. They became obligatory under the Works Councils Act of 1920 (Feurstenberg, 1987). Table 15.6 charts the development of industrial democracy institutions in eleven European countries from 1910 to 1990.

Poole (1986a) has also observed that the distribution of power is decisive in determining which type of participation emerges as dominant. Where trade unions are strong (such as in Britain up to the 1980s), the development of participative machinery has been typically grounded in collective bargaining and organized on the basis of a single channel of representation. By contrast, in cases where the right to form unions has been denied to workers and unions, experimentation with a range of direct forms of participation has typically occurred (IDE, 1981a).

Table 15.6 Introduction of industrial democracy institutions in principal European countries.

Country	1900	1910	1920	1930	1940	1950	1960	1970	1980	1990
Belgium					délégation syndicates X X (C) (S)	works council law	general agreement on délégations syndicates	I (C)	I I (S) (S)	extensions to works councils law
Denmark				co-operative committees X (C)					amendments to company act to provide (S) worker representation on boards	
Finland	labour agreement act X (C)			general agreement X (C)		agreement on shop stewards	X X (C) (C)	agreement on information		
France				Matignon agreement X (S)	X enterprise sections (C) committees syndicates		X X X (S) (S) (F) act encouraging plant-level bargaining		Sudreau Report	
Germany	works council act X (S)			co-determination: Montan industries X	X X works constitution act (S) (S)			I (S)	I co-determination (S) law	
Ireland	shop stewards X (I)				X joint consultation (I) committees					
Italy			commissioni interne (I)			factory councils	X X collective (I) (S) agreement act			

Netherlands	labour act X (S)		works council X act (S)	co-determination (modification to 1950 act)	I X collective (S) (S) agreement act
Norway	workers' councils X (S)		extension of basic agreement (C)		I company act (S) changed to give minority representative rights
Sweden	basic agreement X (F)		X works councils (C) agreement		act X I X co-determination on (S)(S)(S) act public representation
UK	shop stewards X X (I) (I)	Whitley committees	joint production, consultative and advisory committees	extension of shop stewards system (I)	X Bullock (F) report	joint consultation (I)

Key

X = introduction of a new institution

I = reform of existing institution

(I),(C),(S),(F) = mode of introduction, informally (I), by collective agreement (C), by statutory law (S), or facilitative (F)

Source: M. Poole, reprinted with permission © 1993 M. Poole *Industrial Relations: Origins and patterns of national diversity*, Routledge and Kegan Paul.

THE SOCIAL CHAPTER: CONVERGENCE, HARMONIZATION OR DIFFUSION?

In the third and final part of this chapter we review the work done by the European Commission to implement the 'Social Chapter'.

To summarize the argument so far, although several factors have been influential in promoting the 'convergence' or 'harmonization' of industrial relations in Europe, all European countries still have their own individual arrangements for managing the relationships between employers, employees and their respective collective organizations. As a result, there is:

- Wide disparity in the types of working conditions currently in operation in the various countries.
- A big difference in levels of social protection enjoyed by workers between countries.
- International diversity and multiplicity of social security laws and regulations which make it very difficult for governments and organizations to increase the mobility of workers between EU member states.

This is why, in the context of the establishment of a Single European Market, the heads of state of eleven member states of the European Union agreed, on 9 December 1989, to adopt the Community Charter of the Fundamental Social Rights of Workers. Based on earlier texts such as the Social Charter of the Council of Europe and the conventions of the International Labour Organization, this Chapter provides a foundation of social rights which are guaranteed to all EU workers and which, in the words of Papandreou (1992), 'will form a keystone of a social dimension underlying the European model of labour law and, more generally, of the place of work in our society' (p. 5). In itself, the Chapter has no effect on the existing legal situation in the various member countries. It merely states the rights which were the subject of deliberations in the European Council meeting of December 1989, as shown in Appendix 1.

IMPLEMENTATION OF THE CHAPTER

Under the terms of Point 28 of the Chapter, the European Council invited the Commission to submit initiatives relating to the effective implementation of the various rights and principles set out in the Chapter as soon as possible. The response of the Commission was the creation of an action programme containing forty-seven separate proposals for directives on such matters as the re-organization of working time, the freedom of movement of EU workers, the equal treatment of men and women at work, and the co-ordination of vocational training programmes within the community.

For example, in its action programme relating to employment and remuneration, the Commission proposed a set of directives concerning the organization of working time which, on the one hand, respected the need for organizations to be flexible, and, on the other, contained a basic set of minimum provisions regarding employment and remuneration (see Illustration 15.19).

These directives are accompanied by specific proposals to meet three specific needs:

1. To improve the functioning of the internal market and to make the labour market more transparent within the context of economic and social cohesion (based on Article 100a of the EEC Treaty).
2. To improve living and working conditions for workers (based on Article 100 of the EEC Treaty).

Illustration 15.19 **Range of directives relating to employment and remuneration.**

- Daily and weekly rest periods, shift work, night work, and working conditions for children and pregnant women.
- Training and employment of disabled people.
- Co-ordination and rationalization of vocational training programmes such as Comett, Eurotecnet, Erasmus, Lingua, Tempus, Petra and IRIS.

- Establishment of a European works council in community-scale undertakings for the purposes of informing and consulting employees.
- Usage of various forms of employee participation in company profits and trading results.
- Protection of workers from the risks related to exposure to asbestos at work.

3. To protect the health and safety of people at work (based on Article 118a of the EEC Treaty).

Of these proposals, only those based on Article 118a had been adopted by the Council of Ministers by mid-1992. Work on the proposal based on Article 100a is progressing slowly, and very little progress has been made on the proposals based on Article 100 of the EEC Treaty. This latter set of proposals has been rejected by the European Parliament.

We shall now outline the implementation of the Social Chapter in relation to four issues: employment contracts, redundancy, immigration, equal opportunities, and free movement of labour.

Labour contracts

Faced with the considerable development of very varied forms of employment contracts other than those of an open-ended type, the EU Commission takes the view that there should be a Community framework ensuring a minimum of consistency between these various forms of contract in order to avoid the danger of distortions of competition and to increase the transparency of the labour market at community level. Hence, in its application of the Chapter, the Commission has proposed a number of fundamental provisions in respect of certain employment relationships, such as temporary contracts,

Illustration 15.20 **EU directive on labour contracts.**

Under the directive, all workers should know for whom and where they are supposed to be working and what the essential conditions of the employment relationship are. The essential aim is to create a balance between the interests of workers in being aware of the nature and content of their employment relationship and that of businesses searching for new and more flexible forms of employment relationships geared to the needs of a modern economy. Apart from the renewed potential for 'black work' the emergence of new forms of distance work, work experience schemes and mixed employment training

contracts, more flexible forms of part time and full time working and, in more general terms, the development of new forms of work tend to obscure the situation of large numbers of workers. As a result, conventional concepts of what is meant by workers, employed persons, working time etc. are no longer covered by conventional labour law. The directive makes a contribution to improving the transparency of a labour market which is undergoing change and has the potential for altering the situation of workers employment relationships which generally fall outside tra-ditional patterns.

work experience schemes and part time working arrangements. For instance, on 28 November 1990, the Commission submitted a proposal for a directive requiring formal proof of an employment relationship and this directive was adopted on 14 October 1991 (see Illustration 15.20).

Redundancy

Another initiative presented under the Commission's action programme relating to the implementation of the Chapter is the proposed directive on collective redundancies. On 18 September 1991, the Commission submitted a proposal for an EU directive amending directive 75/129 concerning the approximation of member states' legislation on collective redundancies. It can be seen that the directive addresses some of the fears and concerns raised by the industrial restructuring process we described in Chapter Five (see Illustration 15.21). The proposal widens the field of application of the existing directive as regards redundancies made by decision making centres, but ensures that such centres supply employers with all the information they need to inform and consult workers' representatives and notify the competent public authority of the plans. The proposal also seeks to extend workers' rights as regards information and consultation to cases of redundancy resulting from a court decision. In the approach chosen by the Commission, the proposal offers more flexibility for small businesses by stipulating that member states do not have to provide for worker representation in establishments employing fewer than fifty workers.

Immigration

The need to re-focus Community attention on the immigration issue was emphasized at the Hanover meeting of the European Council of June 1988, which called on the Commission to draw up a report on the social integration of migrant workers, with a view to preparing the ground for a discussion of the matter in the Council.

As regards the social and legal situation of immigrants from non-member countries in each of the twelve member states, the report on the 'Social integration of migrants from non-member countries residing permanently and legally in the member states' gave a first indication of the legal and *de facto* situation of immigrants. A second report entrusted by the Commission to a group of experts and entitled 'Policies on immigration and the social integration of migrants in the European Community' made a major contribution to a more in depth look at this question. The European Council

Illustration 15.21 **The EU's rationale for the collective redundancy directive.**

'Fifteen years of directive 75/129 and the impact of the internal market on business restructuring have made it necessary to amend the original directive. With transnational business restructuring gathering pace on the eve of completion of the internal market, redundancies are increasingly being decided at a higher level of business than that of the direct employer, i.e. by a company exercising control over a group, whether it be situated in the same Member State as the employer or in an entirely different one, or by the central management of a multiple-branch undertaking, with the actual employer being located in a different member state entirely'.

Source: Social Europe (1992, p. 18).

of 14 and 15 December 1990 took note of this latter report and asked the General Affairs Council and the Commission to examine the most appropriate measures and actions that could be taken regarding aid to countries on emigration, entry conditions and for social integration.

With a view to promoting harmonization of social protection as part of a wider move towards economic and social integration, the Commission has also proposed a strategy for the convergence of the member states' various social protection policies. This strategy, as presented in the proposal for a Council recommendation of 27 June 1991, sets out to be flexible, progressive and based on a voluntary approach on the part of member states.

Equality opportunities and childcare

A number of directives are already in place which, when incorporated into national laws and regulations, should guarantee the formal equality of men and women at work, facilitate women's access to the labour market, and improve the status of women in society. The extent to which women have similar career opportunities to men in 37 countries around the world is shown in Figure 15.7. However, there is still some way to go before these laws are implemented. For example, reconciling childcare and child education obligations with parents' employment and training is essential if there is to be true equality of opportunity for men and women. In all the EU member states, demand for childcare facilities exceeds supply, with the lack of good quality and affordable facilities constituting a major obstacle to women finding jobs and playing their full part in work and vocational training. Hence, the Commission intends to take steps to encourage childcare facilities and has already drawn attention to the fact that finance is available in this field under Community support frameworks.

Going beyond specifically targeted measures, the Commission has sought to draw up guidelines for a comprehensive policy on childcare within the Community, along with a programme for the consistent and gradual application of this policy. This resulted in a proposal for a Council recommendation on childcare, adopted by the Commission on 4 July 1991 and presented to the Council on 8 July 1991.

Free movement of labour

Finally, the Commission has sought to encourage the free movement of workers by improving the machinery for providing people in the EU member states with information on job vacancies in other parts of the Community. This is why, on 5 September 1991, the Comission adopted the proposal for a revision of Regulation No 1612/68 on freedom of movement for workers within the Community. In particular, the second part of this Regulation specifies the arrangements for a system of vacancy clearance and for co-operation between the central employment services of the EU member states and the Commission. One of the aims of this system is to provide a high quality employment service to people looking for work in a different member state of the Community. To summarize, completion of the internal market and economic integration have clearly shown the need (given the transnational nature of the problems involved) for co-operation and interaction in areas which have hitherto not been dealt with at a EU level. This is why the Community Charter of Fundamental Social Rights of Workers was adopted by the governments of eleven EU member states in Strasbourg on 8 and 9 December 1989. Since then, a variety of directives have been adopted by

do not have similar career opportunities as men

have similar career opportunities as men

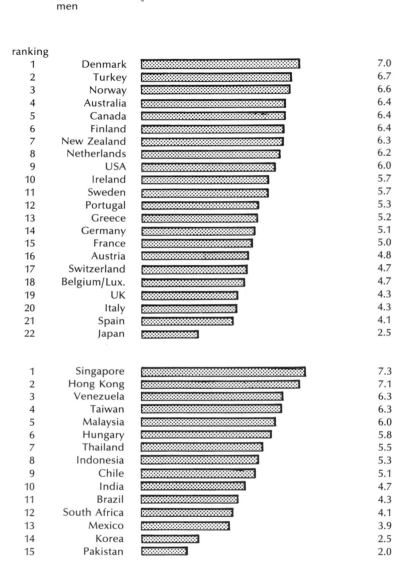

ranking			
1	Denmark		7.0
2	Turkey		6.7
3	Norway		6.6
4	Australia		6.4
5	Canada		6.4
6	Finland		6.4
7	New Zealand		6.3
8	Netherlands		6.2
9	USA		6.0
10	Ireland		5.7
11	Sweden		5.7
12	Portugal		5.3
13	Greece		5.2
14	Germany		5.1
15	France		5.0
16	Austria		4.8
17	Switzerland		4.7
18	Belgium/Lux.		4.7
19	UK		4.3
20	Italy		4.3
21	Spain		4.1
22	Japan		2.5
1	Singapore		7.3
2	Hong Kong		7.1
3	Venezuela		6.3
4	Taiwan		6.3
5	Malaysia		6.0
6	Hungary		5.8
7	Thailand		5.5
8	Indonesia		5.3
9	Chile		5.1
10	India		4.7
11	Brazil		4.3
12	South Africa		4.1
13	Mexico		3.9
14	Korea		2.5
15	Pakistan		2.0

Figure 15.7 Equality of career opportunities for women in 37 countries. *Source*: World Economic Forum (1993), reprinted with permission, © 1993, *Eurobusiness*.

the European Council, which when incorporated in national laws and regulations, create an extensive legal framework of employment protection for workers in the EU.

Nonetheless, at the European Council meeting in Luxembourg on 28 and 29 June 1991, it was noted that 'the progress made in the completion of the internal market has not been accompanied by comparable progress in the field of social policy'. On a number of occasions, both the European Parliament and the Economic and Social Committee have expressed similar opinions and given voice to their concerns about 'the wide gap between the powers available to the Commission under the current legal bases and the ambitions set out in the Charter' (Social Europe, 1992). This has caused the

Commission to propose a revision of the Social Chapter of the Treaty on European Union (the Maastricht Treaty). Whether this is compatible with the current trend towards decentralization of collective bargaining in European countries is not yet clear.

A NEW REGIME FOR INDUSTRIAL RELATIONS OR FRAGMENTED SOCIAL POLICY?

We end this chapter by considering whether the work of the EU represents a new regime for industrial relations, or merely fragmented social policy. Teague (1991) argues that the Social Chapter will not (in the short term) extend existing workers' rights. This significance lies instead in the social and economic arguments that it rejects. The debate about the creation of a social dimension to the Single European Market was characterized by two contrasting models. The 'neo-liberal' approach argued that the European labour market is already too inflexible, rigid and prone to poor employment performance and sluggish economic adjustment. Further labour market regulations would worsen the situation and create a supranational bureaucracy. The 'justification' approach however argued that as European countries implement the Single European Act a range of unfair competitive pressures will emerge creating social dumping and too many 'losers' from the moves to deepen market integration. Teague (1991) argues that the Social Chapter constitutes a third model. It marks the first step towards a new institutional tier being drafted onto the national industrial relations systems. Instead of replacing national arrangements, the Social Chapter attempts to establish a symbiosis by strengthening the co-ordination procedures in the European labour market. It is driven by two premises. First, market integration alone will not bring about sufficient co-ordination of European employment systems. Second, continuing diversity of national industrial relations rules out many positive integration measures intended to create centralization or harmonization. Future employment interventions will therefore be subtler in form, creating:

- Greater communality between existing national rules rather than replacing member state arrangements.
- Policy convergence around steps in the same direction, rather than conformity around approach.
- Diffusion of initiatives aimed at Europeanizing national industrial relations systems rather than attempts at harmonization.

THE SOCIAL POLICY INSTITUTIONAL FRAMEWORK IN THE EU

The EU social policy framework is made up of a wide range of institutions and arrangements (see Figure 15.8). It involves civil servants from EU member states as well as representatives from trade unions and employers' organizations in deliberations aimed at:

- Developing concertive initiatives amongst national labour market institutions.
- Setting an EU agenda for social and labour affairs.
- Creating a body of labour law.
- Establishing a dialogue between trade unions and employers' organizations.

Many of the EU-led labour market initiatives have fallen short of early expectations

Figure 15.8 The social policy institutional framework. *Source*: reprinted from *Human Resource Management Journal*, **2(1)**, 1–21, P. Teague, 'Human resource management, labour market institutions and European integration', copyright © 1991, with kind permission of John Wiley and Sons, Inc.

and a catalogue of administrative, legal and political difficulties (such as lack of resources and imprecise policy objectives) have limited the impact of many EU labour market directives (Brewster and Teague, 1989). No clear channels exist whereby discussions at the EU level can be fed into national deliberations.

The Social Chapter, which is not legally binding, therefore ensures that integration of European industrial relations systems and regulatory arrangements will be a slow and incremental process, although scope exists for the importance of the various social policies to increase gradually. However, the success of the Social Chapter is far from guaranteed. It is not yet apparent that European organizations and trade unions will see the European Union as a strategic site for industrial relations decision making. If this is not the case, then European HRM will be hampered by haphazard trappings and unco-ordinated social and employment initiatives.

CONCLUSION

There has been considerable change in many areas of European HRM as the various chapters of this book have made clear. The last, and perhaps most rigid area, is that of industrial relations. However, even in this area, perhaps the most institutionally and culturally sensitive of all aspects of HRM, there has been something of a managerial revolution. The relationship between workers, employers and their respective collective organizations has changed quite markedly since the 1970s. In considering these changes, the following key learning points should be borne in mind.

LEARNING POINTS FROM CHAPTER FIFTEEN

1. There has been a general decline in the political strength and presence of trade unions in almost every European country. This trend has been most evident in Britain where there has been a weakening of union influence on government policy making, a lower degree of union recognition accorded by employers and a reduced role of union officials in serving the needs of their members.

2. The level of trade union membership has declined to a large extent in countries such as Spain and France, and to a lesser extent in other European countries. Economic recession and increased unemployment have played a part in this, but up to 30 per cent of the fall in trade union membership remains unexplained by changes in the business cycle. Unfavourable demographic and political trends and events have accelerated the decline in membership.

3. The degree of unity between trade unions varies across Europe. There has been a growth in the number of independent unions, internal divisions, and militant offshoots (such as the Italian 'cobas'). This lack of unity has been caused by strained relations with political parties and an increasing diversity of interests among workers. Employers may take advantage of the decline in union power, but to date have favoured a co-operative relationship based on a new realism as opposed to confrontation.

4. Trade unions are structured differently across Europe, typically on a craft, industry or conglomerate (for example, religious or political) basis. There has also been a difference in the pattern of strikes. In general, there has been a decline in the number of strikes since the mid-1970s, the number of man days lost per thousand employees has fallen significantly and there has been a shift in the nature of disputes. Macroeconomic explanations of this strike activity are overly simplistic and ignore the role of state intervention and mediation agencies.

5. The European context for HRM differs from that in the US by having a greater and more active level of direct intervention by the state in the management and conduct of industrial relations. Government intervention has increased in most European countries.

6. The economic and political transformations of the 1980s have also changed the way in which industrial relations are managed. Unions now play a more restricted advisory role rather than a strong representational role. Collective bargaining and employee relations have been decentralized to the lowest level, mainly to company or plant level. Single employer bargaining has increased and the incidence and impact of centralized national and industry-level bargaining has been undermined. The reasons why this has happened include strong competition for the supply of labour, informal agreements to match the ability of more prosperous organizations to pay, greater capital intensity, a growing number of multinational organizations and the requirement for increased flexibility.

7. The demise of industrial relations has been mirrored by the rise of HRM and a more individualized approach to many areas of the employment relationship. Significant changes occurred in the 1980s not only in the coverage of labour negotiations but also in their content, including a focus on flexibility, a demand for shorter hours, more participation and an internationalization of industrial relations.

8. Although many employers have resisted a growth in indirect participation of employees through collective structures such as trade unions, direct participation has increased both through change in work design and in new forms of problem solving such as

quality circles. Many organizations have begun to bypass unions in order to deal with employees directly.

9. The emergence of truly global organizations has increased pressure by trade unions to counter their considerable power and ability to transplant management policies from one country to another. Attempts by unions to exert influence over transnational organizations have generally not met with success.

10. Despite such common trends, key differences have emerged across Europe in terms of the trade union density and structure, the union response to the economic crisis, managerial styles in industrial relations, collective bargaining levels, the level of industrial conflicts and strikes and the system of industrial democracy and employee participation.

11. The highest levels of trade union membership are found in countries such as Sweden, Finland, Ireland and Belgium. Moderate levels of membership exist in Germany, Switzerland, Italy and the Netherlands, and low levels of unionization in Britain, France and Spain.

12. Union responses to the economic climate have ranged from outright refusal to play any part in the management of crisis amongst employers (e.g. in France), to attempts to intervene at the organization, sector or national level in order to relieve the economic crisis (e.g. in Italy), to defensive strategies in the face of job insecurity (e.g. in Britain) through to collaborative strategies in areas such as incomes policies and social programmes (e.g. in Germany and Sweden). There are clear cultural differences in the style of labour relations.

13. Cross-national comparisons of the frequency, size and duration of industrial stoppages show considerable diversity. In countries like Ireland the pattern has been one of a few long stoppages. In Italy, Finland and Spain the number of people participating in stoppages has been high, whilst in France and Portugal the number of stoppages has been high. Belgium, Denmark, the Netherlands, Norway and Sweden have seen a relatively low incidence of strike activity, whilst in Britain no one pattern has been dominant.

14. There have been three waves of industrial democracy in Europe, with the latest wave bringing an extension of ownership rights, both to management and employees, through the growth of financial participation in stock option schemes, management and employee buy-outs, stock ownership, producer co-operatives and wage earner funds. Participation has also increased through more devolved managerial decision making.

15. Whilst several factors have served to promote convergence or harmonization of industrial relations across Europe, all European countries still have their own institutional arrangements for managing the employment relationship. The Social Chapter has the potential to form the keystone of a new social dimension. Implementation of a range of forty-seven directives on matters such as the re-organization of working time, the freedom of movement of EU workers and the equal treatment of men and women has begun. These directives are intended to improve the working of the internal market, to make labour more transparent within the European Union, to improve living and working conditions and to protect health and safety.

16. The extent to which the Social Chapter represents a new regime for industrial relations or merely fragmented social policy has yet to be determined. It will not, however, significantly extend workers rights or replace existing national rules or institutions in the short term. Considerable diversity in industrial relations is likely to remain for the foreseeable future.

PART FOUR

Future Issues in European Human Resource Management

CHAPTER SIXTEEN

Emerging HRM Issues in the Late 1990s

Thinking European, acting through processes of transition

A NEED TO UNDERSTAND THE EUROPEAN PERSPECTIVE

What are the main conclusions from this book? There have been three major themes that have emerged from the material:

1. A need to understand human resource management (HRM) from a European perspective.
2. An underlying process of transition that has generated new patterns of convergence and divergence in European HRM.
3. The emergence of new concepts of organization and structure which are creating a new set of HRM imperatives.

The first theme has been the need to understand HRM from a European perspective. In Chapter One we argued that attention has shifted away from the traditional and specialist areas of personnel management towards broader strategic issues as organizations attempt to change their culture, redesign their structure and resource a more appropriate set of skills and competencies. It has become necessary for organizations to improve the link between the processes through which they consider HRM issues and plan organizational strategy. In order to do this, a broad range of HRM policies have to be considered. The fierce debate about the benefits of HRM that took place in Britain in the 1980s will probably take place within European organizations throughout the 1990s. Political influences, the level of leadership within European organizations and the extent to which European personnel functions can manage their credibility will all play a role in determining how successful organizations are in achieving many of the changes in practice they must make. A wide range of people-related business issues will be faced by European organizations in the 1990s, such as cost competitiveness, changes in structure, the need to enhance organizational competitiveness, the need to develop employee competence and the need to manage cultural diversity. These will place a premium on effective HRM practices. However, whilst US concepts of HRM are clearly relevant to the European context, it is essential that European organizations adapt Anglo-Saxon models of HRM to their own situation.

Why is this the case? Whilst there is no such thing as a single European pattern of HRM and marked differences exist between European countries in terms of their practices as a composite group, European countries are sufficiently alike to be distinguished from the US. In considering whether to adopt US management tools or techniques, European organizations have to consider their more restricted levels of autonomy, an industrial history which has produced a lower exposure to market processes, a greater emphasis on the role of the group over the individual, the increased role of social partners in the employment relationship, and higher levels of government intervention. Whilst the HRM issues being dealt with in Europe are remarkably similar to those faced in the US, these issues have historically been handled along different lines. Moreover, the competence, career paths and professional background of HRM managers varies across Europe. German HRM professionals, with their strong legalistic background, have a very different mindset in comparison to their less formal Anglo-Saxon colleagues, whilst the financial backgrounds of many Dutch and Italian HRM professionals produces yet a different focus. The desire to devolve responsibility for HRM issues to line managers also varies considerably across Europe, as does the level of strategic influence of HRM professionals. It is not possible to tell whether these differences are caused by cultural constraints, or simply represent different levels and stages of the industrialization process across Europe. Nevertheless, patterns of HRM in Europe showed a high degree of consistency in the early 1990s, in that the areas of communality remained so and areas of national variation persisted. From a strategic perspective, there appears to be a common emphasis on the need to promote levels of empowerment, the role of communication, the need to improve horizontal management processes, the use of information technology to help structure the organization, the strategic role of recruitment, the importance of training and career management, and the need for a closer link between pay and performance. However, there are still diverse practices in the extent to which organizational cultures based on diversity and equality of opportunity are promoted, a philosophy of centralization is emphasized in organizational structures, flexible work practices are adopted, customer service is emphasized, measured and rewarded, and innovation and creativity are rewarded. In facing the simultaneous patterns of both convergence and divergence within European HRM practice, organizations have to decide whether they wish to create a European form of HRM, or a form of HRM that will be effective in Europe. There is a difference. In order to do this it is necessary to understand those factors that determine current national differences.

Despite the increasing internationalization of European organizations, many national differences in institutional systems still exist in the mid-1990s. The roles of the state, financial sectors, national systems of education and training and labour relations systems have combined to create unique 'business recipes' or 'logics of managerial action' in each country which guide much management practice. Economic activities and resources are controlled and co-ordinated differently, as are market connections and the development of skills within organizations. Certain European business recipes, such as that evidenced in Germany, appear to be more tightly integrated and consistent and are therefore more likely to be enduring of external pressures for change. Paradoxically, it is these same business recipes that are coming under most philosophical pressure for change. In relation to other parts of the world, the social, legislative and welfare context also influences many areas of HRM in Europe, as do the lower levels of organizational autonomy, a preference for co-determination, a greater emphasis on corporate and social responsibility, the ever present likelihood of state intervention and attempts to 'socially engineer' organizations. The relative size and strength of the private and public sectors and differences in the degree of integration between public and private sector have helped to create national differences in existing HRM practices, as have differences in the typical size of organizations. All these factors make it clear that management theories and practices – particularly those concerned with HRM – are constrained by national cultures.

We developed a number of historical and cultural insights into the various processes, philosophies and problems of national models of HRM in Europe throughout Part One of the book and in Chapter Ten. These insights will maintain their potency for many years to come. This is because national culture will shape the behaviour and structure the perceptions that European managers have of the world and the possible solutions to the current threats faced by their organizations. There are differences in the attitudes that European managers have towards the exercise of authority, the extent to which they will delegate power and the degree to which they will allow themselves to be forced into taking a short-term perspective. European managers approach the 1990s with different assumptions about appropriate pay systems and the importance of distributive justice within them, the need for centralization and vertical hierarchies within their organizational structures, the extent to which they can facilitate effective performance management through the manager–subordinate relationship and their openness towards job and career mobility. In attempting to control such differences, organizational cultures have historically magnified differences in national culture.

Despite the fact that Sweden has more multinational organizations *per capita* than any other European country – with Asea Brown Boveri, Tetra Laval, Ericsson and Electrolux as prime examples – the eventual collapse of the planned merger between Volvo and Renault under the weight of stakeholder power and objections to the perceived national roles led many to question whether the Nordic countries would be able to achieve closer integration with Continental Europe. At the same time the aborted Alcazar project merger between Scandinavian Airlines System (SAS) and the three other carriers of KLM, Swissair and Austrian Airlines led to concerns over the workability of transnational mergers. Two business heroes of the 1980s – Pehr Gyllenhammar and Jan Carlson – suffered as a result of their avowed Europeanism. All things being equal, the creation of transnational organizations that move beyond nationality in terms of employee attitudes and values may remain a myth for several years to come.

EUROPEAN HRM IN TRANSITION

However, all things are not equal. Despite the many obstacles and provisos that must be associated with the emergence of a European brand of HRM, it seems that a fundamental transition is taking place. Global competition is forcing organizations continually to work with and learn from people worldwide. International organizational behaviour and HRM in the 1990s is shifting from a perspective of cultural influence, compromise and adaptation, to one based on collaboration and cross-cultural learning. The current standing of many national models of HRM in Europe is under extreme threat from transitions in the shape and nature of organizations and developments in the business environment. The business environment is changing in a way that suggests that there is no going back for any of us.

The second theme that has linked the material together has therefore been the notion of transition. Differences in HRM do not seem quite as stark when European organizations consider their future. There is a degree of convergence taking place. A wide range of pressure points in the business environment have created an irresistible force for change in Europe. As a consequence, HRM practices are in a period of transition under the influence of two imperatives: a pan-European requirement to create new organizational structures and HRM systems that are capable of surviving rapid and 'discontinuous' change; and a common collection of strategic pressures (such as globalization, rationalization, business integration and social and demographic problems) that are reshaping – indeed possibly superseding – national differences in HRM. These pressures for change will not only shape the context for European HRM, but will increasingly determine its content. The material covered in Chapter Four demonstrated that strategically-minded HRM specialists, personnel directors and senior line managers have to anticipate a wide range of business trends, understand their implications and implement new policies and practices in order to 'continuously improve' their organizations. In doing this they will need to maintain sensitivity to the issues covered in Part One of the book.

Throughout the book we have endeavoured to analyse and describe European HRM against the touchstone of business transition. It is inevitable that radical changes in the content of HRM in European organizations will take place. Whilst deep philosophical divisions over the eventual future for Europe will remain, most commentators agree that the essence of the problem is the need to find a balance between international competitiveness and the maintenance of national cultures. European countries are now quite tightly integrated with as much as 83 per cent of investment and consumption covered by production from within Europe. An active and unique economic, business and social policy is therefore a possibility. Yet, few believe that Europe can ignore issues of international competitiveness. In the mid-1990s four reports from UNICE (the European employers' federation), the European Round Table (a network of forty industrialists from the leading organizations), the European Group of Socialist Parties in the European Parliament and the Delors White Paper for the European Commission (a wide range of political constituencies) all agreed on a common diagnosis of Europe's problems. Fundamental changes are expected in the balance of trade and global competition, the balance between savings and investment, the harnessing of new technology, the harmonization of national and pan-European economic policy and increased flexibility in the labour market. Why? Because Europe is plagued by lower levels of productivity in comparison to its worldwide competitors and has a large trade deficit.

Many European organizations now believe that they will have to create a different competitive means as they redefine their problem of poor competitiveness. As a result, there will be considerable change in levels of competitiveness. National business models will also come under extreme threat as the 1990s recession (which has been the deepest in Europe for sixty years) dents European optimism. European organizations are under pressure to improve their productivity because producing goods and services in Europe is relatively expensive. High levels of taxation, strong trade unions, a web of employment legislation and high levels of social welfare provision have combined to produce perhaps the world's best standard of living and quality of life. However, the removal of trade barriers, the globalization of trade and advances in production techniques in the Far East means that Europe's underlying quality differential can no longer be guaranteed. Many technological innovations now sweep around the world within a three year period. Whilst the final internal economic architecture of Europe that will face this challenge has yet to emerge, there has already been a process of asset redistribution on a pan-European scale in the run up to the SEM and this has triggered new developments in HRM. Organization structures, work practices, employee training and development needs, levels of international mobility, career development patterns and performance management requirements have all been influenced. At the same time there has been an extensive process of restructuring and rationalization as European organizations responded to the growing international competitive threat. In the process, distinctive national models of HRM have been challenged by powerful and generic patterns of industrial sector competitive dynamics. Some transnational organizations have exported jobs across the EU to cheaper wage economies or to countries outside the EU on the grounds of relative labour costs, market expansion or technological deregulation. Historical differences in levels of state ownership have been eroded as a massive process of privatization has swept across Europe and beyond. Policies of retrenchment, control of public expenditure, and restructuring of labour markets have led to reductions in employment, new patterns of HRM, and industrial unrest.

There has also been a massive transformation of Central and East European economies, although the social costs have been extremely high and the process of change is expected to be long, slow and painful. Europe faces a destiny of either greater integration across the whole Union, or the creation of a two-tier Europe, in which high wages in the first tier countries would be paid for by high performance products, but in other areas jobs would be lost to the cheaper second tier countries. The second more loosely integrated tier would only be able to attract investment for low-skilled, low-wage production at the cost of higher inflation, fluctuating interest rates and uneven economic growth. Consequently, the overall position of Europe could deteriorate further.

On top of these economic pressures a series of social and demographic pressures have combined to create a mosaic of influences on European HRM policies and practices. Conflicting arguments abound as to whether Europe should equalize differentials in social costs, reduce working time in an attempt to share out what employment there is, or significantly reduce social entitlement in a response to competitive pressure. Most likely, all three processes will occur, changing HRM policies and practices all the more. Unemployment levels have risen across Europe, and whilst there are large differences in unemployment between industrial sectors, geographical regions and demographic groups, concerted efforts at job creation have done little to dent the rising tide of unemployment and the increasing pressure this has put on social costs and social unrest. Declining birth rates may ease unemployment pressures in the short term, but increase them in the longer term as skills shortages are experienced and the size and purchasing power of domestic markets are reduced. Age-dependency ratios are also set to increase significantly, with pension funds and employee contributions to social funds coming under immense pressure. Few analysts believe that current social welfare systems can sustain the drain on their funds. The social, employment and HRM implications of the ensuing 'age wars' are only just beginning to dawn on Europeans. More women are joining the workforce, helping to fuel pressure on the need for more flexible time patterns of employment and slowly influencing management styles and career patterns within European organizations.

A pan-European trend towards flexibility of employment is eroding historical differences in employment protection and social legislation. Deregulation, attacks on employment rigidity and the availability of new patterns of work have all attracted new entrants to the labour force and opened up internal labour markets. However, at a societal level this organizational flexibility may result in a pauperization, not just a peripheralization, of employment and an increase in divisions between socially-protected workers and those in unprotected jobs. Levels of education and training are increasing as European countries cope with skill shortages. Complex patterns of skills shortage in some areas exist hand-in-hand with a marked over-supply of labour in others. This is generating new patterns of labour mobility. Employee attitudes are hardening towards immigration and the transfer of employment. Moreover, the values and expectations of the workforce are also changing. Employment is playing less of a central role in the lives of many people and European organizations face conflicting pressures from a new generation of highly educated workers who want more opportunities for development, autonomy, flexibility and meaningful work and the mass of employees whose levels of commitment and job satisfaction are falling. The net result is an increasingly instrumental attitude to work, which will make the process of creating change in European organizations all the more intricate.

The combination of these social and economic pressures is leading to numerous changes in HRM provision across European organizations. Wage disparities are being reduced, bargaining structures decentralized, the role of trade unions is changing and organizations are faced with paradoxical trends of deregulation in some areas but increasing employment legislation in others. The most pressing HRM issues are the need to create flatter and more flexible European-wide organization structures, a stronger emphasis on external customers, and greater sensitivity to national cultural differences whilst attempting to converge HRM policies. In response to these issues, European organizations are pursuing common policies aimed at enhancing their management skills, promoting flexibility, encouraging participation, creating new career paths, building international workforces and attempting to develop an organizational capability for the future.

In doing this, there is both competition between European countries through their involvement in foreign direct investment and a process of industrial restructuring. European economies are becoming dominated increasingly by large multinational organizations. The new economic environment for Europe in the 1990s has created the need for a new form of organization – the transnational organization – which recognizes new resources and capabilities, captures them and then leverages the advantages on a worldwide scale. The prospect of transnational organizations is seen by many as a possible new source of European competitive advantage, because it may spur performance beyond the limits of national competitiveness. Whilst these developments may eventually lead to a new European model of management, they are already creating new HRM imperatives. In addition to the emergence of a flexible cadre of international managers capable of implementing complex strategies, European organizations are developing stronger co-ordinating centres. Long-lasting decisions are being made about what should be managed centrally and what is best managed locally. The answers are being determined on an industry basis, again superseding national models of HRM.

More immediately, a process of integration of European industry is being driven by high levels of foreign direct investment. In its broadest sense this represents a competition between workers, governments, organizations, markets and business systems, with clear winners and losers. Mergers and acquisitions have become more intense as European economic space is re-organized and clear geographical and sectoral patterns of capital flow can be detected. Associated with this restructuring, there has been a process of shareholder democratization and legislative reform. The basis of effective corporate performance is being questioned within European organizations as a battle between competing forms of capitalism. Various forms of strategic alliance have also proved a popular option as European organizations attempt to access new markets, technologies or resources, create economies of scale, share the costs and risks of technological innovation, create barriers to takeovers, or slowly exit from non-core businesses.

This integration of European business through foreign direct investment, either in the form of mergers and acquisitions or strategic alliances, is affecting patterns of European HRM in four ways. There are changes in the overall employment levels and structure of industries. New dynamics of business networking have created different mindsets and reference points for HRM decisions. Different patterns of HRM practices are created in foreign-owned organizations as core techniques are transferred from the acquirer. Finally, the need to tackle specific HRM problems that are associated with the actual process of merging and integration generates new policies and practices. The 1990s may be characterized by a period of industry shake-outs, restructuring and a consolidation of the position of the survivors. These new dynamics of competition within each industrial sector will further accelerate transition in national models of HRM. However, European HRM may also undergo a period of revolution, not just transition. As a final theme we provide an analysis of the most likely revolutionary changes that may structure developments in HRM in the 1990s and beyond.

NEW STRUCTURAL CONCEPTS FOR THE 1990s: NEW HRM IMPERATIVES

The third theme of the book has been the emergence of new ground rules. New concepts are irrevocably changing the nature of HRM in organizations. Most of these new concepts are driven by a change in the structure of organization. Ludo van Heyden of INSEAD argues that the 1990s will be a decade not of resource scarcity, but of excess capacity – an era of power for the consumer and purchaser but not for the producer or supplier. In each layer – whether it be suppliers, producers, distributors or consumers – trade liberalization is creating a new tranche of competitors. No one organization can dominate all aspects of competition and so faces a host of competitors from several different industrial backgrounds and each operating to their own competitive logic. This is happening at a time of 'consumer satiation' with a reduced overall demand for physical goods – certainly in the European market. He asks the question: how many lap top computers can you carry in your suitcase? As the decade of consumerism (the 1980s) has passed, the problem European organizations face in the 1990s is 'customer scarcity', not resource scarcity. Organizations are not short of technology, or production capacity, cash, capital or people. Finding customers, retaining them and continuing the relationship with them will be the core problem faced by all European organizations. In this environment, the development of distinctive business concepts will be the main shaping force of HRM practices. However, whilst innovations will come from organizational practice, new paradigms for management thinking, industrial sector-specific solutions and learning from regional perspectives, Europe is best viewed as a collection of regions. We therefore need to be sensitive to the way that small and medium-sized organizations adapt the general developments in HRM and management thinking outlined in this final chapter so that they work on a local scale. What are these new developments? What are the driving forces that are breaking down national patterns of HRM at the organizational level?

In Chapter Eight we analysed the complex pressures facing European organizations as they change their structure. We now consider the processes that will be used to reassess and plan future organization designs. We discussed the Anglo-Saxon origins of HRM at length in Chapter One, and then pointed to some key differences in implementation in Chapter Two. In the field of organization and work structuring a similar situation applies. A host of new concepts and buzz words have appeared in the American management literature, very quickly moving into the UK, and through consultancy practice into the major European multinational organizations.

There are three major processes at the organizational level that are forcing a change in HRM and overriding historical patterns of activity (see Illustration 16.1). These concepts are now discussed as part of our overall conclusions.

Illustration 16.1   **Three major processes that are reshaping national patterns of HRM at the organizational level.**

- Downsizing and delayering, driven by natural gains in productivity and the push-down of information in organizations.
- Business process thinking and the 'reengin-

eering' of work to create new organizational designs.
- The creation of new business networks within the economic chain.

DOWNSIZING AND DELAYERING: PROACTIVE AND REACTIVE RESTRUCTURING

The first phenomenon at the organizational level that is reshaping and breaking down national patterns of HRM is the process of downsizing and delayering within organizations. In Chapters Four and Five we pointed to the likelihood of significant rationalization of European business, reductions in employment, and simplifications of management structures. In Chapter Eleven we pointed out that as the process of rationalization speeds up, it will become even more difficult for organizations to resource their international assignments, encourage career mobility and accelerate the process of internationalization. Therefore, one of the most pressing problems for European organizations in structural terms is how to cope with the problem of downsizing and rationalization (Cameron, Freeman and Mishra, 1991; Heister, Jones and Benham, 1988; Kozlowski, Chao, Smith, and Hedlund, 1993; Schneier, Shaw and Beatty, 1993; Tylczak, 1991; Vollmann and Brazas, 1993). Downsizing is a separate process to broader issues of change across the organizational life cycle and the management of organizational decline. It is a deliberate decision to reduce the workforce that is intended to improve organizational performance (Kozlowski *et al.*, 1993) and so may occur in the absence of overt processes of decline.

The era of the large organization, ever increasing in its scope and level of employment has ended as organizations realize they cannot afford to own and control all they need to deliver success (Doorley, 1993). Indeed, the brake was put on growth in the size of organizations by the early 1970s. *The Economist* (1990b) cites work on the size of organizations in the US, the UK and Germany by T. Huppes (see Figure 16.1). It can be seen that in the UK the average size of organizations for the years 1930, 1969, 1975 and 1990 was 30, 94, 61 and 31 employees respectively. In Germany the average size of organizations in 1951, 1974 and 1990 was 64, 89 and 75 employees respectively, i.e. a similar pattern to the UK with less marked downsizing up to 1990. In the US the average number of employees per organization fell by 20 per cent from 1975 to 1985.

Vollmann and Brazas (1993) describe some of the findings from IMD's long-term research project 'Manufacturing 2000' in relation to the debate on the effectiveness of downsizing strategies. They point out that downsizing is often equated with sudden, drastic levels of redundancy. It is the most visible part of reactive restructuring and rationalization. This need not be the case. Reactive restructuring is based on downsizing. Proactive restructuring includes downsizing, but also adds value to work by diverting effort to activities that add customer value to the organization's products and processes. It is given the less threatening name of 'rightsizing'.

There are two powerful structural forces that are reducing the requirement for labour and driving the need for 'downsizing' across several US and European industries (especially manufacturing) and make continued high levels of 'downsizing' or

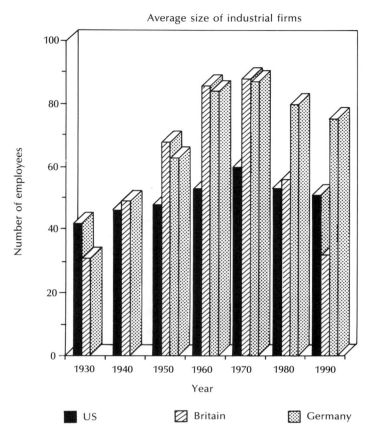

Average size of industrial firms

US   Britain   Germany

Figure 16.1 Average size of organizations in US, UK and Germany.

'rightsizing' inevitable (Vollmann and Brazas, 1993). The first driving force is 'natural productivity' defined as growth in sales output per hour of labour input as a result of technological improvements in processes, product designs and component materials. High technology industries can see gains of 20 per cent plus year on year. Lower rates exist for other industries. If sales cannot increase fast enough to compete with these gains, the result is a reduced labour requirement and downsizing. Deferring a response can lead to the need for traumatic actions, as Philips found out in the early 1990s.

The second driving force is 'information push-down' whereby advances in information technology (IT) and information management transform the underlying decision processes of the organization (one of the basic building blocks of organization). These changes in structure and way in which work is carried out reduce the need for service staff (those who advise, counsel or co-ordinate but do not either lead or operate) drastically. As layers are cut out from the organization, the information previously residing with the service staff is pushed down the hierarchy in the organization. A range of surveys have revealed the extent of change in the US. Some 66 per cent of organizations with more than 5,000 employees reduced the size of their workforce in the latter half of the 1980s (Greenberg, 1988). The process has moved away from blue collar workforces to white collar workers. Over 85 per cent of the Fortune 1000 organizations downsized their white collar workforce between 1987 and 1991, with more than 50 per cent downsizing in 1990 alone. One million US managers lost their jobs in 1990 and 50 per cent took pay cuts of 30–50 per cent to get new jobs (Cameron, Freeman and Misthra, 1991). This shift of downsizing strategies to white collar workforces is also evident in Europe (Melcher and Levine, 1990) and significant reductions in employment and the number of management levels have been seen not just in the UK, but across many European organizations. As we argued in Chapter Four, comparable levels of rationalization are anticipated in Europe, with the automobile, chemical, steelmaking and financial service sectors leading the way.

As the 1990s advance, the pressure on US and European organizations to maintain competitive cost structures and improve productivity will continue to grow. In Chapter Eight we described the long process of structural change in the Bayer Group as it evolved from a functional to a product-based structure. In January 1993 this process was continued, but with the additional ingredient of 'delayering'. Six management layers were reduced to four layers, the number of business groups were reduced from 23 to 21, with a new direct reporting relationship to the board, and a fall of 10 per cent in the number of management-grade employees was announced (Hasell, 1993). The focus of research to help managers understand how to manage this process has been on the reactions of individuals who have lost their jobs, the psychological impact of unemployment and the reactions of survivors to the process of downsizing. There is less known about the impact of the many different mechanisms for downsizing on individual reactions and the eventual impact on the organization. Knowledge is based on experience, which is both recent and stems mainly from the US and UK, two countries that pursued these strategies over the 1980s. The impact on European managers in the 1990s is unknown. Moreover, there has been increasing criticism of downsizing strategies in the US which may apply to the European experience if they are pursued for productivity reasons alone (Schneier, Shaw and Beatty, 1993). Major US organizations (such as Kodak, General Motors, Chrysler, Pratt and Whitney, General Electric, Unisys, Digital and IBM) responded to productivity pressures by 'downsizing', 'restructuring' and 'rightsizing' in the 1980s and cutting the size of the workforce. However, such responses tended only to treat the symptoms of poor productivity, too many people, rather than its likely cause, the amount of work and the way it is done. Schneier *et al.* (1993) cite surveys by the Society for Human Resource Management in the US of 1,468 'downsized' organizations which found that in 50 per cent of cases levels of productivity either stayed the same or worsened. Similar findings emerged from work by the American Productivity and Quality Center and other researchers. Less than half of the organizations that downsized reduced their expenses, less than a third increased profits, and only one-fifth increased productivity.

Vollmann and Brazas (1993) point to the corrosive effect downsizing has on the psychological contract between employer and employee (see Figure 16.2). The relatively low productivity gains that have been achieved from downsizing in the US and UK can, in part, be explained by the hidden social costs that result from a more instrumental approach to work (see Chapter Four) and changed employee behaviours. After three years of economic downturn and rising unemployment in the UK in the early 1990s, occupational psychologists began to talk of 'recession fatigue' which creates a negative, devil may care attitude to messages from employers. This more instrumental approach is reflected in proactive behaviours such as higher levels of absenteeism and abuse of sick leave, more theft and shrinkage and acts of sabotage to important resources such as databases. Few organizations publicly admit to such behaviour, but it happens none the less and carries high cost. There is also a set of reactive behaviour, such as: higher levels of stress and the natural loss of effectiveness that goes along with this; legitimate stress-related illness and high absenteeism; and a

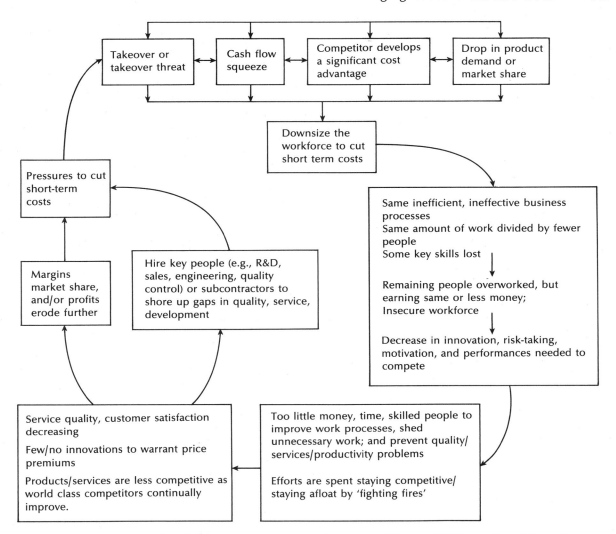

Figure 16.2 The vicious cycle of downsizing. *Source*: Vollmann and Brazas (1993), reprinted from *European Management Journal*, **11(1)**, 18–29, T. Vollmann and M. Brazas, 'Downsizing', © 1993, with kind permission from Pergamon Press Ltd, Headington Hill Hall, Oxford, OX3 0BX, UK.

staff turnover 'timebomb' where large numbers of disillusioned staff (typically of younger age) leave the organization at the first sign of economic recovery to exact revenge for miserable times past. Then there are the costs of non-conformance: recruitment or training costs to cover unplanned staff loss or absence; development time to bring staff back to full productivity in new roles; and re-work necessitated by confused work process in the aftermath of re-organization. It is not surprising that Schneier, Shaw and Beatty (1993) reported such low productivity gains. Illustration 16.2 provides an example of using business process redesign to combat such productivity issues.

Downsizing exercises tend to be associated with a number of approaches aimed at improving productivity. The relative advantages and disadvantages of each have been summarized by Schneier, Shaw and Beatty (1993) and are shown in Table 16.1. Each of these approaches has different implications for the structure of organizations. We

Table 16.1 **Productivity improvement approaches.**

Approach*	Description	Potential advantages*	Potential disadvantages*	Impacts on dimensions of structure**
1 Hiring freeze	Company ceases hiring, with very few exceptions	(a) Can de done at no cost to company (b) Simple to implement (c) May have minimal negative impact on morale of employees	(a) May not have a significant impact on productivity (b) May preclude opportunities to obtain needed skills, fresh perspective	↓ Professionalism
2 Financial separation incentives	Certain employees offered financial incentives to leave or retire early	(a) All terminations are voluntary (b) May be relatively painless way of reducing white collar employees	(a) May lead to loss of value employees (b) May be expensive (c) May not have a significant impact on productivity	↓ Professionalism ↓ Hierarchy of authority
3 Budgetary controls	Strict controls are placed on increasing overhead expenses; detailed substantiation required for expenditures	(a) Good 'preventive maintenance' approach keeps expenses under control (b) May instil strong sense of fiscal management	(a) May not provide enough impact for companies with currently excessive overheads (b) May inappropriately restrict some high value, high leverage, high potential units if applied uniformly across the company	↑ Formalization ↑ Standardization ↑ Centralization
4 'Mandated' lay-offs	Workforce reduced by specific percentage or number, across entire company, or within division or unit	(a) May be quick way to achieve expense reduction (b) May target those with performance problems, if done carefully	(a) May not have lasting impact on productivity (or on costs or profits) (b) May not address root causes of decreased white collar productivity (c) May have negative effects on employee morale	↓ Specialization ↓ Hierarchy of authority ↓ Complexity ↓ Professionalism

			Impact on dimensions of structure
5 Time and motion studies	Studies aimed at analysing and then streamlining worker activities to increase efficiency/speed (most typically conducted with production workers)	(a) Analyses workers' actions and processes, identifying causes of problems (e.g. delays, inaccuracies) (b) May lead to lasting change	(a) Scope is generally confined to a few organizational processes (b) May not have a significant impact on organization's overall productivity	↑ Formalization ↑ Specialization ↑ Standardization
6 Task analysis	Emphasis on analysis of work, often by external party; outputs of white collar (overhead) jobs and units analysed to assess their costs and their 'value' to customers; redundant or low-value tasks that can be eliminated, reduced, or improved are identified; often a target overhead reduction (e.g. 30–40 percent) is provided	(a) Utilizes data-based process to identify redundant, low-value work (b) Focuses on reducing work and, if appropriate, reducing number of white collar employees	(a) Some improvements may be difficult to implement (b) The organization's key processes (potential causes for low production) may remain unchanged (c) Can take a relatively long time	↓ Formalization ↓ Specialization ↑ Standardization ↓ Complexity ↑ Professionalism
7 Business process re-engineering/ work effectiveness	Emphasis on data gathering and implementation; internal 'customer–supplier' teams identify improvement opportunities and implement solutions; work processes mapped, identifying underlying causes of problems, reducing the amount of work, improving processes and related systems (e.g. measurement; reward)	(a) Solutions are developed by those involved in the process, making them more easily implementable (b) May address barriers (e.g. structure, systems, skills) to lasting effectiveness/ productivity	(a) May be slow to implement (b) Requires organizational leadership, commitment, and discipline	↓ Formalization ↓ Specialization ↑ Standardization ↑ Hierarchy of authority ↓ Complexity ↓ Centralization ↑ Professionalism

* Illustrative not exhaustive

** Where a dimension of structure is not mentioned it is either because it is not affected, or it could be changed in either direction

Source: After Schneier, Shaw and Beatty (1993), adapted to include impact on dimensions of structure. Reprinted from C. Schneier, D. Shaw and R. Beatty, 'Companies' attempts to improve performance while containing costs: quick fix versus lasting change', *Human Resource Planning*, **15(3)**, © 1993, with kind permission of the Human Resource Planning Society.

Illustration 16.2 **Business process redesign to combat work overload after downsizing.**

In the US growing competition and downsizing have extended the work week at the expense of productivity and morale. In the aftermath of a downsizing exercise fewer people remain and have to pick up the slack of workers who have left, resulting in higher stress levels and more works' compensation claims. Job demands increase both in volume and in quality. A survey of 21,400 employees by a US consulting firm found that 95 per cent of employees worked longer than the 40 hour workweek, with 57 per cent working an extra 6–20 hours a week, with a 10 hour workday becoming the norm. Since 1970 the average US worker puts in an extra 100 more hours a year (a whole month) of extra time into employment. US employees work 320 hours longer a year than French and German employees. As part of a co-ordinated response to the workload and stress issues associated with downsizing, some US organizations, such as Merck & Co., have redesigned work routines at the organizational level. The redesign of business processes lessens the work pressures on remaining staff but, of course, forever removes the need to employ new staff.

have added a link in Table 16.1 back to the seven structural dimensions of organizations identified by Daft (1992) and described in Chapter Eight.

NEW WAYS OF COMPETING AND VIEWING STRUCTURE: BUSINESS PROCESS RE-ENGINEERING

This leads us to the second phenomenon at the organizational level that is reshaping HRM – the growth of 'business process' thinking. In Chapter Eight we described a series of underlying principles of organization such as communications and interaction nodes or levels of managerial discretion. Traditionally these have been used to help shape organizations. However, Ulrich and Lake (1990) point out that many CEOs believe that simply doing more of what worked in the 1980s – restructuring, delayering and the mechanistic top down measures – will no longer work. Organizations are therefore trying increasingly to blur the boundaries between functions, people, the organization and its suppliers and customers. The most appropriate organizational design is not an organization chart, but a stable 'business process' which can be used to clarify reporting relationships, responsibilities and control systems. We noted in Chapter Eight that the smoothest examples of implementing pan-European organization structures occurred when issues of purpose, power, people and business process were left to the last (Blackwell, Bizet, Child and Hensley, 1992), but were nevertheless addressed.

A growing number of organizations are therefore adopting a new approach to structuring the organization and managing its performance called 'Business Process Re-engineering' (BPR) or 'Process Management' (Denton, 1991; Hammer, 1990; Hammer and Champy, 1993; Johansson, McHugh, Pendlebury and Wheeler, 1993; and Morris and Brandon, 1993). This approach represents a synthesis of business and systems management and aims to create dramatic improvements in response times, service and quality by cutting across departmental demarcations and formal organization boundaries. Johansson, McHugh, Pendlebury and Wheeler (1993), four international (Anglo-American) consultants from Coopers and Lybrand, have articulated some of the broad business implications of Hammer's (1990) original notions of BPR.

The 1980s saw a host of improvements to the business process within international organizations, such as:

- Total quality management (TQM).
- Just-in-time production (JIT).
- Manufacturing resource planning (MRP II).

These changes in business philosophy have been used to improve operations in areas as diverse as new product design teams, distribution networks and the application of advanced technology. However, the changes in philosophy engendered by TQM, JIT and MRP II have not been enough because in many instances they continued to encourage an internal focus. This is ill-suited to development of the transnational organization discussed in Chapter Five. Although many European organizations have managed to achieve dramatic operational efficiencies by improving productivity and reducing lead times, product inventories and cost of quality, these improvements have not been spread throughout the entire organization or industrial sector. TQM, JIT and MRP II programmes have frequently been led by managers who are functional specialists. The initiatives have been hampered by information systems and performance management systems that were still designed along functional lines (Kaplan and Murdock, 1991). Whilst individual functions may have been 'optimized', this has often been at the expense of the whole organization.

Despite the fact that most Western organizations are more quality-conscious, they remain '. . . highly bureaucratic, with departments acting individually and "throwing over the wall" to the next department, designs, information, product, and most of all problems. Different functions measure work and success in different ways and, therefore, have different goals and objectives. . .'.   Johansson *et al.* (1993, p. 7).

Given the level of competitive threat highlighted throughout this book, it is not surprising that BPR holds a number of attractions for the large European multinationals. The current evolution and development of organization structures has been fraught with difficulties. Structures are seen increasingly as obstacles to change, not drivers of it. Yet intense competition is demanding a quantum improvement in performance in terms of quality, time and cost. BPR offers the opportunity to close competitive performance gaps rapidly, rather than having to chase for 'continual improvements'. Organizations can establish world class performance and create the rules of the game for their industry, it is claimed. They may also redefine and strengthen the basic capabilities that have determined their historical success. Finally, BPR can reinforce a collaborative (rather than a competitive) behavioural set within the organization. Consultancies parade these attractions and tempt organizations with radical performance improvements, such as:

- Taking out up to 70 per cent of the people and 90 per cent of the time in some business processes by shifting from a functional hierarchy to a team-managed process.
- Improving quality from a 5 per cent level of defects or rejects to a defect level of one part per 10,000.
- Reducing administrative process costs by 50 per cent.
- Increasing customer satisfaction by 35–95 per cent.

EVOLVING BUSINESS RECIPES: CONVERGENCE TOWARDS UNDERLYING BUSINESS PROCESSES?

Despite the current focus on the topic, process thinking is not a new phenomenon. Johansson *et al.* (1993) drew upon the work of Italian consultant Giorgio Merli (1987) to explain the different international paths taken towards the development of a process orientation. The national business systems or recipes outlined in Chapter Three are not static. They have developed over time, and are now converging (see Figure 16.3). After the Second World War both Japanese and Anglo-Saxon organizations concentrated on securing supply through bureaucratic production strategies and non-participative management styles. Rapid growth saw the development of a bureaucratic and functional type of structure. Japanese organizations focused this bureaucracy on their production systems (with the assumption that if they got this right, market share would follow), with leading organizations like the Toyota Motor Company introducing a management system in the 1960s that was the forerunner of the JIT improvements that were initiated in the West only by the 1980s. Anglo-Saxon organizations took a more immediate market driven approach to capitalize on the high levels of growth in the 1960s and early 1970s. The 1973 oil crisis saw Japanese organizations, still production driven but with a high emphasis on getting the underlying business processes right, start to move towards a stronger marketing orientation. Sony, Toyota, Nissan and Honda all appeared in US markets in force at this time and soon followed into

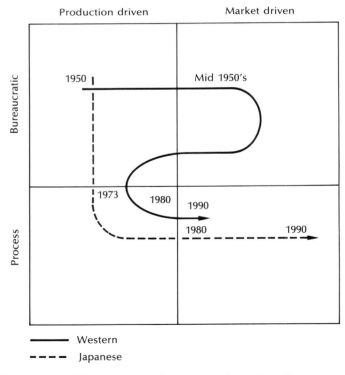

Figure 16.3 Japanese and Western use of process orientation. *Source*: reproduced from *Business Process Re-engineering: Breakpoint strategies for market dominance* by H. Johansson, P. McHugh, A. Pendlebury and W. Wheeler, copyright © 1993, by permission of John Wiley and Sons, Inc.

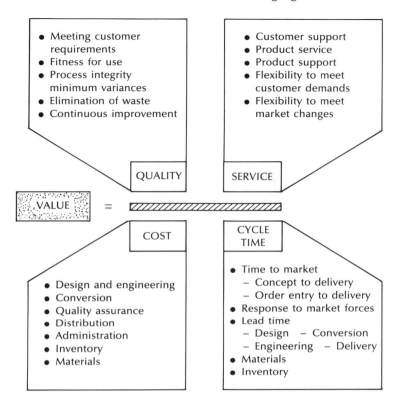

Figure 16.4 New value-based performance indices that shape corporate governance. *Source*: reproduced from *Business Process Re-engineering: Breakpoint strategies for market dominance* by H. Johansson, P. McHugh, A. Pendlebury and W. Wheeler, copyright © 1993, by permission of John Wiley and Sons, Inc.

European markets. Anglo-American organizations (who were less affected by the tripling of oil prices) still tried to compete for shrinking markets in a market driven bureaucratic way (the formula that had given US multinationals so much success in the 1950s). By the late 1970s and early 1980s Anglo-Saxon organizations were under severe competitive threat, and began to imitate and then adapt Japanese-influenced concepts such as TQM and JIT, concentrating far more on their production facilities and the overall business process.

However, this new philosophy was still being used in a tactical sense. Increasingly, it was appreciated that a (global) market driven perspective to business processes (i.e. improvements that could result in radical strides within the marketplace) represented the most powerful goal. Four 'value-metrics' guide corporate governance and may be used to quantify an organization's efforts in this area of global competition (see Figure 16.4).

WHAT DOES BUSINESS PROCESS RE-ENGINEERING ENTAIL?

BPR sounds attractive, but what does it really entail and can it be implemented within European – or indeed any international – organizations? Schneier, Shaw and Beatty (1993) draw a number of useful distinctions between total quality (TQ) approaches and BPR approaches (which they term 'work effectiveness'). These are shown in Table 16.2. As we outlined in our discussion of the co-ordinating mechanisms and modes of organizations in Chapter Eight, most work is traditionally carried out through functional divisions and hierarchical structures. Organizations break work down into a sequence of separate and narrowly defined tasks so that people can be organized and segregated into functions, such as sales or production, which are separately administered across a number of hierarchical layers. As a result, work and information within the organization flows across these boundaries step by step. This arrangement was well suited to work throughout most of the 1900s when the main goals of organizations were to achieve cost efficiency, growth and control (Woolfe, 1991) and has become ingrained into many organizational cultures. Yet in a post-industrial environment those organizations that survive tend to pursue the goals of innovation, quality and service. In order to deliver such goals, they have to rethink the way they

Table 16.2 **Comparing total quality (TQ) and business process re-engineering (BPR)*.**

Possible similarities	Possible differences	Potential common problems**
1. Cost reduction, quality improvement, performance improvement, and/or culture change are objectives	1. BPR takes a 'zero-based' approach to processes (i.e. first asks if the process should be eliminated)	1. Emphasis on process activity, versus results
2. Top management support is advocated as necessary	2. TQ may seek to improve existing processes. It typically emphasizes and may begin with use of a specific set of tools (e.g. SPC, cause and effect diagrams); BPR uses any and all tools (including TQ tools) as a means for improvement	2. Event-drive, versus integrated into culture/fabric/daily operations of organization
3. Workflow focus		3. Staff- or consultant-, versus user-driven
4. Empowerment advocated	3. BPR advocates attacking 'head-on' any cultural or systematic 'sacred cows' (e.g. organization reporting relationships, performance measures, rewards) that may block implementation: TQ usually operates within a function or department, hence some barriers to improvements are outside of the function's or department's control	4. Initiative broad, versus obtaining early success to build credibility
5. Logical, data-based approach utilized		
6. Continuous improvement advocated		
7. Determining and meeting customer expectations advocated	4. TQ may (initially) be focused on skill-building via classroom training; BPR is focused on designing and conducting forums where candid communication takes place, followed up with actions on the job; training may be used but not necessarily as a critical or initial activity	
8. Teams typically relied upon to produce significant improvements		
9. Follow-up advocated	5. BPR has often begun in white-collar work; TQ has often begun in operations/manufacturing	

TQ and BPR can be compatible and even interdependent
performance improvement approaches

* The lists are generalizations; both TQ and BPR may be conceived and implemented differently from the above in any given setting
** Applicable to most large-scale change initiatives
Source: reprinted from C. Schneier, D. Shaw and R. Beatty, 'Companies' attempts to improve performance while containing costs: quick fix versus lasting change', *Human Resource Planning*, **15**(3), 1–26, © 1993, with kind permission of the Human Resource Planning Society.

structure activities and work by concentrating instead on the business processes that cut across traditional functional boundaries. It has been argued that as European organizations migrate from a domestic to a pan-European or global structure, they need to break down traditional kinds of organization by linking and re-building their structure and operations from a process-orientated perspective (Woolfe, 1991).

BPR as a philosophy uses tools and techniques already developed as part of TQM and JIT initiatives, re-packages them and then applies them as part of a broader business perspective and vision. It represents a conscious effort to re-shape the organization behind a new vision of the marketplace and the customer and attempts to redefine business processes, organization structures and technology in a way that facilitates the streamlining, deletion or change in the way in which work is done (Oliver, 1993). BPR is therefore best defined as the means by which an organization can achieve radical change in performance by the application of tools and techniques that focus on the organization as a set of customer-orientated core business processes rather than a set of functions (Johansson *et al.*, 1993).

But what exactly do the management writers and consultants mean by a 'business process'? The business process perspective views an organization's activities as a single and continuous operation. Fundamental processes (usually originating in manufacturing areas but equally applicable to the delivery of a service) provide the real basis for competitive strength. A core business process combines both physical activity with information flow in order to address the needs of the marketplace. Most organizations or industries are best viewed as competing on no more than six or seven such processes. These 'processes' represent '. . . a set of linked activities that take an input and transform it to create an output' (Johansson *et al.*, 1993). A business process therefore emerges from:

- Identifying a tangible result or output that is required in the organization.
- Analysing the set of work activities that need to be involved.
- Identifying the most effective way of linking those activities.

Such processes may be physical, involve paperwork, be undertaken by computer, or may be a logical sequence of events. Woolfe (1991) gives the example of the process of taking a customer order. When an organization is structured along traditional functions such as sales, credit control, accounts and so forth, the process involves receiving the order, checking customer credit, pricing the order, scheduling production and confirming delivery in separate functions – which means that perhaps two hours of work takes up to six days to deliver because the work flows across functions, sits in queues, and involves each new function wasting time understanding the information that surrounds the task, stopping and restarting the work. Yet if the same activities are undertaken much at the same time, under the control of an individual or a dedicated team, the same two hours' work is carried out with no additional time elapsing and indeed probably quicker because hand-over tasks are no longer necessary, fewer controls are required and steps can be self-monitored. By organizing around a team that is directly accountable for delivering the output of the process (in this case taking a customer order) customer service is improved. However, the real benefits come from putting control over the process under a single umbrella, viewing the work as a simultaneous set of actions as opposed to a sequential flow from one action to another. Seeing the whole allows improvements to be made to the structure of work because it becomes easier to identify and eliminate unnecessary steps (such as making sure the right people talk to each other, only appropriate information is considered, decisions are made at the right level, and technology is used to carry out mundane steps or control basic steps).

By re-framing the work process and organization structure along such principles, radical improvements in performance become possible (see Figure 16.5). This offers the hope of breaking the vicious cycle of downsizing (see Figure 16.6). There are three main motivations for organizations to pursue a BPR approach, all of which could be seen in the description of the strategic pressures shaping European HRM in Part Two:

- A desire for cost reductions.
- Pressure to renew competitiveness in order to achieve parity with competitors or establish best practice.
- A desire for competitive dominance.

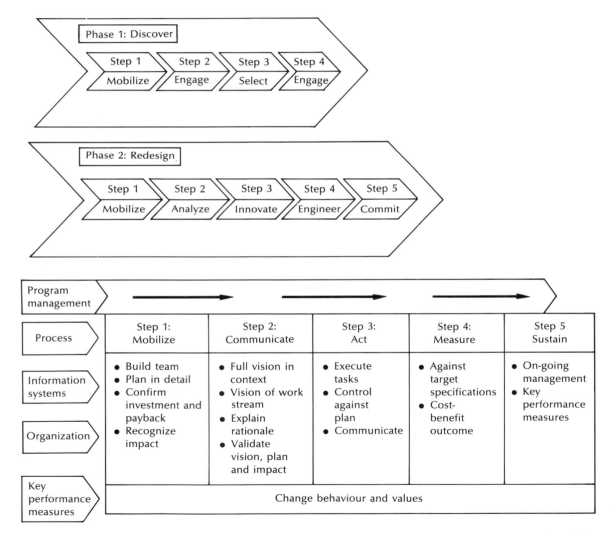

Figure 16.5 Three phases in a basic business process re-engineering approach. *Source:* reproduced from *Business Process Re-engineering: Breakpoint strategies for market dominance* by H. Johansson, P. McHugh, A. Pendlebury and W. Wheeler, copyright © 1993, by permission of John Wiley and Sons. Inc.

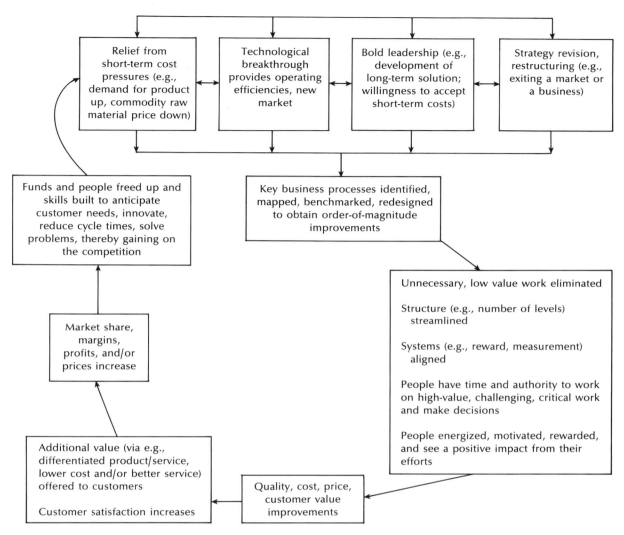

Figure 16.6 Breaking the vicious cycle of downsizing. *Source*: Vollmann and Brazas (1993), reprinted from *European Management Journal*, **11(l)**, 18–29, T. Vollmann and M. Brazas, 'Downsizing' © 1993, with kind permission from Pergamon Press Ltd, Headington Hill Hall, Oxford, OX3 0BX, UK.

AVOIDING THE TRAP OF TAYLORISM

The key to BPR is the ability to build an extensive understanding of the activities that constitute core business processes. This usually relies on 'process mapping' and 'data modelling' techniques, which have been developed over a long period, starting with the work of Frederick Taylor on productivity. Is BPR just a more up-to-date version of Taylorism, a reductionist and rationalizing approach to work study that will result in poorly designed jobs from a human point of view (see Chapter Twelve for the discussion of job design and the relative levels of adoption of Taylorist principles in work structuring across Europe)? There most certainly is a danger that the approach may just be used this way. Many process mapping techniques, whilst appearing

Table 16.3 **Range of analysis techniques that can constitute a business process re-engineering intervention.**

Type of information	Typical tools and techniques	Main application
Work study methods	Flow diagrams String diagrams Travel charts Process charts Multiple activity charts	Scientific methods of observation, data collection and analysis to improve productivity
Organization and method studies		Office operations analysed to achieve equal loading and efficient utilization of time
Process control	Computer flow charts using conventions such as International Definition (IDEF)	Dynamic characteristics of production facilities analysed to gather data to control outputs by adjusting inputs to the system
Process simulation	Computer programs using languages such as SIMAN (event-driven simulation language) or CINEMA (an animation tool)	Complex, highly automated processes are modelled on computers to test for responses to a range of operating conditions
Business modelling	Accounting models Marketing and pricing models Distribution modelling techniques Stochastic simulators	Business results simulated on mathematical and statistical models to gain an understanding of the impact of major environmental influences on the corporate plan
Systems engineering and analysis		Flow diagrams used to define procedural operations where computers or telecommunications affect some of the process

modern, operate on reductionist principles and do not pick up the complexity of human operation. The range of analysis techniques used in a typical BPR intervention are shown in Table 16.3. Indeed, Johansson *et al.* (1993) point out that in using BPR to structure organizations and work, there is a temptation to either suffer from 'paralysis by analysis' or to concentrate on simple reductionist improvements. For BPR to have any real benefits, a clear vision of the new process has to be set in place, and a variety of critical questions considered.

The pitfalls of process mapping are outlined in Illustration 16.3 whilst the potential benefits are highlighted in Illustration 16.4. It is in the answer to such questions that national cultural differences across Europe will come to the fore.

Illustration 16.3 **Pitfalls of process mapping: critical questions to bear in mind.**

■ Is the complexity necessary? ■ Are simplifications possible? ■ Are there too many interdepartmental transfers? ■ Are people empowered to fulfil their function? ■ Is the process effective?	■ Is work carried out efficiently? ■ Are costs appropriate? ■ Is there significant variability in load? ■ What drives process cost? ■ How is quality assured?

Source: Johansson *et al.* (1993).

Illustration 16.4 **Potential benefits of a business process re-engineering perspective.**

■ Encourages managers to see beyond their current mental models or images of organization by challenging the way work is done. ■ Links improvement and change efforts to strategic objectives and high-level performance goals. ■ Incorporates changes to the entire chain of related activities and presents an opportunity to re-align strategy, business processes, technology and people. ■ Identifies 'upstream' activities that drive 'downstream' performance.	■ Encourages thinking along defunctionalized and customer-orientated lines. ■ Involves an immediate radical change in operation and corporate governance, rather than continuous improvement mentality which may not improve European competitiveness quickly enough. ■ Facilitates organizational solutions that create more value for less effort, rather than just reducing the size of functions to cut costs. ■ Maximizes the potential of the individual and the team.

IMPLEMENTATION OF BUSINESS PROCESS RE-ENGINEERING IN EUROPE

In Chapter One we pointed out that it was a changing basis of competition that led towards the development of HRM. We are now seeing a common drive towards structuring organizations around their core business processes in the same way. Of course, the methods by which organizations may choose to implement this goal will reflect and draw upon national strengths and weaknesses in their existing HRM. We first touched upon the topic of BPR in Chapter Four with the description of re-engineering work at Sweden's ICA. It is clear that this North American import is being adapted by European organizations in order to overcome a different set of cultural impediments. However, Woolfe (1991) has reported a number of examples of process redesign examined as part of Butler Cox's Foundation research programme involving 400 of Europe's largest organizations (see Illustration 16.5).

BPR may have profound effects on European management thinking, as did the JIT approach in 1978 when it attacked the foundations of functional Taylorism, forced organizations to reconsider work as a continuous flow of activity linked to real demand and facilitated a managerial approach driven by concepts of speed and quality, i.e. a focus on how organizations competed, not on what they did (Johansson, McHugh, Pendlebury and Wheeler, 1993). It is an approach that matches transnational thinking:

... In the past, new concepts or approaches tend to gain acceptance in different time periods within each region. BPR seems to break this norm. There is a realization that no matter where

ustration 16.5 **European examples of business process re-engineering.**

Zeppelin Metallwerke, a German construction equipment dealer, distributes Caterpillar equipment. At any point in time its customers have more than 20,000 earth moving machines in the field, requiring Zeppelin to track over 100,000 different parts and get them quickly to their customers. The process was labour intensive, prone to errors, and administered at each of twenty-three branches. Zeppelin redesigned its parts order fulfilment process, centrally recording orders and controlling access to inventory, location of parts, distribution to staff, and accounting. The time taken to get replacement parts to customers was cut by a factor of four, and Zeppelin guarantees next day delivery on 98 per cent of its parts.

Siemens, the German electronic firm, redesigned its engineering parts purchasing process and reduced the work required to replace a component order by 33 per cent of effort and 66 per cent of elapsed time.

SAS, the Scandinavian airline, replaced its step-by-step check in process with one that required each member of a fifteen-strong check-in team to access all relevant flight information for passengers including transfer details, stopovers, flight times and meal requests. Any one team can now respond fully to passenger enquiries.

Ford Motor Company in the United States reduced the number of staff employed to order components, receive parts and pay suppliers from 500 to under 100. The lengthy procedure of matching invoices to purchase orders was replaced by a system of payment on delivery of parts to the receiving bay. The redesigned process is now being adopted by Ford's subsidiaries in Europe.

Source: Woolfe (1991).

a business is located or headquartered, the necessity for a step change in performance will be a prerequisite for leapfrogging the competition.

> Johansson, McHugh, Pendlebury and Wheeler (1993, p. xii)

Organizations are being driven in this direction through developments in politics, economics, legislation and regulation. However, the most potent pressures for this type of thinking actually come from the customer, competitors, cost pressures, technology shifts and new stakeholders. Only the last of these forces differs for Continental European organizations in comparison to Anglo-Saxon organizations. BPR as a technique may be used to structure work at both the job level and the organizational level, but it is likely to have its most significant impact on European HRM when it is used to structure work at the organizational level. The attraction of BPR to European organizations is two-fold:

1. A tool to achieve competitive advantage in organizational redesign, restructuring and rationalization in a post-merger phase.
2. A tool to reduce the labour cost element in automated processes, thereby overcoming the need to transfer labour across Europe because of social labour cost pressures.

In Chapter Five we described the widespread process of business integration taking place in Europe largely through mergers and acquisitions and the associated need to rationalize operations on a new basis in order to achieve competitiveness. After a period of growth through acquisition there is often a need to restructure corporate operations. A good example of using BPR in Europe in order to absorb and then make the most out the process of business integration is Asea Brown Boveri (see Illustration 16.6). The solutions that European organizations adopt to resolve their problems of competitiveness – the business recipe they choose to attack each core business process within the organization – will probably have the greatest shaping influence on HRM over the 1990s.

Illustration 16.6 **The customer focus campaign: redesigning a global/local organization at Asea Brown Boveri.**

The sheer scale and complexity of the restructuring taking place in European organizations can be exemplified by Asea Brown Boveri (ABB). ABB was created out of the merger of Sweden's Asea and Switzerland's Brown Boveri Group, headed by Percy Barnevik. ABB purchased several competitors in geographical markets and then rationalized the businesses, particularly where local product content was not an issue and so manufacturing capacity could be paired.

In the three years following the merger of Asea and Brown Boveri, 33 group managers at the corporate centre and 51 top managers from the business areas had to manage between 70 to 75 acquisitions and a 91 per cent increase in total employment. Higher performance standards, a rapidly shifting environment and constraints on resources all contributed to a significant heightening of managerial demands, placing a premium on the need to develop a systematic, co-ordinated and focused process to prioritise decisions.

In 1993 ABB had more than 50 business areas, grouped into eight business segments with a worldwide scale. Each of the business area leaders has to rationalize and optimize the business on a global scale based on cost and quality standards. ABB also has a national organization for each industrialized country with its own structure and career paths. It therefore operates 1100 companies involved in the manufacture, service, or sale of products across the 50 business areas. Each company president reports to both the business area and national President.

In 1990 Percy Barnevik introduced the Customer Focus Campaign (CFC) which was involved with the redesign and improvement of customer servicing processes. It was also known as The Global Campaign for Time-Based Management and Total Quality Management. ABB had an orderflow system dominated by national interests and the needs of domestic economies of host countries. However, having acquired so many organizations, ABB sought to rationalize efforts by improving processes focused on the customer.

A senior manager at the Orlikon headquarters in Zurich led a worldwide task force of some 40 managers from the main operating countries. Consultants were brought in to advise on appropriate tools and techniques. Each country-based or product-based CFC team determined its own core business processes and set about redesigning them to ensure they were more customer responsive. All business unit CEOs were given objectives in their annual appraisals to run one full process-orientated project a year.

The Abacus measurement system requires each of the 1100 business units to report each month and other systems required reporting on lead times, cost and quality. This enhances competition among managers and co-operation in solving joint process problems.

On a micro-level some radical improvements were made, such as the reduction of lead times in Swedish manufacturing plants. However, on a macro-level progress has been slow because of varying levels of skill and commitment. It is likely that BPR considerations will continue to inform decisions made by ABB to restructure its operations throughout the 1990s.

Source: Johansson, McHugh, Pendlebury and Wheeler (1993); Nielsen and Rötiss (1991).

HRM IMPLICATIONS OF BUSINESS PROCESS RE-ENGINEERING

The choice of business process within an industry and focus of changes in it will become a more powerful determinant of HRM than national HRM practice. However, there are a number of 'structural imperatives' associated with BPR (see Illustration 16.7) and in order to make these work, numerous other areas of the HRM system have to be adapted. Financial rewards and recognition that are not team-based will have to be removed whilst pay systems that encourage knowledge and competency will need to be introduced. Career paths will take on new dimensions, with process leadership becoming as powerful a goal as functional leadership.

The management literature has always been littered with examples of new and attractive sounding concepts that subsequently fall into disrepute because of poor

ation 16.7 **Structural imperatives associated with process-orientated business recipes.**

Restructuring becomes a continuous process, as opposed to a grand design initiated by new leadership or poor performance.
- Re-organization of activities in order to minimize:
  – waste,
  – 'non-value-adding' activities.
- Closer alignment and balancing of operations to market demand.
- Quality principles built into each action, not just into the structure.

- Every business activity that is structured should have a connection upstream (towards suppliers) and downstream (towards customers).
- Greater attention to the depth and structure of information that employees are exposed to in order to be truly effective.
- Multi-discipline self-managing teams managed by corporate value added performance indices, measured by cost, quality, time and service.

implementation or inappropriate cultural fit. Because BPR traverses several management functions it presents major management challenges. In order to make BPR work as a management tool, change has to be created in a series of areas and implementing such changes implies the following major shifts:

- Viewing the organization as a series of business processes, not functions.
- Moving towards more flexible and adaptable teamworking to cover the work process from beginning to end.
- Affording individual team members greater discretion and wider roles and equipping them to respond to more fulfilling roles.
- Capitalizing on information systems to redesign work by providing support, guide work routines, and facilitate decision making.

Process redesign approaches to work structuring will only be successful to the extent that they make the most of, and understand the implementation issues associated with, all these four elements. There are also implications for several other areas of HRM covered in this book. The most brutal assessment of BPR (if it is only used to achieve short term productivity and cost savings) is that it requires organizations to motivate employees to design out their jobs and careers and then willingly implement the changes. A lot more thought has to go into the HRM aspects of BPR. Indeed, Oliver (1993) acknowledges that pure BPR spells massive trouble for people and organizations: '... change, upheaval, expenditure, re-visiting, revising, re-building, re-structuring, re-skilling, re-organizing and, another unpleasant "re" word, redundancy'. Organizations and management institutions are beginning to realize that there will be significant HRM implications resulting from BPR, not least of which is how to motivate people into a process which may design themselves out of a job:

Grave new world

[Change is not without inconvenience because] ... 'Better' in business means enhanced efficiency, greater productivity, higher quality and superior competitiveness ... There will be many people who will declare themselves 're-engineered' with a wry smile. It lacks the implied slur of 'redundant' ... There is the possibility that those released from certain functions could be used to generate growth elsewhere – the economic climate permitting. At the moment, it is a possibility rather than a probability. Those re-engineered out of their jobs will have the satisfaction of knowing they have collaborated in producing a more robust company; better able to survive: a cerebral satisfaction at best and no consolation.   (Oliver, 1993)

As organizations examine their core processes anew, the barriers that used to insulate one function from another are removed. The sense of mystery about what other people do is lost, and everyone needs to understand what is going on. Communication has to become comprehensive.

Experience in the US has also shown that there are a wide range of educational, training and other HRM issues associated with the implementation of re-engineered organizations. In many organizations implementation will be a continuous process lasting from five to ten years. The most obvious issues are shown in Illustration 16.8. Process working therefore not only undermines conventional organization structures and national patterns of HRM, it also threatens individuals in terms of their status and traditional patterns of career progression. This will create immense implementation problems in Europe, where, as we argued in Chapter Eleven, career and management development systems are steeped in national institutional arrangements. BPR perhaps requires a revolution in HRM, not just a transition (see Illustration 16.9) and this may be beyond the capability of most European organizations for several years to come. It is not surprising then that there are many who say that business processes are inherited and not designed, so meddle with them at your peril!

Re-organizing a work department or team around underlying business processes is radical enough, so the concept of redesigning the organization and its whole structure around business processes is extremely threatening. Despite the growing number of successes from redesigning business processes, it is hard for many people to think of doing work this way. Managers are not accustomed to thinking about cross-functional processes and those processes they do recognize are frequently seen as fundamental to the way the business works. One way or another, BPR will be debated throughout the 1990s.

THE NETWORK ORGANIZATION

Finally, we briefly consider the third development at the organizational level that is re-shaping the nature of HRM and breaking down national differences. This is the development of informal business networks and changes to supply chain management.

Illustration 16.8 **HRM issues that have to be resolved in order to make BPR effective.**

- Dissemination of information about missions and objectives associated with underlying business processes.
- Using organization-wide business processes to help manage performance and provide guidance over activity.
- New reward systems that link pay to the possession of broader competencies or to customer-related performance measures.
- Convincing employees that they have permission to exercise new authorities.
- Providing managers with the knowledge to make correct decisions.
- Upskilling remaining employees to the level of competence needed by the process.
- Reducing the number of layers, levels, and roles within the organization without designing out important decision making capabilities.
- Confusion over leadership roles as vertical hierarchies are reduced.
- Re-allocation of workload to employees/units designed out of the process.
- A shift of focus in HRM policies from the individual to their time, in order to encourage more attractive trade-offs between income and time, such as the purchase of extra vacation days, extended leave, flexible hours and sabbaticals from salary and credit ratings.

Illustration 16.9   **Key areas of change in order to implement business process re-engineering.**

Enabler	Impact or receptive environments
People	■ Higher levels of empowerment. ■ Cross-functional business process knowledge. ■ Enhanced teamworking.
Management and leadership	■ Replacement of functional executives by directors of core business processes. ■ Technically knowledgeable senior leaders, operational leaders maintain coaching role. ■ Lower role for finance and marketing background.
Organizational culture	■ Strong articulation of mission, values and organization climate. ■ Teamwork prevalent at all levels. ■ Focus on range of stakeholder perspectives, i.e. shareholders, customers, suppliers. ■ International and global market leadership.
Structure/ functionalism	■ Fewer vertical layers in the organization. ■ High levels of de-functionalization consistent with corporate strategy. ■ Transfer of more and more business processes outside function control. ■ Small cadres of functional experts acting as advisers to business process teams.
Inventive management of new assets	■ Redirection of excess capacity rather than cost cutting and rationalization. ■ Extension of asset management philosophy from financial and physical assets towards people, brands, intellectual property etc.
Performance management	■ Performance indicators for developing, enhancing, renewing and regenerating the new assets. ■ Business performance indicators geared towards quality, lead time, cost and service. ■ Examination of performance indicators to remove conflicting pressures.

Source: after Johansson, McHugh, Pendlebury and Wheeler (1993).

The network metaphor for organizing has been used recently to describe new social exchanges, inter-organizational relations, the development of entrepreneurial organizations and processes of industrial change (Johannisson, 1987). Miles and Snow (1986) argued that the search for a competitive response to turbulent changes in the business environment is producing a new organizational form which they called the 'dynamic network'. Historically, ways of doing business have been determined by ways of organizing and major competitive advances have been achieved by companies that invested or quickly applied a new form of organization and management. These new forms – as with the international division, function, geographic, product and matrix forms of co-ordination – tend to emerge from a variety of experimental actions taken by innovative organizations. The increased use of joint ventures, subcontracting and licensing activities across international borders seen in the 1980s have heralded a dynamic network (see Figure 16.7).

Each individual organization (component) within the network may bring with it its distinctive competence so that a properly constructed network can display the technical specialization of a functional structure, the market responsiveness of a product division, and the balanced characteristics of a matrix structure. The dynamic network becomes an extremely flexible structure, able to accommodate complexity whilst maximizing specialized competence. It operates by essentially leasing entire workforces

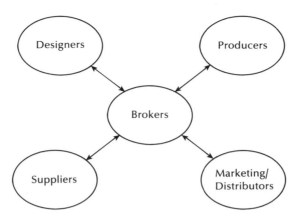

The Network involves five separate roles of designer, producer, marketing/distributors and suppliers

Vertical Disaggregation   Functions such as product design and development, manufacturing, marketing and distribution are performed by independent organizations within a network

Brokers assemble or locate business groups. A single broker may play a lead role and sub contract needed services, or linkages may be formed between equal partners

Market Mechanics such as contracts and payment for results hold the major functions together rather than planning and control mechanisms

Full Disclosure Information Systems are used as a substitute for time-consuming trust building based on experience

Figure 16.7   The principles of a dynamic network structure. *Source*: Miles and Snow (1986). Copyright 1986 by the Regents of the University of California. Reprinted from the *California Management Review*, vol. 28, no. 3, by permission of the Regents.

– a characteristic already seen in construction, large-scale media projects, hotel management and retail sales sectors. As a principle of organization, it can also operate within a single organization as part of a parallel process to the formal structure. Organizations such as IBM and Texas Instruments have used internal venturing (intrapreneurship) and innovation teams, operating on these principles, rapidly to develop new products. A more obvious example of a flexible network structure is the Italian organization of Benetton (see Illustration 16.10). Analysing the HRM patterns of such experiments may reveal the shape of the next transitions in store.

THE VIRTUAL ORGANIZATION

Taken at their highest level of conceptualization, both process management and business networks cut across not only departments, functions and separate manufacturing plants, but also across whole organizations within any business supply chain (Johansson, McHugh, Pendlebury and Wheeler, 1993). Combine this with the network structure outlined above and it is not surprising to see that many business futurists now point to the 'virtual organization' as the management model of tomorrow. Organizations will only survive by rapidly forming and reforming business relationships. The virtual organization implies permanent revolution, as networks of

Illustration 16.10 **A co-operative flexible organization: Benetton.**

Benetton has grown over a period of 35 years into a $1.9 billion organization by following two objectives: economies of scale and manufacturing flexibility based on subcontracting. It subcontracts 95 per cent of its activities in manufacturing to 700 independent or partially owned 'Indotti'. Purchasing of raw materials is centralized – making Benetton the world's largest purchaser of wool – as is final distribution of finished products. The only functions kept inhouse are those where expensive high technology provides economies of scale, such as complex chemical processes for creating colours. Benetton allows its own plant managers to run subcontracting outfits on a part time basis. The subcontractors are specialized and do not need overheads such as salesmen, market-ing and finance. Subcontractors are guaranteed a 10 per cent profit margin on average costs and so are motivated to improve their profits by reducing their costs. Downstream sales and distribution is a negotiated flexible contract. Except for ten flag-stores, the network of shops is owned by 1,000 entrepreneurs, highly motivated to get the market mood right. They buy inventory from Benetton but cannot return stock. Eighty entrepreneur-agents use their capital to set up the retail network in each country and act as a link between the Benetton corporate centre and the clients (shop owners) and final consumers. Therefore, at each stage of the business process Benetton has made the decision to make or buy.

Source: Ketelhöhn (1993).

small organizations and people are brought together to undertake business projects guided by an attractive entrepreneurial vision. It appears to be the logical end state of the process of re-structuring, rationalization, merging and demerging, downsizing and outsourcing sweeping through Europe in the 1990s. Protagonists argue that the joint ventures, strategic alliances, outsourcing the extended customer–supplier links (see Chapter Five) will develop into more spontaneous partnerships, ordered by high speed communications networks, and common technical standards for information transfer.

Organizations and their structures have always been more flexible and fluid than the various typologies used in the management literature would suggest. The increasing impact of information technology, which has blurred previous distinctions between units both within and outside a specific company, has directed attention away from the purely physical artefacts of an organization design. Harrington (1991) has analysed the impact of information technology on organization structure. He draws a distinction between the physical aspects of structure – akin to those aspects detailed in Chapter Eight – and the perceptual or virtual aspects of structure which form the basis of the logical links between actions carried out, and the meaning that individual managers give to it.

Byrne (1993) points to a number of different perspectives on the topic. Jan Hopland from DEC used the term 'virtual' to describe an enterprise that can marshal more resources than it has on its own by using both internal and external collaborations. Roger Nagel, a US consultant, focuses on the use of technology to execute a wide array of temporary alliances with others to grasp specific market opportunities. Davidow and Malone (1992) encompass a range of ideas from empowerment through to just-in-time inventories. However, the metaphor for the concept has computing origins. The term 'virtual' derives from the type of memory that makes a computer act as if it has more storage capacity than it really has. In the same vein, the virtual corporation is expected to assemble numerous collaborations only when they are needed. The virtual corporation is a temporary network of independent companies able to share costs, skills and access to global markets and contribute what they are best at by capitalizing on the power of information (Byrne, Brandt and Port, 1993).

Suppliers, customers and even erstwhile rivals will create, it is proposed, fluid and flexible organizations, with no central office, formal hierarchy or vertical integration. Each company only contributes what it regards as its 'core competencies', mixing and matching what it does best with other organizations and entrepreneurs. The drive towards this form of organization comes from two pressures. The concept of time as a primary basis of competition has led to the realization that organizations that attempt to own, manage and control all their activities run out of time. Secondly, as organizations also compete on the basis of their underlying resources and capabilities, the value of these becomes more explicit and the cost of competing outside these capabilities more onerous.

At the moment the virtual corporation only exists in the minds of futurists. However, Byrne, Brandt and Port (1993) cite several examples of organizations leading the way. Corning Inc. of the US has nineteen partnerships that accounted for 13 per cent of its revenue in 1992. The Chairman, James Houghton, expects the trends to develop. John Sculley, Chairman of Apple Computer Inc. sees the concept taking off over the next 10–20 years on the back of a new cadre of entrepreneurial industries and companies. Apple entered into a year long agreement with Sony to build its low-end Powerbook computers, combining Sony's core competences in miniaturization with Apple's competences in marketing. The linkage served the purpose of getting a new product out quickly. Apple's strategy of developing partnerships is also seen as a key contribution to its high revenues per employee (at $437,100 per employee in 1992, four times those of DEC and twice those of IBM).

MCI, the US long distance telephone company, allied its core competencies in network integration and software development with the strengths of other companies who make telecommunications equipment. The package of 'one stop' hardware and services combining the talents of up to a hundred other companies saved MCI $300 to $500 million a year in capital (Byrne, Brandt and Port, 1993). IBM's planned break-up into independent businesses and ABB's highly decentralized structure are presented as tentative moves towards the virtual corporation as are rapid competitive attacks such as those achieved by the Danish hearing-aid manufacturer, Otikon. Such developments, if they truly are the forerunner of the virtual corporation, carry significant managerial implications, placing emphasis on the negotiation, business relationship, team building and motivation skills of managers. The relationship between ideas about commitment, competence and employee costs and values and models of HRM will also have to be reconceptualised.

Although developments in collaboration signal the potential for the virtual corporation, they do not prove its feasibility. The concept relies on computers allowing teams of people in different companies routinely to work together concurrently (not sequentially) on computer networks, signing electronic contracts to enable immediate work. Concurrent working within organizations is causing enough headaches, let alone across them. It is also important not to confuse the progress made through joint ventures and partnerships with the advent of the 'virtual corporation'. The two need not necessarily follow, particularly as the practical constraints and implementation issues associated with the 'virtual corporation' are not insignificant (Byrne, 1993). Antitrust policies, intellectual property laws, and the tendency of managers to devalue work by outsiders or undervalue the benefits of shared resources will act as clear obstacles. Despite the spate of corporate downsizings, lay-offs of middle managers and reductions in management layers during the 1980s many organizations were left in the 1990s with the same organization structures (Byrne, Brandt and Port, 1993) and low gains in productivity. There are also strategic risks associated with the 'virtual corporation'. Proprietary information or technology may escape and the launch of strategically vital products may be hampered by the poor (and uncontrolled) performance of a collaborator. Such entangled organizations are more likely to stumble and so the virtual organization is likely to remain in the realm of futurists for some time to come.

A RETURN TO THE INDUSTRIAL RELATIONS DIMENSION

In discussing forces of revolution, not just transition, in European HRM, we would be remiss not to return to the industrial relations dimension.

It will be the need to manage the present that will bring a sense of reality back into the transition taking place in European HRM. In the opening chapter we argued that HRM as a philosophy tends to entail a move towards direct communication with and management of the workforce, substituting the need to deal with collective bodies such as trade unions. The last chapter showed that the industrial relations scene has indeed already been transformed within Europe. However, the scale of change in the way that people are managed is leading to a new period of industrial unease. Figure 16.8 shows the number of employees involved in strikes each year as a proportion of the number involved in strikes in 1982. By the early 1990s – before the full impact of new patterns of HRM had been felt or understood – a marked rise in militancy in countries such

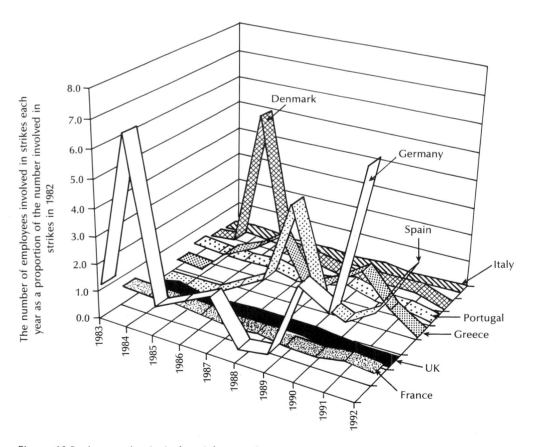

Figure 16.8 A new rise in industrial unrest?.

as Germany and Spain could be detected and unrest in France and Italy was also increasing. The need to devote renewed attention to the management of industrial relations may yet take European organizations by surprise.

European industry is suffering an unaccustomed feeling of discomfort, or indeed crisis, as organizations in the industrial heartland of Europe sense a growing air of crisis and catastrophe greater than at any time since the the end of the Second World War, fuelled by the global recession of the early 1990s, the burdensome costs of integration and pressure on social costs and the rising economic power of Asia (Hasell, 1993). The sense of crisis may subside of its own accord, but it has signalled a marked shift in European thinking as past practices are questioned. In order for the transition in European HRM to continue, we can best conclude with a quote from a leading German industrialist:

... Crisis is a productive state. We just have to remove the sense of catastrophe that goes with it.   Manfred Schneider, Chairman of the Board of Management, (paraphrasing the Swiss writer Max Frisch) in Hasell (1993, p. 60).

References

Abe, H. and Wiseman, R.L. (1983) A cross-cultural confirmation of the dimensions of intercultural effectiveness. *International Journal of Intercultural Relations*, **7**, 53–68.

Abernathy, W., Clark, K.B. and Kantrow, A.M. (1981) The new industrial competition. *Harvard Business Review*, **59**(5), 69–77.

Aboud, A. (1992) France: acquisition of a private company. *Mergers and Acquisition International*, **12** (9), 8–10.

Abranavel, R. and Ernst, D. (1992) Mergers and acquisitions versus alliances: strategic choices for European national champions. *Mergers and Acquisitions Europe*, **4**(4), 39–48.

Ackermann, K.F. (1986) A contingency model of HRM strategy – empirical research findings reconsidered. *Management Forum*, **6**, 65–83.

Adler, N.J. (1981) Re-entry: managing cross-cultural transitions. *Group and Organizational Studies*, **6**(3), 341–56.

Adler, N.J. (1983) Cross-cultural management research: the ostrich and the trend. *Academy of Management Review*, **8**, 226–32.

Adler, N.J. (1984) Women in international management: where are they? *California Management Review*, **26**(4), 122–32.

Adler, N.J. (1986) *International dimensions of organizational behavior*, Boston: Kent Publishing Company.

Adler, N.J. (1991) *International dimensions of organizational behavior*, Boston: PWS–Kent.

Adler, N.J. and Bartholomew, S. (1992) Academic and professional communities of discourse: generating knowledge on transnational human resource management. *Journal of International Business Studies*, **3**(3), 551–69.

Adler, N.J. and Ghader, F. (1989) International business research for the twenty-first century: Canada's new research agenda. In A. Rugman (ed.) *Research in global strategic management: A Canadian perspective*, Greenwich: JAI Press.

Adler, N.J. and Laurent, A. (1986) Unpublished results from the *Cultural synergy survey*. Collected at INSEAD in 1980–83 and in 1982 at major American and Canadian multinationals.

Adler, P.S. and Cole, R.E. (1993) Designed for learning: a tale of two autoplants. *Sloan Management Review*, **35**, 85–94.

Aijeruke, M. and Boddewyn, J. (1970) Socioeconomic indicators in comparative management. *Administrative Science Quarterly*, **15**, 453–8.

Akimune, I. (1991) Japan's direct investment in the EC. In M. Yoshitomi (ed.) *Japanese direct investment in Europe*, London: Avebury.

Amado, G., Faucheux, C. and Laurent, A. (1991) Organizational change and cultural realities: Franco-American contrasts. *International Studies of Management and Organization*, **21**(3), 62–95.

Amblard, H., Abramovici, N.-B., Livian, Y.-F., Poirson, P. and Roussillon, S. (1989) *Management des ressources humaines*, Paris: Eyorolles.

Amoroso, B. (1990) Development and crisis of the Scandinavian model of labour relations in Denmark. In G. Baglioni and C. Crouch (eds) *European industrial relations: The challenge of flexibility*, London: Sage.

Andersen, J., Cour C. la, Svendsen, L.K., Kiel, O., Kamp, M. and Larsen, H.H. (1993) Denmark. In C. Brewster, A. Hegewisch, J.T. Lockhart, and L. Holden (eds) *The European human resource management guide*, London: Academic Press.

Anderson, N. and Shackleton, V. (1986) Recruitment and selection: a review of developments in the 1980s. *Personnel Review*, **15**(4), 19–26.

Arbose, J. (1992) Belgium: company defences must be redrawn. *International Management*, **47**(7), 23.

Argyris, C. (1982) *Reasoning, learning and action*. San Francisco: Jossey Bass.

Arkin, A. (1992a) At work in the powerhouse of Europe: personnel management in Germany. *Personnel Management*, **24**(2), 32–5.

Arkin, A. (1992b) The land of social welfare: personnel management in Denmark. *Personnel Management*, **24**(3), 33–5.

Armstrong, A. (1991) Management skills and performance audit. *Asia Pacific Human Resource Management*, Summer 1991, 25–39.

Armstrong, M. (1987) A case of the emperor's new clothes. *Personnel Management*, **19**(8), 30–5.

Armstrong, M. (1988) *A handbook of personnel management practice*, 3rd edition, London: Kogan Page.

Armstrong, M. (1992) (ed.), *Strategies for human resource management*, London: Kogan Page.

Armstrong, P.J. (1984) Work, rest or play? Changes in time spent at work. In P. Marstrand (ed.) *New technology and the future of work and skills*, London: Francis Pinter.

Arnold, J., Robertson, I.T. and Cooper, C.L. (1991) *Work psychology: Understanding human behaviour in the workplace*, London: Pitman.

Arvey, R.D., Miller, H.E., Gould, R. and Burch, P. (1987) Interview validity for selecting sales clerks. *Personnel Psychology*, **40**, 1–12.

Ashenfelter, O. and Johnson, G. (1969) Bargaining theory, trade unions and industrial strike activity. *American Economic Review*, **59**.

Ashton, D. (1986) Handling cultural diversity. In A. Mumford (ed.) *Handbook of management development*, London: Gower.

Atkinson, J. (1984) Manpower strategies for flexible organizations. *Personnel Management*, **16**(8), 28–31.

Bacharach, S. (1989) Organizational theories: some criteria for evaluation. *Academy of Management Review*, **14**, 496–515.

Baglioni, G. (1991) Industrial relations in Europe in the 1990s. In G. Baglioni and C. Crouch (eds) *European industrial relations: the challenge of flexibility*, London: Sage.

Baglioni, G. and Crouch, C. (1991) (eds) *European industrial relations: the challenge of flexibility*, London: Sage.

Bain, G. and Elsheikh, F. (1976) *Union growth and the business cycle: an econometric analysis*, Oxford: Basil Blackwell.

Baird, L., Meshoulam, I. and DeGive, G. (1983) Meshing human resource planning with strategic business planning: a model approach. *Personnel*, **60**, 14–25.

Baker, H., Miller, T. and Ramsperger, B. (1981) An inside look at corporate mergers and acquisitions. *MSU Business Topics*, Winter, 49–57.

Ball, D.A. and McCulloch, W.H. (1990) *International business*, 4th edition, Boston: Irwin.

Ball, G. (1992) The Spartan profession: personnel management in Greece. *Personnel Management*, **24**(9), 40–4.

Bamber, G.J. and Lansbury, R. (1987) *International and comparative industrial relations*, London: Unwin Hyman.

Bamber, G.J. and Whitehouse, G. (1992) International data on economic, employment and human resource issues. *International Journal of Human Resource Management*, **3**(2), 353–69.

Bandrowski, J. (1991) Restructuring is a continuous process. *Long Range Planning*, **24**(1), 10–14.

Barham, K., Fraser, J. and Heath, I. (1987) *Management for the future*, Ashridge: Ashridge Management College, FME.

Barney, J. (1991) Firm resources and sustainable competitive advantage. *Journal of Management*, **17**(1), 99–120.

Barsoux, J.-L. (1992) Following the leaders. *International Management*, **47**(7), 40–1.

Barsoux, J.-L. and Lawrence, P. (1990) *Management in France*, London: Cassell.

Barsoux, J.-L. and Lawrence, P. (1991) The making of a French manager. *Harvard Business Review*, **69**(4), 58–67.

Bartlett, C. (1992) Christopher Bartlett on transnationals: an interview. *European Management Journal*, **10**(3), 271–6.

Bartlett, C., Doz, Y. and Hedlund, G. (1990) *Managing the global firm*, London: Routledge.

Bartlett, C. and Ghoshal, S. (1989) *Managing across borders*. Boston: Hutchinson.

Bartlett, C. and Ghoshal, S. (1992) What is a global manager? *Harvard Business Review*, **70**(5), 124–32.

Baxter, A. and Bollen, B. (1992) Deals stay on track in Europe and Britain. *Mergers and Acquisitions International*, October, 2–5.

Beamish, P.W., Killing, J.P., Lecraw, D.J. and Crookell, H. (1991) *International management: Text and cases*, Boston: Irwin.

Bean, R. (1985) *Comparative industrial relations*, Beckenham: Croom Helm.

Beaumont, P.B. (1991a) The US human resource management literature: a review. In G. Salaman (ed.) *Human resource strategies*, Milton Keynes: Open University.

Beaumont, P.B. (1991b) HRM and international joint ventures: some evidence from Britain. *Human Resource Management Journal*, **4**(1), 90–101.

Beer, M. (1980) *Organization change and development*, Santa Monica, Cal.: Goodyear.

Beer, M., Eisenstat, R. and Spector, B. (1990) Why change programs don't produce change. *Harvard Business Review*, (**68**)6, 158–66.

Beer, M., Lawrence, P.R., Mills, D.Q. and Walton, R.E. (1985) *Human resource management*, New York: Free Press.

Beer, M., Spector, B., Lawrence, P., Mills, D. and Walton, R.E. (1984) *Managing human assets*, New York: Free Press.

Beer, S. (1972) *Brain of the firm*, New York: Herder & Herder.

Ben-Shakar, G., Bar-Hillel, M., Bilu, Y., Ben-Abba, E. and Flug, A. (1986) Can graphology predict occupational success? Two empirical studies and some theoretical ruminations. *Journal of Applied Psychology*, **71**, 645–53.

Ben-Shakar, G. (1989) Non-conventional methods in personnel selection. In P. Herriot (ed.) *Assessment and selection in organizations: Methods and practice for recruitment and appraisal*, Chichester: John Wiley.

Benedetti, C. (1992) Mega-competitors in the global battle: requirements for success. In *World competitiveness report 1992*, Geneva: World Economic Forum.

Bennett, D. and Karlsson, U. (1992) Work organization as a basis for competition: the transition of car assembly in Sweden. *International Studies of Management and Organization*, **22**(4), 49–60.

Berger, L. (1991) Trends and issues for the 1990s: creating a viable framework for compensation designs. In M. Rock and L. Berger (eds) *The compensation handbook*, New York: McGraw-Hill.

Berger, S. (1980) The traditional sector in France and Italy. In S. Berger and M. Piore (eds) *Dualism and discontinuity in industrial societies*, Cambridge: Cambridge University Press.

Berggren, C. (1992) *Alternatives to lean production*, Ithaca, New York: ILR Press.

Bernardin, H.J. (1986) Subordinate appraisal: a valuable source of information about managers. *Human Resource Management*, **25**, 421–39.

Bernardin, H.J. and Russell, J. (1993) *Human resource management: An experiential approach*, London: McGraw-Hill.

Bernhard, H.B. and Ingolis, C.A. (1988) Six lessons for the corporate classroom. *Harvard Business Review*, **66**(5), 40–51.

Bessant, J.R. and Grunt, M. (1985) *Management and manufacturing innovation in the UK and West Germany*, Aldershot: Edward Elgar.

Besse, D. (1992) Finding a new raison d'être: personnel management in France. *Personnel Management*, **24**(8), 40–3.

Bethell-Fox, C.E. (1989) Psychological testing. (ed.) *Assessment and selection in organizations: methods and practice for recruitment and appraisal*, Chichester: John Wiley.

Bevan, S. and Fryatt, J. (1988) *Employee selection in the U.K.* Sussex: Institute of Manpower Studies.

Black, J.S. (1990) The relationship of personal characteristics with the adjustment of Japanese expatriate managers. *Management International Review*, **30**, 119–34.

Black, J.S. and Gregersen, H. (1991) Antecedents to cross-cultural adjustment for expatriates in Pacific Rim assignments. *Human Relations*, **44**(5), 497–515.

Black, J.S. and Mendenhall, M. (1990) Cross-cultural training effectiveness: a review and theoretical framework for future research. *Academy of Management Review*, **15**, 113–36.

Black, J.S. and Mendenhall, M. (1991) The U-curve adjustment hypothesis revisited: a review and theoretical framework. *Journal of International Business Studies*, **22**(2), 225–48.

Black, J.S. and Oddou, G. (1991) Towards a comprehensive model of international adjustment: an integration of multiple theoretical perspectives. *Academy of Management Review*, **16**, 291–317.

Black, J.S., Gregersen, H.B. and Mendenhall, M.E. (1992) Toward a theoretical framework of repatriation adjustment. *Journal of International Business Studies*, **23**, 737–59.

Black, J.S., Mendenhall, M.E. and Oddou, G. (1991) Towards a comprehensive model of international adaptation: an integration of multiple theoretical perspectives. *Academy of Management Review*, **16**(2), 291–318.

Blackwell, N., Bizet, J-P., Child, P. and Hensley, D. (1991) Shaping a pan-European organization. *McKinsey Quarterly*, **1991**(2), 94–111.

Blackwell, N., Bizet, J-P., Child, P. and Hensley, D. (1992) Creating European organizations that work. *McKinsey Quarterly*, **1992**(2), 31–43.

Blanpain, R. (1974) The influence on labour management decision-making: a comparative legal survey. *Industrial Law Journal*, **3**.

Blanpain, R. and Köhler, E. (1988) (eds) *Legal and contractual limitations to working-time in the European Community member states*. Deventer, Kluwer: European Foundation for the Improvement of Living and Working Conditions.

Bleeke, J. and Ernst, D. (1992) The way to win in cross-border alliances. *McKinsey Quarterly*, **1992**(1), 113–33.

Blum, A.A. (1987) Industrial democracy and management. *International Studies of Management and Organization*, **17**(2), 3–9.

Blunt, P. (1990) Recent developments in HRM: the good, the bad and the ugly. *International Journal of HRM*, **1**(1), 45–59.

Boam, R. and Sparrow, P.R. (eds) (1992) *Designing and achieving competency: A competency-based approach to developing people and organizations*, London: McGraw-Hill.

de Boer, C. (1978) The polls: attitudes towards work. *Public Opinion Quarterly*, **42**, 414–23.

Boerlijst, G. and Meijboom, G. (1989) Matching the individual and the organization. In P. Herriot (ed.) *Assessment and selection in organizations: Methods and practice for recruitment and appraisal*. Chichester: John Wiley.

Bognanno, M. and Sparrow, P.R. (1994) Integrating HRM strategy using culturally-defined competencies at British Petroleum: cross-cultural implementation issues. In J.M. Hiltrop and P.R. Sparrow (eds) *European human resource management: A casebook*, Hemel Hempstead: Prentice Hall.

Boldy, D., Jain, S. and Northey, K. (1993) What makes an effective European manager? *Management International Review*, **33**(2), 157–69.

Bollinger, D. and Hofstede, G. (1987) *Les différences culturelles dans le management*. Paris: Les Editions d'Organization.

Boltanski, L. (1982) (ed) *Les cadres: La formation d'un groupe social*, Paris: de Minuit.

Bosch, F.A.J. van den, and Prooijen, R.A. van (1992a) The competitive advantage of European nations: the impact of national culture, a missing element in Porter's analysis? *European Management Journal*, **10**(2), 173–7.

Bosch, F.A.J. van den, and Prooijen, R.A. van (1992b) European management: an emerging competitive advantage of European nations. *European Management Journal*, **10**(4), 445–8.

Bosch, G. (1988) Der bundesdeutsche Arbeitsmarkt im internationalen Vergleich; 'Eurosklerose oder Modell Deutschland'? *WSI Mitteilungen*, **3**, 176–85.

Bournois, F. (1991a) *La gestion des cadres en Europe*, Paris: Editions Liaisons.

Bournois, F. (1991b) Gestion des RH en Europe: données comparées. *Revue française de gestion*, Mars–avril–mai.

Bournois, F. (1992) The impact of 1993 on management development in Europe. *International Studies of Management and Organization*, **22**(1), 3–6.

Bournois, F. (1993) France. In C. Brewster, A. Hegewisch, J.T. Lockhart, and L. Holden (eds) *The European human resource management guide*. London: Academic Press.

Bournois, F. and Chauchat, J.-H. (1990) Managing managers in Europe. *European Management Journal*, **8**(1), 3–18.

Bournois, F. and Metcalfe, P. (1991) Human resource management of executives in Europe: structures, policies and techniques. In C. Brewster and S. Tyson (eds) *International comparisons in human resource management*, London: Pitman.

Bournois, F. and Roussillon, S. (1992) The concept of 'highflier' executives in France: the weight of the national culture. *Human Resource Management Journal*, **3**(1), 37–56.

Boxall, P.F. (1991) Strategic human resource management: beginnings of new theoretical sophistication? *Human Resource Management Journal*, **2**(3), 60–79.

Boyatzis, R. (1982) *The competent manager*, New York: John Wiley.

Boyatzis, R. (1991) Building on competence: the effective use of managerial talent. In G. Salaman (ed.) *Human resource strategies*, London: Sage.

Boyer, R., (1988) *In search of labour market flexibility: European economies in transition*, Oxford: Clarendon Press.

Bressand, A. and Nicolaïdis K. (1990) Regional integration in a networked world economy, In W. Wallace (ed.) *The dynamics of European integration*. London: Royal Institute of International Affairs.

Brett, J., Stroh, L. and Reilly, A. (1990) *Impact of societal shifts and corporate changes on employee relocation*, Washington, DC: Employee Relocation Council.

Brewster, C. (1993) European human resource management: reflection of, or challenge to, the American concept? In P. Kirkbride (ed.) *Human resource management in the new Europe of the 1990s*, London: Routledge.

Brewster, C. and Bournois, F. (1991) Human resource management: a European perspective. *Personnel Review*, **20**(6), 4–13.

Brewster, C. and Hegewisch, A. (1993) Personnel management in Europe: a continent of diversity. *Personnel Management*, **25**(1), 36–40.

Brewster, C. and Larsen, H.H. (1993) Human resource management in Europe: evidence from ten countries. *International Journal of Human Resource Management*, **3**(3), 409–34.

Brewster, C. and Teague, P. (1989) *EC social policy and Britain*, London: Institute of Personnel Management.

Brewster, C. and Tyson, S. (1991) (eds) *International comparisons in human resource management*, London: Pitman.

Brewster, C., Hegewisch, A. and Lockhart, J.T. (1991) Researching human resource management: methodology of the Price Waterhouse Cranfield Project on European trends. *Personnel Review*, **20**(6), 36–40.

Brewster, C., Hegewisch, A. and Lockhart, J.T. (1993) The United Kingdom of Great Britain and Northern Ireland. In C. Brewster, A. Hegewisch, J.T. Lockhart and L. Holden (eds) *The European human resource management guide*, London: Academic Press.

Brewster, C., Hegewisch, A. and Mayne, L. (1993) Trends in European HRM: signs of convergence? In P. Kirkbride (ed.) *Human resource management in the new Europe of the 1990s*, London: Routledge.

Brewster, C., Hegewisch, A., Lockhart, J.T. and Holden, L. (eds) (1993) *The European human resource management guide*, London: Academic Press.

Brislin, R., Cushner, C., Cherrie, C. and Yong, M. (1986) *Intercultural interactions: A practical guide*. Beverly Hills, Cal.: CA Publications.

British Institute of Management/Manpower (1992) *Long term U.K. employment policies*, Corby: British Institute of Management.

Bronder, C. and Pritzl, R. (1992) Developing strategic alliances: a conceptual framework for successful co-operation. *European Management Journal*, **10**(4), 412–21.

Brooke, M.Z. and Remmers, H.L. (1977) (eds) *The international firm*. London: Pitman.

Brown, W. (1981) *The changing contours of British industrial relations*, London: Basil Blackwell.

Brown, W. and Sisson, K (1984) Current trends and future possibilities. In M. Poole *et al.* (eds) *Industrial relations in the future*, London: Routledge & Kegan Paul.

Bruns, W. (1992) *Performance measurement, evaluation, and incentives*, Boston: Harvard Business School Press.

Bruton, K. (1990) The business culture in Spain. In C. Randlesome (ed.) *Business cultures in Europe*, Oxford: Heinemann.

Buchanan, D. and Boddy, D. (1982) Advanced technology and the quality of working life: the effects of word processing on video typists. *Journal of Occupational Psychology*, **55**, 1–11.

Buelens, M., De Clerq, J., Graeve, B.D. and Vanderheyden, K. (1993) Belgium. In C. Brewster, A. Hegewisch, J.T. Lockhart, and L. Holden (eds) *The European human resource management guide*, London: Academic Press.

Buono, A.F. and Bowditch, D. (1989) *The human side of mergers and acquisitions*, San Francisco: Jossey-Bass.

Burns, T. and Stalker, G.M. (1961). *The management of innovation*, London: Tavistock.

Burrell, G. and Morgan, G. (1979) *Sociological paradigms and organizational analysis*, London: Heinemann Educational Books.

Butler, R. (1991) *Designing organizations: A decison-making perspective*, London: Routledge.

Byrne, J. (1993) The futurists who fathered the ideas. *Business Week*, No. 3292–622, February 8th, 41.

Byrne, J., Brandt, R. and Port, O (1993) The virtual corporation. *Business Week*, No., 3292–622, February 8th, 36–40.

Calori, R. (1993) Brasseries Kronenbourg. In G. Johnson and K. Scholes (eds) *Exploring corporate strategy*: Text and cases, 3rd edition, Hemel Hempstead: Prentice Hall.

Cameron, K.S., Freeman, S.J. and Mishra, A.K. (1991). Best practices in white-collar downsizing: managing contradictions. *Academy of Management Executive*, **5**(3), 57–73.

Camuffo, A. and Costa, G. (1993) Strategic human resource management – Italian style. *Sloan Management Review*, **34**(2), 59–67.

Caplan, J. (1992) It's the climate that counts: personnel management in Italy. *Personnel Management*, **24**(4), 32–5.

Carson, I. (1992) Europe's pension deficit. *International Management*, October, 80–3.

Carter, J.C. (1989) Moving managers internationally: the need for flexibility. *Human Resource Planning*, **12**(1), 43–7.

Carty, P. (1993) Headhunters cross frontiers. *The European Business News*, 12th–15th August, No. 0170, 45.

Cascio, W.F. (1982) *Applied psychology in personnel management*, Reston, Virginia: Reston Publishing Co.

Cascio, W.F. (1986) *Managing human resources*, London: McGraw-Hill.

Caudron, S. (1993) Master the compensation maze. *Personnel Journal*, **72**(6), 64a–64o.

Cecchini, P., Catinat, M. and Jacquemin, A. (1988) *The European challenge 1992 – the benefits of a Single Market*. Aldershot: Wildwood House.

Cella, G. and Treu, T. (1982) National trade union movements. In R. Blanpain (ed.) *Comparative labour law and industrial relations*, Deventer, Holland: Kluwer.

Chandler, A.D. (1990) *Scale and scope*, Cambridge Mass.: Harvard University Press.

Cherns, A. (1982) Culture and values: the reciprocal influence between applied social science and its cultural and historical context. In N. Nicholson and T.D. Wall (eds) *The theory and practice of organizational psychology*, London: Academic Press.

Cherrington, D. (1987) *Personnel management: The management of human resources*, 2nd edition, New York: Allyn & Bacon.

Child, J. (1981) Culture, contingency and capitalism in the cross-national study of organizations. In B.M. Staw and L.L. Cummings (eds) *Research in organizational behaviour*, **3**, Greenwich: JAI Press.

Church, A.T. (1982) Sojourner adjustment. *Psychological Bulletin*, **9**, 540–72.

Clague, L. and Krupp, N. (1978) International personnel: the repatriation problem. *Personnel Administrator*, **23**, 29–33.

Clark, F. (1992) *Total career management: Strategies for creating management careers*, London: McGraw-Hill.

Clark, T. (1993) Selection methods used by executive search consultancies in four European countries: a survey and critique. *International Journal of Selection and Assessment*, 1(1), 41–9.

Clegg, H. (1976) *Trade unionism under collective bargaining: A theory based on comparisons of six countries*, Oxford: Basil Blackwell.

Cockerill, A. (1989) The kind of competence for rapid change. *Personnel Management*, 21(9), 52–6.

Conrad, P. and Pieper, R. (1990) Human resource management in the Federal Republic of Germany. In R. Pieper (ed.) *Human resource management: An international comparison*, Berlin: de Gruyter.

Constable, J. and McCormick, R. (1987) *The making of British managers*, London: British Institute of Management/Confederation of British Industry.

Cook, F. (1991) Merit pay and performance appraisal. In M. Rock and L. Berger (eds) *The compensation handbook*, New York: McGraw-Hill.

Cooper, R. (1974) *Job motivation and job design*, London: Institute of Personnel Management.

Cooper, J. and Giacomello, G. (1993) Italy. In C. Brewster, A. Hegewisch, J.T. Lockhart, and L. Holden (eds) *The European human resource management guide*. London: Academic Press.

Copeland, L. and Griggs, L. (1985) *Going international*, New York: Random House.

Coulson-Thomas, C. (1990) *Professional development of and for the Board*, London: Institute of Directors.

Coulson-Thomas, C. (1992) *Creating the global company: Successful internationalization*, London: McGraw-Hill.

Coulson-Thomas, C. and Wakeham, A. (1991) *The effective Board: Current practice, myths and realities*, London: Institute of Directors.

Courpasson, D. (1989) Les entreprises bancaires: nouvelles competences et resources humaines, Working paper. Groupe ESC Lyon.

Courpasson, D. and Livian, Y.-F. (1991) Training for strategic change: some conditions of effectiveness: a case in the banking sector of France. *Paper at 6th Workshop on Strategic Human Resource Management*, March 1991, EIASM, St Gallen.

Crabb, S. (1992) Salaries and the Single Market, *Personnel Management*, 24(6), 21.

Craggs, S. (1993) Master of the universe. *International Management*, 48(6), 25–6.

Cressey, P. (1991) Total quality management and worker participation. *European Participation Monitor P+*, No. 2, 3–7.

Crouch, C. (1991) The United Kingdom: rejection of compromise. In G. Baglioni and C. Crouch (eds) *European industrial relations: The challenge of flexibility*, London: Sage Publications.

Crowe, D. (1992) A new approach to reward management. In M. Armstrong (ed.) *Strategies for human resource management*, London, Kogan Page.

Crozier, M. (1971) *Le phénomène bureaucratique*, Paris: Sevil.

Cummings, T.G. and Huse, E.F. (1989) *Organization development and change*, 4th edition, St. Paul, Minn.: West Publishing.

Cummings, T. and Molloy, E. (1977) *Improving productivity and the quality of work life*, New York: Praeger.

Curnow, B. (1989) Recruit, retrain and retain: personnel management and the three R's. *Personnel Management*, 21(11), 40–7.

Curson, C. (1986) *Flexible patterns of work*, Wimbledon: Institute of Personnel Management.

Cyert, R.M. and March, J.G. (1963) *A behavioural theory of the firm*, Englewood Cliffs, NJ: Prentice Hall.

Czinkota, M., Rivoli, P. and Ronkainen, I. (1992) *International Business*, 2nd edition, Orlando: Dryden Press.

Dachler, H.P. (1989) Selection and the organizational context. In P. Herriot (ed.) *Assessment and selection in organizations: methods and practice for recruitment and appraisal*, Chichester: John Wiley.

Dadfar, H. and Gutavsson, P. (1992) Competition by effective management of cultural diversity: the case of international construction projects. *International Studies of Management and Organization*, 22(4), 81–92.

Daft, R.L. (1992) *Organization theory and design*, 4th edition, St. Paul, Minn.: West Publishing.

Dale, M. and Iles, P. (1992) *Assessing management skills: A guide to competencies and evaluation techniques*, London: Kogan Page.

Daniel, W.W. and Millward, N. (1983) *Workplace industrial relations in Britain*, London: Heinemann.

Davidow, W. and Malone, M (1992). *The virtual corporation: Structuring and revitalising the corporation for the 21st century*, New York: Harper Business.

Davies, D.R. and Sparrow, P.R. (1985) Age and work behaviour. In N. Charness (ed.) *Ageing and human performance*, Chichester: John Wiley.

Davis, L.E. (1966) The design of jobs, *Industrial Relations*, **6**, 21–5.

Davis, L.E. (1979) Job design: historical overview. In L.E. Davis and J.C. Taylor (eds) *Design of jobs*, Santa Monica, Cal: Goodyear Publishing.

Davis, S.M. (1984) *Managing corporate culture*, Cambridge, Mass.: Ballinger.

Dayan, J.L., Gehin, J.P. and Verdier, E. (1986) La formation continue dans l'industrie. *Formation-Emploi*, **16**, 7–36.

Deal, T. and Kennedy, A. (1982) *Corporate cultures: the rites and rituals of corporate life*, Reading: Addison-Wesley.

Della Rocca, G. and Prosperetti, L. (1991) (eds) *Salari e producttivitá: Esperienze internazionale e italiane*, Milan: Franco Angeli.

Denton, D.K. (1991) *Horizontal management: Beyond total customer satisfaction*, New York: Lexington Books.

Derr, C.B. (1986) *Managing the new careerists*, San Francisco: Jossey-Bass.

Derr, C.B. (1987) Managing high potentials in Europe: some cross-cultural findings. *European Management Journal*, **5**(**2**), 72–80.

Derr, C.B. and Laurent, A. (1989) The internal and external career: a theoretical and cross-cultural perspective. In M. Arthur, P.R. Lawrence and D.T. Hall (eds) *Handbook of career theory*, Cambridge: Cambridge University Press.

Derr, C.B. and Oddou, G. (1991) Are US multinationals adequately preparing future American leaders for global competition? *International Journal of Human Resource Management*, **2**(**2**), 227–44.

Derr, C.B. and Oddou, G. (1993) Internationalising managers: speeding up the process. *European Management Journal*, **11**(**4**), 435–42.

Derr, C.B., Wood, J., Walker, M. and Despres, C. (1992) *The emerging role of the HR manager in Europe*, IMD report prepared for the European Association for Personnel Management, Lausanne: IMD.

Desatnick, R.L. and Bennet, M.L. (1978) *Human resource management in the multinational company*, New York: Nichols Publication Company.

Dickson, M. (1988) The world turned upside down. *Mergers and Acquisitions*, March, 15–17.

Dijck, J.J.J. van (1992) Transnationalization of economic and social life in Europe. In J.J.J. van Dijck and A.A.L.G. Wentick (eds) *Transnational business in Europe, Economic and social perspectives*, Tilburg: Tilburg University.

Dixon, P. and Hedley, B. (1992) Currency union: what companies need to do differently to win. *European Business Journal*, **4**(**1**), 25–33.

Doeringer, P. (1981) Industrial relations research in international perspective. In P. Doeringer (ed.) *Industrial relations in international perspective: Essays on research and policy*, London: Macmillan.

Doorley, T.L. (1993) Teaming up for success. *Business Quarterly*, **57**(**4**), 99–103.

Dopson, S., Risk, A. and Stewart, R. (1992) The changing role of the middle manager in the U.K. *International Studies of Management and Organization*, **22**(**1**), 40–53.

Dowling, P.J., Schuler, R.S. and Welch, D.E. (1994) *International dimensions of human resource management*, 2nd edition, Belmont, Cal.: Wadsworth Publishing Co.

Drakeley, R. (1989) Biographical data. In P. Herriot (ed.) *Assessment and selection in organizations: Methods and practice for recruitment and appraisal*, Chichester: John Wiley.

Drenth, P.J.D. (1988) Psychologische selectie en discriminateie. *Gedrag en Organisatie*, **1**(**3**), 12–22.

Drenth, P.J.D. (1989) Psychological testing and discrimination. In P. Herriot (ed.) *Assessment and selection in organizations: Methods and practice for recruitment and appraisal*, Chichester: John Wiley.

Driver, M.J. (1980) Career concepts and organizational change. In C.B. Derr (ed.) *Work, family and the career*, New York: Praeger.

Driver, M.J. (1982) Career concepts: a new approach to career research. In R. Katz (ed.) *Career issues in human resource management*, Englewood Cliffs, NJ: Prentice Hall.

Drucker, P.F. (1954) *The practice of management*, New York: Harper & Row.

Duncan, R. (1979) What is the right organization structure? Decision tree analysis provides the answer. *Organizational Dynamics*, 7(4), 59–80.

Dyas, G.P. and Thanheiser, H. (1976) *The merging European enterprise. Strategy and structure in French and German industry*, London: Macmillan.

Dyson, K. (1986) The state, banks, and industry: the West German case. In A. Cox (ed). *The state, finance and industry*, Brighton: Wheatsheaf Books.

Easterby-Smith, M. (1992) European management education: the prospects for unification, *Human Resource Management Journal*, 3(1), 24–36.

Eberwein, W. and Tholen, J. (1993) *Euro-manager or splendid isolation? An Anglo German comparison*, Berlin: de Gruyter.

Economist (1990a) Information technology survey. *The Economist*, June 16, 315 (No. 7659), 5–38.

Economist (1990b) Average number of employees. *The Economist*, December 15th, 317 (No. 7605), 89–90.

Economist (1992a) Europe's sale of the century. *The Economist*, July 4th, 324 (No. 7766), 71–2.

Economist (1992b) The elusive Euro-manager. *The Economist*, November 7th, 325 (No. 7784), 2–81.

Economist (1993a) Getting Europe back to work. *The Economist*, August 28th, 328 (No. 7826).

Economist (1993b) Musical chairs. *The Economist*, August 17th, 328 (No. 7820), 69.

Economist Intelligence Unit (1991) *Business comparisons: An analytical and statistical survey of Europe and the USA*, London: EIU.

Edstrom, A. and Galbraith, J. (1977) Alternative policies for international transfers of managers. *Management International Review*, 17, 11–22.

Ekvall, G. (1980) Industrial psychology in Sweden. In X. Zamek-Gliszezynska (ed.) *Work psychology in Europe*, Warsaw: Polish Scientific Publishers.

Elizur, R., Borg, I., Hunt, R. and Beck, I.N. (1991) The structure of work values: a cross cultural comparison. *Journal of Organizational Behaviour*, 12(1), 21–38.

Ellegard, K., Engstrom, T. and Nilsson, K. (1991) *Reforming industrial work: Principles and realities in the planning of Volvo's car assembly plant in Uddevalla*, Stockholm: Swedish Work Environment Fund.

Ellert, J. and Killing, K. (1992) Nestlé case study. *IMD Case Study GM 432* Lausanne: International Institute for Management Development.

Emery, F.E. (ed.) (1969) *Systems thinking*, Harmondsworth: Penguin.

Estivill, J and de la Hoz, J. (1991) Transition and crisis: the complexity of Spanish industrial relations. In G. Baglioni and C. Crouch (eds) *European industrial relations: The challenge of flexibility*, London: Sage.

Ettlie, J. (1986) Implementing manufacturing technology: lessons from experience. In D. Davis and Associates (eds) *Managing technological innovation*, San Francisco: Jossey-Bass.

Eurobusiness (1989) Europe's top 500 companies: the Eurobusiness ranking. *Eurobusiness*, November, 27–38.

Euromonitor (1993) *European marketing data and statistics, 28th edition*, London: Euromonitor.

European Business News (1993) Job-cutter's axe chips away at power of labour. *The European*, 21st October 1993, No 0180, 40–1.

European Parliament News (1993) Hoover jobs switch row. *European Parliament News*, 8th–12th February 1993, 4.

Eurostat (1989) *Europe in figures: Deadline 1992*, Brussels: European Community.

Eurostat (1991) *A social portrait of Europe*, Brussels: European Community.

Evans, A. and Curson, C. (1986) Overtime and its alternatives. In C. Curson (ed.) *Flexible patterns of work*, Wimbledon: Institute of Personnel Management.

Evans, P. (1992a) Management development as glue technology. *Human Resource Planning*, **15**(1), 85–106.

Evans, P. (1992b) Developing leaders and management development. *European Management Journal*, **10**(1), 1–9.

Evans, P. and Doz, Y. (1989) The dualistic organization. In P. Evans, Y. Doz and A. Laurent (eds) *Human resource management in international firms*, London: Macmillan.

Evans, P., Doz, Y. and Laurent, A. (1989) (eds) *Human resource management in international firms: Change, globalisation and innovation*, London: Macmillan.

Evans, P., Lank, E. and Farquhar, A. (1989) Managing human resources in the international firm: lessons from practice. In P. Evans, Y. Doz and A. Laurent (eds) *Human resource management in international firms: Change, globalization and innovation*, London: Macmillan.

Eyraud, F. (1993) Equal pay and the value of work in industrialised countries, *International Labour Review*, **132**(1), 33–49.

Farnham, D. and Pimlott, J. (1987) *Understanding industrial relations*, London: Cassell.

Fayol, H. (1949) *General and industrial management*, London: Pitman.

Feldman, D.C. and Tompson, H.B. (1992) Entry shock, culture shock: socializing the new breed of global managers. *Human Resource Management*, **31**(4), 345–62.

Feltham, R. (1989) Assessment centres. In P. Herriot (ed.) *Assessment and selection in organizations: Methods and practice for recruitment and appraisal*, Chichester: John Wiley.

Ferguson, I.R.G. (1973) *Management by objectives in Deutschland*, Frankfurt: Herder & Herder.

Ferner, A. and Hyman, R. (1992a) IR on the continent: a model of co-operation? *Personnel Management*, **24**(8), 32–5.

Ferner, A. and Hyman, R. (eds) (1992b) *Industrial relations in the new Europe*. Oxford: Basil Blackwell.

Feurstenberg F. (1987) The Federal Republic of Germany. In G. Bamber and R. Lansbury (eds) *International and comparative industrial relations*, London: Unwin Hyman.

Filella, J. (1991) Is there a Latin model in the management of human resources? *Personnel Review*, **23**(6), 14–23.

Filella, J. (1992) Waiting to join the mainstream: personnel management in Spain. *Personnel Management*, **24**(7), 28–31.

Filella, J. and Soler, C. (1993) Spain. In C. Brewster, A. Hegewisch, J.T. Lockhart, and L. Holden (eds) *The European human resource management guide*, London: Academic Press.

Findley, A. and Stewart, A. (1986) Manpower policies of British firms with offices in the Middle East. *Liverpool papers in human geography, No. 24*, Liverpool: University of Liverpool.

Finlay, P. (1991) Overmanning: Germany versus Britain. *Management Today*, August 1991, 43–7.

Finney, M. and Von Glinlow, M.A. (1988) Integrating academic and organization approaches to developing the international manager. *Journal of Management Development*, **7**(2).

Fiol, C.M. (1991) Managing culture as a competitive resource: an identity-based view of sustainable competitive advantage. *Journal of Management*, **17**(1), 191–211.

Fisher, C.D., Schoenfeldt, L.F. and Shaw, J.B. (1990) *Human resource management*, Boston: Houghton Mifflin.

Fitz-enz, J. (1981) Human resources: a different perspective. *Personnel Journal*, **60**(2), 118–20.

Flamholtz, E. (1974) Human resource accounting: a review of theory and research. *Journal of Management Studies*, **11**, 44–61.

Fletcher, C. and Williams, R. (1992) The route to performance management. *Personnel Management*, **24**(10), 42–7.

Fletcher, S. (1992) *Competence-based assessment techniques*, London: Kogan Page.

Folletti, S., Giacomello, G. and Cooper, J. (1991) Recruitment, reform and the Italian labour market. *Personnel Review*, **20**(6), 24–7.

Fombrun, C.J. (1983) Strategic management: integrating the human resource systems into strategic planning. *Advances in strategic management. Vol. 2*, Greenwich, Conn.: JAI Press.

Fombrun, C.J. (1984) The external context of human resource management. In C. Fombrun, N. Tichy and M.A. Devanna (eds) *Strategic human resource management*, New York: John Wiley.

Fombrun, C.J., Tichy, N.M. and Devanna, M.A. (1984) *Strategic human resource management*, New York: John Wiley.

Fonda, N. (1989) Management development: the missing link in sustained business performance. *Personnel Management*, 21(12), 50–3.

Forsberg, B. and Söderström, M. (1991) Strategic competence analysis as a tool for business development for the 1990s. *Paper at 6th Workshop on Strategic Human Resource Management*, March 1991, EIASM, St Gallen.

Forster, N. (1990) A practical guide to management of job changes and relocation. *Personnel Review*, 19(4), 26–35.

Forster, N. (1992) International managers and mobile families: the professional and personal dynamics of trans-national career pathing and job mobility in the 1990s. *International Journal of Human Resource Management*, 3(3), 605–24.

Fowler, A. (1990) Performance management: the MBO of the '90s. *Personnel Management*, 22(7), 47–51.

Fox, S. (1992a) The European learning community: towards a political economy of management learning. *Human Resource Management Journal*, 3(1), 70–6.

Fox, S. (1992b) What are we? The constitution of management in higher education and human resource management. *International Studies of Management and Organization*, 22(3), 71–93.

Franck, G. (1990) Mergers and acquisitions: competitive advantage and cultural fit. *European Management Journal*, 8(1), 40–3.

Freeman, J. (1982) Organizational life cycles and natural selection processes. In B.M. Staw and L. L. Cummings (eds) *Research in organizational behaviour*, Greenwich, Conn.: JAI Press.

Frère, M. (1991) Participative management at Aérospatiale. *European Participation Monitor P +*, No. 2, 15–18.

Frost, P.J., Moore, L.F., Louis, M.R., Lundberg, C.C. and Martin, J. (eds) (1985) *Organizational culture*, Beverly Hills, Cal.: Sage.

Galbraith, J. (1974) Organization design: an information processing view. *Interfaces*, 4, 28–36.

Galbraith, J. (1977) *Organization design*, Reading, Mass.: Addison-Wesley.

Garratt, B. (1991) Learning and change in corporate culture: an integrative approach using British and Dutch experiences. *European Business Journal*, 3(3), 25–30.

Gaugler, E. and Wiltz, S. (1993) Germany. In C. Brewster, A. Hegewisch, J.T. Lockhart, and L. Holden (eds) *The European human resource management guide*, London: Academic Press.

Geertz, C. (1973) *The interpretation of cultures: Selected essays*, New York: Basic Books.

Gentil, B. (1988) La gestion des ressources potentielles en cadres de haut niveau. *L'enjeu humain de l'entreprise*, Collection les enjeux de l'enterprise. CEPP, 403–6.

George, J. (1986) Appraisal in the public sector: dispensing with the big stick, *Personnel Management*, 18(5), 32–5.

Gershuny, J. (1985) Economic development and change in the mode of provision of services. In N. Redclift and E. Mingione (eds) *Beyond employment*, Oxford: Basil Blackwell.

Gertsen, M. (1990) Intercultural competence and expatriates. *International Journal of Human Resource Management*, 1(3), 341–62.

Ghoshal, S. and Haspeslagh, P. (1990) The acquisition and integration of Zanussi by Electrolux: a case study. *European Management Journal*, 8(4), 414–33.

Ghoshal S. and Haspeslagh, P. (1993) Electrolux: the acquisition and integration of Zanussi. In G. Johnson and K. Scholes (eds) *Exploring corporate strategy: Text and cases*, 3rd edition, Hemel Hempstead: Prentice Hall.

Gibbons, P. (1993) *Saville Holdsworth Ltd. international validation study: Project outline*, June 1993.

Gibson, N. (1990) CMB: role model or rarity? *Eurobusiness*, 2(12), 16–19.

Ginzberg, E. (1982) The mechanization of work. *Scientific American*, 247(3), 66–75.

Glass, P. (1990) Skills required for effective performance by hospital managers. *Asia Pacific Human Resource Management*, February 1990, 24–40.

Godkin, L., Braye, C.E. and Craunch, C.L. (1989) US-based cross-cultural management research in the eighties. *Journal of Business and Economic perspectives*, 15(2), 37–45.

Goetschy, J. and Rojot, J. (1987) France. In G. Bamber and R. Lansbury (eds) *International and comparative industrial relations*, London: Unwin Hyman.

Goldsmith, W. and Clutterbuck, D. (1984) *The winning streak*. London: Weidenfeld & Nicholson.

Goldstein, I.L. (1986) *Training in organizations: Needs assessment, development and evaluation*, 2nd edition, Monterey, Cal.: Brooks-Cole.

Gomez-Mejia, L. and Balkin, D. (1987) Determinants of managerial satisfaction with the expatriation and repatriation process. *Journal of Management Development*, 6(1), 7–17.

Gomez-Mejia, I.R. and Welbourne, T. (1991) Compensation strategies in a global context. *Human Resource Planning*, 14(1), 29–42.

Goodstein, L.D. and Burke, W.W. (1991) Creating successful organization change. *Organizational Dynamics*, 19(4), 5–17.

Gospel, H. (ed.) (1991) *Industrial training and technological innovation: A comparative and historical study*, London: Routledge.

Gospel, H. and Littler, C.R. (1983) *Managerial strategies and industrial relations: An historical and comparative study*, London: Heinemann.

Gourevitch, P., Martin, A., Ross, G., Allen, C., Bornstein, S. and Markovits, A. (1984) *Unions and economic crisis*, London: Allen & Unwin.

Graham, H.T. (1978) *Human resources management*, 2nd edition, Plymouth: MacDonald & Evans.

Grahl, J. and Teague, P. (1991) European level collective bargaining: a new phase? *Relations Industrielles*, 46, 1.

Grant, R.M. (1991) The resource-based theory of competitive advantage: implications for strategy formulation. *California Management Review*, 33(3), 114–35.

Gray, S.J. and McDermott, M.C. (1987) International mergers and takeovers: a review of trends and recent developments. *European Management Journal*, 6(1), 26–43.

Greenberg, E.R. (1988) Downsizing and worker assistance: latest AMA survey results, *Personnel* 65(11), 49–53.

Grenig, J.E. (1991) The dismissal of employees in the United States. *International Labour Review*, 130(5), 569–81.

Grindley, J. (1986) Mergers and acquisitions: (1) Premerger human resources planning. *Personnel*, 63(9), 28–36.

Grinyer, P.H., Mayes, D. and McKiernan, P. (1987) *Sharpbenders: The secrets of unleasing corporate potential*, Oxford: Basil Blackwell.

Grünberg, L. (1986) Workplace relations in the economic crisis: a comparison of a British and a French automobile plant. *Sociology*, 20(4), 503–31.

Grønhaug, K. and Nordhaug, O. (1992) Strategy and competence in firms. *European Management Journal*, 10(4), 438–44.

Guest, D. (1987) Human resource management and industrial relations. *Journal of Management Studies*, 24(5), 503–21.

Guest, D. (1990) Human resource management and the American dream. *Journal of Management Studies*, 27(4), 377–97.

Gunnigle, P. (1993) Ireland. In C. Brewster, A. Hegewisch, J.T. Lockhart, and L. Holden (eds) *The European human resource management guide*, London: Academic Press.

Guptara, B. (1989) Under negotiation. In R. Hill *We Europeans*, London: Europublications, 4th edition, 1993.

Guterl, F. and Gross, N. (1993) On the continent a new era is also dawning. *International Business Week*, No. 3310-640, 41.

Gutteridge, T.G. (1986) Organizational career development systems: the state of practice. In D.T. Hall (ed.) *Career development in organizations*, London: Jossey-Bass.

Gyllenhammer, P.G. (1977) *People at work*, Reading, Mass.: Addison-Wesley.

Hackett, E., Mirvis, P. and Sales, A. (1991) Women's and men's expectations about the impact of new technology at work. *Group and Organization Studies*, 16(1), 60–81.

Hackman, J.R. (1987) The design of work teams. In J. Lorsch (ed.) *Handbook of organizational behaviour*, Englewood Cliffs, NJ: Prentice Hall.

Hackman, J.R. and Oldham, G.R. (1976) *Work redesign*, Reading, Mass.: Addison-Wesley.

Hackman, J.R. and Oldham, G.R (1980) Motivation through the design of work: test of a theory. *Organizational Behaviour and Human Performance*, **16**, 250–79.

Hagedoorn, J. and Schot, J. (1988) *Cooperation between companies and technological development*, Delft: TNO.

Hale, A. and Tijmstra, S. (1990) *European management education*, Geneva: Interman.

Hall, D.T. (1986) Breaking career routines: midcareer choice and identity development. In D.T. Hall (ed.) *Career development in organizations*, London: Jossey-Bass.

Ham, J. van, Paauwe, J. and Williams, R. (1986) Personnel management in a changed environment. *Personnel Review*, **15**(3), 3–7.

Hambleton, R.K. and Bollwark, J. (1991) Adapting tests for use in different cultures: technical issues and methods. *ITC Bulletin*, 3–33.

Hamel, G. and Prahalad, C.K. (1989) Strategic intent. *Harvard Business Review*, **67**(3), 63–76.

Hamel, G. and Prahalad, C.K. (1991) Corporate imagination and expeditionary marketing. *Harvard Business Review*, **69**(4), 81–92.

Hamill, J. (1984) Labour relations decision-making within multinational corporations, *Industrial Relations Journal*, **15**.

Hamill, J. (1992a) Employment effects of changing multinational strategies in Europe. *European Management Journal*, **10**(3), 334–40.

Hamill, J. (1992b) Pan-europeanization: myth or reality. *European Management Journal*, **10**(4), 477–84.

Hammer, M. (1990) Re-engineering work: don't automate, obliterate. *Harvard Business Review*, **68**(4), 104–112.

Hammer, M. and Champy, J. (1993) *Re-engineering the corporation: A manifesto for a business revolution*, London: Nicholas Brearley.

Hammett, J. (1984) The changing work environment: high technology and the baby boomers challenge management to adapt. *Employment Relations Today*, **11**(3), 297–304.

Hampden-Turner, C. (1981) *Maps of the mind*, New York: Macmillan.

Hampden-Turner, C. (1990) *Corporate culture*, London: Economist Books.

Hampden-Turner, C. and Trompenaars, F. (1993) *The seven cultures of capitalism*, London: Piatkus.

Handy, C. (1976) *Understanding organizations*, London: Penguin.

Handy, C. (1987) *The making of managers: A report on management education, training and development in the United States, West Germany, France, Japan and the U.K.*, London: NEDO/MSC.

Handy, C. (1989), *The future of work*, Oxford: Basil Blackwell.

Handy, C., Gordon, C., Gow, I. and Randlesome, C. (1988) *Making managers*, London: Pitman.

Handy, L. and Barham, K. (1989) Crossing cultural borders, *Eurobusiness*. February, 29–31.

Hannaway, C. (1992) Why Irish firms are smiling: personnel management in Ireland. *Personnel Management*, **24**(5), 38–41.

Hansson, J. (1988) *Creative human resource management: Competence as strategy*, Stockholm: Prisma.

Harding, S. (1991) *Employee attitudes towards their employers: A European perspective*, London: International Survey Research.

Harding, I. (1993) High-fliers can't take off. *The European Business News*, 29th April 1993, 47.

Harpaz, I. (1989) Non-financial employment commitment: a cross-national comparison, *Journal of Occupational Psychology*, **62**(2), 147–50.

Harrington, J. (1991) *Organizational structure and information technology*, Hemel Hempstead: Prentice Hall.

Harris, P.R. and Moran, R.T. (1987) *Managing cultural differences*, Houston: Gulf Publishing.

Harrison, R. (1992) *Employee development*, London: Institute of Personnel Management.

Hart, H. (1993) Workgroups in Sweden: an overview. *European Participation Monitor P +* , No. 5, 12–18.

Harvey, M.G. (1982) The other side of foreign assignments: dealing with the repatriation problem. *Columbia Journal of World Business*, **17**(1), 53–9.

Harvey, M.G. (1985) The executive family: an overlooked variable in international assignments. *Columbia Journal of World Business*, **20**(1), 84–93.

Hasell, N. (1993) The view from Bayer. *Management Today*, November 1993, 60–4.

Hassid, J. (1980) *Greek industry and the EEC: A study of the impact from entry, Vol. 1*. Athens: Institute of Economics and Industrial Research.

Hayes, C., Anderson, A. and Fonda, N. (1984) *Competence and competition: Training and education in the Federal Republic of Germany, the United States and Japan*, London: NEDO/MSC.

Hazzard, M.S. (1981) *Study of the repatriation of the American international executive*, New York: Korn/Ferry International.

Heath, R. (1993a) German shareholders fight for their rights. *European Business News*, 28th January 1993, 35.

Heath, R. (1993b) Old faces enter the boardroom. *European Business News*, 18th February 1993, 38.

Hedberg, B., Nystrom, P.C. and Starbuck, W.H. (1976) Camping on seesaws: prescriptions for a self-designing organization. *Administrative Science Quarterly*, **21**, 41–64.

Heister, W.J., Jones, W.D. and Benham, P.O. (1988) *Confronting challenges and choosing options*, London: Jossey Bass.

Hendry, C., Pettigrew, A.M. and Sparrow, P.R. (1988) Changing patterns of human resource management. *Personnel Management*, **20**(11), 37–47.

Hendry, C. (1991) International comparisons of human resource management: putting the firm in the frame. *International Journal of Human Resource Management*, **2**(3), 415–40.

Hendry, C. (1993) *Human resource strategies for international growth*, London: Routledge.

Hendry, C. and Pettigrew, A.M. (1986) The practice of strategic human resource management. *Personnel Review*, **15**(5), 3–8.

Hendry, C. and Pettigrew, A.M. (1987) Banking on HRM to respond to change. *Personnel Management*, **19**(11), 29–32.

Hendry, C. and Pettigrew, A.M. (1990) Human resource management: an agenda for the 1990s. *International Journal of Human Resource Management*, **1**(1), 17–43.

Hendry, C., Pettigrew, A.M. and Sparrow, P.R. (1989) Linking strategic change, competitive performance and human resource management: results of a U.K. empirical study. In R. Mansfield (ed.) *Frontiers of management research*, London: Routledge.

Henzler, H.A. (1992a) Managing the merger: a strategy for the new Germany. *McKinsey Quarterly*, **1992**(2), 63–77.

Henzler, H.A. (1992b) The new era of Eurocapitalism. *Harvard Business Review*, **70**(4), 57–68.

Herzberg, F. (1968) One more time: how do you motivate employees? *Harvard Business Review*, **46**(1), 53–62.

Herzberg, F. and Zautra, Z. (1976) Orthodox job enrichment: measuring true quality in job satisfaction. *Personnel*, **53**, 54–68.

Heyer, S. and Lee, R. (1991) Rewiring the corporation. *Journal of Business Strategy*, **12**(4), 40–5.

Hibbs, D. (1976) Industrial conflict in advanced industrial societies, *American Political Science Review*, **70**, 1033–58.

Hickson, D.J. (ed.) (1993) *Management in western Europe: Society, culture and organization in twelve nations*, Berlin: de Gruyter.

Hilb, M. (1992) The challenge of management development in Western Europe in the 1990s. *International Journal of Human Resource Management*, **3**(3), 575–84.

Hilb, M. and Wittmann, S. (1993) Switzerland. In C. Brewster, A. Hegewisch, J.T. Lockhart, and L. Holden (eds) *The European human resource management guide*, London: Academic Press.

Hill, R. (1993) *We Europeans*, London: Europublications, 4th edition.

Hill, S. (1990) *Why quality circles had to fail, but TOM might succeed*, mimeo, London: London School of Economics.

Hilton, P. (1992) Using incentives to reward and motivate employees. *Personnel Management*, **24**(9), 49–52.

Hiltrop, J.-M. (1991a) HRM in European banking: challenges and difficulties. *European Management Journal*, **9**(1), 36–42.

Hiltrop, J.-M. (1991b) Human resource practices of multinational organizations in Belgium. *European Management Journal*, **9**(4), 404–11.

Hiltrop, J.-M. (1992) Just-in-time manufacturing: implications for the management of human resources. *European Management Journal*, **10**(1), 49–55.

Hiltrop, J.-M. (1993) European HRM: strategic pressures driving European HRM. *European Management Journal*, **11**(4), 424–42.

Hiltrop, J.-M. and Janssens, M. (1990) Expatriation: challenges and recommendations. *European Management Journal*, **8**(1), 19–26.

Hindle, T. (1990a) Cross-border takeovers: proof that the single market is here. *EuroBusiness*, **2**(5), 13–16.

Hindle, T. (1990b) British hares, continental tortoises? *EuroBusiness*, **2**(9), 33–6.

Hinterhuber, H.H. and Stumpf, M. (1990) Human resource management in Italy. In R. Pieper (ed.) *Human resource management: An international comparison*, Berlin: de Gruyter.

Hirsh, W. (1984) *Career management in the organisation*, Report No. 96. Falmer: Institute of Manpower Studies.

Hofheinz, P. (1992) Can Europe compete? *Fortune*, 14th December 1992, 47–54.

Hofstede, G. (1980) *Culture's consequences: International differences in work-related values*, Beverly Hills: Sage. Reprinted 1984.

Hofstede, G. (1991) *Cultures and organizations: Software of the mind*. London: McGraw-Hill.

Hofstede, G. (1992) Cultural dimensions in people management: the socialization perspective. In V. Pucik, N. Tichy and C. Barnett (eds) *Globalizing management: creating and leading the competitive organization*. Chichester: John Wiley.

Hofstede, G. (1993) Cultural constraints in management theories. *Academy of Management Executive*, **7**(1), 81–93.

Hofstede, G. and Bond, M. (1988) The Confucius connection: from cultural roots to economic growth. *Organizational Dynamics*, **16**(4), 4–21.

Hogg, C. (1988) Human resource management and the international market place. *Manpower Policy and Practice*, **3**(4), 25–34.

Hogg, C. and Tugwell, J. (1988) *Expatriates, Factsheet No. 8*, Wimbledon: Institute of Personnel Management.

Holden, L. (1991) European trends in training and development. *International Journal of Human Resource Management*, **2**(2), 113–31.

Holden, L. and Livian, Y. (1992) Does strategic training policy exist? *Personnel Review*, **21**(1), 12–23.

Holdsworth, R. (1991) Appraisal. In F. Neale (ed.) *Handbook of performance management*, London: Institute of Personnel Management.

Holland, J.L. (1985) *Making vocational choices*, 2nd edition, Englewood Cliffs, NJ: Prentice Hall.

Holmes, G. (1990) Alternatives to acquisitions: when alliances make sense. *Mergers and Acquisitions Europe*, **2**.

Holmes, G. (1993) Return of the heavyweights. *Mergers and Acquisitions International*, February 1993, 19–28.

Hoogendoorn, J. (1992) New priorities for Dutch HRM: personnel management in Holland. *Personnel Management*, **24**(12), 42–6.

Hoogendoorn, J., Van der Wal, T.H. and Spitsbaard, T.W. (1993) Holland. In C. Brewster, A. Hegewisch, J.T. Lockhart, and L. Holden (eds) *The European human resource management guide*, London: Academic Press.

Hooghiemstra, T. (1990) Management of talent. *European Management Journal*, **8**(2), 142–9.

Horovitz, J.H. (1980). *Top management control in Europe*, New York: St Martin's Press.

Horowitz, J.H. and Jurgens-Panak, M. (1992) *Total customer satisfaction*, London: Pitman.

van Houten, G. (1989) The implications of globalism: new management realities at Philips. In P. Evans, Y. Doz and A. Laurent (eds) *Human resource management in international firms*, London: Macmillan.

Howard, C. (1980) The returning overseas executive: culture shock in reverse. *Human Resource Management*, **13**(2), 22–6.

Hui, C.H. (1990) Work attitudes, leadership and managerial behaviour in different cultures. In R.W. Brislin (ed.) *Applied cross-cultural psychology*, Newbury Park: Sage.

Humes, S. (1993) *Managing the multinational: Confronting the global-local dilemma*, Hemel Hempstead: Prentice Hall.

Hunsaker, P. and Coombs, M. (1988) Mergers and acquisitions: managing the emotional issues. *Personnel*, **65(3)**, 56–63.

Hunt, J., Lees, S., Grumbler, J. and Vivien, P. (1987) *Acquisitions: The human factor*, London: London Business School.

Hunter, J.E. and Hunter, R.F. (1984) Validity and utility of alternative predictors of performance. *Psychological Bulletin*, **96**, 72–98.

Hutton, S.P. and Lawrence, P.A. (1979) *The work of production managers: Case studies at manufacturing companies in West Germany*, London: Department of Industry.

Hyde, D., Ellert, J. and Killing, J.P. (1991) The Nestlé takeover of Rowntree: a case study. *European Management Journal*, **9(1)**, 1–17.

IDE Research Group (1981a) *European industrial relations*, Oxford: Clarendon Press.

IDE Research Group (1981b) *Industrial democracy in Europe*, Oxford: Clarendon Press.

Iles, P. (1992) Centres of excellence? Assessment and development centres, managerial competence, and human resource strategies. *British Journal of Management*, **3(2)**, 79–90.

Incomes Data Service (1990a) *European management guide to recruitment*, Wimbledon: Institute of Personnel Management.

Incomes Data Service (1990b) *European management guide to employment terms and conditions*, Wimbledon: Institute of Personnel Management.

Incomes Data Service (1991) *European management guide to industrial relations*, Wimbledon: Institute of Personnel Management.

Incomes Data Service (1992) *European management guide to pay and benefits*, Wimbledon: Institute of Personnel Management.

Incomes Data Service (1993a) *European management guide to training and development*, Wimbledon: Insitute of Personnel Management.

Incomes Data Service (1993b) New appraisal scheme at IBM emphasizes customer satisfaction. *Incomes Data Service Report 642*, 2.

Industriemagazin (1987) Prognos, AG, Institut fur Arbeitsmarkt-und Berufsforschung. *Industriemagazin*, April 1987, 174.

Institute of Manpower Studies (1988) *Employee selection in the UK*, Report Number 160. Brighton: IMS.

Institute of Personnel Management (1992) Salaries and the single market, *Personnel Management*, **24(6)**, 21.

International Management (1992a) Eurotrends. *International Management*, **47(7)**, 12.

International Management (1992b) Germany: the housing costs keep managers at home. *International Management*, **47(10)**, 20–1.

D'Irbarne, P. (1989 *La logique de l'honneur*, Paris: Seuil.

Iterson, A. van and Olie, R. (1992) European business systems: the Dutch case. In R.D. Whitley (ed.) *European business systems: Firms and markets in their national contexts*, London: Sage.

Jackson, S.E., Schuler, R.S., and Rivero, J.C. (1989) Organizational characteristics as predictors of personnel practices. *Personnel Psychology*, **42(4)**, 727–86.

Jackson, T. (1990) Creating a Euro-workforce: what are real issues? *European Management Journal*, **8(2)**, 223–6.

Jackson, T. (1993) *Organizational behaviour in international management*, Oxford: Butterworth-Heinemann.

Jacobs, E. (1973) *European trade unionism*, New York: Holmes & Meier.

Jakob, H.J. (1990) From national to European – how to make it happen? *European Management Journal*, **8(2)**, 192–7.

Janssens, M. (1994a) International job transfers: a comprehensive model of expatriate managers' cross-cultural adjustment. *Unpublished PhD thesis*, Leaven: Katholieke Universiteit Leuven.

Janssens, M. (1994b) Evaluating international managers' performance: parent company standards as a control mechanism. *International Journal of Human Resource Management* (in press).

Janz, T. (1982) Initial comparisons of behaviour description interviews versus unstructured interviews. *Journal of Applied Psychology*, **67**, 577–80.

Javetski, W., Glasgall, W., Melcher, R., Oster, P. and Kiefer, S. (1992). Continental drift: now a two-tiered economy may evolve. *International Business Week*, 5th October 1992, 14–16.

Jay, P. (1967) *Management and Machiavelli*, London: Hodder & Stoughton.

Jemison, D. and Sitkin, S. (1986) Corporate acquisitions: a process perspective. *Academy of Management Review*, **11**, 145–63.

Johannisson, B. (1987) Beyond process and structure: social exchange networks, *International Studies of Management and Organization*, **17**(1), 3–23.

Johansson, H.J., McHugh, P., Pendlebury, A.J. and Wheeler, W.A. (1993) *Business process re-engineering: Breakpoint strategies for market dominance*, Chichester: John Wiley.

Johnson, G. and Scholes, K. (1993) *Exploring corporate strategy: Text and cases*, 3rd edition, Hemel Hempstead: Prentice Hall.

Johnston, J. (1991) An empirical study of the repatriation of managers in U.K. multinationals. *Human Resource Management Journal*, **4**(1), 102–9.

Jones, H.G. (1984) Decentralization in Swedish companies. *Journal of Industrial Affairs*, **12**(1), 11–18.

Jones, H.G. (1986) Structural changes in Swedish management. *European Management Journal*, **4**(2), 133–42.

Jones, H.G. (1991) Motivation for higher performance at Volvo. *Long Range Planning*, **24**(5), 92–104.

Joshi, H. and Davies, H. (1992) Day care in Europe and mothers' forgone earnings. *International Labour Review*, **132**(6), 561–79.

Kakabadse, A. (1991) *The wealth creators: Top people, top teams and executive best practice*, London: Kogan Page.

Kakabadse, A. (1993) The success levers for Europe: the Cranfield executive competencies survey. *Journal of Management Development*, **12**(8).

Kanellopoulos, C. (1990) *Personnel management and personnel managers in Greece*, Athens: Greek Productivity Centre.

Kaplan, R.B. and Murdock, L. (1991) Rethinking the corporation: core process redesign. *The McKinsey Quarterly*, **1991**(2), 27–55.

Kassalow, E. (1982) Industrial democracy and collective bargaining: a comparative view, *Labour and Society*, 7.

Katz, D. and Kahn, R.L. (1978). *The social psychology of organizations*, New York: John Wiley.

Kaufman, B. (1982) The determinants of strikes in the United States, 1900–1977, *Industrial and Labor Relations Review*, 35.

Keenan, A. (1992) Graduate recruitment and the Single European Market. *European Management Journal*, **10**(4), 485–93.

Kelly, L., Whatley, A. and Worthley, R. (1991) Self-appraisal, life goals and national culture: an Asian-Western comparison. *Asia Pacific Journal of Management*, **7**(2), 41–58.

Kendall, D.W. (1981) Repatriation: an ending and a beginning. *Business Horizons*, **24**(6), 21–5.

Kennedy, C. (1992) ABB: model merger for the new Europe. *Long Range Planning*. **25**(5), 10–17.

Kennedy, T. (1978) *European labour relations*, London: Associated Business Programmes.

Kern, H. and Schumann, M. (1989) New concepts of production in German plants. In P.J. Katzenstein (ed.) *Industry and politics in West Germany: Toward the third West German Republic*, Cornell: Cornell University Press.

Kerr, J. (1982) Assigning managers on the basis of the life cycle. *Journal of Business Strategy*, **2**(4), 58–65.

Ketelhöhn, W. (1993) What do we mean by co-operative advantage? *European Management Journal*, **11**(1), 30–7.

Kidger, P. (1991) The emergence of international human resource management. *International Journal of Human Resource Management*, **2**(2), 149–63.

Kilmann, R.H., Saxton, M.J. and Serra, R. (1985) (eds) *Gaining control of the corporate culture*, San Francisco: Jossey-Bass.

Kimberley, J.R. and Miles, R.H. (1980) *The organizational life cycle*, San Francisco: Jossey-Bass.

King, A.Y.C. and Bond, M.H. (1985) The Confucian paradigm of man: a sociological view. In W. Tseng and D. Wu (eds) *Chinese culture and mental health: An overview*, New York: Academic Press.

Kinnie, N. and Lowe, D. (1990) Performance related pay on the shopfloor. *Personnel Management*, **21(11)**, 45–9.

Klein, J., Edge, G. and Kass, T. (1991) Skill-based competition. *Journal of General Management*, **16(4)**, 1–15.

Kleingartner, A. and Anderson, C.S. (1987) (eds) *HRM in high technology firms*, Lexington, Mass.: Lexington Books.

Klimoski, R.J. and Rafaeli, A. (1983) Inferring personal qualities through handwriting analysis, *Journal of Occupational Psychology*, **56**, 191–202.

Knights, D., Morgan, G. and Murray, F. (1992) Business systems, consumption and change: personal financial services in Italy. In R.D. Whitley (ed.) *European business systems: Firms and markets in their national contexts*, London: Sage.

Kobrin, S.J. (1988) Expatriate reduction and strategic control in American multinational corporations. *Human Resource Management*, **27(1)**, 63–75.

Kochan, T.A. and Capelli, P. (1984) The transformation of the industrial relations and personnel function. In P. Osterman (ed.) *Internal labour markets*, Boston, Mass.: MIT Press.

Koopman-Iwema, A.M. and Flechsenberger, D. (1984) Works councils: the Dutch and German case. In A.M. Koopman-Iwema and R.A. Roe (eds) *Work and organizational psychology – European perspectives*, Lisse: Swets & Zeitlinger.

Korn-Ferry International (1990) *Board of directors: Seventeenth annual study*, New York: KFI.

Kotter, J. and Heskett, J. (1992) *Corporate culture and performance*, New York: Free Press.

Kotter, J. and Leahey, J. (1990) Changing the culture at British Airways. *Harvard Business School Case No. 491–009.*

Kozlowski, S.W., Chao, G.T., Smith, E.S., and Hedlund, J. (1993) Organizational downsizing: strategies, interventions and research implications. In C. Cooper and I. Robertson (eds) *International Review of Industrial and Organizational Psychology. Volume 9*, Chichester: John Wiley.

Kravaritou-Marnitakis, Y. (1988) *New forms of work: Labour law and social security aspects in the European Community*, Dublin: European Foundation for the Improvement of Living and Working Conditions.

Kreiner, K. (1989) Culture and meaning: making sense of conflicting realities in the workplace, *International Studies of Management and Organization*, **19(3)**, 64–81.

Kristensen, P.H. (1992) Strategies against structure: institutions and economic organization in Denmark. In R.D. Whitley (ed.) *European business systems: Firms and markets in their national contexts*, London: Sage.

Kroeber, A. and Kluckhohn, C. (1952) Culture: a critical review of concepts and definitions, *Cambridge: Papers of the Peabody museum of archeology and ethnology*, Harvard University, 1–223.

Krol, R van de (1993) The Netherlands' invisible army. *International Management*, **48(2)**, 44–5.

Landa, O. (1990) Human resource management: in Czechoslovakia – management development a key issue. In R. Pieper (ed.) *Human resource management: An international comparison*, Berlin: de Gruyter.

Landy, F.J. and Rastegary, H. (1989) Criteria for selection. In M. Smith and I. Robertson (eds) *Advances in selection and assessment*, Chichester: John Wiley.

Lane, C. (1989) *Management and labour in Europe*, Aldershot: Edward Elgar.

Lane, C. (1992) European business systems: Britain and Germany compared. In R. Whitley (ed.) European business systems: Firms and markets in their national contexts, London: Sage.

Lane, H.W. and DiStefano, J.J. (1988). *International management behaviour: From policy to practice*, Ontario: Nelson.

Lange, K. and Johnsen, P. (1993) Norway. In C. Brewster, A. Hegewisch, J.T. Lockhart, and L. Holden (eds) *The European human resource management guide*, London: Academic Press.

Lange, P., Ross, G. and Vannicelli, M. (1982) *Unions, change and crisis: French and Italian union strategy and the political economy, 1945–80*, London: Allen & Unwin.

Larsson, R. (1989) *Organizational integration of mergers and acquisitions: A case survey of realization of synergy potentials*, Lund: Lund University Press.

Latham, G.P. and Saare, L.M. (1984) Do people do what they say? Further studies on the situational interview, *Journal of Applied Psychology*, **69**, 569–73.

Lauermann, E. (1992) British Airways in Europe: a human resources viewpoint of development. *European Management Journal*, **10** (1), 85–6.

Laurent, A. (1981) Matrix organizations and Latin cultures: a note on the use of comparative data in management education. *International Studies of Management and Organization*, **10**(4), 101–14.

Laurent, A. (1983) The cultural diversity of western conceptions of management. *International Studies of Management and Organization*, **13**(1–2), 5–96.

Laurent, A. (1986) The cross-cultural puzzle of international human resource management. *Human Resource Management*, **25**(1), 91–102.

Laurent, A. (1991) Managing across cultures and national borders. In S. Makridakis (ed.) *Single Market Europe: Opportunities and challenges for business*, San Francisco: Jossey-Bass.

Lawler, E. (1981) *Pay and organizational development*, Wokingham: Addison-Wesley.

Lawrence, P. (1980) *Managers and management in West Germany*, London: Croom Helm.

Lawrence, P. (1991) The personnel function – an Anglo-German comparison. In C. Brewster and S. Tyson (eds) *International comparisons in human resource management*, London: Pitman.

Lawrence, P. (1993a) Human resource management in Germany. In S. Tyson, P. Lawrence, P. Poirson, L. Manzolini and C.S. Vincente (eds) *Human resource management in Europe: Strategic issues and cases*, London: Kogan Page.

Lawrence, P. (1993b) Management development in Europe: a study in cultural contrast. *Human Resource Management Journal*, **3**(1), 11–23.

Lawrence, P. and Lorsch, J.W. (1967) *Organization and environment*, Cambridge: Harvard Graduate School of Business Administration.

Ledford, G. (1991) The design of skill-based pay plans. In M. Rock and L. Berger (eds) *The compensation handbook*, New York: McGraw-Hill.

Lee, J.A. (1966) Cultural analysis in overseas operations, *Harvard Business Review*. **44**(2), 106–14.

Lefkoe, P. (1987) Why so many mergers fail. *Fortune*, 20th July.

Legge, K. (1989) Human resource management: a critical analysis. In J. Storey (ed.) *New perspectives on human resource management*, London: Routledge.

Lengnick-Hall, C.A. and Lengnick-Hall, M.L. (1988) Strategic human resources management: a review of the literature and a proposed typology. *Academy of Management Review*, **13**, 454–70.

Lessem, R. and Neubauer, F. (1994) *European management systems: Towards unity out of cultural diversity*, London: McGraw-Hill.

Levinson, D.J., Darrow, C.N., Klein, E.B., Levinson, M.H. and McKee, B. (1978) *Seasons of a man's life*, New York: Knopf.

Levy-Leboyer, C. and Sperandio, J.C. (1987) *Traite de psychologie du travail*, Paris: Presses de psychologie du travail. Paris: Presses Universitaires de France.

Lewis, W.W. and Harris, M. (1992) Why globalization must prevail: an economic rationale for the inevitable defeat of protectionism. *McKinsey Quarterly*, **1992**(2), 114–31.

Lilja, K., Räsänen, K. and Tainio, R. (1992) A dominant business recipe: the forestry sector in Finland. In R.D. Whitley (ed.) *European business systems: Firms and markets in their national contexts*, London: Sage.

Lindell, M. (1991) How managers should change their style in a business life cycle. *European Management Journal*, **9**(3), 271–9.

Lindell, M. and Rosenqvist, G. (1990) Is there a third management style? *Working Paper No. 204*, Helsinki: Swedish School of Economics and Business Administration.

Lipietz, A. (1988) L'Europe: dernier recours pour une relance mondiale. *Le Monde Diplomatique*, May 1988.

Livy, B. (1988) *Corporate personnel management*, London: Pitman Books.

Littler, C. (1982) *The development of the labour process in capitalist societies*. London: Heinemann.

Lloyd, T. and Skeel, S. (1992) Why Germans like the best of British. *Management Today*, December 1992, 38–52.

Loher, B., Noe, R., Moeller, N. and Fitzgerald, M. (1985) A meta-analysis of the relation of job characteristics to job satisfaction. *Journal of Applied Psychology*, **70**, 280–9.

London Business School (1990) *Continental mergers are different*, London: London Business School.

London, M., Wohlers, A.J. and Gallagher, P. (1990) A feedback approach to management development. *Journal of Management Development*, **9**(6), 17–31.

Long, P. (1986) *Performance appraisal revisited*, London: Institute of Personnel Management.

Longenecker, C. and Gioia, D. (1988) Neglected at the top: executives talk about executive appraisal. *Sloan Management Review*, **29**(2), 41–7.

Lorbiecki, A. (1993) Unfolding European management development. *Management Education and Development*, **24**(1), 5–13.

Lorenz, C. (1993) Second thoughts about moving in. *Financial Times*, 1st February, 11.

Louis, M. (1986) Sourcing workplace cultures: why, when and how. In R. Kilman, M. Saxton and R. Serpa (eds) *Gaining control of the corporate culture*, San Francisco: Jossey-Bass.

Luffman, G., Sanderson, S., Lea, E. and Kenny, B. (1991) *Business policy: An analytical introduction*, Oxford: Basil Blackwell.

Lutz, B. (1981) Education and employment: contrasting evidence from France and the Federal Republic of Germany. *European Journal of Education*, **16**, 73–86.

Mabey, C. (1989) The majority of large companies use occupational tests. *Guidance and Assessment Review*, **5**(3), 1–4.

Macleod, G. and Wyndham, J. (1991) Developing the competent manager. *Asia Pacific Human Resource Management*, Winter 1991, 69–78.

MacMillan, I.C. and Schuler, R.S. (1985) Gaining a competitive edge through human resources. *Personnel*, **62**(4), 24–9.

Magnet. M. (1984) Acquiring without smothering. *Fortune*, November 12th, 22–30.

Mahoney, J.T. and Panadian, J.R. (1992) The resource-based view within the conversation of strategic management. *Strategic Management Journal*, **13**(2), 363–80.

Maitland, I. (1983) *The causes of industrial disorder: A comparison of a British and German factory*, London: Routledge & Kegan Paul.

Manzolini, L. (1993) Environmental dynamics and the organizational innovation process: implications for human resource management in Italy. In S. Tyson, P. Lawrence, P. Poirson, L. Manzolini and C.S. Vincente (eds) *Human resource management in Europe: Strategic issues and cases*, London: Kogan Page.

Marceau, J. (1992) Small country business systems: Australia, Denmark and Finland compared. In R. Whitley (ed.) *European business systems*, London: Sage.

Marciniak, F. (1991) VW circles as a component in total quality management, *European Participation Monitor P+*, No. 2, 11–14.

Marginson, P., Edwards, P.K., Martin, R., Purcell, J. and Sisson, K. (1988) *Beyond the workplace: Managing industrial relations in the multi-establishment enterprise*, Oxford: Basil Blackwell.

Marks, M.L and Mirvis, P. (1985) Merger syndrome: management by crisis. Part Two, *Mergers and Acquisitions*, **12**(2), 50–5.

Marsden, D. (1991) Le politiche retributive aziendali. Il ruolo e la diffusione del 'merit pay'. In Asap Unità studi *1990: Rapporto sui salari*, Milan: Franco Angeli.

Martin, P. and Nicholls, J. (1987) *Creating a committed workforce*, London: Institute of Personnel Management.

Mathis, R.L. and Jackson, J.H. (1992) *Personnel: Contemporary perspectives and applications*, 5th edition, St. Paul, Minn.: West Publishing.

Maurice, M. (1980) Societal differences in organizing manufacturing units. *Organization Studies*, **1**, EGOS.

Maurice, M., Sorge, A. and Warner, M. (1980) Societal differences in organizing manufacturing units. *Organization Studies*, **1**(1), 63–91.

Mayo, A. (1991) *Managing careers: Strategies for organizations*, Wimbledon: Institute of Personnel Management.

McAfee, R.B. and Champagne, P.J. (1988) Employee development: discovering who needs what. *Personnel Administrator*, **33**(2), 92–8.

McBeath, G. (1990) *Practical management development*, Oxford: Basil Blackwell.

McClelland, D.C. (1987) *Human motivation*, Cambridge: Cambridge University Press.

McCulloch, S. (1993) Recent trends in international assessment. *International Journal of Selection and Assessment*, **1**(1), 59–61.

McDermott, M.C. (1993) Restructuring in the domestic appliances industry: implications for Maytag Corporation and its European operations. *European Management Journal*, **11**(3), 347–52.

McEvoy, G. (1991) Publication trends in international human resource management: the decade of the 1980s. *Working paper*, Utah State University, 1–21.

McEvoy, G. and Beatty, R.W. (1989) Assessment centres and subordinate appraisals of managers: a seven year examination of predictive validity. *Personnel Psychology*, **42**, 37–52.

McEvoy, B. and Cascio, W. (1985) Strategies for reducing employee turnover: a meta-analysis, *Journal of Applied Psychology*, **70**, 342–53.

Meaning of Work International Team (1987) *The meaning of work*. New York: Academic Press.

Medoff, J. and Abraham, K. (1980) Experience, performance and earnings. *Quarterly Journal of Economics*, December, 703–36.

Melcher, R., Levine, J.B. and Oster, P. (1992) The best laid plans of multinationals. *International Business Week*, 5th October 1992, 17–18.

Melcher, R. and Levine, J.B. (1990) Fired. Now Europe is singing the white-collar blues. *Business Week*, November 26th, 70–1.

Mendenhall, M. and Oddou, G. (1987) The dimensions of expatriate acculturation: a review. *Academy of Management Review*, **10**, 39–47.

Mendenhall, M., Dunbar, E. and Oddou, G. (1987) Expatriate selection, training and career-pathing: a review and critique. *Human Resource Management*, **26**(3), 331–45.

Mendes, P. (1992) A product of the country's history: personnel management in Portugal. *Personnel Management*, **24**(6), 40–3.

Mergers and Acquisitions Europe (1991a) Crossborder deals in Europe surge to $60 billion, overtakings the U.S. *Mergers and Acquisitions Europe*, **3**(1), 36–41.

Mergers and Acquisitions Europe (1991b) Towards 2000: days of reckoning for France's strategic acquirers. *Mergers and Acquisitions Europe*, **3**(1), 7–9.

Mergers and Acquisitions Europe (1992a) Crossborder transactions in Europe throttled back to $40 billion. *Mergers and Acquisitions Europe*. **4**(1), 7–14.

Mergers and Acquisitions Europe (1992b) Japanese acquisitions in the EC. *Mergers and Acquisitions Europe*, **4**(5), 20–31.

Mergers and Acquisitions Europe (1992c) Europe's top acquirers: the bottom line. *Mergers and Acquisitions Europe*, **4**(6), 22–30.

Mergers and Acquisitions Europe (1992d) Dealmaker of the year: Elf Aquitaine. *Mergers and Acquisitions Europe*, **4**(1), 18–23.

Merit, A. (1992) Putting humanity back into human resource. *Personnel Management*, **24**(1), 24–7.

Merkle, J.A. (1980) *Management and ideology: The legacy of international scientific management movement*, Los Angeles: University of California Press.

Merli, G. (1987) *Total manufacturing management: production organization for the 1990s*, London: Productivity Press.

Meyer, H-D. (1993) The cultural gap in long-term international work groups: a German–American case study. *European Management Journal*, **11**(1), 93–101.

Meyer, H-D. (1990) Human resource management in the German Democratic Republic: problems of availability and the use of manpower potential in the sphere of the high qualification spectrum in a retrospective view. In R. Pieper (ed.) *Human resource management: An international comparison*, Berlin: de Gruyter.

Miles, J. and Greenberg, J. (1992) *Cultural diversity as a challenge to achieving distributive justice within the European Community*. Unpublished paper.

Miles, R. and Snow, C. (1984) Designing strategic human resource systems. *Organizational Dynamics*, **12**(2), 36–52.

Miles, R. and Snow, C. (1986) Organizations: new concepts for new forms. *California Management Review*, **28**(3), 62–73.

Mill, C. (1991) Job prospects remain grim. *Personnel Management*, **23**(10), 93–5.

Millen, A. (1990) How 'small' can also be 'international'. *Eurobusiness*, February 1990, 35–9.

Miller, D. and Friesen, P.H. (1984) *Organizations: A quantum view*, Englewood Cliffs, NJ: Prentice Hall.

Miller, E.L. (1972) The selection decision for an international assignment: a study of the decision-maker's behaviour. *Journal of International Business Studies*, 3(2), 49–65.

Mills, D.Q. and Friesen, B. (1992) The learning organization. *European Management Journal*, 10(2), 146–56.

Mills, G. (1985) *On the board*, London: Allen & Unwin.

Millward, N. and Stevens, M. (1986) *British workplace industrial relations 1980–84*, Aldershot: Gower.

Mintzberg, H. (1979) *The structuring of organizations*, Hemel Hempstead: Prentice Hall.

Mintzberg, H. (1983) *Power in and around organizations*, New York: Prentice Hall.

Mintzberg, H. (1991) Effective organization. *Sloan Management Review*, 32, 54–68.

Misumi, J. (1993) Attitudes to work in Japan and the West. *Long Range Planning*, 26(4), 66–71.

Mitchell, D. (1993) Corporate Europe at the crossroads, *EIU European Trends*. (2), 53–8.

Mohrman, S. (1991) *Human resource strategies for lateral integration in high technology settings*, Los Angeles: CEO publication.

Moore, M.L. and Dutton, P. (1978) Training needs analysis: review and critique. *Academy of Management Review*, 3, 532–45.

Morgan, G. (1986) *Images of organization*, London: Sage.

Morgan, G. (1989) *Riding the waves of change: Developing managerial competencies for a turbulent world*, Oxford: Jossey-Bass.

Morris, D. and Brandon, J. (1993) *Re-engineering your business*, London: McGraw-Hill.

Mosley, C. and Bryan, J. (1992) A competency approach to performance management. In R. Boam and P. Sparrow (eds) *Designing and achieving competency: A competency-based approach to developing people and organizations*, London: McGraw-Hill.

Mosley, H. (1990) The social dimension of European integration. *International Labour Review*, 129(2), 143–70.

Moss-Kanter, R. (1983) *The change masters*, New York: Simon & Schuster.

Moss-Kanter, R. (1989) *When giants learn to dance*, Hemel Hempstead: Simon & Schuster.

Moss-Kanter, R. (1991) Transcending business boundaries: 12,000 world managers view change. *Harvard Business Review*, 69(3), 151–64.

Muchinsky, P.M. (1986) Personnel selection methods. In C.L. Cooper and I.T. Robertson (eds) *International review of industrial and organizational psychology*, Chichester: John Wiley.

Mueller, F. and Purcell, J. (1992) The Europeanization of manufacturing and the decentralization of bargaining: multinational management strategies in the European automobile industry. *International Journal of Human Resource Management*, 3(1), 15–34.

Mullins, S. (1993) Privatization at all costs? Spreading the word. *Mergers and Acquisitions International*, 13(5), 25–9.

Mumford, A. (1989) *Management development: Strategies for action*, Wimbledon: Institute of Personnel Management.

Murdoch, V.J. (1992) Assessment centres: through the glass brightly. *Asia Pacific Journal of Human Resources*, Spring 1992, 29–41.

Murphy, K. (1992) Performance measurement and appraisal: motivating managers to identify and reward performance. In W. Bruns (ed.) *Performance measurement evaluation, and incentives*, Boston: Harvard Business School Press.

Naisbitt, J. and Aburdene, P. (1990) *Megatrends 2000*, London: Sidgwick & Jackson.

Napier, N.K. (1989) Mergers and acquisitions: human resource issues and outcomes. *Journal of Management Studies*, 26(3), 271–89.

Napier, N.K. and Peterson, R.B. (1991) Expatriate re-entry: what do repatriates have to say? *Human Resource Planning*, 14(1), 18–28.

Naulleau, G. and Harper, J. (1993) A comparison of British and French management cultures: some implications for management development practices in each country. *Management Education and Development*, 24(1), 14–25.

Naylor, T.H. (1985) International strategy matrix. *Columbia Journal of World Business*, 20, 11–19.

Neal, F. (ed.) (1991) *The handbook of performance management*, London: Institute of Personnel Management.

Negrelli, S. and Santi, E. (1991) Industrial relations in Italy. In G. Baglioni and C. Crouch (eds) *European industrial relations: The challenge of flexibility*, London: Sage.

Nicholas, J. (1982) The comparative impact of organization development interventions on hard criteria measures. *Academy of Management Review*, 7, 531–42.

Nicolaides, P. (1992) Foreign direct investment, its causes, its contribution and some of its consequences. *Business Strategy Review*, 3(2), 1–16.

Nicolaides, P. and Thomsen, S. (1991) The impact of 1992 on direct investment in Europe. *European Business Journal*, 3(2), 8–16.

Nielsen, J.A. and Rötiss, J. (1991) European organization: corporate design. *The McKinsey Quarterly*, 1991(2), 112–24.

Nikas, C. (1991) Aspects of labour mobility between eastern and western European countries. *European Research*, November, 1–5.

Noble Lowndes (1993) *The 1993 guide to pensions and labour law in Europe*, Croydon: Noble Lowndes.

Norsted, J. and Aguren, S. (1975) *The Saab-Scandia Report*, Stockholm: Swedish Employers Federation.

O'Reilly, B. (1992) Your new global workforce. *Fortune*, December 14th, 62–70.

O'Reilly, J. (1992) The societal construction of labour flexibility: employment strategies in retail banking in Britain and France. In R. Whitley (ed.) *European business systems*, London: Sage.

Oberg, K. (1960) Culture shock: adjustment to a new cultural environment. *Practical Anthropologist*, 7, 177–82.

Oddou, G. (1991) Managing your expatriates: what successful firms do. *Human Resource Planning Journal*, 14(4), 301–8.

Oddou, G. and Derr, C.B. (1991) European MNC strategies for internationalising managers: current and future trends. *National Academy of Management Meeting*, August 12, Miami, Florida.

OECD (1991) *Employment outlook*, Paris: Organization for Economic Co-operation and Development.

Ohmae, K. (1990) *The borderless world*, New York: Harper Business.

Ohmae, K. (1992) Designing alliances that work. *McKinsey Quarterly*, 1992(1), 118–19.

Olian, J.D. and Rynes, S.L. (1984) Organizational staffing: integrating practice with strategy. *Industrial Relations*, 23(2), 170–83.

Oliver, J. (1993) Shocking to the core, *Management Today*. August, 18–22.

Östman, L. (ed.) (1977) *Payment by results*, Stockholm: Swedish Employers' Federation.

Otley, D. (1992) United Bank: a case study on the implementation of a performance-related reward scheme. In W. Bruns (ed.) *Performance measurement, evaluation and incentives*, Boston, Mass.: Harvard Business School Publications.

Ott, S. (1989) *The organizational culture perspective*, Pacific Grove, Cal.: Brooks Publishing.

Ouchi, W. (1981) *Theory Z*, Reading, Mass.: Addison-Wesley.

Paoletti, F. (1993) Telespazio: the telecommunications sector. In S. Tyson, P. Lawrence, P. Poirson, L. Manzolini and C.S. Vicente (eds) *Human resource management in Europe: Strategic issues and cases*. London: Kogan Page.

Papalexandris, N. (1988) Factors affecting management staffing and development: the case of Greek firms. *European Management Journal*, 6(1), 67–72.

Papalexandris, N. (1991) A comparative study of human resource management in selected Greek and foreign-owned subsidiaries in Greece. In C. Brewster and S. Tyson (eds) *International comparisons in human resource management*, London: Pitman.

Papalexandris, N. (1993) Greece. In C. Brewster, A. Hegewisch, J.T. Lockhart, and L. Holden (eds) *The European human resource management guide*, London: Academic Press.

Papandreou, V. (1992) Community charter of the fundamental social right of workers. In *Social Europe: first report on the application of the community charter of the fundamental social rights of workers*, Luxembourg: Office for Official Publications of the Commission of the European Communities.

Parasuraman, A., Berry, L. and Zeithalm, A. (1991) Perceived service quality as a customer-based performance measure. *Human Resource Management*, **32**(4), 335–65.

Parkes, C. (1993) No time like the present. *Financial Times*, 8th March 1993, 30.

Parry, I. (1993) The big three hide from green groups. *The European Business News*, 20th May 1993, 40.

Pascale, R. (1985) The paradox of 'corporate culture': reconciling ourselves to socialization. *California Management Review*, **27**(2), 26–41.

Pascale, R.T. and Athos, A.G. (1982) *The art of Japanese management*, New York: Simon & Schuster.

Pavitt, K. and Patel, P. (1988) The international distribution and determinants of technological activity. *Oxford Review of Economic Policy*, **4**(4), 35–55.

Payne, R.L. (1991) Taking stock of corporate culture, *Personnel Management*. **23**(7), 26–9.

Pearson, R. (1991) *The human resource: Managing people and work in the 1990s*, London: McGraw-Hill.

Pedler, M., Burgoyne, J. and Boydell, T. (1991) *The learning company: A strategy for sustainable development*, London: McGraw-Hill.

Peltonen, T. (1993) Managerial career patterns in transnational corporations: an organizational capability approach. *European Management Journal*, **11**(2), 248–57.

Peng, T.K., Peterson, M.F. and Shyi, Y.-P. (1990) Quantitative methods in cross-national management research: trends and equivalence issues. *Journal of Organizational Behaviour*, **12**(1), 87–107.

Pennings, J.M. (1993) Executive reward systems: a cross-national comparison. *Journal of Management Studies*, **30**(2), 261–80.

Personnel Management (1991) German apprenticeship scheme introduced for sixth-formers by Hoechst. *Personnel Management*, **23**(5), 9.

Peters, T. (1979) Beyond the matrix organization. *Business Horizons*, **22**(3), 15–27.

Peters, T. and Waterman, R. (1982) *In search of excellence*, New York: Harper & Row.

Pettigrew, A. (1973) *The politics of organizational decision-making*, London: Tavistock.

Pettigrew, A. (1985) *The awakening giant: Continuity and change in ICI*, Oxford: Basil Blackwell.

Pettigrew, A. and Whipp, R. (1991) *Managing change for competitive success*, Oxford: Basil Blackwell.

Pettigrew, A., Hendry, C. and Sparrow, P.R. (1989) *Training in Britain: employers perspectives on human resources*, London: HMSO.

Pettigrew, A., Hendry, C. and Sparrow, P.R. (1990) *Corporate strategy change and human resource management*, Research and Development Report No. 63. Sheffield: Employment Department.

Pettigrew, A., Sparrow, P.R. and Hendry, C. (1988) The forces that trigger training. *Personnel Management*, **20**(12), 28–32.

Pfeffer, J. (1978) *Organization design*, Arlington Heights, Ill.: AHM.

Pfeffer, J. (1981) *Power in organizations*, Marshfield: Pitman.

Phatak, A. (1974) *Managing multinational corporations*, New York: Praeger.

Phillips, N. (1992) *Managing international teams*. London: Pitman.

Philpott, L. and Sheppard, L. (1992) Managing for improved performance. In M. Armstrong (ed.), *Strategies for human resource management*, London: Kogan Page.

Pieper, R. (1990) (ed.) *Human resource management: An international comparison*, Berlin: de Gruyter.

Pinaud, H. (1992) A French trade unionist's view of the changes affecting management in Europe. *International Studies of Management and Organization*, **22**(1), 30–9.

Pinder, M. (1990) *Personnel management for the Single European Market*, London: Pitman.

Piore, M.J. and Sabel, C. (1984) *The second industrial divide*, New York: Basic Books.

Poirson, P. (1993) The characteristics and dynamics of human resource management in France. In S. Tyson, P. Lawrence, P. Poirson, L. Manzolini and C.S. Vincente (eds) *Human resource management in Europe: Strategic issues and cases*, London: Kogan Page.

Poole, J. (1993) Economic aches and political pains. *EuroBusiness*, **1**(6), 85–8.

Poole, M. (1986a) *Industrial relations: Origins and patterns of national diversity*, London: Routledge & Kegan Paul.

Poole, M. (1986b) *Towards a new industrial democracy: Workers' participation in industry*, London: Routledge & Kegan Paul.

Poole, M. (1990) Editorial: human resource management in an international perspective. *International Journal of Human Resource Management*, 1(1), 1–15.

Poortinga, Y.H., Coetsier, P., Meuris, G., Miller, K.M., Samsonowitz, V., Seisdedos, N. and Schlegal, J. (1982) A survey of attitudes towards tests among psychologists in six Western European countries. *International Review of Applied Psychology*, 31, 7–34.

Popper, M. (1993) The Anglo-Saxon invasion. *Mergers and Acquisitions International*, 13(2), 14–18.

Porter, B and Parker, W. (1992) Culture change. *Human Resource Management*, 33(2), 45–68.

Porter, M.E. (1980) *Competitive strategy*, New York: Free Press.

Porter, M.E. (1985) *Competitive advantage*, New York: Free Press.

Porter, M.E. (1990) *The competitive advantage of nations*, London: Macmillan.

Porter, M.E. (1992) A note on culture and competitive advantage. *European Management Journal*, 10(2), 178.

Prahalad, C.K. and Doz, Y. (1987) *The multinational mission*. New York: Free Press.

Prewitt, L.B. (1982) The emerging field of human resources management. *Personnel Administrator*, May 1982, 81–7.

Pryor, R. (1985) A fresh approach to performance appraisal. *Personnel Management*, 17(6), 38–9.

Pucik, V. (1988) Strategic alliances, organizational learning and competitive advantage: the HRM agenda. *Human Resource Management*, 27(1), 77–93.

Pucik, V. (1992) *Globalizing management*, New York: McGraw-Hill.

Pucik, V. and Katz, J.H. (1986) Information, control and human resource management in multinational firms. *Human Resource Management*, 25, 121–32.

Pugh, D.S. (1976) The Aston approach to the study of organizations. In G. Hofstede and M.S. Kassen (eds) *European contributions to organization theory*, Assen, The Netherlands: Van Gorvan.

Pugh, D.S., Hickson, D.J. and Hinings, C.R. (1969). An empirical taxonomy of work organizations. *Administrative Science Quarterly*, 14, 115–26.

Purg, D. (1990) Human resource management in Yugoslavia: problems and perspectives. In R. Pieper (ed.) *Human resource management: An international comparison*, Berlin: de Gruyter.

Pye, A.J. and Mangham, I.L. (1987) *Review of management training working party no. 3*, London: British Institute of Management/Confederation of British Industry.

Rafaeli, A. and Klimoski, R.J. (1983) Predicting sales success through handwriting analysis: an evaluation of the effects of training and handwriting sample content. *Journal of Applied Psychology*, 68, 212–17.

Ramsey, H. (1992) Swedish and Japanese work methods – comparisons and contrasts. *European Participation Monitor P+*, Issue No. 3, 37–40.

Randall, G.A., Packard, P.M., Shaw, R.L. and Slater, A.J. (1984) *Staff appraisal*, London: Institute of Personnel Management.

Randlesome, C. (1989) *Making middle managers? Aspects of the German Chambers of Industry and Commerce*, Cranfield School of Management Working Paper SWP 19/89.

Randlesome, C. (1990a) *Business cultures in Europe*, Oxford: Heinemann.

Randlesome, C. (1990b) The business culture in West Germany. In C. Randlesome (ed.) *Business cultures in Europe*, Oxford: Heinemann.

Randlesome, C. (1993) Ein Kampf: the German struggle with the MBA. *European Management Journal*, 11(3), 353–6.

Ranney, J. and Cardner, C. (1984) Sociotechnical systems in two office settings. *Office, Technology and People*, 44, 33–42.

Rappoport, C. (1992) Europe looks ahead to hard choices. *Fortune*, 14th December 1992, 22–31.

Räsänen, K. (1991) Making history/breaking history: the dynamics of organizational transformation. *International Studies of Management and Organization*, 21(4), 3–8.

Räsänen, K. and Whipp, R. (1992) National business recipes: a sector perspective. In R. Whitley (ed.) *European business systems: Firms and markets in their national contexts*, London: Sage.

Redman, T. and Snape, E. (1992) Upward and onward: can staff appraise their managers? *Personnel Review*, 21 (7), 32–46.

Reed, R. and DeFillippi, R.J. (1990) Causing ambiguity, barriers to imitation, and sustainable competitive advantage. *Academy of Management Review*, **15**, 88–102.

Regout, S. (1992) New forms of work organization – a typology. *European Participation Monitor* P+, Issue No. 3, 31–4.

Rehder, R.R. (1992a) Building cars as if people mattered: the Japanese lean system vs. Volvo's Uddevalle system. *Columbia Journal of World Business*, **27**, 57–70.

Rehder, R.R. (1992b) Sayonara, Uddevalla? *Business Horizons*, **35**(6), 8–18.

Rehn, G. and Viklund, B. (1991) Changes in the Swedish model. In G. Baglioni and C. Crouch (eds) *European industrial relations: The challenge of flexibility*, London: Sage.

Reich, R. (1991) Who is them? *Harvard Business Review*, **68**(1), 53–64.

Reicheld, F. and Sasser, W. (1990) Zero defections: quality comes first. In C. Lovelock (ed.) *Managing services*, New York: Prentice Hall.

Reilly, R.R. and Chao, G.T. (1982) Validity and fairness of some alternative employee selection procedures. *Personnel Psychology*, **35**, 1–62.

Rice, A.K. (1958) *Productivity and social organisation: The Ahmedabad experiment*, Tavistock: London.

Riley-Adams, R. (1993) Hands across the sea. *International Management*, **48**(6), 23–4.

Roberts, K. (1981) The sociology of work entry and occupational choice. In A.G. Watts, D.E. Super and J.M. Kidd (eds) *Career development in Britain*, Cambridge: Hobson's Press.

Robertson, I.T. and Makin, P.J. (1986) Management selection in Britain: a survey and critique. *Journal of Occupational Psychology*, **59**(1), 45–57.

Robertson, I.T. and Smith, M. (1985) *Motivation and job design: Theory, research and practice*, London: Institute of Management.

Robertson, I.T. and Smith, M. (1989) Personnel selection methods. In M. Smith and I. Robertson (eds) *Advances in selection and assessment*, Chichester: John Wiley.

Rodriguez, J. (1991) Spanish customs. *Personnel Management*, **23**(4), 23.

Roe, R.A. (1989) Designing selection procedures. In P. Herriot (ed.) *Assessment and selection in organizations: Methods and practice for recruitment and appraisal*, Chichester: John Wiley.

Rojot, J. (1990) Human resource management in France. In R. Pieper (ed.) *Human resource management: An international comparison*, Berlin: de Gruyter.

Romero, F. (1990) Cross-border population movements. In W. Wallace (ed.) *The dynamics of European integration*, London: Royal Institute of International Affairs.

Ronen, S. (1986) *Comparative and multinational management*, New York: John Wiley.

Ronen, S. and Shenkar, O. (1985) Clustering countries on attitudinal dimensions: a review and synthesis. *Academy of Management Review*, **10**(7), 445–54.

Roomkin, J.M. (1989) (ed.) *Managers as employees: An international comparison of the changing character of managerial employment*, Oxford: Oxford University Press.

Roos, J. and von Krogh, G. (1992) Figuring out your competence configuration. *European Management Journal*, **10**(4), 422–7.

Ross, J.D. (1981) A definition of HRM. *Personnel Journal*, **60**(10), 781–3.

Rossett, A. (1990) Overcoming obstacles to needs assessment. *Training*, **27**(3), 36, 38–41.

Roth, S. (1993) Lean production in German motor manufacturing. *European Participation Monitor* P+, No. 5, 35–9.

Rousseau, D.M. (1990) New hire perceptions of their own and their employer's obligations: a study of psychological contracts. *Journal of Organizational Behaviour*, **11**, 389–400.

Saari, L., Johnson, T., McLaughlin, S. and Zimmerle, D. (1988) A survey of management training and education practice in U.S. companies. *Personnel Psychology*, **41**, 731–45.

Sabel, C. (1982) *Work and politics*, Cambridge: Cambridge University Press.

Sadler, P. and Milmer, K. (1993) *The talent-intensive orgnization: Optimisng your company's human resource strategies*, London: Economist Intelligence Unit.

Saias, M. (1989) Compétitivité et stratégies des enterprises face à l'horizon 93. *Revue française de gestion*, May 1989.

Salaman, G. (1991) (ed.) *Human resource strategies*, Milton Keynes: Open University.

Samovar, L.A., Porter, R.E. and Jain, N.C. (1981) *Understanding intercultural communication*, Belmont, Cal.: Wadsworth.

Sasseen, J. (1992) Cap Gemini's twin challenge. *International Management*, **47**(10), 28–31.

Sasseen, J. (1993) Disney's bungle book. *International Management*, **48**(6), 26–7.

Sathe, V. (1985) *Culture and related corporate realities*, Homewood Ill.: Irwin.

Saunderson, A. (1993a) Cut jobs, cut costs to forestall VW's crisis. *European Business News*, 21st January 1993, 35.

Saunderson, A. (1993b) German bankers shake their industrial chains. *European Business News*, 25th March 1993, 34.

Schein, E.H. (1971) The individual, the organization and the career: a conceptual scheme. *Journal of Applied Behavioural Science*, **7**, 401–26.

Schein, E.H. (1975) How career anchors hold executives to career paths. *Personnel*, **52**(3), 11–24.

Schein, E.H. (1978) *Career dynamics*, Reading, Mass.: Addison-Wesley.

Schein, E.H. (1981) Coming to a new awareness of organizational culture, *Sloan Management Review*, **22**(4), 3–16.

Schein, E.H. (1982) Individuals and careers. *Technical report 19*. Office of Naval Research.

Schein, E.H. (1983) The role of the founder in creating organizational culture. *Organizational Dynamics*, **12**(2), 13–28.

Schein, E.H. (1985) *Organizational culture and leadership*, San Francisco: Jossey-Bass.

Schein, E.H. (1989) Organizational culture: what it is and how to change it. In P. Evans, Y. Doz and A. Laurent (eds) *Human resource management in international firms: Change, globalization, innovation*. Basingstoke: Macmillan.

Schein, E.H. and Van Maanen, J. (1977) Career development. In J.R. Hackman and J.L. Suttle (eds) *Improving life at work*, Santa Monica: Goodyear.

Schmitt, N., Gooding, R.Z., Noe, R.A. and Kirsch, M. (1984) Meta-analysis of validity studies published between 1964 and 1982 and the investigation of study characteristics. *Personnel Psychology*, **37**, 407–22.

Schneider, S., (1988) National vs. corporate culture: implications for human resource management. *Human Resource Management*, **27**(2), 231–46.

Schneier, C.E., Shaw, D.G. and Beatty, R.W. (1991) Performance measurement and management: a tool for strategy execution, *Human Resource Management*, **30**(4), 279–303.

Schneier, C.E., Shaw, D.G. and Beatty, R.W. (1993) Companies' attempts to improve performance while containing costs: quick fix versus lasting change. *Human Resource Planning*, **15**(3), 1–26.

Scholz, C. (1987) Corporate culture and strategy – the problem of strategic fit, *Long Range Planning*. **20**(4), 78–87.

Schön, D. (1983) *The reflective practitioner*, New York: Basic Books.

Schroder, M. (1989) *Managerial competence: the key to excellence*, Dubique, Ill.: Kendall & Hunt.

Schuler, R.S. (1990) Repositioning the human resource function: transformation or demise? *Academy of Management Executive*, **40**(3), 49–60.

Schuler, R.S. (1992a) Linking the people with the strategic needs of the business. *Organizational Dynamics*, Summer, 18–32.

Schuler, R.S. (1992b) *Managing human resources*, 4th edition, St Paul, Minn.: West Publishing.

Schuler, R.S. and Huber, V.L (1993) *Personnel and human resource management*, 5th edition, St Paul, Minn.: West Publishing.

Schuler, R.S. and Jackson, S.E. (1987) Linking competitive strategies with human resource management practices. *Academy of Management Executive*, **1**(3), 207–19.

Schuler, R.S. and Jackson, S.E. (1988) Customerization: the ticket to better HR business. *Personnel*, **65**(6), 36–44.

Schuler, R.S., Dowling, P.J. and de Cieri, H. (1993) An integrative framework of strategic international human resource management. *International Journal of Human Resource Management*, **5**(4), 717–64.

Schuler, R.S. and Walker, J.W. (1990) Human resources strategy: focusing on issues and actions. *Organizational Dynamics*, Summer, 5–19.

Schultz, M. (1992) Post modern pictures of culture: a post modern reflection on the 'modern notion' of corporate culture, *International Studies of Management and Organization*, **22**(2), 15–39.

Schwab, L. (1987) L'individualisation des salaires. *Les cashiers Français*, Special issue on 'La flexibilité du travail', **231**, 25–9.

Schweiger, D.M. and Weber, K. (1990) Strategies for managing human resources during mergers and acquisitions: an empirical investigation. *Human Resource Planning*, 12(2), 69–86.

Scullion, H. (1992) Strategic recruitment and development of the 'international manager': some European considerations. *Human Resource Management Journal*, 3(1), 57–69.

Segrestin, D. (1990) Recent changes in France. In G. Baglioni and C. Crouch (eds) *European industrial relations: The challenge of flexibility*, London: Sage.

Sellier, F. (1978) France. In J. Dunlop and W. Galenson (eds) *Labor in the twentieth century*, New York: Academic Press.

Sels, A. (1992) The rule of pragmatism in a diverse culture: personnel management in Belgium. *Personnel Management*, 24(11), 46–52.

Semlinger, K. and Mendius, H.G. (1989) *Personalplanung und Personalentwicklung in der gewerblichen Wirtschaft*, RKW: unpublished.

Sengenberger, W. (1984) West German employment policy: restoring worker competition, *Industrial Relations*. 23(3), 323–43.

Seppänen, R. (1993) HRM developments in Finland. *Personnel Management*, 25(6), 32.

Servan-Schreiber, J.-J. (1967) *The American Challenge*, London: Hamish Hamilton.

Shackleton, V. and Newell, S. (1989) Selection procedures in practice. In P. Herriot (ed.) *Assessment and selection in organizations*, Chichester: John Wiley.

Shackleton, V. and Newell, S. (1991) Management selection: a comparative survey of methods used in top British and French companies. *Journal of Occupational Psychology*, 64(1), 23–36.

Shalev, M. (1978) Strikers and the State: a comment, *British Journal of Political Science*, 8.

Shapiro, A.C. (1991) Competitive implications of Europe 1992. *European Management Journal*, 3(3), 3–18.

Sharp, M. (1990) Technology and the dynamics of integration. In W. Wallace (ed.) *The dynamics of European integration*, London: Royal Institute of International Affairs.

Sheard, A. (1992) Learning to improve performance. *Personnel Management*, 24(11), 40–5.

Shenkar, O. and Zeira, Y. (1987) HRM in international joint ventures: directions for research. *Academy of Management Review*, 12, 546–57.

Shenton, G. (1992) Towards a definition of European management. *European Foundation for Management Development Forum*, 92(2), 10–12.

Sheridan, J. (1992) Organizational culture and employee retention, *Academy of Management Journal*, 35(5), 1036–56.

Shimmin, S. (1989) Selection in a European context. In P. Herriot (ed.) *Assessment and selection in organizations: Methods and practice for recruitment and appraisal*, Chichester: John Wiley.

Sibson, R.E. (1983) Strategic personnel planning. *Personnel Administrator*, 28(10), 39–42.

Simon, H.A. (1947) *Administrative behaviour*, New York: Macmillan.

Sisson, K. (1989) *Personnel management in Britain*, Oxford: Basil Blackwell.

Sisson, K., Waddington, J. and Whitston, C. (1991) Company size in the European Community. *Human Resource Management Journal*, 2(1), 94–109.

Smiley, T. (1989) A challenge to the human resource and organizational function in international firms, *European Management Journal*, 7(2), 189–97.

Smircich, L. (1983) Concepts of culture and organizational analysis. *Administrative Science Quarterly*, 28, 339–58.

Smith, M. (1986) Selection: where are the best prophets? *Personnel Management*, 18(11), 63.

Smith, M. and Abrahamsen, M. (1992) Patterns of selection in six countries. *The Psychologist*, 205–7.

Smith, P. (1992) Organizational behaviour and national cultures. *British Journal of Management*, 3, 39–51.

Social Europe (1992) *First report on the application of the community charter of the fundamental social rights of workers*, Luxembourg: Office for Official Publications of the Commission of the European Communities.

Söderström, M. (1993) Personnel management in Sweden: an HRM role struggling for survival. *Personnel Management*, 25(6), 28–33.

Söderström, M. and Syrén, S. (1993) Sweden. In C. Brewster, A. Hegewisch, J.T. Lockhart, and L. Holden (eds) *The European human resource management guide*, London: Academic Press.

Sorge, A. and Streeck, W. (1988) Industrial relations and technical change: the case for an extended perspective. In R. Hyman and W. Streeck (eds) *New technology and industrial relations*, Oxford: Basil Blackwell.

Sorge, A. and Warner, M. (1980) The context of industrial relations in Great Britain and West Germany, *Industrial Relations Journal*, 11(1), 41–50.

Sorge, A. and Warner, M. (1986) *Comparative factory organization and manpower in manufacturing*, Gower: WZB Publications.

Soskice, D. (1978) Strike waves and wage explosions, 1968–1970: an economic interpretation. In C. Crouch and A. Pizzorno (eds) *The resurgence of class conflict in Western Europe since 1968*, London: Macmillan.

Sparrow, P.R. (1986) The erosion of employment in the U.K.: the need for a new response. *New Technology, Work and Employment*, 1(2), 101–12.

Sparrow, P.R. (1988) Strategic HRM in the computer supplier industry. *Journal of Occupational Psychology*, 51, 25–42.

Sparrow, P.R. (1990) International personnel planning pressures at Mogul Oil. In D. Wilson and R. Rosenfeld (eds) *Managing organizations: Text, readings and cases*, London: McGraw-Hill.

Sparrow, P.R. (1991) Developing a human resource management strategy: International Computers. In K. Legge, C. Clegg and N. Kemp (eds) *Case studies in information technology, people and organizations*, Manchester: NCC/ Blackwell.

Sparrow, P.R. (1992) Human resource planning at Engindorf. In D. Winstanley and J. Woodall (eds) *Case studies in personnel*, London: Institute of Personnel Management.

Sparrow, P.R. (1994a) Organizational competencies: creating a strategic behavioural framework for selection and assessment. In N. Anderson and P. Herriot (eds) *Handbook of assessment and appraisal*, Chichester: John Wiley.

Sparrow, P.R. (1994b) The psychology of strategic management: emerging themes of diversity and managerial cognition. In C. Cooper and I. Robertson (eds) *International review of industrial and organizational psychology, Volume 9*, Chichester: John Wiley.

Sparrow, P.R. (1994c) The evolution of HRM strategies in International Computers Ltd. from 1981–91. In J.M. Hiltrop and P.R. Sparrow (eds) *European human resource management: A casebook*, London: Prentice Hall.

Sparrow, P.R. and Bognanno, M. (1993) Competency requirement forecasting: issues for international selection and assessment. *International Journal of Selection and Assessment*, 1(1), 50–8.

Sparrow, P.R. and Hendry, C. (1988) Acquisitions and mergers: good HRM stategy counts, *Manpower Policy and Practice*, Summer. 15–19.

Sparrow, P.R. and Pettigrew, A. (1987) Britain's training problems: the search for a strategic human resources management approach. *Human Resource Management*, 26, 109–27.

Sparrow, P.R. and Pettigrew, A. (1988a) How Halfords put its HRM into top gear. *Personnel Management*, 20(6), 30–4.

Sparrow, P.R. and Pettigrew, A. (1988b) Contrasting HRM responses in the changing world of computing. *Personnel Management*, 20(3), 40–5.

Sparrow, P.R., Schuler, R.S. and Jackson, S.E. (1994) Convergence or divergence: human resource practices and policies for competitive advantage worldwide. *International Journal of Human Resource Management*, 5(2), 267–99.

Spencer, L.M. and Spencer, S.M. (1993) *Competence at work: Models for superior performance*, Chichester: John Wiley.

Sperl, R. (1988) Cross-border transfers of employees: an expensive business. *Proceedings of 4th CBI/Employee Relocation Council International Conference*, London: CBI/ERC.

Spineux, A. (1991) Trade unionism in Belgium: the difficulties of a major renovation. In G. Baglioni and C. Crouch (eds) *European industrial relations: The challenge of flexibility*, London: Sage.

Staber, U. and Bögenhold, D. (1993) Self-employment: a study of seventeen OECD countries. *Industrial Relations Journal*, 24(2), 126–37.

Staehle, W. and Schirmer, F. (1992) Lower-level and middle-level managers as the recipients and actors in human resource management. *International Studies of Management and Organization*, 22(1), 67–89.

Stamp, G. (1990) A matrix of working relationships. *Individual and organizational unit work paper*, Uxbridge: Brunel Institute of Organization and Social Studies.

Stanton, M. (1992) Organization and human resource management: the European perspective. In M. Armstrong (ed.) *Strategies for human resource management: A total business approach*, London: Kogan Page.

Steele, M. (1993) The European brewing industry 1992. In G. Johnson and K. Scholes (eds) *Exploring corporate strategy: Text and cases*, 3rd edition, London: Prentice Hall.

Stening, B.W. (1979) Problems of cross-cultural contact: a literature review, *International Journal of Intercultural Relations*. 3, 269–313.

Storey, J. (1989) (ed.) *New perspectives on human resource management*, London: Routledge.

Storey, J. (1992a) *Developments in the management of human resources: An analytical review*, Oxford: Basil Blackwell.

Storey, J. (1992b) Making European managers: an overview. *Human Resource Management Journal*, 3(1), 1–10.

Strauss, G. (1979) Workers participation: symposium introduction. *Industrial Relations*, 18, 247–61.

Streeck, W. (1987) The uncertainties of management in the management of uncertainty: employers, labour relations and industrial adjustment in the 1980s. *Work, Employment and Society*, 1(3), 281–309.

Strongin Dodds, L. (1992) Merger in a cold climate. *International Management*, May 1992, 62–5.

Super, D.E. (1957) *The psychology of careers*, New York: Harper & Row.

Super, D.E. (1980) A life-span, life-space approach to career development. *Journal of Vocational Behaviour*, 13, 282–98.

Susman, G. (1976) *Autonomy at work*, New York: Praeger.

Syrett, M. and Gratton, L. (1989) Grooming managers for the 21st century. *Eurobusiness*, 2(3), 32–4.

Taillieu, T. (1990) International career orientations of young European graduates. *Conference paper at the fifth workshop on strategic human resources management*, 6th–9th March, Leuven University.

Taoka, G.M. and Beeman, D.R. (1991) *International business: Environments, institutions and operations*, New York: Harper Collins.

Taylor, F.W. (1911) *Principles of scientific management*, New York: Harper & Row.

Teague, P. (1989) *The European Community*: The social dimension, London: Kogan Page.

Teague, P. (1991) Human resource management, labour market institutions and European integration. *Human Resource Management Journal*, 2(1), 1–21.

Thompson, P., Wallace, T. and Flecker, J. (1992) The urge to merger: organizational change in the merger and acquisitions process in Europe. *International Journal of Human Resource Management*, 3(2), 285–306.

Thomsen, S. (1992) Integration through globalization. *National Westminster Bank Quarterly Review*, 5(2), 32–40.

Thomsen, S. and Woolcock, S. (1993) *Direct investment and European integration: Competition among firms and governments*, London: Royal Institute of International Affairs.

Thom, G. (1992) The Single European Market and labour mobility, *Industrial Relations Journal*. 23(1), 14–25.

Thurley, K. (1990) Towards a European approach to personnel management. *Personnel Management*, 22(9), 54–7.

Thurley, K. and Wirdenius, H. (1989) *Towards European management*, London: Pitman.

Thurley, K. and Wirdenius, H. (1991) Will management become 'European'? Strategic choices for organizations. *European Management Journal*, 9(2), 127–34.

Thurley, K. and Wood, S. (eds) (1983) *Industrial relations and management strategy*, Cambridge: Cambridge University Press.

Thurow, L. (1992) *Head to head*, London: Nicholas Brealey.

Tichy, N.M., Fombrun, C.J. and Devanna, M.A. (1982) Strategic human resource management. *Sloan Management Review*, 23(2), 47–61.

Tichy, N. and Nisberg, J. (1978) When does work restructuring work? Organizational innovations at Volvo and G.M. *Organizational Dynamics*, **5**, 73.

Thierry, H. (1987) De effectiviteit van prestatiebeloning. *Economisch-Statistische Berichten*, **2–9**, 804–9.

Tijmstra, S. and Casler, K. (1992) Management learning for Europe. *European Management Journal*, **10**(1), 30–8.

Tollgerdt-Andersson, I. (1993) Attitudes, values and demands on leadership – a cultural comparison. *Management Education and Development*. **24**(1), 48–57.

Torbiorn, I. (1982) *Living abroad: Personal adjustment and personnel policy in overseas setting*, New York: John Wiley.

Torrington, D. (1988) How does HRM change the personnel function? *Personnel Review*, **17**(6), 3–9.

Torrington, D. (1994) *International human resource management: Think globally, act locally*, Hemel Hempstead: Prentice Hall.

Torrington, D. and Blandamer, W. (1992) Competency, pay and performance management. In R. Boam and P. Sparrow (eds) *Designing and achieving competency: A competency-based approach to developing people and organizations*, London: McGraw-Hill.

Torrington, D. and Hall, L. (1991) *Personnel management: A new approach*, 2nd edition, Hemel Hempstead: Prentice Hall.

Torrington, D. and Mackay, L. (1986) Will consultants take over the personnel function? *Personnel Management*, **18**(2), 34–7.

Torrington, D., Mackay, L. and Hall, L. (1985) The changing nature of personnel management. *Employment Relations*, **7**(5), 10–16.

Towers Perrin (1992) *Priorities for gaining competitive advantage: A worldwide human resource study*, London: Towers Perrin.

Trepo, G. (1975) Mise en place d'une D.P.O.: le role crucial de la direction. *Direction et gestion*, **1**, 25.

Treu, T. (1992) Labour flexibility in Europe. *International Labour Review*, **131**(4), 497–512.

Treu, T. (1981) Italy. In R. Blanpain (ed.) *Comparative labour law and industrial relations*, Deventre: Kluwer.

Trice, H. (1985) Rites and ceremonials in organizational cultures. In S. Bachrach and S. Mitchell (eds) *Perspectives in organizational sociology: Theory and research*, Greenwich: JAI Press.

Trice, H. and Beyer, J. (1984) Studying organization culture through rites and ceremonials. *Academy of Management Review*, **9**, 653–9.

Trice, H. and Beyer, J. (1986) Using six organizational rites to change culture. In R. Kilman, M. Saxton and R. Serpa (eds) *Gaining control of the corporate culture*, San Francisco: Jossey-Bass.

Trist, E. and Bamforth, K.W. (1951). Some social and psychological consequences of the longwall method of coal getting, *Human Relations*, **4**, 3–38.

Trompenaars, F., (1993) *Riding the waves of culture*, London: Economist Books.

Tung, R.L. (1981) Selection and training for personnel for overseas assignments. *Columbia Journal of World Business*, **16**(1), 68–78.

Tung, R.L. (1982) Selection and training procedures of U.S., European and Japanese multinationals. *California Management Review*, **25**, 57–71.

Tung, R.L. (1988) *The new expatriates: Managing human resources abroad*, Cambridge, Mass.: Ballinger.

Turner, P. (1991) Capital flows in the 1980s. *Bank for International Settlements Economic Papers 3*, Basle: Bank for International Settlements.

Tylczak, L. (1991) *Downsizing without disaster*, London: Kogan Page.

Tyson, S. (1983) Personnel management in its organizational context. In K. Thurley and S. Wood (eds) *Industrial relations and management strategy*, Cambridge: Cambridge University Press.

Tyson, S. (1985) Is this the very model of a modern personnel manager? *Personnel Management*, **17**(4).

Tyson, S. (1993) Human resource management in the United Kingdom. In S. Tyson, P. Lawrence, P. Poirson, L. Manzolini and C.S. Vincente (eds) *Human resource management in Europe: Strategic issues and cases*, London: Kogan Page.

Tyson, S. and Brewster, C. (1991) Conclusions: comparative studies and the development of human resource management. In C. Brewster and S. Tyson (eds) *International comparisons in human resource management*, London: Sage.

Tyson, S., Lawrence, P., Poirson, P., Manzolini, L. and Vincente, C.S. (eds) (1993) *Human resource management in Europe: Strategic issues and cases*, London: Kogan Page.

Ulrich, D. and Lake, D. (1990) *Organizational capability: Competing from the inside out*, New York: John Wiley.

Umstot, D., Bell, C.H. and Mitchell, T.R. (1976). Effects of job enrichment and task goals on satisfaction and productivity: implications for job design. *Journal of Applied Psychology*, **61**, 367–79.

Usunier, J.-C. (1990) French international business education: a pessimistic view. *European Management Journal*, **8**(3), 388–93.

Uvalic, M., (1991) The PEPPER Report. *Commission of the European Communities and the European University Institute*, Brussels.

Välikangas, L. (1992) Executive summary. In *World competitiveness report: 1992*, Geneva: World Economic Forum.

Vandamme, J. (1984) *Pour une nouvelle politique sociale en Europe*, Paris: Economica.

Vanderbroeck, P. (1992) Long-term human resource development in multinational organizations. *Sloan Management Review*, **34**(1), 95–99.

Vandermerwe, S. (1992) *Scandinavian Airlines re-visited: customer relationships through services*, IMD case study No. M416-7. Lausanne: IMD.

Vandermerwe, S. (1993) A framework for constructing Euro-networks, *European Management Journal*, **11**(1), 55–61.

Vandermerwe, S. and L'Huillier, M.A. (1989). Euro-consumers in 1992. *Business Horizons*, **32**(1), 34–40.

Van Maanen, J. and Schein, E.H. (1979) Towards a theory of organizational socialization. In B.M. Staw (ed) *Research in organizational behaviour. Vol. 1*. Greenwich, Conn.: JAI Press.

Vermot-Gaud, C. (1990) *Détecter et gérer les potentials humains dans l'entreprise*, Paris: Editions Liaisons.

Vernon, R. and Wells, L.T. (1991) *The manager in the international economy*, 6th edition, Englewood Cliffs, NJ: Prentice Hall.

Very, P., Berthelier, M. and Calori, R. (1993) A note on the world automobile industry. In G. Johnson and K. Scholes (eds) *Exploring corporate strategy: Text and cases*, Hemel Hempstead: Prentice Hall.

Vincente, C.S. (1993) Human resource management in Spain: strategic issues, the economic and social framework. In S. Tyson, P. Lawrence, P. Poirson, L. Manzolini and C.S. Vincente (eds) *Human resource management in Europe: Strategic issues and cases*, London: Kogan Page.

Vickerstaff, S. (1992) (ed) *Human resource management in Europe: Text and cases*, London: Chapman & Hall.

Visser, J. (1990) Continuity and change in Dutch industrial relations. In G. Baglioni and C. Crouch (eds) *European industrial relations: The challenge of flexibility*, London: Sage.

Vollmann,, T. and Brazas, M. (1993) Downsizing. *European Management Journal*, **11**(1), 18–29.

Walker, J. (1980) *Human resource planning*, New York: McGraw-Hill.

Walker, J. (1992) *Human resource strategy*, London: McGraw-Hill.

Wall, T., Kemp, N., Jackson, P. and Clegg, C. (1986). Outcomes of autonomous work groups: a long-term field experiment. *Academy of Management Journal*, **29**, 280–304.

Walton, R.E. and Lawrence, P.R. (eds) (1985) *HRM trends and challenges*, Boston: Harvard Business School Press.

Walton, R.E. and Schlesinger, L. (1979) Do supervisors thrive in participative work systems? *Organizational Dynamics*, **8**, 25–38.

Wanous, J.D. (1974) Individual differences and reactions to job characteristics. *Journal of Applied Psychology*, **59**, 616–22.

Warr, P. (1982) A national study of non-financial employment commitment. *Journal of Occupational Psychology*, **55**, 297–312.

Wassell, T. (1993a) Half a millennium of sex battle ahead. *The European Business News*, 29th April 1993, 40.

Wassell, T. (1993b) Job-cutter's axe chips away at power of labour. *The European Business News*, 21st October 1993, No. 0180, 40–41.

Watson, D. (1993) European industrial policy–fact or fantasy? *European Business Journal*. 5(3), 8–17.

Weber, M. (1947) *The theory of social and economic organizations*, London: Oxford University Press.

Weber, R. (1969) Convergence or divergence. *Columbia Journal of World Business*, 4(3), 75–83.

Welfens, P. (1992) Foreign investment in the East European transition. *Management International Review*, 32, 199–218.

Whetton, D.A. and Cameron, K.S. (1984) *Developing management skills*, Glenview, Ill.: Scott Foresman.

Whipp, R. (1991) Human resource management, strategic change and competition: the role learning. *International Journal of Human Resource Management*, 2(2), 165–91.

Whitley, R.D. (ed.) (1992) *European business systems: Firms and markets in their national contexts*, London: Sage.

Wickens, P. (1987) *The road to Nissan*, London: Macmillan.

Wiener, M.J. (1981) *English culture and the decline of the industrial spirit 1850–1980*, Harmondsworth: Penguin.

Wijk, van G. (1987) Strategic reorientation and organizational redesign: the impact of new technologies, *International Studies of Management and Organization*, 17(4), 3–5.

Wilhelm, W. (1992) Changing corporate culture – or corporate behavior? How to change your company. *Academy of Management Executive*, 6, 72–7.

Wilkins, A. (1984) The creation of company cultures: the role of stories and human resource systems, *Human Resource Management*, 23(1), 41–60.

Wilkins, M. (1974) *The maturing of multinational enterprise: American business abroad from 1914 to 1970*, Cambridge, Mass.: Harvard University Press.

Williams, P. (1991) Strategy and objectives. In F. Neale (ed.) *Handbook of performance management*, Wimbledon: Institute of Personnel Management.

Wilpert, B. and Rayley, J. (1983) *Anspruchund Wirklichkeit der Mitbestimmung*, Frankfurt: Campus.

Wilsher, P. (1993) Nestlé Rowntree: a bittersweet tale. *Management Today*, March 1993, 54–7.

Wilson, C. (1992) *A strategy of change: Concepts and controversies in the management of change*, London: Routledge.

Wilson, D.C. and Rosenfeld, R. (1990) *Managing organizations: Text, readings and cases*, London: McGraw-Hill.

Wissema, H. (1992) *Unit management*, London: Pitman.

Witte, K de, (1989) Recruiting and advertising. In P. Herriot (ed.) *Assessment and selection in organizations: Methods and practice for recruitment and appraisal*, Chichester: John Wiley.

Wolff, C.J. de (1989) The changing role of psychologists in selection. In P. Herriot (ed.) *Assessment and selection in organizations: Methods and practice for recruitment and appraisal*, Chichester: John Wiley.

Womark, J.P., Jones, D.T. and Roos, D. (1990) *The machine that changed the world*, New York: Rawson.

Wood, S. (1986) Personnel management and recruitment. *Personnel Review*, 15(2), 3–11.

Wood, S. and Peccei, R. (1990) Preparing for 1992: business versus strategic human resource management. *Human Resource Management Journal*, 1(1), 63–89.

Woodley, C. (1990) The cafeteria route to compensation. *Personnel Management*, 22(5), 42–5.

Woodruffe, C. (1990) *Assessment centres: Identifying and developing competence*, Wimbledon: Institute of Personnel Management.

Woolfe, R. (1991) Managing and redesigning business processes to achieve dramatic performance improvements. *European Business Journal*, 20–8.

World Economic Forum (1990) *The world competitiveness report: 1990*, Geneva: World Economic Forum.

World Economic Forum (1993) *The world competitiveness report: 1993*, Geneva: World Economic Forum.

Wright, P.M. and McMahan, G.C. (1992) Theoretical perspectives for strategic human resource management. *Journal of Management*, **18**(2), 295–320.

Wright, V. (1991) Performance-related pay. In F. Neale (ed.) *Handbook of performance management*, Wimbledon: Institute of Personnel Management.

Young, S. and Hamill, J. (eds) (1992) *Europe and the multinationals: Issues and responses for the 1990s*, Aldershot: Edward Elgar.

Zeira, Y. and Banai, M. (1985) Selection of expatriate managers in MNSc: the host environment point of view. *International Studies of Management and Organization*, **15**(1), 33–51.

Zeira, Y. and Harari, E. (1977) Managing third country nationals in multinational corporations. *Business Horizons*, **19**, 83–8.

Zuboff, S. (1988) *In the age of the smart machine*, New York: Basic Books.

Subject Index